The Municipal Year Book

2008

The authoritative
source book of
local government data
and developments

PRESS

The Municipal Year Book

2008

Washington, DC

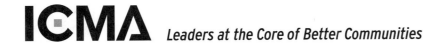

ICMA advances professional local government worldwide. Its mission is to create excellence in local governance by developing and advancing professional management of local government. ICMA, the International City/County Management Association, provides member support; publications, data, and information; peer and results-oriented assistance; and training and professional development to more than 9,000 city, town, and county experts and other individuals and organizations throughout the world. The management decisions made by ICMA's members affect 185 million individuals living in thousands of communities, from small villages and towns to large metropolitan areas.

Volume 75, 2008

ISBN: 978-0-87326-721-2
ISSN: 0077-2186
43493

Library of Congress Catalog Card Number: 34-27121

The views expressed in this *Year Book* are those of individual authors and are not necessarily those of ICMA.

Suggested citation for use of material in this *Year Book*: Jane S. Author [and John N. Other], "Title of Article," in *The Municipal Year Book 2008* (Washington, D.C.: ICMA, 2008), 00–000.

Table of Contents

B The Intergovernmental Dimension

Acknowledgments

The Municipal Year Book, which provides local government officials with information on local government management, represents an important part of ICMA's extensive research program. Each year, ICMA surveys local officials on a variety of topics, and the data derived from their responses constitute the primary information source for the *Year Book.* Authors from local, state, and federal government agencies; universities; and public interest groups as well as ICMA staff prepare articles that describe the data collected and examine trends and developments affecting local government.

We would like to express our appreciation to the thousands of city and county managers, clerks, finance officers, personnel directors, police chiefs, fire chiefs, and other officials who patiently and conscientiously responded to ICMA questionnaires. It is only because of their time-consuming efforts that we are able to provide the information in this volume.

In addition, I would like to thank the ICMA staff who have devoted countless hours to making the *Year Book* so valuable. Ann I. Mahoney is the director of publishing; Christine Ulrich is the editorial director; and Jane C. Cotnoir is the *Year Book* editor. Other ICMA staff members who contributed to this publication are Evelina Moulder, director of survey research and information management; Valerie Hepler, director of publications production; Sebia Clark, program analyst; and Nedra James, editorial assistant. Finally, thanks go to Sandra F. Chizinsky, ICMA consulting editor.

Robert J. O'Neill Jr.
Executive Director
ICMA

Inside the *Year Book*

Local government concerns are increasingly complex and sophisticated, and the need for familiarity with a broad range of issues is unsurpassed. Furthering the knowledge base needed to better manage local government is one of ICMA's top goals. Through survey-based research; a summary of selected best practices in local government; a brief review of local-state relations, congressional actions, and Supreme Court decisions in 2007; up-to-date salary and expenditure data; and wideranging directories, this edition of *The Municipal Year Book* provides some of the most important and timely information available on issues of importance to local government.

MANAGEMENT TRENDS AND ISSUES

Local Government Employee Health Insurance Programs

The cost of offering health care benefits to employees and retirees continues to increase for local governments. To reduce these costs, some employers have strengthened preventive care programs, offered incentives to employees to stop smoking, and taken other steps to improve employees' overall health. This article (A1), based on a survey conducted by ICMA staff and the ICMA Health Care Advisory Group and sponsored by CIGNA, identifies local government employers' top employee health concerns, programs that they have instituted to address those concerns, the types of benefits they are currently offering, and approaches they have taken to pay for those benefits.

Cooperation and Conflict in Governmental Decision Making in Mid-Sized U.S. Cities

The presence of cooperation and conflict in the decision-making process can have a significant impact on the final decision that emerges. Factors that have been identified as being predictive of these dynamics in local government decision making include a city's form of government, population size, location (urban or suburban), fiscal condition, socioeconomic conditions, and methodology of council elections. Focusing on mid-sized cities in the United States and using statistical analysis to test various assumptions about the causes and levels of cooperation and conflict, this article (A2) finds that form of government is most predictive of the levels of cooperation and conflict in the decision-making process, and that the existence of a professional management position—whether in the council-manager form or in a mayor-council form with a chief administrative officer—is directly related to lower levels of conflict and higher levels of cooperation.

Local Government Use of Customer Service Systems

For local governments, interaction with the public they serve is critical to engaging citizens in the community. A centralized customer service (311) system provides a vehicle through which residents can make their needs known to their local government and receive information back about the status of their requests. A 311 system also enables a local government to gather information for performance management, neighborhood problem solving, and capital budgeting. Using the findings of a national survey of local governments, this article (A3) explores the implementation of customer service systems and examines how local governments are using these systems to respond to citizen needs and strengthen their relationships with constituents.

Local Government Approaches to Active Living, 2007

The rapid rise in obesity rates among children and adults and the associated health problems and costs have made the obesity epidemic a high-profile issue in America. Many cities and counties are addressing this issue by tackling two of its root causes: declining activity levels and poor diets. In 2004, ICMA and the National Association of Counties (NACo) surveyed municipal and county governments to find out their interests, needs, and programming related to active living. ICMA and NACo partnered again in 2007, conducting parallel surveys to gauge changes since 2004 as well as to explore local government efforts to make healthy foods accessible and to combat youth obesity. This article (A4), which presents findings from the 2007 surveys, also highlights the tools and strategies that local governments consider to be most helpful in addressing active living goals and the barriers that impede their efforts.

Municipal Form of Government: Trends in Structure, Responsibility, and Composition

ICMA has been conducting a survey on municipal form of government for many years. The longitudinal data that emerge allow researchers to examine how the form and structure of city government have changed over time. Some changes are noticeable, such as the increase in chief appointed official positions in all forms of government; some are more nuanced, such as the characteristics that indicate a blurring of distinctions among traditional forms of government. With the findings from the 2007 survey, as summarized in this article (A5), ICMA adds another set of data to the picture of these and other developing trends.

Award-Winning Innovations in Local Government, 2007

Governments in the 21st century must continually adapt and innovate to meet increasingly diverse and complex challenges, ranging from threats of natural disaster and terrorist attack, to pressure from technically savvy citizens demanding better and more efficient services, to the burden of increased mandates from federal and state governments. This article (A6) presents 23 of the "Top 100" programs recognized by the Innovations in American Government (IAG) Awards program of Harvard University's Ash Institute for Democratic Governance and Innovation. These entries, which cover a range of policy areas, reflect innovations at the local level that indicate the following trends: a focus on prevention (of drug abuse, illness, youth criminality, etc.), governance by network, new uses of information technology and data, and a growing interest in sustainability and conservation. The article concludes by identifying three principles that are shared by local governments that embrace innovation and continually strive to improve citizen services: move from red tape to no tape, develop strategic partnerships, and increase citizen participation through technology.

THE INTERGOVERNMENTAL DIMENSION

State-Local Relations:
Authority and Finances

In recent years, local officials throughout the country have had reason to be concerned about how state mandates, prohibitions, and preemptions affect their authority, and about the lack of state fiscal support for local government. Of particular concern in 2007 were developments in the areas of property tax reform, cable franchising, and eminent domain. For example, legislation limiting local governments' use of eminent domain passed in Connecticut as well as in several other states, including Ohio, Virginia, and Wyoming. This article (B1) provides an overview of conditions and developments in the areas of local authority and finance; it also considers significant ballot measures, judicial decisions, and legislation.

Actions Affecting Local Government:
First Session of the 110th Congress

When the Democrats took control of both the House of Representatives and the Senate following the 2006 elections, their leaders pledged to push through an ambitious agenda to counter 12 years of Republican control, starting with the passage of several top-priority bills within the first 100 hours. Although the White House and congressional Republicans successfully opposed many of the Democrats' goals, such as linking funding to a timeline for the withdrawal of troops from Iraq, by the end of the session, the Democrats had secured an increase in the minimum wage from $5.15 to $7.25 by 2009 and a new ethics bill. As summarized in this article (B2), other congressional achievements included a law to implement many of the recommendations put forth by the 9/11 Commission. Congress also passed the CLEAN Energy Act, setting new standards for fuel consumption, use of biofuels, and energy efficiency in buildings and appliances.

Recent Supreme Court Cases
Affecting Local Government

During its 2006–2007 session, the U.S. Supreme Court dealt with such issues as solid-waste flow-control ordinances, time limits on discrimination claims, the use of racial classifications in school assignments, the execution of mentally ill defendants, the interplay of federal environmental statutes, and the lawfulness of searches and seizures under the Fourth Amendment. This article (B3) reviews the major holdings in these and other cases, each of which has implications for state and local governments. For example, because drug abuse by students is a serious problem and the government has an interest in stopping it, and in light of the special characteristics of the school environment, which have long allowed significant limitations on students' First Amendment rights, the Court ruled that it is permissible for school officials to discipline students for speech that can be reasonably regarded as encouraging the use of illegal drugs. For each case the authors provide concise yet comprehensive information about the background, legal precedents, and reasoning behind the Court's decision.

STAFFING AND COMPENSATION

One of the most basic managerial concerns is compensation. This section provides salary data for a variety of positions held by local officials.

The first two articles in this section look at the salaries of 23 municipal positions (C1) and 23 county positions (C2). These articles are based on information obtained in July 2006 through SurveyNavigator™ for ICMA, a Web-based interactive version of the annual salary survey that is managed and operated by The Waters Consulting Group, Inc.

The third article, "Police and Fire Personnel, Salaries, and Expenditures for 2007" (C3), presents the following for both police and fire departments in tabular form: total personnel, the number of uniformed personnel, minimum crew per fire apparatus, entrance and maximum salaries, information on longevity pay, and a breakdown of departmental expenditures. Data from the 2007 survey are compared with those from 2006.

DIRECTORIES

The directories section (D1) comprises 10 tables that provide the names of nearly 70,000 contacts in U.S. local government.

A special directory in the *Year Book* is "Professional, Special Assistance, and Educational Organizations Serving Local and State Governments" (D2). The 80 organizations that are included provide educational and research services to members and others, strengthening professionalism in government administration.

ORGANIZATION OF DATA

Most of the tabular data for *The Municipal Year Book 2008* were obtained from public officials through questionnaires developed and administered by ICMA. ICMA maintains databases with the result of these surveys. All survey responses are reviewed for errors. Extreme values are identified and investigated; logic checks are applied in the analysis of the results.

Government Definitions

A municipality, by census definition, is a "political subdivision within which a municipal corporation has been established to provide general local government for a specific population concentration in a defined area." This definition includes all active governmental units officially designated as cities, boroughs (except in Alaska), villages, or towns (except in Minnesota, New York, New England, and Wisconsin), and it generally includes all places incorporated under the procedures established by the several states.

Counties are the primary political administrative divisions of the state. In Louisiana these units are called parishes. Alaska has county-type governments called boroughs. There are certain unorganized areas of some states that are not included in the *Year Book* database and that have a county designation from the Census Bureau for strictly administrative purposes. These comprise 12 areas in Alaska, 2 areas in South Dakota, 5 areas in

Table 1   U.S. LOCAL GOVERNMENTS, 2002

Local governments	87,849
County	3,034
Municipal	19,431
Town or township	16,506
School district	13,522
Special district	35,356

Note: The Census Bureau updates the number of local governments every five years in the years ending in 2 and 7. The vast majority of municipal governments are under 2,500 in population and are not included in the ICMA database.

Rhode Island, 8 areas in Connecticut, and 1 area in Montana.[1]

According to the U.S. Bureau of the Census, in January 2002 there were 87,849 governments in the United States (Table 1).

Municipality Classification

Table 2 details the distribution of all municipalities of 2,500 and over in population by population, geographic region and division, metro status, and form of government.

Population   This edition of the *Year Book* generally uses the 2000 Census Bureau figures for placing local governments in the United States into population groups for tabular presentation. The population categories are self-explanatory.

Geographic Classification   Nine geographic divisions and four regions are used by the Bureau of the Census (Figure 1). The nine divisions are *New England*: Connecticut, Maine, Massachusetts, New Hampshire, Rhode Island, and Vermont; *Mid-Atlantic*: New Jersey, New York, and Pennsylvania; *East North-Central*: Illinois, Indiana, Michigan, Ohio, and Wisconsin; *West North-Central*: Iowa, Kansas, Minnesota, Missouri, Nebraska, North Dakota, and South Dakota; *South Atlantic*: Delaware, the District of Columbia, Florida, Georgia, Maryland, North Carolina, South Carolina, Virginia, and West Virginia; *East South-Central*: Alabama, Kentucky, Mississippi, and Tennessee; *West South-Central*: Arkansas, Louisiana, Oklahoma, and Texas; *Mountain*: Arizona, Colorado, Idaho, Montana, Nevada, New Mexico, Utah, and Wyoming; and *Pacific Coast*: Alaska, California, Hawaii, Oregon, and Washington.

The geographic regions are consolidations of states in divisions: *Northeast:* Connecticut, Maine, Massachusetts, New Hampshire, New Jersey, New York, Pennsylvania, Rhode Island, and Vermont; *North Central:* Illinois, Indiana, Iowa, Kansas, Michigan, Minnesota, Missouri, Nebraska, North Dakota, Ohio, South Dakota, and Wisconsin; *South:* Alabama, Arkansas, Delaware, the District of Columbia, Florida, Georgia, Kentucky, Louisiana, Maryland, Mississippi, North Carolina, Oklahoma, South Carolina, Tennessee, Texas, Virginia, and West Virginia; and *West:* Alaska, Arizona, California, Colorado, Hawaii, Idaho, Montana, Nevada, New Mexico, Oregon, Utah, Washington, and Wyoming.

Metro Status   Metro status refers to the status of a municipality within the context of the U.S. Office of Management and Budget (OMB) definition of a metropolitan area. A metropolitan area is typically "a core area containing a large popu-

Table 2   CUMULATIVE DISTRIBUTION OF U.S. MUNICIPALITIES WITH A POPULATION OF 2,500 AND OVER

Classification	Population								
	2,500 and over	5,000 and over	10,000 and over	25,000 and over	50,000 and over	100,000 and over	250,000 and over	500,000 and over	Over 1,000,000
Total, all cities	7,194	5,163	3,268	1,440	657	247	68	32	9
Population group									
Over 1,000,000	9	9	9	9	9	9	9	9	9
500,000–1,000,000	23	23	23	23	23	23	23	23	. . .¹
250,000–499,999	36	36	36	36	36	36	36	. . .	. . .
100,000–249,999	179	179	179	179	179	179	. . .	. . .	. . .
50,000–99,999	410	410	410	410	410	. . .	. . .	. . .	. . .
25,000–49,999	783	783	783	783	. . .	. . .	. . .	. . .	. . .
10,000–24,999	1,828	1,828	1,828	. . .	. . .	. . .	. . .	. . .	. . .
5,000–9,000	1,895	1,895	. . .	. . .	. . .	. . .	. . .	. . .	. . .
2,500–4,999	2,031	. . .	. . .	. . .	. . .	. . .	. . .	. . .	. . .
Geographic region									
Northeast	1,963	1,454	887	322	109	33	8	4	2
North-Central	2,105	1,452	915	371	147	44	14	5	1
South	2,052	1,390	843	354	176	77	23	13	3
West	1,074	867	623	393	225	93	23	10	3
Geographic division									
New England	729	554	352	137	46	12	1	1	
Mid-Atlantic	1,234	900	535	185	63	21	7	3	2
East North-Central	1,410	1,024	668	266	103	30	8	5	1
West North-Central	695	429	248	105	44	14	6	. . .	. . .
South Atlantic	879	600	386	168	86	34	9	4	. . .
East South-Central	441	308	169	56	22	12	3	2	. . .
West South-Central	732	481	287	130	68	31	11	7	3
Mountain	385	273	160	93	52	27	8	3	1
Pacific Coast	689	594	463	300	173	66	15	7	2
Metro status									
Central	540	539	539	504	360	175	65	31	9
Suburban	4,256	3,248	2,110	812	290	72	3	1	. . .
Independent	2,398	1,376	619	124	7	. . .	. . .	. . .	. . .
Form of government									
Mayor-council	3,131	2,007	1,175	486	235	98	39	21	6
Council-manager	3,520	2,756	1,869	902	409	144	27	10	3
Commission	143	110	71	25	8	5	2	1	. . .
Town meeting	338	235	107	6	. . .	. . .	. . .	. . .	. . .
Rep. town meeting	62	55	46	21	5	. . .	. . .	. . .	. . .

¹(. . .) indicates data not applicable or not reported.

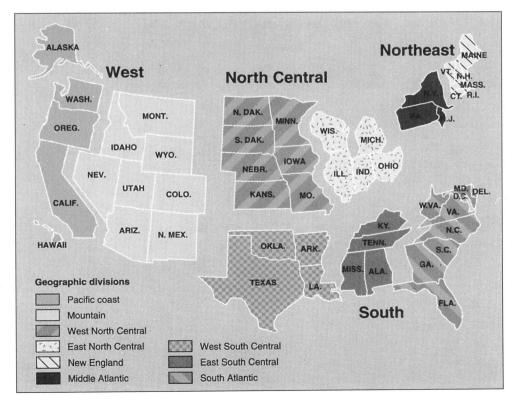

Figure 1   *U.S. Bureau of the Census geographic regions and divisions*

ALASKA

West   **North Central**   **Northeast**

WASH.   MONT.   N. DAK.   MINN.   MAINE   VT. N.H. MASS.

OREG.   IDAHO   WYO.   S. DAK.   WIS.   N.Y.   CT. R.I.

NEV.   UTAH   COLO.   NEBR.   IOWA   MICH.   PA.   N.J.

CALIF.   ARIZ.   N. MEX.   KANS.   MO.   ILL. IND. OHIO   MD. DEL. D.C.

HAWAII   OKLA.   ARK.   KY.   W.VA. VA.   N.C.

    TEXAS   LA.   TENN.   S.C.

    MISS. ALA.   GA.

    FLA.

South

Geographic divisions

- Pacific coast
- Mountain
- West North Central
- East North Central
- New England
- Middle Atlantic
- West South Central
- East South Central
- South Atlantic

lation nucleus, together with adjacent communities having a high degree of economic and social integration with that core."² There are three levels of classification: metropolitan statistical areas, consolidated metropolitan statistical areas, and primary metropolitan statistical areas.

The current standards require that each newly qualifying *metropolitan statistical area* (MSA) must include *either* at least one city with a population of 50,000 or more, *or* a Census Bureau–defined urbanized area of at least 50,000 *and* a total metropolitan population of at least 100,000 (75,000 in New England).³ The county (or counties) that contains the largest city becomes the central county (counties), along with any adjacent counties that have at least 50% of their population in the urbanized area surrounding the largest city in the MSA. Additional outlying counties are included in the MSA if they meet the specified requirement of commuting to the central counties and other selected requirements of metropolitan character (such as population density and percentage urban). In New England, the MSAs are defined in terms of cities and towns rather than counties.

An area that meets the requirements for an MSA and has a population of 1,000,000 or more may be recognized as a *consolidated metropolitan statistical area* (CMSA) if separate component areas can be identified within the entire area as meeting statistical criteria specified in the standards and if local opinion indicates support for the component areas. If recognized, the component areas are designated *primary metropolitan statistical areas* (PMSAs). Like the CMSAs that contain them, PMSAs comprise entire counties, except in New England, where they comprise cities and towns. If no PMSAs are recognized, the entire area is designated an MSA.

As of June 30, 1999, there were 258 MSAs and 18 CMSAs, comprising 73 PMSAs in the United States.

The largest city in each MSA/CMSA is designated a *central city*. Additional cities qualify if specified requirements are met for population size and commuting patterns. The title of each MSA consists of the names of up to three of its central cities and the name of each state into which the MSA extends. However, the name of a central city with fewer than 250,000 in population and less than one-third of the population of the area's largest city is not included in the MSA title unless local opinion supports its inclusion. Titles of PMSAs are also typically based on central city names but may consist of county names.

Form of Government Form of government relates primarily to the organization of the legislative and executive branches of municipalities and townships.

In the *mayor-council* form, an elected council or board serves as the legislative body. The head of government is the chief elected official, who is generally elected separately from the council and has significant administrative authority.

Many cities with a mayor-council form of government have a city administrator who is appointed by the elected representatives (council) and/or the chief elected official and is responsible to the elected officials. Appointed city administrators in mayor-council governments have limited administrative authority: they often do not directly appoint department heads or other key city personnel, and their responsibility for budget preparation and administration, although significant, is subordinate to that of the elected officials.

Under the *council-manager* form, the elected council or board and chief elected official (e.g., the mayor) are responsible for making policy. A professional administrator appointed by the council or board has full responsibility for the day-to-day operations of the government.

The *commission* form of government operates with an elected commission performing both legislative and executive functions, generally with departmental administration divided among the commissioners.

The *town meeting* form of government is a system in which all qualified voters of a municipality meet to make basic policy and elect officials to carry out the policies.

Under the *representative town meeting* form of government, the voters select a large number of citizens to represent them at the town meeting(s). All citizens can participate in the meeting(s), but only the representatives may vote.

County Classification

Counties are the primary political administrative divisions of the states. The county-type governments in Alaska are called boroughs. Table 3 details the distribution of counties throughout the nation, using the same geographic and population categories as Table 2.

Metro Status For counties, metro status refers to the status of a county within the context of the OMB definition of an MSA. "Metro" means that a county is located within an MSA; "nonmetro" indicates that it is located outside the boundaries of an MSA.

Counties that are located in an MSA are classified in a way similar to that for cities. *Central* counties are those in which central cities are located. *Suburban* counties are the other counties located within an MSA. Counties not located in an MSA are considered *independent*.

Table 3   CUMULATIVE DISTRIBUTION OF U.S. COUNTIES

Classification	All counties	Population								
		2,500 and over	5,000 and over	10,000 and over	25,000 and over	50,000 and over	100,000 and over	250,000 and over	500,000 and over	Over 1,000,000
Total, all counties	3,039	2,925	2,752	2,366	1,497	859	476	201	91	28
Population group										
Over 1,000,000	28	28	28	28	28	28	28	28	28	28
500,000–1,000,000	63	63	63	63	63	63	63	63	63	. . .[1]
250,000–499,999	110	110	110	110	110	110	110	110	. . .	. . .
100,000–249,999	275	275	275	275	275	275	275	. . .	. . .	. . .
50,000–99,999	383	383	383	383	383	383	. . .	. . .	. . .	. . .
25,000–49,999	638	638	638	638	638	. . .	. . .	. . .	. . .	. . .
10,000–24,999	869	869	869	869	. . .	. . .	. . .	. . .	. . .	. . .
5,000–9,999	386	386	386	. . .	. . .	. . .	. . .	. . .	. . .	. . .
2,500–4,999	173	173	. . .	. . .	. . .	. . .	. . .	. . .	. . .	. . .
Under 2,500	114	. . .	. . .	. . .	. . .	. . .	. . .	. . .	. . .	. . .
Geographic region										
Northeast	189	189	188	183	174	129	85	45	19	3
North-Central	1,054	1,007	914	747	445	229	125	45	19	7
South	1,372	1,346	1,301	1,152	684	365	178	66	28	7
West	424	383	349	284	194	136	88	45	25	11
Geographic division										
New England	45	45	45	43	40	24	14	6	2	. . .
Mid-Atlantic	144	144	143	140	134	105	71	39	17	3
East North-Central	437	436	433	407	298	165	94	33	15	5
West North-Central	617	571	481	340	147	64	31	12	4	2
South Atlantic	545	543	535	482	314	192	101	39	17	3
East South-Central	360	358	356	323	175	73	27	7	2	. . .
West South-Central	467	445	410	347	195	100	50	20	9	4
Mountain	276	245	215	159	93	54	32	14	7	2
Pacific Coast	148	138	134	125	101	82	56	31	18	9
Metro status										
Central	457	457	457	457	454	439	377	195	89	28
Suburban	341	339	338	331	283	177	68	6	2	. . .
Independent	2,241	2,129	1,957	1,578	760	243	31	. . .	. . .	. . .
Form of government										
County commission	2,188	2,085	1,919	1,580	886	404	174	59	24	4
Council-manager/administrator	372	366	364	350	288	213	143	69	36	14
Council–elected executive	479	474	469	436	323	242	159	73	31	10

[1](. . .) indicates data not applicable.

Form of Government For counties, form of government relates to the structural organization of the legislative and executive branches of counties; counties are classified as being with or without an administrator. There are three basic forms of county government: commission, council-administrator, and council–elected executive.

The *commission* form of government is characterized by a governing board that shares the administrative and, to an extent, legislative responsibilities with several independently elected functional officials.

In counties with the *council-administrator* form, an administrator is appointed by, and responsible to, the elected council to carry out directives.

The *council–elected executive* form features two branches of government: the executive and the legislative. The independently elected executive is considered the formal head of the county.

The use of varying types of local government is an institutional response to the needs, requirements, and articulated demands of citizens at the local level. Within each type of local government, structures are developed to provide adequate services. These structural adaptations are a partial result of the geographic location, population, metropolitan status, and form of government of the jurisdiction involved.

Consolidated Governments

The Bureau of the Census defines a consolidated government as a unit of local government in which the functions of a primary incorporated place and its county or minor civil division have merged. There are several categories of consolidations: city-county consolidations that operate primarily as cities (Table 4), consolidated cities (Table 5), and counties that maintain certain types of offices

Table 4 LEGALLY DESIGNATED CITY-COUNTY CONSOLIDATED GOVERNMENTS OPERATING AS CITIES

State	Consolidated government
Alaska.	City and Borough of Anchorage
	City and Borough of Juneau
	City and Borough of Sitka
California . . .	City and County of San Francisco
Colorado. . . .	City and County of Denver
Hawaii.	City and County of Honolulu
Kansas	Kansas City and Wyandotte County
Kentucky. . . .	City of Louisville and Jefferson County
Montana	Anaconda–Deer Lodge
	Butte–Silver Bow

Note: The Census Bureau counts Butte–Silver Bow also as a consolidated city.

Table 5 CONSOLIDATED CITIES

State	Consolidated city
Connecticut.	City of Milford
Florida.	City of Jacksonville
Georgia.	Athens–Clarke County
	City of Columbus
	Augusta–Richmond County
Indiana	City of Indianapolis
Tennessee	Nashville–Davidson

Note: The Census Bureau treats these as consolidated cities.

Table 6 COUNTIES THAT MAINTAIN OFFICES AS PART OF ANOTHER GOVERNMENT

State	County	Other government
Florida.	Duval	City of Jacksonville
Georgia	Clarke	Athens–Clarke County
	Muscogee	City of Columbus
	Richmond.	Augusta–Richmond County
Indiana	Marion	City of Indianapolis
Kentucky	Lexington–Fayette Urban County	Lexington–Fayette
Louisiana.	Parish of East Baton Rouge.	City of Baton Rouge
	Parish of Lafayette.	City of Lafayette
	Parish of Orleans	City of New Orleans
	Terrebonne Parish	City of Houma
Massachusetts	County of Nantucket	City of Nantucket
	County of Suffolk	City of Boston
New York.	County of Bronx	New York City
	County of Kings	New York City
	County of New York	New York City
	County of Queens	New York City
	County of Richmond	New York City
Pennsylvania.	County of Philadelphia	City of Philadelphia

but as part of another city or township government (Table 6). One city-county consolidation operates primarily as a county: the City and Borough of Yakutat in Alaska. In addition, the District of Columbia is counted by the Census Bureau as a city, a separate county area, and a separate state area. To avoid double counting in survey results, ICMA counts the District of Columbia only as a city.

Independent Cities

The Census Bureau defines independent cities as those operating outside of a county area and administering functions commonly performed by counties (Table 7). The bureau counts independent cities as counties. For survey research purposes, ICMA counts independent cities as municipal, not county governments.

USES OF STATISTICAL DATA

The Municipal Year Book uses primary and secondary data sources. ICMA collects and publishes the primary source data. Secondary source data are data collected by another organization. Most of the primary source data are collected through survey research. ICMA develops questionnaires on a variety of subjects during a given year and then pretests and refines them to increase the validity of each survey instrument. Once completed, the surveys are sent to officials in all cities above a given population level (e.g., 2,500 and above, 10,000 and above, etc.). For example, the city managers or chief administrative officers receive the *Organizational Structure and Decision Making* survey, and finance officers receive the *Police and Fire Personnel, Salaries, and Expenditures* survey.

ICMA conducts the city, county, and councils of government salary surveys and the *Police and Fire Personnel, Salaries, and Expenditures* survey every year. Other research projects are conducted every five years, and some are one-time efforts to provide information on subjects of current interest.

LIMITATIONS OF THE DATA

Regardless of the subject or type of data presented, data should be read cautiously. All policy,

Table 7 INDEPENDENT CITIES

State	Independent city
Maryland	Baltimore City
Missouri	St. Louis
Nevada	Carson City
Virginia.	Alexandria
Virginia.	Bristol
Virginia.	Buena Vista
Virginia.	Charlottesville
Virginia.	Chesapeake
Virginia.	Clifton Forge
Virginia.	Colonial Heights
Virginia.	Danville
Virginia.	Emporia
Virginia.	Fairfax
Virginia.	Falls Church
Virginia.	Franklin
Virginia.	Fredericksburg
Virginia.	Galax
Virginia.	Hampton
Virginia.	Harrisonburg
Virginia.	Hopewell
Virginia.	Lexington
Virginia.	Lynchburg
Virginia.	Manassas
Virginia.	Martinsville
Virginia.	Newport News
Virginia.	Norfolk
Virginia.	Norton
Virginia.	Petersburg
Virginia.	Poquoson
Virginia.	Portsmouth
Virginia.	Radford
Virginia.	Richmond
Virginia.	Roanoke
Virginia.	Salem
Virginia.	Staunton
Virginia.	Suffolk
Virginia.	Virginia Beach
Virginia.	Waynesboro
Virginia.	Williamsburg
Virginia.	Winchester

political, and social data have strengths and limitations. These factors should be considered in any analysis and application. Statistics are no magic guide to perfect understanding and decision making, but they can shed light on particular subjects and questions in lieu of haphazard and subjective information. They can clarify trends in policy expenditures, processes, and impacts and thus assist in evaluating the equity and efficiency of alternative courses of action. Statistical data are most valuable when one remembers their imperfections, both actual and potential, while drawing conclusions.

For example, readers should examine the response bias for each survey. Surveys may be sent to all municipalities above a certain population threshold, but not all of those surveys are necessarily returned. Jurisdictions that do not respond are rarely mirror images of those that do. ICMA reduces the severity of this problem by maximizing the opportunities to respond through second and (sometimes) third requests. But although this practice mitigates the problem, response bias invariably appears. Consequently, ICMA always includes a "Survey Response" table in each article that analyzes the results of a particular survey. This allows the reader to examine the patterns and degrees of response bias through a variety of demographic and structural variables.

Other possible problems can occur with survey data. Local governments have a variety of record-keeping systems. Therefore, some of the data (particularly those on expenditures) may lack uniformity. In addition, no matter how carefully a questionnaire is refined, problems such as divergent interpretations of directions, definitions, and specific questions invariably arise. However, when inconsistencies or apparently extreme data are reported, every attempt is made to verify these responses through follow-up telephone calls.

TYPES OF STATISTICS

There are basically two types of statistics: descriptive and inferential.

Descriptive

Most of the data presented in this volume are purely descriptive. Descriptive statistics summarize some characteristics of a group of numbers. A few numbers represent many. If someone wants to find out something about the age of a city's workforce, for example, it would be quite cumbersome to read a list of several hundred numbers (each representing the age of individual employees). It would be much easier to have a few summary descriptive statistics, such as the mean (average) or the range (the highest value minus the lowest value). These two "pieces" of information would not convey all the details of the entire data set, but they can help and are much more useful and understandable than complete numerical lists.

There are essentially two types of descriptive statistics: measures of central tendency and measures of dispersion.

Measures of Central Tendency These types of statistics indicate the most common or typical value of a data set. The most popular examples are the mean and median. The mean is simply the arithmetic average. It is calculated by summing the items in a data set and dividing by the total number of items. For example, given the salaries of $15,000, $20,000, $25,000, $30,000, and $35,000, the mean is $25,000 ($125,000 divided by 5).

The mean is the most widely used and intuitively obvious measure of central tendency. However, it is sensitive to extreme values. A few large or small numbers in a data set can produce a mean that is not representative of the "typical" value. Consider the example of the five salaries above. Suppose the highest value was not $35,000 but $135,000. The mean of the data set would now be $45,000 ($25,000 divided by 5). This figure, however, is not representative of this group of numbers because it is substantially greater than four of the five values and is $90,000 below the high score. A data set such as this is "positively skewed" (i.e., it has one or more extremely high scores). Under these circumstances (or when the data set is "negatively skewed" with extremely low scores), it is more appropriate to use the median as a measure of central tendency.

The median is the middle score of a data set that is arranged in order of increasing magnitude. Theoretically, it represents the point that is equivalent to the 50th percentile. For a data set with an odd number of items, the median has the same number of observations above and below it (e.g., the third value in a data set of 5 or the eighth value in a data set of 15). With an even number of cases, the median is the average of the middle two scores (e.g., the seventh and eighth values in a data set of 14). In the example of the five salaries used above, the median is $25,000 regardless of whether the largest score is $35,000 or $135,000. When the mean exceeds the median, the data set is positively skewed. If the median exceeds the mean, it is negatively skewed.

Measures of Dispersion This form of descriptive statistics indicates how widely scattered or spread out the numbers are in a data set. Some common measures of dispersion are the range and the interquartile range. The range is simply the highest value minus the lowest value. For the numbers 3, 7, 50, 80, and 100, the range is 97 (100 − 3 = 97). For the numbers 3, 7, 50, 80, and 1,000, it is 997 (1,000 − 3 = 997). Quartiles divide a data set into four equal parts similar to the way percentiles divide a data set into 100 equal parts. Consequently, the third quartile is equivalent to the 75th percentile, and the first quartile is equivalent to the 25th percentile. The interquartile range is the value of the third quartile minus the value of the first quartile.

Inferential

Inferential statistics permit the social and policy researcher to make inferences about whether a correlation exists between two (or more) variables in a population based on data from a sample. Specifically, inferential statistics provide the probability that the sample results could have occurred by chance if there were really no relationship between the variables in the population as a whole. If the probability of random occurrence is sufficiently low (below the researcher's preestablished significance level), then the null hypothesis—that there is no association between the variables—is rejected. This lends indirect support to the research hypothesis that a correlation does exist. If they can rule out chance factors (the null hypothesis), researchers conclude that they have found a "statistically significant" relationship between the two variables under examination.

Significance tests are those statistics that permit inferences about whether variables are correlated but provide nothing directly about the strength of such correlations. Measures of association, on the other hand, indicate how strong relationships are between variables. These statistics range from a high of +1.0 (for a perfect positive correlation), to zero (indicating no correlation), to a low of −1.0 (for a perfect negative correlation).

Some common significance tests are the chi square and difference-of-means tests. Some common measures of association are Yule's Q, Sommer's Gamma, Lambda, Cramer's V, Pearson's C, and the correlation coefficient. Anyone seeking further information on these tests and measures should consult any major statistics textbook.[4]

Inferential statistics are used less frequently in this volume than descriptive statistics. However, whenever possible, the data have been presented so that the user can calculate inferential statistics whenever appropriate.

SUMMARY

All social, political, and economic data are collected with imperfect techniques in an imperfect world. Therefore, users of such data should be continuously cognizant of the strengths and weaknesses of the information from which they are attempting to draw conclusions. Readers should note the limitations of the data published in this volume. Particular attention should be paid to the process of data collection and potential problems such as response bias.

---

[1]The terms *city* and *cities,* as used in this volume, refer to cities, villages, towns, townships, and boroughs.

[2]See census.gov/population/www/estimates/aboutmetro. html.

[3]The vast majority of the text describing metropolitan areas has been taken from the Web site cited in footnote 2.

[4]For additional information on statistics, see Tari Renner's *Statistics Unraveled: A Practical Guide to Using Data in Decision Making* (Washington, D.C.: ICMA, 1988).

A Management Trends and Issues

Local Government Employee Health Insurance Programs

Evelina R. Moulder
ICMA

Selected Findings

As one way to gain control over health care benefit costs, local governments are offering employees preventive programs, the most prevalent of which are fitness programs (42%), smoking cessation programs (35%), and programs to address obesity (33%).

More local governments reported that they offer PPO plans (74%) than reported HMO, POS, or indemnity plans.

Nearly two-thirds of local governments (62%) purchase health insurance independently rather than through an association/coalition (20%) or a state plan (11%).

By all accounts, the cost of health care benefits continues to increase for local governments, which typically offer such benefits to employees. In addition, benefits for retirees have often been negotiated through union contracts and are offered to many other employees as well. Some employers have taken steps to reduce the cost of health care benefits by strengthening preventive care programs and offering incentives to employees to stop smoking and take other steps to improve their overall health. A few creative approaches to benefits have been introduced that are tailored to individual needs and circumstances, such as offering plans with high deductibles. Because the cost of health care benefits is a critical issue for local governments, ICMA staff worked with the ICMA Health Care Advisory Group to develop a survey of local government employee health insurance programs. The survey was sponsored by CIGNA.

SURVEY METHODOLOGY

The survey was mailed to all municipalities with a population of 2,500 and above and to all counties with an elected executive or a chief appointed official (CAO). Table 1/1 shows the total recipients and the response rates by population and geographic division. The overall response rate of 28% was somewhat lower than anticipated, a fact that can probably be attributed to the length of the survey (six pages rather than four), the complexity of the survey, and the amount of information that the respondent had to obtain to complete the survey.

HEALTH INSURANCE BENEFITS

Although local governments are unable to offer salaries that compete with those in the private sector, the health insurance benefits often offset that disparity and thus are an important recruiting tool.

Virtually all local governments (99%) offer health insurance to employees (not shown). The few that do not are in the same population groups as those that reported similarly in ICMA's 2003

Table 1/1   SURVEY RESPONSE

Classification	No. of cities[1]/ counties surveyed (A)	Respondents No.	Respondents % of (A)
Total	8,013	2,243	28
Population group			
Over 1,000,000	33	13	39
500,000–1,000,000 ...	66	13	20
250,000–499,999	111	40	36
100,000–249,999	339	132	39
50,000–99,999	561	192	34
25,000–49,999	936	302	32
10,000–24,999	2,001	610	31
5,000–9,999	1,936	476	25
2,500–4,999	2,019	463	23
Under 2,500	11	2	18
Geographic division			
New England	739	146	20
Mid-Atlantic	1,287	222	17
East North-Central	1,518	446	29
West North-Central ...	764	272	36
South Atlantic	1,217	441	36
East South-Central ...	479	103	22
West South-Central ...	789	196	25
Mountain	453	161	36
Pacific Coast	767	256	33

[1]For a definition of terms, please see "Inside the *Year Book*," x.

health care survey.[1] When contacted in 2003, the local governments that did not offer insurance explained that they could not negotiate a reasonable rate because they had so few employees.

TOP THREE HEALTH CONCERNS

The cost of premiums is determined in part by the health issues that are present among an employee group. The top three health concerns reported by respondents to this survey were obesity/weight management, heart disease, and stress management (Table 1/2).

Generally, among the population groups and geographic divisions, between 40% and 50% reported obesity/weight management as the top concern (not shown). However, stress management was not reported as one of the top three concerns

by any respondents in local governments with a population 500,000 and above, even though it is overall one of the top concerns.

There are some interesting geographic variations. The highest percentage reporting smoking as a concern, for example, is in the East South-Central division, which includes Alabama, Kentucky, Mississippi, and Tennessee. This division also has the highest percentage (73%) reporting cancer as the number one concern, compared with 40% overall. This may reflect a relationship between smoking and cancer. Depression, although reported overall by only 169 local governments, shows noticeably higher percentages reporting in the Mountain and East South-Central divisions than in the other divisions. Hypertension is one of the primary concerns that respondents wrote in under "other."

Because many of the top concerns are related—especially with stress as a factor in obesity and smoking—these are probably important areas for further program development.

PROGRAMS TO ADDRESS HEALTH CONCERNS

With obesity/weight management, heart disease, and stress management identified as the top three concerns reported by respondents, it is noticeable that only 33% of local governments reported programs to address obesity, and even fewer (29%) have programs to reduce heart disease (Table 1/3). About half of the local governments surveyed either do not plan to introduce programs to address these concerns or are unsure as to whether they will. However, fitness programs were reported by the highest percentage of local governments (42%), and given that fitness helps manage obesity, there may be more attention being paid to obesity than the specific data show. Disease prevention programs are offered by 35% of local governments, which may address obesity as well. (Stress management was not covered in questions about programs to manage health concerns.)

Generally, the larger the local government, the more likely it is to offer any of these programs (not shown). The percentages reporting offering

Table 1/2   TOP THREE HEALTH CONCERNS

Health concern	Total reporting as one of the top three concerns (A)	#1 concern No. reporting	#1 concern % of (A)	#2 concern No. reporting	#2 concern % of (A)	#3 concern No. reporting	#3 concern % of (A)
Obesity/weight management	1,139	527	46	325	29	287	25
Heart disease	930	350	38	330	36	250	27
Stress management	852	388	46	233	27	231	27
Disease prevention	666	303	46	158	24	205	31
Smoking	623	240	39	198	32	185	30
Cancer	585	236	40	182	31	167	29
Diabetes	539	143	27	203	38	193	36
Low back pain	433	176	41	110	25	147	34
Nutrition	240	59	25	74	31	107	45
Depression	169	33	20	57	34	79	47
Asthma	25	7	28	9	36	9	36
At-risk pregnancies	21	11	52	5	24	5	24

Note: Percentages may exceed 100% because of rounding.

Table 1/3   PROGRAMS TO ADDRESS HEALTH CONCERNS

Health concern	Total reporting (A)	Program offered now No. (A)	Program offered now % of (A)	In next 12 months % of (A)	In 1–3 years % of (A)	In 3–5 years % of (A)	Do not plan to consider % of (A)	Not sure % of (A)
Obesity/weight . . . . management	1,780	594	33	12	7	1	18	29
Heart disease	1,623	464	29	10	6	1	21	34
Fitness	1,662	703	42	11	5	1	15	26
Disease prevention . . .	1,655	523	32	9	6	1	20	33
Smoking	1,744	601	35	12	6	1	19	28
Cancer	1,538	331	22	6	5	1	23	44
Diabetes	30	26	86	7	7	0	0	0
Low back pain	1,555	387	25	6	5	1	22	41
Nutrition	1,661	496	30	11	6	1	21	31
Depression	1,595	484	30	5	5	1	22	37
Asthma	1,531	291	19	3	3	1	30	44
At-risk pregnancies . . .	1,518	252	17	3	3	1	33	44

Note: Percentages may exceed 100% because of rounding.

Table 1/4   HEALTH INSURANCE BENEFITS

Type of plan	Current employee plans No. reporting (A)	Current employee plans % of (A)	Early retiree plans No. reporting (B)	Early retiree plans % of (B)	Retirees 65+ plans No. reporting (C)	Retirees 65+ plans % of (C)
Total	2,165	100	1,631	100	1,800	100
Medical						
Health maintenance organization (HMO)	855	40	449	28	438	24
Point of service (POS)	414	19	229	14	194	11
Preferred provider organization (PPO)	1,592	74	802	49	644	36
Indemnity	184	9	102	6	96	5
Health reimbursement arrangement (HRA)						
with underlying medical	126	6	36	2	29	2
Medicare Advantage	—	—	—	—	62	3
Medicare Supplement	—	—	—	—	286	16
Other						
Stand-alone HRA (without medical plan)[1]	—	—	6	*	10	1
Health savings account (HSA)[2]	219	10	50	3	—	—
Pharmacy	1,549	72	711	44	—	—
Medicare Part D Pharmacy—ER PDP[3]	—	—	—	—	286	16
Medicare Part D Pharmacy—Subsidy[3]	—	—	—	—	139	8
Dental	1,830	85	62	41	529	29
Employee assistance program (EAP)	1,229	57	216	13	129	7
Other	451	21	145	9	137	8
Do not offer benefits	—	—	575	35	735	41

* = Less than 0.5%.
[1]A stand-alone HRA is an account funded by the employer for the employee's health care expenses during retirement. An employer can elect to contribute funds before, upon, or after retirement, and in addition to or in lieu of coverage.
[2]An HSA is an account funded by the employee for future health care expenses. The employee can choose the fund for current health expenses or allow the fund to grow.
[3]Medicare Part D Pharmacy—ER PDP (Emergency Room Prescription Drug Plan)/Subsidy—Supplemental Pharmacy program is available to Medicare beneficiaries.

these programs typically decrease among smaller population groups, although this decrease is not as pronounced with fitness programs.

Geographically, the local governments in the Pacific Coast division generally show the highest percentages reporting programs to address the various health concerns (not shown). Curiously, even though smoking is a top concern in the East South-Central division, responses indicate that the localities in this division are the least likely to offer a program to address this issue. On the other hand, 35% of local governments overall are offering programs to help employees stop smoking. According to an article in the *New York Times* from October 26, 2007,

> Many businesses are seeking to reduce their medical bills by paying for programs to help employees stop smoking. A decade ago, such programs were rare. But recent surveys indicate that one-third of companies with at least 200 workers now offer smoking cessation as part of their employee benefits package. Among the nation's biggest companies, the number may be nearly two-thirds of employers.[2]

HEALTH INSURANCE BENEFITS

The survey covered plans for current employees, early retirees, and retirees age 65 and over. The plans for each are shown and discussed separately below.

Current Employee Plans
Among the major types of medical plans—health maintenance organization (HMO), point of service (POS), preferred provider organization (PPO), and indemnity—the PPO plan is clearly the option offered by the highest percentage of local governments reporting (74%), followed by HMOs (40%) (Table 1/4).

When the availability of employee plans is viewed by population groups, PPOs are offered by more than 80% of jurisdictions with a population above 50,000 (not shown). HMOs are offered by about 75% and POS plans are offered by about 50% of governments with a population of 500,000 and over. The two counties reporting with a population under 2,500 indicated that only HMOs are offered. The percentage reporting any plan decreases with population size.

As for the geographic divisions, the availability of PPOs is generally high across all the divisions except New England, and was noted by more than 80% of local governments in the Pacific Coast, East South-Central, and West South-Central divisions (not shown). The highest percentage of jurisdictions offering an HMO is in the Pacific Coast division (66%). Among respondents in the New England division, a higher percentage (59%) offer HMOs than offer PPO or POS plans (49% and 48%, respectively). Since local governments in New England tend to be smaller in population than those in other geographic divisions, there may be some economies of scale with HMOs to be gained by this group. These localities also show the highest percentage reporting indemnity plans (24%).

Dental plans, reported by 85% overall, were reported by 100% of all local governments with a population of 250,000 and over. In general, dental plans were reported by higher percentages of local governments across all population groups than were pharmacy plans, reported by 72% overall.

Under "other," quite a few respondents wrote in vision (eye care) plans, and a few wrote in flexible spending accounts.

Early Retiree Plans
Overall, 35% of local governments do not offer early retiree health benefits (Table 1/4), and smaller local governments show the highest percentages of jurisdictions reporting this fact (not shown): among local governments with a population under 10,000, 50% or more do not offer early retiree plans. Among the larger local governments, the majority offer several plans—HMO, POS, PPO; however, PPO plans are reported by the highest percentage overall (49%), which is not surprising because this is the type of plan most commonly offered to local government employees.

As with the plans offered for current employees, a higher percentage of local governments (49%) reported offering early retirees a PPO plan than any other type of medical health benefit; the local governments in the Pacific Coast division show the highest percentage (49%) offering an HMO to early retirees; and 60% of these Pacific Coast localities offer early retirees a PPO (not shown). Overall, slightly more than 40% of all respondents reported offering early retirees a dental plan and 44% offer a pharmacy plan.

Retiree Age 65+ Plans
Although a majority of local governments offer insurance benefits to retirees (Table 1/4), smaller local governments and those in the East South-Central and Mountain divisions show the highest percentages that do not offer retiree health benefits (not shown).

PPO plans are offered to retirees by the highest percentage of local government respondents (36%), followed by HMO plans at 24%. Although overall only 5% of those reporting offer indemnity plans to retirees, local governments in the New England and Mid-Atlantic divisions show the highest percentages in this regard (16% and 13%, respectively) (not shown). Indemnity plans tend to be the most expensive, and it may be that they are offered as part of a contractual agreement.

Under "other," some respondents wrote in "COBRA" (Consolidated Omnibus Budget Reconciliation Act), which is not a plan but a legal obligation. "Vision" appeared frequently.

PAYING FOR RETIREE HEALTH CARE BENEFITS

Of the 1,378 providing information on payment methods for retiree health benefits, 25% reported that these benefits are fully paid by the local government; 41% reported that they are partially paid by the local government, and 54% reported that they are available to retirees at cost (Figure 1/1). Because these percentages exceed 100%, it is clear that many local governments have more than one

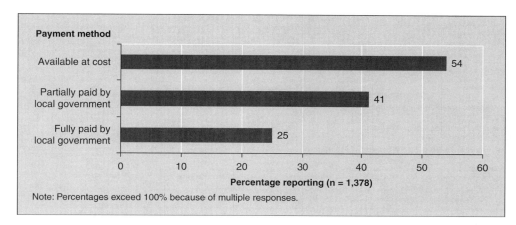

Figure 1/1 *Payment method for retiree health benefits*

kind of arrangement. Some arrangements may be contractual; others may be related to tenure or position. Population does not seem to be a factor in determining how benefits are paid for, although among the 13 local government respondents in the population group 500,000–1,000,000, only one reported that the benefits are fully paid by the local government (not shown).

Within these statistics there are some interesting geographic variations (not shown). For instance, 61% of local governments in the Mid-Atlantic division reported paying in full for the retiree benefits, compared with 25% overall. By contrast, the Mountain division shows one of the lowest percentages reporting that the local government pays for benefits (12%); however, this division also shows 80% reporting that benefits are available to retirees at cost, compared with 54% overall. The West North-Central division shows the next highest percentage reporting that retiree benefits are available at cost (79%) and the lowest percentage reporting that they are paid in full by the local government (8%).

Health Savings Accounts and Health Reimbursement Arrangements
Table 1/4 shows that only 219 local governments reported offering a health savings account (HSA), and only 126 reported offering a health reimbursement arrangement (HRA) with an underlying medical plan to current employees. Apart from the fact that these plans have distinct requirements, the HRA is paid for by the employer only, whereas the HSA is funded with employee contributions. As shown in Table 1/5, the percentage of those local governments indicating that over the next five years they might consider offering an HSA with

a high deductible is higher than that of those who reported the possible consideration of an HRA.

Additional Programs and Product Offerings
Among the various programs listed in Table 1/6, health risk assessment questionnaires and disease management programs are offered by the highest percentages of those reporting (28% and 23%, respectively).

Health risk assessment questionnaires are offered by the majority of local governments with a population of 250,000 and over, and by close to 40% of localities in the New England and Pacific Coast divisions (not shown). Disease management programs also are offered by the majority of local governments with a population of 250,000 and over, as well as by nearly 50% of local governments with a population of 50,000–249,999. The percentage offering disease management programs decreases consistently among smaller local governments. More than half of the geographic divisions show slightly above-average percentages reporting such programs, with the highest percentage (36%) in the South Atlantic division.

Although the overall number of local governments reporting the use of health coaches is low (277), close to 50% of those in the 250,000–1,000,000 population range reported the use of health coaches (not shown).

The two programs that the highest percentages of local governments are considering offering over the next five years are the online health plan enrollment for employees and rewards for employees engaging in wellness or disease prevention programs (21% each). Online enrollment reduces some of the manual work involved in processing applications, presumably reducing the cost of

Table 1/5   HSA AND HRA PLANS

		Program not currently offered but may be considered				
Plan/product	Total reporting (A)	In next 12 months % of (A)	In 1–3 years % of (A)	In 3–5 years % of (A)	Do not plan to consider % of (A)	Not sure % of (A)
HSA with high deductible	1,607	7	15	5	34	39
HRA *with* underlying medical plan	1,549	6	10	4	37	44
Stand-alone HRA *without* medical plan	1,504	3	5	1	46	45

Note: Percentages may exceed 100% because of rounding.

Table 1/6 ADDITIONAL PROGRAMS AND PRODUCT OFFERINGS

Plan/product	Total reporting (A)	Program offered now		Program not currently offered but may be considered				
		No.	% of (A)	In next 12 months % of (A)	In 1–3 years % of (A)	In 3–5 years % of (A)	Do not plan to consider % of (A)	Not sure % of (A)
Affordable but limited benefits plan for employees not eligible for existing plans	1,684	52	3	1	2	1	66	26
Onsite clinic	1,724	59	3	1	1	1	77	16
Disease *management* programs	1,742	398	23	6	6	2	34	30
Health adviser/coach	1,712	277	16	5	5	2	44	29
Online health plan enrollment for employees	1,719	288	17	7	11	3	33	30
Health risk assessment questionnaire	1,792	509	28	9	7	2	26	29
Rewards to employees for using high-quality, cost-efficient providers	1,724	113	7	4	7	2	37	43
Rewards to employees for engaging in wellness or disease *prevention* programs ...	1,751	313	18	9	9	3	28	34
Online tools to help employees select a plan and allow them to enroll online	1,741	202	12	6	11	3	37	32
Online tools to allow employees to customize their benefits	1,727	67	4	3	6	3	48	36

Note: Percentages may exceed 100% because of rounding.

premiums. Rewards for employees who are engaged in wellness or disease prevention programs may give local governments the greatest financial benefit because a reduction in hospitalizations should, at a minimum, produce a smaller percentage of increase in premiums over time.

Of the 509 respondents that reported the use of a health risk assessment questionnaire, 468 answered the question about whether they use incentives to encourage employees to complete it, and of those, 40% reported that they do (not shown). The assessments can be used to educate employees about their health, and to develop or recommend preventive programs to meet their needs.

GASB REGULATIONS

Retiree health care benefits represent a significant expenditure over time. The Government Accounting Standards Board (GASB), which establishes accounting standards for state and local governments, requires that local governments

disclose the costs of unfunded nonpension retiree benefits. The majority of respondents to this survey (68%) reported familiarity with GASB regulations (Table 1/7). Not surprisingly, the larger local governments show higher percentages reporting familiarity than do the smaller ones, but even among smaller local governments at least 62% are familiar with GASB. Among the geographic divisions, local governments in New England reported the highest percentage (84%) having familiarity with GASB regulations.

Level of GASB liability
Respondents were asked about their local government's likely level of GASB liability—that is, the level at which the government is responsible for unfunded nonpension retiree benefits. Of the 1,412 who answered the question, 44% said the likely level was less than $10 million, 15% said $10 million to $100 million, 3% said more than $100 million, nearly 26% were unsure, and 12% indicated that GASB does not apply (not shown). Not sur-

Table 1/7 FAMILIARITY WITH GASB REGULATIONS

Classification	No. reporting (A)	Yes	
		No.	% of (A)
Total	2,118	1,432	68
Population group			
Over 1,000,000	13	12	92
500,000–1,000,000 ...	13	12	92
250,000–499,999	39	34	87
100,000–249,999	128	96	75
50,000–99,999	182	130	71
25,000–49,999	282	192	68
10,000–24,999	577	407	71
5,000–9,999	458	283	62
2,500–4,999	424	266	63
Under 2,500	2	0	0
Geographic division			
New England	139	116	84
Mid-Atlantic	210	131	62
East North-Central ...	422	296	70
West North-Central ...	259	167	65
South Atlantic	410	281	69
East South-Central ...	98	54	55
West South-Central ..	184	119	65
Mountain	153	94	61
Pacific Coast	243	174	72

Table 1/8 APPROACHES TO MANAGING GASB LIABILITY

Health concern	Total reporting (A)	Offer now		Program not currently offered but may be considered				
		No.	% of (A)	In next 12 months % of (A)	In 1–3 years % of (A)	In 3–5 years % of (A)	Do not plan to consider % of (A)	Not sure % of (A)
Discontinue early retiree medical benefits for								
New hires	935	75	8	5	5	3	48	32
Current employees	834	45	5	2	2	2	57	33
Current retirees	815	32	4	1	1	1	61	33
Discontinue 65+ retiree medical benefits for								
New hires	1,075	65	6	5	4	2	53	31
Current employees	737	45	6	2	3	2	56	32
Current retirees	717	38	5	1	1	1	60	32
Substitute current retiree plan with voluntary plan can access through the local government for								
New hires	1,119	46	4	3	3	1	52	37
Current employees	994	36	4	2	3	1	53	37
Current retirees	985	35	4	2	2	1	56	36
Funding an HRA or HSA for								
New hires	1,154	97	8	7	8	4	38	35
Current employees	1,038	84	8	7	9	4	38	35
Current retirees	1,004	27	3	4	5	2	51	36
Reduce retiree benefits (e.g., by moving to Medicare Advantage) for								
New hires	1,106	44	4	4	4	1	46	41
Current employees	1,003	38	4	3	4	1	47	41
Current retirees	991	37	4	2	3	1	49	41
Health coaching for current employees	1,141	131	12	5	5	2	38	39
Prefund retiree medical liability	1,143	67	6	6	6	3	40	40

Note: Percentages may exceed 100% because of rounding.

prisingly, population size is related to the amount of estimated liability: localities with higher populations reported higher liability, which is probably attributable to the higher number of employees and retirees in larger local governments.

Approaches to Managing Liability

Table 1/8 presents various programs that can help local governments manage their liability for retiree health benefits. The vast majority of local governments do not have any of these programs in place, and apart from funding an HSA or HRA for new hires or current employees, offering health coaching for current employees, and prefunding retiree medical liability (as well as four other options that were less likely to be considered), the majority have no plans to consider any of them. It is noteworthy, however, that although only 67 local governments reported that they currently prefund retiree medical liability, 164 reported that they will consider it at some point in the next five years.

When the responses are examined by population group and geographic division, some interesting variations are evident. Thirteen percent of local governments with a population of 500,000 and greater indicated that they plan to consider reducing the retiree benefits for current employees over the next 1–3 years, compared with 4% overall considering this change (not shown). Nine percent in the Mid-Atlantic division also reported planning to consider this option within 1–3 years. Some of the larger local governments are also considering reducing benefits for current retirees in 1–3 years.

Prefunding Retiree Liability

As Table 1/9 shows, a majority of local governments are reportedly unsure about how they can prefund retiree liability. Among the options, a VEBA—Voluntary Employees' Beneficiary Association—is the choice indicated by the highest percentage, albeit a small one. As described on the Internal Revenue Service's Web site, VEBAs are trusts that are exempt from tax under the provisions of IRC [Internal Revenue Code] section 501(c)(9). A VEBA is a "welfare benefit fund . . . through which the employer provides welfare benefits to employees and their beneficiaries. While welfare benefit funds can also be taxable trusts, most welfare benefit funds apply for exempt status as VEBAs in order to reduce or eliminate income taxes at the trust level. . . . The most common types of welfare benefits are medical, dental, disability, severance and life insurance benefits."[3]

Another option, an Integral Part Trust, is a tax-exempt vehicle that holds employer and employee assets that are used to provide health care benefits to employees.[4] And a third option is other post-employment benefits (OPEB) bonds, which are bonds sold to fund a local government's liability for unfunded retiree health benefits.

Respondents had an opportunity to write in "other" types of funding vehicles they might use. Although more than 600 checked "other," only 21 actually described what that other might be. A few wrote in "cash," and one or two respondents wrote in "fund" or "trust."

Table 1/9   OPTIONS FOR PREFUNDING RETIREE LIABILITY

Prefunding vehicle	No. reporting (A)	Definitely would use % of (A)	Probably would use % of (A)	Probably would not use % of (A)	Definitely would not use % of (A)	Not sure % of (A)
Voluntary Employees' Beneficiary Association (VEBA)	818	6	8	6	13	67
Integral Part Trust	814	3	8	7	14	69
Other post-employment benefits (OPEB) bonds	805	1	4	9	18	68

Note: Percentages may exceed 100% because of rounding.

DECISION-MAKING AUTHORITY FOR HEALTH BENEFIT SELECTION

Overall, the highest percentage of respondents reporting on who makes the final decision when selecting health plans indicated that the selection is made by an elected official (53%), followed by the CAO/manager (42%) (Figure 1/2).

Larger local governments were more likely than smaller ones to report the human resource (HR) manager as the decision maker (not shown). Local governments in the Pacific Coast (21%) and Mountain (23%) divisions also show higher percentages reporting the HR manager as the decision maker.

PURCHASING OPTIONS

The majority of local government respondents (62%) purchase health insurance independently

rather than through an association/coalition (20%) or a state plan (11%) (Table 1/10). This is true regardless of population size, but there are noteworthy variations among the geographic divisions.

The majority of New England local governments reported purchasing through an association/coalition, an approach that is used by more than 50% of reporting jurisdictions only in the New England division. The Pacific Coast division shows 35% purchasing independently (the lowest percentage using that method), 28% purchasing through a coalition, and 30% purchasing through a state plan. Local governments in California, which is in that division, show a comparatively high number purchasing through the state plan (CALPERS), as can be seen on Table 1/11, which presents the number of responding local governments in each state that reported purchasing through the state plan.

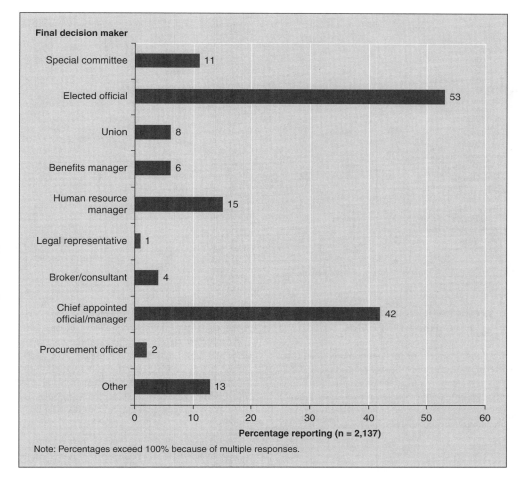

Final decision maker

	Percentage reporting (n = 2,137)
Special committee	11
Elected official	53
Union	8
Benefits manager	6
Human resource manager	15
Legal representative	1
Broker/consultant	4
Chief appointed official/manager	42
Procurement officer	2
Other	13

Note: Percentages exceed 100% because of multiple responses.

Figure 1/2   *Entity that makes the final health plan decision*

Table 1/10   METHOD OF PURCHASING HEALTH INSURANCE

Classification	No. reporting (A)	Independently		Through an association/ coalition		Through the state plan		Other	
		No.	% of (A)	No.	% of (A)	No.	% of (A)	No.	% of (A)
Total	2,148	1,336	62	437	20	226	11	149	7
Population group									
Over 1,000,000	13	11	85	0	0	0	0	2	15
500,000–1,000,000	13	13	100	0	0	0	0	0	0
250,000–499,999	39	32	82	1	3	1	3	5	13
100,000–249,999	129	101	78	8	6	10	8	10	8
50,000–99,999	185	122	66	16	9	23	12	24	13
25,000–49,999	290	193	67	50	17	32	11	15	5
10,000–24,999	582	359	62	133	23	58	10	32	6
5,000–9,999	463	263	57	119	26	46	10	35	8
2,500–4,999	432	241	56	109	25	56	13	26	6
Under 2,500	2	1	50	1	50	0	0	0	0
Geographic division									
New England	141	54	38	79	56	2	1	6	4
Mid-Atlantic	213	104	49	57	27	32	15	20	9
East North-Central	428	279	65	83	19	40	9	26	6
West North-Central	262	205	78	40	15	7	3	10	4
South Atlantic	429	303	71	58	14	44	10	24	6
East South-Central	92	63	69	4	4	13	14	12	13
West South-Central	188	139	74	24	13	7	4	18	10
Mountain	153	104	68	25	16	8	5	16	11
Pacific Coast	242	85	35	67	28	73	30	17	7

Note: Percentages may not total 100% because of rounding.

Table 1/11   RESPONDING LOCAL GOVERNMENTS THAT PURCHASE THROUGH THE STATE PLAN, SHOWN BY STATE

State	Number of local governments purchasing through state plan
Alabama	9
Alaska	1
Arkansas	1
California	**71**
Delaware	2
Georgia	1
Hawaii	1
Illinois	10
Kansas	3
Maine	2
Michigan	6
New Jersey	19
New Mexico	7
New York	13
North Carolina	3
North Dakota	4
Oklahoma	2
South Carolina	15
Tennessee	4
Texas	4
Utah	1
Virginia	21
West Virginia	2
Wisconsin	24

Table 1/12   SELF-FUNDED OR FULLY INSURED HEALTH PLANS

Classification	No. reporting (A)	Self-funded		Fully insured		Some of each		Not sure	
		No.	% of (A)	No.	% of (A)	No.	% of (A)	No.	% of (A)
Total	2,144	467	22	1,340	63	303	14	34	1
Population group									
Over 1,000,000	13	4	31	4	31	5	39	0	0
500,000–1,000,000	13	4	31	2	15	7	54	0	0
250,000–499,999	39	17	44	15	39	7	18	0	0
100,000–249,999	130	65	50	46	35	19	15	0	0
50,000–99,999	182	82	45	74	41	26	14	0	0
25,000–49,999	288	97	34	166	58	24	8	1	*
10,000–24,999	585	123	21	361	62	92	16	9	2
5,000–9,999	457	44	10	326	71	78	17	9	2
2,500–4,999	435	31	7	345	79	44	10	15	3
Under 2,500	2	0	0	1	50	1	50	0	0
Geographic division									
New England	139	28	20	83	60	25	18	3	2
Mid-Atlantic	206	36	18	139	68	28	14	3	2
East North-Central	425	103	24	253	60	64	15	5	1
West North-Central	263	50	19	158	60	49	19	6	2
South Atlantic	427	118	28	265	62	38	9	6	1
East South-Central	99	29	29	65	66	4	4	1	1
West South-Central	191	51	27	116	61	19	10	5	3
Mountain	155	36	23	76	49	41	27	2	1
Pacific Coast	239	16	7	185	77	35	15	3	1

Note: Percentages may not total 100% because of rounding.
* = Less than 0.5%.

SELF-FUNDED OR FULLY INSURED HEALTH PLANS

Sixty-three percent of local governments reported offering fully insured health plans (Table 1/12). This percentage is almost identical to the percentage reported in ICMA's 2003 employee benefit health care survey.[5] Some of the larger local governments show a greater tendency to have a combination of self-funded and fully insured plans, as does one county that reported with a population under 2,500.

Arrayed by geographic division, the responses show that no more than approximately 30% of localities in any division reported self-funded health insurance, whereas 60% or more in all divisions except the Mountain division reported being fully insured; the Mountain division shows 49% to be fully insured.

SUMMARY

The challenges that local governments face in paying for health care benefits for employees mirror those faced by private sector and nonprofit firms. Contractual agreements with unions sometimes limit flexibility for a period of time, but there are steps that local governments can take to reduce the costs. Whether by implementing preventive programs, cost sharing, or a combination of options, local governments can gain some control. In general, the greater the number of employees covered by a plan, the greater the leverage the buyer has in negotiating costs. By purchasing through the state employees' plan or by forming purchasing consortia, local governments have an opportunity to negotiate a better rate than they do as single entities. Engaging employees in preventive programs also holds promise, not only in reducing costs but also in increasing employee longevity.

[1] Evelina R. Moulder, "Local Government Health Care Plans: Customers, Costs, and Options for the Future," in *The Municipal Year Book 2004* (Washington, D.C.: ICMA, 2004), 27.

[2] Matt Freudenheim, "Seeking Savings, Employers Help Smokers Quit," *New York Times,* October 26, 2007, A1, available at nytimes.com/2007/10/26/business/26smoking.html?_r=1&hp&oref=slogin.

[3] Internal Revenue Service, "New Vehicle Dealership Audit Technique Guide 2004—Chapter 13: Voluntary Employees' Benefit Associations (12-2004)," available at irs.gov/businesses/corporations/article/0,,id=137741,00.html.

[4] *Employee Benefit Plan Review* 58, no. 6 (December 2003): 24.

[5] Moulder, "Local Government Health Care Plans," 29, 30.

^A2

Cooperation and Conflict in Governmental Decision Making in Mid-Sized U.S. Cities

Karl Nollenberger
Illinois Institute of Technology

Selected Findings

Form of government is the only statistically significant factor to account for levels of conflict and cooperation in the decision-making process.

Both council-manager cities and mayor-council cities that have a professional chief administrative officer (CAO) are more likely to have less conflict and more cooperation than mayor-council cities without a CAO.

The process of decision making in local government can have a significant impact on the substance of the final decision that emerges. This process is often defined by the levels of conflict and cooperation that accompany it. Conflict results from negative interactions, which include blocking behavior when some participants seek to impose their preferences on others. Alternatively, cooperation means positive interactions or active contributions that strive to take participants' preferences into account. However, the absence of conflict does not necessarily mean the presence of cooperation, nor does the absence of cooperation necessarily mean the presence of conflict.

Form of government—specifically, the roles and responsibilities of officials—has been identified as one of the factors predictive of conflict and cooperation in the decision-making process. Other factors that have been identified include (1) population size of the city, (2) location of city (stand-alone urban or suburban), (3) fiscal condition of the city, (4) socioeconomic conditions in the community, and (5) methodology of council elections. In an effort to identify those factors that have the most influence in this regard, this article focuses on mid-sized cities in the United States to examine the relationship between patterns of conflict and cooperation in the governmental decision-making process.

THE IMPORTANCE OF MID-SIZED CITIES

In the public administration and political science communities, relatively little attention has been paid to the study of mid-sized cities in the United States—those cities that are between 40,000 and 250,000 in population. Larger cities have received much more attention and analysis, and many of the findings that have emerged from the studies of larger cities have been applied to mid-sized cities without regard for how size affects city governance. Thus, to set the stage for an analysis of cooperation and conflict within the decision-making process, it is first necessary to recognize the unique aspects of local government in mid-sized cities.

Despite the fact that mid-sized cities are the centers of urban growth in the United States, "the medium-sized civil community has been substantially neglected as a focus of study. This neglect is all the more a problem in light of the statistical findings on the optimal size city, which suggests that cities in this size range achieve optimum performance on most measures."[1]

The mid-sized city can be the center of a hinterland or it can be part of a larger metropolitan area. It has an industrial base of its own, with each individual enterprise having importance to the community, and it has the ability to develop a cultural life of its own, such as art museums and theater. At around 40,000 people, a community's governmental institutions become professionalized. Up to around 250,000 people, everyone in the community knows someone who knows someone who is actively involved in local government decision making. While these localities are too big for community-wide face-to-face relationships, they are small enough to allow people to have direct relationships with the actors in the community affairs arena. And while the governmental institutions are large enough to be complex and to have specialists in management, they are small enough to make it incumbent upon those specialists to deal directly with the public rather than hide behind a bureaucracy. Further, the civil community in this population range still relies on volunteer services, so there is a unique lay-professional relationship in the governmental sphere. In short, civil communities of 40,000–250,000 "are large enough to be functional, given the demands for services placed upon them today, yet small enough to be democratic in the sense of offering significant possibilities for meaningful political communication and participation."[2]

LEADERSHIP AND MANAGEMENT IN LOCAL GOVERNMENT

"Leadership is one of the world's oldest preoccupations. The understanding of leadership has figured strongly in the quest for knowledge."[3] Management, by comparison, traces its roots to the Industrial Revolution, when it became necessary to organize (manage) resources for the production of an end product. The boundary between leadership and management has been the subject of much discussion. While there are some clear distinctions between the two functions, John W. Gardner, founder of Common Cause and one of the nation's foremost advocates for social action, concluded that "every time I come across first-class managers they turn out to have quite a lot of leader in them."[4]

The multitude of jurisdictions and the diverse settings that exist in American culture have had a significant impact on the patterns of leadership and management that are found in local government today. City governments in the United States operate under one of five types of governmental structure: weak mayor-council, strong mayor-council, commission, town meeting, or council-manager. The weak mayor-council form tends to be found primarily in small jurisdictions—those with populations of less than 5,000—while the commission and town meeting forms are infrequently found in cities today. The two primary forms of government for cities over 50,000 are the strong mayor-council and the council-manager.

Because the complexity of urban issues in the 21st century has challenged the traditional concepts of leadership and management in local government, it is important to understand the roles that elected officials and professionals play in this arena.

Leadership in Strong Mayor-Council Government

In the literature reviewing the strong mayor-council form of government, the acquisition and use of power is seen as the dominant feature of the mayor's role. J. L. Pressman's 1972 research on the city of Oakland is often regarded as a basis for measuring mayoral leadership. The research was done at the time of the "urban crisis," when mayoral leadership was widely heralded as a way to address the crisis because, although few mayors have *all* the resources necessary to deal with the tasks facing them, an effective mayor can use the brokerage function to accumulate influence and power. Pressman outlined seven resources that a successful mayor would be able to call upon:

- Sufficient city government finances and staff
- City jurisdiction in social program areas, such as education, housing, redevelopment, and job training
- Mayoral jurisdiction within city government in these social program areas.
- Sufficient salary to enable the mayor to spend full time on the job
- Sufficient staff support for policy planning, speech writing, intergovernmental relations, and political work
- Ready vehicles for publicity, such as friendly newspapers or television stations
- Politically oriented groups that could be mobilized to help achieve particular goals.[5]

Pressman also acknowledged that in addition to these resources, the mayor's personality is a potential source of influence.

Apart from the fact that the personal attributes (experience, financial support, time and energy commitment, and media savvy) of the individual in office can affect his or her leadership strengths, James Svara suggests that the ideal mayor in the strong mayor-council form of government operates in the style of an entrepreneur or innovator.[6] Using a power-oriented approach, this mayor looks for creative solutions and accumulates resources to build coalitions and gain leverage. The resources are both formal (e.g., appointment of department heads, development of the budget, direction of departments, veto authority) and informal (e.g., support of the political party or community elite, strong popular backing, private backers indebted to the mayor for various reasons). As it happens, however, trends in the political system—for example, a decrease in political party influence, a splintering of the community elite, increases in interest groups, the diversity of council members, implementation of civil service, purchasing reforms, and court actions on hiring—have reduced many of these informal resources.

Nevertheless, Rob Gurwitt suggests that the appeal of the strong mayor form of government has brought the age of municipal reform, as it was known in the 20th century, to an end.[7] The reason is pure politics and the demand for more of it. According to Gurwitt, the issue of responsiveness is more important today than are the issues of economy and efficiency, which make up the foundation of the council-manager form of government. He posits that the strong mayor form facilitates professional management as well as responsiveness because in many cases, the strong mayor city has a professional administrator reporting to the mayor.

The strong mayor form with a professional chief administrative officer (CAO) has not been the subject of much research to date, despite the fact that in 2002, 39% of the mayor-council cities over 50,000 in population reported the existence of a CAO.[8] Regardless of the legal standing of the CAO position, the role of the CAO in a strong mayor city largely depends on the appointing and confirmation power of the mayor and on the CAO's relationship with the mayor, as well as on the environment in the community.

Leadership in Council-Manager Government

The role of the mayor in the council-manager plan requires a rethinking of the standard assumptions of that role. In contrasting mayor-council government to council-manager government, Chet Newland makes three main distinctions:

1. Mayor-council government emphasizes separation of powers with the focus on mayoral leadership, and administration is more fragmented and ad hoc. Council-manager government facilitates more collaborative civic authority, combined with coordinated, institutionalized administration.
2. Transactional politics is the ideal of the mayor-council form, facilitating brokerage among different interests. Transformational politics is the ideal of the council-manager form, seeking a collaborative, community-wide orientation.
3. Politically sensitive administration is the ideal in the mayor-council form with non-routinization to facilitate responsiveness. Professionally expert administration is the ideal in council-manager government, with neutrally equal access and responsiveness.[9]

In the strong mayor form of government, the separation of powers "predisposes officials to conflict";[10] since both the mayor and the council represent the general polity, there may be conflict over mission, goals, and policies as well as over administrative boundaries. Reflecting a commonly held interpretation of urban politics, Edward Banfield and James Q. Wilson asserted nearly a half century ago that "politics arises out of conflict, and it consists of the activities . . . by which conflict is carried on."[11] Yet according to Svara, conflict is not the only condition for advancing the governmental process.[12]

Whereas power is the basis for the mayor-council form of government, cooperation is the basis for the council-manager form. The most important elements in a cooperative arrangement are common goals, coordinated efforts, and the sharing of rewards. In a council-manager city, there is no separation of powers: the council possesses all authority except for what is delegated to the manager. Unlike in a mayor-council city, where the mayor is the key initiator of action, the mayor in a council-manager city may take on that role alone or share it with the city council and manager. Primarily, though, the mayor serves as facilitator, promoting communication and effective interaction in the process and providing a greater sense of purpose—"a guiding force in city government who helps ensure that all other officials are performing as well as possible and that all are moving in the right direction."[13] The mayor or chairperson provides political leadership, and the manager provides professional leadership.

Responding to charges of weakness, the council-manager form has adapted over time.[14] Whereas the original reform movement called for five-member councils, at-large elections, and a mayor chosen from among the council, many cities have adopted larger councils, have gone to district elections (17% use them exclusively), and have adopted the direct election of the mayor (76%) (see "Municipal Form of Government" in this edition of the *Municipal Year Book,* pages 27–33). In addition, some cities have expanded the mayor's authority to include veto power, the power to appoint council committees and advisory boards, review of the budget for submission to the council, preparation of an annual report to the community, and initiation of the hiring or termination of the manager. Yet the form remains a parliamentary system with involvement by the whole council and the manager.

In either form of government, the council serves as representative, governing official, supervisor, and judge. As a representative, it speaks on behalf of the constituents. In its governing role, it legislates and gives direction. In its supervisory capacity, it appoints and supervises staff. And as a judge, it resolves disputes. In the strong mayor form, however, the council is more likely to play the representative and the legislative ratification roles, whereas in the council-manager form, the council can define its role as it sees fit, serving in whatever capacity it chooses. As Svara sees it, the council's role in the strong mayor form of government is as a counterweight, while in the council-manager form it is that of a senior partner.[15]

Clearly, the relationship between the city manager and the council is extremely important for the success and proper operation of local government. The manager's role in aiding the council to do its work is as important as the role the manager plays in administration. The real issue seems to be not whether the manager is a leader but what type of leader the manager is. The nature of the local community is a major factor in that analysis. Local government professionals have reported that the biggest difference in their work over the past ten years has been the increase in their degree of participation in public policy making and problem solving.[16] The manager has become a facilitator to help promote problem solving and develop consensus among interests. Fifty-six percent of managers in a 1985 survey indicated that policy making was their major role, up from 22% in 1965.[17] In a survey done in 1997, 79% of city managers in cities over 100,000 in population indicated that their most important role in local government was policy and council relations.[18] Managers must be able to read situations and create the opportunities to solve problems. In a successful council-manager local government, all members of the governing body as well as the manager are part of the process of developing cohesion within the group.

CONFLICT AND COOPERATION AND THE DECISION-MAKING PROCESS

In his research into public sector organizations, Svara summarizes a position on conflict by noting that "disagreement becomes conflict . . . when incompatible goals cause some participants to seek to impose their preferences on others."[19] Alternatively, cooperation, as defined at the beginning of this article, means positive interactions or active contributions that seek to accommodate participants' preferences. When cooperation is predominant, elected and administrative officials may be assumed to have compatible goals. Low cooperation results from the absence of positive interactions, or from the presence of contributions that fail to meet expectations or are lower than preferred. When interactions become negative, such as blocking behavior and activities that disregard the preferences of other participants, the result is conflict. Low conflict results from the absence of negative interactions and the presence of a low level of activity. Yet, as has been noted, the absence of conflict does not necessarily mean the presence of cooperation, nor does the absence of cooperation necessarily mean the presence of conflict.

In his examination of conflict and cooperation published in 1988, Svara sought to determine (1) whether form of government is really an indicator of more fundamental differences and (2) whether the council-manager form truly allows for more cooperation or an absence of conflict.[20] He began by assuming that "conflict is more likely associated with greater population size, less growth (as an indicator of economic conditions), higher proportions of minorities in the population, lower education attainment, lower government bond rating, larger councils, more district seats, and partisan elections." Through his research on 12 cities, Svara found that "council-manager cities not only experience less conflict but manifest a pattern of interaction that can be characterized as cooperation." He further noted that council-manager governments are more often found in large, medium, and small cities rather than in very large ones; that they are more prevalent in suburban and rural areas than in central cities; and that they generally enjoy higher income, greater growth, and a better quality of life than cities that use other forms of government. However, he also acknowledged that this research, while "more than a case study of a single community," was "less than an analysis of a large sample of randomly selected cities."[21]

As previously noted, form of government has been identified as one of the factors predictive of conflict and cooperation in the decision-making process. Other factors have also been researched to determine whether they have an impact on the roles of leadership and the exercise of policy development in a city organization. These other factors are population size of the city; location of the city (central city versus suburban as it relates to media attention); fiscal condition of the city; socioeconomic conditions in the community, such as ethnicity levels, income levels, and growth; and methodology of council elections, such as size of the council, election type (district versus at large elections), and partisanship.[22] But in all cases the research has analyzed how conflict and cooperation are related to just one, two, or maybe three factors and has not controlled for the potential influence of the other factors on their findings. Standing alone, a factor may appear to have an impact on the decision-making process that is proven to be noncausal when controlled for other factors. Thus, it is important to analyze all factors simultaneously and to control for those that may contribute to the levels of conflict and cooperation in that process. Accordingly, the research for this article builds on past research efforts involving individual and paired case studies to create a sample of randomly selected cities with a database of the potentially predictive factors in order to assess the levels of conflict and cooperation.

SURVEY ASSUMPTIONS AND DESIGN

The governmental process includes the functions of policy decision making, implementation of the decisions that are made, and management of organizational resources. The roles of the mayor, council members, and city manager/CAO and their contributions to organizational issues can vary significantly among cities. This variation, along with what those officials understand their roles to be, can create conflict or foster cooperation in the decision-making process. To measure the levels of conflict and cooperation in the process requires some assumptions on the causes of these dynamics; these assumptions will be tested against a comparison of the relationship of the dependent variables of conflict and cooperation in individual cities with the independent variables that may predict the levels of conflict and cooperation. In other words, does one independent variable (such as form of government or partisanship of elections) have a greater relationship to the levels of conflict or cooperation in a city than the other independent variables?

The primary assumption is that where expectations among the mayor, council members, and city manager/CAO differ regarding the involvement of each in policy development and city management, conditions are ripe for conflict, whereas expectations that are commonly held among all participants support cooperation. The level of cooperation and conflict is based on the level of congruence found among the mayor, city council, and manager/CAO in their preferred roles as well as in their expectations of each other's roles in decision making and policy development.

The research presented here has examined the dependent variables of conflict and cooperation within the context of the following tensions:

1. **Tension based on weak relationships among elected officials.** There is less conflict and more cooperation when the relationship between the mayor and the city council is characterized by unity. To measure this relationship, the survey included questions on the following three factors.

   - *Level of cohesion or divisiveness on the council:* More factions equal more conflict.
   - *Mayor-council relations:* Less amiable relationships equal less cooperation.
   - *Trust in and support for mayor by council:* More trust and support equal more cooperation.

2. **Tension based on how each set of officials perceives and fills its roles and functions.** When elected officials assume roles in long-term goal setting and broad oversight, they reinforce cooperation. When council members concentrate on the more intangible, abstract areas of goal setting and oversight—that is, when they (and the mayor in council-manager cities) focus on long-term matters, refrain from administrative details, and provide performance feedback—the level of cooperation is high; when their involvement in these areas is lower than preferred, however, the level of cooperation is lower and the manager does not get the clear direction that is needed to do his or her job. Yet this does not necessarily mean there will be conflict. On the other hand, when council members concentrate more highly on tangible, concrete areas of policy and administration, the attention to detail that is required *is* likely to lead to conflict. And while low involvement is associated with low levels of conflict, that does not necessarily mean cooperation.

As the quality of performance in specific role functions decreases, there will be more conflict and less cooperation among the parties; conversely, higher levels of performance enhance the relationships and cooperation. To measure levels of performance, the survey included questions on the roles of policy maker and policy implementer. For policy maker (mayor and council) performance, it examined

- *Establishment of priorities and long-term goals:* Effective long-term goal setting equals more cooperation.
- *Council appraisal and performance feedback to mayor or manager:* More feedback equals more cooperation.
- *Attention to real problems in the city rather than to administrative details and minutia:* A focus on important issues equals less conflict.

For policy implementer (mayor/staff or city manager) performance (dependent on form of government), it examined

- *Accomplishment of goals set by council:* More goals accomplished equals more cooperation.
- *Provision of alternatives:* More policy analysis and alternatives equals more cooperation.
- *High standards of personal conduct:* Higher standards equals less conflict.

The roles of mayor, council member, and city manager/CAO are all important to the decision-making process in their own right. The survey was undertaken to gain insight into how the individuals occupying these positions perceive their own roles and those of the other entities in the process. The survey instruments were all identical except for four questions with 16 subquestions that were unique to the form of government or role/position being surveyed. Each question on conflict and cooperation was scored according to how the answer related to the tensions outlined above; the scoring was done on a zero-to-one basis, with zero being the low and one being the high level of conflict or cooperation. An index variable was created for each survey instrument. The resultant database includes the scores for all surveyed mayors, responding council members, and city managers/CAOs where the position exists.

As has been noted, six factors have been identified that can affect the level of conflict and cooperation in the local governmental process.

This research used a multivariate model to correlate 11 independent variables for these factors, by city, to the level of conflict and cooperation measured by survey instruments in those cities. Those factors and their independent variables are shown below. The relationship of these independent variables to the levels of conflict and cooperation among the responding cities provides the basis for the analysis that follows.

Size of city
- Census population data for cities between 50,000 and 250,000 population

Location of city
- Central city or suburban city

Fiscal condition of city
- Bond ratings by Moody's, Standard & Poor's, and Fitch

Socioeconomic conditions
- Ethnicity: Heterogeneity of the city (percentage of white population)
- Income level: Average family income
- Growth in the city: Population of growth or decline between 1990 and 2000
- Educational level in the community: Percentage of college graduates

Methodology of council elections
- Size of the city council
- Election type: District versus at-large council elections
- Partisan versus nonpartisan elections

Institutional form of government
- Mayor-council and mayor/council-manager.

METHODOLOGY

The research for this project was conducted in all 562 cities with more than 50,000 and less than 250,000 in population, as determined by the 2000 census. Questionnaires were distributed to mayors, city council members, and city managers/CAOs (where they exist) during the months of March through October of 2006; similar survey instruments were used in order to assess respondents' perspectives of conflict and cooperation in the governmental process. Since responses from all three parts of the decision-making triangle were crucial for the analysis, the survey was administered first to the mayor and city manager/CAO and then to council members in the cities where responses were received from the mayoral position. An example of some of the survey questions and the scoring is shown in the appendix. The survey process described above resulted in a significant response rate from all three parts of the triangle (Table 2/1).

Of the 265 mayors who responded, 74 were from strong mayor-council cities, which constitute 34% of the total base of responding cities (190 of 562). Of those 74 cities, those that elicited a response from the CAO, if there was one, as well as from the mayor were the mayor-council cities in which surveys were also distributed to the council members. The council member response rate was 42% overall (i.e., from both mayor-council and council-manager cities), but it differed by city. Table 2/2 shows the number of cities in which at least 29% of members of the entire council responded; in three cities, 100% of the council members responded.

Table 2/1 SURVEY RESPONSE

City type	No. of cities surveyed (A)	Mayors reporting		Council members reporting		City managers/chief administrative officers reporting	
		No.	% of (A)	No.	% of (A)	No.	% of (A)
Total	562	265	47	745	42	266	54
Strong mayor	190	74	39	275	41	55	47
Council-manager	372	191	51	470	42	211	56

Table 2/2 COUNCIL MEMBER RESPONSES IN CITIES EXCEEDING 29%

City type	Total	29–34%	35–39%	40–49%	50–74%	75–100%
Total	165	27	9	21	86	22
Strong mayor	59	11	5	16	25	2
Council-manager	106	16	4	5	61	20

All cities where 29% or more of the council members responded are included in the database. The 36 cities for which council member responses were between 29% and 39% were analyzed to confirm that they are not significantly different from the remainder of the database because of this lower response rate. Ultimately, a total of 165 cities produced responses from the mayor, at least 29% of the council members, and the CAO where one existed, and thus met the triangle response requirements needed to measure the levels of conflict and cooperation within the governmental decision-making process.

Comparison of Survey Base with Total Cities
A statistical analysis was done to determine whether the qualifying cities are reflective of all cities in the population range of 50,000–250,000—that is, whether they are skewed toward higher or lower income levels, greater or lesser diversity, faster or slower growth, more or less educated populations, mayor-council or council-manager form of government, partisan or nonpartisan elections, at-large or district elections, central city or suburban cities, and larger or smaller city councils. From the results of an Independent Samples test, it was concluded that the differences between the qualifying cities and the nonqualifying cities for the independent variables of growth, educational level, median household income, and council size are not significant. However, the independent variables of population and ethnicity show some significant differences. The difference in population is not considered to be relevant within this research effort because the cities were all in the 50,000–250,000 population range. As for ethnicity, the overall percentage of whites in all cities in the population range is 70.74% while that among the qualifying cities is 76.26%, and while statistically significant, the difference is not considered a major detraction to the results of the overall analysis.

As can be seen from the listing of factors and variables, four of the independent variables—city location, form of government, election type, and partisanship—have two alternatives. A statistical analysis of these variables in the qualifying cities compared with these variables in all the cities within the population range shows a statistical difference for city location and election type, while form of government and partisanship are statistically the same. Specifically, the database of qualifying cities is more likely than the total cities in the population group of 50,000–250,000 to include central cities and cities with district elections.

Descriptive Analysis of Qualifying Cities
Before undertaking a statistical analysis of the effects of the independent variables on the levels of conflict and cooperation in the decision-making process, it was necessary to test the database of qualifying cities for unusual characteristics that might influence the subsequent analysis. This process included looking for outliers (cities that are different enough from the rest of the sample to affect the analysis), testing for multicollinearity (the presence of two independent variables that may be correlated to a high enough degree that they have similar effects on the dependent variable), identifying curvilinear relationships (necessary because multiple regression forecasts a straight line, which requires linearity in results), and looking for heteroscedasticity (which usually results from data that include heterogeneous subunits, such as median household income and different populations). After it was determined that there was no leverage exerted in the regression by outliers, that none of the variance inflation factors indicated any significant level of multicollinearity or curvilinearity, and that there was no condition of heteroscedasticity, all 165 qualifying cities were retained in the database for the full regression analysis.

As has been noted, the regression analysis used seven continuous and four dichotomous variables. The descriptive statistics of the seven continuous variables for the 165 cities are shown in Table 2/3. The four dichotomous variables have the characteristics shown in Table 2/4.

FINDINGS

When measuring the levels of conflict and cooperation in the decision-making process within organizations, consideration must be given to the influence of the different players and their roles. In other words, does the mayor have an equal impact on the creation of conflict and/or cooperation as the city council as a group and the city manager/CAO, or do these players contribute to these conditions to

Table 2/3 DESCRIPTIVE STATISTICS OF CONTINUOUS VARIABLES

Variables	Minimum	Maximum	Average
Population in 2000 . . .	50,269	227,818	87,314
Growth: % change in population, 1990–2000	−20.80	275.80	18.0
Ethnicity: % white population	4.26	97.30	76.3
Educational level: % college graduates	8.63	74.40	28.3
Median household income	$21,180	$100,411	$44,538
Council size: # members	5	20	8
Bond rating score	1	10	4.6

Table 2/4 DESCRIPTIVE STATISTICS OF DICHOTOMOUS VARIABLES

Variables	No.	Percentage
Form of government		
Mayor-council	59	35.8
Council-manager	106	64.2
Election type		
At large	65	39.4
District	100	60.6
Partisanship		
Nonpartisan	141	85.5
Partisan	24	14.5
City location		
Central city	97	58.8
Suburb	68	41.2

Table 2/5 WEIGHTING OF ROLES IN DECISION MAKING: THREE ALTERNATIVES

Alternatives	Form of government	Roles as weighted		
		Mayor	City manager/chief administrative officer (CAO)	City council
Alternative #1	All	33% with CAO 50% if no CAO	33% CAO . . .	33% with CAO 50% if no CAO
Alternative #2	Mayor-council	40% with CAO 50% if no CAO	10% CAO . . .	50% . . .
	Council-manager	33%	33% city manager	33%
Alternative #3	All	1/X of total X responses	1/X of total X responses	Each response is 1/X of total X responses

In a multiple regression analysis, the regression coefficients are interpreted for their effects on the dependent variables while controlling for the effect of all the independent variables included in the regression. Regression analysis shows the significance of the relationships between the independent variables and the dependent variables, with lower scores being more significant than higher scores. Social science research uses .05 and .10 as the levels of statistical significance for relationships to exist.)

As shown in Table 2/6, the form-of-government independent variable explains the generation of conflict with a significance of .000 in Alternative 2. The next closest independent variable is educational level, with a significance level of .084. These results indicate that the council-manager form of government generates less conflict in the decision-making process than the mayor-council form. In the database, the council-manager form was coded differently from the mayor-council form, and the regression analysis shows these differences to be the most significant of all the relationships with independent variables when related to the levels of conflict and cooperation. The form-of-government independent variable also explains the generation of cooperation with a significance of .000 in Alternative 2. Again, the next closest independent variable is educational level, with a significance level of .238. The council-manager form of government fosters more cooperation in the decision-making process than the mayor-council form.

Multiple regression analysis also makes it possible to determine whether there are other variables not identified in the model that are affecting the dependent variables. The statistical analysis, as reflected in the coefficient of determination, is interpreted as "the percentage of variation in the dependent variable that is explained by the independent variable."[24] In Alternative 2, the coefficient of determination for conflict in the decision-making process is 12.6%, which is less than the moderate assessment level of 20%–40% in social science research and thereby indicates the presence of factors in the generation of conflict that the model has not identified. But of the factors that have been identified, form of government is the most significant. On the other hand, the coefficient of determination for cooperation is 31.0%, which is within the 20%–40% moderate level of the causation factors for cooperation but also indicates the possible presence of other factors that would account for cooperation in the decision-making process.

Table 2/6 REGRESSION ON CONFLICT AND COOPERATION: ALTERNATIVE 2

Variable	Significance	
	Conflict	Cooperation
City size, 2000	.536	.558
Growth in city	.739	.944
Ethnicity	.725	.813
Education level	.084	.238
Income level	.442	.704
Form of government	**.000**	**.000**
Council size	.155	.779
Election type	.800	.570
Partisanship	.660	.836
City location	.997	.869
Financial condition	.602	.302
Coefficients of determination	12.6%	31.0%

An analysis of the average conflict and cooperation scores by roles in the two forms of government is helpful in understanding the results of the regression analysis. As shown in Table 2/7, the average scores for the levels of conflict in the council-manager form of government are less than they are in the mayor-council form, while the average scores for levels of cooperation are higher.

Of particular interest in these scores are the levels of conflict and cooperation in the mayor-council form of government in cities with a CAO compared with those levels in cities without a CAO. The cities with a CAO show less conflict and more cooperation for council members than do those without a CAO. The conflict level for mayors is slightly higher, but that for cooperation is higher as well. As a result of this finding, the form-of-government independent variable in the database was extended to three forms of government—council-manager, mayor-council with CAO, and mayor-council without CAO—to recognize these differences and test the results.

With this modification, the coefficient of determination for conflict increases from 12.6% to 14.0%, explaining more of the variation in the dependent variable, while form of government is still at the significance level of .000 (see Table 2/8). Educational level is still the next closest independent variable with a significance level of .099. At the same time, the coefficient of determination for cooperation decreases from 31.0% to 27.7%, with a significance level still at .000. And again, educational level is the closest independent variable with a significance level of .311. The recognition of the mayor-council form with a CAO separate from the mayor-council form without a CAO

different degrees? To address this issue of impact, the roles of these different officials were weighted on the basis of three alternative scenarios, as shown in Table 2/5. A composite index for conflict and cooperation was created for each city based upon these alternative weightings, and a multiple regression analysis for both dependent variables—conflict and cooperation—was performed against the 11 independent variables using the three alternatives. This approach made it possible to determine whether the weightings had any significant impact on the results of the regression analysis.

It would be reasonable to assume that the mayor in a city would be accorded more significance in the decision-making process than each individual council member, given the mayor's visibility and level of authority; this assumption would favor Alternatives 1 and 2 over Alternative 3. The role of the CAO in the mayor-council form of government, where the position reports to the mayor, would indicate less influence for that role as well in the process. Alternative 2, which weights the level of decision making for the different positions by form of government and groups the council members as one unit, seems to provide the best description of the relative roles for the players in decision making. While each of the three alternatives shows similar results for the multiple regression, this research has focused on Alternative 2.

(Multiple regression is a statistical technique used to test the robustness of the bivariate relationships among variables when they are controlled for other variables.[23] The multiple regression modeling tries to control for all identifiable independent variables that are affecting the dependent variables and to assess the relevance of those effects.

Table 2/7   AVERAGE CONFLICT AND COOPERATION MEASURES, BY ROLES

Dependent variable	All cities	Council-manager	Mayor-council		
			All	With CAO	Without CAO
Conflict					
Mayor	0.2059	0.1829	0.2473	0.2512	0.2435
Council	0.2677	0.2427	0.3126	0.2866	0.3378
City manager/CAO	0.2155	0.2108	0.2326	0.2326	n/a
Cooperation					
Mayor	0.8005	0.8385	0.7322	0.7451	0.7198
Council	0.7226	0.7553	0.6637	0.6854	0.6428
City manager/CAO	0.7785	0.7864	0.7449	0.7499	n/a

n/a = not applicable.

Table 2/8   REGRESSION ON CONFLICT AND COOPERATION: ALTERNATIVE 2 WITH THREE FORMS OF GOVERNMENT

Variable	Significance	
	Conflict	Cooperation
City size—2000	.457	.493
Growth in city	.619	.894
Ethnicity	.682	.778
Education level	.099	.311
Income Level	.392	.570
Form of government	**.000**	**.000**
Council size	.142	.550
Election type	.822	.522
Partisanship	.744	.518
City location	.978	.900
Financial condition	.740	.351
Coefficients of determination	14.0%	27.7%

Table 2/9   REGRESSION ON CONFLICT AND COOPERATION: ALTERNATIVE 2, WITH THREE FORMS OF GOVERNMENT AND ONLY SIX INDEPENDENT VARIABLES

Variable	Significance	
	Conflict	Cooperation
City size, 2000	.523	.475
Education level	.088	.239
Income level	.281	.339
Form of government	**.000**	**.000**
Council size	.107	.318
Financial condition	.711	.326
Coefficients of determination	16.4%	29.6%

increases the overall viability of the regression analysis and slightly increases the strength of the conflict predictive value while slightly decreasing the cooperation predictive value. It would appear from this analysis, then, that while institutional form of government is a major predictor of the levels of conflict and cooperation in the decision-making process, the existence of a CAO in the mayor-council form increases the likelihood of less conflict and more cooperation, whereas the lack of a city manager or CAO increases the likelihood of more conflict and less cooperation.

To further refine the regression, the five independent variables that exceeded the .500 significance level for both conflict and cooperation and did not have any significant impact on the levels of conflict and cooperation were eliminated. Those variables are election type, city location, ethnicity, partisanship, and growth. This elimination further increases the coefficient of determination for conflict from 14.0% to 16.4% and for cooperation from 27.7% to 29.6%, while the conflict and cooperation variables for form of government are both still significant at .000 (see Table 2/9). This alternative appears to be the most robust model for the prediction of conflict and cooperation at this time. While the predictive value of the coefficient of determination for conflict at 16.4% is less than the moderate level of 20%–40%, the predictive value for cooperation at 29.6% is in the middle of the moderate range. Educational level is the next closest variable having influence on both conflict

and cooperation, but at .239 it is not statistically significant for cooperation, and at .088 it is significant for conflict only at the .10 significance level. Thus, form of government is the only identified independent variable that has a statistically significant relationship with the levels of conflict and cooperation in the decision-making process.

SUMMARY AND IMPLICATIONS

Of the factors identified in this analysis, the form of government proved to be the only statistically significant causal factor for the levels of conflict and cooperation in the decision-making process. In particular, this study found that the mayor-council form of government generates more conflict and less cooperation in decision making than the council-manager form, and that the council-manager form generates more cooperation and less conflict than the mayor-council form. In addition, it found that the mayor-council form with a CAO position has less conflict and more cooperation than the mayor-council form without a CAO.

It is interesting to note that if bivariate analysis is performed on the independent variables and the dependent variables of conflict and cooperation, the independent variables of form of government, election type, and council size (for both conflict and cooperation) and of partisanship, income level, and financial condition (for cooperation) show some levels of significance. However, form of government is the only significant factor in multiple regression when the analysis is controlled for the other variables.

While it could be argued that cities with less tendency for conflict and more tendency for cooperation are more likely to adopt a form of government that includes a city manager or CAO, it is more plausible that the existence of the professional managerial position helps to reduce conflict and increase cooperation. The council-manager form of government, a product of the 20th century in the United States, enjoyed its greatest period of growth after World War II. The role of the city manager in policy development and decision making has been more pronounced in the last quarter of the 20th century and the first decade of this century.

The mayor-council form of government, in which the mayor sees leadership as the acquisition and use of power, functions through the separation of powers and thus creates an environment for competition and disagreement similar to that found on the national level. In the council-manager form, on the other hand, the mayor's role is of presiding officer of the city council; having little independent power, the mayor serves more as a facilitator to promote communication and effective interaction in the decision-making process, and so the relationship between the mayor and the council members requires more cooperation and less conflict. And since the city manager is hired and fired by the whole council, not by one individual, the security of his or her position depends on a favorable relationship with the entire council. Thus, with the increased involvement of local government professionals in policy making over the past decade, the manager, like the mayor, has had to become a facilitator to help promote problem solving and develop consensus among interests. Finally, with the city council functioning as the ultimate decision maker, the council-manager form of government produces an environment characterized by higher levels of cooperation and lower levels of conflict within the decision-making process.

While the mayor-council form of government with a CAO has not been the subject of much research to date, the results of this research show that in working with the city council, the local government professional in a mayor-council city may play a role similar to the role he or she plays in a council-manager city. Conceivably, mayor-council cities that are more prone to cooperation and less prone to conflict are more likely to create a professional management position; however, it is more likely that the professional position is what helps to reduce conflict and enhance cooperation between officials included in the decision-making process.

There may be additional factors affecting conflict and cooperation that have not been identified yet, perhaps because measures of the independent variables are not sophisticated enough to identify them. But among the factors that have been identified, form of government is the only one that is statistically significant, with the council-manager form and the mayor-council form with a CAO generating less conflict and more cooperation than the mayor-council form without a CAO. The research conducted for this study shows that the existence of a professional management position in mayor-council cities is directly related to lower levels of conflict and higher levels of cooperation, and this research needs to be built upon to assess the significance of this finding.

[1] Daniel J. Elazar, *The Closing of the Metropolitan Frontier—Cities of the Prairie Revisited* (New Brunswick, N.J.: Transaction Publishers, 2002), 3.

[2] Daniel J. Elazar, *Cities of the Prairie* (Lanham, N.J.: University Press of America, 1970), 437.

[3] Bernard Bass, *Handbook of Leadership,* 3rd ed. (New York: The Free Press, 1990), 3.

[4] John W. Gardner, *On Leadership* (New York: The Free Press, 1990), 3.

[5] J. L. Pressman, "Preconditions of Mayoral Leadership," *American Political Science Review* 66, no. 2 (1972): 512.

[6] James H. Svara, "Conflict and Cooperation in Elected-Administrative Relations in Large Council-Manager Cities," *State and Local Government Review* 31 (Fall 1999): 173–189.

[7] Rob Gurwitt, "The Lure of the Strong Mayor," *Governing* 6, no. 10 (July 1993): 36–41, available at governing.com/archive/1993/jul/mayor.txt.

[8] Kimberly L. Nelson, "Assessing the CAO Position in a Strong-Mayor Government," *National Civic Review* 91 (Spring 2002): 41–54.

[9] Chester Newland, "Managing from the Future of Council-Manager Government," in *Ideal and Practice in Council-Manager Government,* ed. H. George Frederickson, 2nd ed. (Washington, D.C.: ICMA, 1994), 278.

[10] James H. Svara, *Official Leadership in the City: Patterns of Conflict and Cooperation* (New York: Oxford University Press, 1990), 45.

[11] Edward C. Banfield and James Q. Wilson, *City Politics* (New York: Vintage Books, 1963), 5.

[12] Svara and Associates, *Facilitative Leadership.*

[13] Ibid., xxvii.

[14] William J. Hansell, "Evolution and Change Characterize Council-Manager Government," *Public Management* 82, no. 8 (August 2000): 17–21.

[15] Svara and Associates, *Facilitative Leadership.*

[16] John Nalbandian, "Facilitating Community, Enabling Democracy: New Roles for Local Government Managers," *Public Administration Review* 59, no. 3 (May/June 1999): 187–197.

[17] John Nalbandian, *Professionalism in Local Government* (San Francisco: Jossey-Bass, 1991).

[18] James H. Svara, "The Shifting Boundary between Elected Officials and City Managers in Large Council-Manager Cities," *Public Administration Review* 59 (January/February 1999):48.

[19] Svara, *Official Leadership in the City,* 28.

[20] James H. Svara, "Conflict, Cooperation, and Separation of Powers in City Government," *Journal of Urban Affairs* 10, no. 4 (1988): 367.

[21] Ibid., 359–360.

[22] Peggy Heilig and Robert J. Mundt, *Your Voice at City Hall* (Albany: State University of New York Press, 1984); Heywood T. Sanders, "The Government of American Cities: Continuity and Change in Structure," in *The Municipal Year Book 1982* (Washington, D.C.: International City Management Association, 1982), 178–186; James R. Bowers and Wilbur C. Rich, *Governing Middle-Sized Cities: Studies in Mayoral Leadership* (Boulder, Colo.: Lynne Rienner Publishers), 2000; Martin Shefter, *Political Crisis Fiscal Crisis: The Collapse and Revival of New York City* (New York: Columbia University Press, 1992); Doris A. Graber, *Mass Media and American Politics,* 7th ed. (Washington, D.C.: CQ Press, 2006); James H. Svara, "The Mayor in Council-Mayor Cities: Recognizing Leadership Potential," *National Civic Review* 75, no. 5 (September/October 1986): 271–283, 305; Svara, "Conflict, Cooperation, and Separation of Powers"; Svara, *Official Leadership in the City;* Chester A. Newland, "Public Executives: Imperium, Sacerdotium, Collegium? Bicentennial Leadership Challenges," in *Public Administration Review* 47 (January/February 1987): 45–56; Newland, "Managing from the Future."

[23] Evan M. Berman, *Essential Statistics for Public Managers and Policy Analysts* (Washington, D.C.: CQ Press, 2002), 124

[24] Ibid., 122.

APPENDIX

SURVEY QUESTIONS AS INDICATORS OF CONFLICT AND COOPERATION: MAYORS

Cooperation: Positive interaction or active contributions that match preferences. Low cooperation is the absence of positive interaction or the presence of contributions that fail to meet expectations.

Mayor-council form. Listed below are activities that are usually performed by the mayor in mayor-council cities. For each, indicate how you would rate your performance—is your performance very good, good, satisfactory, poor, or very poor? Check the appropriate box.

Rate the mayor's performance:	Very good	Good	Fair	Poor	Very poor
a. Providing the council with sufficient alternatives for making policy decisions	1.0	.75	.50	.25	0
b. Accomplishing the goals established by the council	1.0	.75	.50	.25	0
c. Insuring that city government is open to the participation of all groups in the community	1.0	.75	.50	.25	0
d. Providing the council with sufficient information and performance measures to assess the effectiveness of programs and services	1.0	.75	.50	.25	0
f. Seeking to improve the efficiency of city government	1.0	.75	.50	.25	0
g. Interacting with other local governments and the federal and state government	1.0	.75	.50	.25	0
h. Promoting economic development of the city	1.0	.75	.50	.25	0

Council-manager form. Listed below are activities that are usually performed by the mayor in council-manager cities. For each, indicate how you would rate your performance—is your performance very good, good, satisfactory, poor, or very poor? Check the appropriate box.

Rate the mayor's performance:	Very good	Good	Fair	Poor	Very poor
a. Serving as a spokesperson for city government and representing the city in dealings with the public	1.0	.75	.50	.25	0
b. Promoting communication within the council	1.0	.75	.50	.25	0
c. Promoting a positive relationship between the council and the manager	1.0	.75	.50	.25	0
d. Helping the council set goals and priorities	1.0	.75	.50	.25	0
e. Helping the council adopt policies	1.0	.75	.50	.25	0
f. Seeking to improve the efficiency of city government	1.0	.75	.50	.25	0
g. Interacting with other local governments and the federal and state government	1.0	.75	.50	.25	0
h. Promoting economic development of the city	1.0	.75	.50	.25	0

Conflict: Negative interactions, including blocking behaviors and activities that disregard others' preferences. Low conflict is the absence of negative interactions and the presence of a low level of activity.

7. In your judgment, what percent of the council decisions that you consider important are made unanimously or nearly unanimously?

Over 75% 0.0   50–74% 0.67   25–49% 0.33   Fewer than 25% 1.0

8. In general, would you say that there are blocks or factions on the council that consistently vote in the same way on a number of issues? Put an X by your response.

☐ No, there are no real divisions within the council. 0.0   ☐ Yes, there are some divisions but they are not very strong. 0.50

☐ Yes, there are sharp divisions within the council. 1.0

A 3

Local Government Use of Customer Service Systems

Evelina R. Moulder
ICMA

Selected Findings

While only 15% of the 710 survey respondents reported using a centralized customer service system, 34% (190) are considering implementing one.

When asked about the driving force behind implementation of the system, the highest percentage of respondents (43%) identified improving service despite increased cost.

Only 42 local governments (57%) reported that nonemergency police departments are integrated into the centralized call system; however, of the 28 that reported measuring nonemergency calls to 911 since the system was implemented, 43% reported a decrease in those calls.

For local governments, interaction with the public they serve is critical to engaging citizens in the community. Typically, local government services are provided as residents expect: trash is picked up, streetlights function, and potholes are filled, so residents have no need to contact their local government regarding these services. But if something goes wrong, they will make contact. If this contact produces a negative experience, it can create an impression that is difficult for the local government to overcome. A satisfying customer service experience, however, can engender positive feelings about the local government and encourage further citizen involvement with the community.

To this end, a centralized customer service system provides a vehicle through which residents can make their specific needs known to their local government and receive information back about the status of their requests. The ongoing information feedback from the customer to the local government and back to the customer can produce a positive experience that leads to engagement in the community and with the local government at a broader level.

Centralized customer service systems also enable local governments to access the information they need to inform their performance management, identify problems specific to a neighborhood, and provide direction for the capital budget.

ICMA conducted a national local government customer service systems (311) survey to explore the successful implementation of these systems and examine how they are being used to respond to citizen needs and strengthen local government-constituent relationships. ICMA will use the results of this survey to develop case studies, reports, conference sessions, and workshops that will benefit local governments as they explore implementing a 311 system.

SURVEY METHODOLOGY

A paper survey was mailed to city managers and chief administrative officers (CAOs) in munici-

palities with a population of 25,000 and over and to all counties with a CAO or a chief elected executive. The survey was also available for completion online. Of the 2,287 jurisdictions contacted, 710 responded for a survey response rate of 31% (Table 3/1).

LOCAL GOVERNMENT IMPLEMENTATION

While only 104 of the 710 survey respondents reported use of a centralized customer service system, the results also show that 34% (190) are considering implementing one (not shown). All these local governments have populations of 25,000 and over. A somewhat higher percentage of local governments in the West region (41%) indicated plans to implement a system than did those in the other three regions. Figure 3/1 shows the reasons that respondents gave for not implementing a centralized system.

These reasons point to several areas in which local governments need assistance—notably, implementing the application process and obtaining a 311 designation, demonstrating the necessity of such a system, and making elected officials aware of the benefits that a customer service system can bring. Clearly cost is a major concern, and there are demonstrable savings to be achieved from implementation, such as a reduction in calls to 911

Table 3/1   SURVEY RESPONSE

Classification	No. of cities[1]/ counties surveyed (A)	Respondents	
		No.	% of (A)
Total	2,287	710	31
Population group			
500,000 and over	99	24	24
100,000–499,999	450	160	36
25,000–99,999	1,498	456	30
2,500–24,999	240	70	29
Geographic region			
Northeast	394	88	22
North-Central	556	165	30
South	795	242	30
West	542	215	40

[1]For a definition of terms, please see "Inside the *Year Book*," x.

and improved customer service, information, reporting, and management. The results of this survey also show that the difficulty in obtaining a 311 designation is across the board (between 31% and 38% in all four regions) and not limited to a few states (not shown).

Driving Force Supporting Implementation
Improving service despite increased cost was cited by the highest percentage of respondents (43%) who identified the driving force behind implementation of the system (Figure 3/2). Seven local governments attributed implementation primarily to pressure from elected officials, which is possibly related to public pressure and expectations for customer service. None of the respondents reported inspiration from another agency.

Coverage
Only seven local governments reported that their systems cover more than one jurisdiction (not shown). Of these, four are county governments.

Call Intake Software Technology
A slight majority of local government respondents (52%) use some form of off-the-shelf call intake technology (not shown). Most have added modifications to or customized the package. Of the 90 local governments reporting, 16 have systems developed by in-house staff without the use of consultants.

Departmental Integration into the Centralized System
Of the local governments that provided information on which departments are integrated into their centralized customer service system (Table 3/2), more than 80% identified

- Public works (95%)
- Code enforcement (88%)
- City/county management/administration (84%)
- Parks and recreation (81%).

These departments are obvious candidates for inclusion because they handle problems that usually require a repair (public works and code enforcement) or specific information about programs, locations, and services (parks and recreation). The city or country administrative offices are often the

Funding for this study comes from the Alfred P. Sloan Foundation, which makes grants to advance science, technology, and the quality of American life.

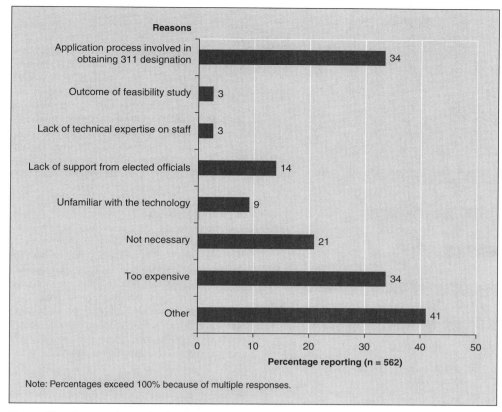

Figure 3/1   *Reasons for not implementing a centralized customer service system*

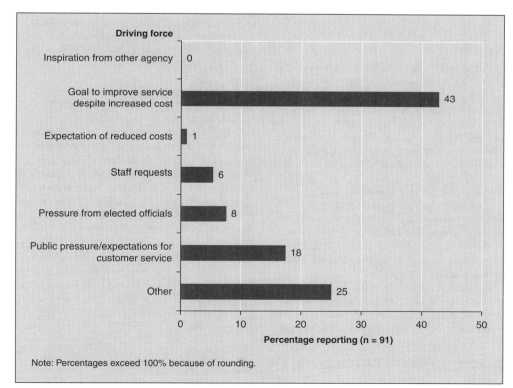

Figure 3/2   *Driving force behind implementation of a centralized customer service system*

TABLE 3/2   DEPARTMENTAL INTEGRATION INTO CENTRALIZED SYSTEM

Department	No. reporting (A)	Departments are integrated	
		No.	% of (A)
City/county management/ administration	82	69	84
Elected officials' offices .	79	46	58
Parks and recreation ...	78	63	81
Code enforcement	80	70	88
Refuse collection and disposal	76	59	78
Public works	81	77	95
Animal control	78	42	54
Health/social services ...	71	19	27
Water	75	50	67
Nonemergency police ...	74	42	57

Note: Not all respondents answered each question about integration, so the base used to calculate the percentages is different for each department.

ported a decrease in calls to 911 (not shown). However, ICMA has anecdotal information that the need for specially trained dispatch staff who can distinguish an emergency from a nonemergency makes integration of emergency services into the centralized system challenging.

The survey collected information about the number of calls received for information or services specific to each of these departments, but the extreme variation in numbers and the few local governments that provided information make this information unusable.

Routing and Tracking Requests Internally

According to 89% of the local government respondents, the routing and tracking of requests is handled within the centralized system, and for the vast majority of those localities, departments are alerted when a request is submitted (not shown). Moreover, 92% of respondents reported that their centralized systems are updated to reflect job status. There is, however, some variation in *how* a system is updated. For 67% of the 79 local governments responding to this question, the system is updated directly. At least six local governments reported both direct system updates and updates to work orders, which are then updated in the centralized system.

Nine local governments reported that routing and tracking is handled by department-specific work order systems. Of those, six update the central customer service system with job status information.

CUSTOMER USE OF CENTRALIZED SERVICE SYSTEMS

It almost goes without saying that whatever advantages such a system may provide will depend on the system's accessibility for its customers, its responsiveness to and efficiency in handling customer calls, and its ability to track and keep customers informed of its progress in handling the problem—all the things that add up to a positive and satisfying customer service experience.

first place that these calls are received, as are calls for general information.

It is somewhat surprising that a higher percentage of local governments have not integrated the nonemergency police into the system, because

reducing the number of nonemergency calls to police dispatchers is often touted as a benefit. Twenty-eight local governments have measured nonemergency calls to 911 since the centralized system was implemented, and of these, 43% re-

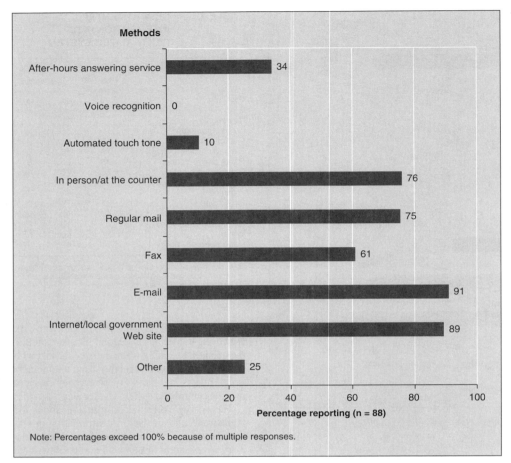

Methods

Note: Percentages exceed 100% because of multiple responses.

Figure 3/3   *Methods of contacting the system*

Accessing the System

Customers often have different needs or preferences when it comes to communicating with a service provider. Each local government provides more than one way to access the system, with e-mail and Web access reported by the highest percentages (Figure 3/3). None of the local governments indicated the use of voice recognition.

Close to 44% of the 92 local governments reporting, including the two localities with a population of 500,000 and over, do not use a single access number (not shown). Of those that do, 9% use 311 and nearly 19% use a single access, or hotline, number *other than* 311. Local governments in the Northeast region, none of which reported using 311, show the highest percentage reporting the use of an alternative single hotline number. Date of implementation does not seem to have been influential in whether there is a single access number. As for the remaining respondents, 15% reported a Web-based access system under "other," so those responses were recoded as a distinct answer, and the remaining 14% who reported "other" described a system with multiple access points, such as the telephone, the Web, or contact with a person.

Who Handles the Calls?

In 38% of the local governments reporting, central call staff are trained to handle the calls, while another 28% reported that central call staff make a record of the call and then put the caller in touch with the responsible department (not shown). Thirty-five percent reported "other" descriptions, including customers entering the "call" into a Web-based system with information routed to the responsible department, or the department taking the call and then entering it into a centralized system. The responses in "other" reflect the fact that not all systems are centralized with call center staff.

Requests for Service Received

The survey included a question about the types of requests received by the centralized customer service system. The objective of this question was to determine the proportion of calls that come in for service, for information, for general comments, etc.

Requests for service top the list (Table 3/3). Whether this would be true in the absence of a centralized system is unknown, but centralized customer service systems are designed to manage service calls, so the high percentage of calls suggests that a strong correlation exists between design and use.

When the responses are reviewed by population size, it is notable that of the 49 local governments reporting with a population of 25,000–99,999, 13 indicated that they receive no requests for *information* about local government services (not shown). Yet all 13 of them reported receiving requests for *service,* and all but one reported receiving complaints about graffiti and the like. It would be interesting to learn whether any characteristics of their system would explain the lack of requests for information received by the system.

Tracking Methods

Quality customer service involves not only taking a call for service but also providing feedback to the customer about the status of the request. To facilitate such quality service, local governments need a system that includes customer tracking capability. When asked if they track contact and local information, however, only 63 of 71 local governments answering the question indicated that they track the street address of the issue, and only 58 reported tracking the street address of the caller (Figure 3/4).

The survey also asked whether the local government uses geographic information system (GIS) technology. But the question did not specifically link the use of GIS to tracking, so some local governments may have answered it without relating it to their system's centralized customer service tracking capability. That said, 35 of the 79 local governments responding to the question (44%) reported that their system does use GIS (not shown).

Customer Response Mechanism

Eighty-two local governments reported that their system includes a customer response mechanism through which it can provide such information as estimated repair time or notification that the repair has been made. Of those, 62 reported the type of response mechanism they use (Figure 3/5). A majority of respondents (71%) issue a tracking number, which enables the customer to follow the progress of the issue resolution. Several local governments use multiple response mechanisms, such as providing issue-specific information (e.g., the estimated date of resolution) to the operator to pass along to the customer, sending out an automated e-mail with a copy of the request and additional information, and sending out an automated e-mail at different stages of issue resolution.

Table 3/3   TYPES OF CALLS/REQUESTS FOR SERVICE

Type of call/request	No. reporting (A)	No. reporting on type of request	% of (A)
Requests for service such as pothole repair, burned-out streetlights	85	84	99
Requests for information about local government services, schedules, etc.	85	72	85
Complaints about graffiti, vacant lots	82	75	92
Suggestions, general feedback, or comments on a specific issue	75	61	81

Note: Not all respondents answered each question about types of calls or services requested, so the base used to calculate the percentages is different for each type shown.

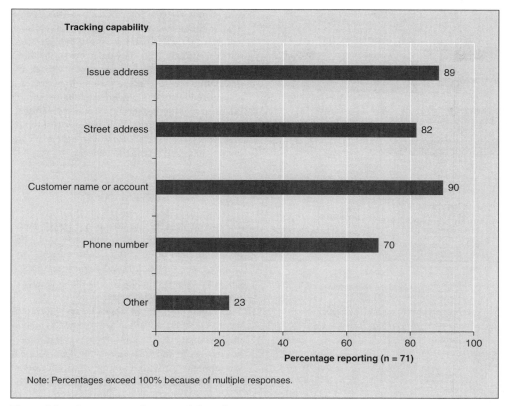

Note: Percentages exceed 100% because of multiple responses.

Figure 3/4 *Customer tracking capability of system*

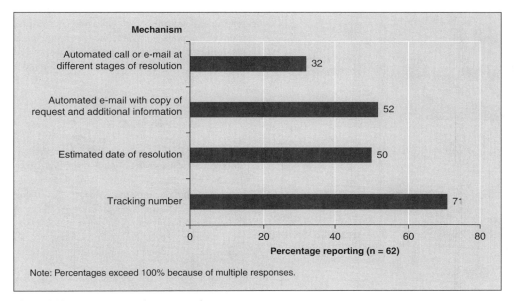

Note: Percentages exceed 100% because of multiple responses.

Figure 3/5 *Response mechanism used*

The next question on the survey asked how the response was communicated, which may have been confusing because the previous question asked whether the system has a response mechanism and gave automated e-mail as an example. As it happens, the highest percentage of respondents answering the question (46%) reported e-mail as the method of communicating a response to a user request (not shown). Close to 43% indicated that the response is communicated in accordance with customer preference, and 42% reported that the response is communicated in the same manner in which it was received. Responses by phone (34%) and regular mail (27%) were reported by the fewest local governments.

MANAGEMENT USES

The use of a centralized customer service system brings several other issues into play, among them being the capabilities and value of the system beyond customer service, and financial considerations.

Reporting Capabilities and Use

Centralized customer service systems can support management decisions, policies, and strategies. Reports generated from the system are a starting point for this support. If managers are able to receive information about service requests by geographic area, for example, they can identify patterns in problems that seem concentrated in a particular location and take steps to address those problems. The time taken to complete a system request is useful for establishing benchmarks and evaluating the processes and procedures involved in the response. Being able to access information on repeat requests allows a manager to look at why that problem reoccurs and create policies to reduce its occurrence or even eliminate it.

Figure 3/6 shows the reporting capability identified by local governments with centralized customer service systems. Twenty-six of the localities that use reports for performance measurement indicated that they have all four of the reporting capabilities covered in the survey (not shown).

Reporting functionality depends on two things: (1) the data necessary for the report must be in the system, and (2) the reporting program must be written to pull the data into a report. But while 81 of the 84 respondents reported that their system is capable of generating reports on the types of service requests received, this reporting functionality seems to be underused (Figure 3/7). For example, although 79% (64) indicated that they use the information for performance measurement, only 45 of them said that they have the capability to generate reports on both the time it takes to complete a service request and the number of repeat requests received—two indicators that would seem to be inputs for performance measures. It may be that the data are available in the systems but the reporting programs have not yet been written.

The two least reported uses of the report information are for capital maintenance planning and annual reports. However, such reports could probably provide local governments with valuable information to use in the capital planning process.

Using the information with citizen groups is an essential step in the customer service feedback loop. If, for example, the public works staff know that a particular problem occurs with higher frequency in a particular neighborhood and can use the reports to show that the frequency has significantly decreased, they would have a great communication tool. Also, by using data on problems in a particular neighborhood, they may be able to engage the community residents in solving the problem themselves. And identifying problems *by* neighborhood enables comparisons to be made *across* neighborhoods that may show what is different and what works.

Without information about customer satisfaction, a local government is unable to determine the full value of its system. However, only 47% of those reporting said that they use customer satisfaction surveys to determine the level of satisfaction with the centralized customer service

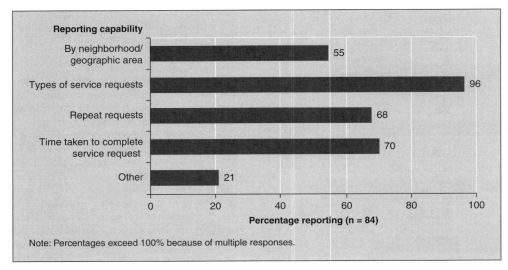

Figure 3/6   *Reporting capability of system*

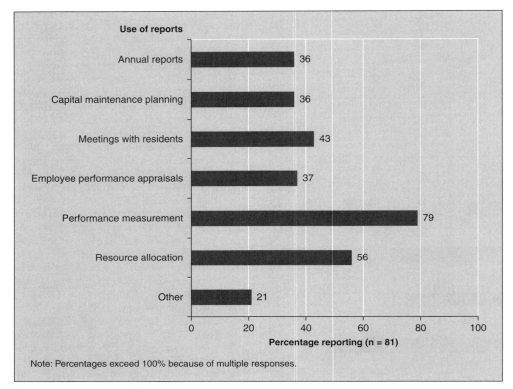

Figure 3/7   *Use of system reports*

system (not shown). Some of the localities that do not conduct a customer satisfaction survey indicated that they use other means to evaluate customer satisfaction, but they did not describe those means. For those survey respondents who identified public pressure as the driving impetus for a centralized system, a citizen satisfaction survey is a good tool for measuring the public reaction to the system's implementation, yet only 6 of the 16 that reported public pressure also reported conducting a citizen satisfaction survey.

SYSTEM COST

The survey included questions about development, capital, and operating expenditures. Few respondents provided information on these issues, and among those that did, the expenditures in each category vary significantly. For this reason, the information is difficult to use.

The first category of expenditures, "development and implementation," was defined as including "planning, design, consulting, and staff time," not hardware and software costs. Twelve local governments provided amounts, which ranged from $1,000 to over $4 million (not shown). The next category, capital expenditures, includes software and hardware purchased to implement the system. Among the 30 respondents who provided amounts, the lowest amount reported was $8,000, and the highest was $525,000. Finally, annual operating expenditures were described as staffing, training, supplies, software, and noncapital hardware, and the 35 local governments who responded in this category reported a low of $1,350 and a high of $350,000.

SUMMARY

The survey results show that although implementation of centralized customer service systems to date has been limited, local governments are interested in implementing them. In fact, the number interested in their implementation is greater than the number currently reporting their use. As more local governments launch these systems, we can anticipate more robust use of the functionality.

A 4

Local Government Approaches to Active Living, 2007

Christine Shenot
ICMA

> **Selected Findings**
>
> *The top three actions that local governments say they could take to combat health problems related to obesity are developing a cohesive system of parks and trails (50%), using zoning to support mixed land uses (37%), and requiring neighborhood streets to be designed with pedestrians and cyclists in mind (33%).*
>
> *Respondents rated parents as the most valuable partner in fighting youth obesity (92%); however, when asked whether they are working with parents in this regard, only 38% said yes.*

Americans hear more about the obesity epidemic every day. They wake up to front-page newspaper articles about the health implications, and see similar stories on television when they turn on the evening news. The topic of obesity—once relegated to medical and public health journals—has even been made the subject of popular television shows, such as *Shaq's Big Family Challenge* and *The Biggest Loser.*

Why has the issue gained such a high profile? One major reason is that over the past quarter century, obesity rates among children as well as adults have risen rapidly. Two out of three American adults today are overweight, and as the Centers for Disease Control and Prevention (CDC) reported in late November 2007, more than 72 million U.S. adults—34% of the U.S. population—are obese.[1] It was just ten years ago that obesity rates topped 20% for the first time and that was in three states, with every other state reporting rates in the range of 10% to 19%.[2]

The rapid rise of obesity and overweight among youth has been even more striking. In 2002, 16% of children and teenagers aged 6 to 19 were overweight, compared with only 4% of children aged 6 to 11 and 6% of adolescents in the early 1970s.[3] And the numbers appear likely to keep increasing. According to the Institute of Medicine, about one-third of American children and adolescents today are either obese or at risk of becoming obese.[4]

Another reason that obesity is getting so much attention is the associated health problems and costs. Obesity brings an increased risk of diabetes and other serious health problems, such as heart disease. It has become the second leading cause

of preventable death, behind smoking. And the annual costs of obesity in 2000 were estimated at $117 billion: $61 billion spent on treating health problems and $56 billion spent in indirect costs related to lost productivity, sick time, and other nonmedical expenditures.[5]

Public health authorities have sounded the alarm on the health consequences for children in particular, with pediatricians reporting increases in formerly adult conditions such as Type II diabetes and high blood pressure. Health experts warn that if current trends continue, one out of every three children born in the United States today will develop diabetes, and these children will die at a younger age than their parents.

Many cities and counties are addressing the issue by tackling two of the root causes of the trend: declining activity levels and poor diets. Local governments can do much to promote active living by using land use and zoning authority, for example, to encourage more pedestrian-friendly designs and a mix of land uses so as to put homes and/or offices in proximity to schools, parks, and shopping. Much has been learned in recent years about how community design affects physical activity levels and obesity; research has shown that people who live in compact neighborhoods with connected streets and a mix of shops and businesses do more walking than those who live in areas that are less pedestrian-friendly—and consequently enjoy the health benefits that come from that lifestyle.[6] On the food side of the equation, many local governments are supporting farmers' markets and community gardens to provide urban residents with better access to healthy food.

Despite the continued grim headlines about obesity, however, there are signs that the heightened public awareness might soon bring change. When the CDC announced that more than one-third of American adults are obese, many news reports highlighted another notable finding: the fact that the rate of obesity did not rise significantly from 2003–2004 to 2005–2006. Similarly, the CDC also reported in November 2007 that the prevalence of regular physical activity among American adults increased between 2001 and 2005: from 43% to nearly 47% among women, and from 48% to nearly 50% among men.[7]

Clearly, the nation's obesity epidemic and associated chronic health problems present huge challenges for local government, and evidence has shown that local government leaders are not only aware of and responsive to the obesity epidemic, but also looking into opportunities to do more. In 2004, ICMA surveyed municipal governments to find out their interests, needs, and programming related to active living, which refers not to exercise and fitness programs but to a way of life that incorporates physical activity into daily routines, such as walking to school or working in the garden. ICMA repeated the survey in 2007 in an effort to gauge changes over those three years and to get a similar read on new topics—namely, access to healthy food and initiatives to address youth obesity—that were not addressed by the first survey.

As with the 2004 survey, the National Association of Counties (NACo) partnered with ICMA to conduct a parallel survey of counties in 2007, which will be discussed briefly at the end of this article. In both cases, although NACo's survey reflects a different respondent perspective—that of elected county officials instead of appointed municipal officials—its findings are similar to ICMA's. Both groups of respondents have become more attuned over these three years to the role that local government can play in addressing obesity. Both groups also emphasize the importance of promoting active living over that of ensuring access to healthy foods, which indicates that responses to this epidemic are still evolving. Municipal and county leaders also cite similar challenges or barriers to their ability to promote active living and to address youth obesity, and they identify similar tools and strategies as the most helpful in this regard.

SURVEY METHODOLOGY

The new survey, *Active Living Approaches by Local Government, 2007,* was designed not only to update the findings from 2004, when ICMA and NACo focused primarily on active living, but also to gain a bigger picture of the issue: to better understand how local government leaders view

ICMA and the National Association of Counties (NACo) produced the *Active Living Approaches by Local Government, 2007* survey with support from the Robert Wood Johnson Foundation through its Leadership for Healthy Communities program, formerly known as Active Living Leadership. This national program is a partnership effort of ICMA, NACo, and other organizations working with local, state, and school leaders to create healthier communities by ensuring access to healthy foods, increasing opportunities for physical activity, and improving the social environments that shape how kids perceive healthy eating and active living. For more information, go to leadershipforhealthycommunities.org/.

their role in promoting active living and healthy eating, and to learn what actions they have undertaken to build healthier communities, which stakeholders have been most helpful to them in this regard, and what resources they have needed to aid them in their efforts.

As it did in 2004, ICMA developed the 2007 survey questions jointly with NACo. The new survey contained 3 of the 11 questions asked in 2004, as well as 10 new ones. Most of the new questions either focused on food access and youth obesity—both critical parts of the same "healthy communities" equation—or made changes to previous questions to get a more complete picture of what local governments are doing and who they are working with to promote active living and healthy eating. As with the first survey, the questions were designed to gauge awareness of and commitment to addressing these issues, as well as to identify challenges and the best ways to overcome them.

ICMA mailed a paper version of the survey in June 2007 to chief administrative officers in 3,264 municipalities (cities, towns, townships, villages, etc.) with populations of 10,000 or more. A second round of surveys was distributed via e-mail in July. These mailings generated a total of 518 responses for an overall response rate of 16% (Table 4/1). NACo e-mailed and faxed the survey in June to chief elected officials (CEOs) of 400 randomly selected counties. Because of a poor initial response, NACo e-mailed the survey to another 800 randomly selected CEOs in September and advertised the survey on an electronic mailing list of 580 county and noncounty individuals who are interested in health issues affecting local governments. In total, NACo received 86 responses from county representatives for a response rate of less than 7%. Each organization included similar introductory material, with the survey printed on its own stationery.

The ratio of responses received by ICMA and NACo in 2007 was similar to that received in 2004:

in 2007, ICMA received 16.6 responses for every NACo response compared with 13.3 in 2004.[8] Both organizations saw their response rates drop significantly from 2004 to 2007, with ICMA receiving about a 47% lower response rate in 2007 and NACo receiving about a 56% lower response rate.

AWARENESS AND COMMITMENT

The 2007 survey results indicate a growing awareness of the role that local governments can play in combating obesity. Virtually all the municipal officials responding to a question about their role said that it is important for local government to encourage and provide opportunities for residents to be physically active (Table 4/2). Of those, 70% said it is "very important," compared with 65% who said so in 2004 (not shown). Similarly, 70% of the respondents who answered a question about their residents' priorities indicated that opportunities for physical activity are important to residents, while 22% indicated that it is an emerging issue (not shown). The findings on both questions vary only slightly across population groups and geographic regions, although respondents from the

West show the highest percentages reporting that the local government role in encouraging and providing opportunities for physical activity is very important and that residents consider opportunities for physical activity to be an important issue.

While nearly all municipal officials indicated that it is a local government's responsibility to improve opportunities for physical activity, the survey results show more mixed responses on the question of how important it is for local government to ensure convenient access to healthy foods through grocery stories, farmers' markets, and community gardens. Twenty-five percent of the respondents to this question described that role as very important, and 56% said that it is somewhat important (Table 4/3). However, nearly one out of five said it is either not very important (12%) or not important at all (7%), despite the fact that among those who provided information about the availability of healthy foods, a majority said that this benefit is only somewhat accessible (48%) or not very accessible (9%) in their communities (not shown).

The difference in the responses regarding a local government's role in promoting active living on one hand and promoting healthy eating on

Table 4/1 SURVEY RESPONSE

Classification	No. of municipalities surveyed (A)	No. reporting No.	No. reporting % of (A)
Total	3,264	518	16
Population group			
250,000 and over	68	4	6
50,000–249,999	588	102	17
10,000–49,999	2,608	412	16
Geographic region			
Northeast	886	89	10
North-Central	914	162	18
South	841	138	16
West	623	129	21
Metro status			
Central	539	94	17
Suburban	2,106	326	16
Independent	619	98	16
Form of government			
Mayor-council	1,172	103	9
Council-manager	1,868	403	22
Commission	71	2	3
Town meeting	107	6	6
Representative town meeting	46	4	9

Table 4/2 IMPORTANCE OF LOCAL GOVERNMENT ENCOURAGING AND PROVIDING OPPORTUNITIES FOR RESIDENTS TO BE PHYSICALLY ACTIVE

Classification	No. reporting (A)	Very important % of (A)	Somewhat important % of (A)	Not very important % of (A)	Not at all important % of (A)
Total	516	70	29	1	0
Population group					
250,000 and over	4	100	0	0	0
50,000–249,999	102	74	27	0	0
10,000–49,999	410	69	30	1	0
Geographic region					
Northeast	88	67	33	0	0
North-Central	161	65	34	1	0
South	138	72	26	2	0
West	129	78	22	1	0
Metro status					
Central	94	80	20	0	0
Suburban	324	67	32	2	0
Independent	98	72	28	0	0

Note: Percentages may exceed 100% because of rounding.

Table 4/3 IMPORTANCE OF LOCAL GOVERNMENT EFFORTS TO ENSURE CONVENIENT ACCESS TO HEALTHY FOODS

Classification	No. reporting (A)	Very important % of (A)	Somewhat important % of (A)	Not very important % of (A)	Not at all important % of (A)
	513	25	56	12	7
Population group					
250,000 and over	4	50	25	25	0
50,000–249,999	101	29	55	10	6
10,000–49,999	408	23	57	13	7
Geographic region					
Northeast	88	36	52	8	3
North-Central	160	19	58	15	8
South	137	20	56	18	7
West	128	29	57	6	8
Metro status					
Central	93	25	58	15	2
Suburban	325	24	54	13	9
Independent	95	25	62	8	4

Note: Percentages may not total 100% because of rounding.

the other indicates greater confidence in a local government's ability to influence how active people are than to influence what they eat. One telling survey finding emerged from a question in which municipal officials were asked to review a list of 18 possible actions that a local government could take to address obesity and its related health problems, and to select the top three actions they could take that would have the greatest impact on those problems. As shown in Figure 4/1, the 294 respondents to the question favored developing a cohesive system of parks and trails (50%), using zoning to support a mix of land uses (37%), and requiring neighborhood streets to be designed with pedestrians and cyclists in mind (33%).

Each of these choices also ranks high in terms of municipalities that have already taken action. Among respondents who chose zoning and street

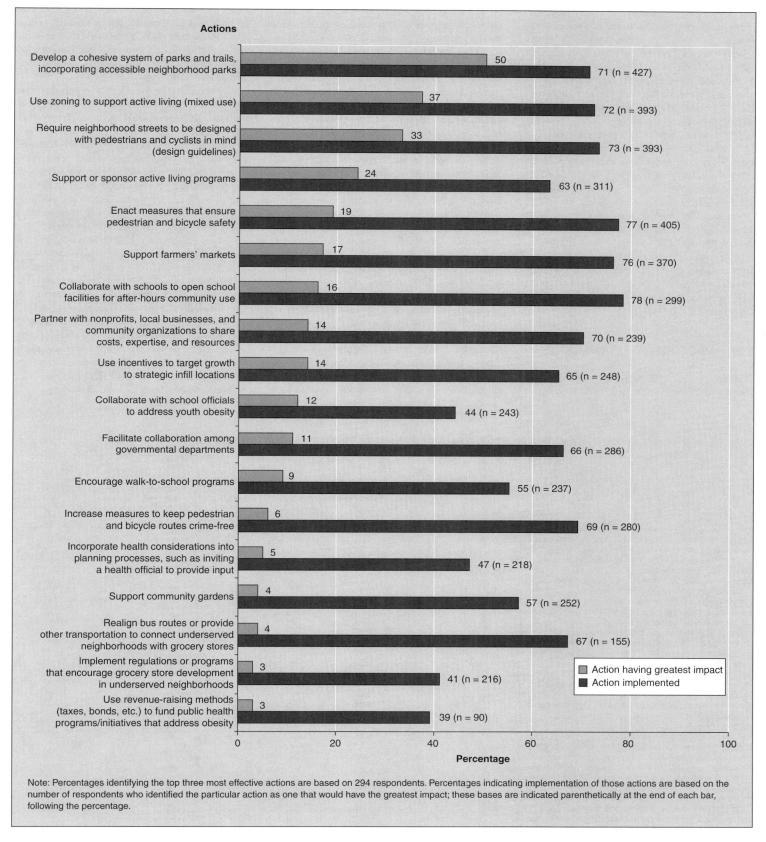

Actions

Action	Greatest impact	Action implemented
Develop a cohesive system of parks and trails, incorporating accessible neighborhood parks	50	71 (n = 427)
Use zoning to support active living (mixed use)	37	72 (n = 393)
Require neighborhood streets to be designed with pedestrians and cyclists in mind (design guidelines)	33	73 (n = 393)
Support or sponsor active living programs	24	63 (n = 311)
Enact measures that ensure pedestrian and bicycle safety	19	77 (n = 405)
Support farmers' markets	17	76 (n = 370)
Collaborate with schools to open school facilities for after-hours community use	16	78 (n = 299)
Partner with nonprofits, local businesses, and community organizations to share costs, expertise, and resources	14	70 (n = 239)
Use incentives to target growth to strategic infill locations	14	65 (n = 248)
Collaborate with school officials to address youth obesity	12	44 (n = 243)
Facilitate collaboration among governmental departments	11	66 (n = 286)
Encourage walk-to-school programs	9	55 (n = 237)
Increase measures to keep pedestrian and bicycle routes crime-free	6	69 (n = 280)
Incorporate health considerations into planning processes, such as inviting a health official to provide input	5	47 (n = 218)
Support community gardens	4	57 (n = 252)
Realign bus routes or provide other transportation to connect underserved neighborhoods with grocery stores	4	67 (n = 155)
Implement regulations or programs that encourage grocery store development in underserved neighborhoods	3	41 (n = 216)
Use revenue-raising methods (taxes, bonds, etc.) to fund public health programs/initiatives that address obesity	3	39 (n = 90)

Legend: Action having greatest impact / Action implemented

Percentage (0, 20, 40, 60, 80, 100)

Note: Percentages identifying the top three most effective actions are based on 294 respondents. Percentages indicating implementation of those actions are based on the number of respondents who identified the particular action as one that would have the greatest impact; these bases are indicated parenthetically at the end of each bar, following the percentage.

Figure 4/1   *Actions selected as having the greatest impact on obesity-related health problems and actions implemented*

design guidelines as the actions that would have the greatest impact in fighting obesity, 72% said that they have already implemented mixed-use zoning and 73% said that they have implemented street design guidelines; further, among those who identified parks and trails as an effective strategy, 71% said they are already developing such amenities (Figure 4/1). Again, these three strategies, which are more traditionally aligned with a local government's oversight of development, were the top three selected as the ones that local governments could take to have the greatest impact on health problems related to obesity. Yet local government support for farmers' markets, an action that 76% of both municipal and county respondents have already taken (see Table 4/4), was included by only 17% as one of the top three strategies.

Asked to select the two most important reasons for local governments to take a leadership role in fighting obesity, nearly 89% of the 423 municipal government respondents who answered the question selected "improving the quality of life for constituents" (not shown). The second most popular reason points to local governments' own bottom line as 53% selected "reducing health insurance/absenteeism costs to local governments and business." These are the two primary reasons among NACo's county respondents as well, the percentages being 84% and 49%, respectively (not shown).

ADDRESSING CHALLENGES

Findings from the 2007 survey provide an illuminating look at the barriers that local government leaders reportedly face in their efforts to promote active living, and their perspective on this issue has changed somewhat since 2004. From among eight possible barriers, the one identified by the largest percentage of respondents in 2007 is the same as that identified in 2004: a lack of funding, staff, or resources. This barrier was identified by 60% of those responding to this question, which reflects a decrease of 7 percentage points since 2004 (Figure 4/2). The second most common barrier, identified by 47% of the respondents (an increase of 7 percentage points since 2004), is that the community has not articulated physical activity as a priority. The third most-cited barrier, identified by 37% of the respondents in 2007, is the fact that encouraging physical activity is not regarded as the role of local government.

In addition to the smaller proportion of respondents who said they are stymied by a lack of funding or other resources, some notable changes are discernible between the findings from 2004 and those from 2007. Specifically, a greater percentage in 2007 cited a lack of knowledge in designing and implementing an effective active living initiative (roughly 30%, compared with only about 18% in 2004); 23% indicated there is no political will to support active living initiatives, up from just 13% in 2004; and the 37% who noted that encouraging physical activity is not regarded as a role of local government is up from 28% in 2004 (Figure 4/2).

When asked to rank eight possible tools and strategies in order of their helpfulness in addressing these barriers, only 65 municipal officials responded. Those who did, however, reveal a clear preference for resources that would improve their own ability to address the challenges. Ranked on an 8-point scale, with 1 being most helpful and 8 being least helpful, the following tools and strategies garnered the most responses ranking them as 1, 2, or 3: increased training and education on the subject (66%), sample policies and programs (63%), and best practices and case studies (60%). Considered to be less helpful are access to local experts, funders, and community groups (35%); research statistics showing the benefit of active living (28%); and facilitated connection with peers or with school officials (12% and 26%, respectively) (not shown).

Municipal leaders have a similar perspective of the barriers that a local government faces in its efforts to address youth obesity, although they place considerably more emphasis on how the issue is perceived by the public. The greatest challenge, identified by 71% of the respondents to this question, is that the community has not articulated youth obesity as a priority issue. A lack of funding, staff, or resources is the second most commonly cited challenge at 60%, and 46% of the respondents said that encouraging physical activity and healthy eating among children is not regarded as the role of local government (not shown). When asked to use the same 8-point scale to rank the helpfulness of specific tools and strategies in addressing youth obesity, the 79 respondents to this question focused on the same three approaches they had identified for the previous question on active living: the largest percentage of respondents (72%) ranked sample policies and programs as a 1, 2, or 3; the two other most popular choices are best practices and case studies (62%) and increased training and education (57%) (not shown).

Table 4/4   IMPLEMENTATION PLANS FOR ACTIONS TO ADDRESS HEALTH PROBLEMS RELATED TO OBESITY

Actions	ICMA				NACo	
	No. citing action as having greatest impact (A)	Feasible to implement in next year % of (A)	Planning to implement % of (A)	Have implemented % of (A)	No. citing action as having greatest impact (B)	Have implemented % of (B)
Collaborate with schools to open school facilities for after-hours community use	299	14	8	78	45	64
Enact measures that ensure pedestrian and bicycle safety	405	9	14	77	51	63
Support farmers' markets	370	14	11	76	70	76
Require neighborhood streets to be designed with pedestrians and cyclists in mind (design guidelines)	393	11	17	73	48	54
Use zoning to support active living (mixed use)	393	10	18	72	45	38
Develop a cohesive system of parks and trails, incorporating accessible neighborhood parks	427	8	21	71	57	79
Partner with nonprofits, local businesses, and community organizations to share costs, expertise, and resources	239	21	11	70	59	63
Increase measures to keep pedestrian and bicycle routes crime-free	280	18	13	69	39	62
Realign bus routes or provide other transportation to connect underserved neighborhoods with grocery stores	155	24	9	67	32	47
Facilitate collaboration among governmental departments	286	25	9	66	61	62
Use incentives to target growth to strategic infill locations	248	12	23	65	32	41
Support or sponsor active living programs	311	25	13	63	63	54
Support community gardens	252	30	13	57	47	53
Encourage walk-to-school programs	237	27	19	55	37	51
Incorporate health considerations into planning processes, such as inviting a health official to provide input	218	34	19	47	40	70
Collaborate with school officials to address youth obesity (data sharing, planning processes, task forces, after-school physical activity and/or nutrition programs)	243	33	24	44	58	48
Implement regulations or programs that encourage grocery store development in underserved neighborhoods	216	37	22	41	20	25
Use revenue-raising methods (taxes, bonds, etc.) to fund public health programs/initiatives that address obesity	90	48	13	39	32	38

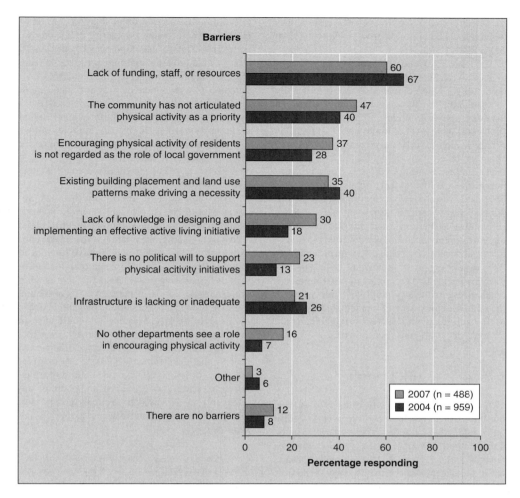

Barriers

Figure 4/2 *Barriers to promoting active living behaviors*

PARTNERING ON YOUTH OBESITY

The 2007 survey results make clear that local governments are still in the process of defining their role in addressing youth obesity and determining the best way to go about it. In response to the general question previously cited about the actions a local government can take that would have the greatest impact on health problems related to obesity, only between 9% and 16% of respondents checked the three actions related to schools. However, among all 18 possible actions that have been implemented, collaborating with schools to open school facilities for after-hours community use is the one that has been implemented by the largest proportion of respondents (78%) (Table 4/4). Beyond that, 55% of those who identified encouraging walk-to-school programs as having the greatest impact said that they have already done so, and 44% of those who selected collaborating with school officials to address youth obesity through data sharing, planning processes, etc., said that they have implemented such agreements.

One of the more notable findings from the survey came in response to a two-part question about how valuable different stakeholders are in assisting local governments in their efforts to combat youth obesity and whether the local governments are currently working with those stakeholders. The survey first asked respondents to rate 14 potential stakeholder partners—from parents and faith-based organizations to youth sports clubs and the private sector—on a scale from 1 (most valuable) to 5 (least valuable). Not surprisingly, the largest percentage of respondents chose parents as the most valuable partner in fighting youth obesity (92%); the only other stakeholders to be ranked most valuable by a majority of respondents are parks and recreation departments (59%) and schools (57%) (Table 4/5).

But in their answers to the second question—about whether they are currently working with these stakeholders—respondents indicated that some untapped opportunities exist for local governments in their efforts to reverse the trend of youth obesity. More than eight out of every ten officials who answered this question with regard to parks and recreation facilities said they are currently working with them; in contrast, only 38% of the respondents who answered with regard to parents said yes, as did only 59% of those who answered with regard to schools (Table 4/5). Local governments could build on efforts to address youth obesity by exploring opportunities to partner with parents and schools. With children, the first step can be as simple as replacing junk food

Table 4/5   VALUE OF STAKEHOLDERS IN COMBATING YOUTH OBESITY

| | Municipal officials (ICMA survey) | | | | | | | | County officials (NACo survey) | | | | | | | |
| | No. reporting (A) | Ranking, % of (A) | | | | | Currently working with | | No. reporting (C) | Ranking, % of (C) | | | | | Currently working with | |
Stakeholder		1	2	3	4	5	No. reporting (B)	% of (B)		1	2	3	4	5	No. reporting (D)	% of (D)
Parks and recreation...................	476	59	31	9	1	0	407	81	77	56	36	5	0	3	59	75
Youth sports clubs......................	464	39	43	16	2	*	391	61	66	33	49	30	2	2	58	31
Community organizations	457	26	33	32	8	1	385	60	78	33	45	15	4	3	60	73
Schools................................	465	57	36	7	1	*	403	59	79	68	27	4	1	0	64	67
Planners	454	15	27	35	16	7	379	57	78	35	30	21	9	6	57	53
Public health agencies	455	38	35	21	5	2	386	51	80	65	29	4	3	0	64	86
Transportation.........................	445	9	27	36	16	12	377	41	75	29	33	17	13	7	58	41
Parents	467	92	5	2	*	*	396	38	78	87	10	3	0	0	62	53
Private sector	447	14	29	37	15	5	379	36	72	19	51	15	10	4	59	34
Medical professionals	454	35	42	18	4	1	386	33	78	53	33	13	1	0	59	64
Food providers	444	25	30	25	14	6	366	17	70	40	29	19	9	0	57	30
Faith-based organizations...............	446	11	19	45	19	6	371	16	76	18	41	30	9	1	59	29
Extension services	425	4	19	37	27	13	361	16	77	34	35	22	8	1	61	66
Athlete/famous role models..............	445	12	32	32	16	8	373	13	76	21	32	21	13	9	56	7

Note: Percentages may not total 100% because of rounding.
* = Less than 0.5%.

and sugary drinks in school vending machines with healthy snacks, bottled water, and fruit juice. Other actions could include adding family nutrition education as a goal in after-school programs, making sure that kids have safe places to play and safe routes to walk or bike to school, and partnering with schools on a community health and fitness event. Communities across the country are pursuing all these changes. And the elected officials and professional managers who lead local government can work with schools, parents, and other partners to bring the same simple goals to other spheres of community life.

COMPARISON WITH NACO SURVEY RESULTS

Overall, ICMA's 2007 survey found that the strong support for active living seen in 2004 continues to grow among chief administrators and other nonelected officials in local government, and that most municipalities are focusing their efforts in the traditional realm of planning and community design, parks and trails, and support for farmers' markets. Some are also working with schools, primarily to help make school facilities available for after-hours community use.

The elected county officials who returned NACo's survey provided similar feedback. Just as 99% of ICMA's respondents said that it is either very important or somewhat important for local government to encourage and provide opportunities for residents to engage in physical activity, 95% of NACo's respondents made the same assessment. However, compared with ICMA's municipal leaders, NACo's county officials revealed a more marked change from 2004 to 2007 in how strongly they feel about the county's role (Table 4/6). The proportion of county respondents who described a local government's responsibility to encourage and provide opportunities

Table 4/6 IMPORTANCE OF LOCAL GOVERNMENT ENCOURAGING AND PROVIDING OPPORTUNITIES FOR RESIDENTS TO BE PHYSICALLY ACTIVE, 2004 AND 2007

	2004	2007	Change in percentage points
ICMA			
Very Important	64.8	70.3	+5.50
Somewhat Important	32.9	28.7	−4.20
Not very important	2.0	1.0	−1.00
Not at all important	0.3	0.0	−0.30
NACo			
Very Important	64.3	84.0	+19.7
Somewhat Important	31.0	10.5	−20.5
Not very important	4.0	3.5	−0.5
Not at all important	0.8	1.2	+0.4

for active living as very important, versus somewhat important, jumped from 64% to 84% in those three years.

The majority of municipal and county respondents also said that it is important for local governments to ensure convenient access to healthy food, but here, too, there were differences between the two groups. Municipal officials did not attribute the same level of importance to a focus on healthy eating as they did to active living: only about a quarter of municipal respondents answering this question described food access as a very important local government responsibility, whereas 56% said it is somewhat important (Table 4/3). Among county officials, however, 67% of those responding to the same question said that ensuring convenient access to healthy foods is a very important local government role, with an additional 29% describing it as somewhat important (not shown). Yet the two groups are more in alignment when assessing the availability of healthy food in their communities: 44% of municipal respondents to this question said it is very accessible, as did 40% of county officials (not shown).

CONCLUSION

The trend of rising obesity rates is rooted in lifestyle changes that have evolved over the course of a couple of generations. These changes can be traced to multiple causes—the way communities are built and designed, the way people get around and children get to school, the way they spend their free time, and, in many homes, the time and money available to prepare meals. Reversing this trend will be extremely challenging.

The fight against obesity has to be built around public education, and it starts with youth. It requires getting back to a way of living that enables people to strike the right energy balance between the food that is taken in and the calories that are expended. Over the past decade, the phrase "active living" has come into regular use to describe the routine activity that comes in the course of daily life—whether it's walking to the office, doing yard work on a Saturday, taking the dog for a walk, playing with the kids in a park, or going shopping downtown. The point is simple: activity doesn't have to be structured exercise in order to have health benefits. At the same time, healthy eating isn't just about avoiding too many potato chips or too much ice cream. It's about getting a balanced diet and eating more fresh nutritious food. It's about making it easier for someone living on food stamps to purchase produce at a farmers' market.

As public awareness of the obesity epidemic increases, appointed and elected officials from cities and counties are becoming more attuned to the broad-based role that local government can play in creating healthy communities, more committed to action, more innovative in their approaches to tackling the problem, and more proactive in their efforts

to build partnerships around shared community interests. The growing popularity of mixed-use, pedestrian-friendly development since the 1990s, along with a growing commitment to revitalizing older neighborhoods and providing multiple transportation options in more densely developed areas, all complement the heightened focus on active living. And growing support for farmers' markets and community gardens is just one indication that municipal and county officials are beginning to see more of a local government role in making sure that all residents have convenient access to affordable, healthy food.

Local elected and appointed officials are uniquely positioned to provide the vision and leadership needed at the community level to make active living and healthy eating a shared community goal. They know they will have to work at multiple levels—with multiple partners—to forestall the impending health crisis that looms, with more than one-third of Americans being obese and a similar proportion of children being either obese or at risk of obesity. Success will come with an integrated, multidisciplinary approach, one that benefits from the leadership of elected officials and professional management—and one that involves all levels of local government, including transportation, parks and recreation, and planning departments, as well as state agencies, community groups, businesses, nonprofit organizations, and schools.

---

[1] Centers for Disease Control and Prevention (CDC), "Obesity among Adults in the United States—No Statistically Significant Change since 2003–2004," *NCHS Data Brief*, no. 1 (November 2007), available at cdc.gov/nchs/data/databriefs/db01.pdf.

[2] CDC Behavioral Risk Factor Surveillance System, "U.S. Obesity Trends 1986–2006," available at cdc.gov/nccdphp/dnpa/obesity/trend/maps/.

[3] CDC, National Center for Health Statistics, "Prevalence of Overweight among Children and Adolescents: United States, 1999–2002," available at cdc.gov/nchs/products/pubs/pubd/hestats/overwght99.htm.

[4] Institute of Medicine of the National Academies, *Progress in Preventing Childhood Obesity: How Do We Measure Up?* (Washington, D.C.: The National Academies, 2006), available at iom.edu/?id=37007.

[5] CDC provides a variety of data and information, including the estimated costs of obesity-related chronic diseases, in "Preventing Obesity and Chronic Diseases through Good Nutrition and Physical Activity," available at cdc.gov/nccdphp/publications/factsheets/Prevention/obesity.htm; see also the U.S. Department of Health and Human Services, "Overweight and Obesity: At a Glance," available at surgeongeneral.gov/topics/obesity/calltoaction/fact_glance.htm.

[6] Summaries of research conducted on the relationships among the built environment, physical activity, and obesity are available through the Robert Wood Johnson Foundation, Active Living Research, at activelivingresearch.org/resourcesearch/summaries; see also activelivingresearch.org/index.php/What_We_are_Learning/117.

[7] CDC, "Prevalence of Regular Physical Activity among Adults—United States, 2001 and 2005," *Morbidity and Mortality Report Weekly*, November 23, 2007, 1209–1212, available at cdc.gov/mmwr/preview/mmwrhtml/mm5646a1.htm?s_cid=mm5646a1_e.

[8] Nadejda Mishkovsky, "Local Government Approaches to Active Living," *The Municipal Year Book 2005* (Washington, D.C.: ICMA, 2005), 9–13.

A5

Municipal Form of Government: Trends in Structure, Responsibility, and Composition

Evelina R. Moulder
ICMA

Selected Findings

The current survey results show a slight increase since 2001 in the percentage reporting the council-manager form, as well as a slight decrease in the percentage reporting the mayor-council form.

The percentage of municipalities that reported a position for a CAO, often titled "city manager" or "chief administrative officer," has increased four percentage points since 2001.

Only larger cities, those with a population of 250,000 and above, show a majority of cities reporting term limits for council members.

ICMA has been conducting a survey on municipal form of government for many years. The longitudinal data that emerge allow researchers to compare over time the changes in the form and structure of city government. Sometimes the changes are noticeable, such as the increase in chief appointed official (CAO) positions in all forms of government, and sometimes they are more nuanced, such as the characteristics that point to a loosening of the boundaries of traditional forms of government. This year ICMA adds another set of data to extend the picture of these and other developing trends.

SURVEY METHODOLOGY

The *Municipal Form of Government, 2006* survey was mailed in August 2006 to all municipalities with a population of 2,500 and over and to those under 2,500 that are in the ICMA database (there are thousands of municipalities under 2,500 in population). A second mail was sent to those municipalities that did not respond to the first mail. The final response rate was 47% (Table 5/1), which is lower than in previous years. Anecdotal information suggests that local governments are inundated with surveys and have become less likely to respond.

DEFINITIONS AND FINDINGS

The *Municipal Form of Government, 2006* survey used the following definitions for the five forms of government:

- *Mayor-council:* An elected council or board serves as the legislative body. The chief elected official (CEO) is the head of government, with significant administrative authority, generally elected separately from the council.
- *Council-manager:* An elected council or board and CEO (e.g., mayor) are responsible for making policy with advice of the CAO. A professional administrator appointed by the board or council has full responsibility for the day-to-day operations of the government.
- *Commission:* Members of a board of elected commissioners serve as heads of specific departments and collectively sit as the legislative body of the government.

Table 5/1 SURVEY RESPONSE

Classification	No. of municipalities[1] surveyed (A)	No responding No.	No responding % of (A)
Total	8,278	3,864	47
Population group			
Over 1,000,000	9	2	22
500,000–1,000,000. .	23	9	39
250,000–499,999 . . .	36	17	47
100,000–249,999 . . .	179	100	56
50,000–99,999	408	227	56
25,000–49,999	780	424	54
10,000–24,999	1,826	883	48
5,000–9,999	1,889	868	46
2,500–4,999	2,011	839	42
Under 2,500	1,117	495	44
Geographic region			
Northeast	2,155	807	37
North-Central	2,463	1,227	50
South	2,415	1,120	46
West	1,245	710	57
Geographic division			
New England	845	401	48
Mid-Atlantic.	1,310	406	31
East North-Central . .	1,573	748	48
West North-Central. .	890	479	54
South Atlantic	1,099	575	52
East South-Central . .	494	170	34
West South-Central .	823	376	46
Mountain.	470	266	57
Pacific Coast.	774	443	57
Metro status			
Central	540	283	52
Suburban	4,949	2,361	48
Independent	2,789	1,220	44

[1]For a definition of terms, please see "Inside the *Year Book*," x.

- *Town meeting:* Qualified voters convene to make basic policy and to choose a board of selectmen. The selectmen and elected officers carry out the policies established by the government.
- *Representative town meeting:* Voters select citizens to represent them at the town meeting. All citizens may attend and participate in debate, but only representatives may vote.

Among municipalities, the council-manager and mayor-council forms of government are the most prevalent, reported by 55% and 34% of respondents, respectively (Table 5/2). The town meeting, a form of government found especially in New England, was reported by 5% overall and by 49% of New England municipalities. Less than 1% reported the commission or representative town meeting form of government.

Included on Table 5/2 is a column for those local governments that did not report their form of government. Although their answers to some of the other questions on the survey may suggest a particular form of government, any assumptions that might be drawn would be unreliable.

When compared with the forms of government reported in the 2001 survey, the current results show a slight increase in the percentage reporting the council-manager form, as well as a slight decrease in the percentage reporting the mayor-council form. In 2001, 53% reported the council-manager form and 38%, the mayor-council form of government.[1]

Only 11 of the 32 municipalities with a population of 500,000 and over responded to the survey, and one of them did not answer the form-of-government question, so for larger cities, it is not possible to draw conclusions about the relationship between population size and form of government. Among cities with a population of 5,000–249,999, however, the majority reported the council-manager form of government, as did a bare majority of those under 2,500 in population. As previously noted, there are thousands of municipalities with a population below 2,500; because ICMA's database contains only a small proportion of those jurisdictions, the data on them cannot be considered reflective of that cohort.

According to a majority of respondents overall (57%) and all cities with a population of 500,000 and above, their form of government is established in the charter (Figure 5/1).

Position of Chief Appointed Official

The percentage of municipalities that reported a position for a CAO, often titled "city manager" or "chief administrative officer," has increased four percentage points since 2001.[2] As shown in Table 5/3, there are some variations by population, geographic division, and form of government.

In the majority of cities that have a CAO (68%), the official is appointed by the council (Table 5/4), although again there are variations by geographic division and form of government. In particular, mayor-council and commission localities show the

Table 5/2   MUNICIPAL FORM OF GOVERNMENT

Classification	No. reporting (A)	Mayor-council % of (A)	Council-manager % of (A)	Commission % of (A)	Town meeting % of (A)	Representative town meeting % of (A)	Did not report % of (A)
Total	3,864	34	55	1	5	1	4
Population group							
Over 1,000,000	2	0	100	0	0	0	0
500,000–1,000,000	9	44	44	0	0	0	11
250,000–499,999	17	65	35	0	0	0	0
100,000–249,999	100	27	70	0	0	0	3
50,000–99,999	227	26	67	1	*	1	5
25,000–49,999	424	31	63	1	1	1	4
10,000–24,999	883	29	59	1	5	1	4
5,000–9,999	868	33	54	1	7	1	4
2,500–4,999	839	43	44	1	7	1	5
Under 2,500	495	39	50	*	5	0	6
Geographic division							
New England	401	11	29	*	49	4	7
Mid-Atlantic	406	46	42	4	0	1	8
East North-Central	748	42	50	1	*	1	5
West North-Central	479	52	44	1	0	0	3
South Atlantic	575	23	73	1	0	0	4
East South-Central	170	67	28	1	0	0	5
West South-Central	376	29	69	*	0	0	2
Mountain	266	40	58	0	0	0	3
Pacific Coast	443	17	80	0	0	0	3
Metro status							
Central	283	35	60	*	0	0	4
Suburban	2,360	32	55	1	5	1	5
Independent	1,220	38	52	1	6	*	3

Note: Percentages may not total 100% because of rounding.
* = Less than 0.5%.

Table 5/3   POSITION OF CHIEF APPOINTED OFFICIAL

Classification	No. reporting (A)	Yes No.	Yes % of (A)
Total	3,788	3,216	85
Population group			
Over 1,000,000	2	2	100
500,000–1,000,000	9	6	67
250,000–499,999	17	12	71
100,000–249,999	99	89	90
50,000–99,999	223	192	86
25,000–49,999	418	358	86
10,000–24,999	866	758	88
5,000–9,999	851	725	85
2,500–4,999	824	661	80
Under 2,500	479	413	86
Geographic division			
New England	398	319	80
Mid-Atlantic	393	314	80
East North-Central	731	571	78
West North-Central	469	422	90
South Atlantic	565	540	96
East South-Central	165	94	57
West South-Central	371	313	84
Mountain	262	224	86
Pacific Coast	434	419	97
Metro status			
Central	277	222	80
Suburban	2,310	2,005	87
Independent	1,201	989	82
Form of government			
Did not report	106	86	81
Mayor-council	1,319	834	63
Council-manager	2,106	2,099	100
Commission	35	22	63
Town meeting	194	154	79
Representative town meeting	28	21	75

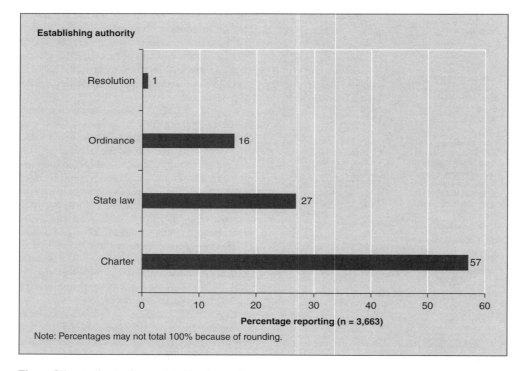

Figure 5/1   *Authority for establishing form of government*

ordinance, or home rule change that has been proposed by citizens through a petition process can be placed on the ballot, the council must consider it. Vote results are then binding on the local government. In contrast, the *direct* initiative requires that any change proposed by the citizens through a petition process be placed directly on the ballot for a vote. The direct initiative can be nonbinding, in which case citizens can place a question on the ballot for voter approval or rejection, but implementation of the initiative is not binding on the local government.

A majority of municipalities (58%) reported providing for initiatives, although population size seems to influence the prevalence of this option (Table 5/6). The cities with a population of 500,000 and above all offer citizens this opportunity, but among cities reporting with a population under 5,000, less than 50% do. The percentages vary even more by geographic division, as the highest percentages providing for initiatives are cities in the New England (81%) and Pacific Coast (79%) divisions, and the lowest are East South-Central division cities (26%), followed by cities in the South Atlantic and West North-Central divisions (38% and 39%, respectively).

Among forms of government, the town meeting municipalities show the highest percentage providing for initiatives (85%), followed by the representative town meeting (65%) and council-manager cities (62%).

Legislative Referendum   Legislative referendum allows the council to place any question on the

lowest percentages reporting appointment solely by the council and the highest percentages showing appointment involving the elected official.

Provision for Initiative, Referenda, and Recall
There are various provisions that allow citizens or the council to introduce items on a ballot. These

provisions are initiative, referenda, and recall (Table 5/5).

Initiative   Through an initiative, citizens can place charter, ordinance, or home rule changes on the ballot by collecting the required number of signatures on a petition. There are three types of initiatives: indirect, direct, and nonbinding. The *indirect* provision requires that before any charter,

Table 5/4   APPOINTMENT OF CHIEF APPOINTED OFFICIAL

		Appointed by			Nominated by		
Classification	No. reporting (A)	Chief elected official % of (A)	Council % of (A)	Chief elected official and council combined % of (A)	Chief elected official and approved by council % of (A)	Council and approved by chief elected official % of (A)	Other % of (A)
Total	3,159	4	68	19	9	*	1
Population group							
Over 1,000,000	2	0	50	50	0	0	0
500,000–1,000,000 . . .	5	20	40	40	0	0	0
250,000–499,999	12	25	42	8	25	0	0
100,000–249,999	89	6	63	27	3	0	1
50,000–99,999	188	3	67	23	6	0	0
25,000–49,999	351	3	69	19	9	*	*
10,000–24,999	748	4	70	16	10	*	1
5,000–9,999	709	5	69	16	9	*	1
2,500–4,999	651	3	65	21	9	0	1
Under 2,500	404	3	68	22	7	*	*
Geographic division							
New England	314	7	85	5	1	0	2
Mid-Atlantic	300	6	65	14	14	0	1
East North-Central	565	5	54	24	16	*	1
West North-Central . . .	414	2	62	24	11	1	1
South Atlantic	527	1	74	21	3	*	*
East South-Central . . .	96	8	51	25	15	0	1
West South-Central . . .	305	2	71	23	4	0	1
Mountain	225	4	58	24	13	0	1
Pacific Coast	413	3	80	12	4	0	*
Metro status							
Central	216	7	64	22	7	0	1
Suburban	1,963	4	67	19	10	*	1
Independent	980	3	71	19	7	*	1
Form of government							
Mayor-council	833	10	43	23	21	*	2
Council-manager	2,049	1	77	19	4	0	*
Commission	22	0	50	27	9	0	14
Town meeting	150	12	79	6	0	0	3
Representative town meeting	21	0	86	0	10	5	0
Did not report	84	7	73	10	10	0	1

Note: Percentages may not total 100% because of rounding.
* = Less than 0.5%.

Table 5/6   PROVISION FOR INITIATIVE AND INITIATIVE PROCESS

		Has provision for initiative		Type of initiative process			
Classification	No. reporting (A)	No.	% of (A)	No. reporting (B)	Indirect % of (B)	Direct % of (B)	Nonbinding % of (B)
Total	3,603	2,073	58	1,902	49	49	15
Population group							
Over 1,000,000	2	2	100	2	50	50	0
500,000–1,000,000 . . .	9	9	100	9	44	56	22
250,000–499,999	17	15	88	15	33	73	13
100,000–249,999	97	83	86	71	59	45	13
50,000–99,999	214	161	75	147	63	44	14
25,000–49,999	404	284	70	260	50	50	14
10,000–24,999	823	501	61	462	52	49	15
5,000–9,999	810	466	58	435	46	48	16
2,500–4,999	773	368	48	333	43	54	14
Under 2,500	454	184	41	168	49	48	15
Geographic division							
New England	385	313	81	297	45	52	22
Mid-Atlantic	363	153	42	134	42	42	38
East North-Central	692	433	63	401	41	53	21
West North-Central . . .	446	174	39	161	58	42	6
South Atlantic	543	204	38	190	58	38	10
East South-Central	149	38	26	35	37	54	14
West South-Central . . .	350	233	67	210	54	49	6
Mountain	252	190	75	175	57	50	8
Pacific Coast	423	335	79	299	53	57	8
Form of government							
Mayor-council	1,222	566	46	516	46	48	21
Council-manager	2,034	1,263	62	1,163	54	48	10
Commission	34	17	50	15	27	60	27
Town meeting	188	159	85	148	36	57	26
Representative town meeting	26	17	65	14	7	43	57
Did not report	99	51	52	46	37	61	20

Table 5/5   PROVISION FOR INITIATIVE, REFERENDA, AND RECALL

Provision	No. reporting (A)	Has provision % of (A)
Initiative	3,603	58
Legislative referendum . . .	3,497	76
Popular referendum	3,189	45
Recall	3,311	60

ballot for voter approval or rejection. The results may be binding or nonbinding. Slightly more than 75% of municipalities reported a provision for legislative referenda, with population size seeming to influence the responses. Among population groups, for example, the larger the group, the higher the percentage reporting this provision. All cities reporting with a population of 500,000 and above offer legislative referenda compared with 68% of those with a population under 2,500 (not shown). Among geographic divisions, close to 60% of cities in the East South-Central division do not have legislative referenda, compared with 24% overall. Among forms of government, the town meeting and council-manager forms show the highest percentages offering this type of provision (88% and 79%, respectively).

For those municipalities that reported providing for a legislative referendum, the survey included a follow-up question to determine which items must be placed on the ballot. Figure 5/2 shows the percentage reporting each item. Bond measures and charter amendments were reported by the highest percentages (67% and 56%, respectively), with the percentage reporting bond measures increasing among the smaller local governments (not shown). The East South-Central and Mid-Atlantic divisions show the lowest percentages indicating that bond measures must be placed on the ballot for voter approval; the council-manager and town meeting forms of government show the highest percentages, followed by mayor-council cities. There is more variation by population and geographic division regarding charter amendments, with no discernable pattern emerging.

Popular Referendum   Popular referendum allows citizens to collect signatures on a petition to place on the ballot any charter, ordinance, or home rule change that has been adopted by the local government *before* the change can take effect. Approximately 45% of municipalities reported this option for citizens, with cities in larger population groups showing higher percentages than smaller cities. Among geographic divisions, there seems to be a greater tendency in the East and West to make this option available than in the central part of the country, although the Mid-Atlantic division cities show a relatively low percentage reporting it (Figure 5/3). Among forms of government, the town meeting cities show the highest percentage reporting popular referendum (67%), followed by council-manager cities (48%) (not shown).

Recall   Recall allows citizens to collect signatures for a petition to place on the ballot a question of whether an elected official should be removed

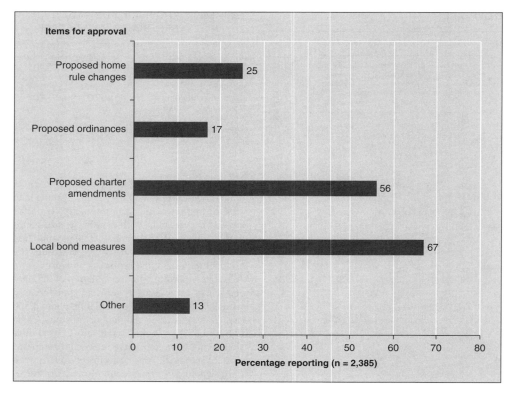

Figure 5/2   *Items that must be placed on the ballot for voter approval or rejection*

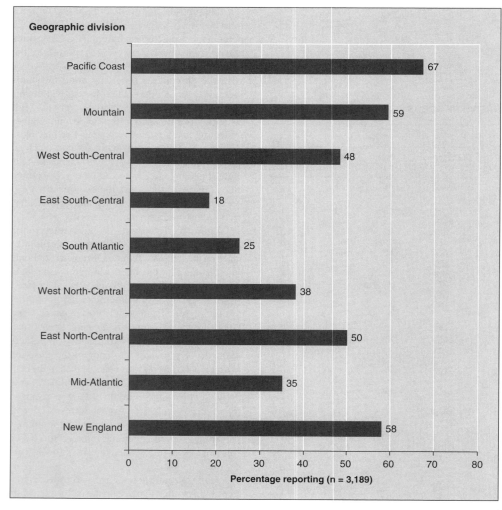

Figure 5/3   *Popular referendum provided on the ballot, by geographic division*

from office before his or her term has expired. Sixty percent of municipalities reported a provision for recall, with the highest percentages seen among larger local governments. Among the geographic divisions, Pacific Coast cities show the highest percentage by far reporting this provision (90%), followed by the Mountain and West South-Central divisions at 78% (not shown).

Among forms of government, the council-manager localities show the highest percentage with a provision for recall at 67%, followed by cities with the commission form (55%); however, only 31 cities with the commission form answered the question (not shown). Mayor-council cities show 52% with a provision for recall.

Change in Structure or Form of Government
With the various opportunities for citizens to place items on the ballot, it is not surprising that some changes in either the structure or form of local government were introduced between January 2001 and when the survey was conducted in 2006. Table 5/7 shows the attempted changes in structure or form of government reported on the survey and results of the attempt. Among the proposed changes, 50% or more respondents reported that approval was obtained to increase or decrease the number of council or board members, to change the method of electing the CEO, to decrease the power/authority of the CEO, and to add the position of CAO.

As might be anticipated, the changes in form of government typically involve mayor-council and council-manager localities because these represent the largest proportion of local governments. Overall, 23 cities reported a proposed change in form of government to mayor-council, 5 of which (5%) reported that the proposals were approved (Table 5/8).

The highest number of municipalities proposing a change in form of government (70) reported a proposed change to the council-manager form; of those, 35 (50%) reported that the proposals were approved.

The Chief Elected Official
Some local governments, primarily mayor-council cities (31%), have positions for both a mayor *and* a council president or board chair (not shown). At least 92% of all survey respondents with the town meeting and representative town meeting forms of government reported a council president or board chair position, but no more than 8% reported the position of mayor. Survey respondents were instructed to answer the questions that followed based on the position of mayor if they have one, or on the position of council president or chair if they do not have a mayor.

Election   Although in the majority of cities (76%), voters elect the mayor or council president/board chair directly, there are some variations by population, geographic division, and form of government (Table 5/9). For instance, in all cities with a population of 250,000 and above, the voters directly elect the CEO. Below that population cutoff, there is not a great deal of variation in the percentages reporting direct election.

When the data are arrayed by geographic division, however, it is noticeable that almost half of the New England cities reported that the council

Table 5/7 PROPOSED CHANGES IN STRUCTURE OR FORM OF GOVERNMENT

Proposed changes	No. reporting change was proposed (A)	Change was not approved % of (A)	Change was approved % of (A)
Change . . .			
From at-large to ward or district elections	38	40	42
From ward or district to at-large elections	23	39	48
To a mixed system with some at-large and some ward or district elections. . . .	20	45	45
The mix between the number of council members elected at large and the number elected by ward or district	19	47	37
The method of election of the chief elected official.	33	29	56
Who appoints the chief appointed official.	4	1	0
The form of government.	118	44	45
Increase . . .			
The number of council or board members	58	35	59
The powers/authorities of the chief elected official.	24	50	42
Decrease . . .			
The number of council or board members	22	36	55
The power/authority of the chief elected official	27	30	56
Add the position of chief appointed official (the appointed professional administrator)	71	21	72
Eliminate the position of chief appointed official (the appointed professional administrator)	17	53	29

Note: Not all who reported that the change was proposed answered whether it was approved, which explains why the percentages do not total 100%.

Table 5/8 CHANGES IN FORM OF GOVERNMENT: NUMBER OF PROPOSALS ATTEMPTED AND APPROVED

		Change to								
		Mayor-council		Council-manager		Commission		Town meeting		Representative town meeting
Change from	No. reporting	Att.	App.	Att.	App.	Att.	App.	Att.	App.	Att.	App.
Mayor-council.	55			55	25	0	0	0	0	0	0
Council-manager . . .	20	19	2			0	0	1	0	0	0
Commission	7	1	1	6	5			0	0	0	0
Town meeting.	8	1	1	7	3	0	0			0	0
Representative town meeting	5	2	1	2	2	0	0	1	0		

Note: Att. = attempted, app. = approved.

Table 5/9 SELECTION OF CHIEF ELECTED OFFICIAL

Classification	No. reporting (A)	Voters elect directly % of (A)	Council selects from among its members	Council member receiving the most votes	Council members rotate into the position % of (A)	Other % of (A)
Total	3,629	76	22	1	2	*
Population group						
Over 1,000,000	2	100	0	0	0	0
500,000–1,000,000	8	100	0	0	0	0
250,000–499,999.	17	100	0	0	0	0
100,000–249,999.	99	87	11	0	2	0
50,000–99,999.	218	75	23	1	1	0
25,000–49,999.	400	73	25	1	2	0
10,000–24,999.	819	71	27	*	2	*
5,000–9,999.	816	77	22	*	1	*
2,500–4,999.	778	79	18	*	2	1
Under 2,500.	472	79	19	1	1	*
Geographic division						
New England	340	44	49	1	5	1
Mid-Atlantic	384	66	32	1	1	*
East North-Central.	706	83	16	1	*	*
West North-Central	463	90	10	*	*	0
South Atlantic	550	83	15	1	1	*
East South-Central	159	87	13	0	0	0
West South-Central	353	89	10	*	0	1
Mountain	259	88	12	0	0	*
Pacific Coast	415	54	40	1	6	0
Form of government						
Mayor-council	1,262	96	3	*	*	*
Council-manager.	1,999	67	30	1	2	*
Commission.	34	56	41	3	0	0
Town meeting	158	46	46	0	8	1
Representative town meeting . . .	25	44	44	0	12	0
Did not report.	151	70	27	2	1	1

Note: Percentages may not total 100% because of rounding.
* = Less than 0.5%.

selects the CEO from among its members, as did 40% of cities in the Pacific Coast division.

In cities with a mayor-council form of government, 96% reported that voters directly elect the mayor. By contrast, in council-manager cities, 67% reported that voters directly elect the mayor, while 30% reported that the council selects the CEO from among its members.

Almost 86% of local governments reported that the position of CEO is officially part time, although a majority of larger local governments (those with a population of 250,000 and above) indicated that the position is full time (not shown). Ninety-five percent of respondents in council-manager cities reported that the CEO's position is part time, compared with 72% of respondents in mayor-council cities.

Terms of Office A four-year term was reported by the highest percentage of respondents, followed by a two-year term (Table 5/10). Four-year terms were generally reported by higher percentages of larger cities than smaller cities and by 87% of cities in the East South-Central division (not shown). Council-manager cities show the highest percentage reporting two-year terms (41%), and mayor-council cities show the highest percentage reporting four-year terms (68%). The town meeting and representative town meeting local governments show percentages way above the average reporting a one-year term (44% and 52%, respectively).

The vast majority (91%) of cities do not have legal limits on the number of terms allowed for the position of CEO (not shown); generally, those cities that do have term limits are larger. Where term limits are imposed, the majority (54%) of cities show a limit of two terms, followed by 28% reporting three terms.

Responsibilities and Authority of the Chief Elected Official

Although the distinctions are not consistent across local governments, typically CEOs have varying degrees of responsibility and authority, depending on the form of government.

Serving on the Council and Voting in Meetings The CEO serves on the council in 72% of reporting cities overall, but noticeably in only 44% of mayor-council cities (not shown). A slim majority of those cities in which the CEO is on the council reported that the official receives supplemental compensation for the additional duties involved (not shown).

Although 72% of council-manager and approximately 90% of commission, town meeting, and representative town meeting local government respondents reported that the CEO can vote on all issues before the council, in only 26% of mayor-

Table 5/10 LENGTH OF TERM FOR CHIEF ELECTED OFFICIAL

Length of term	Percentage reporting (n = 3,361)
1 year	14
2 years	35
3 years	6
4 years	45
Other.	1

council cities does the CEO have this authority (Table 5/11). Among mayor-council cities, however, 55% reported that the CEO is permitted to vote to break a tie while 17% reported that the CEO is never permitted to vote.

Budget Responsibility Since 1996, there has been a small but steady drop in the percentage of cities reporting that the CEO has the authority to develop and make recommendations for the budget submitted to council—from 13% in 1996[3] to 12% in 2001[4] and 11% in 2006. At the same time, the percentage reporting that the authority lies with the CAO has increased noticeably—from 57% in 2001 to 65% in 2006. As Table 5/12 shows, even among mayor-council and commission forms of government, the CAO has this responsibility more often than the CEO.

The survey also covered several areas of authority of the CEO, including

- Assigning council members to chair or serve on committees
- Appointing citizens to serve on advisory or quasi-judicial authorities, boards, or commissions
- Receiving the annual budget developed by the CAO
- Preparing the annual budget
- Making an annual report to the council.

Approximately 75% of respondents reported that the CEO has the authority to assign council members to chair or serve on committees, and slightly more reported the authority to appoint citizens to serve on advisory or quasi-judicial authorities, boards, or commissions (not shown). However, just 50% reported that the CEO has the authority to make an annual report to council, and less than a majority (42%) reported that the CEO is authorized to receive the annual budget.

Election and Terms of Council Members
Among the questions that ICMA staff are often asked are whether the political party of a candidate for the council is placed on the ballot and whether council members have term limits. The survey results show that while political party is on the ballot in only 20% of cities reporting overall, it is on the ballot in 87% of cities in the Mid-Atlantic geographic division—an anomaly that was reflected in the 2001 survey results as well (not shown).

Elections: At Large and Ward/District
Although two-thirds of local government respondents (66%) reported that council members are elected at large, cities with a population of 250,000 and above tend to show election by ward, or district, or by a combination of the two methods. Another interesting variation is that cities on the coasts show higher percentages reporting at-large elections than do those in the middle of the country. For example, only 45% in the West North-Central geographic division reported at-large elections compared with 81% and 89% in the New England and Pacific Coast divisions, respectively (not shown).

Approximately 17% of those reporting indicated that they use of elections by ward/district, and 17% show a combination of at-large and ward/district elections. The highest percentages reporting elections by ward/district alone are in the West North-

Table 5/11 VOTING AUTHORITY OF CHIEF ELECTED OFFICIAL

Classification	No. reporting (A)	On all issues % of (A)	Only to break a tie % of (A)	Never % of (A)	Other % of (A)
Total	3,564	57	34	7	2
Population group					
Over 1,000,000	2	100	0	0	0
500,000–1,000,000	8	50	0	50	0
250,000–499,999	17	35	6	59	0
100,000–249,999	99	74	10	14	2
50,000–99,999	215	71	16	11	2
25,000–49,999	392	63	23	10	4
10,000–24,999	807	62	28	9	2
5,000–9,999	793	56	38	4	1
2,500–4,999	769	45	49	5	1
Under 2,500	462	54	41	5	1
Geographic division					
New England	320	78	10	10	2
Mid-Atlantic	374	57	32	9	2
East North-Central	685	52	37	9	3
West North-Central	452	41	41	16	2
South Atlantic	548	57	39	4	*
East South-Central	159	47	40	11	3
West South-Central	347	46	50	2	1
Mountain	262	54	42	3	1
Pacific Coast	417	81	17	1	1
Form of government					
Mayor-council	1,231	26	55	17	3
Council-manager	1,986	72	25	2	1
Commission	33	88	9	3	0
Town meeting	143	91	6	2	1
Representative town meeting	22	91	5	5	0
Did not respond	149	62	33	5	1

Note: Percentages may not total 100% because of rounding.
* = Less than 0.5%.

Table 5/12 AUTHORITY TO DEVELOP AND MAKE RECOMMENDATIONS FOR THE BUDGET SUBMITTED TO THE COUNCIL

Classification	No. reporting (A)	Chief elected official % of (A)	Chief appointed official % of (A)	Chief elected and chief appointed officials, combined % of (A)	Chief financial officer % of (A)	Finance committee % of (A)	Other % of (A)
Total	3,549	11	65	8	10	1	5
Population group							
Over 1,000,000	1	0	100	0	0	0	0
500,000–1,000,000	8	50	38	0	0	0	13
250,000–499,999	16	31	44	6	19	0	0
100,000–249,999	96	14	79	5	2	0	0
50,000–99,999	210	12	73	5	7	0	3
25,000–49,999	395	14	71	4	9	0	2
10,000–24,999	807	12	67	8	10	1	4
5,000–9,999	793	10	63	7	12	1	6
2,500–4,999	766	11	57	11	11	2	8
Under 2,500	457	7	69	7	8	1	8
Geographic division							
New England	363	15	58	8	5	4	10
Mid-Atlantic	362	12	50	12	18	2	6
East North-Central	675	13	55	10	15	1	7
West North-Central	451	4	74	7	9	1	6
South Atlantic	540	6	83	4	5	0	1
East South-Central	157	34	36	12	10	1	8
West South-Central	350	17	71	7	3	*	1
Mountain	244	8	62	5	14	*	11
Pacific Coast	407	6	79	4	10	0	2
Form of government							
Mayor-council	1,212	26	34	13	17	2	9
Council-manager	2,007	2	87	3	6	*	2
Commission	33	3	33	12	30	3	18
Town meeting	176	10	47	14	7	7	16
Representative town meeting	26	4	58	12	8	0	19
Did not respond	95	12	56	7	13	0	13

Note: Percentages may not total 100% because of rounding.
* = Less than 0.5%.

Table 5/13   NUMBER OF STANDING COMMITTEES

Classification	No. reporting (A)	1–2 % of (A)	3–5 % of (A)	6–10 % of (A)	11–15 % of (A)	More than 15 % of (A)
Total	1,968	17	43	30	6	4
Population group						
Over 1,000,000	2	0	50	50	0	0
500,000–1,000,000	7	0	14	43	29	14
250,000–499,999	10	10	30	40	10	10
100,000–249,999	59	7	39	34	12	9
50,000–99,999	128	13	34	38	9	6
25,000–49,999	232	13	36	35	9	7
10,000–24,999	441	15	40	34	7	4
5,000–9,999	445	16	47	27	6	4
2,500–4,999	413	22	46	26	2	3
Under 2,500	231	22	52	22	4	*

Note: Percentages may not total 100% because of rounding.
* = Less than 0.5%.

Table 5/14   AREAS OF COMMITTEE USE

Areas of committee use	Percentage reporting (n = 3,523)
Zoning	86
Planning	84
Parks and recreation	66
Economic development	41
Libraries	41
Historic preservation	39
Housing	30
Growth	29
Beautification	27
Code enforcement	25
Environmental issues	22
Transportation	21
Finance	20
Architectural review	19
Airports	18
Civil service	17
Cable TV	17
Art	15
Community-police relations	14
Charter review commissions . . .	12
Ethics	8

Central (34%) and East South-Central (33%) divisions.

Terms of Office   Regardless of whether council members are elected at large or by ward/district, the majority of respondents reported four-year terms (62% and 65%, respectively) (not shown). Noticeable variation occurs in the New England and the West South-Central divisions, where percentages reporting four-year terms for both at-large and ward/district elections are much lower than those in other divisions. Both of these divisions show the highest percentages reporting two- or three-year terms.

Only 9% of respondents overall reported a limit on the number of terms that a council member may serve (not shown). Only larger cities—those with a population of 250,000 and above—show a majority of cities reporting term limits for council members. Cities with the council-manager form of government were more likely to report term limits (13%) than were cities with other forms of government (not shown).

Almost 85% of those reporting indicated that terms of office are staggered, a practice that provides some continuity. Yet among larger local governments—those with a population of 500,000 and above—the percentage reporting staggered terms is much lower: 46% (not shown).

Committees and Citizen Boards
Fifty-four percent of councils often use standing committees—permanent bodies with set memberships and regularly scheduled meetings—to consider specific policy matters. Population size seems to be a factor in the number of standing committees used, with the number generally increasing among the larger local governments (Table 5/13).

Ninety-five percent of municipalities reported using citizen authorities, boards, or commissions. Virtually all local governments that provided information about the process—whether the members are elected or appointed—indicated that the members are appointed. When the data are viewed by demographic classifications, however, interesting variations emerge: in the population group 500,000–1,000,000, three of the eight cities reporting indicated that the members are elected, as did 41% of municipalities in the New England geographic division (not shown). In New England, that may be a function of the town meeting and representative town meetings forms of government, which are more prevalent there. In fact, when the data are presented by form of government, the town meeting and representative town meeting forms show much higher percentages with elected members of citizen groups (56% and 46%, respectively).

The citizen boards or commissions typically serve several functions: the majority of local governments reported that they serve an advisory role (89%), but 41% of respondents reported a decision-making role for them and 31% reported a quasi-judicial role (not shown). Respondents with the town meeting and representative town meeting forms of government show percentages well above average reporting a decision-making role for these groups.

Table 5/14 shows the functional areas in which citizen groups are used, with planning and zoning reflecting the highest percentages of municipalities reporting use.

SUMMARY

The 2006 survey results show an increase in the percentage of municipalities reporting a position for a CAO, and the number of proposed and approved changes in form of government from mayor-council to council-manager is noteworthy. Local governments will continue to adapt to community needs, retaining and expanding upon structures that have proven to be successful.

[1]Susan A. MacManus and Charles S. Bullock, III, "The Form, Structure, and Composition of America's Municipalities in the New Millennium," in *The Municipal Year Book 2003* (Washington, D.C.: ICMA, 2003), 6.

[2]Ibid., 13.

[3]Tari Renner and Victor S. DeSantis, "Municipal Forms of Government: Issues and Trends," in *The Municipal Year Book 1998* (Washington, D.C.: ICMA, 1998), 30–41.

[4]MacManus and Bullock, "America's Municipalities in the New Millennium," 11.

A6

Award-Winning Innovations in Local Government, 2007

Stephen Goldsmith

Ash Institute for Democratic Governance and Innovation
John F. Kennedy School of Government
Harvard University

Selected Findings

To prevent asthma hospitalizations by combating factors that exacerbate disease factors in the home, the Boston Public Health Commission launched the Healthy Homes initiative, providing home visits for education on asthma self-management strategies, and environmental monitoring and inspection for families of asthmatic children.

In Coral Gables, Florida, residents and visitors are enjoying the nation's first Park-by-Phone program, which enables them to pay for parking simply by punching a few numbers into their cell phone keypads.

As part of Seattle's Climate Protection Initiative, a variety of programs aimed at environmental conservation, Seattle City Light, which provides electricity to 370,000 residential and commercial customers, has become the first public utility in the country to achieve "zero net emissions" of greenhouse gases.

In recent years, local governments in the United States have encountered a growing series of challenges in the face of a steady decrease in funding; such challenges have included threats of natural disaster and terrorist attack, as well as pressure from technically savvy citizens demanding better and more efficient services, 24 hours per day. Add the burden of increased mandates from federal and state governments, and it is clear why municipal and county government resources are continually being stretched to the limit.

Yet despite these seemingly insurmountable obstacles, many local government officials are demonstrating that they are up to the challenge. Increasingly, they are not only devising creative strategies for solving the most pressing public concerns, but also transforming the way that government does business. Other local officials are exploring and adapting strategies traditionally reserved for the private sector to make their work more effective, efficient, and accountable. Using the latest technological trends, most officials approach their citizens as customers and continually find ways to improve upon their customer service. Almost all have recognized that the agencies they lead cannot "go it" alone, and so they develop strategic partnerships with other agencies, jurisdictions, and service providers in the private and nonprofit sectors.

Last year, Harvard University's Innovations in American Government (IAG) Awards Program celebrated 20 years of recognizing the best and most groundbreaking programs at all levels of government in the United States. Over the years, IAG has received applications from more than 25,000 government programs and awarded more than $20 million in grants to over 400 initiatives. These grants are designed to promote and broaden excellence and creativity in the public sector. In 2007, six jurisdictions received the top prize of $100,000 for initiatives that are truly creative, significant in scope, measurably effective, and transferable to other jurisdictions. More than 1,000 government units apply for these awards every year, demonstrating that jurisdictions nationwide are not content to maintain the status quo, and that innovation is necessary as government agencies strive to adapt and respond to a frequently changing environment.

Each year, IAG applicants exemplify the current and prevailing breakthroughs in government innovation. Among the top local initiatives in 2007 are developments reflecting the following public sector breakthroughs:

- *A focus on prevention.* A notable trend apparent among this past year's applicants is the emphasis on prevention as a means of achieving better outcomes and saving money on services. Preventive measures have been undertaken in such diverse policy areas as special education, substance abuse treatment, juveniles at risk of dropping out of school or entering the criminal justice system, and environmental monitoring of at-risk homes to counter incidences of asthma. Successful measures in these areas can result in long-term cost savings if citizens' need of public services is reduced. However, potential savings and improved outcomes will often be realized in an agency or area of responsibility other than where the actual prevention has taken place, so many agencies lack the motivation or incentive to take this route. Territoriality, lack of direct

Innovations in American Government Awards Program

The Innovations in American Government Awards Program operates on an annual cycle, with applications due in the fall. Each year, it receives an average of 1,000 applications from federal, state, county, city, tribal, and territorial programs.

Eligibility
Programs and initiatives that are administered under the authority of one or more governmental entities in the United States are eligible to apply. A program must be currently in operation and have existed for one year prior to the date of submission. Public-private and public-nonprofit partnerships, and union initiatives, are eligible as long as there is significant governmental involvement and oversight; applications from such programs must be submitted by the partnering governmental entity.

Criteria
Throughout the selection process, evaluators, site visitors, and the National Selection Committee evaluate each application on four criteria: novelty, effectiveness, significance, and transferability.
  Novelty is the degree to which a program demonstrates a leap in creativity. Effectiveness *is measured by tangible results.* Significance *is the extent to which a program successfully addresses an important problem of public concern; the program should respond to a problem of national import and scope, make substantial progress in diminishing the problem within its jurisdiction, or change the organizational culture or the traditional approach to management or problem solving.* Transferability *is the degree to which a program, or aspects of it, shows promise of inspiring successful replication by other governmental entities.*

Applications for the 2009 Innovations in American Government Awards can be made at innovationsaward.harvard.edu.

financial benefit, and fear of not receiving credit for the hard work can all get in the way.

- *Better governance by network.* A trend seen in recent years has been a fundamental shift from traditional, command-and-control, hierarchical government bureaucracies to government by and through partnerships. Such joint ventures take the form of interagency partnerships, regional collaborations, and outsourcing of certain tasks to private and nonprofit agents who are better equipped to accomplish them. Interagency or cross-government partnerships are most effective when the problems at hand require a multidisciplinary approach, such as providing services to families who require a combination of medical, educational, and legal support. Regional partnerships among cities or counties can be useful when the resources of a single jurisdiction are limited. Nonprofit and private partnerships can be instrumental in filling a void in areas where the government lacks expertise or credibility. A community- or faith-based organization may be better equipped to manage social services programs, while the private sector may excel in providing technical assistance or building infrastructure. Innovative government agencies around the country are finding that leveraging partnerships and collaborations, both within government and between other sectors of society, enables them to produce more public value.

- *New uses for information technology and data.* In the early years of the technology revolution, many of the e-government and related innovations were system automations, in which computers and information technology were used to automate tasks that had traditionally been performed manually. Today, public officials are using the latest technological advances to transform how they govern and to improve service delivery, particularly by improving customer access to services. In the future, the digitization of information will allow governments to collect, analyze, and make more information available to their own organizations and the public to facilitate decision making. It will also enable governments to reallocate community resources, and to monitor and reengineer services in order to improve response times and performance outcomes—as measured, for example, by such health indicators as asthma-related emergency room visits.

- *Emphasis on sustainability and conservation.* In the past, when the federal government directed environmental policy, local governments were primarily concerned with trash pickup and landfills. Today, local leaders have begun to look at issues of energy consumption and environmental sustainability. For example, they are developing incentives, such as the imposition of additional fees on new construction that is not energy efficient, and finding creative ways to collaborate with private and community stakeholders to address mounting resource challenges. This work reflects a shift in which local governments are taking on major global issues, such as climate change, that were previously the sole domain of the federal government.

Below are 23 examples of innovations at the local level that reflect some of the above break-throughs. They show how city and county officials are pushing the boundaries and using new tools to create public value and better serve their constituencies. These programs were included among the Top 100 programs recognized by the IAG Awards Program for the 2007 award year.[1]

AFFORDABLE HOUSING

Housing Loan Fund
City of McAllen, Texas (pop. 126,411)[2]

Affordable Homes of South Texas (AHSTI), in McAllen, Texas, is a community-based nonprofit organization that provides affordable housing and administers the Housing Loan Fund program. Established in 1976 with a $200,000 Community Development Block Grant (CDBG) from the U.S. Department of Housing and Urban Development (HUD), AHSTI uses both public and private funding to provide affordable mortgage packages for low-income families. It achieves this by leveraging public funding to encourage private donations; private and public sources finance all of AHSTI's mortgages in equal parts.

For families with a $56,000 mortgage, AHSTI offers a payment schedule consisting of two 10-year periods. The program provides financing from private sources—mainly a consortium of local banks—for the first 10-year payment. The loan recipient pays back $28,250 with a 6% interest rate. CDBGs, as well as funding from HUD's HOME Investment Partnership Program, finance the second 10-year payment of $28,250, also with a 6% interest rate. By blending public and private sources, AHSTI offers low-income families a 20-year mortgage with an effective interest rate of 3%.

AHSTI also maximizes the benefit of its grant funding to its loan recipients by using other cost-saving strategies—namely, the internalization of all development activities. By employing in-house mortgage lenders, land developers, and construction staff, AHSTI eliminates the need for external contracting.

The numbers substantiate its achievement. Between October 1995 and May 2006, AHSTI's mortgage loan portfolio jumped from $5.7 million to $26 million, a 350% increase; during that same period, delinquency on those loans dropped from 20% in 1995 to 3.6% in 2006. As of late 2006, AHSTI had provided the opportunity of homeownership to more than 2,500 McAllen residents.

Contact name: Robert A. Calvillo
Contact organization: Affordable Homes of South Texas
E-mail: rcalvillo@ahsti.org
Web site: ahsti.org

Land Banking Program for Affordable Housing
City of Eugene, Oregon (pop. 146,356)

In the late 1970s, Eugene, Oregon, identified a lack of suitable land as the principal obstacle to affordable housing for its low-income residents. The city responded by purchasing various sites in areas across the city, which were "banked" or reserved for future construction of affordable housing. Since its first purchase in 1979, the Land Banking Program for Affordable Housing has acquired nearly 90 acres of land and earmarked it for the development of affordable housing. As of fall 2006, developers have built 510 affordable housing units for residents of Eugene.

The program has enabled Eugene to regain control over neighborhood development by preventing pockets of wholly low-income communities and by ensuring that new housing be located near public schools, public transportation, and prospective places of employment. The Land Bank creates continuous opportunities for local developers, who engage in a competitive bidding process for each site. This method enhances the quality of housing and resident services. A 2006 survey of Eugene's affordable housing occupant population reported that 73% of respondents were satisfied or extremely satisfied with their overall living situation.

Eligible residents are those experiencing severe housing hardships—expending more than 50% of their household income on housing costs. Between 2005 and 2009, the city will build an average of 100 additional units on Land Bank sites to meet the needs of its 7,000 residents who qualify for the low-cost housing.

Contact name: Stephanie Jennings
Contact organization: Planning and Development Division, City of Eugene, Oregon
E-mail: stephanie.a.jenning@ci.eugene.or.us
Web site: eugene-or.gov

Urban Land Reform Initiative
Genesee County, Michigan (pop. 441,966)

Before the Genesee County, Michigan, treasury department developed the Urban Land Reform Initiative, the county would auction off tax-delinquent properties to investors. Most speculators would maintain properties as minimally as possible and for only so long as it was economically viable. They would then simply abandon the land, valueless after years of refused maintenance. This practice left behind derelict neighborhoods throughout the county.

The treasury department enacted land banking laws in 1999 as the initial component of its Urban Land Reform Initiative. These laws allow the county to tax foreclose on such properties after two or fewer years—before significant property devaluation occurs—and the state court to ensure clear title exchange. The model restricts the sale of property by speculators seeking personal profit; it also assists property owners with funds to maintain and manage tax-foreclosed properties.

Genesee County has collected $7.2 million over the first five years of the initiative through stronger enforcement of fee collection from delinquent taxpayers. With proceeds from delinquency fees and land sales, it has replaced auctions of tax-foreclosed land with the Genesee Land Bank. Vested with the authority to acquire property through foreclosure, the Land Bank revives and redevelops land in accordance with the best interests and needs of the surrounding community. By fall 2006, the Genesee Land Bank had developed hundreds of units of affordable housing, had renovated numerous homes, and had converted a four-story building—previously vacant for 25 years—in downtown Flint into a new commercial and residential center.

Genesee County has also exercised its control over the tax foreclosure process to assist 1,700 homeowners facing substantial financial hardship. The county treasurer may grant foreclosure postponements to preserve homeownership and, ultimately, support affordable housing.

Contact name: Daniel Kildee
Contact organization: Genesee Land Bank/Treasurer's Office, Genesee County, Michigan
E-mail: dkildee@sbc.global.net
Web site: thelandbank.org

CHILDREN AND FAMILY SERVICES

Educational Advocacy Initiative
Fulton County, Georgia (pop. 960,009)

The National Center on Education Disability and Juvenile Justice (EDJJ) reports that there is an overrepresentation of youth with educational difficulties in the juvenile justice system.[3] According to the EDJJ, between 30% and 70% of youth in the corrections system have learning disabilities, many of which previously went undiagnosed.[4] In July 2004, Juvenile Court of Fulton County, Georgia, embarked on the Education Advocacy Initiative, a three-pronged intervention aimed at expanding the understanding of the link between educational disabilities and the propensity of these youth to become involved with juvenile court.

In the first of the three principal components, an educational advocate works with families and educators to compile an educational history of an adjudicated youth to present to judges and probation officers. This history details how academic, cognitive, or socioemotional difficulties may have affected a student's behavior. The educational advocate also runs workshops for social workers, law enforcement officers, attorneys, social service agency providers, and parents to further the understanding of educational law in relation to the rights of and protections for students with disabilities and other educational needs.

In the second component, the educational advocate provides technical assistance to schools to improve their ability to identify, assess, and resolve the special needs of students. Common outcomes of interventions at the school level include referrals to counseling, student support team services, and special education programs, as well as the development of individual plans to help educators reduce the maladaptive behaviors of their students and increase overall student success.

The third component is a multidisciplinary group known as the Education Advocacy Coordinating Committee (EACC). Composed of representatives from various governmental agencies and educational institutions, the EACC supports the Educational Advocacy Initiative. The committee meets monthly to devise strategies that can help its represented organizations better respond to the needs of court-involved youth with disabilities and to reduce the flow of youth from schools to jails. In this manner, the EACC aims to promote structural reform at the local and state levels to benefit delinquent youth with educational disabilities.

Contact name: Kimberly R. Mills
Contact organization: Juvenile Court of Fulton County, Georgia
E-mail: kimberly.mills@fultoncountyga.gov
Web site: co.fulton.ga.us

Juvenile Justice Continuum of Services and Graduated Sanctions
Luna County, New Mexico (pop. 27,205)

In 1997, in response to the increasing frequency and seriousness of juvenile crime, the 6th Judicial District of New Mexico implemented the Juvenile Justice Continuum of Services and Graduated Sanctions. This comprehensive initiative, which includes punitive components, shifts the focus of the justice system from adjudication and incarceration to intervention and positive youth development to prevent crime. Service offerings address the underlying health, social, and behavioral issues that often foreshadow juvenile delinquency.

On the preventive end of the continuum, the initiative offers after-school, athletic, and scholastic programs, all of which are led by adults who model healthy civic behaviors. Juvenile Justice staff target programming to youth considered to be at risk because of high poverty and unemployment rates, low levels of parental education, and family histories of mental health or substance abuse. Programs address such issues as substance abuse and teen pregnancy prevention, high school graduation incentives, and adult literacy.

The initiative uses a range of responses to juvenile offenses. In lieu of immediate incarceration for offenders, staff may require visits to the probation office, mandatory community service, and participation in mental health and substance abuse treatment programs. Failure to attend meetings or comply with regulations results in further interventions, including drug court, secure schooling, or court-ordered probation. The program reserves detention only for those who do not respond to intervention efforts.

As evidence of its successes, the Juvenile Justice program cites cost savings to the justice system and a reduction in juvenile offenses. Between 1997 and 2006, the program saved the counties of Luna, Grant, and Hidalgo approximately $684,000 in law enforcement costs; it also saved the state of New Mexico roughly $8,100,000 and $10,700,000 in adjudication and long-term juvenile commitment fees, respectively. And as of October 2006, total juvenile offenses had declined by an average of 68%, with a related 58% decrease in the number of juvenile commitments to long-term detention facilities.

Contact name: Rheganne Vaughn
Contact organization: 6th Judicial District, Luna County, New Mexico
E-mail: rheganne_vaughn@lunacountynm.us
Web site: lunacountynm.us

Relative Caregiver Program
Monterey County, California (pop. 410,206)

The Kinship Center, an adoption, foster, and relative care service agency in Monterey County, California, presents a grim picture of the outcomes of youngsters who spend their childhoods passed from household to household as part of California's foster care system. More than half of the children who grow to adulthood without the stability of a permanent family will not graduate from high school. Many are homeless at some point in their lives, and only 10% ever become financially independent.[5]

In 2002, in an effort to foster family cohesiveness in the lives of children whose parents are unable to provide the requisite care, the Kinship Center—with funding from the Monterey County Department of Social and Employment Services—initiated the Relative Caregiver Program. An alternative to foster care, the Relative Caregiver Program supports those relatives, 95% of whom are biological grandparents, who assume parental responsibilities from family members unable to care for their own children. Through the Kinship Center, a relative who serves as a child's principal caretaker is offered a variety of free services, ranging from tutoring to pediatric medicine to clothing and food that has been collected by the center. The center also offers support services, including peer mentoring, support groups, and parent education classes, to assist in transitioning the children back to their parents. Of the 563 families that participated in the Relative Caregiver Program between 2002 and October 2006, 88% made use of the center's food bank, 70% accepted grocery certificates or prepared meals during the holidays, 30% brought their children to the Kinship Center for medical attention, and 30% of new parents participated in ongoing adult education or support groups.

Monterey County now boasts one of the lowest foster care placement rates in California: 3.9 children per 1,000 in Monterey County are placed in foster care compared with 7.8 per 1,000 statewide. By diverting children from the juvenile dependency system, the Relative Caregiver Program not only saves public resources but also promotes permanent familial relations and stable environments for children.

Contact name: Carole Biddle
Contact organization: Kinship Center
E-mail: cbiddle@kinshipcenter.org
Web site: kinshipcenter.org

COMMUNITY AND ECONOMIC DEVELOPMENT

Beaverton Central Plant
City of Beaverton, Oregon (pop. 89,643)

In the mid-1990s, the city of Beaverton, Oregon, set out to reinvigorate its downtown area. With private contractors overseeing design and construction, the city built a mixed-use development known as The Round. The Round made space available to home and business owners; since then, the addition of parking and fitness facilities, new shops and restaurants, an amphitheater, and ample green space has increased its popularity in the community.

To foster growth while committing to energy efficiency and environmental conservation, the city acquired the Central Heating and Cooling Plant. This facility serves as the principal provider of energy to those who live and work at The Round. Owning the plant is part of the active role the city has taken in the public-private effort to redevelop Beaverton's urban core. Through efficient operation of the plant, the city shields its residents from escalating utility rates and encourages them to make greater use of The Round.

The Beaverton Central Plant (BCP) provides centralized heating and cooling, hot water, and systems maintenance, as well as cooling equipment for dedicated computer server rooms used by high-tech firms housed in The Round. Its sophisticated control network drives energy efficiency well beyond that of a conventional plant operating system; greater efficiency reduces overall resource consumption, saving money and mitigating the plant's environmental impact. Current electrical energy savings, for example, are equivalent to the annual consumption of more than 160 homes. The city projects that savings will double once the complex at The Round is completed.

BCP is also a financial success, generating positive cash flow and limiting the cost to taxpayers. With the Oregon State Department of Energy offering the plant financing and tax credits, Beaverton is able to leverage more of its assets to fuel further development.

Contact name: Lonnie Dicus
Contact organization: Beaverton Central Plant
E-mail: ldicus@ci.beaverton.or.us
Web site: beavertonoregon.gov

Inspection Points Program
City of Temecula, California (pop. 93,923)

The city of Temecula, California meets regularly with developers and construction personnel to exchange information on the status of their building projects. At the peak of a 2001 development boom, builders voiced frustration that inadequate inspections were hindering their progress.

In response, the city's building and safety department undertook a study to analyze assessment times and locations, staff availability, and travel requirements. As it evaluated sites, the department noticed a pattern of project development types and corresponding needs, and so it began to assign staff to development projects in line with individual training and experience. The study also enhanced the department's understanding of work schedules so that for any particular project, an inspection could be scheduled at the most appropriate time of day.

The city took the results of this study and initiated the Inspection Points Program to increase efficiency in its building inspection procedures. Assigning inspectors to specific areas has reduced staff commutes and allowed more time for site assessment; in addition, staff continuity has fostered familiarity with sites, thereby eliminating repeated inspection efforts and enabling inspectors to devote more time to the assessment of newly completed work. And knowledge of each facility's particular needs combined with more available staff time has allowed for the scheduling of more inspections later in the day, the result of which has been fewer canceled appointments and increased building approval rates.

The increased number of inspections scheduled later in the day has given construction workers adequate preparation time. In its first year, the

program raised the percentage of projects ready for review when the inspector arrived to 75%, up from the prior readiness rate of 54%; moreover, the inspection passage rate increased from 28% to 50%. The building and safety department's regular and efficient inspection services benefit the development community and the residents of Temecula by expediting building projects in the city.

Contact name: Mark Harold
Contact organization: Temecula Department of Building and Safety
E-mail: Mark.Harold@cityoftemecula.org
Web site: cityoftemecula.org/Temecula/Government/CommDev

Vacant Property Registration Fee Program
City of Wilmington, Delaware (pop. 72,826)

For decades, urban neighborhoods in Wilmington, Delaware, were adversely affected by chronically neglected properties. In 2003, the city devised the Vacant Property Registration Fee Program to deter ownership of vacant property. The program assesses annual registration fees for all properties that are vacant for more than one year. The fees begin at $500 for the first year of vacancy and increase significantly with each subsequent year. To date, the maximum annual fee collected for ownership of a vacant building was $10,500: the property had been vacant for 21 years.

With legal support from the state, Wilmington assesses the fee as a lien against the real estate. Property owners thus cannot avoid the fee if they intend to sell or otherwise use their land. The city imposes additional fines and may press criminal charges against those who try to evade the process. Finally, it puts up for sheriff's sale any properties with excessive unpaid fees, making them available to people or organizations for rehabilitation.

While other municipalities charge administrative fees on vacant properties in order to keep them code compliant, such programs only motivate owners to fulfill the minimum upkeep on vacant lots. Wilmington's program, in contrast, prioritizes active community development, aiming to reduce the number of vacant lots and to build stronger neighborhoods. In its first two years, the program decreased the number of vacant properties in the city from 1,455 to 1,135, a 22% decline. Property owners have spent in excess of $31 million in renovation and new construction. Further, builders have constructed more than 1,000 units of affordable housing in areas that suffer from a severe shortage of livable space.

Contact name: Cynthia Ferguson
Contact organization: Department of Licenses and Inspections, Wilmington, Delaware
E-mail: cferguson@ci.wilmington.de.us
Web site: ci.wilmington.de.us/VacantProperties/index.htm

CRIMINAL JUSTICE AND PUBLIC SAFETY

Coordinated Community Response Project
City of Grand Forks, North Dakota (pop. 50,372)

Domestic violence was a significant problem in Grand Forks, North Dakota. The city's police de-

partment estimated that nearly 900 children, or one in three of all elementary public school students, lived with violence in their homes. The most frequently reported personal injury crimes—of which there were 657 cases in 2005—were committed at home. In a 2004 community assessment, the United Way identified domestic violence as the second most pressing issue affecting the Grand Forks community.

In response, the police department launched the Coordinated Community Response Project. The project brings together 11 governmental and private agencies, including the county sheriff, correction center, state's attorney, child protection and health agencies, and the Community Violence Intervention Center; these agencies work collaboratively to improve efforts to respond to domestic violence.

The police department began by analyzing years of data from monitored police calls and information related to the prosecutions and sentences of perpetrators of domestic violence. This statistical analysis exposed weak links in domestic violence response efforts; it also helped the police develop strategies for improved protection and violence prevention. The department then conveyed these strategies to government and private partners in a series of regular meetings, which provided violence response training and helped foster interagency collaboration. In 2005, 1,417 public and private sector professionals attended these meetings and became familiar with best practices in domestic violence prevention and response.

This inclusive approach toward enhancing the capability of local professionals has had a tangible impact on the incidence and reporting of domestic violence in Grand Forks. The police department reports that since the program began, the number of referrals to the local offender treatment group has risen by nearly 70%. Child abuse or neglect is also now more likely to be reported: the police estimate that 61% of violent incidents involving children were reported in 2005, up from an estimated 30% in 2002.

Contact name: Pete Haga
Contact organization: Grand Forks Police Department
E-mail: phaga@grandforksgov.com
Web site: grandforksgov.com/police

Evacuation Program
City of Hermiston, Oregon (pop. 14,891)

The Umatilla Chemical Depot in Hermiston, Oregon, is one of seven U.S. Army installations that currently store chemical weapons.[6] With the operation of a weapons storage facility comes the responsibility to safeguard the local community in the event of a chemical agent emergency. Assuming that function, the Hermiston police department initiated an extensive evacuation program that makes use of the latest technology to ensure the quickest and most efficient mass exit of the Hermiston population.

This traffic control system takes advantage of all available technological avenues to communicate traffic patterns to evacuees and affect the flow of vehicles out of the city. Video cameras located throughout Hermiston provide police officers with real-time images of roadways, giving them the information they need to direct traffic most effectively. Law enforcement officials are able to post accurate messages on electronic billboards located along city highways, and can communicate the most up-to-date information via radio and television. They also have the capability to drop barricades and alter traffic signals to further direct vehicular flow.

Perhaps the most significant feature of Hermiston's evacuation program is that the police department activates the system and controls its functions on a Wi-Fi network, accessible through any Internet portal with proper passwords. The city introduced this critical feature to allow for the remote control of evacuation procedures by police officers in the field, away from the central dispatch center. Through the use of Wi-Fi and other technologies to monitor and control traffic, the city is able to facilitate the safest and most expeditious evacuation in times of emergency.

Contact name: Daniel James Coulombe
Contact organization: Police Department, City of Hermiston, Oregon
E-mail: dcoulombe@hermiston.or.us

Overt Drug Market Strategy
City of High Point, North Carolina (pop. 97,796)

A decade ago, street-level drug dealing and its attendant criminal activity, from assaults to prostitution, were rife in the city of High Point, North Carolina. The police force was ineffectual, and it alienated the community with the use of strong-arm tactics.

To mend the relationship between law enforcement and community members while combating crime, the city police department adopted a new approach known as the Overt Drug Market Strategy (ODMS). ODMS combines crime mapping and community policing with a new accord with drug dealers.

Police first identify crime-ridden neighborhoods in the city. They then begin a program of aggressive intelligence gathering to identify and build cases against the most active drug dealers. Violent offenders are immediately prosecuted, but the program reserves an alternative strategy for drug dealers who lack a history of violent behavior. Police "call in" these dealers—with the assurance that they will not be arrested—to a meeting where family and community members speak to the damage that the dealers' criminal behavior has caused loved ones and neighbors. The dealers are then offered a second chance: police will "bank" or make inactive the case against them as long as they retire. In addition, the city offers assistance, including educational and vocational training programs, to help dealers who abandon their trade to rejoin society.

While the police department has not eliminated the drug trade in High Point, the Overt Drug Market Strategy has successfully reduced the occurrence of violent crime citywide by 20% over its two-year lifespan.

Contact name: Marty Sumner
Contact organization: Police Department, High Point, North Carolina
E-mail: Marty.sumner@highpointnc.gov
Web site: high-point.net/police

Teen Prostitution Prevention Project
Suffolk County, Massachusetts (pop. 687,610)

The Teen Prostitution Prevention Project (TPPP)—a collaboration of law enforcement, criminal justice, child protection, and youth and medical service agencies—identifies, supports, and ultimately protects teenage prostitutes in Massachusetts.

In 2004, TPPP received funding from the state's Executive Office of Public Safety to create a comprehensive blueprint outlining the commitment of partner agencies to work together toward shared goals. The project then sought to quantify the prevalence and scope of prostituted teenagers in Suffolk County, Massachusetts. A database was created, which now serves as the warehouse for information on youth prostitution. Since this comprehensive data collection project began, TPPP has identified 101 children exploited through prostitution, up from only seven reported cases between 2001 and 2003. Informed by this research, it has created "Responding to Youth Exploited through Prostitution: Guidelines for a Multidisciplinary Intervention," an instruction manual it distributes to response teams charged with taking action to prevent teenage prostitution. The teams comprise representatives of partner organizations.

On the strength derived from its cross-agency partnerships, TPPP has built a community-wide response model to address the problem of youth prostitution. It has based its efforts on the conviction that youth empowerment and offender accountability are not mutually exclusive. TPPP has also transformed the discourse surrounding sex trafficking and exploitation by presenting prostituted youth not as offenders but as victims of adults seeking profit.

Contact name: Susan Goldfarb
Contact organization: Children's Advocacy Center
E-mail: Susan.Goldfarb@suf.state.ma.us

EDUCATION AND TRAINING

Las Artes
Pima County, Arizona (pop. 946,362)

In the summer of 1997, two local artists—backed by a Pima County, Arizona, workforce readiness program—approached Tucson's inner-city community housing residents to elicit their participation in a public works project. The objective of the resultant Las Artes program was twofold: to use ceramic tiles to create durable works of art to celebrate the neighborhood's multiplicity of cultures, and to instill in participants a sense of commitment and responsibility associated with seeing a project through from start to completion.

In this community, 25% of 16- to 19-year-olds and more than 41% of residents over age 25 lack a high school diploma. In response to the low levels of education of many of its participants, Las Artes expanded from a primarily vocational program to one offering educational components. Over time, a participant's attainment of a general education development (GED) diploma became central to

the mission of Las Artes. Youth participants enroll in remedial education classes to bring them to a ninth-grade level. The program also prepares them to take the GED, using educational software tools to develop individualized courses of study, making available private tutoring on weekends, and offering an eight-week intensive course.

While fostering educational opportunities, Las Artes maintains its vocational arts roots. Participants work 30 hours per week creating tile murals; the murals will eventually decorate parks and public buildings throughout Tucson. Las Artes also teaches the elements of research design and methods of artistic production, along with the value of teamwork to meet a deadline. Participants receive a stipend for their efforts plus incentive payments upon the completion of each eight-week phase of the program.

As of October 2006, Las Artes had facilitated GED attainment for 413 out-of-school youth. It also beautified the community with more than 60 public works of art now on display in urban and rural neighborhoods throughout Pima County.

Contact name: Elena West
Contact organization: Community Service Division, Pima County, Arizona
E-mail: Ewest@csd.pima.gov
Web site: pima.gov/ced/CR/LasArtes.html

Will Power to Youth
City of Los Angeles, California (pop. 9,948,081)

The Shakespeare Festival/LA organization offers an arts-based youth development and job-training program known as Will Power to Youth. Each year, 50 to 60 students participate in the program with the support of the city of Los Angeles's Department of Community Development, the California Department of Justice, and the National Endowment for the Arts. Since 1994, Will Power to Youth has served more than 500 youth.

Guided by professional mentor artists, program participants write, produce, and star in an original adaptation of a Shakespearean play. The participants are responsible for every aspect of the theatrical production, including choreography, composition of an original score, and design and construction of the set. Will Power to Youth compensates the young artists, who work full time and fulfill a commitment of 200 hours; program participants earn $6.75 per hour, a wage that lifts the per capita income of their families by approximately 4%.

Vocational and academic activities are fundamental components of Will Power to Youth. The program incorporates 50–70 hours of community- and relationship-building exercises into the production process, in line with the U.S. Department of Labor's measures for workforce skill attainment. Through the program, students may also receive credits toward high school graduation. Program participants achieve a graduation rate upward of 90%, whereas only 30% of Los Angeles United School District high school students typically complete their secondary education. This dual focus on scholastic and workforce skill building, achieved through a performing arts lens, distinguishes Will Power to Youth from other at-risk youth intervention programs.

Contact name: Ben Donenberg
Contact organization: Shakespeare Festival/
   Los Angeles
E-mail: ben@shakespearefestivalla.org
Web site: shakespearefestivalla.org/education/
   will_power_to_youth.php

HEALTH AND SOCIAL SERVICES

Healthy Homes
City of Boston, Massachusetts (pop. 590,763)

Children's Hospital Boston, Massachusetts, reports that asthma is the most widespread chronic condition that affects children in the United States, and the third most common cause of hospitalization for children under age 15.[7] The hospitalization rate in Boston for asthma is more than twice that in Massachusetts, with a disproportionate percentage of patients being black and Latino. The Boston Public Health Commission (BPHC) found a high incidence of asthma-aggravating factors, such as smoking (30%) and infestations of mice or cockroaches (70%), in the homes of the 250 families with asthma sufferers that participated in its Healthy Homes Program.

In an effort to prevent asthma hospitalizations by combating factors that exacerbate disease factors in the home, BPHC launched the Healthy Homes initiative. The initiative provides home visits for education on asthma self-management strategies, and environmental monitoring and inspection for families of asthmatic children. A range of health care providers, including pediatricians, community health center personnel, and school nurses, refer families with children who suffer from asthma. A Healthy Homes staffer visits the families to inspect each room in the house for asthma triggers, such as airborne dust, nitrogen dioxide, and humidity. The staffer then makes environmental improvement recommendations to the family and provides an in-home asthma management toolbox to help put the suggestions into practice. The Home SAFE Kit includes plastic food containers, cockroach traps and mousetraps, hypoallergenic mattress and pillow covers, and videos and resources guides—available in several languages—to educate family members on asthma prevention strategies.

Before Healthy Homes interventions were implemented, 37% of participating families rated their children's asthma as severe or very severe; after participating in the program, only 9% of families rated their children in either of these categories. Participants' reporting of symptom days was consistent with the self-severity ratings. Before the project, 49% of participants described mouse infestation as heavy/very heavy; after prevention suggestions were implemented, only 11% checked this category and 40% reported no rodent infestation at all. Especially striking is that Healthy Homes has achieved these results at low cost: an intervention, which includes supply kits and two home visits, costs only $250 per family. Additional professional pest control services cost about $100 per visit.

On the basis of these outcomes, BPHC has institutionalized the Healthy Homes Program, providing more than 100 asthma home visits to Boston families each year and working closely with its public housing office to offer healthy homes services to residents of public housing.

Contact name: Margaret Reid
Contact organization: Boston Public Health
   Commission, Boston, Massachusetts
E-mail: mreid@bphc.org
Web site: bphc.org

Medication Access Program
Cumberland County, North Carolina (pop. 299, 060)

North Carolina's Cumberland County Medication Access Program (CCMAP) has been providing the uninsured and underinsured with essential prescription medications since 2002. CCMAP distributes medicines donated by local physicians, clinics, and pharmaceutical patient assistant programs, ensuring that county residents with chronic medical conditions who cannot afford remedial treatment (those with an income within 200% of the federal poverty guidelines) have access to requisite medications. As of January 2008, CCMAP dispensed more than $22.6 million in prescription medications to county residents in need.

The Cumberland County Detention Center approached CCMAP as it struggled to finance the high costs of medication for its inmates. Because of the success of CCMAP and its leftover repository of unused medication, the county health department forged a partnership with CCMAP wherein the county purchases medication in bulk and CCMAP staff fill prescriptions to distribute to detainees. CCMAP also donates overstocked pharmaceutical samples directly to the detention center.

The success is evident in the numbers. In fiscal year (FY) 2004, before the joint venture, the county health department spent $295,846 on medicine for inmates. In FY 2005, when CCMAP began to provide medications, the county spent half that amount, $150,299. In FY 2006, the health department realized further cost savings, spending only $94,085 on medication for those incarcerated at the detention center. While seeing to it that those in need have access to necessary medication, the initiative has also saved Cumberland County taxpayer dollars.

Contact name: Catherine Roach
Contact organization: Cumberland County
   Medication Access program
E-mail: croach@capefearvalley.com
Web site: ccmap.org

MANAGEMENT AND GOVERNANCE

Hamlets and Villages
Clackamas County, Oregon (pop. 374,230)

Representatives on the Clackamas County Board of County Commissioners (BCC) noticed a recurring theme in conversations with their constituents: citizens in unincorporated areas felt removed from decision making in their communities. They regretted the lack of opportunity for increased civic engagement and welcomed conduits through which their voices would be heard.

Responding to the call for greater involvement in grassroots governance, the BCC partnered with the consulting firm of Cogan Owens Cogan to create the Hamlets and Villages model. Unlike cities, hamlets and villages are not responsible for direct service provision, and they lack the power to tax in most circumstances. However, they do serve important advisory functions. For example, their elected officials make recommendations to county government on issues of concern to their constituents, such as local public transportation, the building of pedestrian and bike paths, or the construction of a new community center. Hamlet and village representatives also consult on land use and maintain relations with neighboring communities.

An additional and noteworthy feature of this governance model is the criterion for civic participation. Villages and hamlets do not require voter registration for residents to participate in the decision-making process; instead, eligibility for participation comes with residential property or business ownership within the geographical boundary.

As of fall 2006, five close-knit communities east of Portland formed the first recognized operational village. Nearby Beavercreek also assumed formal recognition as a hamlet. Several other communities throughout Clackamas County continue to pursue formal status as either hamlets or villages in an effort to augment civic engagement and citizen empowerment.

Contact name: Kirstin Greene
Contact organization: Cogan Owens Cogan
E-mail: Kirstin.Greene@coganowens.com
Web site: clackamas.us

Park-by-Phone
City of Coral Gables, Florida (pop. 42,794)

To reduce the hassle of finding and paying for parking, the city of Coral Gables initiated the nation's first Park-by-Phone program. In partnership with Clancy Systems, a company that facilitates electronic payments, city residents and visitors may now pay for both on-street parking and surface lot simply by punching a few numbers into their cellular phone keypads.

After registering and paying an annual service fee of $5.95, drivers may park at any metered space by dialing a number identified on the meter and entering the amount of time they wish to purchase. They may also redial the number to add time from any remote location, eliminating the need to return to their cars to feed the meters. At the end of each month, their credit cards are charged for the cost of any parking purchased along with a 10% convenience fee.

Because of its convenience, use of this payment system has grown steadily since it began in June 2005. During a typical month, approximately 6,000 parking transactions will occur through the Park-by-Phone program. The U.S. Conference of Mayors recognized the city of Coral Gables for this program with an Honorable Mention in its City Livability Awards Program.

Contact name: Maria Higgins Fallon
Contact organization: Office of Public Affairs,
   Coral Gables, Florida
E-mail: mfallon@coralgables.com
Web site: coralgables.com

Public Employee Cross-Training
City of Cedar Falls, Iowa (pop. 36,940)

Cedar Falls, Iowa, depends on property taxes to provide basic services to residents and visitors. As the community grew, the city faced a challenge familiar to many municipal governments: the state imposes legal constraints that prohibit property tax increases. Yet current revenues were not enough to adequately provide services to meet the needs of the emergent population.

The city identified new staff hires as an area where it could realize savings. It found that it was more cost-effective to pay current city employees supplemental wages to, for example, augment the firefighting and police forces. So the city of Cedar Falls instituted its Public Employee Cross-Training Program, which prepares staff to serve as reserve officers in the fire and police departments.

As of October 2006, city employees accounted for seven of the ten new reservists at the fire department for a total cost equivalent to that of one full-time firefighter. The police department expanded its reserve unit by three officers, all of them city employees, for less than half the cost of hiring one permanent law enforcement officer. In actual numbers, cross-trained employees serve public safety duty at a maximum cost of $7,750 annually, including benefits, whereas the annual cost of hiring one full-time firefighter or police officer would be between $70,000 and $80,000. The program also financially benefits its participants: not only does the city compensate them for their overtime, but they receive an increased pension package upon retirement as well. Thus, with its Public Employee Cross-Training Program, the city of Cedar Falls increased its capacity to serve and protect its growing population without straining the current budget.

Contact name: Richard Ahlstrom
Contact organization: Cedar Falls Police Department
E-mail: richard.ahlstrom@ci.cedar-falls.ia.us
Web site: cedarfalls.com

TRANSPORTATION, INFRASTRUCTURE, AND THE ENVIRONMENT

Renewable Energy Mitigation Program
City of Aspen, Colorado (pop. 5,728)

The median home size in the United States is 2,434 square feet. The average residence built today in Pitkin County, Colorado, is more than double that size—4,953 square feet—with 10% of new houses exceeding 10,000 square feet. Owners equip many of these houses with amenities that require significant energy input, inflating the energy needs of houses of such great size.

To conserve limited natural resources and reduce the environmental impact of recently constructed and future homes, the city of Aspen and Pitkin County collaborated with the Community Office for Resource Efficiency, a local nonprofit dedicated to promoting energy efficiency and green building. The collaboration created the Renewable Energy Mitigation Program (REMP), a framework in which home builders must choose to either build in accordance with energy codes or

pay a tax to offset excessive energy use. Almost half of all home builders opt to install solar hot water, solar photovoltaic, and geothermal systems. These renewable energy systems enable builders to avoid fees by fulfilling renewable energy requirements while they reduce CO_2 emissions by more than 50,000 tons. Builders that choose not to incorporate renewable energy systems pay a tax in proportion to the size of the building project—from $5,000 to $10,000.

Since its inception, REMP has raised approximately $6 million in energy mitigation fees, which it uses to finance energy-saving infrastructure projects throughout Pitkin County. For example, REMP funds supported the installation of solar hot water systems for Aspen's most recent affordable-housing project, energy-efficient improvements to Aspen's ice-skating and pool facility, and a hydroelectric lighting system for a large hotel garage, which alone will eliminate five million pounds of greenhouse gases over the next 20 years. The REMP program strives to eliminate three tons of carbon from the air for every ton of carbon emitted from energy-inefficient homes in the community.

Contact name: Stephen Kanipe
Contact organization: Community Development Department—City of Aspen, Colorado
E-mail: stephenk@ci.aspen.co.us
Web site: aspencore.org

Seattle Climate Protection Initiative
City of Seattle, Washington (pop. 582,454)

In the winter of 2004–2005, reduced snowmelt from the Cascade Mountains was threatening Seattle's drinking water reservoirs and hydroelectric turbines, as well as increasing the risk of wildfire in the forest areas near the city. In response, Mayor Greg Nickels started the Seattle Climate Protection Initiative (SCPI), a variety of specific programs and efforts aimed at environmental conservation. For example, SCPI requires construction projects to plant two new trees for every tree they remove; it imposes a commercial parking tax to discourage drivers from parking downtown and uses the revenues to promote public transportation; and it mandates that the city offset all emissions from work-related air travel by city employees by investing in alternative energy. In addition, Seattle increased the amount of public money earmarked for sustainable landscaping projects and improvements to pedestrian and bicycle infrastructure. The city also launched a biodiesel program to encourage public buses, Washington State ferries, and city trucks to use cleaner fuel alternatives.

Perhaps SCPI's most drastic improvement is with Seattle City Light (SCL), which provides electricity to 370,000 residential and commercial customers in the city. SCL is the first public utility in the country to achieve "zero net emissions" of greenhouse gases, which it accomplished through a variety of methods: disinvesting in coal power; increasing holdings in wind power; and increasing conservation efforts. SCL offsets its remaining carbon by purchasing external emissions-cutting projects.

Since the inception of SCPI, Seattle has reduced its carbon emissions by 60%. Further, Mayor Nickels has persuaded hundreds of mayors across

the country to voluntarily commit to reducing their carbon emissions to the level recommended in the international Kyoto agreement. Together, this growing group of mayors represents at least 18% of the U.S. population. Their efforts encourage other jurisdictions to look seriously at their own consumption levels.

Contact name: Steve Nicholas
Contact organization: Seattle Office of Sustainability and Environment
E-mail: steve.nicholas@seattle.gov
Web site: seattle.gov/environment

Water System Conservation Program
City of San Antonio, Texas (pop. 1,296,682)

For more than a century, the Edwards Aquifer has supplied San Antonio with pure spring water at a minimal cost to city residents. However, the city's recent massive growth has compromised this inexpensive water supply. In 1992, when local government officials realized that the organizational structure governing water use could not handle the increased strain, the city combined two existing water utilities and one city department to create the San Antonio Water System (SAWS). SAWS manages the water supply and leads conservation efforts with a focus on community-wide education and infrastructure improvement.

SAWS administers a wide variety of programs to reduce water usage. For example, "Plumbers to People" provides leak repair for low-income citizens; in so doing, it conserves water and reduces costs for households less able to afford high plumbing bills. The Seasonal Irrigation Program (SIP), which originated in 1998, sends an e-mail to 4,000 homeowners with advice on the conservative use of water while gardening. A study by SIP found that the e-mails save 36 million gallons of water each year.

Based on predicted consumption trends, estimates are that the SAWS program has saved 175.5 billion gallons of water. At its onset in 1993, SAWS set a per-person water use reduction goal of 12% by 2008. The city reached this goal in 2001, and in 2003, it achieved a per-person water use reduction of 20%.

Contact name: Dana Nichols
Contact organization: Conservation Department, San Antonio, Texas
E-mail: dana.nichols@saws.org
Web site: saws.org

CONCLUSION

Governments in the 21st century must continually adapt and innovate to meet the increasingly diverse and complex challenges that epitomize the environments in which they serve. In order to meet their community's future demands to provide more services with fewer tax dollars, local officials must redefine how they see their roles in the community, retrain and reorganize themselves to confidently fulfill that new role, and reallocate assets within the community to increase public value. Through 20 years of evaluating government innovation, the IAG Awards Program has identified three principles shared by local governments that embrace innovation in their efforts to continually improve citizen services:

- *Move from red tape to no tape.* Rigid bureaucratic systems and unnecessary rules designed to protect and maintain the status quo stifle innovation. These regulatory limits also produce massive amounts of paperwork, which require so much time to locate that they discourage the application of informed discretion. The most effective government agencies work across traditional silos, using rules to protect equity and fairness and to reward results, not processes. Innovative leaders increasingly deploy decision support systems to analyze digital information in order to make services quicker and more responsive.
- *Develop strategic partnerships.* The steady increase in demand for services, matched only by the steady decrease in available resources, continues to challenge counties and municipalities across the country. Government cannot successfully meet all of its current and future responsibilities alone; it must rely on a network of nongovernmental partners—private firms, nonprofit organizations, faith- and community-based groups—to help define and achieve goals to benefit its constituents. Creative and effec-

tive leaders in all sectors, represented by the programs highlighted above, transform government's role from direct service provider to generator of public value.

- *Increase citizen participation through technology.* Recent advances in technology enable government agencies to be more accountable, to be transparent, and to improve performance. Collaborative technologies currently popular on the Internet—think Facebook and Wikipedia—allow the most savvy local governments to capture the talent, creativity, and experiences of its citizens by encouraging participatory problem solving and civic engagement. These tools might also help officials to anticipate and address risks ranging from natural disasters to terrorist attacks. The 9/11 Commission criticized government's failure to "imagine" the terrorist threat. What if we had thousands brainstorming possible terrorist attacks rather than a disjointed few?

Over the last 20 years, globalization and technological advances have forced local governments to face a multitude of complex changes. However, the primary purpose of government—to create public value for citizens—remains unchanged. Local government officials must continue to create public value while simultaneously responding to new challenges. Innovation enables public of-

ficials to perform at a level that allows citizens to have confidence in their government, a confidence critical to the health of democracy. Public officials must question old models and rules in order to adapt to new realities; in the place of those old models and rules we see new ideas and innovations born of necessity. If the responses we receive to the upcoming year's IAG Awards competition are any indication, local government officials will continue to rise to the occasion.

---

[1]Unless otherwise noted, all statistics come from applications for the 2007 Innovations in American Government Awards Program.

[2]All populations are 2006 estimates from the U.S. Bureau of the Census.

[3]Sue Burrell and Loren Warboys, "Special Education and the Juvenile Justice System," *Juvenile Justice Bulletin* (Washington, D.C.: Office of Juvenile Justice and Delinquency Prevention, U.S. Department of Justice, July 2000), available at ncjrs.gov/html/ojjdp/2000_6_5/contents.html (accessed December 27, 2007).

[4]As cited in the 2007 Innovations in American Government Awards application of the Education Advocacy Initiative.

[5]Kinship Center, *Annual Report, 2005–2006;* for more information, go to kinshipcenter.org/adoption_child_california_family.html (accessed December 27, 2007).

[6]U.S. Army Chemical Materials Agency Web site, at cma.army.mil/umatilla.aspx (accessed December 27, 2007).

[7]Children's Hospital Boston, at childrenshospital.org/az/Site2174/mainpageS2174P0.html (accessed December 27, 2007).

B The Intergovernmental Dimension

B 1

State-Local Relations: Authority and Finances

David R. Berman
Senior Research Fellow, Morrison Institute
Arizona State University

Selected Findings

In response to complaints from local governments, the West Virginia legislature passed a bill that will allow five cities or metropolitan governments to experiment with home rule for up to five years, beginning in 2008.

Under a 2007 Colorado law, firefighters with any of five types of cancer (not including lung cancer, which is usually caused by smoking) are presumed to have gotten the cancer on the job and are therefore eligible for workers' compensation.

In 2007, legislation limiting local governments' use of eminent domain passed in Connecticut as well as in several other states, including Ohio, Virginia, and Wyoming.

Early in 2007, speaking before a conference of the Missouri Municipal League, the state attorney general articulated what local officials knew to be true: "There is a growing and alarming trend in our state for state government to try to usurp your local control authority."[1] In recent years, local officials in Missouri and elsewhere have had reason to be concerned about how state mandates, prohibitions, and preemptions affect their authority, and about the lack of state fiscal support for local government.[2] Of particular concern in 2007 were developments in the areas of property tax reform, eminent domain, and cable franchising. This article provides an overview of conditions and developments in the areas of local authority and finance; it also considers significant ballot measures, judicial decisions, and legislation.

LOCAL AUTHORITY

In the mid-19th century, state legislatures were, in effect, "spasmodic city councils" that directly controlled the actions of local officials and interfered at will in local government affairs. In response, local officials and others began a long quest for home rule, which increases a local government's ability to initiate action and gives it greater protection from state interference in local affairs. Over the years, the view that local governments should have home rule has gained ground: some degree of home rule is available for municipalities in 48 states, and county governments have such powers in 37 of the 48 states with viable county governments.[3]

Home rule status has done little, however, to change or even challenge fundamental assumptions about the legal status of municipal or other local governments. Even home rule jurisdictions have few of the protections against arbitrary state action that private corporations, also chartered by the state, commonly enjoy. Although municipalities and counties with home rule authority are generally better off than those without, local governments with or without home rule have only limited power to initiate action and must spend much time and energy trying to ward off mandates, preemptions, and prohibitions that would further limit their authority.

Home Rule

Although judges have claimed, at various times and in various places, that there is an inherent right of local self-government, the dominant legal view has been that municipalities, counties, and other local units are the "legal creatures" of their states. In the words of Judge John F. Dillon, a much-quoted 19th-century authority on municipal law,

> *Municipal corporations owe their origin to, and derive their powers and rights wholly from, the legislature. It breathes into them the breath of life, without which they cannot exist. As it creates, so it may destroy. If it may destroy, it may abridge and control. . . . We know of no limitation of this right so far as corporations themselves are concerned. They are, so to phrase it, the mere tenants at will of the legislature.[4]*

Consistent with this view, courts have commonly limited the power of local governments by applying what has come to be known as "Dillon's Rule of strict construction":

> *It is a general and undisputed proposition of law that a municipal corporation possesses and can exercise the following powers, and no others: First, those granted in express words; second, those necessarily or fairly implied in or incident to the powers expressly granted; third, those essential to the accomplishment of declared objects and purposes of the corporation—not simply convenient, but indispensable. Any fair, reasonable doubt concerning the existence of power is resolved by courts against the corporation, and the power is denied.[5]*

In Dillon's Rule states, local governments must obtain specific legislative authority for virtually everything they wish to do. As a result, state legislators are busy passing bills that affect one or a few local governments and are immersed in minor local matters at the expense of policy issues of statewide interest. In New Hampshire, for example, municipalities have been compelled to secure state legislative approval for routine decisions— such as whether they could impose a user fee for trash removal, post warning signs on frozen ponds, or allow their citizens to pay municipal bills by credit card. In Arkansas, another Dillon's Rule state, the legislature busied itself in 2007 by giving municipalities specific powers—such as the authority to remove vehicles abandoned in the right of way.

To circumvent Dillon's Rule, several states have constitutional provisions or statutes that allow local governments to obtain home rule. The traditional and most common form of home rule (1) gives local governments that qualify under state constitutional or statutory provisions (e.g., a municipality over a certain population size) the right to make decisions without specific grants of authority on local matters and (2) limits the power of the state to intervene in local matters. In practice, however, courts have found it difficult to distinguish between what is a local affair and what is of statewide concern, and they have usually resolved uncertainties in favor of the states.

In other states where home rule exists, Alaska being an example, state statutes or constitutions avoid the problem of distinguishing between state and local concerns by taking a devolution-of-powers approach, under which local units are authorized to carry out any function or exercise any power not expressly forbidden or preempted by the state (in essence, a reversal of Dillon's Rule). Even in these states, however, courts have tended to interpret the law to limit municipal action to what the courts define as the sphere of local affairs, and they often overturn municipal ordinances on the grounds that such ordinances relate to a "statewide" rather than a "local" matter.[6] And in many of the states that have some form of official home rule, courts nevertheless continue to apply Dillon's Rule to limit the scope of municipal power.[7]

In addition to the protections afforded by home rule, local governments are protected in most states by constitutional prohibitions on special, or local, legislation—that is, acts that affect only a particular local jurisdiction. State constitutions commonly classify municipalities and counties by criteria such as population or total property value, and they require that the legislature treat all jurisdictions in the same category equally. Prohibitions on local legislation, however, offer only limited protection, largely because legislatures are permitted to refine the scheme to the point where only one jurisdiction falls into a classification. Because of the classification schemes, state legislatures often have nearly as much freedom in dealing with their large cities as they did under the system of special legislation.

In some states, particularly in the South, local laws are common. For example, of the 139 bills that passed in the 2005 regular session of the Alabama legislature, 80 were local bills relating to such matters as fire protection fees, traffic laws, and the sale of draft beer. In Alabama, South Carolina, and other southern states, there is also a strong tradition of giving state legislators a great deal of control over legislation affecting the localities they represent. This practice effectively compels local elected officials to constantly go back to the legislative delegation for additional authority.

In 1973, South Carolina voters adopted a constitutional "home rule" amendment that prohibits special legislation. Since then, in keeping with the amendment, governors have regularly vetoed special legislation, but the legislature has just as routinely overridden the vetoes. Thus, the amendment has done little to prevent needless or harmful legislative interference in the affairs of specific local governments. To make matters worse, the South Carolina Supreme Court has interpreted the amendment in such a way as to prevent the legislature from delegating more authority to individual local governments. In 2007, for example, the court ruled in a 3–2 decision that a 2005 law transferring the power to appoint members of a recreation commission from Richland County's legislative delegation to the Richland County Council violated the constitutional prohibition on special legislation. To comply with the court ruling, the legislature would have to pass legislation applying to all counties or all local governments. Coming up with general legislation of this nature is far more difficult than acting through special legislation.

A recent study undertaken in North Carolina suggests that local governments' need for specific legislative authority to take action "limits flexibility, efficiency, and predictability." The author recommends that the legislature (1) use broad language when drafting enabling legislation, (2) clarify the broad construction standard that courts must use to review challenges to local authority, and (3) delegate greater discretion to local entities. Unless changes are made, local authority in North Carolina will continue to depend on court decisions and special legislation.[8]

The battle for broader grants of local discretion has been a difficult one in recent years. In 2000, for example, New Hampshire local officials failed to secure voter approval for a constitutional amendment that would have given municipalities the authority to pass their own laws in areas where the state has not acted. The New Hampshire Municipal Association and several local officials led the fight for the amendment, contending that cities and towns should not have to constantly secure state legislative approval for routine decisions. Business groups were prominent in opposition, contending that local home rule would lead to more regulations and a crazy quilt of conflicting local laws. Also in 2000, Michigan voters rejected a proposed constitutional amendment that would have required a two-thirds vote of the legislature (rather than a simple majority, as under previous law) to eliminate or preempt local ordinances or charter provisions. Conflicts between the state legislature and the city of Detroit over a host of matters—and a growing perception among local officials that the legislature was eager to impose its will on all local governments—powered the drive for the constitutional amendment. As in other states, the issue found local officials and their organizations on one side, and business groups—such as state and local chambers of commerce—on the other.

Vermont is another state where legislators have been reluctant to relinquish control. As they had in the past several legislative sessions, Vermont legislators refused in 2007 to consider a proposal offered by the Vermont League of Cities and Towns (VLCT) to streamline legislative approval of municipal charters. The measure would have reduced the role of the legislature in reviewing changes to municipal charters that had been approved by local voters. Currently, charter changes must be submitted to the legislature for approval in the form of a bill. Over the years, the legislature has often altered charter amendments in ways that were contrary to the actions of the voters. In other cases, locally approved changes have failed to go into effect simply because the legislature did not get around to voting on them. The proposed legislation would have allowed charter changes to go into effect unless (1) concerns were raised by the attorney general, six senators, or 30 representatives, and (2) the legislature elected to review the concerns.

Also in 2007, Vermont legislators once again virtually ignored a league-sponsored constitutional amendment that would have given municipalities the authority to take any local action that is not specifically prohibited by state law. From the VLCT's point of view, "Vermont's great paradox is that, despite its tradition and reputation of direct democracy and robust local control, it is among the most centralized states in terms of the power relationship" between the municipalities and the state.[9] Over the years, legislators have been reluctant to devolve authority to Vermont municipalities and have forced municipalities to constantly engage in a struggle to retain what little authority they do have. Victories have come largely in the form of specific grants of power to specific municipalities—for example, the right of particular cities to appoint the municipal treasurer or constable. This strategy of "incremental home rule" has brought some gains, but the results are a far cry from general home rule powers.

In West Virginia, the need for home rule has been a rallying point for municipal officials: as the leader of the state municipal league declared in 2006, "Cities have to be able to have the power to govern themselves. . . . Every time we take a step, the state tells us how to take it."[10] This situation, however, may be greatly improving. In 2007, in response to complaints from local governments, the West Virginia legislature passed a bill that will allow five cities or metropolitan governments to experiment with home rule for up to five years, beginning in 2008. A special panel will select the five jurisdictions for the pilot program; officials in those jurisdictions will have the authority to make decisions on a range of matters—including taxation, personnel, and administration—that are currently beyond their authority without specific legislative approval.

On average, about one-fifth of the hundreds of measures introduced yearly in state legislatures significantly affect local government authority, finances, personnel management, structure, or physical boundaries. Given the importance of state legislative decisions to local governments' well-being, it comes as no surprise to find that local elected officials regularly take their case to state lawmakers. Sometimes they are on the offensive, trying to secure needed changes from the legislature. Perhaps even more often, though, local officials are on the defensive, trying to prevent cuts in state funding or to fend off costly mandates and unnecessary regulations. Often, local officials simply seek greater clarity in state law: in 2007 in Utah, for example, a legislative committee attempted to clear up confusion in state statutes concerning the roles of the mayor, the council, and administrators in local governance.

Some state legislation is the result of a genuine desire to make local government more accountable, effective, and efficient. For example, state legislators have long felt responsible for protecting citizens from dishonest or incompetent local officials. They also feel a duty to address problems that spill over local boundary lines, and to ensure fair treatment for all citizens with regard to education and other services. In an effort to maintain the health of the state's economy, many legislators have come to the aid of distressed localities. And in nearly every session, state legislators tinker with laws that they think will improve local government operations or service delivery. Nevertheless, in some cases, such tinkering, particularly in the case of mandates, may originate in a desire to shift program costs. And in the case of prohibitions, legislative action is often a matter of acceding to the demands of interest groups that are eager to avoid local taxes or regulations.

Mandates

State officials often rely on their legislative and regulatory authority to compel local units to follow certain procedures, make changes in existing programs, or assume new program responsibilities.[11] These state mandates—whether in the form of statutes, executive orders, or administrative regulations—often create unfunded costs for local governments. Some mandates cost relatively little money, but their aggregate effects can be staggering, and the big-ticket items—in areas such as health care, education, land use, and environmental protection—can overwhelm local government budgets. Even when local officials sympathize with the goals of state mandates, they are aware that all mandates distort local priorities and restrict local managerial flexibility. Nevertheless, local officials appear willing to live with most mandates if those mandates are at least partially funded; given local governments' financial constraints, they are hard put, without state funding, to both provide mandated services and address local priorities.[12]

Mandates on local government are valuable to state lawmakers because they allow them to claim credit for providing programs and services while avoiding burdens on their own budgets and the negative feedback that comes from levying taxes to support them. The matters addressed by mandates range from the important to the inconsequential, with the latter outnumbering the former.[13] In some cases, local governments face direct orders to spend at a certain level. In Wisconsin, for example, municipalities that have libraries must, by state law, provide annual library funding that is at least equal to the average amount spent for this purpose in the previous three years.[14] New Jersey municipalities have had to live with a similar law. Yet in both Wisconsin and New Jersey, the state government is simultaneously pressuring local governments to reduce expenditures.[15]

From the local perspective, mandates that require local governments to raise revenues for state agencies are especially irksome. In 2007, for example, the Arkansas legislature required municipalities to collect 30 cents from municipal water customers and to give this revenue to the state health department to fund its water testing program. Local officials argue that such programs should be funded by state general revenues.

Some expensive mandates are the products of end runs by local government employees, who succeed in securing benefits through state legislation that they could not obtain through collective bargaining: for example, some states require local governments to pay police officers and firefighters what some observers consider to be overly generous pension benefits. Although retirement benefits are set by state law, they are paid for out of local funds. In a number of states—Florida, Illinois, Kentucky, New Jersey, Pennsylvania, and West Virginia among them—police and firefighter pension funds are underfunded or run the risk of being so. In some states, such as Michigan, wages and benefits for police officers and firefighters are determined by arbitrators appointed under the provisions of state law and are therefore outside the control of local elected officials. Moreover, the arbitrators' decisions tend to have a ripple effect, setting a higher standard for wages and benefits for other employees.[16]

Municipal officials in New York State have long opposed the Wicks Law, which includes bidding requirements that drive up construction costs, and the Taylor Law, which places key decisions about personnel costs for police and firefighters beyond the control of local officials. As Ernest J. Strada, president of the New York Conference of Mayors, testified in the summer of 2007, "Real efficiencies cannot be achieved at the local level without the ability to reasonably control expenses—particularly personnel and construction expenses—two of the biggest cost drivers for municipal governments."[17]

The International Association of Firefighters and other groups are supporting an ongoing nationwide effort that may prove very expensive for local governments: the creation of a presumptive eligibility for workers' compensation for firefighters with certain forms of cancer. Under a 2007 Colorado law, for example, firefighters with any of five types of cancer (not including lung cancer, which is usually caused by smoking) are presumed to have gotten the cancer on the job and are therefore eligible for workers' compensation. It is not necessary for them to demonstrate that their cancer was work related: the burden is shifted to the local government—which must prove, by a preponderance of the medical evidence, that the cancer was *not* work related. The law could dramatically increase the workers' compensation insurance premiums paid by local governments; it also opens the door for employees in other high-risk occupations to demand similar protections. In 2007, Oregon local officials fended off a similar proposal, which the League of Oregon Cities estimated would have increased workers' compensation rates for cities by 234%.[18]

When it comes to mandates, courts have been inclined to defer to the judgment of the legislatures, making it difficult for localities to challenge state mandates in the courts.[19] Nevertheless, local governments have had some success in securing voter support for measures that are intended to reduce the number of mandates, or that require the states to pick up the costs of implementation. Voters appear to view such measures as a means of reducing local property taxes and preserving local control over spending priorities.[20]

Local officials and their associations regularly try to fend off mandates—or, failing this, to limit their financial impact. Local governments have sometimes obtained a pledge of additional state funds to cover the costs of new mandates—although, over time, states have not always been willing or able to live up to their agreements. Local governments have also sometimes succeeded in gaining the authority to raise the revenues needed to meet the costs of a new mandate; this outcome is not all that desirable, however, because local officials who raise taxes in order to comply with a mandate risk incurring the wrath of their taxpayers for programs demanded by the state.

Local officials have secured a number of legislative and administrative reforms that focus on the mandate process. Several states have statutory or constitutional provisions that limit their ability to impose mandates on local governments. Some laws call for full or partial state reimbursement of the costs of new mandates; others require that the state pick up the costs for mandated programs or give localities the authority to raise taxes to finance them. Under Proposition 1A, adopted by California voters in 2004, if the state fails to provide reimbursement within a year, local agencies may stop providing the mandated service. Explaining this provision, a representative for the California State Association of Counties said, "They've always said that they know they owe us the money, but the problem has been that they didn't ever allow us to not perform the mandate."[21]

More than 40 states have fiscal note requirements that call for state agencies (in some places, commissions on intergovernmental relations) to estimate the costs that state laws or regulations impose on localities. Several states combine fiscal notes with a requirement that the state reimburse localities, in full or in part, for the expense of undertaking the mandated activity. Other states use fiscal notes simply to call attention to the costs incurred by local governments. When employed alone (i.e., without a reimbursement requirement), fiscal notes appear to have only a limited effect on legislative behavior. Even if legislators are made more aware of the financial burden they are passing on to local governments, they will not necessarily refuse to impose the costs—which are, after all, assumed not by the state but by local governments. As an anti-mandate strategy, the primary value of fiscal notes seems to be in providing local governments with lobbying ammunition. At times, too, fiscal notes have been criticized for failing to even come close to anticipating the actual costs of mandates.

As a deterrent to unfunded mandates, a statutory or constitutional requirement for reimbursement is more effective than a simple requirement for cost estimates. Moreover, reimbursement requirements added to the state constitution with the backing of the voters may initially be more effective in influencing legislative behavior than those created by statute. Legislatures in some states have simply ignored reimbursement requirements (there is no penalty for doing so) or have gotten around them by earmarking as mandate reimbursement a part of the funding already allocated for state aid to localities—in effect, deducting mandate reimbursement costs from local aid programs.[22] Overall, extensive funding for mandates does not appear to be the major effect of reimbursement provisions; instead, the provisions seem more likely to deter mandates or to cause them to be modified so that they are less expensive.[23]

In addition to fiscal notes and reimbursement requirements, states have considered or adopted a variety of other anti-mandate measures, including the following:

- Requiring an agency to compile and annually update a catalog that lists all mandates and shows the fiscal impact of new mandates
- Requiring state agencies to regularly review current mandates to determine whether any of them can be relaxed or eliminated
- Encouraging agencies to implement new mandates in a few localities, on an experimental basis, to determine their effectiveness and impacts before they are implemented statewide
- Enabling the governor to suspend mandates at the request of local governments (acting individually or together), should mandates be found to impose an unreasonable burden.

For local governments, the mandate problem remains something of a no-win situation: even if a state decides to relinquish a long-standing requirement that localities provide a particular service, municipalities or counties may have no choice but to fund and provide the service anyway, because their citizens want it continued.

Prohibitions and Preemptions

Along with demands that they do certain things, local governments confront a range of "thou shall not" directives. Legislative acts prohibiting local governments from taking certain actions often reflect a particular group's desire to minimize, if not completely avoid, government taxation or regulation. In particular, local officials are continuously on guard against state legislation that would exempt certain businesses from local sales taxes or completely preempt local sales tax authority. In 2006, for example, the Oklahoma legislature considered no fewer than 36 requests for sales tax exemptions, many of which were granted. One Oklahoma municipal official likened the stream of sales tax exemptions to "death by a thousand duck bites."[24]

Tax Exemptions State legislators are attracted to certain proposals—such as raising the homestead exemption on property taxes or granting sales tax exemptions—both because they are politically popular and because they carry no costs to the state. But tax exemptions can significantly reduce the flow of funds into local treasuries and can be as financially devastating as unfunded mandates. From the point of view of local officials, a preferable arrangement is the one approved by Florida voters in 2006, under which local governments may, at their discretion, increase homestead exemptions for low-income senior citizens, but are not required to do so.

Local officials generally seek, but do not always receive, a guarantee of state reimbursement for any local revenues that are lost because of a state tax-exemption measure. When money lost as the result of exemptions is not reimbursed, local officials have to make up the difference by drawing on their own revenue sources, usually the property tax. And when the state grants exemptions from taxes on business property, local governments must often make up the difference by shifting the burden to those who own residential properties. In some places, such shifts have been dramatic.

Tobacco and Guns Some of the historic battles over preemption have involved the regulation of tobacco and guns. When it comes to tobacco, half the states preempt local ordinances that address youths' access to tobacco (laws that concern, for example, penalties for minors, the posting of signs, the fines that can be imposed on retailers who violate the law, and restrictions on vending machines and on the distribution of samples), and more than 20 states have laws preempting clean indoor-air ordinances. Because it is easier and less expensive than going from locality to locality, the tobacco industry has directed its efforts at the state level. Anti-smoking coalitions, however, have enjoyed more success at the local level.[25]

Laws in about a dozen states prevent localities from passing anti-smoking measures that are more restrictive than state standards. In addition, state legislatures often exempt various venues—such as taverns, casinos, lounges, and bowling alleys—from local as well as state smoking restrictions. Because of pressure from the tobacco industry and from groups such as restaurant associations, statewide smoking regulations are often less demanding than the local ordinances they replace.

In 2006, tobacco companies adopted a strategy of trying to head off stringent anti-smoking initiatives by offering voters competing but less restrictive measures. In Arizona and Ohio, the proposals supported by tobacco groups had relatively weak coverage (e.g., they would not have applied to bars) and would have struck down all local anti-smoking measures that were stricter than the state standard. The proposals supported by health groups would have imposed more stringent nonsmoking rules and would also have allowed local governments to adopt even stricter regulations. Voters in both states favored the measures sponsored by health groups.

In 2007, Illinois, Maryland, Minnesota, New Hampshire, New Mexico, and Oregon adopted statewide smoking bans in bars, restaurants, and/or other public places, while the Virginia General Assembly rejected a statewide ban on smoking in bars and restaurants. Some of these laws—Minnesota's, for example—set a minimum statewide standard and allow local governments to adopt stricter policies if they so choose. Also in 2007, North Carolina legislators authorized municipalities and counties to restrict smoking in buildings that they own or lease, and on public transportation vehicles (the latter change partially removed an existing preemption).

Court decisions in 2007 regarding local smoking regulations were inconsistent. In Pennsylvania, a state appeals court ruled that the state's 1988 Clean Indoor Air Act denies most local governments the right to impose stricter anti-smoking regulations than the state does; Philadelphia appears to be the only exception. On the other hand, a circuit court judge in South Carolina concluded that a state clean-air law adopted in 1990 did not prevent the municipality of Sullivan Island from banning smoking in bars, restaurants, and workplaces.

Thanks in large part to the National Rifle Association, 46 states prohibit or restrict local gun control ordinances. Some states prohibit local jurisdictions from imposing firearm ordinances that are more restrictive than state laws (Alaska imposed such a restriction in 2005), and others have rescinded local ordinances to ensure uniform firearms laws statewide. In five states, preemption has come through judicial rulings rather than by statute. A growing number of states (which now make up a majority) have restricted local governments' authority to regulate the open carrying of guns and to determine where guns can be banned. In response to the events surrounding Hurricane Katrina, at least 20 states passed legislation in 2006 and 2007 that prohibits local governments from attempting, during emergencies or natural disasters, to confiscate weapons from citizens who are legally permitted to possess them.

Late in 2006, Ohio governor Bob Taft vetoed a measure amending the state's concealed-carry law on the grounds that it had the effect of preempting a wide range of local gun regulations, some 80 in number, including assault-weapon bans in several municipalities. The veto was overridden in the legislature only a few hours after it was made. In another turn in the story, however, the Ohio Supreme Court agreed late in 2007 to hear a challenge brought by local officials, who charged that the law is unconstitutional because it is not general in nature and thus conflicts with municipal home rule rights.

Eminent Domain Courts have long recognized that under the power of eminent domain, local governments have broad authority to regulate the use of private property in the interests of public safety, health, and welfare. Specifically, local governments may confiscate private property for "public use" if the owner receives "just compensation." In recent years, however, eminent domain has been called into question: the issue is what constitutes public use. Traditionally, the power to take private land for public use has been restricted to purposes such as the revitalization of blighted areas or the construction of roads and public buildings that will be owned or primarily used by the general public. The notion that public use should encompass takings for the purpose of general public benefits, such as increased tax revenues or economic development, is more controversial.

In 2005, in *Kelo v. City of New London,* the U.S. Supreme Court confirmed, by a 5–4 vote, a Connecticut Supreme Court decision that had upheld the right of a city to take private homes through eminent domain and sell the property for private development. The decision did not give municipalities new powers, but it did confirm the existence of a power that some local governments had been exercising within the political limits established in their communities. Writing for the majority, Justice Paul Stevens noted that "promoting economic development is a traditional and long-accepted function of government" and that "local officials, not federal judges, know best in deciding whether a development project will benefit the community." The Court noted, however, that there was nothing in its decision to prevent states from restricting municipal use of the power of eminent domain.

The *Kelo* decision was in keeping with the rulings of several state courts that had defined public use broadly; other state courts, however, had limited local governments' power to confiscate private property for economic development. At the time of the decision, courts in about a dozen states had already prohibited state and local governments from using eminent domain to promote economic development unless the goal was to eliminate blight.

The *Kelo* decision came too late to significantly affect state legislative action in 2005; by the waning months of that year, however, many lawmakers were poised to take action, even in states where private property owners were already protected from the unreasonable use of eminent domain powers. By the fall of 2007, legislatures in more than 30 states had adopted legislation restricting the use of eminent domain, and in several states, voters adopted ballot measures that have the same effect. In 2007, legislation limiting local governments' use of eminent domain passed in Connecticut, where it all started, and in several other states, including Ohio, Virginia, and Wyoming. The Connecticut legislation prohibits the taking of property when the primary goal is to increase local tax revenues. It also includes a number of procedural safeguards on the use of eminent domain: for example, both the taking and the development plan must be approved by a two-thirds majority of the local legislative body. In addition, property owners must receive 125% of the average of two appraisals for their property.

Some states, including North Carolina, have restricted eminent domain in the context of urban redevelopment by specifying that the authority may be exercised only to take a parcel that is blighted. Other states have gone further, coupling restrictions on private use with narrower definitions of what constitutes "blight"—in effect, allowing condemnation only when the property poses a threat to public health and safety. Alabama, one of the first states to respond to *Kelo,* initially prohibited the use of eminent domain for economic development but made an exception for blighted properties. In 2006, the state moved to close that loophole by making it more difficult to designate property as blighted. In Colorado in 2006, the legislature required that blight be proven by "clear and convincing evidence," as opposed to "a preponderance of the evidence," which is a less demanding standard of proof. Meanwhile, a 2006 Minnesota law that defines blight to emphasize significant violations of housing, maintenance, and building codes restricts the ability of a governmental authority to assemble property for redevelopment.

In 2007, following a pattern set by several other states, Virginia passed legislation allowing local governments to take property for public use only if it is blighted, not simply because it is in a blighted area. With the governor's help, however, the definition of blight was broadened from a condition threatening "public health and safety" to one threatening "public health or safety." In Ohio, legislation passed in 2007 requires 70% of an area to be blighted before it can become subject to eminent domain; local officials had favored a proposal that called for a 50% threshold. The version approved by the legislature did, however, make it easier to designate a property as blighted than did the other alternatives being considered. To the relief of local officials, a proposed constitutional amendment giving the state the power to override local laws regarding eminent domain failed to clear the legislature. Also in 2007, a takings measure failed to get through the Colorado legislature, and Washington State voters turned down a highly restrictive takings measure.

In response to the *Kelo* decision, several states have altered the eminent domain process—by, for example, requiring that property owners receive earlier notification and more complete information. Georgia and Utah now require that decisions regarding the use of eminent domain for redevelopment purposes be made by the governing body of a county or municipality, rather than by appointed officials working for housing authorities or similar bodies. Some states have increased the amount of compensation given to people whose property is condemned. In Indiana, for example, if the condemned property is a person's primary residence, the owner is required to receive 150% of fair-market value. A constitutional amendment approved by Louisiana voters in September 2006 requires that state and local governments compensate landowners for "the highest and best use" of their property, a much more expensive standard than had previously been employed.

At least 40 states now have broad constitutional or statutory prohibitions on state and local governments' authority to take property and transfer it to a private party for economic development. Local officials throughout the nation contend that

many of the proposed and adopted measures are dangerously broad and constitute an overreaction to the Supreme Court decision. In their view, eminent domain has been used prudently to benefit the public—and only after serious discussion and public debate. Some local officials are concerned that overreactions to the Court's decision will make it more difficult for local governments to attract new businesses and pursue community revitalization projects.

In several states, various groups, some of which have a national base, have drawn upon the current outcry against eminent domain to promote a broader campaign for the protection of property rights. As part of this effort, property-rights advocates have been active in the courts, challenging zoning and other governmental restrictions on the use of private property by contending that such regulations diminish the value of their property and thus amount to unconstitutional takings. The goal of such litigation is to discourage local regulations by requiring localities to compensate property owners who are financially damaged by them. Property-rights advocates, real estate agents, and developers have also pushed for state legislation and for voter-approved propositions that would require property owners to be compensated if state or local regulations limit the use of private property. Measure 37, approved by Oregon voters in 2004, was the result of such an effort. Under that measure, if zoning or other land use decisions diminish property values, state and local governments must either reimburse property owners or lift the restrictions. Local governments have generally chosen to waive restrictions in order to settle claims against them under Measure 37. One result of Measure 37 was to open the door to the creation of large residential, commercial, and industrial developments on farm- and forestland. In 2007, Oregon voters modified the measure to curb such development through zoning restrictions and through limitations on the number of homes that landowners can build on their property as compensation for a regulatory taking.

In 2006, "*Kelo*-plus" propositions—measures that both limit eminent domain and restrict takings (along the lines of Measure 37)—were on the ballot in Arizona, California, and Idaho. Voters approved the proposition in Arizona but turned down those in California and Idaho. After passage of the Arizona proposition, a spokesperson for the Arizona Municipal League said that it "will have the effect of seriously slowing down or virtually stopping new zoning."[26] Opponents of takings measures have argued that such measures have the potential not only to severely cripple the enforcement of zoning regulations, but also to undermine environmental controls, smoking bans, living-wage laws, and restrictions on adult entertainment.

Telecommunications For some time, phone companies have been pressuring state legislatures for bills that would move cable-franchising authority to the state level, and they have succeeded in about a dozen states. Previously, cable companies negotiated individual franchise contracts with each municipality in which they wished to operate; this arrangement allowed localities to collect fees and to subject the cable companies to local regulations. Local officials

are concerned that where statewide franchising bills become law, localities will not only lose franchise fees and regulatory authority, but also be unable to protect public rights-of-way and respond to consumer complaints. Another concern is that cable companies operating under state franchises will bypass low-income areas or small rural populations that they consider unprofitable. Local franchise agreements commonly avoid such problems through "build-out" provisions that require companies to provide services in every neighborhood. Local agreements also ensure that companies provide services such as educational and government-access channels; these, too, could be lost in the shift of franchising authority to the state level.

In 2005, the Texas legislature established a model for future action by approving a statewide franchise system. In response to local concerns, the legislature grandfathered existing franchise agreements and directed that future fees from statewide franchises be transferred to local governments. However, not all states that have shifted authority to state agencies have safeguarded local revenues, and only about half the states that have moved cable-franchising authority to the state level have included build-out provisions. A California law adopted in 2006, for example, includes such provisions: although it transfers cable-franchising authority held by local agencies to the state's public utility commission, local authorities continue to oversee customer service, retain limited control over rights-of-way, and receive a 5% franchise fee.

Among the states that moved cable franchising to the state level in 2007 were Florida, Georgia, Illinois, Missouri, Ohio, and Utah. The Cable and Video Competition Law of 2007, adopted in Illinois, imposes state franchising but (1) requires cable providers to pay municipalities up to a 5% franchise fee, (2) requires cable providers to help pay for the cost of operating local government and public-access channels, (3) imposes regulations and fees on cable providers' use of rights-of-way, and (4) has extensive consumer protection provisions regarding matters such as installation, rate increases, and termination of service. The legislation passed in Georgia includes several similar provisions. In Missouri, the new cable competition bill allows companies to bypass local governments and to provide cable service anywhere in the state, with the approval of the state public service commission. Although the law requires providers to expand services into rural areas, it is written in such a way that it will likely take years for services to reach some of these areas. The measure may also lead to the loss of some consumer protections and some public-access channels. In Colorado, on the other hand, Quest failed in its effort to obtain a statewide permit to sell cable services. Statewide cable franchising also failed in Tennessee in 2007.

Residency Requirements Beyond the financial and regulatory areas, prohibitions and preemptions involve everyday local government decisions on personnel and other internal matters. Of importance in several states in recent years have been the efforts, sometimes supported by groups of local employees such as police and firefighters, to eliminate local residency requirements for municipal workers. In 1999, the Minneapolis Police

Federation led a successful effort in the state legislature to repeal the authorization for locally enacted residency requirements in Minneapolis and St. Paul. A similar decision by the Michigan legislature, which ended the long-established local practice of requiring municipal employees to live inside municipal boundaries, helped prompt an unsuccessful effort to secure a constitutional amendment that would have made it tougher for the legislature to restrict or eliminate local laws.

In several states, legislatures have prohibited local residency requirements for schoolteachers. In 2000, for example, city council members in Providence, Rhode Island, voiced their displeasure with a recent state law that exempted teachers from the city's residency requirement, which was embedded in the city's charter. A year later, the Pennsylvania legislature prohibited Philadelphia and Pittsburgh from requiring teachers to live in the districts where they work. Currently, the issue of residency requirements is alive and well in Ohio, where some municipalities have challenged a state law that prohibits municipalities from requiring their employees to live within municipal limits. The municipalities are arguing that their home rule powers give them the authority to set residency requirements. In 2007, however, courts rejected this argument in cases involving Akron and Cleveland, both of which are home rule cities.

Supporters of state actions to end residency requirements argue that the state has an interest in safeguarding employees' freedom of movement. Supporters also argue that ending residency requirements will help cities attract teachers, public safety officers, and other needed workers. Those in favor of residency requirements contend that being a part of the community they serve strengthens public employees' job performance and commitment to the community—which, in turn, helps foster positive attitudes among community residents toward municipal workers. Supporters of residency requirements also view them as a means of keeping well-paid, middle-class people in cities, and cite as an additional virtue the fact that residency requirements can help reduce response times during emergencies. More generally, state prohibitions are criticized on the grounds that decisions regarding local residency requirements, whatever their merits, should be made not by the state, but by the local governments involved.

LOCAL FINANCES

Financing is an area in which local officials have relatively little control: the local government revenue base is largely what state officials want it to be. The state not only confers local revenue sources, but may also reduce them or divert them to state uses. In recent years, with the states straining for revenues and being locked into costly "untouchables" (such as education and health care), local officials have had to fight "takeaways"— state attempts to deprive them of revenue sources that local governments have long relied on. At the same time, state aid has been unreliable, to say the least. Although states have shown some tendency to assume more of the costs of government, this shift has often led to a loss of local con-

trol. States have also encouraged consolidation and service sharing at the local level as a means of achieving savings.

Financial Controls

State constitutions and statutes impose controls on nearly all aspects of local financial management: assessment, taxation, indebtedness, budgeting, accounting, auditing, and fiscal reporting. In the area of taxation, for example, states may prohibit certain types of local taxes (e.g., a sales tax or a graduated income tax) and may limit increases in tax rates or property tax assessments. In a half-dozen states, the amount of total revenue that can be raised is tied to such measures as inflation, population, and growth in personal income, and all funds raised over the limit have to be refunded to taxpayers. In some states, total expenditures are tied to a growth index. Finally, many states require voter approval for tax increases and for spending increases above a certain level.

Other state-imposed limitations on local finances have to do with local borrowing; such limitations may, for example, require a public referendum to permit the issuance of bonds, restrict the purposes for which localities may borrow, or limit the amount of debt that localities can incur. Debt limits apply to general-obligation bonds and may be expressed either as specific dollar amounts or as a percentage (from 15% to 25%) of the value of the property within the jurisdiction. One effect of debt limits is to encourage local governments to turn to more costly revenue bonds, which are supported only by the revenues derived from the project for which the money is borrowed.

Many state restrictions grew out of the Great Depression of the 1930s, which caused local financial operations to collapse throughout the nation. During this period, several states placed in receivership cities that faced financial emergencies. The depression brought a multitude of measures at the state level that were designed to head off future problems; it also gave birth to the idea of giving a state agency complete control over the financial management of all municipalities, although this actually occurred only in the few states where municipal default problems had been extensive. Among the powers given to state agencies in these places—of which New Jersey was one—was the authority to review local budgets before their adoption and to order changes to avoid a deficit.

New Jersey continues to exercise unique financial controls over local governments; North Carolina and Ohio are other prime examples of states where state agencies continuously monitor local government finances in an attempt to keep local governments from falling into financial distress. Monitoring is useful in that it helps to detect and correct problems early on; moreover, monitoring can act as a form of credit enhancement, making investors more comfortable with municipal bonds and encouraging them to give the bonds a higher rating.

A more recent wave of restrictions has centered not so much on keeping local governments out of financial difficulty as on reducing local governments' demands on taxpayers. Several citizens' groups have taken their case to the voters and succeeded in obtaining passage of restrictive

measures. Tax protesters—such as Howard Jarvis in California during the 1970s and 1980s and, more recently, Bill Sizemore in Oregon and Douglas Bruce in Colorado—have been able to tap a groundswell of anti-tax sentiment in their states and lead successful initiative campaigns for strong anti-tax measures. Elsewhere, in an effort to preempt the tax-protest movement in their states and to shape the nature of reform, state lawmakers have adopted similar, but less severe, tax and expenditure limitations (TELs).[27]

California voters set the pace in 1978 when they approved Jarvis's Proposition 13, which capped local property tax rates and limited increases in assessed property value unless the property was sold. As the result of a series of propositions adopted since 1978, California now requires that virtually all local revenue-raising actions (taxes, fees, charges) be approved by at least two-thirds of the voters. In Oregon, changes in the pattern of state-local financial relations began in November 1990, when voters adopted Sizemore's Measure Number 5, which severely restricted the amount that could be raised by municipalities, counties, and special districts and forced several communities to make dramatic cutbacks in their services. Measure 47, sponsored by an Oregon property taxpayers' group and approved by voters in 1996, further limited property taxes, although a subsequent vote modified some of the force of the measure.

Under Bruce's constitutional amendment, known as the Taxpayers' Bill of Rights (TABOR) and adopted by Colorado voters in 1992, voters must approve (1) any new state or local tax or any increase in an existing tax and (2) any state or local spending increase that exceeds a certain limit. The limits on state spending are tied to inflation and to changes in population; those on local government spending are tied to changes in population and in property values. Neither state nor local spending can increase by more than 6% annually, and revenues that exceed the amount that state or local governments can spend must be refunded to taxpayers unless voters decide otherwise. In November 2005, confronted by a state budget crisis, the governor and the legislature asked voters to lift the state spending limits for five years, allowing the state government to keep $3.7 billion in revenues that existing taxes are expected to generate; this money would otherwise have had to be returned to taxpayers. Close to 52% of the voters approved this proposal, known as Referendum C. As a result of the voters' action, the legislature had an extra $800 million in 2006 for education, transportation, and health care— areas in which it had been forced to cut back because of recessionary conditions and limited funds.

The Colorado vote and the decision of California voters, in November 2005, to turn down a proposition that would have limited state spending (to the level of the prior year, plus a percentage equivalent to the average revenue growth for the three previous years) represented setbacks to the spending-limit approach. National groups, including Americans for Limited Government and Americans for Tax Reform, have continued to promote Colorado's TABOR plan or versions thereof in better than a dozen states, but have had little to show for their efforts.

Because of a variety of obstacles, including adverse court decisions, only three TABOR proposals made it to the ballot in 2006—in Maine, Nebraska, and Oregon. In yet another indication of a weakening in the TABOR movement, voters in all three states turned down the measures. The measure voted on in Maine was similar to the one that had been adopted by Colorado voters in 1992, and applied revenue and expenditure limits to local as well as to state government (the others did not). Although Maine already had a law limiting state and local spending, proponents of the TABOR measure claimed that the existing law was too weak.

Despite evidence of decreasing interest in TABOR proposals, anti-tax sentiment continues to run strong in some quarters. For example, the idea surfaced for a time in the Florida legislature early in 2007. And, as noted later in this article, many of the current anti-tax efforts are focused on the property tax: groups in several states have proposed constitutional or statutory provisions that would limit increases in property tax rates, property assessments, and overall property tax levies.

The primary effect of the tax revolt of the past three decades has been to cut into local revenues. In some jurisdictions, however, there has been a secondary effect: because local officials have found it more difficult to meet matching requirements for state and federal grants, their ability to attract intergovernmental aid has been compromised. Often, local officials succeed in reducing their losses through productivity improvements or through targeted revenue increases, such as new or increased fees. Because of such steps, TELs appear to have had little effect on total spending. They have, however, affected the composition of local revenues; specifically, they have decreased local governments' long-term reliance on the property tax and increased reliance on state aid and on locally collected fees and sales taxes. Generally, TELs also appear, over the long run, to encourage centralization of authority at the state level and to increase local governments' dependence on regressive revenue sources, such as fees and sales taxes.[28]

Locally Collected Revenues
Local governments in the United States raise around 65% of their total revenues. Most of the outside revenue—some 31% of total revenues—comes from the states, while the federal government contributes the remaining 4%. Of the revenue that local governments raise on their own, about 46% is provided by the property tax, 10% comes from locally adopted sales taxes, 3% from individual income taxes, and about 38% from charges and miscellaneous fees.[29] Municipalities have the most diversified revenue structure and, compared with counties, are far less dependent on state aid and the property tax.

The Property Tax Historically, the property tax has been a rich and relatively stable source of income that local officials could pretty much call their own, increasing or decreasing the tax rate depending on their budgetary needs. However, this tax has become increasingly unpopular.[30] Public-choice theorists like the property tax because it gives citizens a highly visible "tax price" for the public services that are being offered, thus clarifying their choices. Yet, one might argue, it is the very visibility of the tax that makes it unpopular and encourages local officials to turn to less visible revenue sources.[31] State and local officials commonly debate over who is responsible for the increases in property tax levels: state officials point to local governments' failure to tighten their belts sufficiently, and local officials contend that the state is responsible because it has cut state aid, forcing localities to turn to the property tax, and has not allowed localities to seek out other locally collected revenue sources.

Some of the pressure to abandon the property tax has come not from the state legislature but from court decisions. Courts in about half the states have found that reliance on the local property tax to finance education discriminates against students in areas where property values are the lowest and thus violates state constitutional provisions.

State legislatures have used a number of methods to force or encourage local units to cut expenses, which indirectly reduces pressure on the property tax: among other means, state have imposed spending caps, set limitations on retirement benefits for local government workers, and encouraged sharing or consolidation of local services. States have also used more direct methods: granting property tax rebates, and freezing or capping increases in property tax rates or property assessments. However, severe state-imposed limits on property taxes make it more difficult for local officials to meet increased costs, including those costs mandated by the state, and ultimately lead to cutbacks in local services. Limits are easier to live with if they are accompanied by increases in state aid and/or by greater access to revenues from other local sources; giving voters the opportunity to override the limits also makes them more palatable.

Targeted relief and "tax swapping" (substituting one tax for another) are other common state responses to property tax pressure. Several states have adopted programs that provide tax relief for certain population groups on the basis of factors such as age, income, and disability. As noted earlier, some states have homestead exemption programs, under which a portion of the value of a home belonging to a member of a targeted group is exempt from the property tax. Still others have "circuit-breaker" programs that protect against property tax overload. Such programs provide automatic tax relief when property taxes exceed a certain percentage of household income; the critical percentage and the definition of household income vary from state to state, and tax relief generally comes in the form of direct tax reductions or rebates.[32]

States that cut property taxes generally replace at least some of the lost revenues through tax swapping or by temporarily drawing on state budget surpluses. Cutbacks are sometimes accompanied by increases in state aid. Sometimes, too, local governments are given increased authority to raise revenues by other means, such as a local income tax. Several states have limited property tax cuts or rebates to primary residences or owner-occupied homes and excluded vacation homes and investment property.

Given the extent of local government dependence on the property tax, whether and how states decide to replace revenues that are lost because of state-imposed property tax cuts are matters of vital concern to local governments. Although sales tax revenues are the most common replacement for property taxes, other sources have not been ignored. In 2006, Texas lawmakers turned to a broad-based business tax to replace property tax revenues. In 2007, after allowing citizens to deduct up to $1,000 in property tax payments from their income taxes, North Dakota legislators filled the void by increasing taxes on oil and gas production. Also in 2007, South Dakota legislators offset a property tax reduction by increasing taxes on tobacco.

In 2007, more than half the states took some action intended to reduce the pressure on local property taxes. In New Jersey, the state with the highest property taxes in the country, the legislature limited the ability of municipalities, counties, and school districts to increase property taxes by more than 4% annually (the recent average had been close to 7%) without voter approval. Also in 2007, the Indiana legislature provided $300 million in property tax relief and gave local governments the option of increasing local income taxes to replace the lost revenue. Late in 2007, the Wisconsin legislature extended limits on property tax increases for another two years; thanks to the governor's use of line-item veto power, however, the law was modified: property taxes may increase by up to 3.86% before falling back, in 2008, to a maximum annual increase of 2%.

Florida lawmakers in 2007 used the threat of losing state aid to encourage localities to roll back property taxes to 2006 levels (revenues generated by new construction were excluded). The law requires localities to reduce their property taxes by up to 9% (depending on their recent property tax revenue history), and it applies to all local governments except those with severe financial difficulties and those that have experienced very slow growth in property tax levels. Higher tax rates are permitted, however, through a supermajority vote of the city council or county commission, or through a voter referendum. Thus far, the law has prompted several communities to raise fees, to freeze or lay off staff, and to cut programs—especially quality-of-life programs such as libraries, parks, and special events. Local officials argue that decisions about taxes and service levels should rest primarily with voters and local officials, and that the law amounts to state interference.

In 2007, pursuant to a constitutional amendment passed the previous year, Tennessee lawmakers created the Property Tax Freeze Program, which allows municipal and county governments to freeze the property tax of low-income seniors at 2007 levels. Applicants must be 65 or older, and must meet income requirements that vary from county to county, depending on the average income of residents between 65 and 74 in each county. Because local governments will not be reimbursed for the lost property tax revenue, those that wish to implement the program will likely have to reduce service levels or make up the funding in some other way.

Late in 2007, the Washington Supreme Court upheld a lower court decision that had held unconstitutional Initiative 747, a 2001 measure that limited the annual growth in property tax revenue to 1%. Also in 2007, Texas voters approved several propositions offering property tax relief, including a 10% limit on increases in property assessments and a property tax exemption for disabled veterans. Meanwhile, New Jersey municipal officials were disappointed by the voters' rejection of Public Question 1, which would have amended the constitution to dedicate a portion of the sales tax to property tax relief.

On January 29, 2008, a smorgasbord of tax relief measures was placed on the Florida ballot, including a general property tax cut, a doubling of the homestead exemption for nonschool taxes, and a provision that would allow homeowners to take up to $500,000 of the savings provided by the existing 3% cap on property assessment with them when they move and buy a new home in the state. All the measures have been harshly criticized by local officials, who fear a massive loss of revenue. Because the proposed measures were part of a constitutional amendment, a 60% vote was required to secure their approval.

Local Sales Taxes Thirty-eight states allow the local sales tax. Many states permit counties, municipalities, and special districts to levy the tax, while some restrict that right to either municipalities or counties. The sales tax has the advantage of shifting, or "exporting," part of the tax burden to nonresidents but tends to be regressive in its overall impact. Another disadvantage is that reliance on the sales tax encourages the "fiscalization of land use," also known as "zoning for dollars": land use decisions that favor sales tax–generating developments, such as shopping centers, rather than housing or other nonretail activities.

The quest for sales tax revenue not only conditions land use decisions but often throws local governments into intense, sometimes ruinous, competition for developments like shopping centers. In many cases, jurisdictions compete by attempting to offer retail developers the largest tax rebate. In some places, however, state legislatures have sought to prevent rebate offers, which they see as needless giveaways, by threatening to cut off state aid. Under an Arizona bill passed in 2007, for example, municipalities in certain high-growth counties that offer tax rebates to retail developers are penalized by losing state-shared revenue that is equivalent in amount to the incentive given to developers. Local officials in the Phoenix metropolitan area pledged to avoid competing with each other by agreeing to share revenues from developments along common borders, but they failed to implement their agreements. While often acknowledging the ill effects of competition, local officials in Arizona and elsewhere believe that the root of the problem is a state-structured tax system that forces them to be excessively dependent on the sales tax. Many view tax rebates as an important economic development tool.

Income Taxes, User Fees, and Impact Fees Of the 18 states that authorize local income taxes, only a few—in particular, Ohio and Pennsylvania—rely on the tax to a significant extent. Apparently,

many jurisdictions are afraid that a local income tax would hurt the development of the local economy.[33] Several localities, however, have taken advantage of new authority to collect fees for various services, such as police, fire, and ambulance. User fees have become a popular means of financing water and sewer service, transportation, and other services. The notion that the direct user of a service should pay for it appears to be popular throughout the country. Because of this view, user fees are a relatively acceptable way of raising revenue. Local officials also find user fees attractive because they can usually be levied without permission from the state legislature. However, some courts have declared user fees (such as transportation utility fees, which are fees charged to private property owners to finance road repairs or improvements in their area) to be disguised taxes and therefore invalid in the absence of specific state authorization.

Close to half the states authorize local governments to impose impact fees on developers to help offset the costs engendered by the construction or expansion of roads, sewers, and parks. A study by the Brookings Institution found that impact fees have been a valuable tool for financing local infrastructure: in addition to making up for declines in federal and state assistance for construction projects, such fees have helped local governments avoid greater reliance on the property tax and have also made it possible to sustain community growth.[34]

Because those who benefit from the improvements pay for them, local officials see impact fees as an equitable means of helping to offset the costs of development. Builders commonly argue, however, that impact fees are excessive and far beyond the actual cost of providing new infrastructure. In recent years, several states have sided with builders' associations and enacted legislation that requires impact fees to be (1) reasonable and (2) related to reliable estimates of the impact of particular developments.

Meanwhile, builders' associations around the country have been waging state-level campaigns against various types of development fees. In 2004, as the result of such pressure, the Minnesota legislature passed a law requiring municipalities that charge a fee for reviewing or processing a development application to establish a demonstrable link between the fee levied and the actual cost of providing the service. In 2006, courts in Mississippi and North Carolina invalidated impact fees for the reason that localities needed state enabling legislation to collect them. Also in 2006, at the request of the Wisconsin Builders Association, the Wisconsin legislature passed a law that limits the types of facilities that can be funded with impact fees.

Protecting Existing Revenue Sources In recent years, many localities have struggled not only to obtain new local revenue sources but also to protect the ones they have. For example, local governments have had to fight off tax exemptions adopted at the state level that reduce the intake from local property, sales, and other taxes. As noted earlier, fighting exemptions is often a losing battle. Another problem is that legislatures have, at times, simply dipped into local tax revenues and used

them for their own purposes. This approach has been especially common in California—where, beginning in 1992, municipalities, counties, and special districts lost close to $3 billion a year in property taxes because the legislature decided to draw on this source to pay for education. In the course of the decade, the legislature took away other local taxes and fees—for example, on alcohol, cigarettes, and mobile homes—often without reimbursing local governments.

In 2003, faced with a $38 billion deficit, the California legislature took half of the municipal governments' sales tax revenues to balance the budget, promising (as it had in the past) to make it up later. In response, a coalition of local officials began an initiative campaign that ultimately resulted in a constitutional amendment, Proposition 1A, approved by California voters in 2004. Under Proposition 1A, the state is prohibited from borrowing property tax revenues from local governments unless the governor declares a fiscal emergency and two-thirds of the legislature agrees to the loan. In addition, the borrowed funds must be paid back, with interest, within five years. The proposition also prohibits the state from reducing local government sales tax revenues, and allows local governments to stop providing any mandated service for which the state fails to provide reimbursement within a year. With the greater security offered by Proposition 1A, several California cities decided in 2005–2006 to ask their voters to approve half-cent sales tax measures. Some local officials said that without passage of Proposition 1A, they would not have gone to the voters: "Why pass a sales tax increase if the state is just going to take it away?"[35]

In 2007, South Carolina local officials were able to fend off state efforts to take fines paid by motorists who had been caught by stoplight cameras (which had been used to support the operation of the camera systems) and deposit them in a state fund for schools. The Texas legislature, on the other hand, decided that municipalities must share such fines with the state. In Missouri, municipalities won a major victory when a bill that had passed in the House failed in the Senate; the bill would have prevented municipalities from going to court to collect taxes from cell phone companies. After failing to secure passage of the bill, the cell phone companies announced that they would negotiate a settlement with the municipalities. The resolution of this six-year-long battle could bring in hundreds of millions in municipal revenues.

State Assistance

State financial aid to local governments consists of grants and shared taxes. Grants are usually for specific programs in areas such as education or transportation, although most states also provide unrestricted grants for general purposes. Much of the unrestricted aid comes to local governments as compensation for a state action—for example, to compensate for a state-required property tax exemption that reduces local revenues—or to help local governments pay for state-mandated services. In the case of shared taxes, states act as tax collectors, returning all or a portion of the yield to local governments according to an allocation formula or on the basis of the revenues' origin. Sales, income, and gasoline taxes are among the state taxes that are often shared. As they do with grants, states earmark much of the shared revenue for specific purposes—requiring, for example, that localities spend their share of the state gas tax on highway or street improvements. Some shared revenue, however, is unrestricted and can be spent as local officials see fit.

State aid is a major source of local revenue, accounting for more than one-third of all local general revenues. Over the years, the bulk of state aid (since 1975, between 60% and 64%) has gone to education.[36] A majority of the aid goes to school districts; counties come in second, and municipalities wind up third. More than 80% of all funds for education go to independent school districts; the rest go to municipal or county governments in the few states—including Maryland, North Carolina, and Virginia—where these units, rather than independent school districts, have responsibility for school systems. Counties receive the bulk of the state funds earmarked for welfare, health, and hospitals, while state aid for highways is relatively equally distributed between counties and municipalities. Municipalities receive 58% of the general, unrestricted support funds.[37] Overall, state aid has a modest equalizing effect, only somewhat reducing the revenue gap between poorer and wealthier localities. On the other hand, states often assist financially distressed local governments when the need arises.

Although vital to local governments, state aid is not dependable—a characteristic that makes it more difficult for local governments to plan budgets and borrow money. The amount tends to ebb and flow with legislative moods and changing economic conditions. Because state aid is based largely on sales and income taxes, it can be relatively high in times of prosperity but also relatively low when the economy is in trouble. Even in times of widespread prosperity, however, aid may be limited because it competes poorly with demands for tax relief and for other expenditures. Moreover, even in good economic times, state aid may not fare well because lawmakers, for ideological or political reasons, do not look favorably on the aid system; as a Wisconsin legislator declared nearly a decade ago, "I don't view my role as being an ATM machine for local governments."[38]

During the early 2000s, financial pressures prompted state officials to cut back aid, and legislatures were particularly inclined to reduce funds for schools and general local government assistance.[39] In New York, for example, where local revenue sharing comes through several aid programs, state aid declined from $1.1 billion in 1988–1989 to $800 million in 2003–2004.[40] In 2004, Alaska eliminated its municipal revenue-sharing program, an action that has had a particularly drastic impact on many of the state's smallest cities.

The state aid picture in 2007 was, as always, a mixed bag. The Wisconsin legislature froze shared-revenue payments for 2008 and 2009 at 2007 levels. Michigan lawmakers preserved revenue sharing but also froze payments at 2007 levels. This was a positive sign only in that for the previous six years, the state had reduced the amount of funding provided under the shared-revenue program (which has been fully funded only three times in the past 16 years). Because of these and other reductions in state aid, Michigan localities have been forced to cut services and raise property taxes.[41] In New Jersey, meanwhile, local officials complained about a cut of several million dollars in the Extraordinary Aid Program, which provides funding for communities on the basis of need.[42] In Arkansas, on the other hand, municipalities and counties received a chunk of the state's nearly $1 billion in surplus revenues to spend pretty much as they wished. The state's municipalities received a total of $12 million, and the counties received another $12 million.

The New York state budget for 2007–2008 includes an additional $200 million in Aid and Incentives for Municipalities. The funds awarded to municipalities under this program vary with the municipalities' level of fiscal distress, but jurisdictions that receive amounts over a certain level must use the funds to (1) minimize or reduce the property tax burden, (2) invest in development programs that increase tax growth, or (3) invest in technology with the aim of reducing operating expenditures. The state budget also includes $25 billion for the Shared Municipal Services Incentives program, which encourages municipalities to economize and improve services through consolidations and cooperative arrangements.

State lawmakers in New York and elsewhere have increasingly looked on state aid as a way to encourage local government to share or consolidate services. Some—perhaps many—state lawmakers, however, are critical of state aid on principle: they see no reason for the state to raise money that local officials spend and have suggested that, as an alternative, the state give local officials greater authority to raise revenues. Critics of this approach argue that it overlooks the wide variation in localities' tax bases and revenue-raising ability. Increased authority to raise revenues is unlikely to be of much value in a jurisdiction with a limited tax base. State aid, on the other hand, can enable jurisdictions with lower tax bases to afford at least a minimal level of services. Because of structural changes in their economies, some jurisdictions have a particularly strong need for continued intergovernmental aid.

On the question of state aid, the debate has often proceeded as one might expect: state officials find state aid programs objectionable because they are the ones who must suffer the pain of raising revenues, while local officials get credit for providing the services that the aid supports. Along with this view comes the suspicion that local officials seek the aid only because they are afraid to ask their own taxpayers to support services and because they want to use state money to keep local tax rates low. Local officials, for their part, see state aid as justified because it offsets costly state mandates and makes up for state laws that limit local governments' ability to raise revenues. With state mandates in mind, local officials argue that when it comes to claiming credit for programs financed by other governments in order to keep their taxes low, the states are the guilty parties.

What happens when states decide to cut aid? Here is one local official's answer: "It's not rocket science. . . . It's pretty much raise taxes or cut services. That's what it boils down to."[43] Generally, municipal officials say that they are most likely to cut funds for general government (administration and personnel) or leisure and culture (parks and recreation, libraries), and least likely to cut funds for public safety (police, fire, and emergency medical services).[44] But whatever adjustments are made to compensate for cutbacks in state aid tend to be short-term: rather than abandon or drastically revamp programs, local officials often try to maintain service levels by making temporary adjustments in funding—such as drawing on budget reserves, delaying capital purchases or construction projects, or cutting employee expenses—and hoping that these will suffice until aid is restored.[45] In recent years, many localities have attempted to cope by imposing new fees or increasing old ones.

State Assumption of Financial Responsibility

Considering state aid in isolation gives an incomplete and somewhat misleading picture of state efforts to ease financial pressures on local governments. For example, a state that provides minimal direct aid to local governments may actually provide more indirect aid than many or most states by assuming the cost of expensive functions that, in other states, are borne by local governments. Looking across the nation, the state share of total state and local spending is relatively high in Alaska, Vermont, and West Virginia and relatively low in Florida, Nebraska, and Tennessee.[46] Much of the difference among states has to do with the proportion of spending on education that is borne by the state government.

Transferring educational funding to the states has been an effective means of ensuring equity and providing overall support. It has also, however, created other difficulties. For one, it makes financial support of education less stable by tying it to the ups and downs in the fiscal health of the state—and, often, to revenue sources that are less dependable than the property tax, especially in a recessionary period. Pinning school funding to the sales tax, for example, makes support for education volatile. Even in good times, moreover, the level of support can vary significantly because education has to compete with a host of other demands on state funds.

The growth in state financial aid also has disadvantages for educators: namely, increases in state regulations and caps on local educational expenditures. States have become increasingly involved with curriculum, class size, and special education—and, in the interest of accountability, are more and more likely to impose statewide academic standards and mandated tests. As state funding of education has grown, so has state meddling in the details of educational policy. As one state legislator put it, "When we control the money, it's hard to get out of the details."[47] Overall, while local school officials are busier than ever before, their authority, particularly at the district level, has been increasingly undercut.

In recent years, states have not only picked up more of the costs of education but have also taken on more financial responsibility for courts and corrections, health care for indigent citizens, mental health care, and cash welfare assistance. Generally, state assumption of expenditures can reduce the spending disparities that result from reliance on the local property tax and free up local property tax revenues for other local functions. Yet the price is likely to be a loss of local control and perhaps a decline in service quality. In fact, some programs that are now under state administration may be better off under direct local control. Some observers have suggested, for example, that a decentralized court system, which can allow more flexibility in judicial administration, may be preferable to a court system financed and administered by the state. Instead of assuming full financial and administrative responsibility for courts, states could provide relief through grants-in-aid and cost reimbursement plans but could give local governments some control over the administration of the system.

Consolidation and Cooperation

In the interest of cost savings, states have occasionally encouraged the consolidation of local government units or greater service sharing between local governments. The consolidation of school districts, for example, has been viewed as a means of achieving economic efficiency and lowering property taxes, and such consolidations are currently being contemplated in a number of states, including Arizona and New Jersey. In 2007, legislatures in Maine and South Dakota shrunk the number of school districts from more than 150 to about 80.

Rather than restructure local governments, state lawmakers have generally encouraged pragmatic responses to problems that spill over boundary lines. They have, for example, encouraged the transfer of functions among jurisdictions (e.g., from city to county), elaborate systems of interlocal contracts and agreements, local government participation in metropolitan or regional councils of governments, and the creation of special districts and authorities to deal with specific issues. States generally play a positive role in encouraging cooperative activities, and much can be accomplished through state passage of joint powers acts, which encourage cooperative ventures. In recent years, several states, including New Jersey and Wisconsin, have used financial grants to encourage local governments to consolidate fire protection and other services, or to share costs for functions such as road construction and sanitation.

Local officials have shown a particular inclination to seek out partnerships with other local governments. Indeed, over the years, the tensions and uncertainties of dealing with the federal and state governments have encouraged local officials to look to each other for support and to come together to address common problems and operate more economically. As of 2003, for example, there were 3,332 cooperative agreements between local government entities in New York.[48] Local officials value the cooperative approach as a means of retaining local identity while preserving their ability to address problems that transcend their boundaries or are beyond their individual financial or technical capabilities.

CONCLUDING NOTE

Although home rule remains important as a legal concept, the world of local officials is filled with state mandates, preemptions, and prohibitions. In addition, state aid programs—especially those under which state revenues are shared with local governments for unrestricted purposes—have become endangered.

The absence of broad and clear grants of local discretion means that local government authority is unstable—continually defined and redefined through litigation and through an endless flow of narrowly focused local legislation. States would do well to clarify and strengthen home rule, and to increase, when possible, local discretion to deal with matters that are of no great concern to the state or that should be decided in light of the needs and priorities of particular communities. State intervention carries the double risk of transferring control to authorities that have little knowledge of local problems and of contributing to the neglect of what are properly state duties.

To a large extent, the real issues of state-local relations revolve around financial matters, rather than around abstract concerns about local home rule. Local officials want more control over their revenue decisions. They also want more state aid, in part to make up for what they see as unfair state policies. In a broad sense, state and local governments are in the same boat when it comes to gathering revenues: both are subject to the ups and downs in the general economy and to shifts in public attitudes regarding taxing and spending. Still, states can take a number of steps to increase the financial stability of local governments. The Massachusetts Municipal Association has suggested, for example, that as a first priority, state and local officials in that state "must forge a new and enduring state-local fiscal partnership" through two means: "a fixed share of state collections dedicated to the support of local government services" and a reduction in the "over-reliance on the property tax."[49]

States could, for example, greatly ease the pressure on local property taxes by eliminating various mandates and tax exemptions and by expanding local revenue-raising powers. Mandate relief and increased revenue authority could go a long way toward helping localities to become more self-sufficient. State governments can also help local officials meet their financial responsibilities by extending aid, picking up the costs of certain functions, and encouraging greater efficiency and greater cost sharing among local governments. Finally, states can ease local governments' financial burdens by taking steps to move municipal employees into a state-administered health insurance program, as Massachusetts did in 2007.

In building a revenue structure, localities need state cooperation to secure a balanced set of taxes—including sales or income taxes, which are plentiful when the economy is good but lose value when it is bad, and a property tax, which comes in handy during a recession but is not as responsive as other taxes to economic growth. Since the potential revenue bases of local jurisdictions vary widely, state aid is needed to upgrade and, through careful targeting, to equalize service levels.

---

[1]Attorney General Jay Nixon, quoted in David A. Lieb, "Missouri Officials Disagree over Limits on Local Control," *Columbia Daily Tribune,* 27 February 2007, available at columbiatribune.com/2007/Feb/20070227News011.asp.

[2]See, for example, Christiana Brennan and Christopher Hoene, "The State of America's Cities, 2006: The Annual Opinion Survey of Municipal Officials," *Research Brief on American Cities* (March 2006); and Michael A. Pagano and Christopher W. Hoene, "City Fiscal Conditions in 2006," *Research Brief on American Cities* (October 2006).

[3]U.S. Advisory Commission on Intergovernmental Relations (ACIR), *Local Government Autonomy: Needs for State Constitutional Statutory and Judicial Clarification* (Washington, D.C.: U.S. Government Printing Office [GPO], October 1993); see also Dale Krane, Platon N. Rigos, and Melvin B. Hill Jr., *Home Rule in America: A Fifty-State Handbook* (Washington, D.C.: CQ Press, 2001).

[4]*City of Clinton v. Cedar Rapids and Missouri River Railroad,* 24 Iowa 455 at 475 (1868).

[5]John F. Dillon, *Commentaries on the Law of Municipal Corporations* (Boston: Little, Brown, 1911), 145.

[6]Gordon L. Clark, *Judges and the Cities* (Chicago: University of Chicago Press, 1985), 78–79.

[7]See Jesse J. Richardson Jr., Meghan Zimmerman Gough, and Robert Puentes, "Is Home Rule the Answer? Clarifying the Influence of Dillon's Rule on Growth Management" (paper prepared for the Brookings Institution Center on Urban and Metropolitan Policy, January 2003); and David J. Barron, "Reclaiming Home Rule," *Harvard Law Review* 116 (June 2003): 2348–2386.

[8]Frayda S. Bluestein, "Do North Carolina Local Governments Need More Home Rule?" *North Carolina Law Review* 84 (September 2006): 1983.

[9]"Local Democracy in Vermont," *Vermont League of Cities and Towns: Weekly Legislative Report* 8 (23 February 2007): 1, available at vlct.org/d/advocacy/wl07_08.pdf.

[10]Danny Jones, mayor of Charleston, quoted in Justin D. Anderson, "Jones Vows to Fight for W. Va. Cities; Mayor's Goal as President Is to Gain Home Rule for Municipalities," *Charleston Daily Mail,* 21 August 2006, 1D.

[11]What is included in the definition of a mandate varies from state to state. The Connecticut ACIR, for example, counts not only statutes or administrative regulations that directly require actions on the part of local governments, but also those that require actions if a local government chooses to perform a service that it is not actually required to perform. See Connecticut ACIR, *Compendium of Statutory and Regulatory Mandates on Municipalities in Connecticut* (Hartford: Connecticut ACIR, 2003). Some states regard prohibitions and preemptions as mandates; these are considered in a separate section of this article.

[12]State of Minnesota, Office of the Legislative Auditor, *State Mandates on Local Governments* (St. Paul, January 2000); see also Lawrence J. Grossback, "The Problem of State-Imposed Mandates: Lessons from Minnesota's Local Governments," *State and Local Government Review* 34 (Fall 2002): 183–197.

[13]A study of Kansas completed in the mid-1990s, for example, suggests that the state had a compelling interest in the adoption and enforcement of only about 100 of the 941 mandates it was imposing on local governments at the time. About 300 of those mandates were obsolete and widely ignored. One of these—more than a century old—required counties to pay the burial expenses of Civil War veterans and limited this payment to $20 per headstone. See Edward Flentje, "State Mandates as Family Values?" *Current Municipal Problems* 22 (1996): 510–512.

[14]See Amy Rinard, "Library Funds Jump as Cities Feel Crunch," *Milwaukee Journal Sentinel,* 16 May 2005, B1.

[15]See William G. Dressel Jr., "Property Tax Session Only a Start on Needed Reform," *Asbury Park Press* (Neptune, N.J.), 2 September 2007, opinion section.

[16]Task Force on Local Government Services and Fiscal Stability, *Final Report to the Governor* (State and Local Government Team, Michigan State University Extension, May 2006), available at web1.msue.msu.edu/slg.

[17]Ernest J. Strada, "Successful Strategies to Improve the Efficiency and Competitiveness of Local Government Entities in New York State," testimony before the New York State Commission on Local Government Efficiency and Competitiveness, June 13, 2007, Saratoga Springs, N.Y., 3, available at nycom.org/mn_news/documents/Testimonyfor LocalGovCommission.doc.

[18]League of Oregon Cities, "Senate Passes Cancer Presumption," *Legislative Bulletin* (1 June 2007): 1.

[19]Robert M. M. Shaffer, "Comment: Unfunded State Mandates and Local Governments," *University of Cincinnati Law Review* 64 (Spring 1996): 1057–1088.

[20]Susan A. MacManus, "Mad about Mandates: The Issue of Who Should Pay for What Resurfaces in the 1990s," *Publius* 21 (Summer 1991): 59–75; see also Shaffer, "Unfunded State Mandates."

[21]Pat Leary, quoted in Alexa H. Bluth, "Cities May Get Some Clout," *Sacramento Bee,* 25 October 2004, 1A, available at dwb.sacbee.com/content/politics/story/11210833p-12126658c.html.

[22]See Richard H. Horte, "State Expenditures with Mandate Reimbursement," in *Coping with Mandates: What Are the Alternatives?* ed. Michael Fix and Daphne Kenyon (Washington, D.C.: Urban Institute Press, 1990), 23; and Janet M. Kelly, *State Mandates: Fiscal Notes, Reimbursement, and Anti-Mandate Strategies* (Washington, D.C.: National League of Cities, 1992).

[23]Virginia Legislature, Joint Legislative Audit and Review Commission, *Intergovernmental Mandates and Financial Aid to Local Governments,* House Document no. 56 (Richmond: 1992).

[24]Janet Pearson, "City Gets Serious about Finding New Revenue," *Tulsa World,* 9 July 2006, G1.

[25]Peter D. Jackson, Jeffrey Wasserman, and Kristiana Raube, "The Politics of Antismoking Legislation," *Journal of Health Politics, Policy, and Law* 18 (Winter 1993): 787–819.

[26]Christian Parker, "Eminent Domain Issue Passes, Gets OK from Supreme Court," *Arizona Capitol Times,* 10 November 2006, 3–4.

[27]See, generally, National Conference of State Legislatures (NCSL), *State Tax and Expenditure Limits, 2005* (Denver: NCSL, 2005).

[28]ACIR, *Tax and Expenditure Limits on Local Governments* (Washington, D.C.: GPO, March 1995); see also Phillip G. Joyce and Daniel R. Mullins, "The Changing Fiscal Structure of the State and Local Public Sector: The Impact of Tax and Expenditure Limitations," *Public Administration Review* 51 (May–June 1991): 240–253; Daniel E. O'Toole and Brian Stipak, "Coping with State Tax and Expenditure Limitations: The Oregon Experience," *State and Local Government Review* 30 (Winter 1998): 9–16; Alvin D. Sokolow, "The Changing Property Tax and State-Local Relations," *Publius* 28 (Winter 1998): 165–187; and Jocelyn M. Johnston, Michael A. Pagano, and Philip A. Russo Jr., "State Limits and State Aid: An Exploratory Analysis of County Revenue Structure," *State and Local Government Review* 32 (Spring 2000): 86–97.

[29]U.S. Bureau of the Census, *State and Local Government Finances 2004–2005* (Washington, D.C.: GPO, 2007).

[30]Richard L. Cole and John Kincaid, "Public Opinion on U.S. Federal and Intergovernmental Issues in 2006: Continuity and Change," *Publius* 36 (Summer 2006): 443–459.

[31]This argument is made, for example, by Wallace E. Oates in "Local Property Taxation: An Assessment," *Land Lines* (May 1999).

[32]For a detailed analysis, see Stanley Chervin, *Property Tax Reduction and Relief Programs* (Nashville: Tennessee Advisory Commission on Intergovernmental Relations, June 2007).

[33]David Brunori, *Local Tax Policy: A Federalist Perspective* (Washington, D.C.: Urban Institute Press, 2003).

[34]Arthur C. Nelson and Mitch Moody, *Paying for Prosperity: Impact Fees and Job Growth* (Washington, D.C.: Brookings Institution, June 2003).

[35]Paul Brown, councilman, San Luis Obispo, quoted in Sally Connell, "Prop. 1A Greased Way for Tax Votes," *Tribune* (San Luis Obispo, Calif.), 13 August 2006, A1.

[36]While the record varies from state to state, by some measurements state aid to education has generally declined in recent years. When one controls for inflation, for example, state aid per pupil dropped in the nation as a whole between 2002 and 2005: see Suho Bae and Thomas Gais, "State Fiscal Report: State-Specific Data Reveal Growing Differences in Education Resources since the Last Recession," *Rockefeller Institute Policy Brief* (12 July 2007).

[37]See David R. Berman, *Local Government and the States: Autonomy, Politics and Policy* (Armonk, N.Y.: M. E. Sharpe, 2003).

[38]Representative John Gard, quoted in Amy Rinard, "State Lawmakers Cool to More Local Funding," *Milwaukee Journal Sentinel,* 9 April 1999, 1.

[39]See, for example, Andrew Reschovsky, "The Impact of State Government Fiscal Crises on Local Governments and Schools," *State and Local Government Review* 36 (Spring 2004): 86–102.

[40]Office of the New York State Comptroller, *Revenue Sharing in New York State* (Albany, 2005).

[41]See Task Force on Local Government Services and Fiscal Stability, Report to the Governor, May 2006, available at www.cityofypsilanti.com; "Focus on Building Opportunity in State," *Detroit Free Press,* 10 October 2007; Michigan Municipal League, "Communities Count: Revenue Sharing," February 2007, available at mml.org/legislative/papers/rev-shrng-feb07.pdf.

[42]Dressel, "Property Tax Session."

[43]Quoted in Kevin McDermott and Patrick J. Powers, "Illinois Cities Protest Plan to Cut Revenue Sharing," *St. Louis Post-Dispatch,* 11 May 2002, 12.

[44]Christopher Hoene, *Local Budget and Tax Policy in the U.S.: Perceptions of City Officials* (Washington, D.C.: National League of Cities, 2005).

[45]John R. Bartle, "Coping with Cutbacks: City Response to Aid Cuts in New York State," *State and Local Review* 28 (Winter 1996): 38–48.

[46]Congressional Quarterly, *State and Local Source Book 2005* (Washington, D.C.: Congressional Quarterly, 2006), 38.

[47]Quoted in Robert C. Johnson and Jessica L. Sandham, "States Increasingly Flexing Their Policy Muscle," *Education Week* 18, no. 31 (1999): 19–20.

[48]Strada, "Successful Strategies."

[49]Massachusetts Municipal Association (MMA), "Rebuilding a Strong and Lasting State-Local Financial Relationship," in *Our Communities and Our Commonwealth: Partners for Progress and Prosperity* (Boston: MMA, November 2006), 1.

THE *YEAR BOOK* STATE CORRESPONDENTS

Alabama
Perry C. Roquemore Jr.
Executive Director
Alabama League of Cities

Arkansas
Ken Wasson
Assistant Director
Arkansas Municipal League

Georgia
Mike Stewart
Assistant Director for Administration
Association County Commissioners
  of Georgia

Ashley Meggitt
Policy Analyst
Association County Commissioners
  of Georgia

Illinois
Dawn S. Peters
Executive Director
Illinois Municipal League

Maryland
Candace L. Donoho
Director of Government Relations
Maryland Municipal League

Thomas C. Reynolds
Manager, Research and Information
  Management
Maryland Municipal League

Massachusetts
Matthew G. Feher
Senior Legislative Analyst
Massachusetts Municipal Association

Missouri
Patrick Bonnot
Staff Associate, Legislation
Missouri Municipal League

New Hampshire
Cordell Johnson
Government Affairs Attorney
Local Government Center

New York
Barbara VanEpps
Director of Intergovernmental Finance
New York State Conference of Mayors

North Carolina
Andrew L. Romanet Jr.
General Counsel
North Carolina League of Municipalities

Pennsylvania
Richard Schuettler
Deputy Executive Director
Pennsylvania League of Cities and
  Municipalities

Shaun Kroeck
Legislative Analyst
Pennsylvania League of Cities and
  Municipalities

South Carolina
Faidra T. Smith
Administration Manager/Public Information
  Coordinator
Town of Hilton Head Island

Texas
Monty Wynn
Assistant Director of Legislative Services
Texas Municipal League

Vermont
Steven E. Jeffrey
Executive Director
Vermont League of Cities and Towns

David Gunn
Senior Administrative Services Assistant
Vermont League of Cities and Towns

B 2

Actions Affecting Local Government: First Session of the 110th Congress

Lydia Bjornlund
Bjornlund Communications

Selected Findings

The CLEAN Energy Act sets new standards for fuel consumption, use of biofuels, and energy efficiency in buildings and appliances; the act also creates two new grant programs for local governments.

Congress secured a minimum wage increase from $5.15 to $7.25 by 2009—the first increase since 1997.

President Bush followed through on his threat to veto reauthorization of the State Children's Health Insurance Program, decrying its exorbitant price tag. He also threatened to veto both the House and the Senate versions of the farm bill reauthorization unless Congress substantially reduces its cost.

The 2006 elections brought Democratic majorities to the House of Representatives and the Senate, and House Speaker Nancy Pelosi (D-Calif.) and Senate Majority Leader Harry M. Reid (D-Nev.) pledged to jointly push an ambitious agenda to counter 12 years of Republican control. The new leadership planned to assume immediate control with the passage of several top-priority bills in the first 100 hours.

U.S. policy in Iraq remained at the top of the agenda for most of the first session, but Democrats made little headway in forging a new direction and ultimately gave up on their efforts to link funding to a timeline for the withdrawal of troops from Iraq. Congress also failed to pass legislation on immigration, domestic surveillance, and other core issues. It did make headway in other areas, however, including homeland security and a comprehensive energy package.

As has become all too common for the federal government, the 2007 Congress allowed federal funding to lapse, thereby requiring several continuing resolutions to keep the government operating. Just before recessing on December 21, 2007, it passed a whopping $555 billion omnibus spending bill for 11 appropriations that remained for fiscal year (FY) 2008. In essence, the bill split the difference between the Democrats' total proposed spending and the administration's request, cutting overall discretionary spending by $10.6 billion. The bill funds the Iraq war well into 2008.

President Bush expressed criticism of the bill, even as he signed it into law five days later. "I am disappointed in the way the Congress compiled this legislation, including abandoning the goal I set early this year to reduce the number and cost of earmarks by half," the president said in a statement. "Instead, the Congress dropped into the bill nearly 9,800 earmarks that total more than $10 billion. These projects are not funded through a merit-based process and provide a vehicle for wasteful government spending."[1]

The only spending measure to become law prior to this omnibus appropriations was the FY 2008 appropriations for the Department of Defense, which the president signed on November 13, 2007.

HOMELAND SECURITY

During the first half of 2007, Congress followed through on its pledge to continue to implement the recommendations of the 9/11 Commission. As one of the first measures enacted by both chambers at the start of 110th Congress, the Implementing the 9/11 Commission Recommendations Act of 2007 (P.L. 110-53) revises the distribution of key Department of Homeland Security (DHS) grants to state and local governments, and creates a new interoperable communications grant program for those governments. Provisions establish the Urban Area Security Initiative (UASI) to provide grants to assist high-risk metropolitan areas in preventing, preparing for, protecting against, and responding to terrorist acts, based on an assessment of the relative threat, vulnerability, and consequences from terrorist acts faced by eligible metropolitan areas (defined as the 100 most populous metropolitan statistical areas in the United States). The legislation also requires screening of all cargo on passenger planes and container ships, strengthens privacy and civil liberties oversight of executive branch programs, expands existing nuclear nonproliferation programs, and implements policy changes for improving U.S. diplomacy efforts.

The legislation passed both in both chambers in January but stalled as lawmakers struggled to hammer out various differences between the House and Senate versions and to address White House objections. Finally, on August 3, 2007, President Bush signed legislation to implement many of the recommendations put forth by the 9/11 Commission (P.L. 110-53).

On another note, both the House and the Senate passed FY 2008 funding bills for DHS in the summer of 2007. The Senate bill (S. 1644) proposed a total of $40.6 billion for DHS operations and activities, $2.3 billion more than the president's budget and almost $5.8 billion more than FY 2007 levels. It also included $177 million more in discretionary spending than the House version of the legislation (H.R. 2638), while providing roughly $142 million less in funds for programs for state and local first responders, including the State Homeland Security Program, the Law Enforcement Terrorism Prevention Program, Citizen Corps, and the Metropolitan Medical Response System.

Following the passage of the Senate bill on July 26, a conference committee was appointed to resolve differences, and pundits expected the final version to be the first spending bill enacted for FY 2008. But both bills exceeded the White House's proposed budget, and President Bush threatened to veto the legislation unless it was scaled back to be more in line with his budget. In the end, this appropriations bill was folded into the omnibus appropriations bill that was signed into law on December 26, 2007. The funding for state and local programs, a Federal Emergency Management Agency initiative, is set at $3.18 billion, which is $1.48 billion above the administration's request and $406.3 million above the FY 2007 level. The bill also provides $750 million for the Assistance to Firefighters Grant Program, which is $450 million above the administration's request and $88 million above the FY 2007 level, as well as $820 million in discretionary funds for the UASI, to be used primarily for port security grants and rail and transit security grants.

U.S. Troop Readiness, Veterans' Care, Katrina Recovery Act

Debate over the war in Iraq dominated the first six months of 2007, often becoming emotional and contentious. Democrats had hoped to use their majority power to force the Bush administration to set deadlines for the withdrawal of troops from Iraq, and passed an Iraq spending bill (HR 1591) that included a schedule for all troops to be withdrawn by August 2008. President Bush vetoed the bill, warning that this would not give the fledgling democracy in Iraq enough time to stabilize.

Congress responded to the veto by removing provisions for troop withdrawal from a similar bill. Whereas the first bill had narrowly passed the House in a vote that split along party lines, this subsequent legislation had more bipartisan support. Emergency appropriations for FY 2007 passed the House with a 280–142 vote and the Senate with an 80–14 vote, and the U.S. Troop Readiness, Veterans' Care, Katrina Recovery, and Iraq Accountability Appropriations Act, 2007

(P.L. 110-28) was signed into law on May 25, 2007, just days before existing funds would be exhausted.

The majority of funds in the $120-billion emergency appropriations act—almost $100 billion—were intended to continue military operations in Iraq and Afghanistan through September 30. The bill also established 18 benchmarks for progress that the Iraqi government was required to meet in order to continue to receive aid for reconstruction. These benchmarks include reopening talks on the Iraqi constitution, passing a new oil law, reversing the purge of former Baathists from government, and dismantling sectarian Shi'ite militias. Democrats, including Speaker Pelosi and Senator Reid, called the benchmarks "woefully weak." "We are moving backward," said Sen. Russell Feingold (D-Wis.). "Instead of forcing the president to safely redeploy our troops, instead of coming up with a strategy providing assistance to a post-redeployment Iraq, and instead of a renewed focus on the global fight against al-Qaeda, we are faced with a spending bill that kicks the can down the road and buys the administration time."[2]

The final bill also included $17 billion in unrelated domestic spending, including $6.4 billion for hurricane recovery in the Gulf Coast and $3 billion in relief aid to farmers suffering from drought and other natural disasters.

Minimum Wage

Democrats attached the "Fair Minimum Wage Act" as a provision to P.L. 110-28, increasing the hourly minimum wage from $5.15 to $7.25 by 2009. Democrats had fought for a minimum-wage increase for several years, and attaching it to the Iraq war funding ensured that they succeeded in fulfilling their campaign promises. In addition, Title VII sets forth the first federal mandate of tamper-resistant prescription pads for Medicaid reimbursement, which the Bush administration believes could save taxpayers $355 million.

Protect America Act

Just prior to the 2007 summer recess, the Republican minority persuaded enough Democrats to join in support of the Protect America Act to secure its passage. The measure allows federal agencies to eavesdrop, without first getting a warrant, on foreign suspected terrorists who contact sources in the United States by Internet or phone communications. The act removes the prohibition on warrantless spying on Americans abroad; further, it gives the government wide powers to order communication service providers, such as cell phone companies and Internet service providers, to make their networks available to government eavesdroppers, shielding them from liability. The temporary legislation, which would expire in 180 days, was signed by President Bush on August 5, 2007 (P.L 110-55).

A number of Democrats joined with civil liberties organizations to oppose the act and have vowed to take a tougher line when the measure comes up for renewal. Congress deferred further discussion on permanent legislation until January 2008.

THE ENVIRONMENT

As Democrats took over control of Congress, they included energy legislation and environmental issues in their "100-Hour Plan": their top-priority measures to be addressed during the first 100 hours of the 110th Congress.

CLEAN Energy Act of 2007

The CLEAN Energy Act of 2007 (H.R. 6) passed the House without amendment in January 2007. It was then combined with a more comprehensive Senate bill (S. 1419), which passed the Senate on June 21. After further amendments and negotiation between the House and Senate, a revised bill passed both houses and was signed into law on December 19, 2007.

The stated purpose of the Energy Independence and Security Act of 2007 (P.L.110-140) is "to move the United States toward greater energy independence and security, to increase the production of clean renewable fuels, to protect consumers, to increase the efficiency of products, buildings, and vehicles, to promote research on and deploy greenhouse gas capture and storage options, and to improve the energy performance of the Federal Government, and for other purposes." However, the legislation that was passed was quite different from the Democrats' initial vision. As introduced, the bill sought to cut subsidies to and tax deductions for the petroleum industry in order to promote petroleum independence and the use of alternative forms of energy, but the tax reforms were dropped when they faced significant opposition by Senate Republicans.

As enacted, the 822-page legislation will change U.S. energy policy in several areas. First, it requires automakers to boost gas mileage to 35 miles per gallon by 2020—a 40% increase over current levels, marking the first time in 32 years that fuel efficiency requirements have been raised. The bill also mandates the expanded use of ethanol and other biofuels; the 36 billion gallons that are required to be added to the nation's gasoline supply by 2022 amount to five times the current levels. The American Council for an Energy-Efficient Economy projects that by 2030, the bill will reduce energy use by 7% and carbon dioxide emissions by 9% over current levels.

Second, the legislation increases energy-efficiency standards for appliances and buildings, outlaws the sale of most incandescent lightbulbs by 2014, and requires new and renovated federal buildings to be "carbon neutral" by 2030. Finally, it increases federal research on carbon sequestration technologies.

The new legislation creates two new grant programs for local governments. The Energy Efficiency and Conservation Block Grant Program authorizes $2 billion annually over five years to help localities address energy efficiency and emissions concerns according to emission allocation levels. A second grant program creates demonstration grants to help local governments implement cost-effective technologies in local government buildings. The funding will be allotted through a cost-sharing program in which the federal government will assume 40% of expenses for new energy-saving efficiencies and the local government will assume the rest. The local government's cost burden will be waived, however, for severely economically distressed localities.

America's Climate Security Act

The 110th Congress also paid unprecedented attention to reducing the effect of greenhouse emissions on the environment. Early in the year, a select committee was convened in the House to focus on global warming. Dozens of hearings were held on the issue, and numerous bills were introduced and considered. Manik Roy, director of congressional affairs for the Pew Center on Global Climate Change, called this "explosion of activity" evidence that "Congress is finally wrestling with the real issues."[3]

Supporters within Congress agreed that there is growing pressure for such legislation. "With all the irrefutable evidence we now have corroborating that climate change is real, dangerous, and proceeding faster than many scientists predicted, this is the year for Congress to move this critical legislation," explained Sen. Joe Lieberman (I-Conn.). "If we fail to start substantially reducing greenhouse gas emissions in the next couple of years, we risk bequeathing a diminished world to our grandchildren. Insect-borne diseases such as malaria will spike as tropical ecosystems expand; hotter air will exacerbate the pollution that sends children to the hospital with asthma attacks; food insecurity from shifting agricultural zones will spark border wars; and storms and coastal flooding from sea-level rise will cause mortality and dislocation."[4] John Warner (R-Va.) joined with Lieberman to draw from various proposals to craft the America's Climate Security Act (S. 2191), which was introduced on October 18, 2007. In early December, the Environment and Public Works Committee approved this bill—the ninth energy bill to be introduced in 2007—with an 11–8 vote that split largely along party lines.

Like several of the other bills introduced in 2007, the legislation would establish a cap-and-trade system to put a market price on carbon. Proponents believe that a such a system, which has been successfully used to reduce acid rain, would drive greater efficiency and new technologies while reducing greenhouse gas emissions. Specifically, the reduction in emissions would be 10% by 2020 and 70% by 2050.

To build flexibility into the legislation to make it responsive to changes in science and the market, the measure would establish a cap-and-trade program, administered by two new federal boards. The program would set a cap on the amount of emissions permitted from each specific group of polluters; these limits, which must be lower than a company's current emissions level, would get tougher every year after 2012. The allowed emissions would then be divided up into individual permits, which carry a financial value. Utilities and industries would be granted these permits, which they could sell or trade in order to continue operating profitably.[5]

Supporters of the legislation will face an uphill battle to secure its passage. Several Republicans joined forces with utilities, oil companies, and manufacturers to oppose the measure. James M. Inhofe (R-Okla.), the bill's chief critic on the

Senate Environment and Public Works Committee, argued that the measure would impose an unacceptable price on American industry, homeowners, and consumers and could cost 2.3 million jobs over the next decade. On the other side of the debate, environmentalists argued that the legislation does not go far enough.

IMMIGRATION REFORM

Congress continued to struggle with legislation to address illegal immigration. The Clear Law Enforcement for Criminal Alien Removal (CLEAR) Act (H.R. 842) was introduced by Rep. Charles Norwood (R-Ga.) on February 6, 2007, just a week before his death. H.R. 842 would provide for enhanced federal, state, and local assistance in the enforcement of immigration laws, amend the Immigration and Nationality Act of 1965, and authorize appropriations to carry out the State Criminal Alien Assistance Program.

Of particular interest to local governments is the CLEAR Act's provisions designed to force local government law enforcement personnel to play a stronger role in the enforcement of immigration laws and the apprehension of illegal aliens. The act states that "state and local law enforcement personnel, in the course of their routine duties, have the inherent authority to investigate, apprehend, or transfer to federal custody aliens in the United States (including interstate transportation of such aliens to detention centers) in order to assist in the enforcement of U.S. immigration laws." State and local governments oppose the legislation, arguing that taking on expanded responsibilities for enforcing immigration laws would draw local resources from more critical public safety needs. Some local government leaders also claim that such legislation would undermine the relationship between the local government and immigrant communities, resulting in distrust and fear among legal as well as illegal immigrants. Communities with large numbers of immigrants fear that people would not provide information to police or report crimes because they would fear deportation.

The bill has languished in the House Subcommittee on Immigration, Citizenship, Refugees, Border Security, and International Law since March 2007, but proponents have vowed to make sure that it reaches the House floor for consideration.

FARM BILL REAUTHORIZATION

The basic framework of the nation's agricultural policy dates back to the 1930s, when the first farm price and income support programs were established as an emergency response to the economic distress of agricultural communities during the Great Depression. Subsequent farm bills have continued to focus on traditional commodities, primarily field crops, dairy, sugar, and, until recently, tobacco; other livestock and specialty crops, including fruits and vegetables, receive only limited direct support.

With the current farm bill—the Farm Security and Rural Investment Act of 2002—due to expire in 2007, Congress struggled to come to consensus on reauthorization legislation. The Bush administration released its proposal for a new farm bill at the end of January, while the congressional agriculture committees and various stakeholder groups crafted their own proposals.

The House of Representatives passed its new farm bill—the Farm, Nutrition, and Bioenergy Act (H.R. 2419)—on July 27, 2007. The bill intended to provide for the continuation of agricultural programs in place since the 2002 farm bill (lawmakers enact a new farm bill every five years) and addressed many issues, including subsidies for farmers and ways to provide the federal government with authority to prevent states from banning certain foods, such as genetically engineered produce. At the time that this provision was added, Arkansas, California, and Missouri had passed laws creating state committees that review whether genetically engineered rice should be grown in the state. If the 2007 farm bill passed, these would be preempted.

In November, after months of negotiations, the Senate Agriculture, Nutrition and Forestry Committee finally brought to the floor its proposal, the Food and Energy Security Act (S. Amdt. 3500). The rural development title would provide $400 million in budget authority for several initiatives intended to protect and enhance rural communities, including community facilities such as day care centers, rural hospitals, and libraries. It would also provide mandatory funding to help alleviate the current backlog for building or expanding wastewater treatment plants. In addition, it would enhance rural broadband initiatives and create two new programs—one to assist rural communities with planning grants and one to provide technical assistance for entrepreneurs.

Other provisions of the farm bill address areas in which the public well-being is at stake: rural communities, natural resources and the environment, and food assistance and nutrition. In fact, roughly 60% of the farm bill appropriation covers nutrition programs, such as food stamps, designed to ensure that no Americans go hungry. The Food Stamp program provides a monthly benefit amount to eligible low-income families that can be used to purchase food; eligibility is based on household income and assets. Roughly 26.3 million people receive benefits, but experts suspect that many eligible people are not enrolled in the program.

Critics of the current legislation say that funding for food stamps and nutrition programs has not kept up with cost-of-living increases, resulting in a growing number of Americans who cannot afford to feed their families. The 2007 farm bill would address these concerns by adjusting food stamp payments and treating families with children more generously. In the nutrition title, for example, the current asset limit, which is $2,000 or $3,000 for households with elderly or disabled members, would be indexed for inflation at $100 increments; the standard for food stamps would be increased to $140 per family and indexed for inflation; the dependent care deduction would increase to $175 a month; and the child care deduction for children under two years of age

would increase by $200 a month. The minimum monthly benefit would increase from $10 in the current farm bill to $18, indexed for inflation. The new bill would exempt individual retirement accounts and education savings accounts from the asset limit. And the eligibility time limit for single unemployed adults would change from three months to six months out of every three years, but states would have the option to hold it at three months.

In addition to these and other food stamp changes, the nutrition title increases the National School Lunch Act's Food and Vegetable Program so that each state, as well as the District of Columbia, is entitled to a minimum grant of 1% of the total funds.

The 1,600-page bill has been widely criticized, not only for some of the controversial provisions but also for its $288 billion price tag. The Bush administration has threatened to veto the legislation because of its cost. "Farm equity has risen approximately $200 billion per year for the past five years," the White House said in a recent statement. "Despite this strength, the bill continues to increase price supports and send farm subsidies to people who are among the wealthiest 2 percent of American tax filers. . . . Payments should be targeted to those who really need them."[6]

Physicians and nutritionists have added their voice to the opposition of the farm bill, saying that subsidizing crops such as grain and sugar beets contributes to the steadily rising levels of childhood obesity and diabetes. They are particularly critical of the subsidy for corn, a crop that is often converted into high-fructose corn syrup and fatty processed foods that undermine the nation's health. Environmentalists are also actively fighting the bill, seeking changes that would reduce crop subsidies in favor of funding for agriculture conservation programs; they argue that, by focusing on large-scale production of basic crops, subsidies encourage heavy use of pesticides and fertilizers that damage and exhaust the soil. A final group of opponents to the farm bill argue that the legislation is an outdated system of handouts that favor large-scale operators and make it increasingly hard for family farms to compete.

The farm bill passed the House in July, but stalled in the Senate as Democrats and Republicans debated how to handle more than 260 amendments that had been proposed to the bill. The Senate passed a revised bill just prior to adjourning in December, but there remain important differences between the two bills that must be ironed out. Congress is expected to revisit the legislation early after the break, but President Bush has threatened to veto both versions of the bill unless lawmakers can substantially reduce the cost. In the meantime, a temporary extension of the 2002 farm bill remains in place.

REAUTHORIZATION OF SCHIP

The State Children's Health Insurance Program (SCHIP) was created by the Balanced Budget Act of 1997. The law builds on Medicaid and authorizes states to provide health care coverage to "targeted low-income children" who are not uninsured and are not eligible for Medicaid. States receive an enhanced federal match and have three years to spend each year's allotment. In 2005, an estimated 6 million children were covered at one point in time at a cost of $7 billion, $5 billion of which was federal funds.

With SCHIP scheduled to expire on September 30, 2007, the 110th Congress considered reauthorization legislation. Funding levels quickly emerged as the biggest stumbling block. Other issues addressed included who should be covered under SCHIP, how funds should be distributed across states, how best to reach eligible children who are not enrolled in the program, and what the scope of SCHIP benefits should be.

The House and Senate agreed to a reauthorization bill (H.R. 976) that would expand the program by $35 billion over five years, bringing the total to $60 billion. It would provide coverage for nearly 4 million uninsured children, while continuing coverage for 6.6 million already on the rolls. The spending would be offset by a $1.00 increase in the federal tax on cigarettes. On October 3, President Bush used his constitutional prerogative for just the fourth time and vetoed the SCHIP reauthorization bill.

Although the Senate had passed the bill with a veto-proof majority, the House roll-call vote of 273–156 was 13 votes short of the two-thirds majority needed to override the president's veto. Democrats countered by introducing a slightly revised version on October 25. To appease Republicans, the revised Children's Health Insurance Program (CHIP) bill would set the top income limit to 300% of the federal poverty level; strengthen provisions to ensure that illegal immigrants are not eligible for coverage; and phase out coverage for adults (except for pregnant women) in one year. Both the House and the Senate approved the revised bill (with a vote of 273–156 in the House and 64–30 in the Senate), but President Bush vetoed this legislation as well.

LOCAL PREPAREDNESS ACQUISITION ACT

On July 27, 2007, Rep. Ed Towns (D-N.Y.) and Rep. Brian Bilbray (R-Calif.) introduced the Local Preparedness Acquisition Act (H.R. 3179) "to amend title 40, United States Code, to authorize the use of Federal supply schedules for the acquisition of law enforcement, security, and certain other related items by State and local governments." Extending cooperative purchasing to the U.S. General Services Administration's (GSA) Schedule 84, which includes law enforcement, firefighting, and security products and services, the bill would thereby provide state and local governments with the option of purchasing fire alarm systems, bomb detection equipment, perimeter security and video surveillance systems, and countless other homeland security goods and services at GSA-approved reduced prices.

The government has enjoyed significant savings through cooperative purchasing as evidenced by the growth in cooperative purchasing sales from $5 million in FY 2003 to more than $217 million in FY 2006. In 2006, Congress expanded cooperative purchasing for goods and services related to recovery from natural disasters and terrorist attacks.

Local and state governments rallied in support of H.R. 3179, arguing that it would provide volume pricing and decrease duplication of effort by state and local government contract managers to make public sector procurement more cost-effective. Moreover, it would save taxpayers millions of dollars, reduce red tape for local governments and businesses, and ensure the delivery of life safety and homeland security equipment and services to local government entities.

On September 7, H.R. 3179 was referred to the Subcommittee on Government Management, Organization, and Procurement. Proponents believe that the bill stands a good chance of passage, particularly because the cooperative purchasing is voluntary for both local and state governments and does not require any federal appropriations.

METHAMPHETAMINE REMEDIATION RESEARCH ACT

On December 21, 2007, President Bush signed into law the Methamphetamine Remediation Research Act of 2007 (P.L. 110-143). The bill requires the U.S. Environmental Protection Agency (EPA) to develop voluntary health-based cleanup guidelines for counties to use to ensure that former methamphetamine (meth) lab sites are safe and free from contamination. The legislation also enacts two new research programs: Funding is provided for the National Institute of Science and Technology to develop equipment that local enforcement agencies can use to detect active meth labs and to measure the labs' contamination levels. Funding is also provided to the National Academy of Sciences to study the long-term health impacts of meth exposure on first responders and children rescued from meth labs. The act directs EPA to work with state and local agencies during all phases of implementation.

LEGISLATION TO WATCH

While Congress continues to struggle with major public policy issues, a number of other pieces of legislation of importance to state and local governments that have been pushed to the back burner are likely to be revisited. The legislation to watch in the upcoming months include bills addressing crime control and prevention, housing and homelessness, public lands and rural communities, and collective bargaining for public safety employees.

Crime Control and Prevention

In October 2007, Sen. Joe Biden Jr. (D-Del.), chairman of the Senate Subcommittee on Crime and Drugs, released an ambitious, comprehensive, and wide-ranging anti-crime package, partly in reaction to evidence that violent crime is increasing nationwide. "It should be a surprise to no one that crime is up for the second year in a row," Senator Biden said as he introduced his crime bill. "The federal government has taken its focus off of street crime since 9/11, asking law enforcement to do more with less. Fewer police on the street protecting communities, plus fewer FBI agents focused on crime control, plus fewer federal law enforcement dollars equals more crime—it's as simple that. We need to meet this problem head-on, with a comprehensive approach that blends traditional crime-fighting tools with 2007 technology."[7]

The Crime Control and Prevention Act of 2007 (S. 2237) includes more than $6 billion in grants for law enforcement and crime prevention programs; it also incorporates several other crime bills, including the Gang Abatement and Prevention Act, which creates a new federal offense of "street gang crime"; the Cyber Security Act, which adds conspiracy to commit cyber crimes and expands the definition of cyber extortion; the Restitution for Crime Victims Act, which includes pretrial restraint of substitute assets; and the Violence against Children Act, which increases the penalties for violent crimes against minors.

Of particular interest to local governments are provisions that would strengthen the Community-Oriented Policing program, authorize more agents for the FBI and Drug Enforcement Administration (DEA), and outline a new housing assistance program to attract and retain federal law enforcement officers. In addition, Biden's bill would establish a national commission to examine and analyze the intergovernmental dimensions of jailing the nonviolent mentally ill.

The bill has an entire title on prevention, with particular emphasis on protecting children and providing resources to communities to deal with pre-crime intervention, violent crimes, and gangs. These resources include changes to Head Start, a strengthening of programs that target babies and the very young, and specific gang abatement programs. The bill also has provisions for juvenile justice programs, including grants for specialized training programs for juvenile court justices. The National Association of Counties (NACo) and other organizations have long argued that implementing a wide range of community-based health and human services programs would be more beneficial for nonviolent offenders who suffer from mental illnesses and less costly for county taxpayers. Key provisions of the bill include

- Reauthorization of the Office of Community Oriented Policing Services at $1.15 billion per year, with $600 million set aside for hiring over the next six years
- Addition of 1,000 FBI agents to focus on traditional crime
- Addition of 500 DEA agents to fight drug trafficking
- Focus on the reduction of recidivism, including more than $1 billion for substance abuse treatment programs, academic and vocational education programs, housing and job counseling programs, and mentoring for offenders who are approaching release or have already been released
- Creation of a National Commission on Crime Intervention and Prevention Strategies to identify intervention and prevention programs that are most ready for replication around the country,

and to provide resources and guidance to state and local law enforcement on how to implement those strategies in a direct and accessible format
- Funding for prevention and treatment programs targeting abuse of prescription and over-the-counter drugs, including new grant programs tailored to emerging drug threats and regulation of Internet pharmacies
- Renewal of the ban on assault weapons and increased regulation of gun show sales
- Updating of current federal laws relating to child exploitation and violence against children, drug possession and trafficking, firearms, computer crimes, intellectual property, and victims rights.

Biden's crime bill enjoys the support of many leading law enforcement groups, including the International Association of Chiefs of Police and the National Association of Police Organizations. Local government advocates will likely watch carefully as the bill moves through Congress.

Housing and Homelessness

Late in the session, debate on the Community Partnership to End Homelessness Act (S. 1518) was scheduled in the Senate. The bill would reauthorize for five years the McKinney-Vento Homeless Assistance Act (initially passed in 1987) and would consolidate several competitive grant programs for assistance to the homeless (the Supportive Housing Program, the Shelter Plus Care Program, and the Moderate Rehabilitation/Single Room Occupancy Program) into a single program. Proponents believe this will make program administration more efficient.

The bill also seeks to make the programs more flexible, particularly programs in rural communities. Under the new requirements, a rural community could use funds for homelessness prevention and housing stabilization, in addition to transitional housing, permanent housing, and supportive services. The application process for these funds would be streamlined to be more consistent with the capacities of rural homelessness programs. Communities could apply for the Community Homelessness Prevention and Housing Stability Program to serve people who have moved frequently for economic reasons, are doubled up, are about to be evicted, live in severely overcrowded housing, or otherwise live in an unstable situation that puts them at risk of homelessness. In addition, the definition for chronic homelessness would be expanded.

Other provisions of the bill seek to strengthen accountability for results. Funding would be based on a community's demonstrated need, past performance, plans to improve performance, leveraging, and other factors. Communities that demonstrate results—reducing the number of people who become homeless, the length of time people are homeless, and recidivism back into homelessness—would be allowed to use their homeless assistance funding more flexibly and to serve groups that are at risk of becoming homeless.

The legislation would authorize $1.8 billion for FY 2008. The Congressional Budget Office estimates that implementing this legislation would cost about $7.7 billion over the next five years,

assuming the appropriation of the necessary amounts; the Joint Committee on Taxation estimates that enacting S. 1518 would reduce revenues by $7 million over the 2008–2012 period and by $22 million over the next 10 years.

Another bill addressing the nation's housing issues was sent to the floor by the House Financial Services Committee in October. The Mark-to-Market Extension and Enhancement Act of 2007 (H.R. 3965) would extend the U.S. Department of Housing and Urban Development's Mark-to-Market Program to 2012. This program allows owners of Section 8 properties with above-market-rate rents to restructure their mortgages to offer rents at a more competitive rate. The extension proposal would expand eligibility for Mark-to-Market restructuring to further the preservation of affordable housing in a cost-effective manner. Additional provisions address the preservation and rehabilitation needs of homes damaged by Hurricanes Katrina, Rita, and Wilma, or by other natural disasters.

Public Lands and the Secure Rural Schools and Community Self-Determination Act

The Secure Rural Schools and Community Self-Determination Act (P.L. 106-393) was signed into law on October 30, 2000. The act addresses the decline in recent years in revenue received from timber harvest on federal land, revenue that has historically been shared with counties. In 2006, President Bush proposed to phase out the Secure Rural Schools program and to pay for it by selling 300,000 acres of national forest land—a proposal that met with overwhelming bipartisan opposition. Amid the controversy, Congress failed to reauthorize the Secure Rural Schools legislation, electing instead to pass a one-year extension.

Legislation was introduced in both Houses of Congress early in the session (H.R. 17; S. 380). Proponents of the legislation tacked on the re-authorization bill as an amendment to other bills, including the energy bill, but the reauthorization provision was stripped from this bill just prior to its passage. Rural counties, particularly in the Pacific Northwest, have made the multi-year reauthorization of the Secure Rural Schools and Self-Determination Act a priority.

Payments in Lieu of Taxes

The Payments in Lieu of Taxes (PILT) program is intended to help offset the loss of taxes in counties with a national park, wildlife refuge, or other federal land, and to reimburse them (at least partially) for the costs they bear in providing services on these federal lands. The program was conceived in 1978 and is currently funded on a yearly basis—consistently on a level less than authorized. Local government lobbying organizations continue to lobby for PILT funding to be provided at authorized levels.

Collective Bargaining for Public Safety Officers

The Public Safety Employer-Employee Cooperation Act of 2007 (H.R. 980/S. 2123) would establish minimum standards for state collective

bargaining laws for public safety officers. Such standards would include

- The right to join a union and have the union recognized by the employer
- The right to bargain over wages, hours, and working conditions
- A dispute resolution mechanism, such as fact finding or mediation
- Enforcement of contracts through state courts.

State and local government lobbying groups have joined together to oppose the act, which would require all state and local governments to engage in collective bargaining with their public safety employees. The legislation proposes having the Federal Labor Relations Authority (FLRA) establish guidelines and criteria for collective bargaining for state and local public safety employees, and authorizes the FLRA to determine whether the collective bargaining agreements of each state fit within guidelines. Should the FLRA find that a state is not in compliance, it will give the state a set amount of time to comply with FLRA collective bargaining regulations. If the state does not comply, the FLRA will oversee collective bargaining agreements within that state. The Senate version of the bill exempts jurisdictions with populations of less than 5,000 or fewer than 25 public safety employees.

LOOKING FORWARD

The enthusiasm with which Democrats stormed the house in January 2007 had waned by the end of the session. While they achieved some of their goals, including an increase in the minimum wage, a new ethics bill, and energy legislation, the White House and congressional Republicans stood firm in opposition to many of the other changes the new majority party had pledged to bring about. At year's end, Congress had done little to address some of the thorny issues that have plagued the nation for many years, including immigration reform, trade policies, antiterrorism strategies, and—perhaps most critical—the war in Iraq. Congress will likely revisit the issue of warrantless wiretapping of foreign entities, as allowed temporarily by the Protect America Act. It also will be forced to grapple with the proposed fence along the Mexican border, which was authorized by the Secure Fence Act of 2006.

Even when Congress had managed to pass major legislation, the threat of a veto loomed large—a threat that President Bush carried out as promised on several key pieces of legislation, as he remained steadfast in his attempts to chip away at discretionary funding and any bills that he believed to be too expensive. He has vowed to continue to push for reduced spending and to oppose any efforts to increase taxes.

At the same time, determined to protect his legacy, Bush is urging Congress to reauthorize the No Child Left Behind law before he leaves office. The legislation, which was passed six years ago and is considered one of his major legislative accomplishments, requires annual testing of children in grades three through eight and once in high school to ensure proficiency in reading and math. Experts say the law has succeeded in identifying failing schools and pockets of students who are struggling, but critics oppose the law's emphasis on standardized testing to determine a school's success. Bush has threatened to veto any reform that "weakens the accountability system" in the act.[8]

State and local governments have called upon the federal government to strengthen intergovernmental relations and accountability by continuing to work with them on homeland security, poverty, crime, and the many other issues that beset our nation and our communities. They continue to call on the federal government to provide adequate funding for mandates and to fully fund PILT.

Although there were moments of bipartisanship, by year's end, lawmakers once again began to engage in contentious debate, pointing fingers at one another to place blame for the lack of progress. In the coming year, Congress will likely continue to seek common ground on immigration reform, trade policy, antiterrorism legislation, and—foremost—the war in Iraq. There are several areas that it will have to revisit: the farm bill, the Protect America Act, and No Child Left Behind will lapse if Congress does not resolve their reauthorization. But with the 2008 elections putting these and other issues before the eyes of the public, lawmakers are unlikely to take risks, making it unlikely that they will be able to make progress in traditionally divisive areas. Although Democrats and Republicans will need to put aside their differences to see reform, many pundits are already looking ahead to 2009—when a new team of lawmakers has been determined by elections—for a chance to bring about major changes.

---

[1]Ben Feller, "Bush Signs $555 Billion Spending Bill," *Washington Times,* 27 December 2007, available at washingtontimes.com/apps/pbcs.dll/article?AID=/20071227/NATION/403431131/1001.

[2]Shailagh Murray, "Congress Passes Deadline-Free War Funding Bill," *Washington Post,* 25 May 2007, A01, available at washingtonpost.com/wp-dyn/content/article/2007/05/24/AR2007052402570.html.

[3]Tim Bentley, "Congressional Action on Climate Change," *Daily Report,* September 20, 2007, available at dailyreportonline.com.

[4]"Lieberman-Warner Introduce America's Climate Security Act," *eNewsUSA,* 18 October 2007, available at enewsusa.blogspot.com/2007/10/lieberman-warner-introduce-americas.html.

[5]Jason Mathers and Michelle Manion, "Cap-and-Trade Systems," *Catalyst* 4, no. 1 (Spring 2005), available at ucsusa.org/publications/catalyst/page.jsp?itemID=27226959.

[6]Nicole Gaouette, "Farm Bill Affects More Than Just Land and Furrows," *Los Angeles Times,* 2 December 2007, available at latimes.com/news/printedition/asection/la-na-farmqa2dec02,1,3158710.story?coll=la-news-a_section.

[7]Office of Joseph R. Biden Jr., "Press Release: Biden Unveils Most Comprehensive Anti-Crime Legislation in Over a Decade," 25 October 2007, available at biden.senate.gov/newsroom/details.cfm?id=286107

[8]Maria Glod, "Congress Is Urged to Enhance 'No Child' Law," *Washington Post,* 8 January 8, 2008, A03, available at washingtonpost.com/wp-dyn/content/article/2008/01/07/AR2008010701823.html?hpid=sec-education.

Recent Supreme Court Cases Affecting Local Government

Shea Riggsbee Denning, Jodi Harrison,
Robert P. Joyce, Laurie L. Mesibov, and
Richard Whisnant
School of Government
University of North Carolina at Chapel Hill

Selected Findings

Pay that is currently low because of having been set low long ago cannot be the basis of a discrimination claim under Title VII of the Civil Rights Act.

The special characteristics of the school environment and the governmental interest in stopping drug abuse allow school officials to discipline students for speech that can be reasonably regarded as encouraging the use of illegal drugs.

Public entities can direct private firms to dispose of solid waste at particular facilities without violating the commerce clause, provided that the designated facilities are public.

The 2006–2007 term of the U.S. Supreme Court yielded decisions on a number of issues important to local governments. Among the matters addressed by the Court were solid-waste flow-control ordinances, time limits on discrimination claims, the use of racial classifications in school assignments, the execution of mentally ill defendants, the interplay of federal environmental statutes, and the lawfulness of searches and seizures under the Fourth Amendment. Many of the Court's opinions were decided by five-member majorities, with Justice Kennedy providing the swing vote that determined whether the Court's opinion was that shared by the conservative justices (Chief Justice Roberts and Justices Alito, Scalia, and Thomas) or by the liberal bloc (Justices Breyer, Ginsburg, Souter, and Stevens).

CONSTITUTIONALITY OF SOLID-WASTE FLOW-CONTROL ORDINANCES

Public entities can direct private firms to dispose of solid waste at particular facilities without violating the commerce clause, provided that the designated facilities are public.

In *C & A Carbone, Inc., v. Clarkstown* (511 U.S. 383 [1994]), the U.S. Supreme Court struck down a "flow control" ordinance that had required private collection firms to dispose of waste at particular facilities, on the grounds that the collection and disposal of solid waste by private firms was protected by the commerce clause of the Constitution, and that state and local governments were therefore not free to direct disposal to particular facilities. After the *Carbone* decision, most local governments moved away from attempting to control the flow of solid waste collected by private firms; one result was the proliferation of large, private, regional landfills, which now handle much of the municipal solid waste in the country. In *United Haulers Association, Inc., v. Oneida-Herkimer Solid Waste Management Authority* (127 S.Ct.

Where quotations from the Court's rulings include internal citations from other decisions, those citations have been omitted.

1786 [2007]), the Court created an exception to *Carbone* that will likely eviscerate the earlier opinion. Under the new ruling, governments can require waste generated within their jurisdictions to be disposed of at designated facilities, as long as those facilities are publicly owned.

Chief Justice Roberts wrote the opinion for the six-justice majority. Justice Alito dissented, joined by Justices Stevens and Kennedy, on the grounds that the case was controlled by *Carbone*. Justices Scalia and Thomas concurred in the judgment, but each wrote separately to explain his views on the commerce clause. For Justice Scalia, the "dormant" commerce clause, which has been held to limit state regulation of commercial activity, applies only in a limited set of cases, not including this case. For Justice Thomas, there is no such thing as a "dormant" commerce clause.

Local governments in the state of New York had never fully acquiesced to *Carbone*. In New York, as in other states, flow control has been important to waste planning because it allows more certain (and thus less expensive) financing of the large, capital-intensive solid-waste disposal facilities now required under environmental laws. In 1995, United Haulers Association, Inc., a trade association of solid-waste haulers, some of whose members had their own disposal facilities, sued Oneida and Herkimer counties, arguing that in light of *Carbone*, it was unconstitutional for the counties to require waste collected in their jurisdictions to be disposed of at particular facilities. Tipping fees at the facility designated by the Oneida-Herkimer Solid Waste Management Authority were in the range of $89 per ton, and the waste haulers claimed that they could dispose of waste at other facilities for $37 to $55 per ton, including transportation.

The district court viewed *Carbone* as controlling, and ruled in favor of the haulers. The Court of Appeals for the Second Circuit reversed, following a line of its own cases that had upheld a distinction between publicly owned and privately owned facilities for commerce clause purposes. On remand, the district court upheld the local ordinances, finding not only that they did not impose an unreasonable burden on interstate commerce, but that they imposed no cognizable burden at all. The Second Circuit

affirmed. The Supreme Court agreed to hear the case to resolve conflicts among this case; other, similar Second Circuit cases; and cases from the Sixth Circuit, which followed *Carbone*.

The Court affirmed the Second Circuit's judgment and upheld the ordinances. Chief Justice Roberts distinguished *Carbone* from the United Haulers case on the grounds that *Carbone* dealt with a central concern of the commerce clause: preventing state and local governments from showing favoritism toward private businesses within their own jurisdictions. The United Haulers case, however, involved a publicly owned facility and therefore deserved a different commerce clause test. "Disposing of trash has been a traditional government activity for years, and laws that favor the government in such areas—but treat every private business, whether in-state or out-of-state, exactly the same—do not discriminate against interstate commerce for purposes of the Commerce Clause." So, instead of the "rigorous scrutiny" the Court uses for local regulation that appears to favor private in-state firms, the proper analysis is the "balancing test" of *Pike v. Bruce Church, Inc.* (397 U.S. 137, 142 [1970]): is the burden imposed on interstate commerce clearly excessive in relation to the local benefits? Noting that local governments have health, safety, environmental, and financial interests in flow control, including the encouragement of recycling, the Court upheld the Oneida-Herkimer ordinances.

RESTRICTIONS ON STUDENT SPEECH IN A SCHOOL SETTING

The special characteristics of the school environment and the governmental interest in stopping drug abuse allow school officials to discipline students for speech that can be reasonably regarded as encouraging the use of illegal drugs.

In 2002, the Olympic Torch Relay went along the street in front of a high school in Juneau, Alaska. Students were allowed to leave the school grounds to watch, and school officials considered their attendance at the parade a school-sponsored event. Joseph Frederick, a high school senior, and some friends unfurled a banner that said "BONG HiTS 4 JESUS." The principal, Deborah Morse, demanded that the banner be taken down, but Frederick refused. The principal then took the banner down herself and suspended Frederick for ten days. The superintendent and the school board upheld the suspension.

Frederick sued, alleging that the school board and the principal had violated his First Amendment rights. The district court ruled in favor of the board. The Court of Appeals for the Ninth Circuit reversed, ruling that because the school punished Frederick without demonstrating that his speech created a risk of substantial disruption of a school activity, it had violated his rights. The court also ruled that Morse was not entitled to qualified immunity from liability for damages because she knew, or should have known, that her actions were unconstitutional. The U.S. Supreme Court agreed to decide whether Frederick had a First Amendment right to display his banner—and, if so, whether that right was so clearly established that the principal could not claim immunity and therefore could be personally liable for monetary damages.

In *Morse v. Frederick,* 127 S.Ct. 2618 (2007), the Court, in an opinion written by Chief Justice Roberts, rejected Frederick's argument that this was not a school speech case. It then held that a principal may, consistent with the First Amendment, restrict student speech at a school event when the speech is reasonably viewed as promoting illegal drug use. In considering whether the banner promoted illegal drug use, the Court explained that at least two interpretations of the words—that they constitute an imperative encouraging viewers to smoke marijuana or, alternatively, that the words celebrate drug use—demonstrate that the banner promoted such use. The pro-drug interpretation gains further support from the paucity of alternative meanings the banner might bear. In any case, the Court found that the banner was not part of a political debate about the criminalization of drug possession.

Drug abuse by students is a serious problem, and the government has an interest in stopping it. In light of that interest, and in light of the special characteristics of the school environment, which have long allowed significant limitations on students' First Amendment rights, the principal's actions were reasonable, given the circumstances and the necessity for a quick decision on her part. However, the Court refused to expand the school's authority to discipline students for any personal speech that is merely inconsistent with the school's educational goals. Because the Court found that the First Amendment did not protect Frederick's speech, there was no need to address the issue of qualified immunity.

Justice Alito wrote a concurring opinion designed to protect students' political speech. He supported the Court's opinion only to the extent that it allows a public school to restrict speech that a reasonable observer would interpret as advocating illegal drug use. The opinion, in his view, provides "no support for any restriction of speech that can plausibly be interpreted as commenting on any political or social issue."

LIMITS ON SPEECH

The free-speech interests of a school must be balanced against the interests of the athletic association that it has voluntarily joined.

In *Tennessee Secondary School Athletic Association v. Brentwood Academy,* 127 S.Ct. 2489 (2007), the football coach at a private high school sent a letter to a group of eighth-grade boys that encouraged them to come to spring football practice and told them that it "would definitely be to [their] advantage" to do so. The Tennessee Secondary School Athletic Association, to which the school belonged, imposed a penalty on the school, holding that the letter violated a rule that prohibited member schools from using "undue influence" in recruiting students for their athletic programs. Did the penalty infringe on the school's First Amendment free-speech rights? (The question could arise only if the athletic association could be characterized as a governmental entity. A private entity cannot violate the First Amendment; only a government can. The Supreme Court had held in an earlier stage of this case that the athletic association was in fact acting as a governmental entity.)

The Court held that the free-speech interests of the school in communicating with prospective football players must be balanced against the interests that the athletic association was attempting to protect. Those interests were to safeguard students against exploitation, to preserve fair competition among schools, and to ensure that athletics remained secondary to academics. In that balance, the Court held, the interests protected by the athletic association prevail.

In this case, the balance was in favor of the athletic association in large part because the regulated speech was directed at particular individuals (the prospective football players). "[T]here is a difference of constitutional dimension," the Court said, "between rules prohibiting appeals to the public at large and rules prohibiting direct, personalized communication in a coercive setting." The school would be much more protected in communicating to people generally about its athletic programs.

PARENTS' RIGHTS UNDER THE INDIVIDUALS WITH DISABILITIES EDUCATION ACT

Parents of children with disabilities, as well as the children themselves, have rights under the Individuals with Disabilities Education Act, and are entitled to sue, with or without an attorney, to have these rights enforced.

The Individuals with Disabilities Education Act (IDEA) offers federal funds to states in return for the state's promise to educate students in accordance with the requirements of IDEA. IDEA requires states to identify students with disabilities and to provide them with a free appropriate public education (FAPE). Each student's FAPE must be described in an Individualized Education Program (IEP) developed by a team of educators, parents, and other individuals. Parents who are dissatisfied with a proposed or current IEP may file an administrative complaint. If the complaint is not resolved in their favor, parents may sue in state or federal court.

The parents of Jacob Winkelman, a child with autism spectrum disorder, believed that the school district's proposed IEP did not offer Jacob a FAPE. They went unsuccessfully through IDEA's administrative review process; acting *pro se* (without legal representation), they then sued the school district in federal district court. The district court dismissed the case, and the Winkelmans appealed to the Court of Appeals for the Sixth Circuit, which also dismissed their appeal. According to the appeals court, (1) IDEA grants rights only to children, not to parents; and (2) IDEA does not change the long-standing general prohibition against nonlawyer parents representing their minor children in federal court. The parents then appealed to the U.S. Supreme Court.

In *Winkelman v. Parma City School District,* 127 S.Ct. 1994 (2007), the Supreme Court, by a vote of 7–2, held that IDEA grants parents independent, enforceable rights, rejecting the school district's argument that the only purpose for parental involvement is to facilitate vindication of their child's rights. Under IDEA, parental rights include entitlement to a FAPE for their child, as well as rights involving procedural and reimbursement-related matters. In reaching this conclusion, the Court noted that one of IDEA's goals is to ensure that the "rights of children with disabilities and parents of such children are protected." IDEA's interlocking statutory provisions allow extensive parental involvement in the development of the IEP and, at a parent's request, expansive review of decisions related to a child's FAPE. It would be inconsistent with this statutory scheme to bar parents from asserting their own rights in federal court. In addition, a determination that IDEA gives parents independent, enforceable rights imposes no new substantive condition or obligation on states.

The Court did not address the question of whether parents may represent their children in court without legal counsel because in this case the parents were representing themselves, not their child. The law is settled that individuals have the right to pursue their own claims in federal court without legal representation.

The dissent agreed that parents have the right to act *pro se* when they seek reimbursement for private school expenses or redress for violations of their own procedural rights, but that they do not have this right when, as in this case, they seek a judicial determination that their child's FAPE is substantively inadequate.

CONSTITUTIONALITY OF RACIAL CLASSIFICATIONS IN SCHOOL ASSIGNMENTS

The U.S. Supreme Court found that two school districts' voluntary plans to assign students to schools on the basis of race failed to meet the strict scrutiny standard.

The equal protection clause of the Fourteenth Amendment prohibits governmental entities, including school boards, from engaging in discrimination on the basis of race. Race-based decisions are subject to strict scrutiny, the most demanding standard of court review. To meet that standard, the government must demonstrate that it is seeking to achieve a compelling interest, and that the means it has selected to further that interest are narrowly tailored to achieve it.

Many U.S. Supreme Court cases, most notably *Brown v. Board of Education,* 347 U.S. 483 (1954), have dealt with the use of race by public school boards—in particular, with the actions that school boards take to address illegal segregation. The Supreme Court decision in *Parents Involved in Community Schools v. Seattle School District No. 1* and *Meredith v. Jefferson County Board of Education,* 127 S.Ct. 2738 (2007), joins two lower court cases—one from Seattle, Washington, and the other from Jefferson County (Louisville and surrounding areas), Kentucky. Both districts had adopted plans under which it was possible that some decisions about which school a student would attend would be based solely on the student's race (as defined by the district: in Seattle, students are either "white" or "nonwhite," and in Jefferson County they are either "black" or "other"). Neither district was under a court order to desegregate its schools; both had adopted race-based policies voluntarily. Thus, the Court was deciding what a school board *may* do, not what it *must* do.

The Court found that neither district met the burden of showing that the interest it sought to achieve—racial diversity—justified the chosen means: enrollment decisions that discriminated among individual students solely on the basis of race. The Court stated that "[c]lassifying and assigning schoolchildren according to a binary conception of race is an extreme approach," especially when racial diversity is not binary, and requires much more than "an amorphous end" to justify it. In the Court's view, instead of starting from a demonstration of the level of diversity that provides purported educational benefits, the Seattle and Jefferson County school boards had developed plans to achieve a particular type of racial balance. The Court rejected this approach because to accept racial balance—standing alone—as a compelling state interest "would justify imposing racial proportionality throughout American society"—which, the Court said, was contrary to its precedents. In addition, narrow tailoring requires "serious, good faith consideration of workable race-neutral alternatives." Neither district had demonstrated that it had considered methods other than explicit racial classification to achieve its goals.

In a concurring opinion that provided the fifth vote, Justice Kennedy rejected Seattle's and Jefferson County's plans because they were not narrowly tailored, not because he rejected the importance of diversity. He said that school districts do have a compelling interest in promoting diversity that justifies giving some consideration to race, even in the absence of past discrimination. To this end, schools may deal with unequal educational opportunities through race-conscious measures that address the problem in a general way—that is, without treating individual students differently solely on the basis of their race. For example, school boards may draw attendance zones and select sites for new schools in such a way as to further racial diversity.

The dissent said that Supreme Court precedent allowed voluntary integration plans with race-based student assignments, and that not all governmental use of racial classifications should automatically be treated in the same way—that is, subject to the same level of strict scrutiny.

The practical impact of the ruling is unclear because of the split between Justice Kennedy and the four justices who made up the judgment of the Court. However, school boards that want to make decisions about individual students solely on the basis of their race should (1) be specific about the intended benefits, (2) develop plans that reflect the true racial diversity of the district, (3) explain why less intrusive means would not be successful, and (4) assign a duration to the plan. Even school districts that have taken these steps should be prepared to face a legal challenge. Race-conscious strategies designed to achieve specific benefits—such as those that take demographics into account in selecting a site for a new school—are more likely to go unchallenged or to be upheld.

This decision is expected to have little or no impact on higher-education admissions plans designed to further diversity, an issue that was the subject of Supreme Court rulings in 2003.

TIME LIMITS ON DISCRIMINATION CLAIMS

Pay that is currently low because of having been set low long ago cannot be the basis of a discrimination claim under Title VII of the Civil Rights Act.

If an employer decides to pay a female employee less than a male employee for the same work because of the female's sex, that is an intentionally discriminatory act that can serve as the basis of a lawsuit under Title VII of the Civil Rights Act, provided that the employee files the discrimination charge with the Equal Employment Opportunity Commission (EEOC) within 180 or 300 days (depending on the state) of receiving the discriminatory pay. But what if an employee has just realized that her pay is lower than that of male employees because of the cumulative effect of past discriminatory practices, and not because of any current intentional discrimination? Can she pursue a claim under Title VII? According to the U.S. Supreme Court ruling in *Ledbetter v. Goodyear Tire & Rubber Co.,* 127 S.Ct. 2162 (2007), the answer is no.

When Lily Ledbetter retired from Goodyear after 18 years as a supervisor, she realized for the first time that she had been paid substantially less than the other comparable supervisors, all of whom were men. She filed a charge with the EEOC and eventually undertook a lawsuit under Title VII. Ledbetter's claim was that because of her sex, her salary had been set lower many years before, and that the subsequent application of the salary plan caused her salary to remain lower. A jury agreed with her, and Goodyear appealed.

The Supreme Court held that Ledbetter's opportunity to challenge the low salary expired 180 days after the original salary was set. The fact that her pay continued to be low as a result of an initial discriminatory act does not mean that she can challenge the low pay now. "[C]urrent effects alone cannot breathe life into prior, uncharged discrimination," the Court said. "[S]uch effects in themselves have no present legal consequences."

A vigorous dissent by Justice Ginsburg pointed out that because information about pay is often kept confidential, an employee may not initially realize that an employer has intentionally set her pay low. Moreover, intentional discrimination may take the form of small discrepancies that add up to significant differences over time. Nonetheless, a majority of the Court held that in order for a charge of pay discrimination to provide a basis for a Title VII lawsuit, the intentionally discriminatory act must occur within the filing period; the current effects of previous discrimination are an inadequate basis for a suit.

CHALLENGES TO CONGRESSIONAL REDISTRICTING

Citizens who are not specially injured, but who are merely affected in the same way as citizens generally, may not sue to block a state's congressional redistricting plan.

In the United States, there is no such thing as a "federal election." There are elections for federal offices, of course: president and vice president, U.S. senator, and member of the U.S. House of Representatives. Those elections are conducted by the states, however, and not by the federal government. Thus, they are state elections for federal offices.

The Constitution provides that the manner of conducting elections for the U.S. Senate and U.S. House "shall be prescribed in each State by the Legislature thereof," subject to regulation by Congress. That is, each state legislature decides how elections will be conducted in that state. This provision is known as the elections clause.

Every ten years, after the federal census, states redraw the districts for electing members of the U.S. House in order to take into account the new population numbers. The purpose of the redistricting is to preserve the principle of "one person one vote."

After the 2000 census, the Colorado legislature was unable to agree on a redistricting plan, so a state court drew up a plan, and the court's plan was used in the 2002 election. In 2003, the legislature enacted a plan that it intended to use in 2004. Under the state constitution, however, congressional districts cannot be redrawn more than once per census. The Colorado Supreme Court held that because the legislative plan was the second one adopted, it was invalid. Thus, despite the fact that the elections clause requires the manner of election to be "prescribed in each State by the *Legislature* thereof," Colorado had a court-devised plan that foreclosed the use of the legislative plan.

Was the use of the court plan a violation of the elections clause? That question was put to issue in a lawsuit brought by four Colorado citizens. In *Lance v. Coffman*, 127 S.Ct. 1194 (2007), the U.S. Supreme Court did not address the question of whether the use of the court plan violated the elections clause. Instead, it held that the four citizens who brought the lawsuit lacked the standing to challenge the use of the court redistricting plan.

The Court explained its refusal to allow the citizens' suit to go forward by stating that courts should not hear "generalized grievances." Citizens who challenge a government action must be able to show some kind of harm that is special to them, and that differs from the harm that they claim citizens generally are suffering. The requirement of specialized harm "ensures that courts exercise power that is judicial in nature" and is addressed to the resolution of specific conflicts. The Court noted that the claim in this case—that the state was not properly following the elections clause—"is precisely the kind of undifferentiated, generalized grievance about the conduct of the government that we have refused to countenance in the past." The government's conduct affected the citizens who brought the suit in the same way that it affected citizens generally, and so could not be heard.

LIMITS OF FOREIGN SOVEREIGN IMMUNITY

The Foreign Sovereign Immunities Act of 1976 does not bar a local government from seeking a declaration of the validity of tax liens against property owned by a foreign government.

Pursuant to the Foreign Sovereign Immunities Act of 1976 (FSIA), foreign governments are generally immune from suit. Foreign sovereigns do not, however, enjoy absolute immunity from civil action. Such governments remain subject to the jurisdiction of state and federal courts in any case in which "rights in immovable property situated in the United States are in issue" (28 U.S.C. §1605(a)(4)). In *Permanent Mission of India v. City of New York,* 127 S.Ct. 2352 (2007), the U.S. Supreme Court determined that complaints filed by the city in an effort to obtain declarations of the validity of its tax liens against properties owned by India and the People's Republic of Mongolia were actions to determine rights in immovable property—and, as such, were not precluded by the FSIA.

The governments of India and the People's Republic of Mongolia own multistory buildings in New York City that are used in part for diplomatic offices and in part to house diplomatic employees who rank below the level of ambassador. Under New York law, real property that is owned by a foreign government and that is used exclusively for diplomatic offices or to house an ambassador or a minister plenipotentiary to the United Nations is exempt from taxation; any portion of such property used for other purposes is subject to taxation. The city of New York levied property taxes against the Permanent Mission of India and the Ministry for Foreign Affairs of the People's Republic of Mongolia for those portions of their New York City buildings that were used to house lower-level diplomatic employees. Both foreign governments refused to pay the taxes, which constituted liens against their respective properties. As of February 1, 2003, India owed about $16.4 million in unpaid property taxes and interest, and Mongolia about $2.1 million.

Although the city was aware that it could not foreclose on the properties to enforce its tax liens because the FSIA allows no exception for enforcement actions, in April 2003 the city filed complaints in state court seeking declaratory judgments to establish the validity of the liens. The city explained that even though a declaration that the liens were valid would not allow it to foreclose on the property, foreign governments traditionally pay taxes that have been declared by a court to constitute valid liens, that the federal government of the United States can reduce aid to countries that refuse to pay valid court judgments, and that tax liens are enforceable against subsequent purchasers. India and Mongolia removed the cases to federal court, and argued in that forum that the FSIA rendered them immune from the city's actions. The district court ruled against the foreign governments, concluding that they were subject to suit under the "immovable property" exception. India and Mongolia appealed, and a unanimous panel of the Court of Appeals for the Second Circuit affirmed. The foreign governments petitioned for review by the Supreme Court, which affirmed the lower court's ruling.

The Court began by noting that under the FSIA, a foreign state is presumptively immune from suit unless a specific exception applies. The Court then examined the scope of the immovable-property exception. India and Mongolia contended that the exception applied only to actions contesting the right to ownership or possession of property, while the city argued that the exception encompassed additional rights, such as the determination of tax liens. Noting that the text of §1605(a)(4) did not limit the term "rights" to include only the rights to title, ownership, or possession, or exclude cases in which the validity of a lien was in issue, the Court proceeded to determine whether an action seeking a declaration that a tax lien is valid places "rights in immovable property . . . in issue." Because a tax lien runs with the land and is enforceable against subsequent purchasers, it reduces the market value of the property to which it is attached. Such a lien thereby interferes with the right to convey property, which the Court characterized as "one of the quintessential rights of property ownership." Thus, the Court concluded, a suit to establish the validity of a lien implicates "rights in immovable property."

Moreover, the Court explained that its interpretation of the "immovable property" exception was supported by the FSIA's codification of a restrictive view of sovereign immunity, pursuant to which a sovereign is immune from suit for sovereign or public (but not private) acts, and by international law at the time of the enactment of the FSIA. The Court noted that property ownership is not an inherently sovereign function, and that a foreign sovereign's immunity has not traditionally extended to " 'an action to obtain possession of or establish a property interest in immovable property' " (citing Restatement [Second] of Foreign Relations Law of the United States §68[b], at 205 [1965]). Because a suit to have a tax lien declared valid is an action to establish an interest in immovable property, the Court reasoned that the city's suits against the foreign governments would not have been barred at the time of the FSIA's enactment.

Several facets of the case may render its application and use in practice a rarity. First, only a limited number of state and local governments have within their jurisdictions real property owned by foreign governments. Second, the FSIA governs only the immunity question; state and local laws govern whether such property is taxable. If the property is exempt under state or local law, the immunity question never arises. Third, even if a state or local government succeeds in establishing the tax liability of a foreign government, the state or local government may not enforce such liability by foreclosing on the property. Thus, its ability to secure payment from a foreign government for tax liability is, in reality, quite hampered.

AUTHORITY OF THE U.S. ENVIRONMENTAL PROTECTION AGENCY TO REGULATE GREENHOUSE GASES

Massachusetts and other states have special standing to challenge federal government inaction—in particular, the refusal of the U.S. Environmental Protection Agency to regulate greenhouse gases under the Clean Air Act.

In *Massachusetts v. Environmental Protection Agency,* 127 S.Ct. 1438 (2007), a closely divided U.S. Supreme Court crafted a new rule of standing and concluded that the U.S. Environmental Protection Agency (EPA) has the authority to regulate greenhouse gas emissions under §202(a)(1) of the Clean Air Act. Because of concern about global climate change, environmental groups had petitioned EPA to begin rule making for greenhouse gases. EPA denied the petition on three grounds: (1) it lacked the authority to regulate these gases; (2) even if it had the authority, it was unwise to regulate because the role of greenhouse gases in global warming is uncertain; and (3) regulation of greenhouse gases would conflict with the president's policy on climate change. The Commonwealth of Massachusetts and several other state and local governments intervened to seek judicial review in the U.S. Court of Appeals for the District of Columbia. The D.C. Circuit panel upheld EPA's decision in a split decision, with each of the three judges offering a separate opinion. In light of the "unusual importance of the underlying issue," the Supreme Court agreed to hear the case. Justice Stevens delivered the Court's opinion, joined by the liberal bloc (Justices Souter, Ginsburg, and Breyer) and Justice Kennedy. Chief Justice Roberts and Justice Scalia both filed dissenting opinions—and, along with the rest of the conservative bloc (Justices Thomas and Alito), joined each others' opinions.

The majority's explanation of standing is novel and potentially important to state and local governments. First, Stevens distinguished *Lujan v. Defenders of Wildlife,* 504 U.S. 555 (1992), in which the Court had found that in the absence of concrete, particularized injuries to a plaintiff, there is no standing: "[S]tates are not normal litigants for the purposes of federal jurisdiction." Citing and then quoting extensively from Justice Kennedy's concurrence in *Lujan,* the majority went on to note Justice Holmes's opinion in *Georgia v. Tennessee Copper Co.,* 206 U.S. 230, 237 (1907), which recognized the quasi-sovereign interests of states in protecting their citizens from pollution. Given this quasi-sovereign status, as well as Congress's creation of a statutory procedure for challenging inaction on the part of EPA, the Court found that Massachusetts deserved "special solicitude" in its standing analysis. The majority then worked through the well-established requirements for standing (injury, causation, and redressability), but without deep concern for the question that most bothered the dissenters: whether federal courts have a role in reviewing the policy choices of federal agencies. The majority found that the risk of an increase in the sea level was sufficient to qualify as an injury to Massachusetts; it also found that the possibility that EPA regulations on greenhouse gas emissions might slow down global warming was enough to establish a remedy for this injury.

The majority focused mostly on the question of standing; as to whether the Clean Air Act authorizes EPA to regulate, the Court had "little trouble finding that it does." Justice Stevens acknowledged that EPA has discretion to decide whether to issue rules on greenhouse gases, but found that the agency's stated rationale for its failure to start rule making was "arbitrary and capricious."

Chief Justice Roberts's dissent challenged the novelty of and reasoning behind the majority's analysis of standing. Justice Scalia, in a separate dissent, challenged the majority's ruling on the matter of administrative law: that is, whether EPA's rationale for inaction was adequate. All four dissenters believed that the case was not justiciable, and that EPA had given a reasonable basis for refusing to regulate greenhouse gases.

All the justices acknowledged the importance of climate change as a policy matter. But this case illustrates the deep differences on the Court regarding the proper role of courts in general, with the dissenters believing that standing should be used to restrict judicial review of choices made by the political and executive branches.

RESOLVING THE CONFLICT BETWEEN THE CLEAN WATER ACT AND THE FEDERAL ENDANGERED SPECIES ACT

In deciding whether to transfer permitting authority to a state, the U.S. Environmental Protection Agency is not required to consider potential impacts on federally threatened or endangered species.

National Association of Home Builders v. Defenders of Wildlife, 127 S.Ct. 2518 (2007), resolves a conflict between two federal environmental laws: the Clean Water Act (specifically, the act's provisions for transferring permitting authority from the federal government to the states), and the Endangered Species Act (specifically, the act's provisions requiring federal agencies to consult with the U.S. Fish and Wildlife Service before taking actions that might harm threatened or endangered species). Justice Alito wrote the majority opinion and was joined by the conservative bloc (Chief Justice Roberts, and Justices Scalia and Thomas) and Justice Kennedy. Justice Stevens dissented, and was joined by Justices Souter, Ginsburg, and Breyer; Justice Breyer wrote a separate, additional dissent.

The state of Arizona sought the authority to run the National Pollutant Discharge Elimination System (NPDES) permitting program in Arizona; under §402(b) of the Clean Water Act, the U.S. Environmental Protection Agency (EPA) "shall approve" a transfer of permitting authority to a state if the state meets nine criteria. EPA concluded that Arizona met the criteria and approved the transfer. Defenders of Wildlife sought judicial review of this approval, noting that §7(a)(2) of the Endangered Species Act requires federal agencies such as EPA to consult with the U.S. Fish and Wildlife Service to ensure that a proposed agency action is unlikely to jeopardize a threatened or endangered species. Defenders of Wildlife claimed that Arizona would issue more NPDES permits, which would lead to more development and would thereby threaten at least two endangered species: the cactus ferruginous pygmy-owl and the Pima pineapple cactus. The National Association of Home Builders intervened in support of EPA's decision.

In the Ninth Circuit Court and the U.S. Supreme Court, the case turned entirely on the legal relationship between §402(b) of the Clean Water Act and §7(a)(2) of the Endangered Species Act. Was the list of nine criteria for permit transfer authority in the Clean Water Act an exclusive list, or did §7(a)(2) provide, in effect, a tenth criterion that a state must meet? The five-member Supreme Court majority held that the nine criteria listed in the Clean Water Act were the exclusive requirements that a state must meet, and thus upheld EPA's decision to give Arizona the power to issue NPDES permits.

Among other arguments, Defenders of Wildlife had claimed that because EPA regional offices had at one time taken the position that the NPDES delegation process was subject to the consultation requirements in §7(a)(2) of the Endangered Species Act, EPA's action was arbitrary and capricious. Justice Alito rejected this argument, holding that as long as they follow required procedures, agencies can change their minds during a decision-making process without rendering their final decision arbitrary and capricious.

To reconcile the apparently contradictory requirements of the Clean Water Act and the Endangered Species Act, the majority simply held that the Clean Water Act cannot be implicitly amended by a later statute (such as the Endangered Species Act) without a clearer indication of

congressional intent to amend. The Court then turned to rules issued by the Fish and Wildlife Service regarding §7(a)(2), which interpret the consultation requirement to apply only to "discretionary" actions of federal agencies. The Court held that this interpretation was a reasonable one, entitled to deference under *Chevron U.S.A., Inc., v. Natural Resources Defense Council, Inc.,* 467 U.S. 837, 843 (1984). This agency rule thus also supported a decision in favor of EPA.

Justice Stevens's dissent argued forcefully that a prior decision of the Court, *TVA v. Hill,* 437 U.S. 153 (1978), known as the snail darter case, had already established that "the [Endangered Species Act] 'reveals a conscious decision by Congress to give endangered species priority over the "primary missions" of federal agencies,' " and thus §7(a)(2) trumped the "exclusivity" of the nine criteria in §402(b) of the Clean Water Act. The dissent found no support in the statutes, or in prior Court decisions, for a distinction between "discretionary" and "mandatory" federal action that would limit the reach of §7. It offered two other ways to harmonize the provisions at issue in this case. Justice Breyer joined the Stevens dissent, and in his separate dissent noted that even nominally "exclusive" lists of agency criteria for decisions always have room for some agency discretion, and thus that EPA's job in applying the nine criteria in §402 of the Clean Water Act could be interpreted to include some consideration for endangered species.

CRUEL AND UNUSUAL PUNISHMENT

The execution of a prisoner whose mental illness prevents him from comprehending the meaning and purpose of the punishment to which he has been sentenced violates the Eighth Amendment.

More than two decades ago, the U.S. Supreme Court held in *Ford v. Wainwright,* 477 U.S. 399 (1986; plurality opinion), that the Eighth Amendment prohibits states from executing a defendant who is insane. Some years later, Congress enacted the Antiterrorism and Effective Death Penalty Act of 1997 (AEDPA); under the AEDPA, claims presented for the first time in a second or subsequent application for writ of habeas corpus must be dismissed unless they fall within narrowly defined exceptions. Because a prisoner's claim that mental illness renders him incompetent to be executed cannot be evaluated by a court until an execution date is set, and because an execution date cannot be set until after the time for filing an initial petition for writ of habeas corpus has expired, there was some question as to whether the AEDPA barred a claim of incompetency raised at the first opportunity that it could be decided.

The Supreme Court held in *Panetti v. Quarterman,* 127 S.Ct. 2842 (2007), that the AEDPA did not bar such a claim. This procedural ruling cleared the way for the Court to consider two matters: (1) whether the process afforded by state law conformed to the minimum due process requirements established in *Ford,* and (2) the legal issue central to the substance of Panetti's claim—namely, whether the execution of a defendant whose mental illness prevents him from comprehending the meaning and purpose of the punishment to which he has been sentenced violates the Eighth Amendment. In a 5–4 decision, with Justice Kennedy writing for the majority, the Court determined that the execution of such a defendant would be unconstitutional.

Scott Panetti was convicted and sentenced to death in a Texas state court in 1995 for murdering the parents of his estranged wife. After the state trial court set a date for his execution, Panetti filed motions in state court alleging that he was incompetent to be executed, requesting a competency hearing, and seeking funds to hire a mental health expert. The state court judge appointed two mental health experts without input from Panetti or the state, who determined that Panetti " 'knows that he is about to be executed, and that his execution will result in his death [and] has the ability to understand the reason he is to be executed.' " The court-appointed experts stated that Panetti's uncooperative and bizarre behavior was intentional and calculated and that he " 'could answer questions about relevant legal issues . . . if he were willing to do so.' " On the basis of these reports, and without a hearing, the state court ruled that Panetti had failed to show that he was incompetent to be executed.

Panetti then sought habeas relief in the federal courts. Despite finding that the state court proceedings were constitutionally inadequate, the federal district court denied relief, arguing that Panetti had failed to meet the standard of incompetency required by precedent from the Court of Appeals for the Fifth Circuit. The lower court explained that the " 'Fifth Circuit test for competency to be executed requires the petitioner know no more than the fact of his impending execution and the factual predicate for the execution.' " The Court of Appeals affirmed, and the Supreme Court agreed to review the case.

After determining that the AEDPA's prohibition of claims raised for the first time in a second habeas petition did not preclude its consideration of Panetti's incompetency claim, the Court addressed another procedural hurdle. Federal law generally prohibits the granting of an application for writ of habeas corpus if the claim raised was adjudicated on its merits in state court, as Panetti's incompetency claim was. An exception applies if the adjudication of the claim in state court resulted in a decision that was contrary to or involved an unreasonable application of clearly established federal law.

Because the opinion of the Court in *Ford* was stated in a plurality opinion, with Justice Powell concurring with the judgment and with portions of the plurality opinion, but writing a separate concurring opinion defining the procedures required by due process more narrowly than the plurality had, Justice Powell's concurrence (as the more narrow holding) constituted clearly established law on the incompetency standard. Justice Powell's opinion in *Ford* requires a state to provide certain minimum procedures to a prisoner raising a *Ford*-based competency claim. Once the prisoner has made a substantial threshold showing of

insanity, the state must provide the prisoner with an opportunity to be heard and to present evidence and argument from counsel, including expert psychiatric evidence that may differ from the state's psychiatric evidence. Justice Powell's *Ford* opinion further provided "substantial leeway" for states to adopt a process that best balances the various interests.

In *Panetti,* the Court found that the state court's competency determination violated this clearly established law. Panetti made a substantial showing of incompetency, yet the state court afforded him no competency hearing and based its determination on the examinations of psychiatrists that it had appointed, without affording Panetti adequate means to submit expert evidence in response, thus engaging in the very type of adjudication that Justice Powell had warned, in *Ford,* would invite arbitrariness and error. Because the state court failed to adhere to clearly established law, the Supreme Court considered Panetti's competency claim on its merits, without deferring to the state court's determination of competency.

Thus, the Court arrived at the following issue: if a prisoner suffers from a mental illness that prevents him from rationally understanding why he is to be executed, is that prisoner competent? An expert witness had testified on Panetti's behalf in the federal district court proceedings that Panetti's mental problems were indicative of "schizo-affective disorder" and that Panetti believed his execution was " 'part of spiritual warfare . . . between the demons and the forces of the darkness and God and the angels and the forces of light.' " This expert testified that although Panetti claimed to understand that the state wished to execute him for committing murder, he actually believed that the stated reason was a sham and that that the state really wanted to execute him to stop him from preaching.

This evidence was irrelevant under the competency standard established by the Fifth Circuit Court of Appeals, which required only that a prisoner know the following: (1) he committed the crime in question, (2) he is going to be executed, and (3) the reason given by the state for the execution is the commission of the aforementioned crime. However, the Supreme Court rejected the standard of the Fifth Circuit as amended, holding that the Constitution places a substantive restriction on the state's power to take the life of a prisoner who is insane. The Court explained that according to the plurality opinion in *Ford,* the Eighth Amendment prohibits the state from executing anyone whose mental illness prevents him from comprehending the reasons for the penalty or its implications. Justice Powell's concurrence in *Ford* held that the Eighth Amendment forbids the execution only of those who are unaware of the punishment they are about to suffer and why they are to suffer it. In *Panetti,* the Court determined that the Fifth Circuit's approach was inconsistent with *Ford,* regardless of whether the determination of competency depends on whether a prisoner *is able to comprehend* why he is being punished or on whether a prisoner *is unaware* of why he is being punished.

The Court noted that in the controlling part of his Ford opinion (i.e., the portion that received

five votes), Justice Marshall had set forth several principles as underlying the Court's ruling; among those was the fact that the execution of someone who is insane offends humanity, provides no example to others, and serves no retributive purpose. In the view of the *Panetti* Court, these principles were jeopardized by the Fifth Circuit's standard for determining competency; accordingly, the Court rejected the notion that a prisoner may not demonstrate incompetency once a court has found that he can identify the stated reason for his execution. Because a prisoner's awareness of the stated rationale for his impending execution is not the same as a rational understanding of it, the Court held that the district court should have considered Panetti's argument that he suffers from a severe, documented mental illness that is the source of gross delusions that prevent him from comprehending the meaning and purpose of the punishment to which he has been sentenced. Differentiating Panetti's case from circumstances in which a lack of understanding may result from a misanthropic personality or an amoral character, the Court explained that "[g]ross delusions stemming from a severe mental disorder may put an awareness of a link between a crime and its punishment in a context so far removed from reality that the punishment can serve no proper purpose."

While rejecting the standard employed by the Fifth Circuit to evaluate competency appeals, the Court declined "to set down a rule governing all competency determinations." Instead, the Court remanded the matter to the district court for further development of the record and factual findings, and with directions to conduct a proper Eighth Amendment analysis.

Justice Thomas wrote a stinging dissent, joined by Chief Justice Roberts and by Justices Scalia and Alito, that accused the majority of imposing rational understanding as an additional constitutional requirement not required by *Ford* and that characterized the majority opinion as a "half-baked holding that leaves the details of the insanity standard for the district court to work out."

EXECUTION OF SEARCH WARRANTS

Ordering unclothed occupants from bed and holding them at gunpoint for less than five minutes without allowing them to dress is not an unreasonable search under the Fourth Amendment.

On December 11, 2001, Los Angeles County sheriff's deputy Dennis Watters obtained a search warrant for two houses in Lancaster, California, where he believed he could find suspects in a fraud and identity-theft ring. All of the suspects were African American, and one had registered a 9-millimeter Glock handgun. Deputy Watters had obtained information indicating that the suspects lived in the first house described in the warrant. Watters did not know that Max Rettele had purchased the house in September—and that Rettele, his girlfriend, Judy Sadler, and her 17-year-old son, Chase

Hall, all of whom are white—had moved into the house thereafter.

At 7:15 a.m. on December 19, 2001, Watters and six other deputies knocked on Rettele's door. Hall opened the door, and the deputies ordered him to lie face down on the ground. With their guns drawn, the deputies then went into Rettele and Sadler's bedroom and ordered the couple to get out of bed. The couple protested that they had no clothes on. The deputies held them at gunpoint, and for one to two minutes did not allow them to cover their nude bodies. By the time the deputies allowed the couple to dress and leave the bedroom, the officers had realized their mistake.

Rettele and Sadler filed suit in district court against Los Angeles County, the Los Angeles County Sheriff's Department, Deputy Watters, and other members of the sheriff's department, alleging that their Fourth Amendment rights had been violated by the unreasonable search and detention. The district court held that the warrant was properly obtained and that the search was reasonable—and that, in the alternative, any Fourth Amendment rights the deputies had violated were not clearly established and that the deputies were therefore entitled to qualified immunity. The Court of Appeals for the Ninth Circuit reversed, holding that a reasonable jury could conclude that the search and detention were " ' "unnecessarily painful, degrading, or prolonged," and involved "an undue invasion of privacy," ' " and that a reasonable deputy should have known that the search and detention were unlawful.

The Supreme Court agreed to hear the case and reversed in a *per curiam* opinion. At the outset, the Court quickly rejected the court of appeals' view that because Rettele, Sadler, and Hall were white, and the suspects were African Americans, the deputies should immediately have realized that they were not the suspects identified in the warrant and thus posed no threat. The Court stated that when the deputies ordered Rettele and Sadler from bed, they did not know whether the suspects might also have been in the house. Citing *Michigan v. Summers,* 452 U.S. 692 (1981), in which the Court held that officers executing a search warrant for contraband may detain occupants while a conducting a search and may take reasonable action to ensure their own safety during a search, the Court concluded that because blankets and bedding can conceal a weapon, and one of the suspects was known to carry a firearm, the orders to Rettele and Sadler were permissible to protect the safety of the deputies. Moreover, the Court noted that Rettele and Sadler were detained no longer than was necessary to ensure the officers' safety. Because warrants are issued on the basis of probable cause rather than absolute certainty, the Court recognized that the innocent have been and will continue to be searched on the basis of valid warrants. When police officers execute a valid warrant and act reasonably to protect themselves, the Fourth Amendment is not violated—even where, as in this case, residents may suffer frustration and embarrassment.

THE RIGHT TO CHALLENGE A SEIZURE AT A TRAFFIC STOP

A passenger in a car that is stopped by a police officer is, like the driver, seized within the meaning of the Fourth Amendment and may therefore challenge the constitutionality of the stop.

Early on the morning of November 27, 2001, sheriff's deputies in Sutter County, California, pulled over a car driven by Karen Simeroth to verify the legitimacy of a temporary operating permit displayed on her vehicle. The deputy who approached the car saw Bruce Brendlin, whom he recognized as "one of the Brendlin brothers," sitting in the passenger seat. The deputy returned to his car, called for backup, and verified that Brendlin was a parole violator subject to an outstanding warrant for his arrest. After additional officers arrived, the deputy returned to the passenger side of Simeroth's car, pointed his gun at Brendlin, told him to get out of the car, and placed him under arrest. In the course of the arrest, deputies searched Brendlin and found a syringe cap. The officers then patted down Simeroth and discovered syringes and a plastic bag containing a green leafy substance. She was also placed under arrest. Officers then searched the car and found materials used to produce methamphetamine. Brendlin was charged with possession and manufacture of methamphetamine. He moved to suppress the evidence obtained in the searches of his person and the car, arguing that it resulted from the unlawful seizure of his person in the traffic stop, which the officers made without probable cause or reasonable suspicion. The U.S. Supreme Court held unanimously that from the moment the police stopped Simeroth's car, Brendlin was "seized" within the meaning of the Fourth Amendment.

When a law officer, by means of physical force or show of authority, terminates or restrains a person's freedom of movement, the person thus seized is entitled to challenge the government's action under the Fourth Amendment, which prohibits "unreasonable searches and seizures." However, without actual submission on the part of the person seized, no seizure occurs. When it is unclear whether the police intended to restrain an individual and whether that person submitted to their authority, the test is whether a reasonable person would have believed himself free to end the encounter with the police. In *Brendlin v. California,* 127 S.Ct. 2400 (2007), the Supreme Court concluded that in Brendlin's circumstances "any reasonable passenger would have understood the police officers to be exercising control to the point that no one in the car was free to depart without police permission."

Brendlin had initially challenged the seizure in the California Supreme Court, which had ruled that he was not seized until he was formally arrested; the ruling was based on three arguments, each of which was specifically rejected by the U.S. Supreme Court. First, the California court had found that Brendlin was not seized because the deputy who stopped the car intended only to investigate Simeroth and did not direct a show of authority toward Brendlin. The Supreme Court reasoned that this analysis improperly shifted the focus from the intent of the police, as objectively manifested by their behavior, to the police's subjective motive in stopping the car. The Court explained, citing *Michigan v. Chesternut* (486 U.S. 567, 575 n. 7, 108 S.Ct. 1975, 1981 n. 7 [1988]) that the "intent that counts under the Fourth Amendment is the 'intent [that] has been conveyed to the person confronted' " and that "the criterion of willful restriction on freedom of movement is no invitation to look to subjective intent when determining who is seized."

Second, the Supreme Court criticized the California court's assumption that a passenger in a car cannot submit to a show of authority because only the driver controls the moving vehicle. Brendlin submitted to the officers' show of authority by staying inside the car after it was stopped.

Third, the Supreme Court dismissed the state court's concerns that a ruling in favor of Brendlin " 'would encompass even those motorists following a vehicle subject to a traffic stop who, by virtue of the original detention, are forced to slow down and perhaps even come to a halt in order to accommodate that vehicle's submission to police authority.' " An occupant of a car that is stuck in traffic because another car has been pulled over does not believe that a show of authority is being directed at him or his car. Furthermore, traffic jams resulting from traffic stops do not call for a precautionary rule to avoid the " 'arbitrary and oppressive interference by [law] enforcement officials with the privacy and personal security of individuals' that the Fourth Amendment was intended to limit." In contrast, the Supreme Court noted that a ruling that a passenger in a private car is *not* seized in a traffic stop would create troublesome consequences. Under such a rule, law enforcement officers would have an incentive to stop cars with passengers regardless of whether they had probable cause or reasonable suspicion of illegal activity, and, in the process, would indisputably violate the driver's Fourth Amendment rights.

Given that in all federal courts of appeal and in every state court other than those in California, Colorado, and Washington, the interpretation of the Fourth Amendment is consistent with the Supreme Court's interpretation in *Brendlin,* the Court's decision is unlikely to mandate a change in practice or procedure in most locales.

EXHAUSTION REQUIREMENTS OF THE PRISON LITIGATION REFORM ACT

Although the Prison Litigation Reform Act requires prisoners to exhaust prison grievance procedures before filing suit, it does not (1) require that the complaint include proof that administrative remedies have been exhausted; (2) permit suit only against defendants named in the complaint; or (3) require dismissal of the entire action in the event that the exhaustion requirement is not met for part of the action.

The Prison Litigation Reform Act (PLRA) provides that "no action shall be brought with respect to prison conditions . . . by a prisoner confined in any jail, prison, or other correctional facility until such administrative remedies as are available are exhausted" (42 U.S.C. §1997e[a]). Three Michigan prison inmates (Lorenzo Jones, Timothy Williams, and John Walton) brought suits against the Michigan Department of Corrections. All three suits were dismissed for failure to properly exhaust administrative remedies under the PLRA.

Jones's suit was dismissed because he did not attach to his complaint proof that he had exhausted administrative remedies. Williams's suit was dismissed because during the grievance process, he did not identify by name all of the defendants he later named in his lawsuit. Walton's case was dismissed for the same reason. In all three cases, the lower courts also listed as an alternative basis for dismissal a "total exhaustion" requirement—under which, if any part of the plaintiff's complaint does not comply with the exhaustion requirements of the PLRA, the entire complaint would be dismissed. In each case, the Sixth Circuit Court affirmed the lower court's dismissal. The U.S. Supreme Court granted review to consider the propriety of the dismissal of the prisoners' cases under the exhaustion requirements of the PLRA. In *Jones v. Bock,* 127 S.Ct. 910 (2007), the Court held that the specific procedural requirements approved by the Sixth Circuit were not required by the PLRA.

First, the Sixth Circuit required prisoner-litigants to attach to their complaints proof that they had exhausted administrative remedies before bringing suit. The Court rejected this requirement, pointing out that it was not mandated by the PLRA. It also held that the requirement conflicted with the general rule of pleading, which requires only "a short and plain statement of the claim" (F.R.Civ.P. 8[a]). The Court conceded that adding such a requirement might make it easier for courts to deal with prisoner litigation, but said that the courts should avoid attempting to improve the statute by adding requirements that do not appear in the statute.

Second, the Sixth Circuit required the prisoner to identify in the first step of the grievance process any and all individuals who would later be named as defendants in his or her lawsuit. Again, the

Court rejected this requirement, finding that it had no basis in the PLRA. Further, the Court noted that when Jones, Williams, and Walton had filed their grievances, the procedures in place at the Michigan Department of Corrections did not require that every potential defendant be named. Thus, the Court held that the plaintiffs could not be found to have failed to exhaust this procedural requirement because the procedure did not exist at the time they filed their grievances.

Third, the Sixth Circuit applied a "total exhaustion" rule. In this instance, the Court found that the language of the PLRA did offer some support for the Sixth Circuit's view, because it stated that "no action shall be brought" until administrative procedures were exhausted. Nevertheless, the Court found that the phrase "no action shall be brought" was mere "boilerplate language" that in other circumstances, such as statutes of limitation, did not mandate the dismissal of an entire case. The Court held that "as a general matter, if a complaint contains both good and bad claims, the court proceeds with the good and leaves the bad" (127 S.Ct. at 924). It therefore held that if a suit presented both exhausted and unexhausted claims, a court should dismiss the claims that were not properly exhausted but proceed with the claims that were properly exhausted.

In closing, the Court noted that it understood and sympathized with the procedural difficulties presented to lower courts by the flood of prisoner suits. It nevertheless refused to allow courts to address this problem by adding onerous pleading rules that were not required by the PLRA.

PLEADING REQUIREMENTS

Federal Rule of Civil Procedure 8(2)(a) requires only a short and plain statement of the claim.

William Erickson, an inmate at the Colorado state prison, was enrolled in a hepatitis treatment program that required him to self-inject medication. Proper use and disposal of the syringes was a requirement for continued participation. Asserting that he had used a syringe to inject drugs, the prison suspended Erickson from the program.

Erickson sued under 42 U.S.C. §1983, alleging that his removal from the program amounted to cruel and unusual punishment under the Eighth Amendment. Erickson denied the prison's allegation of drug abuse and claimed that his suspension from the program caused him to suffer injury because of his untreated illness.

Both the district court and the Court of Appeals for the Eighth Circuit agreed that the case should be dismissed because it offered only "conclusory allegations" that the plaintiff had suffered or was suffering an injury. The Supreme Court granted review and reversed. In *Erickson v. Pardus,* 127 S.Ct. 2197 (2007), the Court pointed out that Federal Rule of Civil Procedure 8(2)(a) requires only "a short and plain statement of the claim showing that the pleader is entitled to relief." The Court held that Erickson's case had given the lower court adequate notice of the claim and the grounds it rested upon. While declining to discuss the merits of Erickson's claims, the Court nevertheless held that those claims should not have been dismissed on summary judgment.

Justice Scalia stated that he would not have granted review in the case. Justice Thomas dissented on the ground that he would limit Eighth Amendment claims to injuries relating to the criminal sentence only.

SUMMARY

The Supreme Court's Fourth Amendment jurisprudence during the 2006–2007 term was predictable, but most of its other rulings were not. Cases addressing issues from economics to human rights continue to be decided by the slimmest of majorities, with vehement criticism from dissenting justices. Decisions this term defined parameters and set forth standards that will assist local governments across the country in their attempts to control the flow of solid waste, assign students to schools, establish tax liens, and evaluate claims of employment discrimination, among other activities. How the Court will rule on the issues to come before it in the future remains uncertain, given the deep division between the views of the conservative and liberal justices.

C Staffing and Compensation

C 1

Salaries of Municipal Officials, 2007

Rollie O. Waters and Joyce C. Powell
The Waters Consulting Group, Inc.

Selected Findings

The highest percentage of increase in average salary using the same cities from 2006 to 2007 is for the position of chief administrative officer (CAO)/city manager (5.3%); the second highest is for the position of chief financial officer (5.2%).

The highest average salary shown is for the combined position of CAO/city manager ($93,464).

Average salaries for all city positions but three—chief elected official, treasurer, and health officer—are highest in the West region. The position of primary assistant manager/CAO shows the greatest shift in salaries by region, with the lowest average salary in the Northeast ($69,149) and the highest in the West ($117,250), a difference of $48,101.

This article and the accompanying tables present the results of ICMA's 2007 survey of salaries of local government officials in cities. In 2007, the survey instrument collected salary information on 23 positions that are common to municipal and county governments, as well as on 52 management and professional positions. Data reported in the *Municipal Year Book* covers the 23 positions of local government officials.

Local government salaries are affected by several variables other than individual expertise, including population, geographic region, and service delivery. Cities that have ports, military bases, or universities and that are full service will typically have higher salaries than those that do not have these characteristics.

SURVEY METHODOLOGY

This is the fourth year that ICMA has offered SurveyNavigator™ for ICMA, a Web-based interactive version of the annual survey. This system is managed and operated by The Waters Consulting Group, Inc. Prior to SurveyNavigator™, data were collected in the summer and fall months and made available in a summary format through ICMA's *Municipal Year Book*, which is published in the spring of the following year. A printed version and a disk of the survey data were also made available for a fee through the ICMA bookstore. The online version, SurveyNavigator™ for ICMA, is updated weekly as changes are made by each participating local government.

In July 2007, survey notices were mailed to all municipal and county governments with populations of 2,500 and above and to those under 2,500 that are recognized by ICMA as having a council-manager form of government or as providing for an appointed general management (chief administrative officer, or CAO) position. The survey notice gave the Web address for SurveyNavigator™ (surveynavigator.com/icma) and provided a unique identification number and password for the local government choosing to participate. A second, abbreviated paper survey

was mailed and/or e-mailed to those local governments that had not responded to the first mailing or had not provided the information online. The overall city response rate to the 2007 survey was 22% as of December 20, 2007 (Table 1/1). However, the structure of the new online survey tool allows for weekly updates and additional

Table 1/1   SURVEY RESPONSE

Classification	No. of cities[1] surveyed (A)	Respondents No.	Respondents % of (A)
Total	8,675	1,897	22
Population group			
Over 1,000,000	9	4	44
500,000–1,000,000 . .	23	6	26
250,000–499,999 . . .	36	6	17
100,000–249,999 . . .	179	39	22
50,000–99,999	407	88	22
25,000–49,999	775	160	21
10,000–24,999	1,821	375	21
5,000–9,999	1,883	345	18
2,500–4,999	2,003	431	22
Under 2,500	1,539	443	29
Geographic region			
Northeast	2,134	195	9
North-Central	2,669	704	26
South	2,660	855	32
West	1,212	143	12
Geographic division			
New England	838	78	9
Mid-Atlantic	1,296	117	9
East North-Central . .	1,550	287	19
West North-Central . .	1,119	417	37
South Atlantic	1,170	372	32
East South-Central . .	492	58	12
West South-Central . .	998	425	43
Mountain	455	66	15
Pacific Coast	757	77	10
Form of government			
Mayor-council	3,945	754	19
Council-manager	4,126	1,067	26
Commission	152	28	18
Town meeting	387	38	10
Representative town meeting	65	10	15
Metro status			
Central	540	130	24
Independent	3,346	936	28
Suburban	4,789	831	17

[1]For a definition of terms, please see "Inside the *Year Book*," x.

data to be entered at any time by participating local governments.

AVERAGE SALARIES

Using the exact same cities and titles to ensure comparability between 2006 and 2007, Table 1/2 shows the percentage of change in average salary for all 23 positions over the preceding year. This year the highest increase in average salary is 5.3% for the position of chief administrative officer (CAO)/city manager, followed by 5.2% for the position of chief financial officer.

When all data from 2007 are used irrespective of the cities that reported in 2006, the highest average salary shown is for the combined position of CAO/city manager ($93,464) (Table 1/3), which is consistent with prior years and not surprising given the level of responsibility that the position holds. The next highest average salary is for the primary assistant manager/CAO ($85,181), followed closely by the average salary for the engineer ($83,153).

Population size has a major influence on local government salaries, in part because larger populations usually require more services to meet citizen demands and thus require more employees to provide those services. The complexity of managing cities with larger populations requires a salary commensurate with the level of expertise and experience demanded of the job. It is useful to examine average salaries by population group because such a breakout provides a picture of change in the average salary for smaller cities (see Table 1/3).

Geographic region also affects salaries. Historically, the highest salaries are typically found in the West, and this data collection cycle shows no exception. For twenty of the twenty-three positions included in the survey, the highest average salary among all cities is found in the West region (Table 1/4). The positions for which the highest average salary was not reported in the West region are chief elected official (Northeast region), treasurer (South region), and health officer (insufficient data reported from the West region for analysis).

Table 1/2   CHANGE IN AVERAGE SALARY, 2006 TO 2007

Position	2006 average salary ($)	2007 average salary ($)	Percentage of change (%)
Chief administrative officer/city manager	99,583	104,857	5.3
Chief elected official	41,596	42,327	1.8
Chief financial officer	76,907	80,892	5.2
Chief law enforcement official	78,108	81,703	4.6
Chief librarian	63,201	64,869	2.6
Clerk	53,273	55,315	3.8
Economic development director	79,141	81,680	3.2
Engineer	82,043	84,578	3.1
Fire chief	78,915	82,530	4.6
Health officer	67,559	69,113	2.3
Human resources director	72,365	74,959	3.6
Human services director	73,144	75,178	2.8
Information services director	76,220	78,635	3.2
Parks and recreation director	70,526	73,127	3.7
Parks superintendent	55,432	57,169	3.1
Planning director	73,177	75,683	3.4
Primary assistant manager/CAO	85,652	88,396	3.2
Public safety director	81,006	83,502	3.1
Public works director	78,075	80,859	3.6
Purchasing director	63,545	65,432	3.0
Recreation director	57,676	59,391	3.0
Risk manager	63,912	65,991	3.3
Treasurer	60,938	62,790	3.0

Note: This table compares the average pay change for position using the exact same cities and titles used in *The Municipal Year Book 2007*. Where cities that reported last year did not report this year, they were excluded from the calculations for both years shown above.

A close look at the average salaries on a regional basis for the positions of public works director and economic development director provides a clear example of this regional influence. For the position of public works director (Table 1/5), the highest average salary for 2007 ($90,996) is found in the West region. This is $23,082 higher than the lowest average salary for the same position ($67,914), found in the South. For the position of economic development director (Table 1/6), the lowest average salary is in the North-Central region ($62,880) and the highest is in the West ($106,558), a difference of $43,678.

Figure 1/1 illustrates the variation among geographic regions for several positions. Of interest is the average salary for the chief law enforcement official in the Northeast ($83,180), which is the highest average salary for this position next to that shown for the West ($92,610).

City governments often want to know the competitiveness of their salary ranges in addition to the competitiveness of their salaries. Table 1/7 shows the average salary range minimums, maximums, and spreads for all 23 full-time positions

Table 1/3   AVERAGE SALARY ($) FOR POSITION, BY POPULATION GROUP, 2007

Job title	Total	Greater than 1,000,000	500,000–1,000,000	250,000–499,999	100,000–249,999	50,000–99,999	25,000–49,999	10,000–24,999	5,000–9,999	2,500–4,999	Under 2,500
Chief admin. officer/city manager	93,464	220,784	206,874	188,407	165,513	143,370	130,088	105,493	86,543	71,333	61,341
Chief elected official	39,812	143,690	35,153	43,112	55,064	40,186	43,489	41,064	33,341	23,448	34,697
Chief financial officer	76,848	144,166	150,412	126,069	115,688	104,772	96,670	78,560	64,900	54,882	46,909
Chief law enforcement official	72,684	162,114	154,064	132,031	127,152	111,721	102,240	84,391	67,833	55,610	48,360
Chief librarian	56,332	125,754	127,275	108,935	102,808	88,404	72,580	60,470	47,611	34,502	28,394
Clerk	49,903	104,361	101,077	94,992	81,786	68,228	65,780	54,269	49,366	41,793	36,388
Economic development director	74,451	120,360	123,777	110,740	116,559	95,237	85,387	72,570	58,413	48,567	35,930
Engineer	83,153	95,968	135,109	93,309	98,250	94,937	88,844	74,439	73,170	53,813	79,273
Fire chief	77,188	140,210	143,150	123,392	119,087	106,425	94,275	76,954	56,958	51,025	47,764
Health officer	67,687	136,118	155,359	115,796	89,913	78,456	59,733	54,747	46,485	22,601	—
Human resources director	74,151	122,016	132,736	118,199	103,317	94,765	82,401	62,503	51,703	43,406	28,809
Human services director	69,550	129,043	106,668	135,774	99,019	82,158	70,463	63,700	44,668	42,637	35,292
Information services director	79,538	120,543	139,392	125,340	104,480	92,043	81,210	66,639	59,536	45,449	44,781
Parks and recreation director	69,308	148,262	116,558	124,400	107,306	91,641	87,199	68,443	53,018	43,197	35,364
Parks superintendent	52,506	83,916	63,194	83,165	69,884	66,538	59,182	49,635	42,118	33,491	31,247
Planning director	76,009	130,619	127,160	122,036	101,177	93,486	85,726	71,471	64,136	53,402	53,410
Primary assistant manager/CAO	85,181	144,908	139,290	128,378	117,175	112,648	93,558	79,801	63,199	57,077	57,367
Public safety director	74,750	156,245	—	117,075	85,681	88,873	90,418	73,617	66,816	58,214	59,901
Public works director	71,165	150,551	157,840	133,715	118,235	107,517	98,154	79,425	65,279	54,476	47,043
Purchasing director	62,811	101,155	101,314	89,847	72,536	66,302	65,135	49,453	43,731	34,968	33,039
Recreation director	55,990	103,148	78,660	88,702	76,244	72,500	64,318	53,683	39,794	32,981	34,417
Risk manager	67,496	79,057	95,288	85,051	76,485	67,571	64,994	57,186	60,325	—	—
Treasurer	48,998	105,941	97,630	92,496	83,981	71,183	63,137	53,580	47,710	38,986	38,982

Table 1/4   AVERAGE SALARY ($) FOR POSITION, BY REGION, 2007

Job title	Total	Northeast	North-Central	South	West
			Region		
Chief admin. officer/city manager	93,464	81,698	86,619	95,478	124,822
Chief elected official	39,812	55,212	36,821	38,023	40,559
Chief financial officer	76,848	68,921	75,290	75,654	94,547
Chief law enforcement official	72,684	83,180	70,014	69,738	92,610
Chief librarian	56,332	59,157	48,420	59,751	70,379
Clerk	49,903	50,229	47,915	48,729	65,661
Economic development director	74,451	67,557	62,880	76,693	106,558
Engineer	83,153	72,142	78,189	84,741	96,753
Fire chief	77,188	68,975	77,634	74,017	100,521
Health officer	67,687	58,332	71,455	72,809	—
Human resources director	74,151	66,658	74,785	71,108	91,713
Human services director	69,550	64,598	66,027	68,734	107,190
Information services director	79,538	70,005	79,564	77,591	96,046
Parks and recreation director	69,308	58,999	65,257	69,659	94,442
Parks superintendent	52,506	55,639	55,007	48,662	66,433
Planning director	76,009	66,236	76,745	74,621	87,987
Primary assistant manager/CAO	85,181	69,149	77,738	85,658	117,250
Public safety director	74,750	63,484	74,651	74,131	101,566
Public works director	71,165	69,803	71,102	67,914	90,996
Purchasing director	62,811	60,855	67,406	61,384	69,832
Recreation director	55,990	47,084	50,746	57,815	74,160
Risk manager	67,496	65,747	71,186	63,053	86,800
Treasurer	48,998	47,600	44,633	59,696	55,532

Table 1/5   AVERAGE SALARY FOR PUBLIC WORKS DIRECTOR, BY REGION, 2006 AND 2007

Region	2006		2007	
	No. reporting	Average salary ($)	No. reporting	Average salary ($)
Total	1,698	72,904	1,312	71,165
Northeast	251	78,061	144	69,803
North-Central .	566	71,397	485	71,102
South	690	65,616	577	67,914
West	191	96,923	106	90,996

Table 1/6   AVERAGE SALARY FOR ECONOMIC DEVELOPMENT DIRECTOR, BY REGION, 2006 AND 2007

Region	2006		2007	
	No. reporting	Average salary ($)	No. reporting	Average salary ($)
Total	474	75,751	337	74,451
Northeast	57	69,749	24	67,557
North-Central .	162	66,144	121	62,880
South	173	75,473	154	76,693
West	82	99,489	38	106,558

surveyed in 2007. The positions of human services director and engineer have the greatest range spread (49%), and the position of CAO/city manager has the least range spread (36%). Figure 1/2 shows the actual average salaries for six selected positions in conjunction with the average ranges for those positions.

Table 1/8 lists the average, median, and first- and third-quartile salaries for all 23 positions for which there were enough responses to compute the information. For some positions, such as recreation director in cities with populations over 1 million, fewer than three cities reported, so no calculation could be made.

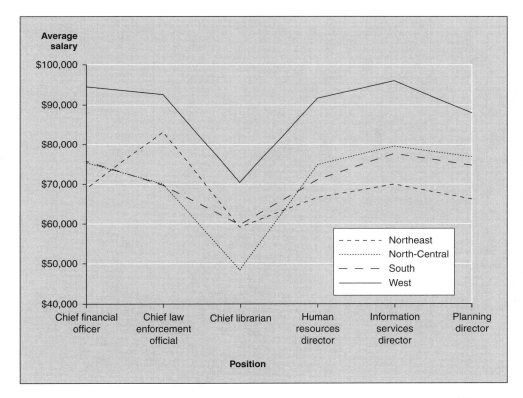

Figure 1/1   *Average salaries for six selected municipal positions, by geographic region, 2007*

Table 1/7   AVERAGE PAY STRUCTURE RANGES, 2007

Position	No. reporting	Average minimum ($)	Average maximum ($)	Average range spread (%)
Chief administrative officer/city manager .	1,399	72,204	98,079	36
Chief elected official	346	53,250	76,139	43
Chief financial officer	931	63,772	89,844	41
Chief law enforcement official	1,505	62,317	87,441	40
Chief librarian	415	53,503	76,338	43
Clerk	1,344	44,441	62,576	41
Economic development director	337	62,677	89,366	43
Engineer	427	64,743	96,227	49
Fire chief	786	65,463	94,407	44
Health officer	105	55,855	80,309	44
Human resources director	535	61,786	89,356	45
Human services director	120	61,683	92,025	49
Information services director	360	61,412	89,889	46
Parks and recreation director	634	58,972	84,554	43
Parks superintendent	428	45,751	67,834	48
Planning director	535	60,899	87,429	44
Primary assistant manager/CAO	411	69,025	98,726	43
Public safety director	129	63,025	89,386	42
Public works director	1,312	61,593	86,066	40
Purchasing director	174	50,531	74,644	48
Recreation director	280	48,926	69,807	43
Risk manager	163	52,324	77,653	48
Treasurer	366	46,349	64,153	38

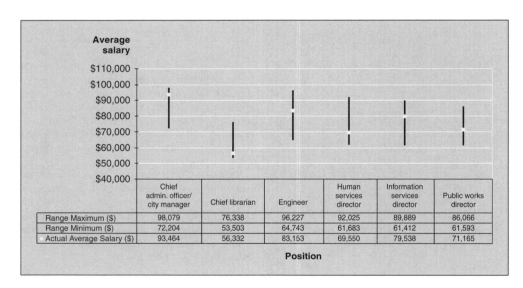

	Chief admin. officer/ city manager	Chief librarian	Engineer	Human services director	Information services director	Public works director
Range Maximum ($)	98,079	76,338	96,227	92,025	89,889	86,066
Range Minimum ($)	72,204	53,503	64,743	61,683	61,412	61,593
Actual Average Salary ($)	93,464	56,332	83,153	69,550	79,538	71,165

Position

Figure 1/2   *Actual average salaries and salary ranges for six selected municipal positions, 2007*

Table 1/8   SALARIES OF MUNICIPAL OFFICIALS: JULY–DECEMBER 2007

Salary data for the municipal positions in this table are based on information reported by municipal officials between late July 2007 and mid December 2007. Data are reported by position title only. Although job responsibilities are generally similar, the titles do not necessarily indicate identical duties and responsibilities.

This table includes salaries for only full-time personnel. Salaries are presented by ten population groups and are further classified by geographic region, city type, and form of government. In some instances, form-of-government information

is missing; therefore, the number of municipalities reporting by form of government might not always match the total number of municipalities reporting.

Classifications having fewer than three municipalities reporting are excluded because meaningful statistics cannot be computed. Consequently, the number reporting in some subcategories does not always equal the total reporting. The median represents either the value of the middle observation or, when there is an even number of observations, the mean of the two middle observations.

vations. The first- and third-quartile observations represent the value of the observation below which 25% and 75% of the number of observations fall, respectively, and are calculated around the median, such that an equal number of observations fall between the median and the first quartile and between the median and the third quartile.

(. . .) indicates that fewer than three municipalities reported, so meaningful statistics cannot be computed.

Title of official	Number of municipalities reporting	Mean ($)	First quartile ($)	Median ($)	Third quartile ($)
All cities					
Chief admin. officer/city manager					
Total	1,399	93,464	65,674	88,932	114,361
Geographic region					
Northeast	129	81,698	57,000	80,000	108,990
North-Central	495	86,619	65,844	83,000	105,000
South	661	95,478	65,779	90,000	119,370
West	114	124,822	91,500	114,590	150,000
Metro type					
Central	113	142,439	116,175	137,245	159,307
Suburban	748	98,390	71,895	93,770	119,905
Independent	538	76,328	56,416	73,020	94,069
Form of government					
Mayor-council	370	78,521	58,025	75,002	96,029
Council-manager	985	99,755	69,996	95,150	123,000
Commission	12	79,526	61,921	76,000	84,547
Town meeting	26	74,072	48,837	70,216	94,959
Rep. town meeting . .	6	94,055	66,769	96,558	121,452
Chief elected official					
Total	346	39,812	14,838	25,775	56,141
Geographic region					
Northeast	39	55,212	30,608	45,094	75,473
North-Central	123	36,821	15,000	24,000	52,477
South	146	38,023	13,510	24,912	51,875
West	38	40,559	14,999	21,868	70,032
Metro type					
Central	69	54,683	17,369	32,423	84,784
Suburban	177	38,488	15,000	24,000	54,308
Independent	100	31,894	13,064	24,797	46,339
Form of government					
Mayor-council	201	45,585	18,000	37,416	68,006
Council-manager	125	28,460	12,099	15,635	26,000
Commission	10	37,274	20,063	26,000	51,141
Town meeting	9	69,125	59,973	67,322	74,546
Chief financial officer					
Total	931	76,848	56,875	74,452	94,984
Geographic region					
Northeast	85	68,921	51,360	69,502	88,270
North-Central	305	75,290	58,767	74,833	92,352
South	446	75,654	54,112	72,657	94,530
West	95	94,547	67,587	89,787	115,068
Metro type					
Central	114	101,870	88,663	96,471	114,153
Suburban	515	79,426	60,939	77,128	97,858
Independent	302	63,007	48,410	63,098	75,154
Form of government					
Mayor-council	257	66,272	47,204	66,958	83,138
Council-manager	646	81,146	62,016	77,865	99,278
Commission	8	69,010	54,000	70,138	80,635
Town meeting	15	75,982	62,097	78,750	91,926
Rep. town meeting . .	5	80,308	73,698	74,000	92,000
Chief law enforcement official					
Total	1,505	72,684	50,172	67,536	90,867
Geographic region					
Northeast	140	83,180	60,272	81,630	101,758
North-Central	545	70,014	50,724	65,416	86,850
South	715	69,738	47,046	62,837	87,294
West	105	92,610	65,291	81,013	117,790
Metro type					
Central	123	107,430	90,429	101,628	121,296
Suburban	735	80,944	58,289	77,438	100,256
Independent	647	56,696	43,671	53,536	66,994

Title of official	Number of municipalities reporting	Mean ($)	First quartile ($)	Median ($)	Third quartile ($)
All cities continued					
Form of government					
Mayor-council	576	62,988	44,488	57,608	76,689
Council-manager	870	78,896	55,262	74,323	98,419
Commission	28	68,115	55,775	60,869	85,944
Town meeting	24	79,006	60,506	82,238	97,841
Rep. town meeting . .	7	95,114	82,656	97,677	103,574
Chief librarian					
Total	415	56,332	36,718	53,238	72,417
Geographic region					
Northeast	69	59,157	46,350	59,893	73,278
North-Central	161	48,420	33,670	43,035	59,155
South	143	59,751	37,056	55,125	78,544
West	42	70,379	41,251	61,770	95,566
Metro type					
Central	51	86,577	72,100	85,670	101,805
Suburban	196	59,903	39,052	56,643	76,599
Independent	168	42,983	31,138	40,199	53,708
Form of government					
Mayor-council	134	45,811	29,127	39,278	61,169
Council-manager	244	62,130	40,095	56,643	77,910
Commission	6	67,115	46,461	56,983	91,127
Town meeting	25	52,214	42,522	55,565	62,311
Rep. town meeting . .	6	61,863	58,998	63,426	71,698
Clerk					
Total	1,344	49,903	35,814	46,460	61,011
Geographic region					
Northeast	124	50,229	35,910	51,584	63,068
North-Central	412	47,915	35,465	45,398	59,552
South	706	48,729	35,376	45,174	58,487
West	102	65,661	45,605	61,047	82,500
Metro type					
Central	114	68,273	53,399	64,086	78,606
Suburban	636	54,839	41,305	52,929	66,866
Independent	594	41,092	32,359	39,570	48,759
Form of government					
Mayor-council	506	42,416	31,246	39,616	51,729
Council-manager	789	54,713	40,914	51,409	65,412
Commission	16	48,945	39,948	45,579	53,223
Town meeting	26	48,910	37,131	53,182	58,481
Rep. town meeting . .	7	54,788	45,334	51,900	64,468
Economic development director					
Total	337	74,451	55,098	71,356	92,793
Geographic region					
Northeast	24	67,557	51,814	68,384	87,635
North-Central	121	62,880	49,097	62,256	77,304
South	154	76,693	56,652	71,455	95,759
West	38	106,558	84,597	107,327	129,284
Metro type					
Central	55	95,363	76,435	93,839	114,274
Suburban	184	78,754	60,429	74,465	94,290
Independent	98	54,635	37,351	51,998	67,754
Form of government					
Mayor-council	100	64,560	46,364	61,645	79,597
Council-manager	228	79,078	59,079	74,057	96,039
Town meeting	6	61,921	45,280	62,396	81,833
Engineer					
Total	427	83,153	68,560	82,020	97,274
Geographic region					
Northeast	39	72,142	58,219	74,362	85,268
North-Central	133	78,189	66,288	79,046	92,518
South	198	84,741	69,509	84,386	98,418
West	57	96,753	77,551	91,701	121,308

Table 1/8   SALARIES OF MUNICIPAL OFFICIALS: JULY–DECEMBER 2007
continued

Title of official	Number of municipalities reporting	Distribution of 2007 salaries Mean ($)	First quartile ($)	Median ($)	Third quartile ($)
All cities continued					
Metro type					
Central	101	88,627	77,662	87,880	98,680
Suburban	220	86,534	72,449	86,720	102,144
Independent	106	70,919	59,414	71,910	81,551
Form of government					
Mayor-council	103	74,850	62,448	80,039	88,462
Council-manager	309	86,614	71,063	84,641	99,615
Commission	5	65,131	66,288	71,978	74,234
Town meeting	6	64,239	46,575	65,538	75,271
Rep. town meeting . .	4	80,499	78,149	80,997	83,347
Fire chief					
Total	786	77,188	55,646	73,532	96,115
Geographic region					
Northeast	58	68,975	50,167	71,101	92,474
North-Central	235	77,634	58,459	77,850	95,571
South	420	74,017	52,415	70,017	91,648
West	73	100,521	69,473	97,194	125,258
Metro type					
Central	119	102,299	86,977	98,508	116,048
Suburban	395	81,865	59,251	80,929	104,093
Independent	272	59,409	47,151	58,844	70,621
Form of government					
Mayor-council	217	66,398	48,000	61,707	84,786
Council-manager	530	82,016	60,235	78,133	103,188
Commission	16	70,448	51,113	61,680	100,518
Town meeting	17	65,074	49,556	68,215	91,623
Rep. town meeting . .	6	93,192	91,210	94,312	97,224
Health officer					
Total	105	67,687	42,743	61,860	83,784
Geographic region					
Northeast	35	58,332	40,158	56,934	76,457
North-Central	23	71,455	47,541	67,477	86,400
South	47	72,809	40,352	65,520	90,855
Metro type					
Central	34	94,264	72,619	82,874	119,751
Suburban	49	58,492	39,868	58,094	75,910
Independent	22	47,092	30,155	41,787	53,703
Form of government					
Mayor-council	22	55,742	26,858	48,485	73,281
Council-manager	65	73,732	45,229	66,835	90,510
Town meeting	12	54,422	24,834	57,671	77,980
Rep. town meeting . .	5	63,905	58,656	63,376	70,221
Human resources director					
Total	535	74,151	53,549	72,360	93,621
Geographic region					
Northeast	33	66,658	54,383	67,509	79,019
North-Central	124	74,785	56,724	76,335	93,357
South	314	71,108	51,210	68,681	92,712
West	64	91,713	66,165	83,335	119,527
Metro type					
Central	117	89,836	76,875	86,706	103,432
Suburban	272	77,366	55,468	75,236	97,065
Independent	146	55,591	40,112	54,311	68,171
Form of government					
Mayor-council	126	59,570	38,752	57,628	80,523
Council-manager	393	79,137	60,132	77,106	97,660
Commission	6	64,714	47,778	58,098	73,760
Town meeting	7	64,241	56,695	61,700	72,966
Rep. town meeting . .	3	75,374	73,264	79,019	79,307
Human services director					
Total	120	69,550	49,318	66,215	85,262
Geographic region					
Northeast	21	64,598	49,407	60,811	78,080
North-Central	17	66,027	38,800	57,542	88,736
South	76	68,734	50,063	67,042	83,684
West	6	107,190	84,420	105,975	128,389
Metro type					
Central	32	87,661	64,887	83,825	106,064
Suburban	63	69,680	54,885	70,380	85,035
Independent	25	46,037	35,237	42,204	52,188
Form of government					
Mayor-council	19	54,491	35,305	45,322	67,786
Council-manager	93	73,233	52,303	72,708	87,108
Town meeting	8	62,501	56,405	60,495	68,878
Information services director					
Total	360	79,538	60,180	77,461	95,667
Geographic region					
Northeast	33	70,005	60,661	72,450	84,772
North-Central	80	79,564	62,729	80,070	92,640
South	204	77,591	58,554	74,386	95,156
West	43	96,046	70,654	93,530	121,395

Title of official	Number of municipalities reporting	Distribution of 2007 salaries Mean ($)	First quartile ($)	Median ($)	Third quartile ($)
All cities continued					
Metro type					
Central	104	91,419	74,000	86,478	103,900
Suburban	182	80,874	62,525	79,900	95,602
Independent	74	59,555	49,388	58,042	67,671
Form of government					
Mayor-council	64	74,837	58,802	72,823	87,208
Council-manager	283	81,300	61,975	79,172	97,483
Commission	3	46,625	43,988	51,750	51,825
Town meeting	5	71,356	75,882	77,542	79,460
Rep. town meeting . .	5	67,916	60,767	79,595	84,772
Parks and recreation director					
Total	634	69,308	48,142	65,964	87,534
Geographic region					
Northeast	48	58,999	44,458	61,917	69,947
North-Central	199	65,257	45,046	61,513	85,073
South	340	69,659	49,677	66,650	89,061
West	47	94,442	65,299	89,665	119,058
Metro type					
Central	102	90,841	72,503	89,753	103,780
Suburban	326	74,063	53,631	71,362	92,120
Independent	206	51,119	37,989	48,895	62,262
Form of government					
Mayor-council	155	56,507	39,590	52,992	72,018
Council-manager	459	74,154	53,406	70,824	92,486
Commission	5	62,899	35,000	41,520	101,504
Town meeting	12	52,152	36,126	59,190	67,327
Rep. town meeting . .	3	68,453	57,752	68,287	79,072
Parks superintendent					
Total	428	52,506	38,870	51,162	64,687
Geographic region					
Northeast	27	55,639	44,062	52,007	69,226
North-Central	112	55,007	41,300	55,171	67,431
South	247	48,662	35,096	46,593	59,793
West	42	66,433	50,757	67,138	79,958
Metro type					
Central	80	61,538	49,145	60,163	68,593
Suburban	202	56,818	42,005	57,733	70,070
Independent	146	41,593	32,723	40,662	50,137
Form of government					
Mayor-council	112	45,179	33,247	44,211	55,119
Council-manager	304	54,985	40,556	53,366	66,466
Commission	6	51,273	40,447	54,365	62,030
Town meeting	3	57,029	44,654	47,348	64,564
Rep. town meeting . .	3	72,767	69,399	74,485	76,993
Planning director					
Total	535	76,009	57,063	72,521	90,632
Geographic region					
Northeast	50	66,236	53,704	63,043	79,451
North-Central	119	76,745	62,038	74,164	90,341
South	298	74,621	55,526	71,440	90,292
West	68	87,987	63,540	80,566	113,513
Metro type					
Central	101	89,781	73,542	88,992	103,000
Suburban	296	78,393	60,398	75,152	94,348
Independent	138	60,814	49,161	59,220	69,694
Form of government					
Mayor-council	114	68,427	54,844	68,138	82,697
Council-manager	401	78,755	58,820	75,400	95,216
Commission	5	70,964	62,000	63,059	64,584
Town meeting	12	60,406	51,646	56,783	70,071
Rep. town meeting . .	3	67,813	61,922	79,019	79,307
Primary asst. manager/CAO					
Total	411	85,181	61,930	80,592	107,904
Geographic region					
Northeast	39	69,149	53,651	67,085	86,298
North-Central	115	77,738	63,072	76,775	92,201
South	214	85,658	61,143	81,510	110,852
West	43	117,250	89,570	114,442	142,213
Metro type					
Central	70	109,290	91,492	111,165	119,795
Suburban	253	84,794	61,104	80,413	103,176
Independent	88	67,117	54,917	66,361	80,341
Form of government					
Mayor-council	74	66,133	47,881	61,800	85,894
Council-manager	324	90,274	66,851	85,127	111,450
Commission	4	60,532	55,227	57,027	62,332
Town meeting	6	69,841	52,249	70,502	85,569
Rep. town meeting . .	3	68,500	62,225	62,657	71,854
Public safety director					
Total	129	74,750	56,845	71,502	91,935

Table 1/8   SALARIES OF MUNICIPAL OFFICIALS: JULY–DECEMBER 2007
continued

Title of official	Number of municipalities reporting	Distribution of 2007 salaries			
		Mean ($)	First quartile ($)	Median ($)	Third quartile ($)
All cities continued					
Geographic region					
Northeast	9	63,484	44,222	48,769	87,192
North-Central	74	74,651	59,007	71,465	95,980
South	41	74,131	59,000	72,289	86,452
West	5	101,566	76,440	79,970	91,349
Metro type					
Central	13	97,047	70,622	93,473	117,075
Suburban	85	75,184	56,845	75,496	93,036
Independent	31	64,209	50,052	67,896	80,910
Form of government					
Mayor-council	56	65,548	43,842	65,492	83,576
Council-manager	71	82,903	67,722	81,702	97,672
Public works director					
Total	1,312	71,165	50,064	66,882	87,957
Geographic region					
Northeast	144	69,803	52,000	69,997	84,186
North-Central	485	71,102	52,938	67,300	86,850
South	577	67,914	45,964	62,629	84,190
West	106	90,996	62,397	84,588	116,724
Metro type					
Central	105	104,429	87,963	99,972	116,214
Suburban	704	76,272	55,793	73,260	93,750
Independent	503	57,073	43,230	54,539	68,030
Form of government					
Mayor-council	460	62,570	46,057	59,449	76,196
Council-manager	802	76,106	53,516	72,031	95,343
Commission	18	64,765	54,314	58,972	77,859
Town meeting	24	71,909	56,528	70,340	86,440
Rep. town meeting . .	8	82,229	72,814	83,940	95,649
Purchasing director					
Total	174	62,811	51,128	64,311	75,012
Geographic region					
Northeast	16	60,855	53,683	63,844	73,006
North-Central	23	67,406	56,943	68,135	80,064
South	121	61,384	45,921	62,858	72,480
West	14	69,832	54,827	68,905	84,488
Metro type					
Central	71	72,377	60,426	69,885	79,757
Suburban	72	61,171	51,670	63,290	70,905
Independent	31	44,710	30,024	37,704	53,005
Form of government					
Mayor-council	38	54,086	32,752	56,310	72,956
Council-manager	133	65,433	54,568	65,376	75,116
Recreation director					
Total	280	55,990	39,753	56,206	69,300
Geographic region					
Northeast	50	47,084	35,764	46,746	59,949
North-Central	75	50,746	31,637	51,753	64,738
South	121	57,815	44,384	58,372	71,030
West	34	74,160	49,387	70,181	96,578
Metro type					
Central	53	66,737	53,336	64,987	77,339
Suburban	158	59,013	41,594	59,820	72,491
Independent	69	40,814	31,000	40,386	47,699
Form of government					
Mayor-council	65	50,287	34,221	50,895	62,886
Council-manager	196	59,164	42,998	58,676	72,928
Commission	3	51,638	39,331	46,575	61,414
Town meeting	12	38,746	31,779	38,754	42,740
Rep. town meeting . .	4	48,165	37,761	56,478	66,883
Risk manager					
Total	163	67,496	52,809	67,297	80,940
Geographic region					
Northeast	5	65,747	57,904	71,491	73,259
North-Central	29	71,186	60,591	73,609	80,870
South	109	63,053	47,904	61,695	75,804
West	20	86,800	70,899	93,723	100,156
Metro type					
Central	75	66,979	53,941	67,470	77,998
Suburban	66	74,374	60,928	72,412	86,876
Independent	22	48,622	38,546	45,263	52,490
Form of government					
Mayor-council	24	59,605	44,623	59,873	68,102
Council-manager	136	68,613	53,053	69,116	81,913
Treasurer					
Total	366	48,998	33,140	45,321	61,038
Geographic region					
Northeast	65	47,600	29,061	45,305	59,792
North-Central	200	44,633	32,115	42,278	55,820
South	73	59,696	41,097	56,052	75,705
West	28	55,532	40,284	51,208	76,748

Title of official	Number of municipalities reporting	Distribution of 2007 salaries			
		Mean ($)	First quartile ($)	Median ($)	Third quartile ($)
All cities continued					
Metro type					
Central	39	80,655	66,816	78,801	98,379
Suburban	144	49,523	33,565	48,208	61,730
Independent	183	41,839	31,306	41,392	49,981
Form of government					
Mayor-council	180	41,976	29,485	39,876	49,368
Council-manager	157	57,302	41,000	55,473	71,378
Commission	12	49,154	33,125	46,194	61,920
Town meeting	13	39,831	23,789	36,174	52,000
Rep. town meeting . .	4	68,411	56,535	68,866	80,742
Over 1,000,000					
Chief admin. officer/city manager					
Total	3	220,784	197,298	230,088	248,922
Geographic region	. . .	. . .	. . .	. . .	. . .
Metro type					
Central	3	220,784	197,298	230,088	248,922
Form of government	. . .	. . .	. . .	. . .	. . .
Chief elected official					
Total	4	143,690	80,997	132,379	195,072
Geographic region					
South	3	162,254	118,381	176,762	213,381
Metro type					
Central	4	143,690	80,997	132,379	195,072
Form of government					
Council-manager	3	132,665	73,998	87,996	168,998
Chief financial officer					
Total	4	144,166	136,594	139,275	146,847
Geographic region					
South	3	137,450	135,663	137,525	139,275
Metro type					
Central	4	144,166	136,594	139,275	146,847
Form of government					
Council-manager	3	147,622	139,275	141,024	152,670
Chief law enforcement official					
Total	3	162,114	148,154	168,504	179,270
Geographic region					
South	3	162,114	148,154	168,504	179,270
Metro type					
Central	3	162,114	148,154	168,504	179,270
Form of government	. . .	. . .	. . .	. . .	. . .
Chief librarian					
Total	3	125,754	121,000	122,000	128,632
Geographic region					
South	3	125,754	121,000	122,000	128,632
Metro type					
Central	3	125,754	121,000	122,000	128,632
Form of government	. . .	. . .	. . .	. . .	. . .
Clerk					
Total	4	104,361	101,433	104,593	107,521
Geographic region					
South	3	101,748	99,642	103,224	104,593
Metro type					
Central	4	104,361	101,433	104,593	107,521
Form of government					
Council-manager	3	107,128	104,593	105,961	109,081
Economic development director					
Total	3	120,360	110,341	113,520	126,960
Geographic region					
South	3	120,360	110,341	113,520	126,960
Metro type					
Central	3	120,360	110,341	113,520	126,960
Form of government	. . .	. . .	. . .	. . .	. . .
Engineer					
Total	3	95,968	86,797	102,048	108,180
Geographic region					
South	3	95,968	86,797	102,048	108,180
Metro type					
Central	3	95,968	86,797	102,048	108,180
Form of government	. . .	. . .	. . .	. . .	. . .
Fire chief					
Total	4	140,210	126,250	136,112	150,072
Geographic region					
South	3	132,411	125,836	126,663	136,112
Metro type					
Central	4	140,210	126,250	136,112	150,072
Form of government					
Council-manager	3	145,277	136,112	145,560	154,584
Health officer					
Total	3	136,118	133,708	136,308	138,624

Table 1/8   SALARIES OF MUNICIPAL OFFICIALS: JULY–DECEMBER 2007
continued

Title of official	Number of municipalities reporting	Distribution of 2007 salaries			
		Mean ($)	First quartile ($)	Median ($)	Third quartile ($)
Over 1,000,000 continued					
Geographic region					
South	3	136,118	133,708	136,308	138,624
Metro type					
Central	3	136,118	133,708	136,308	138,624
Form of government	. . .	. . .	. . .	. . .	. . .
Human resources director					
Total	4	122,016	109,883	115,875	128,009
Geographic region					
South	3	112,760	108,765	111,000	115,875
Metro type					
Central	4	122,016	109,883	115,875	128,009
Form of government					
Council-manager	3	127,178	115,875	120,750	135,267
Human services director					
Total	3	129,043	115,355	124,848	140,634
Geographic region	. . .	. . .	. . .	. . .	. . .
Metro type					
Central	3	129,043	115,355	124,848	140,634
Form of government					
Council-manager	3	129,043	115,355	124,848	140,634
Information services director					
Total	4	120,543	103,007	119,807	137,343
Geographic region					
South	3	115,943	100,739	105,274	125,813
Metro type					
Central	4	120,543	103,007	119,807	137,343
Form of government					
Council-manager	3	111,939	100,739	105,274	119,807
Parks and recreation director					
Total	4	148,262	116,450	144,714	176,526
Geographic region					
South	3	140,442	115,192	117,708	154,326
Metro type					
Central	4	148,262	116,450	144,714	176,526
Form of government					
Council-manager	3	158,446	142,198	171,720	181,332
Parks superintendent					
Total	. . .	. . .	. . .	. . .	. . .
Geographic region	. . .	. . .	. . .	. . .	. . .
City type	. . .	. . .	. . .	. . .	. . .
Form of government	. . .	. . .	. . .	. . .	. . .
Planning director					
Total	4	130,619	112,178	131,880	150,321
Geographic region					
South	3	124,231	110,380	113,976	132,954
Metro type					
Central	4	130,619	112,178	131,880	150,321
Form of government					
Council-manager	3	136,167	128,284	149,784	150,858
Primary asst. manager/CAO					
Total	3	144,908	113,268	157,590	182,889
Geographic region	. . .	. . .	. . .	. . .	. . .
Metro type					
Central	3	144,908	113,268	157,590	182,889
Form of government					
Council-manager	3	144,908	113,268	157,590	182,889
Public safety director					
Total	. . .	. . .	. . .	. . .	. . .
Geographic region	. . .	. . .	. . .	. . .	. . .
City type	. . .	. . .	. . .	. . .	. . .
Form of government	. . .	. . .	. . .	. . .	. . .
Public works director					
Total	4	150,551	143,579	159,198	166,170
Geographic region					
South	3	145,574	134,241	152,916	160,578
Metro type					
Central	4	150,551	143,579	159,198	166,170
Form of government					
Council-manager	3	144,654	134,241	152,916	159,198
Purchasing director					
Total	4	101,155	93,096	99,196	107,255
Geographic region					
South	3	106,381	99,196	102,756	111,753
Metro type					
Central	4	101,155	93,096	99,196	107,255
Form of government					
Council-manager	3	100,621	90,556	95,636	108,193
Recreation director					
Total	. . .	. . .	. . .	. . .	. . .
Geographic region	. . .	. . .	. . .	. . .	. . .
City type	. . .	. . .	. . .	. . .	. . .
Form of government	. . .	. . .	. . .	. . .	. . .

Title of official	Number of municipalities reporting	Distribution of 2007 salaries			
		Mean ($)	First quartile ($)	Median ($)	Third quartile ($)
Over 1,000,000 continued					
Risk manager					
Total	3	79,057	72,622	77,520	84,724
Geographic region					
South	3	79,057	72,622	77,520	84,724
Metro type					
Central	3	79,057	72,622	77,520	84,724
Form of government	. . .	. . .	. . .	. . .	. . .
Treasurer					
Total	. . .	. . .	. . .	. . .	. . .
Geographic region	. . .	. . .	. . .	. . .	. . .
City type	. . .	. . .	. . .	. . .	. . .
Form of government	. . .	. . .	. . .	. . .	. . .
500,000–1,000,000					
Chief admin. officer/city manager					
Total	4	206,874	191,086	201,558	217,346
Geographic region					
South	4	206,874	191,086	201,558	217,346
Metro type					
Central	4	206,874	191,086	201,558	217,346
Form of government					
Council-manager	4	206,874	191,086	201,558	217,346
Chief elected official					
Total	3	35,153	26,230	32,423	42,712
Geographic region					
South	3	35,153	26,230	32,423	42,712
Metro type					
Central	3	35,153	26,230	32,423	42,712
Form of government					
Council-manager	3	35,153	26,230	32,423	42,712
Chief financial officer					
Total	4	150,413	131,251	148,722	167,883
Geographic region					
South	4	150,413	131,251	148,722	167,883
Metro type					
Central	4	150,413	131,251	148,722	167,883
Form of government					
Council-manager	4	150,413	131,251	148,722	167,883
Chief law enforcement official					
Total	4	154,064	149,369	152,810	157,506
Geographic region					
South	4	154,064	149,369	152,810	157,506
Metro type					
Central	4	154,064	149,369	152,810	157,506
Form of government					
Council-manager	4	154,064	149,369	152,810	157,506
Chief librarian					
Total	. . .	. . .	. . .	. . .	. . .
Geographic region	. . .	. . .	. . .	. . .	. . .
City type	. . .	. . .	. . .	. . .	. . .
Form of government	. . .	. . .	. . .	. . .	. . .
Clerk					
Total	4	101,077	99,587	110,745	112,235
Geographic region					
South	4	101,077	99,587	110,745	112,235
Metro type					
Central	4	101,077	99,587	110,745	112,235
Form of government					
Council-manager	4	101,077	99,587	110,745	112,235
Economic development director					
Total	4	123,777	122,173	124,428	126,032
Geographic region					
South	4	123,777	122,173	124,428	126,032
Metro type					
Central	4	123,777	122,173	124,428	126,032
Form of government					
Council-manager	4	123,777	122,173	124,428	126,032
Engineer					
Total	4	135,109	125,723	134,218	143,604
Geographic region					
South	4	135,109	125,723	134,218	143,604
Metro type					
Central	4	135,109	125,723	134,218	143,604
Form of government					
Council-manager	4	135,109	125,723	134,218	143,604
Fire chief					
Total	4	143,150	139,254	142,436	146,332
Geographic region					
South	4	143,150	139,254	142,436	146,332
Metro type					
Central	4	143,150	139,254	142,436	146,332

Table 1/8   SALARIES OF MUNICIPAL OFFICIALS: JULY–DECEMBER 2007
continued

Title of official	Number of municipalities reporting	Distribution of 2007 salaries			
		Mean ($)	First quartile ($)	Median ($)	Third quartile ($)
500,000–1,000,000 continued					
Form of government					
Council-manager	4	143,150	139,254	142,436	146,332
Health officer					
Total	3	155,359	140,038	159,408	172,704
Geographic region					
South	3	155,359	140,038	159,408	172,704
Metro type					
Central	3	155,359	140,038	159,408	172,704
Form of government					
Council-manager	3	155,359	140,038	159,408	172,704
Human resources director					
Total	4	132,736	126,692	137,194	143,238
Geographic region					
South	4	132,736	126,692	137,194	143,238
Metro type					
Central	4	132,736	126,692	137,194	143,238
Form of government					
Council-manager	4	132,736	126,692	137,194	143,238
Human services director					
Total	. . .	. . .	. . .	. . .	. . .
Geographic region	. . .	. . .	. . .	. . .	. . .
City type	. . .	. . .	. . .	. . .	. . .
Form of government	. . .	. . .	. . .	. . .	. . .
Information services director					
Total	3	139,392	129,236	151,084	155,394
Geographic region					
South	3	139,392	129,236	151,084	155,394
Metro type					
Central	3	139,392	129,236	151,084	155,394
Form of government					
Council-manager	3	139,392	129,236	151,084	155,394
Parks and recreation director					
Total	3	116,558	105,592	109,183	123,838
Geographic region					
South	3	116,558	105,592	109,183	123,838
Metro type					
Central	3	116,558	105,592	109,183	123,838
Form of government					
Council-manager	3	116,558	105,592	109,183	123,838
Parks superintendent					
Total	3	63,194	57,421	60,300	67,520
Geographic region					
South	3	63,194	57,421	60,300	67,520
Metro type					
Central	3	63,194	57,421	60,300	67,520
Form of government					
Council-manager	3	63,194	57,421	60,300	67,520
Planning director					
Total	4	127,160	121,580	129,101	134,681
Geographic region					
South	4	127,160	121,580	129,101	134,681
Metro type					
Central	4	127,160	121,580	129,101	134,681
Form of government					
Council-manager	4	127,160	121,580	129,101	134,681
Primary asst. manager/CAO					
Total	4	139,290	130,371	159,338	168,257
Geographic region					
South	4	139,290	130,371	159,338	168,257
Metro type					
Central	4	139,290	130,371	159,338	168,257
Form of government					
Council-manager	4	139,290	130,371	159,338	168,257
Public safety director					
Total	. . .	. . .	. . .	. . .	. . .
Geographic region	. . .	. . .	. . .	. . .	. . .
City type	. . .	. . .	. . .	. . .	. . .
Form of government	. . .	. . .	. . .	. . .	. . .
Public works director					
Total	. . .	. . .	. . .	. . .	. . .
Geographic region	. . .	. . .	. . .	. . .	. . .
City type	. . .	. . .	. . .	. . .	. . .
Form of government	. . .	. . .	. . .	. . .	. . .
Purchasing director					
Total	4	101,314	97,251	101,627	105,690
Geographic region					
South	4	101,314	97,251	101,627	105,690
Metro type					
Central	4	101,314	97,251	101,627	105,690
Form of government					
Council-manager	4	101,314	97,251	101,627	105,690

Title of official	Number of municipalities reporting	Distribution of 2007 salaries			
		Mean ($)	First quartile ($)	Median ($)	Third quartile ($)
500,000–1,000,000 continued					
Recreation director					
Total	. . .	. . .	. . .	. . .	. . .
Geographic region	. . .	. . .	. . .	. . .	. . .
City type	. . .	. . .	. . .	. . .	. . .
Form of government	. . .	. . .	. . .	. . .	. . .
Risk manager					
Total	4	95,288	86,847	93,779	102,220
Geographic region					
South	4	95,288	86,847	93,779	102,220
Metro type					
Central	4	95,288	86,847	93,779	102,220
Form of government					
Council-manager	4	95,288	86,847	93,779	102,220
Treasurer					
Total	. . .	. . .	. . .	. . .	. . .
Geographic region	. . .	. . .	. . .	. . .	. . .
City type	. . .	. . .	. . .	. . .	. . .
Form of government	. . .	. . .	. . .	. . .	. . .
250,000–499,999					
Chief admin. officer/city manager					
Total	6	188,407	182,664	194,364	206,197
Geographic region					
South	3	193,468	185,609	191,500	200,343
Metro type					
Central	6	188,407	182,664	194,364	206,197
Form of government					
Council-manager	5	198,579	191,500	197,228	209,186
Chief elected official					
Total	3	43,112	18,480	20,760	56,568
Geographic region	. . .	. . .	. . .	. . .	. . .
Metro type					
Central	3	43,112	18,480	20,760	56,568
Form of government	. . .	. . .	. . .	. . .	. . .
Chief financial officer					
Total	5	126,069	125,590	126,608	140,130
Geographic region	. . .	. . .	. . .	. . .	. . .
Metro type					
Central	5	126,069	125,590	126,608	140,130
Form of government					
Council-manager	4	126,189	118,948	133,369	140,611
Chief law enforcement official					
Total	5	132,031	134,014	136,981	138,082
Geographic region					
South	3	126,288	120,391	136,981	137,532
Metro type					
Central	5	132,031	134,014	136,981	138,082
Form of government					
Council-manager	4	131,536	128,686	137,532	140,382
Chief librarian					
Total	. . .	. . .	. . .	. . .	. . .
Geographic region	. . .	. . .	. . .	. . .	. . .
City type	. . .	. . .	. . .	. . .	. . .
Form of government	. . .	. . .	. . .	. . .	. . .
Clerk					
Total	5	94,992	93,330	99,089	103,279
Geographic region					
South	3	102,456	101,184	103,279	104,139
Metro type					
Central	5	94,992	93,330	99,089	103,279
Form of government					
Council-manager	4	95,408	92,882	101,184	103,709
Economic development director					
Total	4	110,740	90,916	108,276	128,100
Geographic region	. . .	. . .	. . .	. . .	. . .
Metro type					
Central	4	110,740	90,916	108,276	128,100
Form of government					
Council-manager	3	106,610	88,413	93,420	118,212
Engineer					
Total	5	93,309	55,049	109,948	117,650
Geographic region	. . .	. . .	. . .	. . .	. . .
Metro type					
Central	5	93,309	55,049	109,948	117,650
Form of government					
Council-manager	4	104,609	96,223	113,799	122,185
Fire chief					
Total	5	123,392	114,317	124,199	127,229
Geographic region					
South	3	120,866	117,685	124,199	125,714
Metro type					
Central	5	123,392	114,317	124,199	127,229

Table 1/8   SALARIES OF MUNICIPAL OFFICIALS: JULY–DECEMBER 2007
continued

Title of official	Number of municipalities reporting	Distribution of 2007 salaries			
		Mean ($)	First quartile ($)	Median ($)	Third quartile ($)
250,000–499,999 continued					
Form of government					
Council-manager	4	125,660	120,942	125,714	130,432
Health officer					
Total	3	115,796	98,198	105,887	128,439
Geographic region	. . .	. . .	. . .	. . .	. . .
Metro type					
Central	3	115,796	98,198	105,887	128,439
Form of government	. . .	. . .	. . .	. . .	. . .
Human resources director					
Total	5	118,199	114,652	116,958	129,155
Geographic region					
South	3	113,822	106,156	114,652	121,904
Metro type					
Central	5	118,199	114,652	116,958	129,155
Form of government					
Council-manager	4	118,509	110,404	121,904	130,009
Human services director					
Total	. . .	. . .	. . .	. . .	. . .
Geographic region	. . .	. . .	. . .	. . .	. . .
City type	. . .	. . .	. . .	. . .	. . .
Form of government	. . .	. . .	. . .	. . .	. . .
Information services director					
Total	4	125,340	117,848	125,896	133,388
Geographic region	. . .	. . .	. . .	. . .	. . .
Metro type					
Central	4	125,340	117,848	125,896	133,388
Form of government					
Council-manager	3	124,055	113,097	122,598	134,285
Parks and recreation director					
Total	4	124,400	114,984	125,996	135,411
Geographic region					
South	3	115,537	108,196	121,773	125,996
Metro type					
Central	4	124,400	114,984	125,996	135,411
Form of government					
Council-manager	4	124,400	114,984	125,996	135,411
Parks superintendent					
Total	4	83,165	76,425	89,760	96,501
Geographic region					
South	3	82,079	69,763	93,097	99,904
Metro type					
Central	4	83,165	76,425	89,760	96,501
Form of government					
Council-manager	4	83,165	76,425	89,760	96,501
Planning director					
Total	5	122,036	109,726	119,629	129,754
Geographic region	. . .	. . .	. . .	. . .	. . .
Metro type					
Central	5	122,036	109,726	119,629	129,754
Form of government					
Council-manager	4	125,114	116,891	124,692	132,915
Primary asst. manager/CAO					
Total	4	128,378	113,421	118,924	133,881
Geographic region	. . .	. . .	. . .	. . .	. . .
Metro type					
Central	4	128,378	113,421	118,924	133,881
Form of government					
Council-manager	3	133,121	117,465	123,697	144,064
Public safety director					
Total	. . .	. . .	. . .	. . .	. . .
Geographic region	. . .	. . .	. . .	. . .	. . .
City type	. . .	. . .	. . .	. . .	. . .
Form of government	. . .	. . .	. . .	. . .	. . .
Public works director					
Total	4	133,715	131,324	133,707	136,098
Geographic region	. . .	. . .	. . .	. . .	. . .
Metro type					
Central	4	133,715	131,324	133,707	136,098
Form of government					
Council-manager	3	134,127	131,399	134,936	137,260
Purchasing director					
Total	4	89,847	86,027	93,065	96,885
Geographic region	. . .	. . .	. . .	. . .	. . .
Metro type					
Central	4	89,847	86,027	93,065	96,885
Form of government					
Council-manager	3	89,908	85,791	96,465	97,305
Recreation director					
Total	. . .	. . .	. . .	. . .	. . .
Geographic region	. . .	. . .	. . .	. . .	. . .
City type	. . .	. . .	. . .	. . .	. . .
Form of government	. . .	. . .	. . .	. . .	. . .

Title of official	Number of municipalities reporting	Distribution of 2007 salaries			
		Mean ($)	First quartile ($)	Median ($)	Third quartile ($)
250,000–499,999 continued					
Risk manager					
Total	3	85,051	82,233	86,573	88,630
Geographic region	. . .	. . .	. . .	. . .	. . .
Metro type					
Central	3	85,051	82,233	86,573	88,630
Form of government	. . .	. . .	. . .	. . .	. . .
Treasurer					
Total	4	92,496	82,741	98,378	108,134
Geographic region	. . .	. . .	. . .	. . .	. . .
Metro type					
Central	4	92,496	82,741	98,378	108,134
Form of government					
Council-manager	3	92,898	81,277	105,465	110,802
100,000—249,999					
Chief admin. officer/city manager					
Total	31	165,513	141,076	160,860	184,682
Geographic region					
North-Central	4	154,990	136,284	151,793	170,500
South	18	160,892	151,169	160,634	174,878
West	7	192,938	163,916	191,339	213,292
Metro type					
Central	21	162,971	140,000	154,000	171,127
Suburban	10	170,852	149,770	178,688	189,769
Form of government					
Mayor-council	6	117,085	106,033	120,169	128,116
Council-manager	24	177,642	152,615	171,875	190,854
Chief elected official					
Total	27	55,064	22,350	34,895	89,432
Geographic region					
North-Central	6	50,206	21,525	27,300	84,776
South	11	52,071	20,290	27,000	83,226
West	8	46,288	23,475	35,988	55,344
Metro type					
Central	18	52,936	21,750	28,800	92,309
Suburban	9	59,322	24,000	37,080	83,452
Form of government					
Mayor-council	7	96,853	83,226	104,937	115,317
Council-manager	18	37,518	18,424	25,431	36,810
Chief financial officer					
Total	34	115,688	103,133	110,172	123,563
Geographic region					
North-Central	5	103,606	98,018	101,504	109,476
South	19	111,104	104,343	108,950	119,626
West	8	133,327	116,397	125,517	148,634
Metro type					
Central	22	112,899	104,217	110,172	118,838
Suburban	12	120,801	102,498	117,126	129,863
Form of government					
Mayor-council	7	107,309	99,100	105,570	109,491
Council-manager	25	118,524	107,520	116,384	125,736
Chief law enforcement official					
Total	38	127,152	111,884	127,722	140,004
Geographic region					
Northeast	3	150,351	126,750	136,500	167,027
North-Central	6	115,627	106,005	111,311	130,904
South	21	120,332	109,367	121,500	132,261
West	8	144,999	130,871	148,825	153,110
Metro type					
Central	26	122,004	111,025	119,553	138,317
Suburban	12	138,306	129,825	133,426	149,944
Form of government					
Mayor-council	9	126,635	95,184	117,000	141,835
Council-manager	27	128,498	117,796	130,440	138,084
Chief librarian					
Total	19	102,808	93,418	101,504	110,025
Geographic region					
North-Central	3	103,594	99,761	101,504	106,382
South	12	93,389	82,798	100,400	102,387
West	3	137,706	127,376	128,438	143,402
Metro type					
Central	12	99,279	87,830	103,174	109,407
Suburban	7	108,859	99,170	100,836	113,941
Form of government					
Council-manager	15	103,681	93,418	100,836	109,060
Clerk					
Total	34	81,786	63,883	84,596	93,263
Geographic region					
North-Central	6	79,760	66,952	80,532	89,815
South	19	75,324	59,382	74,244	89,058
West	7	98,512	89,345	96,232	108,859

Table 1/8   SALARIES OF MUNICIPAL OFFICIALS: JULY–DECEMBER 2007
continued

Title of official	Number of municipalities reporting	Distribution of 2007 salaries			
		Mean ($)	First quartile ($)	Median ($)	Third quartile ($)
100,000–249,999 continued					
Metro type					
Central	21	77,590	60,000	78,258	89,987
Suburban	13	88,564	83,017	89,640	95,674
Form of government					
Mayor-council	5	77,792	58,449	91,520	92,581
Council-manager	27	83,240	68,174	86,174	95,953
Economic development director					
Total	18	116,559	103,451	116,047	128,423
Geographic region					
South	11	111,015	101,832	116,133	125,120
West	4	138,454	124,179	133,368	147,644
Metro type					
Central	13	110,565	101,493	110,147	127,126
Suburban	5	132,141	119,254	123,114	137,881
Form of government					
Mayor-council	5	111,544	105,624	110,147	115,960
Council-manager	13	118,487	103,427	119,254	134,119
Engineer					
Total	30	98,250	81,705	97,028	114,052
Geographic region					
North-Central	5	90,051	78,964	81,600	97,539
South	16	97,065	81,747	95,821	108,337
West	7	116,212	106,932	120,988	126,400
Metro type					
Central	20	92,576	78,641	93,661	106,074
Suburban	10	109,598	96,772	110,670	124,717
Form of government					
Mayor-council	6	91,645	81,705	87,769	102,222
Council-manager	23	100,867	91,696	100,029	120,354
Fire chief					
Total	35	119,087	104,801	119,096	127,667
Geographic region					
North-Central	6	110,361	102,684	104,801	121,443
South	20	112,741	98,756	114,644	123,455
West	7	144,863	133,986	151,258	156,409
Metro type					
Central	25	113,522	99,125	114,192	123,406
Suburban	10	132,998	124,062	128,165	139,029
Form of government					
Mayor-council	7	106,312	90,563	108,612	115,425
Council-manager	26	123,640	113,598	123,347	128,312
Health officer					
Total	12	89,913	75,985	89,682	115,158
Geographic region					
South	10	84,635	73,331	83,270	100,007
Metro type					
Central	9	90,558	77,312	88,164	115,606
Suburban	3	87,977	74,461	102,943	108,975
Form of government					
Council-manager	10	91,335	77,578	89,682	111,992
Human resources director					
Total	38	103,317	93,533	101,755	112,328
Geographic region					
Northeast	3	103,853	97,800	102,000	108,980
North-Central	6	100,831	86,540	102,374	115,836
South	21	98,157	90,543	99,183	109,046
West	8	118,528	102,826	117,438	130,130
Metro type					
Central	25	99,138	93,420	100,402	107,040
Suburban	13	111,354	95,656	111,955	121,008
Form of government					
Mayor-council	9	93,654	84,888	93,510	95,992
Council-manager	27	106,917	97,754	105,216	114,264
Human services director					
Total	12	99,019	80,620	100,533	119,690
Geographic region					
South	9	98,405	81,660	92,622	115,668
Metro type					
Central	9	95,905	77,501	92,622	117,000
Suburban	3	108,363	98,664	115,668	121,714
Form of government					
Mayor-council	3	88,715	69,193	81,660	104,710
Council-manager	9	102,454	84,406	108,443	117,000
Information services director					
Total	35	104,480	93,318	101,555	119,495
Geographic region					
Northeast	3	107,667	103,520	115,000	115,480
North-Central	4	102,440	95,560	102,290	109,170
South	19	96,216	76,088	98,528	106,333
West	9	121,770	100,620	123,571	129,348

Title of official	Number of municipalities reporting	Distribution of 2007 salaries			
		Mean ($)	First quartile ($)	Median ($)	Third quartile ($)
100,000–249,999 continued					
Metro type					
Central	22	107,012	91,608	106,093	124,737
Suburban	13	100,195	94,596	98,528	106,897
Form of government					
Mayor-council	9	103,363	92,040	105,768	107,040
Council-manager	26	104,866	94,861	101,088	123,436
Parks and recreation director					
Total	32	107,306	97,444	105,819	117,775
Geographic region					
North-Central	5	107,343	101,064	101,504	112,757
South	20	99,745	87,973	100,666	112,306
West	5	137,586	118,944	142,100	144,773
Metro type					
Central	20	103,274	94,530	101,418	115,401
Suburban	12	114,026	98,214	113,572	123,723
Form of government					
Mayor-council	7	91,309	80,467	98,280	99,963
Council-manager	23	112,190	99,009	111,336	123,210
Parks superintendent					
Total	26	69,884	59,813	67,863	81,164
Geographic region					
North-Central	5	75,781	64,168	81,515	84,672
South	15	64,923	59,046	64,236	71,185
West	5	83,774	76,340	84,255	88,893
Metro type					
Central	17	65,596	56,992	64,168	74,000
Suburban	9	77,983	75,420	80,112	84,672
Form of government					
Mayor-council	6	66,188	57,372	63,441	74,347
Council-manager	18	70,787	61,052	70,678	83,219
Planning director					
Total	27	101,177	87,519	105,461	117,779
Geographic region					
North-Central	3	94,948	83,038	87,404	103,086
South	17	97,052	74,040	105,396	117,152
West	5	114,818	103,184	105,461	133,070
Metro type					
Central	17	97,652	87,634	105,396	115,960
Suburban	10	107,170	84,800	107,431	130,221
Form of government					
Mayor-council	5	93,832	87,404	89,080	108,950
Council-manager	21	102,089	87,634	105,461	118,406
Primary asst. manager/CAO					
Total	25	117,175	107,700	120,000	140,565
Geographic region					
South	15	112,179	109,591	118,248	137,027
West	6	144,144	132,352	152,840	166,417
Metro type					
Central	17	114,470	111,483	118,248	127,464
Suburban	8	122,922	87,790	141,387	149,927
Form of government					
Mayor-council	3	80,917	61,375	73,932	96,966
Council-manager	22	122,119	112,200	121,908	140,974
Public safety director					
Total	3	85,681	68,378	75,833	98,061
Geographic region	. . .	. . .	. . .	. . .	. . .
Metro type					
Central	3	85,681	68,378	75,833	98,061
Form of government	. . .	. . .	. . .	. . .	. . .
Public works director					
Total	34	118,235	101,945	116,877	130,680
Geographic region					
Northeast	3	111,809	107,713	115,960	117,980
North-Central	5	111,183	104,553	112,416	120,494
South	18	107,545	98,070	110,158	118,287
West	8	149,106	125,482	151,256	170,266
Metro type					
Central	22	117,842	102,060	116,087	125,722
Suburban	12	118,957	103,281	118,538	136,175
Form of government					
Mayor-council	9	108,875	97,843	105,013	115,960
Council-manager	24	121,651	106,596	119,036	132,615
Purchasing director					
Total	24	72,536	65,879	73,693	79,425
Geographic region					
North-Central	4	74,771	69,676	74,899	79,994
South	15	71,616	64,764	72,480	78,414
West	4	71,540	63,192	73,082	81,430
Metro type					
Central	16	71,406	61,921	73,520	78,633
Suburban	8	74,796	70,287	75,414	83,421

Table 1/8   SALARIES OF MUNICIPAL OFFICIALS: JULY–DECEMBER 2007
continued

Title of official	Number of municipalities reporting	Mean ($)	First quartile ($)	Median ($)	Third quartile ($)
100,000–249,999 continued					
Form of government					
Mayor-council	5	69,485	67,071	70,008	70,380
Council-manager	18	73,406	62,771	76,698	81,141
Recreation director					
Total	18	76,244	60,580	76,562	80,985
Geographic region					
South	11	66,946	59,124	69,544	77,270
West	4	105,811	90,089	101,403	117,125
Metro type					
Central	12	69,153	58,461	70,772	78,607
Suburban	6	90,425	77,322	79,164	102,286
Form of government					
Mayor-council	5	70,819	58,512	77,667	81,428
Council-manager	12	78,504	62,268	74,436	82,986
Risk manager					
Total	29	76,485	67,284	77,293	86,985
Geographic region					
North-Central	4	74,644	68,576	73,913	79,981
South	17	72,078	67,284	75,000	83,229
West	8	86,768	79,991	93,723	97,182
Metro type					
Central	18	75,571	70,649	76,548	84,848
Suburban	11	77,979	64,469	86,103	90,625
Form of government					
Mayor-council	5	65,870	59,017	63,765	69,996
Council-manager	22	79,131	72,122	84,309	92,466
Treasurer					
Total	17	83,981	61,166	85,620	100,822
Geographic region					
North-Central	3	79,670	73,840	89,877	90,604
South	8	85,408	61,662	71,059	113,501
West	4	74,791	58,763	73,393	89,421
Metro type					
Central	11	93,260	74,643	95,935	109,630
Suburban	6	66,970	57,030	64,729	72,442
Form of government					
Mayor-council	4	90,878	86,402	98,379	102,854
Council-manager	12	81,191	59,788	71,059	96,076
50,000–99,999					
Chief admin. officer/city manager					
Total	81	143,370	123,380	138,055	156,979
Geographic region					
North-Central	22	127,442	120,072	126,595	133,728
South	43	146,673	130,612	149,520	158,843
West	15	159,112	119,226	142,472	193,637
Metro type					
Central	47	133,048	117,485	128,000	150,000
Suburban	33	159,018	134,971	148,242	176,460
Form of government					
Mayor-council	13	114,705	105,095	115,600	123,188
Council-manager	68	148,850	127,761	148,046	158,610
Chief elected official					
Total	44	40,186	13,794	21,963	66,454
Geographic region					
North-Central	15	41,386	16,312	24,720	63,203
South	19	32,866	13,098	15,828	37,828
West	8	44,921	13,195	25,567	80,937
Metro type					
Central	28	48,994	14,799	37,828	80,937
Suburban	15	25,581	13,186	15,028	24,808
Form of government					
Mayor-council	16	76,877	64,804	81,581	97,383
Council-manager	28	19,220	12,970	14,534	20,585
Chief financial officer					
Total	79	104,772	92,760	102,100	116,035
Geographic region					
North-Central	22	106,461	96,436	105,782	111,730
South	41	100,860	93,600	99,002	111,650
West	14	116,702	89,191	110,212	145,602
Metro type					
Central	48	96,750	87,984	95,889	105,840
Suburban	30	118,108	104,893	113,905	131,957
Form of government					
Mayor-council	16	93,619	87,265	92,545	105,780
Council-manager	63	107,605	94,818	104,730	119,670
Chief law enforcement official					
Total	81	111,721	98,020	109,759	121,467
Geographic region					
North-Central	24	111,362	100,339	115,551	118,484
South	41	106,318	95,553	104,057	118,976
West	14	129,037	99,014	120,999	150,108

Title of official	Number of municipalities reporting	Mean ($)	First quartile ($)	Median ($)	Third quartile ($)
50,000–99,999 continued					
Metro type					
Central	50	102,162	91,685	100,301	111,740
Suburban	31	127,139	115,388	120,000	128,514
Form of government					
Mayor-council	17	99,325	91,244	98,435	109,400
Council-manager	64	115,014	99,839	114,292	125,460
Chief librarian					
Total	29	88,404	70,901	89,630	102,912
Geographic region					
North-Central	8	82,507	79,003	88,007	96,287
South	10	83,346	67,415	85,300	93,504
West	9	100,960	73,688	97,912	125,980
Metro type					
Central	18	78,217	68,040	76,629	91,991
Suburban	10	108,963	96,038	106,011	123,522
Form of government					
Mayor-council	9	81,413	67,086	85,670	94,078
Council-manager	20	91,550	72,700	92,689	110,865
Clerk					
Total	79	68,228	56,710	67,860	79,296
Geographic region					
North-Central	23	65,846	61,077	68,489	74,046
South	40	68,164	57,514	67,684	79,044
West	14	72,503	51,990	70,665	99,980
Metro type					
Central	46	64,043	53,419	62,154	72,568
Suburban	32	74,520	64,199	76,200	88,468
Form of government					
Mayor-council	15	55,267	42,153	57,200	72,487
Council-manager	64	71,265	59,089	69,247	82,973
Economic development director					
Total	38	95,237	76,001	86,981	114,204
Geographic region					
North-Central	8	78,789	76,121	79,295	83,107
South	17	87,802	66,300	85,451	97,824
West	12	117,339	106,787	128,000	132,641
Metro type					
Central	18	83,804	70,551	81,618	95,826
Suburban	20	105,528	81,942	105,785	129,530
Form of government					
Mayor-council	8	85,536	73,175	84,357	96,204
Council-manager	30	97,824	77,447	89,996	125,755
Engineer					
Total	70	94,937	81,676	92,107	104,479
Geographic region					
North-Central	18	92,825	91,735	96,357	100,631
South	38	91,796	80,896	89,109	103,769
West	12	109,732	81,892	106,099	136,456
Metro type					
Central	41	85,411	80,039	87,880	95,487
Suburban	28	109,361	94,859	108,684	125,874
Form of government					
Mayor-council	12	85,968	80,910	83,345	89,073
Council-manager	58	96,792	84,869	95,718	105,903
Fire chief					
Total	81	106,426	93,648	106,330	114,354
Geographic region					
North-Central	23	107,197	100,643	106,811	114,291
South	42	101,841	91,655	102,766	112,118
West	14	121,453	97,910	109,197	153,284
Metro type					
Central	51	98,593	89,946	97,157	106,878
Suburban	29	121,474	107,994	113,340	128,460
Form of government					
Mayor-council	18	97,921	90,470	98,362	107,730
Council-manager	63	108,855	94,348	106,642	118,984
Health officer					
Total	13	78,456	68,634	76,764	88,055
Geographic region					
North-Central	4	93,185	81,259	86,400	98,325
South	7	78,663	64,131	76,764	85,158
Metro type					
Central	8	77,142	70,754	77,766	86,445
Suburban	5	80,559	68,634	70,805	88,055
Form of government					
Council-manager	11	83,944	69,720	78,768	89,802
Human resources director					
Total	79	94,765	80,494	92,422	104,099
Geographic region					
North-Central	21	96,690	85,062	97,011	103,176
South	42	90,752	80,132	90,066	100,486
West	15	104,627	75,196	83,040	138,653

Table 1/8   **SALARIES OF MUNICIPAL OFFICIALS: JULY–DECEMBER 2007**
continued

Title of official	Number of municipalities reporting	Distribution of 2007 salaries			
		Mean ($)	First quartile ($)	Median ($)	Third quartile ($)
50,000–99,999 continued					
Metro type					
Central	47	86,332	77,078	83,040	96,446
Suburban	31	108,264	93,693	102,918	126,205
Form of government					
Mayor-council	15	81,013	74,000	81,246	85,706
Council-manager	64	97,989	81,929	95,532	107,506
Human services director					
Total	17	82,158	75,012	83,244	87,643
Geographic region					
South	14	77,958	74,931	81,498	86,419
Metro type					
Central	11	76,608	68,995	81,000	85,050
Suburban	6	92,332	85,262	87,213	91,601
Form of government					
Council-manager	17	82,158	75,012	83,244	87,643
Information services director					
Total	72	92,043	80,519	91,322	102,736
Geographic region					
North-Central	17	89,251	80,579	85,000	98,356
South	40	91,958	80,443	94,782	102,736
West	13	96,541	63,584	86,027	124,080
Metro type					
Central	44	86,653	78,403	86,466	97,525
Suburban	27	102,213	85,465	98,356	119,779
Form of government					
Mayor-council	14	76,977	72,902	78,559	84,907
Council-manager	58	95,679	82,077	95,862	107,145
Parks and recreation director					
Total	64	91,641	77,223	88,921	104,063
Geographic region					
North-Central	15	97,724	87,276	95,514	106,089
South	41	86,389	73,947	85,010	95,532
West	7	112,434	85,210	104,862	141,801
Metro type					
Central	40	84,409	73,005	82,215	93,232
Suburban	23	104,356	87,953	104,501	115,690
Form of government					
Mayor-council	10	80,598	70,806	81,505	90,507
Council-manager	54	93,686	79,071	90,661	104,980
Parks superintendent					
Total	55	66,538	55,313	67,662	72,720
Geographic region					
North-Central	14	77,387	69,896	74,345	78,107
South	30	58,238	52,699	59,001	65,399
West	10	76,007	66,876	69,600	91,733
Metro type					
Central	32	61,499	52,131	60,819	68,756
Suburban	23	73,549	67,980	71,598	77,503
Form of government					
Mayor-council	9	72,369	67,662	71,232	75,718
Council-manager	46	65,397	54,771	64,698	71,792
Planning director					
Total	69	93,486	80,442	90,100	103,350
Geographic region					
North-Central	17	96,728	90,100	92,929	102,078
South	38	89,890	79,230	88,910	101,537
West	13	100,519	76,267	86,154	134,450
Metro type					
Central	43	85,061	77,451	86,154	91,545
Suburban	25	109,225	92,929	104,616	129,650
Form of government					
Mayor-council	13	79,950	70,000	83,600	88,992
Council-manager	56	96,628	82,398	92,329	106,683
Primary asst. manager/CAO					
Total	55	112,648	101,585	111,000	122,310
Geographic region					
North-Central	15	103,587	94,721	105,857	116,799
South	30	113,724	102,479	112,419	124,035
West	10	123,010	103,095	111,406	132,126
Metro type					
Central	28	107,271	100,896	108,524	116,018
Suburban	27	118,223	102,418	120,337	132,174
Form of government					
Mayor-council	5	94,216	100,582	102,667	103,176
Council-manager	50	114,491	102,479	112,419	124,035
Public safety director					
Total	8	88,873	70,078	92,411	100,647
Geographic region					
North-Central	4	99,368	92,683	101,257	107,942
South	3	74,053	64,343	68,445	80,959

Title of official	Number of municipalities reporting	Distribution of 2007 salaries			
		Mean ($)	First quartile ($)	Median ($)	Third quartile ($)
50,000–99,999 continued					
Metro type					
Central	4	81,703	68,027	82,047	95,724
Suburban	3	97,606	84,241	100,037	112,187
Form of government					
Mayor-council	4	78,921	68,027	80,986	91,880
Council-manager	4	98,824	92,139	101,257	107,942
Public works director					
Total	70	107,517	94,997	104,157	117,766
Geographic region					
North-Central	20	109,543	98,985	113,253	117,717
South	35	102,183	92,057	99,972	112,651
West	13	121,572	102,921	113,784	137,196
Metro type					
Central	39	98,230	89,215	97,307	104,948
Suburban	30	120,027	110,398	115,519	130,662
Form of government					
Mayor-council	16	92,637	83,635	94,760	99,369
Council-manager	54	111,926	97,613	110,067	122,807
Purchasing director					
Total	42	66,302	56,395	66,246	72,476
Geographic region					
North-Central	6	66,738	59,926	64,974	67,676
South	31	67,594	58,065	66,903	73,231
West	3	57,382	50,703	53,022	61,881
Metro type					
Central	30	65,417	55,993	66,246	70,526
Suburban	11	70,345	61,880	68,640	80,820
Form of government					
Mayor-council	7	58,316	49,242	53,022	70,003
Council-manager	35	67,899	58,618	66,903	72,303
Recreation director					
Total	41	72,500	57,090	67,300	83,264
Geographic region					
North-Central	10	79,481	67,190	78,025	85,909
South	20	63,354	53,125	59,820	71,123
West	10	86,227	66,785	80,540	112,467
Metro type					
Central	24	66,097	55,143	65,484	71,816
Suburban	16	83,066	59,946	84,535	99,992
Form of government					
Mayor-council	11	63,945	54,307	62,159	71,977
Council-manager	30	75,636	59,694	70,924	85,909
Risk manager					
Total	47	67,571	54,468	65,219	79,964
Geographic region					
North-Central	9	76,995	69,953	79,129	81,619
South	31	62,967	53,941	60,453	69,229
West	6	82,826	51,107	87,060	105,910
Metro type					
Central	33	59,372	52,000	56,100	68,432
Suburban	14	86,899	72,500	83,642	98,592
Form of government					
Mayor-council	6	67,240	60,193	64,259	71,790
Council-manager	41	67,620	54,143	67,180	80,004
Treasurer					
Total	16	71,183	68,044	75,109	79,361
Geographic region					
North-Central	4	75,062	70,787	73,717	77,992
South	8	60,653	55,123	66,123	74,675
West	3	91,550	81,815	85,613	98,317
Metro type					
Central	12	67,440	68,044	72,547	77,136
Suburban	4	82,411	73,109	80,120	89,422
Form of government					
Mayor-council	5	64,542	62,280	78,017	78,801
Council-manager	11	74,201	70,278	74,241	78,812
25,000–49,999					
Chief admin. officer/city manager					
Total	146	130,088	111,682	131,461	144,606
Geographic region					
Northeast	13	112,439	108,000	115,684	124,041
North-Central	49	122,575	108,270	120,973	138,146
South	68	135,169	119,906	135,582	150,659
West	16	145,838	100,268	140,979	181,828
Metro type					
Central	26	122,257	109,411	123,605	137,113
Suburban	95	136,206	115,822	136,500	153,418
Independent	25	114,980	98,855	116,459	130,416
Form of government					
Mayor-council	17	106,108	89,500	105,000	116,459
Council-manager	125	134,274	115,000	133,956	145,948

Table 1/8 continued **SALARIES OF MUNICIPAL OFFICIALS: JULY–DECEMBER 2007**

Title of official	Number of municipalities reporting	Distribution of 2007 salaries			
		Mean ($)	First quartile ($)	Median ($)	Third quartile ($)
25,000–49,999 continued					
Chief elected official					
Total	46	43,489	14,027	21,361	73,689
Geographic region					
Northeast	4	81,320	72,699	98,513	107,134
North-Central	17	39,676	13,702	20,000	71,749
South	19	33,434	12,232	17,369	40,755
West	6	60,913	19,536	59,756	99,776
Metro type					
Central	11	50,098	14,867	26,656	79,559
Suburban	26	39,318	14,027	19,253	61,762
Independent	9	47,461	15,000	54,855	71,160
Form of government					
Mayor-council	19	62,122	21,709	71,749	90,322
Council-manager	25	29,813	12,000	15,000	25,750
Chief financial officer					
Total	128	96,670	84,673	95,706	109,151
Geographic region					
Northeast	11	81,263	72,221	87,179	95,788
North-Central	41	96,869	87,356	96,408	108,534
South	61	97,723	79,372	95,556	111,956
West	15	103,145	90,943	97,562	118,834
Metro type					
Central	26	89,309	78,934	88,705	91,668
Suburban	80	103,137	92,687	102,684	115,367
Independent	22	81,857	70,632	78,308	93,272
Form of government					
Mayor-council	19	84,260	73,917	87,179	94,952
Council-manager	107	99,169	87,120	99,323	112,098
Chief law enforcement official					
Total	136	102,240	87,945	101,511	115,262
Geographic region					
Northeast	14	104,237	94,979	103,845	109,956
North-Central	44	100,205	88,973	100,494	111,543
South	69	101,352	87,086	101,021	115,000
West	9	115,888	97,562	117,790	134,559
Metro type					
Central	29	92,565	83,356	91,083	96,678
Suburban	83	110,358	100,494	107,016	123,078
Independent	24	85,856	78,528	81,882	95,529
Form of government					
Mayor-council	23	94,418	84,298	93,360	99,781
Council-manager	109	104,236	91,589	104,628	118,626
Chief librarian					
Total	68	72,580	60,536	72,387	83,910
Geographic region					
Northeast	12	74,204	61,797	74,255	85,230
North-Central	14	73,506	63,677	69,565	86,664
South	37	70,387	57,257	71,821	80,453
West	5	82,313	70,057	77,277	99,683
Metro type					
Central	13	71,268	57,859	73,986	81,603
Suburban	44	74,655	64,050	73,172	84,898
Independent	11	65,829	56,128	62,428	69,670
Form of government					
Mayor-council	8	$60,233	46,574	62,897	71,351
Council-manager	58	$74,183	61,710	72,417	84,531
Clerk					
Total	133	65,780	52,637	65,940	77,512
Geographic region					
Northeast	12	64,658	53,794	60,299	73,426
North-Central	42	61,857	52,437	65,420	71,217
South	66	66,212	51,808	67,184	78,983
West	13	77,298	60,898	69,898	88,777
Metro type					
Central	27	58,741	46,239	58,755	69,423
Suburban	86	70,399	58,487	70,930	78,803
Independent	20	55,421	46,307	53,352	65,934
Form of government					
Mayor-council	18	61,029	41,988	64,942	74,237
Council-manager	113	66,599	54,386	66,514	77,812
Economic development director					
Total	63	85,387	69,450	88,051	97,589
Geographic region					
North-Central	19	76,344	60,244	76,775	93,888
South	33	85,957	70,093	90,314	97,264
West	9	106,730	88,051	104,520	124,161
Metro type					
Central	11	77,424	69,324	77,625	81,196
Suburban	45	89,426	71,687	93,682	98,820
Independent	7	71,938	58,806	71,145	88,863

Title of official	Number of municipalities reporting	Distribution of 2007 salaries			
		Mean ($)	First quartile ($)	Median ($)	Third quartile ($)
25,000–49,999 continued					
Form of government					
Mayor-council	12	82,215	68,323	87,921	95,879
Council-manager	51	86,133	69,450	90,108	97,589
Engineer					
Total	113	88,844	78,000	89,148	98,384
Geographic region					
Northeast	10	71,150	70,036	76,932	81,967
North-Central	32	89,038	79,380	90,447	98,063
South	57	88,872	78,000	89,148	97,895
West	14	100,927	89,773	99,034	122,760
Metro type					
Central	25	84,727	78,853	83,576	91,074
Suburban	69	92,162	79,501	92,518	102,000
Independent	19	82,212	74,917	81,498	92,389
Form of government					
Mayor-council	18	83,726	74,878	85,078	91,769
Council-manager	92	90,261	78,047	90,196	99,617
Fire chief					
Total	123	94,275	80,952	92,525	108,682
Geographic region					
Northeast	7	93,227	84,750	92,761	103,787
North-Central	45	91,185	80,940	89,200	98,508
South	61	94,048	78,595	91,938	111,593
West	10	110,302	98,511	112,550	125,251
Metro type					
Central	25	86,488	80,940	83,805	91,938
Suburban	73	101,673	90,172	104,978	115,000
Independent	25	80,462	68,839	77,245	93,124
Form of government					
Mayor-council	19	85,080	74,450	85,170	93,967
Council-manager	100	96,298	81,913	94,488	111,592
Health officer					
Total	22	59,733	49,675	61,629	70,100
Geographic region					
Northeast	7	64,292	55,649	70,221	75,092
North-Central	6	65,122	62,757	67,156	69,172
South	9	52,595	39,868	55,953	61,860
Metro type					
Central	7	67,144	63,690	66,835	73,457
Suburban	12	56,186	39,294	57,514	68,746
Independent	3	56,632	49,838	55,953	63,087
Form of government					
Mayor-council	3	71,463	68,607	69,737	73,457
Council-manager	17	55,994	43,722	56,934	65,520
Human resources director					
Total	133	82,401	63,837	82,022	97,374
Geographic region					
Northeast	11	69,983	61,101	72,635	79,893
North-Central	39	78,742	63,101	83,886	93,116
South	67	81,925	63,199	81,845	98,118
West	16	101,853	84,450	111,673	119,527
Metro type					
Central	26	75,644	60,945	78,219	86,475
Suburban	85	87,594	67,888	89,457	103,932
Independent	22	70,326	57,351	67,007	84,450
Form of government					
Mayor-council	21	69,442	56,031	63,137	86,524
Council-manager	108	85,541	67,459	85,604	99,817
Human services director					
Total	27	70,463	60,831	67,464	84,520
Geographic region					
Northeast	5	82,646	74,840	82,832	89,240
North-Central	4	76,175	71,585	86,767	91,358
South	16	64,916	55,265	63,902	72,020
Metro type					
Central	6	70,359	60,542	63,865	82,933
Suburban	16	75,692	62,154	77,267	85,909
Independent	5	53,855	49,052	50,400	66,619
Form of government					
Council-manager	25	70,641	61,675	67,464	84,240
Information services director					
Total	99	81,210	68,197	82,022	91,908
Geographic region					
Northeast	9	73,525	63,654	71,125	84,772
North-Central	29	82,177	75,695	83,302	92,015
South	52	79,486	65,652	79,000	90,375
West	9	95,738	82,022	93,530	112,608
Metro type					
Central	22	73,725	60,891	72,363	82,316
Suburban	64	86,218	73,466	85,743	95,506
Independent	13	69,219	51,750	66,830	84,968

Table 1/8   SALARIES OF MUNICIPAL OFFICIALS: JULY–DECEMBER 2007
continued

Title of official	Number of municipalities reporting	Distribution of 2007 salaries			
		Mean ($)	First quartile ($)	Median ($)	Third quartile ($)
25,000–49,999 continued					
Form of government					
Mayor-council	11	71,640	59,027	67,754	84,139
Council-manager	85	82,709	69,709	82,548	92,695
Parks and recreation director					
Total	105	87,199	70,390	86,144	100,506
Geographic region					
Northeast	6	73,641	66,923	70,566	80,076
North-Central	30	87,053	73,813	88,262	100,771
South	58	86,406	70,499	83,960	98,728
West	11	99,173	87,904	99,683	114,955
Metro type					
Central	24	79,799	66,250	79,475	90,532
Suburban	69	92,319	80,280	92,685	103,376
Independent	12	72,558	61,672	68,559	82,644
Form of government					
Mayor-council	15	75,654	64,949	80,923	84,999
Council-manager	89	89,115	71,223	89,461	101,717
Parks superintendent					
Total	90	59,182	47,300	59,325	68,680
Geographic region					
Northeast	7	63,837	54,425	69,470	73,539
North-Central	20	61,599	53,851	63,289	68,715
South	55	55,159	44,585	53,400	64,362
West	8	76,724	64,678	76,529	87,029
Metro type					
Central	18	52,312	44,847	49,959	62,447
Suburban	57	63,611	53,400	62,686	72,594
Independent	15	50,591	38,724	48,318	59,886
Form of government					
Mayor-council	11	52,062	42,399	50,094	61,134
Council-manager	76	60,046	48,503	60,217	68,865
Planning director					
Total	103	85,726	72,630	86,740	96,732
Geographic region					
Northeast	9	77,702	75,199	76,417	89,046
North-Central	27	83,621	70,517	83,686	95,120
South	54	85,230	72,399	86,404	97,318
West	13	97,710	85,422	95,400	113,498
Metro type					
Central	23	77,861	67,305	78,200	89,676
Suburban	64	91,728	79,057	90,539	100,812
Independent	16	73,023	59,379	68,537	83,822
Form of government					
Mayor-council	15	77,117	65,691	76,417	93,682
Council-manager	86	87,551	75,511	87,508	97,962
Primary asst. manager/CAO					
Total	76	93,558	73,497	94,088	109,618
Geographic region					
Northeast	8	86,111	77,873	88,205	96,518
North-Central	18	92,467	79,725	93,349	106,120
South	43	91,130	65,092	94,422	114,188
West	7	119,789	87,477	114,442	159,097
Metro type					
Central	13	85,736	66,248	84,687	103,360
Suburban	53	96,289	76,775	96,062	111,197
Independent	10	89,254	73,346	86,163	109,602
Form of government					
Mayor-council	6	97,001	93,061	103,415	110,671
Council-manager	68	93,741	73,150	94,088	109,601
Public safety director					
Total	19	90,418	80,910	95,321	101,791
Geographic region					
North-Central	12	96,278	92,208	98,113	105,833
South	4	84,698	71,738	85,184	98,144
Metro type					
Suburban	13	95,827	88,517	98,106	107,931
Independent	4	74,635	70,327	80,910	85,219
Form of government					
Mayor-council	4	81,989	75,970	80,663	86,682
Council-manager	14	96,327	89,372	97,985	107,232
Public works director					
Total	139	98,154	84,236	98,328	113,287
Geographic region					
Northeast	15	87,654	80,515	89,046	93,646
North-Central	48	100,011	90,248	98,558	110,813
South	62	96,177	80,449	98,570	112,073
West	14	111,794	99,223	116,790	121,800
Metro type					
Central	28	93,114	81,694	92,754	101,981
Suburban	91	103,606	89,439	105,706	118,449
Independent	20	80,404	67,955	77,479	94,441

Title of official	Number of municipalities reporting	Distribution of 2007 salaries			
		Mean ($)	First quartile ($)	Median ($)	Third quartile ($)
25,000–49,999 continued					
Form of government					
Mayor-council	20	87,667	79,459	86,087	97,753
Council-manager	116	100,251	85,458	102,938	114,437
Purchasing director					
Total	46	65,135	57,919	65,912	71,806
Geographic region					
Northeast	7	62,283	56,758	60,515	66,980
North-Central	6	65,868	58,458	71,326	74,997
South	29	62,917	57,848	63,327	69,700
West	4	85,104	77,324	87,999	95,780
Metro type					
Central	12	66,350	63,565	69,639	72,839
Suburban	28	67,322	59,587	64,024	69,807
Independent	6	52,496	35,659	40,169	64,197
Form of government					
Mayor-council	6	68,314	61,972	72,457	77,509
Council-manager	39	65,413	57,990	65,376	70,679
Recreation director					
Total	60	64,318	54,734	62,673	69,862
Geographic region					
Northeast	8	59,791	53,255	60,801	67,263
North-Central	13	63,125	56,992	61,547	68,744
South	33	63,238	53,622	62,026	69,300
West	6	78,874	63,998	75,837	96,850
Metro type					
Central	9	55,186	48,710	56,820	61,175
Suburban	43	68,540	59,390	65,322	75,590
Independent	8	51,894	44,392	53,377	59,702
Form of government					
Mayor-council	5	62,982	62,905	64,660	68,744
Council-manager	53	64,739	55,104	62,026	70,017
Risk manager					
Total	40	64,994	52,770	64,841	73,365
Geographic region					
Northeast	3	67,551	64,698	71,491	72,375
North-Central	8	63,943	57,198	62,101	73,501
South	25	59,550	49,139	62,569	70,656
West	4	99,210	94,691	97,961	102,480
Metro type					
Central	12	57,031	50,376	55,915	64,576
Suburban	24	72,337	61,743	71,162	80,309
Independent	4	44,827	37,139	40,663	48,351
Form of government					
Mayor-council	5	54,338	42,155	59,266	63,611
Council-manager	35	66,517	53,311	69,800	73,537
Treasurer					
Total	23	63,137	48,100	69,472	78,712
Geographic region					
Northeast	4	80,078	78,077	80,742	82,743
North-Central	12	53,678	47,019	53,310	70,429
South	5	82,308	75,705	76,957	82,748
Metro type					
Central	6	63,505	48,505	62,563	81,903
Suburban	12	62,034	47,259	70,266	79,420
Independent	5	65,345	57,200	69,472	76,957
Form of government					
Mayor-council	4	45,294	37,487	46,518	54,325
Council-manager	17	66,481	49,420	75,250	82,465
10,000–24,999					
Chief admin. officer/city manager					
Total	302	105,493	91,373	104,347	118,078
Geographic region					
Northeast	35	104,133	87,879	104,475	119,153
North-Central	111	100,648	89,914	101,854	110,409
South	139	106,190	91,476	104,580	121,580
West	17	134,229	110,000	131,914	150,000
Metro type					
Central	5	109,423	94,458	105,575	116,175
Suburban	191	109,753	95,561	107,513	122,906
Independent	106	97,632	89,003	98,881	106,729
Form of government					
Mayor-council	71	95,131	85,650	98,036	107,182
Council-manager	219	109,126	95,199	105,900	120,981
Commission	5	85,637	82,000	82,400	89,787
Town meeting	6	109,282	96,212	107,169	122,640
Chief elected official					
Total	106	41,064	15,769	37,416	63,303
Geographic region					
Northeast	20	55,141	38,389	44,828	73,870
North-Central	45	40,359	17,508	31,159	62,896

Table 1/8 continued — SALARIES OF MUNICIPAL OFFICIALS: JULY–DECEMBER 2007

Title of official	Number of municipalities reporting	Mean ($)	First quartile ($)	Median ($)	Third quartile ($)
10,000–24,999 continued					
South	38	36,388	13,274	19,950	58,386
West	3	17,034	14,684	14,941	18,338
Metro type					
Suburban	70	42,332	16,873	32,477	64,610
Independent	34	38,286	15,356	39,125	55,304
Form of government					
Mayor-council	66	47,565	24,418	45,063	67,880
Council-manager	29	20,622	12,000	13,494	19,562
Commission	4	23,113	17,888	20,825	26,050
Town meeting	6	77,175	68,903	74,095	82,112
Chief financial officer					
Total	284	78,560	66,944	77,627	90,750
Geographic region					
Northeast	38	75,491	64,402	76,443	91,140
North-Central	100	79,113	71,366	81,802	91,054
South	130	76,479	64,044	74,594	86,002
West	16	99,294	80,468	97,730	113,238
Metro type					
Central	4	79,345	67,160	79,802	91,987
Suburban	184	81,374	69,249	81,772	94,651
Independent	96	73,133	63,473	72,872	82,484
Form of government					
Mayor-council	81	72,416	60,445	74,705	85,744
Council-manager	190	80,984	67,917	78,931	91,945
Commission	3	65,425	61,638	67,275	70,138
Town meeting	8	87,021	84,730	87,575	96,359
Chief law enforcement official					
Total	329	84,391	70,536	83,013	97,448
Geographic region					
Northeast	46	95,556	78,178	95,499	106,311
North-Central	119	84,518	73,870	85,842	96,191
South	149	78,794	65,952	76,243	89,419
West	15	104,733	82,191	102,043	125,031
Metro type					
Central	5	84,913	78,237	79,058	82,389
Suburban	209	90,633	76,648	90,856	102,712
Independent	115	73,023	62,404	72,369	82,506
Form of government					
Mayor-council	109	80,654	64,809	80,724	94,058
Council-manager	201	85,879	72,450	83,521	97,000
Commission	7	70,542	59,403	68,000	86,696
Town meeting	9	96,838	89,891	98,430	100,299
Rep. town meeting	3	115,383	103,574	108,733	123,867
Chief librarian					
Total	93	60,470	47,490	57,179	72,509
Geographic region					
Northeast	23	68,947	59,094	65,453	78,677
North-Central	30	62,189	53,631	59,336	71,816
South	35	52,538	39,342	46,635	59,779
West	5	66,685	47,490	51,209	88,525
Metro type					
Suburban	58	62,259	50,015	59,094	75,170
Independent	33	55,922	46,104	53,970	64,967
Form of government					
Mayor-council	22	64,853	52,253	64,771	74,883
Council-manager	58	57,458	44,952	53,737	66,624
Town meeting	9	69,412	61,432	65,453	81,991
Clerk					
Total	269	54,269	43,279	53,523	64,000
Geographic region					
Northeast	41	56,132	48,312	56,500	66,136
North-Central	72	52,530	43,262	54,341	63,060
South	141	52,461	42,284	51,493	61,119
West	15	74,520	58,593	72,450	81,838
Metro type					
Central	6	48,201	45,288	47,823	50,583
Suburban	171	57,462	46,090	58,565	67,988
Independent	92	48,730	41,520	48,690	55,981
Form of government					
Mayor-council	72	50,434	37,611	54,826	63,835
Council-manager	180	55,434	44,976	53,127	64,373
Commission	3	55,224	44,541	47,561	62,076
Town meeting	11	58,985	54,574	58,155	63,499
Rep. town meeting	3	58,201	53,184	60,700	64,468
Economic development director					
Total	96	72,570	63,105	72,000	83,417
Geographic region					
Northeast	11	60,915	55,353	67,266	76,201
North-Central	35	73,117	64,410	73,355	78,885
South	44	73,065	60,324	71,611	87,379
West	6	87,115	71,831	89,826	99,182
10,000–24,999 continued					
Metro type					
Suburban	67	73,348	60,852	72,000	85,587
Independent	27	70,520	64,920	72,000	80,886
Form of government					
Mayor-council	27	68,793	60,693	71,448	77,992
Council-manager	63	74,715	64,668	72,000	84,870
Town meeting	3	56,600	41,144	60,000	73,757
Engineer					
Total	132	74,439	61,891	74,439	85,762
Geographic region					
Northeast	18	79,885	59,505	75,835	92,260
North-Central	50	71,954	62,296	74,882	83,915
South	54	72,466	61,571	71,466	83,414
West	10	87,710	72,110	91,349	97,560
Metro type					
Central	3	61,640	59,742	65,354	65,396
Suburban	76	78,558	66,500	80,274	92,201
Independent	53	69,256	57,148	67,698	77,632
Form of government					
Mayor-council	39	71,572	57,148	77,632	86,288
Council-manager	85	75,935	63,000	73,733	84,872
Town meeting	4	77,590	68,307	73,873	83,155
Fire chief					
Total	249	76,954	63,855	73,780	87,560
Geographic region					
Northeast	23	78,568	67,138	76,066	92,724
North-Central	88	78,163	64,182	77,873	89,763
South	126	73,625	61,314	70,706	82,859
West	12	99,944	76,936	92,693	112,941
Metro type					
Central	5	78,925	72,613	76,243	89,383
Suburban	146	83,298	69,148	83,398	95,355
Independent	98	67,402	59,016	66,603	74,657
Form of government					
Mayor-council	77	71,058	58,332	73,308	84,686
Council-manager	157	79,047	65,431	73,537	86,832
Commission	5	79,374	65,004	73,179	100,212
Town meeting	7	85,193	74,138	91,623	95,554
Rep. town meeting	3	95,502	93,280	95,866	97,906
Health officer					
Total	38	54,747	38,287	51,200	73,286
Geographic region					
Northeast	17	63,041	49,637	60,631	77,874
North-Central	8	57,671	45,929	49,866	70,726
South	13	42,101	27,600	38,028	42,739
Metro type					
Suburban	25	56,555	42,743	58,656	75,910
Independent	12	48,792	35,263	41,787	53,076
Form of government					
Mayor-council	11	50,263	34,277	46,072	60,659
Council-manager	17	53,444	37,057	42,739	61,511
Town meeting	7	63,894	57,671	75,281	78,085
Rep. town meeting	3	57,223	54,147	58,656	61,016
Human resources director					
Total	173	62,503	48,578	62,691	74,940
Geographic region					
Northeast	16	57,938	52,193	60,234	69,186
North-Central	46	63,792	51,475	64,069	77,558
South	101	61,728	47,632	61,511	72,360
West	10	71,701	62,390	67,346	81,103
Metro type					
Central	6	66,343	50,986	59,613	84,146
Suburban	96	65,849	52,658	64,896	78,228
Independent	71	57,654	45,810	58,790	68,539
Form of government					
Mayor-council	46	52,738	39,520	49,990	63,149
Council-manager	118	66,675	54,240	65,617	76,656
Town meeting	6	60,686	55,658	60,234	68,824
Human services director					
Total	32	63,700	51,043	60,115	78,851
Geographic region					
Northeast	8	66,042	60,241	60,717	68,761
North-Central	6	65,891	40,431	51,432	82,260
South	17	60,573	47,607	58,488	77,184
Metro type					
Suburban	22	72,366	58,831	72,123	84,581
Independent	9	44,304	35,237	37,929	52,188
Form of government					
Mayor-council	6	55,151	40,431	51,432	59,994

Table 1/8   SALARIES OF MUNICIPAL OFFICIALS: JULY–DECEMBER 2007
continued

Title of official	Number of municipalities reporting	Mean ($)	First quartile ($)	Median ($)	Third quartile ($)
10,000–24,999 continued					
Council-manager	21	65,433	52,188	58,884	82,572
Town meeting	5	66,677	60,368	60,622	65,811
Information services director					
Total	96	66,639	55,909	62,752	74,851
Geographic region					
Northeast	12	69,071	60,577	72,821	78,022
North-Central	23	66,859	57,433	60,606	74,293
South	54	64,415	53,575	61,146	72,990
West	7	78,901	67,331	74,744	87,528
Metro type					
Central	5	63,383	57,372	67,640	74,421
Suburban	56	71,387	58,359	69,399	80,244
Independent	35	59,506	52,013	60,008	67,179
Form of government					
Mayor-council	21	65,038	53,200	60,008	74,421
Council-manager	68	67,124	56,907	63,092	73,756
Town meeting	4	68,699	67,389	76,712	78,022
Parks and recreation director					
Total	190	68,443	55,708	66,650	79,691
Geographic region					
Northeast	25	59,459	50,402	62,251	68,287
North-Central	65	68,713	55,598	71,523	81,584
South	95	68,446	56,181	65,916	77,052
West	5	109,810	102,313	107,110	113,076
Metro type					
Central	6	71,688	60,283	67,788	76,842
Suburban	116	72,059	59,869	69,783	85,786
Independent	68	61,990	53,138	61,802	71,346
Form of government					
Mayor-council	42	61,454	48,602	61,258	75,932
Council-manager	139	70,721	57,100	67,963	84,267
Town meeting	7	69,016	61,484	66,415	71,221
Parks superintendent					
Total	137	49,635	39,030	47,358	58,542
Geographic region					
Northeast	15	53,960	44,280	51,300	64,759
North-Central	38	54,684	46,159	55,322	64,519
South	77	45,003	36,621	44,000	51,809
West	7	63,913	54,203	63,910	73,038
Metro type					
Central	4	52,051	42,071	49,914	59,895
Suburban	74	52,981	40,529	52,181	64,830
Independent	59	45,275	38,354	45,636	52,952
Form of government					
Mayor-council	36	46,945	38,155	46,506	55,119
Council-manager	95	50,429	39,291	47,358	59,074
Commission	3	41,910	35,057	53,114	54,365
Planning director					
Total	150	71,471	59,967	68,193	81,268
Geographic region					
Northeast	24	65,976	57,004	63,903	77,450
North-Central	40	70,836	62,131	67,846	79,364
South	80	71,683	59,937	69,068	81,997
West	6	94,862	79,956	106,998	122,045
Metro type					
Central	4	70,266	63,096	64,859	72,030
Suburban	93	74,718	62,771	71,746	84,968
Independent	53	65,865	55,827	63,059	72,264
Form of government					
Mayor-council	35	67,436	60,176	67,740	74,431
Council-manager	103	73,644	60,129	69,628	85,384
Town meeting	9	63,389	53,428	63,532	76,735
Primary asst. manager/CAO					
Total	132	79,801	65,581	77,968	91,607
Geographic region					
Northeast	15	73,297	60,644	67,085	83,954
North-Central	51	76,311	66,457	77,850	85,948
South	60	80,251	64,769	78,909	93,397
West	6	121,217	109,494	122,862	137,180
Metro type					
Suburban	99	82,328	65,937	80,000	96,230
Independent	32	71,953	65,287	71,782	83,556
Form of government					
Mayor-council	24	69,439	56,621	72,509	86,377
Council-manager	104	82,105	67,113	79,924	92,228
Town meeting	3	88,806	78,269	89,452	99,666
Public safety director					
Total	48	73,617	62,070	72,623	91,587

Title of official	Number of municipalities reporting	Mean ($)	First quartile ($)	Median ($)	Third quartile ($)
10,000–24,999 continued					
Geographic region					
Northeast	3	85,818	65,887	87,192	106,436
North-Central	32	71,251	62,070	71,465	91,216
South	13	76,626	64,200	72,958	93,100
Metro type					
Suburban	35	73,775	51,799	77,155	92,730
Independent	12	73,079	67,672	71,348	76,508
Form of government					
Mayor-council	19	63,989	40,711	69,108	84,221
Council-manager	28	81,187	70,716	73,994	93,693
Public works director					
Total	318	79,425	67,742	78,749	92,388
Geographic region					
Northeast	48	80,432	70,315	78,559	89,158
North-Central	122	83,011	71,597	83,362	95,145
South	134	73,620	61,286	72,532	84,328
West	14	100,277	78,931	98,560	116,724
Metro type					
Central	5	85,523	73,775	84,190	97,947
Suburban	206	83,221	71,491	81,156	95,921
Independent	107	71,831	61,641	72,252	83,362
Form of government					
Mayor-council	102	76,551	65,929	77,919	89,570
Council-manager	197	80,682	67,275	78,567	93,876
Commission	6	68,860	62,862	76,722	79,538
Town meeting	10	86,837	79,980	86,945	98,900
Rep. town meeting ..	3	90,942	81,335	85,670	97,914
Purchasing director					
Total	25	49,453	36,747	52,840	63,901
Geographic region					
Northeast	6	56,604	55,577	63,844	70,213
South	17	43,942	32,388	43,947	55,164
Metro type					
Suburban	15	52,349	41,016	55,164	65,397
Independent	9	42,532	28,912	37,704	54,968
Form of government					
Mayor-council	9	48,497	25,871	52,840	67,233
Council-manager	15	49,064	37,277	51,384	56,131
Recreation director					
Total	77	53,683	43,400	52,000	63,987
Geographic region					
Northeast	18	54,699	45,339	54,216	65,393
North-Central	26	48,284	31,260	49,257	63,005
South	28	55,323	43,407	52,108	66,328
West	5	68,920	51,132	63,987	82,896
Metro type					
Central	3	53,942	49,470	50,803	56,844
Suburban	52	57,078	42,341	59,068	68,540
Independent	22	45,625	43,402	44,819	49,375
Form of government					
Mayor-council	23	45,893	34,270	50,814	57,646
Council-manager	47	57,954	44,661	57,090	70,239
Town meeting	5	47,883	36,637	42,593	67,085
Risk manager					
Total	31	57,186	41,622	52,994	74,887
Geographic region					
North-Central	7	67,822	53,214	74,833	80,291
South	22	50,879	40,251	45,573	58,922
Metro type					
Suburban	16	64,798	51,166	61,124	80,002
Independent	13	45,380	36,252	44,970	45,947
Form of government					
Mayor-council	6	43,656	37,280	42,905	45,822
Council-manager	24	59,112	44,248	53,274	75,031
Treasurer					
Total	57	53,580	40,392	54,431	71,378
Geographic region					
Northeast	18	49,850	34,080	52,800	59,522
North-Central	26	53,622	40,113	57,594	72,233
South	13	58,658	41,489	49,096	73,320
Metro type					
Suburban	37	54,002	34,500	54,495	71,504
Independent	18	50,207	40,666	46,108	61,070
Form of government					
Mayor-council	27	46,046	29,172	42,966	60,240
Council-manager	21	62,339	46,752	59,792	73,632
Commission	3	54,970	42,140	62,280	71,455
Town meeting	4	48,036	39,889	48,653	56,800

Table 1/8   **SALARIES OF MUNICIPAL OFFICIALS: JULY–DECEMBER 2007**
continued

Title of official	Number of municipalities reporting	Mean ($)	First quartile ($)	Median ($)	Third quartile ($)
5,000–9,999					
Chief admin. officer/city manager					
Total	272	86,543	72,988	85,086	100,150
Geographic region					
Northeast	37	74,343	57,000	73,000	91,344
North-Central	83	86,092	77,515	83,640	95,108
South	129	87,359	70,000	89,856	102,504
West	23	103,224	88,288	94,092	115,713
Metro type					
Suburban	151	90,025	74,059	89,268	103,615
Independent	121	82,198	70,000	81,910	92,400
Form of government					
Mayor-council	85	79,430	68,506	80,000	91,344
Council-manager	174	91,549	75,556	90,000	102,985
Town meeting	10	70,900	47,671	70,216	89,229
Chief elected official					
Total	59	33,341	15,000	24,912	46,824
Geographic region					
Northeast	4	44,270	34,175	49,553	59,647
North-Central	23	26,557	12,210	16,560	32,669
South	25	41,791	24,000	35,141	53,373
West	7	19,207	15,000	21,000	21,500
Metro type					
Suburban	28	38,296	14,750	24,000	53,780
Independent	31	28,865	15,000	26,689	44,073
Form of government					
Mayor-council	45	32,898	15,000	27,745	45,854
Council-manager	9	28,400	14,000	18,684	21,000
Town meeting	3	53,026	49,553	59,539	59,756
Chief financial officer					
Total	182	64,900	51,194	65,481	75,375
Geographic region					
Northeast	16	57,700	36,756	59,237	72,765
North-Central	61	65,521	56,423	66,914	76,988
South	85	64,120	49,500	64,764	73,937
West	20	72,076	58,439	68,673	81,014
Metro type					
Suburban	95	68,074	54,143	68,500	78,237
Independent	87	61,433	49,539	61,963	72,606
Form of government					
Mayor-council	54	60,959	48,447	64,342	73,947
Council-manager	121	66,412	52,272	66,728	77,128
Town meeting	4	72,184	57,361	68,322	83,145
Chief law enforcement official					
Total	294	67,833	54,266	66,615	77,800
Geographic region					
Northeast	34	81,276	60,148	75,012	100,535
North-Central	96	68,287	57,722	67,825	75,171
South	139	62,413	48,190	60,258	72,085
West	25	77,942	68,894	75,730	81,013
Metro type					
Suburban	145	74,972	59,546	72,322	85,635
Independent	149	60,886	50,285	61,000	69,597
Form of government					
Mayor-council	114	65,607	50,138	65,142	74,975
Council-manager	162	69,003	56,970	67,132	78,461
Commission	9	64,066	56,685	57,992	71,244
Town meeting	8	79,160	73,726	77,816	82,701
Chief librarian					
Total	76	47,611	39,349	47,816	54,621
Geographic region					
Northeast	18	48,201	40,529	49,336	58,518
North-Central	29	48,163	43,884	50,000	54,342
South	19	43,421	31,362	42,390	48,774
West	10	52,912	40,306	51,919	62,478
Metro type					
Suburban	32	49,322	39,979	51,722	57,780
Independent	44	46,367	38,548	45,756	52,553
Form of government					
Mayor-council	28	46,075	37,087	47,004	53,577
Council-manager	38	47,809	40,007	47,121	55,061
Town meeting	7	53,684	49,336	51,986	57,297
Clerk					
Total	237	49,366	38,917	48,624	58,501
Geographic region					
Northeast	27	48,934	35,924	49,200	60,739
North-Central	61	48,698	40,373	49,464	58,396
South	129	48,042	38,771	45,838	55,452
West	20	60,523	45,289	55,009	68,492
Metro type					
Suburban	121	52,735	43,026	52,000	62,407
Independent	116	45,851	37,500	44,317	54,000

Title of official	Number of municipalities reporting	Mean ($)	First quartile ($)	Median ($)	Third quartile ($)
5,000–9,999 continued					
Form of government					
Mayor-council	80	46,583	35,641	44,317	58,627
Council-manager	143	51,070	41,139	49,720	59,024
Commission	4	45,877	39,167	44,600	51,310
Town meeting	8	48,709	42,252	49,526	57,168
Economic development director					
Total	56	58,413	45,047	57,364	65,835
Geographic region					
Northeast	6	68,283	46,478	74,840	91,039
North-Central	24	56,610	49,302	57,933	66,893
South	22	49,847	42,509	48,515	59,430
West	4	101,547	82,321	106,277	125,503
Metro type					
Suburban	29	65,571	51,252	65,000	73,590
Independent	27	50,726	42,680	48,921	59,340
Form of government					
Mayor-council	17	51,527	35,292	57,866	64,875
Council-manager	36	60,930	48,082	57,086	67,567
Town meeting	3	67,241	52,582	64,792	80,675
Engineer					
Total	47	73,170	60,779	72,500	81,558
Geographic region					
Northeast	3	69,923	52,976	72,973	88,396
North-Central	18	70,347	64,575	72,239	78,738
South	20	75,290	59,347	74,242	84,833
West	6	76,197	63,351	75,392	85,820
Metro type					
Suburban	24	74,650	61,189	74,769	88,269
Independent	23	71,626	60,032	71,919	79,687
Form of government					
Mayor-council	15	70,129	63,564	74,838	80,381
Council-manager	30	76,070	60,604	72,737	86,226
Fire chief					
Total	161	56,958	45,800	54,972	67,862
Geographic region					
Northeast	15	53,068	42,047	52,919	69,742
North-Central	48	56,347	48,835	53,518	64,439
South	82	54,512	43,415	53,978	62,937
West	16	74,968	58,794	69,639	80,357
Metro type					
Suburban	77	60,950	49,094	57,566	74,172
Independent	84	53,298	43,581	52,062	60,751
Form of government					
Mayor-council	56	49,725	41,597	49,740	57,560
Council-manager	93	61,087	51,155	58,517	71,448
Commission	6	49,833	48,079	49,147	55,530
Town meeting	5	64,649	68,215	71,269	75,705
Health officer					
Total	6	46,485	30,245	35,208	47,761
Geographic region					
Northeast	4	52,123	29,388	40,268	63,004
Metro type					
Independent	4	49,593	30,122	35,208	54,679
Form of government					
Town meeting	3	59,498	39,044	50,536	75,471
Human resources director					
Total	75	51,703	38,165	49,216	62,837
Geographic region					
North-Central	9	39,848	37,200	42,249	44,634
South	54	50,945	37,676	51,099	61,526
West	11	62,047	42,203	64,872	67,172
Metro type					
Suburban	34	55,301	39,734	52,149	64,917
Independent	41	48,719	35,048	48,935	57,408
Form of government					
Mayor-council	22	40,650	29,224	38,165	49,064
Council-manager	52	55,728	41,769	52,796	64,887
Human services director					
Total	23	44,668	37,109	42,204	53,386
Geographic region					
Northeast	6	41,432	29,377	43,213	45,509
North-Central	3	50,703	38,674	54,894	64,828
South	14	44,762	39,036	41,610	50,342
Metro type					
Suburban	13	45,682	41,268	43,920	54,894
Independent	10	43,351	29,159	40,231	44,850
Form of government					
Mayor-council	7	38,071	23,727	35,318	47,955
Council-manager	13	45,712	39,445	42,204	51,879
Town meeting	3	55,542	44,272	46,038	62,059

Table 1/8   SALARIES OF MUNICIPAL OFFICIALS: JULY–DECEMBER 2007
continued

Title of official	Number of municipalities reporting	Mean ($)	First quartile ($)	Median ($)	Third quartile ($)
5,000–9,999 continued					
Information services director					
Total	27	59,536	46,998	53,266	67,492
Geographic region					
Northeast	3	57,563	45,352	61,224	71,604
North-Central	3	52,299	49,296	52,437	55,370
South	19	61,627	46,960	53,266	73,369
Metro type					
Suburban	12	58,946	44,734	56,209	71,412
Independent	15	60,009	47,881	52,437	62,476
Form of government					
Mayor-council	3	54,628	52,229	58,304	58,864
Council-manager	22	60,552	47,861	52,852	68,474
Parks and recreation director					
Total	123	53,018	41,111	49,122	61,978
Geographic region					
Northeast	10	49,664	38,831	47,017	61,920
North-Central	39	51,756	43,962	50,000	59,476
South	61	51,761	38,178	47,954	61,933
West	13	65,285	54,000	67,914	73,620
Metro type					
Suburban	64	56,953	45,918	57,684	68,267
Independent	59	48,750	37,843	47,208	56,353
Form of government					
Mayor-council	44	48,741	39,752	47,883	57,693
Council-manager	76	56,428	43,255	52,807	65,496
Parks superintendent					
Total	58	42,118	31,233	42,886	51,172
Geographic region					
North-Central	18	40,167	30,021	42,327	51,398
South	30	40,530	30,836	40,090	49,171
West	8	51,881	42,795	54,355	59,311
Metro type					
Suburban	23	43,998	35,500	46,868	53,213
Independent	35	40,882	30,882	40,019	49,088
Form of government					
Mayor-council	22	38,316	27,464	38,862	47,196
Council-manager	35	44,512	34,013	44,492	52,715
Planning director					
Total	98	64,136	50,470	62,000	73,918
Geographic region					
Northeast	11	53,029	45,562	53,457	58,383
North-Central	19	66,947	53,628	66,347	76,857
South	53	62,754	50,262	59,831	74,277
West	15	73,601	54,916	67,786	74,914
Metro type					
Suburban	63	66,604	51,501	63,004	75,581
Independent	35	59,692	49,566	57,491	68,266
Form of government					
Mayor-council	26	61,254	53,824	62,107	73,918
Council-manager	69	65,906	50,262	62,280	74,500
Primary asst. manager/CAO					
Total	55	63,199	47,998	63,700	79,168
Geographic region					
Northeast	10	48,446	38,700	45,917	57,320
North-Central	10	59,803	49,531	59,390	70,707
South	29	62,958	51,750	65,724	77,600
West	6	94,612	86,005	91,894	93,875
Metro type					
Suburban	35	63,223	47,998	59,283	78,584
Independent	20	63,156	53,145	66,361	79,143
Form of government					
Mayor-council	13	49,485	37,679	47,677	59,496
Council-manager	39	68,110	55,313	68,954	81,845
Public safety director					
Total	22	66,816	53,376	64,632	74,372
Geographic region					
North-Central	14	61,916	53,376	62,664	70,493
South	7	79,843	64,782	75,496	83,348
Metro type					
Suburban	17	71,323	60,000	68,954	75,496
Independent	5	51,491	35,759	51,500	60,611
Form of government					
Mayor-council	10	59,583	46,193	59,502	67,584
Council-manager	12	72,844	63,348	69,846	77,048
Public works director					
Total	252	65,279	52,451	63,332	75,468
Geographic region					
Northeast	35	64,945	50,272	60,437	75,570
North-Central	85	66,499	58,944	65,962	73,495
South	111	62,902	48,628	60,858	75,080
West	21	73,465	62,000	69,069	84,168

Title of official	Number of municipalities reporting	Mean ($)	First quartile ($)	Median ($)	Third quartile ($)
5,000–9,999 continued					
Metro type					
Suburban	145	68,954	56,942	66,331	77,850
Independent	107	60,299	47,929	59,316	69,284
Form of government					
Mayor-council	91	61,226	49,185	62,032	68,604
Council-manager	143	68,223	56,436	65,768	77,799
Commission	7	57,815	50,959	57,640	64,647
Town meeting	9	65,119	57,448	57,818	70,586
Purchasing director					
Total	15	43,731	31,858	37,500	50,277
Geographic region					
South	13	44,624	32,716	37,500	50,132
Metro type					
Suburban	4	39,772	36,068	37,026	40,730
Independent	11	45,170	30,024	40,343	50,588
Form of government					
Mayor-council	5	29,959	24,807	29,047	32,716
Council-manager	10	50,617	36,789	46,516	50,888
Recreation director					
Total	38	39,794	30,342	38,455	46,337
Geographic region					
Northeast	11	39,360	26,539	40,914	51,016
North-Central	12	39,561	30,716	35,452	45,150
South	13	40,698	30,264	37,900	45,000
Metro type					
Suburban	24	40,384	30,068	39,505	45,150
Independent	14	38,782	30,389	37,704	46,337
Form of government					
Mayor-council	9	41,635	27,206	35,861	58,850
Council-manager	22	41,701	31,468	40,685	46,337
Town meeting	5	35,305	37,508	40,000	40,914
Risk manager					
Total	6	60,325	48,629	53,310	60,035
Geographic region					
South	5	60,091	47,846	50,979	55,641
Metro type					
Independent	5	60,091	47,846	50,979	55,641
Form of government					
Council-manager	6	60,325	48,629	53,310	60,035
Treasurer					
Total	61	47,710	35,000	48,416	57,300
Geographic region					
Northeast	15	45,754	33,166	42,725	54,458
North-Central	27	47,536	40,389	47,520	55,207
South	13	51,688	47,867	52,938	62,288
West	6	44,765	29,139	47,258	49,991
Metro type					
Suburban	25	47,749	33,216	48,416	56,307
Independent	36	47,684	40,697	48,357	58,547
Form of government					
Mayor-council	22	42,887	32,189	46,701	50,857
Council-manager	30	52,858	41,778	51,469	64,602
Commission	3	36,441	31,250	35,000	40,911
Town meeting	5	44,350	31,350	42,725	64,796
2,500–4,999					
Chief admin. officer/city manager					
Total	302	71,333	57,944	68,758	83,426
Geographic region					
Northeast	31	57,274	48,874	57,419	64,885
North-Central	114	72,983	63,182	70,030	83,267
South	141	69,955	55,014	68,504	80,560
West	16	98,955	85,373	96,198	105,185
Metro type					
Suburban	148	75,778	62,710	74,870	87,596
Independent	153	67,016	55,014	65,000	74,736
Form of government					
Mayor-council	109	67,210	57,500	67,913	77,000
Council-manager	183	74,451	60,133	70,061	85,964
Town meeting	8	59,618	50,722	61,564	69,497
Chief elected official					
Total	43	23,448	12,456	16,107	26,469
Geographic region					
Northeast	7	20,300	11,728	12,746	21,219
North-Central	12	22,970	12,000	18,552	26,207
South	20	21,460	12,456	17,291	24,998
West	4	40,331	14,792	24,610	50,150
Metro type					
Suburban	21	26,871	12,456	20,508	26,988
Independent	22	20,181	12,000	14,280	25,633

Table 1/8   SALARIES OF MUNICIPAL OFFICIALS: JULY–DECEMBER 2007
continued

Title of official	Number of municipalities reporting	Distribution of 2007 salaries			
		Mean ($)	First quartile ($)	Median ($)	Third quartile ($)
2,500–4,999 continued					
Form of government					
Mayor-council	39	24,582	12,456	18,474	27,747
Council-manager	4	12,390	11,700	12,000	12,690
Chief financial officer					
Total	142	54,882	42,240	52,753	66,034
Geographic region					
Northeast	13	46,229	40,310	43,394	53,794
North-Central	52	56,123	47,306	56,356	68,005
South	66	52,074	41,353	47,833	61,061
West	11	76,091	65,930	68,220	86,484
Metro type					
Suburban	84	56,520	41,480	56,356	67,231
Independent	57	52,777	42,888	50,740	59,322
Form of government					
Mayor-council	53	50,408	41,000	48,214	59,806
Council-manager	85	58,257	43,902	55,789	67,074
Town meeting	3	51,607	46,118	46,710	54,648
Chief law enforcement official					
Total	330	55,610	46,101	53,548	62,590
Geographic region					
Northeast	33	57,857	47,000	56,000	64,356
North-Central	130	58,294	49,189	57,460	63,493
South	149	51,410	42,609	49,553	58,208
West	18	66,883	51,208	63,437	75,033
Metro type					
Suburban	148	61,530	50,544	59,636	73,682
Independent	181	50,735	43,505	49,870	57,242
Form of government					
Mayor-council	155	52,745	44,104	51,903	60,721
Council-manager	163	58,247	48,369	54,859	64,991
Commission	7	52,676	39,562	55,124	56,844
Town meeting	5	62,579	53,642	56,000	58,375
Chief librarian					
Total	72	34,502	28,331	34,277	39,948
Geographic region					
Northeast	11	36,338	19,383	35,000	50,523
North-Central	42	35,585	29,793	36,271	40,034
South	14	27,815	25,305	28,902	31,778
West	5	40,085	33,675	37,368	42,952
Metro type					
Suburban	26	35,083	28,349	34,627	40,806
Independent	46	34,173	28,488	34,150	38,765
Form of government					
Mayor-council	36	33,282	27,177	34,127	39,021
Council-manager	28	35,453	28,983	33,499	40,533
Town meeting	8	36,663	20,276	38,389	46,884
Clerk					
Total	275	41,793	34,200	41,728	48,368
Geographic region					
Northeast	33	39,599	29,910	40,000	47,600
North-Central	82	43,375	35,419	42,599	50,889
South	144	40,082	34,328	39,603	46,453
West	16	53,613	41,469	49,429	61,896
Metro type					
Suburban	125	44,172	34,957	43,470	51,900
Independent	149	39,838	32,690	39,539	46,446
Form of government					
Mayor-council	131	39,866	31,751	39,713	46,898
Council-manager	133	44,177	35,800	43,347	49,386
Commission	5	39,625	39,539	43,470	43,596
Town meeting	6	32,831	24,897	33,593	42,987
Economic development director					
Total	38	48,567	37,591	49,509	60,417
Geographic region					
North-Central	17	45,882	37,024	48,056	52,000
South	16	47,703	35,212	46,662	62,603
West	3	65,957	61,568	61,707	68,222
Metro type					
Suburban	14	53,006	44,358	56,240	63,697
Independent	24	45,978	36,834	47,871	52,201
Form of government					
Mayor-council	18	46,667	34,835	48,549	51,999
Council-manager	20	50,278	38,724	52,217	61,575
Engineer					
Total	20	53,813	39,360	56,074	63,773
Geographic region					
Northeast	4	38,486	27,248	36,620	47,858
North-Central	8	57,709	51,183	58,508	64,490
South	4	49,215	22,461	36,860	63,614
West	4	65,948	60,431	62,012	67,529

Title of official	Number of municipalities reporting	Distribution of 2007 salaries			
		Mean ($)	First quartile ($)	Median ($)	Third quartile ($)
2,500–4,999 continued					
Metro type					
Suburban	11	55,054	40,686	57,090	65,240
Independent	9	52,297	42,100	55,058	63,320
Form of government					
Mayor-council	10	55,288	37,120	59,317	62,349
Council-manager	9	53,477	50,232	51,500	65,132
Fire chief					
Total	86	51,025	39,425	48,857	58,521
Geographic region					
Northeast	6	34,180	23,113	33,987	47,277
North-Central	18	49,545	45,983	52,762	58,272
South	52	48,366	38,128	47,675	52,199
West	10	77,617	60,652	69,084	96,263
Metro type					
Suburban	42	54,979	44,110	49,806	61,685
Independent	44	47,250	34,084	47,529	53,922
Form of government					
Mayor-council	24	47,889	37,691	49,144	57,816
Council-manager	57	53,309	41,546	48,797	60,382
Town meeting	4	34,276	19,407	35,597	50,466
Health officer					
Total	5	22,601	15,155	15,600	20,516
Geographic region					
Northeast	4	24,463	14,629	18,058	27,892
Metro type					
Independent	3	27,417	16,116	20,516	35,268
Form of government	...	...	...	...	...
Human resources director					
Total	21	43,406	35,000	40,164	51,210
Geographic region					
South	18	41,471	35,065	39,935	50,227
Metro type					
Suburban	11	48,214	37,644	42,516	53,924
Independent	10	38,116	30,177	35,363	45,860
Form of government					
Mayor-council	8	44,913	32,738	35,421	53,435
Council-manager	13	42,478	35,464	41,605	51,210
Human services director					
Total	3	42,637	39,252	43,569	46,488
Geographic region	...	...	...	...	...
Metro type	...	...	...	...	...
Form of government					
Council-manager	3	42,637	39,252	43,569	46,488
Information services director					
Total	12	45,449	40,527	51,027	55,290
Geographic region					
South	8	49,606	49,091	52,278	55,290
Metro type					
Suburban	5	46,404	45,880	50,326	52,828
Independent	7	44,767	34,133	51,727	56,798
Form of government					
Mayor-council	3	42,015	35,668	45,386	50,047
Council-manager	9	46,594	45,880	51,727	57,036
Parks and recreation director					
Total	85	43,197	34,005	42,084	49,331
Geographic region					
Northeast	4	30,644	28,930	32,456	34,170
North-Central	32	41,358	34,944	40,600	47,512
South	46	43,532	34,540	43,047	49,922
West	3	74,412	60,623	62,684	82,337
Metro type					
Suburban	31	51,462	42,539	49,284	59,976
Independent	53	38,455	28,499	38,336	46,752
Form of government					
Mayor-council	25	36,924	28,836	37,308	43,849
Council-manager	56	47,059	38,262	47,080	54,065
Town meeting	3	29,881	25,879	31,981	34,934
Parks superintendent					
Total	36	33,491	28,433	33,108	37,620
Geographic region					
North-Central	12	35,984	28,991	35,494	41,053
South	19	31,372	27,248	30,462	33,647
West	4	33,757	32,602	34,508	35,664
Metro type					
Suburban	12	34,154	29,261	35,036	40,012
Independent	24	33,159	27,941	32,328	34,979
Form of government					
Mayor-council	17	33,801	26,469	33,936	40,000
Council-manager	19	33,214	29,332	31,990	34,769

Table 1/8   SALARIES OF MUNICIPAL OFFICIALS: JULY–DECEMBER 2007
continued

Title of official	Number of municipalities reporting	Distribution of 2007 salaries			
		Mean ($)	First quartile ($)	Median ($)	Third quartile ($)
2,500–4,999 continued					
Planning director					
Total	59	53,402	41,738	50,596	59,521
Geographic region					
Northeast	3	46,386	42,570	44,608	49,313
North-Central	11	54,613	50,732	52,244	58,243
South	37	51,223	39,573	47,821	57,512
West	8	64,444	50,712	61,215	70,247
Metro type					
Suburban	34	58,197	49,207	55,463	66,853
Independent	24	47,292	40,235	44,281	52,587
Form of government					
Mayor-council	17	54,335	44,608	52,244	60,700
Council-manager	41	53,000	40,464	50,594	57,512
Primary asst. manager/CAO					
Total	38	57,077	41,101	58,500	64,422
Geographic region					
North-Central	14	55,656	47,393	58,865	64,321
South	18	55,944	37,831	58,500	62,772
West	4	74,408	52,377	71,402	93,433
Metro type					
Suburban	20	60,740	48,054	59,539	72,702
Independent	18	53,007	39,736	56,886	62,076
Form of government					
Mayor-council	19	54,687	39,914	58,500	65,754
Council-manager	17	61,365	48,830	60,000	64,917
Public safety director					
Total	20	58,214	42,836	52,242	71,610
Geographic region					
North-Central	8	55,246	38,482	46,668	62,899
South	8	60,509	46,042	59,962	73,822
Metro type					
Suburban	12	62,386	46,679	60,922	77,595
Independent	8	51,956	40,320	46,668	58,693
Form of government					
Mayor-council	12	54,754	40,293	46,273	71,270
Council-manager	8	63,404	49,107	59,962	73,822
Public works director					
Total	271	54,476	44,823	52,789	63,360
Geographic region					
Northeast	33	52,554	46,705	50,671	61,325
North-Central	101	58,754	50,628	58,165	65,000
South	118	49,148	39,007	47,386	55,271
West	19	68,170	55,018	66,040	68,372
Metro type					
Suburban	132	57,737	47,522	56,944	67,607
Independent	138	51,361	42,143	50,084	58,914
Form of government					
Mayor-council	119	53,400	44,950	52,219	63,450
Council-manager	146	55,322	43,803	52,932	63,094
Town meeting	4	56,610	49,201	51,851	59,261
Purchasing director					
Total	8	34,968	24,978	30,482	43,924
Geographic region					
South	5	28,467	22,836	25,693	27,747
Metro type					
Suburban	5	33,922	25,693	33,216	43,915
Independent	3	36,710	24,945	27,747	43,994
Form of government					
Mayor-council	3	26,065	22,490	22,836	28,026
Council-manager	5	40,309	27,747	43,915	43,950
Recreation director					
Total	32	32,981	26,879	33,667	37,188
Geographic region					
Northeast	8	29,055	13,346	33,910	38,069
North-Central	10	28,811	25,602	29,632	34,002
South	9	34,301	28,233	35,000	38,900
West	5	45,226	30,727	33,943	47,008
Metro type					
Suburban	12	36,038	26,718	31,137	42,901
Independent	20	31,147	27,696	33,913	35,813
Form of government					
Mayor-council	9	35,577	33,943	34,221	46,743
Council-manager	22	32,786	26,350	30,980	35,355
Risk manager					
Total	. . .	. . .	. . .	. . .	. . .
Geographic region	. . .	. . .	. . .	. . .	. . .
City type	. . .	. . .	. . .	. . .	. . .
Form of government	. . .	. . .	. . .	. . .	. . .
Treasurer					
Total	82	38,986	27,804	39,324	48,017

Title of official	Number of municipalities reporting	Distribution of 2007 salaries			
		Mean ($)	First quartile ($)	Median ($)	Third quartile ($)
2,500–4,999 continued					
Geographic region					
Northeast	21	33,919	23,920	27,798	47,076
North-Central	37	40,031	30,413	39,956	47,694
South	15	40,438	27,477	34,860	46,382
West	9	44,090	35,135	43,596	57,600
Metro type					
Suburban	38	37,972	27,869	38,941	46,893
Independent	44	39,861	27,664	40,106	48,739
Form of government					
Mayor-council	43	36,318	27,811	35,592	46,855
Council-manager	32	43,859	30,098	41,752	53,871
Commission	4	40,986	33,625	41,213	48,575
Town meeting	3	22,576	20,272	23,789	25,487
Less than 2,500					
Chief admin. officer/city manager					
Total	252	61,341	47,685	56,645	71,949
Geographic region					
Northeast	10	52,654	33,838	46,458	73,603
North-Central	110	58,854	48,055	57,491	69,836
South	114	61,255	47,315	56,392	72,478
West	18	81,913	50,916	69,027	101,984
Metro type					
Suburban	120	66,071	49,996	61,979	80,613
Independent	132	57,041	46,710	54,505	65,502
Form of government					
Mayor-council	67	58,530	47,229	56,300	70,104
Council-manager	181	62,532	47,700	59,685	72,800
Chief elected official					
Total	11	34,697	14,450	36,000	43,077
Geographic region					
North-Central	4	34,376	30,114	38,760	43,022
South	6	38,825	18,525	32,207	43,129
Metro type					
Suburban	8	34,077	12,714	26,050	43,022
Independent	3	36,349	32,207	38,614	41,624
Form of government					
Mayor-council	7	32,379	20,950	38,614	43,077
Council-manager	4	38,753	12,403	24,400	50,750
Chief financial officer					
Total	69	46,909	35,642	45,672	52,695
Geographic region					
Northeast	3	55,999	51,821	52,282	58,319
North-Central	22	47,249	38,871	47,855	53,981
South	35	41,956	31,065	40,000	48,142
West	9	62,311	39,942	60,702	79,868
Metro type					
Suburban	30	49,099	37,667	47,855	58,351
Independent	39	45,225	32,799	44,782	52,161
Form of government					
Mayor-council	25	43,737	31,200	45,000	51,360
Council-manager	44	48,712	36,780	46,684	55,342
Chief law enforcement official					
Total	285	48,360	39,253	45,614	55,245
Geographic region					
Northeast	8	56,916	39,343	53,098	72,520
North-Central	124	47,659	40,362	46,800	53,016
South	137	46,908	38,115	43,995	53,889
West	16	61,947	46,313	57,763	70,381
Metro type					
Suburban	107	54,333	44,350	49,226	63,147
Independent	178	44,769	37,386	43,267	51,222
Form of government					
Mayor-council	147	44,294	36,715	43,260	48,740
Council-manager	134	52,794	43,148	49,353	59,137
Chief librarian					
Total	52	28,394	19,241	28,654	35,344
Geographic region					
North-Central	35	29,676	24,881	30,621	36,060
South	10	21,031	17,784	19,572	22,117
West	5	31,923	13,520	34,195	45,120
Metro type					
Suburban	19	26,480	17,015	30,621	33,453
Independent	33	29,497	20,659	27,663	37,028
Form of government					
Mayor-council	28	25,132	18,419	23,318	31,140
Council-manager	22	33,025	26,376	32,930	37,109
Clerk					
Total	304	36,388	29,116	34,585	42,163

Table 1/8   SALARIES OF MUNICIPAL OFFICIALS: JULY–DECEMBER 2007
continued

Title of official	Number of municipalities reporting	Distribution of 2007 salaries			
		Mean ($)	First quartile ($)	Median ($)	Third quartile ($)
Less than 2,500 continued					
Geographic region					
Northeast	7	29,689	21,135	29,183	33,947
North-Central	124	37,685	30,104	35,973	42,931
South	157	34,978	28,649	34,324	40,619
West	16	43,105	32,794	39,752	58,300
Metro type					
Suburban	88	40,439	33,508	39,043	46,146
Independent	216	34,738	28,472	33,509	40,222
Form of government					
Mayor-council	183	34,843	28,620	33,678	40,957
Council-manager	118	38,734	30,856	36,716	45,459
Economic development director					
Total	17	35,930	31,140	36,361	37,482
Geographic region					
North-Central	15	34,521	29,563	36,361	37,395
Metro type					
Suburban	4	34,319	22,751	33,735	45,303
Independent	13	36,426	33,280	36,361	37,308
Form of government					
Mayor-council	11	37,941	34,820	37,308	42,643
Council-manager	6	32,243	28,775	32,962	35,948
Engineer					
Total	3	79,273	76,289	77,865	81,553
Geographic region					
West	3	79,273	76,289	77,865	81,553
Metro type	...	...	...	...	...
Form of government	...	...	...	...	...
Fire chief					
Total	38	47,764	37,281	44,901	56,926
Geographic region					
Northeast	3	41,851	37,998	42,315	45,936
North-Central	5	56,731	34,179	58,126	59,685
South	27	45,326	37,563	41,000	54,615
West	3	60,668	52,077	57,042	67,446
Metro type					
Suburban	18	49,895	39,732	49,957	56,926
Independent	20	45,846	36,275	40,240	49,724
Form of government					
Mayor-council	14	45,736	35,521	39,833	46,490
Council-manager	23	48,920	37,936	48,551	58,905
Health officer					
Total	...	...	...	...	...
Geographic region	...	...	...	...	...
City type	...	...	...	...	...
Form of government	...	...	...	...	...
Human resources director					
Total	3	28,809	23,847	24,289	31,511
Geographic region	...	...	...	...	...
Metro type	...	...	...	...	...
Form of government					
Mayor-council	3	28,809	23,847	24,289	31,511
Human services director					
Total	...	...	...	...	...
Geographic region	...	...	...	...	...
City type	...	...	...	...	...
Form of government	...	...	...	...	...
Information services director					
Total	8	44,781	34,651	39,138	47,902
Geographic region					
South	4	37,613	34,435	39,138	42,316
Metro type					
Suburban	5	40,363	32,195	36,225	42,051
Independent	3	52,143	39,290	43,110	60,480
Form of government					
Council-manager	6	43,290	33,014	38,760	42,845
Parks and recreation director					
Total	24	35,364	27,960	36,832	41,687
Geographic region					
North-Central	12	34,385	25,214	37,596	40,418
South	10	35,590	29,792	34,265	40,102
Metro type					
Suburban	11	36,998	29,727	36,432	46,780
Independent	13	33,981	28,630	37,232	39,012
Form of government					
Mayor-council	11	37,465	35,372	38,106	41,823
Council-manager	12	32,450	22,444	33,390	37,500
Parks superintendent					
Total	17	31,247	21,860	28,781	38,925
Geographic region					
North-Central	4	36,812	34,659	40,699	42,852
South	13	29,534	20,796	28,193	35,858

Title of official	Number of municipalities reporting	Distribution of 2007 salaries			
		Mean ($)	First quartile ($)	Median ($)	Third quartile ($)
Less than 2,500 continued					
Metro type					
Suburban	4	28,857	20,546	28,162	36,473
Independent	13	31,982	21,860	28,781	38,925
Form of government					
Mayor-council	10	28,390	21,062	25,570	35,739
Council-manager	7	35,327	25,307	35,858	40,699
Planning director					
Total	16	53,410	42,489	47,863	63,835
Geographic region					
South	10	48,067	40,830	46,098	53,323
West	6	62,314	45,026	57,169	74,561
Metro type					
Suburban	7	58,273	49,511	53,560	65,902
Independent	9	49,627	35,126	43,319	49,316
Form of government					
Council-manager	14	55,216	43,388	50,964	64,627
Primary asst. manager/CAO					
Total	19	57,367	42,322	55,307	72,564
Geographic region					
North-Central	4	47,786	40,398	48,218	55,606
South	11	55,515	44,330	55,307	72,564
Metro type					
Suburban	11	54,182	42,322	53,256	65,583
Independent	8	61,747	42,287	56,199	76,678
Form of government					
Mayor-council	3	44,995	40,864	49,680	51,468
Council-manager	14	59,539	41,893	56,199	76,794
Public safety director					
Total	6	59,901	45,333	52,272	78,339
Geographic region					
South	3	60,197	47,070	50,543	68,498
Metro type					
Suburban	5	61,772	43,596	54,000	86,452
Form of government					
Mayor-council	3	46,048	42,072	50,543	52,272
Council-manager	3	73,753	65,024	86,452	88,832
Public works director					
Total	218	47,043	38,485	44,962	54,074
Geographic region					
Northeast	8	44,355	34,572	41,702	54,340
North-Central	102	48,587	41,090	47,077	56,343
South	92	43,966	35,615	43,048	49,632
West	16	56,238	42,755	51,209	69,045
Metro type					
Suburban	88	50,861	42,375	47,627	58,112
Independent	130	44,459	36,890	43,286	50,644
Form of government					
Mayor-council	101	44,869	37,710	43,596	52,624
Council-manager	114	48,811	39,298	46,523	55,596
Purchasing director					
Total	...	...	...	...	...
Geographic region	...	...	...	...	...
City type	...	...	...	...	...
Form of government	...	...	...	...	...
Recreation director					
Total	9	34,417	26,244	29,064	34,155
Geographic region					
Northeast	3	30,953	28,875	34,155	34,633
Metro type					
Suburban	5	27,091	26,988	29,064	31,140
Independent	4	43,575	25,581	30,200	48,193
Form of government					
Council-manager	6	38,392	26,430	28,026	32,883
Risk manager					
Total	...	...	...	...	...
Geographic region	...	...	...	...	...
City type	...	...	...	...	...
Form of government	...	...	...	...	...
Treasurer					
Total	102	38,982	30,214	36,534	44,707
Geographic region					
Northeast	4	48,176	35,619	45,824	58,380
North-Central	89	38,064	29,952	36,483	44,574
South	5	31,262	26,000	27,700	36,584
West	4	59,876	46,923	63,794	76,748
Metro type					
Suburban	22	46,393	36,277	41,939	54,959
Independent	80	36,945	29,485	35,256	43,742
Form of government					
Mayor-council	73	37,420	29,882	35,627	43,700
Council-manager	28	43,156	32,622	41,650	52,356

C 2

Salaries of County Officials, 2007

Rollie O. Waters and Joyce C. Powell
The Waters Consulting Group, Inc.

Selected Findings

The highest percentages of increase in average salary from 2006 to 2007 are for the positions of chief law enforcement official (5.5%); clerk, information services director, and treasurer (4.8%); and parks superintendent (4.6%).

The highest average salary shown is for the combined position of chief administrative officer/county manager ($100,074).

Geographically, the highest average salaries are almost evenly split between the West and Northeast regions; for the majority of titles, the lowest average salaries are found in the North-Central region.

This article and the accompanying tables present the results of ICMA's 2007 survey of salaries of local government officials in counties. In 2007, the survey instrument collected salary information on 23 positions that are common to municipal and county governments.

SURVEY METHODOLOGY

This is the fourth year that ICMA has offered SurveyNavigator™ for ICMA, a Web-based interactive version of the annual survey. This system is managed and operated by The Waters Consulting Group, Inc. Prior to SurveyNavigator™, data were collected in the summer and fall months and made available in a summary format through ICMA's *Municipal Year Book,* which is published in the spring of the following year. A printed version and a disk of the survey data were also made available for a fee through the ICMA bookstore. The online version, SurveyNavigator™ for ICMA, is updated weekly as changes are made by each participating local government.

In July 2007, survey notices were mailed to all municipal and county governments with populations of 2,500 and above and to those under 2,500 that are recognized by ICMA as having a council-manager form of government or as providing for an appointed general management (chief administrative officer, or CAO) position. The survey notice gave the Web address for SurveyNavigator™ (surveynavigator.com/icma) and provided a unique identification number and password for the local government choosing to participate. A second, abbreviated paper survey was mailed and/or e-mailed to those local governments that had not responded to the first mailing or had not provided the information online. The overall county response rate to the 2007 survey was 18% as of December 20, 2007 (Table 2/1). However, the structure of the new online survey tool allows for weekly updates and additional data to be entered at any time by participating local governments.

AVERAGE SALARIES

Using the exact same cites and titles to ensure comparability between 2006 and 2007, Table 2/2 shows

Table 2/1   SURVEY RESPONSE

Classification	No. of counties surveyed (A)	Respondents No.	Respondents % of (A)
Total	3,040	538	18
Population group			
Over 1,000,000	28	7	25
500,000–1,000,000 . .	63	10	16
250,000–499,999 . . .	110	23	21
100,000–249,999 . . .	276	38	14
50,000–99,999	383	56	15
25,000–49,999	638	84	13
10,000–24,999	869	164	19
5,000–9,999	386	78	20
2,500–4,999	173	48	28
Under–2,500	114	30	26
Geographic region			
Northeast	190	9	5
North-Central	1,054	202	19
South	1,372	287	21
West	424	40	9
Geographic division			
New England	46	2	4
Mid-Atlantic	144	7	5
East North-Central . .	437	49	11
West North-Central . .	617	153	25
South Atlantic	545	63	12
East South-Central . .	360	8	2
West South-Central . .	467	216	46
Mountain	276	32	12
Pacific Coast	148	8	5
County type			
Metro	799	135	17
Nonmetro	2,241	403	18
Form of government			
County commission . .	2,191	425	19
Council-manager/ admin	371	60	16
Council–elected executive	478	53	11
Metro status			
Central	458	77	17
Independent	2,241	403	18
Suburban	341	58	17

the percentage of change in average salary for all 23 positions over the preceding year. Overall, the highest percentages of increase in average salary from 2006 to 2007 are for the positions of chief law enforcement official (5.5%); clerk, information services director, and treasurer (4.8%); and parks superintendent (4.6%). The lowest percentages of

increase in average salary are for the positions of fire chief and human services director (2.0%).

Many factors influence the salaries of top local government officials. One is the type of services delivered. Some county services, for example, include an airport and/or a seaport. Some counties provide refuse collection and disposal for all cities and towns within their boundaries; others provide park and recreation services, but the solid-waste collection is provided by the cities within the county.

Another factor influencing local government salaries is population. This is true, in part, because larger populations usually mean larger budgets, more services to meet citizen demands, and more employees to be managed. The complexity of managing counties with larger populations requires a salary commensurate with the level of expertise and experience demanded of the job. An example of the variation in average salaries among population groups is shown in Table 2/3, where the difference between the highest and lowest average salaries for the chief financial officer position is $81,426.

Regional variations also affect average salaries. The highest average salaries in 2007 appear almost evenly distributed between the West and Northeast regions; for the majority of titles, the lowest average salaries are found in the North-Central region (Table 2/4). Figure 2/1 shows the regional differences and similarities in average salaries for six selected positions.

County governments often want to know the competitiveness of their salary ranges in addition to the competitiveness of their salaries. Table 2/5 shows the average salary range minimums, maximums, and spreads for all 23 full-time positions surveyed in 2007. The position of recreation director has the greatest range spread (58%), and the position of chief elected official has the least range spread (31%). Figure 2/2 shows the actual average salaries for six selected positions in conjunction with the average ranges for those positions.

Table 2/6 lists the average, median, and first- and third-quartile salaries for all 23 positions for which there were enough responses to compute the information. For some positions, such as parks and recreation director in counties with populations over 1 million, fewer than three counties reported, so no calculation could be made.

Table 2/2 CHANGE IN AVERAGE SALARY, 2006 TO 2007

Position	2006 average salary ($)	2007 average salary ($)	Percentage of change (%)
Chief admin. officer/county manager	108,021	112,848	4.5
Chief elected official	41,677	43,453	4.3
Chief financial officer	82,773	85,554	3.4
Chief law enforcement official	66,837	70,494	5.5
Chief librarian	65,462	66,959	2.3
Clerk	50,279	52,671	4.8
Economic development director	76,439	78,517	2.7
Engineer	76,033	78,736	3.6
Fire chief	76,063	77,614	2.0
Health officer	68,138	69,970	2.7
Human resources director	76,028	78,564	3.3
Human services director	77,733	79,280	2.0
Information services director	80,594	84,444	4.8
Parks and recreation director	68,344	70,326	2.9
Parks superintendent	42,380	44,348	4.6
Planning director	70,745	72,570	2.6
Primary assistant manager/CAO	91,207	93,836	2.9
Public safety director	62,560	65,057	4.0
Public works director	83,877	86,886	3.6
Purchasing director	65,933	67,950	3.1
Recreation director	46,638	47,837	2.6
Risk manager	60,302	62,230	3.2
Treasurer	52,584	55,105	4.8

Note: This table compares the average pay change for position using the exact same counties and titles used in *The Municipal Year Book 2007*. Where counties that reported last year did not report this year, they were excluded from the calculations for both years shown above.

Table 2/3 AVERAGE SALARY FOR CHIEF FINANCIAL OFFICER, BY POPULATION GROUP, 2007

Population group	No. reporting	Average salary ($)
Total	140	75,378
Over 1,000,000	4	129,856
500,000–1,000,000	7	122,855
250,000–499,999	18	104,197
100,000–249,999	18	95,079
50,000–99,999	22	74,038
25,000–49,999	29	61,708
10,000–24,999	30	54,309
5,000–9,999	8	48,430
2,500–4,999[1]	—	—
Under 2,500[1]	—	—

[1]Because meaningful statistics cannot be computed for classifications having fewer than three counties reporting, no average salary data are available for this population group.

Table 2/4 AVERAGE SALARY ($) FOR POSITION, BY REGION, 2007

Job title	Total	Region			
		Northeast	North-Central	South	West
Chief admin. officer/county manager	100,074	99,832	91,600	109,327	100,617
Chief elected official	44,712	35,043	32,378	48,437	46,604
Chief financial officer	75,378	100,827	73,633	74,071	78,215
Chief law enforcement official	65,753	87,980	64,375	67,066	65,221
Chief librarian	63,115	84,140	85,503	59,799	50,824
Clerk	45,963	52,730	41,850	46,548	54,141
Economic development director	67,709	77,306	51,053	79,817	54,535
Engineer	79,213	98,054	78,535	78,700	81,432
Fire chief	67,248	—	35,074	69,764	74,269
Health officer	65,705	81,609	58,718	75,896	76,331
Human resources director	71,431	77,613	70,735	68,669	88,273
Human services director	75,085	77,998	82,020	60,763	82,626
Information services director	77,351	82,063	70,441	80,153	80,939
Parks and recreation director	67,329	88,966	59,420	71,241	87,101
Parks superintendent	49,858	53,682	50,661	49,959	44,082
Planning director	67,028	63,787	59,110	74,683	68,766
Primary assistant manager/CAO	79,105	78,165	82,698	75,708	86,136
Public safety director	65,095	93,521	52,898	67,785	75,364
Public works director	78,731	80,402	78,020	80,573	74,684
Purchasing director	66,795	66,093	63,668	66,041	92,165
Recreation director	52,482	—	33,640	54,434	53,081
Risk manager	59,278	53,237	59,095	58,191	64,938
Treasurer	47,726	62,729	49,203	44,880	54,856

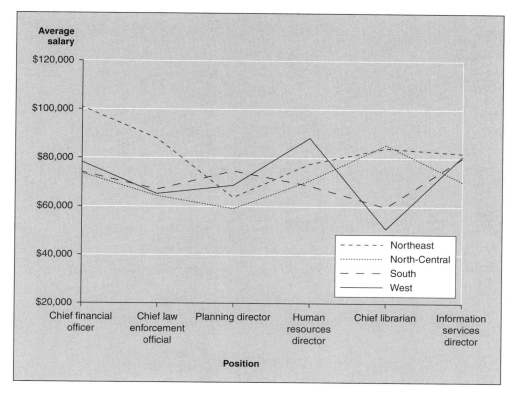

Figure 2/1   *Average salaries for six selected county positions, by geographic region, 2007*

Table 2/5   AVERAGE PAY STRUCTURE RANGES, 2007

Position	No. reporting	Average minimum ($)	Average maximum ($)	Average range spread (%)
Chief admin. officer/county manager	165	75,539	109,590	45
Chief elected official	269	44,084	57,818	31
Chief financial officer	140	61,963	92,151	49
Chief law enforcement official	334	60,884	93,698	54
Chief librarian	45	63,620	92,315	45
Clerk	327	36,485	52,898	45
Economic development director	51	60,157	93,203	55
Engineer	130	62,812	93,033	48
Fire chief	36	59,745	92,695	55
Health officer	104	57,889	85,029	47
Human resources director	153	56,814	84,449	49
Human services director	91	60,971	87,338	43
Information services director	132	61,491	90,344	47
Parks and recreation director	94	54,439	81,611	50
Parks superintendent	41	45,325	70,696	56
Planning director	109	57,681	85,493	48
Primary assistant manager/CAO	59	67,029	99,658	49
Public safety director	36	53,064	81,476	54
Public works director	121	67,032	99,734	49
Purchasing director	57	48,256	71,032	47
Recreation director	22	40,228	63,474	58
Risk manager	58	47,657	71,550	50
Treasurer	400	46,004	64,547	40

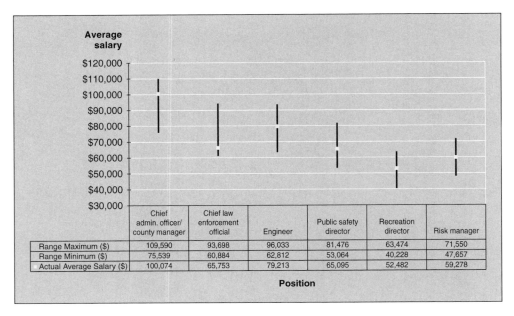

Figure 2/2   *Actual average salaries and salary ranges for six selected county positions, 2007*

Table 2/6   SALARIES OF COUNTY OFFICIALS: JULY–DECEMBER 2007

Salary data for the county positions in this table are based on information reported by county officials between late July 2007 and mid December 2007. Data are reported by position title only. Although job responsibilities are generally similar, the titles do not necessarily indicate identical duties and responsibilities.

For the position of county manager, data are shown for only those counties recognized by ICMA as having the council-manager form of government. For the position of chief administrative officer, data are shown for all other reporting counties.

Salaries are presented by ten population groups and are further classified by geographic region

and form of government. In some instances, form-of-government information is missing; therefore, the number of counties reporting by form of government might not always match the total number of counties reporting. For all positions, only full time positions are reported on the table.

Classifications having fewer than three counties reporting are excluded because meaningful statistics cannot be computed. Consequently, the number reporting in some subcategories does not always equal the total reporting. Quartiles are not shown when only three counties reported. The median represents either the value of the middle observation or, when there is an even

number of observations, the mean of the two middle observations. The first- and third-quartile observations represent the value of the observation below which 25% and 75% of the number of observations fall, respectively, and are calculated around the median, such that an equal number of observations fall between the median and the first quartile and the median and the third quartile.

(. . .) indicates that fewer than three counties reported, so meaningful statistics cannot be computed.

		Distribution of 2007 salaries			
Title of official	No. of counties reporting	Mean ($)	First quartile ($)	Median ($)	Third quartile ($)
All counties					
Chief admin. officer/county manager					
Total	165	100,074	74,099	96,800	124,120
Geographic region					
North East	7	99,832	82,805	97,639	116,845
North-Central	75	91,600	71,794	88,435	114,279
South	68	109,327	76,454	100,971	136,766
West	15	100,617	80,975	97,023	116,324
County type					
Metro	75	126,506	99,094	124,442	144,804
Nonmetro	90	78,048	64,991	80,370	98,186
Form of government					
Commission	76	78,299	56,666	75,299	97,244
Council-manager/admin	58	123,027	95,450	117,312	141,914
Council–elected executive	31	110,515	87,607	102,948	130,526
Chief elected official					
Total	269	44,712	26,928	39,444	55,344
Geographic region					
North East	6	35,043	14,763	15,888	30,319
North-Central	55	32,378	18,654	24,701	34,757
South	187	48,437	32,358	43,164	59,850
West	21	46,604	27,819	40,733	61,963
County type					
Metro	79	60,804	34,985	59,316	82,423
Nonmetro	190	38,021	25,636	36,137	46,775

		Distribution of 2007 salaries			
Title of official	No. of counties reporting	Mean ($)	First quartile ($)	Median ($)	Third quartile ($)
All counties continued					
Form of government					
Commission	220	44,088	27,993	39,435	53,467
Council-manager/admin	20	37,983	22,429	33,021	50,472
Council–elected executive	29	54,087	22,771	46,710	76,881
Chief financial officer					
Total	140	75,378	51,107	71,466	95,679
Geographic region					
North East	5	100,827	82,258	93,236	129,434
North-Central	58	73,633	49,391	68,210	94,620
South	59	74,071	51,550	69,702	93,905
West	18	78,215	53,396	85,525	96,250
County type					
Metro	63	96,264	74,973	95,393	112,435
Nonmetro	77	58,290	43,500	55,985	72,003
Form of government					
Commission	69	63,365	43,500	58,716	82,632
Council-manager/admin	44	88,562	62,891	84,486	109,238
Council–elected executive	27	84,593	69,049	82,258	103,426
Chief law enforcement official					
Total	334	65,753	44,597	62,546	79,413
Geographic region					
North East	6	87,980	66,153	72,232	83,133
North-Central	187	64,375	47,689	62,571	76,492
South	108	67,066	39,870	59,547	85,078
West	33	65,221	48,597	59,166	77,850

Table 2/6 **SALARIES OF COUNTY OFFICIALS: JULY–DECEMBER 2007**
continued

Title of official	No. of counties reporting	Distribution of 2007 salaries			
		Mean ($)	First quartile ($)	Median ($)	Third quartile ($)
All counties continued					
County type					
Metro	92	91,251	68,480	89,843	105,333
Nonmetro	242	56,059	41,487	53,349	69,307
Form of government					
Commission	238	56,958	41,509	53,349	67,903
Council-manager/admin	58	92,328	74,277	87,842	109,260
Council–elected executive ..	38	80,273	61,509	76,406	93,410
Chief librarian					
Total	45	63,115	35,464	58,000	90,588
Geographic region					
North-Central	8	85,503	56,110	94,993	103,310
South	27	59,799	29,872	51,587	88,874
West	9	50,824	22,000	40,968	65,395
County type					
Metro	19	89,178	66,467	94,786	108,505
Nonmetro	26	44,069	27,599	39,268	56,397
Form of government					
Commission	25	40,474	27,486	37,568	48,714
Council-manager/admin	13	94,278	84,140	94,786	116,800
Council–elected executive ..	7	86,100	70,602	98,352	98,821
Clerk					
Total	327	45,963	33,615	40,804	51,647
Geographic region					
North East	7	52,730	39,575	47,666	70,746
North-Central	100	41,850	31,988	39,732	47,901
South	189	46,548	33,507	40,812	51,626
West	31	54,141	38,733	46,728	64,741
County type					
Metro	100	59,319	45,200	52,082	68,989
Nonmetro	227	40,080	31,905	37,740	44,909
Form of government					
Commission	255	43,534	32,758	39,908	49,174
Council-manager/admin	35	56,871	40,202	51,668	68,319
Council–elected executive ..	37	52,389	36,757	44,818	59,827
Economic development director					
Total	51	67,709	43,951	60,935	85,456
Geographic region					
North East	5	77,306	44,401	58,123	103,978
North-Central	14	51,053	38,447	48,502	59,521
South	24	79,817	59,998	71,026	98,806
West	8	54,535	32,601	52,457	77,536
County type					
Metro	21	89,613	64,771	83,000	105,807
Nonmetro	30	52,377	38,447	48,438	62,844
Form of government					
Commission	21	52,884	36,330	43,500	59,913
Council-manager/admin	16	82,468	63,346	72,682	98,031
Council–elected executive ..	14	73,080	52,033	67,921	96,085
Engineer					
Total	130	79,213	69,838	80,430	90,581
Geographic region					
North East	3	98,054	88,479	101,165	109,185
North-Central	64	78,535	69,946	81,985	89,224
South	56	78,700	69,246	79,868	92,736
West	7	81,432	73,591	77,752	88,556
County type					
Metro	67	84,179	74,606	82,560	98,009
Nonmetro	63	73,932	67,500	78,222	87,662
Form of government					
Commission	87	76,324	67,500	79,536	89,110
Council-manager/admin	27	87,782	75,397	85,516	103,143
Council–elected executive ..	16	80,459	71,506	78,108	92,984
Fire chief					
Total	36	67,248	43,350	61,941	79,826
Geographic region					
North-Central	3	35,074	17,549	24,000	47,062
South	30	69,764	44,545	61,941	78,996
West	3	74,269	64,001	82,002	88,403
County type					
Metro	22	74,790	42,183	70,583	81,850
Nonmetro	14	55,396	44,545	51,545	69,585
Form of government					
Commission	17	55,395	38,091	45,182	59,733
Council-manager/admin	11	81,966	69,045	78,072	88,021
Council–elected executive ..	8	72,200	46,724	67,600	79,349
Health officer					
Total	104	65,705	39,543	61,651	82,678

Title of official	No. of counties reporting	Distribution of 2007 salaries			
		Mean ($)	First quartile ($)	Median ($)	Third quartile ($)
All counties continued					
Geographic region					
North East	6	81,609	64,077	69,389	101,571
North-Central	64	58,718	39,092	53,089	78,607
South	22	75,896	41,992	71,464	86,987
West	12	76,331	50,380	65,406	110,929
County type					
Metro	41	88,603	64,082	81,846	114,181
Nonmetro	63	50,803	37,630	49,381	62,708
Form of government					
Commission	64	53,285	37,445	50,041	63,720
Council-manager/admin	19	98,115	76,800	93,220	115,622
Council–elected executive ..	21	74,230	56,817	69,676	87,866
Human resources director					
Total	153	71,431	49,440	66,624	93,236
Geographic region					
North East	8	77,613	59,450	75,097	93,693
North-Central	56	70,735	50,346	64,896	90,979
South	77	68,669	46,740	62,254	81,628
West	12	88,273	78,214	87,058	97,506
County type					
Metro	91	82,908	61,302	80,604	103,808
Nonmetro	62	54,585	40,754	54,757	64,749
Form of government					
Commission	79	64,117	42,758	57,621	79,046
Council-manager/admin	44	82,636	61,765	81,407	98,063
Council–elected executive ..	30	74,256	59,880	70,138	86,512
Human services director					
Total	91	75,085	59,050	74,643	90,749
Geographic region					
North East	5	77,998	61,242	77,474	78,470
North-Central	48	82,020	65,767	77,925	92,940
South	29	60,763	32,000	58,297	77,927
West	9	82,626	61,880	90,673	103,248
County type					
Metro	34	93,215	74,587	92,745	116,618
Nonmetro	57	64,271	52,800	66,000	78,470
Form of government					
Commission	55	64,506	49,762	64,170	79,548
Council-manager/admin	21	93,334	74,569	84,987	116,600
Council–elected executive ..	15	88,327	73,929	78,470	107,725
Information services director					
Total	132	77,351	53,285	74,033	93,125
Geographic region					
North East	4	82,063	76,823	81,775	87,015
North-Central	40	70,441	47,655	65,765	83,598
South	74	80,153	54,533	75,741	95,823
West	14	80,939	69,197	78,489	90,951
County type					
Metro	85	87,947	63,456	86,794	106,971
Nonmetro	47	58,189	46,625	54,666	72,069
Form of government					
Commission	73	69,868	47,250	63,426	82,743
Council-manager/admin	33	93,539	75,960	89,795	113,256
Council–elected executive ..	26	77,818	61,109	74,619	89,458
Parks and recreation director					
Total	94	67,329	43,255	61,924	82,987
Geographic region					
North East	3	88,966	77,348	77,831	95,017
North-Central	45	59,420	39,797	47,568	76,967
South	39	71,241	48,054	62,213	85,498
West	7	87,101	73,391	82,002	99,067
County type					
Metro	44	85,828	59,848	82,559	106,075
Nonmetro	50	51,050	39,416	46,231	62,960
Form of government					
Commission	44	55,382	36,928	45,583	62,650
Council-manager/admin	31	80,110	56,940	78,913	94,502
Council–elected executive ..	19	74,140	47,898	74,090	90,519
Parks superintendent					
Total	41	49,858	38,539	47,351	62,733
Geographic region					
North-Central	17	50,661	37,450	43,740	67,730
South	18	49,959	40,752	46,998	53,654
West	4	44,082	37,664	47,616	54,035
County type					
Metro	21	61,451	50,434	62,733	69,096
Nonmetro	20	37,686	30,171	40,805	45,116

Table 2/6   SALARIES OF COUNTY OFFICIALS: JULY–DECEMBER 2007
continued

Title of official	No. of counties reporting	Distribution of 2007 salaries Mean ($)	First quartile ($)	Median ($)	Third quartile ($)
All counties continued					
Form of government					
Commission	16	37,746	26,494	36,788	44,360
Council-manager/admin	16	57,490	47,525	52,793	68,010
Council–elected executive . .	9	57,824	44,748	55,876	62,733
Planning director					
Total	109	67,028	43,757	65,000	83,734
Geographic region					
North East	5	63,787	42,530	58,123	66,082
North-Central	44	59,110	38,301	54,028	71,857
South	44	74,683	56,661	69,946	89,837
West	16	68,766	42,802	66,679	87,942
County type					
Metro	48	82,739	68,034	78,579	95,192
Nonmetro	61	54,666	37,852	52,499	65,000
Form of government					
Commission	50	56,753	38,002	50,260	64,950
Council-manager/admin	34	75,313	60,170	76,112	89,896
Council–elected executive . .	25	76,312	61,576	71,044	92,946
Primary asst. manager/CAO					
Total	59	79,105	49,725	75,632	107,311
Geographic region					
North-Central	22	82,698	51,069	78,839	114,832
South	31	75,708	49,124	75,632	101,407
West	4	86,136	63,288	79,391	102,239
County type					
Metro	32	103,014	79,250	101,407	121,024
Nonmetro	27	50,768	29,271	47,261	67,958
Form of government					
Commission	18	44,916	27,100	31,719	57,990
Council-manager/admin	30	96,172	72,380	95,515	118,900
Council–elected executive . .	11	88,504	63,437	75,935	102,650
Public safety director					
Total	36	65,095	45,680	62,426	75,820
Geographic region					
North-Central	12	52,898	38,113	50,106	62,512
South	18	67,785	48,257	62,968	75,634
West	4	75,364	67,499	78,172	86,037
County type					
Metro	17	81,066	64,369	75,760	103,114
Nonmetro	19	50,805	40,258	52,429	62,426
Form of government					
Commission	14	48,208	37,300	45,430	60,700
Council-manager/admin	14	76,288	59,019	66,613	99,070
Council–elected executive . .	8	75,059	59,456	74,643	82,916
Public works director					
Total	121	78,731	52,597	75,429	104,206
Geographic region					
North East	6	80,402	68,077	77,197	89,675
North-Central	50	78,020	43,538	81,270	105,180
South	49	80,573	52,847	74,197	106,957
West	16	74,684	43,907	76,305	96,525
County type					
Metro	58	99,043	75,810	98,284	117,185
Nonmetro	63	60,031	40,860	56,947	77,023
Form of government					
Commission	60	64,025	40,346	56,131	81,460
Council-manager/admin	38	99,496	80,102	97,435	119,037
Council–elected executive . .	23	82,787	69,703	76,866	97,834
Purchasing director					
Total	57	66,795	47,347	63,689	82,002
Geographic region					
North East	4	66,093	44,882	58,110	79,321
North-Central	15	63,668	51,795	60,902	77,367
South	35	66,041	45,208	62,341	88,520
West	3	92,165	84,896	87,790	97,247
County type					
Metro	42	74,073	59,031	73,374	90,747
Nonmetro	15	46,416	36,831	42,640	48,233
Form of government					
Commission	22	53,059	38,693	46,389	58,795
Council-manager/admin	21	79,552	68,554	77,324	88,088
Council–elected executive . .	14	69,245	49,930	63,908	85,906
Recreation director					
Total	22	52,482	33,588	52,564	56,626
Geographic region					
South	19	54,434	33,896	53,976	60,690
County type					
Metro	7	74,575	55,014	56,817	86,329
Nonmetro	15	42,173	31,841	35,000	53,574

Title of official	No. of counties reporting	Distribution of 2007 salaries Mean ($)	First quartile ($)	Median ($)	Third quartile ($)
All counties continued					
Form of government					
Commission	7	52,414	32,780	35,000	54,284
Council-manager/admin	9	56,720	34,512	56,052	67,409
Council–elected executive . .	6	46,205	38,770	51,897	54,045
Risk manager					
Total	58	59,278	42,663	55,777	72,587
Geographic region					
North-Central	21	59,095	38,196	67,684	75,005
South	27	58,191	43,939	54,619	62,471
West	8	64,938	47,320	65,240	75,628
County type					
Metro	38	65,844	47,215	62,042	77,875
Nonmetro	20	46,803	34,896	41,899	56,000
Form of government					
Commission	23	50,739	36,645	46,322	54,678
Council-manager/admin	21	68,669	58,656	67,684	77,927
Council–elected executive . .	14	59,221	42,663	57,983	69,720
Treasurer					
Total	400	47,726	33,475	42,734	57,161
Geographic region					
North East	6	62,729	57,316	59,960	63,466
North-Central	167	49,203	35,740	44,653	59,111
South	196	44,880	31,418	40,033	50,606
West	31	54,856	41,439	49,914	65,088
County type					
Metro	98	65,908	48,923	60,492	79,857
Nonmetro	302	41,825	31,552	39,105	48,351
Form of government					
Commission	331	44,079	32,160	40,607	50,792
Council-manager/admin	34	72,373	59,323	71,800	83,685
Council–elected executive . .	35	58,273	40,221	53,174	67,002
Over 1,000,000					
Chief admin. officer/county manager					
Total	5	190,079	162,000	186,840	192,846
Geographic region					
South	3	215,400	189,843	192,846	229,679
County type					
Metro	5	190,079	162,000	186,840	192,846
Form of government	. . .	. . .	. . .	. . .	. . .
Chief elected official					
Total	4	112,797	110,516	131,583	133,864
Geographic region					
South	3	107,146	93,115	133,416	134,313
County type					
Metro	4	112,797	110,516	131,583	133,864
Form of government	. . .	. . .	. . .	. . .	. . .
Chief financial officer					
Total	4	129,856	110,207	118,979	138,628
Geographic region	. . .				
County type					
Metro	4	129,856	110,207	118,979	138,628
Form of government	. . .	. . .	. . .	. . .	. . .
Chief law enforcement official					
Total	4	142,088	118,695	125,246	148,639
Geographic region	. . .	. . .	. . .	. . .	. . .
County type					
Metro	4	142,088	118,695	125,246	148,639
Form of government	. . .	. . .	. . .	. . .	. . .
Chief librarian					
Total	. . .	. . .	. . .	. . .	. . .
Geographic region	. . .	. . .	. . .	. . .	. . .
County type	. . .	. . .	. . .	. . .	. . .
Form of government	. . .	. . .	. . .	. . .	. . .
Clerk					
Total	5	103,163	63,168	107,844	120,084
Geographic region					
South	3	133,232	113,964	120,084	145,926
County type					
Metro	5	103,163	63,168	107,844	120,084
Form of government					
Commission	3	133,232	113,964	120,084	145,926
Economic development director					
Total	. . .	. . .	. . .	. . .	. . .
Geographic region	. . .	. . .	. . .	. . .	. . .
County type	. . .	. . .	. . .	. . .	. . .
Form of government	. . .	. . .	. . .	. . .	. . .

Table 2/6   SALARIES OF COUNTY OFFICIALS: JULY–DECEMBER 2007
continued

Title of official	No. of counties reporting	Mean ($)	First quartile ($)	Median ($)	Third quartile ($)	Title of official	No. of counties reporting	Mean ($)	First quartile ($)	Median ($)	Third quartile ($)
Over 1,000,000 continued						**Over 1,000,000 continued**					
Engineer						County type					
Total	4	100,604	78,703	100,736	122,637	Metro	4	98,187	90,747	91,669	99,110
Geographic region						Form of government	...	...	...	...	...
South	3	93,715	77,206	80,200	103,466	**Recreation director**					
County type						Total	...	...	...	...	...
Metro	4	100,604	78,703	100,736	122,637	Geographic region	...	...	...	...	...
Form of government	...	...	...	...	...	County type	...	...	...	...	...
Fire chief						Form of government	...	...	...	...	...
Total	...	...	...	...	...	**Risk manager**					
Geographic region	...	...	...	...	...	Total	3	99,674	80,315	82,911	110,651
County type	...	...	...	...	...	Geographic region	...	...	...	...	...
Form of government	...	...	...	...	...	County type					
Health officer						Metro	3	99,674	80,315	82,911	110,651
Total	3	128,923	122,821	137,894	139,511	Form of government	...	...	...	...	...
Geographic region	...	...	...	...	...	**Treasurer**					
County type						Total	3	134,621	105,582	117,767	155,233
Metro	3	128,923	122,821	137,894	139,511	Geographic region					
Form of government	...	...	...	...	...	South	3	134,621	105,582	117,767	155,233
Human resources director						County type					
Total	7	123,741	105,668	119,445	133,246	Metro	3	134,621	105,582	117,767	155,233
Geographic region						Form of government					
South	5	126,995	101,400	119,445	145,219	Commission	3	134,621	105,582	117,767	155,233
County type											
Metro	7	123,741	105,668	119,445	133,246	**500,000–1,000,000**					
Form of government						**Chief admin. officer/county manager**					
Commission	4	128,883	95,634	123,310	156,559	Total	7	154,474	131,930	139,818	171,380
Human services director						Geographic region					
Total	4	131,075	122,725	128,168	136,518	North-Central	4	155,459	136,084	143,477	162,852
Geographic region	...	...	...	...	...	County type					
County type						Metro	7	154,474	131,930	139,818	171,380
Metro	4	131,075	122,725	128,168	136,518	Form of government					
Form of government	...	...	...	...	...	Council-manager/admin	4	170,095	138,598	167,721	199,218
Information services director						**Chief elected official**					
Total	7	138,637	122,718	148,106	152,759	Total	6	74,218	39,906	80,777	106,172
Geographic region						Geographic region					
South	5	149,073	148,106	151,088	154,429	South	3	62,477	43,394	60,910	80,777
County type						County type					
Metro	7	138,637	122,718	148,106	152,759	Metro	6	74,218	39,906	80,777	106,172
Form of government						Form of government					
Commission	4	148,570	141,100	151,268	158,737	Commission	3	64,819	46,907	60,910	80,777
Parks and recreation director						**Chief financial officer**					
Total	...	...	...	...	...	Total	7	122,855	110,342	126,006	133,380
Geographic region	...	...	...	...	...	Geographic region					
County type	...	...	...	...	...	North-Central	4	119,542	113,710	121,542	127,374
Form of government	...	...	...	...	...	County type					
Parks superintendent						Metro	7	122,855	110,342	126,006	133,380
Total	...	...	...	...	...	Form of government					
Geographic region	...	...	...	...	...	Council-manager/admin	4	126,005	118,638	128,741	136,108
County type	...	...	...	...	...	**Chief law enforcement official**					
Form of government	...	...	...	...	...	Total	8	113,657	92,107	118,805	129,294
Planning director						Geographic region					
Total	4	131,738	107,779	129,238	153,196	North-Central	5	107,121	97,606	112,831	124,779
Geographic region	...	...	...	...	...	County type					
County type						Metro	8	113,657	92,107	118,805	129,294
Metro	4	131,738	107,779	129,238	153,196	Form of government					
Form of government	...	...	...	...	...	Council-manager/admin	5	110,332	97,606	124,779	124,779
Primary asst. manager/CAO						**Chief librarian**					
Total	...	...	...	...	...	Total	...	...	...	...	...
Geographic region	...	...	...	...	...	Geographic region	...	...	...	...	...
County type	...	...	...	...	...	County type	...	...	...	...	...
Form of government	...	...	...	...	...	Form of government	...	...	...	...	...
Public safety director						**Clerk**					
Total	...	...	...	...	...	Total	8	66,823	57,637	65,468	81,704
Geographic region	...	...	...	...	...	Geographic region					
County type	...	...	...	...	...	North-Central	3	54,490	37,205	53,183	71,122
Form of government	...	...	...	...	...	South	3	77,581	65,468	68,967	85,388
Public works director						County type					
Total	5	143,109	137,415	138,000	138,988	Metro	8	66,823	57,637	65,468	81,704
Geographic region						Form of government					
South	3	146,185	133,890	137,415	154,095	Commission	3	84,279	75,515	89,060	95,434
County type						Council-manager/admin	3	60,424	56,152	59,121	64,044
Metro	5	143,109	137,415	138,000	138,988	**Economic development director**					
Form of government						Total	3	76,121	62,192	74,381	89,179
Commission	3	146,185	133,890	137,415	154,095	Geographic region	...	...	...	...	...
Purchasing director						County type					
Total	4	98,187	90,747	91,669	99,110	Metro	3	76,121	62,192	74,381	89,179
Geographic region						Form of government	...	...	...	...	...
South	3	100,468	90,473	91,994	106,226						

Table 2/6   SALARIES OF COUNTY OFFICIALS: JULY–DECEMBER 2007
continued

Title of official	No. of counties reporting	Distribution of 2007 salaries			
		Mean ($)	First quartile ($)	Median ($)	Third quartile ($)
500,000–1,000,000 continued					
Engineer					
Total	6	88,432	77,162	90,094	100,930
Geographic region	...	...	...	...	...
County type					
Metro	6	88,432	77,162	90,094	100,930
Form of government	...	...	...	...	...
Fire chief					
Total	...	...	...	...	...
Geographic region	...	...	...	...	...
County type	...	...	...	...	...
Form of government	...	...	...	...	...
Health officer					
Total	4	114,645	100,485	116,512	130,673
Geographic region	...	...	...	...	...
County type					
Metro	4	114,645	100,485	116,512	130,673
Form of government	...	...	...	...	...
Human resources director					
Total	8	103,612	86,065	103,163	112,211
Geographic region					
North-Central	4	99,470	82,379	94,972	112,063
County type					
Metro	8	103,612	86,065	103,163	112,211
Form of government					
Commission	3	104,595	103,163	107,263	107,362
Council-manager/admin	3	98,377	84,334	87,193	106,829
Human services director					
Total	...	...	...	...	...
Geographic region	...	...	...	...	...
County type	...	...	...	...	...
Form of government	...	...	...	...	...
Information services director					
Total	5	118,534	108,852	120,736	130,584
Geographic region					
South	3	130,825	125,660	130,584	135,869
County type					
Metro	5	118,534	108,852	120,736	130,584
Form of government					
Commission	3	120,057	114,794	120,736	125,660
Parks and recreation director					
Total	6	109,347	95,613	108,549	122,899
Geographic region					
North-Central	3	107,960	98,707	104,896	115,680
County type					
Metro	6	109,347	95,613	108,549	122,899
Form of government					
Council-manager/admin	3	115,489	104,233	126,464	132,232
Parks superintendent					
Total	...	...	...	...	...
Geographic region	...	...	...	...	...
County type	...	...	...	...	...
Form of government	...	...	...	...	...
Planning director					
Total	3	98,116	91,073	94,952	103,577
Geographic region	...	...	...	...	...
County type					
Metro	3	98,116	91,073	94,952	103,577
Form of government	...	...	...	...	...
Primary asst. manager/CAO					
Total	3	109,490	105,235	105,633	111,816
Geographic region	...	...	...	...	...
County type					
Metro	3	109,490	105,235	105,633	111,816
Form of government	...	...	...	...	...
Public safety director					
Total					
Geographic region	...	...	...	...	...
County type	...	...	...	...	...
Form of government	...	...	...	...	...
Public works director					
Total	6	110,003	100,055	111,408	115,632
Geographic region					
North-Central	4	112,820	106,714	113,695	119,800
County type					
Metro	6	110,003	100,055	111,408	115,632
Form of government					
Council-manager/admin	3	112,009	103,575	110,614	119,745

Title of official	No. of counties reporting	Distribution of 2007 salaries			
		Mean ($)	First quartile ($)	Median ($)	Third quartile ($)
500,000–1,000,000 continued					
Purchasing director					
Total	3	90,316	79,663	82,002	96,813
Geographic region	...	...	...	...	...
County type					
Metro	3	90,316	79,663	82,002	96,813
Form of government	...	...	...	...	...
Recreation director					
Total	...	...	...	...	...
Geographic region	...	...	...	...	...
County type	...	...	...	...	...
Form of government	...	...	...	...	...
Risk manager					
Total	...	...	...	...	...
Geographic region	...	...	...	...	...
County type	...	...	...	...	...
Form of government	...	...	...	...	...
Treasurer					
Total	6	73,004	62,153	76,112	84,204
Geographic region					
North-Central	3	80,825	78,264	85,280	85,613
County type					
Metro	6	73,004	62,153	76,112	84,204
Form of government					
Commission	3	74,126	68,215	80,976	83,461
250,000–499,999					
Chief admin. officer/county manager					
Total	16	149,409	130,721	144,208	167,626
Geographic region					
North-Central	6	137,227	129,949	141,389	143,466
South	7	160,089	146,642	167,013	174,420
County type					
Metro	16	149,409	130,721	144,208	167,626
Form of government					
Commission	4	113,849	108,231	112,349	117,966
Council-manager/admin	7	160,929	143,124	161,152	173,194
Council–elected executive ..	5	161,729	144,608	155,162	169,465
Chief elected official					
Total	14	70,219	50,181	72,296	93,945
Geographic region					
South	9	71,387	25,794	88,320	98,556
West	3	70,442	57,879	65,605	80,586
County type					
Metro	14	70,219	50,181	72,296	93,945
Form of government					
Commission	7	91,790	76,962	89,076	101,537
Council-manager/admin	4	51,300	44,063	50,209	57,446
Council–elected executive ..	3	45,110	19,882	24,194	59,881
Chief financial officer					
Total	18	104,197	94,893	106,574	114,302
Geographic region					
North-Central	6	107,877	98,156	110,070	120,884
South	7	101,702	97,866	106,645	109,687
West	3	119,742	105,399	115,405	131,916
County type					
Metro	18	104,197	94,893	106,574	114,302
Form of government					
Commission	7	95,839	94,305	95,393	106,574
Council-manager/admin	6	109,468	86,440	112,149	125,970
Council–elected executive ..	5	109,574	109,570	113,636	114,525
Chief law enforcement official					
Total	18	110,820	96,328	108,266	128,593
Geographic region					
North-Central	6	113,958	99,323	118,043	127,640
South	8	117,602	99,265	115,504	139,785
West	3	101,603	97,089	98,610	104,621
County type					
Metro	18	110,820	96,328	108,266	128,593
Form of government					
Commission	7	89,602	85,320	94,167	98,841
Council-manager/admin	6	125,958	122,248	127,432	129,836
Council–elected executive ..	5	122,361	105,900	114,790	141,862
Chief librarian					
Total	8	102,452	93,758	98,821	114,636
Geographic region					
North-Central	3	103,605	97,007	98,813	107,807
South	4	97,623	89,154	94,131	102,601

Table 2/6 continued   SALARIES OF COUNTY OFFICIALS: JULY–DECEMBER 2007

Title of official	No. of counties reporting	Mean ($)	First quartile ($)	Median ($)	Third quartile ($)
250,000–499,999 continued					
County type					
Metro	8	102,452	93,758	98,821	114,636
Form of government					
Council-manager/admin	4	104,656	93,479	106,000	117,178
Council–elected executive ..	3	103,853	98,821	98,829	106,372
Clerk					
Total	15	81,157	70,293	78,874	87,028
Geographic region					
South	9	86,282	67,671	78,874	88,044
West	3	82,641	80,956	83,543	84,777
County type					
Metro	15	81,157	70,293	78,874	87,028
Form of government					
Commission	7	69,815	69,549	78,369	81,011
Council-manager/admin	4	88,710	71,603	78,229	95,335
Council–elected executive ..	4	93,454	74,546	92,412	111,320
Economic development director					
Total	5	84,400	62,940	64,771	105,807
Geographic region					
South	3	84,418	60,979	64,771	98,033
County type					
Metro	5	84,400	62,940	64,771	105,807
Form of government					
Council-manager/admin	3	75,312	60,064	62,940	84,374
Engineer					
Total	16	92,818	81,804	96,360	106,367
Geographic region					
North-Central	4	104,143	102,745	107,032	108,430
South	10	87,858	80,293	89,300	97,909
County type					
Metro	16	92,818	81,804	96,360	106,367
Form of government					
Commission	7	96,995	88,218	98,136	103,440
Council-manager/admin	6	95,864	86,637	101,464	107,899
Council–elected executive ..	3	76,978	67,720	79,537	87,515
Fire chief					
Total	5	89,207	77,084	78,072	81,392
Geographic region					
South	5	89,207	77,084	78,072	81,392
County type					
Metro	5	89,207	77,084	78,072	81,392
Form of government	...	...	...	...	...
Health officer					
Total	12	93,785	77,794	101,354	113,897
Geographic region					
North-Central	4	102,529	92,855	102,360	112,034
South	5	72,573	64,750	70,178	80,333
West	3	117,481	113,275	117,062	121,477
County type					
Metro	12	93,785	77,794	101,354	113,897
Form of government					
Commission	4	77,333	60,865	75,256	91,723
Council-manager/admin	5	95,658	91,759	93,220	111,500
Council–elected executive ..	3	112,601	111,562	113,636	114,157
Human resources director					
Total	21	100,852	93,236	96,903	113,510
Geographic region					
North-Central	5	105,519	96,664	106,142	113,636
South	11	95,896	79,321	94,764	107,143
West	3	115,714	110,953	113,510	119,374
County type					
Metro	21	100,852	93,236	96,903	113,510
Form of government					
Commission	9	97,497	91,552	94,764	106,008
Council-manager/admin	7	106,746	96,783	106,142	113,939
Council–elected executive ..	5	98,640	81,628	108,395	113,636
Human services director					
Total	7	89,941	67,886	85,425	116,612
Geographic region					
North-Central	3	108,783	101,013	116,600	120,462
County type					
Metro	7	89,941	67,886	85,425	116,612
Form of government					
Council-manager/admin	4	96,162	78,643	101,013	118,531
Information services director					
Total	18	106,429	92,738	106,067	116,701
Geographic region					
North-Central	3	109,334	104,351	116,537	117,919
South	11	104,171	90,450	101,521	115,476
West	3	116,124	111,569	116,167	120,701

Title of official	No. of counties reporting	Mean ($)	First quartile ($)	Median ($)	Third quartile ($)
250,000–499,999 continued					
County type					
Metro	18	106,429	92,738	106,067	116,701
Form of government					
Commission	7	102,729	90,450	93,462	115,182
Council-manager/admin	6	108,472	97,272	109,138	118,664
Council–elected executive ..	5	109,157	105,163	106,971	116,537
Parks and recreation director					
Total	12	100,374	83,208	102,856	113,032
Geographic region					
North-Central	4	108,131	106,493	111,394	113,032
South	5	93,425	72,871	85,000	94,394
County type					
Metro	12	100,374	83,208	102,856	113,032
Form of government					
Commission	3	81,873	68,003	77,831	93,722
Council-manager/admin	6	102,613	94,820	103,029	112,112
Council–elected executive ..	3	114,398	93,253	113,636	135,162
Parks superintendent					
Total	5	65,852	60,912	67,571	68,851
Geographic region					
North-Central	3	71,277	68,211	68,851	73,130
County type					
Metro	5	65,852	60,912	67,571	68,851
Form of government					
Council-manager/admin	3	63,646	61,043	67,571	68,211
Planning director					
Total	10	92,324	84,594	88,945	95,200
Geographic region					
North-Central	3	95,882	82,550	87,173	104,860
South	7	90,799	85,908	89,808	94,488
County type					
Metro	10	92,324	84,594	88,945	95,200
Form of government					
Council-manager/admin	5	86,341	83,734	87,173	89,808
Council–elected executive ..	4	103,623	93,954	101,932	111,601
Primary asst. manager/CAO					
Total	7	132,844	117,624	140,405	146,482
Geographic region					
South	4	130,426	117,058	131,035	144,403
County type					
Metro	7	132,844	117,624	140,405	146,482
Form of government					
Council-manager/admin	4	129,778	113,872	128,911	144,817
Council–elected executive ..	3	136,932	130,076	140,405	145,523
Public safety director					
Total	3	103,428	100,851	105,900	107,241
Geographic region					
South	3	103,428	100,851	105,900	107,241
County type					
Metro	3	103,428	100,851	105,900	107,241
Form of government	...	...	...	...	...
Public works director					
Total	12	115,234	106,410	116,029	120,912
Geographic region					
North-Central	4	112,205	105,601	112,593	119,196
South	6	112,617	104,941	111,281	118,561
County type					
Metro	12	115,234	106,410	116,029	120,912
Form of government					
Council-manager/admin	6	121,113	115,893	118,466	123,517
Council–elected executive ..	4	111,196	98,324	107,728	120,600
Purchasing director					
Total	12	82,241	73,199	78,899	102,266
Geographic region					
North-Central	3	78,403	77,668	77,927	78,899
South	7	86,922	71,842	98,272	103,713
County type					
Metro	12	82,241	73,199	78,899	102,266
Form of government					
Commission	3	80,469	67,401	98,272	102,439
Council-manager/admin	5	87,976	77,927	79,871	100,820
Council–elected executive ..	4	76,402	64,541	73,269	85,130
Recreation director					
Total	3	59,146	55,014	56,052	61,731
Geographic region					
South	3	59,146	55,014	56,052	61,731
County type					
Metro	3	59,146	55,014	56,052	61,731
Form of government	...	...	...	...	...

Table 2/6 **SALARIES OF COUNTY OFFICIALS: JULY–DECEMBER 2007**
continued

Title of official	No. of counties reporting	Mean ($)	First quartile ($)	Median ($)	Third quartile ($)
250,000–499,999 continued					
Risk manager					
Total	14	74,350	58,779	75,169	85,257
Geographic region					
North-Central	4	81,273	75,625	82,010	87,659
South	6	66,572	57,450	58,902	72,599
West	3	87,569	78,002	82,748	94,726
County type					
Metro	14	74,350	58,779	75,169	85,257
Form of government					
Commission	3	64,486	55,355	57,048	69,898
Council-manager/admin	6	83,136	77,294	82,010	90,789
Council–elected executive	5	69,724	59,148	68,718	73,255
Treasurer					
Total	16	83,819	77,556	81,522	88,934
Geographic region					
North-Central	4	88,731	81,223	88,978	96,486
South	8	84,292	74,677	80,000	88,934
West	3	82,641	80,956	83,543	84,777
County type					
Metro	16	83,819	77,556	81,522	88,934
Form of government					
Commission	7	73,396	68,638	75,117	79,697
Council-manager/admin	5	84,302	78,976	82,021	83,543
Council–elected executive	4	101,456	90,205	93,769	105,020
100,000–249,999					
Chief admin. officer/county manager					
Total	21	124,911	102,948	124,442	145,000
Geographic region					
North-Central	6	115,773	106,566	119,230	134,473
South	12	135,705	114,261	135,488	161,750
County type					
Metro	19	123,062	99,364	124,442	141,552
Form of government					
Commission	7	88,853	73,098	76,174	99,364
Council-manager/admin	10	152,635	127,737	144,387	175,250
Council–elected executive	4	118,704	116,385	122,946	125,266
Chief elected official					
Total	27	61,718	41,689	60,387	82,423
Geographic region					
North-Central	4	39,624	31,625	38,807	46,806
South	21	65,872	48,778	66,709	82,740
County type					
Metro	26	59,935	39,844	59,851	81,991
Form of government					
Commission	16	73,765	60,119	78,174	90,528
Council-manager/admin	8	37,696	28,639	35,903	46,806
Council–elected executive	3	61,532	38,251	46,710	77,403
Chief financial officer					
Total	18	95,079	82,288	93,012	104,446
Geographic region					
North-Central	5	97,452	82,173	92,360	105,164
South	11	91,071	78,837	93,077	101,096
County type					
Metro	16	95,034	80,797	92,719	106,681
Form of government					
Commission	5	83,500	65,000	82,632	105,164
Council-manager/admin	9	105,485	92,360	97,926	129,434
Council–elected executive	4	86,139	76,262	84,807	94,684
Chief law enforcement official					
Total	21	90,261	79,872	91,846	98,027
Geographic region					
North-Central	6	87,967	76,277	90,063	99,980
South	13	92,649	80,844	91,846	98,027
County type					
Metro	19	88,187	76,620	90,798	96,873
Form of government					
Commission	9	80,191	73,368	80,844	90,798
Council-manager/admin	8	110,313	95,570	99,814	120,664
Council–elected executive	4	72,815	56,200	71,462	88,077
Chief librarian					
Total	6	88,491	72,733	89,463	101,017
Geographic region					
South	4	88,005	63,417	86,013	110,601
County type					
Metro	6	88,491	72,733	89,463	101,017
Form of government					
Council-manager/admin	4	103,785	92,125	98,940	110,601

Title of official	No. of counties reporting	Mean ($)	First quartile ($)	Median ($)	Third quartile ($)
100,000–249,999 continued					
Clerk					
Total	31	59,000	50,592	55,795	64,684
Geographic region					
North-Central	4	51,811	47,784	59,197	63,223
South	25	58,145	50,400	53,616	63,468
County type					
Metro	29	57,966	50,400	54,382	64,272
Form of government					
Commission	20	59,461	51,108	55,088	63,669
Council-manager/admin	8	57,187	44,704	55,744	68,730
Council–elected executive	3	60,768	46,892	59,827	74,174
Economic development director					
Total	5	113,863	99,406	100,051	139,281
Geographic region					
South	3	112,913	99,728	100,051	119,666
County type					
Metro	4	120,198	99,890	119,666	139,974
Form of government					
Council-manager/admin	3	126,914	119,344	139,281	140,668
Engineer					
Total	22	82,075	72,311	79,878	95,683
Geographic region					
North-Central	4	85,577	73,109	87,167	99,635
South	17	81,621	71,415	80,220	89,087
County type					
Metro	21	81,968	71,415	79,536	97,882
Form of government					
Commission	10	71,945	58,547	76,272	80,049
Council-manager/admin	9	92,377	76,452	85,516	104,894
Council–elected executive	3	84,939	78,467	85,519	91,700
Fire chief					
Total	9	82,986	50,421	94,039	94,993
Geographic region					
South	8	81,508	47,917	86,671	97,984
County type					
Metro	7	79,582	45,413	79,304	100,498
Form of government					
Commission	4	58,321	39,178	45,413	64,555
Council-manager/admin	4	104,696	90,355	94,516	108,856
Health officer					
Total	10	95,812	77,142	89,138	119,277
Geographic region					
North-Central	4	94,295	81,185	89,138	102,249
South	5	93,352	56,817	76,880	143,062
County type					
Metro	10	95,812	77,142	89,138	119,277
Form of government					
Commission	3	90,758	59,898	82,271	117,374
Council-manager/admin	4	118,556	109,637	117,579	126,498
Council–elected executive	3	70,542	66,848	76,880	77,404
Human resources director					
Total	31	74,146	52,140	74,123	93,936
Geographic region					
North-Central	5	95,270	90,788	96,096	105,564
South	24	68,600	50,071	62,383	83,787
County type					
Metro	29	72,747	51,840	70,845	93,334
Form of government					
Commission	17	60,172	46,740	52,440	66,624
Council-manager/admin	10	93,322	77,995	94,168	103,197
Council–elected executive	4	85,598	73,303	83,999	96,294
Human services director					
Total	12	87,134	57,875	100,833	111,857
Geographic region					
North-Central	5	111,075	108,022	110,902	114,720
South	6	71,606	43,005	61,454	93,382
County type					
Metro	12	87,134	57,875	100,833	111,857
Form of government					
Commission	5	63,255	40,776	49,692	100,104
Council-manager/admin	5	108,281	108,022	110,902	120,168
Information services director					
Total	31	81,641	66,132	80,728	93,941
Geographic region					
North-Central	6	92,076	80,566	88,053	102,614
South	23	78,748	60,870	78,936	91,089
County type					
Metro	29	81,287	64,704	80,511	94,870

Table 2/6 SALARIES OF COUNTY OFFICIALS: JULY–DECEMBER 2007
continued

Title of official	No. of counties reporting	Distribution of 2007 salaries			
		Mean ($)	First quartile ($)	Median ($)	Third quartile ($)
100,000–249,999 continued					
Form of government					
Commission	17	70,295	57,570	67,560	82,743
Council-manager/admin	10	100,850	86,048	95,124	111,199
Council–elected executive . .	4	81,838	76,929	81,895	86,805
Parks and recreation director					
Total	9	89,155	74,090	88,520	94,611
Geographic region					
South	6	97,037	87,428	93,170	101,704
County type					
Metro	7	88,878	73,074	85,995	99,340
Form of government					
Council-manager/admin	4	98,040	86,810	93,170	104,399
Council–elected executive . .	3	82,868	80,042	85,995	87,258
Parks superintendent					
Total	9	60,774	42,446	51,033	72,015
Geographic region					
South	7	58,174	42,400	49,249	67,218
County type					
Metro	8	63,256	47,548	59,382	74,862
Form of government					
Council-manager/admin	7	60,159	45,801	51,033	69,873
Planning director					
Total	15	82,825	67,748	78,000	96,545
Geographic region					
North-Central	4	89,381	74,810	88,851	103,422
South	10	79,190	63,632	74,480	88,342
County type					
Metro	13	82,417	66,566	77,558	100,144
Form of government					
Commission	4	58,365	56,385	61,061	63,041
Council-manager/admin	7	95,132	80,797	89,925	106,700
Council–elected executive . .	4	85,746	75,401	85,252	95,597
Primary asst. manager/CAO					
Total	11	104,855	87,480	97,976	125,055
Geographic region					
North-Central	4	97,628	70,663	99,720	126,685
South	5	116,721	97,976	119,200	125,257
County type					
Metro	9	104,732	89,407	97,976	124,852
Form of government					
Council-manager/admin	9	112,107	93,730	119,200	125,257
Public safety director					
Total	5	90,913	74,446	75,760	100,160
Geographic region					
South	3	95,947	75,103	75,760	106,697
County type					
Metro	5	90,913	74,446	75,760	100,160
Form of government					
Council-manager/admin	3	104,518	87,960	100,160	118,897
Public works director					
Total	18	94,661	74,682	93,335	112,782
Geographic region					
North-Central	4	107,416	100,508	112,082	118,990
South	12	90,630	68,114	85,585	112,640
County type					
Metro	16	93,649	74,256	89,914	113,396
Form of government					
Commission	5	66,596	52,597	52,847	74,607
Council-manager/admin	10	109,192	88,009	110,855	122,113
Council–elected executive . .	3	93,001	83,075	92,946	102,900
Purchasing director					
Total	17	67,700	55,000	68,142	80,256
Geographic region					
North-Central	5	62,875	58,687	60,060	72,192
South	11	69,815	53,880	68,142	84,632
County type					
Metro	16	66,425	54,440	65,242	77,131
Form of government					
Commission	6	52,972	50,116	53,880	58,795
Council-manager/admin	9	77,124	68,554	76,089	88,088
Recreation director					
Total	4	89,833	62,627	84,906	112,112
Geographic region					
South	4	89,833	62,627	84,906	112,112
County type					
Metro	3	98,256	81,033	105,248	118,976
Form of government	. . .	. . .	. . .	. . .	. . .

Title of official	No. of counties reporting	Distribution of 2007 salaries			
		Mean ($)	First quartile ($)	Median ($)	Third quartile ($)
100,000–249,999 continued					
Risk manager					
Total	11	56,864	47,649	50,461	62,163
Geographic region					
North-Central	3	51,950	42,634	48,516	59,549
South	8	58,706	48,883	53,639	60,667
County type					
Metro	11	56,864	47,649	50,461	62,163
Form of government					
Council-manager/admin	7	61,096	47,649	59,172	67,868
Treasurer					
Total	23	62,513	50,832	57,822	64,406
Geographic region					
South	20	63,134	50,618	58,832	67,203
County type					
Metro	23	62,513	50,832	57,822	64,406
Form of government					
Commission	18	56,594	50,289	55,952	62,089
Council-manager/admin	4	82,304	56,492	70,966	96,779
50,000–99,999					
Chief admin. officer/county manager					
Total	29	97,673	88,878	100,548	112,778
Geographic region					
North-Central	9	107,726	99,806	112,778	118,414
South	16	93,289	83,451	100,971	106,273
County type					
Metro	13	111,232	101,394	112,778	118,414
Nonmetro	16	86,657	80,735	91,139	100,596
Form of government					
Commission	8	85,971	80,996	95,211	99,992
Council-manager/admin	11	110,075	102,168	112,778	117,312
Council–elected executive . .	10	93,394	83,216	92,502	106,722
Chief elected official					
Total	28	52,914	30,342	53,377	71,623
Geographic region					
North-Central	4	54,712	29,490	53,668	78,891
South	20	54,946	46,804	53,377	71,623
County type					
Metro	17	50,534	30,456	52,365	67,462
Nonmetro	11	56,593	36,204	54,389	80,900
Form of government					
Commission	17	59,762	49,304	55,305	71,008
Council-manager/admin	3	18,665	12,770	13,539	21,997
Council–elected executive . .	8	51,206	13,947	56,365	78,891
Chief financial officer					
Total	22	74,038	62,690	72,191	85,290
Geographic region					
North-Central	6	82,692	68,212	86,320	94,593
South	12	67,705	60,593	67,537	75,003
West	3	79,320	74,743	79,300	83,887
County type					
Metro	9	76,359	64,210	70,185	92,300
Nonmetro	13	72,430	62,183	77,422	82,258
Form of government					
Commission	8	66,860	60,593	65,547	72,464
Council-manager/admin	7	82,341	70,816	81,126	94,822
Council–elected executive . .	7	73,937	67,932	74,197	84,279
Chief law enforcement official					
Total	39	75,868	65,718	76,386	87,194
Geographic region					
North-Central	15	83,324	68,982	82,621	101,999
South	20	70,663	58,526	70,314	79,530
West	3	70,073	66,240	67,080	72,409
County type					
Metro	20	81,961	67,480	81,044	101,999
Nonmetro	19	69,454	62,388	71,275	77,910
Form of government					
Commission	20	65,504	55,575	67,277	71,251
Council-manager/admin	11	90,255	78,101	101,998	103,773
Council–elected executive . .	8	81,996	75,428	80,352	87,991
Chief librarian					
Total	5	65,755	51,587	64,002	72,274
Geographic region					
South	5	65,755	51,587	64,002	72,274
County type					
Nonmetro	3	74,071	61,930	72,274	85,313
Form of government					
Council–elected executive . .	3	74,071	61,930	72,274	85,313

Table 2/6 continued   SALARIES OF COUNTY OFFICIALS: JULY–DECEMBER 2007

Title of official	No. of counties reporting	Distribution of 2007 salaries			
		Mean ($)	First quartile ($)	Median ($)	Third quartile ($)
50,000–99,999 continued					
Clerk					
Total	38	47,995	42,597	48,326	55,892
Geographic region					
North-Central	9	50,126	37,315	51,277	60,468
South	24	44,708	41,688	46,549	50,342
West	3	63,267	62,160	64,000	64,741
County type					
Metro	20	49,064	44,216	49,569	53,148
Nonmetro	18	46,808	37,171	47,596	58,318
Form of government					
Commission	21	50,240	44,424	48,864	59,334
Council–manager/admin	5	44,675	32,062	45,403	51,626
Council–elected executive	12	45,451	37,175	48,174	52,940
Economic development director					
Total	8	65,024	56,061	60,709	73,694
Geographic region					
South	5	72,723	60,935	70,288	83,912
County type					
Metro	3	68,956	54,131	70,288	84,447
Nonmetro	5	62,665	58,123	60,482	60,935
Form of government					
Council–elected executive	6	64,904	51,937	59,529	78,168
Engineer					
Total	16	84,571	80,316	90,072	94,639
Geographic region					
North-Central	5	84,131	86,196	87,718	89,530
South	9	83,964	80,855	91,052	94,500
County type					
Metro	8	79,672	75,909	89,385	92,736
Nonmetro	8	89,471	84,322	90,072	96,550
Form of government					
Commission	11	80,774	77,173	87,718	93,054
Council–elected executive	3	93,169	89,172	92,148	96,656
Fire chief					
Total	9	54,675	39,029	59,733	67,966
Geographic region					
South	9	54,675	39,029	59,733	67,966
County type					
Metro	5	49,976	38,435	39,425	59,733
Nonmetro	4	60,549	57,869	66,057	68,738
Form of government					
Commission	4	43,921	38,349	38,930	44,502
Council–elected executive	4	62,107	57,869	67,600	71,838
Health officer					
Total	15	64,940	56,973	63,600	81,486
Geographic region					
North-Central	6	66,080	55,121	61,077	77,284
South	5	59,296	55,391	63,014	81,126
County type					
Metro	6	55,580	56,182	60,322	63,222
Nonmetro	9	71,180	63,014	69,676	83,900
Form of government					
Commission	8	55,638	53,532	56,973	64,070
Council–elected executive	5	73,206	63,014	69,676	84,950
Human resources director					
Total	33	61,422	50,649	62,600	69,935
Geographic region					
North-Central	9	73,629	64,043	69,935	89,482
South	18	53,153	40,204	57,545	62,787
West	4	69,161	63,119	71,829	77,871
County type					
Metro	17	63,020	57,468	62,964	74,197
Nonmetro	16	59,725	50,172	59,847	68,690
Form of government					
Commission	14	55,123	38,429	57,545	65,480
Council–manager/admin	8	73,908	64,028	67,561	89,487
Council–elected executive	11	60,359	55,237	62,600	69,105
Human services director					
Total	14	82,179	77,957	85,383	90,787
Geographic region					
North-Central	7	86,373	81,913	89,119	92,750
South	4	71,482	65,531	73,742	79,692
County type					
Metro	4	87,299	83,816	88,226	91,709
Nonmetro	10	80,131	73,026	81,728	90,398
Form of government					
Commission	5	90,555	90,673	90,825	91,193
Council–elected executive	7	73,990	70,454	77,927	78,258
50,000–99,999 continued					
Information services director					
Total	28	65,287	50,318	70,125	76,101
Geographic region					
North-Central	6	72,187	68,311	74,914	80,139
South	17	59,378	44,370	58,506	70,470
West	3	76,460	73,531	74,661	78,489
County type					
Metro	17	66,230	50,646	70,470	82,318
Nonmetro	11	63,829	53,919	69,780	73,134
Form of government					
Commission	13	60,692	44,370	63,426	74,661
Council-manager/admin	6	72,338	69,585	70,125	74,587
Council–elected executive	9	67,223	49,333	73,868	81,532
Parks and recreation director					
Total	15	65,178	56,894	63,209	77,053
Geographic region					
North-Central	5	63,214	56,287	63,209	78,913
South	8	63,436	55,591	61,048	71,694
County type					
Metro	6	73,683	63,462	76,555	82,066
Nonmetro	9	59,507	49,861	62,213	70,859
Form of government					
Commission	4	56,989	50,852	58,085	64,222
Council-manager/admin	6	71,457	60,841	74,886	82,066
Council–elected executive	5	64,194	62,213	63,209	74,197
Parks superintendent					
Total	8	48,616	43,866	47,616	52,585
Geographic region					
South	3	48,372	40,437	44,748	54,496
County type					
Metro	3	50,619	43,807	51,488	57,866
Nonmetro	5	47,415	44,748	46,218	49,014
Form of government					
Commission	3	43,786	41,172	46,218	47,616
Council–elected executive	4	48,332	43,866	48,118	52,585
Planning director					
Total	19	68,606	63,188	68,204	72,621
Geographic region					
North-Central	5	67,898	68,348	70,038	71,044
South	9	70,228	61,576	67,091	74,197
West	3	69,254	66,579	68,359	71,481
County type					
Metro	9	72,227	67,091	70,038	74,604
Nonmetro	10	65,347	58,986	65,082	68,320
Form of government					
Commission	5	68,537	64,800	68,359	74,604
Council-manager/admin	6	70,728	67,369	68,276	69,616
Council–elected executive	8	67,057	60,713	65,723	71,832
Primary asst. manager/CAO					
Total	12	78,278	63,855	74,430	86,596
Geographic region					
North-Central	6	86,961	72,578	90,102	97,568
South	4	70,434	63,574	69,953	76,813
County type					
Metro	7	86,112	74,715	83,089	97,417
Nonmetro	5	67,311	61,942	64,273	73,229
Form of government					
Council-manager/admin	6	89,243	77,496	90,102	97,568
Council–elected executive	4	67,176	62,319	63,437	68,294
Public safety director					
Total	7	65,565	59,752	62,979	71,848
Geographic region					
South	4	60,492	56,387	60,342	64,448
County type					
Nonmetro	5	64,180	61,798	62,979	68,857
Form of government					
Council-manager/admin	3	63,180	60,342	62,979	65,918
Council–elected executive	3	63,022	57,113	61,798	68,319
Public works director					
Total	18	81,014	68,506	77,197	96,020
Geographic region					
North-Central	5	99,897	97,115	97,755	107,302
South	9	69,699	63,842	67,870	74,197
County type					
Metro	11	87,103	75,863	89,505	97,435
Nonmetro	7	71,446	63,970	67,870	74,495
Form of government					
Commission	5	76,871	70,414	80,569	94,515
Council-manager/admin	7	92,360	76,802	97,115	102,529
Council–elected executive	6	71,231	68,933	73,160	76,199

Table 2/6   SALARIES OF COUNTY OFFICIALS: JULY–DECEMBER 2007
continued

Title of official	No. of counties reporting	Distribution of 2007 salaries			
		Mean ($)	First quartile ($)	Median ($)	Third quartile ($)

50,000–99,999 continued
Purchasing director
Total	12	51,558	45,368	48,630	57,366
Geographic region					
North-Central	3	54,368	51,101	56,243	58,573
South	8	50,991	43,547	48,207	52,420
County type					
Metro	6	55,665	48,148	55,165	60,861
Nonmetro	6	47,451	44,039	46,389	48,940
Form of government					
Commission	5	45,722	43,596	45,959	46,819
Council-manager/admin	3	64,378	60,819	60,902	66,200
Council–elected executive . .	4	49,239	46,599	48,657	51,296
Recreation director					
Total	. . .	. . .	. . .	. . .	. . .
Geographic region	. . .	. . .	. . .	. . .	. . .
County type	. . .	. . .	. . .	. . .	. . .
Form of government	. . .	. . .	. . .	. . .	. . .
Risk manager					
Total	13	52,877	42,967	46,322	67,684
Geographic region					
North-Central	5	58,198	42,967	67,684	68,048
South	5	47,441	45,316	45,351	46,322
County type					
Metro	7	49,052	41,300	45,351	57,003
Nonmetro	6	57,340	45,428	59,189	67,428
Form of government					
Commission	5	43,281	37,285	40,830	46,322
Council-manager/admin	5	61,435	45,351	67,684	73,817
Council–elected executive . .	3	54,609	47,889	52,810	60,429
Treasurer					
Total	40	59,047	47,932	54,639	65,345
Geographic region					
North-Central	12	69,474	53,838	65,753	86,126
South	22	51,900	45,210	48,983	55,269
West	4	61,043	57,488	61,791	65,345
County type					
Metro	26	61,194	48,193	53,942	67,839
Nonmetro	14	55,060	48,471	55,861	61,407
Form of government					
Commission	27	53,186	47,757	51,765	58,808
Council-manager/admin	6	78,906	72,402	87,753	91,006
Council–elected executive . .	7	64,632	51,636	57,551	71,124

25,000–49,999
Chief admin. officer/county manager
Total	33	82,427	72,660	83,075	96,387
Geographic region					
North-Central	24	82,339	77,869	85,948	90,927
South	9	82,663	58,866	76,692	126,545
County type					
Metro	9	85,950	78,383	83,075	89,107
Nonmetro	24	81,106	71,622	83,311	96,767
Form of government					
Commission	16	71,218	62,488	79,092	88,951
Council-manager/admin	14	93,740	77,613	88,645	100,835
Council–elected executive . .	3	89,418	84,280	85,650	92,672
Chief elected official					
Total	39	41,857	26,823	41,117	50,014
Geographic region					
North-Central	14	26,575	20,604	23,317	31,435
South	24	49,933	38,909	46,288	54,842
County type					
Metro	8	48,047	36,827	43,444	56,969
Nonmetro	31	40,259	26,823	38,348	49,494
Form of government					
Commission	33	42,488	33,183	41,180	49,783
Council–elected executive . .	4	31,843	20,173	20,766	32,436
Chief financial officer					
Total	29	61,708	49,249	62,256	72,315
Geographic region					
North-Central	20	57,877	44,680	62,474	69,559
South	8	68,241	50,081	60,706	78,016
County type					
Metro	5	67,512	60,660	62,256	73,243
Nonmetro	24	60,498	48,182	61,721	72,081
Form of government					
Commission	15	57,347	46,511	54,600	68,268
Council-manager/admin	11	68,517	55,438	68,744	73,248
Council–elected executive . .	3	58,545	53,619	62,256	65,326

25,000–49,999 continued
Chief law enforcement official
Total	62	65,992	55,151	69,463	81,937
Geographic region					
North-Central	43	71,123	58,999	73,300	82,478
South	18	52,370	39,204	43,624	58,503
County type					
Metro	14	72,030	58,571	74,128	85,711
Nonmetro	48	64,231	49,424	66,853	78,839
Form of government					
Commission	44	62,461	47,985	59,855	78,097
Council-manager/admin	14	73,426	62,344	73,004	81,702
Council–elected executive . .	4	78,811	73,517	78,816	84,110
Chief librarian					
Total	8	55,645	41,777	55,698	65,408
Geographic region					
South	6	52,216	38,971	48,288	60,292
County type					
Nonmetro	6	54,862	38,971	50,590	69,896
Form of government					
Commission	5	47,716	37,568	43,180	58,000
Council-manager/admin	3	68,858	57,993	62,591	76,590
Clerk					
Total	51	42,983	35,714	42,288	49,348
Geographic region					
North-Central	18	45,528	39,339	47,258	51,323
South	32	40,205	35,003	40,673	48,006
County type					
Metro	13	42,458	35,000	46,710	48,430
Nonmetro	38	43,162	36,435	40,843	49,615
Form of government					
Commission	42	42,503	35,326	41,544	48,731
Council-manager/admin	7	44,264	38,062	40,883	50,049
Economic development director					
Total	6	70,639	69,004	71,128	74,242
Geographic region					
South	4	74,390	70,323	73,107	77,173
County type					
Metro	4	70,394	65,009	71,788	77,173
Form of government					
Council-manager/admin	5	70,512	68,345	70,982	75,231
Engineer					
Total	24	78,337	71,394	82,324	87,136
Geographic region					
North-Central	18	81,866	79,607	85,018	88,177
South	5	63,917	62,082	69,546	69,779
County type					
Metro	8	75,550	73,695	77,963	81,972
Nonmetro	16	79,731	71,336	85,650	88,395
Form of government					
Commission	18	79,402	72,505	85,018	88,177
Council-manager/admin	5	74,835	71,933	75,000	79,248
Fire chief					
Total	4	49,212	40,000	51,136	60,349
Geographic region					
South	3	42,242	34,818	45,182	51,136
County type					
Nonmetro	3	57,465	51,136	57,090	63,607
Form of government	. . .	. . .	. . .	. . .	. . .
Health officer					
Total	19	59,217	45,550	61,506	76,695
Geographic region					
North-Central	16	57,083	48,725	59,343	72,895
County type					
Metro	4	66,729	64,911	66,330	68,148
Nonmetro	15	57,214	31,497	56,000	80,745
Form of government					
Commission	13	56,544	39,200	56,000	70,313
Council-manager/admin	3	71,702	67,128	72,750	76,800
Council–elected executive . .	3	58,314	43,537	66,614	77,240
Human resources director					
Total	30	54,982	43,251	56,963	64,511
Geographic region					
North-Central	21	54,965	47,509	57,926	62,201
South	8	51,035	34,634	47,110	71,138
County type					
Metro	8	59,883	51,826	59,320	66,289
Nonmetro	22	53,200	35,822	55,457	63,301

Table 2/6   SALARIES OF COUNTY OFFICIALS: JULY–DECEMBER 2007
continued

Title of official	No. of counties reporting	Distribution of 2007 salaries			
		Mean ($)	First quartile ($)	Median ($)	Third quartile ($)
25,000–49,999 continued					
Form of government					
Commission	15	51,843	36,842	51,552	64,230
Council-manager/admin	11	60,918	56,420	60,456	72,123
Council–elected executive . .	4	50,432	43,936	53,808	60,305
Human services director					
Total	18	72,078	67,228	76,625	81,966
Geographic region					
North-Central	13	78,249	74,643	80,849	84,042
South	5	56,032	34,465	67,814	74,569
County type					
Metro	4	77,626	74,624	77,321	80,323
Nonmetro	14	70,493	66,258	76,625	83,579
Form of government					
Commission	11	67,714	64,518	75,446	82,668
Council-manager/admin	5	77,084	74,569	80,000	80,849
Information services director					
Total	24	57,275	47,321	55,717	65,657
Geographic region					
North-Central	14	58,272	52,123	55,717	64,497
South	9	53,966	43,081	48,120	63,079
County type					
Metro	7	58,843	50,479	59,486	62,209
Nonmetro	17	56,630	47,344	53,942	65,980
Form of government					
Commission	15	52,384	46,625	53,094	57,322
Council-manager/admin	6	68,597	61,774	69,760	79,747
Council–elected executive . .	3	59,088	55,642	59,486	62,733
Parks and recreation director					
Total	17	53,527	43,030	50,530	64,626
Geographic region					
North-Central	10	53,031	43,273	53,654	63,606
South	7	54,237	37,214	50,530	73,997
County type					
Metro	5	55,424	43,075	59,741	72,993
Nonmetro	12	52,737	42,755	49,049	64,264
Form of government					
Commission	9	50,696	43,030	47,568	61,992
Council-manager/admin	7	61,056	46,802	64,144	73,997
Parks superintendent					
Total	7	40,710	34,847	43,740	48,893
Geographic region					
North-Central	4	37,805	33,757	40,595	44,643
South	3	44,582	41,339	50,434	50,752
County type					
Nonmetro	5	39,417	32,244	43,740	47,351
Form of government					
Commission	4	37,805	33,757	40,595	44,643
Council-manager/admin	3	44,582	41,339	50,434	50,752
Planning director					
Total	21	58,827	47,317	54,246	69,636
Geographic region					
North-Central	14	52,931	44,499	53,154	58,841
South	6	66,832	52,746	63,765	77,588
County type					
Metro	6	59,169	42,924	64,503	73,888
Nonmetro	15	58,690	47,950	53,809	64,194
Form of government					
Commission	12	53,346	45,100	52,269	54,771
Council-manager/admin	7	68,989	57,272	72,660	76,764
Primary asst. manager/CAO					
Total	8	58,613	41,970	53,476	77,677
Geographic region					
South	6	58,182	35,233	53,476	80,876
County type					
Metro	3	74,014	64,063	73,674	83,795
Nonmetro	5	49,372	29,478	46,134	52,499
Form of government					
Commission	3	34,892	29,271	29,478	37,806
Council-manager/admin	4	72,638	53,964	72,068	90,742
Public safety director					
Total	5	39,210	29,815	44,000	46,867
Geographic region					
North-Central	3	46,061	36,908	44,000	54,185
County type					
Metro	3	47,017	38,341	46,867	55,618
Form of government					
Commission	3	28,271	20,407	29,815	36,908

Title of official	No. of counties reporting	Distribution of 2007 salaries			
		Mean ($)	First quartile ($)	Median ($)	Third quartile ($)
25,000–49,999 continued					
Public works director					
Total	13	82,600	66,000	85,635	96,373
Geographic region					
North-Central	7	80,672	66,779	85,635	95,950
South	5	80,969	58,112	78,448	96,373
County type					
Metro	4	75,123	65,197	73,003	82,929
Nonmetro	9	85,923	66,000	95,867	98,197
Form of government					
Commission	5	81,712	66,000	96,034	98,197
Council-manager/admin	7	81,338	62,835	78,448	91,004
Purchasing director					
Total	6	42,225	36,667	38,307	41,214
Geographic region					
South	4	44,922	38,278	40,629	47,272
County type					
Nonmetro	5	37,932	36,504	37,158	39,457
Form of government					
Commission	4	38,125	36,063	37,981	40,043
Recreation director					
Total	. . .	. . .	. . .	. . .	. . .
Geographic region	. . .	. . .	. . .	. . .	. . .
County type	. . .	. . .	. . .	. . .	. . .
Form of government	. . .	. . .	. . .	. . .	. . .
Risk manager					
Total	11	42,528	30,408	38,196	52,110
Geographic region					
North-Central	6	44,977	33,226	41,449	52,228
South	4	37,116	29,537	30,029	37,608
County type					
Nonmetro	10	42,310	30,311	34,883	53,423
Form of government					
Commission	8	38,420	30,122	34,883	45,897
Treasurer					
Total	70	51,833	40,578	48,098	57,625
Geographic region					
North-Central	40	56,427	45,155	52,941	71,650
South	29	44,317	36,147	40,764	48,912
County type					
Metro	16	54,653	46,091	50,464	64,774
Nonmetro	54	50,998	40,193	47,699	55,177
Form of government					
Commission	54	49,241	38,891	46,313	52,590
Council-manager/admin	11	64,123	53,701	71,500	76,649
Council–elected executive . .	5	52,793	52,315	53,174	55,906
10,000–24,999					
Chief admin. officer/county manager					
Total	42	76,733	62,310	78,596	96,604
Geographic region					
North-Central	18	67,539	54,403	68,997	79,480
South	18	84,366	73,151	91,174	98,312
West	5	81,040	49,914	89,167	114,296
County type					
Metro	6	84,655	74,615	93,108	96,604
Nonmetro	36	75,413	60,208	76,716	93,681
Form of government					
Commission	28	68,504	52,649	70,174	83,001
Council-manager/admin	9	95,873	88,296	96,800	99,000
Council–elected executive . .	5	88,363	87,848	90,200	96,015
Chief elected official					
Total	77	39,322	25,683	39,711	50,073
Geographic region					
North-Central	14	24,404	15,822	23,756	28,997
South	54	45,368	35,687	43,436	54,798
West	8	27,620	21,053	26,684	31,386
County type					
Metro	3	29,415	13,930	16,187	38,285
Nonmetro	74	39,723	27,675	39,745	50,038
Form of government					
Commission	73	38,995	25,683	39,444	49,932
Council–elected executive . .	3	55,298	46,958	50,618	61,297
Chief financial officer					
Total	30	54,309	42,029	50,854	62,111
Geographic region					
North-Central	11	50,862	43,029	49,816	55,393
South	15	52,300	36,927	50,500	61,508
West	4	71,322	50,589	77,916	98,648

Table 2/6 SALARIES OF COUNTY OFFICIALS: JULY–DECEMBER 2007
continued

Title of official	No. of counties reporting	Mean ($)	First quartile ($)	Median ($)	Third quartile ($)
10,000–24,999 continued					
County type					
Metro	4	66,081	59,721	68,849	75,209
Nonmetro	26	52,498	41,492	48,998	58,847
Form of government					
Commission	20	50,104	40,816	45,964	58,599
Council-manager/admin	5	55,630	50,500	55,985	58,891
Council–elected executive . .	5	69,807	60,058	74,904	76,125
Chief law enforcement official					
Total	105	58,279	47,571	57,174	69,406
Geographic region					
North-Central	63	59,458	50,444	61,915	68,176
South	32	55,052	40,911	46,789	72,624
West	9	59,523	48,597	50,375	67,470
County type					
Metro	9	66,615	57,174	63,613	74,800
Nonmetro	96	57,497	44,975	55,260	68,515
Form of government					
Commission	85	55,572	44,710	53,796	64,346
Council-manager/admin	11	76,070	73,201	74,800	78,799
Council–elected executive . .	9	62,094	47,571	67,470	71,976
Chief librarian					
Total	7	42,649	29,472	47,111	49,577
Geographic region					
South	4	33,498	28,765	29,472	34,205
County type					
Nonmetro	7	42,649	29,472	47,111	49,577
Form of government					
Commission	7	42,649	29,472	47,111	49,577
Clerk					
Total	99	41,600	33,040	39,423	44,400
Geographic region					
North-Central	29	40,221	33,210	40,360	43,697
South	62	41,393	31,428	37,809	43,486
West	7	49,667	44,355	46,598	51,282
County type					
Metro	9	46,614	37,608	40,385	45,838
Nonmetro	90	41,099	32,202	39,022	43,786
Form of government					
Commission	85	39,654	32,586	38,892	43,697
Council-manager/admin	6	59,125	38,378	45,293	81,969
Council–elected executive . .	8	49,135	33,642	41,872	56,922
Economic development director					
Total	13	48,354	35,467	42,000	56,637
Geographic region					
North-Central	3	41,989	34,665	36,330	46,484
South	7	57,167	41,760	54,529	67,275
West	3	34,156	28,734	35,467	40,234
County type					
Nonmetro	13	48,354	35,467	42,000	56,637
Form of government					
Commission	9	37,995	33,000	36,330	42,000
Council-manager/admin	3	71,861	59,005	63,481	80,526
Engineer					
Total	30	70,197	57,447	75,992	84,338
Geographic region					
North-Central	19	74,274	67,495	77,000	86,275
South	10	60,450	48,354	58,878	76,528
County type					
Metro	4	64,697	53,463	61,253	72,487
Nonmetro	26	71,043	62,903	76,403	84,338
Form of government					
Commission	27	72,324	66,441	76,733	86,275
Fire chief					
Total	4	47,020	45,379	46,624	48,266
Geographic region					
South	4	47,020	45,379	46,624	48,266
County type	. . .	. . .	. . .	. . .	. . .
Form of government	. . .	. . .	. . .	. . .	. . .
Health officer					
Total	20	46,428	37,136	44,938	60,383
Geographic region					
North-Central	16	44,826	39,189	44,938	56,187
South	3	49,647	30,638	31,200	59,433
County type					
Nonmetro	18	45,841	33,869	44,938	58,560
Form of government					
Commission	17	46,741	38,769	44,116	59,747

Title of official	No. of counties reporting	Mean ($)	First quartile ($)	Median ($)	Third quartile ($)
10,000–24,999 continued					
Human resources director					
Total	17	54,104	44,408	50,000	69,326
Geographic region					
North-Central	7	57,386	46,650	49,440	70,460
South	7	42,940	28,413	39,079	59,474
County type					
Nonmetro	16	53,011	43,076	49,720	62,523
Form of government					
Commission	11	51,361	34,952	44,670	70,460
Council-manager/admin	3	52,777	49,720	50,000	54,445
Council–elected executive . .	3	65,493	54,344	60,058	73,924
Human services director					
Total	20	58,523	51,536	61,246	72,878
Geographic region					
North-Central	10	66,432	63,070	66,339	73,113
South	7	41,855	22,969	32,000	59,050
West	3	71,052	54,954	57,803	80,525
County type					
Nonmetro	19	58,283	50,968	59,428	72,996
Form of government					
Commission	16	54,120	45,373	61,246	68,897
Council-manager/admin	3	67,095	59,050	59,210	71,198
Information services director					
Total	17	51,822	42,023	47,759	61,134
Geographic region					
North-Central	8	44,291	41,789	43,431	45,613
South	6	56,885	52,928	62,743	71,169
West	3	61,776	47,779	61,134	75,452
County type					
Nonmetro	15	51,964	41,952	47,759	63,568
Form of government					
Commission	13	46,775	41,086	44,044	53,348
Council–elected executive . .	3	66,666	55,114	59,486	74,628
Parks and recreation director					
Total	25	46,267	34,710	43,793	56,379
Geographic region					
North-Central	13	44,619	37,668	40,535	46,238
South	11	46,475	34,355	46,247	56,845
County type					
Metro	6	46,357	36,174	45,939	56,968
Nonmetro	19	46,238	36,120	43,793	55,608
Form of government					
Commission	17	44,880	34,571	39,797	58,853
Council-manager/admin	5	54,597	46,247	54,838	56,379
Council–elected executive . .	3	40,240	34,704	40,566	45,939
Parks superintendent					
Total	8	30,917	25,610	30,874	39,079
Geographic region					
North-Central	5	33,780	26,747	35,000	38,539
County type					
Nonmetro	8	30,917	25,610	30,874	39,079
Form of government					
Commission	7	29,520	25,484	26,747	36,769
Planning director					
Total	28	46,464	35,566	39,918	57,417
Geographic region					
North-Central	12	36,962	28,482	35,511	44,168
South	10	50,894	36,794	48,371	60,982
West	5	61,704	40,268	55,855	83,206
County type					
Metro	3	50,150	40,909	56,906	62,768
Nonmetro	25	46,022	35,926	39,836	56,427
Form of government					
Commission	18	44,002	34,998	39,418	53,566
Council-manager/admin	5	45,985	35,926	40,000	58,949
Council–elected executive . .	5	55,805	37,132	56,906	68,630
Primary asst. manager/CAO					
Total	12	49,539	32,592	47,863	59,686
Geographic region					
South	9	52,259	29,973	50,987	71,643
County type					
Nonmetro	10	46,283	30,846	44,738	50,356
Form of government					
Commission	6	40,747	28,043	31,719	40,027
Council-manager/admin	5	54,811	48,464	50,987	55,700
Public safety director					
Total	10	48,644	39,389	44,919	54,555

Table 2/6   SALARIES OF COUNTY OFFICIALS: JULY–DECEMBER 2007
continued

Title of official	No. of counties reporting	Distribution of 2007 salaries			
		Mean ($)	First quartile ($)	Median ($)	Third quartile ($)
10,000–24,999 continued					
Geographic region					
North-Central	3	40,757	37,707	38,520	42,690
South	6	53,696	44,258	51,680	61,499
County type					
Nonmetro	8	45,949	38,141	44,117	49,425
Form of government					
Commission	5	44,278	38,520	41,995	46,859
Council-manager/admin	3	48,735	41,623	46,240	54,599
Public works director					
Total	32	55,905	41,449	55,132	65,591
Geographic region					
North-Central	13	63,238	41,238	63,688	84,136
South	13	53,732	42,000	51,900	60,647
West	5	40,639	39,338	42,000	44,542
County type					
Metro	4	57,272	50,319	59,838	66,791
Nonmetro	28	55,709	41,449	53,232	65,591
Form of government					
Commission	23	55,535	41,241	54,564	65,450
Council-manager/admin	4	68,081	59,200	62,757	71,638
Council–elected executive ..	5	47,864	41,238	41,520	51,325
Purchasing director					
Total	3	44,597	23,000	26,000	56,895
Geographic region	...	...	...	...	...
County type					
Nonmetro	3	44,597	23,000	26,000	56,895
Form of government	...	...	...	...	...
Recreation director					
Total	11	38,841	31,059	34,512	42,452
Geographic region					
South	9	39,996	29,838	34,512	49,818
County type					
Nonmetro	10	37,743	30,448	33,896	35,065
Form of government					
Commission	5	36,223	32,280	33,280	35,000
Council-manager/admin	3	44,587	32,175	34,512	51,962
Council–elected executive ..	3	37,457	31,276	35,087	42,452
Risk manager					
Total	...	...	...	...	...
Geographic region	...	...	...	...	...
County type	...	...	...	...	...
Form of government	...	...	...	...	...
Treasurer					
Total	122	43,717	33,787	41,368	49,216
Geographic region					
North-Central	55	46,599	39,005	42,558	55,734
South	57	39,503	31,020	37,128	43,000
West	9	51,296	43,709	46,010	59,467
County type					
Metro	7	48,908	41,731	44,554	54,088
Nonmetro	115	43,401	33,265	40,750	49,116
Form of government					
Commission	108	42,027	33,292	40,519	45,881
Council-manager/admin	6	66,799	60,499	64,768	67,441
Council–elected executive ..	8	49,209	38,288	46,324	62,972
5,000–9,999					
Chief admin. officer/county manager					
Total	8	61,238	46,194	62,410	80,207
Geographic region					
North-Central	5	44,917	26,204	52,857	58,000
County type					
Nonmetro	8	61,238	46,194	62,410	80,207
Form of government					
Commission	7	55,343	39,531	58,000	70,881
Chief elected official					
Total	40	31,758	24,780	31,368	38,950
Geographic region					
North-Central	12	21,758	15,098	19,815	25,007
South	23	33,941	28,113	33,072	38,841
West	4	48,419	40,139	48,617	56,897
County type					
Nonmetro	39	31,702	24,754	30,492	39,545
Form of government					
Commission	36	31,238	24,780	31,194	38,950
Council–elected executive ..	4	36,441	28,562	33,246	41,125
Chief financial officer					
Total	8	48,430	30,506	42,825	66,968

Title of official	No. of counties reporting	Distribution of 2007 salaries			
		Mean ($)	First quartile ($)	Median ($)	Third quartile ($)
5,000–9,999 continued					
Geographic region					
North-Central	3	61,213	57,808	66,617	67,320
South	3	27,383	24,952	25,291	28,768
County type					
Nonmetro	8	48,430	30,506	42,825	66,968
Form of government					
Commission	8	48,430	30,506	42,825	66,968
Chief law enforcement official					
Total	39	48,535	40,160	46,059	52,897
Geographic region					
North-Central	25	48,228	41,664	46,059	51,605
South	7	40,047	30,645	33,588	46,042
West	6	57,250	45,802	50,547	64,089
County type					
Nonmetro	39	48,535	40,160	46,059	52,897
Form of government					
Commission	35	48,031	40,458	47,717	52,897
Council–elected executive ..	4	52,952	39,112	43,011	56,851
Chief librarian					
Total	5	28,135	20,079	27,486	35,464
Geographic region					
West	3	32,170	27,772	35,464	38,216
County type					
Nonmetro	5	28,135	20,079	27,486	35,464
Form of government					
Commission	5	28,135	20,079	27,486	35,464
Clerk					
Total	38	36,339	31,100	36,272	40,408
Geographic region					
North-Central	15	36,515	35,760	37,184	39,982
South	18	34,076	27,917	32,953	36,357
West	4	44,657	37,621	42,634	49,671
County type					
Nonmetro	37	36,500	32,400	36,476	40,544
Form of government					
Commission	34	36,052	30,455	35,760	40,408
Council–elected executive ..	4	38,781	36,420	38,262	40,622
Economic development director					
Total	5	52,581	43,500	44,401	47,000
Geographic region					
North-Central	3	43,834	42,251	43,500	45,250
County type					
Nonmetro	5	52,581	43,500	44,401	47,000
Form of government					
Commission	5	52,581	43,500	44,401	47,000
Engineer					
Total	11	65,787	61,008	70,280	73,392
Geographic region					
North-Central	10	65,212	60,762	70,032	73,530
County type					
Nonmetro	11	65,787	61,008	70,280	73,392
Form of government					
Commission	9	64,334	60,516	69,784	73,668
Fire chief					
Total	...	...	...	...	...
Geographic region	...	...	...	...	...
County type	...	...	...	...	...
Form of government	...	...	...	...	...
Health officer					
Total	11	47,029	39,502	42,135	52,478
Geographic region					
North-Central	8	43,452	39,669	41,838	45,316
County type					
Nonmetro	11	47,029	39,502	42,135	52,478
Form of government					
Commission	8	46,722	38,614	42,828	51,589
Council–elected executive ..	3	47,848	40,874	41,541	51,669
Human resources director					
Total	6	36,866	32,738	36,768	44,342
Geographic region					
North-Central	3	36,506	31,846	40,116	42,971
County type					
Nonmetro	6	36,866	32,738	36,768	44,342
Form of government					
Commission	6	36,866	32,738	36,768	44,342
Human services director					
Total	9	54,568	51,256	61,242	62,916

Table 2/6   SALARIES OF COUNTY OFFICIALS: JULY–DECEMBER 2007
continued

Title of official	No. of counties reporting	Distribution of 2007 salaries			
		Mean ($)	First quartile ($)	Median ($)	Third quartile ($)
5,000–9,999 continued					
Geographic region					
North-Central	5	59,822	52,800	62,916	64,170
County type					
Nonmetro	9	54,568	51,256	61,242	62,916
Form of government					
Commission	9	54,568	51,256	61,242	62,916
Information services director					
Total	. . .	. . .	. . .	. . .	. . .
Geographic region	. . .	. . .	. . .	. . .	. . .
County type	. . .	. . .	. . .	. . .	. . .
Form of government	. . .	. . .	. . .	. . .	. . .
Parks and recreation director					
Total	6	38,527	39,100	40,051	43,312
Geographic region					
North-Central	6	38,527	39,100	40,051	43,312
County type					
Nonmetro	6	38,527	39,100	40,051	43,312
Form of government					
Commission	5	38,129	38,938	39,586	44,244
Parks superintendent					
Total	. . .	. . .	. . .	. . .	. . .
Geographic region	. . .	. . .	. . .	. . .	. . .
County type	. . .	. . .	. . .	. . .	. . .
Form of government	. . .	. . .	. . .	. . .	. . .
Planning director					
Total	6	45,037	37,934	44,491	50,565
Geographic region					
North-Central	3	42,096	37,177	46,452	49,194
County type					
Nonmetro	6	45,037	37,934	44,491	50,565
Form of government					
Commission	6	45,037	37,934	44,491	50,565
Primary asst. manager/CAO					
Total	3	26,013	19,490	27,000	33,030
Geographic region					
North-Central	3	26,013	19,490	27,000	33,030
County type					
Nonmetro	3	26,013	19,490	27,000	33,030
Form of government					
Commission	3	26,013	19,490	27,000	33,030
Public safety director					
Total	4	55,449	47,652	57,623	65,420
Geographic region					
North-Central	3	48,599	41,952	53,352	57,623
County type					
Nonmetro	4	55,449	47,652	57,623	65,420
Form of government					
Commission	4	55,449	47,652	57,623	65,420
Public works director					
Total	7	49,523	39,212	45,558	56,409
Geographic region					
North-Central	4	44,923	39,534	42,747	48,136
County type					
Nonmetro	7	49,523	39,212	45,558	56,409
Form of government					
Commission	6	45,855	38,850	42,747	53,293
Purchasing director					
Total	. . .	. . .	. . .	. . .	. . .
Geographic region	. . .	. . .	. . .	. . .	. . .
County type	. . .	. . .	. . .	. . .	. . .
Form of government	. . .	. . .	. . .	. . .	. . .
Recreation director					
Total	. . .	. . .	. . .	. . .	. . .
Geographic region	. . .	. . .	. . .	. . .	. . .
County type	. . .	. . .	. . .	. . .	. . .
Form of government	. . .	. . .	. . .	. . .	. . .
Risk manager					
Total	. . .	. . .	. . .	. . .	. . .
Geographic region	. . .	. . .	. . .	. . .	. . .
County type	. . .	. . .	. . .	. . .	. . .
Form of government	. . .	. . .	. . .	. . .	. . .
Treasurer					
Total	56	38,167	31,251	37,462	42,911
Geographic region					
North-Central	29	41,386	34,942	39,936	45,320
South	22	31,006	25,560	31,005	35,415
West	4	49,951	44,565	51,614	57,000

Title of official	No. of counties reporting	Distribution of 2007 salaries			
		Mean ($)	First quartile ($)	Median ($)	Third quartile ($)
5,000–9,999 continued					
County type					
Nonmetro	55	38,309	31,494	37,740	43,223
Form of government					
Commission	49	38,061	30,973	37,740	43,845
Council–elected executive . .	7	38,909	34,324	36,000	41,282
2,500–4,999					
Chief admin. officer/county manager					
Total	3	44,701	30,660	40,000	56,392
Geographic region	. . .	. . .	. . .	. . .	. . .
County type					
Nonmetro	3	44,701	30,660	40,000	56,392
Form of government					
Commission	3	44,701	30,660	40,000	56,392
Chief elected official					
Total	21	31,214	25,049	31,439	37,992
Geographic region					
South	18	34,178	29,848	34,403	38,463
County type					
Nonmetro	21	31,214	25,049	31,439	37,992
Form of government					
Commission	20	30,514	25,015	31,097	37,982
Chief financial officer					
Total	. . .	. . .	. . .	. . .	. . .
Geographic region	. . .	. . .	. . .	. . .	. . .
County type	. . .	. . .	. . .	. . .	. . .
Form of government	. . .	. . .	. . .	. . .	. . .
Chief law enforcement official					
Total	24	40,983	31,144	35,213	38,904
Geographic region					
North-Central	14	36,365	31,609	35,020	37,172
South	6	32,115	29,699	32,513	35,472
West	4	70,448	48,735	56,182	77,894
County type					
Nonmetro	24	40,983	31,144	35,213	38,904
Form of government					
Commission	24	40,983	31,144	35,213	38,904
Chief librarian					
Total	4	33,414	22,004	25,924	37,334
Geographic region	. . .	. . .	. . .	. . .	. . .
County type					
Nonmetro	4	33,414	22,004	25,924	37,334
Form of government					
Commission	4	33,414	22,004	25,924	37,334
Clerk					
Total	27	33,744	27,925	31,725	34,151
Geographic region					
North-Central	11	30,222	27,925	30,936	31,737
South	11	30,069	24,568	31,439	33,627
West	5	49,577	34,415	35,140	43,800
County type					
Nonmetro	27	33,744	27,925	31,725	34,151
Form of government					
Commission	27	33,744	27,925	31,725	34,151
Economic development director					
Total	. . .	. . .	. . .	. . .	. . .
Geographic region	. . .	. . .	. . .	. . .	. . .
County type	. . .	. . .	. . .	. . .	. . .
Form of government	. . .	. . .	. . .	. . .	. . .
Engineer					
Total	. . .	. . .	. . .	. . .	. . .
Geographic region	. . .	. . .	. . .	. . .	. . .
County type	. . .	. . .	. . .	. . .	. . .
Form of government	. . .	. . .	. . .	. . .	. . .
Fire chief					
Total	. . .	. . .	. . .	. . .	. . .
Geographic region	. . .	. . .	. . .	. . .	. . .
County type	. . .	. . .	. . .	. . .	. . .
Form of government	. . .	. . .	. . .	. . .	. . .
Health officer					
Total	6	35,403	30,581	33,188	35,313
Geographic region					
North-Central	5	31,689	30,414	31,083	35,292
County type					
Nonmetro	6	35,403	30,581	33,188	35,313
Form of government					
Commission	6	35,403	30,581	33,188	35,313

Table 2/6   SALARIES OF COUNTY OFFICIALS: JULY–DECEMBER 2007
continued

Title of official	No. of counties reporting	Distribution of 2007 salaries			
		Mean ($)	First quartile ($)	Median ($)	Third quartile ($)
2,500–4,999 continued					
Human resources director					
Total	. . .	. . .	. . .	. . .	. . .
Geographic region	. . .	. . .	. . .	. . .	. . .
County type	. . .	. . .	. . .	. . .	. . .
Form of government	. . .	. . .	. . .	. . .	. . .
Human services director					
Total	4	60,433	41,651	56,545	75,328
Geographic region	. . .	. . .	. . .	. . .	. . .
County type					
Nonmetro	4	60,433	41,651	56,545	75,328
Form of government					
Commission	4	60,433	41,651	56,545	75,328
Information services director					
Total	. . .	. . .	. . .	. . .	. . .
Geographic region	. . .	. . .	. . .	. . .	. . .
County type	. . .	. . .	. . .	. . .	. . .
Form of government	. . .	. . .	. . .	. . .	. . .
Parks and recreation director					
Total	. . .	. . .	. . .	. . .	. . .
Geographic region	. . .	. . .	. . .	. . .	. . .
County type	. . .	. . .	. . .	. . .	. . .
Form of government	. . .	. . .	. . .	. . .	. . .
Parks superintendent					
Total	. . .	. . .	. . .	. . .	. . .
Geographic region	. . .	. . .	. . .	. . .	. . .
County type	. . .	. . .	. . .	. . .	. . .
Form of government	. . .	. . .	. . .	. . .	. . .
Planning director					
Total	. . .	. . .	. . .	. . .	. . .
Geographic region	. . .	. . .	. . .	. . .	. . .
County type	. . .	. . .	. . .	. . .	. . .
Form of government	. . .	. . .	. . .	. . .	. . .
Primary asst. manager/CAO					
Total	. . .	. . .	. . .	. . .	. . .
Geographic region	. . .	. . .	. . .	. . .	. . .
County type	. . .	. . .	. . .	. . .	. . .
Form of government	. . .	. . .	. . .	. . .	. . .
Public safety director					
Total	. . .	. . .	. . .	. . .	. . .
Geographic region	. . .	. . .	. . .	. . .	. . .
County type	. . .	. . .	. . .	. . .	. . .
Form of government	. . .	. . .	. . .	. . .	. . .
Public works director					
Total	7	36,205	27,403	30,986	37,432
Geographic region					
North-Central	5	32,131	29,076	30,986	32,000
County type					
Nonmetro	7	36,205	27,403	30,986	37,432
Form of government					
Commission	7	36,205	27,403	30,986	37,432
Purchasing director					
Total	. . .	. . .	. . .	. . .	. . .
Geographic region	. . .	. . .	. . .	. . .	. . .
County type	. . .	. . .	. . .	. . .	. . .
Form of government	. . .	. . .	. . .	. . .	. . .
Recreation director					
Total	. . .	. . .	. . .	. . .	. . .
Geographic region	. . .	. . .	. . .	. . .	. . .
County type	. . .	. . .	. . .	. . .	. . .
Form of government	. . .	. . .	. . .	. . .	. . .
Risk manager					
Total	. . .	. . .	. . .	. . .	. . .
Geographic region	. . .	. . .	. . .	. . .	. . .
County type	. . .	. . .	. . .	. . .	. . .
Form of government	. . .	. . .	. . .	. . .	. . .
Treasurer					
Total	40	33,503	28,226	31,187	34,445
Geographic region					
North-Central	14	29,545	28,258	29,652	30,883
South	21	31,374	26,539	31,764	36,484
West	5	53,526	34,413	43,800	44,115
County type					
Nonmetro	40	33,503	28,226	31,187	34,445
Form of government					
Commission	39	33,325	28,201	30,936	34,110
Less than 2,500					
Chief admin. officer/county manager					
Total	. . .	. . .	. . .	. . .	. . .
Geographic region	. . .	. . .	. . .	. . .	. . .

Title of official	No. of counties reporting	Distribution of 2007 salaries			
		Mean ($)	First quartile ($)	Median ($)	Third quartile ($)
Less than 2,500 continued					
County type	. . .	. . .	. . .	. . .	. . .
Form of government	. . .	. . .	. . .	. . .	. . .
Chief elected official					
Total	13	31,841	25,332	29,122	33,852
Geographic region					
South	12	31,674	24,768	27,634	34,882
County type					
Nonmetro	13	31,841	25,332	29,122	33,852
Form of government					
Commission	13	31,841	25,332	29,122	33,852
Chief financial officer					
Total	. . .	. . .	. . .	. . .	. . .
Geographic region	. . .	. . .	. . .	. . .	. . .
County type	. . .	. . .	. . .	. . .	. . .
Form of government	. . .	. . .	. . .	. . .	. . .
Chief law enforcement official					
Total	14	39,107	32,524	35,895	42,338
Geographic region					
North-Central	8	35,636	32,322	33,448	38,620
West	5	45,853	41,938	42,471	57,090
County type					
Nonmetro	14	39,107	32,524	35,895	42,338
Form of government					
Commission	12	37,328	32,322	33,572	41,316
Chief librarian					
Total	. . .	. . .	. . .	. . .	. . .
Geographic region	. . .	. . .	. . .	. . .	. . .
County type	. . .	. . .	. . .	. . .	. . .
Form of government	. . .	. . .	. . .	. . .	. . .
Clerk					
Total	15	33,794	27,147	34,367	38,067
Geographic region					
North-Central	7	29,885	26,133	31,000	33,218
West	6	38,794	35,472	38,515	44,023
County type					
Nonmetro	15	33,794	27,147	34,367	38,067
Form of government					
Commission	13	32,544	26,917	32,068	35,653
Economic development director					
Total	. . .	. . .	. . .	. . .	. . .
Geographic region	. . .	. . .	. . .	. . .	. . .
County type	. . .	. . .	. . .	. . .	. . .
Form of government	. . .	. . .	. . .	. . .	. . .
Engineer					
Total	. . .	. . .	. . .	. . .	. . .
Geographic region	. . .	. . .	. . .	. . .	. . .
County type	. . .	. . .	. . .	. . .	. . .
Form of government	. . .	. . .	. . .	. . .	. . .
Fire chief					
Total	. . .	. . .	. . .	. . .	. . .
Geographic region	. . .	. . .	. . .	. . .	. . .
County type	. . .	. . .	. . .	. . .	. . .
Form of government	. . .	. . .	. . .	. . .	. . .
Health officer					
Total	4	36,716	36,157	38,887	39,447
Geographic region	. . .	. . .	. . .	. . .	. . .
County type					
Nonmetro	4	36,716	36,157	38,887	39,447
Form of government					
Commission	4	36,716	36,157	38,887	39,447
Human resources director					
Total	. . .	. . .	. . .	. . .	. . .
Geographic region	. . .	. . .	. . .	. . .	. . .
County type	. . .	. . .	. . .	. . .	. . .
Form of government	. . .	. . .	. . .	. . .	. . .
Human services director					
Total	. . .	. . .	. . .	. . .	. . .
Geographic region	. . .	. . .	. . .	. . .	. . .
County type	. . .	. . .	. . .	. . .	. . .
Form of government	. . .	. . .	. . .	. . .	. . .
Information services director					
Total	. . .	. . .	. . .	. . .	. . .
Geographic region	. . .	. . .	. . .	. . .	. . .
County type	. . .	. . .	. . .	. . .	. . .
Form of government	. . .	. . .	. . .	. . .	. . .
Parks and recreation director					
Total	. . .	. . .	. . .	. . .	. . .
Geographic region	. . .	. . .	. . .	. . .	. . .

Table 2/6   SALARIES OF COUNTY OFFICIALS: JULY–DECEMBER 2007
continued

Title of official	No. of counties reporting	Distribution of 2007 salaries			
		Mean ($)	First quartile ($)	Median ($)	Third quartile ($)
Less than 2,500 continued					
County type	. . .	. . .	. . .	. . .	. . .
Form of government	. . .	. . .	. . .	. . .	. . .
Parks superintendent					
Total	. . .	. . .	. . .	. . .	. . .
Geographic region	. . .	. . .	. . .	. . .	. . .
County type	. . .	. . .	. . .	. . .	. . .
Form of government	. . .	. . .	. . .	. . .	. . .
Planning director					
Total	. . .	. . .	. . .	. . .	. . .
Geographic region	. . .	. . .	. . .	. . .	. . .
County type	. . .	. . .	. . .	. . .	. . .
Form of government	. . .	. . .	. . .	. . .	. . .
Primary asst. manager/CAO					
Total	. . .	. . .	. . .	. . .	. . .
Geographic region	. . .	. . .	. . .	. . .	. . .
County type	. . .	. . .	. . .	. . .	. . .
Form of government	. . .	. . .	. . .	. . .	. . .
Public safety director					
Total	. . .	. . .	. . .	. . .	. . .
Geographic region	. . .	. . .	. . .	. . .	. . .
County type	. . .	. . .	. . .	. . .	. . .
Form of government	. . .	. . .	. . .	. . .	. . .
Public works director					
Total	3	47,682	33,809	36,816	56,123
Geographic region	. . .	. . .	. . .	. . .	. . .
County type					
Nonmetro	3	47,682	33,809	36,816	56,123

Title of official	No. of counties reporting	Distribution of 2007 salaries			
		Mean ($)	First quartile ($)	Median ($)	Third quartile ($)
Less than 2,500 continued					
Form of government					
Commission	3	47,682	33,809	36,816	56,123
Purchasing director					
Total	. . .	. . .	. . .	. . .	. . .
Geographic region	. . .	. . .	. . .	. . .	. . .
County type	. . .	. . .	. . .	. . .	. . .
Form of government	. . .	. . .	. . .	. . .	. . .
Recreation director					
Total	. . .	. . .	. . .	. . .	. . .
Geographic region	. . .	. . .	. . .	. . .	. . .
County type	. . .	. . .	. . .	. . .	. . .
Form of government	. . .	. . .	. . .	. . .	. . .
Risk manager					
Total	. . .	. . .	. . .	. . .	. . .
Geographic region	. . .	. . .	. . .	. . .	. . .
County type	. . .	. . .	. . .	. . .	. . .
Form of government	. . .	. . .	. . .	. . .	. . .
Treasurer					
Total	24	27,847	25,086	28,437	31,681
Geographic region					
North-Central	8	29,343	27,253	29,049	30,588
South	12	24,953	19,418	25,991	28,866
West	4	33,541	32,186	35,138	36,493
County type					
Nonmetro	24	27,847	25,086	28,437	31,681
Form of government					
Commission	23	27,507	25,045	28,026	30,753

C 3

Police and Fire Personnel, Salaries, and Expenditures for 2007

Evelina R. Moulder
ICMA

Selected Findings

The average numbers of uniformed personnel are 93 for police and 78 for fire departments.

The average entrance salaries are $40,228 for police and $37,429 for fire personnel.

The mean per capita total departmental expenditures are $242.17 for police and $144.60 for fire departments.

For many police departments across the country, immigration has been a seriously debated topic. There is no debate as to whether there are people in this country illegally; the debate is about the role of police in enforcing federal immigration laws. A position paper produced by the Major Cities' Chiefs Association describes the challenges: "Local police agencies must balance any decision to enforce federal immigration laws with their daily mission of protecting and serving diverse communities, while taking into account: limited resources; the complexity of immigration laws; limitations on authority to enforce; risk of civil liability for immigration enforcement activities and the clear need to foster the trust and cooperation from the public including members of immigrant communities."[1] Immigration and homeland security concerns have become more paramount in the United States than ever before, and police officers face these complex challenges in the performance of their daily responsibilities.

With 1.6 million fires reported in the United States in 2006,[2] and severe wildfires consuming huge swaths of land in California during 2007, fire services have also had extensive demands made upon them. Fire personnel from across the country gave their support during the California wildfires, testing resources at home.

This article examines the current cross-sectional patterns and longitudinal trends in U.S. municipalities' police and fire departmental administrative practices, personnel, salaries, and expenditures.

METHODOLOGY

The data in this research were collected from responses to ICMA's annual *Police and Fire Personnel, Salaries, and Expenditures* survey, which was mailed in January 2007 to 3,263 municipalities with populations of 10,000 or more (Table 3/1). Respondents had a choice of completing and submitting the survey on the Web or by mail. A total of 1,391 jurisdictions completed the survey for an overall response rate of 43%, which is identical to last year's response rate.

Table 3/1   SURVEY RESPONSE, 2007

Classification	No. of municipalities[1] surveyed (A)	Respondents No.	Respondents % of (A)
Total	3,263	1,391	43
Population group			
Over 1,000,000	9	4	44
500,000–1,000,000 ..	23	5	22
250,000–499,999 ...	36	15	42
100,000–249,999 ...	179	85	48
50,000–99,999	409	190	47
25,000–49,999	783	326	42
10,000–24,999	1,824	766	42
Geographic region			
Northeast	886	262	30
North-Central	914	407	45
South	840	410	49
West	623	312	50
Geographic division			
New England	352	101	29
Mid-Atlantic	534	161	30
East North-Central ..	666	278	42
West North-Central ..	248	129	52
South Atlantic	384	205	53
East South-Central ..	169	55	33
West South-Central .	287	150	52
Mountain	160	74	46
Pacific Coast	463	238	51
Metro status			
Central	539	240	45
Suburban	2,105	884	42
Independent	619	267	43

[1]For a definition of terms, please see "Inside the *Year Book*," x.

The survey response patterns are presented in Table 3/1 by population group, geographic region, geographic division, and metropolitan status. There is variation in the response patterns by population size, with a low of 22% in cities with 500,000–1,000,000 in population, and a high of 48% in those with 100,000–249,999. The patterns by geographic division show that Mid-Atlantic and New England jurisdictions were the least likely to return the questionnaires (30% and 29%, respectively), while South Atlantic, West North-Central, West South-Central, and Pacific Coast jurisdictions were the most likely to do so (close to 53% in each). There is minimal variation by metropolitan status.

ADMINISTRATION

Respondents were asked several questions about service provision and delivery. Virtually all the jurisdictions responding to the 2007 survey (97%) indicated that they provide police services, and 85% reported that they provide fire services (not shown)—figures that have remained almost identical for several years. Thirty-two jurisdictions reported having a public safety department. To be counted among these respondents, a city had to report "public safety department" as the type of service for both police and fire (see sidebar).

These data on cities that provide police and fire services do not necessarily mean that all these cities actually deliver each service: 4% of jurisdictions reported contracting with another government for police service delivery (not shown). The highest percentage of cities reporting this arrangement is in the Pacific Coast division (16%). Among the 48 cities that do not provide police services, 42 answered the question about how the services *are* provided, and of those, the majority (31), all of which are under 250,000 in population, reported that the county provides the service (not shown). Four cities reported a regional police service; one reported a special district.

Of the cities that provide fire protection services, the majority (63%) reported having a full-time paid or a full-time and part-time paid fire department, 20% reported a combination of paid and volunteer fire personnel, 12% reported an all-volunteer fire department, and the remaining cities said they contract out for such services or provide them in some other way (not shown). Among the 205 cities that do not provide fire services, 165 provided information on how the services are provided, and of those, 51% reported that services are provided by a special district and 29% indicated that the county provides the service. Regional fire services were reported by 7%.

PERSONNEL

The average size of the full-time paid workforce for both police and fire departments is presented in Table 3/2. The data include both uniformed and

Cities that reported a public safety department (consolidated police and fire)

Auburn	AL
Huntsville	AL
Sunnyvale	CA
Greenacres	FL
Bainbridge	GA
Storm Lake	IA
Easthampton	MA
East Grand Rapids	MI
Escanaba	MI
Fraser	MI
Grand Haven	MI
Grosse Pointe Park	MI
Oak Park	MI
Inver Grove Heights	MN
Ferguson	MO
Maryville	MO
Mexico	MO
Sikeston	MO
West Plains	MO
Kinston	NC
Morganton	NC
Alamogordo	NM
Grants Pass	OR
North Augusta	SC
North Myrtle Beach	SC
Spartanburg	SC
Mitchell	SD
Portland	TX
Southlake	TX
Watauga	TX
Orem	UT
Ashwaubenon	WI

civilian, or nonuniformed, personnel. The average number of total police department employees, 122, represents a decrease in the average number of police personnel reported in 2006, which was 135. The average number of fire personnel is 84, compared with 88 in 2006. As with all averages in this article, these fluctuate depending on which cities report information each year.

The average numbers of full-time paid police employees show a decrease with population size for all reporting jurisdictions. However, because there are relatively few cities over 1,000,000 in population, findings from cities of that size can fluctuate significantly, depending on the cities that responded and their population size. In 2004, five cities responded. In 2005, although Los Angeles, Houston, and Philadelphia returned surveys, only two of these cities provided the number of full-time police personnel. In 2006 only Los Angeles and Philadelphia returned surveys. In 2007, Phoenix, Philadelphia, San Diego, and Dallas returned surveys. Since none of these cities has a population as high as that of Los Angeles, the average number of full-time paid police personnel is noticeably lower in 2007 than it was in 2006.

The average numbers of full-time police personnel by population category in 2007 also differ somewhat from the 2006 figures. For example, cities over 1,000,000 in population show an average of 4,462 police personnel (Table 3/2), compared with 9,996 in 2006; cities in the 500,000–1,000,000 population group show an average of 2,027 police personnel in 2007, compared with 1,775 police employees in 2006; and cities with populations of 25,000–49,999 and 10,000–24,999 show the same averages for police employees as reported in 2006.

The patterns for fire departments are similar to those for police departments: the average numbers of full-time paid fire employees decrease with the population size of the reporting communities and are generally less than or nearly identical to those reported in 2006. For example, cities

over 1,000,000 in population show an average of 1,912 fire employees (Table 3/2), compared with 3,114 in 2006, while cities in the population group of 500,000–1,000,000 show an average of 1,043 fire employees in 2007, compared with 1,026 in 2006. Continuing down in population, the average for communities in the 10,000–24,999 population group (26) is almost identical to the 2006 average (27).

Per capita figures per 1,000 population are important because they "normalize" the data. This is apparent in Table 3/2 because although the average numbers of personnel per capita generally decrease, they are comparable averages.

The cross-sectional patterns by geographic division indicate that municipalities in the Mountain division show the highest average number of full-time police employees (249) and that those in the New England division show the lowest (58) (Table 3/2). Regarding full-time paid fire employees, the highest average number is again in the Mountain division (146), and the lowest average numbers are in the West North-Central and New England divisions (44 and 49, respectively). As in 2006, the South Atlantic and East South-Central divisions, respectively, show the highest average numbers of police and fire full-time paid personnel per capita per 1,000 population.

Not surprisingly, metropolitan status patterns indicate that central cities have larger police and fire departments than either independent or suburban cities. In 2007, central cities averaged 364 full-time paid police department personnel, compared with 72 and 49 for suburban and independent communities, respectively (Table 3/2). The figures for full-time paid fire department personnel show a similar pattern, as the central cities show an average of 209, compared with 53 for suburban cities and 34 for independent cities. These differences, of course, reflect population differences in the communities served and are consistent with the patterns reported in previous surveys. The per capita figures per 1,000 population show the highest per capita full-time paid police and fire department personnel in central and independent jurisdictions.

Figure 3/1 shows the changes over ten years in the average number of full-time employees per 1,000 population for both services.

Table 3/3 presents the average numbers of full-time uniformed, or sworn, personnel in police and fire departments as of January 1, 2007. Among reporting cities, these numbers are 93 for police departments and 78 for fire departments, representing a decrease for both services, probably explained by the lack of response from Los Angeles, which positively skewed the data in 2006. Among the cities with over 1,000,000 in population, the average number of sworn police personnel reported in 2007 is 3,512; in 2006, the figure was 7,966. Predictably, the remaining averages are consistently correlated with the population size of the responding jurisdictions: the police department averages range from 1,343 for cities of 500,000–1,000,000 to 34 for cities of 10,000–24,999, similar to the 2006 figures. The figures per 1,000 population show a high of 2.59 for cities over 1,000,000 in population and a low of 1.78 for cities of 50,000–99,999.

Table 3/2   FULL-TIME PAID PERSONNEL, 2007

Classification	Police			Fire		
	No. reporting	Mean	Per capita per 1,000 population	No. reporting	Mean	Per capita per 1,000 population
Total	1,197	122	2.59	938	84	1.69
Population group						
Over 1,000,000	4	4,462	3.31	4	1,912	1.44
500,000–1,000,000	4	2,027	3.18	3	1,043	1.76
250,000–499,999	13	1,046	2.85	13	504	1.44
100,000–249,999	74	372	2.57	65	243	1.64
50,000–99,999	165	161	2.38	142	136	1.91
25,000–49,999	277	87	2.49	226	59	1.70
10,000–24,999	660	42	2.67	485	26	1.64
Geographic division						
New England	94	58	2.25	79	49	1.74
Mid-Atlantic	138	111	2.16	52	96	1.33
East North-Central	246	84	2.39	214	55	1.49
West North-Central	119	72	2.30	96	44	1.18
South Atlantic	168	160	3.53	148	98	2.27
East South-Central	51	109	3.24	49	81	2.40
West South-Central	141	157	2.85	127	104	1.72
Mountain	61	249	2.86	47	146	1.44
Pacific Coast	179	144	2.19	126	120	1.65
Metro status						
Central	223	364	2.77	212	209	1.82
Suburban	727	72	2.49	504	53	1.60
Independent	247	49	2.72	222	34	1.77

For fire departments in cities over 1,000,000 in population, the average number of sworn personnel reported in 2007 is 1,480, compared with 2,888 in 2006. As with the average number of sworn police personnel, the remaining averages decline from 1,016 for cities in the 500,000–1,000,000 population group to 26 for cities in the 10,000–24,999 population group. The figures per 1,000 population show a high of 1.62 for cities in the 500,000–1,000,000 population range and a low of 1.11 for cities of over 1,000,000.

The variations by geographic division are similar to the patterns seen above for full-time police personnel but differ somewhat from the patterns for fire personnel. The Mountain division shows the highest average number of sworn full-time police personnel (158), followed by the West South-Central division (129), while the New England division shows the lowest (49) (Table 3/3). When per capita per 1,000 population figures are reviewed, the South Atlantic (2.73) and East South-Central (2.56) divisions are the highest, and the Pacific Coast division is the lowest (1.58), which was also the case in 2006. For fire personnel, the Mid-Atlantic and Mountain divisions show the highest average numbers of uniformed personnel

per capita (105 and 107, respectively), while the West North-Central and New England divisions show the lowest (39 and 50, respectively). When per capita per 1,000 population figures are reviewed, the East South-Central division shows the highest average (2.28) and the West North-Central shows the lowest (1.16). The differences by metropolitan status show that independent cities have slightly higher per capita numbers of uniformed personnel in both services than central cities and that suburban communities' per capita numbers are the lowest.

STAFFING REQUIREMENTS FOR FIRE PERSONNEL

All reporting jurisdictions with a population of 250,000 and over reported minimum staffing requirements, as did 82% of reporting jurisdictions overall (not shown). The responses by geographic division indicate that the majority of jurisdictions in all areas of the country have a minimum requirement, and that more than 80% of cities in the South Atlantic, Pacific Coast, East South-Central, Mountain, West South-Central, and East North-Central divisions have requirements or policies advising minimum staffing per shift. This pattern is similar to that reported in previous surveys, as are the differences by metropolitan status, which range from a low of 77% for suburban cities to a high of 95% for central cities.

The average minimum staffing for apparatus—pumpers, ladders, and other equipment—is presented in Table 3/4. For pumpers, ladders, and rescue units, the average minimum crew is highest for cities over 1,000,000 in population.

HOURS WORKED PER SHIFT

Several questions were asked regarding the average number of hours worked per shift and per week for both services. The results, which are not displayed, are as expected. Approximately 76% of jurisdictions reported that their police department employees work 40 hours a week, and 14% reported a 42-hour workweek. Fire departments had more varied responses to the workweek question: 22% indicated that their workweek is 56 hours, and only 6% reported a 40-hour workweek. Sixteen percent reported a 50- to 54-hour workweek in 2007, which is unchanged from 2006.

The average number of hours worked per shift also varies between the services. Forty-one percent of the cities indicated that their police officers work an 8-hour shift, and 46% reported 10- or 12-hour shifts. Fire departments, on the other hand, are most likely to have 24-hour shifts (78%).

SALARY AND LONGEVITY PAY

Tables 3/5 through 3/8 present various salary and longevity pay data for full-time police officers and firefighters.

Minimum and Maximum Salaries
Tables 3/5 and 3/6 present detailed entrance and maximum salary data as well as the average

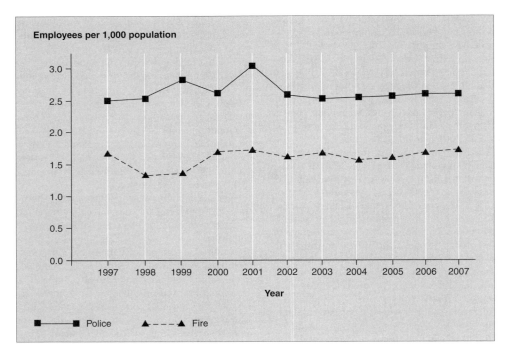

Figure 3/1   *Police and fire trends in employees per 1,000 population, 1997–2007*

Table 3/3   UNIFORMED SWORN PERSONNEL, 2007

Classification	Police			Fire		
	No. reporting	Mean	Per capita per 1,000 population	No. reporting	Mean	Per capita per 1,000 population
Total	1,198	93	2.03	907	78	1.58
Population group						
Over 1,000,000	4	3,512	2.59	4	1,480	1.11
500,000–1,000,000	4	1,343	2.13	4	1,016	1.62
250,000–499,999	13	850	2.25	14	468	1.28
100,000–249,999	75	272	1.86	66	224	1.53
50,000–99,999	165	120	1.78	139	110	1.60
25,000–49,999	276	68	1.93	219	56	1.61
10,000–24,999	661	34	2.14	461	26	1.58
Geographic division						
New England	92	49	1.89	75	50	1.75
Mid-Atlantic	132	101	1.92	45	105	1.35
East North-Central	244	66	1.89	203	53	1.41
West North-Central	120	51	1.84	87	39	1.16
South Atlantic	173	117	2.73	149	103	2.15
East South-Central	52	93	2.56	48	77	2.28
West South-Central	143	129	2.11	128	101	1.65
Mountain	66	158	2.03	49	107	1.22
Pacific Coast	176	101	1.58	123	87	1.24
Metro status						
Central	226	276	2.12	214	195	1.70
Suburban	729	55	1.96	480	45	1.47
Independent	243	39	2.16	213	33	1.71

number of years required to reach the maximum for police officers and firefighters, respectively. In addition to the measures of central tendency (mean and median) for the salary data, the first and third quartiles are included to indicate the degree of dispersion. The annual base salaries are the entrance salaries paid to sworn police officers or firefighters within their first 12 months of employment. Each reported amount excludes uniform allowances, holiday pay, hazardous duty pay, and any other form of additional compen-sation. The maximum is the highest annual base salary paid to uniformed personnel who do not hold any promotional rank.

The median entrance salary for police personnel is $39,341 and the mean is $40,228 (Table 3/5). The median maximum salary for police is $54,637 and the mean is $56,214. The entrance salary for firefighters tends to be lower than that for police, with a median of $36,248 and a mean of $37,429 (Table 3/6). The maximum fire salary median and mean are $49,418 and $50,879, respectively.

For both police and fire, the mean is higher than the median salary. This means that some higher salaries are positively skewing the mean.

The highest average entrance salaries for both police personnel and firefighters are found in sub-urban cities and the Pacific Coast division. The highest average maximum salaries for both groups of personnel are also found in suburban cities, but while the highest average maximum salary for fire-fighters is again in the Pacific Coast division, that for police personnel is in the Mid-Atlantic divi-sion, followed closely by the Pacific Coast divi-sion. The lowest average entrance and maximum salaries for both police personnel and firefighters are found in independent cities and in the East South-Central division. For both services, the dif-ference between the highest and lowest average entrance salaries among the geographic divisions is substantial: $25,165 for police and $24,093 for fire. For police, the difference between the high-est and lowest average maximum salaries among the geographic divisions ($28,258) is even more substantial than that for firefighters ($26,577).

For both police and fire services, an average of seven years of service is required to reach the maximum salary, with larger cities tending to have longer service requirements.

Longevity Pay

Longevity pay is defined as compensation beyond the regular maximum salary based on number of years of service. Longevity serves as an eco-nomic incentive to decrease employee turnover and reward those employees who have already achieved the maximum salary and now have lim-ited opportunities for promotion. Longevity pay can be administered in several ways—a flat dollar amount, a percentage of the base salary, a percent-age of the maximum pay, or a step increase in the basic salary plan.

Table 3/4   MINIMUM CREW PER FIRE APPARATUS, 2007

Classification	Pumpers		Ladders		Rescue units	
	No. reporting	Average minimum crew	No. reporting	Average minimum crew	No. reporting	Average minimum crew
Total	648	3.2	590	2.9	490	2.5
Population group						
Over 1,000,000	4	4.0	4	4.3	3	3.3
500,000–1,000,000	4	3.5	4	3.5	4	2.0
250,000–499,999	15	3.5	15	3.4	11	3.0
100,000–249,999	60	3.5	61	3.2	53	2.7
50,000–99,999	120	3.1	113	3.1	93	2.4
25,000–49,999	160	3.0	153	2.7	116	2.3
10,000–24,999	285	3.1	240	2.9	210	2.6
Geographic division						
New England	41	3.0	35	2.6	30	2.4
Mid-Atlantic	54	3.3	48	3.1	35	3.4
East North-Central	113	3.2	105	2.9	98	2.6
West North-Central	62	3.3	58	3.1	51	2.6
South Atlantic	119	2.9	112	2.7	86	2.2
East South-Central	32	3.3	30	3.0	23	2.6
West South-Central	86	3.2	71	2.7	61	2.5
Mountain	42	3.8	40	3.3	34	2.4
Pacific Coast	99	3.0	91	3.1	72	2.3
Metro status						
Central	188	3.2	184	2.9	146	2.5
Suburban	342	3.1	294	3.0	264	2.5
Independent	118	3.1	112	2.7	80	2.6

Table 3/5   POLICE OFFICERS' ANNUAL BASE SALARY, JANUARY 1, 2007

Classification	Entrance salary					Maximum salary					No. of years to reach maximum	
	No. of cities reporting	Mean ($)	First quartile ($)	Median ($)	Third quartile ($)	No. of cities reporting	Mean ($)	First quartile ($)	Median ($)	Third quartile ($)	No. of cities reporting	Mean
Total	1,213	40,228	32,982	39,341	45,515	1,197	56,214	46,698	54,637	63,982	1,005	7
Population group												
Over 1,000,000	4	41,588	39,395	40,629	42,822	4	61,270	58,508	61,227	63,989	4	8
500,000–1,000,000	5	41,727	35,568	44,266	47,022	5	62,227	53,562	61,296	69,325	5	11
250,000–499,999	14	44,385	37,646	44,434	48,371	14	58,615	52,825	59,306	65,920	11	9
100,000–249,999	75	46,326	36,041	44,250	51,802	75	64,371	55,748	61,668	69,412	70	9
50,000–99,999	167	44,652	36,081	42,372	50,541	165	61,778	52,416	60,341	68,532	144	7
25,000–49,999	280	41,103	35,004	40,194	45,693	275	57,244	48,208	56,041	64,956	238	7
10,000–24,999	668	37,965	31,455	37,886	43,578	659	53,336	44,259	51,043	60,791	533	7
Geographic division												
New England	93	40,144	36,508	39,488	42,887	93	51,217	46,015	49,528	54,184	89	6
Mid-Atlantic	139	41,444	36,331	41,000	46,109	138	69,715	58,628	69,470	79,850	138	5
East North-Central	250	41,652	37,866	41,052	45,649	249	56,062	49,504	56,096	63,294	230	6
West North-Central	120	36,444	31,352	36,484	42,111	118	49,688	44,112	50,044	57,026	93	7
South Atlantic	173	32,930	29,601	32,076	35,568	168	51,740	44,447	50,730	56,943	84	13
East South-Central	50	29,343	26,154	29,631	31,875	52	41,457	36,026	41,422	47,403	43	11
West South-Central	143	34,704	29,508	34,008	39,294	136	46,430	38,442	47,304	54,150	105	9
Mountain	67	40,109	35,026	39,816	43,780	66	55,902	49,447	56,124	62,878	51	10
Pacific Coast	178	54,508	47,175	53,388	60,385	177	69,094	60,849	67,862	76,287	172	5
Metro status												
Central	230	39,901	32,188	38,007	44,748	226	55,888	47,096	54,600	61,636	187	9
Suburban	736	42,480	36,036	41,456	47,322	728	60,218	50,519	59,236	67,887	637	6
Independent	247	33,821	28,510	32,448	38,836	243	44,522	38,337	44,064	50,295	181	9

Tables 3/7 and 3/8 show a range of longevity pay data for police and firefighter personnel, respectively. The tables cover whether personnel can receive longevity pay, the maximum salary they can receive including longevity pay, and the average number of years that is required for them to receive longevity pay.

Sixty-seven percent of all police departments reporting have a system that awards longevity pay to their personnel (Table 3/7). The Mid-Atlantic division shows the highest percentage of cities with longevity pay for police personnel (94%), closely followed by the West South-Central division (92%).

The average maximum salary including longevity pay for police officers is $60,628. The figures range from a low of $57,665 for cities with populations of 10,000–24,999 to a high of $82,459 for cities with populations of 250,000–499,999. Geographic divisions show a clear disparity in this regard. Once again, cities in the East South-Central division show the lowest average maximum of $46,047, while the highest average maximums are $74,564 for Pacific Coast and $74,309 for Mid-Atlantic jurisdictions. And again, suburban cities have a higher average maximum salary with longevity pay ($64,777) than either central ($58,271) or independent ($48,123) cities.

The longevity pay patterns for firefighters (Table 3/8) are similar to those for police officers. Sixty-four percent of jurisdictions reported longevity pay for fire personnel, including 91% of jurisdictions in the West South-Central division

Table 3/6 FIREFIGHTERS' ANNUAL BASE SALARY, JANUARY 1, 2007

| | Entrance salary | | | | | Maximum salary | | | | | No. of years to reach maximum | |
Classification	No. of cities reporting	Mean ($)	First quartile ($)	Median ($)	Third quartile ($)	No. of cities reporting	Mean ($)	First quartile ($)	Median ($)	Third quartile ($)	No. of cities reporting	Mean
Total	894	37,429	30,289	36,248	42,819	880	50,879	42,948	49,418	57,957	733	7
Population group												
Over 1,000,000	3	38,537	36,961	37,001	39,346	3	56,888	54,546	57,704	59,638	3	12
500,000–1,000,000	5	37,887	32,628	36,540	40,443	5	58,721	50,049	54,455	68,612	5	13
250,000–499,999	14	42,742	37,397	42,241	47,431	14	57,576	51,700	55,050	65,103	12	9
100,000–249,999	67	42,519	32,992	40,285	48,784	67	59,419	49,633	58,244	64,326	62	9
50,000–99,999	139	41,997	33,762	40,318	48,225	136	57,445	48,527	56,551	64,768	120	7
25,000–49,999	215	37,857	31,828	37,115	42,884	214	51,466	44,608	50,064	57,612	176	7
10,000–24,999	451	34,884	28,319	33,681	39,992	441	46,931	38,930	46,000	52,968	355	7
Geographic division												
New England	74	37,992	34,750	38,158	40,531	75	47,551	43,722	46,883	50,596	72	6
Mid-Atlantic	47	36,125	32,046	34,319	39,516	45	56,622	46,235	51,056	68,823	47	5
East North-Central	202	40,469	36,202	40,130	44,811	201	53,651	46,563	54,021	59,690	186	6
West North-Central	81	33,555	28,696	32,631	37,631	82	44,989	38,707	45,462	50,014	67	8
South Atlantic	149	30,765	26,594	30,065	33,155	146	46,998	40,227	46,560	52,452	72	13
East South-Central	48	27,920	24,770	27,875	30,781	48	39,474	33,188	38,893	46,381	40	11
West South-Central	129	32,858	27,284	32,000	36,878	120	43,977	37,228	44,758	51,649	96	8
Mountain	44	37,619	34,274	38,214	41,219	44	52,112	47,052	52,594	57,447	35	9
Pacific Coast	120	52,013	45,278	49,709	57,276	119	66,051	58,236	64,548	73,242	118	4
Metro status												
Central	215	37,496	30,528	36,359	41,902	214	52,273	44,854	50,935	57,970	177	9
Suburban	460	40,191	33,020	39,056	45,467	453	54,544	46,332	52,752	61,373	393	6
Independent	219	31,562	26,271	29,900	36,024	213	41,686	35,943	41,014	46,584	163	8

Table 3/7 LONGEVITY PAY FOR POLICE OFFICERS, JANUARY 1, 2007

| | Personnel can receive longevity pay | | | | | Maximum salary including longevity pay | | | | | No. of years of service to receive longevity pay | |
| | | Yes | | No | | | | | | | | |
Classification	No. reporting (A)	No.	% of (A)	No.	% of (A)	No. of cities reporting	Mean ($)	First quartile ($)	Median ($)	Third quartile ($)	No. of cities reporting	Mean
Total	1,230	825	67	405	33	598	60,628	49,940	57,849	68,894	753	6
Population group												
Over 1,000,000	4	3	75	1	25	2	60,712	58,628	60,712	62,797	3	4
500,000–1,000,000	5	5	100	0	0	3	65,316	58,929	63,096	70,593	5	9
250,000–499,999	14	10	71	4	29	5	82,459	58,799	66,334	70,293	9	7
100,000–249,999	76	47	62	29	38	34	69,718	57,376	65,280	71,940	42	8
50,000–99,999	168	106	63	62	37	85	66,153	55,767	63,935	74,514	98	7
25,000–49,999	282	194	69	88	31	142	61,099	50,726	58,870	69,843	169	7
10,000–24,999	681	460	68	221	33	327	57,665	47,198	54,064	65,412	427	6
Geographic division												
New England	94	79	84	15	16	63	52,885	46,781	51,150	56,278	72	8
Mid-Atlantic	143	134	94	9	6	108	74,309	60,084	74,170	85,620	127	6
East North-Central	252	189	75	63	25	142	58,083	50,734	57,809	65,584	175	6
West North-Central	121	64	53	57	47	45	54,033	46,860	53,231	64,365	58	7
South Atlantic	172	83	48	89	52	49	56,448	47,936	55,636	63,989	67	7
East South-Central	52	27	52	25	48	13	46,047	40,000	46,138	53,726	24	7
West South-Central	146	134	92	12	8	86	50,510	41,649	50,132	55,372	126	3
Mountain	68	26	38	42	62	19	56,194	51,528	56,840	63,021	23	5
Pacific Coast	182	89	49	93	51	73	74,564	65,364	71,783	81,492	81	11
Metro status												
Central	230	152	66	78	34	110	58,271	49,506	54,703	63,010	140	6
Suburban	751	516	69	235	31	382	64,777	53,615	63,242	73,452	473	7
Independent	249	157	63	92	37	106	48,123	40,351	46,854	51,908	140	5

Table 3/8   LONGEVITY PAY FOR FIREFIGHTERS, JANUARY 1, 2007

| | Personnel can receive longevity pay | | | | | Maximum salary including longevity pay | | | | | No. of years of service to receive longevity pay | |
| | No. reporting (A) | Yes | | No | | No. of cities reporting | Mean ($) | First quartile ($) | Median ($) | Third quartile ($) | No. of cities reporting | Mean |
Classification		No.	% of (A)	No.	% of (A)							
Total	993	636	64	357	36	416	54,376	45,714	51,866	61,704	559	6
Population group												
Over 1,000,000	3	3	100	0	0	2	58,036	56,203	58,036	59,870	3	4
500,000–1,000,000	5	5	100	0	0	2	61,252	56,400	61,252	66,103	5	6
250,000–499,999	14	7	50	7	50	2	52,650	50,814	52,650	54,486	5	6
100,000–249,999	68	43	63	25	37	33	65,634	50,010	62,650	69,972	40	6
50,000–99,999	145	96	66	49	34	69	61,523	50,696	59,259	69,533	85	6
25,000–49,999	230	154	67	76	33	106	54,984	47,170	53,070	60,554	134	6
10,000–24,999	528	328	62	200	38	202	49,689	42,085	47,835	55,722	287	5
Geographic division												
New England	81	67	83	14	17	53	49,998	45,084	49,621	55,084	62	8
Mid-Atlantic	72	51	71	21	29	33	62,739	49,184	54,369	76,836	42	5
East North-Central	221	169	77	52	24	117	55,621	47,244	55,717	62,675	152	6
West North-Central	100	46	46	54	54	27	47,618	43,788	47,583	50,292	40	5
South Atlantic	154	72	47	82	53	40	51,725	44,070	49,521	56,148	60	6
East South-Central	50	26	52	24	48	13	41,980	34,729	42,073	46,850	23	7
West South-Central	139	126	91	13	9	77	46,109	38,116	47,040	52,801	116	3
Mountain	51	22	43	29	57	13	55,344	51,283	53,232	58,572	18	6
Pacific Coast	125	57	46	68	54	43	74,935	64,688	71,703	81,906	46	9
Metro status												
Central	219	148	68	71	32	97	53,583	46,850	50,696	58,301	133	6
Suburban	541	343	63	198	37	225	58,674	48,339	56,073	65,658	298	6
Independent	233	145	62	88	38	94	44,906	38,514	44,548	49,374	128	5

(the high) and 43% of those in the Mountain division (the low). Central jurisdictions (68%) are slightly ahead of suburban (63%) and independent (62%) jurisdictions in offering longevity pay for firefighters.

The average maximum salary with longevity pay for firefighters is $54,376. Among population groups, the cities with populations of 100,000–249,999 show the highest average maximum salary with longevity pay ($65,634), while those with populations of 10,000–24,999 show the lowest ($49,689). Geographically, Pacific Coast jurisdictions show the highest average maximum salary with longevity pay ($74,935), and East South-Central communities again show the lowest ($41,980). Suburban communities show a higher average maximum salary ($58,674) than either central ($53,583) or independent ($44,906) cities.

Overall, the length of service required for police and firefighters to receive longevity pay is six years for both, which is identical to the number reported in 2006. However, the number of years varies somewhat within the classification categories. In the Pacific Coast division, for example, both groups of personnel serve a well-above-average number of years to qualify for longevity pay: police serve an average of 11 years and firefighters serve an average of 9.

EXPENDITURES

Respondents were asked to provide expenditure (not budget) figures for their department's most recently completed fiscal year. The items include salaries and wages for all department personnel, contributions for employee benefits, capital outlays, and all other departmental expenditures. Average expenditures are presented in Tables 3/9

through 3/15. Per capita expenditures are shown in addition to average expenditures. Per capita presentations are useful because they normalize the information.

Salaries and Wages

Part of ICMA's process of reviewing survey results is to design logic checks that will identify problematic values. One logic check is that total expenditures for salaries and wages must be greater

than the minimum salary for police (or fire) sworn personnel multiplied by the number of sworn personnel reported. For those jurisdictions reporting total expenditures for salaries and wages below that amount, the total salary and wage expenditures amount was removed.

Table 3/9 shows that the average per capita expenditure for civilian and uniformed police personnel in 2007 was $150.19, an increase from the 2006 average of $141.03. As population de-

Table 3/9   EXPENDITURES FOR SALARIES AND WAGES (CIVILIAN AND UNIFORMED), 2007

| | Police | | | Fire | | |
Classification	No. of cities reporting	Mean ($)	Per capita ($)	No. of cities reporting	Mean ($)	Per capita ($)
Total	1,103	7,679,704	150.19	905	5,679,427	99.67
Population group						
Over 1,000,000	4	294,936,537	219.18	4	130,388,187	99.07
500,000–1,000,000	4	126,179,598	197.90	4	67,399,859	107.19
250,000–499,999	14	63,589,067	171.79	15	32,908,304	92.51
100,000–249,999	72	22,648,327	161.19	64	16,928,499	120.43
50,000–99,999	147	9,966,537	144.52	137	10,016,214	137.04
25,000–49,999	248	5,477,834	156.04	207	3,629,655	104.43
10,000–24,999	614	2,348,109	146.64	474	1,367,343	84.16
Geographic division						
New England	83	3,807,141	144.01	72	3,125,378	104.45
Mid-Atlantic	133	7,966,876	166.05	56	5,866,889	80.35
East North-Central	230	5,613,848	151.25	207	3,817,263	98.16
West North-Central	109	4,049,935	131.19	100	2,999,596	60.78
South Atlantic	163	7,712,793	156.97	146	5,316,814	104.27
East South-Central	43	4,523,404	126.23	42	3,745,397	101.59
West South-Central	126	9,389,679	133.66	123	5,942,812	81.81
Mountain	58	15,535,529	157.71	45	9,014,855	76.70
Pacific Coast	158	11,561,057	161.60	114	12,508,591	164.75
Metro status						
Central	208	22,895,793	158.11	205	13,863,739	107.44
Suburban	673	4,757,635	155.82	487	3,996,969	102.81
Independent	222	2,281,535	125.70	213	1,649,253	85.03

creases, average per capita expenditures also generally decrease. So, too, do average salary and wage expenditures for police: from $294,936,537 for cities with populations over 1,000,000 to $2,348,109 for cities of 10,000–24,999 in population (Table 3/9). The average expenditure decrease is more pronounced than the average per capita decrease among population groups, which is to be expected.

Overall, the spread of average per capita salary and wage expenditures is greater for police departments than for fire departments. The average per capita police expenditures show a low of $144.52 in cities of 50,000–99,999 in population and a high of $219.18 in the largest cities (Table 3/9). For firefighters, the average per capita expenditures range from a low of $84.16 for cities with populations of 10,000–24,999 to a high of $137.04 for cities with populations of 50,000–99,999.

Geographically, Mid-Atlantic jurisdictions show the highest average per capita salary and wage expenditure for police personnel ($166.05), and Pacific Coast jurisdictions show the highest for fire ($164.75). Cities in the East South-Central division show the lowest for police ($126.23) and those in the West North-Central division show the lowest for fire ($60.78).

Social Security and Retirement Benefits

The average expenditures for municipal contributions to federal social security and other employee retirement programs are reported in Table 3/10. These expenditures are for both uniformed and civilian personnel. The table shows combined retirement and social security contributions because some states opt out of social security programs for local government employees, relying instead on an employee-sponsored retirement program. Zeros have been removed from the calculations because although zero is a legitimate answer, it skews the averages.

The average per capita expenditure for employee social security and retirement benefits for police in 2007 ($28.93) is up from the 2006 amount ($26.06). Among the population groups, the highest average police per capita expenditure for social security and retirement is in the over-1,000,000 population group, but only one city reported. Geographically, the highest average police department per capita expenditure for these benefits is found in the Pacific Coast division ($40.33); the lowest is in the New England division ($19.49). Suburban cities show a slightly higher average per capita municipal contribution ($30.93) than central cities ($29.69); independent cities show a lower amount ($23.28).

The average per capita expenditure for social security and retirement benefits for fire departments in 2007 was $19.53 (Table 3/10), compared with $17.33 in 2006. The per capita amounts fluctuate among the population groups. Among the geographic divisions, the highest average fire department per capita expenditure for social security and retirement benefits is found in the Pacific Coast cities ($29.04), and the lowest is in the West North-Central ($11.85) cities. Central and suburban cities show the highest average per capita expenditures at $21.81 and $20.12, respectively.

Health, Hospitalization, Disability, and Life Insurance

Table 3/11 shows the average total municipal contributions for health, hospitalization, disability, and life insurance programs. The mean per capita expenditures for 2007 have increased to $24.48 for police and $16.37 for fire. In 2006, they were $23.83 for police and $15.15 for fire.

Total Personnel Expenditures

Table 3/12 shows the total personnel expenditures for civilian and uniformed employees for both police and fire services. These data represent total salaries and wages; contributions for federal social security and other retirement programs; and contributions to health, hospitalization, disability, and life insurance programs. To be included in this table, the jurisdiction had to provide each of these expenditures. Those who reported an amount of zero were excluded from the table. Again, although zero is a legitimate amount, it negatively skews the average.

For fire services in particular, the workforce composition affects personnel expenditures: when

Table 3/10 TOTAL MUNICIPAL CONTRIBUTIONS TO SOCIAL SECURITY AND STATE/CITY-ADMINISTERED EMPLOYEE RETIREMENT SYSTEMS, 2007

Classification	Police No. of cities reporting	Police Mean ($)	Police Per capita ($)	Fire No. of cities reporting	Fire Mean ($)	Fire Per capita ($)
Total	845	1,472,135	28.93	728	1,111,324	19.53
Population group						
Over 1,000,000	1	181,110,985	119.34	2	42,685,219	31.32
500,000–1,000,000	4	18,907,034	29.09	3	12,519,681	18.90
250,000–499,999	7	13,040,736	30.04	9	13,166,511	41.24
100,000–249,999	51	4,673,377	31.95	52	2,983,562	20.26
50,000–99,999	113	2,085,200	30.86	116	1,525,508	22.49
25,000–49,999	192	1,133,386	31.54	168	807,032	22.64
10,000–24,999	477	428,406	26.89	378	264,366	16.55
Geographic division						
New England	39	523,923	19.49	35	406,852	14.94
Mid-Atlantic	91	2,958,513	31.07	41	2,002,503	19.81
East North-Central	149	1,168,330	30.84	157	920,820	21.00
West North-Central	105	777,354	20.55	91	522,313	11.85
South Atlantic	155	1,474,719	32.61	136	1,179,876	23.92
East South-Central	42	853,449	24.26	41	655,045	18.10
West South-Central	122	1,324,003	22.55	112	1,217,521	15.05
Mountain	46	1,692,534	30.66	33	743,546	13.40
Pacific Coast	96	2,028,976	40.33	82	2,102,229	29.04
Metro status						
Central	155	4,268,697	29.69	168	2,903,408	21.81
Suburban	494	1,009,733	30.93	373	686,915	20.12
Independent	196	426,010	23.28	187	347,872	16.28

Table 3/11 TOTAL MUNICIPAL CONTRIBUTIONS FOR HEALTH, HOSPITALIZATION, DISABILITY, AND LIFE INSURANCE PROGRAMS, 2007

Classification	Police No. of cities reporting	Police Mean ($)	Police Per capita ($)	Fire No. of cities reporting	Fire Mean ($)	Fire Per capita ($)
Total	1,007	1,241,861	24.48	832	885,548	16.37
Population group						
Over 1,000,000	3	53,068,827	37.95	3	19,719,654	14.37
500,000–1,000,000	4	16,606,908	26.27	3	8,359,113	12.40
250,000–499,999	13	9,442,217	24.57	13	5,708,293	14.84
100,000–249,999	70	3,675,071	26.37	61	2,285,650	15.87
50,000–99,999	141	1,717,023	24.80	129	1,761,552	23.97
25,000–49,999	227	830,476	23.74	191	584,339	16.60
10,000–24,999	549	390,342	24.37	432	231,617	14.17
Geographic division						
New England	46	673,326	26.53	42	456,325	18.57
Mid-Atlantic	111	1,743,660	28.12	52	1,214,834	14.21
East North-Central	210	987,009	26.69	191	716,751	17.58
West North-Central	105	561,440	18.26	93	354,389	9.66
South Atlantic	159	1,049,873	24.02	141	753,418	15.92
East South-Central	41	806,800	22.51	41	660,224	17.56
West South-Central	131	1,128,594	17.56	124	701,261	11.13
Mountain	54	1,524,482	23.25	43	1,187,947	14.31
Pacific Coast	150	2,197,568	29.92	105	2,030,879	27.52
Metro status						
Central	200	3,473,382	25.22	192	2,030,441	17.66
Suburban	594	801,421	25.51	438	668,373	16.95
Independent	213	374,804	20.90	202	268,239	13.91

the total average personnel expenditures for fire personnel are analyzed by departments with full-time or full-time and part-time paid personnel ($8,806,565) and then by those that are all volunteer ($392,345), the differences are apparent (not shown).

The mean per capita personnel expenditure amounts are $201.17 for police and $127.61 for fire (Table 3/12). For police departments, these amounts generally decline from the larger to the smaller cities. Among the geographic divisions,

the high for police is in the Pacific Coast division ($226.16), followed closely by the Mid-Atlantic division ($225.03); the low is in the West North-Central division ($171.02).

For fire departments, the mean per capita personnel expenditures vary noticeably among population groups—from a high of $156.29 for cities with populations of 100,000–249,999, to a low of $114.09 for cities of 10,000–24,999 in population. Geographically, the average per capita high is again seen in the Pacific Coast division

($171.97), and the low is again seen in the West North-Central division ($81.47). The highest average per capita personnel expenditure for police departments is found in suburban cities; for fire, the highest is in central cities. For both services, independent cities have the lowest average per capita personnel expenditures.

Capital Outlays

Table 3/13 shows departmental expenditures for capital outlays. These outlays include the purchase and replacement of equipment, the purchase of land and existing structures, and construction. The amounts include the capital expenditures within individual departmental budgets as well as those expenditures included in citywide capital budgets designated for departmental programs or equipment. Total capital outlay expenditures may fluctuate dramatically from one year to the next for both police and fire departments. This is because the cost of individual capital projects varies widely among communities as well as within the same community over time. Whereas the number of employees, which relates to population size, determines personnel expenditures, fire equipment such as pumpers will cost the same regardless of the size of the community. The per capita cost for the pumpers will necessarily be higher among cities with fewer people.

The 2007 average municipal capital outlay expenditures per capita were $11.07 for police, an increase from the $8.39 shown in 2006, and $11.09 for fire, which is above the 2006 figure of $8.73. For police, the highest average capital outlay expenditures per capita are in cities with populations of 10,000–24,999 ($11.72) and cities in the Mountain division ($14.91). For fire services, the average capital outlays per capita are highest in cities with populations of 100,000–249,999 ($13.00) as well as cities in the Mid-Atlantic ($15.88) division.

Table 3/12   TOTAL PERSONNEL EXPENDITURES, 2007

Classification	Police			Fire		
	No. of cities reporting	Mean ($)	Per capita ($)	No. of cities reporting	Mean ($)	Per capita ($)
Total	787	9,833,148	201.17	685	7,007,758	127.61
Population group						
Over 1,000,000	1	761,135,858	501.56	2	208,344,535	153.12
500,000–1,000,000	4	161,693,540	253.26	3	85,575,924	129.54
250,000–499,999	7	92,682,207	218.27	9	53,928,977	146.42
100,000–249,999	51	31,066,502	210.98	52	22,692,221	156.29
50,000–99,999	107	13,088,757	192.90	111	9,264,705	137.92
25,000–49,999	181	7,337,433	208.50	162	4,915,425	138.83
10,000–24,999	436	3,139,995	197.57	346	1,840,636	114.09
Geographic division						
New England	33	4,735,830	188.04	29	3,643,315	133.13
Mid-Atlantic	83	15,728,345	225.03	32	13,163,290	137.04
East North-Central	137	8,394,712	204.85	149	5,855,517	131.11
West North-Central	98	5,396,415	171.02	87	4,013,918	81.47
South Atlantic	151	9,665,514	213.32	135	6,731,523	142.04
East South-Central	37	6,654,342	174.28	36	5,275,983	136.38
West South-Central	113	10,198,816	176.22	108	8,237,878	107.26
Mountain	43	12,739,390	214.73	30	7,999,575	109.70
Pacific Coast	92	12,957,224	226.16	79	10,422,544	171.97
Metro status						
Central	152	27,477,007	200.76	164	17,698,806	145.62
Suburban	455	6,610,152	212.90	343	4,377,807	128.18
Independent	180	3,080,905	171.87	178	2,225,407	109.93

Table 3/13   MUNICIPAL EXPENDITURES FOR CAPITAL OUTLAYS, 2007

Classification	Police			Fire		
	No. of cities reporting	Mean ($)	Per capita ($)	No. of cities reporting	Mean ($)	Per capita ($)
Total	1,013	435,590	11.07	847	455,869	11.09
Population group						
Over 1,000,000	4	6,254,020	4.56	4	6,563,299	4.99
500,000–1,000,000	4	2,621,339	4.13	4	1,450,570	2.44
250,000–499,999	9	1,967,864	5.44	12	1,645,687	4.74
100,000–249,999	67	1,442,485	10.97	62	1,548,298	13.00
50,000–99,999	141	756,141	10.78	125	769,556	11.41
25,000–49,999	233	348,236	10.19	193	309,318	9.17
10,000–24,999	555	186,738	11.72	447	184,407	11.87
Geographic division						
New England	74	372,323	9.44	58	334,376	11.70
Mid-Atlantic	109	277,650	7.34	67	354,809	15.88
East North-Central	204	250,151	9.36	189	238,746	8.56
West North-Central	102	233,391	7.64	88	329,504	11.47
South Atlantic	157	548,441	14.47	140	360,284	10.27
East South-Central	41	505,462	14.15	40	436,049	12.34
West South-Central	122	445,632	13.86	114	517,921	11.20
Mountain	57	918,969	14.91	45	987,025	12.35
Pacific Coast	147	646,415	11.13	106	919,762	11.92
Metro status						
Central	196	1,015,049	9.96	187	787,323	7.61
Suburban	612	343,405	12.07	466	440,199	13.04
Independent	205	156,778	9.15	194	174,015	9.77

OTHER EXPENDITURES

Table 3/14 presents the data for all other departmental expenditures not accounted for in the previous tables. These include ongoing maintenance, utilities, fuel, supplies, and other miscellaneous items.

The average per capita expenditures in 2007 were $32.51 for police and $20.89 for fire. These figures represent an increase, albeit slight for fire, in the per capita average expenditures over those reported in 2006.

TOTAL DEPARTMENTAL EXPENDITURES

Table 3/15 shows the combined personnel, capital outlay, and all other departmental expenditures. The average per capita figures for 2007 are $242.17 and $144.60 for police and fire, respectively—an increase over the $219.17 for police personnel and a decrease from the $149.01 for fire personnel reported in 2006.

Not all cities include the same expenditures in their budgets. Of the 823 jurisdictions providing information about services included in the fire department budget, 48% cited ambulance personnel and 51% cited ambulance equipment (not shown). Emergency medical training (EMT) personnel were included by 91%, and EMT equipment was included by 93%. This does not necessarily mean, however, that these are the only jurisdictions that provide EMT and ambulance services; these are just the cities that reported having these services in the fire department budget.

CONCLUSION

This report has examined the cross-sectional and longitudinal patterns found in the responses to ICMA's annual *Police and Fire Personnel, Salaries, and Expenditures* survey. Most of the changes over time in police and fire employment and expenditures have been small, incremental shifts. It is not uncommon for one year to show increases and the next to show decreases in average expenditures.

Although using per capita figures instead of absolute numbers reduces the skew of the data, any analysis of the reported changes must control for population size of the responding jurisdictions. Another influential factor is a significant difference in the number reporting in any population group. Any major increase or decrease in that number can affect the average.

[1]"M.C.C. Immigration Committee Recommendations for Enforcement of Immigration Laws by Local Police Agencies" (June 2006), 5, available at majorcitieschiefs.org/pdfpublic/mcc_position_statement_revised_cef.pdf (accessed January 2, 2008).

[2]U.S. Fire Administration, "QuickStats: The Overall Fire Picture—2006," at usfa.dhs.gov/statistics/quickstats/index.shtm (accessed January 2, 2008).

Table 3/14   ALL OTHER DEPARTMENTAL EXPENDITURES, 2007

Classification	Police			Fire		
	No. of cities reporting	Mean ($)	Per capita ($)	No. of cities reporting	Mean ($)	Per capita ($)
Total.	1,090	1,667,362	32.51	929	1,068,743	20.89
Population group						
Over 1,000,000	4	33,715,084	25.95	4	15,852,549	11.97
500,000–1,000,000	4	32,948,790	50.59	4	20,364,272	33.98
250,000–499,999.	12	14,169,964	37.98	13	6,965,537	19.86
100,000–249,999.	72	5,865,215	40.22	63	2,507,455	17.84
50,000–99,999.	144	2,665,310	38.44	134	2,205,490	29.78
25,000–49,999.	244	1,158,095	32.60	209	754,429	21.83
10,000–24,999.	610	478,778	29.98	502	291,359	18.50
Geographic division						
New England	78	426,167	16.89	72	424,081	15.88
Mid-Atlantic	128	855,742	19.61	81	600,661	13.95
East North-Central	233	973,320	30.13	210	670,471	19.78
West North-Central	105	838,592	23.84	95	376,650	13.02
South Atlantic.	162	2,216,373	41.23	143	1,164,365	25.27
East South-Central.	41	830,200	26.13	41	556,257	17.56
West South-Central	129	1,547,597	26.94	126	867,709	16.20
Mountain	59	2,962,425	40.48	47	1,544,537	17.02
Pacific Coast	155	3,821,285	54.65	114	3,209,290	40.05
Metro status						
Central	207	4,780,445	35.73	203	2,424,643	19.50
Suburban	661	1,071,925	32.63	516	835,990	22.92
Independent.	222	537,521	29.14	210	329,946	17.23

Table 3/15   TOTAL DEPARTMENTAL EXPENDITURES, 2007

Classification	Police			Fire		
	No. of cities reporting	Mean ($)	Per capita ($)	No. of cities reporting	Mean ($)	Per capita ($)
Total	1,055	12,443,188	242.17	904	7,876,417	144.60
Population group						
Over 1,000,000	4	491,389,113	364.32	4	220,558,160	166.98
500,000–1,000,000	4	197,263,670	307.98	4	105,887,757	168.88
250,000–499,999	12	99,036,477	258.51	14	53,877,395	149.11
100,000–249,999	69	37,303,808	264.09	62	23,708,555	168.43
50,000–99,999	141	16,659,560	240.64	130	11,078,451	164.86
25,000–49,999	239	8,488,394	241.38	206	5,493,183	157.54
10,000–24,999	586	3,810,286	238.67	484	2,104,317	130.09
Geographic division						
New England	75	5,414,364	200.91	68	4,230,791	144.06
Mid-Atlantic	124	12,961,637	240.35	78	6,586,425	93.30
East North-Central	221	8,265,598	247.25	202	6,043,966	155.85
West North-Central	104	6,263,592	194.80	96	3,459,384	94.95
South Atlantic	162	12,818,687	267.94	143	8,462,381	173.22
East South-Central	40	7,561,552	208.69	40	6,007,855	164.27
West South-Central	122	14,131,265	212.43	125	8,577,346	125.65
Mountain	59	25,015,962	260.39	45	15,126,518	126.32
Pacific Coast	148	20,655,990	288.41	107	14,603,440	189.89
Metro status						
Central	200	36,741,291	247.14	198	21,550,255	163.73
Suburban	645	7,710,731	251.19	501	4,648,610	142.75
Independent	210	3,837,538	209.74	205	2,557,937	130.65

Table 3/16 **POLICE DEPARTMENT PERSONNEL, SALARIES, AND EXPENDITURES FOR CITIES 10,000 AND OVER: 2007**

This table comprises 1,391 cities 10,000 and over in population (based on U.S. Bureau of the Census 2000 counts). The information in the table was collected in the spring of 2007 in a survey conducted by ICMA. Refer to the accompanying article for the survey methodology. The information is presented in two separate tables—one for police (Table 3/16) and one for fire (Table 3/17). The following definitions apply to both tables.

Type: letter identifies municipal designation: c, city; v, village; b, borough; t, town; tp, township.
Service provision: the number in this column indicates how the service is provided.
1 Full-time paid
2 All volunteer
3 Combined paid and volunteer
4 Public safety department (consolidated police and fire department)
5 Contract with county or other government entity for service
6 Contract with private company for service
7 Other

Full-time paid personnel: the number in this column shows the actual (not authorized) number of full-time paid employees.
Full-time uniformed personnel: the number in this column shows the number of sworn/uniformed employees.

Duty hours per week: shows the average number of hours worked per week.
Minimum base salary ($): shows the minimum base salary paid to full-time sworn/uniformed personnel. This amount does not include uniform allowance, holiday pay, hazard pay, or any other additional compensation.
Maximum base salary ($): shows the maximum base salary paid to full-time sworn/uniformed personnel. This amount does not include uniform allowance, holiday pay, hazard pay, or any other additional compensation.
Longevity pay: shows whether personnel can receive longevity pay: y, yes; n, no.
Maximum salary with longevity ($): shows the maximum salary with longevity pay included.
Years of service for longevity: shows the number of years of service required before personnel can receive longevity pay.
Total expenditures (A) ($): shows total departmental expenditures for the most recently completed fiscal year.
Total personnel expenditures (B) ($): shows total expenditures for salaries and wages (C); city contribution to retirement and social security (D); and city contribution to health, hospitalization, disability, and life insurance programs (E).
(B) as % of (A): shows total personnel expenditures as a percentage of total departmental expendi-

tures. In some instances, the percentage equals or exceeds 100%. For some cities the retirement expenditures are in other accounts, so although they are reported as costs, they do not come out of the departmental budget. This accounts for the percentage in excess of 100.
Salaries and wages (C) ($): shows the amount of salaries and wages for all departmental personnel—regular, temporary, full time, and part time—and of stipends for volunteers. This is a gross amount, including longevity pay, hazard pay, and holiday pay, without deduction of withholding for income tax or employee contributions to social security or retirement coverage.
City contribution to retirement and social security (D) ($): shows city contributions only.
City contribution to insurance (E) ($): shows city contribution to health, hospitalization, disability, and life insurance programs.
Capital outlay (F) ($): Shows amount spent on purchases of equipment, land and existing structures, and construction.
All other (G) ($): shows amount of expenditures other than those described in (B) through (F) above. Expenditures include fuel, utilities, supplies, etc.

(—) Indicates data not reported.

													Reported expenditures (in $000)						
City	State	Type	Service provision	Full-time paid personnel	Full-time uniformed personnel	Duty hours per week	Minimum base salary ($)	Maximum base salary ($)	Longevity pay	Maximum salary with longevity ($)	Years of service for longevity	Total expenditures (A) ($)	Total personnel expenditures (B) ($)	(B) as % of (A)	Salaries and wages (C) ($)	City contribution to retirement and social security (D) ($)	City contribution to insurance (E) ($)	Capital outlay (F) ($)	All other (G) ($)
Over 1,000,000																			
DALLAS	TX	c	1	3,633	3,065	40	41,690	61,572	y	—	1	327,094	—	—	218,441	—	19,851	339	31,243
PHILADELPHIA	PA	c	1	7,462	6,630	40	39,568	51,388	y	56,543	3	811,433	761,136	94	474,219	181,110	105,806	10,923	39,374
PHOENIX	AZ	c	3	4,275	2,461	40	38,875	60,882	y	64,882	7	473,742	—	—	292,698	—	—	8,196	15,467
SAN DIEGO	CA	c	1	2,479	1,893	40	46,217	71,240	n	—	—	353,287	—	—	194,389	—	33,549	5,558	48,776
500,000–1,000,000																			
AUSTIN	TX	c	1	1,935	1,357	40	47,022	76,340	y	78,090	1	198,707	174,788	88	134,733	27,777	12,278	4,283	19,637
EL PASO	TX	c	1	1,505	1,089	40	32,835	53,562	y	54,762	1	105,925	93,935	89	71,190	13,703	9,041	995	10,995
JACKSONVILLE	FL	c	3	2,887	1,648	40	35,568	61,296	y	63,096	17	285,133	218,635	77	169,115	26,129	23,391	2,470	64,028
OKLAHOMA CITY	OK	c	1	—	—	40	44,266	50,613	y	—	20	—	—	—	—	—	—	—	—
SEATTLE	WA	c	—	1,782	1,277	—	48,944	69,325	y	—	7	199,290	159,416	80	129,680	8,018	21,718	2,738	37,135
250,000–499,999																			
ALBUQUERQUE	NM	c	1	1,338	962	40	38,520	43,826	y	54,486	4	115,135	88,724	77	67,172	12,765	8,787	5,621	20,790
ANCHORAGE	AK	c	—	—	—	—	—	—	—	—	—	—	—	—	—	—	—	—	—
ARLINGTON	TX	c	3	727	552	40	45,131	63,526	y	66,334	1	61,912	—	—	43,505	—	5,550	—	5,939
AURORA	CO	c	1	782	636	40	43,737	66,764	y	—	5	66,781	58,940	88	48,656	5,011	5,273	272	7,570
CINCINNATI	OH	c	1	1,331	1,085	40	46,104	55,799	y	58,799	8	—	—	—	85,288	—	—	—	12,091
CLEVELAND	OH	c	1	1,968	1,604	40	48,832	50,812	y	—	—	171,275	159,194	93	116,294	21,852	21,048	—	12,081
LONG BEACH	CA	c	3	1,406	958	40	53,881	66,718	y	70,293	10	180,959	145,593	80	100,203	24,846	20,542	3,296	32,070
MESA	AZ	c	1	1,335	845	40	46,987	63,440	n	—	—	120,618	—	—	84,982	—	11,000	1,477	15,647
NEW ORLEANS	LA	c	3	—	1,404	40	30,732	36,570	y	162,381	1	80,546	80,546	100	60,931	9,693	9,921	—	—
RALEIGH	NC	c	1	807	753	42	32,166	54,723	y	—	5	—	—	—	43,423	—	3,915	4,307	—
RIVERSIDE	CA	c	1	581	389	40	58,716	74,940	n	—	—	74,062	—	—	46,555	—	5,376	1,057	11,218
SANTA ANA	CA	c	3	659	363	40	60,612	73,680	n	—	—	108,131	—	—	59,972	—	11,566	210	27,045
TOLEDO	OH	c	1	811	686	40	41,677	54,808	y	—	26	71,790	—	—	44,996	—	9,378	—	5,608
VIRGINIA BEACH	VA	c	1	986	817	40	37,355	62,814	n	—	—	72,883	61,153	84	47,186	9,998	3,969	82	11,648
WICHITA	KS	c	3	864	—	40	36,938	52,192	y	—	6	64,347	54,625	85	41,084	7,117	6,423	1,389	8,332
100,000–249,999																			
ALLENTOWN	PA	c	1	212	193	40	38,445	51,412	y	53,837	5	28,882	27,406	95	16,233	8,023	3,150	179	1,298
ANN ARBOR	MI	c	1	220	155	40	41,018	65,354	y	65,854	5	24,787	21,869	88	16,604	1,441	3,824	54	2,864
ARVADA	CO	c	1	213	133	40	46,743	64,123	n	—	—	21,916	—	—	13,098	—	2,123	—	5,317
BABYLON	NY	t	—	—	—	—	—	—	—	—	—	—	—	—	—	—	—	—	—
BAKERSFIELD	CA	c	1	489	335	40	49,866	60,738	n	—	—	44,759	—	—	24,950	—	4,920	205	7,082

Table 3/16 continued

POLICE DEPARTMENT PERSONNEL, SALARIES, AND EXPENDITURES FOR CITIES 10,000 AND OVER: 2007

City	State	Type	Service provision	Full-time paid personnel	Full-time uniformed personnel	Duty hours per week	Minimum base salary ($)	Maximum base salary ($)	Longevity pay	Maximum salary with longevity ($)	Years of service for longevity	Total expenditures (A) ($)	Total personnel expenditures (B) ($)	(B) as % of (A)	Salaries and wages (C) ($)	City contribution to retirement and social security (D) ($)	City contribution to insurance (E) ($)	Capital outlay (F) ($)	All other (G) ($)
100,000–249,999 continued																			
BATON ROUGE– EAST BATON ROUGE	LA	c	1	784	623	40	29,200	40,419	y	48,503	10	—	52,699	—	39,670	6,078	6,950	2,952	5,679
BEAUMONT	TX	c	1	309	248	40	40,044	54,444	y	54,644	1	24,130	21,360	89	15,937	2,430	2,993	338	2,433
BELLEVUE	WA	c	1	—	—	40	49,204	68,157	y	—	5	34,060	—	—	19,384	—	3,000	80	9,575
BERKELEY	CA	c	1	278	167	40	80,820	100,584	y	105,613	27	—	—	—	—	—	7,073	146	11,555
BURBANK	CA	c	3	283	158	40	61,884	77,280	n	—	—	—	—	—	22,330	—	— 16,735	—
CAMBRIDGE	MA	c	—	—	—	—	—	—	—	—	—	—	—	—	—	—	—	—	—
CAPE CORAL	FL	c	1	329	215	40	41,496	60,466	n	—	—	31,070	24,264	78	17,152	4,539	2,573	4,262	2,544
CEDAR RAPIDS	IA	c	1	228	194	other	36,525	52,499	y	53,699	5	20,135	16,666	83	11,904	2,879	1,882	448	3,021
CHESAPEAKE	VA	c	1	532	337	40	34,136	67,671	n	—	—	37,241	31,175	84	23,282	4,896	2,996	—	6,066
CHULA VISTA	CA	c	3	370	242	40	60,316	73,315	n	—	—	45,340	41,057	91	27,478	9,859	3,720	198	4,085
CLEARWATER	FL	c	3	387	261	40	41,116	60,892	y	—	0	33,353	26,592	80	21,319	2,327	2,945	335	6,426
COLUMBIA	SC	c	1	370	334	other	29,278	46,845	n	—	—	23,318	19,878	85	15,759	2,750	1,368	479	2,961
COLUMBUS– MUSCOGEE CONSOLIDATED	GA	c	1	465	370	42	30,152	46,797	n	—	—	25,226	21,898	87	15,719	4,359	1,820	803	2,524
CONCORD	CA	c	3	216	156	40	57,001	69,291	—	—	—	35,705	29,009	81	17,853	7,149	4,007	1,013	5,683
CORAL SPRINGS	FL	c	1	—	202	40	48,748	63,877	y	64,516	5	35,336	30,321	86	21,238	5,909	3,174	658	4,357
CORONA	CA	c	1	304	174	40	48,336	65,196	y	66,916	5	35,026	—	—	18,967	—	5,519	114	5,074
DALY CITY	CA	c	1	150	111	40	72,644	88,400	y	89,600	20	19,834	—	—	12,432	—	2,651	734	4,030
DAYTON	OH	c	1	508	408	40	45,916	55,805	y	56,921	20	46,992	42,854	91	31,467	5,951	5,435	805	3,333
DES MOINES	IA	c	1	504	378	40	44,250	57,620	y	60,390	5	55,942	43,170	77	29,691	7,474	6,005	3,288	9,484
DURHAM	NC	c	1	563	492	42	33,039	55,506	n	—	—	38,639	35,368	92	26,862	5,297	3,209	—	3,270
EL MONTE	CA	c	3	226	156	40	50,736	61,668	y	65,364	5	29,982	—	—	18,307	—	2,191	232	3,249
FAYETTEVILLE	NC	c	1	504	345	40	32,500	55,691	y	—	—	33,978	27,365	81	20,371	3,678	3,316	915	5,702
FONTANA	CA	c	3	264	180	40	57,880	76,961	y	—	10	29,953	—	—	18,645	—	5,200	1,700	4,208
FORT COLLINS	CO	c	1	252	188	40	48,982	66,663	n	—	—	27,581	20,705	75	16,460	1,853	2,391	795	6,081
FORT LAUDERDALE	FL	c	1	689	491	40	45,032	63,898	y	71,885	5	87,069	—	—	46,795	—	—	2,056	14,839
FREMONT	CA	c	1	291	187	other	72,007	87,544	y	99,407	19	54,398	39,579	73	28,943	6,836	3,799	275	14,545
FULLERTON	CA	c	1	230	161	40	59,042	73,355	n	—	—	33,662	27,703	82	18,641	5,411	3,651	694	5,265
GRAND PRAIRIE	TX	c	1	319	216	40	46,325	63,639	y	—	—	25,676	22,344	87	16,843	3,580	1,920	350	2,982
GRAND RAPIDS	MI	c	—	—	—	—	—	—	—	—	—	—	—	—	—	—	—	—	—
HAMPTON	VA	c	1	381	275	40	35,620	58,141	y	—	3	—	—	—	—	—	—	—	—
HUNTINGTON	NY	t	—	—	—	—	—	—	—	—	—	—	—	—	—	—	—	—	—
HUNTINGTON BEACH	CA	c	1	358	223	40	62,525	77,438	y	85,182	10	—	—	—	—	—	—	—	—
HUNTSVILLE	AL	c	4	457	349	40	34,944	53,331	y	53,901	5	—	—	—	—	—	—	—	—
INGLEWOOD	CA	c	1	343	185	40	48,492	59,172	y	66,675	7	34,498	28,500	83	21,365	3,121	4,014	2,142	3,856
IRVINE	CA	c	1	234	158	40	54,637	77,450	n	—	—	45,829	—	—	25,326	—	2,385	6	10,802
JOLIET	IL	c	3	371	295	40	40,872	73,604	y	—	15	42,646	40,725	95	31,021	5,481	4,222	—	1,922
LAFAYETTE CONSOLIDATED	LA	c	3	289	223	40	27,540	36,545	y	—	1	19,809	—	—	11,550	—	1,831	531	4,059
LAREDO	TX	c	1	495	421	40	40,622	57,242	y	58,739	1	35,053	31,018	88	22,566	5,080	3,372	52	3,982
LEXINGTON– FAYETTE	KY	c	1	—	639	40	31,799	49,350	n	—	—	52,987	48,250	91	35,240	6,193	6,816	1,664	3,074
LITTLE ROCK	AR	c	1	625	513	40	33,421	49,828	y	51,628	1	52,251	43,732	84	33,424	4,890	5,417	2,957	5,562
McALLEN	TX	c	1	392	259	40	—	—	—	—	—	26,752	21,947	82	16,919	2,608	2,420	1,421	3,383
MESQUITE	TX	c	1	280	219	40	48,744	62,196	y	65,196	1	27,948	23,601	84	17,298	3,951	2,352	1,321	3,025
MOBILE	AL	c	1	755	466	42	26,616	41,280	n	—	—	—	—	—	—	—	—	—	—
NAPERVILLE	IL	c	1	295	188	40	50,138	70,459	y	71,959	10	30,218	25,551	85	21,507	1,053	2,990	106	4,562
NEWPORT NEWS	VA	c	1	578	418	48	33,620	66,535	n	—	—	37,613	30,508	81	24,362	2,937	3,209	—	6,289
NORFOLK	VA	c	1	—	—	40	34,650	55,500	n	—	—	95,137	48,969	51	39,440	6,495	3,034	1,168	45,000
PASADENA	CA	c	3	364	242	40	60,688	74,314	n	—	—	50,628	—	—	30,553	—	7,219	84	6,589
PASADENA	TX	c	1	321	255	40	41,972	61,808	y	—	1	36,336	28,900	80	20,221	4,376	4,302	1,565	5,872
PEMBROKE PINES	FL	c	1	314	247	40	47,320	66,685	y	72,020	10	34,367	30,252	88	19,945	6,797	3,510	1,057	3,058
PEORIA	AZ	c	1	264	87	40	43,748	61,548	n	—	—	25,435	20,219	79	14,780	2,695	2,743	986	4,230
PEORIA	IL	c	1	387	251	40	39,968	60,817	y	65,682	5	30,208	28,204	93	20,259	3,478	4,466	874	1,130
PLANO	TX	c	1	480	340	40	52,867	66,158	y	67,358	1	44,427	39,760	89	29,827	4,991	4,941	106	4,561
POMONA	CA	c	1	319	185	40	58,284	71,172	y	81,492	20	46,491	—	—	25,144	—	3,511	779	10,521
PORTSMOUTH	VA	c	1	—	—	—	—	—	—	—	—	—	—	—	—	—	—	—	—
RAMAPO	NY	t	1	108	108	40	—	—	y	—	—	24,312	22,940	94	13,561	7,363	2,015	211	1,162
ROCKFORD	IL	c	1	334	305	40	39,368	57,306	y	63,037	5	34,665	26,906	78	23,359	3,071	476	476	7,283
SALEM	OR	c	1	252	189	40	45,656	58,219	n	—	—	35,618	28,593	80	19,255	5,621	3,716	310	6,715
SALINAS	CA	c	1	249	170	40	60,912	77,760	n	—	—	35,509	26,451	74	21,103	1,068	4,279	4,535	4,523
SALT LAKE CITY	UT	c	1	575	423	40	36,462	54,600	y	—	6	50,908	41,652	82	29,184	8,899	3,569	356	8,899
SAN BUENAVENTURA (VENTURA)	CA	c	1	176	127	40	58,201	70,745	n	—	—	27,914	—	—	14,424	—	619	155	7,572
SANTA CLARA	CA	c	3	177	128	40	91,272	110,904	y	116,460	10	34,470	—	—	22,736	—	—	—	3,618
SANTA CLARITA	CA	c	5	—	—	—	—	—	—	—	—	—	—	—	—	—	—	—	—
SCOTTSDALE	AZ	c	3	703	425	40	47,965	69,534	n	—	—	72,255	51,128	71	40,539	6,811	3,778	6,145	14,982
SIOUX FALLS	SD	c	1	252	216	40	40,165	57,034	n	—	—	22,148	18,587	84	13,613	2,640	2,333	519	3,042
SPRINGFIELD	MO	c	1	446	303	40	31,554	50,003	y	51,200	5	31,703	25,476	80	18,516	4,986	1,973	719	5,508
ST. PETERSBURG	FL	c	1	782	540	40	40,305	60,891	y	60,891	—	—	—	—	—	—	—	—	—
STAMFORD	CT	c	1	361	300	40	47,042	59,098	y	64,098	5	57,537	—	—	31,199	—	3,505	13,146	2,075

Table 3/16 continued **POLICE DEPARTMENT PERSONNEL, SALARIES, AND EXPENDITURES FOR CITIES 10,000 AND OVER: 2007**

City	State	Type	Service provision	Full-time paid personnel	Full-time uniformed personnel	Duty hours per week	Minimum base salary ($)	Maximum base salary ($)	Longevity pay	Maximum salary with longevity ($)	Years of service for longevity	Reported expenditures (in $000)							
												Total expenditures (A) ($)	Total personnel expenditures (B) ($)	(B) as % of (A)	Salaries and wages (C) ($)	City contribution to retirement and social security (D) ($)	City contribution to insurance (E) ($)	Capital outlay (F) ($)	All other (G) ($)
100,000–249,999 continued																			
STERLING HEIGHTS	MI	c	1	262	—	40	43,908	68,111	y	—	5	25,663	24,338	95	17,346	2,242	4,749	463	863
SUNNYVALE	CA	c	4	285	215	42	76,465	111,145	n	—	—	—	—	—	28,623	—	8,625	35	6,100
SYRACUSE	NY	c	1	567	497	40	35,383	53,048	y	—	—	61,858	58,466	95	36,334	8,858	13,274	799	2,593
TALLAHASSEE	FL	c	1	498	359	40	37,318	61,004	y	63,750	13	41,844	—	—	27,251	—	2,574	46	8,392
TEMPE	AZ	c	1	501	308	40	48,925	66,057	y	67,708	5	64,461	42,035	65	31,620	5,925	4,490	9,491	12,935
THORNTON	IL	tp	—	—	—	—	—	—	n	—	—	—	—	—	—	—	—	—	—
TOPEKA	KS	c	1	346	292	40	33,696	55,910	n	—	—	26,238	21,423	82	17,016	2,431	1,976	72	4,744
VALLEJO	CA	c	1	203	148	40	79,437	110,686	y	132,979	20	35,803	—	—	31,157	—	4,697	94	4,551
VANCOUVER	WA	c	1	231	200	other	53,376	68,124	n	—	—	28,667	21,572	75	18,296	876	2,400	303	6,792
WACO	TX	c	1	307	229	40	39,341	52,101	y	53,301	1	24,128	20,740	86	15,780	3,477	1,483	126	3,261
WEST VALLEY CITY	UT	c	1	229	185	40	34,900	51,865	n	—	—	18,058	—	—	11,204	—	1,974	65	2,841
WESTMINSTER	CO	c	1	260	179	40	—	—	n	—	—	21,776	—	—	16,144	—	2,047	401	2,223
WINSTON-SALEM	NC	c	1	659	288	40	31,008	56,980	n	—	—	45,801	40,663	89	27,336	7,183	6,144	525	4,613
50,000–99,999																			
ABINGTON	PA	tp	1	115	89	40	49,387	69,054	y	71,754	7	12,780	—	—	8,607	—	1,377	78	2,535
ALAMEDA	CA	c	1	136	95	40	70,743	85,981	y	89,420	15	25,005	—	—	14,413	—	1,985	143	4,132
ALHAMBRA	CA	c	1	124	89	40	54,864	66,684	n	—	—	19,759	14,646	74	9,794	2,894	1,956	365	4,748
ANTIOCH	CA	c	3	153	113	other	61,668	74,964	n	—	—	25,533	19,413	76	13,124	3,801	2,488	491	5,630
ARLINGTON HEIGHTS	IL	v	1	150	112	40	46,465	71,915	y	73,515	5	19,152	16,541	86	11,731	2,770	2,040	400	2,210
ASHEVILLE	NC	c	1	233	224	42	28,769	41,325	n	—	—	13,103	12,677	97	9,661	1,571	1,444	82	343
BATTLE CREEK	MI	c	1	132	111	40	37,264	50,203	y	51,203	7	13,457	11,700	87	8,111	1,874	1,715	23	1,734
BAYTOWN	TX	c	1	169	126	40	40,541	40,541	y	55,167	1	14,156	11,948	84	8,491	1,917	1,539	376	1,832
BELLFLOWER	CA	c	5	—	—	40													
BELLINGHAM	WA	c	1	163	109	40	49,548	67,572	y	71,086	5	—	13,775	—	10,382	1,800	1,592	295	4,588
BEND	OR	c	1	124	91	40	46,788	56,928	n	—	—	11,948	10,352	87	6,825	1,807	1,720	287	1,309
BETHLEHEM	PA	c	1	156	149	40	37,246	49,500	y	53,460	4	13,045	—	—	9,241	—	1,423	239	570
BLOOMINGTON	IN	c	1	122	85	48	42,372	42,372	y	42,772	1	9,710	7,408	76	5,637	1,083	687	232	2,070
BLOOMINGTON	MN	c	1	132	113	other	43,860	68,316	n	—	—	17,119	14,966	87	11,053	2,863	1,050	1,598	—
BOSSIER CITY	LA	c	1	233	175	40	32,796	44,168	y	—	3	15,844	12,591	79	9,340	1,810	1,441	1,570	1,682
BOULDER	CO	c	1	273	171	40	44,253	65,565	n	—	—	25,183	—	—	19,756	—	4,454	1,349	4,077
BOWIE	MD	c	1	4	2	40	40,000	121,990	n	—	—								
BROOKLYN PARK	MN	c	1	112	74	42	41,122	58,781	y	64,365	4	12,424	9,991	80	8,163	928	899	10	2,423
BUENA PARK	CA	c	1	133	—	40	56,412	72,072	y	75,676	20	20,970	18,721	89	12,376	4,373	1,971	284	1,965
BURNSVILLE	MN	c	1	84	75	40	47,328	67,500	y	67,500	12	9,446	8,512	90	6,742	731	1,039	11	923
CAMARILLO	CA	c	5	—	—	40													
CARLSBAD	CA	c	3	156	112	40													
CARSON	CA	c	1	206	176	40	76,616	83,311	y	92,862	19								
CARY	NC	t	1	173	140	40	35,401	62,296	n	—	—	14,853	13,009	88	9,971	1,883	1,154	509	1,335
CHINO	CA	c	3	146	99	40	59,040	71,760	n	—	—	24,898	—	—	11,733	—	3,864	395	6,118
CHINO HILLS	CA	c	5	—	—	—													
CLOVIS	CA	c	1	151	100	40	59,364	72,156	n	—	—	20,678	15,920	77	11,078	2,271	2,571	385	4,372
COLERAIN TOWNSHIP	OH	tp	7	38	35	other	41,393	57,134	n	—	—	4,134	—	—	2,185	—	351	136	1,077
COLONIE	NY	t	1	148	104	40	42,289	62,961	y	80,723	5	25,695	10,836	42	8,002	1,951	881	3,019	11,840
CONCORD	NC	c	1	166	148	42	29,623	52,136	y	55,636	11	11,851	8,599	73	6,632	806	1,160	391	2,861
CORVALLIS	OR	c	1	75	51	40	44,519	60,849	n	—	—	9,689	7,054	73	5,084	815	1,154	256	2,380
CUPERTINO	CA	c	—	—	—														
DECATUR	IL	c	1	—	—	40	—	—		—		16,223	—	—	10,293	—	2,395	—	1,482
DELRAY BEACH	FL	c	1	221	149	40	40,322	67,640	n	—	—	24,914	20,690	83	14,387	3,976	2,326	354	3,871
DES PLAINES	IL	c	1	132	105	40	52,293	72,928	y	—	10	—	—	—	—	—	—	—	—
DIAMOND BAR	CA	c	—	—	—														
DOTHAN	AL	c	3	239	157	42	29,390	45,011	n	—	—	14,163	11,849	84	8,273	2,214	1,361	419	1,895
DUBUQUE	IA	c	1	98	93	40	41,995	46,654	y	48,987	6	8,180	6,846	84	5,631	219	995	22	1,313
EDEN PRAIRIE	MN	c	1	87	65	40	47,278	65,395	n	—	—	8,409	7,718	92	6,488	745	484	76	615
EDISON	NJ	tp	1	224	205	40	40,203	107,165	y	122,168	25	—	—	—	26,385	—	—	—	—
EDMOND	OK	c	1	126	105	other	35,810	57,534	y	59,534	4	13,436	9,356	70	7,174	1,317	865	173	3,907
ELGIN	IL	c	1	247	182	other	49,841	68,532	y	69,732	10	29,808	27,296	92	20,012	1,937	5,347	847	1,665
EUCLID	OH	c	1	153	96	40	43,272	52,344	y	56,532	5	—	—	—	—	—	—	—	—
FAIRFIELD	CT	t	1	114	108	—	49,346	57,656	y	61,256	20	12,785	—	—	9,484	3,363	—	1,690	1,458
FARMINGTON HILLS	MI	c	1	169	120	40	40,337	58,075	y	63,882	3	18,029	16,531	92	11,233	3,650	1,646	314	1,184
FEDERAL WAY	WA	c	1	149	120	40	47,016	63,072	y	67,014	5	19,040	14,446	76	10,291	3,071	983	—	4,975
FLAGSTAFF	AZ	c	1	150	104	40	40,424	55,773	n	—	—	13,803	10,995	80	8,332	1,471	1,191	435	2,372
FLOWER MOUND	TX	t	1	106	69	40	46,144	58,387	y	60,187	—	8,428	7,884	94	5,903	975	1,006	10	534
FOLSOM	CA	c	1	114	84	40	59,816	72,697	y	74,514	10	—	—	—	—	—	—	—	—
FORT SMITH	AR	c	3	202	163	40	33,430	39,990	y	40,110	5	13,356	10,152	76	8,512	352	1,287	516	2,688
FREDERICK	MD	c	1	177	140	42	38,196	61,154	n	—	—								
GAITHERSBURG	MD	c	1	51	45	40	42,671	65,285	n	—	—	5,894	4,654	79	3,530	762	361	573	667
GARDENA	CA	c	1	136	83	40	56,640	68,844	y	75,900	26	—	13,183	—	9,074	2,978	1,131	4,362	17,681
GASTONIA	NC	c	1	179	154	other	29,726	54,054	n	—	—	12,195	10,395	85	8,485	919	991	93	1,707
GREELEY	CO	c	1	230	130	40	47,919	66,441	n	—	—	20,379	—	—	—	—	—	—	—
GREENBURGH	NY	t	1	152	122	40	35,079	85,191	y	88,691	7	18,217	16,381	90	12,503	2,415	1,463	245	1,591
GREENVILLE	NC	c	1	210	171	48	31,512	57,845	n	—	—	15,971	11,930	75	8,956	1,199	1,775	745	3,296
GREENVILLE	SC	c	1	231	188	other	26,374	43,368	y	—	5	14,877	13,111	88	9,645	2,052	1,413	435	1,331

Table 3/16 continued POLICE DEPARTMENT PERSONNEL, SALARIES, AND EXPENDITURES FOR CITIES 10,000 AND OVER: 2007

												Reported expenditures (in $000)							
City	State	Type	Service provision	Full-time paid personnel	Full-time uniformed personnel	Duty hours per week	Minimum base salary ($)	Maximum base salary ($)	Longevity pay	Maximum salary with longevity ($)	Years of service for longevity	Total expenditures (A) ($)	Total personnel expenditures (B) ($)	(B) as % of (A)	Salaries and wages (C) ($)	City contribution to retirement and social security (D) ($)	City contribution to insurance (E) ($)	Capital outlay (F) ($)	All other (G) ($)
50,000–99,999 continued																			
GRESHAM	OR	c	3	159	119	—	44,364	59,436	n	—	—	25,575	16,090	63	10,551	2,810	2,729	4,441	5,044
GULFPORT	MS	c	3	256	165	40	29,701	32,349	y	—	1	—	11,370	—	7,853	1,466	2,051	1,008	—
HAMILTON	OH	c	1	154	123	40	40,435	52,208	y	57,429	5	16,461	13,611	83	9,753	1,870	1,988	959	1,891
HARLINGEN	TX	c	1	149	119	40	30,000	40,000	y	41,200	1	—	—	—	4,499	—	—	—	—
HAWTHORNE	CA	c	1	135	84	40	56,652	79,608	y	88,365	27	18,034	—	—	8,534	—	2,224	100	4,458
HESPERIA	CA	c	5	—	—	—	—	—	—	—	—	—	—	—	—	—	—	—	—
HOOVER	AL	c	1	214	154	other	39,666	56,472	n	—	—	22,420	16,616	74	12,950	2,045	1,621	1,998	3,806
HUNTINGTON PARK	CA	c	1	112	69	40	59,500	80,700	y	89,150	20	—	—	—	—	—	—	—	—
IDAHO FALLS	ID	c	1	127	91	40	35,922	48,734	y	51,860	3	10,022	—	—	6,115	—	—	196	874
IRONDEQUOIT	NY	t	1	74	56	40	35,822	63,839	y	68,467	4	7,605	6,889	91	5,329	1,085	475	122	593
JACKSONVILLE	NC	c	1	129	108	42	30,097	52,749	y	—	5	8,300	6,167	74	4,681	792	694	196	1,936
JANESVILLE	WI	c	1	118	105	40	33,607	56,358	y	56,358	—	10,900	9,981	92	6,544	1,678	1,759	163	756
JOHNSON CITY	TN	c	1	170	144	42	29,996	45,179	y	49,337	5	15,930	9,242	58	6,603	1,366	1,272	5,267	1,421
KENNEWICK	WA	c	1	108	89	40	53,400	67,980	n	—	—	16,486	11,229	68	7,634	3,271	324	1,775	3,482
KENOSHA	WI	c	1	198	186	40	44,532	55,284	y	55,584	5	21,796	18,422	85	11,704	3,168	3,550	561	2,813
KETTERING	OH	c	1	114	84	40	47,798	64,542	n	—	—	12,739	10,288	81	7,736	1,497	1,055	267	2,184
KILLEEN	TX	c	3	227	178	40	35,568	52,416	y	54,096	1	16,227	13,945	86	11,033	2,159	753	729	1,552
LA MESA	CA	c	1	105	65	40	53,580	65,112	n	—	—	11,584	9,564	83	6,154	2,188	1,222	609	1,411
LAGUNA NIGUEL	CA	c	5	—	—	—	—	—	—	—	—	—	—	—	—	—	—	—	—
LAKE CHARLES	LA	c	1	186	184	40	26,416		—	y	—	—	14,036	9,901	71	7,570	1,206	1,124	193	3,942
LAKE FOREST	CA	c	5	—	—	—	—	—	—	—	—	—	—	—	—	—	—	—	—
LAKELAND	FL	c	1	340	224	42	37,630	52,962	y	53,442	10	29,110	—	—	18,526	—	1,531	182	6,329
LAKEWOOD	WA	c	1	120	101	40	52,224	62,208	n	—	—	—	—	—	8,563	—	1,566	—	—
LAUDERHILL	FL	c	1	150	118	42	41,325	61,442	y	—	—	13,005	—	—	8,451	—	—	45	1,558
LAYTON	UT	c	1	102	75	40	33,623	55,370	n	—	—	7,493	—	—	6,410	—	—	228	855
LEE'S SUMMIT	MO	c	1	164	89	40	36,323	48,694	n	—	—	—	—	—	8,580	9,214	—	—	—
LIVERMORE	CA	c	1	212	117	40	62,544	75,972	y	79,770	5	—	—	—	—	—	2,775	12	4,049
LONGMONT	CO	c	1	159	124	40	47,832	62,904	y	63,984	2	16,632	14,061	85	10,936	1,166	1,958	513	2,059
LONGVIEW	TX	c	3	194	167	40	36,601	48,128	y	—	1	13,058	10,803	83	7,892	1,715	1,194	118	2,138
LOVELAND	CO	c	1	128	88	40	46,332	61,476	y	63,935	5	13,178	10,583	80	8,040	922	1,621	275	2,320
LOWER MERION	PA	tp	1	142	123	40	50,417	62,248	y	66,917	3	15,840	14,171	89	10,702	900	2,568	212	1,457
LYNCHBURG	VA	c	1	184	161	40	30,618	53,243	n	—	—	12,549	10,924	87	8,328	1,947	648	137	1,488
MARGATE	FL	c	1	194	121	40	44,195	63,580	y	66,580	10	16,433	15,056	92	10,436	2,459	2,160	488	890
MARIETTA	GA	c	1	169	137	40	33,030	49,296	n	—	—	11,615	10,022	86	7,437	1,363	1,221	687	906
McKINNEY	TX	c	1	167	133	40	48,292	61,547	y	62,747	1	13,789	11,631	84	8,659	1,592	1,379	573	1,585
MEDFORD	OR	c	1	143	95	40	42,204	53,904	n	—	—	7,252	—	—	—	2,169	1,768	636	1,711
MELBOURNE	FL	c	—	—	—	—	—	—	—	—	—	—	—	—	—	—	—	—	—
MIDWEST CITY	OK	c	3	119	91	40	38,656	43,190	n	—	—	9,808	7,860	80	6,383	1,337	139	177	1,770
MILPITAS	CA	c	1	113	85	40	72,466	98,434	y	113,298	9	—	—	—	—	—	—	—	—
MINNETONKA	MN	c	1	73	54	42	49,712	60,341	n	—	—	7,554	6,273	83	5,026	617	630	208	1,073
MISSION VIEJO	CA	c	5	—	—	40	—	—	—	—	—	—	—	—	—	—	—	—	—
MISSOULA	MT	c	1	—	96	40	39,816	59,844	y	—	1	9,300	—	—	6,750	—	977	—	—
MISSOURI CITY	TX	c	1	96	69	40	41,500	58,100	y	42,460	1	—	—	—	—	508	16	16	784
MONTEBELLO	CA	c	1	103	74	40	50,904	64,980	n	—	—	15,220	13,145	86	8,539	2,705	1,901	34	2,041
MONTEREY PARK	CA	c	3	107	76	40	58,044	70,548	n	—	—	13,374	—	—	8,716	—	857	94	1,972
MOUNTAIN VIEW	CA	c	1	147	96	40	77,189	93,734	n	—	—	23,924	—	—	15,940	—	2,402	129	2,913
MUNCIE	IN	c	1	115	106	40	40,221	40,221	y	42,509	5	9,972	8,979	90	6,231	1,041	1,707	360	633
MURFREESBORO	TN	c	1	230	183	other	30,937	46,747	y	—	1	16,464	12,299	75	9,488	1,527	1,283	1,208	2,957
NASHUA	NH	c	1	217	162	40	36,240	54,768	y	55,768	7	17,528	—	—	13,677	—	—	2,552	1,299
NEW ROCHELLE	NY	c	1	221	177	other	43,264	73,595	y	80,681	5	27,495	25,341	92	18,824	3,580	2,937	121	2,034
NORMAN	OK	c	1	162	130	other	35,896	51,110	y	51,110	5	14,578	12,098	83	9,073	1,631	1,393	881	1,600
NORTH CHARLESTON	SC	c	1	370	250	other	30,973	43,362	y	43,882	10	22,524	18,599	83	12,531	2,247	3,821	1,313	2,612
NORTH MIAMI	FL	c	1	183	122	40	42,619	63,398	y	69,737	5	16,807	—	—	11,083	2,981	—	115	2,627
NORTH RICHLAND HILLS	TX	c	1	157	113	40	45,263	59,564	y	60,839	1	13,546	10,898	80	8,292	1,149	1,456	25	2,623
NORWALK	CT	c	1	189	173	40	50,665	61,657	y	62,342	8	19,101	17,074	89	14,536	1,902	636	—	2,026
ODESSA	TX	c	1	200	148	40	34,020	38,916	y	—	1	15,543	12,773	82	9,271	2,013	1,489	185	2,585
OGDEN CITY	UT	c	1	161	143	40	31,824	44,486	y	—	10	14,268	10,604	74	7,587	1,632	1,385	241	3,423
OREM	UT	c	4	173	140	40	36,564	54,840	n	—	—	15,998	13,481	84	9,347	2,868	1,265	672	1,844
ORLAND PARK	IL	v	1	125	96	40	52,462	70,005	y	72,705	5	—	—	—	—	—	—	—	—
PALATINE	IL	v	1	132	88	40	53,160	74,149	y	75,149	8	15,462	13,682	88	9,897	1,976	1,809	248	1,531
PALO ALTO	CA	c	3	152	90	40	70,803	86,944	n	—	—	26,851	—	—	15,018	—	2,602	114	6,325
PARMA	OH	c	1	—	—	40	44,348	61,303	y	63,103	5	—	—	—	8,431	—	1,615	—	540
PAWTUCKET	RI	c	1	189	153	40	43,039	50,468	y	55,767	4	—	—	—	—	—	—	—	—
PENSACOLA	FL	c	1	209	175	40	32,011	54,600	y	60,060	5	16,310	—	—	8,330	—	1,035	7	3,960
PETALUMA	CA	c	3	102	75	40	63,772	77,542	n	—	—	—	—	—	8,141	—	2,127	2,293	332
PITTSBURG	CA	c	1	97	71	40	61,236	74,424	n	—	—	16,720	12,103	72	8,601	794	2,707	1,020	—
PLAIN	OH	tp	5	—	—	40	—	—	—	—	—	—	—	—	—	—	—	—	—
PLEASANTON	CA	c	3	115	83	40	67,452	81,996	n	—	—	19,489	16,969	87	10,646	3,774	2,549	354	2,167
PLYMOUTH	MN	c	1	—	—	40	—	—	—	—	—	—	—	—	—	—	—	—	—
POMPANO BEACH	FL	c	—	—	—	—	—	—	—	—	—	—	—	—	—	—	—	—	—
PORT ARTHUR	TX	c	1	146	112	40	36,834	51,232	y	52,432	1	—	—	—	—	—	—	—	—
PORT ST. LUCIE	FL	c	1	309	232	40	38,608	60,208	n	—	—	28,031	22,581	81	16,014	3,473	3,094	1,467	3,983

Table 3/16 continued
POLICE DEPARTMENT PERSONNEL, SALARIES, AND EXPENDITURES FOR CITIES 10,000 AND OVER: 2007

City	State	Type	Service provision	Full-time paid personnel	Full-time uniformed personnel	Duty hours per week	Minimum base salary ($)	Maximum base salary ($)	Longevity pay	Maximum salary with longevity ($)	Years of service for longevity	Reported expenditures (in $000) Total expenditures (A) ($)	Total personnel expenditures (B) ($)	(B) as % of (A)	Salaries and wages (C) ($)	City contribution to retirement and social security (D) ($)	City contribution to insurance (E) ($)	Capital outlay (F) ($)	All other (G) ($)
50,000–99,999 continued																			
PORTLAND	ME	c	1	225	166	40	31,975	45,678	n	—	—	12,299	—	—	10,643	—	—	418	1,238
RANCHO CORDOVA	CA	c	5	—	—	—	—	—		—	—	—	—	—	—	—	—	—	—
RAPID CITY	SD	c	3	130	103	40	36,545	55,598	n	—	—	10,335	8,441	82	6,705	948	787	239	1,655
READING	PA	c	1	207	—	40	49,300	54,637	y	58,871	3	—	—	—	—	—	—	—	—
REDFORD	MI	tp	1	—	75	—	42,872	57,163	y	83,632	5	15,259	13,071	86	5,525	4,892	2,653	1,351	837
REDLANDS	CA	c	3	161	95	40	53,084	64,524	y	67,750	20	23,881	19,110	80	13,156	3,809	2,144	1,130	3,642
REDONDO BEACH	CA	c	3	113	100	40	52,176	63,444	y	74,864	10	25,397	19,763	78	13,340	4,802	1,621	351	5,283
RENTON	WA	c	1	138	94	42	49,884	66,768	y	74,784	5	17,962	12,953	72	10,048	1,175	1,729	226	4,782
RICHARDSON	TX	c	1	237	125	40	—	—	y	—	1	17,338	17,940	103	13,555	3,094	1,291	—	1,398
RICHMOND	CA	c	1	229	157	40	74,868	86,376	y	101,172	5	47,581	32,241	68	21,714	5,453	5,073	3,112	12,228
ROANOKE	VA	c	1	307	254	48	31,213	49,941	n	—	—	28,589	17,286	60	13,227	2,639	1,420	6,424	4,879
ROCKY MOUNT	NC	c	1	177	128	40	30,369	45,553	y	48,513	1	10,817	9,265	86	7,359	1,207	698	347	1,205
ROSEVILLE	CA	c	1	200	128	40	49,010	70,573	y	74,102	10	29,050	—	—	15,546	—	2,759	—	6,248
ROSWELL	GA	c	1	176	140	40	35,000	—	n	—	—	15,137	13,001	86	9,183	1,441	2,377	164	1,971
ROYAL OAK	MI	c	1	104	88	40	39,153	55,228	y	60,750	5	10,821	10,163	94	7,109	1,457	1,596	2	656
SAN LEANDRO	CA	c	1	138	89	40	70,776	103,236	y	—	—	23,404	18,804	80	12,282	5,204	1,318	108	4,492
SAN MARCOS	CA	c	5	—	—	—	—	—		—	—	—	—	—	—	—	—	—	—
SAN MATEO	CA	c	1	145	106	40	67,974	80,995	n	—	—	—	—	—	—	—	—	1,922	2,941
SANDY CITY	UT	c	3	—	117	42	33,592	49,258	n	—	—	11,341	—	—	6,577	—	920	464	2,198
SANDY SPRINGS	GA	c	1	106	—	40	38,000	47,000	n	—	—	—	—	—	—	—	—	—	—
SANTA BARBARA	CA	c	1	206	139	40	60,736	77,989	n	—	—	30,455	—	—	16,768	—	3,074	48	4,669
SANTA CRUZ	CA	c	1	113	97	40	60,756	81,420	y	—	—	—	—	—	—	—	—	—	—
SANTA FE	NM	c	1	178	178	40	35,152	58,536	y	58,536	1	14,600	13,852	95	9,706	2,297	1,849	489	259
SANTA MARIA	CA	c	3	144	65	40	56,189	68,298	n	—	—	17,331	—	—	11,412	—	2,286	145	2,036
SANTA MONICA	CA	c	1	388	204	40	62,148	76,728	y	82,943	5	60,894	—	—	36,548	—	7,401	1,431	5,069
SANTEE	CA	c	—	—	—	—	—	—		—	—	—	—	—	—	—	—	—	—
SARASOTA	FL	c	1	262	196	other	32,920	66,330	y	61,330	12	—	—	—	—	1,990	1,269	99	1,678
SOUTH SAN FRANCISCO	CA	c	—	—	—	—	—	—		—	—	—	—	—	—	—	—	—	—
SPRINGFIELD	OH	c	1	141	122	40	39,811	52,000	y	—	5	1,749	—	—	7,847	—	1,265	1,328	78
ST. CHARLES	MO	c	1	152	108	other	46,887	66,530	n	—	—	—	—	—	—	—	—	—	—
ST. CLAIR SHORES	MI	c	1	98	62	40	38,183	62,058	n	—	—	11,623	10,209	88	7,615	1,730	864	541	872
ST. CLOUD	MN	c	1	121	97	40	44,820	56,064	y	—	5	11,924	9,565	80	7,340	861	1,363	210	2,150
ST. JOSEPH	MO	c	1	162	118	40	29,028	45,863	n	—	—	11,300	9,530	84	6,775	1,948	806	238	1,532
ST. PETERS	MO	c	1	—	—	40	—	—		—	—	—	—	—	—	—	—	—	—
SUFFOLK	VA	c	1	217	161	40	32,785	51,475	n	—	—	16,676	12,497	75	9,196	1,802	1,499	866	3,313
TAYLORSVILLE	UT	c	1	61	55	40	32,968	50,953	y	52,736	12	5,583	4,120	74	2,857	885	378	662	800
TEMPLE	TX	c	1	148	123	40	35,684	50,124	y	51,324	1	10,543	8,760	83	7,071	1,127	562	363	1,420
TROY	MI	c	1	212	134	40	39,219	64,100	y	67,531	4	22,236	16,865	76	12,753	2,304	1,807	291	5,081
TURLOCK	CA	c	1	100	65	40	40,560	57,084	n	—	—	13,141	10,691	81	6,585	2,281	1,825	502	1,948
TUSCALOOSA	AL	c	1	334	260	40	35,917	47,660	y	—	20	21,638	17,973	83	14,584	1,975	1,413	502	3,164
TUSTIN	CA	c	3	147	95	40	62,474	76,287	n	—	—	19,059	—	—	11,735	—	2,319	268	1,612
TYLER	TX	c	1	228	171	40	38,563	56,921	y	58,121	1	17,951	15,494	86	10,053	3,528	1,913	238	2,219
UNION CITY	CA	c	1	104	81	40	69,276	82,956	y	87,104	19	—	—	—	—	—	—	—	—
UPLAND	CA	c	3	127	66	40	57,253	69,592	y	71,332	5	14,336	—	—	7,463	—	411	351	4,768
VACAVILLE	CA	c	1	181	113	40	66,786	81,130	y	85,186	12	24,298	—	—	14,782	—	3,785	263	2,363
VICTORIA	TX	c	1	139	100	40	37,904	62,640	y	—	1	9,684	8,059	83	5,958	1,243	857	123	1,502
VICTORVILLE	CA	c	5	—	—	—	—	—		—	—	—	—	—	—	—	—	—	—
WEST BLOOMFIELD CHARTER TOWNSHIP	MI	tp	1	102	78	40	37,511	60,012	y	66,120	5	12,873	—	—	6,924	—	2,934	1,194	1,298
WEST CHESTER	OH	tp	1	95	82	40	45,369	59,111	y	—	5	10,941	—	—	6,221	—	1,054	1,066	1,948
WEST HARTFORD	CT	t	1	151	132	40	49,712	63,050	n	—	—	16,415	14,962	91	10,850	1,609	2,503	140	1,312
WEST JORDAN	UT	c	1	123	95	40	38,293	48,880	n	—	—	12,527	—	—	7,237	—	1,467	79	2,135
WESTLAND	MI	c	1	111	102	42	40,121	57,317	y	57,317	3	15,489	14,274	92	8,861	2,491	2,921	143	1,072
WHEATON	IL	c	1	92	72	40	51,630	68,541	y	70,541	5	10,926	9,575	88	6,999	1,258	1,317	6	1,345
WHITE PLAINS	NY	c	1	247	202	40	49,148	73,709	y	77,007	5	30,772	28,798	94	21,718	4,505	2,574	83	1,891
WHITTIER	CA	c	1	187	127	48	52,404	68,856	n	—	—	32,125	—	—	13,009	—	3,222	1,116	11,416
WILMINGTON	NC	c	1	300	256	42	30,298	57,109	n	—	—	34,714	15,239	44	12,163	1,839	1,237	15,846	3,629
WYOMING	MI	c	1	113	87	40	46,280	55,578	y	56,578	5	13,505	10,896	81	7,078	1,719	2,099	14	2,594
YAKIMA	WA	c	1	171	126	40	47,048	63,771	y	70,148	4	18,710	14,369	77	11,551	776	2,042	422	3,919
YORBA LINDA	CA	c	5	—	—	—	—	—		—	—	—	—	—	—	—	—	—	—
YUMA	AZ	c	1	253	147	40	42,114	58,961	y	—	—	18,771	15,327	82	12,053	1,914	1,360	529	2,915
25,000–49,999																			
ADDISON	IL	v	1	87	63	40	50,222	68,682	n	—	—	10,570	8,842	84	6,517	1,294	1,030	194	1,534
ALAMOGORDO	NM	c	4	103	63	other	30,201	39,639	n	—	—	—	—	—	—	2,013	615	84	972
ALTAMONTE SPRINGS	FL	c	1	122	99	40	35,000	50,750	n	—	—	9,071	8,065	89	6,280	1,266	518	454	553
ALTOONA	PA	c	1	76	76	40	36,316	48,162	y	53,220	5	—	—	—	3,656	—	—	—	—
ANDERSON	SC	c	3	132	87	40	26,517	39,775	n	—	—	6,698	5,359	80	4,051	671	636	341	999
ANDOVER	MN	c	5	—	—	other	—	—		—	—	—	—	—	—	—	—	—	—
ANKENY	IA	c	1	50	42	other	36,655	51,578	y	53,578	3	4,727	3,881	82	2,559	759	563	150	695
APOPKA	FL	c	1	92	79	40	36,979	55,469	n	—	—	7,490	6,307	84	4,230	1,498	579	356	827
APPLE VALLEY	MN	c	1	59	49	40	43,140	61,620	y	67,164	16	465	—	—	4,866	—	432	561	195

Table 3/16   **POLICE DEPARTMENT PERSONNEL, SALARIES, AND EXPENDITURES FOR**
continued   **CITIES 10,000 AND OVER: 2007**

Reported expenditures (in $000)

City	State	Type	Service provision	Full-time paid personnel	Full-time uniformed personnel	Duty hours per week	Minimum base salary ($)	Maximum base salary ($)	Longevity pay	Maximum salary with longevity ($)	Years of service for longevity	Total expenditures (A) ($)	Total personnel expenditures (B) ($)	(B) as % of (A)	Salaries and wages (C) ($)	City contribution to retirement and social security (D) ($)	City contribution to insurance (E) ($)	Capital outlay (F) ($)	All other (G) ($)
25,000–49,999 continued																			
ATASCADERO	CA	c	1	—	—	40	48,419	58,854	n	—	—	—	—	—	—	—	—	—	—
AUBURN	AL	c	4	112	106	48	31,948	49,837	n	—	—	7,309	6,162	84	5,141	732	288	567	580
AUBURN	NY	c	1	76	68	other	35,999	53,001	y	54,551	4	5,881	—	—	4,572	—	—	153	382
AUBURN	WA	c	3	116	84	40	51,739	65,427	y	71,315	5	16,489	10,618	64	8,258	976	1,384	54	5,817
AVONDALE	AZ	c	1	144	95	40	44,852	64,960	n	—	—	12,486	9,268	74	7,139	1,183	946	481	2,737
BALLWIN	MO	c	1	63	54	40	40,070	58,945	n	—	—	—	—	—	6,782	—	—	—	—
BARTLESVILLE	OK	c	1	77	48	42	—	40,394	y	41,594	5	4,564	3,806	83	2,843	494	469	127	630
BELL	CA	c	1	56	43	40	59,232	72,000	n	—	—	7,111	6,162	87	4,552	1,130	479	116	834
BELLEVILLE	NJ	tp	1	116	107	40	37,184	70,329	y	77,329	7	—	—	—	9,000	—	—	—	—
BELMONT	CA	c	1	45	32	56	—	—	n	—	—	—	—	—	6,782	—	—	—	—
BELOIT	WI	c	1	87	76	40	37,757	55,004	y	—	—	10,734	9,088	85	5,372	1,441	2,274	594	1,052
BETHEL PARK	PA	c	1	44	38	40	44,587	68,595	y	72,882	4	4,574	—	—	3,260	—	746	113	388
BEVERLY	MA	c	1	72	69	40	46,877	51,511	y	52,611	10	5,857	—	—	5,584	—	—	25	247
BEVERLY HILLS	CA	c	1	201	136	40	70,000	82,000	y	—	—	—	—	—	—	956	819	7	2,280
BIG SPRING	TX	c	1	—	—	48	27,828	29,967	y	—	—	3,582	—	—	2,222	—	407	407	596
BLUE SPRINGS	MO	c	1	117	83	40	35,651	53,477	n	—	—	10,617	—	—	7,059	—	—	484	3,074
BONITA SPRINGS	FL	c	—	—	—	—	—	—	—	—	—	—	—	—	—	—	—	—	—
BOTHELL	WA	c	1	79	53	40	49,308	63,984	y	70,382	5	9,506	7,785	82	6,109	705	970	171	1,551
BOWLING GREEN	OH	c	1	56	41	40	40,477	53,310	n	—	—	—	—	—	—	—	784	311	350
BRADENTON	FL	c	1	138	122	40	37,000	59,423	y	—	5	14,711	12,241	83	7,204	3,858	1,179	986	1,483
BREMERTON	WA	c	1	78	63	40	53,432	69,134	y	73,623	26	8,937	—	—	5,323	—	—	157	2,026
BROOKFIELD	WI	c	1	82	64	other	46,796	61,508	n	—	—	7,923	7,130	90	4,876	1,232	1,022	146	647
BROOKLYN CENTER	MN	c	1	58	45	42	42,995	63,228	y	65,532	16	5,774	4,590	80	3,721	434	435	19	1,165
BROOMFIELD	CO	c	1	191	142	40	43,014	63,419	n	—	—	17,251	15,083	87	12,390	1,391	1,302	254	1,914
BUFFALO GROVE	IL	v	1	—	—	40	—	—	—	—	—	—	—	—	—	—	—	—	—
BULLHEAD CITY	AZ	c	1	136	83	40	39,117	56,402	y	57,812	10	12,094	9,508	79	7,159	752	1,596	664	1,923
BURLINGTON	IA	c	1	57	42	40	33,139	44,064	y	45,014	5	4,314	3,748	87	2,531	616	600	72	494
BURLINGTON	NC	c	1	143	109	40	32,253	53,236	y	56,431	5	9,723	7,690	79	6,058	1,344	288	308	1,725
CALEXICO	CA	c	—	—	—	—	—	—	—	—	—	—	—	—	—	—	—	—	—
CAMPBELL	CA	c	—	65	43	40	74,701	96,417	n	—	—	11,479	10,010	87	6,899	1,810	1,301	30	1,439
CAROL STREAM	IL	v	1	88	61	40	48,241	69,583	n	—	—	10,181	8,700	85	6,308	1,258	1,134	210	1,271
CARPENTERSVILLE	IL	v	1	81	53	40	50,064	69,048	y	69,848	1	8,003	—	—	5,962	—	—	136	1,056
CASA GRANDE	AZ	c	1	90	62	40	42,051	57,988	n	—	—	9,721	8,380	86	6,098	1,396	886	220	1,121
CASPER	WY	c	1	—	—	40	—	—	—	—	—	—	—	—	—	—	—	—	—
CEDAR FALLS	IA	c	3	45	28	40	34,794	45,325	y	46,705	4	3,780	3,071	81	2,088	490	492	19	690
CEDAR HILL	TX	c	3	71	61	40	40,000	53,725	y	54,925	1	7,493	5,014	67	3,576	702	735	425	2,054
CHARLOTTESVILLE	VA	c	1	136	112	40	33,904	51,230	n	—	—	14,485	11,807	82	6,541	3,528	1,737	669	2,009
CHELTENHAM	PA	tp	1	114	84	40	52,156	65,194	y	65,594	5	11,510	10,646	92	6,835	1,776	2,035	274	590
CHESTER	PA	c	1	—	97	40	44,924	—	y	52,112	3	9,743	—	—	5,883	—	1,419	349	—
CHESTERFIELD	MO	c	1	91	80	40	43,651	61,112	y	—	20	—	—	—	4,963	691	—	—	—
CLAREMONT	CA	c	1	62	41	40	55,884	67,512	n	—	—	8,570	—	—	4,255	—	1,150	481	1,194
CLEBURNE	TX	c	1	70	53	40	39,246	45,524	y	50,516	1	5,396	4,714	87	3,396	727	590	39	644
CLINTON	IA	c	1	55	46	42	33,802	53,076	n	—	—	4,827	3,912	81	2,613	645	655	—	915
COCONUT CREEK	FL	c	1	126	83	42	40,809	71,452	y	73,731	—	12,003	11,424	95	8,569	2,125	729	56	522
COLLIERVILLE	TN	t	1	125	89	other	25,493	47,317	n	—	—	7,877	6,869	87	5,006	905	958	349	659
COLTON	CA	c	1	121	71	40	54,099	65,742	n	—	—	13,123	—	—	6,607	—	1,876	974	1,208
COLUMBIA	TN	c	3	90	84	40	24,565	37,731	y	—	3	5,739	4,464	78	3,475	645	344	258	1,017
CONROE	TX	c	1	127	96	40	37,900	51,654	y	52,854	1	9,577	8,411	88	6,058	1,228	1,123	71	1,096
CONWAY	AR	c	1	120	98	40	28,434	38,412	n	—	—	7,762	6,222	80	4,565	1,167	490	449	1,091
COPPERAS COVE	TX	c	1	71	54	40	35,006	51,604	y	51,604	1	3,545	3,126	88	2,509	395	222	114	304
CORAL GABLES	FL	c	1	265	179	40	42,843	60,320	y	69,828	10	36,102	30,685	85	18,542	11,355	592	341	5,077
COTTAGE GROVE	MN	c	1	48	39	40	45,032	59,301	y	64,638	4	4,328	3,680	85	2,959	347	374	183	465
COVINGTON	KY	c	1	147	116	40	31,319	47,763	y	—	3	13,744	11,994	87	7,737	2,133	2,123	253	1,497
CYPRESS	CA	c	3	73	56	40	57,252	73,056	n	—	—	13,412	—	—	8,659	—	—	345	3,080
DANA POINT	CA	c	—	—	—	—	—	—	—	—	—	—	—	—	—	—	—	—	—
DANVILLE	VA	c	1	137	128	42	29,941	—	—	—	—	7,784	6,775	87	5,271	651	852	238	771
DE SOTO	TX	c	1	88	69	40	41,232	53,892	y	55,092	1	6,407	5,865	92	4,328	914	623	351	191
DEER PARK	TX	c	1	80	59	40	41,912	57,657	y	62,000	0	—	—	—	—	—	—	—	—
DELAWARE	OH	c	1	66	39	40	40,373	60,403	y	—	5	5,709	—	—	3,400	—	570	40	3,857
DELTA	MI	tp	5	—	—	42	—	—	—	—	—	—	—	—	—	—	—	—	—
DEPTFORD	NJ	c	1	66	66	40	38,062	70,613	y	76,262	4	—	—	—	—	—	—	—	—
DERRY	NH	t	1	70	59	40	39,487	48,650	y	—	5	8,895	6,482	73	5,243	572	666	960	1,453
DOVER	DE	c	1	120	91	40	39,297	81,918	y	—	—	10,993	9,800	89	6,977	1,510	1,313	241	951
DOVER	NH	c	1	75	51	other	42,235	62,806	y	64,406	5	6,114	5,323	87	3,856	450	1,017	175	616
DOWNERS GROVE	IL	v	1	—	—	40	—	—	—	—	—	—	—	—	—	—	—	—	—
DRACUT	MA	t	1	49	48	40	39,407	46,583	y	47,803	—	3,717	—	—	2,859	441	—	176	240
DUBLIN	OH	c	1	88	64	40	45,341	67,557	y	68,931	4	9,202	8,275	90	6,048	1,160	1,067	409	517
DUNCANVILLE	TX	c	1	69	58	40	43,785	56,683	y	57,883	1	7,066	5,647	80	4,197	960	489	209	1,211
DUNEDIN	FL	c	5	—	—	—	—	—	—	—	—	—	—	—	—	—	—	—	—
EAST BRUNSWICK	NJ	tp	1	130	95	40	43,951	88,341	y	98,941	6	15,149	13,501	89	11,169	2,181	150	327	1,322
EAST CLEVELAND	OH	c	3	35	—	40	32,719	40,129	n	—	—	—	—	—	—	—	—	—	—
EASTPOINTE	MI	c	1	52	—	40	39,744	57,175	y	—	5	—	—	—	—	—	—	—	—
EGG HARBOR	NJ	tp	1	128	100	other	36,369	73,634	y	77,316	5	11,922	10,832	91	9,323	1,347	161	163	927

Table 3/16 continued **POLICE DEPARTMENT PERSONNEL, SALARIES, AND EXPENDITURES FOR CITIES 10,000 AND OVER: 2007**

City	State	Type	Service provision	Full-time paid personnel	Full-time uniformed personnel	Duty hours per week	Minimum base salary ($)	Maximum base salary ($)	Longevity pay	Maximum salary with longevity ($)	Years of service for longevity	Total expenditures (A) ($)	Total personnel expenditures (B) ($)	(B) as % of (A)	Salaries and wages (C) ($)	City contribution to retirement and social security (D) ($)	City contribution to insurance (E) ($)	Capital outlay (F) ($)	All other (G) ($)
25,000–49,999 continued																			
ELK GROVE VILLAGE	IL	v	1	111	94	40	49,979	70,241	y	70,991	10	12,416	9,215	74	7,509	670	1,036	426	2,775
ELMWOOD PARK	IL	v	1	40	33	40	47,716	59,921	y	67,303	3	4,645	4,255	92	2,959	995	300	105	285
EMPORIA	KS	c	1	70	50	40	30,720	45,566	n	—	—	3,954	3,411	86	2,764	418	228	56	486
EULESS	TX	c	1	118	82	40	45,678	57,661	y	—	1	9,532	8,817	92	6,987	1,043	786	155	560
EUREKA	CA	c	1	60	42	40	41,412	50,364	y	—	—	7,447	—	—	4,452	—	888	155	1,113
FAIRBORN	OH	c	1	59	43	40	42,661	58,531	y	59,994	5	5,416	4,760	88	3,558	689	513	120	536
FARMERS BRANCH	TX	c	1	104	70	42	46,274	62,987	y	—	1	—	—	—	—	—	—	—	—
FINDLAY	OH	c	1	79	72	40	34,528	50,274	y	53,394	8	7,086	—	—	4,190	—	796	53	1,284
FISHERS	IN	t	1	83	76	40	37,680	52,752	n	—	—	1,725	—	—	3,954	1,035	—	520	1,205
FITCHBURG	MA	c	1	114	91	40	37,793	42,334	y	44,401	5	—	—	—	6,456	—	—	103	501
FOND DU LAC	WI	c	1	75	70	other	38,803	54,405	y	—	—	7,957	6,676	84	4,703	1,215	758	342	939
FOSTER CITY	CA	c	3	51	—	40	—	—	y	—	—	7,660	—	—	6,510	—	—	—	1,151
FREEHOLD	NJ	tp	1	86	70	40	32,000	90,910	y	95,310	1	10,136	9,515	94	7,128	1,050	1,336	150	470
FRIENDSWOOD	TX	c	1	77	56	40	—	—	—	—	—	8,715	4,532	52	3,384	685	462	3,396	787
GALLOWAY	NJ	tp	1	87	73	40	39,280	75,246	y	84,087	5	8,388	7,855	94	5,607	1,198	1,050	161	371
GARFIELD HEIGHTS	OH	c	1	75	63	40	42,926	56,041	y	58,516	5	7,040	—	—	4,941	—	893	—	498
GEORGETOWN	TX	c	1	82	60	40	38,783	57,720	y	61,416	—	40,920	39,060	95	37,888	692	480	806	1,054
GILROY	CA	c	1	103	64	40	70,015	85,105	n	—	—	20,848	—	—	9,281	—	1,877	764	6,574
GLASTONBURY	CT	t	1	72	56	40	50,730	65,606	y	66,106	5	7,283	6,587	90	5,030	785	771	217	479
GLENDORA	CA	c	3	94	52	40	54,172	65,847	n	—	—	11,918	—	—	6,669	—	1,231	113	2,073
GLOUCESTER	MA	c	1	68	63	40	36,811	44,245	y	45,745	20	5,024	—	—	4,746	—	—	44	234
GOLDSBORO	NC	c	1	110	99	42	31,595	48,090	y	50,014	5	6,963	5,617	81	4,279	736	602	246	1,101
GOOSE CREEK	SC	c	3	76	57	40	28,992	44,115	n	—	—	4,226	3,373	80	2,656	327	390	128	724
GRAND BLANC	MI	tp	1	61	43	40	37,176	54,687	y	—	6	5,605	4,927	88	3,256	777	894	61	617
GRAND FORKS	ND	c	1	95	80	40	35,057	52,586	y	53,606	6	6,579	5,842	89	4,574	837	430	125	613
GRANTS PASS	OR	c	4	—	—	40	44,748	61,176	n	—	—	—	—	—	—	—	—	—	—
GREENFIELD	WI	c	3	113	58	other	43,297	59,305	y	59,557	5	—	—	—	—	1,213	907	4,327	669
GREENVILLE	MS	c	1	169	101	40	22,500	26,500	y	—	10	6,295	5,842	93	4,015	1,405	423	386	67
GREENWOOD	IN	c	1	81	51	40	36,264	47,381	y	48,881	—	5,931	4,866	82	3,461	624	780	260	805
GROTON	CT	t	1	68	64	40	45,011	54,766	y	55,006	6	7,248	6,620	91	5,048	244	1,327	61	568
HALTOM CITY	TX	c	1	91	67	40	38,135	48,253	y	—	1	6,345	—	—	4,429	—	456	138	728
HANFORD	CA	c	3	72	53	40	42,099	50,752	n	—	—	6,683	5,317	80	3,692	1,168	457	82	1,283
HANOVER PARK	IL	v	1	72	36	40	47,653	69,534	y	—	—	8,613	6,443	75	4,394	1,366	683	122	2,048
HARRISONBURG	VA	c	3	100	84	40	28,808	43,208	y	—	—	6,259	5,171	83	3,867	798	505	324	764
HAZELWOOD	MO	c	1	80	66	40	41,214	53,580	n	—	—	—	—	—	—	—	—	—	—
HELENA	MT	c	2	70	49	40	35,900	43,628	y	46,207	1	5,758	5,357	93	4,374	447	535	233	168
HENDERSON	KY	c	1	66	58	40	29,907	39,971	y	40,371	—	5,577	4,246	76	2,619	661	965	919	413
HENDERSONVILLE	TN	c	1	91	66	other	30,682	46,685	y	48,585	2	6,166	5,378	87	4,070	855	452	164	624
HILTON HEAD ISLAND	SC	t	5	—	—	—	—	—	—	—	—	—	—	—	—	—	—	—	—
HOLLAND	MI	c	1	74	61	40	41,288	52,749	y	52,749	—	6,374	5,550	87	4,278	551	721	1	823
HOMESTEAD	FL	c	3	145	121	40	43,160	75,174	y	81,188	5	18,826	15,162	81	9,308	3,611	2,243	3,588	76
HUBER HEIGHTS	OH	c	1	68	50	48	41,267	58,591	n	—	—	6,441	5,272	82	3,691	794	787	379	790
HURST	TX	c	1	118	72	40	54,787	59,987	y	62,507	1	12,840	9,242	72	6,802	1,527	912	99	3,499
HUTCHINSON	KS	c	1	108	69	40	33,756	45,660	y	46,860	5	6,127	—	—	4,862	—	—	236	998
INVER GROVE HEIGHTS	MN	c	4	41	34	48	42,050	61,385	y	63,222	4	—	—	—	—	260	262	155	—
ITHACA	NY	c	1	83	69	40	38,651	60,461	y	77,859	10	8,408	7,094	84	5,730	1,232	131	138	1,177
JACKSONVILLE	AR	c	1	83	72	40	27,941	41,911	y	42,511	3	5,035	4,340	86	2,859	922	558	118	577
JAMESTOWN	NY	c	1	72	63	40	40,868	59,316	y	62,131	8	7,036	6,764	96	4,527	1,028	1,209	43	230
JEFFERSONTOWN	KY	c	1	59	50	40	42,608	53,259	y	71,681	4	—	—	—	—	—	—	—	—
KANNAPOLIS	NC	c	1	96	21	42	28,196	43,741	n	—	—	6,229	4,927	79	4,027	446	453	248	1,055
KELLER	TX	c	1	72	67	40	44,200	58,094	y	58,094	1	5,482	4,236	77	3,472	624	139	164	1,081
KINGSPORT	TN	c	1	112	106	40	29,812	41,563	n	—	—	8,525	7,576	89	5,592	1,139	845	3	945
KISSIMMEE	FL	c	1	214	137	42	35,549	54,958	y	55,258	10	15,886	12,658	80	9,131	2,136	1,390	1,227	2,002
KOKOMO	IN	c	1	141	105	40	42,648	43,848	y	46,448	1	12,499	11,131	89	7,658	2,445	1,028	480	889
LA GRANGE	GA	c	1	110	84	42	35,048	45,884	—	—	—	—	—	—	—	—	—	—	—
LA PUENTE	CA	c	5	—	—	—	—	—	—	—	—	—	—	—	—	—	—	—	—
LA VERNE	CA	c	1	69	46	40	55,871	67,912	n	—	—	—	—	—	5,363	—	973	—	—
LACEY	WA	c	3	60	46	other	50,176	65,410	y	68,026	11	6,329	5,120	81	4,161	257	702	165	1,043
LANCASTER	OH	c	1	83	63	40	31,304	51,168	y	—	5	7,352	—	—	4,620	—	1,034	186	521
LAWNDALE	CA	c	5	—	—	40	—	—	—	—	—	—	—	—	—	—	—	—	—
LEAGUE CITY	TX	c	1	122	88	40	46,503	60,456	y	—	1	—	—	—	—	879	352	658	—
LEAVENWORTH	KS	c	1	82	62	other	31,101	46,651	y	47,251	5	5,652	—	—	3,655	4,269	602	—	891
LEAWOOD	KS	c	1	79	58	40	36,000	49,566	y	—	5	9,331	5,797	62	4,506	814	478	2,543	991
LEESBURG	VA	t	1	88	74	40	43,033	71,004	n	—	—	7,920	6,621	84	4,915	985	720	527	773
LENEXA	KS	c	1	127	84	40	37,038	55,849	n	—	—	12,012	10,396	87	7,250	1,880	1,266	384	1,231
LEWISTON	ID	c	1	64	43	40	40,304	60,097	y	52,945	1	—	—	—	—	—	—	—	—
LEWISTON	ME	c	1	94	77	other	29,825	42,301	y	42,298	15	5,541	5,009	90	4,106	172	731	60	472
LIBERTY	MO	c	1	54	34	—	35,143	49,200	n	—	—	4,347	3,703	85	2,764	494	446	179	465
LIMA	OH	c	1	107	82	40	36,192	43,389	y	45,365	8	8,029	—	—	58,040	—	1,524	4	533
LINCOLN PARK	MI	c	1	68	49	40	40,985	55,929	y	—	2	—	—	—	—	—	—	—	—
LINDENHURST	NY	v	—	—	—	—	—	—	—	—	—	—	—	—	—	—	—	—	—
LOMBARD	IL	v	1	89	73	40	49,817	70,193	n	—	—	10,307	8,718	85	6,431	1,618	669	179	1,409

Table 3/16 continued
POLICE DEPARTMENT PERSONNEL, SALARIES, AND EXPENDITURES FOR CITIES 10,000 AND OVER: 2007

City	State	Type	Service provision	Full-time paid personnel	Full-time uniformed personnel	Duty hours per week	Minimum base salary ($)	Maximum base salary ($)	Longevity pay	Maximum salary with longevity ($)	Years of service for longevity	Total expenditures (A) ($)	Total personnel expenditures (B) ($)	(B) as % of (A)	Salaries and wages (C) ($)	City contribution to retirement and social security (D) ($)	City contribution to insurance (E) ($)	Capital outlay (F) ($)	All other (G) ($)
25,000–49,999 continued																			
LOMPOC	CA	c	3	66	45	40	48,708	65,268	n	—	—	8,361	—	—	5,208	—	884	191	951
LONG BEACH	NY	c	1	74	74	40	—	—	y	—	6	10,376	—	—	8,500	1,435	—	150	1,876
LOS ALTOS	CA	c	1	43	29	42	73,032	88,761	n	—	—	7,310	—	—	4,206	—	976	656	1,236
LOS BANOS	CA	c	3	67	42	40	41,940	—	n	—	—	5,941	4,800	81	2,878	1,220	701	326	816
LOWER MAKEFIELD	PA	tp	1	38	34	40	42,016	80,201	y	—	30	5,404	4,980	92	2,734	481	1,765	23	401
LUFKIN	TX	c	1	99	75	40	34,324	60,898	y	63,298	1	6,575	5,542	84	4,087	975	480	318	715
LYNNWOOD	WA	c	1	82	67	40	55,661	67,434	y	70,122	5	19,380	15,837	82	11,958	1,354	2,524	99	3,444
MADERA	CA	c	3	80	58	42	47,832	61,056	n	—	—	7,362	—	—	4,129	—	846	371	691
MADISON HEIGHTS	MI	c	1	86	68	40	40,236	58,477	y	63,155	5	8,858	7,229	82	5,068	1,116	1,044	—	1,629
MANALAPAN	NJ	tp	1	69	68	40	29,000	83,468	y	91,815	5	—	—	—	5,948	—	463	—	233
MANASSAS	VA	c	1	114	89	40	40,186	67,122	n	—	—	12,730	9,302	73	6,992	1,356	954	581	2,847
MANCHESTER	NJ	tp	1	65	—	40	36,238	90,658	y	99,724	10	9,677	9,362	97	6,043	1,219	2,099	—	315
MANHATTAN	KS	c	—	—	—	—	—	—	—	—	—	—	—	—	—	—	—	—	—
MANSFIELD	OH	c	1	145	92	40	34,018	46,626	y	—	1	11,492	10,151	88	7,035	1,778	1,338	204	1,137
MAPLE HEIGHTS	OH	c	1	52	38	40	56,636	56,636	y	59,185	5	—	—	—	—	—	553	429	357
MARION	IA	c	1	47	38	40	35,094	48,753	y	49,953	5	4,505	3,886	86	2,627	671	588	267	352
MARYLAND HEIGHTS	MO	c	3	96	78	42	48,281	63,535	y	—	4	8,336	7,567	91	5,845	980	742	133	636
MARYSVILLE	WA	c	3	75	49	42	51,408	64,092	y	71,783	25	8,714	6,876	79	5,126	594	1,156	—	1,838
MASON CITY	IA	c	1	51	47	other	36,941	47,008	n	—	—	4,473	3,713	83	2,716	687	310	189	570
McCANDLESS	PA	t	1	30	28	40	41,000	67,462	y	70,960	1	2,902	2,568	88	1,931	152	484	106	229
McMINNVILLE	OR	c	3	40	32	40	41,676	53,196	y	54,996	—	4,501	3,812	85	2,523	760	529	122	566
MEDINA	OH	c	1	47	37	40	40,708	51,894	y	52,974	5	—	—	—	—	—	—	—	—
MENLO PARK	CA	c	1	76	48	42	68,828	83,660	n	—	—	9,946	8,644	87	6,706	1,317	620	70	1,231
MENOMONEE FALLS	WI	v	1	70	58	40	48,595	58,932	n	—	—	6,948	6,304	91	4,325	1,089	890	165	479
MICHIGAN CITY	IN	c	1	110	103	40	38,661	38,661	y	—	3	8,452	7,617	90	5,271	1,191	1,154	588	247
MIDLAND	MI	c	1	51	48	42	37,728	58,267	y	62,928	5	5,800	4,684	81	3,128	783	773	71	1,045
MIDVALE	UT	c	1	48	42	40	36,140	50,960	n	—	—	—	—	—	—	—	—	—	—
MILFORD	MA	t	1	55	45	other	47,272	47,272	y	—	—	4,215	—	—	3,804	—	—	410	—
MILTON	MA	t	1	79	53	40	35,279	49,500	y	—	10	5,318	—	—	4,777	—	—	108	433
MINOT	ND	c	1	80	58	40	31,623	50,554	n	—	—	4,610	3,785	82	3,257	247	281	220	605
MISHAWAKA	IN	c	1	130	102	48	45,515	47,515	—	—	—	8,843	—	—	6,317	—	1,338	132	175
MISSION	TX	c	1	158	115	42	36,000	36,000	y	37,200	1	—	—	—	—	861	999	62	793
MOLINE	IL	c	1	108	83	40	40,201	62,073	n	—	—	10,755	9,539	89	6,988	1,293	1,257	—	1,217
MONROE	NC	c	3	90	80	other	30,804	46,883	n	—	—	6,770	5,145	76	4,044	670	430	422	1,203
MONROVIA	CA	c	1	91	63	40	53,151	86,148	y	—	6	12,513	—	—	6,517	—	1,319	91	2,176
MONTCLAIR	NJ	tp	1	—	—	42	28,365	77,867	y	85,654	—	—	—	—	—	—	—	—	—
MOORE	OK	c	3	78	73	40	34,723	48,483	y	50,420	3	492	—	—	3,859	—	476	480	361
MOORHEAD	MN	c	1	59	48	40	39,344	48,978	y	50,937	30	5,843	3,946	68	3,209	372	365	22	1,875
MOORPARK	CA	c	5	—	—	—	—	—	—	—	—	—	—	—	—	—	—	—	—
MOUNT LEBANON	PA	c	1	51	42	40	44,797	71,136	y	73,263	4	6,415	5,522	86	4,209	756	557	7	886
MOUNT PLEASANT	SC	t	1	171	131	40	32,469	48,880	n	—	—	8,792	7,488	85	6,157	1,079	252	287	1,017
MOUNT VERNON	WA	c	1	51	40	40	46,654	58,322	y	69,260	10	5,514	4,287	78	3,371	428	487	138	1,089
MURRIETA	CA	c	3	110	80	40	56,631	68,835	n	—	—	—	—	—	—	—	—	—	—
MUSKEGON	MI	c	1	89	78	40	33,753	50,556	y	52,056	5	8,288	7,042	85	5,001	1,295	746	70	1,176
NATICK	MA	t	1	67	54	40	35,189	47,990	y	49,910	10	—	—	—	4,529	—	—	191	204
NAUGATUCK	CT	t	1	68	56	40	46,998	52,836	y	53,336	5	—	—	—	—	—	—	—	—
NEPTUNE	NJ	tp	1	74	74	40	31,846	87,422	y	89,022	5	9,377	8,892	95	6,922	1,145	825	224	260
NEW ALBANY	IN	c	1	72	69	40	41,519	—	y	54,805	1	6,049	5,749	95	3,969	614	1,165	—	300
NEW BERLIN	WI	c	1	90	71	40	41,614	63,303	n	—	—	9,025	8,496	94	5,878	1,500	1,117	146	383
NEW BRAUNFELS	TX	c	1	114	89	40	35,692	41,380	y	43,330	25	8,450	6,546	77	4,752	981	812	666	1,237
NEW IBERIA	LA	c	—	—	—	—	—	—	—	—	—	—	—	—	—	—	—	—	—
NEW LONDON	CT	c	1	82	66	40	38,110	49,528	y	50,128	5	—	—	—	5,793	—	—	58	—
NEWARK	DE	c	1	79	65	40	41,372	57,265	y	—	15	—	—	—	—	—	—	—	—
NEWARK	OH	c	1	97	78	—	34,070	46,093	y	46,987	4	9,060	7,703	85	5,195	1,451	1,056	—	1,358
NEWPORT	RI	c	1	105	84	40	39,993	49,681	y	82,761	5	12,914	—	—	7,206	—	1,925	187	1,154
NILES	IL	v	1	75	61	40	52,194	71,694	y	74,451	8	10,576	8,676	82	6,449	721	1,506	605	1,294
NORMAL	IL	t	1	92	78	40	39,930	61,430	n	—	—	8,420	6,686	79	4,933	1,245	507	222	1,512
NORTH CHICAGO	IL	c	1	75	57	40	44,382	64,537	n	—	—	6,816	6,210	91	5,224	466	519	—	607
NORTH HUNTINGDON	PA	tp	1	28	—	42	55,951	61,686	y	77,108	3	2,709	—	—	2,026	29	—	—	561
NORTH LAUDERDALE	FL	c	5	—	—	40	—	—	—	—	—	—	—	—	—	—	—	—	—
NORTH ROYALTON	OH	c	1	41	37	40	45,739	56,555	y	58,555	5	4,573	—	—	2,980	—	540	65	445
NORTHAMPTON	MA	c	1	62	43	40	36,534	44,851	y	45,651	5	—	—	—	—	—	—	—	—
NORTHAMPTON	PA	tp	1	47	41	40	47,580	70,678	n	—	—	5,521	4,747	86	3,452	353	942	250	524
NORTHBROOK	IL	v	1	88	63	40	47,802	75,115	y	76,915	5	14,054	11,145	79	7,643	2,315	1,186	879	2,030
NOVATO	CA	c	1	80	58	40	61,812	75,132	y	86,976	10	11,455	—	—	8,053	—	284	52	1,528
NOVI	MI	c	1	97	71	42	43,951	63,982	n	—	—	12,039	9,240	77	6,474	1,628	1,137	408	2,392
O'FALLON	MO	c	1	132	102	40	43,222	59,009	n	—	—	9,992	9,030	90	7,223	1,279	528	308	653
OAK CREEK	WI	c	1	79	58	40	41,086	59,906	n	—	—	7,948	8,226	103	4,720	2,681	825	—	751
OAK PARK	MI	c	4	75	64	other	47,115	67,307	y	69,007	—	9,951	9,443	95	5,910	2,548	984	—	508
OAKLAND PARK	FL	c	—	—	—	—	—	—	—	—	—	—	—	—	—	—	—	—	—
OAKLEY	CA	c	5	—	—	—	—	—	—	—	—	—	—	—	—	—	—	—	—
OCALA	FL	c	1	231	153	40	30,202	46,540	y	47,936	1	20,041	15,725	78	11,546	2,474	1,704	613	3,704
OVIEDO	FL	c	1	81	60	42	34,338	50,464	n	—	—	5,152	4,268	83	3,400	598	270	248	636

Table 3/16 continued   POLICE DEPARTMENT PERSONNEL, SALARIES, AND EXPENDITURES FOR CITIES 10,000 AND OVER: 2007

City	State	Type	Service provision	Full-time paid personnel	Full-time uniformed personnel	Duty hours per week	Minimum base salary ($)	Maximum base salary ($)	Longevity pay	Maximum salary with longevity ($)	Years of service for longevity	Total expenditures (A) ($)	Total personnel expenditures (B) ($)	(B) as % of (A)	Salaries and wages (C) ($)	City contribution to retirement and social security (D) ($)	City contribution to insurance (E) ($)	Capital outlay (F) ($)	All other (G) ($)
25,000–49,999 continued																			
PACIFICA	CA	c	1	53	39	40	65,316	85,728	y	90,012	5	7,352	—	—	4,584	—	—	20	889
PALM BEACH GARDENS	FL	c	1	153	112	other	42,180	71,443	y	78,587	10	17,259	14,071	82	9,673	2,653	1,745	349	2,838
PALM COAST	FL	c	—	—	—		—	—		—		—	—		—	—	—	—	—
PALM SPRINGS	CA	c	1	154	88	40	—	—	y	—	15	—	—		—	—	—	—	—
PANAMA CITY	FL	c	1	141	93	40	30,852	44,735	n	—	—	9,097	6,816	75	4,862	1,219	735	740	1,541
PARADISE	CA	t	1	29	26	other	38,251	48,818	y	51,258	10	3,163	—	—	1,646	—	537	45	188
PASCO	WA	c	1	70	59	40	51,500	62,566	y	68,827	21	8,552	5,492	64	4,493	525	474	161	2,899
PEABODY	MA	c	1	109	92	40	39,208	44,554	y	47,054	5	7,531	—	—	6,918	—	—	119	494
PEACHTREE CITY	GA	c	1	56	52	40	32,508	52,349	n	—	—	5,156	3,948	77	2,924	522	501	460	748
PEARLAND	TX	c	1	130	80	40	40,239	55,700	y	56,660	1	9,570	8,137	85	6,367	1,110	660	527	906
PINELLAS PARK	FL	c	1	134	103	40	37,434	56,931	y	58,354	—	12,702	10,123	80	7,278	1,869	976	315	2,265
PITTSFIELD CHARTER TOWNSHIP	MI	tp	1	42	37	40	38,246	55,105	y	57,005	5	3,939	3,396	86	2,554	384	458	222	320
PLACENTIA	CA	c	1	66	50	40	56,179	72,799	y	74,619	20	15,876	9,704	61	6,059	2,290	1,354	174	5,997
PLAINFIELD	MI	tp	5	—	—	40	—	—		—		—	—		—	—	—	—	—
PLANT CITY	FL	c	1	—	—	42		—		—		—	—		—	—	—	—	—
PLEASANT HILL	CA	c	1	63	42	40	56,916	73,500	y	77,175	13	9,481	7,948	84	5,174	1,700	1,073	373	1,160
PORT HURON	MI	c	1	70	51	40	40,974	54,632	y	60,095	20	7,738	—	—	4,204	—	—	185	907
PORT ORANGE	FL	c	1	110	86	42	30,368	50,710	n	—	—	10,035	6,970	69	4,870	1,532	568	148	2,916
PORTERVILLE	CA	c	3	72	50	other	38,448	46,908	n	—	—	6,098	—	—	3,404	—	—	5	1,162
POWAY	CA	c	5	—	—	42	—	—		—		—	—		—	—	—	—	—
PRESCOTT	AZ	c	3	—	—	40	—	—		—		—	—		—	—	—	—	—
QUINCY	IL	c	1	92	76	40	38,679	54,115	y	55,478	10	13,458	7,312	54	5,206	1,108	998	123	6,024
RANCHO SANTA MARGARITA	CA	c	—	—	—		—	—		—		—	—		—	—	—	—	—
REYNOLDSBURG	OH	c	1	66	51	40	39,873	62,753	y	63,853	4	6,432	—	—	4,077	—	776	188	640
RICHLAND	WA	c	1	60	50	40	55,286	62,550	y	70,168	10	8,328	6,205	75	4,742	463	1,000	103	2,019
RIDLEY	PA	tp	1	32	—	40	58,418	—	y	—	—	—	—	—	2,349	—	263	1,024	—
RIVERTON	UT	c	—	—	—		—	—		—		—	—		—	—	—	—	—
ROCHESTER	NH	c	1	72	40	40	36,075	48,295	n	—	—	5,096	4,541	89	3,517	397	627	67	488
ROCK HILL	SC	c	1	165	116	40	30,410	42,556	n	—	—	10,876	8,197	75	6,270	1,155	771	25	2,654
ROCKLIN	CA	c	1	82	57	40	49,382	63,012	y	—	7	11,130	8,232	74	5,596	1,485	1,151	1,133	1,765
ROME	GA	c	1	126	98	40	28,000	42,000	n	—	—	7,862	5,848	74	4,393	699	756	859	1,155
ROSWELL	NM	c	—	111	87	42	28,421	41,590	y	—	3	—	—	—	—	—	—	—	—
ROUND LAKE BEACH	IL	v	1	50	43	40	46,643	66,291	n	—	—	—	—		—	—	—	—	—
ROY	UT	c	1	44	39	40	30,742	44,907	n	—	—	3,590	2,836	79	2,068	509	259	306	447
SAGINAW	MI	tp	1	47	40	40	34,941	53,090	n	—	—	4,936	3,983	81	2,678	565	740	120	833
SALEM	NH	t	1	75	58	40	36,966	53,231	y	—	—	7,098	6,515	92	4,808	548	1,158	121	462
SALISBURY	NC	c	1	102	82	42	29,042	45,016	n	—	—	6,566	4,845	74	3,606	708	531	67	1,654
SAN DIMAS	CA	c	—	—	—		—	—		—		—	—		—	—	—	—	—
SAN JUAN	TX	c	1	45	35	40	30,181	30,181	y	35,000	20	2,062	1,662	81	1,364	166	132	123	277
SAN LUIS OBISPO	CA	c	1	87	57	40	57,824	78,650	n	—	—	12,162	—	—	7,021	—	1,338	882	915
SAN RAMON	CA	c	7	66	53	40	71,400	89,244	n	—	—	10,507	—	—	—	—	—	—	—
SANDUSKY	OH	c	1	—	—	40	—	—		—		—	—		—	—	—	—	—
SANTA PAULA	CA	c	3	37	27	40	43,790	53,229	y	—	—	4,898	—	—	2,666	—	—	89	698
SEASIDE	CA	c	1	56	42	40	55,844	67,862	y	69,559	10	7,386	—	—	3,993	—	1,010	95	1,160
SEATAC	WA	c	—	—	—		—	—		—		—	—		—	—	—	—	—
SHAKER HEIGHTS	OH	c	1	98	70	40	43,409	64,257	y	66,257	7	21,402	9,184	43	6,985	2,058	139	1,483	10,736
SHERMAN	TX	c	1	64	64	40	36,516	47,664	y	—	1	—	—	—	—	—	—	—	—
SHOREVIEW	MN	c	5	—	—		—	—		—		—	—		—	—	—	—	—
SHREWSBURY	MA	t	1	55	36	other	43,460	49,589	n	—	—	3,660	—	—	3,232	—	—	15	413
SLIDELL	LA	c	1	101	88	40	29,848	47,736	y	48,816	5	6,875	—	—	4,147	—	881	657	426
SOUTHAVEN	MS	c	1	114	92	48	29,120	44,720	y	—	5	—	—	—	—	—	—	—	—
SOUTHINGTON	CT	t	1	77	62	40	49,348	62,800	y	62,800	5	6,922	5,859	85	4,165	927	767	298	765
SPARTANBURG	SC	c	4	139	128	42	28,187	41,504	y	—	5	9,916	8,933	90	6,963	1,132	838	149	834
SPRINGDALE	AR	c	1	140	99	40	29,500	42,961	n	—	—	9,523	7,629	80	5,646	1,236	746	855	1,039
STANTON	CA	c	5	—	—	40	—	—		—		—	—		—	—	—	—	—
STATE COLLEGE	PA	b	1	77	65	40	45,448	56,804	y	61,058	5	6,792	6,018	89	4,742	402	874	136	638
STILLWATER	OK	c	1	106	70	40	30,389	55,120	y	—	—	7,002	6,335	90	5,541	695	99	219	447
STREAMWOOD	IL	v	1	71	59	40	50,463	68,597	y	—	—	8,767	6,880	78	5,143	838	898	1,176	711
SURPRISE	AZ	t	1	—	—	40	—	—		—		—	—		—	—	—	—	—
TEMPLE CITY	CA	c	5	—	—		—	—		—		—	—		—	—	—	—	—
TEXARKANA	TX	c	1	—	99	40	32,898	43,006	y	44,206	1	7,587	5,669	75	4,514	801	353	253	1,664
TEXAS CITY	TX	c	1	103	80	40	30,347	48,651	y	—	1	8,510	6,973	82	5,253	840	879	245	1,292
THE COLONY	TX	c	1	68	46	42	44,040	—	y	—	—	5,044	4,190	83	3,225	649	315	422	432
TIGARD	OR	c	1	78	62	40	45,132	56,688	y	59,400	5	8,805	7,050	80	4,861	1,238	951	245	1,510
TINLEY PARK	IL	v	1	—	77	40	49,608	68,266	y	69,826	5	13,190	11,574	88	8,633	1,485	1,456	615	1,001
TREDYFFRIN	PA	tp	1	60	51	40	38,864	66,157	y	—	4	7,759	6,033	78	4,302	830	901	322	1,404
TROTWOOD	OH	c	1	52	4	40	43,326	57,034	y	—	10	5,479	—	—	3,297	—	501	242	864
TROY	NY	c	1	151	117	40	32,076	45,773	y	47,773	5	12,376	11,181	90	7,922	1,728	1,531	353	842
TUPELO	MS	c	1	127	115	40	31,668	38,319	n	—	—	6,906	6,906	100	5,139	711	1,055	—	—

Table 3/16 continued **POLICE DEPARTMENT PERSONNEL, SALARIES, AND EXPENDITURES FOR CITIES 10,000 AND OVER: 2007**

City	State	Type	Service provision	Full-time paid personnel	Full-time uniformed personnel	Duty hours per week	Minimum base salary ($)	Maximum base salary ($)	Longevity pay	Maximum salary with longevity ($)	Years of service for longevity	Total expenditures (A) ($)	Total personnel expenditures (B) ($)	(B) as % of (A)	Salaries and wages (C) ($)	City contribution to retirement and social security (D) ($)	City contribution to insurance (E) ($)	Capital outlay (F) ($)	All other (G) ($)
25,000–49,999 continued																			
UNIVERSITY PLACE	WA	c	—	—	—	—	—	—	—	—	—	—	—	—	—	—	—	—	—
UPPER ARLINGTON	OH	c	1	62	49	40	41,933	66,123	y	—	30	6,459	—	—	4,381	—	790	138	279
UPPER DUBLIN	PA	tp	1	48	40	40	45,388	69,828	y	—	5	5,324	4,741	89	3,737	142	862	364	218
VALLEY STREAM	NY	v	—	—	—	—	—	—	—	—	—	—	—	—	—	—	—	—	—
VALPARAISO	IN	c	1	—	—	other	39,293	42,059	y	—	3	—	—	—	—	—	—	—	—
WALLA WALLA	WA	c	1	71	40	40	45,792	63,816	n	—	—	—	—	—	—	—	—	—	—
WALNUT	CA	c	5	—	—	—	—	—	—	—	—	—	—	—	—	—	—	—	—
WARMINSTER	PA	tp	1	55	49	other	37,000	64,951	y	66,951	5	6,523	—	—	3,931	—	1,568	202	756
WARREN	OH	c	1	101	82	40	31,325	44,762	y	—	5	10,354	8,327	80	5,416	1,568	1,343	481	1,546
WASHINGTON (GLCSTR)	NJ	tp	1	—	85	other	32,681	76,111	y	86,631	5	—	—	—	—	—	—	—	—
WATERTOWN	MA	t	1	80	69	other	41,853	47,355	y	50,655	30	—	—	—	—	—	—	—	—
WATERTOWN	NY	c	1	69	65	40	39,980	50,159	y	51,209	6	6,091	5,052	83	3,725	791	536	36	1,003
WESLACO	TX	c	1	95	65	40	33,278	33,278	y	41,813	3	5,052	4,666	92	3,469	581	616	—	385
WEST BEND	WI	c	1	71	53	40	44,557	55,814	y	56,474	5	6,354	5,830	92	4,023	1,019	787	82	442
WEST SACRAMENTO	CA	c	1	105	53	40	53,376	64,860	n	—	—	14,249	8,762	61	5,910	2,200	651	3,682	1,805
WEST SPRINGFIELD	MA	t	1	87	80	42	36,508	48,774	y	—	—	—	—	—	—	—	—	—	—
WESTERVILLE	OH	c	1	85	70	40	45,906	65,998	y	67,648	5	9,355	—	—	6,010	—	941	—	1,297
WESTFIELD	MA	c	1	92	78	40	39,488	44,246	y	46,742	5	7,881	7,163	91	5,184	646	1,333	141	577
WESTLAKE	OH	c	1	73	52	40	50,248	59,689	y	62,189	5	6,909	—	—	4,395	—	718	261	744
WESTON	FL	c	5	—	—	—	—	—	—	—	—	—	—	—	—	—	—	—	—
WHEAT RIDGE	CO	c	1	—	77	40	45,089	63,637	n	—	—	7,267	6,482	89	5,860	575	48	86	699
WILDWOOD	MO	c	5	—	—	—	—	—	—	—	—	—	—	—	—	—	—	—	—
WILMETTE	IL	v	1	64	46	40	55,635	69,997	y	77,107	20	8,422	—	—	5,126	—	—	213	891
WILSON	NC	c	1	131	110	40	32,896	49,344	y	51,811	—	10,251	7,580	74	5,651	968	960	210	2,461
WINTER SPRINGS	FL	c	1	89	70	42	32,850	50,015	n	—	—	6,108	4,989	82	3,813	683	493	378	741
WOODRIDGE	IL	v	1	82	57	40	47,866	73,938	n	—	—	7,358	7,207	98	5,644	1,023	539	100	52
YORKTOWN	NY	t	1	65	55	40	—	—	—	—	—	8,271	7,593	92	5,695	1,192	706	205	472
YUBA CITY	CA	c	3	103	69	40	46,512	56,544	n	—	—	11,457	9,586	84	6,255	2,295	1,035	127	1,744
YUCAIPA	CA	c	—	—	—	—	—	—	—	—	—	—	—	—	—	—	—	—	—
ZANESVILLE	OH	c	1	72	56	40	28,600	44,075	y	46,553	5	5,354	—	—	3,155	—	984	32	373
10,000–24,999																			
ABBEVILLE	LA	t	1	39	36	40	19,080	30,240	y	49,644	1	2,722	1,952	72	1,342	166	444	183	587
ACWORTH	GA	c	1	34	33	other	—	—	—	—	—	2,954	2,076	70	1,532	169	373	541	338
ADDISON	TX	t	1	68	12	40	47,819	62,067	y	63,507	1	7,241	5,891	81	4,705	585	601	—	1,350
ADRIAN	MI	c	1	37	33	40	36,104	46,469	n	—	—	2,906	2,485	86	1,786	259	440	70	350
AGOURA HILLS	CA	c	5	—	—	—	—	—	—	—	—	—	—	—	—	—	—	—	—
ALBEMARLE	NC	c	1	55	49	42	28,288	46,384	y	48,703	5	3,370	2,681	80	2,003	321	356	191	497
ALBERT LEA	MN	c	1	29	23	40	44,962	50,531	n	—	—	3,267	2,782	85	2,106	244	432	106	380
ALEXANDER CITY	AL	c	1	65	44	42	21,996	31,434	n	—	—	3,551	2,976	84	2,184	332	460	91	484
ALGONQUIN	IL	v	1	53	46	40	45,976	71,865	y	72,763	9	6,033	4,769	79	3,665	745	358	103	1,162
ALICE	TX	c	1	49	36	40	29,390	34,798	y	35,998	1	2,994	2,651	89	2,051	316	283	47	296
ALLIANCE	OH	c	1	41	37	40	32,947	40,706	y	42,026	4	3,648	—	—	2,242	—	503	266	600
ALPENA	MI	c	1	19	18	40	30,992	40,976	y	43,434	8	1,580	—	—	985	—	250	36	292
ALTOONA	IA	c	3	24	22	42	36,831	47,316	y	—	5	2,151	1,811	84	1,295	209	307	54	286
ALTUS	OK	c	1	53	44	40	24,434	38,094	y	—	—	3,614	2,462	68	1,818	336	307	741	411
AMERICUS	GA	c	1	43	35	40	25,421	35,590	y	—	—	3,021	2,209	73	1,695	196	317	162	651
AMESBURY	MA	t	1	33	31	other	37,425	47,013	y	54,064	10	3,170	—	—	2,913	—	—	—	257
AMHERST	NH	t	1	18	12	40	37,877	48,755	y	—	—	1,652	1,323	80	1,064	115	143	—	329
ANACORTES	WA	c	1	25	21	40	50,327	63,020	y	—	5	3,844	2,533	66	1,954	223	355	105	1,207
ANGLETON	TX	c	3	54	37	40	32,000	43,800	y	—	2	2,894	2,603	90	1,963	483	156	—	175
ANOKA	MN	c	1	34	28	40	42,293	60,419	y	65,853	16	3,589	2,917	81	2,403	291	222	157	515
ANSONIA	CT	c	1	61	44	40	44,180	50,840	y	51,150	5	—	—	—	—	211	171	—	—
ARCATA	CA	c	—	35	24	40	39,288	47,772	y	51,355	5	3,608	—	—	2,021	—	—	18	471
ARLINGTON	WA	c	1	31	26	40	49,404	62,196	y	63,396	5	3,976	2,768	70	1,929	744	95	390	818
ARNOLD	MO	c	1	51	47	40	36,379	50,939	y	52,979	—	4,637	3,567	77	2,547	547	472	554	515
ARROYO GRANDE	CA	c	3	36	27	40	49,524	60,216	y	—	—	5,308	4,356	82	2,909	1,209	237	139	814
ARVIN	CA	c	1	24	—	48	38,000	50,500	y	54,060	3	—	—	—	1,233	—	158	129	607
ASHEBORO	NC	c	1	76	70	42	31,161	47,067	n	—	—	5,101	3,730	73	3,011	320	398	232	1,139
ASHLAND	MA	t	1	32	27	40	34,843	48,081	y	49,081	5	2,495	—	—	2,073	—	—	125	90
ASHLAND	OH	c	1	42	32	40	34,382	41,766	y	43,019	5	2,914	2,568	88	1,909	320	339	93	253
ASHWAUBENON	WI	v	4	57	48	other	44,672	63,762	y	64,362	7	6,910	5,995	87	4,038	982	974	244	671
ATHENS	AL	c	1	54	50	40	26,759	43,260	n	—	—	3,658	2,881	79	2,127	357	397	384	392
ATHENS	OH	c	1	39	26	40	36,858	46,821	y	—	5	—	—	—	1,703	—	—	—	—
ATHENS	TN	c	1	33	30	42	29,546	44,319	n	—	—	1,733	1,363	79	1,067	195	100	30	341
ATWATER	CA	c	3	42	33	40	38,868	49,620	n	—	—	3,782	3,473	92	2,342	699	432	—	308
AUBURN	MA	t	1	43	33	other	38,387	51,369	n	—	—	6,099	—	—	3,825	—	—	103	2,171
AUBURNDALE	FL	c	1	43	32	42	32,853	44,688	y	—	5	2,621	2,107	80	1,598	213	297	157	356
AUGUSTA	ME	c	1	54	38	40	27,893	34,694	y	38,938	5	—	3,198	—	2,342	99	756	—	—
AUSTIN	MN	c	1	32	29	40	43,909	52,832	y	55,209	7	3,390	2,548	75	2,000	222	325	201	641
AVENAL	CA	c	5	—	—	—	—	—	—	—	—	—	—	—	—	—	—	—	—
AVON	CT	t	—	—	—	—	—	—	—	—	—	—	—	—	—	—	—	—	—
AVON LAKE	OH	c	1	33	28	40	46,384	61,693	y	63,343	6	3,498	—	—	2,322	—	355	134	257

Table 3/16
continued

POLICE DEPARTMENT PERSONNEL, SALARIES, AND EXPENDITURES FOR CITIES 10,000 AND OVER: 2007

City	State	Type	Service provision	Full-time paid personnel	Full-time uniformed personnel	Duty hours per week	Minimum base salary ($)	Maximum base salary ($)	Longevity pay	Maximum salary with longevity ($)	Years of service for longevity	Total expenditures (A) ($)	Total personnel expenditures (B) ($)	(B) as % of (A)	Salaries and wages (C) ($)	City contribution to retirement and social security (D) ($)	City contribution to insurance (E) ($)	Capital outlay (F) ($)	All other (G) ($)
10,000–24,999 continued																			
BAINBRIDGE	GA	c	4	53	40	42	28,982	—	n	—	—	2,910	2,437	84	1,870	215	351	28	446
BAINBRIDGE ISLAND	WA	c	1	28	20	40	47,100	72,276	y	74,444	5	3,541	2,259	64	1,723	212	324	511	771
BANNING	CA	c	1	62	53	42	50,753	68,666	n	—	—	6,390	4,911	77	3,368	1,302	241	188	1,291
BARABOO	WI	c	1	31	25	other	38,733	45,835	y	—	3	3,051	2,572	84	1,582	742	248	258	221
BARDSTOWN	KY	c	1	29	23	40	26,790	39,761	n	—	—	1,872	1,557	83	1,082	306	169	86	229
BARRINGTON	IL	v	1	42	34	40	48,693	69,888	n	—	—	5,136	4,187	82	3,318	496	372	—	949
BATAVIA	IL	c	1	52	33	40	51,878	71,531	n	—	—	6,451	5,523	86	3,923	896	704	59	869
BEACH PARK	IL	v	—	—	—	—	—	—	—	—	—	—	—	—	—	—	—	—	—
BEACHWOOD	NJ	b	1	20	18	40	36,278	69,909	n	—	—	1,724	1,684	98	1,329	145	209	—	40
BEACHWOOD	OH	c	1	56	42	40	54,593	67,098	y	68,598	7	6,910	6,087	88	4,404	668	1,015	158	666
BEACON	NY	c	1	34	34	40	49,630	62,583	y	—	17	4,421	—	—	3,331	655	—	201	233
BEAUFORT	SC	c	1	53	48	42	30,402	51,362	y	51,362	2	3,822	3,030	79	2,215	395	420	174	618
BEAUMONT	CA	c	1	44	32	40	53,935	69,056	n	—	—	5,134	—	—	2,540	—	314	346	1,025
BEDFORD	IN	c	1	42	33	40	38,286	39,529	y	48,458	4	—	—	—	—	339	412	195	358
BEL AIR	MD	t	1	43	30	40	37,770	42,162	n	—	—	3,114	2,691	86	2,004	302	383	162	261
BELCHERTOWN	MA	t	1	17	—	40	33,367	43,298	y	43,598	10	1,458	—	—	1,255	—	—	56	147
BELLAIRE	TX	c	1	55	41	40	37,630	51,285	y	52,485	—	4,239	3,710	88	2,695	481	534	195	334
BELLE GLADE	FL	c	—	—	—	—	—	—	—	—	—	—	—	—	—	—	—	—	—
BELLEFONTAINE	OH	c	3	30	23	40	37,253	46,093	n	—	—	2,238	1,928	86	1,480	297	151	126	184
BELTON	MO	c	1	53	42	40	34,202	45,834	y	—	—	4,390	3,516	80	2,647	375	494	246	627
BEMIDJI	MN	c	1	35	30	other	41,974	46,125	n	—	—	2,785	2,288	82	1,791	189	308	115	381
BENTONVILLE	AR	c	1	79	53	40	28,766	46,862	n	—	—	5,189	4,158	80	3,196	601	361	421	609
BEREA	OH	c	1	38	31	40	45,248	56,281	y	—	5	—	—	—	2,671	—	560	—	—
BERKELEY	MO	c	1	60	47	40	31,824	39,811	n	—	5	3,271	2,720	83	2,338	140	242	144	407
BERLIN	CT	t	1	51	39	40	48,256	61,506	y	62,206	5	5,561	5,241	94	3,927	649	663	173	148
BERLIN	NH	c	1	32	24	40	41,101	42,557	y	42,632	5	—	—	—	162	368	62	277	
BETHANY	OK	c	1	37	29	40	31,938	49,167	y	51,367	4	2,783	2,403	86	1,729	387	286	86	295
BETHLEHEM	PA	tp	1	34	34	40	50,968	55,968	y	57,522	5	3,493	3,243	93	2,073	793	376	111	139
BIDDEFORD	ME	c	1	64	45	40	40,310	52,541	y	—	—	4,576	3,924	86	3,022	322	579	69	583
BIG RAPIDS	MI	c	1	19	18	40	38,499	49,066	y	50,366	5	1,994	1,715	86	1,051	465	198	32	248
BIRMINGHAM	MI	c	3	51	35	40	37,760	60,252	y	66,277	5	5,920	5,063	86	3,570	565	927	187	670
BIXBY	OK	c	3	33	22	40	30,565	—	n	—	—	2,076	1,668	80	1,229	173	265	168	240
BLOOMINGDALE	IL	v	1	63	47	40	48,422	71,254	y	71,254	8	6,460	5,975	92	4,688	757	529	108	376
BLUE ASH	OH	c	1	48	37	other	52,749	61,152	y	61,432	3	5,928	—	—	3,805	—	651	221	554
BLYTHE	CA	c	1	39	24	40	46,509	59,550	y	62,800	5	4,386	3,946	90	2,395	903	647	8	432
BLYTHEVILLE	AR	c	—	—	—	—	—	—	—	—	—	—	—	—	—	—	—	—	—
BOONE	IA	c	1	18	17	40	37,389	47,371	n	—	—	2,132	1,405	66	882	236	287	9	718
BORGER	TX	c	1	25	24	40	28,741	32,774	y	33,974	1	1,712	1,378	80	1,019	173	186	105	229
BOULDER CITY	NV	c	1	44	34	40	50,407	64,319	n	—	—	4,394	3,682	84	2,553	706	423	107	606
BOURNE	MA	t	1	41	35	42	33,829	47,316	y	47,841	10	2,836	—	—	2,530	—	—	16	290
BRADLEY	IL	v	1	—	30	40	39,874	58,677	y	—	—	3,127	—	—	1,743	—	—	236	1,148
BRAINERD	MN	c	1	38	25	40	45,507	50,502	y	52,775	8	2,900	2,423	84	1,857	227	338	136	341
BRANDON	MI	tp	5	—	—	—	—	—	—	—	—	—	—	—	—	—	—	—	—
BRECKSVILLE	OH	c	1	39	32	40	46,686	61,479	y	65,229	2	3,445	—	—	2,730	321	—	171	223
BRENTWOOD	CA	c	1	68	54	40	65,522	79,625	n	—	—	14,520	—	—	6,695	—	2,441	113	3,716
BRENTWOOD	TN	c	1	61	58	40	31,900	53,600	y	40,000	5	6,068	4,858	80	3,616	737	504	305	906
BRIDGETON	MO	c	1	66	54	40	37,086	52,770	n	—	—	5,596	4,953	88	3,527	711	714	167	476
BRIGHAM CITY	UT	c	1	33	26	40	39,180	78,478	n	—	—	2,726	1,914	70	1,373	315	225	195	618
BRISTOL	RI	t	1	—	41	40	39,059	50,046	y	54,049	5	4,966	4,635	93	2,515	1,339	780	61	270
BRISTOL	TN	c	1	89	66	40	30,000	37,011	n	—	—	7,647	—	—	4,930	—	733	1,528	78
BROOK PARK	OH	c	1	54	—	40	49,756	62,474	n	—	—	5,856	5,000	85	3,623	702	675	390	465
BROOKINGS	SD	c	1	37	28	40	35,484	43,160	y	45,140	5	2,475	2,182	88	1,612	232	337	109	184
BROWNSBURG	IN	t	1	52	36	40	44,000	47,500	y	—	4	4,299	—	—	2,565	—	—	72	748
BROWNWOOD	TX	c	1	56	35	40	26,604	28,848	y	30,288	1	3,527	2,824	80	1,839	770	215	279	424
BUCKINGHAM	PA	tp	1	23	21	other	35,374	64,953	y	67,553	—	2,826	2,442	86	1,807	253	381	173	211
BUFORD	GA	c	—	—	—	—	—	—	—	—	—	—	—	—	—	—	—	—	—
BURKBURNETT	TX	c	1	26	19	40	26,500	30,000	n	—	—	1,304	1,132	87	845	172	115	39	133
BURLESON	TX	c	1	72	53	40	41,578	54,052	y	—	1	4,970	4,295	86	3,344	617	333	18	657
BURR RIDGE	IL	v	1	34	30	40	45,629	66,162	n	—	—	3,923	3,138	80	2,316	538	283	171	614
BUTLER	PA	c	1	23	23	40	32,033	45,762	y	58,848	4	2,079	—	—	1,236	—	395	42	120
CALABASAS	CA	c	—	—	—	—	—	—	—	—	—	—	—	—	—	—	—	—	—
CALHOUN	GA	c	1	59	50	42	26,632	30,566	n	—	—	—	—	—	—	—	—	—	—
CALLAWAY	FL	c	5	—	—	other	—	—	—	—	—	—	—	—	—	—	—	—	—
CALN	PA	tp	1	20	17	42	44,824	64,034	y	67,384	5	1,928	—	—	1,318	—	292	53	610
CAMAS	WA	c	—	—	—	—	—	—	—	—	—	—	—	—	—	—	—	—	—
CAMBRIDGE	OH	c	1	31	25	40	39,000	39,000	y	40,248	—	2,490	2,151	86	1,260	688	202	37	302
CANANDAIGUA	NY	c	1	30	25	other	42,095	52,885	y	53,910	5	2,242	—	—	1,785	—	—	122	202
CANTON	MA	t	1	43	42	40	38,521	49,870	y	50,670	5	4,084	—	—	3,211	—	454	126	293
CARBONDALE	IL	c	1	78	60	40	36,248	47,377	y	50,968	15	6,519	5,358	82	3,911	892	556	260	900
CARLISLE	PA	b	1	—	33	40	40,810	51,875	y	54,355	4	3,410	—	—	2,257	—	361	237	455
CARRBORO	NC	t	1	41	38	42	34,047	52,772	y	—	5	—	—	—	—	—	—	—	—
CARROLL	IA	c	1	16	15	40	31,436	39,295	y	39,895	5	1,173	984	84	641	178	165	87	102
CARTERET	NJ	b	1	73	63	40	36,346	76,437	y	85,609	5	7,492	—	—	5,136	—	1,772	100	50

Table 3/16 POLICE DEPARTMENT PERSONNEL, SALARIES, AND EXPENDITURES FOR
continued CITIES 10,000 AND OVER: 2007

												Reported expenditures (in $000)							
City	State	Type	Service provision	Full-time paid personnel	Full-time uniformed personnel	Duty hours per week	Minimum base salary ($)	Maximum base salary ($)	Longevity pay	Maximum salary with longevity ($)	Years of service for longevity	Total expenditures (A) ($)	Total personnel expenditures (B) ($)	(B) as % of (A)	Salaries and wages (C) ($)	City contribution to retirement and social security (D) ($)	City contribution to insurance (E) ($)	Capital outlay (F) ($)	All other (G) ($)
10,000–24,999 continued																			
CASCADE CHARTER	MI	tp	—	—	—	—	—	—	—	—	—	—	—	—	—	—	—	—	—
CEDAR CITY	UT	c	1	40	34	40	31,719	44,818	n	—	—	2,921	2,249	77	1,485	365	399	134	538
CENTERVILLE	OH	c	1	57	43	40	45,656	64,293	y	64,773	6	6,119	—	—	3,853	—	598	153	764
CENTRAL POINT	OR	c	1	30	—	40	—	—	—	—	—	3,111	—	—	1,435	—	—	—	94
CENTRALIA	WA	c	3	34	28	42	49,021	58,244	y	60,287	6	3,918	2,915	74	2,303	144	468	136	867
CHAMBERSBURG	PA	b	1	37	33	40	37,814	49,795	y	49,795	1	3,488	2,990	86	1,976	564	450	—	499
CHAMPLIN	MN	c	1	29	25	40	39,317	60,680	y	66,140	4	2,833	2,310	82	1,915	227	168	196	327
CHANHASSEN	MN	c	—	—	—	—	—	—	—	—	—	—	—	—	—	—	—	—	—
CHARLESTON	IL	c	1	35	33	40	32,074	54,302	y	54,302	1	2,549	2,078	82	1,850	47	181	57	414
CHARLTON	MA	t	1	22	18	40	42,887	50,452	y	50,552	11	2,127	1,824	86	1,474	161	188	117	186
CHASKA	MN	c	1	26	23	40	44,370	60,120	y	65,532	4	2,326	2,034	87	1,722	183	128	76	216
CHICKASHA	OK	c	1	40	28	40	23,296	33,606	y	35,286	4	2,287	1,982	87	1,376	225	380	6	299
CHILLICOTHE	OH	c	1	51	46	40	31,408	40,456	y	41,856	2	4,652	3,900	84	2,517	627	755	210	543
CHRISTIANSBURG	VA	t	1	59	35	48	32,982	42,507	y	44,632	14	—	—	—	—	—	—	—	—
CIRCLEVILLE	OH	c	1	34	24	40	30,222	40,206	y	41,406	5	2,691	—	—	1,479	—	366	164	263
CLAREMONT	NH	c	3	27	23	40	35,858	42,874	y	43,374	5	1,829	1,732	95	1,202	131	398	50	47
CLARKSBURG	WV	c	1	43	38	40	26,557	28,915	y	—	2	2,961	2,446	83	1,632	503	311	17	497
CLAWSON	MI	c	1	19	18	40	37,603	56,220	n	—	—	2,001	1,674	84	1,196	264	214	44	283
CLAYTON	CA	c	3	13	11	40	51,564	62,676	n	—	—	1,599	1,294	81	934	341	19	65	240
CLAYTON	MO	c	1	—	51	40	42,649	60,301	n	—	—	4,933	4,293	87	3,220	722	351	110	529
CLEARLAKE	CA	c	1	27	24	42	34,690	42,165	y	46,382	5	3,114	2,572	83	1,511	522	539	236	306
CLEMMONS	NC	v	5	—	—	—	—	—	—	—	—	—	—	—	—	—	—	—	—
CLINTON	NJ	tp	1	27	24	40	40,761	77,457	y	82,879	5	2,378	—	—	1,867	291	—	37	182
CLINTON	UT	c	3	18	16	40	34,673	47,590	n	—	—	1,674	1,099	66	726	172	200	230	345
CLIVE	IA	c	1	26	23	40	39,650	49,569	n	—	—	2,590	1,981	76	1,301	444	234	67	543
COCOA	FL	c	1	90	68	40	31,457	42,457	n	—	—	7,193	5,531	77	3,840	1,035	655	340	1,323
COCOA BEACH	FL	c	1	54	37	40	33,000	48,246	n	—	—	3,990	3,486	87	2,476	629	381	110	393
COFFEYVILLE	KS	c	1	35	28	40	30,306	35,651	n	—	—	1,910	1,690	88	1,231	205	254	123	98
COLCHESTER	CT	t	1	9	8	40	41,080	55,078	y	55,828	6	913	554	61	453	79	21	35	325
COLCHESTER	VT	t	1	34	27	40	37,327	51,411	n	—	—	2,689	2,339	87	1,686	220	433	141	209
COLDWATER	MI	c	1	19	—	40	39,790	45,385	y	—	5	1,685	1,307	78	1,046	78	182	191	187
COLLEGE PARK	GA	c	1	89	69	42	36,604	55,697	y	55,697	—	9,004	7,881	88	6,283	305	1,293	250	873
COLLEGE PARK	MD	c	—	—	—	—	—	—	—	—	—	—	—	—	—	—	—	—	—
COLLINSVILLE	IL	c	1	54	36	40	45,656	52,062	y	57,803	2	5,463	4,642	85	3,454	586	602	128	694
COLUMBUS	NE	c	1	50	35	40	31,656	43,908	n	—	—	3,416	2,736	80	2,149	238	349	121	559
COMMERCE CITY	CO	c	1	104	78	40	46,934	65,399	n	—	—	10,234	—	—	6,930	830	—	—	2,473
CONVERSE	TX	c	1	34	30	40	25,090	—	y	—	1	—	—	—	—	—	—	—	—
CONWAY	SC	c	1	66	49	42	29,601	44,402	y	—	5	3,473	2,878	83	2,069	364	445	112	483
CONYERS	GA	c	1	—	43	40	32,076	45,135	y	—	—	2,784	2,637	95	2,113	296	227	44	103
COOS BAY	OR	c	3	34	23	40	39,432	50,316	y	53,838	15	—	2,728	—	1,768	518	440	—	—
COPLEY	OH	tp	1	23	20	40	42,977	56,748	y	—	3	2,541	1,833	72	1,276	237	320	421	287
CORALVILLE	IA	c	1	34	30	40	35,938	50,846	n	—	—	3,098	2,395	77	1,721	293	381	318	385
CORNELIUS	NC	t	1	—	—	42	21,866	48,075	y	—	—	3,040	2,118	70	1,647	258	213	56	867
CORONADO	CA	c	1	64	44	40	50,150	67,206	n	—	—	9,834	8,908	91	6,634	1,367	907	149	776
CORSICANA	TX	c	1	58	44	40	38,196	45,396	y	47,196	1	3,415	3,093	91	2,420	422	250	—	322
COSHOCTON	OH	c	5	—	—	—	—	—	—	—	—	—	—	—	—	—	—	—	—
COVENTRY	CT	t	1	17	12	40	47,216	57,283	y	58,783	3	3,209	1,613	50	1,098	274	240	1,518	79
COVINGTON	WA	c	—	—	—	—	—	—	—	—	—	—	—	—	—	—	—	—	—
CRAWFORDSVILLE	IN	c	1	47	31	40	35,545	45,678	y	46,849	1	2,836	2,369	84	1,752	338	279	114	353
CRESTWOOD	MO	c	1	41	35	40	45,963	57,198	n	—	—	—	—	—	267	215	—	249
CREVE COEUR	MO	c	1	69	52	40	43,680	62,388	n	—	—	5,101	4,620	91	3,410	711	499	185	296
CROMWELL	CT	t	1	34	25	42	43,722	59,300	n	—	—	4,139	—	—	2,380	—	—	142	215
CROWN POINT	IN	c	1	50	38	40	38,840	48,685	y	49,145	3	4,623	4,060	88	2,825	376	858	249	314
CUMBERLAND	MD	c	1	59	50	40	27,799	44,479	y	44,479	—	4,585	3,781	82	2,362	556	863	266	537
CUMRU	PA	tp	1	25	22	40	57,779	60,090	y	62,890	3	2,810	2,601	93	1,703	391	507	69	140
DAPHNE	AL	t	1	67	38	42	25,819	40,019	n	—	—	4,354	3,298	76	2,436	327	534	302	754
DE BARY	FL	c	5	—	—	48	—	—	—	—	—	—	—	—	—	—	—	—	—
DE LAND	FL	c	1	84	58	42	30,663	44,462	y	45,062	8	6,286	4,733	75	3,371	857	505	122	1,432
DEERFIELD	IL	v	1	53	39	40	52,562	72,699	y	77,788	10	6,611	5,897	89	4,345	927	625	213	501
DEFIANCE	OH	c	3	30	27	40	32,989	45,198	—	—	—	2,650	—	—	1,552	—	332	21	467
DEL CITY	OK	c	1	39	28	40	29,702	37,564	y	—	5	2,405	2,273	95	1,598	311	363	7	125
DEMING	NM	c	1	39	33	42	28,054	35,693	y	38,235	8	2,143	1,730	81	1,331	251	147	140	273
DESTIN	FL	c	—	—	—	—	—	—	—	—	—	—	—	—	—	—	—	—	—
DICKINSON	ND	c	1	41	25	40	29,848	38,896	y	—	1	2,279	2,055	90	1,531	252	271	44	180
DICKINSON	TX	c	1	35	—	42	31,345	39,708	y	40,188	1	4,460	3,590	81	3,219	143	228	154	715
DIXON	CA	c	3	31	25	40	48,516	61,920	y	—	—	3,747	3,011	80	2,023	704	284	132	604
DOUGLAS	GA	c	1	41	33	40	27,343	40,691	n	—	—	2,441	2,085	85	1,418	277	390	83	273
DOVER	NJ	t	1	—	39	other	44,235	82,138	n	—	—	3,513	—	—	3,317	—	—	47	149
DOVER	OH	c	1	22	21	40	43,888	43,888	y	—	7	1,864	—	—	1,206	—	224	—	202
DOVER	PA	tp	1	—	—	—	—	—	—	—	—	—	—	—	—	—	—	—	—
DOYLESTOWN	PA	tp	1	24	22	other	39,110	63,718	y	—	1	2,844	2,397	84	1,705	293	398	121	326
DUMAS	TX	c	3	29	21	42	32,585	42,361	y	44,281	2	1,798	1,422	79	1,119	148	155	52	323
DUMONT	NJ	b	1	32	32	40	40,641	103,664	y	—	—	4,619	—	—	3,642	—	249	—	126

Table 3/16 continued

POLICE DEPARTMENT PERSONNEL, SALARIES, AND EXPENDITURES FOR CITIES 10,000 AND OVER: 2007

City	State	Type	Service provision	Full-time paid personnel	Full-time uniformed personnel	Duty hours per week	Minimum base salary ($)	Maximum base salary ($)	Longevity pay	Maximum salary with longevity ($)	Years of service for longevity	Total expenditures (A) ($)	Total personnel expenditures (B) ($)	(B) as % of (A)	Salaries and wages (C) ($)	City contribution to retirement and social security (D) ($)	City contribution to insurance (E) ($)	Capital outlay (F) ($)	All other (G) ($)
10,000–24,999 continued																			
DUNCAN	OK	c	1	46	42	other	26,719	37,681	y	38,881	3	2,643	2,290	87	2,143	141	6	—	353
DURANGO	CO	c	1	—	—	40	39,889	55,845	n			—	—	—	—	—	—	—	—
DURANT	OK	c	1	46	33	40	27,638	30,191	y	39,248	1	2,444	2,220	91	1,615	312	293	57	167
DURHAM	NH	t	1	21	19	40	36,490	47,868	n	—	—	1,937	1,752	90	1,324	122	305	13	172
EAGLE	ID	c	5	—	—	40	—	—				—	—	—	—	—	—	—	—
EASLEY	SC	c	1	50	39	other	28,214	42,320	n			—	—	—	1,442	—	—	—	—
EAST GRAND RAPIDS	MI	c	4	33	30	other	45,116	54,483	y	55,483	5	3,742	3,298	88	2,163	531	603	27	417
EAST HAMPTON	CT	t	1	18	16	40	45,885	57,616	y	58,241	5	—	—	—	1,125	187	—	—	—
EAST LAMPETER	PA	tp	1	43	39	40	43,448	58,398	y	75,167	4	3,801	3,414	90	2,500	395	518	133	255
EAST LIVERPOOL	OH	c	1	17	—	40	—	—	y	—	2	—	—	—	—	—	—	—	—
EAST LONGMEADOW	MA	t	1	24	23	other	40,978	43,557	y	45,807	10	1,878	—	—	1,606	—	99	5	88
EAST MOLINE	IL	c	1	46	36	40	34,648	50,922	n			4,064	3,659	90	2,553	537	569	69	336
EAST ROCKAWAY	NY	v		—	—							—	—	—	—	—	—	—	—
EASTHAMPTON	MA	t	4	28	27	other	38,510	42,973	n			1,853	—	—	1,631	—	—	127	94
EASTON	MA	t	1	37	31	40	39,940	52,551	y	—	5	3,032	—	—	2,743	—	—	56	232
EATONTOWN	NJ	b	1	47	37	40	42,498	89,885	y	100,671	5	4,318	—	—	4,131	—	—	—	186
EDEN	NC	c	1	57	41	48	29,394	44,538	n			—	—	—	—	297	328	172	576
EL CAMPO	TX	c	1	29	26	40	31,250	44,556	y	46,056	1	1,711	1,339	78	1,118	195	25	124	248
EL CERRITO	CA	c	1	47	38	40	58,178	69,805	y	74,691	7	6,946	5,568	80	3,618	1,238	712	109	1,270
EL DORADO	KS	c	3	28	25	48	26,146	37,641	y	38,601	5	1,523	1,426	94	1,125	145	156	15	82
EL PASO DE ROBLES	CA	c	3	52	41	40	47,856	60,804	n			8,943	6,224	70	3,805	1,370	1,048	201	2,519
EL RENO	OK	c	1	35	28	40	28,267	39,582	y	41,982	3	2,020	1,746	86	1,328	231	188	56	217
ELIZABETH CITY	NC	c	1	58	46	42	32,764	39,712	y	—	1	3,847	2,818	73	2,105	447	265	51	978
ELIZABETHTON	TN	c	1	41	37	42	26,790	30,325	—			—	2,065	—	1,616	310	138	—	—
ELIZABETHTOWN	PA	b	1	18	16	40	43,209	57,612	y	60,112	5	1,838	1,624	88	1,170	194	260	64	150
ELK GROVE	CA	c		—	116	42	55,710	83,565	n			—	—	—	—	—	—	—	—
ELKO	NV	c	3	43	37	other	43,812	55,440	y	56,840	8	4,332	3,583	83	2,493	689	401	105	643
ELKTON	MD	t	1	—	28	42	30,618	51,792	n			2,421	1,980	82	1,538	228	213	87	—
ELLENSBURG	WA	c	1	31	24	40	37,503	46,879	n			3,566	2,634	74	1,890	225	519	—	876
ELMWOOD PARK	NJ	b	1	45	42	42	29,500	100,795	y	117,000	6	4,963	—	—	4,194	—	—	—	230
ENDICOTT	NY	v	1	33	—	40	43,868	52,731	n			3,725	3,361	90	2,253	375	733	95	269
ENNIS	TX	c	3	40	34	40	36,483	45,614	y	47,200	1	3,036	2,695	89	1,931	379	383	81	260
ENTERPRISE	AL	c	3	82	49	42	24,814	37,502	y	34,729	10	—	—	—	2,176	277	—	—	—
ERLANGER	KY	c	1	42	37	40	34,070	51,522	n	—		3,996	3,286	82	2,051	747	488	102	608
ESCANABA	MI	c	4	39	35	42	40,382	50,494	y	—	20	3,328	—	—	2,007	—	—	31	373
EUFAULA	AL	c	1	56	36	40	—	28,995	y	—	20	2,278	1,798	79	1,422	138	237	107	373
EUSTIS	FL	c	1	59	45	42	31,953	48,706	n			3,772	3,331	88	2,417	552	361	29	412
EVERGREEN PARK	IL	v	1	70	58	40	43,068	66,910	n			—	—	—	—	—	—	—	—
EXETER	PA	tp	1	34	32	42	61,611	67,879	y	—	3	—	—	—	2,567	—	—	96	380
FAIRHAVEN	MA	t	1	38	32	40	37,935	43,493	y	—	10	2,451	—	—	2,141	—	—	55	256
FAIRMONT	MN	c	1	20	18	40	50,796	52,145	y	52,145	—	2,127	1,797	84	1,216	345	235	32	298
FARIBAULT	MN	c	1	37	30	40	46,758	51,959	y	54,037	5	3,728	2,967	80	2,173	250	544	135	627
FARMINGTON	CT	t	1	63	44	40	50,180	66,254	n			6,240	5,565	89	4,088	405	1,072	—	675
FARMINGTON	MN	c	1	26	23	40	44,761	60,550	y	66,000	4	—	2,000	—	1,576	182	241	—	566
FARMINGTON	UT	c	1	15	12	40	32,656	46,176	y	46,176	1	1,445	—	—	748	—	—	204	493
FARRAGUT	TN	t		—	—	—	—	—				—	—	—	—	—	—	—	—
FAYETTEVILLE	GA	c	1	47	41	40	31,450	51,173	n			3,303	2,659	81	1,831	360	468	126	518
FENTON	MI	c	1	21	16	40	37,087	53,632	y	—	1	2,053	1,662	81	1,119	183	359	171	220
FERGUSON	MO	c	4	52	—	40	37,400	50,163	n			3,978	—	—	2,878	—	—	588	—
FERGUSON	PA	tp	1	18	18	40	41,303	41,303	y	—	6	1,657	1,215	73	1,000	175	40	130	312
FERNANDINA BEACH	FL	c	1	43	33	48	33,559	47,861	y	49,598	5	4,011	2,783	69	2,009	407	366	276	952
FERNDALE	MI	c	1	57	48	other	45,264	53,910	y	—	5	6,165	—	—	5,643	—	—	10	512
FILLMORE	CA	c	5	—	—	42	—	—				—	—	—	—	—	—	—	—
FLORENCE	KY	c	1	60	56	40	38,029	50,226	y	53,726	5	5,693	4,981	87	3,064	946	969	288	425
FLORENCE	NJ	tp	1	32	26	40	41,311	72,700	y	75,608	3	3,265	2,947	90	2,384	199	364	137	181
FOREST ACRES	SC	c	1	35	34	42	32,539	66,978	y	66,978	3	2,286	1,753	77	1,370	234	148	12	522
FOREST GROVE	OR	c	1	30	28	40	42,888	55,536	n			3,368	2,844	84	1,957	434	452	30	494
FOREST PARK	GA	c	1	93	70	other	30,301	42,421	n			5,514	4,040	73	3,104	263	672	520	953
FOREST PARK	OH	c	1	44	36	40	49,069	59,630	n			4,255	3,492	82	2,561	506	425	199	563
FORREST CITY	AR	c	1	42	34	other	28,844	28,844	y	30,644	5	2,603	2,112	81	1,591	218	303	110	381
FORT MADISON	IA	c	1	21	15	40	28,995	38,272	y	39,352	5	1,541	1,427	93	940	229	257	7	106
FORT MORGAN	CO	c	1	35	28	other	76,731	—	n			—	—	—	—	196	471	198	280
FORT WALTON BEACH	FL	c	1	68	55	42	31,065	53,866	y	54,166	17	4,267	3,874	91	3,074	435	365	81	312
FOSTORIA	OH	c	1	29	24	40	35,402	50,627	y	54,677	5	2,618	—	—	1,226	—	398	125	199
FOUNTAIN	CO	c	1	49	40	40	40,227	60,362	n			4,052	3,337	82	2,632	208	497	193	522
FOUNTAIN HILLS	AZ	t	5	—	—	40	—	—				—	—	—	—	—	—	—	—
FOXBOROUGH	MA	t		—	—							—	—	—	—	—	—	—	—
FRANCONIA	PA	tp	1	14	12	40	64,000	69,000	y	—	5	1,676	1,383	83	1,034	296	52	98	195
FRANKFORT	IN	c	1	43	31	40	36,542	40,198	y	—		—	—	—	—	—	141	100	19
FRANKLIN	IN	c	1	56	40	40	40,898	41,898	y	42,898	1	—	—	—	—	451	531	190	321
FRANKLIN	NJ	tp	1	32	29	40	41,304	71,137	y	—		2,981	2,565	86	1,871	402	293	90	325
FRASER	MI	c	4	52	41	40	40,781	58,053	y	—	5	6,497	6,420	99	4,163	1,329	928	—	77
FREEHOLD	NJ	b	1	—	35	40	34,713	84,969	y	88,819	5	4,985	4,514	91	3,528	300	686	88	383
FREEPORT	TX	c	1	47	30	40	31,751	42,662	y	—	1	—	—	—	—	182	180	96	2,183

Table 3/16 continued   **POLICE DEPARTMENT PERSONNEL, SALARIES, AND EXPENDITURES FOR CITIES 10,000 AND OVER: 2007**

City	State	Type	Service provision	Full-time paid personnel	Full-time uniformed personnel	Duty hours per week	Minimum base salary ($)	Maximum base salary ($)	Longevity pay	Maximum salary with longevity ($)	Years of service for longevity	Total expenditures (A) ($)	Total personnel expenditures (B) ($)	(B) as % of (A)	Salaries and wages (C) ($)	City contribution to retirement and social security (D) ($)	City contribution to insurance (E) ($)	Capital outlay (F) ($)	All other (G) ($)
10,000–24,999 continued																			
FREMONT	OH	c	1	39	33	40	35,818	49,504	n	—	—	3,063	2,763	90	2,045	362	356	80	219
GAFFNEY	SC	c	3	42	38	42	25,049	37,573	n	—	—	2,459	2,024	82	1,481	264	278	—	435
GAINESVILLE	TX	c	1	49	38	40	28,968	—	y	—	1	3,766	3,085	82	2,447	363	274	81	600
GALENA PARK	TX	c	1	23	18	40	37,112	39,545	y	—	1	1,504	1,299	86	906	176	216	49	156
GALLUP	NM	c	1	61	61	42	32,760	41,658	n	—	—	4,348	3,500	81	2,855	462	183	181	666
GALT	CA	c	3	43	22	40	48,384	58,788	y	63,197	15	4,556	3,955	87	2,571	804	579	185	415
GARDEN CITY	NY	v	1	67	54	other	46,233	97,527	y	—	6	10,640	—	—	7,284	3,141	1,001	—	414
GATESVILLE	TX	c	1	21	15	40	25,188	30,721	n	—	—	1,049	852	81	640	93	118	15	183
GENEVA	NY	c	1	41	36	40	38,053	51,640	y	52,740	5	3,338	3,107	93	2,257	477	372	53	178
GILLETTE	WY	c	1	73	49	40	41,662	58,365	n	—	—	10,297	4,785	46	3,464	653	668	65	5,448
GLADSTONE	OR	c	1	18	16	40	42,756	52,080	y	53,382	20	—	—	—	—	—	—	—	—
GOLDEN	CO	c	3	61	45	40	43,600	62,800	n	—	—	6,070	5,051	83	3,923	580	547	121	898
GORHAM	ME	t	1	23	21	40	41,467	46,377	y	46,777	10	1,820	—	—	1,257	—	—	78	388
GRAFTON	MA	t	1	19	19	other	42,567	50,544	y	—	10	1,581	—	—	1,581	—	—	—	—
GRANBY	CT	t	1	18	14	40	50,232	64,064	y	64,814	5	2,049	1,883	92	1,398	236	248	72	94
GRAND CHUTE	WI	t	1	31	27	other	42,661	49,504	n	—	—	3,256	2,708	83	1,930	395	382	141	408
GRAND HAVEN	MI	c	4	37	32	42	42,367	52,033	n	—	—	3,160	2,718	86	2,185	110	422	200	242
GRANDVIEW	MO	c	1	68	62	40	35,092	49,106	y	—	3	4,682	3,679	79	2,972	280	426	381	623
GRASS VALLEY	CA	c	1	39	28	42	42,876	54,840	n	—	—	4,141	3,594	87	2,291	776	526	91	457
GREENACRES	FL	c	4	73	51	42	40,500	—	n	—	—	5,473	4,940	90	3,470	755	715	33	500
GREENFIELD	IN	c	1	52	35	40	39,548	—	n	—	—	—	—	—	—	—	—	290	439
GREENSBURG	IN	c	1	18	—	40	30,200	31,000	y	37,200	1	—	—	—	940	—	123	20	200
GREENWOOD	MS	c	1	61	49	40	20,242	27,851	n	—	—	3,419	2,665	78	2,007	348	310	157	597
GREENWOOD	SC	c	1	59	45	42	27,373	38,355	n	—	—	3,419	2,342	69	1,794	319	229	302	774
GREENWOOD VILLAGE	CO	c	1	83	62	40	46,248	63,540	y	65,040	5	8,032	7,416	92	5,303	1,574	539	565	51
GREER	SC	c	1	—	—	—	—	—	n	—	—	5,073	3,809	75	2,627	462	720	422	842
GRIFFITH	IN	t	1	38	30	40	39,766	48,112	y	—	3	—	—	—	1,977	—	—	116	379
GRISWOLD	CT	t	—	—	—	—	—	—	—	—	—	—	—	—	—	—	—	—	—
GROSSE POINTE PARK	MI	c	4	55	44	42	41,689	59,556	y	61,640	5	3,934	3,861	98	3,302	401	158	—	73
GROSSE POINTE WOODS	MI	c	3	51	38	42	45,669	59,512	y	60,512	5	4,813	4,329	90	3,362	591	375	107	377
GROTON	CT	c	1	38	30	40	47,320	57,429	y	58,204	5	4,535	—	—	—	—	—	—	—
GULFPORT	FL	c	1	39	30	40	38,307	57,462	y	—	5	3,491	2,972	85	2,276	401	294	66	453
GUTTENBERG	NJ	t	1	23	23	40	—	75,633	y	77,146	6	2,864	—	—	2,250	—	72	46	132
GUYMON	OK	c	3	20	13	42	24,617	26,490	n	—	—	1,269	1,045	82	723	139	182	46	178
HADDONFIELD	NJ	b	1	24	23	42	32,337	72,500	y	81,019	5	2,743	2,622	96	2,135	207	280	—	121
HAINES CITY	FL	c	1	69	50	42	32,573	48,859	n	—	—	3,623	3,013	83	2,256	303	453	150	461
HALF MOON BAY	CA	c	1	22	17	40	70,092	85,164	y	89,422	5	4,741	4,018	85	2,302	1,039	676	57	666
HAMBURG	NY	v	1	22	14	40	47,712	63,616	y	66,116	5	1,643	—	—	1,131	161	—	—	62
HAMPTON	NH	t	1	42	34	40	36,046	54,184	n	—	—	—	—	—	—	—	—	—	—
HAMPTON	PA	tp	1	20	17	40	52,960	79,425	y	—	5	2,387	—	—	1,502	—	296	149	235
HANOVER	MA	t	1	33	29	40	42,433	49,426	y	50,426	5	2,927	—	—	2,123	—	185	114	268
HANOVER	NH	t	1	—	—	40	—	—	—	—	—	—	—	—	—	—	—	—	—
HARKER HEIGHTS	TX	c	1	49	38	40	37,182	55,441	y	55,441	1	3,138	2,364	75	1,850	340	174	157	617
HARPER WOODS	MI	c	1	30	26	40	36,170	53,782	y	57,815	4	4,952	—	—	3,115	—	1,090	108	445
HARRISON	PA	tp	1	25	13	40	40,679	58,114	y	59,614	6	—	—	—	—	—	—	37	96
HASTINGS	NE	c	1	48	38	other	30,742	42,827	n	—	—	—	—	—	—	—	—	—	—
HATFIELD	PA	tp	1	31	26	40	37,878	69,636	y	74,000	4	4,294	3,161	74	2,160	865	136	413	721
HAVRE DE GRACE	MD	c	1	36	27	40	35,360	51,955	n	—	—	3,140	2,840	90	1,967	349	523	72	228
HAWAIIAN GARDENS	CA	c	—	—	—	—	—	—	—	—	—	—	—	—	—	—	—	—	—
HAYS	KS	c	1	50	32	40	27,924	47,784	y	51,129	5	—	—	—	1,731	—	—	—	—
HAZEL CREST	IL	v	1	32	26	40	41,812	63,621	y	68,530	5	3,238	—	—	2,351	539	—	148	563
HAZEL PARK	MI	c	1	42	37	40	39,520	56,015	y	—	5	3,764	—	—	2,898	—	476	58	277
HAZLET	NJ	tp	1	50	46	40	50,000	82,409	y	83,759	5	5,961	5,895	99	4,650	752	492	—	66
HAZLETON	PA	c	1	33	30	40	33,135	47,336	y	52,070	2	3,714	3,510	94	1,777	1,211	521	57	148
HEALDSBURG	CA	c	3	29	17	40	59,220	72,264	y	78,045	5	—	—	—	2,324	—	—	—	—
HELENA	AL	c	1	22	21	40	35,152	45,838	y	46,138	1	—	—	—	—	—	—	—	—
HENDERSON	TX	c	3	—	—	40	30,185	33,185	y	34,385	1	2,645	2,219	84	1,598	251	370	172	254
HENDERSONVILLE	NC	c	1	43	31	42	28,827	43,861	y	44,650	5	2,850	2,332	82	1,777	289	266	155	364
HERCULES	CA	c	1	31	28	40	64,932	75,276	y	78,276	10	4,654	—	—	2,318	—	300	52	3,434
HERMISTON	OR	c	3	34	25	40	—	—	n	—	—	2,937	2,512	86	1,567	513	431	420	5
HERMOSA BEACH	CA	c	1	50	38	other	55,092	63,768	y	76,522	5	8,212	5,409	66	3,371	1,649	389	160	2,642
HERNDON	VA	t	1	72	55	40	44,443	72,399	n	—	—	7,860	6,456	82	4,958	913	585	882	523
HEWITT	TX	c	1	30	15	40	28,356	45,888	y	47,088	20	1,606	1,291	80	1,012	169	110	97	218
HIBBING	MN	c	1	31	28	42	38,822	41,550	y	44,880	5	2,666	2,231	84	1,579	180	471	43	392
HIGHLAND VILLAGE	TX	c	1	32	25	40	43,600	53,600	y	—	2	2,378	2,043	86	1,625	169	249	84	251
HILLIARD	OH	c	1	67	49	40	39,285	63,036	y	64,796	5	6,586	—	—	4,224	—	850	48	306
HILLSBOROUGH	CA	c	3	34	25	—	75,530	91,806	n	—	—	5,810	4,836	83	3,065	1,070	701	30	943
HILLSDALE	NJ	b	1	22	20	40	31,696	91,230	n	—	—	—	3,040	—	2,538	193	308	—	—
HILLTOWN	PA	tp	1	22	19	42	46,093	68,001	y	—	5	2,545	—	—	1,532	—	177	418	297
HOLDEN	MA	t	1	25	22	40	39,148	52,584	n	—	—	1,900	—	—	1,621	—	—	100	179
HOLLY HILL	FL	c	1	34	29	40	30,600	48,919	y	—	—	1,995	1,588	80	1,155	202	231	47	360

Table 3/16 continued

POLICE DEPARTMENT PERSONNEL, SALARIES, AND EXPENDITURES FOR CITIES 10,000 AND OVER: 2007

City	State	Type	Service provision	Full-time paid personnel	Full-time uniformed personnel	Duty hours per week	Minimum base salary ($)	Maximum base salary ($)	Longevity pay	Maximum salary with longevity ($)	Years of service for longevity	Total expenditures (A) ($)	Total personnel expenditures (B) ($)	(B) as % of (A)	Salaries and wages (C) ($)	City contribution to retirement and social security (D) ($)	City contribution to insurance (E) ($)	Capital outlay (F) ($)	All other (G) ($)
10,000–24,999 continued																			
HOMER GLEN	IL	v	—	—	—	—	—	—		—	—	—	—	—	—	—	—	—	—
HOPATCONG	NJ	b	1	28	28	40	46,823	75,399	y	80,677	5	—	—	—	—	—	—	—	—
HOPE	AR	c	1	33	18	42	22,880	27,040	y	—	5	1,798	1,508	84	1,075	207	225	84	205
HOPEWELL	PA	tp	1	14	13	40	30,539	50,898	y	51,898	6	1,230	—	—	965	—	181	58	109
HOPEWELL	VA	c	1	77	44	42	32,443	48,663	n	—	—	5,293	4,077	77	3,209	587	280	68	1,148
HOPKINS	MN	c	1	38	25	40	48,640	60,183	y	66,363	4	3,702	2,959	80	2,337	282	340	7	735
HORN LAKE	MS	c	1	68	54	42	—	36,044	y	—	4	—	—	—	—	—	—	—	—
HOWARD	WI	v	5	—	—	—	—	—		—	—	—	—	—	—	—	—	—	—
HUDSON	OH	c	1	35	28	40	40,997	56,493	y	58,093	4	—	—	—	—	—	—	—	—
HUEYTOWN	AL	c	1	—	28	40	21,674	33,655	n	—	—	2,426	2,084	86	1,275	611	197	158	183
HUMBLE	TX	c	1	71	55	40	39,180	52,008	y	—	1	6,373	5,211	82	3,736	671	804	165	996
HUNTERSVILLE	NC	t	1	80	71	42	33,737	52,292	—	—	—	6,091	3,591	59	2,889	356	346	440	2,060
HUNTINGTON	IN	c	1	38	35	other	37,347	37,347	y	47,804	1	2,027	—	—	1,752	—	—	100	175
INDIAN TRAIL	NC	t	—	—	—	—	—	—		—	—	—	—	—	—	—	—	—	—
INDIANOLA	IA	c	1	18	18	40	32,546	44,421	y	—	5	1,909	1,577	83	1,001	283	292	51	281
IPSWICH	MA	t	1	30	23	40	42,376	47,271	y	48,771	5	2,512	—	—	1,940	—	—	105	467
IRONTON	OH	c	1	16	13	40	25,833	28,350	y	—	1	954	—	—	491	—	202	23	113
ISSAQUAH	WA	c	1	57	30	48	51,192	63,144	y	—	5	—	—	—	—	—	—	—	—
JACKSONVILLE	IL	c	1	49	38	40	37,455	48,646	y	51,079	7	2,892	2,625	91	2,321	39	264	174	93
JACKSONVILLE BEACH	FL	c	1	80	61	40	33,550	54,642	n	—	—	6,789	5,281	78	4,272	577	431	299	1,210
JENNINGS	LA	c	1	35	32	42	17,690	—	y	—	1	2,124	1,537	72	1,176	158	203	104	483
KALISPELL	MT	c	1	48	30	40	38,938	51,584	n	—	—	4,658	4,383	94	3,182	732	470	89	185
KATY	TX	c	1	59	1	40	48,000		y	—	1	—	—	—	—	—	—	—	—
KELSO	WA	c	1	33	29	other	46,464	58,956	y	63,672	5	3,788	2,747	73	2,114	217	416	66	975
KENMORE	WA	c	—	—	—	—	—	—		—	—	—	—	—	—	—	—	—	—
KENNETT	MO	c	1	28	23	40	20,400	—	n	—	—	1,202	936	78	727	79	130	39	227
KERNERSVILLE	NC	t	1	82	63	40	29,222	44,302	y	—	—	4,782	3,738	78	2,841	487	410	168	875
KERRVILLE	TX	c	1	73	53	40	36,247	49,607	y	50,327	1	—	—	—	2,648	—	—	—	—
KEWANEE	IL	c	1	31	23	40	36,163	44,987	y	47,487	5	2,240	1,942	87	1,390	171	380	56	242
KILGORE	TX	c	1	41	32	42	31,730	42,852	y	—	1	2,434	1,986	82	1,370	319	296	46	403
KINGMAN	AZ	c	1	86	57	other	38,573	54,277	n	—	—	8,421	6,096	72	4,419	1,575	101	937	1,388
KINGSTON	PA	c	1	—	—	40	—	—		—	—	—	—	—	—	—	—	—	—
KINSTON	NC	c	4	—	—	42	43,118	47,548	y	—	5	5,649	4,453	79	3,186	1,095	172	293	903
KIRKSVILLE	MO	c	1	28	26	40	25,892	29,198	n	—	—	1,508	1,292	86	991	130	171	50	166
KLAMATH FALLS	OR	c	1	46	40	40	41,112	50,472	n	—	—	4,738	3,568	75	2,571	591	405	140	1,031
LA GRANGE	IL	v	3	38	29	42	47,245	67,453	y	—	—	3,354	3,050	91	2,259	520	270	98	206
LA MARQUE	TX	c	3	36	24	40	38,315	50,184	y	50,910	1	2,534	2,112	83	1,573	261	277	75	347
LA PALMA	CA	c	—	—	—	40	52,785	67,369	n	—	—	—	—	—	—	—	—	—	—
LA PORTE	IN	c	1	49	46	40	35,272	35,272	y	—	3	3,510	—	—	1,987	—	587	192	275
LA QUINTA	CA	c	5	—	—	—	—	—		—	—	—	—	—	—	—	—	—	—
LA VISTA	NE	c	1	34	30	40	35,755	50,939	y	53,231	7	2,692	2,250	84	1,735	231	284	170	272
LACKAWANNA	NY	c	1	46	46	40	42,404	50,403	y	51,503	5	4,448	4,278	96	3,156	748	373	30	141
LAFAYETTE	CO	c	1	48	39	40	43,401	60,007	y	62,107	8	8,207	—	—	3,056	—	467	3,672	975
LAGUNA BEACH	CA	c	1	86	50	40	52,716	74,148	n	—	—	—	—	—	—	—	—	—	—
LAKE MARY	FL	c	1	42	37	42	33,874	53,377	y	—	3	3,815	3,025	79	2,232	484	309	33	757
LAKE ST. LOUIS	MO	c	1	42	27	48	39,000	57,000	n	—	—	—	—	—	313	508	33	324	
LAKE STATION	IN	c	1	27	23	40	34,862	44,539	y	47,039	4	—	—	—	—	—	—	—	—
LAKE ZURICH	IL	v	1	64	37	40	48,898	69,966	y	70,966	20	6,624	5,611	85	4,296	614	700	97	916
LARKSPUR	CA	c	—	—	—	—	—	—		—	—	—	—	—	—	—	—	—	—
LAURINBURG	NC	c	1	42	—	42	31,139	46,006	y	—	25	—	—	—	—	—	—	—	—
LEBANON	MO	c	1	38	27	40	25,938	30,772	y	—	5	—	—	—	1,206	—	—	188	139
LEESBURG	FL	c	1	106	73	40	31,254	45,896	n	—	—	8,941	6,733	75	4,495	1,783	455	—	1,308
LEHI	UT	c	1	—	—	other	35,549	50,801	y	50,951	10	3,038	—	—	2,185	—	—	289	564
LEICESTER	MA	t	1	20	16	40	38,121	49,384	y	49,684	5	1,597	—	—	1,218	—	128	67	176
LEMON GROVE	CA	c	5	—	—	40	—	—		—	—	—	—	—	—	—	—	—	—
LEMOORE	CA	c	1	32	26	—	38,100	48,888	n	—	—	3,206	2,372	74	1,743	456	173	114	719
LENOIR	NC	c	1	69	51	42	23,398	—	n	—	—	4,822	3,682	76	2,708	573	401	122	1,017
LEVELLAND	TX	c	1	30	21	40	34,008	34,008	y	35,208	1	1,779	1,441	81	1,064	221	156	118	219
LEXINGTON	NC	c	1	77	61	40	25,669	45,762	y	46,906	3	4,977	4,094	82	3,030	494	569	235	648
LEXINGTON	NE	c	1	17	15	40	27,955	37,814	n	—	—	1,071	910	85	623	78	208	13	147
LILBURN	GA	c	1	—	26	40	37,122	55,684	n	—	—	2,289	1,954	85	1,587	157	209	128	208
LINCOLN	RI	t	1	45	37	40	32,665	48,522	y	52,647	3	3,425	2,957	86	2,110	411	436	175	293
LINDENHURST	IL	v	1	17	15	40	45,598	65,576	n	—	—	2,082	—	—	1,105	—	—	—	—
LINO LAKES	MN	c	1	32	26	40	38,975	60,778	n	—	—	19,741	19,346	98	18,888	221	237	177	218
LITTLE CHUTE	WI	v	1	29	26	40	—	—	y	50,253	27	2,622	2,100	80	1,392	333	374	90	432
LOCKHART	TX	c	1	20	20	40	31,200	43,680	y	—	1	1,720	1,506	88	1,159	186	161	15	199
LOCKPORT	IL	c	1	44	37	40	44,639	60,507	y	62,007	8	6,841	3,700	54	2,634	568	497	101	3,041
LOGAN	PA	tp	1	18	—	40	27,019	49,067	y	50,539	5	1,594	1,384	87	934	213	237	54	156
LOMA LINDA	CA	c	5	—	—	—	—	—		—	—	—	—	—	—	—	—	—	—
LONDONDERRY	NH	t	1	80	65	40	40,848	54,185	y	56,353	10	8,306	7,594	91	5,844	589	1,161	413	299
LOS ALAMITOS	CA	c	1	25	21	40	63,785	77,531	n	—	—	—	—	—	—	—	—	—	—
LOUISVILLE	CO	c	1	—	34	40	47,486	66,830	n	—	—	—	—	—	—	—	—	—	—
LOWER	NJ	tp	1	45	40	42	41,026	79,981	y	86,380	5	—	—	—	—	537	837	172	129

Table 3/16 continued

POLICE DEPARTMENT PERSONNEL, SALARIES, AND EXPENDITURES FOR CITIES 10,000 AND OVER: 2007

City	State	Type	Service provision	Full-time paid personnel	Full-time uniformed personnel	Duty hours per week	Minimum base salary ($)	Maximum base salary ($)	Longevity pay	Maximum salary with longevity ($)	Years of service for longevity	Reported expenditures (in $000)							
												Total expenditures (A) ($)	Total personnel expenditures (B) ($)	(B) as % of (A)	Salaries and wages (C) ($)	City contribution to retirement and social security (D) ($)	City contribution to insurance (E) ($)	Capital outlay (F) ($)	All other (G) ($)
10,000–24,999 continued																			
LOWER GWYNEDD	PA	tp	1	18	17	40	47,861	68,373	y	73,842	5	2,482	2,183	88	1,456	344	382	179	120
LOWER MORELAND	PA	tp	1	28	23	40	48,104	66,167	y	72,783	4	2,440	2,237	92	1,947	43	246	123	80
LOWER SALFORD TOWNSHIP	PA	tp	1	21	19	40	42,247	70,404	y	—	5	2,330	2,093	90	1,545	157	390	58	179
LUMBERTON	NC	c	1	80	69	42	24,663	27,905	y	27,955	1	4,529	3,936	87	2,951	507	478	6	587
LYNDHURST	NJ	tp	1	50	50	40	21,861	91,384	y	96,828	4	7,891	6,271	79	5,408	838	25	75	1,545
LYNN HAVEN	FL	c	1	48	29	42	30,205	47,415	n	—	—	2,673	2,035	76	1,500	300	234	304	333
MACOMB	IL	c	1	28	25	40	—	40,713	y	68,817	2	—	—	—	—	—	—	—	—
MAITLAND	FL	c	1	52	42	40	35,600	54,200	y	—	—	4,107	3,576	87	2,403	778	394	295	235
MANCHESTER	PA	tp	—	—	—	—	—	—		—	—	—	—	—	—	—	—	—	—
MANDEVILLE	LA	c	1	54	38	42	30,292	48,376	n	—	—	4,214	3,374	80	2,301	606	466	277	564
MANSFIELD	MA	t	1	43	31	40	38,391	53,552	y	54,177	5	4,353	—	—	2,976	—	448	144	316
MANVILLE	NJ	b	1	24	—	40	—	—	y	60,000	5	2,684	—	—	2,684	—	—	—	222
MAPLE VALLEY	WA	c	5	—	—	—	—	—		—	—	—	—	—	—	—	—	—	—
MARINETTE	WI	c	1	33	24	40	39,832	44,262	y	47,512	3	2,675	—	—	1,514	345	—	39	774
MARQUETTE	MI	c	1	39	33	40	31,637	42,204	y	42,664	5	2,943	2,686	91	2,075	170	441	7	250
MARQUETTE	MI	tp	5	—	—	other	—	—		—	—	—	—	—	—	—	—	—	—
MARSHALL	MO	c	1	30	22	40	27,893	30,430	n	—	—	1,668	1,386	83	1,085	100	201	27	255
MARSHFIELD	WI	c	3	46	31	other	40,335	50,019	y	50,679	5	3,823	3,545	93	2,371	606	567	73	205
MARTIN	TN	c	1	36	27	42	28,720	35,970	n	—	—	—	—	—	1,338	191	—	295	186
MARYSVILLE	OH	c	1	32	27	40	34,354	50,903	y	51,753	3	2,505	—	—	1,857	—	—	79	216
MARYVILLE	MO	c	4	19	19	40	24,003	38,605	y	—	3	1,232	979	79	756	68	155	37	216
MARYVILLE	TN	c	1	52	47	40	30,492	54,745	n	—	—	4,190	3,235	77	2,263	402	569	58	897
MASON	OH	c	1	44	37	other	—	—	n	—	—	3,790	—	—	2,440	—	480	222	93
MASSAPEQUA PARK	NY	v	—	—	—	—	—	—		—	—	—	—	—	—	—	—	—	—
MATTHEWS	NC	t	1	64	52	42	30,633	45,468	y	—	1	5,075	—	—	4,001	—	—	422	651
MAULDIN	SC	c	1	42	38	40	24,400	30,000	y	30,500	5	—	—	—	—	—	—	—	—
MAUMEE	OH	c	1	58	54	40	43,274	55,056	y	56,856	5	7,091	—	—	3,883	—	789	79	1,643
McCOMB	MS	c	1	61	34	42	27,000	39,000	n	—	—	—	—	—	—	247	309	50	291
McHENRY	IL	c	1	68	51	40	46,000	71,000	n	—	—	6,456	—	—	5,484	—	820	523	972
McKEESPORT	PA	c	1	55	50	40	25,000	44,000	y	48,000	5	—	—	—	—	—	—	—	—
McMINNVILLE	TN	c	1	40	36	other	24,565	36,525	n	—	—	1,796	—	—	1,501	—	—	85	211
MELROSE PARK	IL	v	1	91	76	40	30,000	68,512	y	71,012	15	8,655	—	—	5,676	—	1,149	148	1,133
MENASHA	WI	c	1	—	36	48	39,964	55,150	n	—	—	3,891	3,477	89	2,233	581	663	91	323
MENASHA	WI	t	1	32	25	40	40,788	52,800	n	—	—	2,595	2,392	92	1,648	367	376	75	128
MENOMONIE	WI	c	1	34	27	other	45,324	49,452	y	51,924	4	3,429	2,989	87	2,019	482	488	87	352
MERCER ISLAND	WA	c	1	35	31	40	49,733	66,498	y	74,485	5	4,745	3,711	78	2,843	298	569	95	940
MERRIAM	KS	c	1	32	27	40	37,894	56,841	n	—	—	2,572	2,418	94	1,778	326	313	47	108
METUCHEN	NJ	b	1	—	28	40	39,809	75,436	y	—	10	—	—	—	—	—	—	—	—
MEXICO	MO	c	4	36	34	40	26,000	35,650	n	—	—	2,005	1,706	85	1,239	225	241	79	219
MIAMI	OK	c	3	48	31	40	29,322	36,407	n	—	—	—	—	—	—	—	—	—	—
MIAMI SHORES	FL	v	1	45	22	40	38,740	54,652	y	60,117	15	3,125	2,695	86	2,022	444	229	—	430
MIDDLEBURG HEIGHTS	OH	c	1	38	31	40	44,949	60,611	y	—	5	4,201	—	—	2,808	—	463	119	305
MIDDLETOWN	PA	tp	—	—	—	—	—	—		—	—	—	—	—	—	—	—	—	—
MILFORD	NH	t	1	29	23	40	35,045	49,408	—	—	—	1,708	—	—	1,440	170	—	73	25
MILL CREEK	WA	c	1	24	19	40	45,072	60,384	y	62,196	7	2,698	2,049	76	1,581	193	274	83	567
MILLBURN	NJ	tp	1	56	52	other	44,781	76,817	y	83,402	5	6,664	—	—	5,706	—	—	—	472
MILLBURY	MA	t	1	24	—	40	42,762	72,997	y	—	10	1,993	—	—	1,737	—	33	58	61
MILLEDGEVILLE	GA	c	1	59	42	42	26,051	39,640	n	—	—	3,257	2,505	77	1,687	232	586	309	443
MINEOLA	NY	v	—	—	—	—	—	—		—	—	—	—	—	—	—	—	—	—
MINT HILL	NC	t	1	27	25	42	29,829	118,660	n	—	—	2,205	1,313	60	1,022	127	164	399	493
MITCHELL	SD	c	4	26	24	40	33,605	40,010	y	40,660	6	1,983	1,677	85	1,285	184	208	76	230
MOBERLY	MO	c	1	48	33	40	24,449	31,917	n	—	—	15,204	14,960	98	14,431	194	335	61	182
MONROE	GA	c	1	44	38	42	29,131	43,600	n	—	—	3,028	2,263	75	1,677	371	216	166	599
MONROE	WA	c	1	45	32	other	51,072	62,100	y	—	5	5,483	4,465	81	3,100	1,189	175	581	438
MONTGOMERY	OH	c	1	24	21	40	46,842	60,819	y	—	5	2,402	—	—	1,614	—	297	—	176
MONTROSE	CO	c	1	48	36	40	39,696	50,620	y	51,196	10	4,278	2,910	68	2,199	267	443	330	1,037
MONTVILLE	NJ	tp	1	49	42	48	35,924	84,030	y	89,912	5	5,583	—	—	4,273	—	643	—	307
MOON	PA	tp	1	36	30	42	60,466	72,223	y	74,339	5	4,206	3,639	87	2,788	257	593	72	494
MORGAN CITY	LA	c	1	54	51	42	22,620	22,620	n	—	1	3,002	—	—	1,873	—	296	135	471
MORGANTON	NC	c	4	93	76	48	30,477	45,716	y	47,545	1	—	—	—	1,647	—	—	—	—
MORRO BAY	CA	c	1	—	15	40	47,401	60,497	n	—	—	—	—	—	1,647	—	—	—	—
MOSES LAKE	WA	c	3	35	29	40	43,500	54,384	n	—	—	2,797	2,192	78	1,930	165	96	537	68
MOULTRIE	GA	c	1	49	44	48	—	—		—	—	2,757	1,980	72	1,613	162	204	146	631
MOUNT CLEMENS	MI	c	5	—	—	—	—	—		—	—	—	—	—	—	—	—	—	—
MOUNT PLEASANT	TX	c	1	36	27	40	30,784	41,257	y	—	1	2,221	1,829	82	1,370	278	181	77	315
MOUNTAIN BROOK	AL	c	—	64	53	other	33,509	51,917	y	56,330	20	6,253	4,751	76	3,633	659	459	939	563
MOUNTAIN HOME	AR	c	3	34	25	40	20,363	30,555	y	—	1	1,915	1,736	91	1,116	379	241	51	127
MUNSTER	IN	t	1	50	37	40	37,398	52,354	y	54,679	6	3,992	3,543	89	2,564	492	487	197	253
MURPHYSBORO	IL	c	1	13	13	40	24,509	44,339	n	—	—	—	—	—	700	—	—	—	—
MURRYSVILLE	PA	c	1	21	7	40	46,987	57,467	y	82,946	2	2,526	—	—	1,663	—	480	88	168
MUSCATINE	IA	c	1	40	38	40	32,448	45,698	n	—	—	3,188	2,676	84	1,837	480	359	79	433
MUSCLE SHOALS	AL	t	1	44	35	40	29,561	34,778	n	—	—	2,732	2,361	86	1,621	253	487	98	272
MUSTANG	OK	c	1	26	18	other	30,830	47,458	y	49,668	5	—	—	—	—	—	—	—	—

Table 3/16 continued POLICE DEPARTMENT PERSONNEL, SALARIES, AND EXPENDITURES FOR CITIES 10,000 AND OVER: 2007

City	State	Type	Service provision	Full-time paid personnel	Full-time uniformed personnel	Duty hours per week	Minimum base salary ($)	Maximum base salary ($)	Longevity pay	Maximum salary with longevity ($)	Years of service for longevity	Total expenditures (A) ($)	Total personnel expenditures (B) ($)	(B) as % of (A)	Salaries and wages (C) ($)	City contribution to retirement and social security (D) ($)	City contribution to insurance (E) ($)	Capital outlay (F) ($)	All other (G) ($)
10,000–24,999 continued																			
NATCHITOCHES	LA	c	1	66	56	42	21,840	37,398	y	38,146	20	2,938	2,424	83	1,825	274	325	45	468
NEOSHO	MO	c	1	29	27	40	26,062	56,650	n	—	—	1,551	1,195	77	843	304	48	100	256
NEW BERN	NC	c	1	124	88	42	29,025	63,989	y	63,989	5	8,168	6,368	78	4,692	834	842	237	1,563
NEW BRIGHTON	MN	c	1	32	27	40	39,395	60,609	y	66,063	4	1,574	—	—	—	261	266	349	469
NEW FAIRFIELD	CT	t	7	5	—	40	—	—	—	—	—	—	—	—	—	—	—	—	—
NEW LENOX	IL	v	1	44	40	40	40,740	60,077	n	—	—	3,966	3,371	85	2,399	546	426	126	469
NEW PHILADELPHIA	OH	c	1	26	21	40	39,541	41,954	y	42,434	5	1,728	—	—	1,156	—	199	124	150
NEW PORT RICHEY	FL	c	1	51	36	40	37,638	53,972	n	—	—	4,250	3,453	81	2,544	619	290	284	513
NEW SMYRNA BEACH	FL	c	1	59	48	42	30,685	52,263	y	78,221	5	5,762	3,826	66	2,785	658	382	173	1,763
NEWBERRY	SC	c	1	34	31	42	26,879	40,318	y	—	—	1,718	1,373	80	1,072	174	127	87	258
NEWBURYPORT	MA	c	1	35	32	40	35,459	46,657	y	—	5	2,918	—	—	2,672	—	—	10	51
NEWNAN	GA	c	1	77	65	42	30,243	44,845	—	—	—	5,192	4,302	83	3,128	506	668	161	729
NEWTON	KS	c	1	37	33	42	29,371	38,554	y	39,178	2	2,641	2,240	85	1,692	225	323	—	401
NEWTON	NC	c	1	—	—	42	—	—	—	—	—	—	—	—	—	—	—	—	—
NEWTOWN TOWNSHIP	PA	tp	1	32	28	40	26,512	72,069	n	—	—	6,289	3,332	53	2,445	384	503	85	2,872
NILES	MI	c	1	58	23	40	30,383	50,525	y	51,461	5	—	—	—	—	146	373	33	378
NIXA	MO	c	1	27	23	40	29,661	39,055	y	—	—	1,542	1,211	79	889	132	190	111	220
NORCO	CA	c	5	—	—	—	—	—	—	—	—	—	—	—	—	—	—	—	—
NORFOLK	MA	t	1	17	17	other	—	56,230	y	—	—	1,599	—	—	1,388	—	71	42	98
NORFOLK	NE	c	1	61	40	40	31,848	44,256	n	—	—	4,222	3,511	83	2,606	372	532	321	390
NORTH AUGUSTA	SC	c	4	68	57	other	38,308		n	—	—	4,606	3,825	83	2,941	518	366	270	512
NORTH HAVEN	CT	t	1	55	45	40	44,886	53,268	y	53,743	5	5,810	5,438	94	3,455	906	1,077	50	322
NORTH MANKATO	MN	c	1	14	12	42	42,420	52,260	y	—	—	1,310	1,009	77	811	93	104	83	218
NORTH MYRTLE BEACH	SC	c	4	106	81	42	33,961	50,942	y	53,489	5	9,269	5,851	63	4,398	763	690	2,261	1,158
NORTH PLAINFIELD	NJ	b	1	53	47	40	34,266	82,740	y	87,704	15	6,017	—	—	4,537	—	765	—	85
NORTH READING	MA	t	1	31	30	40	37,116	43,630	y	—	5	—	—	—	2,762	—	—	—	416
NORTH ST. PAUL	MN	c	1	16	15	42	47,918	63,890	n	—	—	1,796	1,527	85	1,181	125	221	60	209
NORTH STRABANE	PA	tp	1	21	21	40	49,483	49,483	y	51,957	2	—	—	—	—	175	288	58	107
NORTON SHORES	MI	c	1	30	28	42	38,859	49,129	y	50,129	23	3,274	2,749	84	1,858	606	284	229	296
OCONOMOWOC	WI	c	1	21	21	40	45,469	57,138	n	—	—	2,502	2,222	89	1,517	336	369	52	228
OLDSMAR	FL	c	—	—	—	—	—	—	—	—	—	—	—	—	—	—	—	—	—
ONALASKA	WI	c	1	27	25	other	41,388	46,213	y	48,524	10	—	—	—	1,480	—	—	—	—
ORANGE	TX	c	1	56	42	42	38,938	48,589	y	49,789	1	4,154	3,828	92	2,631	661	535	185	141
OSKALOOSA	IA	c	1	18	16	40	30,149	38,521	y	39,721	6	1,303	1,155	89	767	207	181	30	118
OSSINING	NY	v	1	66	57	40	40,611	78,151	y	79,451	5	9,265	8,632	93	6,170	1,355	1,106	253	380
OSWEGO	IL	v	1	64	46	40	44,000	69,105	n	—	—	5,257	—	—	3,295	—	594	334	606
OSWEGO	NY	c	1	—	—	40	—	—	—	—	—	—	—	—	—	—	—	—	—
OTTAWA	KS	c	1	28	25	40	32,801	45,926	—	—	—	—	2,091	—	1,479	287	325	—	—
OTTUMWA	IA	c	1	35	35	40	37,773	42,328	y	55,890	5	3,138	2,794	89	1,958	454	382	95	250
OVERLAND	MO	c	1	42	42	40	37,310	48,972	n	—	—	—	—	—	—	—	—	—	—
OWATONNA	MN	c	1	34	32	40	45,062	53,004	n	—	—	3,529	2,662	75	2,094	240	328	211	656
OXFORD	MI	tp	5	—	—	—	—	—	—	—	—	—	—	—	—	—	—	—	—
OXFORD	MS	c	1	63	53	—	28,241	39,092	y	—	3	—	—	—	—	—	—	—	—
OXFORD	OH	c	1	39	26	40	45,168	53,139	y	54,239	5	2,853	2,646	93	1,975	507	163	—	208
OZARK	AL	c	1	38	31	40	20,728	30,440	y	29,193	10	2,249	1,723	77	1,358	158	207	43	482
PAINESVILLE	OH	c	1	37	37	40	43,837	55,948	y	58,648	10	4,134	—	—	2,600	—	304	126	661
PALATKA	FL	c	1	52	39	40	27,772	41,032	y	43,084	10	3,573	2,554	71	1,964	379	210	38	982
PALISADES PARK	NJ	b	1	41	33	40	28,980	97,574	y	114,428	20	5,721	—	—	3,970	—	337	533	310
PALMER	PA	tp	1	34	31	40	49,722	57,936	y	61,412	5	—	—	—	—	—	—	—	—
PALMETTO	FL	c	3	—	34	42	33,236	49,864	y	51,360	14	3,624	2,777	77	2,040	356	380	392	454
PAPILLION	NE	c	1	39	35	40	36,442	52,707	y	54,815	6	3,165	2,617	83	2,021	307	289	45	503
PARK FOREST	IL	v	1	51	34	40	42,049	63,785	n	—	—	5,025	4,337	86	3,319	645	373	149	539
PARKER	CO	t	1	76	55	40	42,000	62,400	n	—	—	7,533	5,628	75	4,700	475	453	602	1,302
PARKLAND	FL	c	5	—	—	—	—	—	—	—	—	—	—	—	—	—	—	—	—
PARLIER	CA	c	1	16	13	40	35,360	77,000	n	—	—	1,500	—	—	1,300	—	160	200	—
PARSONS	KS	c	1	31	24	42	30,807	35,174	n	—	—	—	—	—	995	—	143	—	—
PATCHOGUE	NY	v	—	—	—	—	—	—	—	—	—	—	—	—	—	—	—	—	—
PATTERSON	CA	c	5	—	—	40	—	—	—	—	—	—	—	—	—	—	—	—	—
PATTON	PA	tp	1	17	—	40	42,078	59,571	y	63,262	6	1,717	1,431	83	1,058	183	189	54	231
PAYSON	AZ	t	1	30	16	40	40,641	60,961	n	—	—	—	—	—	—	—	—	—	—
PENDLETON	OR	c	1	28	27	42	38,388	48,576	y	51,004	15	3,189	2,199	69	1,493	428	277	32	958
PENN	PA	tp	1	24	22	40	38,236	57,218	y	62,940	6	1,867	—	—	1,354	—	—	2	386
PEQUANNOCK	NJ	tp	1	35	30	40	38,582	91,985	n	—	—	4,211	3,963	94	2,991	269	703	46	203
PERRYSBURG	OH	c	1	42	33	40	41,475	53,060	y	—	10	3,252	—	—	2,345	—	456	—	480
PEWAUKEE	WI	c	1	30	23	40	44,512	57,408	n	—	—	2,706	2,361	87	1,812	274	274	71	274
PFLUGERVILLE	TX	c	3	65	34	40	—	—	y	—	1	11,526	4,688	41	3,585	680	422	6,309	529
PHOENIXVILLE	PA	b	1	25	—	40	47,559	59,448	n	—	—	2,802	2,681	96	1,927	144	609	25	96
PIEDMONT	CA	c	1	31	19	40	63,384	76,476	n	—	—	—	—	—	—	661	267	—	—
PINECREST	FL	v	1	75	54	40	—	—	—	—	—	3,271	—	—	—	881	979	287	638
PITTSBURG	KS	c	1	53	41	40	25,168	44,637	n	—	—	2,982	2,379	80	2,001	151	226	106	497
PLAINSBORO	NJ	tp	1	41	32	40	45,893	81,302	y	84,852	7	4,086	—	—	3,611	—	—	1	213
PLAINVIEW	TX	c	1	43	36	40	29,515	34,237	y	35,437	1	2,693	2,064	77	1,543	289	232	297	332
PLEASANT GROVE	UT	c	1	38	32	40	34,304	49,683	y	62,046	—	2,967	2,311	78	1,508	445	358	454	202

Table 3/16 continued **POLICE DEPARTMENT PERSONNEL, SALARIES, AND EXPENDITURES FOR CITIES 10,000 AND OVER: 2007**

City	State	Type	Service provision	Full-time paid personnel	Full-time uniformed personnel	Duty hours per week	Minimum base salary ($)	Maximum base salary ($)	Longevity pay	Maximum salary with longevity ($)	Years of service for longevity	Total expenditures (A) ($)	Total personnel expenditures (B) ($)	(B) as % of (A)	Salaries and wages (C) ($)	City contribution to retirement and social security (D) ($)	City contribution to insurance (E) ($)	Capital outlay (F) ($)	All other (G) ($)
10,000–24,999 continued																			
PLEASANT PRAIRIE	WI	v	1	29	27	40	44,990	56,222	n	—	—	2,722	2,385	88	1,661	377	346	107	230
POINT PLEASANT	NJ	b	1	60	41	40	49,966	85,867	y	94,454	7	4,910	4,752	97	3,771	627	353	158	—
POQUOSON	VA	c	3	27	22	40	30,065	41,207	n	—	—	1,953	1,406	72	1,192	196	18	64	482
PORT LAVACA	TX	c	3	25	19	42	28,421	38,452	y	39,652	1	1,331	1,072	81	880	117	74	83	175
PORTLAND	TX	c	4	43	34	40	33,377	35,856	y	37,056	1	—	—	—	—	234	247	72	539
PORTSMOUTH	NH	c	1	91	68	40	39,939	53,778	y	54,831	5	7,450	6,818	92	5,075	602	1,140	135	498
POWDER SPRINGS	GA	c	1	34	27	40	33,042	51,215	n	—	—	2,899	2,121	73	1,711	156	253	272	506
PRATTVILLE	AL	c	1	109	78	40	—	—	n	—	—	5,435	4,565	84	3,555	543	466	—	869
PRESCOTT VALLEY	AZ	t	3	75	60	40	41,583	58,216	n	—	—	—	—	—	—	—	—	—	—
PRINCETON	NJ	b	1	45	35	40	48,223	86,710	y	91,046	5	4,444	—	—	3,326	—	606	79	228
PRIOR LAKE	MN	c	1	26	23	40	43,440	60,492	y	65,936	4	2,603	2,322	89	1,867	216	238	77	203
PROSPECT HEIGHTS	IL	c	1	29	24	40	—	—	y	—	—	3,532	2,793	79	2,412	72	308	375	364
PULLMAN	WA	c	1	39	28	40	46,812	63,372	n	—	—	3,940	—	—	2,193	—	—	—	786
RAMSEY	MN	c	1	27	22	40	40,814	58,723	y	64,008	16	2,394	1,923	80	1,570	187	165	195	276
RANTOUL	IL	v	—	—	—	—	—	—	—	—	—	—	—	—	—	—	—	—	—
RAVENNA	OH	c	1	44	25	40	39,790	50,793	y	—	5	3,543	—	—	1,754	—	359	101	1,009
RAYMORE	MO	c	1	41	2	42	27,839	50,085	n	—	—	2,599	—	—	1,713	—	169	—	315
RED BANK	TN	c	3	24	22	40	30,760	30,760	n	—	—	1,315	—	—	820	135	—	43	317
RED BLUFF	CA	c	3	26	19	40	—	—	n	—	—	5,014	4,314	86	3,500	617	197	78	622
RED WING	MN	c	1	33	27	40	46,738	57,034	y	—	—	2,969	2,446	82	1,847	213	385	75	449
RICHMOND	TX	t	1	40	31	40	32,448	49,892	y	—	1	—	—	—	—	—	—	—	—
RINGWOOD	NJ	b	1	26	21	40	31,633	86,058	y	94,664	5	—	—	—	2,433	218	—	—	135
RIPON	CA	c	3	37	25	40	50,408	61,271	n	—	—	5,457	3,226	59	2,108	685	431	534	1,698
RIVER FALLS	WI	c	1	24	22	40	42,141	51,771	n	—	—	2,295	1,976	86	1,388	289	298	49	270
RIVER FOREST	IL	v	1	33	30	40	46,783	69,220	—	—	—	3,456	3,075	89	2,168	673	234	115	266
RIVERBANK	CA	c	5	—	—	other	—	—	—	—	—	—	—	—	—	—	—	—	—
RIVERSIDE	OH	c	1	35	34	40	43,638	51,480	y	52,312	5	3,277	—	—	1,573	—	294	347	753
RIVERVIEW	MI	c	1	31	—	40	—	—	—	—	—	3,164	2,967	94	2,166	490	311	—	197
ROANOKE RAPIDS	NC	c	1	44	41	42	27,536	40,899	y	41,599	2	2,714	2,269	84	1,871	256	141	180	265
ROBSTOWN	TX	c	3	36	28	40	27,360	34,596	y	35,796	1	1,672	1,396	83	1,127	158	110	—	276
ROCK SPRINGS	WY	c	1	64	43	40	41,637	51,999	n	—	—	5,543	4,848	87	3,514	663	670	200	496
ROCKLEDGE	FL	c	1	64	42	42	30,000	46,000	y	46,800	5	4,352	—	—	3,788	—	—	177	387
ROCKWALL	TX	c	1	82	64	40	45,600	55,400	y	—	1	—	—	—	—	—	—	—	—
ROLLA	MO	c	1	33	29	48	26,677	34,808	n	—	—	2,391	1,608	67	1,223	157	228	130	653
ROLLING MEADOWS	IL	c	1	80	54	40	54,915	78,450	y	80,803	10	—	—	—	—	—	—	—	—
ROSEBURG	OR	c	3	42	37	40	39,984	53,604	n	—	—	4,189	3,524	84	2,235	731	558	14	651
ROSENBERG	TX	c	1	83	61	40	34,320	49,774	y	51,267	1	5,204	4,460	86	3,375	644	441	10	734
ROXBURY	NJ	tp	1	48	—	40	39,294	82,609	y	—	5	5,238	—	—	4,163	—	794	—	232
SAGINAW	TX	c	1	40	32	42	36,476	54,716	y	—	1	2,893	2,202	76	1,806	183	213	564	127
SALEM	OH	c	3	24	23	40	26,021	37,898	y	45,573	5	1,871	—	—	1,121	—	342	—	86
SALISBURY	MD	c	1	114	88	42	33,122	52,171	n	—	—	8,045	6,740	84	4,698	1,265	776	183	1,122
SAN ANSELMO	CA	c	1	23	16	40	56,064	68,148	y	71,555	2	3,482	3,160	91	2,102	844	213	74	248
SAN MARINO	CA	c	1	39	26	40	56,556	65,712	n	—	—	4,225	—	—	2,645	—	230	163	413
SANFORD	NC	c	1	94	77	42	31,457	46,698	y	—	5	6,321	5,139	81	3,997	485	657	84	1,098
SAPULPA	OK	c	1	60	48	40	24,000	31,800	n	—	—	7,106	3,448	49	2,524	302	622	3,373	285
SAUK VILLAGE	IL	v	1	—	—	40	43,703	60,144	n	—	—	2,804	—	—	1,818	—	451	83	292
SCARSDALE	NY	v	1	54	43	other	40,000	81,631	y	—	5	6,906	6,346	92	4,730	1,018	597	299	261
SCHERERVILLE	IN	t	1	49	49	40	39,417	49,098	y	50,898	3	4,871	4,305	88	3,081	609	614	—	566
SCHERTZ	TX	c	3	87	39	40	35,472	46,804	y	—	1	—	—	—	—	310	185	65	291
SCIO	MI	tp	—	—	—	—	—	—	—	—	—	—	—	—	—	—	—	—	—
SCOTCH PLAINS	NJ	tp	1	52	45	42	32,656	82,835	y	91,119	23	4,674	—	—	4,256	—	—	—	418
SCOTTS VALLEY	CA	c	3	28	17	42	44,040	59,016	n	—	—	2,355	2,027	86	1,359	354	314	98	230
SEAL BEACH	CA	c	3	38	29	40	60,408	73,416	y	80,952	10	6,412	5,205	81	3,333	1,531	340	—	1,207
SEBASTIAN	FL	c	3	51	38	40	33,505	55,379	y	68,916	10	4,066	3,378	83	2,424	575	378	255	433
SEDALIA	MO	c	3	55	43	40	26,568	32,192	n	—	—	3,004	2,333	78	1,884	186	263	204	467
SEDONA	AZ	c	1	40	31	other	37,653	54,295	n	—	—	2,578	2,032	79	1,778	98	156	247	299
SEEKONK	MA	t	1	34	32	40	41,949	47,284	y	—	20	3,127	2,921	93	2,196	196	528	31	176
SEGUIN	TX	c	3	60	47	40	35,332	48,736	y	49,936	1	4,011	3,293	82	2,540	450	303	409	309
SELMA	CA	c	3	49	34	40	40,104	48,732	n	—	—	—	—	—	—	478	337	—	906
SEMINOLE	FL	c	5	—	—	—	—	—	—	—	—	—	—	—	—	—	—	—	—
SIDNEY	OH	c	1	52	39	40	41,330	51,043	y	53,595	5	5,073	—	—	3,136	—	521	—	817
SIKESTON	MO	c	4	79	70	other	27,891	33,760	n	—	—	5,170	4,148	80	3,039	459	650	166	855
SILOAM SPRINGS	AR	c	1	46	27	42	28,737	43,545	y	43,665	2	2,622	1,911	73	1,484	278	149	123	588
SIMPSONVILLE	SC	c	1	48	38	42	28,138	42,208	y	—	1	—	—	—	—	—	—	—	—
SNELLVILLE	GA	c	1	—	53	40	33,500	59,968	y	60,968	20	—	—	—	—	—	—	—	—
SNYDER	TX	c	1	20	18	40	30,108	31,932	y	33,132	1	1,203	974	81	743	143	88	78	151
SODDY—DAISY	TN	c	1	29	24	40	32,051	44,883	y	—	—	1,820	1,518	83	1,090	248	180	81	221
SOMERSET	MA	t	1	32	31	40	34,357	42,946	y	44,246	5	2,085	—	—	1,945	—	—	28	139
SOMERSWORTH	NH	c	1	31	22	40	35,568	44,845	y	45,677	5	2,339	2,132	91	1,515	148	469	—	207
SOUTH CHARLESTON	WV	c	1	38	27	40	26,000	32,100	n	—	—	1,920	1,454	76	1,376	13	64	94	372
SOUTH ELGIN	IL	v	1	38	24	40	43,576	62,171	n	—	—	4,060	3,500	86	2,496	609	395	69	491
SOUTH EUCLID	OH	c	1	50	11	40	46,278	65,888	y	—	20	—	—	—	—	—	—	—	—
SOUTH LAKE TAHOE	CA	c	1	60	40	42	48,348	58,767	y	61,118	15	6,969	—	—	3,852	—	1,245	1,255	617

Table 3/16 continued   POLICE DEPARTMENT PERSONNEL, SALARIES, AND EXPENDITURES FOR CITIES 10,000 AND OVER: 2007

City	State	Type	Service provision	Full-time paid personnel	Full-time uniformed personnel	Duty hours per week	Minimum base salary ($)	Maximum base salary ($)	Longevity pay	Maximum salary with longevity ($)	Years of service for longevity	Total expenditures (A) ($)	Total personnel expenditures (B) ($)	(B) as % of (A)	Salaries and wages (C) ($)	City contribution to retirement and social security (D) ($)	City contribution to insurance (E) ($)	Capital outlay (F) ($)	All other (G) ($)
10,000–24,999 continued																			
SOUTH LYON	MI	c	1	—	—	other	—	—	—	—	—	—	—	—	—	—	—	—	—
SOUTH SALT LAKE	UT	c	1	72	56	40	33,348	49,368	n	—	—	5,758	4,566	79	3,172	717	676	379	814
SOUTH SIOUX CITY	NE	c	1	36	28	40	36,254	47,237	y	48,797	10	2,286	1,899	83	1,446	198	254	106	281
SOUTH ST. PAUL	MN	c	1	—	26	42	—	—	y	—	—	—	—	—	—	—	—	—	—
SOUTHLAKE	TX	c	4	—	—	40	44,774	58,420	y	46,274	1	—	—	—	—	—	—	—	—
SPARTA	NJ	tp	1	38	38	42	43,472	105,692	y	127,887	6	5,419	5,142	95	3,800	742	598	131	146
SPEEDWAY	IN	t	3	46	34	40	38,685	45,648	y	47,323	1	3,060	2,718	89	2,065	343	310	—	342
SPENCER	IA	c	1	26	18	42	38,053	45,671	y	46,571	10	1,467	—	—	1,015	296	—	8	148
SPRINGBORO	OH	c	1	28	22	40	37,261	50,357	n	—	—	—	—	—	1,617	—	334	120	—
SPRINGDALE	OH	c	1	44	38	other	50,935	61,903	y	63,653	5	4,529	—	—	2,586	—	69	137	1,237
SPRINGETTSBURY	PA	tp	1	34	29	40	35,549	61,392	y	64,442	5	3,440	2,918	85	2,082	558	278	317	204
SPRINGFIELD	TN	c	1	53	38	42	27,290	37,253	y	—	5	3,151	2,696	86	1,959	323	413	157	298
SPRINGVILLE	UT	c	—	—	9	40	33,413	46,425	n	—	—	2,965	2,125	72	1,361	399	365	368	472
ST. ANN	MO	c	1	53	36	40	38,478	—	y	—	5	—	—	—	—	—	—	—	—
ST. AUGUSTINE	FL	c	1	59	46	40	35,218	51,916	y	—	—	4,674	3,830	82	2,777	632	419	224	621
ST. MARYS	GA	c	1	39	31	42	27,933	39,570	n	—	—	2,218	1,648	74	1,249	131	268	99	471
ST. MARYS	PA	c	1	15	15	40	39,937	46,985	y	49,452	3	1,140	924	81	672	100	151	—	216
STAFFORD	CT	t	1	6	—	40	—	—	y	—	5	—	—	—	—	—	—	—	—
STAFFORD	NJ	tp	1	77	55	40	40,515	88,841	y	99,501	4	8,734	8,469	97	7,492	894	82	—	265
STEPHENVILLE	TX	c	3	45	32	other	32,784	37,315	y	—	1	2,639	2,180	83	1,633	333	214	136	323
STERLING	CO	c	1	18	15	other	32,231	43,042	y	—	—	1,418	1,204	85	844	79	280	112	102
STERLING	IL	c	1	46	29	40	33,006	48,373	n	—	—	2,566	—	—	2,039	—	—	145	382
STONEHAM	MA	t	1	44	36	other	39,846	50,533	n	—	—	—	—	—	3,257	—	450	103	275
STORM LAKE	IA	c	4	21	17	42	30,488	37,586	y	—	3	—	—	—	—	—	—	—	—
STREETSBORO	OH	c	1	—	24	40	51,520	53,165	n	—	—	4,214	—	—	1,836	—	161	294	1,939
STRUTHERS	OH	c	3	15	—	40	40,188	40,188	y	—	25	1,048	—	—	1,048	—	—	—	—
SUDBURY	MA	t	1	32	26	other	41,446	45,255	y	45,755	7	2,316	—	—	2,050	—	—	112	154
SUFFERN	NY	v	1	27	—	40	42,371	92,887	y	—	3	4,166	—	—	2,985	—	380	378	238
SUGAR HILL	GA	c	7	—	—	other	—	—	—	—	—	172	—	—	159	—	—	—	—
SULPHUR	LA	c	1	—	68	40	28,344	—	y	—	1	3,958	—	—	2,296	—	371	284	1,007
SUN PRAIRIE	WI	c	1	70	43	other	39,619	46,376	y	46,851	5	—	—	—	—	195	135	20	187
SUNNYSIDE	WA	c	1	—	—	48	45,444	55,236	y	53,795	20	—	—	—	—	—	—	—	—
SUSANVILLE	CA	c	3	18	—	40	—	—	—	—	—	—	—	—	—	—	—	—	—
SWAMPSCOTT	MA	t	1	36	34	40	35,510	46,015	y	47,970	5	1,971	—	—	1,765	—	—	65	141
SYCAMORE	IL	c	1	31	28	40	41,860	58,362	y	59,612	5	2,552	—	—	1,837	23	—	120	692
SYLACAUGA	AL	c	1	54	42	42	26,000	42,000	y	—	—	—	—	—	—	—	—	—	—
TAKOMA PARK	MD	c	1	65	38	40	39,981	53,175	n	—	—	5,859	4,278	73	3,049	634	595	634	947
TARBORO	NC	t	1	34	28	42	27,358	43,479	y	—	5	2,057	1,760	86	1,344	273	143	232	64
TEMPLE TERRACE	FL	c	1	71	50	42	39,638	62,219	y	—	3	6,296	5,318	84	3,916	851	551	291	687
TERRELL	TX	c	1	51	35	40	36,948	51,980	y	53,800	25	3,880	3,456	89	2,336	803	316	349	75
THIBODAUX	LA	c	1	63	50	42	25,563	40,518	n	—	—	3,263	2,412	74	1,738	319	355	164	687
THOMASVILLE	GA	c	1	66	66	42	23,915	34,420	n	—	—	4,377	3,151	72	2,548	347	255	140	1,086
TIFFIN	OH	c	1	42	29	40	37,170	46,966	y	51,663	4	3,047	—	—	2,011	—	467	62	221
TIFTON	GA	c	1	57	44	other	23,483	35,214	n	—	—	3,097	2,525	82	1,836	377	311	18	555
TINTON FALLS	NJ	b	1	43	42	40	28,137	76,350	y	—	6	5,006	4,454	89	3,770	562	121	100	452
TIVERTON	RI	t	1	40	28	other	36,923	44,482	y	47,596	5	—	—	—	—	—	—	—	—
TONAWANDA	NY	v	1	33	28	40	42,812	52,774	y	54,474	5	—	—	—	2,219	—	—	—	—
TRAVERSE CITY	MI	c	1	35	32	40	37,565	42,702	y	45,698	10	3,585	2,738	76	1,931	513	293	—	847
TROUTDALE	OR	c	1	24	22	40	44,100	58,173	y	60,381	5	2,658	2,037	77	1,395	333	309	83	538
TROY	AL	c	1	—	—	42	—	—	—	—	—	—	—	—	—	—	—	—	—
TROY	OH	c	3	45	41	40	40,174	55,617	y	61,179	5	4,431	4,023	91	2,847	718	457	40	368
TUKWILA	WA	c	1	84	68	40	54,840	66,840	y	—	—	11,127	8,247	74	6,144	734	1,368	74	2,807
TULLAHOMA	TN	c	1	43	38	40	32,350	32,350	y	32,550	5	—	—	—	—	157	455	43	425
TWENTYNINE PALMS	CA	c	5	—	—	—	—	—	—	—	—	—	—	—	—	—	—	—	—
UNIVERSAL CITY	TX	c	1	38	29	40	32,367	45,733	y	—	1	2,079	—	—	1,452	210	—	162	255
UNIVERSITY HEIGHTS	OH	c	3	—	29	40	55,469	61,411	y	65,710	4	4,309	—	—	3,066	—	439	516	368
UNIVERSITY PARK	TX	c	1	49	37	40	49,164	62,748	y	63,948	1	5,146	4,426	86	3,282	709	434	78	641
UPPER ALLEN	PA	tp	1	20	18	40	36,005	49,655	y	—	—	1,991	1,685	85	1,202	267	216	92	214
UPPER GWYNEDD	PA	tp	1	23	20	42	38,234	77,164	y	83,463	5	2,540	2,243	88	1,747	80	416	59	238
UPPER PROVIDENCE	PA	tp	1	23	21	40	50,923	63,654	y	66,154	6	3,242	2,397	74	1,574	324	498	162	684
UPPER ST. CLAIR	PA	tp	1	34	28	40	40,976	66,310	y	70,010	4	4,029	3,668	91	2,585	514	568	124	237
URBANA	OH	c	1	—	22	40	34,442	53,380	n	—	—	2,652	—	—	1,344	—	257	223	262
UVALDE	TX	c	1	50	29	40	30,950	38,064	y	38,116	1	—	—	—	—	448	57	—	247
VAN WERT	OH	c	1	31	23	40	32,386	41,434	y	42,684	5	2,440	—	—	1,429	—	320	210	241
VERNON	NJ	tp	1	35	34	40	54,087	78,596	y	88,301	5	4,552	4,112	90	3,100	597	415	116	324
VERO BEACH	FL	c	1	—	—	40	—	—	—	—	—	6,582	5,612	85	4,354	637	620	175	794
VERONA	NJ	tp	1	38	31	40	53,648	84,980	y	93,478	5	3,558	—	—	2,939	—	—	—	156
VESTAVIA HILLS	AL	c	1	69	67	40	32,885	50,898	y	—	6	4,754	—	—	3,423	—	525	61	492
VIENNA	VA	t	1	—	—	42	—	—	y	—	—	—	—	—	—	—	—	—	—
VIENNA	WV	c	1	—	22	40	—	—	y	—	1	1,494	1,194	80	869	98	226	35	265
VILLA PARK	IL	v	1	53	39	40	52,115	69,662	y	70,312	7	5,801	—	—	3,787	—	589	76	692
WALKER	MI	c	1	46	37	40	37,583	56,096	y	57,596	5	4,201	3,714	88	2,687	572	455	134	353
WALPOLE	MA	t	1	45	40	40	39,523	—	y	59,498	5	3,900	—	—	3,124	—	—	427	314

Table 3/16 continued

POLICE DEPARTMENT PERSONNEL, SALARIES, AND EXPENDITURES FOR CITIES 10,000 AND OVER: 2007

City	State	Type	Service provision	Full-time paid personnel	Full-time uniformed personnel	Duty hours per week	Minimum base salary ($)	Maximum base salary ($)	Longevity pay	Maximum salary with longevity ($)	Years of service for longevity	Total expenditures (A) ($)	Total personnel expenditures (B) ($)	(B) as % of (A)	Salaries and wages (C) ($)	City contribution to retirement and social security (D) ($)	City contribution to insurance (E) ($)	Capital outlay (F) ($)	All other (G) ($)
10,000–24,999 continued																			
WANTAGE	NJ	tp	—	—	—	—	—	—	—	—	—	—	—	—	—	—	—	—	—
WARREN	PA	c	1	18	14	40	30,175	35,500	y	36,700	5	1,210	—	—	782	—	268	22	124
WARREN	RI	t	1	29	23	40	34,644	44,128	y	55,949	5	1,859	—	—	1,631	—	—	50	178
WARRENSBURG	MO	c	1	37	30	40	29,201	44,363	y	—	5	1,991	1,717	86	1,313	201	202	188	87
WARRENSVILLE HEIGHTS	OH	c	3	—	47	40	38,410	55,481	y	56,035	1	4,677	—	—	2,783	—	—	24	739
WARRENVILLE	IL	c	1	37	30	40	44,449	64,929	n	—	—	39,762	—	—	2,458	586	—	84	483
WARRINGTON	PA	tp	1	31	28	42	35,828	66,580	y	69,580	5	3,823	3,470	91	2,262	533	674	78	276
WARSAW	IN	c	1	42	34	40	35,592	39,809	y	47,770	1	3,422	2,856	83	2,053	369	434	106	460
WARWICK	PA	tp	1	21	19	40	39,285	65,164	y	—	4	2,509	2,235	89	1,569	248	417	104	170
WASHINGTON	IL	c	1	23	16	40	35,535	50,336	n	—	—	2,447	1,926	79	1,364	216	346	131	390
WASHINGTON	IN	c	1	27	18	40	31,179	31,720	y	32,720	1	—	—	—	—	149	134	47	94
WASHINGTON (MORRIS)	NJ	tp	1	35	32	40	42,424	79,457	y	81,457	5	3,930	3,773	96	2,930	441	401	34	123
WATAUGA	TX	c	4	44	43	42	37,570	48,395	y	49,835	1	3,284	2,663	81	2,168	255	240	247	373
WATERVILLE	ME	c	1	27	27	42	30,947	40,993	y	43,093	7	—	—	—	—	—	—	—	—
WAXAHACHIE	TX	c	1	64	48	40	39,457	48,865	y	—	1	—	—	—	2,755	—	360	325	—
WAYNESBORO	VA	c	3	59	50	40	28,962	42,193	n	—	—	3,612	2,996	83	2,206	398	392	—	616
WEATHERFORD	TX	c	3	82	57	40	39,437	55,212	y	56,412	1	5,794	4,888	84	3,631	775	481	200	706
WEBSTER GROVES	MO	c	1	—	44	40	—	—	n	—	—	—	—	—	—	—	—	—	—
WEIRTON	WV	c	1	40	37	40	25,646	27,539	y	—	0	2,841	—	—	1,614	—	557	104	299
WEST BRADFORD	PA	tp	—	—	—	—	—	—	—	—	—	—	—	—	—	—	—	—	—
WEST CARROLLTON	OH	c	1	32	25	40	47,382	58,157	n	—	—	4,180	—	—	2,005	—	278	1,025	512
WEST CHESTER	PA	b	1	51	46	40	44,447	64,218	y	77,835	5	4,496	—	—	3,829	—	—	249	418
WEST COLUMBIA	SC	c	1	67	48	42	29,332	85,171	n	—	—	4,425	3,488	79	2,440	441	607	215	722
WEST LAMPETER	PA	tp	1	15	—	40	40,150	53,533	y	56,533	5	1,299	1,111	86	838	95	177	75	114
WEST MANCHESTER	PA	tp	1	29	26	40	43,700	61,347	y	67,482	4	1,981	—	—	1,839	—	—	81	142
WEST NORRITON	PA	tp	1	32	27	42	43,584	67,849	y	—	3	4,153	3,862	93	2,309	752	801	44	247
WEST PLAINS	MO	c	4	27	23	other	22,152	38,616	n	—	—	1,451	1,159	80	889	153	116	57	236
WEST WHITELAND	PA	tp	1	31	29	42	47,542	71,314	y	77,019	5	3,829	3,325	87	2,457	457	410	233	271
WEST WINDSOR	NJ	tp	1	58	46	40	44,090	83,495	y	86,527	6	6,899	6,423	93	4,865	716	842	174	302
WESTBOROUGH	MA	t	1	34	27	40	44,096	49,968	y	56,204	25	2,838	2,665	94	2,267	198	199	93	81
WESTCHESTER	IL	v	1	48	35	40	39,514	64,491	y	—	5	4,154	—	—	3,298	—	—	64	392
WESTERLY	RI	t	—	62	50	40	34,675	89,321	n	—	—	—	—	—	3,702	—	—	—	—
WESTMINSTER	MD	c	1	58	43	40	—	30,080	y	60,680	17	4,129	3,099	75	1,916	614	569	336	694
WESTON	CT	t	1	16	15	40	49,203	69,770	y	71,265	5	2,141	1,943	91	1,453	261	228	49	149
WESTON	MA	t	1	30	25	other	38,584	50,730	y	51,930	5	2,603	—	—	2,312	—	—	40	251
WESTTOWN	PA	tp	1	—	—	40	—	—	—	—	—	—	—	—	—	—	—	—	—
WHITEFISH BAY	WI	v	1	27	24	42	44,504	59,435	y	59,735	5	2,551	2,316	91	1,692	347	276	68	167
WHITEHALL	PA	b	1	20	20	40	48,514	69,305	y	71,384	5	2,197	—	—	1,518	—	256	49	360
WHITEMARSH	PA	tp	1	38	31	40	51,913	71,740	y	—	5	3,824	—	—	2,537	—	554	166	532
WHITPAIN	PA	tp	1	36	29	40	46,125	74,033	y	81,000	5	3,988	3,530	89	2,497	327	705	45	413
WILBRAHAM	MA	t	1	26	25	other	41,997	44,770	y	46,785	10	1,687	—	—	1,493	—	—	45	150
WILLIAMSBURG	VA	c	3	53	35	40	31,512	53,100	n	—	—	3,952	2,946	75	2,220	446	279	517	489
WILLOUGHBY	OH	c	1	59	44	40	47,320	66,331	n	—	—	6,772	—	—	4,265	—	874	447	429
WILLOWICK	OH	c	1	35	25	40	46,675	63,294	y	65,291	5	2,998	—	—	2,148	—	328	—	222
WILSONVILLE	OR	c	5	—	—	40	—	—	—	—	—	—	—	—	—	—	—	—	—
WINCHESTER	KY	c	1	38	34	40	25,888	42,073	y	42,073	4	3,039	2,560	84	1,698	523	338	99	381
WINDHAM	ME	t	1	27	26	40	35,360	44,113	y	45,113	12	1,353	—	—	1,353	—	—	115	78
WINDHAM	NH	t	1	—	18	40	40,188	48,473	n	—	—	2,302	2,098	91	1,639	162	296	45	159
WINDSOR	CA	t	5	—	—	40	—	—	—	—	—	—	—	—	—	—	—	—	—
WINDSOR	PA	tp	7	49	49	—	—	—	—	—	—	—	—	—	—	—	—	—	—
WIXOM	MI	c	1	25	21	40	37,141	59,991	y	62,091	15	2,920	—	—	1,745	—	—	144	405
WOOD DALE	IL	c	1	49	—	40	50,000	72,640	y	73,590	15	—	—	—	—	—	—	—	—
WOOD RIVER	IL	c	1	25	19	42	40,019	48,204	y	51,337	2	2,146	1,496	70	1,232	257	7	218	432
WOODHAVEN	MI	c	1	35	31	40	38,189	69,389	n	—	—	—	—	—	—	—	—	—	—
WOODSTOCK	GA	c	1	49	43	other	31,938	51,057	n	—	—	3,297	2,509	76	1,993	347	169	248	540
WOODSTOCK	IL	c	1	52	38	40	—	—	—	—	—	414	—	—	3,200	—	—	—	556
WOODWARD	OK	c	3	36	26	40	30,215	39,023	y	—	1	—	—	—	—	107	74	17	25
WORTH	IL	v	1	26	24	40	39,114	61,480	y	61,866	20	2,398	—	—	1,650	—	—	63	483
WORTHINGTON	OH	c	1	48	34	40	41,273	63,511	n	—	—	4,875	—	—	3,184	—	677	222	219
WYCKOFF	NJ	tp	1	34	26	40	46,919	99,908	y	109,899	5	4,261	4,091	96	3,083	475	532	8	162
XENIA	OH	c	1	52	45	40	40,165	55,286	n	—	—	5,115	—	—	3,037	—	589	246	645
YANKTON	SD	c	1	26	26	40	31,617	42,775	y	—	5	2,116	1,816	86	1,408	208	199	79	221
YARMOUTH	MA	t	3	70	59	40	40,206	65,832	y	66,782	5	5,485	—	—	4,810	—	240	186	197
YAZOO CITY	MS	c	1	25	—	40	24,919	30,685	n	—	—	2,767	1,952	71	1,408	381	162	170	645
YPSILANTI	MI	c	1	50	40	42	38,944	58,246	n	—	—	4,355	3,943	91	2,512	1,066	364	320	92
YUCCA VALLEY	CA	t	5	—	—	40	—	—	—	—	—	—	—	—	—	—	—	—	—
YUKON	OK	c	1	58	37	40	31,282	47,151	y	48,339	4	—	—	—	—	—	—	—	—
ZEPHYRHILLS	FL	c	1	49	33	42	35,485	53,227	n	—	—	3,191	2,598	81	1,843	438	316	124	468
ZION	IL	c	1	69	52	40	45,810	70,063	y	71,063	20	5,981	—	—	3,849	—	—	261	1,771

Table 3/17   FIRE DEPARTMENT PERSONNEL, SALARIES, AND EXPENDITURES FOR CITIES 10,000 AND OVER: 2007

This table comprises 1,391 cities 10,000 and over in population (based on U.S. Bureau of the Census 2000 counts). The information in the table was collected in the spring of 2007 in a survey conducted by ICMA. Refer to the accompanying article for the survey methodology. The information is presented in two separate tables—one for police (Table 3/16) and one for fire (Table 3/17). The following definitions apply to both tables.

Type: letter identifies municipal designation: c, city; v, village; b, borough; t, town; tp, township.
Service provision: the number in this column indicates how the service is provided.
1   Full-time paid
2   All volunteer
3   Combined paid and volunteer
4   Public safety department (consolidated police and fire department)
5   Contract with county or other government entity for service
6   Contract with private company for service
7   Other

Full-time paid personnel: the number in this column shows the actual (not authorized) number of full-time paid employees.
Full-time uniformed personnel: the number in this column shows the number of sworn/uniformed employees.

Duty hours per week: shows the average number of hours worked per week.
Minimum base salary ($): shows the minimum base salary paid to full-time sworn/uniformed personnel. This amount does not include uniform allowance, holiday pay, hazard pay, or any other additional compensation.
Maximum base salary ($): shows the maximum base salary paid to full-time sworn/uniformed personnel. This amount does not include uniform allowance, holiday pay, hazard pay, or any other additional compensation.
Longevity pay: shows whether personnel can receive longevity pay: y, yes; n, no.
Maximum salary with longevity ($): shows the maximum salary with longevity pay included.
Years of service for longevity: shows the number of years of service required before personnel can receive longevity pay.
Total expenditures (A) ($): shows total departmental expenditures for the most recently completed fiscal year.
Total personnel expenditures (B) ($): shows total expenditures for salaries and wages (C); city contribution to retirement and social security (D); and city contribution to health, hospitalization, disability, and life insurance programs (E).
(B) as % of (A): shows total personnel expenditures as a percentage of total departmental expendi-

tures. In some instances, the percentage equals or exceeds 100%. For some cities the retirement expenditures are in other accounts, so although they are reported as costs, they do not come out of the departmental budget. This accounts for the percentage in excess of 100.

Salaries and wages (C) ($): shows the amount of salaries and wages for all departmental personnel—regular, temporary, full time, and part time—and of stipends for volunteers. This is a gross amount, including longevity pay, hazard pay, and holiday pay, without deduction of withholding for income tax or employee contributions to social security or retirement coverage.
City contribution to retirement and social security (D) ($): shows city contributions only.
City contribution to insurance (E) ($): shows city contribution to health, hospitalization, disability, and life insurance programs.
Capital outlay (F) ($): Shows amount spent on purchases of equipment, land and existing structures, and construction.
All other (G) ($): shows amount of expenditures other than those described in (B) through (F) above. Expenditures include fuel, utilities, supplies, etc.

(—) Indicates data not reported.

City	State	Type	Service provision	Full-time paid personnel	Full-time uniformed personnel	Duty hours per week	Minimum base salary ($)	Maximum base salary ($)	Longevity pay	Maximum salary with longevity ($)	Years of service for longevity	Total expenditures (A) ($)	Total personnel expenditures (B) ($)	(B) as % of (A)	Salaries and wages (C) ($)	City contribution to retirement and social security (D) ($)	City contribution to insurance (E) ($)	Capital outlay (F) ($)	All other (G) ($)
Over 1,000,000																			
DALLAS	TX	c	1	1,915	1,654	50–54	41,690	61,572	y	—	1	190,858	173,574	91	129,973	35,049	8,552	2,357	14,927
PHILADELPHIA	PA	c	1	2,529	2,431	42	37,001	51,388	y	54,369	3	270,412	243,115	90	158,444	50,320	34,350	4,352	22,946
PHOENIX	AZ	c	1	2,083	834	56	36,921	57,704	y	61,704	7	247,296	—	—	132,823	—	—	14,221	11,390
SAN DIEGO	CA	c	1	1,119	999	56	—	—	—	—	—	173,666	—	—	100,313	—	16,257	5,323	14,147
500,000–1,000,000																			
AUSTIN	TX	c	1	1,099	1,040	50–54	40,443	70,954	y	70,954	1	103,571	95,641	92	76,061	12,579	7,000	1,925	6,005
EL PASO	TX	c	1	883	813	56	32,260	50,049	y	51,549	1	70,244	57,762	82	44,432	8,610	4,720	2,823	9,659
JACKSONVILLE	FL	c	3	—	1,139	56	32,628	49,536	y	—	5	120,640	103,324	86	73,598	16,368	13,357	78	17,237
OKLAHOMA CITY	OK	c	1	—	—	—	36,540	54,455	y	—	20	—	—	—	—	—	—	—	—
SEATTLE	WA	c	1	1,146	1,072	other	47,565	68,612	y	—	5	129,097	—	—	75,508	—	—	977	48,556
250,000–499,999																			
ALBUQUERQUE	NM	c	1	681	652	56	41,438	44,787	y	48,977	8	64,455	51,455	80	35,250	5,260	10,945	2,001	11,000
ANCHORAGE	AK	c	1	383	309	56	47,917	65,233	n	—	—	60,423	—	—	30,900	—	—	509	13,620
ARLINGTON	TX	c	1	391	263	56	43,044	60,612	y	—	1	38,452	—	—	25,567	—	—	1,120	3,999
AURORA	CO	c	1	329	311	56	40,179	65,497	n	—	—	29,651	25,588	86	21,026	1,875	2,686	151	3,912
CINCINNATI	OH	c	1	868	826	48	43,610	55,123	y	56,323	8	86,771	79,433	92	56,925	15,871	6,637	449	6,888
CLEVELAND	OH	c	1	920	911	48	45,973	48,332	y	—	—	83,280	79,141	95	55,326	13,396	10,418	—	4,139
LONG BEACH	CA	c	1	528	449	56	50,367	64,713	y	—	—	90,304	70,806	78	50,404	10,439	9,962	734	18,764
MESA	AZ	c	1	478	394	56	40,456	54,642	n	—	—	52,643	—	—	35,980	—	4,436	3,903	6,535
NEW ORLEANS	LA	c	1	—	656	56	—	—	—	—	—	37,341	37,337	100	22,718	7,805	6,813	—	—
RALEIGH	NC	c	1	543	521	56	30,285	50,720	y	—	5	—	—	—	27,342	—	2,897	2,001	—
RIVERSIDE	CA	c	1	238	216	56	52,716	70,596	n	—	—	36,925	—	—	23,188	54,693	2,339	737	5,967
SANTA ANA	CA	c	1	238	109	56	55,488	67,476	n	—	—	46,600	—	—	30,743	—	5,836	258	4,515
TOLEDO	OH	c	1	530	501	48	36,470	54,812	n	—	—	51,630	—	—	31,373	—	5,896	—	4,668
VIRGINIA BEACH	VA	c	3	—	435	56	36,088	54,977	n	—	—	36,086	32,257	89	25,115	5,269	1,873	82	3,747
WICHITA	KS	c	1	419	—	56	34,351	48,537	y	—	6	39,724	29,123	73	21,767	3,886	3,470	7,803	2,797
100,000–249,999																			
ALLENTOWN	PA	c	1	142	140	40	37,296	51,056	y	—	5	14,891	14,500	97	8,832	3,971	1,697	109	283
ANN ARBOR	MI	c	1	92	79	50–54	44,893	61,485	y	61,985	7	12,118	10,683	88	7,609	501	2,573	74	1,361
ARVADA	CO	c		—	—	—	—	—	—	—	—	—	—	—	—	—	—	—	—
BABYLON	NY	t	—	—	—	—	—	—	—	—	—	—	—	—	—	—	—	—	—
BAKERSFIELD	CA	c	1	210	183	56	50,011	60,887	y	63,931	15	21,253	—	—	13,364	—	2,205	96	2,130

Table 3/17 continued   FIRE DEPARTMENT PERSONNEL, SALARIES, AND EXPENDITURES FOR CITIES 10,000 AND OVER: 2007

Reported expenditures (in $000)

City	State	Type	Service provision	Full-time paid personnel	Full-time uniformed personnel	Duty hours per week	Minimum base salary ($)	Maximum base salary ($)	Longevity pay	Maximum salary with longevity ($)	Years of service for longevity	Total expenditures (A) ($)	Total personnel expenditures (B) ($)	(B) as % of (A)	Salaries and wages (C) ($)	City contribution to retirement and social security (D) ($)	City contribution to insurance (E) ($)	Capital outlay (F) ($)	All other (G) ($)
100,000–249,999 continued																			
BATON ROUGE– EAST BATON ROUGE	LA	c	1	578	577	56	26,749	39,282	y	47,138	10	—	40,027	—	30,364	4,059	5,604	1,522	2,864
BEAUMONT	TX	c	1	229	224	48	30,552	47,316	y	48,516	1	18,299	17,032	93	13,028	1,780	2,223	378	889
BELLEVUE	WA	c	1	—	—	other	53,032	67,432	y	70,804	5	27,968	21,491	77	18,187	732	2,572	749	4,532
BERKELEY	CA	c	1	136	125	56	70,524	88,848	n	—	—	25,218	19,345	77	14,657	359	4,329	102	2,539
BURBANK	CA	c	1	142	—	56	66,972	83,628	n	—	—	—	—	—	16,477	—	—	37,487	—
CAMBRIDGE	MA	c	—	—	—	—	—	—		—	—	—	—	—	—	—	—	—	—
CAPE CORAL	FL	c	1	—	232	48	40,285	55,661	n	—	—	23,891	19,908	83	11,781	5,257	2,869	1,918	2,066
CEDAR RAPIDS	IA	c	1	155	146	other	38,942	46,383	y	47,583	5	12,589	11,274	90	8,055	1,989	1,230	—	1,315
CHESAPEAKE	VA	c	3	391	378	56	34,136	58,305	n	—	—	33,822	29,717	88	22,390	4,443	2,883	45	4,060
CHULA VISTA	CA	c	1	153	119	56	52,250	63,510	n	—	—	29,387	27,644	94	20,995	4,636	2,011	18	1,726
CLEARWATER	FL	c	1	221	206	56	35,323	52,486	y	—	0	20,384	16,508	81	12,004	2,697	1,806	851	3,025
COLUMBIA	SC	c	7	449	431	56	27,796	44,474	n	—	—	25,381	22,349	88	17,331	3,070	1,948	140	2,892
COLUMBUS– MUSCOGEE CONSOLIDATED	GA	c	1	361	351	56	27,316	42,396	n	—	—	22,118	20,288	92	14,511	4,164	1,613	96	1,734
CONCORD	CA	c	—	—	—	—	—	—		—	—	—	—	—	—	—	—	—	—
CORAL SPRINGS	FL	c	1	—	139	48	43,109	64,000	y	73,090	5	21,953	15,146	69	10,472	3,097	1,576	4,221	2,585
CORONA	CA	c	1	—	118	56	52,872	64,548	y	65,548	5	19,639	—	—	12,471	—	2,802	47	1,655
DALY CITY	CA	c	1	73	66	56	68,460	83,244	y	85,332	5	12,333	—	—	8,550	—	1,648	456	1,679
DAYTON	OH	c	1	385	340	48	41,059	54,787	y	55,883	5	37,256	—	—	34,065	5,586	4,296	1,012	2,179
DES MOINES	IA	c	1	310	246	50–54	43,480	51,814	y	54,923	5	29,708	26,173	88	17,329	5,012	3,833	1,502	2,032
DURHAM	NC	c	1	282	272	56	27,349	45,699	n	—	—	18,605	16,121	87	12,511	1,925	1,685	603	1,882
EL MONTE	CA	c	5	—	—	—	—	—		—	—	—	—	—	—	—	—	—	—
FAYETTEVILLE	NC	c	1	301	290	56	27,416	46,400	y	49,880	5	17,590	14,009	80	10,505	1,274	2,230	1,259	2,322
FONTANA	CA	c	—	—	—	—	—	—		—	—	—	—	—	—	—	—	—	—
FORT COLLINS	CO	c	1	184	157	56	42,744	73,398	y	—	5	21,532	15,569	72	12,705	1,359	1,505	2,093	3,870
FORT LAUDERDALE	FL	c	1	444	382	48	40,659	59,454	y	69,972	5	57,599	—	—	31,512	—	—	597	9,239
FREMONT	CA	c	1	140	126	56	67,982	82,623	y	92,942	19	30,041	23,244	77	17,321	4,097	1,825	134	6,663
FULLERTON	CA	c	1	94	90	56	49,223	65,955	n	—	—	14,536	12,767	88	9,070	2,553	1,144	124	1,644
GRAND PRAIRIE	TX	c	3	212	204	56	44,305	60,872	y	61,232	1	19,414	16,774	86	12,874	2,703	1,197	1,256	1,384
GRAND RAPIDS	MI	c	—	—	—	—	—	—		—	—	—	—	—	—	—	—	—	—
HAMPTON	VA	c	3	260	244	50–54	35,620	58,141	y	—	3	—	—	—	—	—	—	—	—
HUNTINGTON	NY	t	—	—	—	—	—	—		—	—	—	—	—	—	—	—	—	—
HUNTINGTON BEACH	CA	c	1	174	126	56	54,642	67,683	y	74,451	5	—	—	—	—	—	—	—	—
HUNTSVILLE	AL	c	4	336	317	56	30,264	46,280	y	46,850	5	—	—	—	—	—	—	—	—
INGLEWOOD	CA	c	—	—	—	—	—	—		—	—	—	—	—	—	—	—	—	—
IRVINE	CA	c	—	—	—	—	—	—		—	—	—	—	—	—	—	—	—	—
JOLIET	IL	c	1	213	209	50–54	47,089	73,173	y	—	15	27,539	26,859	98	19,178	4,888	2,793	—	680
LAFAYETTE CONSOLIDATED	LA	c	1	256	224	50–54	21,996	29,500	y	—	1	12,488	—	—	7,877	—	1,448	283	1,348
LAREDO	TX	c	1	341	333	56	36,720	47,349	y	48,660	1	29,718	27,949	94	21,665	3,817	2,467	8	1,769
LEXINGTON– FAYETTE	KY	c	1	561	545	56	31,103	48,429	n	—	—	46,626	43,695	94	31,679	5,377	6,639	1,201	4,698
LITTLE ROCK	AR	c	1	397	391	56	30,792	46,321	y	48,121	1	41,782	29,646	71	21,859	3,501	4,285	9,327	2,179
McALLEN	TX	c	1	167	158	56	—	—		—	—	13,233	9,775	74	7,499	1,358	918	2,090	1,368
MESQUITE	TX	c	1	198	190	56	48,744	62,196	y	65,196	1	21,638	18,581	86	13,769	2,936	1,875	1,664	1,393
MOBILE	AL	c	—	—	—	—	—	—		—	—	—	—	—	—	—	—	—	—
NAPERVILLE	IL	c	1	201	189	50–54	63,880	70,428	y	—	—	23,598	17,945	76	15,322	266	2,357	39	5,614
NEWPORT NEWS	VA	c	1	377	345	56	33,620	66,535	n	—	—	26,441	23,686	90	18,577	2,408	2,700	—	2,154
NORFOLK	VA	c	1	508	493	50–54	33,000	64,104	n	—	—	33,939	—	—	26,309	10,559	2,067	—	1,169
PASADENA	CA	c	1	177	161	56	47,844	74,534	n	—	—	29,674	25,361	85	18,127	3,440	3,793	247	4,066
PASADENA	TX	c	2	15	10	other	34,945	52,417	n	—	—	6,706	1,007	15	703	148	154	2,893	2,806
PEMBROKE PINES	FL	c	1	244	234	other	42,374	59,621	y	64,391	10	30,771	27,482	89	17,476	7,007	2,999	1,315	1,973
PEORIA	AZ	c	1	157	133	56	40,488	56,988	n	—	—	19,500	10,884	56	9,100	484	1,300	6,000	2,600
PEORIA	IL	c	1	209	200	50–54	41,361	58,244	y	62,903	5	24,999	18,866	75	14,311	4,389	164	1,038	2,095
PLANO	TX	c	1	316	305	56	52,428	61,826	y	63,026	1	35,154	30,765	88	23,114	3,780	3,870	377	4,013
POMONA	CA	c	—	—	—	—	—	—		—	—	—	—	—	—	—	—	—	—
PORTSMOUTH	VA	c	1	242	233	50–54	32,983	54,420	y	—	—	—	—	—	—	—	—	—	—
RAMAPO	NY	t	—	—	—	—	—	—		—	—	—	—	—	—	—	—	—	—
ROCKFORD	IL	c	1	280	276	50–54	37,269	55,952	y	61,547	5	35,816	28,132	79	23,299	4,480	353	353	2,742
SALEM	OR	c	1	168	155	56	42,428	62,987	n	—	—	22,067	17,829	81	11,898	3,626	2,305	1,440	2,798
SALINAS	CA	c	1	95	89	56	58,884	75,168	y	78,926	20	14,882	12,079	81	8,853	452	2,774	2,014	789
SALT LAKE CITY	UT	c	1	362	329	56	35,298	55,308	y	—	20	29,028	26,432	91	21,462	2,245	2,724	43	2,552
SAN BUENAVENTURA (VENTURA)	CA	c	1	108	73	56	48,823	62,313	n	—	—	16,565	11,875	72	8,832	2,679	364	383	4,308
SANTA CLARA	CA	c	3	153	145	56	85,416	103,872	y	108,972	10	28,541	—	—	19,646	—	—	43	2,056
SANTA CLARITA	CA	c	5	—	—	—	—	—		—	—	—	—	—	—	—	—	—	—
SCOTTSDALE	AZ	c	1	247	222	56	37,128	35,767	n	—	—	24,307	20,148	83	16,517	2,019	1,611	69	4,091
SIOUX FALLS	SD	c	1	193	187	50–54	36,363	51,796	n	—	—	18,109	—	—	104,763	2,258	1,912	1,999	1,477
SPRINGFIELD	MO	c	1	216	197	56	31,075	46,758	y	47,955	5	15,194	14,181	93	10,275	2,807	1,099	60	952
ST. PETERSBURG	FL	c	1	355	321	—	34,826	54,455	y	54,455	—	—	—	—	—	—	—	—	—
STAMFORD	CT	c	3	280	276	42	41,753	64,017	y	69,017	5	35,720	—	—	23,964	—	1,067	774	4,458

Table 3/17 continued   FIRE DEPARTMENT PERSONNEL, SALARIES, AND EXPENDITURES FOR CITIES 10,000 AND OVER: 2007

City	State	Type	Service provision	Full-time paid personnel	Full-time uniformed personnel	Duty hours per week	Minimum base salary ($)	Maximum base salary ($)	Longevity pay	Maximum salary with longevity ($)	Years of service for longevity	Total expenditures (A) ($)	Total personnel expenditures (B) ($)	(B) as % of (A)	Salaries and wages (C) ($)	City contribution to retirement and social security (D) ($)	City contribution to insurance (E) ($)	Capital outlay (F) ($)	All other (G) ($)
100,000–249,999 continued																			
STERLING HEIGHTS	MI	c	1	106	—	56	39,221	62,776	y	—	5	14,660	13,407	91	9,539	1,295	2,572	562	690
SUNNYVALE	CA	c	4	—	—	56	—	—	—	—	—	—	—	—	—	—	—	—	—
SYRACUSE	NY	c	1	430	399	40	32,371	48,533	y	—	—	39,121	37,597	96	23,970	6,105	7,521	898	627
TALLAHASSEE	FL	c	1	267	247	50–54	31,988	51,213	n	—	—	23,800	—	—	13,918	—	1,344	161	6,378
TEMPE	AZ	c	1	157	135	56	42,191	56,955	y	62,650	5	19,756	15,223	77	12,755	810	1,658	1,866	2,667
THORNTON	IL	tp	—	—	—	—	—	—	—	—	—	—	—	—	—	—	—	—	—
TOPEKA	KS	c	1	249	225	50–54	31,895	60,003	y	62,295	4	18,099	16,693	92	13,315	1,972	1,406	56	1,350
VALLEJO	CA	c	1	104	98	other	88,723	108,525	y	147,744	20	22,534	—	—	21,488	—	3,224	22	1,024
VANCOUVER	WA	c	3	215	181	other	52,164	65,928	n	—	—	25,717	19,480	76	16,148	783	2,548	1,126	5,111
WACO	TX	c	1	191	184	56	36,750	48,666	y	50,010	1	14,494	13,095	90	10,044	2,222	829	—	1,399
WEST VALLEY CITY	UT	c	1	93	87	56	31,500	45,364	n	—	—	7,512	—	—	4,602	—	717	351	923
WESTMINSTER	CO	c	1	137	130	56	—	—	n	—	—	12,035	—	—	8,567	—	1,107	206	1,400
WINSTON-SALEM	NC	c	1	359	197	56	28,050	50,600	n	—	—	20,641	18,939	92	14,035	1,746	3,158	199	1,702
50,000–99,999																			
ABINGTON	PA	tp	2	—	—	—	—	—	y	—	—	—	—	—	—	—	—	—	—
ALAMEDA	CA	c	1	109	104	56	61,802	89,882	y	—	0	23,258	18,282	79	12,611	3,619	2,052	471	4,505
ALHAMBRA	CA	c	1	77	70	56	48,564	62,004	n	—	—	13,616	10,874	80	7,422	2,307	1,144	891	1,851
ANTIOCH	CA	c	—	—	—	—	—	—	—	—	—	—	—	—	—	—	—	—	—
ARLINGTON HEIGHTS	IL	v	1	106	102	other	46,480	71,931	y	73,531	5	14,364	12,915	90	8,465	2,811	1,639	79	1,370
ASHEVILLE	NC	c	1	214	212	56	26,343	32,929	n	—	—	14,804	11,293	76	9,067	989	1,237	45	3,466
BATTLE CREEK	MI	c	1	88	87	50–54	36,354	52,382	y	53,382	7	8,670	7,918	91	5,444	1,274	1,200	67	685
BAYTOWN	TX	c	1	96	92	50–54	38,815	48,727	y	49,303	1	7,472	6,788	91	4,868	1,101	818	128	556
BELLFLOWER	CA	c	—	—	—	—	—	—	—	—	—	—	—	—	—	—	—	—	—
BELLINGHAM	WA	c	1	164	144	other	49,704	63,048	y	66,327	5	19,270	14,834	77	11,978	648	2,208	445	3,991
BEND	OR	c	1	102	66	56	45,804	58,512	n	—	—	11,453	11,226	98	8,085	1,793	1,348	65	405
BETHLEHEM	PA	c	1	114	113	42	32,844	46,941	y	50,696	4	8,452	8,149	96	6,122	987	1,040	108	195
BLOOMINGTON	IN	c	1	109	108	48	40,232	40,232	y	41,732	2	9,252	6,606	71	5,047	946	613	169	2,478
BLOOMINGTON	MN	c	2	3	—	40	—	—	n	—	—	2,376	729	31	694	12	22	—	—
BOSSIER CITY	LA	c	1	219	215	48	27,816	27,816	y	—	3	14,862	9,326	63	6,286	1,728	1,312	622	1,885
BOULDER	CO	c	1	111	105	56	46,543	60,382	y	—	4	11,729	—	—	7,917	—	2,344	—	1,559
BOWIE	MD	c	—	—	—	—	—	—	—	—	—	—	—	—	—	—	—	—	—
BROOKLYN PARK	MN	c	2	83	—	other	—	—	—	—	—	1,703	966	57	768	105	93	6	731
BUENA PARK	CA	c	5	—	—	—	—	—	—	—	—	—	—	—	—	—	—	—	—
BURNSVILLE	MN	c	1	41	39	56	52,020	69,180	y	69,180	4	4,500	3,895	87	3,087	326	481	74	531
CAMARILLO	CA	c	—	—	—	—	—	—	—	—	—	—	—	—	—	—	—	—	—
CARLSBAD	CA	c	—	—	—	—	—	—	—	—	—	—	—	—	—	—	—	—	—
CARSON	CA	c	3	3,994	1,307	56	48,200	71,654	y	87,737	10	—	—	—	432,185	—	75,651	—	—
CARY	NC	t	1	209	195	56	32,115	—	n	—	—	14,593	13,450	92	10,336	1,768	1,346	—	1,143
CHINO	CA	c	—	—	—	—	—	—	—	—	—	—	—	—	—	—	—	—	—
CHINO HILLS	CA	c	7	—	—	—	—	—	—	—	—	—	—	—	—	—	—	—	—
CLOVIS	CA	c	1	74	64	56	56,796	69,036	n	—	—	10,398	8,228	79	5,984	1,237	1,006	314	1,856
COLERAIN TOWNSHIP	OH	tp	1	56	54	50–54	39,300	63,500	n	—	—	9,892	7,690	78	6,520	1,099	71	250	1,952
COLONIE	NY	t	—	—	—	—	—	—	—	—	—	—	—	—	—	—	—	—	—
CONCORD	NC	c	1	168	156	50–54	27,930	49,158	y	52,658	11	12,680	8,434	67	6,553	812	1,069	1,068	3,178
CORVALLIS	OR	c	3	67	64	56	45,210	59,088	n	—	—	8,276	6,293	76	4,621	743	928	417	1,566
CUPERTINO	CA	c	—	—	—	—	—	—	—	—	—	—	—	—	—	—	—	—	—
DECATUR	IL	c	1	—	—	56	41,461	52,910	y	59,259	25	12,433	—	—	7,454	—	2,091	—	928
DELRAY BEACH	FL	c	1	154	145	48	41,889	67,200	n	—	—	19,297	16,340	85	11,156	3,193	1,991	195	2,732
DES PLAINES	IL	c	1	97	96	50–54	48,957	76,222	y	—	10	—	—	—	7,946	—	—	—	—
DIAMOND BAR	CA	c	—	—	—	—	—	—	—	—	—	—	—	—	—	—	—	—	—
DOTHAN	AL	c	1	169	166	56	28,662	43,909	y	—	—	12,335	10,462	85	7,331	2,014	1,116	743	1,130
DUBUQUE	IA	c	1	90	89	56	39,470	46,429	y	49,679	5	10,206	7,182	70	4,917	1,363	902	2,281	742
EDEN PRAIRIE	MN	c	2	9	—	other	53,123	67,288	n	—	—	2,488	964	39	834	76	53	444	1,079
EDISON	NJ	tp	3	148	146	40	31,497	103,332	y	120,123	30	—	—	—	15,683	—	—	—	329
EDMOND	OK	c	1	114	110	56	36,560	54,017	y	56,017	4	12,607	9,030	72	7,253	948	828	1,288	2,289
ELGIN	IL	c	1	132	111	50–54	49,032	65,352	y	66,552	10	17,562	15,817	90	10,434	1,390	3,993	229	1,516
EUCLID	OH	c	1	—	—	48	—	—	—	—	—	8,284	7,757	94	5,328	1,567	862	355	172
FAIRFIELD	CT	t	1	98	96	42	49,562	57,625	y	60,625	25	10,745	—	—	8,480	1,634	—	1,435	729
FARMINGTON HILLS	MI	c	1	48	44	42	37,905	59,689	y	65,658	3	7,211	6,365	88	4,675	1,123	566	44	802
FEDERAL WAY	WA	c	—	—	—	—	—	—	—	—	—	—	—	—	—	—	—	—	—
FLAGSTAFF	AZ	c	1	99	97	56	38,134	52,622	n	—	—	9,552	7,361	77	6,100	479	781	1,478	713
FLOWER MOUND	TX	t	1	69	66	56	44,200	56,028	y	57,828	—	6,352	5,941	94	4,431	748	761	7	404
FOLSOM	CA	c	1	76	69	48	61,364	74,569	y	76,433	10	—	—	—	—	—	—	—	—
FORT SMITH	AR	c	1	129	126	56	27,343	39,923	y	40,283	5	9,148	7,875	86	6,739	142	994	326	947
FREDERICK	MD	c	—	—	—	—	—	—	—	—	—	—	—	—	—	—	—	—	—
GAITHERSBURG	MD	c	—	—	—	—	—	—	—	—	—	—	—	—	—	—	—	—	—
GARDENA	CA	c	5	—	—	—	—	—	—	—	—	—	—	—	—	—	—	—	—
GASTONIA	NC	c	1	141	139	56	27,014	42,016	n	—	—	8,969	7,507	84	6,075	635	796	6	1,456
GREELEY	CO	c	1	109	104	56	41,355	57,974	n	—	—	10,421	—	—	—	—	—	—	—
GREENBURGH	NY	t	—	—	—	—	—	—	—	—	—	—	—	—	—	—	—	—	—
GREENVILLE	NC	c	1	143	140	56	28,771	47,204	y	—	—	9,276	—	—	6,588	—	216	232	751
GREENVILLE	SC	c	1	141	138	50–54	26,374	41,600	y	—	5	9,187	8,403	91	6,099	1,224	1,079	118	666

Table 3/17 continued   FIRE DEPARTMENT PERSONNEL, SALARIES, AND EXPENDITURES FOR CITIES 10,000 AND OVER: 2007

City	State	Type	Service provision	Full-time paid personnel	Full-time uniformed personnel	Duty hours per week	Minimum base salary ($)	Maximum base salary ($)	Longevity pay	Maximum salary with longevity ($)	Years of service for longevity	Total expenditures (A) ($)	Total personnel expenditures (B) ($)	(B) as % of (A)	Salaries and wages (C) ($)	City contribution to retirement and social security (D) ($)	City contribution to insurance (E) ($)	Capital outlay (F) ($)	All other (G) ($)
50,000–99,999 continued																			
GRESHAM	OR	c	1	91	11	56	44,772	63,180	n	—	—	14,589	11,137	76	7,471	2,019	1,647	127	3,325
GULFPORT	MS	c	1	173	117	50–54	25,992	30,671	y	—	1	2,434	8,219	338	5,842	1,111	1,266	56	—
HAMILTON	OH	c	1	113	112	50–54	41,796	54,021	y	59,423	5	11,955	10,926	91	7,581	1,863	1,482	73	955
HARLINGEN	TX	c	1	104	101	56	28,080	33,384	y	34,584	1	—	—	—	3,503	—	—	—	—
HAWTHORNE	CA	c	—																
HESPERIA	CA	c	—																
HOOVER	AL	c	1	152	151	50–54	39,666	56,472	n	—	—	16,379	13,460	82	10,430	1,640	1,388	1,479	1,441
HUNTINGTON PARK	CA	c	—																
IDAHO FALLS	ID	c	1	98	94	56	36,624	49,603	y	51,283	3	11,027	—	—	5,864	—	—	717	997
IRONDEQUOIT	NY	t	2	—															
JACKSONVILLE	NC	c	1	75	71	56	25,950	52,749	y	—	5	4,278	3,524	82	2,645	354	525	20	7,334
JANESVILLE	WI	c	1	91	90	56	34,624	55,910	y	55,910	—	8,788	8,103	92	5,435	1,170	1,497	—	685
JOHNSON CITY	TN	c	1	80	77	56	27,480	41,375	y	45,179	5	12,832	5,557	43	3,994	832	730	6,495	780
KENNEWICK	WA	c	1	76	75	50–54	46,800	61,572	n	—	—	9,529	7,297	77	5,569	1,457	270	977	2,608
KENOSHA	WI	c	1	156	135	48	36,984	55,284	y	55,584	5	18,063	15,907	88	10,425	2,456	3,026	296	1,859
KETTERING	OH	c	3	55	48	other	47,445	62,296	n	—	—	8,153	6,201	76	4,463	1,070	668	—	1,951
KILLEEN	TX	c	1	171	169	50–54	32,448	48,672	y	50,352	1	9,596	10,002	104	6,757	2,363	882	464	985
LA MESA	CA	c	1	51	43	56	45,792	55,656	n	—	—	6,272	6,263	100	4,071	1,498	693	5,328	945
LAGUNA NIGUEL	CA	c	—																
LAKE CHARLES	LA	c	1	174	169	56	23,850	—	y	—	—	11,635	9,594	82	7,447	1,171	974	161	1,880
LAKE FOREST	CA	c	5	—															
LAKELAND	FL	c	1	141	122	50–54	33,155	46,654	y	47,134	10	11,262	9,114	81	7,453	1,013	647	1,017	1,132
LAKEWOOD	WA	c	—																
LAUDERHILL	FL	c	1	104	101	48	48,445	78,012	y	81,132	10	12,782	—	—	10,440	—	1,836	801	850
LAYTON	UT	c	1	49	45	56	33,711	47,196	n	—	—	3,268	—	—	2,858	—	—	97	313
LEE'S SUMMIT	MO	c	1	139	124	56	36,323	48,694	n	—	—	—	—	—	7,786	8,313	—	—	—
LIVERMORE	CA	c	—																
LONGMONT	CO	c	1	90	84	56	42,888	57,492	y	58,572	2	9,837	8,415	86	6,594	669	1,152	146	1,277
LONGVIEW	TX	c	1	161	155	50–54	33,953	40,427	y	—	1	11,846	9,801	83	7,580	1,146	1,075	243	1,802
LOVELAND	CO	c	3	70	61	56	42,937	65,834	y	—	—	6,245	6,116	98	4,519	662	935	129	799
LOWER MERION	PA	tp	3	6	—	40	—	—	y	—	—	3,482	514	15	388	40	85	995	1,973
LYNCHBURG	VA	c	1	181	177	56	30,618	53,243	n	—	—	14,028	11,913	85	9,173	2,126	614	853	1,262
MARGATE	FL	c	1	108	106	56	36,222	57,956	y	60,956	10	12,148	11,048	91	7,658	1,998	1,391	379	720
MARIETTA	GA	c	1	135	131	—	33,022	49,271	n	—	—	11,095	9,219	83	6,752	1,216	1,250	503	1,372
McKINNEY	TX	c	1	147	128	56	48,292	61,547	y	62,747	1	17,716	10,388	59	7,821	1,431	1,135	6,067	1,261
MEDFORD	OR	c	1	70	65	56	47,905	59,911	n	—	—	8,806	7,789	88	5,424	1,282	1,083	46	971
MELBOURNE	FL	c	—																
MIDWEST CITY	OK	c	1	92	86	other	34,101	42,250	n	—	—	8,576	6,949	81	5,982	950	17	616	1,010
MILPITAS	CA	c	1	69	64	56	74,218	90,211	y	96,526	9	—	—	—	—	—	—	—	—
MINNETONKA	MN	c	3	7	7	40	—	—	n	—	—	1,885	891	47	745	74	72	261	732
MISSION VIEJO	CA	c	—																
MISSOULA	MT	c	1	—	73	—	39,780	50,112	y	53,232	2	5,600	—	—	3,750	—	533	—	—
MISSOURI CITY	TX	c	1	59	58	50–54	36,250	—	y	37,210	1	5,399	3,807	71	3,174	631	2	2	1,108
MONTEBELLO	CA	c	1	64	57	56	46,080	58,860	—	—	—	11,490	9,674	84	6,703	1,627	1,343	152	1,663
MONTEREY PARK	CA	c	3	59	55	56	61,896	75,228	y	—	—	7,895	7,469	95	5,804	1,175	490	36	390
MOUNTAIN VIEW	CA	c	1	87	74	56	72,381	87,987	n	—	—	15,494	—	—	10,884	—	1,562	143	946
MUNCIE	IN	c	1	111	110	other	40,221	40,221	y	42,521	5	8,628	8,289	96	5,759	897	1,633	103	236
MURFREESBORO	TN	c	1	182	165	56	30,000	46,747	y	—	1	11,984	10,424	87	7,863	1,347	1,214	227	1,332
NASHUA	NH	c	1	175	171	42	36,953	50,419	y	51,873	7	18,580	—	—	12,766	—	—	5,029	785
NEW ROCHELLE	NY	c	1	157	154	other	34,319	68,198	y	70,498	5	22,147	18,984	86	13,041	3,090	2,852	946	2,217
NORMAN	OK	c	1	129	125	56	37,083	52,801	y	52,801	5	10,751	9,879	92	7,675	999	1,205	199	673
NORTH CHARLESTON	SC	c	1	211	201	56	26,401	36,961	y	37,441	10	11,974	10,512	88	6,797	1,235	2,479	655	1,409
NORTH MIAMI	FL	c	—																
NORTH RICHLAND HILLS	TX	c	1	89	85	56	45,263	59,564	y	60,839	1	8,139	7,211	89	5,613	801	797	20	908
NORWALK	CT	c	1	135	131	42	49,191	59,861	y	60,546	8	14,350	12,680	88	11,770	438	473	—	1,670
ODESSA	TX	c	1	164	154	56	34,020	45,312	y	—	1	11,816	10,044	85	7,283	1,625	1,136	470	1,302
OGDEN CITY	UT	c	3	199	137	56	28,578	44,335	y	—	10	—	—	—	—	1,150	946	36	2,539
OREM	UT	c	4	—	—	56	—	—	—	—	—	—	—	—	—	—	—	—	—
ORLAND PARK	IL	v	—																
PALATINE	IL	v	1	99	69	50–54	45,990	75,890	y	76,890	8	12,434	11,125	89	7,952	1,594	1,579	483	826
PALO ALTO	CA	c	1	115	102	56	62,025	76,149	n	—	—	22,449	17,346	77	12,338	2,120	2,887	307	4,796
PARMA	OH	c	1	—	—	48	44,869	56,658	y	58,458	5	—	10,990	—	7,740	1,797	1,452	—	1,062
PAWTUCKET	RI	c	1	151	148	42	45,398	50,129	y	55,393	5	—	—	—	—	2	2	—	2
PENSACOLA	FL	c	1	161	150	56	24,335	37,812	y	41,593	5	12,074	—	—	6,584	—	661	—	1,841
PETALUMA	CA	c	1	58	56	56	64,790	78,747	n	—	—	—	—	—	4,492	—	1,422	1,386	99
PITTSBURG	CA	c	—																
PLAIN	OH	tp	1	35	29	50–54	33,813	47,985	y	49,685	2	4,066	2,754	68	2,043	443	267	103	1,210
PLEASANTON	CA	c	3	119	112	56	60,396	77,076	n	—	—	24,443	22,711	93	14,655	4,551	3,503	162	1,570
PLYMOUTH	MN	c	3	—	—	other	—	—	—	—	—	—	—	—	—	—	—	—	—
POMPANO BEACH	FL	c	1	199	192	48	42,927	60,404	y	—	—	25,095	—	—	14,235	9,101	—	671	3,947
PORT ARTHUR	TX	c	1	107	—	50–54	39,146	45,858	y	47,058	1	—	—	—	—	—	—	—	—
PORT ST. LUCIE	FL	c	—																

Table 3/17
continued

FIRE DEPARTMENT PERSONNEL, SALARIES, AND EXPENDITURES FOR CITIES 10,000 AND OVER: 2007

City	State	Type	Service provision	Full-time paid personnel	Full-time uniformed personnel	Duty hours per week	Minimum base salary ($)	Maximum base salary ($)	Longevity pay	Maximum salary with longevity ($)	Years of service for longevity	Reported expenditures (in $000)							
												Total expenditures (A) ($)	Total personnel expenditures (B) ($)	(B) as % of (A)	Salaries and wages (C) ($)	City contribution to retirement and social security (D) ($)	City contribution to insurance (E) ($)	Capital outlay (F) ($)	All other (G) ($)
50,000–99,999 continued																			
PORTLAND	ME	c	1	242	234	42	29,047	43,527	n	—	—	14,942	—	—	12,286	—	—	588	2,068
RANCHO CORDOVA	CA	c	—	—	—	—	—	—	—	—	—	—	—	—	—	—	—	—	—
RAPID CITY	SD	c	1	130	122	56	33,918	51,577	n	—	—	7,344	6,370	87	4,916	716	737	367	607
READING	PA	c	3	143	141	42	48,250	51,390	y	—	5	13,646	12,588	92	9,214	1,397	1,976	44	1,015
REDFORD	MI	tp	1	—	40	—	42,846	57,125	y	82,041	5	7,018	—	—	3,678	2,965	1,631	793	643
REDLANDS	CA	c	1	68	4	56	50,383	61,241	y	64,303	20	12,843	11,268	88	7,658	2,560	1,049	179	1,406
REDONDO BEACH	CA	c	1	70	64	48	51,252	61,872	y	71,772	5	13,437	11,159	83	7,569	2,798	792	265	2,013
RENTON	WA	c	1	119	106	other	49,776	66,768	y	74,784	5	13,952	12,352	89	10,210	518	1,623	545	1,055
RICHARDSON	TX	c	1	151	140	56	—	—	y	—	1	15,151	14,145	93	10,903	2,454	787	—	1,007
RICHMOND	CA	c	1	93	87	56	69,732	84,492	y	95,784	5	22,084	17,661	80	12,104	2,736	2,820	13	4,410
ROANOKE	VA	c	1	270	262	56	31,213	49,941	n	—	—	22,221	15,515	70	11,915	2,461	1,139	3,416	3,290
ROCKY MOUNT	NC	c	1	132	114	56	28,923	43,384	y	46,204	5	9,222	7,763	84	6,256	991	515	97	1,362
ROSEVILLE	CA	c	1	108	100	56	50,997	79,967	y	83,965	10	24,619	16,817	68	12,030	3,608	1,178	—	7,802
ROSWELL	GA	c	3	15	10	other	—	—	n	—	—	5,101	3,627	71	3,136	310	180	560	914
ROYAL OAK	MI	c	1	66	60	50–54	38,661	55,226	y	60,748	5	7,075	6,713	95	4,610	1,000	1,103	14	349
SAN LEANDRO	CA	c	5	—	—	—	—	—	—	—	—	—	—	—	—	—	—	—	—
SAN MARCOS	CA	c	1	70	61	56	—	—	—	—	—	11,219	8,699	78	6,457	1,556	685	937	1,583
SAN MATEO	CA	c	1	87	71	56	69,306	82,672	n	—	—	—	—	—	—	—	—	63	1,117
SANDY CITY	UT	c	3	—	74	48	31,800	46,621	n	—	—	6,343	—	—	3,916	—	527	259	954
SANDY SPRINGS	GA	c	1	81	—	50–54	30,000	34,000	n	—	—	—	—	—	—	—	—	—	—
SANTA BARBARA	CA	c	1	115	98	56	53,527	65,164	n	—	—	17,996	15,552	86	10,279	3,801	1,472	334	2,110
SANTA CRUZ	CA	c	1	51	49	56	57,816	77,364	y	—	6	—	—	—	—	—	—	—	—
SANTA FE	NM	c	1	136	130	56	31,053	57,432	y	57,932	1	—	—	—	6,703	—	8,506	2,610	1,133
SANTA MARIA	CA	c	3	49	12	56	54,040	65,687	n	—	—	7,793	6,869	88	5,027	1,095	747	165	759
SANTA MONICA	CA	c	1	109	99	56	59,856	73,896	n	—	—	22,462	20,316	90	14,401	3,952	1,963	745	1,401
SANTEE	CA	c	1	59	51	56	43,616	61,373	n	—	—	8,577	7,386	86	5,167	1,324	894	216	975
SARASOTA	FL	c	—	—	—	—	—	—	—	—	—	—	—	—	—	—	—	—	—
SOUTH SAN FRANCISCO	CA	c	—	—	—	—	—	—	—	—	—	—	—	—	—	—	—	—	—
SPRINGFIELD	OH	c	1	133	131	50–54	40,318	50,918	y	—	5	1,816	—	—	7,434	3,020	1,577	1,270	234
ST. CHARLES	MO	c	1	82	79	56	46,888	61,816	n	—	—	—	—	—	—	—	—	—	—
ST. CLAIR SHORES	MI	c	1	50	24	50–54	40,712	57,401	y	63,141	5	5,801	5,130	88	3,849	835	444	208	463
ST. CLOUD	MN	c	1	61	58	56	42,144	49,800	y	—	5	5,819	5,346	92	3,771	431	1,144	23	450
ST. JOSEPH	MO	c	1	134	131	56	30,032	42,705	n	—	—	10,139	9,414	93	6,254	2,476	684	—	725
ST. PETERS	MO	c	—	—	—	—	—	—	—	—	—	—	—	—	—	—	—	—	—
SUFFOLK	VA	c	3	199	195	56	32,785	51,475	n	—	—	15,897	12,397	78	9,265	1,700	1,432	585	2,915
TAYLORSVILLE	UT	c	—	—	—	—	—	—	—	—	—	—	—	—	—	—	—	—	—
TEMPLE	TX	c	1	102	95	56	33,020	44,250	y	45,450	1	7,250	6,541	90	5,352	809	380	169	539
TROY	MI	c	3	18	13	40	—	—	y	—	—	4,927	1,532	31	1,125	232	174	891	2,504
TURLOCK	CA	c	1	64	44	56	41,916	50,952	n	—	—	5,853	4,536	77	3,104	737	695	349	968
TUSCALOOSA	AL	c	1	229	227	50–54	35,917	47,660	y	—	20	14,099	12,856	91	10,400	1,420	1,036	241	1,002
TUSTIN	CA	c	—	—	—	—	—	—	—	—	—	—	—	—	—	—	—	—	—
TYLER	TX	c	1	136	133	56	36,743	48,091	y	49,291	1	—	—	—	—	—	—	—	—
UNION CITY	CA	c	1	46	43	56	79,968	85,428	y	86,952	19	10,591	9,294	88	6,150	2,051	1,092	291	1,005
UPLAND	CA	c	3	47	36	56	55,810	67,837	y	69,533	5	6,868	4,618	67	3,959	511	148	85	2,165
VACAVILLE	CA	c	1	84	79	56	69,643	84,651	y	88,884	12	16,368	—	—	9,551	—	2,067	1,070	1,579
VICTORIA	TX	c	1	108	102	56	36,359	56,630	y	—	1	8,582	6,658	78	4,882	1,013	763	195	1,728
VICTORVILLE	CA	c	1	78	63	56	46,908	57,156	y	59,537	5	7,228	—	—	4,277	—	1,833	28	1,025
WEST BLOOMFIELD CHARTER TOWNSHIP	MI	tp	1	102	97	50–54	36,144	58,551	y	64,406	5	13,602	—	—	7,277	—	3,057	1,291	1,096
WEST CHESTER	OH	tp	1	51	50	50–54	44,853	58,622	y	—	5	6,764	—	—	4,135	—	861	592	628
WEST HARTFORD	CT	t	1	92	90	42	49,686	62,608	n	—	—	11,667	10,949	94	8,354	1,097	1,497	—	718
WEST JORDAN	UT	c	1	84	81	56	38,293	48,880	n	—	—	8,558	—	—	5,081	—	1,077	550	921
WESTLAND	MI	c	1	80	78	50–54	39,202	56,004	y	56,004	3	10,681	10,152	95	6,068	2,005	2,078	94	435
WHEATON	IL	c	1	33	32	other	46,195	66,560	y	67,560	—	6,758	4,580	68	3,314	787	479	21	2,156
WHITE PLAINS	NY	c	1	172	165	42	48,982	73,544	y	76,836	5	19,377	18,587	96	13,934	2,972	1,681	125	665
WHITTIER	CA	c	—	—	—	—	—	—	—	—	—	—	—	—	—	—	—	—	—
WILMINGTON	NC	c	1	211	204	56	25,407	40,233	n	—	—	13,809	10,548	76	8,270	1,334	943	1,670	1,591
WYOMING	MI	c	1	31	30	50–54	45,130	55,430	y	56,430	5	4,570	3,238	71	2,072	498	667	21	1,311
YAKIMA	WA	c	3	87	84	50–54	47,689	64,636	y	71,099	4	9,458	7,943	84	6,587	352	1,004	705	810
YORBA LINDA	CA	c	—	—	—	—	—	—	—	—	—	—	—	—	—	—	—	—	—
YUMA	AZ	c	1	107	90	56	39,108	54,750	y	—	—	9,664	7,806	81	6,144	987	674	107	1,752
25,000–49,999																			
ADDISON	IL	v	—	—	—	—	—	—	—	—	—	—	—	—	—	—	—	—	—
ALAMOGORDO	NM	c	4	—	—	—	—	—	n	—	—	—	—	—	—	—	—	—	—
ALTAMONTE SPRINGS	FL	c	—	—	—	—	—	—	—	—	—	—	—	—	—	—	—	—	—
ALTOONA	PA	c	1	66	66	42	28,119	46,382	y	51,252	5	—	—	—	3,301	—	—	—	—
ANDERSON	SC	c	1	54	53	50–54	26,517	39,775	n	—	—	2,732	2,475	91	1,872	303	300	—	257
ANDOVER	MN	c	2	3	—	other	—	—	—	—	—	1,068	678	64	387	254	36	78	312
ANKENY	IA	c	1	11	10	56	—	—	y	—	—	2,183	1,509	69	1,085	246	177	293	381
APOPKA	FL	c	1	99	77	56	36,979	55,469	n	—	—	9,228	7,093	77	5,059	1,261	772	1,183	952
APPLE VALLEY	MN	c	2	4	—	other	—	—	—	—	—	298	—	—	594	—	529	43	437

Table 3/17 continued

FIRE DEPARTMENT PERSONNEL, SALARIES, AND EXPENDITURES FOR CITIES 10,000 AND OVER: 2007

City	State	Type	Service provision	Full-time paid personnel	Full-time uniformed personnel	Duty hours per week	Minimum base salary ($)	Maximum base salary ($)	Longevity pay	Maximum salary with longevity ($)	Years of service for longevity	Total expenditures (A) ($)	Total personnel expenditures (B) ($)	(B) as % of (A)	Salaries and wages (C) ($)	City contribution to retirement and social security (D) ($)	City contribution to insurance (E) ($)	Capital outlay (F) ($)	All other (G) ($)
25,000–49,999 continued																			
ATASCADERO	CA	c	1	—	—	56	47,266	57,452	n	—	—	—	—	—	—	—	—	—	—
AUBURN	AL	c	4	43	43	50–54	31,948	49,837	n	—	—	3,851	3,222	84	2,712	377	133	252	376
AUBURN	NY	c	1	72	71	48	35,650	52,487	y	53,837	4	5,679	—	—	4,660	—	—	7	226
AUBURN	WA	c	—	—	—	—	—	—	—	—	—	—	—	—	—	—	—	—	—
AVONDALE	AZ	c	1	57	50	56	41,174	59,632	n	—	—	6,822	5,235	77	4,241	470	523	23	1,565
BALLWIN	MO	c	—	—	—	—	—	—	—	—	—	—	—	—	—	—	—	—	—
BARTLESVILLE	OK	c	1	69	64	56	28,654	36,516	y	37,746	5	4,002	3,722	93	2,812	375	535	2	278
BELL	CA	c	—	—	—	—	—	—	—	—	—	—	—	—	—	—	—	—	—
BELLEVILLE	NJ	tp	1	—	—	42	34,169	68,823	y	80,073	7	—	—	—	6,491	—	—	275	149
BELMONT	CA	c	1	43	40	56	—	—	n	—	—	—	—	—	8,756	—	—	—	—
BELOIT	WI	c	1	63	57	50–54	36,730	51,423	y	—	—	7,969	6,966	87	4,112	938	1,915	410	593
BETHEL PARK	PA	c	2	—	—	—	—	—	—	—	—	171	—	—	—	—	29	—	143
BEVERLY	MA	c	1	72	65	42	46,230	49,040	y	50,140	10	4,949	—	—	4,645	—	—	—	304
BEVERLY HILLS	CA	c	1	91	82	56	70,000	100,153	n	—	—	23,384	15,694	67	10,434	3,607	1,653	68	7,562
BIG SPRING	TX	c	1	—	—	56	26,475	26,475	y	—	—	2,429	2,222	92	1,816	116	291	291	206
BLUE SPRINGS	MO	c	—	—	—	—	—	—	—	—	—	—	—	—	—	—	—	—	—
BONITA SPRINGS	FL	c	—	—	—	—	—	—	—	—	—	—	—	—	—	—	—	—	—
BOTHELL	WA	c	1	55	51	50–54	50,808	72,588	y	79,847	5	7,134	5,793	81	4,738	300	755	333	1,008
BOWLING GREEN	OH	c	1	50	—	50–54	40,236	53,215	n	—	—	—	—	—	—	547	403	—	402
BRADENTON	FL	c	1	76	70	56	34,239	56,710	y	—	5	6,972	—	—	4,498	2,221	601	547	461
BREMERTON	WA	c	1	58	56	50–54	—	—	—	—	—	6,553	—	—	4,588	—	—	—	934
BROOKFIELD	WI	c	1	58	57	56	42,623	61,453	n	—	—	6,786	5,972	88	4,161	881	930	220	593
BROOKLYN CENTER	MN	c	3	2	1	other	—	—	n	—	—	860	549	64	310	201	38	—	310
BROOMFIELD	CO	c	—	—	—	—	—	—	—	—	—	—	—	—	—	—	—	—	—
BUFFALO GROVE	IL	v	1	—	—	48	—	—	—	—	—	—	—	—	—	—	—	—	—
BULLHEAD CITY	AZ	c	—	—	—	—	—	—	—	—	—	—	—	—	—	—	—	—	—
BURLINGTON	IA	c	1	41	41	56	32,823	42,479	y	43,429	5	3,725	3,234	87	2,151	586	497	35	456
BURLINGTON	NC	c	1	91	89	56	30,847	50,878	y	43,931	5	5,372	4,559	85	3,554	826	178	120	693
CALEXICO	CA	c	—	—	—	—	—	—	—	—	—	—	—	—	—	—	—	—	—
CAMPBELL	CA	c	5	—	—	—	—	—	—	—	—	—	—	—	—	—	—	—	—
CAROL STREAM	IL	v	—	—	—	—	—	—	—	—	—	—	—	—	—	—	—	—	—
CARPENTERSVILLE	IL	v	1	41	26	50–54	46,179	62,749	y	63,549	1	4,414	—	—	3,389	—	—	150	462
CASA GRANDE	AZ	c	1	40	39	56	34,134	54,114	n	—	—	7,490	4,740	63	3,734	496	509	2,292	459
CASPER	WY	c	1	75	73	56	39,229	47,693	n	—	—	5,804	5,592	96	4,432	482	677	17	196
CEDAR FALLS	IA	c	3	34	21	48	33,592	43,955	y	45,335	4	2,800	2,503	89	1,636	377	490	8	289
CEDAR HILL	TX	c	1	59	58	56	39,000	52,627	y	53,827	1	5,970	4,329	73	3,120	617	591	652	1,025
CHARLOTTESVILLE	VA	c	3	90	—	56	33,904	51,230	n	—	—	7,730	—	—	4,409	2,489	1,295	558	1,149
CHELTENHAM	PA	tp	2	—	—	other	—	—	—	—	—	—	—	—	—	—	—	—	—
CHESTER	PA	c	1	—	59	48	43,144	—	y	49,184	3	4,812	—	—	3,451	—	988	126	—
CHESTERFIELD	MO	c	—	—	—	—	—	—	—	—	—	—	—	—	—	—	—	—	—
CLAREMONT	CA	c	—	—	—	—	—	—	—	—	—	—	—	—	—	—	—	—	—
CLEBURNE	TX	c	1	54	53	56	40,538	47,407	y	52,207	1	4,757	4,338	91	3,205	591	542	—	419
CLINTON	IA	c	1	45	45	50–54	29,506	48,812	n	—	—	3,753	3,381	90	2,212	616	552	1	371
COCONUT CREEK	FL	c	5	—	—	—	—	—	—	—	—	—	—	—	—	—	—	—	—
COLLIERVILLE	TN	t	3	69	66	56	31,078	47,317	n	—	—	5,638	4,819	85	3,584	640	594	368	451
COLTON	CA	c	1	49	46	—	57,096	63,294	n	—	—	8,906	—	—	4,852	—	1,147	165	946
COLUMBIA	TN	c	1	90	86	50–54	24,876	38,226	y	—	3	5,543	4,894	88	3,815	722	356	75	573
CONROE	TX	c	1	79	72	48	37,500	51,109	y	—	11	6,449	5,575	86	4,068	802	704	128	795
CONWAY	AR	c	1	95	93	50–54	28,434	38,412	n	—	—	6,915	5,278	76	4,226	703	349	349	1,150
COPPERAS COVE	TX	c	3	52	50	other	32,002	47,161	y	47,161	1	2,686	2,323	87	1,873	291	160	8	355
CORAL GABLES	FL	c	1	144	128	48	44,415	62,533	y	72,390	10	22,843	20,557	90	13,488	5,786	1,282	117	2,229
COTTAGE GROVE	MN	c	3	3	3	40	40,800	50,520	n	—	—	760	322	42	273	36	13	1	437
COVINGTON	KY	c	1	119	118	48	32,931	46,251	y	—	3	12,296	—	—	7,300	—	1,862	421	562
CYPRESS	CA	c	—	—	—	—	—	—	—	—	—	—	—	—	—	—	—	—	—
DANA POINT	CA	c	—	—	—	—	—	—	—	—	—	—	—	—	—	—	—	—	—
DANVILLE	VA	c	1	123	122	50–54	28,525	44,646	n	—	—	6,740	5,968	89	4,672	580	715	133	639
DE SOTO	TX	c	1	62	60	50–54	41,820	51,996	y	53,196	1	5,126	4,615	90	3,435	721	460	308	203
DEER PARK	TX	c	2	—	—	other	—	—	y	—	0	—	—	—	—	—	—	—	—
DELAWARE	OH	c	1	44	39	50–54	41,746	62,379	y	—	5	4,632	—	—	2,700	—	469	100	474
DELTA	MI	tp	1	35	30	56	37,559	51,817	y	53,630	5	—	—	—	—	—	—	—	—
DEPTFORD	NJ	tp	—	—	—	—	—	—	—	—	—	—	—	—	—	—	—	—	—
DERRY	NH	t	1	87	76	42	38,963	45,100	y	—	5	9,857	8,055	82	5,958	892	1,204	561	1,241
DOVER	DE	c	3	6	4	40	—	—	n	—	—	949	388	41	271	76	41	358	203
DOVER	NH	c	1	51	49	48	35,359	57,985	y	59,585	5	4,934	4,581	93	3,099	487	994	3	350
DOWNERS GROVE	IL	v	1	—	—	other	—	—	—	—	—	—	—	—	—	—	—	—	—
DRACUT	MA	t	1	42	41	42	30,066	44,254	y	45,084	5	2,856	—	—	2,292	363	—	68	133
DUBLIN	OH	c	—	—	—	—	—	—	—	—	—	—	—	—	—	—	—	—	—
DUNCANVILLE	TX	c	1	52	51	56	40,375	51,706	y	52,906	1	4,822	4,393	91	3,266	771	356	156	273
DUNEDIN	FL	c	1	57	53	56	39,409	56,831	n	—	—	6,244	4,904	79	3,543	772	589	116	1,224
EAST BRUNSWICK	NJ	tp	2	—	—	—	—	—	—	—	—	—	—	—	—	—	—	—	—
EAST CLEVELAND	OH	c	1	53	47	48	24,234	40,457	y	41,782	6	—	—	—	—	137	137	12	—
EASTPOINTE	MI	c	1	25	—	56	45,966	55,966	y	—	5	—	—	—	—	—	—	—	—
EGG HARBOR	NJ	tp	2	2	—	—	—	—	—	—	—	425	124	29	105	17	2	58	208

Table 3/17
continued

FIRE DEPARTMENT PERSONNEL, SALARIES, AND EXPENDITURES FOR
CITIES 10,000 AND OVER: 2007

City	State	Type	Service provision	Full-time paid personnel	Full-time uniformed personnel	Duty hours per week	Minimum base salary ($)	Maximum base salary ($)	Longevity pay	Maximum salary with longevity ($)	Years of service for longevity	Total expenditures (A) ($)	Total personnel expenditures (B) ($)	(B) as % of (A)	Salaries and wages (C) ($)	City contribution to retirement and social security (D) ($)	City contribution to insurance (E) ($)	Capital outlay (F) ($)	All other (G) ($)
25,000–49,999 continued																			
ELK GROVE VILLAGE	IL	v	1	100	83	50–54	47,433	69,056	y	69,881	10	12,078	7,352	61	5,230	779	1,344	340	4,385
ELMWOOD PARK	IL	v	1	26	26	50–54	46,151	61,211	y	68,752	3	3,638	2,982	82	1,901	881	200	20	636
EMPORIA	KS	c	1	54	49	50–54	24,428	45,961	n	—	—	3,296	2,807	85	2,244	358	205	22	467
EULESS	TX	c	1	69	66	56	44,345	56,598	y	—	1	5,597	5,211	93	4,162	625	424	4	382
EUREKA	CA	c	1	38	36	56	36,096	43,896	y	—	—	4,608	—	—	2,403	—	503	195	917
FAIRBORN	OH	c	1	51	50	50–54	38,607	56,215	y	57,620	5	5,233	4,717	90	3,328	819	569	—	516
FARMERS BRANCH	TX	c	1	63	55	56	46,274	57,666	y	—	1	—	—	—	—	—	—	—	—
FINDLAY	OH	c	1	72	71	other	33,920	49,298	y	54,228	10	6,158	5,739	93	4,071	932	736	—	418
FISHERS	IN	t	1	122	117	56	37,680	52,752	n	—	—	1,578	—	—	5,635	1,664	1,268	500	1,078
FITCHBURG	MA	c	1	90	87	42	38,994	43,222	y	—	5	—	—	—	5,988	—	—	—	318
FOND DU LAC	WI	c	1	63	61	56	43,084	52,175	y	53,195	5	7,673	6,026	79	4,276	896	853	745	903
FOSTER CITY	CA	c	1	34	—	48	—	—	y	—	—	6,831	—	—	6,097	—	—	—	734
FREEHOLD	NJ	tp	—	—	—	—	—	—	—	—	—	—	—	—	—	—	—	—	—
FRIENDSWOOD	TX	c	2	—	—	—	—	—	—	—	—	1,598	293	18	226	45	22	72	1,233
GALLOWAY	NJ	tp	2	1	—	other	—	—	n	—	—	1,099	821	75	36	772	12	691	358
GARFIELD HEIGHTS	OH	c	1	—	47	50–54	41,172	54,661	y	57,136	5	4,357	—	—	2,954	—	694	—	219
GEORGETOWN	TX	c	1	58	56	40	33,000	52,051	y	55,747	0	6,793	3,388	50	2,618	474	295	2,729	676
GILROY	CA	c	1	44	40	56	67,086	81,544	n	—	—	7,422	6,515	88	4,416	1,351	748	—	907
GLASTONBURY	CT	t	3	2	1	other	—	—	n	—	—	904	455	50	360	42	52	91	359
GLENDORA	CA	c	—	—	—	—	—	—	—	—	—	—	—	—	—	—	—	—	—
GLOUCESTER	MA	c	1	78	77	42	38,338	46,514	y	48,014	20	5,427	—	—	4,733	—	—	3	244
GOLDSBORO	NC	c	1	81	79	56	28,621	43,555	y	45,297	5	4,205	3,761	89	2,977	367	416	—	444
GOOSE CREEK	SC	c	3	42	37	40	28,992	44,115	n	—	—	2,311	1,917	83	1,523	206	188	15	380
GRAND BLANC	MI	tp	—	—	—	—	—	—	—	—	—	—	—	—	—	—	—	—	—
GRAND FORKS	ND	c	1	66	64	50–54	35,057	52,586	y	53,606	6	4,573	4,306	94	3,294	652	360	8	259
GRANTS PASS	OR	c	4	—	—	56	43,968	60,120	n	—	—	—	—	—	—	—	—	—	—
GREENFIELD	WI	c	1	52	51	56	38,360	58,966	y	59,266	5	4,915	4,410	90	2,832	892	684	119	386
GREENVILLE	MS	c	1	85	81	48	22,500	24,232	y	—	10	3,775	—	—	2,739	1,011	297	270	1
GREENWOOD	IN	c	3	32	30	50–54	38,108	47,381	y	48,881	0	6,610	3,020	46	2,390	366	263	1,624	1,966
GROTON	CT	t	—	—	—	—	—	—	—	—	—	—	—	—	—	—	—	—	—
HALTOM CITY	TX	c	1	50	45	56	38,135	48,253	y	—	1	4,099	—	—	2,797	—	262	345	315
HANFORD	CA	c	3	32	30	56	39,865	48,019	n	—	—	3,014	—	—	1,666	4,478	219	108	426
HANOVER PARK	IL	v	1	36	24	50–54	—	—	y	—	—	8,930	3,167	35	2,384	421	362	5,131	631
HARRISONBURG	VA	c	3	71	70	50–54	28,772	43,201	y	—	—	5,448	4,311	79	3,225	673	412	364	773
HAZELWOOD	MO	c	1	38	36	other	46,683	60,688	n	—	—	—	—	—	—	—	—	—	—
HELENA	MT	c	1	37	36	48	39,934	46,271	y	48,930	1	3,234	2,660	82	2,078	290	292	115	463
HENDERSON	KY	c	1	58	56	56	29,907	39,971	y	40,371	—	5,138	3,983	78	2,534	651	798	862	293
HENDERSONVILLE	TN	c	3	97	94	other	30,682	46,685	y	48,585	2	5,607	4,939	88	3,748	815	376	231	436
HILTON HEAD ISLAND	SC	t	1	145	115	56	33,949	48,377	n	—	—	—	11,877	—	7,616	3,340	920	1,309	—
HOLLAND	MI	c	3	28	27	56	45,282	54,629	y	55,829	5	2,808	2,319	83	1,845	148	326	13	476
HOMESTEAD	FL	c	—	—	—	—	—	—	—	—	—	—	—	—	—	—	—	—	—
HUBER HEIGHTS	OH	c	1	54	51	other	38,312	55,680	n	—	—	6,700	4,957	74	3,354	873	729	1,287	456
HURST	TX	c	1	57	56	50–54	54,246	59,467	y	61,987	1	6,138	5,159	84	3,797	870	492	53	925
HUTCHINSON	KS	c	1	91	90	56	31,740	42,948	y	44,148	5	5,478	—	—	4,576	—	—	508	394
INVER GROVE HEIGHTS	MN	c	4	9	8	other	—	11,817	y	—	—	—	—	—	—	—	—	—	—
ITHACA	NY	c	1	69	67	40	31,949	59,327	y	60,877	10	7,821	6,326	81	4,477	906	943	158	1,337
JACKSONVILLE	AR	c	1	49	48	50–54	25,965	38,947	y	39,547	3	—	—	—	—	758	365	8	1,998
JAMESTOWN	NY	c	1	58	57	42	37,523	63,526	y	65,386	4	6,450	6,290	98	4,187	949	1,153	23	138
JEFFERSONTOWN	KY	c	—	—	—	—	—	—	—	—	—	—	—	—	—	—	—	—	—
KANNAPOLIS	NC	c	3	67	55	50–54	23,201	35,988	n	—	—	3,722	2,561	69	2,078	242	240	512	649
KELLER	TX	c	1	53	51	56	42,049	55,299	y	55,299	1	4,210	3,154	75	2,585	465	103	56	1,000
KINGSPORT	TN	c	1	97	93	56	28,376	39,560	n	—	—	5,973	5,233	88	3,868	790	575	9	731
KISSIMMEE	FL	c	1	110	103	56	33,430	51,688	y	51,988	10	9,925	8,253	83	5,737	1,438	1,077	530	1,142
KOKOMO	IN	c	1	124	121	56	40,136	44,595	y	47,195	3	10,485	9,732	93	6,475	2,198	1,058	165	589
LA GRANGE	GA	c	1	60	58	50–54	27,602	39,761	—	—	—	—	—	—	—	—	—	—	—
LA PUENTE	CA	c	5	—	—	—	—	—	—	—	—	—	—	—	—	—	—	—	—
LA VERNE	CA	c	1	35	33	56	54,373	66,091	n	—	—	—	5,218	—	3,820	910	487	—	—
LACEY	WA	c	—	—	—	—	—	—	—	—	—	—	—	—	—	—	—	—	—
LANCASTER	OH	c	1	95	93	50–54	36,173	48,843	y	—	5	7,980	—	—	4,992	—	1,104	116	254
LAWNDALE	CA	c	—	—	—	—	—	—	—	—	—	—	—	—	—	—	—	—	—
LEAGUE CITY	TX	c	2	6	4	other	—	—	—	—	—	394	275	70	213	37	25	24	—
LEAVENWORTH	KS	c	1	56	55	50–54	30,504	45,756	y	46,356	5	3,782	3,498	92	2,571	363	564	—	285
LEAWOOD	KS	c	1	56	55	50–54	30,371	46,530	y	—	5	4,385	3,845	88	2,943	586	316	225	315
LEESBURG	VA	t	—	—	—	—	—	—	—	—	—	—	—	—	—	—	—	—	—
LENEXA	KS	c	1	91	89	56	34,408	51,234	n	—	—	8,615	8,111	94	5,374	1,562	1,175	164	340
LEWISTON	ID	c	1	51	—	50–54	40,304	60,097	y	52,945	1	—	—	—	—	—	—	—	—
LEWISTON	ME	c	1	79	74	42	29,348	43,742	y	43,724	15	4,802	4,698	98	3,962	100	636	36	704
LIBERTY	MO	c	1	41	39	other	35,143	49,200	n	—	—	3,747	3,224	86	2,299	509	415	524	313
LIMA	OH	c	1	65	64	50–54	37,115	43,419	y	46,168	8	7,212	—	—	4,243	—	1,165	471	351
LINCOLN PARK	MI	c	1	33	29	56	40,247	50,290	y	—	1	—	—	—	—	—	—	—	—
LINDENHURST	NY	v	—	—	—	40	—	—	—	—	—	—	—	—	—	—	—	—	—
LOMBARD	IL	v	1	77	64	50–54	46,522	64,332	n	—	—	9,330	8,131	87	6,111	1,366	654	332	867

Table 3/17 continued **FIRE DEPARTMENT PERSONNEL, SALARIES, AND EXPENDITURES FOR CITIES 10,000 AND OVER: 2007**

												Reported expenditures (in $000)							
City	State	Type	Service provision	Full-time paid personnel	Full-time uniformed personnel	Duty hours per week	Minimum base salary ($)	Maximum base salary ($)	Longevity pay	Maximum salary with longevity ($)	Years of service for longevity	Total expenditures (A) ($)	Total personnel expenditures (B) ($)	(B) as % of (A)	Salaries and wages (C) ($)	City contribution to retirement and social security (D) ($)	City contribution to insurance (E) ($)	Capital outlay (F) ($)	All other (G) ($)
25,000–49,999 continued																			
LOMPOC	CA	c	1	25	21	56	45,420	57,960	n	—	—	3,504	—	—	2,330	—	347	45	315
LONG BEACH	NY	c	3	22	22	40	34,214	86,001	y	93,762	6	2,673	—	—	2,491	435	—	75	182
LOS ALTOS	CA	c	5	—	—	—	—	—	—	—	—	3,020	—	—	—	—	—	—	—
LOS BANOS	CA	c	3	20	17	56	40,368	—	n	—	—	—	—	—	—	272	116	254	345
LOWER MAKEFIELD	PA	tp	2	—	—	—	—	—	—	—	—	1,303	—	—	—	—	—	628	—
LUFKIN	TX	c	1	82	76	48	30,047	45,913	y	48,313	1	5,919	4,797	81	3,759	645	394	496	626
LYNNWOOD	WA	c	1	54	52	48	56,482	66,752	y	71,856	5	13,882	11,104	80	8,770	445	1,889	22	2,755
MADERA	CA	c	5	—	—	other	—	—	—	—	—	2,297	—	—	42	—	16	121	2,113
MADISON HEIGHTS	MI	c	1	37	35	56	40,236	58,032	y	62,675	5	5,146	4,132	80	2,848	682	602	—	1,014
MANALAPAN	NJ	tp	2	—	—	other	—	—	—	—	—	—	—	—	—	—	—	—	—
MANASSAS	VA	c	3	8	8	50–54	40,186	67,122	n	—	—	737	724	98	534	113	76	—	13
MANCHESTER	NJ	tp	2	—	—	other	—	—	y	—	—	—	—	—	—	—	—	—	—
MANHATTAN	KS	c	1	78	68	56	31,857	39,166	n	—	—	5,001	4,174	83	2,872	452	849	153	674
MANSFIELD	OH	c	1	100	98	48	35,050	46,777	y	—	1	10,492	9,155	87	6,292	1,528	1,335	116	1,222
MAPLE HEIGHTS	OH	c	1	43	41	other	53,317	53,317	y	55,717	5	5,488	—	—	2,704	—	732	485	350
MARION	IA	c	1	28	28	56	35,924	44,720	y	45,920	5	2,649	2,357	89	1,563	437	356	157	135
MARYLAND HEIGHTS	MO	c	—	—	—	—	—	—	—	—	—	—	—	—	—	—	—	—	—
MARYSVILLE	WA	c	3	73	67	50–54	46,500	66,453	y	68,446	10	8,291	6,905	83	5,418	486	1,001	53	1,333
MASON CITY	IA	c	1	46	44	56	29,536	44,720	n	—	—	3,966	3,225	81	2,318	600	307	598	143
McCANDLESS	PA	t	2	—	—	—	—	—	—	—	—	—	—	—	—	—	—	—	—
McMINNVILLE	OR	c	3	23	22	56	43,860	55,980	y	57,780	—	4,534	2,491	55	1,702	482	306	33	2,010
MEDINA	OH	c	1	3	2	40	36,088	53,310	y	54,390	5	—	—	—	—	—	—	—	—
MENLO PARK	CA	c	—	—	—	—	—	—	—	—	—	—	—	—	—	—	—	—	—
MENOMONEE FALLS	WI	v	3	15	14	50–54	45,531	59,602	n	—	—	2,028	1,676	83	1,193	289	193	9	343
MICHIGAN CITY	IN	c	1	82	81	56	38,661	38,661	y	—	3	7,313	6,827	93	4,832	1,087	907	273	214
MIDLAND	MI	c	1	46	44	56	32,460	52,373	y	56,562	5	5,360	4,238	79	2,783	687	768	167	955
MIDVALE	UT	c	1	37	34	48	35,906	47,320	n	—	—	—	—	—	—	—	—	—	—
MILFORD	MA	t	1	40	40	48	36,801	45,188	y	—	5	2,903	—	—	2,643	—	—	130	130
MILTON	MA	t	1	59	58	42	33,917	47,653	y	—	10	3,926	—	—	3,652	—	—	46	228
MINOT	ND	c	1	50	48	56	31,623	50,554	n	—	—	2,828	—	—	3,159	159	224	69	216
MISHAWAKA	IN	c	1	108	107	56	45,136	47,771	—	—	—	—	—	—	—	—	991	358	189
MISSION	TX	c	3	63	58	56	32,000	32,000	y	33,200	1	3,394	3,119	92	2,387	358	374	13	262
MOLINE	IL	c	1	70	69	50–54	40,357	62,455	n	—	—	8,755	7,028	80	4,801	1,279	947	—	1,727
MONROE	NC	c	1	87	79	56	29,090	44,204	n	—	—	4,719	3,474	74	2,659	483	332	794	486
MONROVIA	CA	c	1	43	41	56	53,462	79,032	y	—	6	7,584	—	—	4,053	—	442	42	1,426
MONTCLAIR	NJ	tp	1	—	—	48	27,093	77,088	y	84,797	—	—	—	—	—	—	—	—	—
MOORE	OK	c	1	60	57	56	31,259	50,648	y	53,814	3	275	—	—	3,505	—	463	407	98
MOORHEAD	MN	c	1	31	30	56	40,586	45,055	y	46,857	30	3,069	1,999	65	1,586	183	230	536	533
MOORPARK	CA	c	—	—	—	—	—	—	—	—	—	—	—	—	—	—	—	—	—
MOUNT LEBANON	PA	c	3	18	17	40	55,432	73,112	y	74,940	4	3,312	2,043	62	1,455	242	346	373	895
MOUNT PLEASANT	SC	t	1	114	109	50–54	26,142	40,068	n	—	—	5,243	4,543	87	3,837	575	130	201	500
MOUNT VERNON	WA	c	3	37	34	48	46,702	56,732	y	73,134	5	3,742	3,103	83	2,602	157	344	62	577
MURRIETA	CA	c	1	47	40	50–54	59,501	72,323	n	—	—	—	—	—	—	—	—	—	—
MUSKEGON	MI	c	—	—	—	—	—	—	—	—	—	—	—	—	—	—	—	—	—
NATICK	MA	t	1	88	85	42	38,715	48,157	y	50,565	10	161	—	—	5,566	—	—	—	—
NAUGATUCK	CT	t	1	42	37	42	48,018	56,012	y	56,212	15	—	—	—	—	—	—	—	—
NEPTUNE	NJ	tp	—	—	—	—	—	—	—	—	—	—	—	—	—	—	—	—	—
NEW ALBANY	IN	c	1	73	72	56	41,519	55,636	y	55,636	1	7,127	6,936	97	4,828	579	1,529	—	190
NEW BERLIN	WI	c	1	15	13	other	45,762	50,992	n	—	—	2,220	1,844	83	1,407	321	115	50	326
NEW BRAUNFELS	TX	c	1	95	91	48	34,302	39,989	y	41,939	25	7,958	6,480	81	4,697	969	814	271	1,207
NEW IBERIA	LA	c	1	58	12	50–54	26,632	—	y	—	5	—	—	—	—	—	—	—	—
NEW LONDON	CT	c	1	—	70	42	—	50,657	y	51,407	5	—	—	—	4,737	—	—	953	412
NEWARK	DE	c	—	—	—	—	—	—	—	—	—	—	—	—	—	—	—	—	—
NEWARK	OH	c	1	80	78	48	29,786	46,280	y	47,195	4	8,546	7,482	88	5,098	1,280	1,104	—	1,064
NEWPORT	RI	c	1	99	99	42	29,497	41,014	y	75,200	7	13,285	12,007	90	6,492	3,543	1,972	307	970
NILES	IL	v	1	57	55	50–54	—	—	y	—	8	7,552	6,201	82	4,811	319	1,071	841	510
NORMAL	IL	t	1	66	62	50–54	39,852	62,269	n	—	—	5,701	4,926	86	3,365	1,131	429	371	404
NORTH CHICAGO	IL	c	1	33	26	40	36,288	56,211	n	—	—	2,709	2,607	96	2,020	323	264	—	102
NORTH HUNTINGDON	PA	tp	2	—	—	—	—	—	—	—	—	—	—	—	—	—	—	—	—
NORTH LAUDERDALE	FL	c	1	44	43	—	—	—	—	—	—	4,790	3,556	74	2,582	685	289	46	1,188
NORTH ROYALTON	OH	c	1	37	36	other	42,685	56,753	y	58,753	5	4,322	—	—	2,698	—	422	80	519
NORTHAMPTON	MA	c	1	61	52	42	35,843	43,997	y	44,797	5	—	—	—	—	—	—	—	—
NORTHAMPTON	PA	tp	2	—	—	—	—	—	—	—	—	—	—	—	—	—	—	—	—
NORTHBROOK	IL	v	1	75	67	56	44,684	71,087	y	72,887	5	11,629	9,575	82	6,398	1,995	1,182	458	1,596
NOVATO	CA	c	—	—	—	—	—	—	—	—	—	—	—	—	—	—	—	—	—
NOVI	MI	c	1	31	30	48	35,010	57,215	n	—	—	4,708	3,683	78	2,745	478	459	525	460
O'FALLON	MO	c	—	—	—	—	—	—	—	—	—	—	—	—	—	—	—	—	—
OAK CREEK	WI	c	1	53	52	56	41,085	58,560	y	58,800	5	6,329	6,115	97	3,372	2,103	639	—	417
OAK PARK	MI	c	4	—	—	42	—	—	—	—	—	—	—	—	—	—	—	—	—
OAKLAND PARK	FL	c	1	72	68	48	—	—	n	—	—	8,877	7,196	81	5,230	1,317	649	74	1,735
OAKLEY	CA	c	—	—	—	—	—	—	—	—	—	—	—	—	—	—	—	—	—
OCALA	FL	c	1	128	118	50–54	30,128	47,258	y	48,675	1	10,994	8,873	81	6,361	1,459	1,053	470	1,651
OVIEDO	FL	c	1	51	48	56	35,987	56,786	n	—	—	4,323	3,025	70	2,450	336	238	424	874

Table 3/17
continued

FIRE DEPARTMENT PERSONNEL, SALARIES, AND EXPENDITURES FOR
CITIES 10,000 AND OVER: 2007

City	State	Type	Service provision	Full-time paid personnel	Full-time uniformed personnel	Duty hours per week	Minimum base salary ($)	Maximum base salary ($)	Longevity pay	Maximum salary with longevity ($)	Years of service for longevity	Total expenditures (A) ($)	Total personnel expenditures (B) ($)	(B) as % of (A)	Salaries and wages (C) ($)	City contribution to retirement and social security (D) ($)	City contribution to insurance (E) ($)	Capital outlay (F) ($)	All other (G) ($)
25,000–49,999 continued																			
PACIFICA	CA	c	1	33	8	56	63,528	85,092	y	94,512	5	5,815	—	—	3,813	—	—	30	402
PALM BEACH GARDENS	FL	c	1	128	109	48	44,088	38,304	y	56,592	10	15,225	13,354	88	9,427	2,247	1,679	95	1,775
PALM COAST	FL	c	3	48	46	56	31,800	53,700	n	—	—	4,644	3,094	67	1,996	686	412	228	1,322
PALM SPRINGS	CA	c	1	62	58	—	—	—	y	—	—	—	—	—	—	—	—	—	—
PANAMA CITY	FL	c	1	83	77	56	26,594	34,080	n	—	—	5,989	5,096	85	3,480	1,031	585	388	505
PARADISE	CA	t	1	26	24	56	35,439	45,223	y	46,354	10	3,471	3,143	91	1,765	849	529	165	163
PASCO	WA	c	1	51	49	50–54	48,646	60,034	y	62,426	20	6,037	4,870	81	4,320	205	344	263	904
PEABODY	MA	c	1	101	96	42	41,720	44,346	y	46,846	5	5,826	—	—	5,525	—	—	—	301
PEACHTREE CITY	GA	c	3	51	49	48	32,508	52,349	n	—	—	4,507	3,596	80	2,570	532	494	250	661
PEARLAND	TX	c	2	—	—	—	—	—	—	—	—	—	—	—	—	—	—	—	—
PINELLAS PARK	FL	c	1	96	88	56	35,022	53,294	y	54,626	—	10,810	8,239	76	5,809	1,598	832	1,152	1,418
PITTSFIELD CHARTER TOWNSHIP	MI	tp	1	20	20	50–54	34,778	46,719	y	47,919	5	2,321	1,806	78	1,371	182	251	55	461
PLACENTIA	CA	c	—	—	—	—	—	—	—	—	—	—	—	—	—	—	—	—	—
PLAINFIELD	MI	tp	1	15	14	56	33,549	43,593	n	—	—	2,099	1,448	69	1,138	163	145	220	432
PLANT CITY	FL	c	1	—	—	56	—	—	—	—	—	—	—	—	—	—	—	—	—
PLEASANT HILL	CA	c	—	—	—	—	—	—	—	—	—	—	—	—	—	—	—	—	—
PORT HURON	MI	c	1	52	51	56	39,751	53,001	y	58,301	20	5,604	—	—	3,128	—	—	111	549
PORT ORANGE	FL	c	1	67	63	56	33,837	54,163	n	—	—	7,127	5,752	81	3,878	1,435	439	79	1,297
PORTERVILLE	CA	c	1	35	34	56	39,216	47,856	n	—	—	3,011	—	—	1,665	—	—	28	553
POWAY	CA	c	1	55	—	56	47,292	57,732	n	—	—	—	—	—	—	—	—	566	584
PRESCOTT	AZ	c	1	—	—	56	—	—	—	—	—	—	—	—	—	—	—	—	4,131
QUINCY	IL	c	1	69	64	56	34,292	46,563	y	51,219	10	6,463	5,923	92	3,649	1,343	930	15	4,174
RANCHO SANTA MARGARITA	CA	c	—	—	—	—	—	—	—	—	—	—	—	—	—	—	—	—	—
REYNOLDSBURG	OH	c	—	—	—	—	—	—	—	—	—	—	—	—	—	—	—	—	—
RICHLAND	WA	c	1	57	55	other	46,248	60,084	y	63,088	25	5,764	5,121	89	3,939	328	854	263	381
RIDLEY	PA	tp	2	—	—	—	—	—	—	—	—	—	—	—	—	—	—	—	—
RIVERTON	UT	c	—	—	—	—	—	—	—	—	—	—	—	—	—	—	—	—	—
ROCHESTER	NH	c	1	39	34	42	33,654	43,701	n	—	—	3,212	2,857	89	2,061	315	480	—	355
ROCK HILL	SC	c	1	106	100	50–54	27,456	34,417	n	—	—	6,120	4,986	81	3,718	694	573	189	945
ROCKLIN	CA	c	3	39	36	56	50,020	60,803	y	63,843	7	6,066	4,543	75	3,087	763	692	27	1,496
ROME	GA	c	1	156	153	56	28,000	42,000	n	—	—	11,539	8,056	70	6,423	685	948	526	2,956
ROSWELL	NM	c	1	87	86	56	27,948	37,452	y	—	3	—	—	—	—	—	—	—	—
ROUND LAKE BEACH	IL	v	—	—	—	—	—	—	—	—	—	—	—	—	—	—	—	—	—
ROY	UT	c	1	31	30	56	—	—	—	—	—	3,733	2,332	62	1,750	375	206	1,056	345
SAGINAW	MI	tp	2	7	—	other	—	—	—	—	—	1,396	737	53	561	109	66	174	485
SALEM	NH	t	1	63	57	42	37,327	44,242	y	—	5	6,945	6,078	88	4,253	653	1,172	232	635
SALISBURY	NC	c	1	—	66	50–54	24,632	33,009	n	—	—	4,753	3,142	66	2,550	158	434	145	1,466
SAN DIMAS	CA	c	—	—	—	—	—	—	—	—	—	—	—	—	—	—	—	—	—
SAN JUAN	TX	c	3	—	10	50–54	23,420	34,000	y	27,640	—	694	—	—	454	—	—	83	58
SAN LUIS OBISPO	CA	c	1	58	42	56	48,932	66,742	n	—	—	9,970	8,767	88	5,941	1,907	919	504	699
SAN RAMON	CA	c	—	—	—	—	—	—	—	—	—	—	—	—	—	—	—	—	—
SANDUSKY	OH	c	1	53	52	50–54	44,000	79,000	y	47,000	3	—	—	—	—	—	—	—	—
SANTA PAULA	CA	c	3	14	14	56	40,471	49,195	y	—	—	1,717	—	—	918	—	—	33	248
SEASIDE	CA	c	1	26	25	50–54	49,676	60,200	y	61,705	—	3,812	—	—	21,112	—	536	142	384
SEATAC	WA	c	1	155	46	56	—	—	y	—	3	—	—	—	—	—	—	—	—
SHAKER HEIGHTS	OH	c	1	69	66	50–54	40,038	64,259	y	66,259	7	16,384	6,796	41	5,017	1,773	5	1,344	8,192
SHERMAN	TX	c	1	75	74	56	31,404	38,328	y	—	1	—	—	—	—	—	—	—	—
SHOREVIEW	MN	c	6	—	—	—	—	—	—	—	—	—	—	—	—	—	—	—	—
SHREWSBURY	MA	t	1	36	34	42	43,471	49,590	y	49,940	5	2,551	—	—	2,410	—	—	4	137
SLIDELL	LA	c	—	—	—	—	—	—	—	—	—	—	—	—	—	—	—	—	—
SOUTHAVEN	MS	c	1	91	—	56	28,149	45,902	y	—	5	—	—	—	—	—	—	—	—
SOUTHINGTON	CT	t	3	33	31	42	45,172	52,460	y	52,460	5	4,190	3,251	78	2,503	385	363	436	503
SPARTANBURG	SC	c	4	76	74	48	25,499	37,248	y	—	5	5,048	4,641	92	3,539	637	464	136	272
SPRINGDALE	AR	c	1	116	112	other	29,500	42,961	n	—	—	8,154	6,110	75	4,735	706	669	1,202	842
STANTON	CA	c	5	—	—	56	—	—	—	—	—	3,125	—	—	—	—	—	—	6
STATE COLLEGE	PA	b	—	—	—	—	—	—	—	—	—	—	—	—	—	—	—	—	—
STILLWATER	OK	c	1	73	71	56	28,246	45,006	n	—	—	5,985	5,097	85	4,466	548	82	205	683
STREAMWOOD	IL	v	1	46	44	other	49,209	65,633	y	—	—	5,356	4,905	92	3,515	594	795	152	299
SURPRISE	AZ	t	1	—	—	56	—	—	—	—	—	—	—	—	—	—	—	—	—
TEMPLE CITY	CA	c	—	—	—	—	—	—	—	—	—	—	—	—	—	—	—	—	—
TEXARKANA	TX	c	1	81	79	56	32,023	39,707	y	40,907	1	4,698	4,313	92	3,525	522	265	21	364
TEXAS CITY	TX	c	1	60	57	48	30,368	41,730	y	—	1	6,127	3,896	64	3,094	365	438	1,362	869
THE COLONY	TX	c	1	36	3	other	44,040	46,800	y	—	1	4,391	2,871	65	2,223	451	196	1,013	508
TIGARD	OR	c	—	—	—	—	—	—	—	—	—	—	—	—	—	—	—	—	—
TINLEY PARK	IL	v	3	—	—	other	—	—	—	—	—	2,811	2,119	75	1,873	240	5	229	463
TREDYFFRIN	PA	tp	2	—	—	—	—	—	—	—	—	—	—	—	—	—	—	—	—
TROTWOOD	OH	c	1	24	23	48	40,681	56,310	y	—	10	2,612	—	—	2,339	397	309	137	567
TROY	NY	c	1	133	120	40	27,013	45,594	y	47,294	5	12,099	11,551	95	7,936	1,898	1,718	9	539
TUPELO	MS	c	1	90	89	56	26,023	35,700	n	—	—	4,591	4,591	100	3,386	448	757	—	—

Table 3/17 continued FIRE DEPARTMENT PERSONNEL, SALARIES, AND EXPENDITURES FOR CITIES 10,000 AND OVER: 2007

City	State	Type	Service provision	Full-time paid personnel	Full-time uniformed personnel	Duty hours per week	Minimum base salary ($)	Maximum base salary ($)	Longevity pay	Maximum salary with longevity ($)	Years of service for longevity	Total expenditures (A) ($)	Total personnel expenditures (B) ($)	(B) as % of (A)	Salaries and wages (C) ($)	City contribution to retirement and social security (D) ($)	City contribution to insurance (E) ($)	Capital outlay (F) ($)	All other (G) ($)
25,000–49,999 continued																			
UNIVERSITY PLACE	WA	c	—	—	—	—	—	—	—	—	—	—	—	—	—	—	—	—	—
UPPER ARLINGTON	OH	c	1	64	61	50–54	37,021	58,383	y	—	30	7,428	—	—	4,544	—	827	406	162
UPPER DUBLIN	PA	tp	2	—	—	other	—	—	—	—	—	682	—	—	—	—	18	484	181
VALLEY STREAM	NY	v	2	—	—	other	—	—	—	—	—	—	—	—	—	—	—	—	—
VALPARAISO	IN	c	1	—	—	other	41,053	42,059	y	—	3	—	—	—	—	—	—	—	—
WALLA WALLA	WA	c	1	58	52	50–54	44,736	57,096	n	—	—	—	—	—	—	—	—	—	—
WALNUT	CA	c	—	—	—	—	—	—	—	—	—	—	—	—	—	—	—	—	—
WARMINSTER	PA	tp	2	—	—	—	—	—	—	—	—	—	—	—	—	—	—	—	—
WARREN	OH	c	1	78	76	50–54	33,286	47,536	y	—	5	6,967	6,692	96	4,396	1,257	1,039	7	267
WASHINGTON (GLCSTR)	NJ	tp	—	—	—	—	—	—	—	—	—	—	—	—	—	—	—	—	—
WATERTOWN	MA	t	1	99	94	42	38,842	47,369	y	51,042	30	—	—	—	—	—	—	—	—
WATERTOWN	NY	c	1	84	83	40	37,682	47,260	y	48,310	6	6,841	6,340	93	4,464	1,108	767	—	502
WESLACO	TX	c	3	60	57	50–54	32,300	32,300	y	39,000	1	3,307	3,063	93	2,303	401	359	—	244
WEST BEND	WI	c	1	40	40	56	39,905	49,397	y	50,057	5	3,696	3,489	94	2,427	529	533	—	207
WEST SACRAMENTO	CA	c	1	68	58	56	55,620	65,088	n	—	—	8,198	6,924	84	4,626	1,859	438	163	1,111
WEST SPRINGFIELD	MA	t	1	66	64	42	41,001	47,680	y	—	—	—	—	—	—	—	—	—	—
WESTERVILLE	OH	c	1	82	80	50–54	44,887	61,087	y	62,662	5	9,845	8,517	87	6,060	1,375	1,082	—	1,327
WESTFIELD	MA	c	1	89	86	48	35,818	40,317	y	45,798	5	8,160	7,582	93	5,510	717	1,355	120	458
WESTLAKE	OH	c	1	44	42	48	50,249	59,690	y	62,189	5	5,435	—	—	3,573	—	597	30	462
WESTON	FL	c	5	—	—	—	—	—	—	—	—	—	—	—	—	—	—	—	—
WHEAT RIDGE	CO	c	—	—	—	—	—	—	—	—	—	—	—	—	—	—	—	—	—
WILDWOOD	MO	c	5	—	—	—	—	—	—	—	—	—	—	—	—	—	—	—	—
WILMETTE	IL	v	1	46	44	50–54	55,635	69,997	y	77,107	20	6,712	—	—	4,077	—	—	335	252
WILSON	NC	c	1	93	89	56	32,896	49,344	y	51,811	—	6,557	5,309	81	3,962	679	667	74	1,174
WINTER SPRINGS	FL	c	1	52	50	56	31,286	47,633	n	—	—	3,755	3,298	88	2,476	444	377	14	444
WOODRIDGE	IL	v	—	—	—	—	—	—	—	—	—	—	—	—	—	—	—	—	—
YORKTOWN	NY	t	—	—	—	—	—	—	—	—	—	—	—	—	—	—	—	—	—
YUBA CITY	CA	c	3	52	49	56	44,436	67,008	n	—	—	8,347	7,055	85	4,757	1,698	599	121	1,171
YUCAIPA	CA	c	—	—	—	—	—	—	—	—	—	—	—	—	—	—	—	—	—
ZANESVILLE	OH	c	1	45	41	56	32,992	43,982	y	46,095	5	3,861	—	—	2,284	—	662	55	133
10,000–24,999																			
ABBEVILLE	LA	t	1	38	37	56	20,249	—	y	—	—	2,280	1,812	79	1,116	250	446	153	314
ACWORTH	GA	c	—	—	—	—	—	—	—	—	—	—	—	—	—	—	—	—	—
ADDISON	TX	t	1	55	54	56	45,020	58,822	y	60,262	1	5,518	—	—	3,660	—	472	—	931
ADRIAN	MI	c	1	19	19	—	40,589	47,011	n	—	—	1,511	1,307	87	931	109	267	29	175
AGOURA HILLS	CA	c	—	—	—	—	—	—	—	—	—	—	—	—	—	—	—	—	—
ALBEMARLE	NC	c	1	42	39	56	25,626	42,016	y	44,117	5	2,650	2,108	80	1,565	187	356	39	503
ALBERT LEA	MN	c	3	17	13	56	36,717	49,604	n	—	—	1,396	1,229	88	900	102	227	15	152
ALEXANDER CITY	AL	c	1	49	45	50–54	20,696	29,042	n	—	—	3,190	2,426	76	1,746	265	415	317	447
ALGONQUIN	IL	v	—	—	—	—	—	—	—	—	—	—	—	—	—	—	—	—	—
ALICE	TX	c	3	30	30	50–54	27,648	33,506	y	34,706	1	1,719	1,468	85	1,130	175	163	77	175
ALLIANCE	OH	c	1	30	29	48	33,721	40,485	y	41,805	4	2,625	—	—	1,720	—	388	77	435
ALPENA	MI	c	1	25	24	56	—	—	y	—	8	2,442	1,710	70	1,217	146	347	120	611
ALTOONA	IA	c	3	7	6	40	33,384	43,559	y	—	5	843	570	68	426	69	73	50	223
ALTUS	OK	c	1	33	33	48	24,216	38,713	y	—	—	1,950	1,784	91	1,395	187	202	51	115
AMERICUS	GA	c	1	51	49	50–54	24,475	34,265	y	—	—	2,901	2,408	83	1,874	212	321	85	408
AMESBURY	MA	t	1	34	34	42	36,295	45,973	y	52,869	7	—	—	—	—	—	—	159	292
AMHERST	NH	t	3	2	—	other	—	—	y	—	—	399	284	71	225	23	36	—	115
ANACORTES	WA	c	3	23	19	50–54	52,008	59,268	y	—	5	2,395	1,894	79	1,604	95	195	22	479
ANGLETON	TX	c	2	—	—	—	—	—	y	—	5	97	—	—	23	—	—	—	46
ANOKA	MN	c	3	4	4	56	50,145	56,930	y	—	—	910	543	60	457	50	36	116	251
ANSONIA	CT	c	2	1	—	—	—	—	—	—	—	—	102	—	90	8	3	—	—
ARCATA	CA	c	—	—	—	—	—	—	—	—	—	—	—	—	—	—	—	—	—
ARLINGTON	WA	c	3	27	25	50–54	48,756	65,016	y	66,216	5	3,707	2,727	74	2,194	443	90	326	1,083
ARNOLD	MO	c	—	—	—	—	—	—	—	—	—	—	—	—	—	—	—	—	—
ARROYO GRANDE	CA	c	3	8	7	56	44,772	54,420	y	—	—	1,488	1,196	80	806	251	138	164	128
ARVIN	CA	c	—	—	—	—	—	—	—	—	—	—	—	—	—	—	—	—	—
ASHEBORO	NC	c	1	47	46	56	31,161	44,962	n	—	—	2,795	2,359	84	1,848	199	312	35	402
ASHLAND	MA	t	1	24	17	42	38,215	48,881	y	49,931	5	2,121	—	—	1,757	152	—	69	142
ASHLAND	OH	c	1	36	35	50–54	39,965	45,508	y	46,758	7	2,960	2,706	91	1,933	441	331	25	229
ASHWAUBENON	WI	v	4	—	—	—	—	—	—	—	—	—	—	—	—	—	—	—	—
ATHENS	AL	c	1	40	39	40	24,097	39,565	n	—	—	2,403	2,207	92	1,633	273	301	29	167
ATHENS	OH	c	1	23	—	48	32,604	45,187	y	—	5	—	—	—	—	—	—	—	—
ATHENS	TN	c	1	20	18	40	25,274	37,911	n	—	—	1,371	1,077	79	843	145	89	6	288
ATWATER	CA	c	1	14	14	56	33,564	42,840	n	—	—	1,532	1,419	93	847	285	287	75	117
AUBURN	MA	t	1	26	25	48	42,357	52,840	n	—	—	4,261	—	—	2,546	—	—	42	1,673
AUBURNDALE	FL	c	1	22	21	56	29,484	42,111	y	—	5	1,712	1,035	60	723	135	177	431	246
AUGUSTA	ME	c	1	42	40	other	26,726	31,299	y	33,025	5	—	2,513	—	2,012	98	402	—	—
AUSTIN	MN	c	1	10	10	40	40,288	47,961	y	49,399	7	1,174	812	69	539	107	165	8	353
AVENAL	CA	c	—	—	—	—	—	—	—	—	—	—	—	—	—	—	—	—	—
AVON	CT	t	—	—	—	—	—	—	—	—	—	—	—	—	—	—	—	—	—
AVON LAKE	OH	c	1	28	27	50–54	46,314	61,699	y	63,299	6	3,257	2,846	87	2,079	469	297	191	219

Table 3/17 continued FIRE DEPARTMENT PERSONNEL, SALARIES, AND EXPENDITURES FOR CITIES 10,000 AND OVER: 2007

City	State	Type	Service provision	Full-time paid personnel	Full-time uniformed personnel	Duty hours per week	Minimum base salary ($)	Maximum base salary ($)	Longevity pay	Maximum salary with longevity ($)	Years of service for longevity	Total expenditures (A) ($)	Total personnel expenditures (B) ($)	(B) as % of (A)	Salaries and wages (C) ($)	City contribution to retirement and social security (D) ($)	City contribution to insurance (E) ($)	Capital outlay (F) ($)	All other (G) ($)
10,000–24,999 continued																			
BAINBRIDGE	GA	c	4	—	—	42	—	—	—	—	—	—	—	—	—	—	—	—	—
BAINBRIDGE ISLAND	WA	c	—	—	—	—	—	—	—	—	—	—	—	—	—	—	—	—	—
BANNING	CA	c	5	—	—	—	—	—	—	—	—	—	—	—	—	—	—	—	—
BARABOO	WI	c	7	2	2	40	—	—	y	—	3	460	393	85	300	73	19	11	88
BARDSTOWN	KY	c	3	30	10	40	20,800	35,943	n	—	—	—	—	—	—	98	60	36	218
BARRINGTON	IL	v	1	40	38	56	49,827	67,674	n	—	—	4,707	3,962	84	2,964	684	313	162	583
BATAVIA	IL	c	1	24	23	50–54	48,462	66,821	n	—	—	4,086	3,204	78	2,351	495	357	62	820
BEACH PARK	IL	v	—	—	—	—	—	—	—	—	—	—	—	—	—	—	—	—	—
BEACHWOOD	NJ	b	2	42	—	other	—	—	n	—	—	57	—	—	—	—	—	21	36
BEACHWOOD	OH	c	1	43	39	other	54,593	67,098	y	68,598	7	4,886	4,607	94	3,149	721	736	43	236
BEACON	NY	c	3	13	13	48	39,016	46,681	y	—	18	1,783	—	—	847	178	—	616	140
BEAUFORT	SC	c	3	29	22	50–54	25,687	49,162	y	49,162	2	2,199	1,636	74	1,217	190	228	82	480
BEAUMONT	CA	c	—	—	—	—	—	—	—	—	—	—	—	—	—	—	—	—	—
BEDFORD	IN	c	1	38	37	56	38,286	39,529	y	48,458	4	2,465	2,281	93	1,519	307	454	11	175
BEL AIR	MD	t	—	—	—	—	—	—	—	—	—	—	—	—	—	—	—	—	—
BELCHERTOWN	MA	t	3	2	—	40	36,795	52,395	y	52,695	10	285	—	—	204	—	—	10	70
BELLAIRE	TX	c	3	24	23	50–54	36,394	52,968	y	54,168	—	1,967	1,725	88	1,276	228	221	82	160
BELLE GLADE	FL	c	—	—	—	—	—	—	—	—	—	—	—	—	—	—	—	—	—
BELLEFONTAINE	OH	c	3	20	20	56	35,293	46,126	n	—	—	1,844	1,496	81	1,123	269	103	218	130
BELTON	MO	c	1	36	—	other	34,202	45,834	y	—	—	3,504	2,596	74	1,915	303	377	527	381
BEMIDJI	MN	c	3	8	8	48	32,664	42,948	n	—	—	735	589	80	456	47	85	10	144
BENTONVILLE	AR	c	1	—	67	56	29,601	48,588	n	—	—	5,756	4,130	72	3,117	619	394	1,062	564
BEREA	OH	c	1	23	23	50–54	44,970	55,991	y	—	5	1,774	—	—	—	375	—	—	—
BERKELEY	MO	c	1	29	28	56	32,631	38,131	n	—	—	1,657	—	—	1,311	178	—	68	100
BERLIN	CT	t	2	—	—	other	—	—	—	—	—	397	134	34	105	8	21	118	145
BERLIN	NH	c	1	20	20	42	35,097	38,613	y	38,738	5	1,648	1,521	92	1,051	164	306	33	93
BETHANY	OK	c	1	23	22	56	26,562	40,919	y	42,719	3	1,810	1,569	87	1,199	163	207	—	240
BETHLEHEM	PA	tp	2	—	—	other	—	—	y	—	0	—	—	—	—	—	—	—	—
BIDDEFORD	ME	c	3	45	43	42	31,493	36,866	y	39,447	5	3,037	2,621	86	2,040	208	372	42	374
BIG RAPIDS	MI	c	3	10	9	56	36,331	46,044	y	46,044	—	787	719	91	536	91	92	—	68
BIRMINGHAM	MI	c	3	37	37	56	38,099	58,265	y	64,092	5	4,614	3,850	83	2,742	380	727	209	555
BIXBY	OK	c	3	23	21	50–54	27,284	31,605	y	—	—	2,388	1,321	55	976	123	222	933	134
BLOOMINGDALE	IL	v	—	—	—	—	—	—	—	—	—	—	—	—	—	—	—	—	—
BLUE ASH	OH	c	1	31	30	other	57,939	66,555	y	66,835	3	4,137	3,588	87	2,531	535	521	240	309
BLYTHE	CA	c	7	—	—	other	—	—	y	—	—	394	187	47	156	12	19	—	207
BLYTHEVILLE	AR	c	—	—	—	—	—	—	—	—	—	—	—	—	—	—	—	—	—
BOONE	IA	c	3	14	14	48	34,339	43,528	y	44,500	3	1,151	1,112	97	696	192	223	—	39
BORGER	TX	c	1	20	19	50–54	26,516	30,853	y	32,053	1	1,268	1,096	86	834	142	120	53	119
BOULDER CITY	NV	c	1	22	20	56	51,521	62,620	n	—	—	2,454	2,230	91	1,573	435	222	10	214
BOURNE	MA	t	1	38	37	42	33,498	46,349	y	—	10	2,808	—	—	2,134	—	—	175	674
BRADLEY	IL	v	3	—	6	50–54	43,106	46,176	y	—	25	873	—	—	435	—	—	165	274
BRAINERD	MN	c	3	9	8	56	42,981	50,465	y	52,736	8	1,060	848	80	607	122	119	44	168
BRANDON	MI	tp	1	13	12	—	—	—	y	—	—	—	—	—	—	—	—	—	—
BRECKSVILLE	OH	c	1	16	15	50–54	48,175	61,458	y	65,208	2	2,220	—	—	1,488	320	—	—	412
BRENTWOOD	CA	c	—	—	—	—	—	—	—	—	—	—	—	—	—	—	—	—	—
BRENTWOOD	TN	c	1	58	57	40	31,900	53,600	y	40,000	5	5,337	4,298	81	3,145	694	458	527	513
BRIDGETON	MO	c	—	—	—	—	—	—	—	—	—	—	—	—	—	—	—	—	—
BRIGHAM CITY	UT	c	2	—	—	other	—	—	—	—	—	507	—	—	110	—	82	119	187
BRISTOL	RI	t	3	—	2	50–54	40,467	65,000	y	42,490	4	628	244	39	183	30	31	68	316
BRISTOL	TN	c	1	52	46	56	28,600	37,011	n	—	—	3,740	—	—	2,406	—	378	746	26
BROOK PARK	OH	c	1	41	—	48	49,762	63,319	n	—	—	5,017	4,498	90	3,176	783	538	292	227
BROOKINGS	SD	c	3	3	2	40	—	—	—	—	—	483	249	51	149	65	34	3	231
BROWNSBURG	IN	t	3	91	74	50–54	34,009	55,009	y	—	4	6,964	—	—	—	—	—	151	—
BROWNWOOD	TX	c	1	32	32	50–54	26,580	29,544	y	30,984	1	186	—	—	1,101	470	149	157	85
BUCKINGHAM	PA	tp	2	—	—	other	—	—	—	—	—	—	—	—	—	—	—	—	—
BUFORD	GA	c	—	—	—	—	—	—	—	—	—	—	—	—	—	—	—	—	—
BURKBURNETT	TX	c	2	—	—	—	—	—	—	—	—	113	—	—	—	—	—	8	105
BURLESON	TX	c	3	28	27	56	41,578	54,052	y	—	1	2,046	1,647	81	1,281	242	123	5	394
BURR RIDGE	IL	v	—	—	—	—	—	—	—	—	—	—	—	—	—	—	—	—	—
BUTLER	PA	c	1	19	19	42	28,439	43,752	y	53,139	5	2,273	2,096	92	1,078	700	316	25	153
CALABASAS	CA	c	—	—	—	—	—	—	—	—	—	—	—	—	—	—	—	—	—
CALHOUN	GA	c	1	40	40	50–54	26,485	33,430	n	—	—	—	—	—	—	—	—	—	—
CALLAWAY	FL	c	1	14	—	50–54	23,839	40,526	y	—	1	749	654	87	484	54	117	13	82
CALN	PA	tp	3	1	—	40	48,920	48,919	n	—	—	—	—	—	—	—	17	—	208
CAMAS	WA	c	—	—	—	—	—	—	—	—	—	—	—	—	—	—	—	—	—
CAMBRIDGE	OH	c	1	20	20	other	40,000	40,000	y	41,248	—	1,997	1,899	95	1,030	704	164	3	96
CANANDAIGUA	NY	c	3	16	15	40	34,095	43,400	y	44,450	5	1,460	—	—	1,062	—	—	159	159
CANTON	MA	t	1	52	51	42	37,789	48,906	y	49,756	5	5,037	—	—	3,689	—	535	444	368
CARBONDALE	IL	c	1	31	29	50–54	33,448	45,157	y	—	—	2,712	2,237	82	1,507	442	288	17	457
CARLISLE	PA	b	1	1	1	40	—	—	y	—	—	901	—	—	69	—	12	3	812
CARRBORO	NC	t	1	33	32	56	30,848	47,815	y	—	5	—	—	—	—	—	—	—	—
CARROLL	IA	c	2	—	—	other	—	—	n	—	—	1,985	47	2	40	2	5	1,921	17
CARTERET	NJ	b	3	24	20	42	39,662	75,682	y	87,034	5	2,641	—	—	1,795	—	619	50	25

Table 3/17
continued

FIRE DEPARTMENT PERSONNEL, SALARIES, AND EXPENDITURES FOR CITIES 10,000 AND OVER: 2007

City	State	Type	Service provision	Full-time paid personnel	Full-time uniformed personnel	Duty hours per week	Minimum base salary ($)	Maximum base salary ($)	Longevity pay	Maximum salary with longevity ($)	Years of service for longevity	Total expenditures (A) ($)	Total personnel expenditures (B) ($)	(B) as % of (A)	Salaries and wages (C) ($)	City contribution to retirement and social security (D) ($)	City contribution to insurance (E) ($)	Capital outlay (F) ($)	All other (G) ($)
10,000–24,999 continued																			
CASCADE CHARTER	MI	tp	1	17	—	50–54	42,000	68,675	n	—	—	1,884	1,446	77	1,055	194	196	193	245
CEDAR CITY	UT	c	3	7	1	40	29,115	41,139	n	—	—	1,488	394	27	303	36	54	808	286
CENTERVILLE	OH	c	—	—	—	—	—	—	—	—	—	—	—	—	—	—	—	—	—
CENTRAL POINT	OR	c	—	—	—	—	—	—	—	—	—	—	—	—	—	—	—	—	—
CENTRALIA	WA	c	1	22	16	42	47,098	58,872	y	—	—	2,685	1,937	72	1,556	90	290	26	722
CHAMBERSBURG	PA	b	3	20	18	other	34,750	46,235	y	46,235	1	2,231	1,391	62	948	185	259	52	787
CHAMPLIN	MN	c	—	—	—	—	—	—	—	—	—	—	—	—	—	—	—	—	—
CHANHASSEN	MN	c	2	—	—	other	—	—	—	—	—	—	—	—	135	—	—	—	—
CHARLESTON	IL	c	1	31	31	50–54	31,500	52,008	y	52,008	1	2,313	—	—	1,753	—	156	154	387
CHARLTON	MA	t	1	15	14	42	45,313	45,313	y	45,313	—	1,118	918	82	737	80	100	—	200
CHASKA	MN	c	2	—	—	other	—	—	y	—	0	799	346	43	158	175	12	415	195
CHICKASHA	OK	c	1	40	38	56	24,237	34,900	y	36,580	1	2,597	2,082	80	1,620	211	251	25	489
CHILLICOTHE	OH	c	1	45	44	56	35,934	46,097	y	47,447	5	4,805	4,003	83	2,572	778	652	549	254
CHRISTIANSBURG	VA	t	2	1	1	other	69,003	69,003	y	69,003	14	—	—	—	—	—	—	—	—
CIRCLEVILLE	OH	c	1	16	16	56	30,384	34,793	y	35,993	5	1,901	1,453	76	924	267	262	165	283
CLAREMONT	NH	c	1	21	20	42	36,247	39,146	y	39,646	5	1,970	1,527	78	1,002	155	370	321	122
CLARKSBURG	WV	c	1	43	42	50–54	26,557	28,413	y	—	2	3,036	2,367	78	1,536	490	340	196	473
CLAWSON	MI	c	2	—	—	other	—	—	y	—	—	470	389	83	32	332	24	2	79
CLAYTON	CA	c	—	—	—	—	—	—	—	—	—	—	—	—	—	—	—	—	—
CLAYTON	MO	c	1	—	34	56	42,649	60,301	n	—	—	3,691	2,965	80	2,254	487	223	613	113
CLEARLAKE	CA	c	—	—	—	—	—	—	—	—	—	—	—	—	—	—	—	—	—
CLEMMONS	NC	v	—	—	—	—	—	—	—	—	—	—	—	—	—	—	—	19	79
CLINTON	NJ	tp	2	—	—	other	—	—	—	—	—	98	—	—	—	—	—	—	—
CLINTON	UT	c	3	31	8	50–54	39,031	53,574	n	—	—	—	—	—	—	57	102	92	161
CLIVE	IA	c	1	8	6	48	40,075	50,085	n	—	—	1,800	888	49	688	117	82	149	798
COCOA	FL	c	1	37	36	50–54	32,091	46,969	n	—	—	4,242	2,789	66	1,762	802	225	613	594
COCOA BEACH	FL	c	1	29	28	56	36,700	49,440	n	—	—	3,549	2,435	69	1,787	448	199	825	289
COFFEYVILLE	KS	c	1	22	19	56	28,246	36,895	n	—	—	1,242	1,141	92	826	157	157	59	42
COLCHESTER	CT	t	3	6	5	40	32,282	46,072	y	46,822	6	765	400	52	332	37	30	12	353
COLCHESTER	VT	t	2	—	—	—	—	—	—	—	—	—	—	—	—	—	—	—	—
COLDWATER	MI	c	3	15	—	50–54	28,000	38,887	y	—	5	1,264	1,012	80	784	63	164	2	251
COLLEGE PARK	GA	c	1	58	35	50–54	36,604	55,697	y	55,697	—	4,738	—	—	3,139	—	642	34	392
COLLEGE PARK	MD	c	—	—	—	—	—	—	—	—	—	—	—	—	—	—	—	—	—
COLLINSVILLE	IL	c	1	30	28	42	41,802	47,524	y	48,332	4	3,263	2,866	88	2,079	396	390	193	204
COLUMBUS	NE	c	3	12	12	50–54	28,944	41,244	n	—	—	1,225	891	73	648	148	94	64	270
COMMERCE CITY	CO	c	—	—	—	—	—	—	—	—	—	—	—	—	—	—	—	—	—
CONVERSE	TX	c	1	—	—	56	26,460	—	y	—	1	—	—	—	—	—	—	—	—
CONWAY	SC	c	1	32	31	56	25,570	38,356	y	—	5	1,681	1,278	76	933	165	179	117	286
CONYERS	GA	c	—	—	—	—	—	—	—	—	—	—	—	—	—	—	—	—	—
COOS BAY	OR	c	3	16	16	56	41,256	52,644	n	—	—	—	1,495	—	993	289	212	—	—
COPLEY	OH	tp	1	14	12	50–54	42,977	56,748	y	—	3	2,351	1,995	85	1,544	229	221	58	298
CORALVILLE	IA	c	3	2	2	40	—	—	n	—	—	743	187	25	124	19	44	401	154
CORNELIUS	NC	t	2	—	—	—	—	—	—	—	—	—	—	—	—	—	—	—	—
CORONADO	CA	c	1	33	29	56	42,687	57,204	n	—	—	5,766	5,250	91	3,866	874	509	165	360
CORSICANA	TX	c	1	57	53	56	38,040	45,240	y	47,040	1	4,248	3,670	86	2,887	518	265	—	577
COSHOCTON	OH	c	1	18	—	42	26,644	32,519	n	—	—	1,303	—	—	768	—	193	6	92
COVENTRY	CT	t	—	—	—	—	—	—	—	—	—	—	—	—	—	—	—	—	—
COVINGTON	WA	c	—	—	—	—	—	—	—	—	—	—	—	—	—	—	—	—	—
CRAWFORDSVILLE	IN	c	1	37	36	56	36,045	46,582	y	46,582	1	3,014	2,362	78	1,711	332	319	289	363
CRESTWOOD	MO	c	1	27	26	56	47,533	59,152	n	—	—	2,632	—	—	—	228	185	—	438
CREVE COEUR	MO	c	—	—	—	—	—	—	—	—	—	—	—	—	—	—	—	—	—
CROMWELL	CT	t	3	—	—	—	—	—	—	—	—	—	—	—	—	—	—	—	—
CROWN POINT	IN	c	3	21	20	56	38,840	48,685	y	49,145	3	2,176	2,171	100	1,580	212	378	42	176
CUMBERLAND	MD	c	1	62	61	other	27,799	44,479	y	44,479	—	4,408	4,012	91	2,580	381	1,051	103	293
CUMRU	PA	tp	2	—	—	—	—	—	y	—	0	—	—	—	—	—	—	—	—
DAPHNE	AL	t	3	26	26	56	25,819	40,019	n	—	—	1,695	1,210	71	907	122	181	58	427
DE BARY	FL	c	5	—	—	56	—	—	—	—	—	—	—	—	—	—	—	—	—
DE LAND	FL	c	1	38	36	other	28,800	41,760	y	42,360	8	3,341	2,044	61	1,526	306	212	615	682
DEERFIELD	IL	v	—	—	—	—	—	—	—	—	—	—	—	—	—	—	—	—	—
DEFIANCE	OH	c	3	20	20	56	34,008	42,978	—	—	—	1,915	1,592	83	1,136	249	207	145	178
DEL CITY	OK	c	1	26	24	56	30,935	39,451	y	—	5	2,215	2,133	96	1,276	164	693	35	46
DEMING	NM	c	1	—	19	56	27,783	35,348	y	37,866	8	1,141	1,076	94	819	164	92	—	65
DESTIN	FL	c	—	—	—	—	—	—	—	—	—	—	—	—	—	—	—	—	—
DICKINSON	ND	c	3	4	4	40	25,688	33,384	y	—	1	218	—	—	221	52	39	57	68
DICKINSON	TX	c	2	4	4	50–54	—	—	y	—	—	—	—	—	—	—	—	—	—
DIXON	CA	c	3	22	20	56	46,620	59,496	n	—	—	2,976	2,395	80	1,767	378	249	209	392
DOUGLAS	GA	c	3	38	37	56	25,388	38,731	n	—	—	1,987	1,787	90	1,218	224	343	52	149
DOVER	NJ	t	3	6	6	48	42,404	70,623	n	—	—	721	—	—	412	—	—	237	72
DOVER	OH	c	1	16	15	56	—	—	y	—	5	1,607	—	—	970	—	200	—	199
DOVER	PA	tp	2	—	—	—	—	—	—	—	—	—	—	—	—	—	—	—	—
DOYLESTOWN	PA	tp	2	—	—	—	—	—	—	—	—	—	—	—	—	—	—	—	—
DUMAS	TX	c	3	15	—	50–54	24,143	31,385	y	33,305	2	1,023	732	71	575	77	79	97	195
DUMONT	NJ	b	2	—	—	other	—	—	n	—	—	148	—	—	—	—	—	—	148

Table 3/17 continued

FIRE DEPARTMENT PERSONNEL, SALARIES, AND EXPENDITURES FOR CITIES 10,000 AND OVER: 2007

City	State	Type	Service provision	Full-time paid personnel	Full-time uniformed personnel	Duty hours per week	Minimum base salary ($)	Maximum base salary ($)	Longevity pay	Maximum salary with longevity ($)	Years of service for longevity	Total expenditures (A) ($)	Total personnel expenditures (B) ($)	(B) as % of (A)	Salaries and wages (C) ($)	City contribution to retirement and social security (D) ($)	City contribution to insurance (E) ($)	Capital outlay (F) ($)	All other (G) ($)
10,000–24,999 continued																			
DUNCAN	OK	c	1	41	40	50–54	26,154	36,879	y	38,079	3	2,496	—	—	2,247	—	7	—	86
DURANGO	CO	c	—	—	—	—	—	—	—	—	—	—	—	—	—	—	—	—	—
DURANT	OK	c	1	32	30	56	25,611	28,855	y	32,895	1	1,695	1,586	94	1,194	164	228	18	92
DURHAM	NH	t	1	24	23	48	32,793	43,517	n	—	—	2,496	2,153	86	1,612	231	310	30	312
EAGLE	ID	c	—	—	—	—	—	—	—	—	—	—	—	—	—	—	—	—	—
EASLEY	SC	c	3	25	24	56	23,091	34,635	n	—	—	—	—	—	828	—	—	—	—
EAST GRAND RAPIDS	MI	c	4	—	—	other	—	—	—	—	—	—	—	—	—	—	—	—	—
EAST HAMPTON	CT	t	2	—	—	other	—	—	—	—	—	—	—	—	—	—	—	—	—
EAST LAMPETER	PA	tp	2	—	—	other	—	—	—	—	—	791	—	—	—	—	—	437	353
EAST LIVERPOOL	OH	c	1	15	—	50–54	—	—	y	—	2	—	—	—	—	—	—	—	—
EAST LONGMEADOW	MA	t	1	8	—	40	37,530	42,154	y	43,005	5	687	—	—	568	—	13	28	47
EAST MOLINE	IL	c	1	35	31	48	32,788	51,466	n	—	—	3,037	2,751	91	1,860	436	454	74	212
EAST ROCKAWAY	NY	v	2	—	—	other	—	—	—	—	—	—	—	—	—	—	—	—	—
EASTHAMPTON	MA	t	4	27	26	42	33,012	38,861	y	39,361	10	1,567	—	—	1,474	—	—	—	93
EASTON	MA	t	1	37	36	42	38,612	50,805	y	—	5	2,711	—	—	2,396	—	—	77	237
EATONTOWN	NJ	b	2	—	—	—	—	—	n	—	—	77	—	—	11	—	—	—	66
EDEN	NC	c	3	17	—	56	27,994	42,417	n	—	—	1,164	706	61	526	68	111	198	261
EL CAMPO	TX	c	2	—	—	other	—	—	y	—	—	130	—	—	—	—	2	6	96
EL CERRITO	CA	c	1	36	17	56	58,124	70,663	n	—	—	6,034	5,291	88	3,595	1,019	676	444	444
EL DORADO	KS	c	3	18	15	50–54	24,925	35,869	y	36,829	5	926	815	88	631	77	107	9	102
EL PASO DE ROBLES	CA	c	1	25	24	56	45,300	57,552	n	—	—	4,439	3,148	71	2,081	550	517	24	1,266
EL RENO	OK	c	1	20	18	50–54	26,873	37,627	y	40,627	5	1,592	1,098	69	860	107	131	431	63
ELIZABETH CITY	NC	c	1	47	45	56	26,572	39,712	y	—	1	3,075	2,004	65	1,548	260	195	362	709
ELIZABETHTON	TN	c	1	32	32	50–54	24,640	28,470	—	—	—	—	1,483	—	1,149	221	113	—	—
ELIZABETHTOWN	PA	b	—	—	—	—	—	—	—	—	—	—	—	—	—	—	—	—	—
ELK GROVE	CA	c	—	—	—	—	—	—	—	—	—	—	—	—	—	—	—	—	—
ELKO	NV	c	3	22	18	other	42,844	54,173	y	55,573	8	2,138	1,517	71	1,050	297	169	62	559
ELKTON	MD	t	—	—	—	—	—	—	—	—	—	—	—	—	—	—	—	—	—
ELLENSBURG	WA	c	—	—	—	—	—	—	—	—	—	—	—	—	—	—	—	—	—
ELMWOOD PARK	NJ	b	2	—	—	other	—	—	—	—	—	770	—	—	65	—	—	600	112
ENDICOTT	NY	v	1	32	—	42	33,681	38,062	n	—	—	3,435	3,178	93	1,899	410	868	152	105
ENNIS	TX	c	3	29	28	48	37,398	46,754	y	48,481	1	2,355	2,006	85	1,404	286	316	156	193
ENTERPRISE	AL	c	1	39	38	56	24,814	37,502	y	34,729	10	—	—	—	1,204	153	—	—	—
ERLANGER	KY	c	3	15	15	56	—	—	n	—	—	2,632	1,938	74	1,404	352	181	—	667
ESCANABA	MI	c	4	—	—	42	—	—	—	—	—	—	—	—	—	—	—	—	—
EUFAULA	AL	c	1	48	43	50–54	22,020	28,718	y	—	20	1,846	1,626	88	1,283	126	217	16	204
EUSTIS	FL	c	3	26	24	56	29,900	45,500	n	—	—	1,456	1,291	89	954	187	149	9	155
EVERGREEN PARK	IL	v	1	4	4	other	—	—	n	—	—	—	—	—	—	—	—	—	—
EXETER	PA	tp	2	1	—	other	—	—	—	—	—	—	—	—	35	—	—	2	202
FAIRHAVEN	MA	t	1	24	23	42	39,136	42,003	y	—	10	1,623	—	—	1,483	—	—	—	140
FAIRMONT	MN	c	2	32	—	—	—	—	n	—	—	213	128	60	65	22	41	—	84
FARIBAULT	MN	c	1	11	9	56	37,631	50,174	y	52,181	5	1,208	997	83	787	84	126	69	141
FARMINGTON	CT	t	3	8	7	40	40,552	55,635	n	—	—	1,374	1,002	73	778	54	169	—	372
FARMINGTON	MN	c	7	1	1	other	—	—	n	—	—	569	375	66	170	190	14	—	195
FARMINGTON	UT	c	1	1	1	other	—	—	—	—	—	415	—	—	234	—	—	72	109
FARRAGUT	TN	t	—	—	—	—	—	—	—	—	—	—	—	—	—	—	—	—	—
FAYETTEVILLE	GA	c	3	23	22	50–54	31,450	51,173	n	—	—	2,004	1,600	80	1,149	209	241	65	339
FENTON	MI	c	2	1	1	other	—	—	n	—	—	716	375	52	328	10	35	162	178
FERGUSON	MO	c	4	27	—	56	37,400	50,163	n	—	—	1,819	—	—	1,224	—	—	214	—
FERGUSON	PA	tp	—	—	—	—	—	—	—	—	—	—	—	—	—	—	—	—	—
FERNANDINA BEACH	FL	c	1	30	29	56	31,597	54,698	y	55,850	5	2,369	2,024	85	1,446	311	266	40	306
FERNDALE	MI	c	1	32	32	50–54	44,364	56,008	y	—	5	—	—	—	—	—	—	20	402
FILLMORE	CA	c	3	4	4	56	49,316	60,471	n	—	—	—	—	—	—	130	17	87	481
FLORENCE	KY	c	3	49	48	40	35,878	50,702	y	54,202	5	4,831	3,597	74	2,185	691	720	256	978
FLORENCE	NJ	tp	3	6	6	other	44,000	62,000	y	64,000	5	—	—	—	—	—	55	3,651	340
FOREST ACRES	SC	c	—	—	—	—	—	—	—	—	—	—	—	—	—	—	—	—	—
FOREST GROVE	OR	c	3	19	18	56	46,164	57,264	n	—	—	2,397	1,862	78	1,300	281	282	9	526
FOREST PARK	GA	c	1	51	49	50–54	30,301	42,421	n	—	—	3,422	2,871	84	2,132	185	553	86	465
FOREST PARK	OH	c	1	29	28	50–54	39,082	55,277	y	56,935	1	3,447	2,814	82	2,042	454	317	99	534
FORREST CITY	AR	c	3	20	20	other	26,458	26,458	n	—	—	1,311	1,034	79	797	87	150	219	193
FORT MADISON	IA	c	1	18	18	56	27,011	37,623	y	38,703	5	1,378	1,249	91	785	216	247	1	129
FORT MORGAN	CO	c	3	4	1	other	—	—	n	—	—	506	262	52	177	21	64	109	135
FORT WALTON BEACH	FL	c	1	39	37	56	27,659	47,960	y	48,310	17	2,665	2,254	85	1,763	235	255	7	304
FOSTORIA	OH	c	1	24	23	40	30,035	43,597	y	47,085	5	2,192	—	—	1,325	—	321	43	128
FOUNTAIN	CO	c	1	26	25	50–54	36,962	55,390	n	—	—	—	—	—	—	69	203	155	261
FOUNTAIN HILLS	AZ	t	6	—	—	—	—	—	—	—	—	—	—	—	—	—	—	—	—
FOXBOROUGH	MA	t	—	—	—	—	—	—	—	—	—	—	—	—	—	—	—	—	—
FRANCONIA	PA	tp	—	—	—	—	—	—	—	—	—	—	—	—	—	—	—	—	—
FRANKFORT	IN	c	1	49	42	—	36,542	40,198	y	—	—	—	—	—	—	—	220	124	18
FRANKLIN	IN	c	1	47	46	56	40,898	41,898	y	42,898	1	3,175	2,930	92	2,299	209	421	134	299
FRANKLIN	NJ	tp	2	—	—	—	—	—	—	—	—	—	—	—	—	—	—	—	—
FRASER	MI	c	4	—	—	56	—	—	—	—	—	—	—	—	—	—	—	—	—
FREEHOLD	NJ	b	2	—	4	other	—	—	n	—	—	394	195	50	139	12	44	—	209
FREEPORT	TX	c	3	10	10	50–54	28,579	42,662	y	—	1	806	547	68	433	64	49	2	804

Table 3/17 continued **FIRE DEPARTMENT PERSONNEL, SALARIES, AND EXPENDITURES FOR CITIES 10,000 AND OVER: 2007**

City	State	Type	Service provision	Full-time paid personnel	Full-time uniformed personnel	Duty hours per week	Minimum base salary ($)	Maximum base salary ($)	Longevity pay	Maximum salary with longevity ($)	Years of service for longevity	Total expenditures (A) ($)	Total personnel expenditures (B) ($)	(B) as % of (A)	Salaries and wages (C) ($)	City contribution to retirement and social security (D) ($)	City contribution to insurance (E) ($)	Capital outlay (F) ($)	All other (G) ($)
10,000–24,999 continued																			
FREMONT	OH	c	1	25	25	50–54	38,269	45,599	n	—	—	1,947	1,836	94	1,322	279	235	24	86
GAFFNEY	SC	c	3	35	34	50–54	22,378	33,566	n	—	—	1,807	1,432	79	1,048	185	199	—	375
GAINESVILLE	TX	c	3	39	38	50–54	25,622	—	y	—	1	2,840	2,654	93	2,121	312	220	—	187
GALENA PARK	TX	c	3	8	6	50–54	32,714	32,714	n	—	—	689	463	67	336	57	70	132	93
GALLUP	NM	c	1	43	42	50–54	31,634	35,303	n	—	—	2,440	2,116	87	1,594	351	170	—	324
GALT	CA	c	—	—	—	—	—	—		—	—	—	—	—	—	—	—	—	—
GARDEN CITY	NY	v	3	34	34	42	39,370	73,957	y	—	8	5,805	5,452	94	3,414	1,578	460	—	810
GATESVILLE	TX	c	2	—	—	other	—	—	n	—	—	377	—	—	—	—	18	48	309
GENEVA	NY	c	3	21	19	40	40,127	50,760	y	51,860	5	1,990	1,626	82	1,199	236	191	3	361
GILLETTE	WY	c	—	—	—	—	—	—		—	—	—	—	—	—	—	—	—	—
GLADSTONE	OR	c	2	2	—	—	—	—	n	—	—	—	—	—	—	—	—	—	—
GOLDEN	CO	c	3	8	5	other	—	—	n	—	—	1,133	679	60	427	188	64	127	327
GORHAM	ME	t	3	10	7	42	30,838	42,195	n	—	—	1,056	—	—	688	—	—	63	253
GRAFTON	MA	t	2	—	—	other	—	—	n	—	—	—	—	—	377	—	—	—	—
GRANBY	CT	t	—	—	—	—	—	—		—	—	—	—	—	—	—	—	—	—
GRAND CHUTE	WI	t	1	10	9	42	42,929	45,510	n	—	—	1,390	1,078	78	789	153	136	77	235
GRAND HAVEN	MI	c	4	—	—	42	31,848	—	n	—	—	—	—	—	—	—	—	—	—
GRANDVIEW	MO	c	1	38	37	56	32,440	36,449	y	—	3	3,179	2,766	87	2,213	180	373	138	275
GRASS VALLEY	CA	c	1	16	15	56	35,784	43,500	n	—	—	1,930	1,431	74	961	199	271	124	375
GREENACRES	FL	c	4	40	38	56	—	—	n	—	—	3,194	3,063	96	2,136	487	440	10	121
GREENFIELD	IN	c	3	45	45	48	39,548	—	n	—	—	2,917	—	—	2,397	—	—	81	327
GREENSBURG	IN	c	3	35	25	50–54	30,200	31,000	y	37,200	1	—	—	—	—	—	183	—	93
GREENWOOD	MS	c	1	53	52	48	23,103	25,250	n	—	—	2,479	2,270	92	1,704	299	267	10	200
GREENWOOD	SC	c	1	51	50	40	24,211	33,862	n	—	—	2,319	2,146	93	1,656	250	240	63	109
GREENWOOD VILLAGE	CO	c	—	—	—	—	—	—		—	—	—	—	—	—	—	—	—	—
GREER	SC	c	1	—	—	—	—	—	n	—	—	2,889	2,038	71	1,414	250	373	218	633
GRIFFITH	IN	t	2	50	—	—	—	—	y	—	—	—	—	—	141	—	—	—	—
GRISWOLD	CT	t	3	1	—	other	—	—		—	—	—	—	—	—	—	—	—	—
GROSSE POINTE PARK	MI	c	4	—	—	42	—	—		—	—	—	—	—	—	—	—	—	—
GROSSE POINTE WOODS	MI	c	4	—	—	42	—	—		—	—	—	—	—	—	—	—	—	—
GROTON	CT	c	3	17	17	48	36,191	54,184	y	55,084	5	2,208	—	—	—	—	—	—	—
GULFPORT	FL	c	3	14	14	56	35,986	55,526	y	—	5	869	766	88	593	72	100	3	101
GUTTENBERG	NJ	t	—	—	—	—	—	—		—	—	—	—	—	—	—	—	—	—
GUYMON	OK	c	3	15	14	48	26,326	26,326	n	—	—	793	627	79	479	60	87	11	156
HADDONFIELD	NJ	b	3	—	—	40	—	—		—	—	—	—	—	—	—	—	—	—
HAINES CITY	FL	c	1	27	26	56	28,142	42,224	n	—	—	1,714	1,292	75	937	157	197	180	154
HALF MOON BAY	CA	c	—	—	—	—	—	—		—	—	—	—	—	—	—	—	—	—
HAMBURG	NY	v	2	—	—	other	—	—	n	—	—	424	—	—	—	—	—	—	364
HAMPTON	NH	t	1	42	41	42	37,472	50,216	n	—	—	—	—	—	—	—	—	—	—
HAMPTON	PA	tp	2	—	—	—	—	—		—	—	—	—	—	—	—	—	—	—
HANOVER	MA	t	1	52	23	42	39,934	46,332	y	48,332	5	—	—	—	—	—	188	27	243
HANOVER	NH	t	—	—	—	—	—	—		—	—	—	—	—	—	—	—	—	—
HARKER HEIGHTS	TX	c	1	31	30	50–54	—	—	y	—	1	2,167	1,757	81	1,393	257	107	165	245
HARPER WOODS	MI	c	1	12	12	56	37,001	52,495	y	55,645	4	1,945	—	—	1,299	—	455	18	93
HARRISON	PA	tp	2	—	—	—	—	—		—	—	152	—	—	—	—	—	—	152
HASTINGS	NE	c	3	28	25	50–54	28,628	40,112	n	—	—	—	—	—	—	—	—	—	—
HATFIELD	PA	tp	2	—	—	—	—	—		—	—	—	—	—	—	—	—	—	—
HAVRE DE GRACE	MD	c	—	—	—	—	—	—		—	—	—	—	—	—	—	—	—	—
HAWAIIAN GARDENS	CA	c	—	—	—	—	—	—		—	—	—	—	—	—	—	—	—	—
HAYS	KS	c	3	24	23	56	26,568	45,480	y	48,664	5	—	—	—	779	—	—	—	—
HAZEL CREST	IL	v	1	22	17	48	40,586	56,978	y	59,978	5	1,711	—	—	1,264	263	—	26	326
HAZEL PARK	MI	c	1	22	—	50–54	33,865	53,589	y	—	5	2,109	—	—	1,577	—	254	67	190
HAZLET	NJ	tp	—	—	—	—	—	—		—	—	—	—	—	—	—	—	—	—
HAZLETON	PA	c	3	21	21	42	34,306	41,339	y	45,472	2	1,886	1,818	96	975	550	294	40	28
HEALDSBURG	CA	c	3	9	6	56	58,056	70,836	y	75,086	5	—	—	—	940	—	—	—	—
HELENA	AL	c	3	18	17	56	35,152	45,838	y	46,138	1	—	—	—	—	—	—	—	—
HENDERSON	TX	c	3	—	—	48	28,747	31,747	y	32,947	1	1,196	995	83	736	115	144	112	89
HENDERSONVILLE	NC	c	3	17	—	50–54	27,455	41,779	y	42,823	5	1,322	975	74	748	91	135	1	345
HERCULES	CA	c	—	—	—	—	—	—		—	—	—	—	—	—	—	—	—	—
HERMISTON	OR	c	—	—	—	—	—	—		—	—	—	—	—	—	—	—	—	—
HERMOSA BEACH	CA	c	1	20	19	56	49,860	63,636	y	70,000	20	4,459	3,178	71	2,215	747	216	227	1,053
HERNDON	VA	t	—	—	—	—	—	—		—	—	—	—	—	—	—	—	—	—
HEWITT	TX	c	3	5	5	40	28,356	45,888	y	47,088	20	504	196	39	152	25	18	240	68
HIBBING	MN	c	1	26	—	50–54	38,628	45,444	y	49,080	5	3,053	2,262	74	1,588	124	550	550	334
HIGHLAND VILLAGE	TX	c	3	10	9	50–54	—	—	y	—	2	1,647	701	43	562	60	79	498	448
HILLIARD	OH	c	—	—	—	—	—	—		—	—	—	—	—	—	—	—	—	—
HILLSBOROUGH	CA	t	1	31	29	56	69,680	84,774	n	—	—	5,991	5,241	87	3,551	765	925	—	749
HILLSDALE	NJ	b	2	—	—	other	—	—	n	—	—	—	—	—	40	—	—	—	—
HILLTOWN	PA	tp	2	—	—	—	—	—		—	—	—	—	—	—	—	—	—	—
HOLDEN	MA	t	1	9	7	other	38,100	50,808	n	—	—	1,089	—	—	620	—	—	363	107
HOLLY HILL	FL	c	1	16	16	56	29,065	46,465	y	—	0	1,254	1,100	88	807	163	130	21	133

Table 3/17 continued **FIRE DEPARTMENT PERSONNEL, SALARIES, AND EXPENDITURES FOR CITIES 10,000 AND OVER: 2007**

City	State	Type	Service provision	Full-time paid personnel	Full-time uniformed personnel	Duty hours per week	Minimum base salary ($)	Maximum base salary ($)	Longevity pay	Maximum salary with longevity ($)	Years of service for longevity	Total expenditures (A) ($)	Total personnel expenditures (B) ($)	(B) as % of (A)	Salaries and wages (C) ($)	City contribution to retirement and social security (D) ($)	City contribution to insurance (E) ($)	Capital outlay (F) ($)	All other (G) ($)
10,000–24,999 continued																			
HOMER GLEN	IL	v	—	—	—	—	—	—	—	—	—	—	—	—	—	—	—	—	—
HOPATCONG	NJ	b	2	—	—	other	—	—	—	—	—	—	—	—	—	—	—	—	—
HOPE	AR	c	1	16	16	56	18,200	20,384	n	—	—	686	639	93	461	57	120	33	14
HOPEWELL	PA	tp	7	—	—	—	—	—	—	—	—	—	—	—	—	—	—	—	—
HOPEWELL	VA	c	1	43	35	56	32,443	48,663	n	—	—	3,167	2,627	83	2,032	399	196	110	433
HOPKINS	MN	c	2	1	1	other	—	—	n	—	—	777	310	40	276	12	22	—	467
HORN LAKE	MS	c	1	35	35	other	30,584	34,034	y	—	4	—	—	—	—	—	—	—	—
HOWARD	WI	v	3	—	—	40	—	—	—	—	—	—	—	—	—	—	—	—	—
HUDSON	OH	c	3	5	5	other	—	—	n	—	—	1,274	649	51	452	92	104	438	217
HUEYTOWN	AL	c	1	32	32	50–54	21,674	33,655	n	—	—	2,902	2,417	83	1,604	620	193	175	155
HUMBLE	TX	c	1	16	14	56	39,180	52,008	y	—	1	1,541	1,286	83	932	164	190	27	228
HUNTERSVILLE	NC	t	2	—	—	—	—	—	—	—	—	—	—	—	—	—	—	—	—
HUNTINGTON	IN	c	1	41	41	48	37,347	37,347	y	47,804	1	2,118	—	—	1,908	—	—	97	113
INDIAN TRAIL	NC	t	—	—	—	—	—	—	—	—	—	—	—	—	—	—	—	—	—
INDIANOLA	IA	c	3	8	7	—	32,085	44,421	y	—	5	1,014	811	80	550	93	168	38	165
IPSWICH	MA	t	1	18	18	42	42,386	47,271	y	48,171	5	1,239	—	—	1,146	—	—	—	93
IRONTON	OH	c	1	17	17	56	26,749	29,275	y	—	1	1,031	—	—	572	—	254	—	52
ISSAQUAH	WA	c	—	—	—	—	—	—	—	—	—	—	—	—	—	—	—	—	—
JACKSONVILLE	IL	c	1	26	25	50–54	38,578	49,262	y	50,512	7	2,240	1,690	75	1,354	3	332	175	375
JACKSONVILLE BEACH	FL	c	1	31	31	56	31,129	33,051	n	—	—	2,939	2,421	82	1,894	310	216	484	34
JENNINGS	LA	c	3	13	10	50–54	20,394	—	y	—	1	1,120	693	62	490	107	96	47	380
KALISPELL	MT	c	1	37	30	50–54	—	—	n	—	—	3,583	3,358	94	2,394	660	303	56	169
KATY	TX	c	3	2	1	40	48,000	—	y	—	1	—	—	—	—	—	—	—	—
KELSO	WA	c	—	—	—	—	—	—	—	—	—	—	—	—	—	—	—	—	—
KENMORE	WA	c	—	—	—	—	—	—	—	—	—	—	—	—	—	—	—	—	—
KENNETT	MO	c	1	10	10	40	24,000	—	n	—	—	605	442	73	350	40	52	40	124
KERNERSVILLE	NC	t	1	63	61	56	29,222	44,302	y	—	—	3,994	3,080	77	2,410	335	334	48	866
KERRVILLE	TX	c	1	—	42	56	35,177	44,510	y	45,182	1	—	—	—	2,062	—	—	—	—
KEWANEE	IL	c	1	16	15	other	29,104	36,669	y	38,829	5	1,282	1,102	86	699	175	228	103	76
KILGORE	TX	c	1	34	31	50–54	31,730	42,852	y	—	1	1,995	1,610	81	1,131	252	227	199	186
KINGMAN	AZ	c	1	56	51	56	36,736	51,692	n	—	—	5,813	4,858	84	3,621	1,193	44	1,092	1,002
KINGSTON	PA	c	3	23	23	40	31,956	42,608	y	46,868	3	1,485	—	—	1,101	—	238	18	127
KINSTON	NC	c	4	—	48	50–54	43,118	47,548	y	—	5	3,346	2,640	79	1,888	627	125	186	521
KIRKSVILLE	MO	c	1	22	19	50–54	27,358	30,850	n	—	—	1,323	1,011	76	794	85	131	203	110
KLAMATH FALLS	OR	c	—	—	—	—	—	—	—	—	—	—	—	—	—	—	—	—	—
LA GRANGE	IL	v	1	21	20	50–54	46,269	64,049	n	—	—	2,279	2,060	90	1,446	442	171	89	130
LA MARQUE	TX	c	3	19	11	50–54	33,456	46,344	y	46,828	1	1,650	1,128	68	872	138	117	157	365
LA PALMA	CA	c	—	—	—	—	—	—	—	—	—	—	—	—	—	—	—	—	—
LA PORTE	IN	c	1	45	45	50–54	33,092	33,092	y	—	3	3,050	—	—	1,908	—	504	31	194
LA QUINTA	CA	c	5	—	—	—	—	—	—	—	—	—	—	—	—	—	—	—	—
LA VISTA	NE	c	2	1	—	other	—	—	y	—	—	238	53	22	33	4	15	10	176
LACKAWANNA	NY	c	1	47	47	40	37,760	47,802	y	48,802	5	4,913	3,991	81	2,997	656	337	682	240
LAFAYETTE	CO	c	3	14	13	56	—	—	y	—	10	1,086	—	—	423	—	48	34	577
LAGUNA BEACH	CA	c	1	41	40	56	43,344	61,020	n	—	—	—	—	—	—	—	—	—	—
LAKE MARY	FL	c	1	39	37	56	33,575	50,378	y	—	3	3,369	2,803	83	2,081	415	307	9	557
LAKE ST. LOUIS	MO	c	—	—	—	—	—	—	—	—	—	—	—	—	—	—	—	—	—
LAKE STATION	IN	c	2	—	—	other	—	—	—	—	—	—	—	—	—	—	—	—	—
LAKE ZURICH	IL	v	1	54	49	other	49,450	71,258	y	—	—	7,304	6,453	88	5,022	708	724	187	663
LARKSPUR	CA	c	1	17	17	56	61,872	80,508	—	—	—	3,436	—	—	1,507	—	798	4	796
LAURINBURG	NC	c	3	6	—	—	31,139	46,006	y	—	25	—	—	—	—	—	—	—	—
LEBANON	MO	c	1	17	16	50–54	24,283	25,945	y	—	5	—	—	—	601	—	—	94	97
LEESBURG	FL	c	1	69	68	56	33,546	48,485	n	—	—	892	4,614	517	3,121	1,221	271	—	720
LEHI	UT	c	1	—	—	40	34,320	52,166	y	52,316	10	908	—	—	567	—	—	100	242
LEICESTER	MA	t	2	—	—	—	—	—	y	—	—	256	—	—	124	—	37	15	79
LEMON GROVE	CA	c	1	21	20	56	—	—	—	—	—	2,978	—	—	1,829	—	441	84	291
LEMOORE	CA	c	2	—	—	—	—	—	—	—	—	356	64	18	53	9	1	—	294
LENOIR	NC	c	1	59	58	56	21,223	—	n	—	—	3,097	2,644	85	1,953	364	327	—	453
LEVELLAND	TX	c	3	8	8	other	34,026	34,026	y	35,226	1	574	416	72	306	61	48	46	112
LEXINGTON	NC	c	1	48	47	56	20,112	35,856	y	36,752	3	2,902	2,434	84	1,789	288	356	34	433
LEXINGTON	NE	c	2	—	—	other	—	—	n	—	—	348	36	10	13	18	4	248	65
LILBURN	GA	c	—	—	—	—	—	—	—	—	—	—	—	—	—	—	—	—	—
LINCOLN	RI	t	—	—	—	—	—	—	—	—	—	—	—	—	—	—	—	—	—
LINDENHURST	IL	v	—	—	—	—	—	—	—	—	—	—	—	—	—	—	—	—	—
LINO LAKES	MN	c	7	—	—	other	—	—	—	—	—	482	—	—	—	—	—	69	413
LITTLE CHUTE	WI	v	2	—	—	other	—	—	n	—	—	545	69	13	19	41	8	8	469
LOCKHART	TX	c	3	14	—	48	27,229	38,584	y	—	1	927	658	71	509	82	67	125	144
LOCKPORT	IL	c	—	—	—	—	—	—	—	—	—	—	—	—	—	—	—	—	—
LOGAN	PA	tp	2	—	—	other	—	—	—	—	—	337	—	—	—	—	15	46	275
LOMA LINDA	CA	c	1	—	26	56	49,714	61,938	y	65,074	—	3,171	—	—	2,108	—	135	107	416
LONDONDERRY	NH	t	1	48	42	48	38,814	51,034	y	52,734	6	7,126	4,249	60	3,079	448	720	2,351	526
LOS ALAMITOS	CA	c	—	—	—	—	—	—	—	—	—	—	—	—	—	—	—	—	—
LOUISVILLE	CO	c	—	—	—	—	—	—	—	—	—	—	—	—	—	—	—	—	—
LOWER	NJ	tp	—	—	—	other	—	—	—	—	—	—	—	—	—	—	—	—	—

Table 3/17
continued

FIRE DEPARTMENT PERSONNEL, SALARIES, AND EXPENDITURES FOR CITIES 10,000 AND OVER: 2007

City	State	Type	Service provision	Full-time paid personnel	Full-time uniformed personnel	Duty hours per week	Minimum base salary ($)	Maximum base salary ($)	Longevity pay	Maximum salary with longevity ($)	Years of service for longevity	Total expenditures (A) ($)	Total personnel expenditures (B) ($)	(B) as % of (A)	Salaries and wages (C) ($)	City contribution to retirement and social security (D) ($)	City contribution to insurance (E) ($)	Capital outlay (F) ($)	All other (G) ($)
10,000–24,999 continued																			
LOWER GWYNEDD	PA	tp	2	—	—	other	—	—	—	—	—	—	—	—	—	—	—	—	—
LOWER MORELAND	PA	tp	2	—	—	—	—	—	—	—	—	—	—	—	—	—	—	—	—
LOWER SALFORD TOWNSHIP	PA	tp	2	—	—	other	—	—	n	—	1	—	—	—	—	—	—	—	—
LUMBERTON	NC	c	3	—	52	56	22,344	25,912	y	25,962	1	2,769	2,501	90	1,892	311	298	92	175
LYNDHURST	NJ	tp	1	—	—	other	—	—	y	—	0	2,313	—	—	—	50	13	1,700	550
LYNN HAVEN	FL	c	1	21	20	48	22,239	34,944	n	—	—	1,187	976	82	688	164	123	23	189
MACOMB	IL	c	1	20	20	50–54	58,943	42,741	y	66,901	2	—	—	—	—	—	—	—	—
MAITLAND	FL	c	1	44	42	56	33,200	50,600	y	—	—	3,398	3,094	91	1,948	755	389	31	274
MANCHESTER	PA	tp	3	15	2	50–54	32,431	56,999	n	—	—	1,897	1,232	65	803	179	250	410	254
MANDEVILLE	LA	c	—	—	—	—	—	—	—	—	—	—	—	—	—	—	—	—	—
MANSFIELD	MA	t	1	32	31	42	43,374	53,711	y	49,621	5	4,317	—	—	2,464	—	374	594	221
MANVILLE	NJ	b	2	—	—	—	—	—	—	—	—	96	—	—	—	—	—	—	—
MAPLE VALLEY	WA	c	—	—	—	—	—	—	—	—	—	—	—	—	—	—	—	—	—
MARINETTE	WI	c	1	15	14	other	40,123	44,581	y	44,581	3	1,893	1,227	65	1,048	176	2	9	656
MARQUETTE	MI	c	1	26	25	50–54	29,345	39,130	y	39,590	5	1,938	1,742	90	1,186	183	373	—	197
MARQUETTE	MI	tp	2	1	—	—	—	—	—	—	—	290	147	51	114	16	17	28	115
MARSHALL	MO	c	1	18	18	56	27,891	30,427	n	—	—	966	804	83	640	57	107	4	158
MARSHFIELD	WI	c	1	34	27	56	42,387	46,584	y	47,244	5	2,390	2,238	94	1,545	316	377	41	110
MARTIN	TN	c	3	28	28	50–54	24,035	31,035	n	—	—	—	—	—	851	117	—	26	102
MARYSVILLE	OH	c	1	29	28	50–54	37,173	51,820	y	52,670	3	2,601	—	—	1,778	—	—	202	185
MARYVILLE	MO	c	4	—	—	40	21,674	34,882	y	—	3	146	108	74	85	8	15	—	38
MARYVILLE	TN	c	1	38	33	other	27,664	49,670	n	—	—	2,985	2,506	84	1,721	307	478	—	479
MASON	OH	c	1	28	27	50–54	43,214	51,317	n	—	—	3,284	—	—	2,127	—	361	36	368
MASSAPEQUA PARK	NY	v	—	—	—	—	—	—	—	—	—	—	—	—	—	—	—	—	—
MATTHEWS	NC	t	3	6	6	other	30,633	45,468	y	—	1	625	—	—	264	—	—	100	54
MAULDIN	SC	c	1	34	33	other	24,400	30,000	y	30,500	5	—	—	—	—	—	—	—	—
MAUMEE	OH	c	2	20	—	other	—	—	—	—	—	2,598	2,075	80	1,520	192	361	103	420
McCOMB	MS	c	1	44	42	50–54	24,000	37,000	n	—	—	1,679	1,568	93	1,138	215	214	—	110
McHENRY	IL	c	—	—	—	—	—	—	—	—	—	—	—	—	—	—	—	—	—
McKEESPORT	PA	c	1	22	22	48	22,000	46,000	y	50,000	5	—	—	—	—	—	—	—	—
McMINNVILLE	TN	c	1	33	33	other	22,464	34,029	n	—	—	1,306	—	—	1,094	—	—	47	166
MELROSE PARK	IL	v	1	63	62	56	32,000	69,678	y	72,178	15	6,498	—	—	4,045	—	1,130	13	589
MENASHA	WI	c	3	—	—	56	—	—	—	—	—	2,506	—	—	—	—	—	3	2,503
MENASHA	WI	t	3	5	4	40	38,463	47,785	n	—	—	1,013	560	55	438	70	52	311	142
MENOMONIE	WI	c	1	29	28	56	35,064	43,584	y	45,324	4	2,764	2,569	93	1,788	349	432	15	179
MERCER ISLAND	WA	c	1	31	28	48	50,900	70,444	y	76,077	3	4,051	3,598	89	2,916	163	517	33	420
MERRIAM	KS	c	3	22	22	56	33,141	49,712	n	—	—	1,790	1,685	94	1,217	228	240	31	73
METUCHEN	NJ	b	2	—	—	—	—	—	—	—	—	—	—	—	—	—	—	—	—
MEXICO	MO	c	4	—	—	40	—	—	—	—	—	—	—	—	—	—	—	—	—
MIAMI	OK	c	1	30	—	56	28,294	31,370	n	—	—	1,323	—	—	1,126	—	127	22	48
MIAMI SHORES	FL	v	—	—	—	—	—	—	—	—	—	—	—	—	—	—	—	—	—
MIDDLEBURG HEIGHTS	OH	c	1	26	25	48	43,680	60,590	y	—	5	3,068	2,705	88	1,938	448	318	75	288
MIDDLETOWN	PA	tp	2	—	—	—	—	—	—	—	—	199	—	—	—	—	—	—	199
MILFORD	NH	t	3	4	—	40	—	—	—	—	—	398	—	—	285	30	—	8	75
MILL CREEK	WA	c	—	—	—	—	—	—	—	—	—	—	—	—	—	—	—	—	—
MILLBURN	NJ	tp	3	46	45	other	44,781	76,817	y	84,498	5	5,289	—	—	4,396	373	—	45	475
MILLBURY	MA	t	3	—	—	40	—	—	—	—	—	5	—	—	—	—	—	—	—
MILLEDGEVILLE	GA	c	1	39	33	50–54	24,810	37,752	n	—	—	1,819	1,454	80	989	137	327	232	133
MINEOLA	NY	v	2	—	—	other	—	—	—	—	—	710	—	—	—	—	—	40	670
MINT HILL	NC	t	3	4	—	40	31,319	80,314	n	—	—	545	238	44	206	25	7	66	241
MITCHELL	SD	c	4	21	21	50–54	31,349	37,339	y	37,989	6	1,469	1,271	87	962	143	165	37	160
MOBERLY	MO	c	1	25	25	56	18,074	26,810	n	—	—	1,144	1,044	91	753	105	185	43	57
MONROE	GA	c	1	23	22	48	29,131	43,600	n	—	—	1,347	1,212	90	903	196	113	—	135
MONROE	WA	c	—	—	—	—	—	—	—	—	—	—	—	—	—	—	—	—	—
MONTGOMERY	OH	c	1	7	7	50–54	46,049	59,191	y	—	5	1,795	—	—	998	—	132	—	330
MONTROSE	CO	c	—	—	—	—	—	—	—	—	—	—	—	—	—	—	—	—	—
MONTVILLE	NJ	tp	2	—	—	—	—	—	y	—	—	—	—	—	—	—	—	—	—
MOON	PA	tp	2	1	—	—	—	—	—	—	—	—	—	—	—	—	—	—	—
MORGAN CITY	LA	c	3	32	31	other	19,800	19,800	y	—	1	1,845	—	—	1,239	—	258	25	122
MORGANTON	NC	c	4	—	—	48	29,026	43,539	y	45,281	1	—	—	—	—	—	—	—	—
MORRO BAY	CA	c	1	11	10	50–54	42,984	52,260	n	—	—	1,656	—	—	974	—	—	—	143
MOSES LAKE	WA	c	—	—	—	—	—	—	—	—	—	—	—	—	—	—	—	—	—
MOULTRIE	GA	c	1	42	41	48	—	—	—	—	—	2,580	1,871	73	1,466	143	261	358	351
MOUNT CLEMENS	MI	c	3	14	12	56	—	51,106	y	52,806	5	1,699	1,499	88	1,048	140	310	89	111
MOUNT PLEASANT	TX	c	3	23	22	56	28,744	38,520	y	—	1	1,564	1,269	81	965	177	127	24	271
MOUNTAIN BROOK	AL	c	1	63	62	56	33,509	51,917	y	56,330	20	5,718	4,877	85	3,653	662	562	495	346
MOUNTAIN HOME	AR	c	3	24	23	56	26,022	38,254	y	38,887	1	1,317	—	—	994	—	149	166	8
MUNSTER	IN	t	2	—	—	other	—	—	y	—	—	514	247	48	211	35	1	200	67
MURPHYSBORO	IL	c	1	11	11	48	25,684	40,751	y	—	7	—	—	—	494	—	—	—	—
MURRYSVILLE	PA	c	2	—	—	—	—	—	—	—	—	—	—	—	—	—	—	—	—
MUSCATINE	IA	c	1	37	36	56	32,440	45,660	n	—	—	2,951	2,627	89	1,820	492	315	32	292
MUSCLE SHOALS	AL	t	1	30	29	other	29,561	34,778	n	—	—	1,998	1,822	91	1,241	197	384	13	163
MUSTANG	OK	c	3	14	12	56	30,183	42,882	y	45,794	5	—	—	—	—	—	—	—	—

Table 3/17 continued — FIRE DEPARTMENT PERSONNEL, SALARIES, AND EXPENDITURES FOR CITIES 10,000 AND OVER: 2007

City	State	Type	Service provision	Full-time paid personnel	Full-time uniformed personnel	Duty hours per week	Minimum base salary ($)	Maximum base salary ($)	Longevity pay	Maximum salary with longevity ($)	Years of service for longevity	Reported expenditures (in $000)							
												Total expenditures (A) ($)	Total personnel expenditures (B) ($)	(B) as % of (A)	Salaries and wages (C) ($)	City contribution to retirement and social security (D) ($)	City contribution to insurance (E) ($)	Capital outlay (F) ($)	All other (G) ($)
10,000–24,999 continued																			
NATCHITOCHES	LA	c	1	45	44	50–54	19,555	43,641	y	44,514	20	1,989	1,871	94	1,358	215	298	2	115
NEOSHO	MO	c	1	29	26	50–54	21,243	49,372	n	—	—	1,497	1,240	83	829	349	61	109	409
NEW BERN	NC	c	3	68	66	56	27,626	57,969	y	57,969	5	4,362	3,091	71	2,249	402	440	264	1,007
NEW BRIGHTON	MN	c	2	—	—	other	—	—	—	—	—	615	371	60	166	189	17	161	83
NEW FAIRFIELD	CT	t	2	—	—	other	—	—	—	—	—	—	—	—	—	—	—	—	—
NEW LENOX	IL	v		—	—		—	—		—		—	—	—	—	—	—	—	—
NEW PHILADELPHIA	OH	c	1	22	21	56	40,535	42,952	y	43,432	5	1,707	—	—	1,144	—	174	134	144
NEW PORT RICHEY	FL	c	1	25	23	56	32,912	50,595	n	—	—	1,938	1,686	87	1,323	214	150	23	228
NEW SMYRNA BEACH	FL	c	1	50	49	56	31,105	50,116	y	80,052	5	5,842	4,407	75	2,948	1,092	367	378	1,056
NEWBERRY	SC	c	3	20	19	48	25,598	38,398	y	—	—	1,017	865	85	667	113	85	—	152
NEWBURYPORT	MA	c	3	38	34	42	35,631	46,883	y	56,728	5	2,891	—	—	2,614	—	—	52	207
NEWNAN	GA	c	1	43	42	56	30,492	45,244	—	—	—	2,629	2,432	93	1,803	274	355	848	169
NEWTON	KS	c	1	44	43	50–54	29,371	38,554	y	39,178	2	3,158	2,863	91	2,087	308	467	4	291
NEWTON	NC	c		—	—		—	—		—		—	—	—	—	—	—	—	—
NEWTOWN TOWNSHIP	PA	tp	3	10	9	48	36,004	45,781	n	—	—	772	696	90	506	56	134	5	660
NILES	MI	c	1	14	14	50–54	28,840	43,940	y	48,334	5	1,170	964	82	718	189	57	84	121
NIXA	MO	c		—	—		—	—		—		—	—	—	—	—	—	—	—
NORCO	CA	c	1	28	26	56	50,760	62,280	y	66,016	5	—	—	—	2,925	—	—	—	—
NORFOLK	MA	t	1	13	13	42	—	48,550	y	—	—	1,130	—	—	864	—	54	22	190
NORFOLK	NE	c	1	36	30	50–54	29,052	40,356	n	—	—	2,654	2,312	87	1,725	209	378	39	303
NORTH AUGUSTA	SC	c	4	—	—	other	—	—	—	—	—	—	—	—	—	—	—	—	—
NORTH HAVEN	CT	t	3	30	29	42	42,304	51,542	y	56,217	5	3,881	3,435	89	2,129	591	714	30	416
NORTH MANKATO	MN	c	2	—	—	other	—	—	n	—	—	690	165	24	136	23	5	418	107
NORTH MYRTLE BEACH	SC	c	4	44	42	56	28,853	43,279	y	45,443	5	2,454	2,141	87	1,624	281	235	—	313
NORTH PLAINFIELD	NJ	b	3	26	24	42	32,530	80,966	y	85,824	15	2,681	—	—	2,018	—	340	—	53
NORTH READING	MA	t	1	19	18	42	41,736	49,577	y	—	5	1,916	—	—	1,916	—	—	—	—
NORTH ST. PAUL	MN	c	2	3	—	other	—	—	n	—	—	334	169	51	127	12	30	77	88
NORTH STRABANE	PA	tp	3	3	3	40	32,136	35,568	n	—	—	327	156	48	96	16	43	—	171
NORTON SHORES	MI	c	1	17	13	50–54	34,006	45,988	y	46,988	23	2,436	1,566	64	1,069	338	158	670	200
OCONOMOWOC	WI	c	3	3	3	other	47,731	53,574	n	—	—	1,218	276	23	222	31	23	2	940
OLDSMAR	FL	c	1	23	20	56	34,774	49,036	n	—	—	2,330	1,375	59	989	234	151	728	227
ONALASKA	WI	c	1	10	10	56	—	—	y	—	10	—	—	—	483	—	—	—	—
ORANGE	TX	c	1	38	37	50–54	32,879	45,033	y	46,233	1	2,734	2,593	95	1,817	372	403	6	136
OSKALOOSA	IA	c	1	8	8	56	28,696	37,251	y	38,451	6	626	596	95	401	102	92	9	22
OSSINING	NY	v	2	—	—	—	—	—	n	—	—	—	—	—	—	—	—	—	—
OSWEGO	IL	v		—	—		—	—		—		—	—	—	—	—	—	—	—
OSWEGO	NY	c	1	—	—	48	—	—		—		—	—	—	—	—	—	—	—
OTTAWA	KS	c	1	20	18	50–54	31,115	43,572	—	—	—	—	1,245	—	846	163	235	—	—
OTTUMWA	IA	c	1	33	33	50–54	32,148	40,768	y	49,300	5	2,401	—	—	1,463	—	395	6	140
OVERLAND	MO	c		—	—		—	—		—		—	—	—	—	—	—	—	—
OWATONNA	MN	c	1	10	8	50–54	42,864	47,627	n	—	—	1,863	865	46	688	72	105	891	107
OXFORD	MI	tp	1	14	—	50–54	—	—	n	—	—	1,389	—	—	574	—	49	66	523
OXFORD	MS	c	1	—	55	—	29,088	29,960	y	30,559	3	—	—	—	—	—	—	—	—
OXFORD	OH	c	3	1	1	other	74,267	82,519	y	83,594	5	358	271	76	204	32	35	6	80
OZARK	AL	c	1	43	43	56	20,728	30,440	y	29,193	10	1,803	1,583	88	1,206	167	211	—	220
PAINESVILLE	OH	c	1	26	26	48	43,844	57,290	y	59,790	10	2,877	2,389	83	1,812	378	198	188	301
PALATKA	FL	c	1	21	20	56	27,112	40,057	y	42,060	10	1,670	1,307	78	1,026	189	92	—	363
PALISADES PARK	NJ	b	2	—	—	—	—	—	—	—	—	361	—	—	201	—	—	—	160
PALMER	PA	tp	—	1	1	—	—	—	—	—	—	—	—	—	—	—	—	—	—
PALMETTO	FL	c	—	—	—	—	—	—	—	—	—	—	—	—	—	—	—	—	—
PAPILLION	NE	c	3	20	19	56	36,596	48,945	y	50,906	6	2,047	1,335	65	1,023	137	174	—	712
PARK FOREST	IL	v	1	23	20	56	42,975	62,213	n	—	—	2,748	2,398	87	1,750	490	157	114	237
PARKER	CO	t	—	—	—	—	—	—	—	—	—	—	—	—	—	—	—	—	—
PARKLAND	FL	c	5	—	—	—	—	—	—	—	—	—	—	—	—	—	—	—	—
PARLIER	CA	c	5	—	—	other	—	—	—	—	—	—	—	—	—	—	—	—	—
PARSONS	KS	c	1	19	19	50–54	19,721	22,516	n	—	—	—	—	—	740	—	117	—	—
PATCHOGUE	NY	v	—	—	—	—	—	—	—	—	—	—	—	—	—	—	—	—	—
PATTERSON	CA	c	3	11	9	56	39,288	47,760	n	—	—	—	—	—	—	—	101	89	73
PATTON	PA	tp	—	—	—	—	—	—	—	—	—	—	—	—	—	—	—	—	—
PAYSON	AZ	t	1	25	7	—	35,044	52,566	n	—	—	—	—	—	—	—	—	—	—
PENDLETON	OR	c	3	33	20	56	40,489	53,524	y	56,200	15	2,933	2,410	82	1,690	418	301	44	479
PENN	PA	tp	3	13	13	50–54	22,600	43,915	n	—	—	982	—	—	505	—	—	168	274
PEQUANNOCK	NJ	tp	2	—	—	other	—	—	n	—	—	710	23	3	20	2	—	543	144
PERRYSBURG	OH	c	1	22	22	50–54	40,924	54,990	y	—	10	3,395	2,282	67	1,647	385	250	850	263
PEWAUKEE	WI	c	3	12	11	56	46,500	53,228	n	—	—	1,719	1,235	72	933	146	156	236	248
PFLUGERVILLE	TX	c	—	—	—	—	—	—	—	—	—	—	—	—	—	—	—	—	—
PHOENIXVILLE	PA	b	2	—	—	—	—	—	—	—	—	—	—	—	—	—	—	—	—
PIEDMONT	CA	c	1	25	25	56	65,160	74,832	n	—	—	—	3,392	—	2,445	722	225	—	—
PINECREST	FL	c	—	—	—	—	—	—	—	—	—	—	—	—	—	—	—	—	—
PITTSBURG	KS	c	1	33	33	56	22,452	40,884	—	—	—	2,190	—	—	1,527	—	205	—	196
PLAINSBORO	NJ	tp	—	—	—	—	—	—	—	—	—	—	—	—	—	—	—	—	—
PLAINVIEW	TX	c	1	36	36	50–54	29,550	34,222	y	35,422	1	2,763	1,936	70	1,511	227	197	441	386
PLEASANT GROVE	UT	c	1	4	4	40	41,797	60,533	y	77,487	—	606	434	72	350	51	32	123	50

Table 3/17   FIRE DEPARTMENT PERSONNEL, SALARIES, AND EXPENDITURES FOR
continued   CITIES 10,000 AND OVER: 2007

City	State	Type	Service provision	Full-time paid personnel	Full-time uniformed personnel	Duty hours per week	Minimum base salary ($)	Maximum base salary ($)	Longevity pay	Maximum salary with longevity ($)	Years of service for longevity	Reported expenditures (in $000)						
												Total expenditures (A) ($)	Total personnel expenditures (B) ($)	(B) as % of (A)	Salaries and wages (C) ($)	City contribution to retirement and social security (D) ($)	City contribution to insurance (E) ($)	Capital outlay (F) ($)	All other (G) ($)
10,000–24,999 continued																		
PLEASANT PRAIRIE	WI	v	1	17	17	56	39,310	54,144	n	—	—	2,045	1,721	84	1,236	271	214	15	309
POINT PLEASANT	NJ	b	—	—	—	—	—	—	—	—	—	—	—	—	—	—	—	—	—
POQUOSON	VA	c	3	27	26	50–54	30,065	41,207	n	—	—	2,065	1,549	75	1,302	220	27	12	503
PORT LAVACA	TX	c	3	16	16	48	28,421	38,452	y	39,652	1	833	720	86	595	80	44	—	114
PORTLAND	TX	c	4	—	—	48	33,690	35,034	y	36,234	1	993	659	66	479	95	84	161	173
PORTSMOUTH	NH	c	1	60	59	42	35,824	46,821	y	47,912	5	6,431	5,458	85	3,857	602	999	561	412
POWDER SPRINGS	GA	c	—	—	—	—	—	—	—	—	—	—	—	—	—	—	—	—	—
PRATTVILLE	AL	c	1	86	79	48	—	—	n	—	—	5,612	4,704	84	3,642	560	502	380	528
PRESCOTT VALLEY	AZ	t	—	—	—	—	—	—	—	—	—	—	—	—	—	—	—	—	—
PRINCETON	NJ	b	2	—	—	—	—	—	—	—	—	440	—	—	19	—	2	321	95
PRIOR LAKE	MN	c	2	—	—	other	—	—	n	—	—	580	400	69	167	216	16	17	163
PROSPECT HEIGHTS	IL	c	—	—	—	—	—	—	—	—	—	—	—	—	—	—	—	—	—
PULLMAN	WA	c	3	32	31	50–54	44,580	54,228	n	—	—	3,392	—	—	2,098	—	—	96	483
RAMSEY	MN	c	3	3	2	other	50,346	92,105	n	—	—	656	393	60	335	30	27	6	256
RANTOUL	IL	v	—	—	—	—	—	—	—	—	—	—	—	—	—	—	—	—	—
RAVENNA	OH	c	1	20	19	50–54	38,505	48,699	y	—	5	1,932	1,539	80	1,079	246	213	117	276
RAYMORE	MO	c	—	—	—	—	—	—	—	—	—	—	—	—	—	—	—	—	—
RED BANK	TN	c	3	33	10	50–54	28,086	28,086	n	—	—	—	—	—	66	—	160	114	
RED BLUFF	CA	c	3	13	12	—	37,560	51,643	n	—	—	1,800	1,820	101	1,500	252	68	59	300
RED WING	MN	c	3	21	1	56	46,738	57,034	n	—	—	3,589	1,985	55	1,478	160	346	—	1,604
RICHMOND	TX	t	3	26	23	56	27,281	45,128	y	—	1	—	—	—	—	—	—	—	—
RINGWOOD	NJ	b	2	—	—	other	—	—	—	—	—	—	—	—	—	—	—	—	—
RIPON	CA	c	—	—	—	—	—	—	—	—	—	—	—	—	—	—	—	—	—
RIVER FALLS	WI	c	7	—	—	other	—	—	n	—	—	436	—	—	244	13	—	15	163
RIVER FOREST	IL	v	1	23	23	50–54	42,538	68,436	—	—	—	2,463	2,271	92	1,700	355	215	52	140
RIVERBANK	CA	c	4	—	—	—	—	—	—	—	—	—	—	—	—	—	—	—	—
RIVERSIDE	OH	c	3	17	17	56	41,666	54,616	n	—	—	1,772	1,422	80	1,028	210	184	51	299
RIVERVIEW	MI	c	1	1	—	other	—	—	—	—	—	1,277	—	—	1,048	—	20	—	127
ROANOKE RAPIDS	NC	c	1	31	30	42	26,216	38,930	y	39,630	2	2,071	1,379	67	1,137	141	102	598	93
ROBSTOWN	TX	c	3	11	10	50–54	25,836	31,572	y	32,772	1	569	451	79	368	51	31	—	118
ROCK SPRINGS	WY	c	1	36	35	50–54	41,637	51,999	n	—	—	3,516	3,175	90	2,353	369	453	141	200
ROCKLEDGE	FL	c	1	40	39	56	31,500	48,800	y	56,000	5	3,122	—	—	2,647	—	—	281	195
ROCKWALL	TX	c	3	10	—	40	—	—	n	—	—	—	—	—	—	—	—	—	—
ROLLA	MO	c	1	28	27	50–54	26,499	34,575	n	—	—	2,298	1,600	70	1,105	253	241	389	309
ROLLING MEADOWS	IL	c	1	43	41	50–54	54,915	78,450	y	80,803	10	—	—	—	—	—	—	—	—
ROSEBURG	OR	c	1	35	34	56	41,976	51,024	n	—	—	3,511	3,206	91	2,101	689	416	—	305
ROSENBERG	TX	c	3	35	33	50–54	33,761	45,584	y	46,952	1	2,632	2,190	83	1,672	313	206	93	348
ROXBURY	NJ	tp	2	—	—	other	—	—	—	—	—	298	—	—	—	—	—	52	246
SAGINAW	TX	c	1	24	24	—	36,476	54,716	y	—	1	2,158	1,463	68	1,199	123	140	568	126
SALEM	OH	c	1	16	16	50–54	27,123	36,789	y	44,301	5	1,205	1,151	95	708	241	201	10	45
SALISBURY	MD	c	1	66	64	42	32,100	51,631	n	—	—	5,419	4,351	80	2,820	1,002	528	218	850
SAN ANSELMO	CA	c	—	—	—	—	—	—	—	—	—	—	—	—	—	—	—	—	—
SAN MARINO	CA	c	1	21	20	40	—	—	n	—	—	3,294	3,062	93	2,228	776	58	29	202
SANFORD	NC	c	1	52	37	56	29,932	44,434	y	—	5	3,113	2,683	86	2,066	249	368	39	390
SAPULPA	OK	c	1	54	53	56	22,500	29,760	n	—	—	5,043	3,241	64	2,607	330	303	1,659	143
SAUK VILLAGE	IL	v	3	—	—	other	—	—	n	—	—	434	—	—	143	—	12	91	177
SCARSDALE	NY	v	3	52	51	42	20,000	74,350	y	—	5	6,141	5,802	94	4,221	996	584	75	264
SCHERERVILLE	IN	t	1	48	10	40	39,417	49,098	y	50,898	3	—	—	—	—	85	8	13	545
SCHERTZ	TX	c	1	31	29	56	30,275	39,947	y	—	1	1,828	—	—	—	1,436	121	—	115
SCIO	MI	tp	1	4	4	other	46,345	46,345	y	—	1	703	452	64	383	53	16	82	170
SCOTCH PLAINS	NJ	tp	2	—	—	—	—	—	—	—	—	—	—	—	—	—	—	—	—
SCOTTS VALLEY	CA	c	—	—	—	—	—	—	—	—	—	—	—	—	—	—	—	—	—
SEAL BEACH	CA	c	—	—	—	—	—	—	—	—	—	—	—	—	—	—	—	—	—
SEBASTIAN	FL	c	—	—	—	—	—	—	—	—	—	—	—	—	—	—	—	—	—
SEDALIA	MO	c	1	41	41	—	24,022	29,539	n	—	—	2,049	1,893	92	1,511	137	245	45	112
SEDONA	AZ	c	—	—	—	—	—	—	—	—	—	—	—	—	—	—	—	—	—
SEEKONK	MA	t	1	44	22	42	34,420	45,645	n	—	—	—	—	—	112	373	—	133	
SEGUIN	TX	c	3	47	44	50–54	35,332	48,736	y	49,936	1	3,179	2,619	82	2,026	363	229	74	487
SELMA	CA	c	3	30	24	48	37,896	46,068	n	—	—	—	—	—	320	179	—	577	
SEMINOLE	FL	c	1	86	70	56	36,198	52,326	y	53,326	5	9,160	8,025	88	4,994	2,138	893	107	1,029
SIDNEY	OH	c	1	39	38	50–54	40,229	50,675	y	53,209	5	3,759	3,310	88	2,343	585	381	—	448
SIKESTON	MO	c	4	—	—	50–54	—	—	—	—	—	—	—	—	—	—	—	—	—
SILOAM SPRINGS	AR	c	1	42	36	56	27,589	42,033	y	42,513	2	2,874	2,172	76	1,709	308	154	158	544
SIMPSONVILLE	SC	c	1	44	44	other	26,817	40,225	y	—	1	—	—	—	—	—	—	750	—
SNELLVILLE	GA	c	5	—	—	—	—	—	—	—	—	—	—	—	—	—	—	—	—
SNYDER	TX	c	3	9	9	50–54	30,108	31,932	y	33,132	1	698	496	71	380	74	42	59	143
SODDY-DAISY	TN	c	2	—	—	—	—	—	y	—	—	562	—	—	—	—	—	396	166
SOMERSET	MA	t	3	32	31	42	34,531	43,163	y	44,463	5	1,931	—	—	1,854	—	—	—	77
SOMERSWORTH	NH	c	1	17	17	42	33,765	41,081	y	42,121	5	2,060	1,305	63	903	123	278	—	755
SOUTH CHARLESTON	WV	c	1	44	40	50–54	26,000	32,100	n	—	—	2,178	1,605	74	1,526	6	73	74	500
SOUTH ELGIN	IL	v	—	—	—	—	—	—	—	—	—	—	—	—	—	—	—	—	—
SOUTH EUCLID	OH	c	1	33	7	50–54	45,083	64,851	y	—	20	—	—	—	—	—	—	—	—
SOUTH LAKE TAHOE	CA	c	1	41	39	56	38,232	48,331	y	50,539	15	508	—	—	2,732	—	1,053	871	415

Table 3/17 continued **FIRE DEPARTMENT PERSONNEL, SALARIES, AND EXPENDITURES FOR CITIES 10,000 AND OVER: 2007**

City	State	Type	Service provision	Full-time paid personnel	Full-time uniformed personnel	Duty hours per week	Minimum base salary ($)	Maximum base salary ($)	Longevity pay	Maximum salary with longevity ($)	Years of service for longevity	Total expenditures (A) ($)	Total personnel expenditures (B) ($)	(B) as % of (A)	Salaries and wages (C) ($)	City contribution to retirement and social security (D) ($)	City contribution to insurance (E) ($)	Capital outlay (F) ($)	All other (G) ($)
10,000–24,999 continued																			
SOUTH LYON	MI	c	2	—	—	other	—	—	—	—	—	—	—	—	—	—	—	—	—
SOUTH SALT LAKE	UT	c	1	40	40	56	—	—	n	—	—	3,977	3,062	77	2,292	383	387	522	393
SOUTH SIOUX CITY	NE	c	2	—	—	other	—	—	—	—	—	432	—	—	9	—	4	256	152
SOUTH ST. PAUL	MN	c	1	—	17	other	—	—	y	—	—	—	—	—	—	—	—	—	—
SOUTHLAKE	TX	c	4	—	62	56	44,774	58,420	y	46,274	1	—	—	—	—	—	—	—	—
SPARTA	NJ	tp	2	—	—	other	—	—	n	—	—	200	—	—	—	—	—	102	98
SPEEDWAY	IN	t	1	34	34	other	—	—	y	—	1	2,620	2,454	94	1,736	430	287	—	166
SPENCER	IA	c	3	5	5	50–54	32,734	39,603	y	40,503	10	1,874	—	—	261	76	—	1,486	51
SPRINGBORO	OH	c	—	—	—	—	—	—	—	—	—	—	—	—	—	—	—	—	—
SPRINGDALE	OH	c	1	49	25	other	45,446	58,069	y	59,819	5	—	—	—	—	425	43	30	377
SPRINGETTSBURY	PA	tp	3	26	17	50–54	28,983	54,873	y	56,073	5	2,422	2,019	83	1,501	302	215	66	337
SPRINGFIELD	TN	c	1	30	30	50–54	27,290	37,253	y	—	5	1,757	1,508	86	1,076	178	254	90	159
SPRINGVILLE	UT	c	3	—	—	42	37,005	51,415	n	—	—	524	229	44	180	25	23	202	93
ST. ANN	MO	c	—	—	—	—	—	—	—	—	—	—	—	—	—	—	—	—	—
ST. AUGUSTINE	FL	c	1	27	26	56	36,072	52,550	n	—	—	2,394	1,930	81	1,304	404	221	295	168
ST. MARYS	GA	c	3	18	17	56	23,879	36,825	n	—	—	1,178	663	56	552	52	58	138	871
ST. MARYS	PA	c	2	—	—	—	—	—	y	—	0	1,083	—	—	—	—	—	801	282
STAFFORD	CT	t	2	—	—	—	—	—	—	—	—	—	—	—	—	—	—	—	—
STAFFORD	NJ	tp	—	—	—	—	—	—	—	—	—	—	—	—	—	—	—	—	—
STEPHENVILLE	TX	c	1	26	25	other	32,784	37,289	y	—	1	1,929	1,608	83	1,216	254	138	49	272
STERLING	CO	c	3	16	16	50–54	32,023	42,771	y	—	—	1,413	1,045	74	735	110	199	58	310
STERLING	IL	c	1	24	23	50–54	34,114	48,373	n	—	—	1,529	—	—	1,337	—	—	121	72
STONEHAM	MA	t	1	36	35	42	39,846	50,533	n	—	—	—	—	—	2,279	—	365	52	143
STORM LAKE	IA	c	4	2	2	40	—	27,851	y	—	3	—	—	—	—	—	—	—	—
STREETSBORO	OH	c	1	—	16	48	41,947	53,244	n	—	—	2,931	1,450	49	1,106	217	126	189	1,292
STRUTHERS	OH	c	1	9	—	56	39,869	39,869	y	40,694	25	645	—	—	645	—	—	—	—
SUDBURY	MA	t	1	35	33	48	39,983	43,791	y	44,291	7	2,647	—	—	2,339	—	—	43	265
SUFFERN	NY	v	2	—	—	—	—	—	—	—	—	390	—	—	—	—	—	89	301
SUGAR HILL	GA	c	—	—	—	—	—	—	—	—	—	—	—	—	—	—	—	—	—
SULPHUR	LA	c	1	—	66	50–54	28,344	—	y	—	1	3,674	—	—	2,228	—	369	269	807
SUN PRAIRIE	WI	c	—	—	—	—	—	—	—	—	—	—	—	—	—	—	—	—	—
SUNNYSIDE	WA	c	1	13	11	48	39,516	45,744	n	—	—	—	—	—	—	—	—	—	—
SUSANVILLE	CA	c	3	8	—	56	—	—	—	—	—	—	—	—	—	—	—	—	—
SWAMPSCOTT	MA	t	1	38	38	42	37,777	44,534	y	46,134	5	2,538	—	—	2,330	—	—	—	208
SYCAMORE	IL	c	1	29	28	other	44,464	60,856	y	62,106	5	1,939	—	—	1,797	22	—	173	119
SYLACAUGA	AL	c	1	21	21	56	26,000	42,000	y	—	—	—	—	—	—	—	—	—	—
TAKOMA PARK	MD	c	—	—	—	—	—	—	—	—	—	—	—	—	—	—	—	—	—
TARBORO	NC	t	3	23	23	50–54	26,055	43,479	y	—	5	1,247	1,113	89	862	161	90	115	20
TEMPLE TERRACE	FL	c	1	44	39	50–54	32,421	53,999	n	—	—	4,213	3,437	82	2,469	581	387	166	609
TERRELL	TX	c	3	23	23	50–54	35,885	50,482	y	51,682	25	2,026	1,703	84	1,153	392	157	45	110
THIBODAUX	LA	c	2	—	—	—	—	—	—	—	—	398	—	—	—	—	16	23	359
THOMASVILLE	GA	c	1	43	43	56	23,907	34,420	n	—	—	2,744	2,031	74	1,643	220	168	42	671
TIFFIN	OH	c	1	38	37	50–54	32,012	39,832	y	43,815	4	3,181	—	—	1,995	—	502	119	168
TIFTON	GA	c	3	36	28	other	22,360	32,718	n	—	—	2,037	1,620	80	1,186	232	201	16	401
TINTON FALLS	NJ	b	2	—	—	—	—	—	y	—	—	—	—	—	—	—	—	—	—
TIVERTON	RI	t	1	34	34	—	29,486	43,270	y	46,299	5	—	—	—	—	—	—	—	—
TONAWANDA	NY	c	3	28	27	42	33,101	50,862	y	52,562	5	—	1,746	—	1,745	—	—	—	—
TRAVERSE CITY	MI	c	1	31	29	56	34,886	40,011	y	42,806	8	3,057	2,392	78	1,708	470	212	—	665
TROUTDALE	OR	c	5	—	—	—	—	—	—	—	—	—	—	—	—	—	—	—	—
TROY	AL	c	1	—	—	48	—	—	—	—	—	—	—	—	—	—	—	—	—
TROY	OH	c	1	40	39	50–54	40,174	55,617	y	61,179	5	3,989	3,590	90	2,700	508	381	8	391
TUKWILA	WA	c	1	67	63	50–54	54,120	67,644	y	71,703	5	9,294	7,532	81	5,841	322	1,368	538	1,223
TULLAHOMA	TN	c	3	32	30	other	31,329	31,329	y	31,529	5	2,142	1,657	77	1,122	136	399	1	484
TWENTYNINE PALMS	CA	c	—	—	—	—	—	—	—	—	—	—	—	—	—	—	—	—	—
UNIVERSAL CITY	TX	c	1	20	19	other	31,100	43,920	y	—	1	1,236	—	—	766	110	—	71	288
UNIVERSITY HEIGHTS	OH	c	1	—	29	50–54	53,478	59,422	y	63,582	4	3,262	—	—	2,523	—	483	420	256
UNIVERSITY PARK	TX	c	1	35	34	56	46,920	59,904	y	61,104	1	3,901	3,384	87	2,504	565	315	101	415
UPPER ALLEN	PA	tp	2	—	—	other	—	—	—	—	—	—	—	—	—	—	—	—	—
UPPER GWYNEDD	PA	tp	2	—	—	other	—	—	y	—	—	56	—	—	1	—	—	—	55
UPPER PROVIDENCE	PA	tp	2	—	—	—	—	—	—	—	—	373	—	—	—	—	—	68	305
UPPER ST. CLAIR	PA	tp	2	—	—	other	—	—	n	—	—	783	—	—	—	—	17	570	197
URBANA	OH	c	1	—	24	56	38,720	53,252	n	—	—	2,920	—	—	14,763	—	354	240	177
UVALDE	TX	c	3	4	4	48	25,605	38,064	y	38,116	1	323	168	52	121	41	6	—	170
VAN WERT	OH	c	1	21	21	56	32,395	43,571	y	44,821	5	2,220	1,435	65	1,016	180	239	587	197
VERNON	NJ	tp	2	—	—	other	—	—	—	—	—	491	—	—	—	—	—	353	138
VERO BEACH	FL	c	—	—	—	—	—	—	—	—	—	—	—	—	—	—	—	—	—
VERONA	NJ	tp	2	—	—	other	—	—	—	—	—	—	—	—	—	—	—	—	—
VESTAVIA HILLS	AL	c	1	94	92	50–54	32,885	50,898	y	—	6	6,646	—	—	4,889	—	818	22	557
VIENNA	VA	t	—	—	—	—	—	—	—	—	—	—	—	—	—	—	—	—	—
VIENNA	WV	c	2	—	2	other	—	—	y	—	1	341	115	34	70	32	13	63	164
VILLA PARK	IL	v	1	22	21	50–54	48,012	67,024	y	67,524	7	—	—	—	1,898	—	307	122	297
WALKER	MI	c	1	8	7	other	38,000	52,322	y	53,822	5	1,276	999	78	766	133	99	106	170
WALPOLE	MA	t	1	36	34	42	39,524	—	y	63,071	5	3,040	—	—	2,450	—	—	320	241

Table 3/17
continued

FIRE DEPARTMENT PERSONNEL, SALARIES, AND EXPENDITURES FOR CITIES 10,000 AND OVER: 2007

City	State	Type	Service provision	Full-time paid personnel	Full-time uniformed personnel	Duty hours per week	Minimum base salary ($)	Maximum base salary ($)	Longevity pay	Maximum salary with longevity ($)	Years of service for longevity	Reported expenditures (in $000)							
												Total expenditures (A) ($)	Total personnel expenditures (B) ($)	(B) as % of (A)	Salaries and wages (C) ($)	City contribution to retirement and social security (D) ($)	City contribution to insurance (E) ($)	Capital outlay (F) ($)	All other (G) ($)
10,000–24,999 continued																			
WANTAGE	NJ	tp	2	—	—	—	—	—	n	—	—	—	—	—	—	—	—	—	—
WARREN	PA	c	1	18	17	56	27,425	31,987	y	32,627	2	1,352	1,195	88	786	134	276	10	147
WARREN	RI	t	2	1	—	—	—	—	y	—	5	685	—	—	153	—	—	260	272
WARRENSBURG	MO	c	1	22	21	56	23,828	38,504	y	—	5	1,898	1,608	85	1,237	169	201	192	99
WARRENSVILLE HEIGHTS	OH	c	1	36	35	48	32,601	59,769	y	64,551	1	3,458	—	—	2,213	—	—	129	103
WARRENVILLE	IL	c	—	—	—	—	—	—	—	—	—	—	—	—	—	—	—	—	—
WARRINGTON	PA	tp	2	—	—	—	—	—	—	—	—	—	—	—	—	—	—	—	—
WARSAW	IN	c	3	31	30	56	36,002	39,809	y	47,770	1	2,328	2,021	87	1,371	312	337	51	256
WARWICK	PA	tp	2	—	—	—	—	—	—	—	—	—	—	—	—	—	6	—	—
WASHINGTON	IL	c	6	—	—	—	—	—	y	—	—	—	—	—	—	—	—	—	—
WASHINGTON	IN	c	1	17	17	56	31,241	31,689	y	32,689	1	937	802	86	580	119	102	45	90
WASHINGTON (MORRIS)	NJ	tp	2	—	—	—	—	—	—	—	—	572	—	—	—	—	—	440	132
WATAUGA	TX	c	4	19	19	50–54	—	—	y	—	1	1,156	1,026	89	845	103	78	—	130
WATERVILLE	ME	c	1	15	15	56	31,362	37,040	n	—	—	—	—	—	—	—	—	—	—
WAXAHACHIE	TX	c	1	47	46	56	41,828	51,798	y	—	1	—	3,146	—	2,420	475	251	95	520
WAYNESBORO	VA	c	3	29	28	other	27,461	—	n	—	—	1,774	1,429	81	1,049	222	158	—	345
WEATHERFORD	TX	c	3	44	42	56	36,878	51,630	y	52,830	1	3,358	3,020	90	2,267	484	269	17	320
WEBSTER GROVES	MO	c	1	—	37	56	—	—	n	—	—	—	—	—	—	—	—	—	—
WEIRTON	WV	c	3	23	22	48	30,776	33,047	y	—	0	1,778	1,357	76	914	125	317	135	285
WEST BRADFORD	PA	tp	2	—	—	—	—	—	—	—	—	—	—	—	—	—	—	—	—
WEST CARROLLTON	OH	c	3	8	8	48	39,631	55,726	n	—	—	1,437	1,196	83	964	168	63	80	161
WEST CHESTER	PA	b	2	—	—	other	—	—	—	—	—	358	—	—	4	—	—	60	294
WEST COLUMBIA	SC	c	1	24	24	56	26,592	75,580	n	—	—	2,419	1,386	57	986	153	247	848	185
WEST LAMPETER	PA	tp	1	—	—	other	—	—	—	—	—	8	—	—	—	—	—	8	—
WEST MANCHESTER	PA	tp	2	1	—	other	62,897	—	—	—	—	—	—	—	—	—	—	9	257
WEST NORRITON	PA	tp	2	—	—	—	—	—	n	—	—	148	—	—	—	—	—	—	148
WEST PLAINS	MO	c	4	11	11	48	19,926	33,179	n	—	—	735	486	66	362	74	50	125	124
WEST WHITELAND	PA	tp	—	—	—	—	—	—	—	—	—	—	—	—	—	—	—	—	—
WEST WINDSOR	NJ	tp	3	13	12	40	34,964	57,065	y	60,097	5	1,745	1,080	62	627	264	189	490	127
WESTBOROUGH	MA	t	1	35	35	42	43,892	50,535	y	56,849	25	3,190	2,832	89	2,409	211	211	358	220
WESTCHESTER	IL	v	1	28	27	50–54	39,375	62,800	y	63,400	10	2,487	—	—	1,920	—	—	24	196
WESTERLY	RI	t	—	—	—	—	—	—	—	—	—	—	—	—	—	—	—	—	—
WESTMINSTER	MD	c	2	—	—	—	—	—	—	—	—	—	—	—	—	—	—	—	—
WESTON	CT	t	2	—	—	other	—	—	—	—	—	527	—	—	—	—	340	66	121
WESTON	MA	t	1	30	30	42	39,509	49,533	y	59,388	5	2,907	—	—	2,074	—	—	640	193
WESTTOWN	PA	tp	—	—	—	—	—	—	—	—	—	—	—	—	—	—	—	—	—
WHITEFISH BAY	WI	v	—	—	—	—	—	—	—	—	—	—	—	—	—	—	—	—	—
WHITEHALL	PA	b	2	—	—	—	—	—	y	—	0	—	—	—	—	—	—	—	—
WHITEMARSH	PA	tp	2	—	—	—	—	—	—	—	—	—	—	—	—	—	—	—	—
WHITPAIN	PA	tp	1	4	4	40	45,000	47,000	y	78,600	5	498	—	—	327	—	110	—	35
WILBRAHAM	MA	t	1	28	24	42	40,060	44,385	y	45,938	5	1,238	—	—	1,134	—	—	—	104
WILLIAMSBURG	VA	c	1	36	35	56	31,512	53,100	n	—	—	2,910	2,358	81	1,785	356	216	134	418
WILLOUGHBY	OH	c	1	40	38	48	47,260	66,371	n	—	—	5,203	4,761	92	3,379	720	662	179	263
WILLOWICK	OH	c	7	2	1	other	—	—	—	—	—	677	601	89	535	56	10	12	64
WILSONVILLE	OR	c	—	—	—	—	—	—	—	—	—	—	—	—	—	—	—	—	—
WINCHESTER	KY	c	1	56	55	56	25,888	42,073	y	42,073	4	4,711	3,654	78	2,437	767	449	256	801
WINDHAM	ME	t	1	2	2	other	34,635	40,579	y	41,579	12	1,128	—	—	511	—	—	481	97
WINDHAM	NH	t	1	—	19	42	38,277	47,116	y	47,866	25	2,095	1,764	84	1,329	187	247	146	185
WINDSOR	CA	t	—	—	—	—	—	—	—	—	—	—	—	—	—	—	—	—	—
WINDSOR	PA	tp	2	—	—	—	—	—	—	—	—	—	—	—	—	—	—	—	—
WIXOM	MI	c	1	2	1	other	—	—	n	—	—	1,268	—	—	474	—	—	496	227
WOOD DALE	IL	c	—	—	—	—	—	—	—	—	—	—	—	—	—	—	—	—	—
WOOD RIVER	IL	c	1	10	10	50–54	39,865	48,122	y	51,250	2	890	—	—	656	141	—	121	233
WOODHAVEN	MI	c	3	8	7	40	58,968	61,006	n	—	—	—	—	—	—	—	—	—	—
WOODSTOCK	GA	c	1	44	43	56	31,938	51,058	n	—	—	2,892	2,472	85	1,994	322	156	252	394
WOODSTOCK	IL	c	—	—	—	—	—	—	—	—	—	—	—	—	—	—	—	—	—
WOODWARD	OK	c	3	31	17	56	25,616	37,044	y	—	1	—	—	—	—	61	93	256	25
WORTH	IL	v	1	13	13	50–54	38,670	60,889	n	—	—	1,379	—	—	799	—	—	231	183
WORTHINGTON	OH	c	1	41	36	50–54	40,893	55,056	y	56,356	5	5,434	4,473	82	2,906	960	607	545	415
WYCKOFF	NJ	tp	2	—	—	other	—	—	—	—	—	375	—	—	—	—	—	143	117
XENIA	OH	c	1	42	41	56	41,535	52,126	n	—	—	5,166	—	—	2,608	—	538	834	565
YANKTON	SD	c	3	2	2	40	—	—	y	—	5	351	162	46	129	16	17	118	72
YARMOUTH	MA	t	3	65	59	42	38,832	54,906	y	55,731	5	5,859	—	—	4,670	—	300	496	352
YAZOO CITY	MS	c	1	28	—	50–54	27,019	31,788	n	—	—	1,867	1,102	59	800	212	90	450	315
YPSILANTI	MI	c	1	22	21	50–54	34,628	54,260	n	—	—	2,549	2,257	89	1,429	619	208	238	54
YUCCA VALLEY	CA	t	—	—	—	—	—	—	—	—	—	—	—	—	—	—	—	—	—
YUKON	OK	c	3	30	28	48	31,281	47,151	y	48,339	4	—	—	—	—	—	—	—	—
ZEPHYRHILLS	FL	c	3	23	22	50–54	—	—	n	—	—	1,701	1,491	88	1,077	264	150	37	173
ZION	IL	c	1	27	26	56	52,780	72,976	y	73,976	20	3,341	—	—	2,417	—	—	70	854

D Directories

D 1

The *Year Book* Directories

The directories in this section of the *Year Book* contain the names of municipal and county officials in the United States as reported at the end of 2007. In addition, this section includes directories for U.S. state municipal leagues; provincial and territorial associations and unions in Canada; state agencies for community affairs; provincial and territorial agencies for local affairs in Canada; U.S. municipal management associations; international municipal management associations; state associations of counties; and U.S. councils of governments recognized by ICMA.

The names of municipal and county managers and other chief appointed management executives for the United States are shown in Directories 1/9 and 1/10. Information on recognized places, including legal basis, title of position, form of government, and year of recognition, plus the number of administrators the community has had and information on the current administrator, is presented in the annual ICMA publication *ICMA Member Roster* (formerly *Who's Who in Local Government Management*).

Information in Directories 1/1 through 1/8 was obtained from the National League of Cities (1/1), the Federation of Canadian Municipalities (1/2), the Council of State Community Development Agencies (1/3), the Ontario Ministry of Municipal Affairs (1/4), ICMA files (1/5, 1/6, and 1/8), and the National Association of Counties (1/7), and is current as of December 31, 2007, unless otherwise indicated.

Information for Directory 1/9 was obtained from the ICMA database of local government employees. The database comprises all cities 2,500 and over in population and all cities under 2,500 that are recognized by ICMA as having a council-manager form of government or as providing for an appointed general management (chief administrative officer) position. Each July local governments in the database are notified to update their information by completing an online update form. Those that have provided updated information are designated with an asterisk (*). Information for Directory 1/10 was obtained in the same way for all county-type governments in the ICMA database, which in fact includes all U.S. counties.

The phone numbers in Directories 1/9 and 1/10 are for the city hall, municipal building, or county building, or for some municipal or county official such as the manager, clerk, or mayor.

U.S. State Municipal Leagues
Directory 1/1 shows 49 state leagues of municipalities serving 49 states. (Hawaii does not have a league.) Information includes league address and Web site, name of the executive director, phone number, and fax number. State municipal leagues provide a wide range of research, consulting, training, publications, and legislative representation services for their clients.

Provincial and Territorial Associations and Unions in Canada
Directory 1/2 shows the associations and unions serving the provinces and territories of Canada. Included are the association's/union's Web site; the name of the president; and the name and title of a permanent officer along with his or her address, phone number, fax number, and e-mail address.

State Agencies for Community Affairs
Directory 1/3 shows the name, address, and Web site of 48 agencies for community affairs in the United States, as well as that for Puerto Rico. It includes the name and title of the head of the agency, along with the agency phone number and fax number. These agencies of state governments offer a variety of research, financial information, and coordination services for cities and other local governments.

Provincial and Territorial Agencies for Local Affairs in Canada
Directory 1/4 shows agencies for local affairs serving provinces and territories of Canada. The directory lists the name and address of the minister, the minister's phone number and fax number, and the agency's Web site.

U.S. Municipal Management Associations
Directory 1/5 shows the name, president, address, e-mail address, phone number, and fax

number of municipal management associations serving 48 of the United States. (The states of Wyoming, Idaho, Montana, North Dakota, and South Dakota are served by the Great Open Spaces City Management Association; Idaho and South Dakota are also served by their own associations; and neither Hawaii nor Louisiana has an association.)

International Municipal Management Associations
Directory 1/6 shows the name, president, address, e-mail address, phone number, and fax number of municipal management associations serving Canada and 14 other countries.

U.S. State Associations of Counties
Directory 1/7 shows the name, address, Web site, name of the executive director, phone number, and fax number for 53 county associations serving 47 states. (Two associations serve the states of Arizona, South Dakota, Washington, and West Virginia; three associations serve the state of Illinois; and three states—Connecticut, Rhode Island, and Vermont—do not have associations.) Like their municipal league counterparts, these associations provide a wide range of research, training, consulting, publications, and legislative representation services.

U.S. Councils of Governments Recognized by ICMA
Directory 1/8 gives the official name, appointed administrator, and telephone number for 102 councils of governments recognized by ICMA.

Officials in U.S. Municipalities
Directory 1/9 lists, alphabetically by state, all incorporated municipalities in the United States 2,500 and over in population, and those municipalities under 2,500 recognized by ICMA. It shows the current form of government; population (in thousands) according to the 2000 Census of Population; municipal phone number; and names of the mayor, appointed administrator, clerk of the governing board, chief finance

officer, public works director, police chief, and fire chief. Leaders (. .) in the population column mean that the population of the municipality is under 500.

Officials in U.S. Counties

Directory 1/10 lists, alphabetically by state, all county-type governments in the United States. It shows the population (in thousands) according to the 2000 Census of Population; the county telephone number; the name of the board chairman,

county judge, or president; and the names of the appointed administrator, clerk of the governing board, chief financial officer, chief law enforcement official, and director of personnel. Leaders (. .) in the population column mean that the population of the county is under 500.

Other Local Government Directories

The names of municipal officials not reported in the *Year Book* are available in many states through directories published by state municipal leagues,

state municipal management associations, and state associations of counties. Names and addresses of these leagues and associations are shown in Directories 1/1, 1/5, and 1/7. In some states the secretary of state, the state agency for community affairs (Directory 1/3), or another state agency publishes a directory that includes municipal and county officials. In addition, several directories with national coverage are published for health officers, welfare workers, housing and urban renewal officials, and other professional groups.

Directory 1/1 U.S. STATE MUNICIPAL LEAGUES

State	Municipal league, headquarters address, and Web site	Executive director (ED)	Phone number / Fax number
Alabama	Alabama League of Municipalities, 535 Adams Avenue, P.O. Box 1270, Montgomery 36104 alalm.org	Perry C. Roquemore Jr.	334 262-2566 334 263-0200
Alaska	Alaska Municipal League, 217 Second Street, Suite 200, Juneau 99801-1267 akml.org	Kathie Wasserman	907 586-1325 907 463-5480
Arizona	League of Arizona Cities and Towns, 1820 West Washington Street, Phoenix 85007 azleague.org	Kenneth L. Strobeck	602 258-5786 602 253-3874
Arkansas	Arkansas Municipal League, P.O. Box 38, North Little Rock 72115 arml.org	Don A. Zimmerman	501 374-3484 501 374-0541
California	League of California Cities, 1400 K Street, Suite 400, Sacramento 95814 cacities.org	Chris McKenzie	916 658-8200 916 658-8240
Colorado	Colorado Municipal League, 1144 Sherman Street, Denver 80203 cml.org	Sam Mamet	303 831-6411 303 860-8175
Connecticut	Connecticut Conference of Municipalities, 900 Chapel Street, 9th Floor, New Haven 06510-2807 ccm-ct.org	James Finley Jr.	203 498-3000 203 562-6314
Delaware	Delaware League of Local Governments, P.O. Box 484, 1210 White Oak Road, Dover 19903-0475 ipa.udel.edu/localgovt/dllg.html	George C. Wright	302 678-0991 302 678-4777
Florida	Florida League of Cities, P.O. Box 1757, 301 Bronough Street, Suite 300, Tallahassee 32301 flcities.com	Michael Sittig	850 222-9684 850 222-3806
Georgia	Georgia Municipal Association, 201 Pryor Street, S.W., Atlanta 30303 gmanet.com/home	Jim Higdon	404 688-0472 678 686-6289
Idaho	Association of Idaho Cities, 3100 South Vista Avenue, Suite 310, Boise 83705 idahocities.org	Ken Harward	208 344-8594 208 344-8677
Illinois	Illinois Municipal League, 500 East Capitol Avenue, P.O. Box 5180, Springfield 62705-5180 iml.org	Kenneth A. Alderson	217 525-1220 217 525-7438
Indiana	Indiana Association of Cities and Towns, 200 South Meridian, Suite 340, Indianapolis 46225 citiesandtowns.org	Matthew C. Greller	317 237-6200 317 237-6206
Iowa	Iowa League of Cities, 317 Sixth Avenue, Suite 800, Des Moines 50309-4111 iowaleague.org	Alan Kemp	515 244-7282 515 244-0740
Kansas	League of Kansas Municipalities, 300 S.W. Eighth Avenue, Topeka 66603-3912 lkm.org	Don Moler	785 354-9565 785 354-4186
Kentucky	Kentucky League of Cities, 101 East Vine Street, Suite 800, Lexington 40507-3700 klc.org	Sylvia L. Lovely	859 977-3700 859 977-3703
Louisiana	Louisiana Municipal Association, P.O. Box 4327, Baton Rouge 70821 lamunis.org	Tom Ed McHugh	225 344-5001 225 344-3057
Maine	Maine Municipal Association, 60 Community Drive, Augusta 04330 memun.org	Christopher G. Lockwood	207 623-8428 207 626-5947
Maryland	Maryland Municipal League, 1212 West Street, Annapolis 21401 mdmunicipal.org	Scott A. Hancock	410 268-5514 410 268-7004
Massachusetts	Massachusetts Municipal Association, One Winthrop Square, Boston 02111 mma.org	Geoffrey Beckwith	617 426-7272 617 695-1314
Michigan	Michigan Municipal League, 1675 Green Road, Ann Arbor 48105 mml.org	Daniel P. Gilmartin	734 662-3246 734 662-8083
Minnesota	League of Minnesota Cities, 145 University Avenue West, St. Paul 55103-2044 lmnc.org	James F. Miller	651 281-1200 651 281-1299
Mississippi	Mississippi Municipal League, 600 East Amite Street, Suite 104, Jackson 39201 mmlonline.com	George E. Lewis	601 353-5854 601 353-0435
Missouri	Missouri Municipal League, 1727 Southridge Drive, Jefferson City 65109 mocities.com	Gary Markenson	573 635-9134 573 635-9009
Montana	Montana League of Cities and Towns, 208 North Montana Avenue, Suite 201, Helena 59624-1704 mlct.org	Alec N. Hansen	406 442-8768 406 442-9231
Nebraska	League of Nebraska Municipalities, 1335 L Street, Lincoln 68508 lonm.org	L. Lynn Rex	402 476-2829 402 476-7052
Nevada	Nevada League of Cities and Municipalities, 310 South Curry Street, Carson City 89703 nvleague.org	David Fraser	775 882-2121 775 882-2813

Directory 1/1 U.S. STATE MUNICIPAL LEAGUES
continued

State	Municipal league, headquarters address, and Web site	Executive director (ED)	Phone number / Fax number
New Hampshire	New Hampshire Local Government Center, 25 Triangle Park, P.O. Box 617, Concord 03302-0617 nhlgc.org/LGCWebsite/index.asp	John B. Andrews	603 224-7447 603 224-5406
New Jersey	New Jersey State League of Municipalities, 222 West State Street, Trenton 08608 njslom.com	William G. Dressel	609 695-3481 609 695-0151
New Mexico	New Mexico Municipal League, P.O. Box 846, 1229 Paseo de Peralta, Santa Fe 87504-0846 nmml.org	William F. Fulginiti	505 982-5573 505 984-1392
New York	New York State Conference of Mayors and Municipal Officials, 119 Washington Avenue, Albany 12210 nycom.org	Peter A. Baynes	518 463-1185 518 463-1190
North Carolina	North Carolina League of Municipalities, P.O. Box 3069, Raleigh 27602-3069 nclm.org	S. Ellis Hankins	919 715-4000 919 733-9519
North Dakota	North Dakota League of Cities, 410 East Front Avenue, Bismarck 58504-5641 ndlc.org	Connie Sprynczynatyk	701 223-3518 701 223-5174
Ohio	Ohio Municipal League, 175 South Third Street, Suite 510, Columbus 43215 omunileague.org	Susan J. Cave	614 221-4349 614 221-4390
Oklahoma	Oklahoma Municipal League, 201 Northeast 23rd Street, Oklahoma City 73105 oml.org	Carolyn Stager	405 528-7515 405 528-7560
Oregon	League of Oregon Cities, 1201 Court Street, N.E., Suite 200, Salem 97301 orcities.org	Mike McCauley	503 588-6550 503 399-4863
Pennsylvania	Pennsylvania League of Cities and Municipalities, 414 North Second Street, Harrisburg 17101 plcm.org	John A. Garner Jr.	717 236-9469 717 236-6716
Rhode Island	Rhode Island League of Cities and Towns, One State Street, Suite 502, Providence 02908 rileague.org	Daniel L. Beardsley Jr.	401 272-3434 401 421-0824
South Carolina	Municipal Association of South Carolina, P.O. Box 12109, Columbia 29211 masc.sc	Howard Duvall	803 799-9574 803 933-1299
South Dakota	South Dakota Municipal League, 214 East Capitol Avenue, Pierre 57501 sdmunicipalleague.org	Yvonne Taylor	605 224-8654 605 224-8655
Tennessee	Tennessee Municipal League, 226 Capitol Boulevard, Suite 710, Nashville 37219-1894 tml1.org	Margaret Mahery	615 255-6416 615 255-4752
Texas	Texas Municipal League, 1821 Rutherford Lane, Suite 400, Austin 78754-5128 tml.org	Frank J. Sturzl	512 231-7400 512 231-7490
Utah	Utah League of Cities and Towns, 50 South 600 East, Suite 150, Salt Lake City 84102 ulct.org	Ken Bullock	801 328-1601 801 531-1872
Vermont	Vermont League of Cities and Towns, 89 Main Street, Suite 4, Montpelier 05602-2948 vlct.org	Steven E. Jeffrey	802 229-9111 802 229-2211
Virginia	Virginia Municipal League, P.O. Box 12164, Richmond 23241 vml.org	R. Michael Amyx	804 649-8471 804 343-3758
Washington	Association of Washington Cities, 1076 Franklin Street, S.E., Olympia 98501-1346 awcnet.org	Stan Finkelstein	360 753-4137 360 753-0149
West Virginia	West Virginia Municipal League, 2020 Kanawha Boulevard East, Charleston 25311 wvml.org	Lisa Dooley	304 342-5564 304 342-5586
Wisconsin	League of Wisconsin Municipalities, 202 State Street, Suite 300, Madison 53703-2215 lwm-info.org	Dan Thompson	608 267-2380 608 267-0645
Wyoming	Wyoming Association of Municipalities, 315 West 27th Street, Cheyenne 82001 wyomuni.org	George Parks	307 632-0398 307 632-1942

Directory 1/2 PROVINCIAL AND TERRITORIAL ASSOCIATIONS AND UNIONS IN CANADA

Province or territory	Association/union and Web site	President	Permanent officer and contact information
Alberta	Alberta Association of Municipal Districts and Counties aamdc.com	Donald Johnson	Gerald Rhodes, Executive Director 2510 Sparrow Drive Nisku T9E 8N5 Phone: 780 955-3639 Fax: 780 955-3615 E-mail: gerald@aamdc.com
	Alberta Urban Municipalities Association munilink.net/live/	Bob Hawkesworth	John McGowan, Chief Executive Officer 10507 Saskatchewan Drive, N.W. Edmonton T6E 4S1 Phone: 780 433-4431 Fax: 780 433-4454 E-mail: jmcgowan@auma.ca
British Columbia	Union of British Columbia Municipalities civicnet.bc.ca/ubcm	Brenda Binnie	Richard Taylor, Executive Director 10551 Shellbridge Way, Suite 60 Richmond V6X 2W9 Phone: 604 270-8226 Fax: 604 270-9116 E-mail: rtaylor@civicnet.bc.ca

Directory 1/2   PROVINCIAL AND TERRITORIAL ASSOCIATIONS AND UNIONS IN CANADA
continued

Province or territory	Association/union and Web site	President	Permanent officer and contact information
Manitoba	Association of Manitoba Municipalities amm.mb.ca	Ron Bell	Joe Masi, Executive Director 1910 Saskatchewan Avenue West Portage-la-Prairie R1N 0P1 Phone: 204 857-8666 Fax: 204 856-2370 E-mail: amm@amm.mb.ca
New Brunswick	Association Francophone des Municipalités du Nouveau-Brunswick afmnb.org	Jean Lanteigne	Lise Ouellette, Directrice-Générale 702 rue Principale, bureau 322 Petit-Rocher E8J 1V1 Phone: 506 542-2622 Fax: 506 542-2618 E-mail: afmnb@nbaibn.com
	Cities of New Brunswick Association	Joel Richardson	Sandra Mark, Executive Director P.O. Box 1421, Station A Fredericton E3B 5E3 Phone: 506 357-4242 Fax: 506 357-4243 E-mail: cnbacnb@nbnet.nb.ca
Newfoundland and Labrador	Newfoundland and Labrador Federation of Municipalities nlfm.ca/default.php?display=cid96&mid=879	Wayne Ruth	Craig Pollett, Executive Director 460 Torbay Road St. John's A1A 5J3 Phone: 709 753-6820 Fax: 709 738-0071 E-mail: executivedirector@nlfm.ca
Northwest Territories	Northwest Territories Association of Communities nwtac.com	Gordon Van Tighem	Yvette Gonzalez, Chief Executive Officer 5201 50th Avenue, Suite 700 Yellowknife X1A 3S9 Phone: 867 873-8359 Fax: 867 873-3042 E-mail: yvette@nwtac.com
Nova Scotia	Union of Nova Scotia Municipalities unsm.ca	Russell Walker	Kenneth R. B. Simpson, Executive Director 1809 Barrington Street, Suite 1106 Halifax B3J 3K8 Phone: 902 423-8331 Fax: 902 425-5592 E-mail: ksimpson@eastlink.ca
Ontario	Association of Municipalities of Ontario amo.on.ca	Doug Reycraft	Pat Vanini, Executive Director 200 University Avenue, Suite 801 Toronto M5H 3C6 Phone: 416 971-9856 Fax: 416 971-6191 E-mail: pvanini@amo.on.ca
	Federation of Canadian Municipalities fcm.ca	Gloria Kovach	Brock Carlton, Chief Executive Officer 24 Clarence Street, 2nd Floor Ottawa K1N 5P3 Phone: 613 241-5221 Fax: 613 241-7440 E-mail: jknight@fcm.ca
Prince Edward Island	Federation of Prince Edward Island Municipalities fpeim.ca	Bruce MacDougall	John Dewey, Executive Director 1 Kirkdale Road Charlottetown C1E 1R3 Phone: 902 566-1493 Fax: 902 566-2880 E-mail: jdewey@freim.ca
Québec	Union des Municipalités du Québec umq.qc.ca	Jean Perrault	Marc Croteau, Directeur-Général 680 rue Sherbrook Ouest, bureau 680 Montreal H3A 2M7 Phone: 514 282-7700 Fax: 514 282-8893 E-mail: mcroteau@umq.qc.ca
Saskatchewan	Saskatchewan Association of Rural Municipalities sarm.ca/	David Marit	Ken Engel, Executive Director 2075 Hamilton Street Regina S4P 2E1 Phone: 306 757-3577 Fax: 306 565-2141 E-mail: kengel@sarm.ca
	Saskatchewan Urban Municipalities Association suma.org/siteengine/activepage.asp?PageID=1	Allan Earle	Laurent Mougeot, Executive Director 2222 13th Avenue Regina S4P 3M7 Phone: 306 525-3727 Fax: 306 525-4373 E-mail: lmougeot@suma.org
Yukon	Association of Yukon Communities ayc.yk.ca	Doug Graham	Tom Paterson, Executive Director 1114 First Avenue, #15 Whitehorse Y1A 1A3 Phone: 867 668-4388 Fax: 867 668-7574 E-mail: ayced@northwestel.net

Directory 1/3   STATE AGENCIES FOR COMMUNITY AFFAIRS

State or territory	Agency, address, and Web site	Name and title of agency head	Phone number Fax number
Alabama	Department of Economic and Community Affairs, 401 Adams Street, P.O. Box 5690, Montgomery 36103-5690 adeca.state.al.us	Bill Johnson Director	334 242-5591 334 242-5099
Alaska	Department of Commerce, Community and Economic Development, P.O. Box 110800, Juneau 99811-0800 dced.state.ak.us	Emil Notti Commissioner	907 465-2500 907 465-5442
Arizona	Department of Commerce, 1700 West Washington, Suite 600, Phoenix 85007 azcommerce.com	Jan Lesher Director	602 771-1100
Arkansas	Department of Economic Development, One Capitol Mall, Little Rock 72201 1800arkansas.com	Maria Haley Executive Director	501 682-2052 501 682-7394
California	Department of Housing and Community Development, 1800 Third Street, Sacramento 95811-6942 hcd.ca.gov	Lynn L. Jacobs Director	916 445-4775 916 324-5107
Colorado	Colorado Department of Local Affairs, 1313 Sherman Street, Denver 80203 dola.state.co.us	Susan Kirkpatrick Executive Director	303 866-4904 303 866-4317
Connecticut	Department of Economic and Community Development, Business and Housing Development, 505 Hudson Street, Hartford 06106-7107 ct.gov/ecd/site/default.asp	Joan McDonald Commissioner	860 270-8000 860 270-8008
Delaware	State Housing Authority, 18 The Green, Dover 19901 destatehousing.com/	Saundra R. Johnson Director	302 739-4263 302 739-6122
Florida	Department of Community Affairs, 2555 Shumard Oak Boulevard, Tallahassee 32399-2100 dca.state.fl.us	Thomas G. Pelham Secretary	850 488-8466 850 921-9781
Georgia	Department of Community Affairs, 60 Executive Park South, N.E., Atlanta 30329-2231 dca.state.ga.us	Mike Beatty Commissioner	404 679-4940 404 679-0646
Idaho	Department of Commerce, 700 West State Street, Boise 83720-0093 commerce.idaho.gov	Jim Ellick Director	208 334-2470
Illinois	Department of Commerce and Economic Opportunity, James R. Thompson Center, 100 West Randolph, Suite 3-400, Chicago 60601 illinoisbiz.biz	Jack Lavin Director	312 814-7179
Indiana	Indiana Housing and Community Development Authority, 30 South Meridian, Suite 1000, Indianapolis 46204 in.gov/ihfa	Sherry Seiwert Executive Director	317 232-7777 317 232-7778
Iowa	Department of Economic Development, 200 East Grand Avenue, Des Moines 50309 iowalifechanging.com	Mike Tramontina Director	515 242-4700 515 242-4809
Kansas	Department of Commerce, Division of Community Development, 1000 S.W. Jackson Street, Suite 100, Topeka 66612-1354 kdoch.state.ks.us/public	Jean Stinson Acting Director	785 296-3481 785 296-5055
Kentucky	Governor's Office for Local Government, Division of Grants, 1024 Capital Center Drive, Suite 340, Frankfort 40601 gold.ky.gov	Colleen B. Chaney, Acting Commissioner	502 573-2382 502 573-2939
Louisiana	Office of Community Development, Division of Administration, P.O. Box 94095, Baton Rouge 70804-9095 doa.louisiana.gov/cdbg/cdbg.htm	Suzie Elkins Executive Director	225 342-7412 225 342-1947
Maine	Department of Economic and Community Development, 59 State House Station, Augusta 04333-0059 econdevmaine.com	John Richardson Commissioner	207 624-9800 207 287-8070
Maryland	Department of Housing and Community Development, 100 Community Place, Crownsville 21032-2023 dhcd.state.md.us	Raymond Skinner Secretary	410 514-7000 410 987-4070
Michigan	Michigan Economic Development Corporation, 300 North Washington Square, Lansing 48913 medc.michigan.org	Josh Linkner CEO	888 522-0103 517 241-3683
Minnesota	Department of Employment and Economic Development, First National Bank Building, 332 Minnesota Street, Suite E200, St. Paul 55101-1351 deed.state.mn.us	Dan McElroy Commissioner	651 297-7114 651 296-1290
Mississippi	Mississippi Development Authority, P.O. Box 849, Jackson 39205 Mississippi.org	Leland R. Speed Executive Director	601 359-3449 601 359-2832
Missouri	Department of Economic Development, P.O. Box 1157, Jefferson City 65102-1157 ded.mo.gov	Greg Steinhoff Director	573 751-4962 573 526-7700
Montana	Department of Commerce, Local Government Assistance Division, P.O. Box 200501, Helena 59601 commerce.state.mt.us	Anthony Preite Director	406 841-2700 406 841-2701
Nebraska	Department of Economic Development, P.O. Box 94666, 301 Centennial Mall South, Lincoln 68509-4666 neded.org	Richard Baier Director	402 471-3441 402 471-3778
Nevada	Commission on Economic Development, 108 East Proctor Street, Carson City 89701-4240 expand2nevada.com	Tim Rubald Director	775 687-4325 775 687-4450
New Hampshire	Office of Energy and Planning, 57 Regional Drive, Suite 3, Concord 03301-8519 nh.gov/oep	Amy Ignatius Director	603 271-2155 603 271-2615
New Jersey	Department of Community Affairs, P.O. Box 800, 101 South Broad Street, Trenton 08625-0800 state.nj.us/dca	Joseph Doria Jr. Commissioner	609 292-6055 609 984-6696
New Mexico	Department of Finance and Administration, Local Government Division, 402 Don Gaspar, Santa Fe 87501 local.nmdfa.state.nm.us	Robert Apodaca Director	505 827-4950 505 827-4948
New York	Division of Housing and Community Renewal, Hampton Plaza, 38-40 State Street, Albany 12207 dhcr.state.ny.us	Deborah VanAmerongen Commissioner	518 473-2526 518 473-9462
North Carolina	Department of Commerce, 301 North Wilmington Street, Raleigh 27601-1058 commerce.state.nc.us	Jim Fain Secretary	919 733-4151 919 715-9593

Directory 1/3   STATE AGENCIES FOR COMMUNITY AFFAIRS
continued

State or territory	Agency, address, and Web site	Name and title of agency head	Phone number Fax number
North Dakota	Division of Community Services, P.O. Box 2057, 1600 East Century Avenue, Suite 2, Bismarck 58503 state.nd.us/dcs	Paul Govig Director	701 328-5300 701 328-5320
Ohio	Department of Development, 77 South High Street, Columbus 43216-1001 odod.state.oh.us	Lee Fisher Director	614 466-3379 614 644-0745
Oklahoma	Department of Commerce, 900 North Stiles Avenue, Oklahoma City 73104-3234 okcommerce.gov	Natalie Shirley Executive Director	405 815-6552 405 815-5290
Oregon	Department of Economic and Community Development, 775 Summer Street, N.E., Suite 200, Salem 97301-1280 econ.oregon.gov	Bob Repine Director	503 986-0123 503 581-5115
Pennsylvania	Department of Community and Economic Development, 400 North Street, 4th Floor, Commonwealth Keystone Building, Harrisburg 17120-0225 newpa.com/default.aspx?id=223	Dennis Yablonsky Secretary	717 787-3003 717 787-6866
Puerto Rico	Office of the Commissioner of Municipal Affairs, P.O. Box 70167, San Juan 00936-8167 ocam.gobierno.pr	Ángel Castillo Rodriguez Commissioner	787 754-1600 787 753-8254
Rhode Island	Department of Administration, Office of Municipal Affairs, One Capitol Hill, 4th Floor, Providence 02908-5873 muni-info.ri.gov	Norene Shawcross Chief Executive Officer	401 222-5766 401 222-2083
South Carolina . . .	Department of Commerce, 1201 Main Street, Suite 1600, Columbia 29201-3200 sccommerce.com	Joe E. Taylor Jr. Secretary	803 737-0400 803 737-0418
South Dakota	Department of Tourism and State Development, 711 East Wells Avenue, Pierre 57501-3369 sdreadytowork.com	Richard Benda Secretary	605 773-3301 605 773-3256
Tennessee	Housing Development Agency, 404 James Robertson Parkway, Suite 1114, Nashville 37243-0900 state.tn.us/thda	Ted R. Fellman Executive Director	615 741-2400 615 741-9634
Texas	Department of Housing and Community Affairs, P.O. Box 13941, Austin 78711-3941 tdhca.state.tx.us	Michael Gerber Executive Director	512 475-3930 512 469-9606
Utah	Governor's Office of Economic Development, 324 South State Street, Suite 500, Salt Lake City 84111 goed.utah.gov	Jason Perry Executive Director	801 538-8700 801 538-8888
	The Utah Department of Community and Culture, 324 South State Street, Suite 500, Salt Lake City 84111 community.utah.gov	Palmer DePaulis Executive Director	801 538-8700 801 538-8888
Vermont	Department of Housing and Community Affairs, National Life Building, 6th Floor, One National Life Drive, Montpelier 05620-0501 dhca.state.vt.us	John S. Hall Commissioner	802 828-5216 802 828-2928
Virginia	Department of Housing and Community Development, The Jackson Center, 501 North Second Street, Richmond 23219-1321 dhcd.virginia.gov	Bill Shelton Director	804 371-7002 804 371-7090
Washington	Department of Community, Trade and Economic Development, P.O. Box 42525, 128 Tenth Avenue, S.W., Olympia 98504-2525 cted.wa.gov	Julie Wilkerson Director	360 725-4000 360 586-8440
West Virginia	Community Development Office, Capitol Complex, Building 6, 1900 Kanawha Boulevard East, Charleston 25305-0311 wvdo.org	Steve Spence Executive Director	304 558-2234 304 558-0449
Wisconsin	Department of Commerce, 201 West Washington Avenue, Madison 53703-7970 commerce.state.wi.us	Mary P. Burke Secretary	608 266-1018 608 226-8969

Directory 1/4   PROVINCIAL AND TERRITORIAL AGENCIES FOR LOCAL AFFAIRS IN CANADA

Providence or territory	Minister, address, and Web site	Phone number Fax number	Providence or territory	Minister, address, and Web site	Phone number Fax number
Alberta	Hon. Ray Danyluk Alberta Municipal Affairs and Housing Communications Branch 18th Floor, Commerce Place 10155-102 Street Edmonton AB T5J 4L4 municipalaffairs.gov.ab.ca	780 427-2732 780 422-1419	New Brunswick	Hon. Edward Doherty Minister Responsible for Aboriginal Affairs Legislative Assembly of New Brunswick P.O. Box 6000 Fredericton E3B 5H1 gnb.ca/0016/index-e.asp	506 462-5177 506 444-5142
British Columbia	Honourable Ida Chong Minister of Community Services and Minister Responsible for Seniors' and Women's Issues P.O. Box 9056 STN PROV GOVT Victoria V8W 9E2 gov.bc.ca/cserv/index.html	250 387-2283 250 387-4312		Hon. Mary Schryer Minister of Family and Community Services, 4th Floor P.O. Box 6000 Fredericton E3B 5H1 gnb.ca	506 453-2001 506 453-7478
Manitoba	Hon. Oscar Lathlin Minister of Aboriginal and Northern Affairs 344 Legislative Building 450 Broadway Winnipeg R3C 0V8 gov.mb.ca/ana	204 945-3719 204 945-8374	Newfoundland and Labrador	Hon. Dave Denine Minister of Municipal Affairs Main Floor, West Block Confederation Building P.O. Box 8700 St. John's A1B 4J6 gov.nf.ca/mpa	709 729-3048 709 729-0943

Directory 1/4   PROVINCIAL AND TERRITORIAL AGENCIES FOR LOCAL AFFAIRS IN CANADA
continued

Providence or territory	Minister, address, and Web site	Phone number Fax number	Providence or territory	Minister, address, and Web site	Phone number Fax number
Northwest Territories ..	Hon. Jackson Lafferty Minister of Education, Culture, and Employment P.O. Box 1320 Yellowknife X1A 2L9 ece.gov.nt.ca	867 669-2399 867 873-0431		P.O. Box 2000 Charlottetown C1A 7N8 gov.pe.ca/commcul/index.php3	
Nova Scotia	Hon. Jamie Muir Minister of Service and Municipal Relations P.O. Box 1003 Halifax B3J 2X1 gov.ns.ca/snsmr/muns/link	902 424-5200 902 424-0720	Québec	Nathalie Normandeau Ministre des Affaires Municipales 10, rue Pierre-Olivier-Chauveau Québec G1R 4J3 mamm.gouv.qc.ca/accueil.asp	418 691-2050 418 643-1795
Ontario	Hon. Jim Watson Minister of Municipal Affairs and Housing 777 Bay Street, 17th Floor Toronto M5G 2E5 mah.gov.on.ca	416 585-7000 416 585-6470	Saskatchewan	Hon. Pat Atkinson Minister of Public Service Commission 2100 Broad Street Regina SK S4P 1Y5 gov.sk.ca/deptsorgs/overviews/?75	306 787-7339 306 787-3397
Prince Edward Island	Hon. Carolyn Bertram Minister of Community and Cultural Affairs	902 368-5250 902 368-4121	Yukon	Hon. Glenn Hart Minister of Community Services P.O. Box 2703 Whitehorse Y1A 2C6 community.gov.yk.ca/	867 667-5811 867 393-6295

Directory 1/5   U.S. MUNICIPAL MANAGEMENT ASSOCIATIONS

State	Association and Web site	President, address, and e-mail	Phone number Fax number
Alabama	Alabama City/County Management Association accma-online.org/	Donna H. Treslar (until 10/08) City Clerk City of Pelham P.O. Box 1419 Pelham 35124-5419 dtreslar@pelhamonline.com	205 620-6402 205 663-0050
Alaska	Alaska Municipal Management Association akml.org/amma.html	Tim Beck (until 11/08) Assembly Fairbanks North Star Borough P.O. Box 71267 Fairbanks 99707 tbeck@ptialaska.net	907 459-1401 907 459-1224
		Denise Michels (until 11/09) Mayor City of Nome P.O. Box 281 Nome 99762 mayor@ci.nome.ak.us	907 443-5231 907 443-5349
Arizona	Arizona City/County Management Association azmanagement.org/	George A. Pettit (until 2/09) Town Manager Town of Gilbert 50 East Civic Center Drive Gilbert 85296-3463 georgep@ci.gilbert.az.us	480 503-6864 480 497-4943
Arkansas	Arkansas City/County Management Association	Catherine Christie Cook (until 6/08) City Manager City of Hope P.O. Box 667 Hope 71802-0667 catcook@arkansas.net	870 777-6701 870 722-2579
		Jimmy W. Bolt (6/08–6/09) City Manager City of Arkadelphia 700 Clay Street Arkadelphia 71923-5963 jimmy@cityofarkadelphia.com	870 246-9864 870 246-1813
California	City Manager's Department, League of California Cities cacities.org	Jeffrey C. Kolin (until 10/08) City Manager City of Santa Rosa P.O. Box 1678 Santa Rosa 95402-1678 jkolin@ci.santa-rosa.ca.us	707 543-3020 707 543-3030
	Cal-ICMA www2.icma.org/cal-icma	Hilary M. Straus (until 8/08) Assistant to the City Manager City of Citrus Heights 6237 Fountain Square Drive Citrus Heights 95621-5577 hstraus@citrusheights.net	916 727-4713 916 725-5799

Directory 1/5   U.S. MUNICIPAL MANAGEMENT ASSOCIATIONS
continued

State	Association and Web site	President, address, and e-mail	Phone number Fax number
Colorado	Colorado City/County Management Association	Clinton R. Mitchell Kinney (until 02/09) City Manager City of Fruita 325 East Aspen Avenue, Suite 155 Fruita 81521-2203 clint@fruita.org	970 858-3663 970 858-0210
Connecticut	Connecticut Town and City Management Association	Karl Kilduff (until 7/08) Town Administrator Town of Darien 229 Branford Road, Unit 440 North Branford 06471-1318 kkilduff@darienct.gov	203 656-7300 203 656-7389
Delaware	City Management Association of Delaware	Anthony J. DePrima City Manager City of Dover P.O. Box 475 Dover 19903-0475 tdeprima@dover.de.us	302 736-7005 302 736-7002
Florida	Florida City and County Management Association fccma.org/	Barbara Lipscomb (until 6/08) City Manager City of Casselberry Casselberry City Hall 95 Triplet Lake Drive Casselberry 32707-3252 blipscomb@casselberry.org	407 262-7700 407 262-7764
		Edward R. Mitchell (6/08–6/09) City Administrator City of West Palm Beach P.O. Box 3366 West Palm Beach 33402-3366 emitchel@wpb.org	561 822-1400 561 822-1424
Georgia	Georgia City-County Management Association gccma.com	Isaiah Hugley (until 3/09) City Manager Columbus-Muscogee Consolidated Government P.O. Box 1340 Columbus 31902-1340 ihugley@columbusga.org	706 653-4029 706 653-4032
Idaho	Idaho City/County Management Association	Bill Belknap (until 2/08) Assistant City Supervisor City of Moscow P.O. Box 9203 Moscow 83843 bbelknap@ci.moscow.id.us	208 883-7007
Illinois	Illinois City/County Management Association ilcma.org/	Ghida Neukirch (until 7/08) Deputy Village Manager Village of Buffalo Grove 50 Raupp Boulevard Buffalo Grove 60089-2139 gneukirch@vbg.org	847 459-2518 847 459-7906
		Patrick Urich (7/08–7/09) County Administrator County of Peoria 324 Main Street, Room 502 Peoria 61602-1319 purich@co.peoria.il.us	309 672-6056 309 672-6054
Indiana	Indiana Municipal Management Association citiesandtowns.org/content/affiliated/IMMA_DHT.htm	Gary A. Huff (until 11/09) Town Manager Town of Fishers 1 Municipal Drive Town Hall Fishers 46038-1574 huffg@fishers.in.us	317 595-3101 317 595-3110
Iowa	Iowa City/County Management Association	Jeffrey Pomeranz (until 7/08) City Manager Town of Cumberland P.O. Box 46229-0155 Indianapolis 46229-0155	515 222-3612 515 222-3638
		Alan D. Johnson (7/08–7/09) City Manager City of Independence 331 First Street East Independence 50644-2814 citymgr@indytel.com	319 334-2780 319 334-2037

Directory 1/5   **U.S. MUNICIPAL MANAGEMENT ASSOCIATIONS**
continued

State	Association and Web site	President, address, and e-mail	Phone number / Fax number
Kansas	Kansas Association of City/County Management accesskansas.org/kacm/	Courtney W. Christensen (until 1/09) City Administrator City of Mission Hills 6300 State Line Road Prairie Village 66208-1922 cchristensen@missionhillsks.gov	913 362-9620 913 362-0673
		Matthew C. Allen (through 2009) Assistant City Manager City of Garden City 301 North 8th Street Garden City 67846-5340 mallen@garden-city.org	620 276-1160 620 276-1169
Kentucky	Kentucky City/County Management Association kccma.org/	James W. Zumwalt (until 1/09) City Manager City of Paducah P.O. Box 2267 Paducah 42002-2267 jzumwalt@ci.paducah.ky.us	270 444-8503 270 443-5058
Maine	Maine Town and City Management Association mtcma.org	Nathaniel J. Tupper (until 9/08) Town Manager Town of Yarmouth 200 Main Street Yarmouth 04096 ntupper@yarmouth.me.us	207 846-9036 207 846-2403
		Steven A. Dyer (as of 9/08) Town Manager Town of Oakland Oakland Town Office P.O. Box 187 Oakland 04963 sdyer@oaklandmaine.com	207 465-7357 207 465-9118
Maryland	Maryland City and County Management Association	Paul E. Folkers (until 5/08) Assistant Chief Administrative Officer County of Montgomery 101 Monroe Street Rockville 20850-2540 paul.folkers@montgomerycountymd.gov	240 777-2514 240 777-2517
		Elaine M. Murphy (5/08–5/09) City Administrator City of Hyattsville 4310 Gallatin Street Hyattsville 20781-2050 emurphy@hyattsville.org	301 985-5000 301 985-5007
Massachusetts	Massachusetts Municipal Management Association mma.org	Maureen Godsey Valente (until 1/09) Town Manager Town of Sudbury 278 Old Sudbury Road Sudbury 01776-1843 valentem@town.sudbury.ma.us	978 639-3385 978 443-0756
Michigan	Michigan Local Government Management Association mlgma.org	Edward B. Koryzno Jr. (until 2/09) City Manager City of Ypsilanti 1 South Huron Street Ypsilanti 48197-5420 ekoryzno@cityofypsilanti.com	734 483-1810 734 483-7260
Minnesota	Minnesota City/County Management Association mncma.org	David J. Unmacht (until 5/08) County Administrator County of Scott 200 Fourth Avenue West Shakopee 55379-1220 dunmacht@co.scott.mn.us	952 496-8100 952 496-8180
		Kris M. Busse (5/08–5/09) City Administrator City of Owatonna 540 W Hills Circle Owatonna 55060-4701 Kris.busse@ci.owatonna.mn.us	507 444-4300 507 444-4394
Mississippi	Mississippi City/County Management Association	Gary A. Suddith (through 2008) Chief Administration Officer City of Laurel P.O. Box 647 Laurel 39441-0647 garysuddith@laurelms.com	601 428-6411 601 428-6442

Directory 1/5   U.S. MUNICIPAL MANAGEMENT ASSOCIATIONS
continued

State	Association and Web site	President, address, and e-mail	Phone number Fax number
Missouri	Missouri City Management Association	Mark R. Randall (until 6/08) City Administrator City of Pleasant Hill 2007 Hidden Valley Drive Pleasant Hill 64080 admin@pleasanthill.com	816 540-3135 816 540-5141
		Richard R. Noll (5/08–5/09) Assistant City Manager City of Kansas City 414 East 12th Street, 29th Floor Kansas City 64106-2748 rich_noll@kcmo.org	816 513-1408 816 513-1363
Nebraska	Nebraska Association of City and County Management	Lowell D. Johnson City Administrator City of Wayne P.O. Box 8 Wayne 68787-0008 cityadmin@cityofwayne.org	402 375-1733 402 375-1619
Nevada	Local Government Managers Association of Nevada	Susan Schlerf (thru 6/30/08) Assistant City Manager City of Reno P.O. Box 1900 Reno 89505-1900 schlerfs@ci.reno.nv.us	775 334-2020 775 731-2097
New Hampshire	New Hampshire Municipal Management Association nhmanagers.org	John Scruton (until 11/08) City Manager City of Rochester 31 Wakefield Street Rochester 03867 john.scruton@rochesternh.net	603 332-1167 603 335-7565
		Jessie W. Levine (11/08–11/09) Town Administrator Town of New London 375 Main Street New London 03257 townadmin@nl-nh.com	603 526-4821 603 526-9494
New Jersey	New Jersey Municipal Management Association njmma.org/	Joseph L. Verruni (1/08–1/09) Township Administrator Township of Wall 2700 Allaire Road Wall 07719-9570 jverruni@townshipofwall.com	732 449-8444 732 449-8996
New Mexico	New Mexico City Management Association	Andrew P. Wise City Manager City of Lovington P.O. Box 1268 Lovington 88260-5008 pwise@lovington-nm.org	505 396-2884 505 396-6328
New York	New York State City County Management Association nyscma.govoffice.com/	Susan Maggiotto (until 6/08) Deputy Village Manager/Clerk Village of Hastings on Hudson 7 Maple Avenue Hastings-On-Hudson 10706-1039 smaggiotto@hastingsgov.org	914 478-3400 914 478-4624
		Harold J. Porr III (6/08–6/09) Village Administrator Village of Bronxville Village Hall 200 Pondfield Road Bronxville 10708-4832 hporr3@optonline.net	914 337-6500 914 337-2683
North Carolina	North Carolina City and County Management Association ncmanagers.org/	Randy McCaslin (until 7/08) Assistant City Manager City of High Point P.O. Box 230 High Point 27261 Randy.mccaslin@highpointnc.gov	336 883-3291 336 883-3052
		David C. Cooke (7/08–7/09) County Manager County of Wake P.O. Box 550 Raleigh 27602-0550 dcooke@co.wake.nc.us	919 856-5555 919 856-6168

Directory 1/5   **U.S. MUNICIPAL MANAGEMENT ASSOCIATIONS**
continued

State	Association and Web site	President, address, and e-mail	Phone number / Fax number
Ohio	Ohio City/County Management Association ocmaohio.org/	R. Thomas Homan (until 7/08) City Manager City of Delaware 1 South Sandusky Street Delaware 43015-2326 rthoman@delawareaohio.net	740 203-1010 740 203-1024
		Brian Humphress (7/08–7/09) City Manager City of Willard 710 Kennedy Drive Willard 44890-9413 manager@willard-oh.com	419 933-2591 419 933-4545
Oklahoma	City Management Association of Oklahoma oml.org/dbs/CMAO/index.cfm	Steven Whitlock (until 8/08) City Manager City of Coweta P.O. Box 850 Coweta 74429-0850 swhitlock@coweta.lib.ok.us	918 486-2189 918 486-5366
Oregon	Oregon City/County Management Association occma.org/DesktopDefault.aspx	Phillip M. Messina (until 1/09) City Administrator City of Central Point 140 South Third Street Central Point 97502 philm@ci.central-point.or.us	541 664-3321 541 664-6384
Pennsylvania	Association for Pennsylvania Municipal Management apmm.govoffice.com/	Gregory G. Smith (until 5/1/08) Township Manager Township of Moon 1000 Beaver Grade Road Moon Township 15108-2906 gsmith@moontwp.com	412 262-1700 412 262-5344
Rhode Island	Rhode Island City and Town Management Association	Gerald Kempen (until 7/08) Town Administrator Town of Middletown 2 JH Dwyer Drive Middletown 02842-4575 gkempen@middletownri.com	401 849-2898 401 845-0400
South Carolina	South Carolina City and County Management Association iopa.sc.edu/scccma/	Charles Bennett II (until 7/08) City Manager City of North Augusta P.O. Drawer 6400 North Augusta 29861-6400	803 441-4202 803 441-4203
South Dakota	South Dakota City Management Association	Roland VanDerWerff (until 10/08) City Administrator City of Hartford P.O. Box 727 Hartford 57033-0727 cityhart@unitelsd.com	605 528-3427 605 528-3320
Tennessee	Tennessee City Management Association tncma.org/	Mitchell Moore (until 7/08) City Manager City of Athens P.O. Box 849 Athens 37371-0849 mmoore@cityofathenstn.com	423 744-2701 423 744-8866
Texas	Texas City Management Association tcma.org/	Mike Perez (until 7/08) City Manager City of McAllen P.O. Box 220 McAllen 78505-0220 Mrperez@mcallen.net	956 972-7100 956 972-7138
Utah	Utah City Management Association ucma-utah.org/	James Davidson (until 10/08) City Administrator City of Lehi 153 North 100 East Lehi 84043-1852 jpdavidson@lehicity.com	801 768-7100 801 768-7101
Vermont	Vermont Town and City Management Association	Carl Rogers (until 6/08) Town Manager Town of Barre P.O. Box 116 Websterville 05678-0116 crogers@barretown.org	802 479-9331 802 479-9332

Directory 1/5   U.S. MUNICIPAL MANAGEMENT ASSOCIATIONS
continued

State	Association and Web site	President, address, and e-mail	Phone number / Fax number
Virginia	Virginia Local Government Management Association vlgma.org	Sanford Wanner (until 7/08) County Administrator County of James City P.O. Box 8784 Williamsburg 23187-8784 sbwanner@james-city.va.us	757 253-6603 757 253-6833
Washington	Washington City/County Management Association wccma.org	Andrew E. Neiditz (until 9/08) City Manager City of Lakewood 10611 82nd Avenue Court, S.W. Lakewood 98498 aneiditz@cityoflakewood.us	253 589-2489 253 589-3774
		Bunyamin B. Yazici City Manager City of Sammamish 801 228th Avenue, S.E. Sammamish 98075 byazici@ci.sammamish.wa.us	425 836-7902 425 295-0600
West Virginia	West Virginia City Management Association	Mark S. Baldwin City Manager City of Martinsburg 232 North Queen Street P.O. Box 828 Martinsburg 25401-3314	304 264-2131 304 264-2136
Wisconsin	Wisconsin City/County Management Association wcma-wi.org/	Michael K. Davis (until 6/08) City Administrator City of Middleton 7426 Hubbard Avenue Middleton 53562-3118 mdavis@ci.middleton.wi.us	608 827-1050 608 827-1057
		Lisa A. Kuss (6/08–6/09) City Administrator City of Clintonville 50 10th Street Clintonville 54929-1513 lkuss@clintonvillewi.org	715 823-7600 715 823-1352
Wyoming, Idaho, Montana, North Dakota, and South Dakota	Great Open Spaces City Management Association	Bret A. Jones (until 5/08) City Administrator City of Gillette P.O. Box 3003 Gillette, WY 82717-3003 bret@www.ci.gillette.wy.us	307 686-5203 307 686-1593
		David W. Waind (5/08–5/09) City Manager City of Minot 515 2nd Avenue, S.W. Minot, ND 58701-3739 waind@web.ci.minot.nd.us	701 857-4750 701 857-4751

Directory 1/6   INTERNATIONAL MUNICIPAL MANAGEMENT ASSOCIATIONS

State, province, or country	Association and Web site	President, address, e-mail address	Phone number / Fax number
Australia	Local Government Managers Australia (LGMA) lgma.org.au	Paul Arnold National President Local Government Managers Australia P.O. Box 973 Burnie 7320	61-03-9676-2755 61-03-9676-2311
Canada	Canadian Association of Municipal Administrators (CAMA) camacam.ca	Barry Carroll Town of Sackville PO Box 6191, 110 Main Street Sackville, E4L 1G6 b.carroll@sackville.com	506 364-4930 506 364-4976
India	City Managers' Association Gujarat	R. Tripathi President City Managers' Association Gujarat Ahmedabad Municipal Corporation Office West Zone Usmanpura Crossroad, Ahmedabad 380013	91-79-27561184 91-79-27551595

Directory 1/6   **INTERNATIONAL MUNICIPAL MANAGEMENT ASSOCIATIONS**
continued

State, province, or country	Association and Web site	President, address, e-mail address	Phone number Fax number
Ireland	County and City Managers' Association	Michael McLoone Donegal County Manager Floor 2, Cumberland House Fenian Street Dublin 2	35-31-509-9560
Israel	Union of Local Authorities in Israel ulai.org.il	Avi Rabinovitch Deputy Director General 19 Ha'arbaa Street, 10th Floor Tel Aviv 64739 ulais@netvision.net.il	972-3-684-4210 972-3-684-4211
Korea	Korean Urban Management Association kruma.org	Choon Hee Ro Kyonggi Research Institute 179-26, Pajang-Dong, Jangan-Gu Seoul City, Kyonggi Province 440-290 South Korea choonr@kangnam.ac.kr	82-331-222-4800 82-331-224-5434
Mexico	Mexican Association of Municipalities (AMMAC) ammac.org.mx	Ruben Fernandez Executive Director Adolfo Prieto 1634, Colonia Del Valle Distrito Federa 03100 Ammac01@infosel.net.mx	55-55-24-4020 53-56-87-9947
Netherlands	Dutch City Managers Association gemeentesecretaris.nl	Piet J. Buytels President P.O. Box 1501 3100 EA Schiedam Schiedam vgs@vng.nl	31-70-373-8677 31-10-473-5978
New Zealand	New Zealand Society of Local Government Managers solgm.org.nz/default.asp	Rod Titcombe President Manawtu District Council Private Bag 10001 Frilding	04-727-533 04-712-153
Norway	Norwegian Forum of Municipal Executives	Oystein Siversten President Municipality of Lenvik N-9301 Lenvik	47-77-85-01-00 47-77-84-20-39
Slovakia	Slovak City Managers' Association	Andrej Bubenik City Manager MU Podunajke Biskupice Trijicne Nam 1 825 61 Bratislava 211 sekretariat@mupb.sk	421-2-54-248-024 421-2-54-248-264
	Local Government Development Center	Luba Vavrova Program Coordinator Centrum rozvoja samospráv Local Government Development Center Laurinská 2 811 01 Bratislava vavrova@crs.sk	4-21-2-54-248-024 4-21-2-54-248-264
South Africa	Institute for Local Government Management of South Africa ilgm.co.za	B. Biyela President Uthungulu House Ste 2 Private Bag X1025 Uthungulu, Krugerand CBD Richards Bay 3900	27-35-789-1404 27-35-789-1641
Spain	L'Union des Dirigeants Territoriaux de l'Europe (U.Di.T.E.) atam.pt/udite.htm	Adrian Mifsud President Zurrieg Local Council Triq PP Saydon Zurreig ZRQ02 Malta	35-62-164-2974
Sweden	Association of Swedish City Managers	Anna Sandborgh Chair Karlstads kommun Kommunledningskontoret 651 84 Karlstad anna.sandborgh@karlstad.se	46-5-429-5102
United Kingdom	Society of Local Authority Chief Executives (SOLACE) solace.org.uk	Cheryl Miller Chief Executive Hope House 45 Greater Peter Street London SW1P 3LT	08-45-652-4010 08-45-652 4011

Directory 1/7   U.S. STATE ASSOCIATIONS OF COUNTIES

State	State association, address, and Web site	Executive director	Phone number / Fax number
Alabama	Association of County Commissioners of Alabama, 100 North Jackson Street, Montgomery 36104 acca-online.org	O. H. Sharpless	334 263-7594 334 263-7678
Alaska	Alaska Municipal League, 217 Second Street, Suite 200, Juneau 99801-1267 akml.org	Kathie Wasserman	907 586-1325 907 463-5480
Arizona	Arizona Association of Counties, 1910 West Jefferson, Suite 1, Phoenix 85009 azcounties.org	Nicole Stickler	602 252-6563 602 254-0969
	County Supervisors Association of Arizona, 1905 West Washington Street, Suite 100, Phoenix 85009 countysupervisors.org	Craig Sullivan	602 252-5521 602 253-3227
Arkansas	Association of Arkansas Counties, 1415 West Third Street, Little Rock 72201 arcounties.org	Eddie Jones	501 372-7550 501 372-0611
California	California State Association of Counties, 1100 K Street, Suite 101, Sacramento 95814-3932 csac.counties.org	Paul McIntosh	916 327-7500 916 441-5507
Colorado	Colorado Counties, Inc., 800 Grant Street, Suite 500, Denver 80203 ccionline.org	Larry Kallenberger	303 861-4076 303 861-2818
Delaware	Delaware Association of Counties, 12 North Washington Avenue, Lewes 19958-1806	Richard Cecil	302 645-0432 302 645-2232
Florida	Florida Association of Counties, P.O. Box 549, Tallahassee 32302 fl-counties.com	Chris Holley	850 922-4300 850 488-7501
Georgia	Association County Commissioners of Georgia, 50 Hurt Plaza, Suite 1000, Atlanta 30303 accg.org	Jerry Griffin	404 522-5022 404 525-2477
Hawaii	Hawaii State Association of Counties, 4396 Rice Street, Suite 206, Lihue 96766 hawaii-county.com/	Michael Victorino	808 270-7760 808 270-7639
Idaho	Idaho Association of Counties, P.O. Box 1623, Boise 83701 idcounties.org	Daniel Chadwick	208 345-9126 208 345-0379
Illinois	Illinois Association of County Board Members, 413 West Monroe Street, 2nd Floor, Springfield 62704 ilcounties.org	Kelly Murray	217 528-5331 217 528-5562
	Metro Counties of Illinois, 1303 Brandywine Road, Libertyville 60048-3000 co.cook.il.us/secretary/HomePage_Links/collar_counties.htm	Dwight Magalis	847 816-0889 847 247-9915
	United Counties Council of Illinois, 217 East Monroe Street, Suite 101, Springfield 62701-1743 unitedcounties.com/default.asp	W. Michael McCreery	217 544-5585 217 544-5571
Indiana	Association of Indiana Counties, 101 West Ohio Street, Suite 1575 Indianapolis 46204 indianacounties.org	David Bottorff	317 684-3710 317 684-3713
Iowa	Iowa State Association of Counties, 501 S.W. Seventh Street, Suite Q, Des Moines 50309-4540 iowacounties.org	William Peterson	515 244-7181 515 244-6397
Kansas	Kansas Association of Counties, 300 S.W. Eighth Street, 3rd Floor, Topeka 66603 kansascounties.org	Randall Allen	785 272-2585 785 272-3585
Kentucky	Kentucky Association of Counties, 380 King's Daughter Drive, Frankfort 40601-4106 kaco.org	Bob Arnold	502 223-7667 502 223-1502
Louisiana	Police Jury Association of Louisiana, 707 North Seventh Street, Baton Rouge 70802 lpgov.org	Roland Dartez	225 343-2835 225 336-1344
Maine	Maine County Commissioners Association, 11 Columbia Street, Augusta 04330 mainecounties.org	Robert Howe	207 623-4697 207 622-4437
Maryland	Maryland Association of Counties, 169 Conduit Street, Annapolis 21401 mdcounties.org	David Bliden	410 269-0043 410 268-1775
Massachusetts	Massachusetts Association of County Commissioners, c/o Peter Collins, 614 High Street, Dedham 02027-0310	Peter Collins	781 461-6105 781 326-6480
Michigan	Michigan Association of Counties, 935 North Washington Avenue, Lansing 48906 micounties.org	Timothy K. McGuire	517 372-5374 517 482-4599
Minnesota	Association of Minnesota Counties, 125 Charles Avenue, St. Paul 55103-2108 mncounties.org	James A. Mulder	651 789-4325 651 224-6540
Mississippi	Mississippi Association of Supervisors, 793 North President Street, Jackson 39202 masnetwork.org	Jack Gregory	601 353-2741 601 353-2749
Missouri	Missouri Association of Counties, 516 East Capitol Avenue, P.O. Box 234, Jefferson City 65102-0234 mocounties.com	Dick Burke	573 634-2120 573 634-3549
Montana	Montana Association of Counties, 2715 Skyway Drive, Helena 59602-1213 maco.cog.mt.us	Harold Blattie	406 444-4360 406 442-5238
Nebraska	Nebraska Association of County Officials, 625 South 14th Street, Suite 200, Lincoln 68508 nacone.org	Larry Dix	402 434-5660 402 434-5673
Nevada	Nevada Association of Counties, 201 South Roop Street, Suite 101, Carson City 89701 nvnaco.org/NACo	Jeff Fontaine	775 883-7863 775 883-7398
New Hampshire	New Hampshire Association of Counties, 46 Donovan Street, Suite 2, Concord 03301-2624 nhcounties.org	Betsy B. Miller	603 224-9222 603 224-8312
New Jersey	New Jersey Association of Counties, 150 West State Street, Trenton 08608-1105 njac.org	Celeste Carpiano	609 394-3467 609 989-8567
New Mexico	New Mexico Association of Counties, 613 Old Santa Fe Trail, Santa Fe 87501 nmcounties.org	Paul Gutierrez	505 983-2101 505 983-4396
New York	New York State Association of Counties, 111 Pine Street, Albany 12207-2737 nysac.org	Stephen J. Acquario	518 465-1473 518 465-0506
North Carolina	North Carolina Association of County Commissioners, P.O. Box 1488, Raleigh 27602-1488 ncacc.org	David F. Thompson	919 715-2893 919 733-1065

Directory 1/7   U.S. STATE ASSOCIATIONS OF COUNTIES
continued

State	State association, address, and Web site	Executive director	Phone number Fax number
North Dakota	North Dakota Association of Counties, 1661 Capitol Way, Bismarck 58502-0877 ndaco.org	Mark Johnson	701 328-7300 701 328-7308
Ohio	County Commissioners Association of Ohio, 37 West Broad Street, Suite 650, Columbus 43215-4195 ccao.org	Larry L. Long	614 221-5627 614 221-6986
Oklahoma	Association of County Commissioners of Oklahoma City, 429 N.E. 50th Street, Oklahoma City 73105-1815 okacco.com	Gayle Ward	405.516.5313 405.516.5333
Oregon	Association of Oregon Counties, P.O. Box 12729, Salem 97309 aocweb.org	Mike McArthur	503 585-8351 503 373-7876
Pennsylvania	County Commissioners Association of Pennsylvania, P.O. Box 60769, Harrisburg 17106-0769 pacounties.org	Douglas E. Hill	717 232-7554 717 232-2162
South Carolina	South Carolina Association of Counties, 1919 Thurmond Mall, Columbia 2920 sccounties.org	Michael B. Cone	803 252-7255 803 252-0379
South Dakota	South Dakota Association of County Officials, 207 East Capitol Avenue, Suite 8, Pierre 57501 sdcounties.org	Eric Erickson	605 224-1968 605 224-9128
	South Dakota Association of County Commissioners, 222 East Capitol Avenue, Suite 1, Pierre 57501 sdcc.govoffice2.com	Bob Wilcox	605 224-4554 605 224-4833
Tennessee	Tennessee County Services Association, 226 Capitol Boulevard, Suite 700, Nashville 37219-1896 tncounties.org	David Seivers	615 532-3767 615 532-3769
Texas	Texas Association of Counties, 1210 San Antonio Street, Austin 78701 county.org	Karen Norris	512 478-8753 512 478-0519
Utah	Utah Association of Counties, 5397 South Vine Street, Salt Lake City 84107-6757 uacnet.org	L. Brent Gardner	801 265-1331 801 265-9485
Virginia	Virginia Association of Counties, 1001 East Broad Street, Suite LL20, Richmond 23219 vaco.org	James Campbell	804 788-6652 804 788-0083
Washington	Washington Association of County Officials, 206 Tenth Avenue, S.E., Olympia 98501-1333 wacounties.org/waco	Deborah D. Wilke	360 753-7319 360 664-2812
	Washington State Association of Counties, 206 Tenth Avenue, S.E., Olympia 98501 wacounties.org/wsac	Bill Vogler	360 753-1886 360 753-2842
West Virginia	County Commissioners' Association of West Virginia, 2309 Washington Street East, Charleston 25311 polsci.wvu.edu/wv	Vivian G. Parsons	304 345-4639 304 346-3512
	West Virginia Association of Counties, 2211 Washington Street East, Charleston 25311-2218 wvcounties.org	Patti Hamilton	304 346-0591 304 346-0592
Wisconsin	Wisconsin Counties Association, 22 East Mifflin Street, Suite 900, Madison 53703 wicounties.org	Mark D. O'Connell	608 663-7188 608 663-7189
Wyoming	Wyoming County Commissioners Association, P.O. Box 86, Cheyenne 82003 wyo-wcca.org	Joseph Evans	307 632-5409 307 632-6533

Directory 1/8   U.S. COUNCILS OF GOVERNMENTS RECOGNIZED BY ICMA

Local government	Appointed administrator	Phone number
ALABAMA-4		
Birmingham Regional Planning Commission	Charles Ball	205-251-8139
Central Alabama Regional Planning and Development Commission	Bob Grasser	334 262-4300
East Alabama Regional Planning and Development Commission	James W. Curtis	256 237-6741
South Central Alabama Development Commission	Tyson Howard	334 244-6903
ARIZONA-2		
Maricopa Association of Governments	Dennis Smith	602 254-6300
Pima Association of Governments	Gary G. Hayes, AICP	520 792-1093
ARKANSAS-3		
Metroplan	Jim McKenzie	501 372-3300
Northwest Arkansas Regional Planning Commission	Jeff Hawkins	479 751-7125
White River Planning and Development District	Van Thomas	870 793-5233 ext 15
CALIFORNIA-10		
Association of Bay Area Governments	Henry L. Gardner	510 464-7900
Association of Monterey Bay Area Governments	Nicolas Papadakis	831 883-3750
Council of Fresno County Governments ...	Barbara Goodwin	559 233-4148
Sacramento Area Council of Governments	Mike McKeever	916 321-9000
Sacramento Transportation Authority	Brian Williams	916 323-0080
San Diego Association of Governments ...	Kenneth E. Sulzer	619 595-5300
Santa Barbara County Association of Governments	Jim Kemp	805 961-8900
Southern California Association of Governments	Mark Pisano	818 236-1808
Stanislaus Area Association of Governments	Vince Harris	209 558-7830
Western Riverside Council of Governments	Rick Bishop, AICP	909 955-7985
COLORADO-1		
Denver Regional Council of Governments	Jennifer Schaufele	303 455-1000
DISTRICT OF COLUMBIA-1		
Metropolitan Washington Council of Governments	David J. Robertson	202 962-3200
FLORIDA-2		
Solid Waste Authority of Palm Beach County	John Booth	561 640-4000
Tampa Bay Regional Planning Council	Manny L. Pumariega	727 570-5151
GEORGIA-4		
Atlanta Regional Commission	Charles Krautler	404 463-3100
Coastal Georgia Regional Development Center	Vernon D. Martin	912 264-7363
Middle Georgia Regional Development Center	James Tonn	478 751-6160
Southeast Georgia Regional Development Center	Lace Futch	912 285-6097

Directory 1/8   U.S. COUNCILS OF GOVERNMENTS RECOGNIZED BY ICMA
continued

Local government	Appointed administrator	Phone number
IDAHO-1		
Panhandle Area Council	James Deffenbaugh	208 772-0584
ILLINOIS-10		
.Bi-State Regional Commission	Denise Bulat	309 793-6300
Champaign County Regional Planning Commission	Denny Inman	217 328-3313
DuPage Mayors and Managers Conference	Mark Baloga	630 571-0480
Lake County Municipal League	Christine Wilson	847 543-8160
North Central Council of Governments	Nora Fesco-Ballerine	815 875-3396
Northeastern Illinois Planning Commission	Ronald Thomas	312 454-0400
Northwest Municipal Conference	Mark Fowler	847 296-9200
South Central Illinois Regional Planning and Development Commission	Fred Walker	618 548-4234
Southwestern Illinois Metropolitan and Regional Planning Commission	Kevin Terveer	618 344-4250
Tri-County Regional Planning Commission	Terry D. Kohlbuss	309 694-9330
IOWA-1		
Midas Council of Governments	Stephen F. Hoesel	515 576-7183 ext 211
KENTUCKY-4		
Barren River Area Development District	Dot Darby-Paschall	270 781-2381
Big Sandy Area Development District	Sandy Runyon	606 886-2374
Lincoln Trail Area Development District	James E. Greer	270 769-2393
Northern Kentucky Area Development District	John Mays	859 283-1885
MARYLAND-2		
Baltimore Metropolitan Council	Larry Klimovitz	410 732-9570
Tri-County Council For Southern Maryland	David Jenkins	301 274-1922 ext 13
MICHIGAN-1		
Southeast Michigan Council of Governments	Paul Tait	313 961-4266
MISSISSIPPI-1		
Central Mississippi Planning and Development District	F. Clarke Holmes	601 981-1511
MISSOURI-4		
East-West Gateway Coordinating Council	Les Sterman	314 421-4220
Mid-America Regional Council	David A. Warm	816 474-4240
South Central Ozark Council of Governments	James Dancy	417 256-4226
Southeast Missouri Regional Planning District	Thomas Tucker	573 547-8357
NEW MEXICO-2		
Middle Rio Grande Council of Governments	Lawrence Rael	505 247-1750
Southwest New Mexico Council of Governments	Don Rauch	505 388-1509
NEW YORK-1		
Capital District Regional Planning Community	Chungchin Chen	518 453-0850
NORTH CAROLINA-7		
Centralina Council of Governments (Region F)	Albert R. Sharp Jr.	704 372-2416
Eastern Carolina Council of Governments (Region P)	Larry Moolenaar	258 638-3185
Lumber River Council of Governments (Region N)	James Perry	910 618-5533
Piedmont Triad Council of Governments (Region G)	Randall L. Billings	336 294-4950
Triangle J Council of Governments (Region J)	Dee Freeman	919 549-0551
Upper Coastal Plain Council of Government	Greg Godard	252 446-0411
Western Piedmont Council of Governments (Region E)	R. Douglas Taylor	828 322-9191
NORTH DAKOTA-1		
Fargo-Moorhead Metropolitan Council of Governments	Brian Shorten	701 232-3242

Local government	Appointed administrator	Phone number
OHIO-4		
Miami Valley Regional Planning Commission	P. Michael Robinette	937 223-6323
Ohio-Kentucky-Indiana Regional Council of Governments	James Duane	513 621-6300 ext 01
Ohio Mid-Eastern Governments Association	John Quinlan	740 439-4471
Toledo Metropolitan Area Council of Governments	Anthony L. Reams	419 241-9155 ext 179
OKLAHOMA-2		
Association of Central Oklahoma Governments	Zach D. Taylor	405 234-2264
Central Oklahoma Economic Development District	Wayne J. Manley	405 273-6410
OREGON-3		
Lane Council of Governments	George W. Kloeppel	541 687-4283
Mid-Columbia Economic	Lee Curtis	541 296-2266
Oregon Cascades West Council of Governments	William R. Wagner	541 967-8720
SOUTH CAROLINA-3		
Central Midlands Council of Governments	Norman Whitaker III	803 376-5390
South Carolina Appalachian Council of Government	Robert Strother	864 242-9733
Upper Savannah Council of Governments	Patricia C. Hartung	864 941-8050
SOUTH DAKOTA-2		
Northeast Council of Governments	Eric Senger	605 622-2595
Planning and Development District Three	Greg Henderson	605 665-4408
TEXAS-15		
Alamo Area Council of Governments	Gloria Arriaga	210 362-5200
Ark-Tex Council of Governments	L.D. Williamson	903 832-8636
Capital Area Planning Council	Betty Voights	512 916-6000
Central Texas Council of Governments	Jim Reed	254 939-1801
Coastal Bend Council of Governments	John P. Buckner	361 883-5743
Concho Valley Council of Governments	Jeffrey K. Sutton	915 944-9666
Deep East Texas Council of Governments	Walter G. Diggles	409 384-5704
Heart of Texas Council of Governments	Kenneth L. Simmons	254 756-6631
Houston-Galveston Area Council	Jack Steele	713 627-3200
Nortex Regional Planning Commission	Dennis Wilde	940 322-5281 ext 02
North Central Texas Council of Governments	R. Michael Eastland	817 640-3300
Panhandle Regional Planning Commission	Gary Pitner	806 372-3381
South Plains Association of Governments	Tim Pierce	806 762-8721
Texoma Council of Governments	Frances Pelley	903 893-2161
West Central Texas Council of Governments	Brad Helbert	325 672-8544
UTAH-1		
Five County Association of Governments	John Williams	435 673-3548
VIRGINIA-5		
Crater Planning District Commission	Dennis K. Morris	804 861-1666
Hampton Roads Planning District Commission	Arthur L. Collins	757 461-3200
Northern Neck Planning District Commission	Jerry W. Davis	804 333-1900
Northern Virginia Planning District Commission	G. Mark Gibb	703 642-0700
West Piedmont Planning District Commission	Robert Dowd	276 638-3987
WASHINGTON-1		
Benton-Franklin Governmental Conference	Gwen Rasmussen	509 943-9185
WEST VIRGINIA-3		
Bel-O-Mar Regional Council	William C. Phipps	304 242-1800
Mid-Ohio Valley Regional Council	Jim Mylott	304 422-4993
Region One Planning and Development Council	Norman Kirkham	304 431-7225
WISCONSIN-1		
East Central Wisconsin Regional Planning Community	Harlan Kiesow	920 751-4770

Directory 1/9 **OFFICIALS IN U.S. MUNICIPALITIES 2,500 AND OVER IN POPULATION**

Data collection

The names appearing in this directory were obtained from the ICMA database of local government employees. Local governments that have provided updated information are designated by an asterisk (∗). For those that have not, the directories show the names of officials from the most recent update.

Form of government

CM   Council-manager
CO   Commission

MC	Mayor-council
RT	Representative town meeting
TM	Town meeting

Municipal designation

b	borough
c	city
d	district
pl	plantation
t	town
tp	township
v	village

Population

Population figures are rounded; 14,500 will appear as 15.

(..) Less than 500 population

Other codes

. . . Data not reported or not applicable

Jurisdiction	Type	Form of govern-ment	2000 Popu-lation (000)	Main telephone number	Chief elected official	Appointed administrator	Clerk of the governing board	Chief financial officer	Fire chief	Police chief	Public works director
ALABAMA											
Abbeville	c	MC	2	(334) 585-6444	Rhett Taylor	James Giganti	. . .	. . .	Ryan Feggin	Mickey Shelley	Robert Wright
Alabaster	c	MC	22	(205) 664-6800	Steven Rauch	. . .	Marsha Massey	. . .	John Cochran	Larry Rollen	Charles Howell
Albertville	c	MC	17	(256) 891-8282	Carl Pruett	. . .	Carolyn Camp	Jonathan Howard	Johnny Hix	Benny Womack	Chuck Rogers
Alexander City	c	MC	15	(256) 329-6730	Donald McClellan	. . .	Luise Hardman	. . .	Ronnie Betts	James Hardman	M. Brewer
Aliceville	c	MC	2	(205) 373-6611	William McKinzey	J. V. Blakney	Vickie Morrow	. . .	David Jackson	Jeff Mordecai	Ricky Johnson
Andalusia	c	MC	8	(334) 222-3312	Jerry Andrews	. . .	Pam Steele	. . .	Ethan Dorsey	Wilbur Williams	James Hogg
Anniston	c	CM	24	(256) 231-7705	Hoyt Howell	. . .	Alan Atkinson	George Vick	William Fincher	John Dryden	Dale Garrett
Arab	t	MC	7	(256) 586-8128	. . .	. . .	. . .	. . .	. . .	. . .	. . .
Athens	c	MC	18	(256) 233-8727	James Williams	. . .	John Hamilton	. . .	Cliff Christopher	Wayne Harper	James Rich
Atmore	c	MC	7	(251) 368-2253	Howard Shell	. . .	Rebecca Smith	. . .	Gerry McGhee	Jason Dean	Don Whatley
Attalla	c	MC	6	(256) 538-9986	. . .	. . .	. . .	. . .	. . .	. . .	. . .
Auburn	c	CM	42	(334) 501-7260	. . .	Charles Duggan	. . .	Andrea Jackson	Larry Langley	. . .	Jeffery Ramsey
Bay Minette	∗ c	MC	7	(251) 580-1619	William Dobbins	. . .	Rita Findley	. . .	Jesse Gregson	Michael Rowland	Lamar Hadley
Bessemer	c	CO	29	(205) 424-4060	Edward May	. . .	. . .	. . .	Chester Kendrick	Oliver Adams	Frank Thompson
Birmingham	c	MC	242	(205) 254-2431	Bernard Kincaid	. . .	Paula Smith	Michael Johnson	Dwayne Murray	Annetta Nunn	Stephen Fancher
Boaz	c	MC	7	(256) 593-8105	Timothy Walker	. . .	Barbara Walden	. . .	Olen Morrison	Terry Davis	Jackie Pullen
Brent	c	MC	4	(205) 926-4643	Jerry Pow	. . .	Linda Cox	. . .	Dennis Stripling	. . .	Bill Hubbard
Brewton	∗ c	MC	5	(251) 809-1770	Ted Jennings	John Angel	. . .	. . .	Lawrence Weaver	Monte McGougin	Danny Howard
Bridgeport	t	MC	2	(256) 495-3892	. . .	. . .	. . .	. . .	. . .	. . .	. . .
Brighton	c	MC	3	(205) 428-9547	Eddie Cooper	. . .	Viola Jones	. . .	. . .	Samuel Greene	. . .
Brundidge	c	MC	2	(334) 735-2321	Jimmy Ramage	William Thomas	. . .	. . .	. . .	Moses Davenport	Bobby Ellsworth
Calera	c	MC	3	(205) 668-3500	. . .	. . .	. . .	. . .	. . .	. . .	. . .
Centreville	c	MC	2	(205) 926-4995	Debbie Martin	Donald Penny	Tina Crumpler	. . .	. . .	Mike Nichols	Roger Burnett
Chickasaw	c	MC	6	(251) 452-6550	Jim Trout	. . .	Mary McLean	. . .	C. Hollinghead	Sam Rawls	
Childersburg	c	MC	4	(256) 378-5521	Billy Meeks	. . .	Sandra Donahoo	. . .	Douglas Blair	Charles Brown	. . .
Citronelle	c	MC	3	(251) 866-7973	Rannel Presnell	. . .	Diane Barnett	. . .	. . .	Raymond Reid	. . .
Clanton	c	MC	7	(205) 755-1105	Billy Joe Driver	. . .	Debra Orange	. . .	Ashley Teel	James Henderson	. . .
Columbiana	c	MC	3	(205) 669-5800	J. Allan Lowe	. . .	Teresa Collum	. . .	. . .	Michael Lann	Lewis King
Cordova	∗ t	MC	2	(205) 483-9266	Jack Scott	. . .	Elaine Stover	. . .	Dean Harbison	John Bentley	. . .
Cullman	c	MC	13	(256) 775-7124	Donald Green	. . .	Lucille Galin	. . .	Dennis Murray	Kenny Culpepper	Peter Nassetta
Dadeville	c	MC	3	(256) 825-9242	. . .	. . .	. . .	. . .	. . .	. . .	. . .
Daleville	c	MC	4	(334) 598-2345	Wess Etheredge	. . .	Angelia Filmore	. . .	. . .	. . .	Mike Gilley
Daphne	t	CO	16	(251) 621-9000	Fred Small	. . .	David Cohen	Kimberly Briley	Andrew Hanson	David Carpenter	Kenneth Eslava
Decatur	c	MC	53	(256) 341-4500	Don Kyle	. . .	Gail Busbey	Tony Stapler	Charlie Johnson	Joel Gilliam	Brent Mullins
Demopolis	c	MC	7	(334) 289-0577	Austin Caldwell	. . .	Vickie Taylor	. . .	George Davenport	Jeff Manuel	Clarence Brooker
Dothan	c	CM	57	(334) 615-3000	Pat Thomas	Michael West	Pam McCoy	Angela Palmer	Samuel Crawford	John Powell	Jerry Corbin
East Brewton	c	MC	2	(251) 867-6092	Terry Clark	. . .	Karen Singleton	. . .	Joey Shell	Wilson Mallard	William Dunaway
Elba	∗ c	MC	4	(334) 897-2333	James Grimes	Wayne Grantham	. . .	. . .	Danny Jordan	Freddy Hanchey	. . .
Enterprise	∗ c	MC	21	(334) 347-1211	Kenneth Boswell	. . .	Steven Hicks	. . .	Byron Herring	Thomas Jones	James Kilgore
Eufaula	c	MC	13	(334) 689-2000	Jay Jaxon	. . .	Joy White	. . .	Lamar Register	Kenneth Walker	John Lawrence
Evergreen	c	MC	3	(251) 578-1574	. . .	. . .	. . .	. . .	. . .	. . .	. . .
Fairfield	c	MC	12	(205) 788-2492	Larry Langford	. . .	Melvin Turner	. . .	Earl Allred	Laird Sharpe	Daniel Fields
Fairhope	c	MC	12	(251) 928-2136	. . .	. . .	. . .	. . .	. . .	. . .	. . .
Fayette	c	MC	4	(205) 932-5367	Ray Nelson	. . .	Dawn Clapp	. . .	Robert Fulmer	Euel Hall	. . .
Florence	c	MC	36	(256) 760-6400	James Frost	. . .	. . .	Dan Barger	Charles Cochran	Ricky Singleton	. . .
Foley	c	MC	7	(251) 943-1545	R. Timothy Russell	A. Perry Wilbourne	. . .	. . .	James Hinton	James Bryan	. . .
Fort Payne	c	MC	12	(256) 845-1524	J. Stout	. . .	James McGee	. . .	Arthur Hill	John Walker	. . .
Fultondale	c	MC	6	(205) 841-4481	James Lowery	. . .	Jane Hicks	. . .	. . .	Byron Pigg	. . .
Gadsden	c	CO	38	(256) 549-4550	Steve Means	Fred Sington	Iva Nelson	. . .	Stephan Carroll	Richard Crouch	Brian Stovall
Gardendale	∗ c	MC	11	(205) 631-8789	Kenneth Clemons	. . .	Keith Mosley	. . .	Clinton Doss	Mike Walker	Jeff Holliyan
Geneva	c	MC	4	(334) 684-2485	Karen Simmons	. . .	Lisa Johnson	. . .	Ben Latimer	Louis Lindsey	Donald Campbell
Glencoe	t	MC	5	(205) 492-1424	. . .	. . .	. . .	. . .	. . .	. . .	. . .
Graysville	c	MC	2	(205) 674-5643	. . .	. . .	Judy Flippo	. . .	Jeffrey Wesley	. . .	. . .
Greensboro	c	MC	2	(334) 624-8119	John Owens	. . .	. . .	. . .	. . .	Claude Hamilton	. . .
Greenville	∗ c	MC	7	(334) 382-2647	Dexter McLendon	. . .	Linda Vanden Bosch	. . .	Michael Phillips	William Ingram	Milton Luckie
Gulf Shores	c	MC	5	(251) 968-2425	David Bodenhamer	. . .	Renee Moore	Shirley Bowyer	Joseph McClusky	Arthur Bourne	Charles Hamilton
Guntersville	c	MC	7	(256) 571-7560	James Townson	. . .	Betty Jones	. . .	James Brown	J. Scott Walls	Mike Bush
Haleyville	∗ c	MC	4	(205) 486-3121	Larry Albright	. . .	. . .	. . .	Ralph Edwards	Kyle Reogas	Mike Taylor
Hamilton	t	MC	6	(205) 921-2121	Ray Harper	. . .	Sue Page	. . .	Barron Wiginton	Billy Owen	Steve Cox
Hartford	c	MC	2	(334) 588-2245	Gene Brannon	. . .	Vicky Marsh	. . .	. . .	Greg Adams	Jimmy Bottoms
Hartselle	c	MC	12	(256) 773-2535	Clifton Knight	D. Vest	Rita Lee	. . .	Rickey Smith	Ronald Merkh	Byron Turney
Headland	c	MC	3	(334) 693-3365	Donald Smith	Jack Manley	Elizabeth White	. . .	Eric Lawrence	Fred Williams	Daniel Vinson
Heflin	c	MC	3	(256) 463-2290	Anna Berry	Terri Daulton	. . .	. . .	Rudy Rooks	Neil Payne	. . .
Helena	∗ c	MC	10	(205) 663-2161	Charles Penhale	. . .	Peggy Dunaway	. . .	Peter Valenti	Douglas Jones	Brian Hinds
Hokes Bluff	t	MC	4	(205) 492-2414	Tim Langdale	S. Hamilton-Burns	. . .	. . .	Mike Howington	Harvey Scales	Wade Reed
Homewood	c	MC	25	(205) 877-8600	Barry McCulley	. . .	Linda Cook	Danny Panos	John Bresnan	Burke Swearingen	David McAshe
Hoover	c	MC	62	(205) 444-7500	Tony Petelos	. . .	Linda Crump	Robert Yeager	Thomas Bradley	Robert Berry	Thomas Daniel
Hueytown	∗ c	MC	15	(205) 491-7010	Delor Baumann	. . .	Janice Wilhite	. . .	James Shelton	Doug McBee	Willie Hegler
Huntsville	c	MC	158	(256) 427-5000	Loretta Spencer	Terry Hatfield	. . .	Randall Taylor	Phillip Underwood	Rex Reynolds	Michael Abbott
Irondale	c	MC	9	(205) 956-9200	Tommy Alexander	Glenda Crowe	Glenda Cox	. . .	Randy Davis	Jerry McIntosh	Dexter Davis
Jackson	c	MC	5	(251) 246-2461	. . .	Jesse Miller	Betty Powell	. . .	. . .	Charles Burge	Kevin Woodson
Jacksonville	c	MC	8	(205) 435-7611	Jerry Smith	. . .	. . .	Rita Spruiell	Michael Daugherty	Thomas Thompson	Stanley Carr
Jasper	c	MC	14	(205) 221-2100	V. L. Posey	. . .	Kathy Chambless	. . .	Calvin Kluesner	Robert Cain	Glenn Ferguson
Kellyton	t	MC	..	(256) 234-4784	. . .	. . .	. . .	. . .	. . .	. . .	. . .
Lafayette	c	MC	3	(334) 864-9812	Robert Finley	Peter Gardner	. . .	. . .	Anthony Wolkerson	Eddie Ware	. . .
Lanett	∗ c	CM	7	(334) 644-2141	Oscar Crawley	Joel Holley	Deborah Daniel	. . .	Tim Jennings	Teddy Morris	Mike Bass
Leeds	c	MC	10	(205) 699-2585	James Whitfield	. . .	Helen Veasey	. . .	David Courson	Charles Hudson	Neil Loggins

Directory 1/9
continued

OFFICIALS IN U.S. MUNICIPALITIES 2,500 AND OVER IN POPULATION

Jurisdiction	Type	Form of govern-ment	2000 Popu-lation (000)	Main telephone number	Chief elected official	Appointed administrator	Clerk of the governing board	Chief financial officer	Fire chief	Police chief	Public works director
ALABAMA continued											
Lincoln	c	MC	4	(205) 763-7777	Carroll Watson	...	Laura Carmack	...	Mike Wesley	Dennis Surrett	Chip Chandler
Linden	c	MC	2	(334) 295-5051	...	Cheryl Hall	Pamela Duke	...	...	...	Terrence Tyson
Lipscomb	c	MC	2	(205) 428-6374	Simon Speights	Geneva Varnon	...	Deborah Miller	David Horn	Conlin Payne	Charles Burgin
Livingston	*	CM	3	(205) 652-2505	Thomas Tartt	Johnny Meadows	...	...	Terry Peeler	...	James Dial
Luverne	c	MC	2	(334) 335-3741	Joe Sport	...	Charlotte Flynn	...	...	Robert Davis	Guy Simmons
Madison	c	MC	29	(256) 772-5600	Charles Yancura	...	...	Lillie Causey	Ralph Cobb	Cecil Moses	Merlyn Adkins
Marion	c	MC	3	(334) 683-6545	Edward Daniel	...	Carolyn Thomas	...	...	Daron Mack	Jackie Nichols
Midfield	c	MC	5	(205) 923-7578	Carlton McWhorter	James Rhodes	...	...	...	James White	Gary Pratt
Millbrook	c	MC	10	(334) 285-6428	Robert Kelley	...	Teresa Mercer	...	Larry Brown	Kenneth Bradley	...
Mobile	c	MC	198	(251) 208-7777	Samuel Jones	Alfred Stokes	Glenda Morgan	Barbara Malkove	Stephen Dean	Phillip Garrett	John Bell
Monroeville	c	MC	6	(251) 575-2081	Anne Farish	...	Toni McKelvey	...	Eddie Everette	Rudolph Munnerlyn	Robert Sims
Montevallo	c	MC	4	(205) 665-2555	Grady Parker	...	Stephen Gibbs	John Abercrombie	...	Steve Southerland	Raymond Cardwell
Montgomery	c	MC	201	(334) 241-4400	Bobby Bright	...	Brenda Blalock	Lloyd Faulkner	John McKee	John Wilson	...
Moulton	t	MC	3	(256) 974-5191	...	...	Shirley Gilley	...	...	E. Weatherford	...
Mountain Brook	c	CM	20	(205) 870-3532	Lawrence Oden	Sam Gaston	...	Steven Boone	Robert Ezekiel	Johnny Stanley	Eddy Tate
Muscle Shoals	*	CO	11	(256) 383-5675	David Bradford	...	Ricky Williams	...	Paul McDougle	Robert Evans	Butch Fleming
Northport	c	CM	19	(205) 339-7000	Harvey Fretwell	Charles Swann	Martha Walker	...	Daryl Patterson	William Galloway	Larry Boshell
Oneonta	c	MC	5	(205) 274-2127	Danny Hicks	Edward Lowe	...	...	David Osborn	James Chapman	...
Opelika	c	MC	23	(334) 705-5130	Gary Fuller	John Seymour	Robert Shuman	Robert Price	Terry Adkins	Thomas Mangham	Mike Hilyer
Opp	c	MC	6	(334) 493-4572	...	...	...	...	...	...	...
Orange Beach	c	CM	3	(251) 981-6979	Stephen Russo	Jeffrey Moon	Cathy Larrimore	...	Michael Robinson	Robert Vinson	William Silvers
Oxford	t	MC	14	(256) 831-7510	Leon Smith	...	Shirley Henson	...	Eugene Smallwood	Stanley Merrill	...
Ozark	c	MC	15	(334) 774-5393	Willis Bunting	...	William Blackwell	...	Dempson Barefield	Tony Spivey	Steven Price
Pelham	t	MC	14	(205) 620-6400	Bobby Hayes	...	Donna Treslar	Tom Seale	Gary Waters	Douglas Wade	Ken Holler
Pell City	c	MC	9	(205) 338-3330	Adam Stocks	...	Marinda Gipson	...	Michael Sewell	Gregory Turley	Mike Martin
Phenix City	c	CM	28	(334) 291-4706	Jeff Hardin	H. H. Roberts	Martha Harris	Steve Smith	Wallace Hunter	Preston Robinson	...
Piedmont	c	MC	5	(256) 447-9007	Charles Fagan	William Fann	...	...	Robert Holbrook	Jimmy Trammell	...
Pleasant Grove	c	MC	9	(205) 744-7221	...	...	...	...	...	...	...
Prattville	c	MC	24	(334) 361-3609	...	...	...	...	Stanley Gann	Alfred Wadsworth	...
Prichard	c	MC	28	(251) 457-3381	...	...	...	...	...	...	...
Rainbow City	c	MC	8	(256) 442-2511	Terry Calhoun	...	Barbara Wester	...	Melvin Potter	Allan Ragan	...
Rainsville	c	MC	4	(256) 638-6331	Roy Sanderson	...	Judy Lewis	...	Ronnie Helton	Roger Byrd	Rickey Dobbins
Red Bay	*	c MC	3	(256) 356-4473	Jeff Reid	...	Linda Holcomb	...	Thomas Strickland	Patrick Creel	...
Roanoke	c	MC	6	(334) 863-4129	...	...	...	...	...	...	...
Russellville	c	MC	8	(256) 332-6060	Johnny Brown	...	Kimberly Wright	...	Joe Mansell	Chris Hargett	...
Saraland	c	MC	12	(251) 675-5103	Thomas Williams	...	Denise Jernigan	...	Ravon Allen	...	Robert Lee
Satsuma	c	MC	5	(251) 675-1440	William Bush	...	Vicki Miller	...	Carey Parker	David Benefield	James Elmore
Scottsboro	c	MC	14	(256) 574-3100	Louis Price	Derrick Wheeler	Gail Duffey	...	Lonnie Webb	Ralph Dawe	William Johnson
Selma	c	MC	20	(334) 874-2110	James Perkins	...	...	Vickey Locke	Henry Allen	Robert Green	Tommy Smith
Sheffield	c	CO	9	(205) 383-0250	Ian Sanford	...	...	...	Tom Isbell	Warren Aycock	...
Slocomb	c	MC	2	(334) 886-2334	James West	Steve Turkoski	Jo Ann Lindsey	...	Kenneth Ball	...	...
Southside	t	MC	7	(256) 442-9775	Wally Burns	...	Cynthia Osborne	...	...	Charles Diggs	Jimmy Whittemore
Spanish Fort	c	MC	5	(251) 626-4884	W. Carter	Mary Williams	...	...	...	...	...
Stevenson	c	MC	1	(256) 437-3000	J. Ricky Steele	...	...	...	Chad McCrary	Danny Winters	Jimmy Guess
Sumiton	t	MC	2	(205) 648-3262	Harry Ellis	...	Judy Glover	...	David Waid	Terry Burnett	George Woods
Sylacauga	c	MC	12	(256) 401-2400	Sam Wright	...	Patricia Carden	...	Thomas Abrams	Louis Zook	Ralph Woolley
Talladega	c	CM	15	(256) 362-8186	Brian York	Sue Horn	...	Terri St. James	Danny Warrick	Alan Watson	James Swinford
Tallassee	c	MC	4	(334) 283-6571	Robert Payne	...	Barbara Garnett	...	Steve Dennis	Randy Yarbrough	Donald Haynes
Tarrant City	*	c MC	8	(205) 841-2758	Loxcil Tuck	...	...	...	Billy Hewitt	Jesse Sprayberry	James Phillips
Thomasville	*	c MC	4	(334) 636-5827	Sheldon Day	...	Deborah Ballard	...	Mark Sims	William Hicks	Ronnie McClure
Troy	c	CO	13	(334) 566-0177	Jimmy Lunsford	...	Alton Starling	...	Curtis Rhodes	Anthony Everage	Jake Wingard
Trussville	c	MC	12	(205) 655-7478	Eugene Melton	...	Lynn Porter	...	Russell Ledbetter	Don Sivley	Lewis Simpson
Tuscaloosa	c	MC	77	(205) 349-0125	Alvin DuPont	...	Stan McCracken	Mike Wright	Alan Martin	Ken Swindle	Richard Curry
Tuscumbia	*	c CO	7	(256) 383-5463	Billy Shoemaker	...	Carolyn Burns	...	David Cole	Terry Sherron	Hugh Stanley
Tuskegee	c	CM	11	(334) 727-2180	...	Alfred Davis	...	...	...	...	...
Union Springs	c	MC	3	(334) 738-2720	Earl Hinson	Cathy Dickerson	Presetta Walker	...	Tim Shirley	Clarence Wheeler	Billy Gholston
Valley	*	c MC	9	(334) 756-5225	Arnold Leak	James Bryan	Martha Cato	...	...	...	John McConnell
Vernon	c	MC	2	(205) 695-7718	Mary Jones	...	Rebecca Cantrell	...	Larry DuBose	Ted Collins	...
Vestavia Hills	c	MC	24	(205) 978-0100	Charles McCallum	...	Rebecca Leavings	Melvin Turner	Alberto Zaragoza	James Wilson	Perry Glass
Warrior	c	MC	3	(205) 647-0521	Rena Hudson	Nancy Evans	...	...	Tommy Hale	Ray Horn	Frank Coffey
Weaver	c	MC	2	(256) 820-1125	William Kimbrough	...	Teresa Summerlin	...	...	Oscar Bush	Steven Mitchell
Wetumpka	c	MC	5	(334) 567-5147	R. Scott Golden	...	Velma Golden	...	Keith Gilmore	William Pertree	Randy Logan
Winfield	c	MC	4	(205) 487-4337	William West	...	Candace Reed	...	Keith Waldrop	Patrick Creel	...
York	c	MC	2	(205) 392-5231	Howard Kennedy	...	Janice Pringle	...	Cornelius Robinson	...	Ernie Truelove
ALASKA											
Akutan	c	MC	..	(907) 274-7555	Joe Bereskin	Erika Tritremmel	Alexandra Paisley	...	...	...	...
Anchorage	c	MC	260	(907) 343-4431	Mark Begich	...	Barbara Gruenstein	Jeffrey Sinz	John Fullenwider	Walter Monegan	...
Barrow	c	CM	4	(907) 852-5211	Jim Vonderstrasse	...	Gwen Edwardson	Lucy Okpik	...	...	Jeff Leavitt
Bethel	c	CM	5	(907) 543-2047	Hugh Dyment	Don Baird	Sandra Modigh	...	George Young	Ben Dudley	Wayne Ogle
Chignik	c	MC	..	(907) 749-2280	Richard Sharpe	...	...	...	Robert Plumb	Kevin Clayton	...
Cordova	c	CM	2	(907) 424-6200	Edward Zeine	Scott Hahn	Dixie Lambert	...	...	...	...
Dillingham	*	c CM	2	(907) 842-5211	Alice Ruby	Cheryl Taylor	Janice Shilanski	Staci Fieser	Norman Heyano	...	Ramon Roque
Fairbanks	c	MC	30	(907) 459-6881	James Hayes	Mark Boyer	Nancy Deleon	Jeffrey Brunsdon	Warren Cummings	James Welch	Dave Jacoby
Fort Yukon	c	CM	..	(907) 662-2479	Antoinette Peter	Richard Carron	Tina Herbert	Jennifer Cannon	G. Benjamin	Lance Fairchild	Grafton Bergman
Galena	c	CM	..	(907) 656-1301	Russ Sweetsir	Walter Wilcox	Jill Chadbourne	Joseph Smith	...	...	Stephen Grube
Homer	c	CM	3	(907) 235-8121	James Hornaday	Walt Wrede	Mary Calhoun	Regina Harville	Robert Painter	Mark Robl	Carey Meyer
Hoonah	*	c MC	..	(907) 945-3663	Dennis Gray	Jerry Medina	Georgina Glover	...	Bill Wolfe	...	Mike Morrison
Juneau	c	CM	30	(907) 586-5250	Sarah Smith	Roddy Swope	Laurie Sica	Craig Duncan	Michael Doyle	Richard Gummow	Joseph Buck
Kenai	c	CM	6	(907) 283-7535	John Williams	...	Carol Freas	L. Semmens	Scott Walden	Charles Kopp	Keith Kornelis
Ketchikan	c	CM	7	(907) 228-5631	Robert Weinstein	Karl Amylon	Katherine Suiter	Robert Newell	Richard Leipfert	Gerald Sirevog	Harvey Hansen
King Cove	c	CM	..	(907) 497-2340	...	...	Debra Marlar	Mary Munk	Andrew Nault	Charles Kamai	John Sullivan
Kodiak	c	CM	6	(907) 486-8640	Carolyn Floyd	Linda Freed	Debra Marlar	Mary Munk	Andrew Nault	Charles Kamai	John Sullivan
Kotzebue	c	CM	3	(907) 442-3401	Frank Greene	...	Sandra McCafferty	Thomas Graham	Ronald Monson	Paul Nolton	Herman Reich
Mountain Village	c	MC	..	(907) 591-2929	Harry Wilde	Carol Myre	Melanie Dela Rosa	...	...	Ronald Self	...
Nome	c	CM	3	(907) 443-6600	Denise Michels	R. Romenesko	Leslee Wessel	Caroline Kauer	Wesley Perkins	Craig Moates	...
Palmer	c	CM	4	(907) 745-3271	John Combs	Tom Healy	Janette Bower	Allan Ossakow	Daniel Contini	George Boatright	Rick Koch
Petersburg	c	CM	3	(907) 772-4519	Ted Smith	Bruce Jones	...	Ashley Royal	Sam Bunge	Dale Stone	...
Saint Paul	c	CM	..	(907) 546-2331	...	Linda Snow	...	...	...	...	...
Sand Point	c	CM	..	(907) 383-2696	...	...	...	...	...	...	...

Directory 1/9 continued **OFFICIALS IN U.S. MUNICIPALITIES 2,500 AND OVER IN POPULATION**

Jurisdiction	Type	Form of govern-ment	2000 Popu-lation (000)	Main telephone number	Chief elected official	Appointed administrator	Clerk of the governing board	Chief financial officer	Fire chief	Police chief	Public works director
ALASKA continued											
Saxman *	c	MC	..	(907) 225-4166	Joe Williams	K. Ludwig-Johnson	Leona Casey	Nancy Nurmi	...	...	Horace Clark
Seldovia	c	CM	..	(907) 234-7643	Tim Volstad	...	Susan Elzig	...	Kim Buchman	Andy Anderson	...
Seward	c	CM	2	(907) 224-4047	...	...	Jean Lewis	Kristin Erchinger	David Squires	Thomas Clemons	William Casey
Sitka	c	CO	8	(907) 747-1808	Fred Reeder	Hugh Bevan	Colleen Pellett	Dave Wolff	Dave Miller	Bob Gorder	Rich Riggs
Skagway	c	CM	..	(907) 983-2297	Tim Bourcy	Robert Ward	Marjorie Harris	...	Martin Beckner	Dennis Spurrier	Grant Lawson
Soldotna *	c	CM	3	(907) 262-9107	David Carey	Thomas Boedeker	Teresa Fahning	Joan Miller	...	John Lucking	Stephen Bonebrake
St. Mary's	c	CM	..	(907) 438-2617	...	Walton Smith	Geraldine Sparks	Richard Alstrom	...	Lee Lamm	Allan Paukan
Unalakleet	c	CM	..	(907) 624-3531	Doris Ivanoff	...	...	...	...	John Wilson	Jay Freytag
Unalaska	c	CM	4	(907) 581-1251	...	...	Debra Mack	...	...	...	Dave Kemp
Valdez	c	CM	4	(907) 835-4313	...	John Hozey	Sheri Pierce	Tom Schantz	George Keeney	William Comer	Robert Thompson
Wasilla *	c	MC	5	(907) 373-9055	Dianne Keller	Sandra Garley	Kristie Smithers	Susan Colligan	...	Angella Long	Archie Giddings
Whittier	c	CM	..	(907) 472-2327	Lester Lunceford	Rick Hohnbaum	Brenda Krol	Donald Grande	Doug Maliski	...	Jim Spain
Wrangell	c	CM	2	(907) 874-2381	Valery McCandless	Robert Prunella	Christie Jamieson	Jeffery Jabusch	Timothy Buness	Arlen McCloskey	Robert Caldwell
ARIZONA											
Apache Junction	c	CM	31	(480) 982-8002	...	George Hoffman	Kathleen Connelly	J Keith Lewis	...	...	Douglas Dobson
Avondale	c	CM	35	(623) 333-1000	Ronald Drake	Charles McClendon	Linda Farris	Kevin Artz	Paul Adams	Stephen MacKinnon	Janet Stewart
Benson *	c	CM	4	(520) 586-2245	Mark Fenn	Martin Roush	Vicki Vivian	Jim Cox	Keith Spangler	Glenn Nichols	Bradley Hamilton
Bisbee *	c	CM	6	(520) 432-6000	Ronald Oertle	Stephen Pauken	Sharyl Honstein	Dee Flanagan	Jack Earnest	James Elkins	Russell McConnell
Buckeye	t	CM	6	(623) 386-4691	Dustin Hull	Jeanine Guy	Linda Garrison	...	C. Dunnington	...	Ron Long
Bullhead City	c	CM	33	(928) 763-9400	...	Timothy Ernster	Diane Heilmann	Rudy Vera	...	Rodney Head	Douglas Lutz
Camp Verde	t	CM	9	(928) 567-6631	...	Michael Scannell	...	...	...	...	...
Carefree	t	CM	2	(480) 488-3686	Edward Morgan	Jonathan Pearson	Elizabeth Wise	...	...	...	...
Casa Grande *	c	CM	25	(520) 421-8600	Robert Jackson	James Thompson	Gloria Leija	Larry Rains	Scott Miller	Robert Huddleston	Kevin Louis
Cave Creek	t	CM	3	(480) 488-1400	Vincent Francia	Usama Abujbarah	Carrie Dyrek	Marian Groeneveld	...	Adam Stein	Roger Kindsfater
Chandler	c	CM	176	(480) 786-2000	...	W. Pentz	Maria Paddock	...	...	...	Robert Zeder
Chino Valley *	t	CM	7	(928) 636-2646	Karen Fann	William Pupo	Jami Lewis	Linda York	...	Patricia Huntsman	James Confer
Clarkdale *	t	CM	3	(928) 634-9591	...	Gayle Mabery	...	Carlton Woodruff	Jerry Doerksen	Pat Haynie	Steve Burroughs
Clifton	t	CM	2	(928) 865-4146	David McCullar	Ray Pini	E. Castaneda	...	...	...	Nazario Hernandez
Coolidge	c	CM	7	(520) 723-5361	Wilbur Wuertz	Robert Flatley	Norma Ortiz	Lisa Pannella	Michael McHugh	James Palmer	Donald Peters
Cottonwood	c	CM	9	(928) 634-5526	Ruben Jauvegui	...	Marianne Jimenez	Jesus Rodriguez	William Casson	Pat Spence	Timothy Costello
Dewey-Humboldt	t	CM	6	(928) 632-7362	...	...	Debbie Gifford	...	...	...	...
Douglas	c	CM	14	(520) 805-5507	Raymond Borane	Michael Ortega	Leticia Rodriguez	Regina Pace	...	Charles Austin	Carlos De La Torre
Duncan	t	CM	..	(928) 359-2791	Randall Norton	Alan Baker	Cynthia Nichols	...	Kelly Cambern	...	Lupe Madrigal
Eagar	t	CM	4	(928) 333-4128	Sandra Burke	William Greenwood	Judy Slade	Ricky Pinckard	...	Benjamin Garms	Elwin Browning
El Mirage	c	CM	7	(623) 972-8116	Fred Waterman	William Cornwall	Edith Hoover	Larry Price	Scott Alvord	Brian Beamish	Chris Young
Eloy	c	CM	10	(520) 466-9201	Manuel Salas	James McFellin	Mary Ridgell	Brian Wright	...	William Pitman	...
Flagstaff	c	CM	52	(928) 779-7685	Joe Donaldson	Kevin Burke	Elizabeth Burke	Mary Jenkins	Mike Iacona	J. McCann	Bill Menard
Florence	t	CM	17	(520) 868-7500	Patsy Williams	Himanshu Patel	Lisa Garcia	Rebecca Guilin	Donald Lowry	Robert Ingulli	Wayne Costa
Fountain Hills *	t	CM	20	(480) 837-2003	Wallace Nichols	...	Bevelyn Bender	Julie Ghetti	Scott LaGreca	...	Thomas Ward
Gila Bend	t	MC	1	(928) 683-2255	...	...	Beverly Turner	Don Steele	David Birchfield	...	John Smith
Gilbert *	t	CM	109	(480) 503-6000	Steven Berman	George Pettit	C. Templeton	Cindi Mattheisen	Colline Dewitt	Timothy Dorn	Lonnie Frost
Glendale	c	CM	218	(623) 930-2000	Elaine Scruggs	Edward Beasley	Pamela Hanna	Ray Shuey	Mark Burdick	Steve Conrad	Roger Bailey
Globe	c	CM	7	(928) 425-7146	David Franquero	...	...	Teresa Williams	Martin Ricklefs	...	Joe Alvarez
Goodyear	c	CM	18	(623) 932-3910	James Cavanaugh	Stephen Cleveland	Dortzal Cockrum	Larry Price	Mark Gaillard	Peter Nick	Cato Esquivel
Guadalupe *	t	CM	5	(480) 730-3080	Francisco Montiel	Mark Johnson	Rose Mary Arellano	...	Wayne Clement	...	Jim Ricker
Hayden	t	CM	..	(520) 356-7801	...	...	...	...	...	...	...
Holbrook	c	CM	4	(928) 524-6225	Bryan Smithson	David Newlin	Cheryl Millage	...	Jack Brooks	DWayne Hartup	Richard Young
Jerome	t	CM	..	(928) 634-7943	...	...	...	...	...	...	...
Kearny	t	CM	2	(520) 363-5547	Debra Sommers	Gary Eide	Margaret Gaston	...	Kenneth Piggott	Joeseph Martinez	Ramon Camcho
Kingman	c	CM	20	(928) 753-5561	Monica Gates	...	Toni Weddle	Coral Loyd	Charles Osterman	Robert Devries	Jack Kramer
Lake Havasu City	c	CM	41	(928) 453-4143	Mark Nexsen	R. Kaffenberger	Carla Simendich	Gayle Whittle	Dennis Mueller	Daniel Doyle	Kevin Murphy
Litchfield Park	c	CM	3	(623) 935-5033	J. Woodfin Thomas	Darryl Crossman	Mary Evans	Benjamin Ronquillo	...	...	Charles Ransom
Mammoth	t	MC	1	(520) 487-2331	...	...	Patsy Large	...	...	...	Juan Ponce
Marana	t	CM	13	(520) 382-1900	Ed Honea	Michael Reuwsaat	Jocelyn Bronson	Roy Cuaron	...	Richard Vidaurri	Harvey Gill
Maricopa	c	CM	4	(520) 568-9098	...	Kevin Evans	Vanessa Bueras	Roger Kolman	...	...	Bob Jackson
Mesa	c	CM	396	(480) 644-2059	Keno Hawker	Christopher Brady	Barbara Jones	Bryan Raines	Harry Beck	Dennis Donna	Jack Friedline
Miami	t	MC	1	(928) 473-4403	Paul Licano	Robert Mawson	...	...	...	Dan Rodriguez	John Encizo
Nogales	c	MC	20	(520) 287-6571	Albert Kramer	Jaime Fontes	Leticia Robinson	Charles Diamond	Lorenzo Rodriquez	John Kissinger	Manuel Tapia
Oro Valley *	t	CM	29	(520) 229-4700	Paul Loomis	David Andrews	Kathi Cuvelier	...	...	Daniel Sharp	...
Page *	c	CM	6	(928) 645-8861	William Justice	Everett Thomas	Lori Anderson	Linda Watson	Larry Clark	Tom Hain	...
Paradise Valley	t	CM	13	(480) 948-7411	Marvin Davis	...	...	Lenore Lancaster	...	...	William Mead
Parker	t	MC	3	(928) 669-9265	D. L. Wilson	...	Candy Cockrell	Lori Wedemeyer	...	Rod Mendoza	...
Payson	t	CM	13	(928) 474-5242	...	Frederick Carpenter	Silvia Smith	...	Martin deMasi	Gordon Gartner	Colin Walker
Peoria	c	CM	108	(623) 773-7100	John Keegan	Terrence Ellis	Mary Jo Kief	John Wenderski	Robert McKibben	David Leonardo	Neil Mann
Phoenix	c	CM	1321	(602) 262-6609	Phil Gordon	Frank Fairbanks	Mario Paniagua	...	Alan Brunacini	Jack Harris	Mark Leonard
Pinetop-Lakeside *	t	CM	3	(928) 368-8696	Lawrence Vicario	L. Udall	Lu Anne Frost	John Brooksby	...	Sherwood Eldredge	Tommy Thomas
Prescott *	c	CM	33	(928) 777-1100	...	Steven Norwood	Elizabeth Burke	Marklyn Woodfill	Darrell Willis	Randy Oaks	Craig McConnell
Prescott Valley *	t	CM	23	(928) 759-3000	Harvey Skoog	Larry Tarkowski	Diane Russell	William Kauppi	...	Daniel Schatz	Norm Davis
Quartzsite	t	CM	3	(928) 927-4333	Patty Bergen	Jay Howe	Kay Kreun	Barbara Jones	...	Glenn Nichols	T. Collier
Queen Creek *	t	CM	4	(480) 358-3000	Arthur Sanders	W. Kross	Jennifer Robinson	...	...	...	...
Safford	c	CM	9	(928) 348-3100	Van Talley	Huey Long	Sharon French	Carlos Vessels	Mike Rhodes	John Griffin	Robert Porter
Sahuarita *	t	CM	3	(520) 822-8800	Lynne Skelton	James Stahle	Sandra Olivas	A. C. Marriotti	...	John Harris	Robert Welch
San Luis	c	CM	15	(928) 627-2027	Alex Harper	...	...	Kerry Jones	Othon Luna	Heriberto Bejarano	David Ford
Scottsdale	c	CM	202	(480) 312-2491	Mary Manross	Janet Dolan	Carolyn Jagger	Craig Clifford	William McDonald	Alan Rodbell	Alvis Dreska
Sedona *	c	CM	10	(928) 282-3113	Pud Colquitt	Eric Levitt	Cherry Lawson	Barbara Ashley	...	Joe Vernier	...
Show Low	c	CM	7	(928) 532-4001	Gene Kelley	Ed Muder	Ann Kurasaki	Larry Ploughe	...	...	...
Sierra Vista	c	CM	37	(520) 458-3315	Thomas Hessler	Charles Potucek	Jack Cooke	David Felix	Bruce Thompson	David Santor	Michael Hemesath
Snowflake	t	CM	4	(928) 536-7103	John Stewart	Brian Richards	...	...	Brian Hancock	David Adams	Gary Fenstermaker
Somerton *	c	CM	7	(928) 627-8866	Miguel Villalpando	Clifford O'Neill	...	...	Paul DeAnda	Terry Hollis	Eddie Mendez
South Tucson	c	CM	5	(520) 792-2424	Shirley Villegas	...	Dolores Robles	Ruben Villa	Larry Anderson	Sixto Molina	Angel Lopez
Springerville *	t	CM	1	(928) 333-2656	Kay Dyson	Scott Garms	Valentina Cordova	Karen Asquith	Max Sadler	Steve West	Tom Malone
St. Johns	c	CM	3	(928) 337-4517	Cristian Patterson	Gregory Martin	Amy Bigelow	...	Gary Liston	James Zieler	Paul Ramsey
Star Valley *	t	CM	2	(928) 472-7752	Chuck Heron	Vito Tedeschi	Sarah Luckie	...	...	...	...
Superior	t	MC	3	(520) 689-5752	...	Rosalicia Cordova	...	...	...	...	...
Surprise	t	CM	30	(623) 222-1000	...	James Rumpeltes	Sherry Aguilar	Robert Nilles	Michael White	Daniel Hughes	Jerry Huston
Taylor *	t	CM	3	(928) 536-7366	John Cole	Eric Duthie	Kelly Jones	Gus Lundberg	Clay Woods	Jerry Van Winkle	Ron Solomon
Tempe	c	CM	158	(480) 350-8278	Neil Giuliano	Charles Meyer	Kathy Matz	...	Cliff Jones	Ralph Tranter	Howard Hargis
Thatcher	t	CM	4	(928) 428-2290	...	Terrel Hinton	...	...	...	Michael McEuen	...
Tolleson	c	CM	4	(623) 936-7111	Adolfo Gamez	Reyes Medrano	C.Hagen-Hurley	Steven Baumgardt	Donald Garcia	L. Rodriguez	Mark Berrelez
Tucson	c	CM	486	(520) 791-4241	Robert Walkup	Mike Hein	Kathleen Detrick	J. Scott Douthitt	Dan Newburn	Richard Miranda	...

Directory 1/9
continued

OFFICIALS IN U.S. MUNICIPALITIES 2,500 AND OVER IN POPULATION

Jurisdiction		Type	Form of govern-ment	2000 Popu-lation (000)	Main telephone number	Chief elected official	Appointed administrator	Clerk of the governing board	Chief financial officer	Fire chief	Police chief	Public works director
ARIZONA continued												
Wickenburg		t	CM	5	(928) 684-5451	Ron Badowski	Gary Edwards	Donna Vivona	Stephanie Wojcik	Ed Temerowski	Anthony Melendez	Harry Parsi
Willcox		c	CM	3	(520) 384-4271	Marlin Easthouse	Michael Leighton	Christina Whelan	Jeffrey Palmer	. . .	. . .	Ryan Benavides
Williams		c	CM	2	(928) 635-4451	Kenneth Edes	J. Wells	Eleanor Addison	Joe Duffy	Joe Schulte	Frank Manson	Glenn Cornwell
Winslow		c	MC	9	(928) 289-2422	. . .		Linda Samson	Regina Reffner	Boney Candelaria	Stephen Garnett	. . .
Youngtown	*	t	CM	3	(623) 933-8286	Michael LeVault	Lloyce Robinson	Letty Goldberg	Jackie Hoffman	. . .	Dan Connelly	Jesse Mendez
Yuma		c	CM	77	(928) 373-5125	Lawrence Nelson	Mark Watson	Brigitta Stanz	. . .	Gary Fisher	William Robinson	. . .
ARKANSAS												
Alma		c	MC	4	(479) 632-4110	John Ballentine	. . .	Christina Inge	. . .	Steve Meadors	Russell White	Mark Yardley
Arkadelphia		c	CM	10	(870) 246-9864	C. Hollingshead	Jimmy Bolt	. . .	. . .	Jerry Sullivan	Al Harris	. . .
Ashdown		c	MC	4	(870) 898-2622	Hoyt Johnson	. . .	Sandra Patterson	. . .	. . .	Ben McCraw	. . .
Atkins		c	MC	2	(479) 641-2900	. . .		. . .	. . .	. . .	. . .	. . .
Augusta	*	c	MC	2	(870) 347-5656	Jimmy Rhodes	. . .	. . .	. . .	. . .	Charles Allen	. . .
Bald Knob		c	MC	3	(501) 724-6371	Doyle Wallace	. . .	. . .	. . .	Danny Holobaugh	Larry Landis	. . .
Barling		c	CM	4	(479) 452-1556	Jerry Barling	Ray Caruthers	Cindy Walker	. . .	Will Dean	John Roth	Steve Core
Batesville	*	c	MC	9	(870) 698-2400	Rick Elumbaugh	. . .	Denise Johnston	. . .	Danny Russell	. . .	Sanford St. John
Beebe	*	c	MC	4	(501) 882-6295	Michael Robertson	Jackie Young	. . .	. . .	William Nick	S. Wayne Ballew	Dwight Oxner
Benton		c	MC	21	(501) 776-5900	Richard Holland	. . .	Cindy Stracener	. . .	Ben Blankenship	Gary Sipes	. . .
Bentonville		c	MC	19	(479) 271-3191	Terry Coberly	. . .	Suzanne Grider	Stewart Smith	Dan White	James Allen	Britt Vance
Berryville		c	MC	4	(870) 423-4414	Tim McKinney	. . .	Sherry Clark	. . .	Gene Chafin	David Muniz	Dwayne Allen
Blytheville		c	MC	18	(870) 763-3602	. . .		. . .	. . .	Gary Perry	. . .	. . .
Booneville		c	MC	4	(479) 675-3811	Jerry Wilkins	. . .	Melinda Smith	. . .	Mike Talley	Stanley Campbell	. . .
Brinkley		c	CM	3	(870) 734-1382	. . .		. . .	. . .	. . .	. . .	William Lasage
Bryant		c	MC	9	(501) 847-0292	Paul Halley	. . .	Brenda Cockerham	Marilyn Payne	Randy Cox	Frank Gonzales	William Lasage
Cabot	*	c	MC	15	(501) 843-3566	Eddie Williams	Karen Davis	. . .	. . .	Phillip Robinson	Jackie Davis	Jerrel Maxwell
Camden		c	MC	13	(870) 836-6436	Chris Claybaker	. . .	. . .	. . .	William Seaton	Elisha Cochran	Bill Braswell
Carlisle	*	c	MC	2	(870) 552-3120	Ray Glover	. . .	. . .	. . .	Marvin Reid	Eric Frank	Richard Sumner
Cherokee Village		c	MC	4	(870) 257-5522	Ray Maynard	. . .	Susan Maynard	. . .	. . .	. . .	. . .
Clarksville		c	MC	7	(479) 754-6486	Billy Helms	. . .	. . .	. . .	Ron Wylie	Jimmy Ralph	Hugh Harrison
Conway		c	MC	43	(501) 450-6110	Tab Townsell	Donald Crain	Michael Garrett	Perry Faulkner	Bart Castleberry	Jerry Snowden	. . .
Corning		c	MC	3	(870) 857-6001	James Ermert	Allen Warmath	Frances Edwards	. . .	Donnie Kirby	Jim Groning	. . .
Crossett		c	MC	6	(870) 364-4825	Marshall McCormick	. . .	Jesse Walthall	Heath White	James Launius	Thomas Sturgeon	Thomas Goree
Dardanelle	*	c	MC	4	(479) 229-4500	Carolyn McGee	. . .	Mary Martin	. . .	Carl Cross	Montie Sims	. . .
De Queen		c	CM	5	(870) 584-3445	Dale Kesner	. . .	. . .	Donna Jones	. . .	Richard McKinley	. . .
De Witt		c	MC	3	(870) 946-1776	Carroll Lester	Shirley Parker	Liz Ferguson	. . .	Ronnie Danner	Bob Paxton	Bill Paxton
Dermott		c	MC	3	(870) 538-5251	. . .		. . .	. . .	. . .	Carl McCree	. . .
Dumas		c	MC	5	(870) 382-2121	Marion Gill	. . .	Johnny Brigham	. . .	David Byrd	Everett Cox	. . .
Earle		c	MC	3	(870) 792-8909	. . .		. . .	. . .	. . .	. . .	. . .
El Dorado	*	c	MC	21	(870) 881-4865	Mike Dumas	. . .	John Wells	. . .	Floyd McAdoo	Ricky Roberts	Charles Atkinson
England		c	MC	2	(501) 842-3911	Ruth Baker	Tammie Jinks	. . .	. . .	Bob Winkler	Nathan Cook	Roy Talley
Eudora		c	MC	2	(870) 355-4436	. . .		. . .	. . .	. . .	. . .	. . .
Eureka Springs		c	MC	2	(479) 253-9703	Kathy Harrison	. . .	MaryJane Sell	. . .	David Stoppel	Earl Hyatt	. . .
Fayetteville		c	CM	58	(479) 575-8330	Dan Coody	. . .	Sondra Smith	Stephen Davis	Chris Bosch	Rick Hoyt	. . .
Fordyce	*	c	MC	4	(870) 352-2198	William Lyon	. . .	Janice McDaniel	. . .	Roy Moseley	Joe Pennington	. . .
Forrest City		c	MC	14	(870) 633-1315	Larry Bryant	. . .	Marie Todd	. . .	Dan Curtner	Clarence McNeary	Clovis Macon
Fort Smith		c	CM	80	(479) 785-2801	Ray Baker	Randy Reed	Cindy Remler	Kara Bushkuhl	Jerry Tomlin	. . .	Steve Parke
Gosnell		c	MC	3	(870) 532-8544	Dick Reams	. . .	. . .	Nola King	. . .	Michael Kelly	Charles Cobb
Gravette		c	MC	1	(479) 787-5757	. . .		. . .	. . .	. . .	. . .	. . .
Greenwood		c	MC	7	(479) 996-2742	Garry Campbell	. . .	Wilma Cabe	Dallas Melvin	Don Oliver	Keith Jackson	. . .
Gurdon		c	MC	2	(870) 353-2514	Rick Smith	. . .	Tambra Smith	. . .	Jake McBride	. . .	. . .
Hamburg		c	MC	3	(870) 853-5300	Gordon Hennington	. . .	. . .	. . .	Steve Cypert	Tommy Breedlove	Jimmy Hargis
Harrison		c	MC	12	(870) 741-2525	. . .		. . .	. . .	. . .	. . .	. . .
Heber Springs		c	MC	6	(501) 362-3635	Edward Roper	. . .	Norma Martin	. . .	Steve Haile	David Smith	. . .
Helena		c	MC	6	(870) 572-2528	Robert Miller	. . .	Sandra Ramsey	. . .	Reginald Wilson	Vincent Bell	. . .
Hope		c	CM	10	(870) 777-6701	Dennis Ramsey	Catherine Cook	Loreta Hare	Debra Hall	Bo Watkins	William Brinkworth	. . .
Hot Springs		c	CM	33	(501) 321-6800	Mike Bush	Kent Myers	. . .	Linda Baker	Arval Sanders	Gary Ashcraft	Ronald Kohler
Hoxie		c	MC	2	(870) 886-2742	Paul Hendrix	. . .	Katie Smith	. . .	David Mason	Kenny Jones	. . .
Jacksonville		c	MC	29	(501) 982-4671	Tommy Swaim	. . .	Susan Davitt	Paul Mushrush	John Vanderhoof	Larry Hibbs	Jimmy Oakley
Jonesboro		c	MC	55	(870) 933-4640	Hubert Brodell	Larry Johnson	Donna Jackson	Larry Flowers	Rusty Bradley	Floyd Johnson	Guy Lowes
Lake Village		c	MC	2	(870) 265-2228	Joanne Bush	. . .	Harolyn Keith	. . .	. . .	Percy Wilburn	. . .
Little Rock	*	c	CM	183	(501) 371-4510	Mark Stodola	Bruce Moore	Nancy Wood	Robert Biles	Rhoda Kerr	Stuart Thomas	Steve Haralson
Lonoke		c	MC	4	(501) 676-2588	Thomas Privett	. . .	Billie Uzzell	. . .	Scott Williams	Ronald Campbell	Tony Scroggins
Magnolia		c	MC	10	(870) 234-1375	Lane Jean	. . .	Judy Whitelaw	. . .	Herschel Hampton	Robert Gorum	Ricky Wilson
Malvern		c	MC	9	(501) 332-3638	. . .		. . .	. . .	Orlen Wiley	. . .	. . .
Manila		c	MC	3	(870) 561-4437	Melvin Browning	. . .	Rachael Scott	. . .	Don Nunnally	Jackie Hill	. . .
Marianna		c	MC	5	(870) 295-6089	Robert Taylor	. . .	. . .	. . .	Mark Andrews	Walter Johnson	Jack Dilks
Marion		c	MC	8	(870) 739-3071	. . .		. . .	. . .	. . .	. . .	. . .
Marked Tree		c	MC	2	(870) 358-3216	Lawrence Ashlock	. . .	Pamela Wright	. . .	Danny Johnson	Orbie Crum	Clifton Parham
Maumelle	*	c	CM	5	(501) 851-2500	Mike Watson	. . .	Joshua Clausen	Tyler Winningham	George Glenn	Sam Williams	Robert Cogdell
Mc Gehee		c	MC	4	(870) 222-3160	. . .		. . .	. . .	. . .	. . .	. . .
Mena		c	MC	5	(479) 394-3141	George McKee	. . .	Regina Walker	. . .	. . .	Russell Nichols	. . .
Monticello		c	MC	9	(870) 367-4400	David Anderson	. . .	Patricia Nelson	. . .	Raymond Chisom	Tommy Free	Lennie Wood
Morrilton		c	MC	6	(501) 354-3484	Stewart Nelson	. . .	Charlotte Kindle	. . .	. . .	Norbert Gunderman	Charles Edwards
Mountain Home	*	c	MC	11	(870) 425-5116	Ed House	. . .	Cynthia Wynn	. . .	Ken Williams	Carry Manuel	Alma Clark
Nashville		c	MC	4	(870) 845-7400	Mike Reese	. . .	Kelly Sherman	Pam McLaughlin	Jerry Harwell	Larry Yates	. . .
Newport	*	c	MC	7	(870) 523-6568	David Stewart	. . .	Linda Treadway	. . .	Michael Mink	Michael Scudder	Burt Willard
North Little Rock	*	c	MC	60	(501) 975-8855	Patrick Hays	Joseph Smith	Diane Whitbey	Robert Sisson	Joe McCall	Danny Bradley	Bobby Ward
Osceola		c	MC	8	(870) 563-5102	. . .		. . .	. . .	. . .	. . .	. . .
Ozark	*	c	MC	3	(479) 667-2238	. . .		. . .	. . .	. . .	. . .	. . .
Paragould		c	MC	22	(870) 239-7510	Winston Gaskill	. . .	Goldie Wise	. . .	William Brown	Dennis Hyde	Sandra Meeker
Paris		c	MC	3	(479) 963-2450	Jim Clay	. . .	Billy Rhinehart	Jewell White	Edward Boyd	Hershel Hice	Jimmy O'Bar
Pea Ridge		c	MC	2	(479) 451-1424	. . .		. . .	. . .	. . .	. . .	. . .
Piggott		c	MC	3	(870) 598-3791	Gerald Morris	. . .	Judy Parker	. . .	John Harlan	William Alstadt	Teddy Bellers
Pine Bluff		c	MC	55	(870) 543-1840	Francis King	. . .	Sharon Hagan	Edward Bogy	David Parsley	Daniel Moses	. . .
Pocahontas		c	MC	6	(870) 892-3924	Gary Crocker	. . .	. . .	. . .	Scott Baltz	Chad Mulligan	. . .
Prescott		c	MC	3	(870) 887-2210	. . .		. . .	. . .	. . .	. . .	. . .
Rogers		c	MC	38	(479) 621-1117	Stephen Womack	. . .	Sandra Fearman	. . .	Wesley Lewis	Timothy Keck	. . .
Russellville		c	MC	23	(479) 968-2098	Raye Turner	. . .	Kathy Collins	. . .	Dennis Miller	James Bacon	Morgan Barrett
Searcy		c	MC	18	(501) 268-2483	Belinda LaForce	. . .	. . .	. . .	Bill Baldridge	J. R. Thomas	. . .
Sheridan		c	MC	3	(870) 942-3921	. . .		. . .	. . .	. . .	. . .	. . .

Directory 1/9 continued — OFFICIALS IN U.S. MUNICIPALITIES 2,500 AND OVER IN POPULATION

		Type	Form of govern-ment	2000 Popu-lation (000)	Main telephone number	Chief elected official	Appointed administrator	Clerk of the governing board	Chief financial officer	Fire chief	Police chief	Public works director
		c	MC	21	(501) 833-3703	Bill Harmon	. . .	Virginia Hillman	. . .	. . .	James Thomas	Denver Gentry
		c	CM	10	(479) 524-5136	M. L. VanPouke	David Cameron	Peggy Woody	Paul Calloway	Jimmy Harris	Jerry Toler	. . .
S		c	MC	45	(479) 750-8535	Jerry Van Hoose	. . .	Denise Pearce	. . .	E. Duane Atha	Sidney Rieff	Sam Goade
S		c	MC	2	(870) 533-2965	E. W. Johnson	. . .	. . .	. . .	. . .	Robert Drake	. . .
St			MC	9	(870) 673-8817	Harry Richenback	. . .	Mitri Greenhill	Jane Jackson	George Jackson	David Cowart	. . .
Te			CM	26	(870) 779-4991	Horace Shipp	Harold Boldt	Patti Grey	. . .	Bobby Honea	Robert Harrison	Rachael Kaplan
Tru			MC	6	(870) 483-5355	Jack Coggins	Patricia Powell	Patsy Bullock	. . .	Gary Anderson	R. Richardson	Bill Matthews
Var			MC	18	(479) 474-8936	John Riggs	Vivian Mitchell	Barbie Curtis	. . .	Teasie Harris	Kenneth Bell	Don Mullens
Wal			MC	3	(479) 637-3181	Patrick Travers	George Harrod	Betty Hunt	. . .	Jimmy Hudgens	Jimmy Doster	Tomas Starr
Waln			MC	4	(870) 886-6638	Junior Rogers	. . .	Carolyn Hayes	. . .	Wayne Masterson	Dan Webb	. . .
Warre			MC	6	(870) 226-6743	Bryan Martin	. . .	Jeanie Reep	. . .	Howard Edwards	Randy Peek	Steven Rand
West			MC	8	(870) 572-2528	. . .	. . .	. . .	. . .	. . .	. . .	. . .
West M			MC	27	(870) 732-7500	William Johnson	. . .	Phillip Para	Robert Gunter	Arburt Robinson	Robert Paudert	. . .
White H			MC	4	(870) 247-2399	James Morgan	. . .	. . .	. . .	Sandy Castleberry	Noel Foster	. . .
Wynne			MC	8	(870) 238-9171	. . .	. . .	. . .	. . .	. . .	. . .	. . .
CALIFOR												
Adelanto			CM	18	(760) 246-2300	Jim Nehmens	D. Hart	Cindy Herrera	William Aylward	John Salvate	Ron Wren	. . .
Agoura Hi			M	20	(818) 597-7300	. . .	. . .	Kimberly Rodrigues	Georgette Holt	. . .	. . .	. . .
Alameda			M	72	(510) 748-4505	Beverly Johnson	Debra Kurita	Lara Weisiger	Zenda James	James Christiansen	Burnham Matthews	Matthew Naclerio
Albany			M	16	(510) 528-5710	Peggy Thomsen	Beth Pollard	Jackie Bucholz	Joan Streit	Marc McGinn	Larry Murdo	Ann Chaney
Alhambra				85	(626) 570-5095	Talmage Burke	Julio Fuentes	Frances Moore	Howard Longballa	Vincent Kemp	. . .	Mary Swink
Aliso Viejo				40	(949) 425-2500	William Phillips	Mark Pulone	. . .	. . .	Ed Fleming	Richard Paddock	John Whitman
Alturas				2	(530) 233-2512	George Andreasen	. . .	Cary Baker	. . .	Keith Jacques	Ken Barnes	Chester Robertson
American Can				9	(707) 647-4361	Cecil Shaver	Richard Ramirez	Kay Woodson	Pete Kolf	Keith Caldwell	Douglas Koford	Robert Weil
Anaheim				328	(714) 765-5100	. . .	David Morgan	Sheryll Schroeder	William Sweeney	Roger Smith	John Welter	Gary Johnson
Anderson				9	(530) 378-6626	Keith Webster	R Scott Morgan	. . .	L. Watkins-Gallino	. . .	Dale Webb	Richard Barchus
Angels Camp				2	(209) 736-2181	. . .	Timothy Shearer	. . .	. . .	. . .	. . .	. . .
Antioch				90	(925) 779-7000	Don Freitas	. . .	Jolene Martin	John Tasker	. . .	Mark Moczulski	Phil Harrington
Apple Valley				54	(760) 240-7000	. . .	. . .	La Vonda Pearson	Kevin Smith	. . .	. . .	. . .
Arcadia			CM	53	(626) 574-5405	Gary Kovack	. . .	June Alford	. . .	David Lugo	David Hinig	Patrick Malloy
Arcata	*	c	CM	16	(707) 822-5953	Harmony Groves	Michael Hackett	. . .	Janet Luzzi	John McFarland	Randal Mendosa	Doby Class
Arroyo Grande		c	CM	15	(805) 473-5400	Tony Ferrara	Steven Adams	Kelly Wetmore	Angela Kraetsch	Terry Fibich	. . .	Don Spagnolo
Artesia		c	CM	16	(562) 865-6262	Tony Mendoza	Maria Dadian	Daryl Betancur	. . .	. . .	. . .	. . .
Arvin		c	CM	12	(661) 854-3134	Tim Tarver	Alan Christensen	Cecilia Vela	David Powell	. . .	Tommy Tunson	Bob Feulner
Atascadero		c	CM	26	(805) 461-5000	Tom O'Malley	Wade McKinney	. . .	. . .	Kurt Stone	John Couch	Steven Kahn
Atherton		t	CM	7	(650) 752-0500	Kathy McKeithen	Wende Protzman	. . .	John Johns	. . .	Robert Brennan	Duncan Jones
Atwater		c	CM	23	(209) 357-6300	Rudy Trevino	Gregory Wellman	. . .	. . .	Dennis Sparks	Jerry Moore	Frank Lozano
Auburn		c	CM	12	(530) 823-4211	. . .	Robert Richardson	Joseph Labrie	Richard Loomis	Mark D'Ambrogi	. . .	Thomas Fossum
Avalon		c	CM	3	(310) 510-0220	. . .	Thomas Sullivan	Shirley Davy	Betty Jo Garcia	Steven Hoefs	. . .	Pastor Lopez
Avenal	*	c	CM	14	(559) 386-5766	. . .	Melissa Whitten	Nina Garza	Esther Strong	. . .	Dave Putnam	Jerry Watson
Azusa		c	CM	44	(626) 812-5027	C. Cruz-Madrid	Francis Delach	Vera Mendoza	Julie Gutierrez	. . .	King Davis	Bill Nakasone
Bakersfield		c	CM	247	(661) 326-3006	Harvey Hall	Alan Tandy	Pamela McCarthy	Gregory Klimko	Ron Fraze	Eric Matlock	Raul Rojas
Baldwin Park		c	CM	75	(626) 960-4011	Manuel Lozano	Vijay Singhal	Kathryn Tizcareno	Hennie Apodaca	. . .	Mark Kling	Shafique Naiyer
Banning		c	CM	23	(909) 922-3105	Brenda Salas	Randy Anstine	Marie Calderon	Bonnie Johnson	Ted Yarbrough	John Horton	Duane Burk
Barstow	*	c	CM	21	(760) 256-3531	Lawrence Dale	Hector Rodriguez	Joanne Cousino	Gil Olivarez	. . .	Dianne Burns	. . .
Beaumont	*	c	CM	11	(951) 769-8520	Jeff Fox	. . .	Karen Thompson	William Aylward	. . .	Frank Coe	Deepak Moorjani
Bell		c	CM	36	(323) 588-6211	George Cole	Robert Rizzo	. . .	. . .	. . .	Michael Trevis	. . .
Bell Gardens	*	c	CM	44	(562) 806-7700	Jennifer Rodriquez	John Ornelas	Marta Solano	Misty Cheng	. . .	Keith Kilmer	John Oropeza
Bellflower		c	CM	72	(562) 804-1424	Ray Smith	Michael Egan	Debra Bauchop	Tae Rhee	. . .	. . .	. . .
Belmont		c	CM	25	(650) 595-7413	Paul Wright	Jack Crist	Teresa Cook	Thomas Fil	. . .	Greg Janke	Ray Davis
Belvedere		c	CM	2	(415) 435-3838	Barbara Morrison	George Rodericks	. . .	Rebecca Eastman	Rich Pearce	Mark Campbell	. . .
Benicia		c	CM	26	(707) 746-4200	Steven Messina	James Erickson	Linda Purdy	. . .	Ken Hanley	Sandra Spagnoli	. . .
Berkeley		c	CM	102	(510) 981-2489	Tom Bates	. . .	Sherry Kelly	. . .	Reginald Garcia	Roy Meisner	Rene Cardinaux
Beverly Hills		c	CM	33	(310) 285-1000	Mark Egerman	Roderick Wood	Nina Webster	Don Oblander	Pete Bonano	David Snowden	Rob Beste
Big Bear Lake		c	CM	5	(909) 866-5831	Elizabeth Harris	Jeffrey Mathieu	Katherine Jeffries	. . .	Kenneth Hammond	. . .	. . .
Bishop		c	CM	3	(760) 873-5863	Kathryn Henderson	Richard Pucci	. . .	. . .	Ray Seguine	. . .	David Grah
Blue Lake		c	CM	1	(707) 668-5655	. . .	. . .	. . .	. . .	. . .	. . .	. . .
Blythe		c	CM	12	(760) 922-6161	Robert Crain	Lester Nelson	. . .	Helen Colbert	Curtis Crecelius	Robert Grady	James Rodkey
Bradbury	*	c	CM	. .	(626) 358-3218	Jon Barker	Jennifer Vasquez	Claudia Sandana	. . .	. . .	. . .	. . .
Brawley		c	CM	22	(760) 344-9111	. . .	Oscar Rodriquez	Janet Smith	Fredrick Selk	Frank Contreras	Henry Graham	Yazmin Arellano
Brea	*	c	CM	35	(714) 990-7600	Marty Simonoff	Tim O'Donnell	Lucinda Williams	William Gallardo	Alford Nero	Mike Messina	. . .
Brentwood		c	CM	23	(925) 516-5400	Brian Swisher	Donna Landeros	Margaret Wimberly	Pamela Ehler	. . .	Michael Davies	Paul Zolfarelli
Brisbane		c	CM	3	(415) 508-2100	. . .	Clayton Holstine	Sheri Schroeder	. . .	. . .	Thomas Hitchcock	Randy Breault
Brooktrails (Csd)		tp	CM	2	(707) 459-2494	George Skezas	Michael Chapman	. . .	. . .	Daryl Schoeppner	. . .	Wendell Wilson
Buellton		c	CM	3	(805) 688-5177	Victoria Pointer	Steven Thompson	Birgit Cripe	Kathryn Wollin	. . .	. . .	Bill Albrecht
Buena Park		c	CM	78	(714) 562-3500	Steve Berry	. . .	Shalice Reynoso	Sung Hyun	. . .	Gary Hicken	James Biery
Burbank		c	CM	100	(818) 238-5800	Stacey Murphy	Mary Alvord	Margarita Campos	Derek Hanway	Michael Davis	Thomas Hoefel	. . .
Burlingame		c	CM	28	(650) 558-7200	. . .	James Nantell	. . .	Jesus Nava	. . .	Gary Missel	. . .
Calabasas		c	CM	16	(818) 878-4225	Dennis Washburn	Anthony Coroalles	Robin Parker	Gary Lysik	Reginald Lee	. . .	Charles Mink
Calexico		c	CM	27	(760) 768-2110	. . .	Luis Estrada	Lourdes Cordova	Veronica Alvarado	Carlos Escalante	Tommy Tunson	Mariano Martinez
California City		c	CM	8	(760) 373-8661	Larry Adams	. . .	Helen Dennis	Terry Hicks	Mike Antonucci	Wayne Dickerson	Ron Wallace
Calimesa		c	CM	7	(909) 795-9801	Shenna Moqeet	David Lane	. . .	Debbie Cain	Craig Anthony	Ronald Wade	Elroy Kiepke
Calipatria		c	MC	7	(760) 348-2293	. . .	Romualdo Medina	. . .	. . .	Chris Hall	. . .	. . .
Calistoga		c	CM	5	(707) 942-2754	Andrew Alexander	. . .	. . .	. . .	Gary Kraus	Mike Dick	Paul Wade
Camarillo		c	CM	57	(805) 388-5307	Michael Morgan	Jerry Bankston	Deborah Harrington	Anita Lawrence	Robert Roper	Mike Lewis	Thomas Fox
Campbell	*	c	CM	36	(408) 866-2100	. . .	Daniel Rich	Anne Bybee	Jesse Takahashi	. . .	David Gullo	Robert Kass
Canyon Lake		c	CM	9	(909) 244-2955	Cora Barrett	. . .	Kathy Bennett	. . .	. . .	. . .	. . .
Capitola		c	CM	10	(831) 475-7300	Dennis Norton	Richard Hill	Pamela Greeninger	Lauren Lai	. . .	Richard Ehle	Steven Jesberg
Carlsbad		c	CM	78	(760) 602-2440	Claude Lewis	Lisa Hildabrand	. . .	. . .	D. Van Der Maaten	Robert Vales	Lloyd Hubbs
Carmel-By-The-Sea		c	CM	4	(831) 620-2000	Sue McCloud	Richard Guillen	Karen Crouch	. . .	. . .	George Rawson	James Cullem
Carpinteria		c	CM	14	(805) 684-5405	. . .	David Durflinger	Jayne Diza	. . .	. . .	. . .	Dale Lipp
Carson		c	CM	89	(310) 830-7600	. . .	Jerome Groomes	Helen Kawagoe	Jacquelyn Acosta	. . .	. . .	Kenneth Boyce
Cathedral City		c	CM	42	(760) 770-0340	Kathleen DeRosa	Donald Bradley	. . .	. . .	William Soqui	Stanley Henry	Patrick Milos
Ceres		c	CM	34	(209) 538-5700	. . .	Brad Kilger	. . .	. . .	. . .	. . .	Joachim Hollstein
Cerritos		c	CM	51	(562) 860-0311	. . .	Art Gallucci	Josephine Triggs	. . .	. . .	. . .	Hal Arbogast
Chico		c	CM	59	(530) 896-7200	. . .	. . .	Deborah Presson	Jennifer Hennessy	John Brown	Bruce Hagerty	. . .
Chino		c	CM	67	(909) 591-9800	Eunice Ulloa	Patrick Glover	Lenna Tanner	David Cain	. . .	Eugene Hernandez	. . .
Chino Hills		c	MC	66	(909) 364-2600	G. Norton-Perry	Douglas La Belle	Mary McDuffe	Judy Lancaster	. . .	Rick Carr	Patricia Hagler
Chowchilla	*	c	CM	11	(559) 665-8615	. . .	Nancy Red	Gayle Welsh	Connie Wright	Harry Turner	Jay Varney	. . .
Chula Vista		c	CM	173	(619) 691-5096	Shirley Horton	David Garcia	Susan Bigelow	Maria Kachadoorian	Douglas Perry	John Kaheny	John Lippitt

Directory 1/9 continued OFFICIALS IN U.S. MUNICIPALITIES 2,500 AND OVER IN POPULATION

Jurisdiction		Type	Form of govern-ment	2000 Popu-lation (000)	Main telephone number	Chief elected official	Appointed administrator	Clerk of the governing board	Chief financial officer	Fire chief	Police chief	Public works director
CALIFORNIA continued												
Citrus Heights	*	c	CM	85	(916) 725-2448	William Hughes	Henry Tingle	Lillian Hare	Stefani Daniell	. . .	Dan Drummond	Pete Santina
Claremont	*	c	CM	33	(909) 399-5460	. . .	Jeffrey Parker	Lynne Pahner	. . .	. . .	Paul Cooper	. . .
Clayton	*	c	CM	10	(925) 673-7300	William Walcutt	Gary Napper	Laci Jackson	Merry Pelletier	. . .	Dan Lawrence	. . .
Clearlake		c	CM	13	(707) 994-8201	James McMurray	Robert Van Nort	. . .	Barbra Lysher	. . .	Robert Chalk	. . .
Cloverdale		c	CM	6	(707) 894-2521	Gail Pardini-Plass	Nina Regor	M. Winterbottom	Barry Whitely	. . .	Stephen Willis	Robert Crabb
Clovis	*	c	CM	68	(559) 324-2000	Nathan Magsig	Kathleen Millison	John Holt	Robert Woolley	Samuel Aston	Jim Zulim	Mike Leonardo
Coachella		c	CM	22	(760) 398-3502	Eduardo Garcia	Timothy Brown	Isabel Castillon	John Gerardi	Alex Gregg	Colleen Walker	Paul Toor
Coalinga	*	c	CM	11	(559) 935-1533	Trish Hill	Stephen Julian	Cindy Johnson	Robert Barron	Daniel Hernandez	Gerald Galvin	Randy Arp
Colma		t	CM	1	(650) 997-8300	Frossanna Vallerga	Diane McGrath	. . .	. . .	. . .	Robert Lotti	. . .
Colton		c	CM	47	(909) 370-5099	Helen Ramos	Daryl Parrish	Caroline Barrera	Dilu DeAlwis	Tom Hendrix	Kenneth Rulon	John Hutton
Colusa		c	CM	5	(530) 458-4740	Pamela Crippen	. . .	. . .	. . .	Randy Dunn	Lyle Montgomery	Patty Hickle
Commerce		c	CM	12	(323) 722-4805	Hugo Argumedo	Thomas Sykes	Linda Olivieri	Vilko Domic	. . .	. . .	. . .
Compton		c	CM	93	(310) 605-5535	Omar Bradley	. . .	Charles Davis	Marilynn Horne	Milford Fonza	Ramon Allen	Angel Espiritu
Concord		c	CM	121	(925) 671-3000	Helen Allen	Lydia Du Borg	Mary Rae Lehman	Peggy Lefebvre	. . .	David Livingston	Qamar Khan
Corcoran	*	c	CM	14	(559) 992-2151	. . .	Ronald Hoggard	Lorraine Lopez	Joyce Venegas	. . .	. . .	Steven Kroeker
Corning	*	c	CM	6	(530) 824-7034	. . .	Stephen Kimbrough	Lisa Linnet	. . .	Robert Pryatel	Anthony Cardenas	Tom Russ
Corona		c	CM	124	(909) 736-2209	. . .	Beth Groves	Victoria Wasko	. . .	Mike Warren	Richard Gonzales	John Licata
Coronado	*	c	CM	24	(619) 522-7300	Tom Smisek	Mark Ochenduszko	Linda Hascup	Leslie Suelter	Kim Raddatz	Paul Crook	Scott Huth
Corte Madera		t	CM	9	(415) 927-5050	. . .	. . .	. . .	George Warman	Robert Fox	. . .	. . .
Costa Mesa	*	c	CM	108	(714) 754-5350	Alan Mansoor	Allan Roeder	Julie Folcik	Marc Puckett	Michael Morgan	C. Shawkey	William Morris
Cotati	*	c	CM	6	(707) 792-4600	Geoff Fox	Dianne Thompson	Tamara Taylor	Jone Hayes	. . .	Robert Stewart	Steve Nommsen
Covina	*	c	CM	46	(626) 331-0114	John King	Paul Philips	Rosie Fabian	William Stawarski	. . .	Kim Raney	Steve Henley
Crescent City	*	c	CM	4	(707) 464-7483	Dennis Burns	Eli Naffah	L. Nickerson	Joei Sanches	Stephen Wakefield	Douglas Plack	James Barnts
Cudahy		c	CM	24	(323) 773-5143	. . .	George Perez	. . .	Aurora Martinez	. . .	. . .	. . .
Culver City		c	CM	38	(310) 253-6000	Steve Rose	Jerry Fulwood	Tom Crunk	Eric Shapiro	Michael Thompson	Ted Cooke	James Davis
Cupertino		c	CM	50	(408) 777-3227	. . .	David Knapp	Kimberly Smith	David Woo	. . .	. . .	Ralph Qualls
Cypress	*	c	CM	46	(714) 229-6700	Phil Luebben	John Bahorski	Denise Basham	Richard Storey	. . .	Rick Hicks	Doug Dancs
Daly City		c	CM	103	(650) 991-8127	Carol Klatt	Patricia Martel	Maria Cortes	Donald McVey	Ron Myers	. . .	D. P. Gleichenhaus
Dana Point	*	c	CM	35	(949) 248-3500	Diane Harkey	Douglas Chotkevys	Kathy Ward	. . .	Rick Robinson	Mark Levy	Brad Fowler
Danville		t	CM	41	(925) 314-3300	Mike Shimansky	Joseph Calabrigo	Marie Sunseri	Elizabeth Hudson	. . .	. . .	. . .
Davis		c	CM	60	(530) 757-5644	Lois Wolk	William Emlen	Bette Racki	. . .	Rose Conroy	James Hyde	Robert Weir
Del Mar		c	CM	4	(858) 755-9313	Carl Hilliard	L. Brekke-Esparza	Mercedes Martin	Kim Krause	David Ott	. . .	David Scherer
Del Rey Oaks		c	CM	1	(408) 394-8511	Jack Barlich	. . .	. . .	. . .	. . .	Ron Langford	. . .
Delano		c	CM	38	(661) 721-3305	Arthur Armendariz	Abdel Salem	Phyllia Kraft	Narciso Aguda	. . .	James Griggs	Kim Domingo
Desert Hot Springs	*	c	CM	16	(760) 329-6411	Alex Bias	Richard Daniels	Rossie Stobbs	. . .	. . .	Patrick Williams	. . .
Diamond Bar		c	CM	56	(900) 860-2489	. . .	. . .	Lynda Burgess	Linda Magnuson	. . .	. . .	David Liu
Dinuba		c	CM	16	(559) 591-5900	Mike Smith	J. Todd	Linda Barkley	. . .	Myles Chute	Myron Galchutt	Blanca Beltran
Dixon	*	c	CM	16	(707) 678-7000	Mary Ann Courville	Warren Salmons	Janice Beaman	Joan Streit	. . .	Donald Mort	David Melilli
Dos Palos		c	CM	4	(209) 392-2174	Jerry Westlake	Darrell Fonseca	Alice Thompson	Manuela Sousa	Dewayne Jones	Paul Lopez	Hub Ballinger
Downey		c	CM	107	(562) 904-7293	Gary McCaughan	Gerald Caton	. . .	Lowell Williams	Ronald Irwin	Gregory Caldwell	Richard Redmayne
Duarte		c	CM	21	(626) 357-7931	. . .	. . .	. . .	. . .	. . .	. . .	. . .
Dublin	*	c	CM	29	(925) 833-6600	Janet Lockhart	Richard Ambrose	Carolyn Parkinson	. . .	William McCannon	Gary Thuman	Lee Thompson
Dunsmuir	*	c	CM	1	(530) 235-4822	Ivan Young	Patricia Hall	Kathryn Wilson	J. Anderson	Daniel Madilla	Craig Dilley	Carl Morzenti
East Palo Alto		c	CM	29	(650) 853-3100	Rose Gibson	Alvin James	Salani Wendt	Amy Rio	. . .	Wesley Bowling	David Miller
El Cajon		c	CM	94	(619) 441-1776	Mark Lewis	Kathleen Henry	Kathie Rutledge	Michael Shelton	Mike Scott	Cliff Diamond	George Turner
El Centro		c	CM	37	(760) 337-4540	C. Viegas-Walker	Ruben Duran	Rita Noden	John Lau	Chris Petree	Raymond Loera	Terry Hagen
El Cerrito		c	CM	23	(510) 215-4300	Mark Friedman	Scott Hanin	Linda Giddings	Brian Foster	Mark Scott	Scott Kirkand	Dan Clark
El Monte		c	CM	115	(626) 580-2001	Ernest Gutierrez	Juan Mireles	Lorene Gutierrez	Marcie Medina	. . .	Kenneth Weldon	. . .
El Paso De Robles	*	c	CM	24	(805) 227-7276	Frank Mecham	James App	Dennis Fansler	. . .	Ken Johnson	Dennis Cassidy	Douglass Monn
El Segundo		c	CM	16	(310) 524-2300	Kelly McDowell	Jeffrey Stewart	Cynthia Mortesen	. . .	Norm Angelo	Jack Wayt	Steve Finton
Elk Grove		c	CM	17	(916) 683-7111	Rick Soares	James Estep	Peggy Jackson	. . .	. . .	. . .	. . .
Emeryville		c	CM	6	(510) 596-4300	John Flores	. . .	. . .	. . .	Stephen Cutright	Kenneth James	Henry Van Dyke
Encinitas	*	c	CM	58	(760) 633-2600	James Bond	Phillip Cotton	Deborah Cervone	Jennifer Smith	Mark Muir	. . .	Larry Watt
Escalon		c	CM	5	(209) 838-4100	. . .	Carl Greeson	Lisa Nebe	Ricky Gibbs	. . .	Douglas Dunford	. . .
Escondido		c	CM	133	(760) 839-4643	Lori Pfeiler	Clayton Phillips	Marsha Whalen	Gil Rojas	Victor Reed	Duane White	Patrick Thomas
Eureka		c	CM	26	(707) 441-4144	. . .	David Tyson	K. Franco Simmons	Carolyn Thomas	Eric Smith	David Douglas	Mike Knight
Exeter		c	CM	9	(559) 592-9224	Charlie Norman	. . .	. . .	Sheri Emerson	. . .	Clifton Bush	Felix Ortiz
Fairfax		t	CM	7	(415) 453-1584	Lew Tremaine	Linda Kelly	Judith Anderson	Ian Roth	. . .	Ken Hughes	Michael Rock
Fairfield		c	CM	96	(707) 428-7394	Karin MacMillan	. . .	Claudia Archer	Robert Leland	Michael Smith	William Gresham	Charles Beck
Farmersville		c	CM	8	(209) 747-0458	Paul Boyer	. . .	Rosemary Silva	Rene Miller	William Lindquist	Mario Krstic	Eliseo Martinez
Ferndale		c	CM	1	(707) 786-4224	Betsy Anderson	Jay Parrish	Frances Scalvini	. . .	. . .	Lonnie Lawson	Tim Miranda
Fillmore		c	CM	13	(805) 524-3701	Evaristo Barajas	Thomas Ristau	Shirley Spitler	Barbara Smith	Patrick Askren	. . .	John Kozar
Firebaugh		c	CM	5	(559) 659-2043	Marcia Sablan	Jose Ramirez	Dorice Fannon	Patricia Barboza	. . .	Rod Lake	Wilson David
Folsom	*	c	CM	51	(916) 355-7208	Andy Morin	Kerry Miller	Christa Schmidt	. . .	Dan Haverty	Sam Spiegel	Richard Lorenz
Fontana		c	CM	128	(909) 350-7650	Mack Nuaimi	Kenneth Hunt	Beatrice Watson	Lisa Strong	. . .	Frank Scialdone	Curtis Aaron
Fort Bragg		c	CM	7	(707) 961-2823	Jere Melo	Linda Ruffing	C. VanWormer	. . .	. . .	. . .	Dave Goble
Fortuna		c	CM	10	(707) 725-7600	Phil Nyberg	Duane Rigge	. . .	Robert Sousa	Robert Sommerville	Kent Bradshaw	Charles Clark
Foster City		c	CM	28	(650) 286-3200	Marland Townsend	James Hardy	Therese Tahir	Ricardo Santiago	Philip Torre	Randy Sonnenberg	John Lisenko
Fountain Valley		c	CM	54	(714) 593-4400	Laurann Cook	Raymond Kromer	. . .	Elizabeth Fox	. . .	Elvin Miali	Wayne Osborne
Fowler		c	CM	3	(559) 834-3113	. . .	David Elias	Jeannie Davis	Helen Harding	. . .	Darrell Jamgochian	. . .
Fremont		c	CM	203	(510) 494-4660	Gus Morrison	Frederick Diaz	. . .	Dave Millican	William McDonald	Craig Steckler	. . .
Fresno		c	CM	427	(559) 498-4591	Alan Autry	Andrew Souza	Rebecca Klisch	. . .	Michael Smith	Jerry Dyer	. . .
Fullerton		c	CM	126	(714) 738-6310	Don Bankhead	Christopher Meyer	. . .	Glenn Steinbrink	James Reed	Patrick McKinley	Robert Savage
Galt		c	CM	19	(209) 745-4695	C. De La Cruz	Ted Anderson	Liz Aguire	Inez Kiriu	. . .	Doug Matthews	Robert Kawasaki
Garden Grove		c	CM	165	(714) 741-5000	Bill Dalton	George Tindall	Ruth Smith	Kingsley Okereke	Keith Osborn	Joseph Polisar	Keith Jones
Gardena		c	CM	57	(310) 217-9500	Paul Tanaka	Mitchell Lansdell	Maria Marquez	. . .	Thom Glonchak	Rodney Lyons	Harold Williams
Gilroy		c	CM	41	(408) 846-0228	. . .	. . .	Rhonda Pellin	Cindy Murphy	Dale Foster	Gregory Giusiana	Wendie Rooney
Glendale		c	CM	194	(818) 548-2110	Gus Gomez	James Starbird	Doris Twedt	Robert Franz	Richard Hinz	Russell Siverling	Kerry Morford
Glendora	*	c	CM	49	(626) 914-8200	Kenneth Herman	Chris Jeffers	Kathleen Sessman	Mary Solty	. . .	Charles Montoya	David Davies
Goleta		c	CM	55	(805) 961-7500	Jonny Wallis	Daniel Singer	D. Constantino	Zenda James	Martin Johnson	Chris Pappas	Steven Wagner
Gonzales		c	CM	7	(831) 675-5000	Matt Gourley	Rene Mendez	. . .	. . .	Rick Rubbo	Paulette Cudio	Carlos Lopez
Grand Terrace		c	CM	11	(909) 824-6621	Lee Ann Garcia	Thomas Schwab	Brenda Stanfill	Larry Ronnow	. . .	. . .	Jerry Glander
Grass Valley	*	c	CM	10	(530) 274-4309	. . .	. . .	Kristi Bashor	Carol Fish	Jim Marquis	John Foster	. . .
Greenfield		c	CM	12	(831) 674-5591	John Huerta	. . .	. . .	Ann Rathbun	John Sims	Joe Grebmeier	John Alves
Gridley		c	CM	5	(530) 846-5695	Frank Cook	John Slota	. . .	. . .	. . .	Jack Storne	Ed Melton
Grover Beach	*	c	CM	11	(805) 473-4567	Stephen Lieberman	Robert Perrault	D. McMahon	Gayla Chapman	Michael Hubert	James Copsey	. . .
Guadalupe		c	CM	5	(805) 343-1340	Sam Arca	Frank Usher	. . .	Carolyn Cooper	Henry Lawrence	William Tucker	Samuel Angulo
Gustine		c	CM	4	(209) 854-6471	Alfred Souza	Margaret Silveira	. . .	. . .	Gary O'Rear	. . .	Gary Davenport
Half Moon Bay	*	c	CM	11	(650) 726-8270	Naomi Patridge	Marcia Raines	Siobhan Smith	Jud Norrell	. . .	Don O'Keefe	Paul Nagengast
Hanford		c	CM	41	(559) 585-2500	. . .	. . .	Karen McAlister	Tom Dibble	Timothy Teronimo	Carlos Mestas	Gary Misenhimer
Hawaiian Gardens		c	CM	14	(562) 420-2641	Ralph Cesena	Ernesto Marquez	Domenic Ruggeri	Michael Fresques	. . .	. . .	Joe Vasquez

Directory 1/9 continued — OFFICIALS IN U.S. MUNICIPALITIES 2,500 AND OVER IN POPULATION

Jurisdiction	Type	Form of govern-ment	2000 Popu-lation (000)	Main telephone number	Chief elected official	Appointed administrator	Clerk of the governing board	Chief financial officer	Fire chief	Police chief	Public works director
CALIFORNIA continued											
Hawthorne *	c	CM	84	(310) 349-2900	Larry Guidi	Jag Pathirana	Angie English	...	...	Michael Heffner	Arnold Shadbehr
Hayward	c	CM	140	(510) 583-4000	Roberta Cooper	Gregory Jones	Angelina Reyes	Debra Auker	Larry Arfsten	Lloyd Lowe	Robert Bauman
Healdsburg	c	CM	10	(707) 431-3317	Jason Liles	Chet Wystepek	Maria Curiel	Tamera Haas	Randy Collins	Susan Jones	George Hicks
Hemet	c	CM	58	(909) 765-2300	C. Robin Lowe	...	Gene Graves	...	Dave Vanverst	Lee Evanson	Juan Perez
Hercules	c	CM	19	(510) 799-8299	Terry Segerberg	Michael Sakamoto	...	Marie Simons	Gary Boyles	Michael Tye	Sharad Pandya
Hermosa Beach	c	CM	18	(310) 318-0239	Sam Edgerton	Stephen Burrell	Elaine Doerfling	Viki Copeland	Russell Tingley	Greg Savelli	Richard Morgan
Hesperia *	c	CM	62	(760) 947-1000	Jim Lindley	Michael Podegracz	Vicki Soderquist	...	Sid Hultquist	Joe Cusimano	Dale Burke
Highland	c	CM	44	(909) 864-6861	Ross Jones	...	Betty Hughes	Chuck Dantnow	Jim Rissmiller	Sheree Stewart	Ernie Wong
Hillsborough	t	CM	10	(650) 375-7400	D. Regan	A. Constantouros	Rachelle Ungaretti	Edna Masbad	Dave Milanese	Matthew O'Connor	Martha DeBry
Hollister	c	CM	34	(831) 636-4300	...	...	...	Barbara Mulholland	William Garringer	Larry Todd	Clint Quilter
Holtville *	c	CM	5	(760) 356-2912	Ira Hearen	Laura Fischer	...	Rosa Ramirez	David Lantzer	John Myers	Gerald Peacher
Hughson	c	CM	3	(209) 883-4055	Thomas Crowder	Joseph Donabed	Mary Jane Cantrell	...	...	...	Ron Bremer
Huntington Beach *	c	CM	189	(714) 536-5491	...	P. Culbreth-Graft	Joan Flynn	Daniel Villella	Duane Olson	Kenneth Small	Robert Beardsley
Huntington Park *	c	CM	61	(323) 582-6161	Elba Guerrero	Gregory Korduner	Rosanna Ramirez	Don Pruyn	...	Michael Trevis	Neil Poole
Huron	c	CM	6	(559) 945-2241	Ramon Dominguez	Alan Bengyel	...	Tim Przybyia	...	Frank Steenport	Nick Escandon
Imperial	c	CM	7	(760) 355-4371	Mark Gran	Marlene Best	Debra Jackson	John Lau	...	...	Joel Hamby
Imperial Beach	c	CM	26	(619) 423-8300	Jim Janney	Gary Brown	Jacque Hald	...	...	Octavia Parker	Hank Levien
Indian Wells	c	CM	3	(760) 346-2489	...	Greg Johnson	...	Kevin McCarthy	...	...	William Hughes
Indio *	c	CM	49	(760) 391-4000	Ben Godfrey	Glenn Southard	Cynthia Hernandez	Susan Mahoney	Ignacio Otero	Bradley Ramos	Jim Smith
Industry	c	CM	..	(626) 333-2211	David Perez	Philip Iriarte	Jodi Scrivens	Victoria Gallo	...	...	...
Inglewood	c	CM	112	(310) 412-5111	Roosevelt Dorn	Mark Weinberg	Yvonne Horton	...	...	Ronald Bank	William Mahar
Ione	c	CM	7	(209) 274-2412	...	Kimberly Kerr	...	...	Ken Mackey	...	...
Irvine	c	CM	143	(949) 724-6000	Beth Krom	Sean Joyce	Pamyla Means	Sherry Harton	...	...	Marty Bryant
Irwindale	c	CM	1	(626) 430-2200	Manuel Almazan	Robert Griego	...	Abraham Dedios	...	Julian Miranda	Rod Posada
Jackson	c	CM	3	(209) 223-1646	Gene Taylor	Michael Daly	Gisele Cangelosi	...	Mark Morton	Scott Morrison	...
Kerman	c	CM	8	(559) 846-9384	...	Ron Manfredi	Edith Forsstrom	...	...	William Newton	Alan Jacobsen
King City	c	CM	11	(408) 385-3281	...	Michael Powers	...	Jim Larson	...	Nick Baldiviez	Sal Morales
Kingsburg *	c	CM	9	(559) 897-5821	Leland Bergstrom	Donald Pauley	Sue Bauch	...	...	Jim Taylor	...
La Canada Flintridge	c	CM	20	(818) 790-8880	...	Mark Alexander	Kathleen Sessman	...	...	...	Steven Castellanos
La Habra	c	CM	58	(562) 905-9700	...	...	Sharie Apodaca	...	...	Dennis Kies	...
La Habra Heights	c	CM	5	(562) 694-6302	Stan Carroll	Ronald Bates	...	...	John Nielsen	...	...
La Mesa	c	CM	54	(619) 667-1105	Arthur Madrid	Sandra Kerl	Mary Kennedy	Gary Ameling	David Burk	Cliff Resch	Gregory Humora
La Mirada	c	CM	46	(562) 943-0131	Bob Chotiner	Andrea Travis	Susan Ramos	Diane Perkin	...	...	Steve Forster
La Palma *	c	CM	15	(714) 690-3330	Mark Waldman	Dominic Lazzaretto	...	Deborah Moreno	...	Ed Ethell	Ismile Noorbaksh
La Puente	c	CM	41	(626) 855-1500	...	...	Carol Cowley	William Henderson	...	...	William Woolard
La Quinta *	c	CM	23	(760) 777-7000	Don Adolph	Thomas Genovese	...	John Falconer	Dorian Cooley	Colleen Walker	Timothy Jonasson
La Verne	c	CM	31	(909) 596-8726	Jon Blickenstaff	Martin Lomeli	Kathleen Hamm	Ronald Clark	John Breaux	Ronald Ingels	Dan Keesey
Lafayette	c	CM	23	(925) 284-1968	Don Tatzin	Steven Falk	Joanne Robbins	Gonzalo Silva	...	Mike Hubbard	Ron Lefler
Laguna Beach	c	CM	23	(949) 497-3311	Toni Iseman	Kenneth Frank	Verna Rollinger	...	Ken MacLeod	James Spreine	...
Laguna Hills *	c	CM	31	(949) 707-2600	R. Craig Scott	Bruce Channing	Peggy Johns	...	...	...	Kenneth Rosenfield
Laguna Niguel	c	CM	61	(949) 362-4300	Mike Whipple	Timothy Casey	...	Dennis Miura	...	...	K. Montgomery
Lake Elsinore	c	CM	28	(909) 674-3124	Pamela Brinley	Robert Brady	Vicki Kasad	Matt Pressey	...	...	David Sapp
Lake Forest *	c	CM	73	(949) 461-3400	Richard Dixon	Robert Dunek	Sherry Wentz	Liz Andrew	...	...	...
Lakeport	c	MC	4	(707) 263-5615	Richard Lamkin	...	Janel Chapman	...	...	Thomas Engstrom	...
Lakewood	c	CM	79	(562) 866-9771	...	Howard Chambers	Denise Hayward	Larry Schroeder	...	...	...
Lancaster	c	CM	118	(805) 723-6000	Frank Roberts	...	Geri Bryan	Gary Hill	...	...	Jeffrey Long
Larkspur *	c	CM	12	(415) 927-5110	...	Jean Bonander	Cynthia Huisman	Amy Koenig	Robert Sinnott	Phillip Green	Hamid Shamsapour
Lathrop *	c	CM	10	(209) 941-7200	Kristy Sayles	Yvonne Quiring	Arthur Caldeira	Terri Vigna	...	Dolores Delgado	Cary Keaton
Lawndale	c	CM	31	(310) 973-3200	Harold Hofmann	Keith Breskin	Pamela Giamario	Ken Louie	...	...	Marlene Miyoshi
Lemon Grove	c	CM	24	(619) 825-3800	Mary Sessom	Graham Mitchell	Christine Taub	Betty Hofman	Jon Torchia	...	Majed Al-Ghafry
Lemoore	c	CM	19	(559) 924-6700	Thomas Buford	Jeff Briltz	Nanci Lima	Nancy Cota	Eugene Miguel	Kimberly Morrell	David Wlaschin
Lincoln	c	CM	11	(916) 645-3314	Kent Nakata	Gerald Johnson	Pat Avila	...	David Whitt	Brian Vizzusi	John Pedri
Lindsay *	c	CM	10	(559) 562-7103	Ed Murray	Scot Townsend	...	Kenny Walker	...	...	Michael Camarena
Live Oak	c	CM	6	(530) 695-2112	...	Rob Hickey	Melissa Dempsey	Satwant Takhar	C. Vanevenhoven	...	Michael Bohlander
Livermore *	c	CM	73	(925) 960-4100	Marshall Kamena	Linda Barton	Alice Calvert	Monica Potter	William Code	Steven Sweeney	Daniel McIntyre
Livingston	c	CM	10	(209) 394-8041	Gurpal Samra	Richard Warne	Martha Nateras	...	Gordon Wilkerson	William Eldridge	Paul Creighton
Lodi	c	CM	56	(209) 333-6800	Susan Hitchcock	Blair King	Randi Johl	James Krueger	Michael Pretz	Jerry Adams	Richard Prima
Loma Linda	c	CM	18	(909) 799-2810	...	Dennis Halloway	Pamela O'Camb	Rita Shirley-West	...	...	T. Jarb Thaipejr
Lomita *	c	CM	20	(310) 325-7110	Mark Waronek	Tom Odom	Dawn Tomita	...	...	...	Wendell Johnson
Lompoc	c	CM	41	(805) 736-1261	Dick Dewees	Gary Keefe	Jane Green	John Walk	Linual White	William Brown	Larry Bean
Long Beach	c	CM	461	(562) 570-6621	Beverly O'Neill	...	Larry Herrera	Michael Killebrew	David Ellis	Anthony Batts	Christine Andersen
Loomis *	t	CM	6	(916) 652-1840	Tom Millward	Perry Beck	Crickett Strock	Roger Carroll	Dave Wheeler	Dave Harris	Brian Fragiao
Los Alamitos	c	CM	11	(562) 431-3538	Frederick Freeman	...	Sue Vanderpool	...	...	Michael McCrary	...
Los Altos *	c	CM	27	(650) 947-2740	Curtis Cole	Philip Rose	Susan Kitchens	Starla Robinson	...	...	...
Los Altos Hills	t	CM	7	(650) 941-7222	Dean Warshawsky	Carl Cahill	Karen Jost	Sarah Ragsdale	...	...	Henry Louie
Los Angeles	c	MC	3694	(213) 485-2881	Richard Riordan	William Fujioka	J. Carey	...	William Bamattre	Bernard Parks	...
Los Banos	c	CM	25	(209) 827-7000	Michael Amabile	Stephen Rath	...	Melinda Wall	Chet Guintini	Michael Hughes	Ray DeSa
Los Gatos	t	CM	28	(408) 354-6832	Mike Wasserman	...	Marian Cosgrove	Stephen Conway	...	Scott Seaman	...
Lynwood	c	CM	69	(310) 603-0220	Fernando Pedroza	Roger Haley	Andrea Hooper	Christy Valencia	...	...	Paul Nguyen
Madera	c	CM	43	(559) 661-5400	...	David Tooley	Sonia Alvarez	Michael Hartman	...	Michael Kime	Dave Chumley
Malibu	c	CM	12	(310) 456-2489	Andy Stern	...	Lisa Pope	...	...	...	Yugal Lall
Mammoth Lakes	t	CM	7	(760) 934-8989	Rick Wood	Rob Clark	Anita Hatter	Brad Koehn	...	Michael Donnelly	Raymond Jarvis
Manhattan Beach	c	CM	33	(310) 802-5000	Linda Wilson	G. Dolan	Liza Tamura	...	Dennis Groat	Ernest Klevesahl	Neil Miller
Manteca *	c	CM	49	(209) 239-8414	Willie Weatherford	Robert Adams	Joann Tilton	Suzanne Mutimer	George Quaresma	Charles Halford	Mark Houghton
Marina	c	CM	25	(831) 884-1211	I. M.-McCutchon	Anthony Altfeld	Joy Junsay	...	Harold Kelley	...	Charles Johnson
Martinez	c	CM	35	(510) 372-3522	...	Donald Blubaugh	...	...	...	...	...
Marysville	c	CM	12	(530) 749-3901	Bill Harris	Stephen Casey	Billie Fangman	Dixon Coulter	...	Bret Smith	David Lamon
Maywood	c	CM	28	(323) 562-5000	...	Edward Ahrens	Jose Ceja	...	...	Bruce Leflar	...
Mc Farland	c	CM	9	(805) 792-3091	...	...	...	...	...	...	...
Mendota	c	MC	7	(559) 655-3291	Joseph Riofrio	Gabriel Gonzalez	Brenda Carter	...	Doug Hicks	...	Domingo Morales
Menlo Park	c	CM	30	(650) 858-3370	Nicholas Jellins	Glen Rojas	...	Carol Augustine	...	Christopher Boyd	Kent Steffens
Merced	c	CM	63	(209) 385-6834	...	James Marshall	...	Bradley Grant	Kenneth Mitten	Mark Dossetti	John Raggio
Mill Valley	c	CM	13	(415) 388-4033	Christopher Raker	Anne Montgomery	Mary Herr	Eric Erikson	...	...	Wayne Bush
Millbrae	c	CM	20	(650) 259-2334	Robert Gottschalk	Ralph Jaeck	Deborah Konkol	...	Dennis Haag	Thomas Hitchcock	Ron Popp
Milpitas	c	CM	62	(408) 586-3090	Jose Esteves	...	Gail Blalock	Emma Karlen	Bill Weisgerber	Charles Lawson	...
Mission Viejo *	c	CM	93	(949) 470-3000	John Paul Ledesma	Dennis Wilberg	Karen Hamman	...	...	...	Loren Anderson
Modesto *	c	CM	188	(209) 577-5200	Jim Ridenour	...	Jean Zahr	Wayne Padilla	James Miguel	Roy Wasden	Nicholas Pinhey
Monrovia	c	CM	36	(626) 932-5550	Robert Hammond	Scott Ochoa	Linda Proctor	...	C. Donovan	Roger Johnson	David Fike
Montclair	c	CM	33	(909) 626-8571	Paul Eaton	Lee McDougal	Donna Jackson	Richard Beltran	Dan Tapia	Chester Thompson	Marilyn Staats

Directory 1/9 continued — OFFICIALS IN U.S. MUNICIPALITIES 2,500 AND OVER IN POPULATION

Jurisdiction	Type	Form of govern- ment	2000 Popu- lation (000)	Main telephone number	Chief elected official	Appointed administrator	Clerk of the governing board	Chief financial officer	Fire chief	Police chief	Public works director
CALIFORNIA continued											
Monte Sereno	c	CM	3	(408) 354-7635	Erin Garner	Brian Loventhal	A. Chelemengos	Sue L'Heureux	...	...	...
Montebello	c	CM	62	(323) 887-1200	Ed Vasquez	Richard Torres	Robert King	Chickwan Tam	Jim Cox	G. Couso-Vasquez	Ted Spaceff
Monterey	c	CM	29	(831) 646-3765	Daniel Albert	Fred Meurer	Bonnie Gawf	Don Rhoads	Gregory Glass	...	Bill Reichmuth
Monterey Park	c	CM	60	(626) 307-1410	Betty Chu	...	David Barron	David Dong	Cathy Orchard	Jones Moy	Ronald Merry
Moorpark *	c	CM	31	(805) 517-6200	Patrick Hunter	Steven Kueny	...	Johnny Ea	Robert Roper	Bob Brooks	Ken Gilbert
Moraga	t	CM	16	(925) 376-2590	Lori Landis	Philip Vince	...	Jennifer Lau	...	Brad Kearns	Daniel Bernie
Moreno Valley	c	CM	142	(909) 413-3000	...	Robert Gutierrez	Alice Reed	Steve Chapman	...	...	Trent Pulliam
Morgan Hill	c	CM	33	(408) 779-7278	Dennis Kennedy	J. Tewes	Irma Torrez	John Dilles	...	Bruce Cumming	James Ashcraft
Morro Bay *	c	CM	10	(805) 772-6200	Janice Peters	Robert Hendrix	Bridgett Bauer	Susan Slayton	Mike Pond	John DeRohan	Bruce Ambo
Mount Shasta	c	CM	3	(530) 926-7510	Audra Gibson	...	Prudence Kennedy	Theodore Marconi	Joseph Spini	Robert Montz	Darrell Hook
Mountain View	c	CM	70	(650) 903-6309	...	Kevin Duggan	Angee Salvador	Robert Locke	Marc Revere	Scott Vermeer	Cathy Lazarus
Murrieta	c	MC	44	(951) 304-2489	...	Rick Dudley	Kay Vinson	Teri Ferro	Philip Armentrout	Mark Wright	James Kinley
Napa	c	CM	72	(707) 257-9500	Ed Henderson	Michael Parness	Pam Nigliazzo	Jed Christensen	...	Dan Monez	Mike O'Bryon
National City	c	CM	54	(619) 336-4300	Nicholas Inzunza	Chris Zapata	Michael Dalla	Bill Yeoman	Rod Juniel	Adolfo Gonzales	Roberto Saucedo
Needles	c	CM	4	(760) 326-2113	Pete Dwyer	Richard Rowe	...	Virginia Tasker	Robert Lyons	Mark Taylor	...
Nevada City *	c	CM	3	(530) 265-2496	...	Mark Miller	Cathy Barnes	Catrina Andes	Greg Wasley	Louis Trovato	Verne Taylor
Newark	c	CM	42	(510) 790-7267	David Smith	John Becker	F. Miller-Rogers	...	Demetrious Shaffer	Ray Samuels	Dennis Jones
Newman	c	CM	7	(209) 862-3725	John Fantazia	Michael Holland	...	...	Melvin Souza	Michael Brady	Ernie Garza
Newport Beach	c	CM	70	(949) 644-3300	Steve Bromberg	Homer Bludau	Lavonne Harkless	...	Timothy Riley	Robert McDonell	Steve Badum
Norco	c	CM	24	(951) 735-3900	Herbert Higgins	Jeffery Allred	Debra McNay	...	Jack Frye	...	Bill Thompson
Norwalk	c	CM	103	(562) 929-5700	Michael Mendez	Ernie Garcia	Gail Vasquez	James Weber	...	...	Gary Di Corpo
Novato *	c	CM	47	(415) 899-8900	...	Daniel Keen	Shirley Gremmels	...	...	Joseph Kreins	...
Oakdale	c	CM	15	(209) 847-3031	Pat Kuhn	Steven Hallam	Nancy Lilly	Albert Auila	Michael Wilkinson	Gary Hampton	John Word
Oakland	c	MC	399	(510) 238-3301	Jerry Brown	Deborah Edgerly	Ceda Floyd	William Noland	Gerald Simon	Richard Word	...
Oakley *	c	CM	25	(925) 625-7000	Kevin Romick	Bryan Montgomery	Nancy Ortenblad	Paul Abelson	...	Chris Thorsen	...
Oceanside *	c	CM	161	(760) 435-3500	James Wood	Peter Weiss	Barbara Wayne	...	Terry Garrison	Frank McCoy	...
Ojai	c	CM	7	(805) 646-5581	Sue Horgan	Jere Kersnar	Carlon Strobel	Susie Mears	...	Bruce Norris	Mike Culver
Ontario	c	CM	158	(909) 395-2442	Gary Ovitt	Gregory Devereaux	Traci McGinley	Yee Grant	Jim Bowman	James Doyle	Kenneth Jeske
Orange	c	CM	128	(714) 744-5500	Mark Murphy	John Sibley	Cassandra Cathcart	...	Vince Bonacker	Andy Romero	Harry Thomas
Orange Cove	c	CM	7	(559) 626-4488	Victor Lopez	...	June Bracamontes	Ross Holliday	Bob Terry	L. Wright	...
Orinda	c	CM	17	(925) 253-4200	Laura Abrams	Janet Keeter	Judith Hanson	...	...	...	Mark Lowery
Orland *	c	CM	6	(530) 865-1600	Paul Barr	Joseph Riker	...	...	Jeff Gomes	Robert Pasero	Jere Schmitke
Oroville	c	CM	13	(530) 538-2407	...	Sharon Atteberry	...	Diane MacMillan	David Pittman	Mitchel Brown	Eric Teitelman
Oxnard	c	CM	170	(805) 385-7590	Manuel Lopez	Edmund Sotelo	Daniel Martinez	Susan Winder	W. Milligan	Arthur Lopez	Granville Bowman
Pacific Grove *	c	CM	15	(831) 648-3100	Daniel Cort	James Colangelo	...	James Becklenberg	Andrew Miller	Darius Engles	...
Pacifica	c	CM	38	(650) 738-7301	Peter DeJarnatt	...	Kathy O'Connell	Maureen Lennon	Andrew Stark	...	Scott Holmes
Palm Desert	c	CM	41	(760) 346-0611	Jean Benson	Carlos Ortega	Sheila Gilligan	Paul Gibson	...	...	...
Palm Springs	c	CM	42	(760) 323-8200	William Kleindienst	David Ready	Patricia Sanders	Thomas Kanarr	Bary Freet	Gary Jeandron	David Barakian
Palmdale	c	CM	116	(661) 267-5400	...	Stephen Williams	Victoria Hancock	...	...	...	Leon Swain
Palo Alto	c	CM	58	(650) 329-2376	...	Frank Benest	Donna Rogers	...	Nicholas Marinaro	Lynne Johnson	Glenn Roberts
Palos Verdes Estates *	c	CM	13	(310) 378-0383	James Goodhart	Joseph Hoefgen	...	...	...	Dan Dreiling	Allan Rigg
Paradise	t	CM	26	(530) 872-6291	Daniel Wentland	Charles Rough	Frankie Rutledge	Rodney Davenport	Jim Broshears	...	Albert McGreehan
Paramount	c	CM	55	(562) 220-2027	Gene Daniels	...	Lana Chikami	Jose Gomez	...	...	Gil Ferreira
Parlier	c	CM	11	(559) 646-3545	Armando Lopez	Lou Martinez	Dorothy Garza	Patricia Barboza	...	Ismael Soliz	Rudy Vela
Pasadena	c	CM	133	(626) 405-4000	Johnny Isbell	Cynthia Kurtz	...	Steven Stark	...	...	Arlington Rodgers
Patterson	c	CM	11	(209) 892-8000	David Keller	M. Morris	Maricela Vela	Margaret Souza	James Kinnear	Tyrone Spencer	Ignacio Lopez
Perris	c	CM	36	(951) 943-6100	Daryl Busch	Richard Belmudez	Margaret Rey	Ron Carr	Tim Williams	Guy Kestell	Ahmad Ansari
Petaluma	c	CM	54	(707) 778-4340	...	Michael Bierman	Gayle Peterson	William Thomas	Chris Albertson	...	Richard Skladzien
Pico Rivera *	c	CM	63	(562) 942-2000	...	Charles Fuentes	Gloria Orosco	...	...	Michael Rothans	Michael Moore
Piedmont	c	MC	10	(510) 420-3040	...	...	Ann Swift	Mark Bichsel	John Speakman	John Moilan	Larry Rosenberg
Pinole	c	CM	19	(510) 724-9000	Maria Alegria	Belinda Espinosa	Elizabeth Grimes	Catherine Heater	James Parrott	Theodore Barnes	Gordon Freeman
Pismo Beach	c	CM	8	(805) 773-4657	Mary Ann Reiss	Kevin Rice	Lori Grigsby	...	Matt Jenkins	Joseph Cortez	Dennis Delzeit
Pittsburg	c	CM	56	(925) 252-4878	Yvonne Beals	Marc Grisham	Lillian Pride	Marie Simons	...	Aaron Baker	John Fuller
Placentia *	c	CM	46	(714) 993-8117	Scott Brady	Robert Dominguez	Patrick Melia	Steven Brisco	Chip Prather	...	...
Placerville	c	CM	9	(530) 642-5200	...	John Driscoll	...	...	...	Steve Brown	Gary Valladao
Pleasant Hill	c	CM	32	(925) 671-5270	Suzanne Angeli	...	Doris Nilsen	Richard Ricci	...	Michael Phalen	Leary Wong
Pleasanton *	c	CM	63	(925) 931-5048	Jennifer Hosterman	Nelson Fialho	Karen Diaz	David Culver	William Cody	Michael Fraser	Robert Wilson
Plymouth *	c	CM	..	(209) 245-6941	Michael O'Meara	Gene Albaugh	Gloria Stoddard	Jeffrey Gardner	...	Michael Prismich	Selby Beck
Pomona *	c	CM	149	(909) 620-2491	Edward Cortez	Douglas Dunlap	Elizabeth Villeral	Paula Chamberlain	...	James Lewis	Chris Vogt
Port Hueneme *	c	CM	21	(805) 986-6500	Maricela Morales	David Norman	...	Robert Bravo	...	Fernando Estrella	Andres Santamaria
Porterville	c	CM	39	(209) 782-7466	Gordon Woods	John Longley	...	...	S. Guyton	Silver Rodriguez	...
Portola	c	CM	2	(530) 832-4216	Bill Adamson	James Murphy	...	...	Curtis Marshall	...	Bill Whitener
Portola Valley	t	MC	4	(650) 851-1700	...	Angela Howard	Sharon Hanlon	...	...	...	Howard Young
Poway *	c	CM	48	(858) 668-4400	Michael Cafagna	Rodney Gould	L. Shae	Andrew White	...	Todd Frank	Kevin Haupt
Rancho Cordova	c	CM	57	(916) 851-8700	...	Ted Gaebler	Lillian Hare	Donna Silva	...	Thomas McMahon	Cyrus Abhar
Rancho Cucamonga *	c	CM	127	(909) 477-2700	William Alexander	Jack Lam	Debra Adams	Tamara Layne	Peter Bryan	...	...
Rancho Mirage *	c	CM	13	(760) 324-4511	G. Hobart	Patrick Pratt	Elena Keeran	Scott Morgan	...	...	Bruce Harry
Rancho Palos Verdes	c	CM	41	(310) 377-0360	Larry Clark	Carolyn Lehr	...	Dennis McLean	...	...	Dean Allison
Rancho Santa Margarita *	c	CM	47	(949) 635-1800	Jerry Holloway	Steven Hayman	Molly McLaughlin	...	...	Chuck Wilmot	Tom Wheeler
Red Bluff	c	CM	13	(530) 527-2605	Forrest Flynn	Martin Nichols	Gloria Shepard	M. Vanwamerdam	Michael Damon	Al Shamblin	Gary Antone
Redding *	c	CM	80	(530) 225-4065	Dick Dickerson	Kurt Starman	C. Strohmayer	Stephen Strong	Gilbert Fry	Leonard Moty	...
Redlands *	c	CM	63	(909) 798-7510	Jon Harrison	Nabar Martinez	Lorrie Poyzer	Tina Kundig	Jim Drabinski	James Bueermann	Ronald Mutter
Redondo Beach	c	CM	63	(310) 372-1171	Gregory Hill	...	Sandy Forest	Diana Moreno	Anthon Beck	Robert Luman	Sylvia Glazer
Redwood City	c	CM	75	(650) 780-7000	...	Peter Ingram	Patricia Howe	Brian Ponty	Gerald Kohlmann	Carlos Bolanos	...
Reedley	c	CM	20	(559) 637-4200	Ray Soleno	Brian Nakamura	Elizabeth Vines	Lori Oken	David Powell	Douglas Johnson	Rocky Rogers
Rialto	c	CM	91	(909) 820-2525	Grace Vargas	Henry Garcia	Barbara McGee	June Overholt	Stephen Wells	Michael Meyers	Robert Harary
Richmond	c	CM	99	(510) 620-6602	Irma Anderson	William Lindsay	Delores Holmes	James Goins	Michael Banks	Chris Magnus	Willie Haywood
Ridgecrest *	c	CM	24	(760) 499-5000	Marshall Holloway	Harvey Rose	Rita Gable	...	...	...	Dennis Speer
Rio Dell	c	CM	3	(707) 764-3532	...	...	...	...	...	Pat Medina	...
Rio Vista	c	CM	4	(707) 374-6451	...	...	...	Misty Cheng	Keith Tadewald	Larry Profitt	David Melilli
Ripon	c	CM	10	(209) 599-2108	Charles Winn	Everett Compton	Lynette Van Laar	...	...	Richard Bull	Ted Johnston
Riverbank	c	CM	15	(209) 869-7101	Chris Crifasi	Richard Holmer	...	...	...	Art Voortman	Laurie Barton
Riverside	c	CM	255	(951) 826-5553	Ronald Loveridge	...	Colleen Nicol	Paul Sundeen	Dave Carlson	Russ Leach	Siobhan Foster
Rocklin	c	CM	36	(916) 625-5000	George Magnuson	Carlos Urrutia	Barbara Ivanusich	Kimberly Sarkovich	Bill Mikesell	Mark Siemens	Kent Foster
Rohnert Park	c	CM	42	(707) 588-2227	Armando Flores	Stephen Donley	...	Sandra Lipitz	...	...	...
Rolling Hills	c	CM	1	(310) 377-1521	...	Anton Dahlerbruch	Marilyn Kern	Nan Huang	...	...	...
Rolling Hills Estates	c	CM	7	(310) 377-1577	Susan Seamans	Douglas Prichard	...	...	...	...	...
Rosemead *	c	CM	53	(626) 569-2100	John Tran	Oliver Chi	Nina Castruita	...	...	...	...
Roseville	c	CM	79	(916) 774-5475	...	W. Robinson	Sonia Orozco	...	Ken Wagner	Joel Neves	Robert Jensen
Ross	t	MC	2	(415) 453-1453	...	...	...	...	...	...	...

Directory 1/9 continued **OFFICIALS IN U.S. MUNICIPALITIES 2,500 AND OVER IN POPULATION**

Jurisdiction	Type	Form of govern-ment	2000 Popu-lation (000)	Main telephone number	Chief elected official	Appointed administrator	Clerk of the governing board	Chief financial officer	Fire chief	Police chief	Public works director
CALIFORNIA continued											
Sacramento	c	CM	407	(916) 264-5726	Heather Fargo	Ray Kerridge	Valerie Burrowes	Thomas Sinclair	Dennis Smith	Arturo Venegas	Michael Kashiwagi
Salinas	c	CM	151	(831) 758-7254	. . .	David Mora	Ann Camel	John Copeland	Daniel Hernandez	. . .	John Fair
San Anselmo	c	CM	12	(415) 258-4600	. . .	Debra Stutsman	. . .	Janet Pendoley	. . .	Charles Maynard	Rabi Elias
San Bernardino	c	MC	185	(909) 384-5161	Judith Valles	Frederick Wilson	Rachel Clark	Barbara Pachon	Larry Pitzer	. . .	Michael Hays
San Bruno *	c	CM	40	(650) 616-7056	Larry Franzella	Constance Jackson	Carol Bonner	John O'Leary	Dan Voreyer	Lee Violett	Jane Chambers
San Buenaventura (Ventura) *	c	CM	100	(805) 654-7853	Carl Morehouse	Rick Cole	Mabi Plisky	Jay Panzic	Mike Lavery	Pat Miller	Ronald Calkins
San Carlos	c	CM	27	(650) 802-4100	. . .	Mark Weiss	Christine Boland	. . .	Doug Fry	Greg Rothaus	Parviz Mokhtari
San Clemente	c	CM	49	(949) 361-8324	Stephany Dorey	G. Scarborough	Myrna Erway	Thomas Rendina	. . .	. . .	David Lund
San Diego	c	MC	1223	(619) 236-6363	Susan Golding	Jay Goldstone	Charles Abdelnour	. . .	Jeff Bowman	William Lansdowne	. . .
San Dimas	c	CM	34	(909) 394-6200	Curtis Morris	Blaine Michaelis	Ina Rios	. . .	. . .	. . .	Krishna Patel
San Fernando	c	CM	23	(818) 898-1200	Julie Ruelas	Jose Pulido	Elena Chavez	Lorena Quijano	. . .	Anthony Alba	Ron Ruiz
San Francisco	c	MC	776	(415) 557-4800	Willie Brown	Edwin Lee	Gloria Young	Chris Vein	Paul Tabacco	Fred Lau	. . .
San Gabriel	c	CM	39	(626) 308-2800	. . .	P. Paules	Cynthia Trujillo	Thomas Marston	Joseph Nestor	David Lawton	. . .
San Jacinto	c	CM	23	(951) 654-7337	Dale Stubblefield	Barry McClellan	Dorothy Chouinard	Bernard Simon	Bob Michaels	Kevin Vest	Michael Emberton
San Jose	c	CM	894	(408) 277-4000	Ron Gonzales	Debra Figone	Patricia O'Hearn	Scott Johnson	Dale Foster	Tom Wheatley	Katy Allen
San Juan Bautista	c	CM	1	(831) 623-4661	Arturo Medina	Jennifer Coile	Shawna Serna	Janet Locey	Rick Cokley	Curtis Hill	. . .
San Juan Capistrano	c	CM	33	(949) 493-1171	. . .	Dave Adams	Margaret Monahan	Cynthia Russell	. . .	. . .	Amy Amirani
San Leandro	c	CM	79	(510) 577-3358	Sheila Young	John Jermanis	Gayle Petersen	Jesse Balola	. . .	Joseph Kitchen	Robert Rockett
San Luis Obispo	c	CM	44	(805) 781-7100	David Romero	Kenneth Hampian	Lee Price	William Statler	Wolfgang Knabe	Deborah Linden	. . .
San Marcos	c	CM	54	(760) 744-1050	F. Smith	R. Gittings	Susan Vasquez	Liliane Serio	Larry Webb	Kim Quaco	Michael Mercereau
San Marino	c	CM	12	(626) 300-0700	. . .	. . .	Carol Robb	Lisa Bailey	John Penido	Arl Farris	John Alderson
San Mateo	c	CM	92	(650) 522-7260	. . .	Arne Croce	Norma Gomez	Hossein Golestan	Brian Kelly	Susan Manheimer	Larry Patterson
San Pablo	c	CM	30	(510) 215-3000	. . .	Brock Arner	. . .	Bradley Ward	. . .	Douglas Krathwohl	Adele Ho
San Rafael	c	CM	56	(415) 485-3063	Al Boro	. . .	. . .	Kenneth Nordhoff	Robert Marcucci	Michael Cronin	Andy Preston
San Ramon	c	CM	44	(925) 973-2500	. . .	Herbert Moniz	Patricia Edwards	Greg Rogers	. . .	Scott Holder	Joye Fukuda
Sand City	c	CM	. .	(831) 394-3054	David Pendergrass	Kelly Morgan	. . .	. . .	. . .	. . .	. . .
Sanger	c	CM	18	(559) 876-6303	. . .	Eugene Drinkhouse	Barbara Mergan	Carlos Sanchez	Clyde Clinton	Thomas Klose	John White
Santa Ana	c	CM	337	(714) 647-5340	Miguel Pulido	David Ream	Janice Guy	Francisco Gutierrez	Marc Martin	Paul Walters	Jim Ross
Santa Barbara *	c	CM	92	(805) 564-5316	Martha Blum	James Armstrong	Cynthia Rodriguez	Bob Peirson	Ronald Prince	Camerino Sanchez	. . .
Santa Clara	c	CM	102	(408) 615-2080	Patricia Mahan	Jennifer Sparacino	Rod Diridon	Mary Ann Parrot	Phillip Kleinheinz	Stephen Lodge	Stephen Yoshino
Santa Clarita	c	CM	151	(661) 259-2489	. . .	Kenneth Pulskamp	Sharon Dawson	. . .	. . .	. . .	. . .
Santa Cruz	c	CM	54	(831) 420-5040	Emily Reilly	Richard Wilson	Leslie Cook	David Culver	Ron Prince	Steve Belcher	Mark Dettle
Santa Fe Springs *	c	CM	17	(562) 868-0511	Joseph Serrano	Frederick Latham	Barbara Earl	Jose Gomez	Alex Rodriguez	. . .	Donald Jensen
Santa Maria	c	CM	77	(805) 925-0951	Laurence Lavagnino	Tim Ness	. . .	Lynda Snodgras	Frank Ortiz	Danny Macagni	Paul Karp
Santa Monica	c	CM	84	(310) 393-9975	Richard Bloom	P. Ewell	Maria Stewart	Carol Swindell	. . .	James Butts	Craig Perkins
Santa Paula	c	CM	28	(805) 525-4478	Richard Cook	Walter Bobkiewicz	Josie Herrera	Alvertina Rivera	. . .	Stephen MacKinnon	Clifford Finley
Santa Rosa	c	CM	147	(707) 543-3060	Michael Martini	Jeffrey Kolin	. . .	Ronald Bosworth	Tony Pini	Michael Dunbaugh	Rick Moshier
Santee *	c	CM	52	(619) 258-4100	Randy Voepel	Keith Till	Linda Troyan	Tim McDermott	Mike Rottenberg	. . .	. . .
Saratoga	c	CM	29	(408) 868-1200	Norm Kline	Dave Anderson	Cathleen Boyer	. . .	. . .	. . .	John Cherbone
Sausalito *	c	CM	7	(415) 289-4100	Michael Kelly	. . .	. . .	Louise Ho	Denis Walsh	Scott Paulin	Tom Birse
Scotts Valley	c	CM	11	(831) 440-5600	Randy Johnson	Charles Comstock	Judi Coffman	Steve Ando	. . .	Steven Lind	Kenneth Anderson
Seal Beach *	c	CM	24	(562) 431-2527	John Larson	David Carmany	Linda Devine	Greg Beaubien	. . .	Jeff Kirkpatrick	Mark Vukojevic
Seaside	c	CM	31	(831) 899-6700	Ralph Rubio	Ray Corpuz	Joyce Newsome	Daphne Hodgson	Jerry Wombacher	Anthony Sollicito	Diana Ingersoll
Sebastapol *	c	CM	7	(707) 823-1153	. . .	David Brennan	Hollie Fiori	Ronald Puccinelli	John Zanzi	Jeffrey Weaver	Richard Emig
Selma *	c	CM	19	(559) 891-2200	Don Tow	D. B. Heusser	Melanie Carter	Judy Bier	Jeffrey Kestly	Thomas Whiteside	Robert Weaver
Shafter *	c	CM	12	(661) 746-5000	Cathy Prout	John Guinn	Dolores Robinson	Jo Barrick	. . .	Charlie Fivecoat	Mike James
Shasta Lake	c	MC	9	(530) 275-7400	Debra Duryee	Don Moore	Eula Morrow	Carol Martin	. . .	. . .	Dennis Daily
Sierra Madre	c	CM	10	(626) 355-7135	John Buchanan	. . .	N. Shollenberger	. . .	Roger Lowe	Marilyn Diaz	Bruce Inman
Signal Hill *	c	CM	9	(562) 989-7304	. . .	Kenneth Farfsing	. . .	Dennis MacArthur	. . .	Thomas Sonoff	. . .
Simi Valley	c	CM	111	(805) 583-6700	Paul Miller	Michael Sedell	. . .	. . .	. . .	Mark Laynew	Timothy Nanson
Solana Beach	c	CM	12	(858) 720-2400	. . .	David Ott	Angela Ivey	Gavin Cohen	. . .	. . .	. . .
Soledad	c	CM	11	(831) 678-3963	. . .	Noelia Chapa	. . .	. . .	Jesse Casillas	Richard Cox	Clif Price
Solvang *	c	CM	5	(805) 688-5575	Ken Palmer	Bradley Vidro	Lynne Bartz	Dana Waite	. . .	. . .	Tom Rowe
Sonoma *	c	CM	9	(707) 938-3681	Doug McKesson	. . .	Gay Rainsbarger	. . .	Phillip Garcia	Bret Sackett	Al Bandur
Sonora *	c	CM	4	(209) 532-4541	. . .	Greg Applegate	. . .	Karen Stark	Mike Barrows	Mace McIntosh	. . .
South El Monte	c	CM	21	(626) 579-6540	. . .	Gary Chicots	Kathy Gonzales	Maria Zamora	. . .	. . .	. . .
South Gate	c	CM	96	(323) 563-9501	Hector De La Torre	. . .	Carmen Avalos	Kenneth Louie	. . .	. . .	Joseph Comstock
South Lake Tahoe	c	CM	23	(530) 542-6000	. . .	David Jinkens	Suzan Alessi	Christine Vuletich	Michael Chandler	Donald Muren	. . .
South Pasadena *	c	CM	24	(626) 403-7200	. . .	Lilian Myers	Sally Kilby	Josh Betta	Jerry Wallace	Daniel Watson	Shin Furukawa
South San Francisco *	c	CM	60	(650) 877-8500	Joseph Fernekes	Barry Nagel	Sylvia Payne	Jim Steele	Russell Lee	Mark Raffaelli	Terry White
St. Helena	c	CM	5	(707) 967-2792	. . .	. . .	. . .	Tamera Haas	. . .	Bert Johansson	Myke Praul
Stanton	c	CM	37	(714) 379-9222	David Shawver	John Wager	Brenda Green	. . .	. . .	Robert Eason	. . .
Stockton	c	CM	243	(209) 937-8212	Gary Podesto	J Palmer	Katherine Meissner	Mark Moses	William Gillis	Mark Herder	James Giottonini
Suisun City *	c	CM	26	(707) 421-7300	Pete Sanchez	Suzanne Bragdon	Linda Hobson	Mark Joseph	Michael O'Brian	Edmond Dadisho	Fernando Bravo
Sunnyvale *	c	CM	131	(408) 730-7490	. . .	Amy Chan	Gail Borowski	Mary Bradley	. . .	. . .	Marvin Rose
Susanville	c	CM	13	(530) 252-5100	Rodney De Boer	Luann Rainey	Debra Magginetti	Robert Porfiri	Stuart Ratner	C. Gallagher	Craig Platt
Sutter Creek	c	CM	2	(209) 267-5647	Brent Parsons	J. Duke	Judy Allen	. . .	Butch Martin	. . .	George Christner
Taft	c	CM	6	(661) 763-1222	Cliff Thompson	. . .	Louise Hudgens	Teresa Statler	Ken Scott	Bertus Pumphrey	Gary Dabbs
Tehachapi	c	CM	10	(661) 822-2200	Philip Smith	Jason Caudle	Jeanette Kelley	R. Cunningham	Tim McLaughlin	. . .	Dennis Wahlstrom
Temecula *	c	CM	57	(951) 506-5100	Chuck Washington	Shawn Nelson	Susan Jones	Genie Roberts	Glenn Patterson	Jerry Williams	William Hughes
Temple City	c	CM	33	(626) 285-2171	Peter Zovak	Charles Martin	Mary Flandrick	. . .	. . .	. . .	Janice Stroud
Thousand Oaks	c	CM	117	(805) 449-2144	Dennis Gillette	Scott Mitnick	Linda Lawrence	Candis Hong	Michael LaPlant	Dennis Carpenter	Mark Watkins
Tiburon	t	CM	8	(415) 435-7373	. . .	Margaret Curran	Diane Crane	. . .	. . .	Matthew Odetto	Patrick Echols
Torrance	c	CM	137	(310) 618-2960	. . .	LeRoy Jackson	Sue Herbers	Eric Tsao	Rick Bongard	James Herren	Brooks Bell
Tracy	c	CM	56	(209) 831-4100	George Bilbrey	. . .	. . .	Zane Johnston	. . .	David Krauss	Nicholas Pinhey
Truckee	t	CM	13	(530) 582-7700	. . .	. . .	Patricia Osborne	Jill Olsen	. . .	Dan Boon	Daniel Wilkins
Tulare	c	CM	43	(559) 684-4200	Richard Ortega	Darrel Pyle	Anna Vital	Darlene Thompson	Michael Threlkeld	Roger Hill	Lew Nelson
Turlock	c	CM	55	(209) 668-5540	. . .	Tim Kerr	. . .	. . .	Mark Langley	Lonald Lott	Cliff Martin
Tustin	c	CM	67	(714) 573-3000	Tracy Worley	William Huston	Maria Huizar	Ronald Nault	. . .	Steve Foster	Tim Serlet
Twentynine Palms	c	CM	14	(760) 367-6799	. . .	Michael Tree	Charlene Sherwood	Ronald Peck	. . .	. . .	Bobby Matz
Ukiah	c	CM	15	(707) 463-6200	Mark Ashiku	Candace Horsley	Marie Ulvila	Michael McCann	Kurt Latipow	John Williams	Diana Steele
Union City	c	CM	66	(510) 471-3232	Mark Green	Larry Cheeves	. . .	. . .	Gerald Simon	Randy Ulibarri	. . .
Upland	c	CM	68	(909) 931-4100	John Pomierski	Robb Quincey	Stephanie Rios	Stephen Dunn	John Scanlon	Martin Thouvenell	George Turner
Vacaville *	c	CM	88	(707) 449-5100	Leonard Augustine	David Van Kirk	M. Thornbrugh	Ken Campo	Brian Preciado	Rich Word	Dale Pfeiffer
Vallejo	c	CM	116	(707) 648-4527	Anthony Intintoli	Joseph Tanner	Allison Villarante	Frederick Wright	Donald Parker	Robert Nichelini	Mark Akuba
Victorville	c	CM	64	(760) 955-5000	. . .	Jon Roberts	Carolee Bates	. . .	John Becker	. . .	Guy Patterson
Villa Park	c	CM	5	(714) 998-1500	. . .	Kenneth Domer	. . .	. . .	. . .	. . .	. . .
Visalia	c	CM	91	(559) 713-4300	Jesus Gamboa	Steven Salomon	Randy Groom	. . .	George Sandoval	Jerry Barker	Russ Webber
Vista *	c	CM	89	(760) 726-1340	Morris Vance	Rita Geldert	Marci Kilian	. . .	Gary Fisher	Ed Prendergast	Mauro Garcia

Directory 1/9 continued **OFFICIALS IN U.S. MUNICIPALITIES 2,500 AND OVER IN POPULATION**

Jurisdiction	Type	Form of govern-ment	2000 Popu-lation (000)	Main telephone number	Chief elected official	Appointed administrator	Clerk of the governing board	Chief financial officer	Fire chief	Police chief	Public works director
CALIFORNIA continued											
Walnut	c	CM	30	(909) 595-7543	Joaquin Lim	...	Teresa DeDios	Christine Londo	...	...	Mary Rooney
Walnut Creek	c	CM	64	(925) 943-5899	Gary Skrel	Gary Pokorny	...	...	...	Thomas Soberanes	Daniel Richardson
Wasco *	c	CM	21	(661) 758-7200	Larry Pearson	Ronald Mittag	Vickie Hight	John Wooner	Dennis Thompson	Joe Pilkington	Marty Jones
Waterford	c	MC	6	(209) 874-2328	Charles Turner	Charles Deschenes	Lori Martin	...	...	...	Matt Erickson
Watsonville	c	CM	44	(831) 768-3010	Antonio Rivas	Carlos Palacios	L. Washington	Marc Pimentel	Mark Bisbee	Terrence Medina	David Koch
Weed *	c	CM	2	(530) 938-5020	Mel Boroali	Earl Wilson	Deborah Salvestrin	Kelly McKinnis	Darin Quigley	Martin Nicholas	Craig Sharp
West Covina	c	CM	105	(626) 939-8450	Steve Herfert	Andrew Pasmant	Janet Berry	Thomas Bachman	Richard Greene	Frank Willis	Shannon Yauchzee
West Hollywood *	c	CM	35	(323) 848-6400	...	Paul Arevalo	...	Anil Gandhy	...	...	...
West Sacramento *	c	CM	31	(916) 617-4500	...	Toby Ross	Kryss Rankin	Leigh Keicher	Frederick Postel	Dan Drummond	...
Westlake Village	c	CM	8	(818) 706-1613	Christopher Mann	Raymond Taylor	Beth Schott	...	...	...	...
Westminster	c	CM	88	(714) 898-3311	Margie Rice	...	Marian Contreras	Sheri Peasley	...	Andrew Hall	Brad Fowler
Wheatland	c	CM	2	(530) 633-2761	...	Stephen Wright	...	...	...	...	...
Whittier	c	CM	83	(562) 464-3390	David Butler	Stephen Helvey	Kathryn Marshall	Rod Hill	...	David Singer	David Mochizuki
Williams	c	MC	3	(530) 473-2445	...	...	...	...	...	...	...
Willits	c	CM	5	(707) 459-4601	Thomas Lucier	Gordon Logan	Frances Schatz	Patricia Frost	...	John Brown	David Madrigal
Willows *	c	CM	6	(530) 934-7041	James Yoder	Michael Mistrot	Natalie Butler	Timothy Sailsbery	Wayne Peabody	William Spears	Kent Perkes
Windsor	t	CM	22	(707) 838-1000	Debora Fudge	J. Mullan	Maria Delao	...	...	Paul Day	Richard Burtt
Winters	c	CM	6	(530) 795-4910	Harold Anderson	John Donlevy	...	Shelly Gunby	...	Steve Godden	Karen Honer
Woodlake	c	CM	6	(559) 564-8055	Jack Ritchie	Bill Lewis	Ruth Gonzalez	...	...	John Zapalac	Ruben De Leon
Woodland	c	CM	49	(530) 661-5811	...	Mark Deven	Sue Vannucci	Joan Drayton	Karl Diekman	Carey Sullivan	Gary Wegener
Woodside	t	CM	5	(650) 851-6790	...	Susan George	Janet Koelsch	...	...	...	...
Yorba Linda	c	CM	58	(714) 961-7100	...	Tamara Letourneau	Kathie Mendoza	Susan Hartman	...	Michael Messina	Mark Stowell
Yountville *	t	CM	2	(707) 944-8851	Cynthia Saucerman	Steven Rogers	Michelle Price	Richard Stranzl	Ernie Loveless	Doug Koford	Myke Praul
Yreka	c	CM	7	(530) 841-2324	Rory McNeil	Brian Meek	...	Rhetta Hogan	Peter Suter	Brian Bowles	Steven Neill
Yuba City	c	CM	60	(530) 822-4601	Bob Barkhouse	Steven Jepsen	...	Robin Bertagna	Marc Boomgaarden	Richard Doscher	...
Yucaipa	c	CM	41	(909) 797-2489	...	John Tooker	...	...	...	...	Raymond Casey
Yucca Valley	t	CM	16	(760) 369-7207	...	Andrew Takata	Janet Anderson	...	...	...	...
COLORADO											
Alamosa	c	CM	7	(719) 589-2593	Farris Bervig	Nathan Cherpeski	...	Hector Chavez	Donald Clayton	Ron Lindsey	Don Koskelin
Arvada *	c	CM	102	(720) 898-7000	Ken Fellman	Craig Kocian	Christine Koch	Victoria Runkle	...	Don Wick	James Root
Aspen	c	CM	5	(970) 920-5241	Rachel Richards	Steve Barwick	Kathryn Koch	...	...	T. Stephenson	Bob Gish
Aurora	c	CM	276	(303) 739-7000	Paul Tauer	Ronald Miller	Debra Johnson	John Gross	Casey Jones	Ricky Bennett	Darrell Hogan
Avon	t	CM	5	(970) 748-4000	Albert Reynolds	Larry Brooks	Patty McKenny	Scott Wright	...	Jeffrey Layman	Robert Reed
Basalt	t	CM	2	(970) 927-4701	Rick Stevens	Tom Baker	Pamela Schilling	Renae Gustine	...	Keith Ikeda	Betsy Suerth
Bayfield	t	MC	1	(970) 884-9544	James Harrmann	...	...	...	...	Jim Harrington	Robert Ludwig
Berthoud	t	MC	4	(970) 532-2643	Milan Karspeck	James White	Mary Cowdin	...	Steve Charles	William Wegener	Jose Huerta
Black Hawk *	c	CM	..	(303) 582-2292	David Spellman	Richard Lessner	Jeanie Magno	...	Robert Norris	Stephen Cole	Philo Shelton
Boulder *	c	CM	94	(303) 441-3090	Mark Ruzzin	Frank Bruno	Alisa Lewis	Robert Eichem	Larry Donner	Mark Beckner	Maureen Rait
Breckenridge *	t	CM	2	(970) 547-3159	Ernie Blake	Timothy Gagen	Mary Loufek	Judith Ferris	...	Rick Holman	Terry Perkins
Brighton	c	CM	20	(303) 655-2000	Janice Pawlowski	John Bramble	...	Bernadette Kimmey	...	Clint Blackhurst	Terry Benton
Broomfield	c	CM	38	(303) 469-3301	Karen Stuart	George Di Ciero	Russell Ragsdale	Gregory Demko	...	Thomas Deland	Dorian Brown
Brush *	c	MC	5	(970) 842-5001	Daniel Scalise	Monty Torres	Cathryn Smith	Alta Gosselink	Eric Ruhl	Mark Thomas	Rowena Pennell
Buena Vista	t	CM	2	(719) 395-8643	Cara Russell	Jerry L'Estrange	Diane Spomer	...	Darryl Pratt	Jimmy Tidwell	Roy Gertson
Burlington	c	MC	3	(719) 346-8652	Thomas Jacobucci	...	Patricia Maldonado	...	...	Randall Millburn	Tracy Tillman
Calhan	t	MC	..	(719) 347-2586	Gary Reimers	...	Cindy Tompkins	...	...	Buddy Johnson	Ryan Miller
Canon City	c	CM	15	(719) 269-9011	William Jackson	Steven Rabe	Rebecca Worthen	Hasmukh Patel	...	Daniel Shull	...
Carbondale	t	CM	5	(970) 963-2733	Michael Hassig	Tom Baker	Marcia Walter	Nancy Barnett	...	Eugene Schilling	Larry Ballenger
Castle Rock	t	CM	20	(303) 660-1015	...	Mark Stevens	Sally Misare	Pam Brockhaus	Arturo Morales	Joseph Lane	Bob Watts
Centennial	c	MC	107	(303) 734-4567	Randy Pye	J. Wedding-Scott	Gerry Cummins	Charles Montoya	...	Grayson Robinson	...
Central City	c	CM	..	(303) 582-5251	Bruce Schmalzr	Lynnette Hailey	Jennifer Novak	Cheryl McEachran	Gary Allen	James Saunders	Larry Wallerich
Cherry Hills Village	c	CM	5	(303) 789-2541	Doug Scott	Eric Ensey	Jennifer Pettinger	Karen Proctor	...	John Patterson	Kevin Louis
Collbran *	t	MC	..	(970) 487-3751	...	Edith Ann Power	...	...	...	...	...
Colorado Springs	c	CM	360	(719) 385-5900	...	Lorne Kramer	Kathryn Young	Steve Hilfers	Manuel Navarro	Luis Velez	Ronald Mitchell
Commerce City	c	CM	20	(303) 289-3612	...	Gerald Flannery	Judith Ridgeley	Roger Tinklenberg	...	R. Hebbard	Gregg Clements
Cortez *	c	CM	7	(970) 565-3402	Orly Lucero	Jay Harrington	Linda Smith	Kathi Moss	...	Roy Lane	Bruce Smart
Craig	c	CM	9	(970) 824-8151	Don Jones	James Ferree	Shirley Seely	Bruce Nelson	...	Walter Vanatta	William Earley
Crested Butte	t	CM	1	(970) 349-5338	...	Susan Parker	Eileen Hughes	Lois Rozman	...	Thomas Martin	Robert Gillie
Cripple Creek *	c	MC	1	(719) 689-2502	Ed Libby	Bill McPherson	Debra Blevins	...	...	...	...
Dacono	c	MC	3	(303) 833-2317	Wade Carlson	Karen Cumbo	Nancy Elliott	...	...	Thomas Davis	Jon Rabas
Del Norte	t	CM	1	(719) 657-2708	Dennis Murphy	Patsy Moreland	...	...	...	Jeffrey Sailee	Jack Glover
Delta *	c	CM	6	(970) 874-7566	William Seuell	Lanny Sloan	Mary Williams	Tod DeZeeuw	...	Richard Bacher	James Hatheway
Denver	c	MC	554	(303) 640-2613	...	...	Sherry Jackson	Margaret Browne	Roderick Juniel	Jerry Whitman	...
Dillon *	t	CM	..	(970) 468-2403	Barbara Davis	Devin Granbery	Jan Thomas	...	...	John Mackey	J Holgerson
Durango	c	CM	13	(970) 375-5050	Sidny Zink	Ronald LeBlanc	Amy Phillips	Sherry Eilbes	...	Albert Bell	Otha Rogers
Eagle	t	CM	3	(970) 328-6354	Roxie Deane	William Powell	Marilene Miller	...	...	...	Dustin Walls
Eaton *	t	CM	2	(970) 454-3338	Keith McIntyre	Gary Carsten	Erica Bagley	...	...	Randall Jacobson	George Spaedt
Edgewater	c	MC	5	(303) 238-7803	Ronalda Goodner	...	Laura Bock	...	Terry McBride	Dan Keough	Mike Ball
Elizabeth	t	CM	1	(303) 646-4166	Chris LaMay	...	Serena Brooks	...	...	...	Billy Holschuh
Englewood	c	CM	31	(303) 762-2300	Beverly Bradshaw	Gary Sears	Louchrisha Ellis	Francis Gryglewicz	Keith Lockwood	Chris Olson	Kenneth Ross
Erie	t	CM	6	(303) 926-2700	...	Mike Acimovic	...	...	...	Stephen Hasler	Judy Ding
Estes Park *	t	CM	5	(970) 586-5331	John Baudek	Randolf Repola	J. Williamson	Steve McFarland	Scott Dorman	Lowell Richardson	Scott Zurn
Evans	c	CM	9	(970) 339-5344	Harold Weisberg	Aden Hogan	Kim Betz	K. Von Achen	Jon Surbeck	Michael Guthrie	Earl Smith
Federal Heights	c	MC	12	(303) 428-3526	Dale Sparks	David Blanchard	Phyllis Schott	Gordon Maddock	Andrew Marsh	Lester Acker	Donald Pardis
Florence *	c	CM	3	(719) 784-4848	Merle Strickland	Tom Piltingsrud	Dori Williams	Patricia Mock	...	Guy Orazem	Martin Duran
Fort Collins	c	CM	118	(970) 221-6505	Ray Martinez	Darin Atteberry	Wanda Krajicek	Michael Freeman	John Mulligan	Stephen Roy	...
Fort Lupton *	c	MC	6	(303) 857-6694	Shannon Crespin	James Sidebottom	Barbara Rodgers	Claud Hanes	...	...	Ramon Hernandez
Fort Morgan	c	MC	11	(970) 867-4310	Jack Darnell	Michael Nagy	Nancy Lockwood	...	Michael Kirkendall	Keith Kuretich	...
Fountain	c	CM	15	(719) 382-8521	Kenneth Barela	Scott Trainor	Sharon Mosley	Kathleen Kuberka	Darin Anstine	John Morse	Gary King
Fraser	t	CM	..	(970) 726-5491	Dennis Soles	Jeffrey Durbin	Molly McCandless	...	...	...	Allen Nordin
Frederick *	t	CM	2	(303) 833-2388	Eric Doering	Derek Todd	Nanette Fornoff	Marcia Lierman	...	Gary Barbour	Allen Conway
Frisco	t	CM	2	(970) 668-5276	Bernie Zurbriggen	Michael Penny	Jo-Anne Tyson	...	...	Tom Wickman	Timothy Mack
Fruita	c	CM	6	(970) 858-3663	...	Clinton Kinney	...	Margaret Steelman	...	Mark Angelo	Tom Huston
Georgetown	t	CM	1	(303) 569-2555	Lynn Granger	Chuck Stearns	Merinel Williams	...	...	Dave Forristal	Howard Kimbrel
Glendale	c	CM	4	(303) 759-1513	Joe Rice	Jerry Peters	Theresa Teeters	Doris Williams	Richard McGowan	Ken Burge	...
Glenwood Springs *	c	CM	7	(970) 384-6400	Bruce Christensen	Jeffrey Hecksel	Robin Clemons	Michael Harman	Michael Piper	Terry Wilson	Robin Millyard
Golden	c	CM	17	(303) 384-8000	Charles Baroch	Michael Bestor	Susan Brooks	Jeffrey Hansen	John Bales	William Kilpatrick	Daniel Hartman
Granby	t	CM	1	(970) 887-2501	Ted Wang	David Huseman	Debbie Hess	Sharon Spurlin	...	Bill Housley	Scott Holley
Grand Junction	c	CM	41	(970) 244-1512	Bruce Hill	Laurie Kadrich	Stephanie Tuin	...	Rick Beaty	Gregory Morrison	Mark Relph
Grand Lake	c	MC	..	(970) 627-3435	...	Shane Hale	...	...	...	...	...

Directory 1/9 continued — OFFICIALS IN U.S. MUNICIPALITIES 2,500 AND OVER IN POPULATION

Jurisdiction	Type	Form of govern-ment	2000 Popu-lation (000)	Main telephone number	Chief elected official	Appointed administrator	Clerk of the governing board	Chief financial officer	Fire chief	Police chief	Public works director
COLORADO continued											
Greeley *	c	CM	76	(970) 350-9710	Jerry Wones	Roy Otto	Betsy Holder	Timothy Nash	Douglas Forsman	Jerry Garner	...
Greenwood Village	c	CM	11	(303) 773-0252	Nancy Sharpe	James Sanderson	Susan Phillips	Craig Larson	...	...	John Sheldon
Gunnison *	c	CM	5	(970) 641-8070	Stu Ferguson	Kenneth Coleman	Gail Davidson	Wendy Hanson	Dennis Spritzer	Greg Anderson	Tex Bradford
Gypsum *	t	CM	3	(970) 524-7514	Steve Carver	Jeffrey Shroll	Jenny Ellringer	Mark Silverthorn	...	...	Don Eaton
Hayden	t	CM	1	(970) 276-3741	Charles Grobe	Russell Martin	Lisa Johnston	...	...	Cyril Lenahan	Franklin Fox
Hudson *	t	MC	1	(303) 536-9311	Neal Pontius	Joseph Racine	Judy Larson	...	...	...	...
Ignacio	t	CM	..	(970) 563-9494	Katherine Gurule	Miguel Sandoval	Georgann Valdez	...	...	Kirk Phillips	...
Johnstown	t	CM	3	(970) 587-5957	...	...	Diana Seele	...	...	Troy Krenning	Donald Gardner
Julesburg	t	CM	1	(970) 474-3344	Philip Mollendor	...	Murial Nelson	...	Todd Blochowitz	...	Allen Coyne
Kersey *	t	CM	1	(970) 353-1681	Gilbert Marin	Cathy Watson	Julie Piper	...	...	Pat Carey	Derrick Arens
Kremmling	t	CM	1	(970) 724-3249	...	...	Sharon Cesar	...	...	Bob Bodemann	James Hursh
La Jara	t	MC	..	(719) 274-0553	...	William Yohey	...	...	...	...	...
La Junta	c	CM	7	(719) 384-5991	Don Rizzuto	Rick Klein	Jan Schooley	Patty Hurt	Jerald Bradfield	Charles Widup	Joe Kelley
Lafayette *	c	CM	23	(303) 665-5588	Chris Berry	Gary Klaphake	Susan Koster	Robert Wright	Gerald Morrell	Paul Schultz	Doug Short
Lakewood	c	CM	144	(303) 987-7700	Stephen Burkholder	Michael Rock	Margy Greer	...	...	Ron Burns	Richard Plastino
Lamar *	c	CM	8	(719) 336-4376	Nelva Heath	Ronald Stock	Maribeth Kemp	...	...	...	...
Las Animas	c	MC	2	(719) 456-0422	...	...	...	...	...	...	...
Leadville	c	MC	2	(719) 486-0549	Pete Moore	...	Eva Fenske	...	Michael Osborn	James Zoller	Scott Marcella
Limon	t	CM	2	(719) 775-2346	Del Beattie	Joe Kiely	Chris Snyder	...	...	Lynn Yowell	Dave Stone
Littleton	c	CM	40	(303) 795-3720	James Taylor	James Woods	Julie Bower	...	John Mullin	...	Charles Blosten
Lochbuie	t	MC	2	(303) 655-3908	William Norris	...	Stacey Aranda	...	...	G. Mendenhall	Mike Hutto
Lone Tree	c	CM	4	(303) 708-1818	...	Jack Hidahl	...	...	...	...	...
Longmont	c	CM	71	(303) 776-6050	Julia Pirnack	Gordon Pedrow	Valeria Skitt	Jim Golden	Steve Trunck	Mike Butler	...
Louisville	c	CM	18	(303) 335-4500	Charles Sisk	Malcolm Fleming	Nancy Varra	Patty Leslie	...	Bruce Goodman	Thomas Phare
Loveland	c	CM	50	(970) 962-2000	Larry Walsh	Don Williams	Teressa Andrews	...	Michael Chard	Luke Hecker	Keith Reester
Lyons	t	CM	1	(303) 823-6622	Timothy Kyer	Gary Cinnamon	Debra Anthony	Janice Saeger	...	Dan Barber	Scott Daniels
Mancos	t	CM	1	(970) 533-7725	Greg Rath	Thomas Yennerell	Georgette Welage	...	...	...	Robin Schmittel
Manitou Springs	c	CM	4	(719) 685-5596	Bill Koerner	Dan Wecks	Lois Greenman	Fred Burmont	...	Jeff Nohr	Gary Smith
Mead	t	CM	2	(970) 535-4477	Richard Kraemer	Dan Dean	C. Bridgwater	...	...	...	Daniel Dennison
Meeker *	t	CM	2	(970) 878-5344	Steve Loshbaugh	Sharon Day	Lisa Cook	...	...	Bob Hervey	Russell Overton
Milliken	t	CM	2	(970) 587-4331	Linda Measner	Sheryl Trent	Gayle Martinez	Diana Vasquez	...	James Burack	Michael Woodruff
Minturn	t	CM	1	(970) 827-5645	Earle Bidez	...	...	Jay Brunvand	...	Lorenzo Martinez	Floyd Duran
Monte Vista	c	CM	4	(719) 852-2692	Donald Schall	Donald Vanwormer	Lucille Duran	Debbie Phillips	Charles Archer	Jim Gallegos	Randy Martinez
Montrose	c	CM	12	(970) 240-1400	Noelle Hagan	Mary Watt	Sharleen Walker	Shani Wittenberg	...	Tom Chinn	James Hougnon
Monument	t	MC	1	(719) 884-8012	Elizabeth Konarski	...	Anne Holliday	...	...	Joe Kissell	Tom Wall
Morrison	t	MC	..	(303) 697-8749	Kathy Dichter	Jerry Smith	Elizabeth Hedberg	Donna Beckman	...	Robert Wasko	Buck Wenger
Mountain Village	t	MC	..	(970) 369-6412	...	Greg Sparks	...	Steven Wilson	...	...	...
Nederland	t	CM	1	(303) 258-3266	...	James Stevens	Sheridan Garcia	...	...	Ken Robinson	Tim Underwood
New Castle	t	MC	1	(970) 984-2311	Frank Breslin	...	Lisa Cain	Lyle Layton	...	Chris Sadler	...
Northglenn	c	CM	31	(303) 451-8326	Kathleen Novak	Arthur Krieger	Diana Lentz	Brent Worthington	...	Russ VanHouten	...
Orchard City	t	CM	2	(970) 835-3337	Thomas Huerkamp	Isaac Holland	...	...	...	...	...
Ouray	c	CM	..	(970) 325-7211	Pamela Larson	Patrick Rondinelli	Kathy Elmont	...	John Fedel	Glenn Johnson	Daniel Fossey
Pagosa Springs	t	CM	1	(970) 264-4151	Ross Aragon	Mark Garcia	Deanna Jaramillo	...	...	Donald Volger	Chris Gallegos
Palisade	t	CM	2	(970) 464-5602	Douglas Edwards	Tim Sarmo	Tina Darrah	...	Richard Rupp	Carroll Quarles	Frank Watt
Parker	t	CM	23	(303) 805-3117	...	Jeannene Bragg	Carol Baumgartner	Michael Farina	...	...	Michael Sutherland
Platteville *	t	CM	2	(970) 785-2245	Steve Shafer	Nicholas Meier	Leah Heneger	...	...	...	Efren Rodriguez
Pueblo	c	CM	102	(719) 553-2633	Mike Occhiato	David Galli	Gina Dutcher	Robert Hain	Greg Miller	Jim Billings	Tom Cvar
Rangely	t	CM	2	(970) 675-8476	Valerie Mallett	Lance Stewart	Christine Brasfield	Karen Ewall	...	Flint Chambers	John Kenney
Ridgway	t	MC	..	(970) 626-5308	Pat Willits	Greg Clifton	Pam Kraft	...	...	David Scott	Dan Bartashius
Rifle	c	CM	6	(970) 625-2121	...	John Hier	Wanda Nelson	Nancy Black	...	Daryl Meisner	Bill Sappington
Rocky Ford	c	MC	4	(719) 254-7414	Randy Hamilton	Daniel Hyatt	Cheryl Grasmick	Cathy Clevenger	Gary Cox	Frank Gallegos	Cy Chavez
Salida	c	CM	5	(719) 539-4555	...	Steven Golnar	Deanna De Luca	...	...	Darwin Hibbs	Tom Shilling
Sheridan	c	CM	5	(303) 762-2200	Mary Carter	Michael Copp	Arlene Sagee	Judy Dahl	Ronald Carter	Ray Sample	Randy Mouring
Silverthorne	t	CM	3	(970) 262-7300	Lou Delpiccolo	Kevin Batchelder	Patty McKenny	Donna Braun	...	John Patterson	William Linfield
Silverton	t	CM	..	(970) 387-5522	Jim Huffman	Devin Granbery	Linda Davis	...	...	...	Gilbert Archuleta
Snowmass Village	t	CM	1	(970) 923-3777	T. Manchester	Russel Forrest	...	Marianne Rakowski	...	Art Smythe	Hunt Walker
South Fork	t	MC	..	(719) 873-0152	...	...	...	...	...	...	...
Steamboat Springs	c	CM	9	(970) 879-2060	Kathy Connell	Alan Lanning	Julie Jordan	Don Taylor	Robert Struble	...	Jim Weber
Sterling	c	CM	11	(970) 522-9700	Dan Jones	Joseph Kiolbasa	...	Debra Forbes	Robert Olme	Roy Breivik	James Allen
Superior *	t	CM	9	(303) 499-3675	...	Scott Randall	Phyllis Hardin	Paul Nilles	...	...	Jon Hakuaas
Telluride	t	CM	2	(970) 728-3071	John Steel	Frank Bell	Mary Schillaci	Lynne Beck	...	James Kolar	Stanford Berryman
Thornton	c	CM	82	(303) 538-7200	Noel Busck	Jack Ethredge	Nancy Vincent	David Boyd	Gregory Sheehan	James Nursey	Chester Elliot
Timnath *	t	MC	..	(970) 224-3211	...	Becky Davidson	Linda Salas	...	...	...	...
Trinidad	c	CM	9	(719) 846-9843	Joseph Reorda	...	Lydia Shea	Rose Blatnik	James Bulson	Charles Glorioso	Michael Valentine
Vail	t	CM	4	(970) 479-2100	...	Stanley Zemler	Lorelei Donaldson	Judy Camp	John Gulick	Dwight Henninger	Greg Hall
Walsenburg	c	MC	4	(719) 738-1048	Jay Crook	Eric Pearson	Paula Sterkconder	H. C. Summers	Gilbert Pedraza	Glyn Ramsey	...
Wellington	t	CM	2	(970) 568-3381	Donald Irwin	...	...	Mike Cummins	Steve Sarno	...	Bill Bodkins
Westminster	c	CM	100	(303) 430-2400	Edward Moss	J. McFall	Linda Yeager	Tammy Hitchens	Jim Cloud	Daniel Montgomery	Ron Hellbusch
Wheat Ridge	c	CM	32	(303) 234-5900	...	G. Young	Wanda Sang	Patrick Goff	...	Jack Hurst	Timothy Paranto
Windsor *	t	CM	9	(970) 686-7476	Edward Starck	Kelly Arnold	Catherine Kennedy	Dean Moyer	...	John Michaels	Terry Walker
Winter Park	t	CM	..	(970) 726-8081	Harold Teverbaugh	David Torgler	Nancy Anderson	...	...	...	James Cordell
Woodland Park *	c	CM	6	(719) 687-9246	Gary Crane	David Buttery	Cindy Morse	Kellie Case	...	Robert Larson	William Alspach
Wray	c	CM	2	(970) 332-4431	Danny Prather	Stanley Holmes	Ida Peery	...	Terry Jay	Richard Crays	Randy Wells
Yuma	c	CM	3	(970) 848-3878	Robert Harper	Doug Sanderson	Karma Wells	...	Daniel Lehman	Joseph Maier	William Eastin
CONNECTICUT											
Ansonia	c	MC	18	(203) 736-5930	James DellaVolpe	Linda Gentile	Elizabeth Lynch	Joseph Miller	Robert Caruso	Kevin Hale	Joseph Maffeo
Ashford *	t	TM	4	(860) 487-4400	Ralph Fletcher	...	Barbara Metsack	...	Wayne Fletcher	...	Joseph Kalinowski
Avon	t	CM	15	(860) 409-4300	...	Philip Schenck	Caroline La Monica	Margaret Colligan	Jamie DiPace	Peter Agnesi	Bruce Williams
Barkhamsted *	t	TM	3	(860) 379-8285	Michael Fox	Deborah Gilpin	Maria Mullady	...	...	...	Richard Novak
Beacon Falls	t	TM	5	(203) 729-4340	Susan Cable	...	Paula Balanda	...	Theodore Smith	...	Frank Delvecchio
Berlin *	t	TM	18	(860) 828-7002	...	Roger Kemp	Kathryn Wall	Anna Johnson	Steve Waznia	Paul Fitzgerald	...
Bethany	t	TM	5	(203) 393-2100	...	...	...	...	...	...	...
Bethel	t	MC	18	(203) 794-8505	...	...	Sheila Zelensky	...	...	...	...
Bethlehem	t	TM	3	(203) 266-7677	...	...	...	...	...	...	James Kacerguis
Bloomfield *	t	CM	19	(860) 769-3500	Sydney Schulman	Louie Chapman	Marguerite Phillips	Daniel Costello	...	Betsy J. S. Hard	David Gofstein
Bolton	t	MC	5	(860) 649-8066	Robert Morra	Joyce Stille	Susan Depold	Jerry McCall	Jim Preuss	...	Danato Rattazzi
Branford	t	RT	28	(203) 488-8394	John Opie	...	Georgette Laske	James Finch	Jack Ahern	Robert Gill	Edward Masotta
Bridgeport	c	MC	139	(203) 576-7200	...	Michael Feeney	Hector Diaz	...	Michael Maglione	Hector Torress	John Marsillio
Bristol	c	MC	60	(860) 584-7600	...	...	...	...	...	...	...

Directory 1/9 continued **OFFICIALS IN U.S. MUNICIPALITIES 2,500 AND OVER IN POPULATION**

Jurisdiction	Type	Form of govern-ment	2000 Popu-lation (000)	Main telephone number	Chief elected official	Appointed administrator	Clerk of the governing board	Chief financial officer	Fire chief	Police chief	Public works director
CONNECTICUT continued											
Brookfield	t	TM	15	(203) 775-7300	Martin Foncello	. . .	Joan Locke	Richard Haley	Wayne Gravis	Robin Montgomery	Ronald Klimas
Brooklyn	t	TM	7	(860) 779-3411	Donald Francis	. . .	Leona Mainville	Steven Townsend	. . .	. . .	Leonard Albee
Burlington	t	TM	8	(860) 673-6789	Theodore Scheidel	. . .	. . .	. . .	. . .	. . .	Albert Wilusz
Canterbury	t	TM	4	(860) 546-9377	Neil Dupont	. . .	Sheila Mason Gale	. . .	. . .	. . .	David Veit
Canton	t	CM	8	(860) 693-7839	Mary Tomolonius	Paul Fetherston	Linda Smith	Diane Napier	Richard Hutchings	Lowell Humphrey	Walter LeGeyt
Cheshire *	t	CM	28	(203) 271-6660	Matt Hall	Michael Milone	Carolyn Soltis	Patti-Lynn Ryan	Jack Casner	Michael Cruess	J. Michelangelo
Chester	t	TM	3	(860) 526-0013	Martin Heft	Lynne Jacques	Debra Calamari	. . .	. . .	. . .	John Divis
Clinton	t	TM	13	(860) 669-9333	William Fritz	. . .	Karen Marsden	Rosemary Faulkner	Jeff Heser	Joseph Faughnan	Edward Vailette
Colchester	t	TM	14	(860) 537-3461	. . .	. . .	. . .	. . .	. . .	. . .	. . .
Columbia	t	TM	4	(860) 228-0110	Adella Urban	Cindy Laquire	. . .	William Heldmann	. . .	. . .	Peter Naumec
Coventry	t	CM	11	(860) 742-6324	James Clark	John Elsesser	Susan Cyr	Elizabeth Bauer	. . .	Beau Thurnauer	Walter Veselka
Cromwell	t	TM	12	(860) 632-3497	Stanley Terry	. . .	Darlene Di Proto	Edward Alsup	. . .	Anthony Salvatore	Robert Jahn
Danbury	c	MC	74	(203) 797-4598	Mark Boughton	Michael McLachlan	Helena Abrantes	David St. Hilaire	Peter Siecienski	Robert Paquette	William Buckley
Danielson	b	CM	4	(860) 774-2527	Elaine Lippke	. . .	R. Duchesneau	. . .	Richard Levola	. . .	. . .
Darien	t	RT	19	(203) 656-7300	Evonne Klein	Karl Kilduff	Donna Rajczewski	Kathleen Clarke	. . .	Duane Lovello	Robert Steeger
Deep River	t	TM	4	(860) 526-6020	Richard Smith	Gina Sopneski	Jeanne Nickse	. . .	. . .	. . .	. . .
Derby	c	MC	12	(203) 736-1450	Tony Staffieri	. . .	Laura Wabno	. . .	. . .	Andrew Cota	Gary Parker
Durham	t	TM	6	(860) 349-3625	Henry Robinson	. . .	Marjorie Hatch	Maryjane Parsons	Steven Levy	. . .	Ralph Zimbouski
East Granby	t	TM	4	(860) 653-2576	. . .	. . .	. . .	. . .	. . .	. . .	. . .
East Haddam	t	TM	8	(860) 873-5020	Susan Merrow	. . .	Maryjane Plude	. . .	John Blaschik	. . .	Mark Kiefer
East Hampton	t	CM	13	(860) 267-4468	Christopher Goff	. . .	Sandra Wieleba	Jeffery Jylkka	Gregory Voelker	Matthew Reimondo	Robert Drewry
East Hartford	t	MC	49	(860) 291-7200	Timothy Larson	John Choquette	. . .	Michael Walsh	David Dagon	Mark Sirois	Billy Taylor
East Haven	t	MC	28	(203) 468-3204	Joseph Maturo	Arthur DeSorbo	Elizabeth Leary	Paul Rizza	Wayne Sandford	Leonard Gallo	Fred Parlato
East Lyme	t	TM	18	(860) 739-6931	. . .	. . .	. . .	. . .	. . .	. . .	. . .
East Windsor	t	TM	9	(860) 623-8122	Linda Roberts	. . .	Karen Gaudreau	. . .	Blaine Simpkins	Edward DeMarco	Leonard Norton
Easton	t	TM	7	(203) 268-6291	William Kupinse	. . .	W. D. Buckley	Grace Stanczyk	Martin Ohradan	John Solomon	Edward Nagy
Ellington	t	TM	12	(860) 870-3100	Michael Stupinski	. . .	Diane McKeegan	Nicholas Dicorleto	. . .	. . .	Peter Michaud
Enfield *	t	CM	45	(860) 253-6300	. . .	Matthew Coppler	Suzanne Olechnicki	Gregory Simmons	. . .	Carl Sferrazza	Piya Hawkes
Essex	t	TM	6	(860) 767-4348	Peter Webster	. . .	Betty Gaudenzi	. . .	Paul Fazzino	. . .	David Caroline
Fairfield	t	RT	57	(203) 256-3057	Kenneth Flatto	Vincent Como	Marguerite Toth	Paul Hiller	Richard Felner	Joseph Sambrook	Richard White
Farmington	t	CM	23	(860) 675-2300	Arline Whitaker	Kathleen Eagen	Paula Ray	Daniel Costello	. . .	Michael Whalen	John McGrane
Glastonbury	t	CM	31	(860) 657-7710	. . .	Richard Johnson	Joyce Mascena	Diane Waldron	Matthew Nelson	Thomas Sweeney	Daniel Pennington
Granby	t	CM	10	(860) 844-5300	. . .	William Smith	. . .	Barbarajean Sibelli	. . .	David Watkins	James Klase
Greenwich	t	RT	61	(203) 622-7734	R. Bergstresser	John Crary	Carmella Budkins	. . .	Daniel Warzoha	James Walters	Marcos Madrid
Griswold	t	TM	10	(860) 376-7060	Paul Brycki	. . .	Ellen Dupont	William Donovan	. . .	. . .	. . .
Groton	c	MC	10	(860) 446-4103	Dennis Popp	. . .	Debra Patrick	Anthony Timpano	Nick Delia	Larry Gurish	Robert Morse
Groton	t	CM	39	(860) 441-6630	. . .	Mark Oefinger	Barbara Tarbox	Salvatore Pandolfo	. . .	David Vanasse	Gary Schneider
Guilford	t	TM	21	(203) 453-8015	Carl Balestracci	. . .	Janice Teft	Sheila Riegelmann	Charles Herrschaft	Thomas Terribile	John Volpe
Haddam	t	TM	7	(860) 345-8531	Anthony Bondi	. . .	Ann Huffstetler	. . .	. . .	. . .	Philip Goff
Hamden	t	MC	56	(203) 287-2500	Carl Amento	Michael Brandi	Vera Morrison	James Hliva	James Leddy	Robert Nolan	Joseph Celotto
Hartford	c	MC	121	(860) 543-8520	Eddie Perez	Lee Erdmann	Daniel Carey	Thomas Morrison	Charles Teale	Patrick Harnett	Bhupen Patel
Harwinton	t	TM	5	(860) 485-9051	Marie Knudsen	. . .	Patricia Williamsen	. . .	. . .	. . .	John Fredsall
Hebron *	t	TM	8	(860) 228-5971	. . .	Jared Clark	Carla Pomprowicz	Michael Hillsberg	Paul Burton	. . .	Andrew Tierney
Jewett City	b	MC	3	(860) 376-7082	Donald Ouillette	. . .	John Hoddy	. . .	. . .	. . .	Joseph Dudek
Kent	t	TM	2	(860) 927-3433	. . .	. . .	. . .	. . .	. . .	. . .	. . .
Killingly	t	CM	16	(860) 779-5335	Janice Thurlow	Bruce Benway	MaryEllen Heckler	James Day	. . .	. . .	. . .
Killingworth	t	TM	6	(860) 663-1765	David Denoir	. . .	Susan Adinolfo	. . .	. . .	. . .	James Ward
Lebanon	t	TM	6	(860) 642-6100	Daniel McGuire	. . .	Joyce McGillicuddy	Barbara Griffin	Robert Cady	. . .	Ronald Ives
Ledyard	t	MC	14	(860) 464-8740	. . .	Deborah Donlon	Peter Kallan	. . .	. . .	Wesley Johnson	Steven Masalin
Lisbon	t	TM	4	(860) 376-7856	Thomas Sparkman	. . .	Marlene LePine	. . .	. . .	. . .	. . .
Litchfield *	t	TM	8	(860) 567-7550	Leo Paul	. . .	Evelyn Goodwin	Cynthia Politano	Thomas O'Hare	Roger Doyle	James Koser
Madison *	t	TM	17	(203) 245-5603	Thomas Scarpati	. . .	Dorothy Bean	Dorothy Bavin	Robert Gerard	Paul Jakubson	Donald Mac Millan
Manchester	t	CM	54	(860) 647-5235	Steve Cassano	Scott Shanley	Joe Camposeo	Alan Desmarais	Thomas Weber	Gerald Aponte	Mark Carlino
Mansfield	t	CM	20	(860) 429-3336	Elizabeth Paterson	Matthew Hart	Joan Gerdsen	Jeffery Smith	. . .	. . .	Lon Hultgren
Marlborough	t	TM	5	(860) 295-6204	Howard Dean	. . .	Nancy Dickson	. . .	. . .	. . .	Thomas Giola
Meriden	c	CM	58	(203) 630-4123	Joseph Marinan	. . .	Irene Masse	Edward Murphy	William Dunn	Robert Kosienski	Mark Zebora
Middlebury	t	TM	6	(203) 758-1779	Edward St. John	Claudia Tata	Alicia Ostar	Michael Belden	. . .	Patrick Bona	. . .
Middlefield	t	MC	4	(860) 349-7114	Charles Augur	. . .	Donna Golub	Joseph Geruch	Stan Atwell	. . .	John Wyskiel
Middletown	c	MC	43	(860) 344-3487	D. Thornton	. . .	Sandra Hutton	Carl Erlacher	Gary Ouellette	J. Brymer	William Russo
Milford	c	MC	48	(203) 783-3210	. . .	. . .	Alan Jepson	. . .	. . .	. . .	. . .
Monroe	t	MC	19	(203) 452-5400	. . .	. . .	Marsha Motter	Carl Tomchik	William Davin	John Salvatore	Arthur Baker
Montville	t	MC	18	(860) 848-3030	Joseph Jaskiewicz	. . .	Lisa Terry	Katherine Maxwell	. . .	. . .	Donald Bourdeau
Naugatuck	t	MC	30	(203) 729-4571	Timothy Barth	. . .	Sophie Morton	Patricia Porciello	Kerry Flaherty	Dennis Clisham	Henry Witkoski
New Britain *	c	MC	71	(860) 826-3404	Timothy Stewart	Lisa Carver	Peter Denuzze	Robert Curry	Mark Carr	William Gagliardi	. . .
New Canaan	t	TM	19	(203) 972-2350	Richard Bond	Peter Murphy	Claudia Weber	Gary Conrad	. . .	Christopher Lynch	Frank De Nicola
New Fairfield	t	TM	13	(203) 312-5660	Margaret Katkocin	. . .	Diana Peck	Mary Anne Weisner	. . .	. . .	Robert Rzasa
New Hartford	t	TM	6	(860) 379-3389	. . .	. . .	. . .	. . .	. . .	. . .	. . .
New Haven	c	MC	123	(203) 946-8252	John Destefano	. . .	Ronald Smith	Mark Pietrosimone	Michael Grant	Francisco Ortiz	Richard Miller
New London	c	CM	25	(860) 447-5210	Ernest Hewett	Martin Berliner	Michael Tranchida	Donald Goodrich	Ronald Samul	Bruce Rinehart	Edward Steward
New Milford	t	MC	27	(860) 355-6010	Patricia Murphy	. . .	George Buckbee	R. Jankowski	William May	Colin McCormack	Patrick Hackett
Newington *	t	CM	29	(860) 665-8500	Rodney Mortensen	John Salomone	Tanya Lane	Ann Harter	Chris Schroeder	Richard Mulhall	. . .
Newtown	t	MC	25	(203) 270-4201	Herbert Rosenthal	. . .	Cynthia Simon	Benjamin Spragg	William Halstead	Michael Kehoe	Fred Hurley
North Branford	t	CM	13	(203) 315-6000	Jo Anne Wentworth	. . .	Lisa Valenti	Anthony Esposito	Ralph Thomas	Matthew Canelli	Francis Merola
North Canaan	t	TM	3	(860) 824-7313	Douglas Humes	Dorothy Paviol	Carolyn O'Connor	Wheaton Byers	Charles Perotti	. . .	Brad Shook
North Haven	t	TM	22	(203) 239-5321	Kevin Kopetz	. . .	Elinor Pedalino	. . .	Vincent Landisio	James Dicarlo	Richard Branigan
North Stonington	t	TM	4	(860) 535-2877	. . .	. . .	. . .	. . .	Timothy Main	. . .	. . .
Norwalk *	c	MC	82	(203) 854-7716	Richard Moccia	. . .	Mary Roman	Tom Hamilton	Denis McCarthy	Harry Rilling	Harold Alvord
Norwich	c	CM	36	(860) 823-3700	Arthur Lathrop	Alan Bergren	Dee Anne Brennan	Joseph Ruffo	James Walsh	Louis Fusaro	Joseph Loyacano
Old Lyme	t	TM	7	(860) 434-1605	Timothy Griswold	. . .	Irene Carnell	Doris Johnson	. . .	. . .	John Roach
Old Saybrook	t	TM	10	(860) 395-3123	Susan Townsley	. . .	Sarah Becker	. . .	David Heiney	Edmund Mosca	Ronald Baldi
Orange *	t	TM	12	(203) 891-2122	James Zeoli	. . .	Patrick O'Sullivan	Pamela Mangini	Charles Sherwood	Robert Gagne	Edwin Lieberman
Oxford	t	TM	9	(203) 888-2543	Katherine Johnson	Beverly Hanna	. . .	Carl Serus	. . .	. . .	George Swift
Plainfield	t	TM	14	(860) 564-4071	. . .	. . .	. . .	. . .	. . .	. . .	. . .
Plainville *	t	CM	17	(860) 793-0221	C. Wazorko	Robert Lee	Carol Skultety	Robert Metcalf	Raymond Swanson	Daniel Coppinger	Carmen Matteo
Plymouth	t	MC	11	(860) 585-4002	David Denis	. . .	Janet Scoville	Manuel Gomes	Mark Sekorski	. . .	Anthony Lorenzetti
Pomfret	t	TM	3	(860) 974-0191	. . .	. . .	Nora Johnson	. . .	. . .	. . .	. . .
Portland	t	TM	8	(860) 342-6700	Edward Kalinowski	. . .	Bernadette Dillon	. . .	. . .	. . .	Richard Kelsey
Preston *	t	TM	4	(860) 887-5581	Robert Congdon	. . .	Hattie Wucik	. . .	Tom Casey	. . .	Robert Boyd
Prospect	t	MC	8	(203) 758-4461	. . .	. . .	. . .	. . .	. . .	. . .	. . .
Putnam	d	MC	9	(860) 928-5529	. . .	. . .	Lucille Herrick	. . .	. . .	Edward Perron	. . .
Putnam	t	TM	9	(860) 963-6800	Daniel Rovero	Douglas Cutler	Sara D'Elia	. . .	. . .	. . .	Gerard Beausoleil

Directory 1/9 continued **OFFICIALS IN U.S. MUNICIPALITIES 2,500 AND OVER IN POPULATION**

Jurisdiction	Type	Form of govern-ment	2000 Popu-lation (000)	Main telephone number	Chief elected official	Appointed administrator	Clerk of the governing board	Chief financial officer	Fire chief	Police chief	Public works director
CONNECTICUT continued											
Redding	t	TM	8	(203) 938-2002	Natalie Ketcham	...	Michele Grande	Mary Anne Wiesner	...	...	Roger Harker
Ridgefield	t	TM	23	(203) 431-2700	Rudy Marconi	...	Barbara Serfilippi	Jay Wahlberg	Heather Burford	Richard Ligi	Peter Hill
Rocky Hill	t	CM	17	(860) 258-2700	Barbara Surwilo	Barbara Gilbert	Ronald McNamara	John Mehr	Joseph Kochanek	Michael Custer	...
Salisbury	t	TM	3	(860) 435-9140	...	...	...	...	...	...	...
Seymour	t	TM	15	(203) 888-2511	Scott Barton	...	Esther Rozum	Douglas Thomas	Michael Driscoll	Michael Metzler	Dennis Rozum
Sharon	t	MC	2	(860) 364-5789	P. Moeller	...	Linda Amerrghi	...	Thomas Casey	...	...
Shelton	c	MC	38	(203) 924-1555	Mark Lauretti	Sandra Nesteriak	...	Louis Marusic	...	Robert Voccola	William Mooney
Simsbury	* t	TM	23	(860) 658-3230	Thomas Vincent	...	Carolyn Keily	Kevin Kane	James Baldis	Peter Ingvertsen	...
Somers	t	TM	10	(860) 763-8200	Richard Jackson	...	Ann Marie Logan	Edward Sullivan	Bill Meier	...	Kenneth Anderson
South Windsor	* t	CM	24	(860) 644-2511	Matthew Streeter	Matthew Galligan	Gretchen Bickford	Melanie Crucitti	Philip Crombie	Gary Tyler	Michael Gantick
Southbury	t	TM	18	(203) 262-0600	Mark Cooper	...	Virginia Salisbury	...	John Stanko	...	George Metcalf
Southington	t	CM	39	(860) 276-6222	Edward Malczyk	John Weichsel	Leslie Cotton	Emilia Portelinha	R. McDonough	John Daly	Steven Wlodkowski
Sprague	t	TM	2	(860) 822-3000	Dennison Allen	...	Claire Glaude	...	Daniel Nagle	...	Mark Benson
Stafford	t	TM	11	(860) 684-1778	Gordon Frassinelli	Michael Waugh	Carol Davis	...	...	...	Alan Wytas
Stamford	c	MC	117	(203) 977-5397	Dannel Malloy	...	Donna Loglisci	Lisa Reynolds	Robert McGrath	Louis Decarlo	Timothy Curtin
Stonington	t	TM	17	(860) 535-4721	Peter Dibble	George Sylvestre	Cynthia Ladwig	Marianna Stevens	...	Dave Erskine	...
Stratford	t	MC	49	(203) 385-4007	...	...	Patricia Ulatowski	Allen Moore	Ronald Nattrass	Robert Mossman	Michael Hudzik
Suffield	t	TM	13	(860) 668-3838	Robert Skinner	...	Elaine O'Brien	Deborah Cerrato	Thomas Bellmore	Peter Inquertsen	Bruce Williams
Thomaston	t	TM	7	(860) 283-9678	Clifford Brammer	...	...	Susan Whitney	...	Edward Grabherr	Gerald Grohoski
Thompson	* t	TM	8	(860) 923-9561	A. David Babbitt	...	...	Michael Martin	...	...	Leo Adams
Tolland	t	CM	13	(860) 871-3600	...	Steven Werbner	Meg DeVito	Christine Hutton	John Littell	...	John Bock
Torrington	c	MC	35	(860) 489-2228	...	...	...	...	...	...	...
Trumbull	t	MC	34	(203) 452-5000	Raymond Baldwin	...	Vivian Burr	Lynn Heim	Robert Pescatore	James Berry	Paul Kallmeyer
Vernon	t	MC	28	(860) 870-3599	Ellen Marmer	Christopher Clark	...	James Luddecke	Robert Kelley	Rudolf Rossmy	George Fetko
Wallingford	t	MC	43	(203) 294-2070	William Dickinson	...	Rosemary Rascati	James Bowes	Wayne Lefebvre	Douglas Dortenzio	Henry McCully
Washington	t	TM	3	(860) 868-2259	Alan Chapin	...	Sheila Anson	...	Alden Johnson	...	...
Waterbury	c	MC	107	(203) 574-6761	Michael Jarjura	Sheila O'Malley	...	Patrick Jones	James Cavanaugh	Neil O'Leary	John Lawlor
Waterford	t	RT	19	(860) 442-0553	Paul Eccard	...	Robert Nye	Ruth Beers	Bruce Miller	Murray Pendleton	Ronald Cusano
Watertown	t	CM	21	(860) 945-5255	...	...	Virginia Stewart	Frank Nardelli	Larry Black	John Carroll	Roy Cavanaugh
West Hartford	t	CM	60	(860) 561-7460	Jonathan Harris	James Francis	Norma Cronin	Chris Johnson	William Austin	James Strillacci	Dana Hallenbeck
West Haven	c	MC	52	(203) 937-3560	H. Borer	...	Deborah Collins	Richard Legg	...	Ronald Quagliani	Arthur Ferris
Westbrook	t	TM	6	(860) 399-3040	Tony Palermo	...	Lori Baldi	...	Clifford Spencer	...	John Riggio
Weston	t	TM	10	(203) 222-2677	...	Thomas Landry	Cynthia Williams	Richard Darling	...	Anthony Land	Joseph Lametta
Westport	t	RT	25	(203) 341-1000	Diane Farrell	...	Patricia Strauss	Donald Miklus	Denis McCarthy	William Chiarenzelli	Stephen Edwards
Wethersfield	* t	CM	26	(860) 721-2801	Andrew Adil	Bonnie Therrien	Dolores Sassano	Lisa Hancock	Charles Flynn	James Cetran	Michael Turner
Willimantac	c	TM	14	(860) 465-3013	...	...	...	...	...	...	...
Willington	t	TM	5	(860) 429-5649	...	...	...	...	...	...	...
Wilton	* t	TM	17	(203) 563-0100	William Brennan	...	Bettye Ragognetti	Joseph Dolan	Paul Milositz	Edward Kulhawik	Thomas Thurkettle
Winchester	t	CM	10	(860) 379-2713	Maryann Welcome	Steven Angelo	Sheila Sedlack	Henry Centrella	Joseph Beadle	Nicholas Guerriero	Patrick Hague
Windham	t	MC	22	(860) 465-3007	Michael Paulhus	...	Ann Bushey	Robert Buden	John Walsh	Lisa Maruzo-Bolduc	Brad Wojick
Windsor	t	CM	28	(860) 285-1900	Francis Brady	Peter Souza	Kathleen Quin	D. Cunningham	Dale Smith	Kevin Searles	Wayne Radke
Windsor Locks	t	TM	12	(860) 627-1444	Edward Ferrari	...	William Hamel	Barbara Bertrand	...	John Suchocki	Scott Lappen
Winsted	* c	CM	7	(860) 379-2713	Maryann Welcome	Owen Quinn	Sheila Sedlack	Henry Centrella	Robert Shopey	Nicholas Guerriero	Patrick Hague
Wolcott	t	MC	15	(203) 879-4666	...	...	...	...	...	...	...
Woodbridge	t	TM	8	(203) 389-3400	Amey Marrella	Joseph Hellauer	S. Ciarleglio	Anthony Genovese	Andrew Esposito	Dennis Phipps	...
Woodbury	t	TM	9	(203) 263-2141	Richard Crane	...	Rita Connelly	Richard Hubbard	...	...	David Monckton
Woodstock	t	TM	7	(860) 928-0208	Delpha Very	...	Judy Alberts	...	...	...	Dwight Ryniewicz
DELAWARE											
Bethany Beach	t	CM	..	(302) 539-8011	Charles Bartlett	Clifford Graviet	Lisa Kail	Madalyn Forrest	...	...	James Seabrease
Cheswold	t	CM	..	(302) 734-6991	...	...	...	...	...	...	...
Dewey Beach	t	CM	..	(302) 227-6363	Robert Frederick	...	...	...	...	Raymond Morrison	...
Dover	c	CM	32	(302) 736-7073	...	Anthony DePrima	Janice Green	Donna Mitchell	...	Jeffrey Horvath	Scott Koenig
Elsmere	t	CM	5	(302) 998-2215	C. Cavanaugh	John Giles	...	David Jaeger	George Giles	...	Joseph Cherneski
Fenwick Island	t	MC	..	(302) 539-3011	...	Anthony Carson	...	...	...	...	...
Georgetown	* t	CM	4	(302) 856-7391	Michael Wyatt	Eugene Dvornick	Angela Townsend	Frank Adams	...	William Topping	William Bradley
Greenwood	t	MC	..	(302) 349-4534	Donald Donovan	Michael O'Gara	Doris Adkins	...	...	Brian Parsons	...
Harrington	c	MC	3	(302) 398-3530	...	...	Charlyne Hughes	Chris Truitt	...	John Horsman	Alan Moore
Laurel	t	MC	3	(302) 875-2277	John Shwed	...	Donna Adkins	Mary Introcaso	Jeff Hill	Donald McGinty	Allen Atkins
Lewes	c	MC	2	(302) 645-7777	James Ford	Thomas Wontorek	...	...	...	...	...
Middletown	t	MC	6	(302) 378-2711	Kenneth Branner	Morris Deputy	Rebecca Ennis	Louis Vitola	...	...	...
Milford	c	CM	6	(302) 422-6616	Joseph Rogers	Richard Carmean	Teresa Hudson	Jeffrey Portmann	...	E Keith Hudson	...
New Castle	* c	CM	4	(302) 322-9812	John Klingmeyer	Cathryn Thomas	Jill DiAngelo	Marian Delaney	...	Kevin McDerby	M. Christopher
Newark	* c	CM	28	(302) 366-7000	Vance Funk	Carl Luft	Susan Lamblack	Dennis McFarland	...	Paul Tiernan	Richard Lapointe
Newport	t	CM	1	(302) 994-6403	...	Rita Shade	...	...	...	...	...
Ocean View	t	MC	1	(302) 539-9797	Gary Meredith	Kathy Roth	Marie Thomas	...	...	K. McLaughlin	Charles McMullen
Rehoboth Beach	c	CM	1	(302) 227-6181	Samuel Cooper	Gregory Ferrese	...	...	...	Keith Banks	Melbourne Craig
Seaford	* c	CM	6	(302) 629-9173	Daniel Short	Dolores Slatcher	...	June Merritt	...	Gary Morris	Robert Nibblett
Smyrna	t	CM	5	(302) 653-3483	Mark Schaeffer	David Hugg	Carol McKinney	Gary Stulir	...	Richard Baldwin	Joseph Heeger
Wilmington	c	MC	72	(302) 576-2100	James Baker	W. Montgomery	Maribel Ruiz	Ronald Morris	James Ford	Michael Szczerba	Kash Srinivasan
DISTRICT OF COLUMBIA											
Columbia	d	MC	572	(202) 727-1000	Adrian Fenty	Dan Tangherlini	...	Natwar Gandhi	Adrian Thompson	Charles Ramsey	...
FLORIDA											
Alachua	c	CM	6	(386) 462-1231	Bonnie Burgess	...	...	Marcian Brown	...	Robert Jernigan	Oren Paulsen
Altamonte Springs	c	CM	41	(407) 571-8000	Russel Hauck	...	Patsy Wainright	Mark Debord	...	Robert Merchant	John Peters
Apalachicola	c	MC	2	(850) 653-9319	...	Betty Taylor-Webb	...	...	...	Anderson Williams	...
Apopka	c	MC	26	(407) 703-1700	John Land	Richard Anderson	Janice Goebel	...	Randall Fernandez	Charles Vavrek	...
Arcadia	c	CM	6	(941) 494-4114	...	...	...	...	...	...	...
Archer	* c	CM	1	(352) 495-2880	...	James Drymon	...	...	...	...	...
Astatula	t	MC	1	(352) 742-1100	...	...	Maria Montalvo	...	...	Carson Sink	Horace Mauldin
Atlantic Beach	c	CM	13	(904) 247-5800	Donald Wolfson	James Hanson	Donna Bussey	Fredrik Van Liere	...	...	Ricky Carper
Atlantis	* c	CM	2	(561) 965-1744	Manuel Fernandez	Mo Thornton	Joan Cannata-Fox	...	...	Robert Mangold	Steven Hazuk
Auburndale	c	CM	11	(863) 965-5530	Marvin Wiley	Robert Green	...	Shirley Lowrance	Sam Efurd	Dean Longo	Mickey Etherton
Aventura	* c	CM	14	(305) 466-8900	Susan Gottlieb	Eric Soroka	Teresa Soroka	Brian Raducci	...	Steve Steinberg	Alan Levine
Avon Park	c	CM	8	(863) 452-4400	Sharon Schuler	C. Shirey	...	Renee Green	Terry Feickert	Frank Mercurio	Theodore Long

Directory 1/9 continued — OFFICIALS IN U.S. MUNICIPALITIES 2,500 AND OVER IN POPULATION

Jurisdiction	Type	Form of govern-ment	2000 Popu-lation (000)	Main telephone number	Chief elected official	Appointed administrator	Clerk of the governing board	Chief financial officer	Fire chief	Police chief	Public works director
FLORIDA continued											
Bal Harbour	v	CM	3	(305) 866-4633	Daniel Tankleff	Alfred Treppeda	Jeanette Horton	...	...	Thomas Hunker	Robert Weldon
Bartow	c	CM	15	(863) 534-0100	Leo Longworth	George Long	Linda Culpepper	David Wright	James Robinson	Erik Sandvik	William Pickard
Bay Harbor Islands	t	CM	4	(305) 866-6241	Isaac Salver	Ronald Wasson	Marlene Marante	Alan Short	...	John Ross	Joseph Fox
Bay Lake	c	CM	..	(407) 828-2241	Orville Bell	...	...	...	...	...	...
Belle Glade	c	CM	14	(561) 996-0100	Steve Wilson	William Underwood	Debra Buff	...	Stephen Rice	...	...
Belle Isle	c	CM	5	(407) 851-7730	William Brooks	Lawrence Williams	Belinda Bateman	...	...	...	James Sapp
Belleair	t	CM	4	(727) 588-3769	...	Micah Maxwell	Donna Carlen	...	...	...	...
Belleair Beach	c	CM	1	(727) 595-4646	Lynn Rives	Nancy McCollum	...	...	...	...	...
Belleair Bluffs *	c	MC	2	(727) 584-2151	...	...	Debra Sullivan	...	...	...	Robert David
Biscayne Park	v	CO	3	(305) 899-8000	John Hornbuckle	Frank Spence	Ann Harper	Holly Hugdahl	...	Mitchell Glansberg	Joseph Fisher
Blountstown	c	CM	2	(850) 674-5488	...	...	...	...	...	...	...
Boca Raton	c	CM	74	(561) 393-7803	Steven Abrams	Leif Ahnell	Sharma Carannante	Mervyn Timberlake	Bruce Silk	Andrew Scott	R. DiChristopher
Bonifay	c	MC	4	(850) 547-4238	James Sims	...	Shirley Mitchell	...	Roy Messer	Ronnie Bennett	Jack Marell
Bonita Springs *	c	CM	32	(239) 949-6262	...	Gary Price	Dianne Lynn	...	...	...	Daryl Walk
Boynton Beach	c	CM	60	(561) 742-6000	Gerald Broening	Kurt Bressner	Janet Prainito	Diane Reese	William Bingham	Marshall Gage	Jeffrey Livergood
Bradenton	c	MC	49	(941) 708-6200	Wayne Poston	...	...	...	Mark Souders	M. Radzilowski	John Cumming
Brooksville	c	CM	7	(352) 544-5407	Ernest Wever	T. Norman-Vacha	Karen Phillips	S. Baumgartner	James Daugherty	Boyce Tincher	Emory Pierce
Bunnell	c	CM	2	(386) 437-7500	Joann King	Richard Diamond	Ronya Johnson	...	Gary Hughes	Michael Ignasiak	Eric Crandall
Bushnell	c	CM	2	(352) 793-2591	...	Vince Ruano	...	N. Joy Coleman	...	Joyce Wells	Ronald Pitts
Callaway *	c	CM	14	(850) 871-6000	Kenneth Meer	Judy Whitis	Genette Bernal	Alice Bennett	Jack McKinney	...	John Adams
Cape Canaveral *	c	CM	8	(321) 868-1221	Rocky Randels	Bennett Boucher	Susan Stills	...	David Sargeant	Doug Scragg	...
Cape Coral	c	CM	102	(239) 574-0450	Eric Feichthaler	Terrance Stewart	Bonnie Vent	Mark Mason	William Van Helden	Daniel Alexander	Charles Pavlos
Casselberry *	c	CM	22	(407) 262-7700	Robert Goff	Barbara Lipscomb	Thelma McPherson	Mark Glover	Donald Harkins	John Paulis	Eduardo Torres
Chattahoochee	c	CM	3	(850) 663-4046	James Atkins	Elmon Garner	Gayle Lanier	...	...	Edward Pullen	...
Chiefland *	c	MC	1	(352) 493-6711	Matthew Pomeroy	Grady Hartzog	...	...	...	Robert Douglas	...
Chipley	c	CM	3	(850) 638-6350	Tommy McDonald	Jim Morris	Patrice Yates	...	Kevan Parker	Kevin Crews	Charles Barfield
Cinco Bayou	t	CM	..	(850) 833-3405	Norman Frucci	Nell Webb	...	...	...	...	...
Clearwater *	c	CM	108	(727) 562-4055	Frank Hibbard	William Horne	Cynthia Goudeau	Margaret Simmons	Jamie Geer	Sidney Klein	Tracy Mercer
Clermont	c	CM	9	(352) 394-4081	Harold Turville	David Saunders	...	Joseph Van Zile	Carle Bishop	Randall Story	Elbert Davis
Clewiston *	c	CO	6	(863) 983-1484	Mali Chamness	Wendell Johnson	...	Ted Byrd	William Pelham	Don Gutshall	Sean Scheffler
Cocoa	c	CM	16	(321) 639-7585	Judy Parrish	James Holt	Joan Clark	Walter Mack	Arthur Romprey	Phillip Ludos	Michael DeVillo
Cocoa Beach	c	CM	12	(321) 868-3306	Leon Beeler	Charles Billias	L. Kalaghchy	Kenneth Killgore	Scott Shear	James Scragg	Robert Torres
Coconut Creek	c	CM	43	(954) 973-6770	Becky Tooley	John Kelly	Barbara Price	Karen Brooks	...	George Raggio	James Sundermeier
Cooper City	c	CM	27	(954) 434-4300	S. Fardelmann	Christopher Farrell	...	Horacio DeOca	Joseph Lello	Edward Werder	Carl Miller
Coral Gables *	c	CM	40	(305) 446-6800	Don Slesnick	David Brown	Walter Foeman	Donald Nelson	Richard Cook	M. Hammerschmidt	Alberto Delgado
Coral Springs	c	CM	117	(954) 344-1000	John Sommerrer	Michael Levinson	...	David Russek	Donald Haupt	Roy Arigo	Rich Michaud
Crescent City	c	MC	1	(386) 698-2525	Howard Kinsella	Marcus Collins	...	Gay Harris	Allen Peacock	George Penley	Michael Ijames
Crestview	c	MC	14	(850) 682-1560	George Whitehurst	...	Janice Young	Patti Mann	Joseph Traylor	Travis Gillihan	General Cox
Crystal River	c	CM	3	(352) 795-4216	Ronald Kitchen	...	Carol Harrington	Mark Thiele	...	Steven Burch	John Lettow
Cutler Bay	t	CM	37	(305) 234-4262	...	Steven Alexander	...	...	...	...	...
Dade City	c	CM	6	(352) 523-5050	P. Hutchison Brock	Harold Sample	James Class	...	Joey Wubbena	Phillip Thompson	...
Dania Beach *	c	CM	20	(954) 924-3600	Robert Anton	Ivan Pato	Louise Stilson	Patricia Varney	...	Donn Peterson	Dominic Orlando
Davenport *	c	CM	1	(863) 419-3300	Peter Rust	Amy Arrington	Raquel Castillo	...	Donald Pelt	Lloyd Clements	...
Davie	t	CM	75	(954) 797-1000	Thomas Trues	Gary Shimun	Russell Muniz	...	Donald DiPetrillo	John George	Bruce Bernard
Daytona Beach	c	CM	64	(386) 671-8000	Baron Asher	James Chisholm	Jennifer Thomas	James Maniak	Lawrence Taft	Dennis Jones	Stan Lemke
Daytona Beach Shores	c	CM	4	(386) 763-5373	Greg Northrup	Michael Booker	Cheri Schwab	Steve Whitmer	...	Stephan Dembinsky	Fred Hiatt
De Bary	c	CM	15	(386) 668-2040	George Coleman	Maryann Courson	Stacy Tebo	James Seelbinder	...	...	...
De Funiak Springs *	c	CM	5	(850) 892-8500	C. Harold Carpenter	Kim Kirby	Vanessa Mitchell	Sara Bowers	Brian Coley	Michael Adkinson	William Holloway
De Land	c	CM	20	(386) 740-5700	Robert Apgar	Michael Abels	Julie Hennessy	Kevin Lewis	Patrick Kelly	Edward Overman	Marvin Williams
Deerfield Beach	c	CM	64	(954) 480-4200	Albert Capellini	Michael Mahaney	A. Graham-Johnson	Sally Siegel	Gary Lother	George Brennan	Donald Freedland
Delray Beach	c	CM	60	(561) 243-7084	Jeff Perlman	David Harden	Chevelle Nubin	Joseph Safford	Kerry Koen	Joseph Schroeder	...
Deltona	c	CM	69	(386) 561-2100	John Masiarczyk	Steven Thompson	Faith Miller	...	Francis Ennist	...	Glenn Kerns
Destin	c	CM	11	(850) 837-4242	Craig Barker	Gregory Kisela	Dana Williams	Lisa Rolan	...	...	Timothy Shockley
Doral	c	CM	20	(305) 470-6840	...	Sergio Purrinos	...	...	...	...	Eric Carpenter
Dundee *	t	CM	2	(863) 419-3100	Linda Riner-Mizell	Charles Saddler	Stephanie Diaz	Pamela Lawson	Chip Johnson	Sammy Taylor	C. J. Johnson
Dunedin	c	CM	35	(727) 733-4151	John Doglione	Robert DiSpirito	Sandra Woodall	...	Clarence Meyer	...	Douglas Hutchens
Dunnellon	c	CM	1	(352) 465-8500	John Taylor	...	Dawn Bowne	Scott Lippmann	Joseph Campfield	Robert Jackson	...
Eagle Lake	c	CM	2	(863) 293-4141	Suzy Wilson	Patricia Jackson	Dawn Osterhout	...	...	James Sullivan	Brian Fletcher
Eatonville	t	MC	2	(407) 623-1313	...	...	Kathy Williams	Katherina Gibson	...	...	...
Edgewater	c	CM	18	(386) 424-2400	Donald Schmidt	...	Susan Wadsworth	...	Tracy Barlow	Michael Ignasiak	Terry Wadsworth
El Portal	v	MC	2	(305) 795-7880	...	...	Lenore Milan	...	...	...	...
Eustis	c	CM	15	(352) 483-5430	Evelyn Smith	Paul Berg	...	Jim Myers	Roy Tremain	...	John Futch
Fellsmere	c	CM	3	(772) 571-1616	John McCants	Jason Nunemaker	Debbie Krages	Larry Napier	...	Larry Tippins	Bud Roode
Fernandina Beach	c	CM	10	(904) 277-7305	Joe Gerity	Michael Czymbor	Cassandra Mitchell	Patricia Clifford	Daniel Leeper	...	...
Flagler Beach	c	MC	4	(386) 517-2000	Ed Kuhnlein	...	Angela Apperson	Beth Thulin	...	Roger Free	Robert Smith
Florida City	c	CM	5	(305) 247-8221	Otis Wallace	Sylvestor Jackson	Sheila Paul	Desmond Chin	...	Pedro Taylor	Darin Baldwin
Fort Lauderdale *	c	CM	152	(954) 828-5300	Jim Naugle	George Gretsas	Jonda Joseph	Betty Burrell	James Eddy	Bruce Roberts	Albert Carbon
Fort Meade	c	CM	5	(863) 285-1100	...	...	Delores Avery	...	...	Irvin Heathcote	Glenn Curlee
Fort Myers	c	MC	48	(941) 332-6775	Bruce Grady	William Mitchell	Marie Adams	...	Richard Chappelle	...	Emmette Waite
Fort Myers Beach	t	CM	6	(239) 765-0202	Daniel Hughes	Gary Parker	...	Janeen Paulauskis	...	...	Damon Grant
Fort Pierce	c	CM	37	(772) 460-2200	Edward Enns	Dennis Beach	Cassandra Steele	George Bergalis	...	Eugene Savage	Gary Ferch
Fort Walton Beach	c	CM	19	(850) 833-9504	Glenda Glover	Joyce Shanahan	Helen Spencer	...	Michael Dutton	Stephen Hogue	Thomas Murray
Frostproof *	c	CM	2	(863) 635-7855	Larry Sullivan	Tenny Croley	...	Melody Zobel	William Lord	...	Jerry Wilbanks
Fruitland Park	c	CM	3	(352) 360-6727	Christopher Bell	Ralph Bowers	Linda Rodrick	...	Thomas Gamble	J. Isom	John Bostic
Gainesville	c	CM	95	(352) 334-5077	...	Russell Blackburn	Kurt Lannon	Mark Benton	William Northcutt	Norman Botsford	Teresa Scott
Golden Beach	t	MC	..	(305) 932-0744	Michael Addicott	Alexander Diaz	Cathy Szabo	Nina Birnbach	...	Bobby Cheatham	Riley Crews
Golf	v	CM	..	(561) 732-0236	...	Mark Hull	Carol Marciano	...	...	...	Ron Lupo
Graceville	c	CM	2	(850) 263-3250	Guyton Williams	Michael Underwood	Kathleen Turner	...	Tracy Dennis	Daniel Ward	Eddie King
Grant-Valkaria	t	CM	3	(321) 725-0454	...	Matthew Brock	...	...	...	...	...
Green Cove Springs	c	CM	5	(904) 529-2200	Deborah Ricks	Don Bowles	Marjorie Robertson	...	...	Robert Musco	Bob Gamble
Greenacres	c	CM	18	(561) 692-2011	Samuel Ferreri	Wadie Atallah	Sondra Hill	Jeffrey Price	...	...	Dennis Rogan
Greenville	t	CM	..	(850) 948-2251	...	...	...	...	...	...	...
Gretna	c	CM	1	(850) 856-5257	...	Antonio Jefferson	Karen Fitzgerald	Dianne Formman	James Payne	Pepe Forbes	Jimmy Austin
Groveland *	c	CM	2	(352) 429-2141	Matthew Bauman	Ralph Hester	...	Dolly Miller	Willie Morgan	Thomas Merrill	Larry Walker
Gulf Breeze	c	CM	5	(850) 934-5100	Lane Gilchrist	Edwin Eddy	Marita Rhodes	Nancy Millay	Robert Minshull	Peter Paulding	Harold Hatcher
Gulf Stream *	t	CM	..	(561) 276-5116	William Koch	William Thrasher	Rita Taylor	...	...	Garrett Ward	...
Gulfport	c	CM	12	(727) 893-1021	...	Thomas Brobeil	Louise Spence	William Kucera	Brian Brooks	...	...
Haines City *	c	CM	13	(863) 421-3600	Phillip Hinkle	E. Toney-Deal	Cherry Dowdy	Donald Carter	Lon Cheney	Morris West	Ronnie Cotton
Hallandale Beach	c	CM	34	(954) 457-1348	Joy Cooper	Dwayne Good	Edward McGough	Mark Antonio	Daniel Sullivan	Thomas Magill	Jenny Cheretis
Havana	t	CM	1	(850) 539-6493	...	Susan Freiden	...	Karen Myrick	Don Vickers	Brian Mitchell	...
Haverhill	t	MC	1	(561) 689-3070	Joseph Kroll	...	...	...	...	...	...
Hawthorne	c	CM	1	(352) 481-2432	John Martin	Chad Shryock	...	Lakesha McGruder	...	...	William Cuthbert

Directory 1/9 continued — OFFICIALS IN U.S. MUNICIPALITIES 2,500 AND OVER IN POPULATION

Jurisdiction	Type	Form of govern-ment	2000 Popu-lation (000)	Main telephone number	Chief elected official	Appointed administrator	Clerk of the governing board	Chief financial officer	Fire chief	Police chief	Public works director
FLORIDA continued											
Hialeah	c	MC	188	(305) 883-8050	Raul Martinez	. . .	Daniel De Loach	. . .	Otto Drozd	Rolando Bolanos	Armando Vidal
Hialeah Gardens	c	MC	7	(305) 558-4114	Yioset Delacruz	. . .	Maria Joffer	Marcos Piloto	. . .	H. Keith Joy	Phillip Sheffield
High Springs *	c	MC	3	(386) 454-1416	Byran Williams	James Drumm	. . .	Helen McIver	. . .	. . .	LaVerne Hodge
Highland Beach	t	CM	3	(561) 278-4548	Harold Hagelmann	Dale Sugerman	Doris Trinley	Stanley Novak	. . .	Glenn Goss	Jack Lee
Hillsboro Beach *	t	MC	2	(954) 427-4011	Carmen McGarry	. . .	Cathy Deckert	Dan Dodge	. . .	Felix Brugnoni	. . .
Holly Hill	c	CM	12	(386) 248-9420	William Arthur	Joseph Forte	Jeaneen Clauss	Brenda Gubernator	. . .	. . .	Milton Hallman
Hollywood	c	CM	139	(954) 921-3201	Mara Giulianti	Cameron Benson	Patricia Cerny	Carlos Garcia	. . .	James Scarberry	Gregory Turek
Holmes Beach	c	MC	4	(941) 708-5800	Rich Bohnenberger	. . .	Brooke Bennett	Richard Ashley	. . .	Jay Romine	Joe Duennes
Homestead *	c	CM	31	(305) 224-4400	Roscoe Warren	Curtis Ivy	Sheila Paul	Janette Smith	. . .	Alexander Rolle	Julio Brea
Indialantic	t	CM	2	(321) 723-2242	Daniel Trott	Christopher Chinault	Laura Eaton	. . .	Tom Barker	Troy Morris	Ronald Cassedy
Indian Creek *	v	CM	. .	(305) 865-4121	Anne McDougal	Samuel Kissinger	Marilane Lima	. . .	. . .	Clarke Maher	. . .
Indian Harbor Beach *	c	CM	8	(321) 773-3181	Jim Nolan	Jacqueline Burns	Debra Maliska	Richard Anderson	Todd Scaldo	Robert Sullivan	Louis Giacona
Indian River Shores *	t	CM	3	(772) 231-1771	Thomas Cadden	Robert Bradshaw	Laura Aldrich	. . .	. . .	. . .	Edward Morris
Indian Rocks Beach *	c	CM	5	(727) 595-2517	William Ockunzzi	. . .	Deanne O'Reilly	Marty Schless	. . .	. . .	Dean Scharmen
Inverness	c	CM	6	(352) 726-2611	. . .	Frank DiGiovanni	Debbie Davis	Donna Kilbury	. . .	. . .	Russ Kreager
Islamorada Village Of Islands *	v	MC	7	(305) 664-6400	. . .	Gary Word	Beverly Raddatz	Alice Filinovich	. . .	. . .	Myles Milander
Jacksonville	c	MC	735	(904) 630-1178	John Peyton	Alan Mosley	. . .	Calvin Ray	. . .	John Rutherford	Lynn Westbrook
Jacksonville Beach	c	CM	20	(904) 270-1655	Fland Sharp	George Forbes	Heidi Reagan	Harry Royal	Gary Frazier	Bruce Thomason	William Edwards
Jasper *	c	CM	1	(386) 792-1212	Matthew Hawkins	Kent Cichon	Jennifer Cone	Margaret Harper	William Trinder	Jeff McGuire	Walter Davis
Juno Beach *	t	CM	3	(561) 626-1122	Linda Hodgkins	Jeffrey Naftal	Allison Fay	Joseph Lo Bello	. . .	Halifax Clark	Anthony Meriano
Jupiter *	t	CM	39	(561) 746-5134	. . .	Andrew Lukasik	Sally Boylan	. . .	. . .	Frank Kitzerow	Thomas Driscoll
Jupiter Island	t	CM	. .	(772) 545-0100	Joseph Connolly	. . .	Antonia Wickes	Connie Holloman	. . .	. . .	. . .
Kenneth City	t	MC	4	(727) 544-6655	William Smith	. . .	Nancy Beelman	. . .	. . .	James Ernst	Albert Carrier
Key Biscayne	v	CM	8	(305) 365-5511	Joe Rasco	. . .	Conchita Alvarez	. . .	John Gilbert	Michael Flaherty	. . .
Key West	c	CM	25	(305) 292-8202	Jimmy Weekley	James Scholl	Cheryl Smith	Roger Wittenberg	William Wardlow	Gordon Dillion	Richard Knowles
Keystone Heights	c	MC	1	(352) 473-4807	. . .	. . .	. . .	. . .	. . .	. . .	. . .
Kissimmee	c	CM	47	(407) 518-2110	George Gant	Mark Durbin	Linda Jaworski	Amy Ady	Robert King	Mark Weimer	George Mann
Lady Lake	t	CM	11	(352) 751-1505	Michael Francis	William Vance	Deborah Gay	Karen Rickelman	. . .	. . .	Warren Blakeley
Lake Alfred	c	CM	3	(863) 291-5747	Nancy Daley	Jan Shockley	Valerie Way	Amber Pennington	Roger Pridgen	Art Bodenheimer	Larry Harbuck
Lake Buena Vista	c	CM	. .	(407) 828-2241	William Sterner	. . .	. . .	. . .	. . .	. . .	. . .
Lake Butler	c	CM	1	(386) 496-3401	Brantley Crawford	John Berchtold	. . .	. . .	. . .	. . .	Hardy Clyatt
Lake City	c	CM	9	(386) 752-2031	Steven Witt	Grayson Carson	Audrey Sikes	James Minchin	Alphonso Wilson	David Allbritton	William Dow
Lake Clarke Shores	t	CM	3	(561) 964-1515	Robert Shalhoub	Joann Hatton	Jo Plyler	William Thrasher	. . .	William Smith	Kevin Varney
Lake Helen	c	MC	2	(386) 228-2121	Mark Shuttleworth	Don Findell	J. Grammatikas	. . .	. . .	Keith Chester	Rick Mullen
Lake Mary	c	CM	11	(407) 585-1419	. . .	John Litton	Carol Foster	Jacqueline Sova	Craig Haun	Richard Beary	Bruce Paster
Lake Park *	t	CM	8	(561) 881-3300	Paul Castro	Maria Davis	Vivian Mendez	Anne Costello	. . .	. . .	. . .
Lake Wales	c	CM	10	(863) 678-4182	Lee Wheeler	Anthony Otte	Diane Smith	Sylvia Edwards	Thomas Tucker	Mark Levine	Chuck Partlow
Lake Worth	c	CM	35	(561) 586-1600	Rodney Romano	Robert Baldwin	Pamela Lopez	Mark Bates	Paul Blockson	William Smith	Dirk Bane
Lakeland	c	CM	78	(863) 834-6007	. . .	Douglas Thomas	Kelly Koos	Jerry Reynolds	Michael Mohler	Roger Bootnor	Richard Lilyquist
Lantana	t	CM	9	(561) 540-5000	. . .	Michael Bomstein	Darla Levy	Barbara Hastings	. . .	Richard Lincoln	Tom Lundquist
Largo *	c	CM	69	(727) 587-6700	Patricia Gerard	Norton Craig	Diane Bruner	Kimball Adams	. . .	Lester Aradi	Brian Ushers
Lauderdale Lakes	c	MC	31	(954) 535-2700	Samuel Brown	Anita Taylor	. . .	Donald St. Georges	Richard Sievers	. . .	. . .
Lauderdale-By-The-Sea	t	CM	2	(954) 776-0576	Oliver Parker	. . .	Jonda Joseph	Esther Colon	Jon Case	Edward Patten	William Mason
Lauderhill	c	CM	57	(954) 730-3000	. . .	Charles Faranda	Judy Higgins	Kennie Hobbs	Edward Curran	Kenneth Patchnek	Charles Cuyler
Leesburg	c	CM	15	(352) 728-9700	John Christian	Jay Evans	Betty Richardson	William Pfeilsticker	Dennis Sargent	H. Idell	. . .
Lighthouse Point	c	MC	10	(954) 943-6500	Fred Schorr	John Lavisky	Carol Landau	Terry Sharp	David Donzella	Ross Licata	Arthur Graham
Live Oak	c	CM	6	(386) 362-2276	. . .	. . .	William McCullers	Deborah Davis	George Croft	Nolan McLeod	Willard Hewiett
Longboat Key	t	CM	7	(941) 316-1999	. . .	Bruce St. Denis	Jane O'Connor	Terence Sullivan	Julius Halas	Al Hogle	Juan Florensa
Longwood	c	CM	13	(407) 260-3440	Paul Lovestrand	John Drago	Geri Zambri	Carol Rogers	Charles Chapman	Tom Jackson	. . .
Lynn Haven	c	CM	12	(850) 265-2121	Walter Kelley	John Lynch	. . .	. . .	Richard Morrison	David Messer	Robert Olson
Macclenny	c	CM	4	(904) 259-6261	Gary Dopson	Gerald Dopson	. . .	Kathy Woods	Daniel Dugger	. . .	David Mette
Madeira Beach	c	CM	4	(727) 391-9951	Charles Parker	. . .	Denise Schlegel	Monica Mitchell	Derryl O'Neal	. . .	Michael Maxemow
Madison	c	CM	3	(850) 973-5081	. . .	. . .	Lee Hall	. . .	Aubrey Blanton	Fred Davis	. . .
Maitland	c	CM	12	(407) 539-6222	Doug Kinson	Dean Sprague	Maria Waldrop	Sharon Anselmo	Kenneth Neuhard	Gary Calhoun	Anthony Leffin
Malabar *	t	CM	1	(321) 727-7764	T. Eschenberg	B. Wilbanks-Free	Susan Killian	. . .	Joseph Gianantonio	Jack Parker	. . .
Manalapan	t	CM	. .	(561) 585-9477	William Benjamin	Gregory Dunham	. . .	. . .	. . .	. . .	. . .
Mangonia Park	t	CM	1	(561) 848-1235	William Albury	. . .	Sherry Albury	. . .	. . .	Rodney Thomas	Peter LaMendola
Marathon	c	CM	10	(305) 743-0033	John Bartus	Michael Puto	Cindy Ecklund	Peter Rosasco	Hans Wagner	. . .	. . .
Marco Island	c	CM	14	(239) 389-5000	Michael Minozzi	. . .	Laura Litzan	William Harrison	Michael Murphy	Roger Reinke	Vladimir Ryziw
Margate	c	CM	53	(954) 972-6454	Arthur Bross	Leonard Golub	Shirley Baughman	Gail Gargano	. . .	Jerry Blough	James Hinds
Marianna	c	CM	6	(850) 482-4353	Paul Donofro	Louy Harris	Daniele Pippin	. . .	Jack Barwick	Lou Roberts	. . .
Mary Esther	c	CM	4	(850) 243-3566	Margaret McLemore	John Lulue	Lynne Oler	Tim Spellman	Ronald McArtor	. . .	Lee Iferd
Mascotte	c	CM	2	(352) 429-3341	. . .	. . .	Dana Waters	. . .	Randy Brasher	Steven Allen	Henry Sharpe
Melbourne *	c	CM	71	(321) 953-6350	Harry Goode	Jack Schluckebier	Cathleen Wysor	Michelle Ennis	Paul Forsberg	Donald Carey	Robert Klaproth
Melbourne Beach	t	CM	3	(321) 724-5860	William Stacey	James Bursick	Patricia Burke	Jane Antonsen	Jim Hunter	David Syrkus	. . .
Mexico Beach	c	CM	1	(850) 648-5700	. . .	. . .	. . .	. . .	. . .	. . .	. . .
Miami *	c	MC	358	(305) 416-2100	Manuel Diaz	Pedro Hernandez	Priscilla Thompson	Diana Gomez	William Bryson	John Timney	Stephanie Grindell
Miami Beach	c	CM	92	(305) 673-7000	David Dermer	Jorge Gonzalez	Robert Parcher	Patricia Walker	Floyd Jordan	Donald DeLucca	Fred Beckmann
Miami Gardens	c	CM	101	(305) 622-8000	Shirley Gibson	Danny Crew	Ronetta Taylor	Chris Wallace	. . .	. . .	Tom Ruiz
Miami Lakes	t	CM	12	(305) 364-6100	Wayne Slaton	Alex Rey	Debra Eastman	Alfredo Acin	. . .	. . .	Osdel Larrea
Miami Shores	v	CM	10	(305) 795-2207	Al Davis	Thomas Benton	Barbara Fugazzi	Mark Malatak	. . .	Kevin Lystad	Scott Davis
Miami Springs	c	CM	13	(305) 805-5000	Billy Bain	James Borgmann	Magali Valls	Charles Marshall	. . .	H. Dilling	Denise Yoezle
Midway	c	CM	1	(850) 574-2355	Delores Madison	. . .	Frances Harrell	. . .	. . .	Gregory Gardner	. . .
Milton	c	CM	7	(850) 983-5400	Guy Thompson	Donna Adams	Dewitt Nobles	. . .	John Reble	W. Markopoulos	Anthony Thomsen
Minneola	c	CM	5	(352) 394-3598	. . .	. . .	Jan McDaniel	. . .	. . .	. . .	Mark Odell
Miramar	c	CM	72	(954) 967-1500	Lori Mosely	Robert Payton	. . .	John Merrell	James Hunt	Melvin Standley	Vernon Hargray
Monticello	c	MC	2	(850) 342-0153	. . .	Donald Anderson	Julie Clark	. . .	. . .	. . .	. . .
Mount Dora	c	CM	9	(352) 735-7186	James Yatsuk	Michael Quinn	. . .	Robert Brekelbaum	Ronald Snowberger	T Scoggins	Gary Hammond
Mulberry	c	CM	3	(863) 425-1125	Robert Wheeler	Frank Thomas	. . .	Diana Heitman	. . .	Alan Graham	. . .
Naples	c	CM	20	(239) 213-1810	Bonnie MacKenzie	A. Moss	Tara Norman	Ann Marie Ricardi	James McEvoy	Steven Moore	Dan Mercer
Neptune Beach	c	CM	7	(904) 270-2400	Richard Brown	James Jarboe	Lisa Volpe	Steven Ramsey	. . .	. . .	Leon Smith
New Port Richey	c	CM	16	(727) 841-4500	Frank Parker	. . .	Victoria McDonald	Richard Snyder	Daniel Azzariti	Aage Madsen	Thomas O'Neill
New Smyrna Beach	c	CM	20	(386) 424-2100	. . .	Frank Roberts	. . .	Bill Poling	Timothy Hawver	Ronald Pagano	Mel Phillips
Newberry *	c	CM	3	(352) 472-2161	John Glanzer	Keith Ashby	Gayle Pons	. . .	David Rodriguez	. . .	Blaine Suggs
Niceville	c	CM	11	(850) 729-4008	. . .	Lannie Corbin	Daniel Doucet	. . .	Michael Wright	Brian Cruttenden	Bruce Price
North Bay Village *	c	CM	5	(305) 756-7171	. . .	Jorge Forte	Yvonne Hamilton	Robert Lange	. . .	Scott Israel	. . .
North Lauderdale	c	CM	32	(954) 722-0900	Gary Frankel	Richard Sala	Carmela Dyer	Brian Raducci	. . .	. . .	Michael Shields
North Miami	c	CM	59	(305) 893-6511	Joe Celestin	Clarance Patterson	Simon Bloom	Carlos Perez	. . .	G. Boyd-Savage	Mark Collins
North Miami Beach	c	CM	35	(305) 948-2900	Jeffrey Mischon	Keven Klopp	Solomon Odenz	Marilyn Spencer	. . .	William Berger	. . .

Directory 1/9 continued — OFFICIALS IN U.S. MUNICIPALITIES 2,500 AND OVER IN POPULATION

Jurisdiction	Type	Form of govern-ment	2000 Popu-lation (000)	Main telephone number	Chief elected official	Appointed administrator	Clerk of the governing board	Chief financial officer	Fire chief	Police chief	Public works director
FLORIDA continued											
North Palm Beach	v	CM	12	(561) 841-3355	Edward Eissey	. . .	Kathleen Kelly	Shaukat Khan	John Armstrong	Earl Johnson	Thomas Hogarth
North Port	c	CM	22	(941) 426-8484	Barbara Gross	Steven Crowell	Helen Raimbeau	Teresa Gould	William Taaffe	David Yurchuck	Juliana Belia
North Redington Beach	t	MC	1	(727) 391-4848	William Queen	. . .	Sharon Proehl	. . .	. . .	. . .	Bruce Mercer
Oakland	c	CM	. .	(407) 656-1117	Kathy Stark	Maureen Rischitelli	Linda Balsavage	Elaine Strickland	. . .	Timothy Driscoll	Louis Marinaro
Oakland Park	c	CM	30	(954) 561-6250	Caryl Stevens	John Stunson	. . .	Elbert Wrains	Jim Henson	Edward Overman	. . .
Ocala	c	CM	45	(352) 351-6663	Gerald Ergle	Paul Nugent	Valerie Forster	Donald Corley	Danny Gentry	Samuel Williams	John Zobler
Ocean Ridge	t	CM	1	(561) 732-2635	Gail Aaskov	. . .	Karen Hancsak	. . .	. . .	. . .	. . .
Ocoee	c	CM	24	(409) 905-3100	Scott Vandergrift	Robert Frank	Jean Grafton	Wanda Horton	Ronald Strosnider	Steven Goclon	David Wheeler
Okeechobee	c	CM	5	(863) 763-3372	James Kirk	V. Whitehall	Lane Gamiotea	. . .	Herb Smith	Dennis Davis	Donnie Robertson
Oldsmar *	c	CM	11	(813) 749-1100	Jim Ronecker	Bruce Haddock	Lisa Lene	. . .	Scott McGuff	. . .	John Mulvihill
Opa-Locka	c	CM	15	(305) 688-4611	. . .	Newall Daughtrey	Deborah Irby	Winston Mottley	. . .	Ronald Wilson	Amir Shafi
Orange City *	c	CM	6	(386) 775-5400	Albert Erwin	John McCue	Debbie Renner	Christine Davis	Herbert Hoffman	Jeffrey Baskoff	Paul Johnson
Orange Park	t	CM	9	(904) 264-9565	. . .	John Bowles	Joyce Bryan	Dorothy Mollnow	Harvey Silcox	James Boivin	William White
Orchid *	t	CM	. .	(772) 589-7686	Richard Dunlop	Maria Aguilar	Deb Branwell	. . .	. . .	Philip Redstone	. . .
Orlando	c	MC	185	(407) 246-2235	Buddy Dyer	Byron Brooks	Grace Chewning	G. Miller	Donald Harkins	Jerry Demings	. . .
Ormond Beach *	c	CM	36	(386) 676-3202	Frederick Costello	Isaac Turner	Veronica Patterson	Paul Lane	Barry Baker	Michael Longfellow	Judy Sloane
Oviedo	c	CM	26	(407) 977-6000	. . .	Gerald Seeber	Barbara Barbour	Michelle Greco	Wayne Martin	Dennis Peterson	Charles Smith
Pahokee *	t	CM	5	(561) 924-5534	James Sasser	Lillie Latimore	Raquel Diaz	Derrek Moore	. . .	. . .	Art Cobb
Palatka	c	CM	10	(386) 329-0100	Karl Flagg	Elwin Boynton	Elizabeth Jordan	Ruby Williams	. . .	Gary Getchell	. . .
Palm Bay	c	CM	79	(321) 952-3400	. . .	Lee Feldman	Alice Passmore	. . .	Lawrence Hellmann	Paul Rumbley	. . .
Palm Beach	t	CM	10	(561) 838-5410	. . .	Peter Elwell	Mary Pollitt	Jane Skittone	Kent Koelz	Michael Reiter	. . .
Palm Beach Gardens	c	CM	35	(561) 799-4110	Joe Russo	Ronald Ferris	Patricia Snider	Allan Owens	Peter Bergel	Stephen Stepp	Michael Morrow
Palm Coast *	c	CM	32	(386) 986-3700	James Canfield	James Landon	Clare Hoeni	Ray Britt	Michael Beadle	. . .	Bill Gilley
Palm Springs	v	CM	11	(561) 965-4010	John Davis	Karl Umberger	Irene Burroughs	Rebecca Morse	. . .	Jay Pickens	Richard Gift
Palmetto *	c	MC	12	(941) 723-4570	Lawrence Bustle	. . .	James Freeman	Karen Simpson	. . .	James Lowe	C. Lukowiak
Palmetto Bay	v	CM	25	(305) 259-1234	Eugene Flinn	Ron Williams	Meighan Pier	Alfredo Acin	. . .	Michael Mouring	. . .
Panama City	c	CM	36	(850) 872-3009	Girard Clemons	Kenneth Hammons	. . .	. . .	Jerry Prater	David Slusser	Neil Fravel
Parker	c	MC	4	(850) 871-4104	Brenda Hendricks	. . .	Lois La Seur	Frances Littleton	Andrew Kelley	Charles Sweat	William Weakley
Parkland *	c	CM	13	(954) 753-5040	Michael Udine	C. Gardner-Young	Sandra Couzzo	Barbara Hastings	. . .	Paul O'Connell	Jim Berkman
Pembroke Park	t	CM	6	(954) 966-4600	John Lyons	Robert Levy	. . .	G. Rodriguez	Timothy Keefe	. . .	. . .
Pembroke Pines	c	CM	137	(954) 435-6505	Alex Fekete	Charles Dodge	Eileen Tesh	Rene Gonzalez	Vito Splendorio	Dan Giustino	Shawn Denton
Pensacola	c	CM	56	(850) 435-1720	John Fogg	Thomas Bonfield	Shirley White	Richard Barker	James Dixon	John Mathis	Alfred Garza
Perry	c	CM	6	(850) 584-7161	. . .	. . .	. . .	Sarah Drawdy	Rodney Lytle	Herman Putnal	Barney Johnson
Pinecrest	v	CM	19	(305) 234-2121	Gary Matzner	Peter Lombardi	Guido Inguanzo	Gary Clinton	. . .	John Hohensee	Daniel Moretti
Pinellas Park *	c	CM	45	(727) 541-0700	William Mischler	Michael Gustafson	Diane Corna	Ronald Miller	Douglas Lewis	Dorene Thomas	Thomas Nicholls
Plant City *	c	CM	29	(813) 659-4200	Rick Lott	David Sollenberger	Virginia Helper	Martin Wisgerhof	George Shiley	Bill McDaniel	Willie Nabong
Plantation	c	MC	82	(954) 797-2240	Rae Armstrong	. . .	Susan Slattery	Herbert Herriman	Robert Pudney	Larry Massey	Frank Decelles
Polk City *	t	CM	1	(863) 984-1375	Donald Penton	Cory Carrier	Sylvia Sims	Victoria Silva	. . .	. . .	Ronnie Sims
Pompano Beach	c	CM	78	(954) 786-4626	Lamar Fisher	Garland Chadwell	Mary Chambers	Cynthia Mothner	Harry Small	. . .	William Flaherty
Ponce Inlet	t	CM	2	(386) 322-6711	Nancy Epps	Kassandra Blissett	Jeaneen Clauss	. . .	Dan Scales	Steven Thomas	Ralph Schoenherr
Port Orange	c	CM	45	(386) 506-5500	Allen Green	Kenneth Parker	. . .	John Shelley	Thomas Weber	Gerald Monahan	Warren Pike
Port Richey	c	CM	3	(727) 816-1900	Mark Abbott	Richard Reade	Shirley Dresch	Annette Perez	Timothy Fussell	William Sager	Allen Foley
Port St. Joe	c	CM	3	(386) 229-8261	Frank Pate	Lee Vincent	. . .	. . .	John Ford	. . .	Terry McDaniels
Port St. Lucie *	c	CM	88	(772) 871-5225	Patricia Christensen	Donald Cooper	Karen Phillips	Marcia Dedert	Ron Parrish	John Skinner	Donald Freedland
Punta Gorda	c	CM	14	(941) 575-3308	Stephen Fabian	Howard Kunik	Susan Foster	David Drury	Robert Naylor	Charles Rinehart	Richard Keeney
Quincy	c	CM	6	(850) 627-7681	. . .	Willie Banks	Sylvia Hicks	Neva Reed	Leonard Griffiss	Gerald McSwain	Gene Tucker
Redington Beach	t	MC	1	(727) 391-3875	Bob Fountaine	. . .	Larry Bittner	Tim Gregson	. . .	. . .	Mark Davis
Redington Shores	t	MC	2	(727) 397-5538	. . .	Donald Lusk	. . .	. . .	. . .	. . .	. . .
Riviera Beach *	c	CM	29	(561) 845-4000	Shelby Lowe	William Wilkins	Carrie Ward	Jeffrey Williams	Troy Perry	Clarence Williams	Vincent Akhimie
Rockledge	c	CM	20	(321) 690-3978	Larry Schultz	James McKnight	Mary Moist	. . .	Richard Allen	John Shockey	Jimmy Gilliard
Royal Palm Beach	v	CM	21	(561) 790-5100	David Lodwick	David Farber	Mary Anne Gould	Stanley Hochman	Thomas Vreeland	Michael Bruscell	Robert Hill
Safety Harbor	c	CM	17	(727) 724-1555	Pam Corbino	Billy Beckett	Cathy Benson	JoAnne Ryan	William Stout	. . .	Kurt Peters
Sanford *	c	CM	38	(407) 330-5602	Linda Kuhn	Robert Yehl	Janet Dougherty	James Poulalion	Gerard Ransom	Brian Todley	Thomas George
Sanibel	c	CM	6	(239) 472-3700	Stephen Brown	Judith Zimomra	. . .	Renee Lynch	. . .	William Tomlinson	Gates Castle
Sarasota	c	CM	52	(941) 951-3634	Lou Ann Palmer	Robert Bartolotta	Billy Robinson	Gibson Mitchell	. . .	Peter Abbott	William Hallisey
Satellite Beach	c	CM	9	(321) 773-4407	Harold Bolin	Michael Crotty	Barbara Boyens	Brenda Raver	Daniel Rocque	Lionel Cote	Robert Stowe
Sebastian	c	CM	16	(772) 589-5330	Brian Burkeen	Alfred Minner	Sally Maio	Shai Francis	. . .	James Davis	Jerry Converse
Sebring	c	MC	9	(863) 471-5100	George Hensley	Robert Hoffman	Kathy Haley	C Michael Eastman	Brad Batz	Thomas Dettman	. . .
Seminole	c	MC	10	(727) 391-0204	Dottie Reeder	Frank Edmunds	Beverly Brown	Christine Trovato	Daniel Graves	. . .	Allen Godfrey
Sewall's Point	t	MC	1	(772) 287-2455	Jon Chicky	Robert Kellogg	Joan Barrow	. . .	. . .	Larry McCarty	. . .
South Bay	c	CM	3	(561) 996-6751	. . .	Bobby Smith	Virginia Walker	Gloria Ramos	. . .	. . .	Theodore Green
South Daytona	c	CM	13	(386) 322-3068	Joe Piggotte	Joseph Yarbrough	Debolena Moore	C. Campbell	James Quinn	Gary White	Mark Juliano
South Miami	c	CM	10	(305) 663-6338	Anna Price	Yvonne McKinley	Ronetta Taylor	Hakeem Oshikoya	. . .	Cokes Watson	W. Balogun
South Palm Beach	t	CM	. .	(561) 588-8889	Beverly Savin	Rex Taylor	Barbara Nock	. . .	Nicholas Alvaro	. . .	. . .
South Pasadena *	c	CO	5	(727) 347-4171	. . .	. . .	Mary Braisted	James Graham	. . .	. . .	Gary Anderson
Springfield	c	MC	8	(850) 872-7570	Robert Walker	. . .	Rhonda Taylor	. . .	Jeremy Adams	Sam Slay	Lee French
St. Augustine *	c	CM	11	(904) 825-1013	Joseph Boles	William Harriss	Karen Rogers	Mark Litzinger	Michael Arnold	Loran Lueders	. . .
St. Augustine Beach	c	CM	4	(904) 471-2122	. . .	Max Royle	. . .	. . .	. . .	Richard Hedges	Marcus Chattin
St. Cloud *	c	CM	20	(409) 957-7209	Donna Hart	Thomas Hurt	Linda Jaworski	Michael Turner	Charlie Lewis	Mark Faucett	Robert MacKichan
St. Pete Beach	c	CM	9	(727) 367-2735	Ward Friszolowski	Michael Bonfield	Theresa McMaster	Stephen Gallaher	Herman Golliner	Charles Romine	Scott Graubard
St. Petersburg *	c	CO	248	(727) 893-7171	Rick Baker	Patricia Elston	E. Andujar	. . .	James Large	Charles Harmon	Patricia Anderson
Starke	c	CO	5	(904) 964-5027	. . .	. . .	Linda Johns	. . .	Dwayne Hardee	Gordon Smith	Ricky Thompson
Stuart	c	CM	14	(772) 288-5313	Karl Krueger	Daniel Hudson	Cheryl White	. . .	Larry Massing	Edward Morley	Samuel Amerson
Sunny Isles Beach	c	CM	11	(305) 947-0606	David Samson	Anthony Szerlag	Richard Brown	Jean Watson	. . .	Fred Maas	Rick Conner
Sunrise	c	CM	85	(954) 741-2580	Steven Feren	Patrick Salerno	Felicia Bravo	Laura Toebe	Bruce Moeller	David Boyett	Paul Callsen
Surfside	t	CM	4	(305) 861-4863	Paul Novack	W. Higginbotham	Bella Carcasses	Daniel Martinez	. . .	Lawrence Boemler	Chris Cohen
Sweetwater	c	MC	13	(305) 221-0411	Jose Diaz	. . .	Marie Schmidt	Michael Lavin	. . .	Jesus Mencoal	Antero Espinosa
Tallahassee	c	CM	150	(850) 891-0000	John Marks	A. F. Thompson	. . .	David Reid	Thomas Quillin	Walter McNeil	. . .
Tamarac	c	CM	55	(954) 724-1350	Joseph Schreiber	Jeffrey Miller	Marion Swenson	Tammy Clayton	James Budzinski	. . .	. . .
Tampa	c	MC	303	(813) 274-8041	Pam Iorio	Darrell Smith	S. Foxx-Knowles	Bonnie Wise	Dennis Jones	Steve Hogue	Irvin Lee
Tarpon Springs *	c	MC	21	(727) 938-3711	Beverley Billiris	Ellen Posivach	Irene Jacobs	Arie Walker	Stephen Moreno	Mark Lecouris	Juan Cruz
Tavares	c	CM	9	(352) 742-6211	Ted Wicks	John Drury	Nancy Barnett	Lori Houghton	Emory Kendrick	Stoney Lubins	Aaron Mercer
Temple Terrace	c	CM	20	(813) 989-7100	. . .	Kim Leinbach	Sydney Barkholz	Lee Huffstutler	Clyde Hiers	Anthony Velong	Woodrow Garcia
Tequesta	v	CM	5	(561) 575-6200	Jim Humpage	Michael Couzzo	Gwen Carlisle	Jody Forsythe	James Weinand	Stephen Allison	Gary Preston
Titusville *	c	CM	40	(321) 383-5775	Ronald Swank	Mark Ryan	Wanda Wells	Robert Erickson	. . .	Anthony Bollinger	James Herron
Treasure Island	c	CM	7	(727) 547-4575	Mary Maloof	Reid Silverboard	Jennifer Nye	Darren La France	Charles Fant	Joseph Pelkington	Donald Hambidge
Trenton	c	CM	1	(352) 463-4000	. . .	Jered Ottenwess	. . .	. . .	. . .	. . .	. . .
Valparaiso	c	MC	6	(850) 729-5402	John Arnold	Paul Maryeski	Tammy Johnson	. . .	Charles Frank	Joseph Hart	Anthony Piper
Venice *	c	CM	17	(941) 486-2626	R. Hammett	Martin Black	Lori Stelzer	Jeffrey Snyder	John Reed	Julie Williams	Lawrence Heath
Vero Beach	c	CM	17	(772) 978-5151	Sandra Bowdent	. . .	Tammy Vock	Stephen Maillet	. . .	James Gabbard	Clifford Suthard

Directory 1/9 continued **OFFICIALS IN U.S. MUNICIPALITIES 2,500 AND OVER IN POPULATION**

Jurisdiction	Type	Form of government	2000 Population (000)	Main telephone number	Chief elected official	Appointed administrator	Clerk of the governing board	Chief financial officer	Fire chief	Police chief	Public works director
FLORIDA continued											
Waldo	c	MC	..	(352) 468-1001	Frank Davis	Kim Worley	...	Chuck Hall	Edward Burkhalter	Alvin Smith	Bernard Carter
Wauchula	c	MC	4	(863) 773-3131	Henry Graham	Richard Giroux	Crissy Abbott	...	...	William Beattie	Luther McClellan
Wellington	v	CM	38	(561) 791-4000	Thomas Wenham	Charles Lynn	Awilda Rodriguez	Francine Ramaglia	...	...	Kenneth Roundtree
West Melbourne *	c	CM	9	(321) 727-7700	Shirley Bradshaw	David Reynal	Markae Rupp	Charlotte Luikart	...	Brian Lock	Barry Bartolino
West Miami	c	CM	5	(305) 266-1122	V. Yedra Chruszcz	Yolanda Aguilar	Felix Diaz	Mercedez Leon	...	Patrick Kiel	Juan Pena
West Palm Beach *	c	CO	82	(561) 822-1400	Lois Frankel	Edward Mitchell	Blane Kauthen	Thomas Harris	Robert Ridgeway	Delsa Bush	Peter Spatara
West Park	c	CM	12	(954) 963-5955	Eric Jones	Russell Benford	...	...	...	...	...
Weston *	c	CM	49	(954) 385-2000	Eric Hersh	John Flint	Patricia Bates	...	Craig Otten	Greg Page	...
White Springs	t	CM	..	(386) 397-2310	Joseph McKire	Robert Townsend	Shirley Heath	Pam Tomlinson	Gerald Ford	Joe Subic	K. Hutcherson
Wildwood *	c	CM	3	(352) 330-1330	D. Wolf	James Stevens	...	Joseph Jacobs	...	Don Clark	R. Kornegay
Williston	c	CM	2	(352) 528-3060	...	James Coleman	...	...	...	...	...
Wilton Manors	c	CM	12	(954) 390-2100	Jim Stork	Joseph Gallegos	Angela Scott	Lisa Rabon	...	Richard Wierzbicki	David Archacki
Windermere *	t	MC	1	(407) 876-2563	Gary Bruhn	Cecilia Bernier	Dorothy Burkhalter	Linda Harrison	...	Daniel Saylor	Craig McNeal
Winter Garden	c	CM	14	(407) 656-4111	Jack Quesinberry	Michael Bollhoefer	Kathy Golden	Brian Strobeck	John Williamson	George Brennan	Robert Smith
Winter Haven	c	CM	26	(863) 291-5600	Murray Easterling	David Greene	Barbara McKenzie	Calvin Bowen	Tony Jackson	Paul Goward	Anthony Viola
Winter Park	c	CM	24	(407) 599-3292	Kenneth Marchman	...	Cynthia Bonham	Charles Hamil	James White	Douglas Ball	Troy Attaway
Winter Springs	c	CM	31	(407) 327-1800	Paul Parlyka	Ronald McLemore	Andrea Luaces	...	Timothy Lallathin	Daniel Kerr	Kipton Lockcuff
Zephyrhills	c	CM	10	(813) 780-0000	Clifford Mc Duffie	Steven Spina	Linda Boan	Cathy Familo	Robert Hartwig	Russell Barnes	Richard Moore
GEORGIA											
Acworth *	c	MC	13	(770) 974-3112	Thomas Allegood	Brian Bulthuis	Regina Russell	...	...	Michael Wilkie	Mark Hipp
Adel	c	CM	5	(229) 896-4504	Richard Barr	Jerry Permenter	...	...	Jimmy Walker	Scott Gore	Wayne Giddens
Albany	c	CM	76	(229) 431-3234	Willie Adams	Alfred Lott	Sue Hammond	Shirley Smith	James Arrowood	...	Phillip Roberson
Alma	c	CM	3	(912) 632-8072	Roger Boatright	Thomas Deen	Jackie Madders	...	...	Jimmy Carter	...
Alpharetta	c	CM	34	(678) 297-6000	Arthur Letchas	Robert Regus	Marilyn Rainwater	...	Keith Sanders	Ed Densmore	John Moskaluk
Alto	t	MC	..	(706) 778-8035	Audrey Turner	...	Penny Rogers	Lisa Turner	...	James Krockum	Wiley Cook
Americus	c	MC	17	(229) 924-4411	William McGowan	Charlotte Cotton	Charlotte Blanton	...	Stephen Moreno	Michael Yates	Jess Grace
Ashburn	c	MC	4	(229) 567-3431	Robert Hunnicutt	Jerry Grimes	Sandra Lumpkin	Tina Mauldin	Brian Meadows	Ben Sumner	Carlton Webb
Athens–Clarke County	c	CM	90	(706) 613-3090	Erwin Eldridge	W Reddish	Gloria Spratlin	John Culpepper	Wendell Faulkner	Joseph Lumpkin	David Clark
Atlanta	c	MC	416	(404) 330-6377	Shirley Franklin	Lynnette Young	Rhonda Johnson	Richard Anderson	...	Richard Pennington	David Scott
Auburn	c	MC	6	(770) 963-4002	Harold Money	...	Terry McElwee	Dee Hickman	...	...	...
Austell	c	MC	5	(770) 944-4300	Joe Jerkins	...	Carolyn Duncan	Brenda Norton	Timothy Williams	Bob Starrett	Randy Bowens
Avondale Estates	c	CM	2	(404) 294-5400	John Lawson	Ronald Rabun	...	...	...	...	Craig Mims
Bainbridge	c	CM	11	(229) 248-2000	Billy Reynolds	Christopher Hobby	...	Steven McKown	Dennis Mock	...	Tommy King
Barnesville	c	CM	5	(770) 358-0181	James Matthews	Kenneth Roberts	Carolyn Parker	...	Robert Devane	...	William Johnson
Baxley	c	CM	4	(912) 367-8300	Steve Rigdon	Jeffrey Baxley	Von Spell	...	Jim Ammons	James Godfrey	Gary Patterson
Blackshear	c	MC	3	(912) 449-7000	Preston Hampton	...	Myra Bolden	...	...	George Smiley	Herbert Barber
Blakely	c	MC	5	(229) 723-3677	Ric Hall	...	...	...	Kenneth Jones	...	James Allen
Bowdon	c	MC	1	(770) 258-8980	...	...	...	...	...	Burl Langley	Jerry Langley
Braselton	t	CM	1	(706) 654-3915	...	Jennifer Scott	...	...	...	...	...
Bremen	c	MC	4	(770) 537-2331	Barbara Rivers	Kim Jones	...	Beverly Cash	Raymond Morton	Larry Henbree	...
Brunswick	c	CM	15	(912) 267-5500	Bradford Brown	Roosevelt Harris	Georgia Marion	James Bradley	Lee Stewart	Thomas Cowan	John Butts
Buford	c	CM	10	(770) 945-6761	Phillip Beard	Bryan Kerlin	...	Mike Brown	...	Nelson Stanley	Lamar Sudderth
Cairo *	c	CM	9	(229) 377-1722	R. VanLandingham	William Whitson	Carolyn Lee	Cecil Rash	Roderick Jolivette	Keith Sandefur	Charles Stokes
Calhoun	c	MC	10	(706) 602-5670	Jimmy Palmer	Kelly Cornwell	...	Cathy Harrison	Leonard Nesbitt	Therrell Goswick	...
Camilla	c	CM	5	(229) 336-2220	Alfred Powell	Michael Scott	Kathy Baker	Jimmy Douglas	David Irwin	Raybun Folsom	James Watson
Canton	c	CM	7	(770) 704-1500	Cecil Pruett	...	Diana Threewitt	Robert Logan	Dean Floyd	Billy Cantrell	Larry Wilson
Carrollton	c	CM	19	(770) 830-2000	Wayne Garner	Casey Coleman	...	Jim Triplett	Jimmy Bearden	Joel Richards	Mike Green
Cartersville *	c	CM	15	(770) 387-5616	Michael Fields	Samuel Grove	Sandra Cline	...	Norris Westbrooks	Michael McCain	Bobby Elliott
Cedartown	c	CM	9	(770) 748-3220	John Barrett	Barry Atkison	Carol Crawford	...	Sammy Stephens	Keith Barber	...
Centerville *	c	MC	4	(478) 953-4734	Harold Edwards	Patrick Eidson	Krista Bedingfield	Dwight Williams	Frank Wadsworth	Michael Sullivan	Mike Brumfield
Chamblee	c	MC	9	(770) 986-5010	Evelyn Kennedy	Kathy Brannon	Rebecca Craven	...	...	...	William Hannon
Chatsworth	c	MC	3	(706) 695-2834	Jerry Sanford	...	Wilma Nolan	...	Richard Keefer	Terry Martin	Everett Jones
Clarkston	c	MC	7	(404) 296-6489	Lee Swaney	...	Tracy Ashby	Juliette Paxton	...	Tony Scipio	Mike Shipman
Claxton	c	MC	2	(912) 739-1712	Perry DeLoach	Gayle Durrence	...	...	Larry Rogers	Edward Oglesbee	...
Cochran	c	MC	4	(478) 934-6346	Charles Killebrew	...	Matthew Turknett	...	Glenn Lord	Robert Schmitz	Keith White
College Park	c	CM	20	(404) 767-1537	Jack Longino	...	Lakeitha Reeves	...	Henry Argo	Gary Yandura	Charles Brewer
Colquitt	c	CM	1	(229) 758-3412	Luther Clearman	Cory Thomas	Vicki Phillips	...	Craig Tully	Scott Worsley	Sam Gardner
Columbus-Muscogee Consolidated *	c	CM	178	(706) 653-4000	...	Isaiah Hugley	Tiny Washington	Pamela Hodge	Jeff Meyer	Richard Boren	Gary Stickles
Commerce	c	CM	5	(706) 335-3164	Charles Hardy	Clarence Bryant	Shirley Willis	Kathy Clark	Johnny Eubanks	John Gaissert	Thomas Harvey
Conyers	c	CM	10	(770) 483-4411	Randal Mills	Antony Lucas	Patricia Smith	...	...	David Cathcarat	Brad Sutton
Cordele	c	CM	11	(229) 273-3102	...	Jean Burnette	...	Allen Fulford	Eugene Stephens	William Orrick	James Watson
Cornelia	c	CM	3	(706) 778-8585	Don Higgins	Dee Anderson	Janie Henderson	...	Frankie Smith	Rick Darby	David Ward
Covington	c	CM	11	(770) 385-2000	Sam Ramsey	Frank Turner	John Grotheer	Linda Walden	Don Floyd	Stacey Cotton	Steve Horton
Cuthbert	c	MC	3	(229) 732-3161	...	...	...	...	...	...	...
Dahlonega	c	CM	3	(706) 864-6133	...	William Lewis	Janet Jarrard	...	...	...	Michael Patterson
Dallas	c	CM	5	(770) 443-8110	...	Ken Elsberry	Sarah Ruff	Lloyd Williamson	...	Scot Halter	Kendall Smith
Dalton *	c	MC	27	(706) 278-9500	Raymond Elrod	James Sanders	B. Chattam	Cindy Jackson	Barry Gober	James Chadwick	Benny Dunn
Darien	c	MC	1	(912) 437-6686	David Bluestein	Christopher Cook	Colleen Jolley	...	...	...	Donnie Howard
Dawson	c	CM	5	(229) 995-4444	Robert Albritten	David Bell	Sheri Howard	...	Don Laye	Ernest Webb	...
Decatur *	c	CM	18	(404) 370-4102	William Floyd	Peggy Merriss	Karen Des Islets	...	Jerry Malone	Michael Booker	David Junger
Donalsonville *	c	MC	2	(229) 524-2118	David Fain	H. Shingler	Linda Gray	...	E. Brooks	Jimmy Holt	Donald Gambrell
Doraville	c	MC	9	(770) 451-8745	Ray Jenkins	...	Betty Cloer	...	...	Tommy McElroy	...
Douglas *	c	CM	10	(912) 384-3302	Tony Paulk	Terrell Jacobs	Wynetta Gaskins	Joyce Cliett	Timothy White	Clifford Thomas	Anthony Kirkland
Douglasville *	c	CM	20	(770) 920-3000	Mickey Thompson	William Osborne	Joyce Stone	Karin Callan	...	J. Whisenant	Greg Roberts
Dublin	c	CM	15	(478) 272-1620	...	George Roussel	...	Joseph Kinard	Robert Drew	Wayne Cain	Jimmy Sawyer
Duluth *	c	CM	22	(770) 476-3434	Shirley Lasseter	Euel McLemore	Teresa Lynn	Ken Sakmar	...	Randall Belcher	Audrey Turner
East Dublin	c	MC	2	(478) 272-6883	George Gornto	Larry Drew	Terrie Drew	...	Doyle Tanner	William Luecke	H. Scarborough
East Point	c	CM	39	(404) 209-5160	Patsy Hilliard	...	Bobbie Jones	William Epps	...	Frank Brown	Derek Bogan
Eastman *	c	CM	5	(478) 374-7721	Woody Woodward	James Wright	Bea Edge	...	Carl Johnson	Furman Wiggins	Royce Williams
Eatonton	c	MC	6	(706) 485-3311	John Reid	Martin Elmore	Sarah Abrams	...	Steve Reid	Kent Lawrence	Michael Roberts
Elberton	c	CM	4	(706) 213-3100	Iola Stone	Lanier Dunn	Cindy Churney	Lynn Saxon	Russell Guest	Mark Welsh	Jimmy Welborn
Fairburn	c	CM	5	(770) 964-2244	Betty Hannah	James Williams	R. Truskolaski	...	Jim Fleming	Mackie Carson	Karl Johnson
Fayetteville *	c	MC	11	(770) 719-4183	Kenneth Steele	William Morton	Judy Stephens	Lorri Robinson	Alan Jones	Jeff Harris	Charles Stanley
Fitzgerald	c	CM	8	(229) 426-5060	Gerald Thompson	Henry Tyson	Linda Saunders	Kathy Young	Roger Coleman	William Smallwood	Waymon Walker
Forest Park *	c	CM	21	(404) 366-4720	Corine Deyton	Johnny Parker	...	M. Blandenburg	Eddie Buckholts	Dwayne Hobbs	Michael Gippert
Forsyth	c	MC	3	(478) 994-5649	James Pace	...	Janice Hall	...	Walter Carter	Benjamin Ponder	Alvin Randall
Fort Oglethorpe	c	CM	6	(706) 866-2544	Judson Burkhart	Jim Dinley	Harold Silcox	Pam Travillian	Bruce Ballew	Larry Black	Phillip Parker
Fort Valley	c	MC	8	(478) 825-8261	John Ezell	Richard Little	...	Linda Peterman	Gary Moye	...	George Clark

Directory 1/9 continued OFFICIALS IN U.S. MUNICIPALITIES 2,500 AND OVER IN POPULATION

Jurisdiction	Type	Form of govern-ment	2000 Popu-lation (000)	Main telephone number	Chief elected official	Appointed administrator	Clerk of the governing board	Chief financial officer	Fire chief	Police chief	Public works director
GEORGIA continued											
Gainesville *	c	CM	25	(770) 535-6887	Robert Hamrick	Bryan Shuler	Denise Jordan	Melody Marlowe	. . .	Roy Hooper	Adrian Niles
Garden City	c	MC	11	(912) 966-7777	Andy Quinney	Brian Johnson	Rhonda Ferrell	Robert Krause	James Crosby	David Lyons	Thomas Cannon
Glennville *	c	MC	3	(912) 654-2461	Jean Bridges	Amy Murray	Teresa Pazderski	. . .	Bobby Brannen	Mickey Anderson	Stan Dansby
Gordon	t	MC	2	(478) 628-2222	Kenneth Turner	. . .	Towana Brown	. . .	Terry Eady	Mike Hall	George Wynn
Grantville	c	CM	1	(770) 583-2289	. . .	Johnny Roberts	. . .	. . .	. . .	. . .	. . .
Greensboro	c	MC	3	(706) 453-7967	Glenn Wright	Larry Postell	. . .	. . .	Fred Cook	Ossie Mapp	Bill Shirley
Griffin *	c	CM	23	(770) 229-6400	Bill Landrum	Kenny Smith	. . .	. . .	Tommy Jones	Frank Strickland	Brant Keller
Grovetown	c	MC	6	(706) 863-4576	. . .	. . .	. . .	. . .	. . .	. . .	. . .
Hampton	c	CM	3	(770) 946-4306	. . .	. . .	. . .	. . .	. . .	. . .	. . .
Hapeville	c	MC	6	(404) 669-2100	C. Martin	. . .	. . .	Michael Rast	William Edwards	Dewey Attaway	James Griffith
Hartwell	c	CM	4	(706) 376-4756	Matt Beasley	David Aldrich	Jean Turner	Joan Hughes	Terry Vickery	Cecil Reno	Dennis White
Hawkinsville *	c	CM	3	(478) 892-3240	Henry Cravey	Jerry Murkerson	Evelyn Herrington	. . .	Leslie Sewell	Samuel Tripp	Johnny Gordon
Hazlehurst *	c	MC	3	(912) 375-6680	Wayne Fountain	. . .	Ethelyn Creech	. . .	Charles Wasdin	Steve Land	Jeff Jones
Helen	c	CM	. .	(706) 878-2733	. . .	Jerry Elkins	Kimberly Smith	Terri Caporale	. . .	Ted Ray	Joseph Hewell
Hinesville *	c	MC	30	(912) 876-3564	Thomas Ratcliffe	Billy Edwards	Sarah Lumpkin	Kimberly Davis	Lamar Cook	George Stagmeier	. . .
Hogansville	c	CM	2	(706) 637-8629	Wilson St. Clair	Randall Jordan	Dianne Carter	. . .	. . .	Hilton Odom	. . .
Holly Springs	c	MC	3	(770) 345-5546	Tim Downing	Anthony Griffin	Marie Johnson	. . .	. . .	Ken Ball	. . .
Homerville	c	MC	2	(912) 487-2375	Carol Chambers	Albert Thornton	Shirley Delk	. . .	Danny Strickland	Mark Register	. . .
Jackson	c	MC	3	(770) 775-7535	Charles Brown	. . .	Lara Brewer	. . .	Harvey Norris	Michael Riley	Dawson Heath
Jefferson	c	CM	3	(706) 367-7207	. . .	David Clabo	. . .	. . .	Don Elrod	Darren Glenn	. . .
Jesup	c	CM	9	(912) 427-1313	Herb Shaw	Richard Deal	Onda Woodard	. . .	Julian Brinkley	Wayne Hutcheson	Eddie Williams
Jonesboro	c	MC	3	(770) 478-3800	Joy Day	. . .	Joan Jones	Stacey Inglis	. . .	Jim Roberts	Sam Durrance
Kennesaw	c	MC	21	(770) 424-8274	Leonard Church	Lewis Kennedy	Debra Taylor	Kenneth Turner	. . .	Tim Callahan	Woody McFarlin
Kingsland	c	MC	10	(912) 729-5613	Kenneth Smith	Gwendolyn Mungin	Shirley Bryan	Tamra Edwards	Morris Peeples	J Franks Waits	William Coleman
La Fayette *	c	CM	6	(706) 639-1501	Neal Florence	Johnnie Arnold	Brenda Anderson	. . .	. . .	. . .	Richard Moore
La Grange	c	CM	25	(706) 883-2010	Jeff Lukken	Thomas Hall	. . .	. . .	Chris Smith	Louis Dekmar	David Brown
Lake City	c	MC	2	(404) 366-8080	Willie Oswalt	Gerald Garr	. . .	. . .	. . .	David Colwell	Eddie Robinson
Lavonia	c	CM	1	(706) 356-8781	Ralph Owens	Gary Fesperman	Angela Greer	. . .	Jones Beasley	Randy Shirley	. . .
Lawrenceville	c	MC	22	(770) 963-2414	. . .	. . .	. . .	. . .	. . .	. . .	. . .
Lilburn *	c	MC	11	(770) 921-2210	Jack Bolton	Thomas Combiths	Kathy Maner	. . .	. . .	John Davidson	. . .
Lithonia	c	MC	2	(770) 482-8136	Marcia Glenn	. . .	. . .	. . .	. . .	Manuel Norrington	. . .
Loganville	c	CM	5	(770) 466-1165	Gene Matthews	Bill Jones	Michelle Deaton	. . .	. . .	. . .	. . .
Louisville	c	CM	2	(478) 625-3166	Julian Veatch	James Rhodes	Lona Lane	. . .	Joe Cox	. . .	Tony Richbourg
Lyons	c	MC	4	(912) 526-8606	John Moore	Rick Hartley	Lynn Rowland	. . .	. . .	Rickey Newsome	Darel Corley
Macon	c	MC	97	(478) 751-7400	Clarence Ellis	Regina McDuffie	. . .	Kelly Clark	James Hartley	Rodney Monroe	Dexter White
Madison	c	CM	3	(706) 342-1251	. . .	. . .	. . .	. . .	. . .	. . .	. . .
Manchester	c	CM	3	(706) 846-3141	Dorsey Wilson	Grady McCalmon	Nancy Thompson	. . .	Fred Schmalz	Ron Jackson	Ralph Pearson
Marietta *	c	CM	58	(770) 794-5562	Bill Dunaway	William Bruton	Stephanie Guy	. . .	Jackie Gibbs	Dan Flyn	. . .
Mc Donough	c	MC	8	(770) 957-3915	Richard Craig	James Lee	. . .	. . .	Don Crowell	Preston Dorsey	Gary Barham
Mc Rae	c	MC	2	(229) 868-6051	. . .	. . .	. . .	. . .	. . .	. . .	. . .
Metter *	c	MC	3	(912) 685-2527	William Trapnell	Joseph Mosley	Angela Conner	. . .	Jason Douglas	William Hooper	Garland Hendrix
Milledgeville	c	MC	18	(478) 414-4092	Floyd Griffin	E. Wood	. . .	Frances Hatcher	Jerome Dietrich	Woodrow Blue	Jack Graham
Millen	c	MC	3	(478) 982-6100	. . .	James Knight	Cynthia Bragg	. . .	. . .	Dennis Simmons	Clay Boulineau
Milton	c	CM	20	(678) 242-2500	. . .	C. Lagerbloom	J. Marchiafava	. . .	. . .	. . .	. . .
Monroe	c	MC	11	(770) 267-7536	Greg Thompson	Julian Jackson	. . .	Renee Prather	Wayne Chancey	Marvin Glass	Hugh Worley
Montezuma	c	MC	3	(478) 472-8144	. . .	. . .	. . .	. . .	. . .	. . .	. . .
Morrow	c	CM	4	(770) 961-4002	James Millirons	John Lampl	Brenda Allen	Tom Sawyer	. . .	. . .	Jeffrey Eady
Moultrie	c	CM	14	(229) 985-1974	William McIntosh	. . .	. . .	Gary McDaniel	Kenneth Hannon	Frank Lang	Albert Ward
Nashville *	c	MC	4	(229) 686-5527	Travis Harper	Mandy Luke	Johnny Hall	. . .	Buck Warren	John Clayton	. . .
Newnan *	c	CM	16	(770) 253-2682	L. Brady	Richard Bolin	Della Hill	Katrina Cline	William Whitley	Douglas Meadows	Michael Klahr
Norcross	c	MC	8	(770) 448-2122	Lillian Webb	Warren Hutmacher	Carol Dennen	Douglas Chastain	. . .	Richard Miller	Brad Cole
Ocilla	c	MC	3	(229) 468-5141	Donald Royal	Greg Giddens	Alicia Roberts	. . .	Mark Taibi	Billy Hancock	Roosevelt George
Palmetto	c	CM	3	(770) 463-3377	. . .	. . .	. . .	. . .	. . .	. . .	. . .
Peachtree City *	c	CM	31	(770) 487-7657	Harold Logsdon	Bernard McMullen	. . .	Paul Salvatore	Ed Eiswerth	. . .	Tom Corbett
Pelham	c	MC	4	(229) 294-7900	Chester Shelnutt	James Davis	Letitia Smith	Ralph Williams	James Creech	Neal McCormick	Roger Barfield
Pembroke	c	MC	2	(912) 653-4413	. . .	. . .	. . .	. . .	. . .	. . .	. . .
Perry	c	CM	9	(478) 988-2700	James Worrall	R. Lee Gilmour	. . .	Brenda King	Gary Hamlin	George Potter	. . .
Pooler	c	CM	6	(912) 748-7261	Earl Carter	Dennis Baxter	Maribeth Lindler	Linda Smith	Nolan Salter	Clarence Chan	Robert Byrd
Port Wentworth	c	MC	3	(912) 964-4379	Tim Holbrook	Phillip Claxton	Janet Hendrick	Judith Harrelson	James Jackson	James Melvin	Tommy Thomas
Powder Springs *	c	CM	12	(770) 943-1666	Patricia Vaughn	Charles Nickerson	Betty Brady	Regina Auld	. . .	Larry Richardson	Rodger Swaim
Quitman	c	CM	4	(229) 263-4166	. . .	. . .	. . .	. . .	. . .	. . .	. . .
Richmond Hill	c	CM	6	(912) 756-3632	. . .	Michael Melton	. . .	. . .	. . .	. . .	. . .
Rincon	c	CM	4	(912) 826-5745	Ken Lee	Phillip Barton	Wanda Hendrix	Brett Bennett	Corey Rahn	. . .	Tim Bowles
Riverdale *	c	CM	12	(770) 997-8989	Phaedra Graham	Iris Jessie	Stephanie thomas	. . .	William Hayes	Thetus Knox	. . .
Rockmart	c	CM	3	(770) 684-5454	. . .	Jeffery Ellis	. . .	. . .	Larry Carter	. . .	. . .
Rome	c	CM	34	(706) 236-4400	Ronald Wallace	John Bennett	Joseph Smith	Sheree Shore	Bobbie McKenzie	Hubert Smith	W Kirk Nulan
Rossville	c	MC	3	(706) 866-1325	Johnny Baker	. . .	Sherry Foster	. . .	William Eaves	. . .	Phillip Morton
Roswell	c	MC	79	(770) 641-3713	Jere Wood	Katherine Love	Sue Creel	Julia Luke	Ricky Spencer	T. Williams	Stuart Moring
Sandersville *	c	MC	6	(478) 552-2525	. . .	William Goforth	. . .	. . .	. . .	. . .	. . .
Sandy Springs	c	CM	85	(770) 730-5600	Eva Galambos	John McDonough	. . .	Steven Rapson	Jack McElfish	Eugene Wilson	Angelia Parham
Savannah *	c	CM	131	(912) 651-6484	Otis Johnson	Michael Brown	Dyanne Reese	Richard Evans	Charles Middleton	Daniel Flynn	Billy Jones
Sky Valley	c	CM	. .	(706) 746-2204	Steve Brett	Darrell Jones	Mandi Cantrell	. . .	. . .	Ralph Woods	Jerry Dills
Smyrna	c	MC	40	(770) 434-6600	A. Bacon	Wayne Wright	Melinda Dameron	Claudia Edgar	. . .	Stanley Hook	Scott Stokes
Snellville	c	MC	15	(770) 985-3500	Brett Harrell	. . .	. . .	. . .	. . .	. . .	. . .
Social Circle	c	CM	3	(770) 464-2380	James Burgess	Douglas White	. . .	Susan Roper	Steve Shelton	Jeff Johnson	. . .
Soperton	c	MC	2	(912) 529-6173	. . .	. . .	. . .	. . .	. . .	. . .	. . .
Springfield	c	MC	1	(912) 754-6666	. . .	. . .	. . .	. . .	. . .	. . .	. . .
St. Marys *	c	MC	13	(912) 510-4000	Deborah Hase	William Shanahan	Darlene Roellig	Jennifer Brown	Robert Horton	Tim Hatch	Bobby Marr
Statesboro	c	CM	22	(912) 764-5468	William Hatcher	George Wood	Judy McCorkle	Cindy West	Joe Beasley	Stan York	Bobby Colson
Stone Mountain	c	CM	7	(770) 498-8984	Gary Peet	. . .	Denise Hicks	. . .	. . .	Chancy Troutman	Jim Tavenner
Sugar Hill	c	CM	11	(770) 945-6716	Gary Pirkle	Robert Hail	Jane Whittington	Kelley Canady	. . .	. . .	. . .
Summerville	c	MC	4	(706) 857-0900	. . .	. . .	. . .	. . .	. . .	. . .	. . .
Suwanee *	c	MC	8	(770) 945-8996	Nick Masino	Marvin Allen	. . .	Amelia Sakmar	. . .	Michael Jones	James Miller
Swainsboro *	c	MC	6	(478) 237-7025	Charles Schwabe	. . .	. . .	Melissa Kirby	Mike Strobridge	Johnny Shuman	Michael Connolly
Sylvania	c	CM	2	(912) 564-7411	Margaret Evans	H. Carter Crawford	Judy Hill	Belinda Whirley	Gary Weaver	Mark Tretheway	Dennis Daley
Sylvester	c	MC	5	(229) 776-8505	William Yearta	Danny Lucas	Deborah Bridges	. . .	Thomas Marchman	Tony Strenth	Jimmy Fowler
Tallapoosa	c	CM	2	(770) 574-2345	Micajah Bagwell	Philip Eidson	Carolyn Brown	Donna Cain	Stephen McClain	David Godfrey	. . .
Thomaston	c	CM	9	(706) 647-4242	Hays Arnold	Patrick Comiskey	. . .	Dennis Truitt	James Lifsey	Dan Greathouse	. . .
Thomasville	c	CM	18	(229) 228-7673	. . .	. . .	. . .	. . .	. . .	. . .	. . .
Thomson *	c	MC	6	(706) 595-1781	Robert Knox	Donald Powers	Dianne Landers	Tammy Haire	Rick Sewell	John Hathaway	Peter Ruddick
Thunderbolt	t	MC	2	(912) 354-5533	James Petrea	M. Lumpkin-Lotson	Rose McCombs	. . .	Lawton Smith	Stephen Smith	Fred Corey

Directory 1/9 continued — OFFICIALS IN U.S. MUNICIPALITIES 2,500 AND OVER IN POPULATION

Jurisdiction	Type	Form of govern- ment	2000 Popu- lation (000)	Main telephone number	Chief elected official	Appointed administrator	Clerk of the governing board	Chief financial officer	Fire chief	Police chief	Public works director
GEORGIA continued											
Tifton *	c	CM	15	(229) 382-6231	Paul Johnson	Michael Vollmer	Rona Martin	Carmina Turner	James Flippo	James Smith	Cal Carpenter
Toccoa	c	CM	9	(706) 886-8451	Ferrell Morgan	William Morse	Josephine Gleason	Emory Stephens	Rodney Burdette	Jackie Whitmire	Randy Smith
Tybee Island *	c	CM	3	(912) 786-4573	Jason Buelterman	Diane Schleicher	Vivian Woods	John Redmond	Clifton Sasser	James Price	Joe Wilson
Tyrone *	t	CM	3	(770) 487-4038	Sheryl Lee	Barry Amos	...	...	...	Brandon Perkins	Renee Holt
Union City	c	CM	11	(770) 964-2288	Ralph Moore	...	Barbara Steward	Theresia McDearis	Kenneth Collins	Michael Isome	Buddy Landrum
Valdosta	c	CM	43	(229) 259-3500	James Rainwater	Larry Hanson	J. Marchiafva	Richard Hamlen	James Rice	Charles Simons	...
Varnell	c	MC	1	(706) 694-8800	...	Jestin Johnson	...	...	...	...	...
Vidalia	c	CM	10	(912) 537-7661	...	William Torrance	...	...	...	...	...
Vienna *	c	MC	2	(229) 268-4744	Willie Davis	Gail Bembry	...	Debra Spring	Chuck Ellis	David Musselwhite	Larry Allen
Villa Rica	c	CM	4	(770) 459-7000	J Collins	...	...	Cindy Samples	...	Michael Mansour	...
Warner Robins	c	MC	48	(478) 929-1111	Donald Walker	...	Carolyn Robbins	...	Robert Singletary	Daniel Hart	Joe Musselwhite
Washington	c	CM	4	(706) 678-3277	Willie Burns	Michael Eskew	Debbie Danner	...	Alan Poss	Michael Davis	...
Waycross	c	CM	15	(912) 287-2912	Robert Odum	Peter Pyrzenski	Jerry Grimes	Larry Gattis	Cedric Scott	Tony Tanner	Sam Ray
Waynesboro	c	CM	5	(706) 554-8000	Martin Dolin	Jerry Coalson	...	...	Ronnie Baxley	Karl Allen	...
West Point	c	MC	3	(706) 645-2226	...	George Moon	...	...	...	...	...
Winder	c	MC	10	(770) 867-3106	...	...	Jane Skelton	George Beck	Raymond Mattison	Stanley Rodgers	...
Woodbine	c	CM	1	(912) 576-3211	W Burford Clark	Sandra Rayson	...	...	...	...	...
Woodstock	c	CM	10	(770) 926-8852	William Dewrell	...	Rhonda Pezzello	Gena Kelley	Jerry Smith	David Schofield	Jarvis Middleton
Wrightsville	c	MC	2	(478) 864-3303	Phillip Boatright	...	Jewell Parker	Ralph Holmes	Stan Garnto	Steve Gresham	Lamar Lague
HAWAII											
Hilo	c	MC	45	(808) 961-8361	...	...	...	...	...	...	...
Honolulu	c	MC	836	(808) 523-4809	Mufi Hannemann	Jeff Coelho	...	Mary Waterhouse	Attilio Leonardi	Boisse Correa	Eric Takamura
IDAHO											
American Falls	c	MC	4	(208) 226-2569	...	...	...	...	...	...	...
Ammon	c	MC	6	(208) 529-4211	C. Ard	...	Aleen Jensen	...	Clarence Nelson	...	David Wadsworth
Blackfoot	c	MC	10	(208) 785-8600	Mike Virtue	...	Suzanne McNeel	...	...	R. Moore	Ron Harwell
Boise	c	MC	185	(208) 384-3850	David Bieter	Jade Riley	Annette Mooney	John Faw	Renn Ross	Michael Masterson	Charles Mickelson
Bonners Ferry	c	MC	2	(208) 267-3105	Darrell Kerby	Stephen Boorman	...	...	Larry Owsley	...	...
Buhl	c	MC	3	(208) 543-5650	Barbara Gietzen	...	Sharon Sheets	...	Mark Grimes	Ronald Romero	R. Himmelberger
Burley	c	MC	9	(208) 678-2224	Jon Anderson	Mark Mitton	Melanie Haynes	...	Phil Heiner	...	Leon Bedke
Caldwell	c	MC	25	(208) 455-3000	Richard Winder	...	Betty Keller	...	Bruce Allcott	...	Gordon Law
Chubbuck	c	MC	9	(208) 237-2400	...	...	...	...	...	...	...
Coeur D'Alene	c	MC	34	(208) 769-2300	...	Wendy Hague	Susan Weathers	Troy Tymesen	Kenneth Gabriel	Thomas Cronin	...
Driggs	c	MC	1	(208) 354-2362	Louis Christensen	...	Sarah McMillon	Amy Smith	...	...	...
Eagle	c	MC	11	(208) 939-6813	Richard Yzaguirre	...	Sharon Moore	...	...	...	...
Emmett	c	MC	5	(208) 365-6050	Ronald Morgan	...	...	...	Shannon Crays	Blaine Hyde	Bruce Evans
Garden City	c	MC	10	(208) 377-1831	...	...	...	...	...	...	...
Gooding	c	MC	3	(208) 934-5669	Herb Stroud	...	Carmen Korsen	...	...	Paul Brown	Todd Bunn
Grangeville	c	MC	3	(208) 983-2851	Terry Vanderwall	...	Donna Forsman	...	Roy Powell	Wayne Sedam	Kenneth Gortsema
Hayden	c	MC	9	(208) 772-4411	Ron McIntire	Jay Townsend	Vicki Rutherford	Lila Erickson	...	...	Wade Holecek
Heyburn	c	MC	2	(208) 679-8158	George Anderson	...	Linda Dayley	...	Mike Brown	George Warrell	Scott Spevak
Idaho Falls	c	MC	50	(208) 529-1248	Linda Milam	...	Rose Anderson	Robert Holm	Dean Ellis	Kent Livsey	Chad Stanger
Jerome *	c	MC	7	(208) 324-8189	Charles Correll	Travis Rothweiler	Katherine Cone	...	James Auclaire	Dan Hall	Robert Culver
Kellogg	c	MC	2	(208) 786-9131	Roger Mangum	...	Sandy Nearing	...	Dale Costa	John Crawford	James Sharp
Ketchum	c	MC	3	(208) 726-3841	Ed Simon	...	Sandra Cady	...	Greg Schwab	Cory Lyman	Brian Christiansen
Kimberly	c	MC	2	(208) 423-4151	...	Polly Hulsey	...	...	...	...	...
Lewiston	c	CM	30	(208) 746-3671	Jeff Nesset	John Krauss	Becky O'Connor	Barbara Clark	Steven Cooper	Jack Baldwin	Chris Davies
McCall	c	CM	2	(208) 634-7142	Kirk Eimers	Lindley Kirkpatrick	Dan Irwin	...	...	Jerry Summers	William Keating
Meridian	c	MC	34	(208) 888-4433	Robert Corrie	...	William Berg	Stacy Kilchenmann	Kenneth Bowers	Richard Worley	Gary Smith
Montpelier	c	MC	2	(208) 847-0824	George Lane	...	Renee Bird	...	David Barnson	David Higley	Donald Toomer
Moscow	c	MC	21	(208) 883-7000	Marshall Comstock	Gary Riedner	Stephanie Kalasz	Donald Palmer	Donald Strong	Daniel Weaver	Les MacDonald
Mountain Home	c	MC	11	(208) 587-2104	Joe McNeal	...	Nina Patterson	...	Philip Gridley	Tommy Berry	Wayne Shepherd
Nampa	c	MC	51	(208) 465-2220	R Tom Dale	...	Diana Lambing	Todd Bunderson	Ron Anderson	Curtis Homer	...
Orofino	c	MC	3	(208) 476-4725	...	Rick Laam	Virginia Davis	...	...	Ronnie Pomerinke	Floyd Williams
Payette	c	MC	7	(208) 642-6024	Mark Heleker	John Franks	...	...	Jeff Sands	Mark Clark	...
Pocatello *	c	MC	51	(208) 234-6163	Roger Chase	...	Rhonda Johnson	David Swindell	Kevin Quick	...	Greg Lanning
Post Falls	c	MC	17	(208) 773-3511	Clay Larkin	Eric Keck	Christene Pappas	Shelly Enderud	...	Clifford Hayes	Terry Werner
Preston	c	MC	4	(208) 852-1817	Jay Heusser	...	Jerry Larsen	...	...	Scott Shaw	Scott Martin
Rathdrum	c	MC	4	(208) 687-0261	Brian Steele	Brett Boyer	Judy Hollenbeck	...	...	Robert Moore	Chet Anderson
Rexburg	c	MC	17	(208) 359-3020	Shawn Larsen	...	Blair Kay	Richard Horner	Spencer Larsen	Lynn Archibald	Farrell Davidson
Rigby	c	MC	2	(208) 745-8111	John Anderson	...	Anna Bidwell	...	...	Larry Anderson	Douglas Nelson
Rupert	c	MC	5	(208) 436-9600	Audrey Neiwerth	...	Linda Price	Colleen Severson	Larry Pool	Kenneth Fedders	Robert Russmann
Salmon	c	MC	3	(208) 756-3214	Stanley Davis	...	...	...	Bob Perry	Jody Seybold	Mickey Verbeck
Sandpoint *	c	MC	6	(208) 263-3310	Raymond Miller	...	Maree Peck	...	Robert Tyler	Mark Lockwood	Kody Van Dyk
Shelley	c	MC	3	(208) 357-3390	Eric Christensen	...	Sandy Gaydusek	...	...	Alan Dial	Rick Anderson
Soda Springs	c	MC	3	(208) 547-2600	Kirk Hansen	Lee Godfrey	Tausha Vorwaller	...	...	Joe Rice	Craig Hill
St. Anthony *	c	MC	3	(208) 624-3494	Willard Beck	...	Taci Stoddard	...	Dave Fausett	James Smith	Scott Butigan
St. Maries	c	MC	2	(208) 245-2577	...	...	...	...	...	...	...
Sun Valley	c	CM	1	(208) 622-4438	David Wilson	Virginia Egger	Janis Wright	Michelle Fosterton	Jeffrey Carnes	Cameron Daggett	Bill Whitesell
Twin Falls *	c	CM	34	(208) 735-7251	Lance Clow	Thomas Courtney	Sharon Bryan	Gary Evans	Ronald Clark	Jim Munn	Jackie Fields
Weiser	c	MC	5	(208) 549-1965	...	...	...	...	...	...	...
ILLINOIS											
Abingdon	c	MC	3	(309) 462-3182	Michael Brackett	...	B. Joanne Batson	...	...	William Robinson	Kirt Links
Addison	v	MC	35	(630) 543-4100	Lorenz Hartnig	Joseph Block	Lucille Zucchero	Roseanne Benson	...	Timothy Hayden	Gregory Brunst
Aledo	c	MC	3	(309) 582-7241	Lee Celske	Patrick Burelle	Brenda Rick	...	Dennis Litwiler	Steve Struble	Jewel Bucy
Algonquin *	v	CM	23	(847) 658-2700	John Schmitt	William Ganek	Gerald Kautz	John Walde	...	Russell Laine	Robert Mitchard
Alsip *	v	MC	19	(708) 385-6902	Patrick Kitching	...	Deborah Venhuizen	Greg Palumbo	Charles Geraci	Robert Troy	Vincent Cullen
Alton	c	MC	30	(618) 463-3599	Donald Sandidge	...	Mary Gibson	Stephanie Elliott	Timothy Spaulding	Christopher Sullivan	James Hernandez
Anna	c	MC	5	(618) 833-8528	Steve Hartline	Steven Guined	...	...	James Cross	Gordon Hopp	Russell Sullivan
Antioch	v	MC	8	(847) 395-1000	Marilyn Shineflug	Michael Haley	Candi Rowe	...	Dennis Volling	Charles Fagan	Bill Smith
Arcola *	c	MC	2	(217) 268-4966	Larry Ferguson	Bill Wagoner	Carol Turner	...	Bob Clark	Michael Phillips	Jack Logan
Arlington Heights *	v	CM	76	(847) 368-5000	...	William Dixon	Edwina Corso	Thomas Kuehne	Glenn Ericksen	Gerald Mourning	Scott Shirley
Arthur	v	MC	2	(217) 543-2927	...	...	...	...	...	...	...
Auburn	c	MC	4	(217) 438-6151	...	...	...	...	...	...	...
Aurora	c	MC	142	(630) 892-8811	David Stover	...	...	Brian Caputo	...	...	...

Directory 1/9 continued OFFICIALS IN U.S. MUNICIPALITIES 2,500 AND OVER IN POPULATION

Jurisdiction	Type	Form of govern-ment	2000 Popu-lation (000)	Main telephone number	Chief elected official	Appointed administrator	Clerk of the governing board	Chief financial officer	Fire chief	Police chief	Public works director
ILLINOIS continued											
Bannockburn	v	MC	1	(847) 945-6080	Michael Grutza	. . .	Frances Picchietti	Linda McCulloch	. . .	Kevin Tracz	. . .
Barrington *	v	CM	10	(847) 304-3400	Karen Darch	Denise Pieroni	Ron Koppelmann	Maggie Bosley	James Arie	Jeffrey Lawler	. . .
Barrington Hills	v	MC	3	(847) 551-3000	. . .	. . .	. . .	. . .	. . .	. . .	. . .
Bartlett	v	CM	36	(630) 837-0800	. . .	Valerie Salmons	Linda Gallien	. . .	. . .	Daniel Palmer	Paul Kuester
Bartonville	v	MC	6	(309) 633-2053	. . .	. . .	. . .	. . .	. . .	. . .	. . .
Batavia	c	MC	23	(630) 879-1424	Jeff Schielke	William McGrath	Maude Volk	Peggy Colby	William Darin	Dennis Anderson	Gary Larson
Beach Park	v	CM	10	(847) 746-1770	Milt Jensen	Kenneth Lopez	Laurie Cvengros	. . .	. . .	. . .	. . .
Beardstown	c	MC	5	(217) 323-3110	Robert Walters	. . .	Brian Ruch	. . .	Robert Brown	Thomas Schlueter	Todd Harmeyer
Beecher *	v	CM	2	(708) 946-2261	Paul Lohmann	Robert Barber	Janett Conner	. . .	David Lagesse	Jeffrey Weissgerber	Harold Cowger
Belleville	c	MC	41	(618) 233-6810	Mark Kern	. . .	Linda Fields	Nancy Boeckman	Mike Hawthorne	James Rokita	. . .
Bellwood	v	MC	20	(708) 547-3500	Donald Lemm	Roy McCampbell	Booker Brown	I. Lagen	Andre Harvey	Greg Moore	John Antonovich
Belvidere	c	CM	20	(815) 544-2612	Frederic Brereton	. . .	Shauna Arco	Pat Chamberlin	David Worrell	Jan Noble	Craig Lawler
Bensenville	v	CM	20	(630) 766-8200	John Geils	Jim Johnson	Patricia Johnson	Thomas Truty	Jack Barba	. . .	Paul Quinn
Benton	c	CO	6	(618) 439-6131	. . .	. . .	. . .	. . .	. . .	. . .	. . .
Berkeley	v	MC	5	(708) 449-8840	Michael Esposito	Lawrence DiRe	Janice McCulloch	. . .	. . .	Timothy Griffin	Robert Larem
Berwyn	c	MC	54	(708) 788-2660	Michael O'Connor	. . .	Tom Pavlik	. . .	Richard Kalivoda	Carl Dobbs	. . .
Bethalto	v	MC	9	(618) 377-8051	Steve Bryant	. . .	Martha Smith	. . .	John Nolte	Alan Winslow	Joseph Ricci
Big Rock	v	CM	. .	(630) 556-4365	. . .	Richard Saks	. . .	. . .	. . .	. . .	. . .
Bloomingdale	v	MC	21	(630) 893-7000	Robert Iden	Daniel Wennerholm	Harriet Ford	Gary Szott	. . .	Timothy Goergen	Mike Marchi
Bloomington	c	CM	64	(309) 434-2509	Stephen Stockton	Thomas Hamilton	Tracey Covert	Brian Barnes	Keith Ranney	Roger Aikin	. . .
Blue Island	c	MC	23	(708) 396-7065	. . .	Michael Anastasia	Pamela Frasor	Linda Martin	David Haywood	Joseph Kosman	Arthur Dertz
Bolingbrook	v	CM	56	(630) 226-8400	Roger Claar	James Boan	Carol Penning	Kirk Openchowski	Charles Peterson	Kenneth Each	Michael Drey
Bourbonnais *	v	CM	15	(815) 937-3570	Robert Latham	Gregg Spathis	Brian Simeur	Nancy Bertrand	. . .	Joseph Beard	Mike Chamness
Bradley	v	MC	12	(815) 932-2125	Jerry Balthazor	. . .	Michael LaGesse	. . .	Steve Wilder	Don Kufner	Carl Erickson
Braidwood	c	CO	5	(815) 458-2333	Wayne Saltzman	. . .	James Hubbard	Lisa Heglund	. . .	Robert Andreina	Aubrey Glisson
Breese	c	MC	4	(618) 526-7731	Donald Maue	Robert Venhaus	. . .	. . .	. . .	James Hummert	Matthew Johnson
Bridgeview	v	MC	15	(708) 594-2525	John Oremus	Frank Bilich	Anne Cusack	Claudette Struzik	Terrence Lipinski	Vladimir Ivkovich	William Green
Broadview *	v	MC	8	(708) 681-3600	Henry Vicenik	. . .	Patricia Williams	Lester Swintek	John Tierney	Raymond Pelletier	Anthony Sacco
Brookfield	v	CM	19	(708) 485-7344	Thomas Sequens	Riccardo Ginex	Kelly Mesich	. . .	Charles La Greco	. . .	. . .
Buffalo Grove	v	CM	42	(847) 459-2500	Elliot Hartstein	William Brimm	Janet Sirabian	. . .	Timothy Sashko	Steven Balinski	Gregory Boysen
Burbank	c	MC	27	(708) 599-5500	. . .	. . .	. . .	. . .	. . .	. . .	. . .
Burnham	v	MC	4	(708) 862-9150	. . .	. . .	. . .	. . .	. . .	. . .	. . .
Burr Ridge	v	CM	10	(630) 654-8181	Jo Irmen	Steven Stricker	. . .	Jerry Sapp	. . .	Herbert Timm	Howard Heil
Bushnell	c	MC	3	(309) 772-2521	Jack Promisson	. . .	. . .	. . .	. . .	Merv Hilliard	Dan Cortelyou
Cahokia	v	MC	16	(618) 337-9500	Frank Bergman	. . .	Norma Jones	Betty Sharp	David Nulsen	Richard Watson	John Torry
Cairo	c	MC	3	(618) 734-4127	James Wilson	. . .	Brenda Miller	. . .	Michael Brey	James Wright	Ronnie Harris
Calumet City	c	MC	39	(708) 891-8100	. . .	. . .	. . .	. . .	. . .	. . .	. . .
Calumet Park	v	MC	8	(708) 389-0850	Buster Porch	. . .	Geraldine Galvin	. . .	Thomas Battistella	Mark Davis	Robert Talaski
Cambridge	v	MC	2	(309) 937-2570	Dwaine VanMeenen	Michael Palmer	. . .	. . .	. . .	. . .	Ed Dole
Canton	c	MC	15	(309) 647-0020	Jerry Bohler	. . .	Nancy Whites	. . .	John Stanko	Donald Edwards	Clifford O'Brien
Carbondale	c	CM	20	(618) 549-5302	Brad Cole	Jeffrey Doherty	Janet Vaught	Ernest Tessone	Jeffery Anderson	Robert Finney	Edward Reeder
Carlinville	c	MC	5	(217) 854-4076	Robert Schwab	. . .	Judy Decker	. . .	Bill Healy	David Haley	MaryBeth Bellm
Carlyle	c	MC	3	(618) 594-2468	Van Johnson	Bill Gruen	Janine Ehlers	. . .	. . .	Kent Newkirk	. . .
Carmi	c	MC	5	(618) 382-8118	. . .	. . .	. . .	. . .	. . .	. . .	. . .
Carol Stream	v	CM	40	(630) 665-7050	Ross Ferraro	Joseph Breinig	. . .	Stan Helgerson	. . .	Rick Willing	John Turner
Carpentersville *	v	CM	30	(847) 426-3439	Bill Sarto	Craig Anderson	Terri Wilde	Lisa Happ	John Schuldt	David Neumann	Robert Cole
Carriers Mills *	v	MC	1	(618) 994-2035	Louis Shaw	. . .	Kim Martin	. . .	Jeff Parks	William Duncan	. . .
Carrollton	c	MC	2	(217) 942-5517	Francis Baker	. . .	Denise Snyder	Patricia Seely	David Steinacher	Mike Kiger	Mike Snyder
Carterville	c	MC	4	(618) 985-2252	Charles Mausey	. . .	Joyce Carney	. . .	William Talley	Monty Jeralds	. . .
Cary	v	CM	15	(847) 639-0003	Steve Lamal	Cameron Davis	. . .	Kevin Dahlstrand	. . .	Ronald Delelio	Bradley Fleck
Casey	c	MC	2	(217) 932-2700	. . .	. . .	. . .	. . .	. . .	. . .	. . .
Caseyville	v	MC	4	(618) 344-1234	George Chance	. . .	Jack Piesbergen	. . .	. . .	. . .	Gerard Scott
Centralia	c	CM	14	(618) 533-7625	Robert Demijan	Grant Kleinhenz	. . .	William Agee	Richard Page	Robert Arnony	Donald Copple
Centreville	c	MC	5	(618) 332-1021	. . .	. . .	. . .	. . .	. . .	. . .	. . .
Champaign *	c	CM	67	(217) 403-8700	Gerald Schweighart	Steven Carter	Marilyn Banks	Richard Schnuer	Dave Penicook	R.T. Finney	Dennis Schmidt
Channahon	v	CM	7	(815) 467-6644	Joseph Cook	James Bowden	Eileen Clark	Robert Guess	. . .	Steve Admonis	Edward Dolezal
Charleston	c	CO	21	(217) 345-8428	Roscoe Cougill	R. Smith	Melinda Bennett	Tamara Moshtagh	Darrell Nees	Ted Ghibellini	Dean Barber
Chatham	v	MC	8	(217) 483-2451	Thomas Gray	. . .	Patrick Schad	Sherry Dierking	. . .	Roy Barnett	Meredith Branham
Cherry Valley	v	MC	2	(815) 332-3441	. . .	David Nord	. . .	. . .	. . .	. . .	. . .
Chester	c	MC	5	(618) 826-2326	Marty Bert	. . .	Nancy Eggemeyer	. . .	Michael Lochhead	Donal McKinney	D. Hartenberger
Chicago	c	MC	2896	(312) 744-0308	Richard Daley	. . .	. . .	Steve Lux	. . .	. . .	. . .
Chicago Heights	c	CO	32	(708) 756-5305	Angelo Clambrone	Rick Doggett	. . .	. . .	Ted Brown	Karla Osentowski	Albert Marconi
Chicago Ridge	v	MC	14	(708) 425-7700	Eugene Siegel	. . .	Charles Tokar	. . .	Randall Grossi	T. Baldermann	John Lind
Chillicothe	c	MC	5	(309) 274-5056	Donald White	. . .	. . .	. . .	. . .	Steve Maurer	Clyde Crabel
Christopher	c	MC	2	(618) 724-7648	Gary Bartolotti	. . .	Jacquelyn Murry	. . .	Charles Lutes	. . .	Dennis Gunter
Cicero	t	MC	85	(708) 656-3600	Betty Maltese	. . .	Marylin Colpo	Donald Schultz	James Smetana	Thomas Rowan	Sam Jelic
Clarendon Hills	v	CM	7	(630) 323-3500	Diane Hiller	Robert Bahan	Dawn Tandle	Kathy Redding	Brian Leahy	L. Patrick Anderson	John Hays
Clinton	c	CO	7	(217) 935-9438	Roger Cyrulik	. . .	R. Wickenhauser	. . .	Jeff Pearl	Mike Reidy	Steve Lobb
Coal City	v	MC	4	(815) 634-8608	Gerald Pierard	Philip Middleton	Pamela Noffsinger	. . .	Harold Holsinger	Vernon Larson	James Hutchings
Coal Valley	v	MC	3	(309) 799-3604	Stanley Engstrom	. . .	Deanna Burnett	. . .	John Diamond	Larry Buechler	Ross Hall
Collinsville	c	CM	24	(618) 346-5200	Stan Schaeffer	Robert Knabel	Louis Jackstadt	Tamara Ammann	James Twyman	Scott Williams	. . .
Colona *	c	MC	5	(309) 792-0571	Danny McDaniel	. . .	Lories Graham	Mary Carlson	. . .	Timothy Krebs	Rick Crew
Columbia	c	MC	7	(618) 281-7144	Lester Schneider	Anthony Traxler	Wesley Hoeffken	Eugene Schorb	Michael Roediger	Joseph Edwards	. . .
Country Club Hills	c	CM	16	(708) 798-2616	Dwight Welch	Dorothy Steward	Deborah McIlvain	Alison Brothen	Garrick Kasper	William Brown	Edward Meinheit
Countryside	c	MC	5	(708) 354-7270	Carl LeGant	Edward Bailey	Shirley Herberts	. . .	. . .	Timothy Swanson	Robert Fullar
Crest Hill	c	MC	13	(815) 741-5100	Nicholas Churnovic	John Tomasoski	Christine Vershay	. . .	. . .	James Ariagno	David Fell
Crestwood	v	MC	11	(708) 371-4800	Chester Stranczek	Frank Gassmere	Nancy Benedetto	. . .	William Boman	John Hefley	Frank Scaccia
Crete	v	MC	7	(708) 672-5431	Michael Einhorn	Thomas Durkin	Kathleen Wantuch	. . .	Lyle Bachert	Paul Van Deraa	Philip Hameister
Creve Coeur	v	MC	5	(309) 699-6714	Eugene Talbot	. . .	. . .	Richard Gilliatt	Fred Lang	Michael Button	. . .
Crystal Lake	c	CM	38	(815) 459-2020	Aaron Shepley	Gary Mayerhofer	Roger Dreher	. . .	James Moore	. . .	Eric Lecuyer
Danville	c	MC	33	(217) 431-2200	Robert Jones	. . .	Janet Myers	Ron Neufeld	Thomas Lane	Robert Dietzen	Don Cheesman
Darien	c	MC	22	(630) 852-5000	. . .	Bryon Vana	Joanne Coleman	. . .	. . .	Robert Pavelchik	Daniel Gombac
De Kalb	c	CM	39	(815) 748-2000	Greg Sparrow	Mark Biernacki	Donna Johnson	Douglas Haywood	Pete Polarek	William Feithen	Richard Monas
Decatur	c	CM	81	(217) 428-2805	Paul Osborne	Stephen Garman	Celeste Harris	Beth Couter	Leslie Albert	Mark Barthelemy	Stephen Swanson
Deer Park	v	CM	3	(847) 726-1648	Richard Karl	James Connors	Sandra Smith	. . .	. . .	. . .	. . .
Deerfield *	v	CM	18	(847) 945-5000	Steven Harris	Kent Street	. . .	. . .	. . .	John Sliozis	Barbara Little
Des Plaines *	c	CM	58	(847) 391-5300	Anthony Arredia	. . .	Donna McAllister	Bob Simpson	Randy Jaeger	James Prandini	Matthew Duskett
Dixmoor	v	MC	3	(708) 389-6121	. . .	. . .	. . .	. . .	. . .	. . .	. . .
Dixon	c	MC	15	(815) 288-1485	Donald Sheets	Rita Crundwell	Kathe Swanson	. . .	Mike Wilcox	Robert Short	Mike Stichter
Dolton	v	CM	25	(708) 201-3268	. . .	. . .	Judith Evans	. . .	Robert Kapusta	. . .	Robert Myers
Downers Grove	v	CM	48	(630) 434-5500	Brian Krajewski	Cara Pavlicek	April Holden	Rita Trainor	Philip Ruscetti	Robert Porter	David Barber

Directory 1/9 continued — OFFICIALS IN U.S. MUNICIPALITIES 2,500 AND OVER IN POPULATION

Jurisdiction	Type	Form of government	2000 Population (000)	Main telephone number	Chief elected official	Appointed administrator	Clerk of the governing board	Chief financial officer	Fire chief	Police chief	Public works director
ILLINOIS continued											
Du Quoin	c	CO	6	(618) 542-3841	John Rednour	...	Mell Smigielski	Cha Hill	Buddy Crain	James Booker	Raymond Spencer
Dupo	v	MC	3	(618) 286-3280	Ronnie Dell	...	Bruce Feltmeyer	...	Kerrey Foster	...	Randy Hamilton
Dwight	v	MC	4	(815) 584-3077	James Mixen	Kevin McNamara	Mary Ann Denker	...	Mark Baker	Timothy Henson	David Bozarth
East Alton	v	MC	6	(618) 259-7714	Fred Bright	...	Lori Palmer	...	Larry Ringering	Richard Brown	Denny Weber
East Dubuque	c	CM	1	(815) 747-3416	Geoffrey Barklow	Al Griffiths	Nancy Roepke	...	Joe Heim	Steven O'Connell	Mark Fluhr
East Dundee *	v	MC	2	(847) 426-2822	Daniel O'Leary	Frank Koehler	Sue Norton	...	...	Terry Mee	T. J. Moore
East Hazel Crest	v	CM	1	(708) 798-0213	Thomas Brown	Patricia Lazuka	...	...	William Vallow	Ray Robertson	Rory Maltrotto
East Moline *	c	MC	20	(309) 752-1584	John Thodos	Richard Keehner	Arletta Holmes	James Hughes	Robert DeFrance	Victor Moreno	Bruce Willemarck
East Peoria	c	CO	22	(309) 698-4750	Charles Dobbelaire	James Brimberry	Veona Dinkins	...	Roger Aylward	Edward Papis	Rick Jeremiah
East St. Louis	c	CM	31	(618) 482-6811	...	...	...	...	...	...	...
Edwardsville	c	MC	21	(618) 962-7530	Gary Niebur	Bennett Dickmann	Patty Theide	...	J. Brian Wilson	David Bopp	Timothy Harr
Effingham	c	CO	12	(217) 342-5301	Robert Utz	...	Rick Goeckner	...	Nicholas Althoff	John Lange	...
El Paso	c	MC	2	(309) 527-4005	Ronald Mool	Richard Gresham	David Fever	...	...	Jeffrey Price	...
Elburn	v	MC	2	(630) 365-5060	James Willey	...	Susan Schoo	Barbara Carlson	Marty Strausberger	Edward Kelley	Michael Anderson
Eldorado *	c	CO	4	(618) 273-6566	Rocky James	...	Pat Mahoney	...	Michael McKinnies	Shannon Deuel	...
Elgin	c	CM	94	(847) 931-6100	Edward Schock	Olufemi Folarin	Dolonna Mecum	James Nowicki	John Henrici	William Miller	John Loete
Elk Grove Village	v	CM	34	(847) 357-4019	...	Raymond Rummel	Ann Walsh	Christine Tromp	...	Stephen Schmidt	Thomas Cech
Elmhurst	c	CM	42	(630) 530-3000	Thomas Marcucci	Thomas Borchert	Janet Edgley	Marilyn Gaston	Michael Kopp	Steven Neibauer	Michael Hughes
Elmwood Park	v	CM	25	(708) 452-7300	Peter Silvestri	John Dalicandro	Elsie Sutter	John Lannefeld	Kerry Hjellum	Frederick Braglia	Peter Terzo
Elwood	v	MC	1	(815) 423-5011	...	Aimee Ingalls	...	...	...	...	...
Eureka	c	MC	4	(309) 467-2113	Scott Punke	Anne Sandvik	Marilyn Walter	...	Craig Neal	Alan Misener	James Lehman
Evanston	c	CM	74	(847) 328-2100	Lorraine Morton	Julia Carroll	Mary Morris	...	Alan Berkowsky	Frank Kaminski	David Jennings
Evergreen Park	v	MC	20	(708) 422-1551	James Sexton	...	Catherine Aparo	...	Edward Clohessy	Michael Saunders	William Lorenzs
Fairbury *	c	MC	3	(815) 692-2743	Robert Walter	Leroy McPherson	Brenda Defries	...	...	Jack Wiser	...
Fairfield	c	MC	5	(618) 842-3871	Wayne Borah	Kennett Foley	Tina Hutchcraft	...	Michael Pottorff	William Winter	...
Fairview Heights	c	MC	15	(618) 489-2000	Gail Mitchell	Donald Greer	Harvey Noubarian	...	...	Ed Delmore	Robert Hotz
Farmer City	c	MC	2	(309) 928-3412	...	...	...	...	...	...	...
Farmington	c	MC	2	(309) 245-2011	Cyril Stobaugh	Roger Woodcock	...	...	...	William Lally	Brad Dilts
Flora	c	CO	5	(618) 662-8313	Lewis Wolfe	Erik Bush	Becky Wiley	Debra Zimmerman	Bruce Dickey	Ed McCormick	David Thompson
Flossmoor *	v	CM	9	(708) 798-2300	Roger Molski	Bridget Wachtel	Pam Hudson	Scott Bordui	Daniel Hornback	John Lancaster	Greg Buenzow
Ford Heights	v	MC	3	(708) 758-3131	Saul Beck	...	Audrey Coulter	Angelia Smith	Gregory Dillard	Percy Coleman	Rufus Fisher
Forest Park *	v	CO	15	(708) 366-2323	Anthony Calderone	Michael Sturino	Vanessa Moritz	Judy Kovacs	Stephen Glinke	James Ryan	Robert Kutak
Forsyth *	v	CM	2	(217) 877-9445	Harold Gilbert	Austin Edmondson	Kathy Mizer	...	...	...	Larry Coloni
Fox Lake	v	MC	9	(847) 587-2151	...	...	...	...	...	Edward Gerretsen	Ronald Hoehne
Fox River Grove	v	MC	4	(847) 639-3170	Katherine Laube	Arthur Osten	Donna Brouder	...	Robert Kreher	Robert Polston	...
Frankfort	v	CM	10	(815) 469-2177	Jim Holland	Jerald Ducay	Kate Romani	Sandra Babka	...	Rob Piscia	Terry Kestel
Franklin Park	v	MC	19	(847) 671-4800	Daniel Pritchett	...	Susan Szymanski	Elliott Becker	David Traiforos	Randall Petersen	Joseph Thomas
Freeburg	v	CM	3	(618) 539-5545	Allen Watters	...	Mary Grau	Bryan Vogel	...	Melvin Woodruff	Ronald Dintelmann
Freeport *	c	MC	26	(815) 235-8200	George Gaulrapp	...	Latacia Ishmon	Craig Joesten	Kevin Countryman	Jerry Whitmore	Craig Lebaron
Fulton	c	CM	3	(815) 589-2616	Paul Sikkom	...	La Vonne Huizonga	...	David Damhoff	Harvey Meade	Randy Balk
Galena	c	MC	3	(815) 777-1050	...	...	...	...	...	Gerald Westemeier	James Rigdon
Galesburg *	c	CM	33	(309) 345-3628	Gary Smith	Dane Bragg	Anita Carlton	Gloria Osborn	John Cratty	David Christensen	Larry Cox
Galva *	c	MC	2	(309) 932-2555	Thomas Hartman	David Dyer	Rhonda Siegel	...	Denny Tarleton	Jerry Clark	Myron Townsend
Geneseo *	c	MC	6	(309) 944-6419	Patrick Eberhardt	Eric Wiederhold	Tracey Kotecki	Teresa Savage	...	Thomas Piotrowski	J. Van De Woestyne
Geneva *	c	MC	19	(630) 232-7494	Kevin Burns	Philip Page	Lynn Landberg	...	Stephen Olson	William Kidwell	Thomas Talsma
Genoa	c	MC	4	(815) 784-2327	David Rood	...	Judith Zmich	David Jepson	Ronald Anderson	Donald Smith	Richard Gentile
Georgetown	c	MC	3	(217) 662-2525	...	...	...	...	...	Michael Vice	...
Gibson City	c	MC	3	(217) 784-5872	Brady Peters	Janet Davis	Vickie Lorenzen	...	...	Christopher Decker	John Stauffer
Gilberts *	v	MC	1	(847) 428-2861	Tom Wajda	Raymond Keller	Darlene Mueller	...	...	Michael Joswick	...
Gillespie	c	MC	3	(217) 839-2919	Dan Fisher	...	Jonella Rolando	...	Larry Norville	Richard Hearn	...
Glen Carbon	v	MC	10	(618) 288-1200	Robert Jackstadt	...	Peggy Goudy	Richard Jett	...	David Bradford	Tom Sedlacek
Glen Ellyn *	v	CM	26	(630) 469-5000	Gregory Mathews	Curtis Barrett	Patricia O'Connor	Jon Batek	S. Raffensparger	Philip Norton	James Foster
Glencoe	v	CM	8	(847) 835-4114	Scott Feldman	Paul Harlow	...	David Clark	...	...	David Mau
Glendale Heights	v	MC	31	(630) 260-6000	Linda Jackson	Donna Becerra	Jo Ann Borysiewicz	Benjamin Abrazaldo	...	...	Richard Dime
Glenview	v	CM	41	(847) 904-4370	Lawrence Carlson	Lawrence Hileman	...	Daniel Wiersma	Dan Bonkowski	William Fitzpatrick	William Porter
Glenwood	v	MC	9	(708) 753-2400	...	...	...	Linda Brunette	...	...	Gerald Brossmer
Godfrey	v	MC	16	(618) 466-3324	Michael Campion	...	Pamela Whisler	...	...	...	Victor Stipes
Granite City	c	MC	31	(618) 452-6235	Ronald Selph	Mike Sparks	Judith Whitaker	Mac McTaggart	Ed Hagnauer	David Ruebhausen	...
Grayslake *	v	MC	18	(847) 223-8515	Timothy Perry	Michael Ellis	Cynthia Lee	Michael Peterson	...	Larry Herzog	...
Greenville *	c	CM	6	(618) 664-1644	Alan Gaffner	David Willey	Margaret Iberg	...	...	Lou Lorton	Bill Grider
Gurnee	v	MC	28	(847) 623-7650	Donald Rudny	James Hayner	Mary Jo Kollross	Patricia Wesolowski	Fred Friedl	Robert Jones	...
Hamilton	c	MC	3	(217) 847-2936	Stephen Woodruff	...	Michelle Dorethy	...	Steve Helenthal	Walter Sellens	...
Hampshire *	v	MC	2	(847) 683-2181	Jeffrey Magnussen	Eric Palm	Linda Vasquez	Kathyrn Michael	...	Thomas Atchison	John Bidinger
Hanover Park *	v	CM	38	(630) 372-4200	Rodney Craig	Marc Hummel	Sherry Craig	Harry Sakai	Craig Haigh	Ronald Moser	Howard Killian
Harrisburg *	c	MC	9	(618) 253-7451	Valerie Mitchell	...	Tracey Martin	...	Bill Summers	...	...
Harvard	c	MC	7	(815) 943-6468	Ralph Henning	David Nelson	Andy Wells	...	...	Kenneth Mrozek	James Carbonetti
Harvey	c	CO	30	(708) 210-5300	...	...	...	...	...	...	...
Harwood Heights	v	MC	8	(708) 867-7200	Margaret Fuller	...	Dianne Larson	...	...	Martin Podosek	...
Havana *	c	MC	3	(309) 543-6580	Dale Roberts	...	Ruby Miller	Harold Palmer	John Kachanuk	Kevin Noble	Don Henderson
Hawthorn Woods *	v	MC	6	(847) 438-5500	Keith Hunt	...	...	...	...	Jennifer Paulus	Daniel Marcinko
Hazel Crest	v	CM	14	(708) 335-9600	Robert Donaldson	Robert Palmer	Florine Robinson	...	Charles Jackson	Claudell Ervin	Tim Fassnacht
Henry	c	MC	2	(309) 364-3056	...	...	Doris Goldner	...	...	Michael Surrells	Thomas Maubach
Herrin	c	MC	11	(618) 942-3175	Edward Quaglia	...	Marlene Simpson	Jody Deaton	Mike Steh	...	Joe Lapinski
Hickory Hills	c	MC	13	(708) 598-4800	Roy Faddis	...	Joann Jackson	...	...	...	Larry Boettcher
Highland *	c	CM	8	(618) 654-9891	Joseph Michaelis	Mark Latham	Barbara Bellm	Sharon Rusteberg	Michael Kilgore	Terrence Baney	Joseph Gillespie
Highland Park *	c	CM	31	(847) 432-0800	Michael Belsky	David Limardi	Shirley Fitzgerald	Elizabeth Spencer	Alan Wax	Paul Shafer	Mary Anderson
Highwood	c	MC	4	(847) 432-1924	Vincent Donofrio	...	Susan Druktenis	...	Thomas Lovejoy	John Kearin	Jeff Ponsi
Hillsboro	c	CO	4	(217) 532-5566	William Baran	...	David Booher	Geoff Trost	Joe Lyerla	Gary Satterlee	D. McCammack
Hillside	v	MC	8	(708) 449-6450	Joseph Tamburino	Russell Wajda	Patrick O'Sullivan	...	Michael Kuryla	Frank Alonzo	Joseph Pisano
Hinsdale *	v	CM	17	(630) 789-7000	Michael Woerner	David Cook	Barbara Grigola	...	Patrick Kenny	Bradley Bloom	George Franco
Hoffman Estates	v	CM	49	(847) 882-9100	William McLeod	James Norris	Virginia Hayter	M. Du Charme	James Eaves	Clinton Herdegen	Ken Hari
Homer Glen *	v	MC	22	(708) 301-0632	James Daley	...	Gale Skrobuton	John Sawyers	...	...	...
Hometown	c	MC	4	(708) 424-7500	Donald Roberton	...	Mary Jo Hacker	...	...	Fred Knoblauch	Joseph Madden
Homewood *	v	CM	19	(708) 798-3000	Richard Hofeld	Mark Franz	Gayle Campbell	Dennis Bubenik	Al Schullo	Larry Burnson	John Schaefer
Hoopeston	c	MC	5	(217) 283-5833	Samuel Ault	...	Gail Lane	William Goodwine	Gregory Shipman	Mark Drollinger	...
Huntley	v	CM	5	(847) 669-9600	Charles Sass	Carl Tomaso	Rita McMahon	...	...	Randall Walters	Jim Schwartz
Indian Head Park	v	CM	3	(708) 246-3080	...	Raymond Garritano	...	David Brink	...	...	Edward Santen
Inverness	v	MC	6	(847) 358-7740	John Tatooles	Curtis Carver	Patricia Ledvina	...	...	...	...
Island Lake	v	MC	8	(847) 526-8764	Charles Amrich	...	Kriss Becker	...	...	John Fellmann	William Kootstra
Itasca	v	MC	8	(630) 773-0835	Claudia Gruber	David Williams	Carole Schreiber	...	...	Edward Votava	Ross Hitchcock

Directory 1/9 continued **OFFICIALS IN U.S. MUNICIPALITIES 2,500 AND OVER IN POPULATION**

Jurisdiction	Type	Form of govern- ment	2000 Popu- lation (000)	Main telephone number	Chief elected official	Appointed administrator	Clerk of the governing board	Chief financial officer	Fire chief	Police chief	Public works director
ILLINOIS continued											
Jacksonville *	c	MC	18	(217) 479-4600	Ronald Tendick	. . .	Andy Ezard	. . .	Rick Kluge	Donald Cook	. . .
Jerseyville	c	CO	7	(618) 498-3312	Yvonne Hartmann	. . .	Catherine Ward	. . .	. . .	Bill Bridges	. . .
Johnston City	c	MC	3	(618) 983-6544	Richard Carter	. . .	Jean Hatfield	. . .	Thomas Burton	Jerald Kobler	Carl Reed
Joliet *	c	CM	106	(815) 724-4020	Arthur Schultz	John Mezera	Janet Traven	Robert Fraser	Richard Marose	Frederick Hayes	. . .
Justice	v	MC	12	(708) 458-2520	Melvin Van Allen	. . .	Kathleen Svoboda	Michelle Jones	Ronald Szarzynski	Paul Wasik	Philip Depaola
Kankakee	c	MC	27	(815) 933-0500	Donald Green	. . .	Anjanita Dumas	James Spice	Ronald Young	Michael Kinkade	Bert Dear
Kenilworth *	v	CM	2	(847) 251-1666	. . .	Bradly Burke	Robert Hastings	Maryann VanDyke	. . .	John Petersen	Ignazio Fiorentino
Kewanee	c	CM	12	(309) 852-2611	James Burns	James Snider	Cari Goff	Debra Johnson	Tom Weston	James Dison	Mike Rapczak
Kildeer	v	CM	3	(847) 438-6000	. . .	Laurel Schreiber	. . .	. . .	. . .	Jeffrey Lilly	. . .
Knoxville	c	MC	3	(309) 289-2814	Phil Myers	. . .	Margaret Bivens	. . .	. . .	Rick Pecsi	. . .
La Grange	v	CM	15	(708) 579-2300	Elizabeth Asperger	Robert Pilipiszyn	Robert Milne	Lou Cipparrone	David Fleege	Michael Holub	Kenneth Watkins
La Grange Park	v	CM	13	(708) 354-0225	Susan Tutt-Parsons	Bohdan Proczko	Kerry Brunette	Pierre Garesche	Dean Maggos	Daniel McCollum	Julius Hansen
La Salle	c	MC	9	(815) 223-4586	Arthur Washkowiak	. . .	V. Kochanowski	Joanne Milby	William Bacidore	Thomas Kramarsic	Samuel McNeilly
Lake Barrington	v	CM	4	(847) 381-6010	. . .	Christopher Martin	. . .	. . .	. . .	. . .	. . .
Lake Bluff *	v	CM	6	(847) 234-0774	Christine Letchinger	R. Irvin	Michael Klawitter	Susan Griffin	David Graf	William Gallagher	Thomas Cahill
Lake Forest	c	CM	20	(847) 234-2600	S. Michael Rummel	Robert Kiely	. . .	K. Reinertsen	W. Michael Hosking	Joseph Buerger	Thomas Naatz
Lake In The Hills	v	MC	23	(847) 960-7400	Ed Plaza	Gerald Sagona	Denise Wasserman	Pete Stefan	. . .	. . .	Fred Mullard
Lake Zurich	v	CM	18	(847) 438-5141	John Tolomei	Bob Vitas	Gloria Palmblad	Jeff Martynowicz	T. Mastandrea	William Urry	Dave Heyden
Lakemoor	v	MC	2	(815) 385-1117	. . .	. . .	. . .	. . .	. . .	. . .	. . .
Lakewood	v	CM	2	(815) 459-3025	Blair Picard	Catherine Peterson	Janice Hansen	Wendy Gregoria	. . .	. . .	Barry Wickersheim
Lansing	v	MC	28	(708) 895-7200	. . .	. . .	. . .	. . .	. . .	. . .	. . .
Lawrenceville	c	MC	4	(618) 943-2116	Henry Kijonka	. . .	Dorothy Theriac	. . .	. . .	David White	Christopher Kelly
Lebanon	c	MC	3	(618) 537-4976	Matthew Berberich	Tom Lenz	Pamela Koshko	. . .	Richard Rutherford	Michael Donovan	Penny Pinkstaff
Lemont	v	MC	13	(630) 257-1590	John Piazza	Gary Holmes	Charlene Smollen	Jean Nona	. . .	K. Shaughnessy	Daniel Fielding
Leroy	c	MC	3	(309) 962-3031	Jane Engblom	. . .	Sue Marcum	. . .	. . .	. . .	. . .
Lewistown	c	MC	2	(309) 547-4300	Kendall Miller	. . .	Melodee Rudolph	. . .	. . .	Jeffrey Schnetzler	. . .
Libertyville *	v	CM	20	(847) 362-2430	Jeffrey Harger	Kevin Bowens	Sally Kowalt	Patricia Wesolowski	Richard Carani	Patrick Carey	John Heinz
Lincoln *	c	MC	15	(217) 735-2815	Elizabeth Davis	. . .	Melanie Riggs	. . .	James Davis	Stuart Erlenbush	Tracy Jackson
Lincolnshire	v	CM	6	(847) 883-8600	Brett Blomberg	Robert Irvin	B. Mastandrea	Stanley Roelker	. . .	Randall Melvin	Frank Tripicchio
Lincolnwood *	v	MC	12	(847) 673-1540	Peter Moy	Timothy Wiberg	Beryl Herman	Ronald Pfeiffer	Michael Hansen	Daniel Gooris	Manuel Castaneda
Lindenhurst	v	CM	12	(847) 356-8252	James Betustak	James Stevens	. . .	. . .	. . .	Jack McKeever	Wesley Welsh
Lisle	v	MC	21	(630) 271-4100	Joseph Broda	Gerald Sprecher	. . .	. . .	. . .	Michael Damico	Ray Peterson
Litchfield	c	MC	6	(217) 324-5253	. . .	. . .	. . .	. . .	William Bergen	. . .	James Kirby
Lockport	c	MC	15	(815) 838-0549	Frank Mitchell	Tim Schloneger	Maria Esposito	Janice Colvin	. . .	Jim Antole	Mike Greenan
Lombard	v	CM	42	(630) 620-5700	William Mueller	William Lichter	. . .	Leonard Flood	George Seagraves	Raymond Byrne	David Gorman
Long Grove	v	CM	6	(847) 634-9440	Anthony Dean	David Lothspeich	Caroline Liebl	. . .	. . .	. . .	Robert Block
Loves Park	c	MC	20	(815) 654-5030	Darryl Lindberg	. . .	Robert Burden	. . .	Philip Foley	Patrick Carrigan	Robert Martin
Lynwood *	c	MC	7	(708) 758-6101	Eugene Williams	. . .	Roy Valle	. . .	. . .	David Palmer	Robert Myers
Lyons	v	MC	10	(708) 447-8886	Marie Vachata	Roy Witherow	Edward Metz	Erin Leahy	Gordon Nord	Dan Babich	Greg Koch
Machesney Park *	v	MC	20	(815) 877-5432	Linda Vaughn	Bob Mullins	Lori Mitchell	. . .	. . .	. . .	Paul Shepperd
Macomb	c	MC	18	(309) 833-2575	Mick Wisslead	. . .	Melanie Falk	. . .	Clarence John	Mike Galloway	Terry Wrestler
Madison	c	MC	4	(618) 876-6268	John Bellcoff	. . .	William Weidner	Jeanne Weidner	Charles Foley	Steven Skoklo	Robert Robbins
Mahomet *	v	CM	4	(217) 586-4456	Deb Braunig	Mell Smigielski	Cheryl Sproul	. . .	. . .	Jerry Gamble	. . .
Manhattan	v	CM	3	(815) 478-3483	William Borgo	Marian Gibson	Mattie Becker	Kevin Sing	Jack Fitgerald	Timothy Barker	. . .
Manteno *	v	CM	3	(815) 468-8224	Timothy Nugent	Craig Blanchette	Cheryl Moseley	. . .	. . .	Bernie Thompson	. . .
Marengo	c	MC	6	(815) 568-7112	Donald Lockhart	Scott Hartman	Diane Schwoch	. . .	. . .	Les Kottke	Donald Craney
Marion *	c	MC	16	(618) 997-6281	. . .	. . .	. . .	. . .	Anthony Rinella	Gene Goolsby	. . .
Marissa	v	MC	2	(618) 295-2351	Steuart McClintock	. . .	Carol Smith	. . .	. . .	Michael Kerperien	William Yates
Markham	c	MC	12	(708) 331-4905	Evans Miller	. . .	Theresa Cannon	. . .	. . .	Eric Lymore	Daniel Costello
Marquette Heights	c	MC	2	(309) 382-3455	David Redfield	. . .	Ron Worrent	. . .	Ronald Smith	Roger Pentecost	Daniel Crum
Marseilles	c	CM	4	(815) 795-2133	. . .	. . .	. . .	. . .	. . .	. . .	. . .
Marshall	c	MC	3	(217) 826-2112	. . .	. . .	. . .	. . .	. . .	. . .	. . .
Maryville *	v	MC	4	(618) 345-7028	Larry Gulledge	. . .	Thelma Long	Marvin Brussatti	Kevin Flaugher	Richard Schardan	Patrick Presson
Mascoutah	c	CM	5	(618) 566-2965	Gerald Daugherty	Terry Draper	Kathleen Schuetz	L. Weidenbenner	Dean Juenger	. . .	Daniel Schrempp
Mason City *	c	MC	2	(217) 482-3669	David Knieriem	. . .	Karla Daubs	David Rodgers	. . .	David Coulter	L. Dixon
Matteson	v	MC	12	(708) 283-4900	Mark Stricker	Lafayette Linear	Dorothy Grisco	Gregory Meyers	Edwin Wilkens	Norman Burnson	Vincent Laoang
Mattoon	c	CO	18	(217) 235-5654	David Carter	. . .	Susan O'Brien	. . .	Bruce Grafton	. . .	David Wortman
Maywood	v	CM	26	(708) 344-1200	. . .	. . .	Ralph McNabb	. . .	Marvin Cox	Luis Morales	Ray Easley
Mc Cook	v	MC	. .	(708) 447-9030	Raymond Tobolski	. . .	Charles Sobus	Renee Botica	Joseph Myrick	Frank Wolfe	Richard Paeth
Mc Henry	c	MC	21	(815) 363-2100	Susan Low	Douglas Maxeiner	Janice Jones	. . .	. . .	Thomas O'Meara	Jon Schmitt
Melrose Park	v	MC	23	(708) 343-4000	Ronald Serpico	. . .	Barbara Jasinski	John Gregor	James Cernauske	Vito Scavo	Ralph Tolomei
Mendota	c	MC	7	(815) 539-7459	Steve Bowne	. . .	Wendy Morris	. . .	Dennis Rutishauser	Tom Smith	Ken Arjes
Metropolis	c	MC	6	(618) 524-4016	Beth Clanahan	. . .	. . .	. . .	Michael Childers	. . .	. . .
Midlothian *	v	MC	14	(708) 389-0200	Thomas Murawski	. . .	Michael Woike	Denise Borne	William Sheehy	Vincent Schavone	Richard Hansen
Milan	v	MC	5	(309) 787-8500	Duane Dawson	Steven Seiver	Barbara Lee	. . .	. . .	. . .	David Pannell
Millstadt	v	MC	2	(618) 476-1514	Alvin Mehrtens	Larry Toenses	Linda Lehr	. . .	Kurt Pellmann	Edward Wilkinson	Stan Jarvis
Minonk	c	MC	2	(309) 432-2558	Bill Koos	. . .	Jim Liner	. . .	. . .	William Butler	Charlie McGuire
Minooka	v	MC	3	(815) 467-2151	Jason Briscoe	James Grabowski	. . .	. . .	. . .	. . .	. . .
Mokena	v	CM	14	(708) 479-3900	Robert Chiszar	John Downs	Jane McGinn	Barbara Shryock	. . .	Stephen Pollak	Louis Tiberi
Moline *	c	CM	43	(309) 797-0747	Donald Welvaert	Lewis Steinbrecher	Lynn Segura	Kathleen Carr	. . .	Gary Francque	Michael Waldron
Momence	c	MC	3	(815) 472-2001	. . .	. . .	. . .	. . .	. . .	. . .	. . .
Monee	v	MC	2	(708) 534-8635	Timothy O'Donnell	. . .	Kathy Buchmeier	. . .	. . .	Russel Caruso	Ron Wolf
Monmouth	c	MC	9	(309) 734-2141	John Reitman	Eric Hanson	Susan Trevor	. . .	James Conard	Roger Johnson	. . .
Montgomery	v	MC	5	(630) 896-8080	Marilyn Michelini	Anne Marie Gaura	Barbara Argo	Jeff Zoephel	. . .	Dennis Schmidt	Mike Pubentz
Monticello	c	MC	5	(217) 762-2583	. . .	Floyd Allsop	. . .	. . .	. . .	John Miller	. . .
Morris	c	MC	11	(815) 942-0103	. . .	. . .	. . .	. . .	. . .	. . .	. . .
Morrison *	c	MC	4	(815) 772-7657	Roger Drey	Tim Long	Melanie Schroeder	. . .	. . .	Ernest Huling	Gary Tresenriter
Morton *	v	MC	15	(309) 266-5361	Norman Durflinger	David Strohl	Joseph Nohl	. . .	Joe Kelley	Nick Graff	Bob Wraight
Morton Grove	v	CM	22	(847) 965-4100	Richard Krier	Joe Wade	Carol Fritzshall	Scot Neukirch	Tom Friel	George Incledon	Andy DeMonte
Mount Carmel	c	CO	7	(618) 262-4822	George Woodcock	Merle Weems	Mark Bader	M. Mollenhauer	Steve Partee	Jimmy Seaton	. . .
Mount Morris	v	MC	3	(815) 734-6425	Steven Mongan	. . .	Sandra Blake	. . .	. . .	Gregory Pickett	. . .
Mount Prospect *	v	CM	56	(847) 392-6000	Irvana Wilks	Michael Janonis	Lisa Angell	David Erb	Michael Figolah	John Dahlberg	Glen Andler
Mount Vernon *	c	CM	16	(618) 242-5000	David Keen	Ronald Neibert	Jacqlyn Sharp	Merle Hollmann	James Brown	Chris Mendenall	Elbert Cain
Mount Zion	v	CM	4	(217) 864-5424	Donald Robinson	Paul Ruff	Tammy Mense	. . .	. . .	Douglas Dunn	Jerry Potts
Mundelein	v	MC	30	(847) 949-3200	Marilyn Sindles	John Lobaito	Pamela Keeney	. . .	Randy Justus	Raymond Rose	Kenneth Miller
Murphysboro	c	MC	13	(618) 684-4961	Ron Williams	Gene Biby	. . .	. . .	Kevin Reeves	Jeff Bock	Dale Noble
Naperville	c	CM	128	(630) 420-6111	A. Pradel	. . .	Suzanne Gagner	Doug Krieger	John Wu	David Dial	David Van Vooren
Nashville	c	MC	3	(618) 327-3058	Raymond Kolweier	. . .	Lloyd Dinkelman	. . .	Alan Hohlt	James Shew	Thomas McFeron
New Baden *	v	MC	3	(618) 588-3813	Timothy Hoerchler	Robert Nielsen	Janet Kuhn	. . .	. . .	. . .	. . .
New Lenox	v	MC	17	(815) 485-6452	Michael Smith	Lewis Loebe	Marcia Englert	K. Auchstetter	. . .	Dan Martin	Ronald Sly
Newton	c	MC	3	(618) 783-8451	Ross McClane	. . .	Jean Ghast	. . .	. . .	Mike Swick	. . .

Directory 1/9 continued — OFFICIALS IN U.S. MUNICIPALITIES 2,500 AND OVER IN POPULATION

Jurisdiction	Type	Form of govern-ment	2000 Popu-lation (000)	Main telephone number	Chief elected official	Appointed administrator	Clerk of the governing board	Chief financial officer	Fire chief	Police chief	Public works director
ILLINOIS continued											
Niles	v	CM	30	(847) 588-8000	Nicholas Blase	George Van Geem	Marlene Victorine	Scot Neukirch	Barry Mueller	Dean Strzelecki	Scott Jochim
Nokomis	c	MC	2	(217) 563-2514	Joseph Gasparich	. . .	Mary Scheller	Joe Murphy	. . .	Thomas Kearns	Terry Hill
Normal	t	CM	45	(309) 454-2444	Christopher Koos	Mark Peterson	Wendellyn Briggs	Ronald Hill	Leland Watson	Kent Crutcher	Michael Hall
Norridge *	v	MC	14	(708) 453-0800	Earl Field	. . .	J. Dunne Bernardi	. . .	. . .	Charles Ghiloni	. . .
North Aurora	v	MC	10	(630) 897-8228	Mark Ruby	Susan McLaughlin	. . .	Margaret Dolasinski	. . .	Thomas Fetzer	Michael Glock
North Chicago	c	MC	35	(847) 596-8600	Leon Rockingham	Deborah Waszak	Lori Collins	John Gantz	Theodore Wilder	Michael Newsome	. . .
North Riverside	v	MC	6	(708) 447-4211	Richard Scheck	Guy Belmonte	Charmaine Kutt	. . .	Raymond Martinek	Anthony Garvey	Tim Kutt
Northbrook	v	CM	33	(847) 272-5050	Mark Damisch	John Novinson	Lona Lovis	Jeff Rowitz	James Reardon	. . .	James Reynolds
Northfield	v	CM	5	(847) 446-9200	Donald Whiteman	Stacy Sigman	. . .	Vivian Perenchio	Michael Nystrand	William Lustig	. . .
Northlake	c	CM	11	(708) 343-8700	Jeffrey Sherwin	. . .	Joanne Floistad	William Kabler	. . .	Dennis Koletsos	Dale Roberts
Oak Brook	v	CM	8	(630) 990-3000	Kevin Quinlan	David Niemeyer	Linda Gonnella	Darrell Langlois	James Bodony	Thomas Sheahan	Michael Meranda
Oak Forest	c	MC	28	(708) 687-4050	Patrick Gordon	Steven Jones	Patricia Kolar	Colleen Julian	Lindsay Laycoax	John Koch	John Stanly
Oak Lawn	v	CM	55	(708) 636-4400	Ernest Kolb	Larry Deetjen	Alice Powers	Gail Paul	Thomas Moran	Robert Smith	. . .
Oak Park	tp	CM	52	(708) 383-8005	F Boulanger	Sharon Hammer	Gregory White	. . .	. . .	. . .	. . .
Oak Park	v	CM	52	(708) 383-6400	. . .	Thomas Barwin	Sandra Sokol	Gregory Peters	Gerald Beeson	Joseph Mendrick	John Wielebnicki
Oakbrook Terrace	c	CM	2	(630) 941-8300	Thomas Mazaika	Martin Bourke	Elaine Deluca	. . .	. . .	Mark Collins	Daniel Tuttle
O'Fallon	c	MC	21	(618) 624-4500	Gary Graham	Walter Denton	Philip Goodwin	Dean Rich	Brent Saunders	. . .	Dennis Sullivan
Oglesby	c	MC	3	(815) 883-3389	. . .	. . .	. . .	. . .	. . .	. . .	. . .
Olney	c	CM	8	(618) 395-7302	Kelly Henby	Robert Ferguson	Belinda Henton	. . .	Gary Foster	Elton Wood	David Berry
Olympia Fields	v	MC	4	(708) 503-8000	Linzey Jones	David Mekarski	Jeffery Cohn	Cynthia Saenz	. . .	Jeff Chudwin	Joe Alexa
Oregon	c	CO	4	(815) 732-6321	James Barnes	. . .	Julienne Crowley	Howard Rattner	. . .	Thomas Miller	J. Dolan
Orland Hills *	v	MC	6	(708) 349-6666	Kyle Hastings	John Daly	Mikki Burke	. . .	. . .	David Laveck	Micheal Worley
Orland Park	v	CM	51	(708) 403-6100	Daniel McLaughlin	Ellen Baer	David Maher	. . .	. . .	. . .	Peter Casey
Oswego	v	CM	13	(630) 554-3287	Craig Weber	Gary Adams	Jeanne Hoch	Mark Pries	. . .	Dwight Baird	Gerald Weaver
Ottawa	c	MC	18	(815) 433-0161	Robert Eschbach	. . .	Elizabeth Taylor	. . .	Richard Scott	Brian Zeilmann	. . .
Palatine	v	CM	65	(847) 358-7500	. . .	Reid Ottesen	. . .	. . .	Norman Malcolm	John Koziol	Andrew Radetski
Palos Heights	c	MC	11	(708) 361-1800	Robert Straz	Daniel Nisavic	Mary Carik	. . .	. . .	George Yott	Gerald Martin
Palos Hills	c	MC	17	(708) 598-3400	Gerald Bennett	. . .	Rudy Mulderink	. . .	. . .	Paul Madigan	Dave Weakley
Palos Park	v	CM	4	(708) 671-3700	Carolyn Baca	Patricia Jones	Annette Mucha	. . .	. . .	Joseph Miller	Larry Miller
Pana	c	MC	5	(217) 562-3626	Larry Chaney	. . .	Terry Klein	. . .	Jerry Blackwell	Mike Harris	. . .
Paris	c	CM	9	(217) 465-7601	Craig Smith	Paul Ruff	Cathy Higgins	. . .	Herman Taylor	Ronald Humphrey	. . .
Park City	c	MC	6	(847) 623-5030	Steve Pannell	. . .	. . .	. . .	. . .	Michael Luff	. . .
Park Forest *	v	CM	23	(708) 748-1112	John Ostenburg	Thomas Mick	Dawn Robinson	Mary Dankowski	Bob Wilcox	Thomas Fleming	Kenneth Eyer
Park Ridge *	c	CM	37	(847) 318-5200	Howard Frimark	Timothy Schuenke	Betty Henneman	Diane Lembesis	Edward Dubowski	Jeffrey Caudill	Joe Saccomanno
Pawnee	v	MC	2	(217) 625-2951	. . .	. . .	. . .	. . .	. . .	. . .	. . .
Paxton *	c	MC	4	(217) 379-4022	James Kingston	. . .	Penny Stevens	Julie Burgess	Dennis Kingren	Robert Bane	Randall Haack
Pekin	c	CM	33	(309) 477-2300	Lyndell Howard	Dennis Kief	Sue McMillan	Robert Reis	John Janssen	Timothy Gillespie	. . .
Peoria	c	CM	112	(309) 494-8575	David Ransburg	. . .	Mary Haynes	James Scroggins	Roy Modglin	John Stenson	Stephen Van Winkle
Peoria Heights	v	MC	6	(309) 686-2385	Earl Carter	Thomas Horstmann	Dyrke Maricle	. . .	Howard Gorman	Larry Hawkins	Kevin Mattlingly
Peotone	v	MC	3	(708) 258-3279	Richard Benson	George Gray	Donna Werner	. . .	John Young	Terry Budds	Thomas Blogg
Peru	c	MC	9	(815) 223-0061	Donald Baker	. . .	Judith Heuser	. . .	Russell Reed	Glenn Fredrickson	Donald Kowalczyk
Phoenix	v	MC	2	(708) 331-2636	Terry Wells	. . .	Johnnie Lane	. . .	Brandon Turner	Melvin Davis	Robert Matthews
Pinckneyville	c	CO	5	(618) 357-6916	Joseph Shirk	. . .	. . .	John Hammack	Jerry Smith	Paul Day	Fred Pabst
Pingree Grove	v	CM	. .	(847) 464-5533	. . .	James Bassett	. . .	. . .	. . .	. . .	. . .
Pittsfield	c	MC	4	(217) 285-4484	John Hayden	. . .	Cindy Prentice	. . .	Michael Braungardt	Michael Bradshaw	. . .
Plainfield	v	CM	13	(815) 436-7093	Richard Rock	Christopher Minick	Susan Janick	. . .	. . .	Donald Bennett	Allen Persons
Plano	c	MC	5	(630) 552-8275	. . .	. . .	Deanna Brown	. . .	. . .	Steven Eaves	John McGinnis
Pontiac	c	CM	11	(815) 844-3396	Scott McCoy	Robert Karls	Sharon Dunham	. . .	Dennis McDugle	R. Newsome	Christopher Brock
Pontoon Beach	v	MC	5	(618) 931-6100	Harold Denham	. . .	Susan Daugherty	Scott Oney	Dan Kreher	Gary Wallace	. . .
Posen	v	MC	4	(708) 385-0139	Kevin Whitney	. . .	Veronica Grabowski	George Klotz	Robert Steele	Terence Urbaniak	Patrick Griffin
Princeton	c	CO	7	(815) 875-2631	Keith Cain	. . .	Clyde Wray	. . .	Terry Himes	Thomas Root	Steven Wright
Prospect Heights *	c	CM	17	(847) 398-6070	Rodney Pace	Pamela Arrigoni	William Kearns	Mohan Rao	. . .	Bruce Morris	Adam Boeche
Quincy	c	MC	40	(217) 228-4500	Charles Scholz	Rick Meehan	Janet Hutmacher	Ann Scott	James Doellman	Michael De Voss	. . .
Rantoul	v	MC	12	(217) 893-1661	. . .	David Johnston	Jeremy Reale	Scot Brandon	Ken Waters	Paul Farber	G. Hazel
Red Bud	c	MC	3	(618) 282-2315	. . .	Pamela Kempfer	. . .	. . .	. . .	Theodore Stellhorn	David Diewald
Richmond	v	MC	1	(815) 678-4040	. . .	Timothy Savage	. . .	. . .	. . .	. . .	. . .
Richton Park	v	CM	12	(708) 481-8950	. . .	Motiryo Keambiroiro	. . .	Constance Hoger	Michael Spain	. . .	. . .
River Forest	v	CM	11	(708) 366-8500	Frank Paris	Steven Gutierrez	Susan Conti	Lynette Tuggle	James Eggert	Nicholas Weiss	Gregory Kramer
River Grove	v	MC	10	(708) 453-8000	Thomas Tarpey	. . .	Joseph Compell	. . .	Loren Lariviere	Dennis Raucci	Brent Leder
Riverdale	v	MC	15	(708) 841-2200	Zenovia Evans	William Cooper	Joyce Forbes	. . .	Gregory Knoll	Peter Satriano	Jerry Townsend
Riverside *	v	CM	8	(708) 447-2700	Harold Wiaduck	Kathleen Rush	Arlene Blaha	Kevin Wachtel	Kevin Mulligan	Eugene Karczewski	Michael Hullihan
Riverton	v	MC	3	(217) 629-9122	Joe Rusciolelli	. . .	Connie Blissett	. . .	. . .	David Smith	Charles Stone
Riverwoods	v	MC	3	(847) 945-3990	. . .	. . .	. . .	. . .	. . .	Morris Weinstein	Russell Kraly
Robbins	v	CM	6	(708) 385-8940	Irene Brodie	Beverly Gavin	Palma James	. . .	Charles Lloyd	Robert Warren	. . .
Robinson	c	MC	6	(618) 544-7616	Gary Davis	Laquita Hasty	Sandrea Jared	. . .	Darrell Akers	David Marqua	William Calvert
Rochelle	c	CM	9	(815) 562-6161	Chet Olson	Ken Alberts	Bruce McKinney	Bob Withrow	Thomas McDermott	Robbie Buck	. . .
Rochester	v	CM	2	(217) 498-7192	. . .	Linda Shaw	Lisa Sandidge	. . .	. . .	William Marass	Wayne Beck
Rock Falls *	c	MC	9	(815) 564-1366	David Blanton	Richard Downey	William Wescott	. . .	James Larson	Humberto Perez	. . .
Rock Island	c	CM	39	(309) 732-2000	Mark Schwiebert	John Phillips	Jeanne Paggen	William Scott	Jerry Shirk	Terrence Dove	Robert Hawes
Rockford *	c	MC	150	(815) 987-5500	Lawrence Morrissey	James Ryan	. . .	Andres Sammul	Donald Robertson	Chet Epperson	Tim Hanson
Rolling Meadows *	c	CM	24	(847) 394-8500	Kenneth Nelson	Thomas Melena	Lisa Hinman	James Egeberg	Philip Burns	Steve Williams	Fred Vogt
Romeoville	v	CM	21	(815) 886-7200	Sandra Guiden	Steve Gulden	Maureen Ley	. . .	. . .	. . .	William Taylor
Roselle *	v	CM	23	(630) 980-2000	Gayle Smolinski	Jeffrey O'Dell	Linda McDermott	Pamela Figolah	Robert Gallas	James Kruger	Robert Burns
Rosemont	v	MC	4	(847) 825-4404	. . .	. . .	. . .	. . .	. . .	. . .	. . .
Round Lake *	v	MC	5	(847) 546-5400	Bill Gentes	Marc Huber	Jeanne Kristan	Steve Shields	. . .	Clifton Metaxa	Davis Clark
Round Lake Beach	v	MC	25	(847) 546-2351	Richard Hill	David Kilbane	Sylvia Valadez	Julian McDonough	Paul Maplethorpe	Douglas Larsson	Curtis Cashman
Round Lake Park	v	MC	6	(847) 546-2790	. . .	. . .	Linda Lucassen	Lee Howard	Paul Maplethorpe	Bruce Johnson	George Johnson
Rushville *	c	MC	3	(217) 322-3833	Scott Thompson	. . .	Stacey Briney	. . .	Vic Menely	Rocky Root	Drew Seal
Salem *	c	CM	7	(618) 548-2222	Leonard Ferguson	Thomas Christie	C Jane Marshall	Marilyn Shetley	. . .	Ron Campo	John Pruden
Sandwich	c	MC	6	(815) 786-9321	Tom Thomas	. . .	Barbara Olson	Carmen Dixon	Richard Kell	Richard Olson	. . .
Sauk Village	v	MC	10	(708) 758-3330	Roger Peckham	Richard Dieterich	Elizabeth Selvey	Beverly Sterrett	Christopher Sewell	Thomas Lacheta	Michael Wall
Savanna	c	MC	3	(815) 273-2251	William Lease	. . .	Walter Shrake	. . .	Shawn Picolotti	Mike Moon	John Lindeman
Savoy	v	MC	4	(217) 359-5894	Robert McCleary	Richard Helton	Billie Krueger	Clarence Well	Michael Forrest	. . .	Frank Rentchler
Schaumburg	v	CM	75	(847) 895-4500	Al Larson	Kenneth Fritz	Marilyn Karr	Douglas Ellsworth	David Schumann	Richard Casler	Steven Weinstock
Schiller Park	v	MC	11	(847) 678-2550	Anna Montana	Kevin Barr	Claudia Irsuto	Kenneth Kowitz	Thomas Deegan	Robert Radak	Ronald Sieracki
Shelbyville	c	CO	4	(217) 774-5531	. . .	. . .	. . .	. . .	. . .	. . .	. . .
Shorewood *	v	MC	7	(815) 725-2150	Richard Chapman	Kurt Carroll	Julia Russell	Sue Berg	Kerry Sheridan	Robert Puleo	Roger Barrowman
Silvis *	c	MC	7	(309) 792-9181	Lyle Lohse	. . .	Barbara Fox	. . .	David Leibovitz	William Hawbaker	James Grafton
Skokie	v	CM	63	(847) 673-0500	George Van Dusen	Albert Rigoni	Marlene Williams	Robert Nowak	Ralph Czerwinski	. . .	Max Slankard
South Beloit	c	CO	5	(815) 389-3023	Randy Kirichkow	. . .	. . .	. . .	Kenneth Morse	Larry Schultz	. . .
South Chicago Heights	v	MC	3	(708) 755-1880	David Owen	Paul Peterson	Melinda Villarreal	. . .	Angelo Petrarca	Ronald Diederich	Tony Renzetti

Directory 1/9 continued — OFFICIALS IN U.S. MUNICIPALITIES 2,500 AND OVER IN POPULATION

Jurisdiction	Type	Form of government	2000 Population (000)	Main telephone number	Chief elected official	Appointed administrator	Clerk of the governing board	Chief financial officer	Fire chief	Police chief	Public works director
ILLINOIS continued											
South Elgin	v	CM	16	(847) 742-5780	Jim Hansen	Larry Jones	Margaret Gray	Arthur Skibley	...	Christopher Merritt	Chuck Behm
South Holland	v	MC	22	(708) 210-2900	Don DeGraff	J. Wynsma	...	...	James Wiley	Warren Millsaps	Chris Niehof
South Jacksonville	v	MC	3	(217) 245-4803	Gordon Jumper	Katherine Simpson	Linda Douglass	...	David Hickox	Richard Evans	John Green
Sparta	c	CO	4	(618) 443-2917	W. Baue	...	Shirley Reimer	...	Bruce Dahlem	Alan Young	...
Spring Valley *	c	MC	5	(815) 664-4221	James Narczewski	...	Rebecca Hansen	...	Gene Scheri	Michael Miroux	John Schultz
Springfield	c	MC	111	(217) 789-2000	Timothy Davlin	...	Cecilia Langford	Thomas Langford	Ronald Hasara	Donald Kliment	Richard Berning
St. Charles	c	MC	27	(630) 377-4400	Donald Dewitte	Brian Townsend	Nancy Garrison	Pam Colby	Alan Schullo	James Lamkin	Mark Koenen
Staunton	c	MC	5	(618) 635-2233	Michael Arnold	...	Marilyn Herbeck	...	...	Ronnie Masinelli	...
Steger	v	CM	9	(708) 754-3395	Louis Sherman	Conrad Kiebles	Carmen Recupito	...	Elmer Joyce	Richard Stultz	John Gilkison
Sterling	c	CM	15	(815) 632-6621	Ted Aggen	Scott Shumard	Marie Rombouts	Cindy Wilson	Arlyn Oetting	Ronald Potthoff	Vernon Gottel
Stickney	v	MC	6	(708) 749-4400	...	...	...	...	...	...	...
Stone Park	v	MC	5	(708) 345-5550	...	Guiseppe Capece	Maria Castrejon	...	Brian Lewis	...	Jim Chillemi
Streamwood	v	CM	36	(630) 837-0200	Billie Roth	Gary O'Rourke	Kittie Kopitke	David Richardson	John Nixon	Alan Popp	John White
Streator	c	CM	14	(815) 672-2517	Raymond Schmitt	Paul Nicholson	Pamela Leonard	...	William Wissen	Jeffery Anderson	Ralph Hermann
Sugar Grove *	v	CM	3	(630) 466-4507	Sean Michels	Brent Eichelberger	Cynthia Welsch	Justin VanVooren	...	Bradley Sauer	Anthony Speciale
Sullivan	c	CO	4	(217) 728-4383	Leon Lane	...	Floyd Buckalew	...	...	Joe Thompson	...
Summit	v	MC	10	(708) 563-4800	Joseph Strzelczyk	...	Andrew Zambrycki	...	John Nemeth	Chuck Wasko	Dan Trapp
Swansea	v	MC	10	(618) 234-0044	Charles Gray	Cheryl Moody	Lauren O'Neill	...	John McGuire	Steve Krakowiecki	Frank Nadler
Sycamore *	c	MC	12	(815) 895-0786	Ken Mundy	F. Nicklas	Candace Smith	...	William Riddle	Donald Thomas	Fred Busse
Taylorville	c	MC	11	(217) 287-7946	James Montgomery	...	Pam Peabody	Nancy France	Charles Doherty	Gregory Brotherton	Denny Macke
Thornton *	tp	MC	180	(708) 596-6040	Frank Zuccarelli	Deborah Kopec	J. Davis-Rivera	...	...	...	...
Thornton *	v	MC	2	(708) 877-4456	Jack Swan	Jason Wicha	Cheryl Bult	...	Brian Kolosh	...	Ronald Bannon
Tinley Park *	v	MC	48	(708) 444-5000	Edward Zabrocki	Scott Niehaus	Frank German	...	Kenneth Dunn	Michael O'Connell	Dale Schepers
Trenton *	c	MC	2	(618) 224-7323	Robert Koentz	...	Carol Gajewski	...	...	Michael Jones	Roger Maue
Troy	c	MC	8	(618) 667-9924	Thomas Caraker	R. Klaustermeier	Mary Chasteen	...	...	...	Alan Secrest
Tuscola	c	MC	4	(217) 253-2112	Daniel Kleiss	James Hoel	Beth Leamon	...	Steve Hettinger	Craig Hastings	Denny Cruzman
University Park *	v	CM	6	(708) 534-6451	Alvin McCowan	David Litton	Dorothy Jones	David Sevier	...	Melvin Easley	Ben Adcock
Urbana	c	MC	36	(217) 384-2458	Tod Satterthwaite	...	Phyllis Clark	Ronald Eldridge	Rex Mundt	Eddie Adair	William Gray
Vandalia	c	MC	6	(618) 283-1196	...	...	Peggy Bowen	...	...	Robert McCart	John Moyer
Venice	c	MC	2	(618) 877-2412	Tyrone Echols	...	Wilbert Glasper	Jacob Young	Thomas Brent	James Newsome	Anthony Matthews
Vernon Hills	v	CM	20	(847) 367-3700	Roger Byrne	Michael Allison	...	Larry Nafrin	...	Mark Fleischhauer	E. Laudenslager
Villa Grove	c	MC	2	(217) 832-4721	Ronald Hunt	...	Brandy Hopkins	...	Ross Elston	Dennis Gire	Steven Duke
Villa Park	v	CM	22	(630) 834-8500	...	Robert Niemann	...	Eric Dubrowski	Robert Wilson	Ronald Ohlson	Vydas Juskelis
Virden	c	MC	3	(217) 965-5805	...	...	...	...	...	...	...
Wadsworth	v	MC	3	(847) 336-7771	...	Moses Amidei	...	...	...	...	...
Warrenville	c	CM	13	(630) 393-9427	Vivian Lund	John Coakley	Emily Larson	...	...	Robert La Deur	...
Washington	c	MC	10	(309) 444-3196	Gary Manier	Robert Morris	Carol Moss	Joan Baxter	...	William Witmer	...
Washington Park	v	MC	5	(618) 874-2040	Robert Moore	L. Cannon-Connor	C. Hollingsworth	Sherman Sorrell	James Brown	Johnnie Matt	Lee McNatt
Waterloo *	c	MC	7	(618) 939-8600	Thomas Smith	...	Barbara Pace	Shawn Kennedy	...	James Trantham	Timothy Birk
Watseka	c	MC	5	(815) 432-2711	...	...	...	...	...	...	...
Wauconda	v	MC	9	(847) 526-9600	J. Eschenbauch	Daniel Quick	Mary Taylor	Zaida Torres	...	George Roberts	Jeffrey Maute
Waukegan *	c	MC	87	(847) 599-2500	Richard Hyde	Raymond Vukovich	Wayne Motley	Lyndon Bruessel	Patrick Gallagher	William Biang	William Johnston
West Chicago	c	CM	23	(630) 293-2200	Michael Fortner	Michael Guttman	Nancy Smith	Linda Martin	...	Gerald Mourning	Robert Flatter
West Dundee	v	CM	5	(847) 551-3800	Larry Keller	Joseph Cavallaro	Barbara Haines	David Danielson	Larry McManaman	Edward Dennis	Richard Monas
West Frankfort *	c	MC	8	(618) 932-3262	Marion Presley	...	Janice Biggs	Christopher McPhail	Wes Taylor	Michael Dinn	...
West Peoria *	c	MC	4	(309) 674-1993	James Dillon	John Carlson	Carole Stephens	Diana Jarbo	...	...	Henry Strube
Westchester *	v	CM	16	(708) 345-0020	Paul Gattuso	Carl Goldsmith	Kathryn Hayes	...	Richard Belmonte	Matt Evans	...
Western Springs	v	CM	12	(708) 246-1800	John Lynch	Patrick Higgins	Jeanine Jasica	...	Frank Benak	William Rypkema	...
Westmont	v	CM	24	(630) 829-4400	William Rahn	Ronald Searl	Virginia Szymski	Lisa Van Bogget	Frank Trout	James Ramey	Steve May
Westville	v	MC	3	(217) 267-2507	...	...	...	...	...	Jeff Keeling	...
Wheaton	c	CM	55	(630) 260-2000	C. James Carr	Donald Rose	Emily Consolazio	Mark Horton	Greg Berk	Mark Field	Joseph Knippen
Wheeling *	v	CM	34	(847) 459-2600	Judy Abruscato	J. Rooney	Elaine Simpson	M. Mondschain	Keith MacIsaac	John Stone	Anthony Stavros
White Hall	c	MC	2	(217) 374-2345	Harold Brimm	...	Sue Reno	...	Garry Sheppard	Robert McMillen	Jay Howard
Willow Springs	v	MC	5	(708) 467-3700	Alan Nowaczyk	Bruce Trego	Sue Fredrickson	...	Larry Moran	Roger Alexander	James Chevalier
Willowbrook *	v	MC	8	(630) 323-8215	Gary Pretzer	Philip Modaff	Leroy Hansen	Sue Stanish	...	Edward Konstanty	Tim Halik
Wilmette	v	CM	27	(847) 251-2700	C. Canning	Michael Earl	...	Robert Amoruso	...	George Carpenter	Donna Jakubowski
Wilmington	c	MC	5	(815) 476-2175	Tony McGann	Sheryl Puracchio	James Johnston	Nick Narducci	Al Zlomie	James Metta	Gary Van Duyne
Winfield	v	CM	8	(630) 933-7100	John Kirschbaum	William Barlow	...	...	...	Douglas Riner	Tye Loomis
Winnetka	v	CM	12	(847) 501-6000	Michael Duhl	Douglas Williams	...	Edward McKee	Scott Smith	Joseph DeLopez	Steven Saunders
Winthrop Harbor	v	MC	6	(847) 872-3846	Robert Loy	...	Jana Lee	...	Michael Stried	Joel Brumlik	John Hogan
Wood Dale	c	CM	13	(630) 766-4900	Kenneth Johnson	Frank Williams	Shirley Siebert	Robert Broznowski	...	...	Craig Wright
Wood River	c	CM	11	(618) 251-3100	David Ayres	...	Janet Sneed	Nancy Schneider	Steve Alexander	Jim Schneider	Steve Palen
Woodridge *	v	MC	30	(630) 852-7000	William Murphy	John Perry	Eileene Nystrom	Deborah Freischlag	...	Geoffrey Korous	Christopher Bethel
Woodstock *	c	CM	20	(815) 338-4300	Brian Sager	Timothy Clifton	Meghan Haak	Roscoe Stelford	...	Robert Lowen	John Isbell
Worth	v	MC	11	(708) 448-1181	Edward Guzdziol	...	Bonnie Price	...	Donald Stefaniak	Patrick O'Connor	W. Demonbreun
Yorkville	c	MC	6	(630) 553-4350	Arthur Prochaska	...	Jackie Milschewski	Traci Pleckham	...	Harold Martin	Eric Dhuse
Zion *	c	CO	22	(847) 746-4000	Lane Harrison	...	Judy Mackey	...	David Labelle	Larry Booth	Ron Colangelo
INDIANA											
Albany	t	MC	2	(765) 789-6112	James Miller	...	Marita Fields	...	Darrin Mays	Shannon Henry	...
Alexandria	c	MC	6	(765) 724-2541	Steve Skaggs	...	...	Janet Lynch	Mike Hensley	Jack Malston	...
Anderson	c	MC	59	(765) 646-9685	J. Lawler	...	Marie Riggs	Morris Long	Jerry Quire	Ronald Rheam	Wilbur Miller
Angola	c	MC	7	(260) 665-2514	Richard Hickman	...	Debra Twitchell	...	Raymond Meek	Jon Parrish	...
Attica	c	MC	3	(765) 762-2467	Harold Long	...	Tracy Smith	...	Jack O'Farrell	Timothy Quinn	Robert Smith
Auburn	c	MC	12	(260) 925-6450	Norman Yoder	...	Rebecca Fuller	...	Jerry Bauermeister	Martin McCoy	...
Aurora	c	MC	3	(812) 926-1777	Richard Ullrich	...	Richard Eaglin	...	...	Noel Houze	...
Austin	t	MC	4	(812) 794-2877	...	...	...	...	...	...	...
Avon	t	MC	6	(317) 272-0948	...	Thomas Klein	...	...	...	Jeff Ritorto	Ryan Canion
Batesville *	c	MC	6	(812) 933-6100	Rick Fledderman	Beth West	Michele Balser	...	Todd Schutte	Stan Holt	...
Bedford	c	MC	13	(812) 279-6555	John Williams	...	Donna Brumbaugh	...	Carl Beauchamp	Dave Jarrard	John Dalton
Beech Grove	c	MC	14	(317) 788-4975	J. Wiley	...	...	Richard Brown	Dennis Buckley	Michael Johnson	Philip Gurganus
Berne	c	MC	4	(260) 589-8526	Blaine Fulton	...	Gwendolyn Maller	...	Armando Velasco	Richard Crider	...
Bicknell	c	MC	3	(812) 735-4636	Gordon Stinebaugh	...	Cindi Parkhill	...	Wayne Bement	Jeff Chambers	...
Bloomington	c	MC	69	(812) 339-2261	John Fernandez	James McNamara	Regina Moore	Thomas Guevara	Jeffrey Barlow	Michael Hostetler	John Freeman
Bluffton	c	MC	9	(260) 824-0612	Ted Ellis	...	...	Nancy Hewitt	David Brinneman	Tamera Schaffer	...
Boonville	c	MC	6	(812) 897-1230	Pamela Henrickson	...	...	...	Steven Byers	Roy Harmon	...
Brazil	c	MC	8	(812) 443-2221	Kenneth Crabb	...	Ruth Mohr	Carolyn Latham	Robert Bennett	Terry Harrison	James Sheese
Bremen	t	MC	4	(574) 546-2471	Thomas Keller	...	Janet Anglemyer	...	Jerry Lanning	Matthew Hassel	...
Brookville	t	CO	2	(765) 647-3322	Michael Biltz	...	...	...	...	Bruce Baker	...
Brownsburg *	t	CM	14	(317) 852-1120	Mike Green	Mark White	Jeanette Brickler	...	William Rosemeyer	David Galloway	...
Brownstown	t	MC	2	(812) 358-5500	Leroy Warren	...	Rebecka Stovall	...	...	Paul Starr	...
Butler	c	MC	2	(260) 868-5200	Floyd Coburn	William Miller	...	...	Brian Moore	Steven Mosser	Ron Walter

Directory 1/9 continued — OFFICIALS IN U.S. MUNICIPALITIES 2,500 AND OVER IN POPULATION

Jurisdiction	Type	Form of govern-ment	2000 Popu-lation (000)	Main telephone number	Chief elected official	Appointed administrator	Clerk of the governing board	Chief financial officer	Fire chief	Police chief	Public works director
INDIANA continued											
Carmel	c	MC	37	(317) 571-2400	James Brainard	...	...	...	Douglas Callahan	Michael Fogarty	John Duffy
Cedar Lake	t	CM	9	(219) 374-7000	Claudia Mentrak	Joan Boyer	...	...	...	Barry Wornhoff	William Maleckar
Chandler	t	CM	3	(812) 925-6882	Donald Wilkey	...	...	...	...	Kenneth Musgrave	Robert Coghill
Charlestown	c	MC	5	(812) 256-7126	George Hall	James Knoebel	...	...	...	Ernest Crumpton	...
Chesterfield	t	RT	2	(765) 378-3331	Don Carpenter	Chris Parrish	...	...	Gary Hutton	Moses Beeman	...
Chesterton	t	RT	10	(219) 926-1641	...	...	...	...	...	...	...
Cicero	t	MC	4	(317) 984-4900	Michael Mauro	...	Janice Unger	...	Steven Peachey	Garry Cook	Jerry Cook
Clarksville	t	CO	21	(812) 283-1504	John Minta	...	...	...	...	...	...
Clinton	c	MC	5	(765) 832-9880	Ronald Shepard	...	...	...	Tim Cottrell	Paul Curry	...
Cloverdale	t	MC	2	(765) 795-6033	...	...	...	...	...	...	...
Columbia City	c	MC	7	(260) 244-5141	...	...	...	...	...	...	...
Columbus	c	MC	39	(812) 376-2570	Fred Armstrong	...	John Baughn	...	Gary Henderson	Matthew McCord	James Norris
Connersville	c	MC	15	(765) 825-4211	Max Ellison	...	...	...	James Bennett	Jim Holbrook	...
Corydon	t	MC	2	(812) 738-3958	Fred Cammack	...	...	Janet Frederick	Tony Ross	Richard Yetter	...
Covington	c	MC	2	(765) 793-3423	Bradley Crain	Richard Rennick	Debby Gurley	...	Richard Talbert	Tony Knecht	...
Crawfordsville	c	MC	15	(765) 364-5150	John Zumer	...	Nellie Thompson	...	Todd Barton	Kurt Knecht	...
Crown Point	c	MC	19	(219) 662-3235	Daniel Klein	...	Patti Olson	...	Gary Huys	Keith Hefner	Jay Olson
Cumberland	t	MC	5	(317) 894-3580	Sandra Cottey	D. Sheridan	Linda Jeter	...	...	Michael Crooke	Arthur Gale
Danville	t	CM	6	(317) 745-3001	Myron Anderson	Gary Eakin	Paula Frye	...	Mark Morgan	Garry Edwards	Rob Roberts
De Motte	t	MC	3	(219) 987-3831	...	John Dyke	...	...	...	William Arnold	Dick Higgins
Decatur	c	MC	9	(260) 724-7171	...	...	...	...	...	...	...
Dunkirk	c	MC	2	(765) 768-6565	Thomas Johnson	...	...	Jane Kesler	Steve Fields	Arnold Clevenger	...
Dyer	t	MC	13	(219) 865-6108	Dennis Hawrot	Joseph Neeb	...	Tom Hoffman	Jeff Zendzian	Donald Horvat	Jay Steinmetz
East Chicago	c	MC	32	(219) 392-1600	George Pabey	...	...	...	...	...	...
Edinburg *	t	CM	4	(812) 526-3512	Bill Davis	...	Jackie Smith	...	Allen Smith	Patrick Pankey	John Drybread
Elkhart	c	MC	51	(574) 294-5471	David Miller	...	Sue Beadle	Clara Mishler	William Johnson	Pamela Westlake	Eric Horvath
Ellettsville	t	RT	5	(812) 876-3860	Patrick Stoffers	...	...	Sandra Hash	Jim Davis	Ron McGlockin	Mike Farmer
Elwood	c	MC	9	(765) 552-5076	Jerry Werline	...	...	...	Milt Gough	Tom Elder	...
Evansville	c	MC	121	(812) 436-4934	...	...	...	...	...	...	...
Fairmount	t	TM	2	(765) 948-4632	Melba Root	...	...	...	Rick Clevenger	Brian Reneau	...
Fishers	t	CM	37	(317) 595-3111	Scott Faultless	Gary Huff	...	...	Brian Lott	George Kehl	Jeffrey Heiking
Fort Branch *	t	CM	2	(812) 753-3824	...	...	...	...	...	...	...
Fort Wayne	c	MC	205	(260) 427-1111	Graham Richard	David Ridderheim	Sandra Kennedy	Alvin Moll	Timothy Davie	Russell York	Gregory Meszaros
Fortville	t	CM	3	(317) 485-4044	Stephen Gipson	...	Margie Manship	...	Kitridge Arnold	Mike Shepherd	Tony Shaw
Frankfort	c	MC	16	(765) 654-5715	Roy Scott	...	...	Marilyn Chittick	Charles Toney	William Moudy	...
Franklin	c	MC	19	(317) 736-3609	N. Blankenship	Norma Brewer	Janet Alexander	...	Michael Herron	John Borges	Rick Littleton
Garrett	c	MC	5	(260) 357-3836	...	...	...	...	...	...	...
Gary	c	MC	102	(219) 881-1300	Scott King	Geraldine Tousant	Suzette Raggs	Husain Mahmoud	Robert Walker	Garnett Watson	...
Gas City	c	MC	5	(765) 677-3080	Eugene Linn	...	...	...	David Linn	James Cassidy	...
Goshen	c	MC	29	(574) 533-8621	Allan Kauffman	Jolinda Fradenburg	...	Nancy Hoke	John Alheim	Michael Kettlebar	...
Greencastle	c	MC	9	(765) 653-9211	Nancy Michael	...	...	Pamela Jones	Bill Newgent	Tom Sutherlin	...
Greendale	c	CM	4	(812) 537-2125	Douglas Hedrick	Steven Lampert	Mary Lynch	...	Edwin Noel	DeWayne Uhlman	...
Greenfield	c	MC	14	(317) 477-4310	Patricia Elmore	...	Larry Breese	...	Lewis McQueen	Rick Hoy	...
Greensburg *	c	MC	10	(812) 663-8582	Frank Manus	...	...	L. June Ryle	Scott Chasteen	Bill Meyerose	...
Greenwood	c	MC	36	(317) 887-5604	Charles Henderson	...	Jeannine Myers	...	Steven Dhondt	Joseph Pitcher	...
Griffith	t	MC	17	(219) 924-7500	Stan Dobosz	...	Ronald Szafarczyk	...	...	Ronald Kottka	Rick Konopasek
Hammond	c	MC	83	(219) 853-6300	Thomas McDermott	...	Gerald Bobos	Tony Bonaventura	Louis Covelli	John Cory	Thomas Golfis
Hanover *	t	MC	2	(812) 866-2131	Debbie Kroger	...	Lucy Anderson	...	...	Marshal Lovins	...
Hartford City	c	MC	6	(765) 348-0412	...	...	...	...	...	...	...
Hebron	t	MC	3	(219) 996-4641	Peter Breuckman	...	...	...	David Wilson	Steven Sibbrell	Steven Martin
Highland *	t	MC	23	(219) 838-1080	Daniel Dernulc	...	...	...	William Timmer	Peter Hojnicki	John Bach
Hobart	c	MC	25	(219) 942-1940	Linda Buzinec	...	...	...	William McCorkle	Robert Paulson	Tony Boren
Huntingburg	c	MC	5	(812) 683-2211	Gail Kemp	...	...	Thomas Ellsworth	Glen Kissling	Ron Bowling	...
Huntington	c	MC	17	(260) 356-1400	...	...	...	...	...	...	...
Indianapolis–Marion County	c	MC	731	(317) 327-5200	Bart Peterson	...	Jean Milharcic	Robert Clifford	Louis Dezelan	Michael Spears	Kumar Menon
Jasper	c	MC	12	(812) 482-4255	...	...	...	...	...	...	...
Jeffersonville	c	MC	27	(812) 285-6405	Thomas Galligan	...	Peggy Wilder	...	Charles Smith	Michael Pavey	...
Kendallville	c	MC	9	(260) 347-2452	Suzanne Handshoe	...	Marsha Kiersey	...	Michael Riehm	Kevin Jones	...
Knox	c	MC	3	(574) 772-4553	...	...	...	...	...	...	...
Kokomo	c	MC	46	(765) 456-7470	Matt McKillip	...	Brenda Ott	Phillip Williams	Patrick Donoghue	Thomas Dinardo	Joseph Ewing
La Porte	c	MC	21	(219) 362-8220	...	...	...	Teresa Ludlow	Andy Snyder	David Gariepy	...
Lafayette *	c	MC	56	(765) 807-1000	Tony Roswarski	...	Cindy Murray	Michael Jones	James Morrow	James Roush	Jennifer Bonner
Lake Station	c	MC	13	(219) 962-3111	Shirley Wadding	...	Martha Kroledge	...	Ron Good	Rich Arnold	Marshall Gilliana
Lawrence	c	MC	38	(317) 549-4803	Thomas Schneider	...	...	Annetta Sweat	Mark Delong	Joseph Carter	Billy Gann
Lawrenceburg	c	MC	4	(812) 532-3553	W. Cunningham	Thomas Steidel	Jackie Stutz	...	Randy Abner	Bernard Hunefeld	Charles Davis
Lebanon *	c	MC	14	(765) 482-1201	James Acton	...	Debra Ottinger	...	James Stevenson	Tom Garoffolo	...
Ligonier	c	MC	4	(574) 894-4113	Charles Musselman	...	Helen Gerke	...	Paul Pfenning	John Durham	...
Linton	c	MC	5	(812) 847-7754	Tommy Jones	...	...	...	Lonnie Eberhardt	Troy Jerrell	...
Logansport	c	MC	19	(574) 753-4745	Richard Hettinger	Richard Farrer	...	Ruth Helms	Ronald Holcomb	Patrick Shively	Klaus Hemberger
Loogootee	c	MC	2	(812) 295-3200	Brian Ader	...	...	Bettye Norris	...	Kelly Rayhill	...
Lowell	t	CM	7	(219) 696-7794	Ray Raszewski	Rick Dal Corobbo	Judith Walters	Marcia Carlson	Jack Eskridge	David Wilson	Michael Lush
Madison	c	MC	12	(812) 265-8300	Albert Huntington	...	...	...	Steve Horton	Robert Wolf	...
Marion	c	MC	31	(765) 662-9931	William Henry	...	Kathi Kiley	Karen Browder	...	...	William McHaney
Markle *	t	MC	1	(260) 758-3193	Tamra Boucher	Darcy Long	Carolyn Hamilton	...	Duane Brumbaugh	John Markley	Rick Asher
Martinsville	c	MC	11	(765) 342-6012	Shannon Buskirk	Roger Layman	...	...	Timothy Fraker	Frans Hollanders	...
Mccordsville *	t	CM	1	(317) 335-3151	Jennifer Williams	Tonya Galbraith	Cathy Gardner	...	...	Harold Rodgers	Ron Crider
Merrillville	t	CM	30	(219) 769-5711	Richard Hardaway	Timothy Brown	R. Ann Antich-Carr	...	Edward Yerga	Nicholas Bravos	Bruce Spires
Michigan City *	c	MC	32	(219) 873-1400	Charles Oberlie	...	Thomas Fedder	John Schaefer	David Lamb	Bernhard Neitzel	Anthony Metzcus
Middletown	t	CM	2	(765) 354-2268	...	...	...	...	...	...	...
Mishawaka	c	MC	46	(574) 258-1600	...	...	Debbie Block	Edwina Kintner	Dale Freeman	Anthony Hazen	Philip Miller
Mitchell	c	MC	4	(812) 849-3831	Jerry Hancock	...	Mark Kern	...	Larry Caudell	Morris Chastain	...
Monticello	c	MC	5	(574) 583-5712	Mary Walters	...	...	...	Michael Keever	Kevin Harris	...
Mooresville	t	MC	9	(317) 831-1608	...	...	...	Sandra Perry	Leslie Farmer	Timothy Viles	Joe Beikman
Mount Vernon	c	MC	7	(812) 838-3317	Jackson Higgins	...	Cristi Wolfe	...	Roger Waters	Glenn Boyster	E. Stucki
Muncie	c	MC	67	(765) 747-4846	Daniel Canan	...	Ruth Dorer	Mary Ann Kratochuil	Gary Lucas	Joseph Winkle	Michael Winkle
Munster	t	CM	21	(219) 836-6900	John Edington	Thomas DeGiulio	...	David Shafer	...	Nikola Panich	James Knesek
Nappanee	c	MC	6	(574) 773-2112	Larry Thompson	...	Kimberly Ingle	...	Donald Abel	Raymond Carich	...
New Albany	c	MC	37	(812) 948-5333	James Garner	Sally Mastrolia	Marcey Wisman	Kathlyn Garry	Ronald Toran	Merle Harl	Anthony Toran
New Castle	c	MC	17	(765) 521-6803	...	...	...	...	...	...	...
New Chicago	t	MC	2	(219) 962-1157	Roger Pelfrey	...	Sherry Hall	...	Lawrence Barniville	James Gunning	...

Directory 1/9 continued — OFFICIALS IN U.S. MUNICIPALITIES 2,500 AND OVER IN POPULATION

Jurisdiction	Type	Form of govern-ment	2000 Popu-lation (000)	Main telephone number	Chief elected official	Appointed administrator	Clerk of the governing board	Chief financial officer	Fire chief	Police chief	Public works director
INDIANA continued											
New Haven	c	MC	12	(260) 748-7050	Terry McDonald	. . .	Paula Staak	Brenda Adams	John Bennett	Michael Sweet	David Jones
New Whiteland *	t	CM	4	(317) 535-9487	John Perrin	. . .	. . .	Maribeth Alspach	Brian Hedrick	Ed Stephenson	James Lasiter
Newburgh	t	CM	3	(812) 853-3578	. . .	. . .	. . .	. . .	. . .	. . .	. . .
Noblesville *	c	MC	28	(317) 776-6328	John Ditslear	Rusty Bodenhorn	. . .	. . .	Kenneth Gilliam	Richard Russell	. . .
North Manchester *	t	MC	6	(260) 982-9800	Don Rinearson	Dan Hannaford	Miriah Tobias	. . .	Dan Renz	David Young	John Mugford
North Vernon	c	MC	6	(812) 346-5907	John Hall	. . .	Roger Short	. . .	Richard McGill	Jack Hatton	. . .
Oakland City	c	MC	2	(812) 749-3222	Lee Ayers	. . .	Judy Cochrane	. . .	David Corn	Tom Rowe	. . .
Paoli	t	MC	3	(812) 723-2739	Johnny Henderson	. . .	Carolyn Clements	. . .	James Hickman	Ronald Shrout	. . .
Peru	c	MC	12	(765) 472-2344	Richard Blair	. . .	Jackquan Gray	. . .	Danny Sparks	William Raber	William Giornto
Petersburg	c	MC	2	(812) 354-8511	Jon Craig	. . .	Tammy Selby	. . .	Philip Taylor	Joe Hill	. . .
Plainfield *	t	MC	18	(317) 839-2561	Robin Brandgard	Richard Carlucci	Wes Bennett	. . .	Byron Anderson	Jeff Mitny	Jason Castetter
Plymouth	c	MC	9	(574) 936-2124	Jack Greenlee	. . .	Toni Hutchings	. . .	Wayne Smith	T. Chamberlin	. . .
Portage	c	MC	33	(219) 762-7784	Sammie Maletta	. . .	. . .	Felix Kimbrough	Michael Brown	David Reynolds	. . .
Porter	t	CM	4	(219) 926-2771	. . .	. . .	. . .	. . .	Lewis Craig	James Spanier	Karl Bauer
Portland	c	MC	6	(260) 726-9395	James Hedges	. . .	Barbara Blackford	. . .	Michael Thomas	Bart Darby	. . .
Princeton	c	MC	8	(812) 385-4428	George Taylor	. . .	Shirley Robb	. . .	Robert Embree	Nick Michas	. . .
Rensselaer	c	MC	5	(219) 866-5213	Susan Smith	. . .	. . .	Frieda Bretzinger	Le Moyne Koehler	William Sammons	. . .
Richmond *	c	MC	39	(765) 983-7200	Sally Hutton	. . .	Karen Chasteen	Tammy Glenn	Michael Crawley	Kris Wolski	Greg Stiens
Roanoke	t	MC	1	(260) 672-8116	. . .	. . .	. . .	. . .	. . .	. . .	. . .
Rochester	c	MC	6	(574) 223-2510	Philip Thompson	. . .	. . .	Carla Smith	Michael Gearhart	Greg Halfast	. . .
Rockville	t	CM	2	(765) 569-6253	Parke Swaim	. . .	Imogene Rahn	. . .	John Malone	Dewey White	. . .
Rushville	c	MC	5	(765) 932-2672	. . .	. . .	. . .	. . .	. . .	. . .	. . .
Salem	c	MC	6	(812) 883-4265	Judy Chastain	. . .	Patricia Persinger	. . .	Michael Mead	Brian Ratts	. . .
Santa Claus *	t	MC	2	(812) 937-2551	Ronald Smith	. . .	. . .	Kim Christensen	Edward Hagedorn	Henry Brown	Russ Luthy
Schererville *	t	CM	24	(219) 322-2211	Michael Troxell	Robert Volkmann	. . .	Janice Malinowski	Joseph Kruzan	David Dowling	Jeffrey Huet
Scottsburg	c	MC	6	(812) 752-4343	William Graham	Sue Barnett	. . .	. . .	Richard Kern	Delbert Meeks	Dennis Nicholas
Sellersburg	t	MC	6	(812) 246-3821	. . .	. . .	. . .	. . .	. . .	. . .	. . .
Seymour	c	MC	18	(812) 522-4020	John Burkhart	Martha McIntire	. . .	Fred Lewis	. . .	. . .	Dave Stark
Shelbyville	c	MC	17	(317) 398-6624	Frank Zerr	. . .	. . .	Rodney Meyerholtz	Kurt Lockridge	Kehrt Etherton	. . .
South Bend	c	MC	107	(574) 235-9216	Stephen Luecke	. . .	Loretta Duda	Frederick Ollett	Luther Taylor	Thomas Fautz	Gary Gilot
Speedway	t	MC	12	(317) 241-2566	. . .	. . .	. . .	. . .	. . .	. . .	. . .
Spencer *	t	MC	2	(812) 829-3213	Dean Bruce	. . .	. . .	Linda Simmerman	Pete Hodge	Larry Smith	Shelley Edwards
St. John *	t	MC	8	(219) 365-4800	Michel Fryzel	Stephen Kil	Sherry Sury	. . .	Fred Willman	Fred Frego	Robert Pharazyn
Sullivan	c	MC	4	(812) 268-6077	Timothy Boles	. . .	Sue Pitts	. . .	Shawn McKinney	David Story	. . .
Syracuse	t	CM	3	(574) 457-3348	Brian Woody	. . .	Julie Kline	. . .	Mickey Scott	Tony Ciriello	Clint Houseworth
Tell City	c	MC	7	(812) 472-2349	P. Goffinet	. . .	. . .	. . .	Dennis Kessans	David Faulkenberg	. . .
Terre Haute	c	MC	59	(812) 244-2320	Judy Anderson	Luke Anderson	Charles Hanley	Margaret Lemont	John Brighton	James Horrall	Robin Drummy
Tipton	c	MC	5	(765) 675-7561	. . .	. . .	. . .	. . .	. . .	. . .	. . .
Trail Creek	t	MC	2	(219) 872-2422	Daniel Tompkins	. . .	Anne Dobbs	. . .	. . .	Eugene Pierce	. . .
Union City	c	MC	3	(765) 964-6534	Phillip DeHaven	. . .	Brenda Campbell	. . .	Timothy Troxell	Monte Poling	. . .
Upland	t	MC	3	(765) 998-7439	. . .	. . .	. . .	. . .	. . .	. . .	. . .
Valparaiso	c	MC	27	(219) 462-1161	Jon Costas	William Hanna	S. Emerson-Swihart	. . .	David Nondorf	Michael Brickner	William Oeding
Vincennes *	c	MC	18	(812) 882-7285	Terry Mooney	Jane Rode	. . .	Beverly Marsh	Joe Yochum	Robert Dunham	Kirk Bouchie
Wabash	c	MC	11	(260) 563-4171	. . .	. . .	. . .	. . .	. . .	. . .	. . .
Warsaw	c	MC	12	(574) 372-9545	Ernest Wiggins	. . .	. . .	. . .	Matthew Warren	Steven Foster	Lacy Francis
Washington *	c	MC	11	(812) 254-5575	David Abel	. . .	Elaine Wellman	. . .	David Chapman	Michael Healy	. . .
West Lafayette	c	MC	28	(765) 775-5100	Jan Mills	. . .	Judith Rhodes	. . .	Philip Drew	Daniel Marvin	David Downey
Westfield *	t	MC	9	(317) 896-5570	Teresa Skelton	Jerry Rosenberger	Cindy Gossard	. . .	Keith Smith	Bryan Foster	. . .
Whiting	c	MC	5	(219) 659-3100	Robert Bercik	. . .	Margaret Drewniak	. . .	Michael Mantich	David Tobias	. . .
Winchester	c	MC	5	(765) 584-6845	Jack Fowler	. . .	Marilyn Pash	. . .	Bill Yost	Michael Burk	. . .
Winona Lake	t	CM	3	(574) 267-7581	David Delp	Craig Allebach	Retha Hicks	. . .	Roger Gelbaugh	Malcolm Gilbert	. . .
Yorktown *	t	CM	4	(765) 759-4003	Steve Lowry	Tim Kelty	. . .	M. Sidey	Kyle Pickering	Richard St. John	Peter Olson
Zionsville *	t	MC	8	(317) 873-5410	Richard Crane	Edward Mitro	John Yeo	. . .	. . .	Richard Dowden	. . .
IOWA											
Adel *	c	CM	3	(515) 993-4525	James Peters	Chad Bird	Pat Gilliland	. . .	Matt Ireland	Jim McNeill	. . .
Albia	c	MC	3	(641) 932-2129	Nancy Spaur	. . .	. . .	. . .	Bill Murphy	Kenneth Powers	Thomas Murphy
Algona	c	MC	5	(515) 295-2411	Lynn Kueck	Cole O'Donnell	Rexann McEnroe	. . .	Chuck Bell	Kevin Bangert	Chad Schaeffer
Alton	c	MC	1	(712) 756-4314	Norman Beltman	. . .	Stacie Dykstra	. . .	Bill Schnee	Jim Schwieson	. . .
Altoona	c	MC	10	(515) 967-5136	Timothy Burget	Jeffery Mark	Randy Pierce	. . .	Jerry Whetstone	John Gray	Vern Willey
Ames	c	CM	50	(515) 239-5101	. . .	Steven Schainker	Diane Voss	Duane Pitcher	Clinton Petersen	Loras Jaeger	Paul Wiegand
Anamosa	c	MC	5	(319) 462-6055	Carl Chalstrom	Patrick Callahan	Suzanne Marek	. . .	Mike Schaffer	Richard Stivers	Gary Kula
Ankeny *	c	CM	27	(515) 965-6400	Steve Van Oort	Carl Metzger	Pamela De Mouth	Dennis Bockenstedt	Rex Mundt	. . .	Jolee Belzung
Atlantic *	c	CM	7	(712) 243-4810	John Krogman	Ronald Crisp	Deb Field	. . .	Mark McNees	Roger Muri	. . .
Audubon	c	MC	2	(712) 563-3269	. . .	. . .	. . .	. . .	. . .	. . .	. . .
Bancroft	c	MC	. .	(515) 885-2382	. . .	. . .	. . .	. . .	. . .	. . .	. . .
Belle Plaine	c	MC	2	(319) 444-2200	James Daily	Bill Daily	Kaye Buch	. . .	Russ Spading	Mike Smith	. . .
Belmond	c	CM	2	(641) 444-3386	Jerry Greenwood	Lee Waltzing	. . .	. . .	Wayne Bruggeman	Linn Larson	Mark Dirks
Bettendorf	c	CM	31	(563) 344-4000	. . .	Decker Ploehn	. . .	Carol Barnes	Gerald Voelliger	Phillip Redington	Wallace Mook
Bloomfield	c	MC	2	(641) 664-2260	Hazel Nardini-Cral	. . .	Marilyn McElderry	. . .	Robert Hongland	. . .	Richard Wilcox
Bondurant	c	MC	1	(515) 967-2418	. . .	Mark Arentsen	. . .	. . .	. . .	. . .	. . .
Boone	c	CM	12	(515) 432-4211	John Slight	Brent Trout	. . .	. . .	Ed Knight	William Skare	Larry Green
Buffalo	c	MC	1	(563) 381-2226	Jack Carson	William Bowers	. . .	. . .	Terry Adams	Gage Adams	Dwain Bollman
Burlington	c	CM	26	(319) 753-8124	Timothy Scott	Bruce Slagle	K. Salisbury	. . .	Thomas Clements	David Wunnenberg	James Grabow
Camanche	c	MC	4	(563) 259-8342	Gary Kampe	. . .	Carol Balster	. . .	Aubrey Wilson	Robert Houzenga	Dave Rickertson
Carlisle	t	MC	3	(515) 989-3224	Dennis Woodruff	Neil Ruddy	. . .	. . .	Larry Dennis	. . .	Steve O'Braza
Carroll *	c	CM	10	(712) 792-1000	Robert Christensen	Gerald Clausen	. . .	Laura Schaefer	Greg Schreck	Jeff Cayler	Randall Krauel
Carter Lake	c	MC	3	(712) 347-6320	Emil Hausner	. . .	Doreen Mowery	. . .	Douglas Brown	Shawn Kannedy	Ronald Rothmeyer
Cascade *	c	MC	1	(563) 852-3114	Tim Stecklein	Randy Lansing	Shelley Annis	. . .	Rick Kremer	Fred Heim	Paul McDermott
Cedar Falls	c	MC	36	(319) 273-8600	Jon Crews	. . .	Gary Hesse	Jennifer Rodenbeck	Steve Mitchell	Richard Ahlstrom	Bruce Sorensen
Cedar Rapids *	c	CM	120	(319) 286-5555	Kay Halloran	James Prosser	Ann Ollinger	Casey Drew	Stephen Havlik	Michael Klapphölz	David Elgin
Centerville	c	MC	5	(641) 437-4339	John Williams	. . .	Kristen May	. . .	Robert Bozwell	Dan Howington	. . .
Chariton	c	CM	4	(641) 774-5991	John Braida	Nels Christensen	Ruth Ryun	. . .	Brian Davis	James Baker	. . .
Charles City *	c	CM	7	(641) 257-6300	James Erb	Thomas Brownlow	Trudy O'Donnell	. . .	Roy Schwickerath	Mike Wendel	. . .
Cherokee *	c	MC	5	(712) 225-5749	Dennis Henrich	. . .	Debra Taylor	. . .	Jack Olson	Steve Schuck	. . .
Clarinda	c	CM	5	(712) 542-2136	Gordon Kokenge	Gary Walter	. . .	. . .	Roger Williams	Keith Brothers	Kelly Parrott
Clarion	c	CM	2	(515) 532-2847	John Ofstethun	Vicky Boyington	. . .	. . .	Ron Piotrowski	Steve Henigar	James Redemske
Clear Lake	c	MC	8	(641) 357-5267	Kirk Kraft	Scott Flory	Gail Robinson	Linda Nelson	. . .	Daniel Jackson	Joseph Weigel
Clinton	c	CM	27	(563) 242-2144	. . .	Gary Boden	. . .	Deborah Neels	Mark Regenwether	Brian Guy	. . .
Clive *	c	CM	12	(515) 223-6220	Les Aasheim	Dennis Henderson	Pamela Shannon	. . .	Rickey Roe	. . .	Bartley Weller

Directory 1/9 continued — OFFICIALS IN U.S. MUNICIPALITIES 2,500 AND OVER IN POPULATION

Jurisdiction	Type	Form of govern-ment	2000 Popu-lation (000)	Main telephone number	Chief elected official	Appointed administrator	Clerk of the governing board	Chief financial officer	Fire chief	Police chief	Public works director
IOWA continued											
Colfax	c	MC	2	(515) 674-4096	Jeff Jones	...	Kathy Mathews	...	Mike Noftsger	Jon Huggins	...
Coralville	c	CM	15	(319) 248-1700	...	Kelly Hayworth	Nancy Beuter	...	David Stannard	Barry Bedford	...
Council Bluffs	c	MC	58	(712) 328-4601	Thomas Hanafan	...	Olga Ramirez	Terry Mauer	Alan Byers	James Wilkinson	Michael Wallner
Cresco	c	MC	3	(563) 547-3101	Ronda Hughes	John Lloyd	...	...	Neal Stapelkamp	Mark Kissinger	Dennis Cauwels
Creston	c	MC	7	(641) 782-2000	Larry Wynn	Joseph Parker	Mary Moore	...	Roger Nurnberg	W. Heatherington	Tom Myers
Davenport	c	CM	98	(563) 326-7711	Charles Brooke	Craig Malin	Jackie Ragsdale	Alan Guard	Mark Frese	Michael Bladel	...
De Witt *	c	MC	5	(563) 659-3811	Donald Thiltgen	Steven Lindner	Catherine Benthin	Deanna Rodriguez	John Burken	Gene Ellis	Larry Kloth
Decorah	c	MC	8	(563) 382-3651	Victor Fye	Jerry Freund	Wanda Hemesath	...	...	Tom Courtney	...
Denison	c	MC	7	(712) 263-3143	Ken Livingston	Gregory Seefeldt	Marcia Bretey	...	Mike McKinnon	Rod Bradley	...
Denver	c	CM	1	(319) 984-5642	Gene Leonhart	Larry Farley	...	...	Ron Milius	Terry Dehmlow	John Foust
Des Moines	c	CM	198	(515) 283-4141	T. M. F. Cownie	Richard Clark	Diane Rauh	Allen McKinley	Phillip Vorlander	William McCarthy	William Stowe
Dubuque *	c	CM	57	(563) 589-4110	Roy Buol	M. Van Milligen	Jeanne Schneider	Kenneth TeKippe	E. Brown	Kim Wadding	Donald Vogt
Dyersville	c	MC	4	(563) 875-7724	James Heavens	Mick Michel	Tricia Maiers	...	Merlin Clemen	Martin Botts	David Vorwald
Eagle Grove	c	CM	3	(515) 448-4343	Myron Amdahl	...	...	Susan Maier	...	Tom Anderson	Carroll Sabin
Eldora	c	CM	3	(641) 939-2393	Timothy Hoy	...	Eric Weinkoetz	Joyce Lawler	Bruce Harvey	Dave Twedt	Dale Seaton
Eldridge	c	MC	4	(563) 285-4841	John Strazewski	John Dowd	Denise Benson	...	David Ploessl	Martin Stolmeier	Brian Wessel
Elkader	c	MC	1	(563) 245-2098	Bob Garms	Jennifer Cowsert	...	...	Mike Anderson	Marvin Duff	Jerry Gamm
Emmetsburg	c	MC	3	(712) 852-4030	Myrna Heddinger	John Bird	Jill Kliegl	...	...	Eric Hanson	William Dickey
Estherville	c	CM	6	(712) 362-7771	Lyle Hevern	...	Vaughn Brua	...	David Knox	Paul Farber	...
Evansdale	c	MC	4	(319) 232-6683	John Mardis	...	Jane Walters	...	Kent Smock	Michael Burke	...
Everly *	c	MC	..	(712) 834-2691	Bud Meyer	...	Cheryl Hoye	Janice Thompson	Brian Kahl	...	Bruce Harden
Fairfield	c	MC	9	(641) 472-6193	Edward Malloy	John Brown	...	...	R. Hickenbottom	Randy Cooksey	...
Forest City	c	MC	4	(641) 585-4597	George Wilson	...	Paul Boock	...	Mark Johnson	Daniel Davis	...
Fort Dodge	c	MC	25	(515) 576-4551	William Patterson	David Fierke	Penny Clayton	...	John Webster	Thomas Francis	Al Dorothy
Fort Madison *	c	CM	10	(319) 372-7700	Steven Ireland	...	Suellen Mead	...	Joey Herren	...	Steven Hayes
Garner *	c	MC	2	(641) 923-2588	Kenton Mick	Brent Hinson	Daisy Huffman	...	...	Thomas Kozisek	...
Gilbert	c	MC	..	(515) 233-2670	...	John Lloyd	...	...	...	...	...
Glenwood	c	MC	5	(712) 527-4717	Dyle Downing	Mary Smith	...	...	...	John O'Connor	Perry Cook
Glidden	c	MC	1	(712) 659-3010	Cynthia Kerkhoff	Loren Lodge	Suzanne Danner	...	Thomas Weber	...	Robert Bock
Graettinger	c	MC	..	(712) 859-3359	Brian Bonstead	...	Sandra Henderson	...	Wayne Anderson	Kevin Olson	...
Grimes	c	MC	5	(515) 986-3036	...	...	...	...	...	...	...
Grinnell	c	CM	9	(641) 236-2600	Gordon Canfield	Russell Behrens	Pamela Rupe	...	Jerry Barns	Jody Matherly	Glenn Baker
Grundy Center	c	MC	2	(319) 824-6118	Jack Stomberg	...	...	...	Gerald Hoffman	Terry Oltman	James Copeman
Guttenberg *	c	CM	1	(563) 252-1161	Gerald Block	Thomas Blake	...	...	Fred Schaub	George Morteo	...
Hampton	c	CM	4	(641) 456-4853	Pat Sackville	...	Robbi Stevens	...	...	Michael Gillette	...
Harlan	c	MC	5	(712) 755-5137	Gary Christiansen	Terry Cox	Susan Lambert	...	Roger Bissen	Frank Clark	...
Hawarden	c	MC	2	(712) 551-2565	Ricard Porter	Jason Metten	...	Sharole Rens	Jon Strong	Michael DeBruin	Thomas Kane
Hiawatha *	c	CM	6	(319) 393-1515	Thomas Patterson	David Van Dee	Kimberly Downs	Laurie Hebl	Michael Nesslage	Richard Pierce	Rodney Jasa
Holstein	c	MC	1	(712) 368-4898	Mary Gross	Mark Baker	...	...	Dan Ehler	...	...
Humboldt *	c	CM	4	(515) 332-3435	Steven Samuels	Lorie Bennett	Gloria Christensen	...	Tony Hosford	Jon Reed	...
Huxley	c	MC	2	(515) 597-2561	Nels Nord	John Haldeman	Lee Ruddick	...	Kevin Deaton	Mark Pote	Jeff Peterson
Ida Grove *	c	MC	2	(712) 364-2428	Dennis Ernst	...	Cindy Murray	...	Matt Wunschel	...	...
Independence	c	MC	6	(319) 334-2780	Frank Brimmer	Alan Johnson	Debra Lynn	...	...	D. Rasmussen	...
Indianola	c	CM	12	(515) 961-9410	Jerry Kelley	Tim Zisoff	...	...	Brian Seymour	Steve Bonnett	...
Iowa City *	c	CM	62	(319) 356-5000	Arthur Wilburn	...	Marian Karr	Kevin O'Malley	Andrew Rocca	Samuel Hargadine	Richard Fosse
Iowa Falls *	c	CM	5	(641) 648-2527	Rocky LaValle	Brian Weuve	Angie Graves	...	Rick Gustin	Ron Kuhfus	Merlin Clock
Jefferson	c	CM	4	(515) 386-3111	...	...	Diane Kennedy	...	...	...	...
Johnston	c	MC	8	(515) 278-2344	Brian Laurenzo	James Sanders	S. Reynolds	Teresa Rotschafer	Jim Krohse	Doug Nichols	Dave Cubit
Kalona	c	CM	1	(319) 656-2910	Jean Gustafson	Douglas Morgan	Karen Christner	...	Steve Yotty	...	...
Keokuk *	c	MC	11	(319) 524-2050	David Gudgel	...	Donna Eilers	...	Mark Wessel	Thomas Crew	...
Knoxville *	c	CM	7	(641) 828-0550	Jon Lenger	Richard Schrad	Jody Meyer	...	Barry Reynolds	Dan Losada	Jeffrey May
Lake View	c	MC	1	(712) 657-2634	Robert Schmidt	Scott Peterson	...	...	LeRoy Olerich	Ted Helmich	Jack De Bourgh
Lamoni	c	MC	2	(641) 784-6311	...	Kirk Bjorland	...	...	Travis Jeanes	Dale Killpack	...
Laurens	c	MC	1	(712) 841-4526	...	...	Eloise Enger	...	Clarence Siepker	Rodney Watkins	Larry Barley
Le Claire	c	CM	2	(563) 289-5441	...	Ed Choate	...	...	...	...	...
Le Mars	c	CM	9	(712) 546-7018	Virgil Van Beek	Scott Langel	Beverly Langel	Bill Cole	Wayne Schipper	Stuart Dekkenga	Charlie Eufers
Lisbon	c	MC	1	(319) 455-2459	Michael Williams	Sandra Deahl	...	...	Michael Svatosch	Ricky Scott	Tom Hoke
Madrid	c	MC	2	(515) 795-3930	Pat Regan	Todd Kilzer	Joni Drake	...	...	Tim Brown	...
Manchester	c	CM	5	(563) 927-3636	...	Timothy Vick	...	...	...	...	...
Manning	c	MC	1	(712) 655-2176	Ron Colling	Jordan Fuller	...	...	Robert Ehlers	Larry Lesle	Tom Wittrock
Mapleton	c	MC	1	(712) 881-1351	Ray Friedrichsen	...	Mavis Skow	...	Jerry Bumstead	John Holton	Mike Hahn
Maquoketa	c	CM	6	(563) 652-2484	Tom Messerli	Brian Wagner	Judith Carr	...	Mark Beck	Brad Koranda	Dave Popp
Marengo	c	CM	2	(319) 642-3232	Joe Seye	Carl Schumacher	...	Barbara Barrick	Steven Meier	Galen Moser	Stuart Stukey
Marion	c	CM	26	(319) 377-1581	Victor Klopfenstein	Lon Pluckhahn	...	Wesley Nelson	Terry Jackson	Harry Daugherty	Tom Newbanks
Marquette	c	MC	..	(563) 873-3735	John Ries	Michael Puksich	Maryanne Trudo	...	...	Randy Grady	Ken Grennier
Marshalltown *	c	CM	26	(641) 754-5704	Gene Beach	Richard Hierstein	Shari Coughenour	...	Larry Squiers	David Walker	Lynn Couch
Mason City *	c	CM	29	(641) 421-3600	Roger Bang	Brent Trout	...	Kevin Jacobson	Bob Platts	David Ellingson	William Stangler
Missouri Valley *	c	MC	2	(712) 642-3502	Randy McHugh	Craig Borlin	...	...	Keith Holtz	Ed Murray	Bob Reisland
Mitchellville	c	CM	1	(515) 967-2935	Michael Kendall	Warren Hall	Andrew Lent	...	Dwayne Heckman	Charles Sickels	Daniel Miers
Monroe	c	MC	1	(641) 259-2319	...	Carol Diekema	...	...	...	...	...
Monticello *	c	MC	3	(319) 465-6435	Gerald Wilbricht	Douglas Herman	Sally Hinrichsen	...	Mark Stoneking	Ryan Evans	Dana Edwards
Mount Pleasant	c	MC	8	(319) 385-1470	John Freeland	Brent Schleisman	Florence Olomon	...	...	Terry Sammons	Christopher Bittle
Mount Vernon	c	MC	3	(319) 895-8742	Paul Tuerler	Michael Beimer	...	...	Mike Buser	Mark Winder	...
Muscatine	c	CM	22	(563) 264-1550	Richard O'Brien	A. J. Johnson	...	...	Steven Dalbey	Gary Coderoni	Randall Hill
Nevada *	c	CM	6	(515) 382-5466	Gearold Gull	Elizabeth Hailey	T. Peterson-Smith	...	Dana Wipperman	Mike Tupper	...
New Hampton	c	MC	3	(641) 394-5906	...	...	Suellen Kolbet	...	...	Michael Anderson	...
Newton *	c	CM	15	(641) 792-2787	Charles Allen	David Watson	Candice Brown	...	Ed Clements	Thomas Wardlow	David Stewart
Nora Springs *	c	CM	1	(641) 749-5315	...	Deborah Gaul	...	...	...	Adam Nerlien	Daniel Grauerholz
North Liberty	c	CM	5	(319) 626-5700	...	Ryan Heiar	Mary Mitchell	...	Eric Vandewater	James Warkentin	Donald Colony
Norwalk	c	MC	6	(515) 981-0228	Jerry Starkweather	Mark Miller	Jennifer Sease	...	Thomas Fleming	Ed Kuhl	Dean Yordi
Oelwein *	c	CM	6	(319) 283-5440	Larry Murphy	Steven Kendall	...	...	Wallace Rundle	Jeremy Logan	...
Onawa	c	MC	3	(712) 433-1181	Neil Leapley	...	Chris Hogan	...	...	Gary Addy	Jeffery Sander
Orange City	c	CM	5	(712) 707-4885	Daryl Beltman	Duane Feekes	Janet Brown	Kent Anderson	Dennis Vander Wel	Dann DeVries	Ted Loucks
Osage	c	MC	3	(641) 732-3709	Steven Cooper	...	Cathy Penney	...	Kurt Angell	Russell Stocker	Jerry Dunlay
Osceola *	c	CM	4	(641) 342-2377	Fred Diehl	William Kelly	Nancy Carmichael	...	Donald McCuddin	Martin Duffus	...
Oskaloosa *	c	CM	10	(641) 673-9431	David Dixon	...	Marilyn Miller	...	Francis Glandon	John McGee	David Neubert
Ottumwa *	c	MC	24	(641) 683-0625	Dale Uehling	...	P Ann Cullinan	Michael Heffernan	Steven O'Connor	James Clark	Larry Seals
Panora	c	CM	1	(641) 755-2164	Steven Baker	Jim Marwedel	...	Joyce Calmer	Matt Harmon	Marty Arganbright	Jerry Buttler
Pella *	c	MC	9	(641) 628-4173	D. Dobernecker	Michael Nardini	Ronda Brown	...	Doug Van Gorkum	M. Marcinkowski	Denny Buyert
Perry	c	MC	7	(515) 465-2481	Viivi Shirley	Butch Niebuhr	Jeanette Peddicord	Susie Moorhead	Chris Hinds	Daniel Brickner	Jack Butler
Pleasant Hill	c	MC	5	(515) 262-9368	Mark Langerud	Donald Sandor	Joni Haag	...	Reylon Meeks	...	Gary Patterson
Pocahontas *	c	MC	1	(712) 335-4841	George Tuttle	Gregory Fritz	Joan De Wall	...	Jim Malecek	Byron Essing	...
Polk City	c	MC	2	(515) 984-6233	Mary Burton	Gary Mahannah	Sharon Nickles	...	Jason Morse	Mark Bowersox	Mike Schulte

Directory 1/9 continued — OFFICIALS IN U.S. MUNICIPALITIES 2,500 AND OVER IN POPULATION

Jurisdiction	Type	Form of govern-ment	2000 Popu-lation (000)	Main telephone number	Chief elected official	Appointed administrator	Clerk of the governing board	Chief financial officer	Fire chief	Police chief	Public works director
IOWA continued											
Red Oak	c	MC	6	(712) 623-6510	James Johnson	Brad Wright	Mary Bolton	...	Rick Askey	Drue Powers	...
Reinbeck	c	MC	1	(319) 788-6404	Lon Larsen	Quentin Mayberry	...	...	...	...	...
Rock Rapids	c	MC	2	(712) 472-2553	Keith Benson	Jordan Kordahl	...	...	Chris Bixenman	Blythe Bloemendaal	Bret Huisman
Rock Valley	c	MC	2	(712) 476-5707	Kent Eknes	Tom Van Maanen	Judy Vant Hul	...	...	Monte Warburton	Myron Van Ginkel
Rolfe	c	MC	..	(712) 848-3124	Gay Stover	Thomas Smith	...	...	...	...	...
Sac City	c	CM	2	(712) 662-7593	Glen Duncan	Jeffrey Fiegenschuh	...	...	John Phillips	John Zimmerman	...
Sanborn	c	MC	1	(712) 729-3842	...	...	...	...	...	...	...
Sergeant Bluff	c	MC	3	(712) 943-4244	...	...	Candice Litras	...	Michael Thompson	Dave McFarland	Roger Groves
Sheldon	c	CM	4	(712) 324-4651	Scott Wahlstrom	Scott Wynja	Arlene Budden	...	Jerry Meyers	Lyle Balkema	Eldor Schuerman
Shenandoah	c	CM	5	(712) 246-4411	Gregg Connell	Byron Harris	...	...	Ron Fox	Kevin Hughes	...
Sibley *	c	CM	2	(712) 754-2541	Betty Kingston	...	Diane Gruis	...	Jim Wiersma	...	Dennis Davids
Sioux Center *	c	CM	6	(712) 722-0761	Dennis Walstra	...	...	B. Van Schouwen	David Holland	Paul Adkins	Murray Hulstein
Sioux City	c	CM	85	(712) 279-6200	K. Van De Steeg	Paul Eckert	...	...	...	Joseph Frisbie	Dave Dorsett
Solon	c	MC	1	(319) 624-3755	Rick Jedlicka	...	Connie Evans	...	...	...	Scott Kleppe
Spencer *	c	MC	11	(712) 580-7200	Reynold Peterson	...	Donna Fisher	...	Douglas Duncan	Mark Lawson	Mark White
Spirit Lake *	c	CM	4	(712) 336-1871	Eric Nielsen	Mark Stevens	...	...	Dave Kollasch	Jeff Hanson	Todd Dolphin
Storm Lake *	c	CM	10	(712) 732-8000	Jon Kruse	Patti Moore	...	Paul Hoye	Mike Jones	...	Patrick Kelly
Story City	c	MC	3	(515) 733-2121	Harold Holm	Mark Jackson	Pat Twedt	...	Scott Nibe	Brian Haffner	Bruce Henrichs
Stratford *	c	CM	..	(515) 838-2311	Michael Nepereny	...	...	...	...	...	Larry Runyan
Strawberry Point *	c	CM	1	(563) 933-4482	Gene Rima	Deanna Dement	...	...	Jeff Robinson	Eldon Melssen	...
Tama	c	MC	2	(641) 484-3822	Richard Gibson	...	...	...	Rod Anderson	...	Stuart Eisentrager
Tipton	c	MC	3	(563) 886-6187	Donald Young	Dick Schrad	John Foley	Lorna Fletcher	John Miller	Roger Hakeman	Doug Boldt
University Heights	c	MC	..	(319) 337-6900	...	...	...	...	...	...	...
Urbandale	c	CM	29	(515) 278-3900	Robert Andeweg	Robert Layton	Debra Mains	Nicci Lamb	Jerry Holt	David Hamlin	David McKay
Vinton	c	MC	5	(319) 472-4707	John Watson	Andrew Lent	Cindy Michael	...	Scott Geissinger	Jeff Tilson	...
Washington	c	MC	7	(319) 653-6584	Edward Brown	David Plyman	Jeff Rosien	...	William Hartsock	...	...
Waterloo *	c	MC	68	(319) 291-4522	Timothy Hurley	...	Nancy Eckert	Michelle Weidner	Doug Carter	Tom Jennings	...
Waukee *	c	CM	5	(515) 987-4522	William Peard	Jeffrey Kooistra	...	...	...	Larry Phillips	John Gibson
Waukon	c	MC	4	(563) 568-3492	Dwight Jones	...	Diane Sweeney	...	...	Loren Fiet	...
Waverly	c	CM	8	(319) 352-4252	Ivan Ackerman	Richard Crayne	JoEllen Raap	Jack Bachhuber	Daniel McKenzie	Richard Pursell	Michael Cherry
Webster City	c	CM	8	(515) 832-9151	Eugene Gray	Ed Sadler	Patricia Nokes	Kasie Doering	Mike Lund	Michael McConnell	...
Wellman *	c	CM	1	(319) 646-2154	Ryan Miller	David Ross	Donna Wade	...	James Seward	...	...
West Bend	c	MC	..	(515) 887-2181	Laura Montag	...	Lisa Sewell	...	...	Richard Jergens	Thomas Hartman
West Branch *	c	MC	1	(319) 643-5888	...	Kyle Soukup	Debra Fiderlein	Betty Ellerhoff	Richard Stoolman	...	Brian Brennan
West Burlington	c	CM	3	(319) 752-5451	Hans Trousil	Dan Gifford	Terrie Simonson	...	...	Alex Oblein	Randy Fry
West Des Moines	c	CM	46	(515) 222-3600	Eugene Meyer	Jeffrey Pomeranz	Fern Stewart	...	Donald Cox	Jack O'Donnell	Larry Read
West Liberty	c	CM	3	(319) 627-2418	William Phelps	Chris Ward	...	...	Curt Newcomb	Hank Priest	Russell Garner
West Point	c	MC	..	(319) 837-6313	Paul Walker	Claron White	Mary Winnike	...	...	...	Fred Boeding
West Union	c	MC	2	(563) 422-3320	...	...	...	...	...	...	...
Wilton	c	MC	2	(563) 732-2115	Dick Summy	Mark Anderson	Lori Brown	...	Darrell Janssen	Steve Mallinger	Bryan Devore
Windsor Heights	c	MC	4	(515) 279-3662	Ned Miller	Marketa Oliver	...	...	Albert Hunter	Gary Walters	John Wiedman
Winterset	c	MC	4	(515) 462-1422	James Olson	Mark Nitchals	...	...	R. Truckenbrod	Ken Burk	...
KANSAS											
Abilene	c	CM	6	(785) 263-2550	Kenneth Peterson	Mark Arbuthnot	Penny Soukup	Janelle Dockendorf	Bob Sims	Bryan Dunlap	Clifford Gibbs
Andover	c	MC	6	(316) 733-1303	Benjamin Lawrence	Jeffrey Bridges	...	Elizabeth Boast	Jimmy Shaver	Randall Harris	Leslie Mangus
Anthony	c	CO	2	(620) 842-5434	John Schott	Donald Heidrick	...	...	Kenny Hudson	John Blevins	Grant Sechler
Arkansas City	c	CM	11	(620) 441-4400	Janet English	Douglas Russell	...	Steven Archer	Eddie Moore	Dan Given	Clay Randel
Atchison	c	CM	10	(913) 367-5500	Daniel Garrity	...	Phyllis Walton	Sheldon Hamilton	Michael McDermed	Michael Wilson	Roger Denton
Augusta *	c	CM	8	(316) 775-4510	Kristey Williams	William Keefer	Erica Jones	...	Raymond Marbut	...	...
Baldwin City	c	CM	3	(785) 594-6427	Gary Walbridge	Jeffrey Dingman	Peggy Nichols	...	Allan Craig	Michael McKenna	Bill Winegar
Basehor *	c	MC	2	(913) 724-1370	Chris Garcia	Carl Slaugh	Mary Ann Mogle	...	...	Terry Horner	Milton Myracle
Baxter Springs	c	MC	4	(620) 856-2114	...	...	Donna Wixon	...	William Ellsworth	David Edmondson	Robert Kirby
Bel Aire	c	MC	5	(316) 744-2451	Brian Withrow	Arthur Lasher	...	Erica Stock	...	John Daily	Terry Dreiling
Belleville	c	CM	2	(785) 527-2288	Bradley Chatfield	Allen Bachelor	Karen Dreesen	...	Duffy Strnad	Gary Frint	...
Beloit *	c	MC	4	(785) 738-3551	Phillip Roberts	Douglas Gerber	Charlene Abell	...	Steve Rugg	Frank Gent	Lloyd Littrell
Bonner Springs *	c	CM	6	(913) 422-1020	Clausie Smith	John Helin	Rita Hoag	Matilda La Plante	Clinton Long	John Haley	Kevin Bruemmer
Burlingame *	c	MC	1	(785) 654-2414	Brenda Dorr	Steven Huffles	Christina Lewis	...	Jim Strohm	Jon Shaffer	Josh Welch
Burlington	c	MC	2	(620) 364-5334	Rick Raymer	...	Daniel Allen	...	...	Doug Jones	...
Caney	c	MC	2	(620) 879-9800	...	Donald Whitman	...	...	...	Rick Pell	...
Cedar Vale	c	MC	..	(620) 758-2244	...	...	Barbara Denney	...	...	...	John Hodgden
Chanute *	c	CM	9	(620) 431-5200	Leroy Chard	Randall Riggs	Joan Howard	James McEwen	...	...	...
Cheney *	c	CM	1	(316) 542-3622	Tim Rosenhagen	Zachary Mohr	Jimmie Diskin	...	Brad Ewy	Howard Bishop	Randall Oliver
Cherryvale	c	CM	2	(620) 336-2776	John Wright	John Cocking	...	...	Paul Newton	Tommy Wilson	Eric Eli
Clay Center	c	MC	4	(785) 632-5454	...	...	Calvin Wohler	...	Jon Siemers	Bill Robinson	Billy Callaway
Clearwater	c	MC	2	(620) 584-2311	James Walker	Kent Brown	Cheryl Wright	...	Marvin Schauf	Michael Friday	Ernie Misak
Coffeyville	c	CM	11	(620) 252-6121	...	Jeffrey Morris	Donna Schoonover	...	Gregory Allen	Joe Humble	Don Males
Colby *	c	CM	5	(785) 460-4400	Ken Bieber	Carolyn Armstrong	Deanna Pabst	...	Robert McLemore	...	Chris Bieker
Columbus	c	CM	3	(620) 429-2159	John Brassart	Evan Capron	Janice Blancett	...	Don Kirk	Charles Sharp	Henry Burton
Concordia	c	CM	5	(785) 243-2670	Joe Jindra	...	Cheryl Lanoue	...	Larry Eubanks	Danny Parker	Ron Copple
Council Grove	c	CM	2	(620) 767-5417	...	...	...	...	...	...	...
De Soto	c	MC	4	(913) 583-1182	David Anderson	Patrick Guilfoyle	...	Bonnie Bennett	Kevin Ritter	...	...
Derby *	c	CM	17	(316) 788-1519	Dion Avello	Kathleen Sexton	...	Jean Epperson	Brad Smith	Jay Reyes	Robert Mendoza
Dodge City *	c	CM	25	(620) 225-8100	Kent Smoll	Ken Strobel	...	Nannette Pogue	Dan Williamson	John Ball	Joseph Finley
Douglass	c	MC	1	(316) 747-2109	...	KaLyn Nethercot	...	...	...	...	...
Edgerton *	c	MC	1	(913) 893-6231	Frankie Cross	David Dillner	Rita Moore	...	Max Sielert	Larry Shoop	Mike Mabrey
Edwardsville	c	MC	4	(913) 441-3707	Stephanie Eickhoff	Douglas Spangler	Phyllis Freeman	...	Clifton Lane	Steven Vaughan	...
El Dorado *	c	CM	12	(316) 321-9100	Tom McKibban	Herbert Llewellyn	Kendra Waite	Dee Anne Grunder	Ken Nakaten	Tom Boren	Brad Meyer
Elkhart	c	MC	2	(620) 697-2171	...	...	Carolea Wellen	...	...	Loren Youngers	Leo Davis
Ellinwood	c	MC	2	(620) 564-3161	Frank Koelsch	...	Kim Schartz	...	Chris Komarek	Kevin PeKarek	Daryle Nielsen
Ellsworth	c	MC	2	(785) 472-5566	Robert Homolka	Jonathan Mitchell	Margaret Shepherd	...	Bob Kepka	David Smith	...
Emporia *	c	CM	26	(620) 342-5105	Tom Meyers	M. Zimmerman	Susan Mendoza	Larry Bucklinger	Jack Taylor	...	Ron Childers
Eudora *	c	MC	4	(785) 542-4111	Thomas Pyle	Cheryl Beatty	Donna Oleson	...	Randy Ates	Bill Long	...
Eureka	c	CO	2	(620) 583-6511	James Bobey	...	Rebecca Schaffer	...	Doug Williams	Lowell Parker	Larry Fritts
Fairway *	c	MC	3	(913) 262-0350	John St. Clair	...	Charlotte Robards	...	...	John Simmons	Bill Stogsdill
Fort Scott	c	CM	8	(620) 223-0550	Garold Billionis	...	Diane Clay	Susan Brown	...	...	Eric Bailey
Fredonia	c	CO	2	(620) 378-2231	Max Wilson	...	...	...	John Settle	Doug McKenna	Junior Hufford
Frontenac	c	CM	2	(620) 231-9210	James Kennedy	Paul Bruneiti	Richard Cicero	...	Mike Hagerty	Carl Flora	...
Galena	c	MC	3	(620) 783-5265	...	...	Deborah Kitch	...	Bill Hall	Cameron Arthur	Leroy Webster
Garden City	c	CM	28	(620) 276-1160	Gary Fuller	Robert Halloran	Stacey Frizzell	Melinda Hitz	Allen Shelton	James Hawkins	Sam Curran
Gardner *	c	MC	9	(913) 856-7535	...	Stewart Fairburn	...	Laura Gourley	...	...	David Greene
Garnett	c	CM	3	(785) 448-5496	Michael Norman	...	...	Joyce Martin	Harold Miller	James Bond	...

Directory 1/9 continued — OFFICIALS IN U.S. MUNICIPALITIES 2,500 AND OVER IN POPULATION

Jurisdiction		Type	Form of govern-ment	2000 Popu-lation (000)	Main telephone number	Chief elected official	Appointed administrator	Clerk of the governing board	Chief financial officer	Fire chief	Police chief	Public works director
KANSAS continued												
Girard		c	CO	2	(620) 724-8918	Maurice Harley	Michael West	. . .	Coralie Bennett	Ronald Scales	Danny Fields	David Crumpacker
Goddard		c	MC	2	(316) 794-2441	. . .	. . .	Karen Bailey	. . .	. . .	Doyle Dyer	Randy Brooks
Goodland		c	CM	4	(785) 899-4500	Richard Billinger	Kenneth Hill	Mary Volk	. . .	Dean Jensen	Raymond Smee	Chuck Lutters
Great Bend		c	MC	15	(620) 793-4111	Mike Allison	Howard Partington	Wayne Henneke	. . .	Mike Napolitano	Dean Akings	Don Craig
Greensburg		c	MC	1	(620) 723-2751	. . .	. . .	. . .	. . .	. . .	. . .	Michael Hayes
Halstead		c	CM	1	(316) 835-2286	. . .	J. Hatfield	Dianne Mueller	. . .	Jim VanSchaick	Austin Hamilton	Pat Adams
Hays		c	CM	20	(785) 628-7320	Kent Steward	Toby Dougherty	. . .	Mark Loughry	Gary Brown	James Braun	Brenda Herrman
Haysville		c	MC	8	(316) 529-5900	Bruce Armstrong	Carol Neugent	Carol McBeath	Beverly Rodgers	. . .	Michael McElroy	Randal Dorner
Herington		c	CM	2	(785) 258-2271	Gary Schrader	Lloyd Matthes	Debbie Wendt	. . .	Kenneth Staatz	Gordon Schroeder	. . .
Hesston		c	MC	3	(620) 327-4412	John Waltner	John Carder	. . .	. . .	Lelyn Peters	Kurt Ford	Kirk Matz
Hiawatha		c	MC	3	(785) 742-7417	Crosby Gernon	Elizabeth Ladner	Vivian Constable	. . .	Gary Shear	Evans Woehlecke	Rick Koenig
Hill City		c	MC	1	(782) 421-2264	. . .	. . .	Debbie Budig	. . .	. . .	. . .	. . .
Hillsboro		c	MC	2	(620) 947-3162	. . .	Lawrence Paine	. . .	. . .	. . .	. . .	. . .
Hoisington	*	c	CM	2	(620) 653-4125	Clayton Williamson	Allen Dinkel	Donita Crutcher	. . .	James Sekavec	Kenton Doze	Paul Zecha
Holton		c	CM	3	(785) 364-2721	Janet Zwonitzer	Glenn Rodden	Pat McClintock	. . .	Tony Raaf	David Lanning	. . .
Horton		c	CM	1	(785) 486-2681	Dale White	Levi Henry	Candice Schmitt	. . .	Gary Behrnes	Richard Luzier	. . .
Hugoton	*	c	MC	3	(620) 544-8531	Jack Rowden	Thomas Hicks	. . .	. . .	. . .	Steven Lewis	Alton Banker
Humboldt		c	MC	1	(620) 473-3232	Mike Rickner	. . .	Rachel Mueller	. . .	Kent Barfoot	Daniel Onnen	Patricia Sanchez
Hutchinson		c	CM	40	(620) 694-2620	. . .	John Deardoff	. . .	Carl Myers	Robert Forbes	James Heitschmidt	Dennis Clennan
Independence		c	CM	9	(620) 332-2500	Dale Bunn	Paul Sasse	. . .	Anthony Royse	Dale Rail	Lee Bynum	. . .
Iola	*	c	CM	6	(620) 365-4900	Billy Maness	Judith Brigham	. . .	. . .	Donald Leapheart	James Kilby	. . .
Junction City		c	CM	18	(785) 238-3103	. . .	Rodney Barnes	Colleen Woodruff	. . .	Michael Ryan	Robert Story	. . .
Kechi	*	c	MC	1	(316) 744-9287	. . .	Mac Manning	Laura Hill	. . .	. . .	Jason Doll	Larry Kallenberger
Kingman		c	MC	3	(620) 532-3111	Brad Frisbie	. . .	Cindy Conrardy	. . .	S. Drosselmeyer	John Braden	R. Robinson
Kinsley		c	CM	1	(620) 659-3611	Mike Herrmann	Jay Dill	Karen Myers	. . .	Larry Myers	Tom Burns	John Baker
La Crosse		c	CM	1	(785) 222-2511	Gerald Washburn	Duane Moeder	Sherri Stevens	. . .	. . .	. . .	. . .
Lake Quivira		c	MC	. .	(913) 631-5300	Patrick McAnany	. . .	. . .	. . .	. . .	Maurice McCarthy	. . .
Lansing		c	MC	9	(913) 727-3233	Kenneth Bernard	Michael Smith	. . .	William Lundberg	. . .	Steve Wayman	John Young
Larned	*	c	CM	4	(620) 285-8500	Robert Pivonka	Donald Gaeddert	Pam Corby	. . .	Jack Clock	Charles Orth	. . .
Lawrence		c	CM	80	(785) 832-3000	David Dunfield	David Corliss	Frank Reeb	Ed Mullins	James McSwain	William Olin	Charles Soules
Leavenworth	*	c	CM	35	(913) 680-2606	Larry Dedeke	J. Miller	Karen Logan	Daniel Williamson	Steve Moody	Lemoine Doehring	Michael McDonald
Leawood	*	c	MC	27	(913) 339-6700	Peggy Dunn	Scott Lambers	Debra Harper	Kathleen Rogers	Ben Florance	John Meier	Joseph Johnson
Lenexa		c	MC	40	(913) 477-7500	Michael Boehm	J. Wade	Mary Sue Fry	Doug Robinson	Kenneth Hobbs	Ellen Hanson	Ronald Norris
Liberal		c	CM	19	(620) 626-0102	. . .	. . .	Debra Giskie	Toby Miller	. . .	Vernon Jordan	Jim Coffey
Lindsborg	*	c	MC	3	(785) 227-3355	John Magnuson	Gregory Du Mars	J. Lovett-Sperling	Larry Lindgren	Willard Keding	. . .	Timothy Dunn
Louisburg		c	MC	2	(913) 837-5371	. . .	. . .	. . .	. . .	. . .	. . .	. . .
Lyons		c	MC	3	(620) 257-2320	Clarence Moses	John Sweet	Jodi Oakley	. . .	Greg Moss	Chris Detmer	David Kendrick
Madison		c	CO	. .	(620) 437-2556	Samuel Wine	. . .	Beth Dains	. . .	. . .	. . .	Dale Haney
Maize		c	MC	1	(316) 722-7561	Clair Donnelly	. . .	Jean Silvestri	. . .	. . .	Matthew Jensby	Ron Smothers
Manhattan		c	CM	44	(785) 587-2489	Mark Taussig	Ron Fehr	Gary Fees	Bernie Hayen	Jim Woydziak	. . .	Chuck Williams
Marysville		c	MC	3	(785) 562-5331	. . .	Rick Shain	Paula Holle	. . .	. . .	Todd Ackerman	Gerald Gellinger
Mc Cracken		c	CM	. .	(785) 394-2229	. . .	. . .	. . .	. . .	. . .	. . .	. . .
Mc Pherson		c	CO	13	(620) 245-2535	William Goering	Gary Meagher	. . .	Richard Janousek	Dennis Thrower	Michael Alkire	Stephen Schmidt
Meade		c	MC	1	(620) 873-2091	. . .	Dean Cordes	Crystal Heddlesten	. . .	. . .	. . .	. . .
Medicine Lodge		c	CM	2	(620) 886-3908	Steven Etheridge	Theodore Hauser	W. Kimball	. . .	Dennis Lunsford	Brian Miller	Gary Uhler
Merriam		c	MC	11	(913) 322-5500	. . .	. . .	. . .	Maureen Rogers	Gerald Montgomery	Kenneth Sissom	Randall Carroll
Minneapolis		c	MC	2	(785) 392-2176	Virginia Hoover	Lowell Parrish	. . .	. . .	Michael Smith	Lanny Zadina	. . .
Mission		c	MC	9	(913) 676-8350	Laura McConwell	Michael Scanlon	Martha Sumrall	. . .	. . .	Randall Wilson	Stephen Weeks
Mission Hills	*	c	MC	3	(913) 362-9620	David Fromm	C. Christensen	Jill Clifton	. . .	. . .	. . .	. . .
Mulvane		c	MC	5	(316) 777-1143	James Ford	Kent Hixson	Patty Gerwick	. . .	Judi Patterson	David Williams	Gary Rambo
Neodesha		c	CM	2	(620) 325-2828	Casey Lair	J. D. Cox	E. Boecker	. . .	Charles Reynolds	Danny Thayer	Gerald Lour
Newton		c	CM	17	(316) 284-6003	Willis Heck	. . .	. . .	Ronald Ahsmuhs	Gary Denny	James Daily	Suzanne Loomis
Norton		c	MC	3	(785) 877-5000	. . .	Rob Lawson	Darla Ellis	. . .	. . .	Lynn Menagh	Dan Bainter
Oakley		c	CM	2	(785) 672-3611	Frank Munk	. . .	Rose Wessel	. . .	Timothy Martin	Danny Shanks	James Glassman
Oberlin		c	MC	1	(785) 475-2217	. . .	. . .	. . .	. . .	Bill Cathcart	. . .	. . .
Olathe		c	CM	92	(913) 971-8600	Michael Copeland	John Wilkes	Debra Gragg	. . .	George Bentley	Janet Thiessen	Rick Biery
Osage City	*	c	CM	3	(785) 528-3714	Steve Haller	Brian Silcott	Linda Jones	. . .	. . .	Fred Nech	Mike Gilliland
Osawatomie	*	c	CM	4	(913) 755-2146	Norma Stephens	Bret Glendening	Ann Elmquist	. . .	James Maxwell	. . .	Stephen Coffelt
Oswego		c	MC	2	(620) 795-4433	Murl Bringle	. . .	Cheri Peine	. . .	. . .	George Elliott	Kevin Frogley
Ottawa	*	c	CM	11	(785) 229-3600	. . .	Richard Nienstedt	. . .	Scott Bird	Jeff Carner	Dennis Butler	Donald Haney
Overland Park		c	CM	149	(913) 895-6000	Ed Eilert	John Nachbar	Marian Cook	Kristy Stallings	. . .	John Douglass	Robert Lowry
Paola	*	c	CM	5	(913) 259-3600	Artie Stuteville	John Wieland	Dan Droste	. . .	Andy Martin	David Smail	Gerry Bieker
Park City	*	c	MC	5	(316) 744-2026	Dee Stuart	Jack Whitson	Carol Jones	. . .	. . .	. . .	Rick Norman
Parsons		c	CM	11	(620) 421-7000	. . .	Donald Cawby	Deborah Lamb	. . .	Tim Hay	Gary Baldwin	Darrell Moyer
Phillipsburg		c	MC	2	(785) 543-5234	. . .	. . .	. . .	. . .	. . .	. . .	. . .
Pittsburg	*	c	CM	19	(620) 231-4100	Bill Rushton	Allen Gill	Tammy Nagle	Jon Garrison	Donald Elmer	Mendy Hulvey	William Beasley
Plainville		c	MC	2	(785) 434-2841	Shirley Hendrex	. . .	James Dryden	. . .	William Strouse	Gary Knight	Bob Wise
Pleasanton		c	CM	1	(913) 352-8257	. . .	. . .	. . .	. . .	. . .	. . .	. . .
Prairie Village		c	MC	22	(913) 381-6464	Ronald Shaffer	Quinn Bennion	Joyce Mundy	Jamie Shell	. . .	Charles Grover	Robert Pryzby
Pratt		c	CM	6	(620) 672-5571	Jeff Taylor	E Howard	LuAnn Kramer	Betsy Koontz	David Kramer	Lonnie McCollum	Larry Koontz
Roeland Park		c	MC	6	(913) 722-2600	Lori Hirons	John Carter	Anthony Pluta	. . .	. . .	Rex Taylor	Patrick Mundis
Rose Hill		c	MC	3	(316) 776-2712	Daniel Woydziak	Joel Pile	Kathy Dinkel	. . .	. . .	Robert Sage	Robert Edwards
Russell		c	CM	4	(785) 483-6311	Neal Farmer	. . .	Karen Gates	. . .	Earl Hemphill	Leo Thomas	Frank Peirano
Sabetha		c	CO	2	(785) 284-2158	Norman Schmitt	Douglas Allen	Linda Lehman	. . .	Benjamin Johnson	Michael Hill	. . .
Salina	*	c	CM	45	(785) 309-5710	Don Marrs	Jason Gage	LieuAnn Elsey	Rodney Franz	J. Larry Mullikin	James Hill	. . .
Scott City		c	MC	3	(620) 872-5322	Henry Strecker	. . .	Brenda Davis	. . .	Kenneth Hoover	. . .	Mike Todd
Sedgwick		c	MC	1	(316) 772-5151	Donald DeHaven	Jaclyn Reimer	Janise Enterkin	. . .	Richard Ludowese	Ray Huff	Frank Preston
Seneca		c	CM	2	(785) 336-2747	. . .	. . .	Jane Strathman	. . .	. . .	. . .	Brian Rusche
Shawnee		c	CM	47	(913) 631-2500	James Allen	Carol Gonzales	. . .	H Lee Meyer	Jeff Hudson	Charles Clark	Ronald Freyermuth
Spring Hill		c	CM	2	(913) 592-3664	Mark Squire	Jonathan Roberts	Beverly Hayden	Pamela Jackson	. . .	Paul Kalmar	Rory Hale
St. Marys		c	CM	1	(785) 437-2311	Mary Denton	. . .	Katherine De Mars	. . .	James Keating	Jimmy Hostetler	Jerry Eichem
Sterling	*	c	CM	2	(620) 278-3423	Lee Sankey	Rod Willis	Sandra Fankhauser	. . .	Rodney Smith	Ed Truelove	Andy Prebble
Stockton		c	CO	1	(785) 425-6703	. . .	. . .	Sandra Rogers	. . .	Alec Hrabe	Donald Jenkins	. . .
Tonganoxie		c	CM	2	(913) 845-2620	David Taylor	Michael Yanez	. . .	. . .	David Bennett	Kenneth Carpenter	Butch Rodgers
Topeka		c	CM	122	(785) 368-3867	William Bunten	Norton Bonaparte	Brenda Younger	Jim Langford	Howard Giles	Ronald Miller	Mike Teply
Tribune		c	MC	. .	(620) 376-4278	. . .	. . .	Meredith Johnson	. . .	. . .	. . .	. . .
Ulysses		c	MC	5	(620) 356-4600	Ed Wiltse	Bud Newberry	Mary Smith	. . .	. . .	Alan Olson	Ruben Flores
Valley Center		c	MC	4	(316) 755-7310	Michael McNown	Irvin Creech	Kristine Polian	. . .	Lonnie Tormey	Kelly Parks	Richard Dunn
Wamego		c	CM	4	(785) 456-9119	Errol Carley	. . .	Elizabeth Kern	. . .	Phillip Stultz	Michael Baker	Claude Asbury
Wellington		c	CM	8	(620) 326-3631	Stanley Gilliland	Adam Collins	Rose Miller	. . .	John Lloyd	Michael Keller	Rodney Conwell
Westwood		c	MC	1	(913) 362-1550	Karen Johnson	. . .	Kathleen McMahon	. . .	. . .	Carlos Wells	John Sullivan
Wichita		c	CM	344	(316) 268-4531	Carlos Mayans	. . .	Patricia Graves	Kelly Carpenter	Lawrence Garcia	Norman Williams	Stephen Lackey
Winfield		c	CM	12	(620) 221-5500	Phil Jarvis	Warren Porter	. . .	Diane Rosecrans	Curtis Wilson	Jerry DeVore	Russ Tomevi

Directory 1/9 continued

OFFICIALS IN U.S. MUNICIPALITIES 2,500 AND OVER IN POPULATION

Jurisdiction	Type	Form of government	2000 Population (000)	Main telephone number	Chief elected official	Appointed administrator	Clerk of the governing board	Chief financial officer	Fire chief	Police chief	Public works director
KENTUCKY											
Alexandria	c	MC	8	(859) 635-4125	Daniel McGinley	...	Karen Barto	...	Jeffrey Pohlman	Michael Ward	Sam Trapp
Anchorage	c	MC	2	(502) 245-4654	Peyton Hoge	...	Christine Franklin	...	Joe Frith	James Edington	Arthur Gullett
Ashland	c	CM	21	(606) 327-2000	Stephen Gilmore	...	Deborah Musser	Tony Grubb	Mark Osborne	Thomas Kelley	Steve Corbitt
Barbourville	c	MC	3	(606) 546-6197	W. Hauser	James Tye	...	...	...	...	James Baker
Bardstown	c	MC	10	(502) 348-5947	Henry Spalding	...	Lonnie Parrott	...	Phillip Parrott	John Johnson	William Burba
Bardwell	c	MC	..	(270) 628-5415	...	...	...	...	...	...	...
Beaver Dam	c	CO	3	(270) 274-7106	David Taylor	Larry Carter	Brenda Dockery	...	Jerrel Shephard	...	Roscoe Simpson
Bellevue	c	MC	6	(859) 431-8866	John Meyer	...	...	Mary Scott	John Daly	Rick Sears	Randy Grosch
Benton*	c	MC	4	(270) 527-8677	Steve Cary	...	Michele Edwards	...	Harry Green	Gary West	...
Berea	c	MC	9	(859) 986-8528	Steven Connelly	Randall Stone	...	...	Randy Rigsby	Buford Brumley	Timothy Taylor
Bowling Green	c	CM	49	(270) 393-3000	Elaine Walker	Kevin DeFebbo	...	Jeff Meisel	...	Doug Hawkins	Emmett Wood
Calvert City	c	MC	2	(270) 395-7138	Lynn Jones	John Ward	Troy Truitt	...	Fred Ross	John Nelson	Ron Sutter
Campbellsville	c	MC	10	(270) 465-7011	Brenda Allen	...	...	...	Allen Johnson	William Cassell	...
Carrollton*	c	MC	3	(502) 732-7060	Ann Deatherage	...	Becky Pyles	...	Randall Tharp	Michael Willhoite	Ronald Knight
Catlettsburg	c	MC	1	(606) 739-4533	Roger Hensley	...	Pauline Hunt	Charles Hedrick	Linzy Runyon	Mark Plummer	Roger West
Central City	c	CM	5	(270) 754-5097	Hugh Sweatt	David Rhoades	Joely Berg	...	Jerrold Moore	Steven Osteen	Wendell Shadowen
Columbia	c	MC	4	(270) 384-2501	Patrick Bell	...	Carolyn Edwards	...	Michael Glasgow	Mark Harris	...
Corbin	c	CM	7	(606) 528-0669	James Williamson	Bill Cannon	Erin Blount	...	Gary Disney	John Mullins	James Foley
Covington	c	CM	43	(859) 292-2133	Denny Bowman	John Fossett	Carol Little	Gregory Engelman	Joseph Heringhaus	Albert Bosse	Geoffrey Warneford
Crestview Hills	c	MC	2	(859) 341-7373	Paul Meier	Daniel Groth	...	C. Monhollen	...	Paul Herbst	James Connelly
Cumberland	c	MC	2	(606) 589-2106	...	...	...	...	...	...	...
Cynthiana	c	CO	6	(859) 234-7150	James Brown	...	Charleen McIlvan	...	Greg Lemons	David McGuffin	Leroy Conner
Danville	c	CM	15	(859) 238-1200	John Bowling	...	Donna Peek	Spencer Rodgers	Mike Thomas	...	Tony Griffin
Dawson Springs	c	MC	2	(270) 797-2781	Stacia Peyton	...	Denise Ridley	...	Terry Warren	Bill Crider	John McChesney
Dayton	c	MC	5	(859) 491-1600	Kenneth Rankle	Dennis Redmond	Donna Leger	...	Denny Lynn	Mark Brown	Donald Riley
Douglass Hills	c	MC	5	(502) 245-3600	Sherl Fetter	...	Henrietta Barker	...	...	...	...
Edgewood	c	MC	9	(859) 331-5910	John Link	Roger Rolfes	Jeanette Kemper	...	...	Anthony Kramer	Stanley Goetz
Elizabethtown	c	MC	22	(270) 765-6121	David Willmoth	Charles Bryant	Mary Chaudoin	Stephen Park	Michael Hulsey	Ruben Gardner	William Owen
Elsmere	c	MC	8	(859) 342-7911	...	...	Melissa Andress	...	...	Timothy Greene	Charles Turner
Erlanger*	c	MC	16	(859) 727-2525	Thomas Rouse	William Scheyer	Linda Carter	Greg Engleman	Tim Koenig	Marc Fields	Rick Bogard
Flatwoods	c	MC	7	(606) 836-9661	...	...	Sarah Armstrong	...	...	Noel Gallion	Fred Dean
Flemingsburg	c	MC	3	(606) 845-5951	Louie Flanery	...	Joy Roark	...	Jerry McCloud	Danny Carpenter	James Compton
Florence	c	MC	23	(859) 371-5491	Diane Whalen	Patricia Wingo	Joseph Christofield	Linda Chapman	Marc Muench	Thomas Kathman	Robert Townsend
Fort Mitchell	c	CM	8	(859) 331-1212	...	...	...	...	...	...	...
Fort Thomas*	c	MC	16	(859) 441-1055	Mary Brown	Donald Martin	Melissa Kelly	Fred Ewald	Mark Bailey	Michael Daly	Ronald Dill
Fort Wright	c	MC	5	(606) 311-1700	Cindy Pinto	...	Jody Anderson	...	Ron Becker	Mark Brow	Tim Maloney
Frankfort	c	CM	27	(502) 875-8500	William May	Anthony Massey	Shirley Brown	James Rogers	Wallace Possich	Ted Evans	Dennis Minks
Franklin	c	CM	7	(270) 586-4497	Jim Brown	...	Kathy Stradtner	Barbara O'Bryan	Shelia Butterbaugh	James Powell	Clifton Beecher
Fulton	c	CM	2	(502) 472-1320	Eddie Crittendon	...	Helen Lee	Lisa Owens	Shawn Bixler	Terry Powell	Richard Tidwell
Georgetown	c	MC	18	(502) 863-9800	Everette Varney	...	Sue Lewis	Michele Pogrotsky	Robert Bruin	Greg Reeves	R. C. Linton
Glasgow	c	MC	13	(270) 651-5131	Charles Honeycutt	Leslie Settle	...	...	James Wingfield	...	Jack Chadwell
Grayson	c	CO	3	(606) 474-6651	Leda Dean	...	Martha Lemaster	...	Gregory Felty	Willard Hill	...
Greenville	c	MC	4	(502) 338-3966	...	...	...	...	...	...	...
Harlan	c	MC	2	(606) 573-2912	Daniel Howard	...	Bobbie Stark	...	William Simms	Roy Hatfield	Kenneth Hicks
Harrodsburg	c	MC	8	(859) 734-2383	...	...	...	...	M. Hockersmith	...	...
Hartford	c	MC	2	(502) 298-3612	...	...	...	...	...	...	...
Hazard	c	CM	4	(606) 436-3171	...	...	...	...	...	...	...
Henderson	c	CM	27	(270) 831-1200	Henry Lackey	Benjamin Saag	Carolyn Williams	Robert Gunter	Terrence Lewis	Mack Brady	X. R. Royster
Hickman*	c	CM	2	(270) 236-2535	Charles Murphy	...	Donna Haney	...	Jackie Duncan	Tony Grogan	...
Highland Heights	c	MC	6	(859) 441-8575	Charles Roettger	...	...	...	...	Carl Mullen	Albert Harris
Hillview*	c	MC	7	(502) 957-5280	James Eadens	...	Betty Bradbury	...	...	Raymon Wilburn	William Pepper
Hodgenville	c	MC	2	(270) 358-3832	Charles Hazle	...	...	...	...	...	...
Hopkinsville	c	MC	30	(270) 890-0265	Richard Liebe	Glenn Abee	Christine Upton	Robert Martin	Fagan Pace	Kermit Yeager	Rick Deason
Hurstbourne	c	CO	3	(502) 426-4808	W. Bardenwerper	Ronald Howard	Katherine Petricek	...	...	Ed Porter	...
Independence	c	MC	14	(859) 356-5302	Thomas Kriege	...	Patricia Taney	Amy Guenther	...	...	Jeffrey Smith
Irvine	c	MC	2	(606) 723-2554	C. Williams	...	...	...	Anthony Murphy	James Crowe	...
Jackson	c	MC	2	(606) 666-7069	Michael Miller	...	Angela Combs	...	Roger Friley	Clyde Caudill	Ralph Cundiff
Jeffersontown*	c	MC	26	(502) 267-8333	Clay Foreman	...	Frank Greenwell	Jim Leidgen	...	Richard Sanders	...
Jenkins	c	MC	2	(606) 832-2141	Robert Shubert	...	Sandra Puckett	...	Richard Corbett	Bill Tackett	...
La Grange	c	MC	5	(502) 222-1433	Elsie Carter	...	Sharon Herndon	...	...	Kevin Collett	Keith Crowder
Lakeside Park	c	MC	2	(859) 341-6670	Frank Smith	...	...	...	...	...	Robert Haglage
Lancaster	c	MC	3	(859) 792-2241	...	...	...	...	...	...	...
Lawrenceburg	c	MC	9	(502) 839-5372	Bobby Sparrow	...	...	...	Robert Hume	Harold Burris	Larry Hazlett
Lebanon	c	MC	5	(270) 692-6272	Gary Crenshaw	...	Joyce Ford	...	Richard Mattingly	Eugene Young	Robert Thompson
Leitchfield*	c	MC	6	(270) 259-4034	William Thomason	...	Erin Embry	...	Carl Smith	Bart Glenn	Darrell Harrell
Lexington-Fayette	c	MC	225	(859) 258-3000	...	...	Liz Deaton	James Deaton	Robert Hendricks	Anthany Beatty	...
London	c	MC	5	(606) 864-4169	Kenneth Smith	...	Connie McKnight	...	Ernest Clark	Elijah Hollon	Steven Edge
Louisville–Jefferson County	c	MC	256	(502) 574-2003	Jerry Abramson	...	Bobbi Holsclaw	Jane Driskell	Gregory Frederick	Robert White	Jim Adkins
Ludlow	c	MC	4	(859) 491-1233	Ed Schroeder	...	...	...	Terry Bandy	Ray Murphy	...
Madisonville*	c	MC	19	(270) 824-2100	Karen Cunningham	Lloyd Merrell	Gina Munger	Steven Ramsey	Tommy Williams	Ronald Hunt	Dennis Farris
Marion	c	MC	3	(270) 965-2266	...	...	...	...	...	...	...
Mayfield	c	MC	10	(502) 247-1971	...	...	...	...	...	...	...
Maysville	c	CM	8	(606) 564-9411	David Cartmell	...	Sharon Swisher	Romie Griffey	John Gantley	Van Ingram	...
Middlesborough	c	MC	10	(606) 248-5600	Ben Hickman	James Pursifull	Teresa Massengill	...	Tim Wilder	Jeff Sharpe	Leeman Moyers
Monticello	c	MC	5	(606) 348-0167	Thurston Frye	...	...	...	Jerry Ferrell	Glen Rose	Leroy Mikel
Morehead	c	MC	5	(606) 784-8505	Bradley Collins	...	Diana Lindsey	...	Charles Walker	Gary Gardner	Dwain Wilson
Morganfield	c	MC	3	(270) 389-2525	Jerry Freer	David Presser	...	...	Earl Woods	Tom Carmon	...
Mount Sterling	c	MC	5	(859) 498-8725	Gary Williamson	...	...	...	...	Michael Schnell	Steve Lane
Mount Washington	c	MC	8	(502) 538-4216	...	...	Christi Franklin	...	...	Leo Oliver	...
Murray	c	MC	14	(502) 762-0309	...	...	...	...	...	...	...
Newport	c	CM	17	(859) 292-3682	Thomas Guidugli	Philip Ciafardini	...	...	Larry Atwell	Thomas Fromme	Christopher Novak
Nicholasville	c	CO	19	(859) 885-1121	Sam Corman	...	Roberta Warren	James Hood	...	Barry Waldrop	Thomas Calkins
Olive Hill	c	MC	1	(606) 286-5532	James Short	...	Don Everman	...	Rod Stephens	Daniel Tackett	Virgil Jordan
Owensboro*	c	CM	54	(270) 687-8545	Tom Watson	Robert Whitmer	Carol Blake	James Fulkerson	Ron Heep	John Kazlauskas	Anthony Cecil
Paducah	c	CM	26	(270) 444-8504	William Paxton	James Zumwalt	...	Jonathan Perkins	Redell Benton	Randy Bratton	...
Paintsville	c	MC	4	(606) 789-2600	Robin Cooper	...	Virgie Castle	Robert Conley	Bob Dixon	Doug Wallen	Larry Herald
Paris	c	CM	9	(859) 987-2110	Donald Kiser	Robert Casher	Cheryl Marsh	...	Michael Withrow	Michael Kendall	Gary Barbee
Park Hills	c	MC	2	(859) 431-6252	Michael Hellmann	...	...	...	Regis Huth	Ricardo Smith	Dennis Finke
Pikeville	c	CM	6	(606) 437-5100	Steven Combs	Donovan Blackburn	Karen Harris	...	...	...	Greg May
Pineville	c	MC	2	(606) 337-2958	...	...	...	...	...	...	...

Directory 1/9   **OFFICIALS IN U.S. MUNICIPALITIES 2,500 AND OVER IN POPULATION**
continued

Jurisdiction	Type	Form of govern- ment	2000 Popu- lation (000)	Main telephone number	Chief elected official	Appointed administrator	Clerk of the governing board	Chief financial officer	Fire chief	Police chief	Public works director
KENTUCKY continued											
Prestonsburg	c	MC	3	(606) 886-2335	Jerry Fannin	...	Peggy Bailey	...	Chester Davis	Stanley Farler	William Harris
Princeton	c	MC	6	(270) 365-9575	...	...	...	...	...	...	...
Prospect *	c	MC	4	(502) 228-1121	...	Ann Simms	...	...	...	Marvin Wilson	...
Providence	c	MC	3	(270) 667-5463	Jerry Fritz	...	Sara Stevens	...	Jimmy Oakley	Archie Benton	Ralph Alexander
Radcliff	c	MC	21	(270) 351-4714	...	...	...	...	...	...	...
Richmond	c	CM	27	(859) 623-1000	Ann Durham	David Evans	Betty Houghton	Janet Herbst	Fred Brandenburg	David Harkleroad	Hershell Sparks
Russell	c	MC	3	(606) 836-9666	Donald Fraley	...	Joyce Conley	...	Harry Thomas	Phillip Caskey	...
Russellville	c	MC	7	(270) 726-5000	Shirley Yassmy	...	...	Jennifer Knight	John Williamson	James Pendergraff	...
Scottsville	c	MC	4	(502) 237-3238	...	...	...	...	...	...	...
Shelbyville	c	MC	10	(502) 633-5000	David Eaton	...	Inez Harris	...	...	John Kubran	Albert Minnis
Shepherdsville *	c	MC	8	(502) 543-2923	Sherman Tinnell	...	Tammy Owen	...	Brad Whittaker	Doug Puckett	Jesse Walls
Shively	c	MC	15	(502) 449-5000	Sherry Conner	...	Mitzi Kasitz	...	Wendell Vincent	Ralph Miller	John Haywood
Somerset	c	MC	11	(606) 679-6366	J. P. Wiles	...	David Godsey	James Hogg	James Latham	David Biggerstaff	James Fisher
Southgate	c	MC	3	(859) 441-0075	Charles Melville	...	Rose Welscher	...	...	Michael Hall	R. Sanzenbacker
Springfield	c	MC	2	(859) 336-5440	Mike Haydon	Laurie Smith	...	...	Troy Logsdon	Fred Armstrong	Glenn Mattingly
St. Matthews	c	MC	15	(502) 895-9444	Arthur Draut	...	Gretchen Kaiser	...	...	Norman Mayer	Bill Kaiser
Stanford	c	MC	3	(606) 365-4500	Eddie Carter	...	Sandra Gooch	...	Leroy Lunsford	Keith Middleton	John Lasure
Stanton	c	MC	3	(606) 663-4459	...	...	...	...	...	...	...
Taylor Mill	c	MC	6	(859) 581-3234	Mark Kreimborg	Jill Bailey	Karen Griffith	...	Dennis Halpin	Steve Knauf	Marc Roden
Tompkinsville	c	MC	2	(502) 487-6776	...	...	Clarnell Emberton	...	...	Johnny Graves	Tom Baker
Union	0	MC	2	(859) 384-1511	...	Warren Moore	...	...	...	...	...
Versailles	c	MC	7	(859) 873-5491	...	...	Allison White	...	Frankie Shuck	William Love	Bartley Miller
Villa Hills	c	MC	7	(859) 341-1515	Dennis Stein	...	Sue Kramer	...	George Bruns	Michael Brown	Derick Yelton
Vine Grove *	c	MC	4	(270) 877-2422	Donovan Smith	...	Cary Broussard	...	Steve New	Steven Manning	Burlin Martin
Williamsburg	c	MC	5	(606) 549-6033	Roger Harrison	...	...	Teresa Black	James Privett	Denny Shelley	Truman Prewitt
Williamstown	c	MC	3	(859) 824-3633	Glenn Caldwell	Douglas Beckham	Vivian Link	...	Les Whalen	Bobby Webb	...
Wilmore	c	MC	5	(859) 858-4411	Harold Rainwater	...	C. Brandenburg	...	Jeffrey Anderson	Stephen Boven	David Carlstodt
Winchester	c	CM	16	(859) 744-7017	Dodd Dixon	Kenneth Kerns	Marilyn Rowe	...	Daniel Castle	William Jackson	Norman Howard
LOUISIANA											
Abbeville *	t	MC	11	(337) 893-8550	Mark Piazza	...	Kathleen Faulk	...	Elvin Michaud	Rick Coleman	Clay Menard
Alexandria	c	MC	46	(318) 449-5020	Edward Randolph	Delores Brewer	Nancy Thiels	David Crutchfield	Paul Smith	Darren Coutee	...
Amite City	t	MC	4	(985) 748-9850	...	...	...	...	...	...	...
Arcadia	t	MC	3	(318) 263-8456	Jesse Smith	...	...	...	Randy Wright	Victor Rogers	...
Baker	c	MC	13	(985) 778-0300	...	J. E. Carroll	Jean Byers	Julie Pittman	...	Sid Gautreaux	Glynn Cavin
Baldwin	t	MC	2	(337) 923-7523	Wayne Breaux	...	Sonya Charles	...	Gene St. Germain	Gerald Minor	...
Ball	t	MC	3	(318) 640-9605	Roy Hebron	...	Willie Bishop	...	...	Spencer Williams	...
Basile	t	MC	1	(337) 432-6692	Berline Sonnier	...	Vickie Briscoe	...	Mike Arnold	Allen Ivory	...
Bastrop	c	MC	12	(318) 283-0250	...	...	...	...	...	...	...
Baton Rouge–East Baton Rouge	c	MC	227	(225) 389-3129	Bobby Simpson	Paul Thompson	...	David Medlin	Edwin Smith	Pat Englade	Fred Raiford
Berwick	t	MC	4	(985) 384-8858	...	...	...	...	...	...	...
Bogalusa	c	MC	13	(985) 732-6211	Mervin Taylor	Gerald Bailey	...	...	...	...	Billy Daniels
Bossier City	c	MC	56	(318) 741-8500	Lorenz Walker	Allen Austin	Dorothy Thornton	Charles Glover	Samuel Halphen	Ken Halphen	Gary Neathery
Breaux Bridge	c	MC	7	(337) 332-1840	Jack Delhomme	...	Pattie Du Puis	...	...	...	Frank Leblanc
Broussard	c	MC	5	(337) 837-6681	Charles Langlinais	...	Tina Denais	...	Danny Denais	Brannon Decou	Larry Champagne
Bunkie	t	MC	4	(318) 346-7663	Gerard Moreau	...	...	...	Joseph Frank	Mary Fanara	Louis Redmon
Carencro	t	MC	6	(337) 896-8481	...	...	...	...	...	...	...
Church Point	t	MC	4	(337) 684-5693	Roger Boudreaux	...	...	...	...	Albert Venable	James Landry
Covington	c	MC	8	(985) 892-1811	Candace Watkins	...	Lynne Moore	...	Richard Badon	Jerome Di Franco	Thomas Mayronne
Crowley	c	MC	14	(337) 783-4103	I. delaHoussaye	Margaret Young	Judy Istre	...	William Schmaltz	Kendall Gibson	Albert John
De Quincy	t	MC	3	(337) 786-8241	...	...	Tammy Pinder	...	...	Michael Suchanek	Bobby Dahlquist
De Ridder	c	MC	9	(337) 462-8900	Gerald Johnson	...	Penelope Simmons	Ginny Brand	Marvin Whiddon	Ricky Johnson	Hershell Nutt
Delhi	t	MC	3	(318) 878-3792	...	...	...	...	...	...	...
Denham Springs	c	MC	8	(225) 665-8121	James De Laune	Ellis Chavers	Lerline Barnett	...	Robert Wascom	Jeffrey Wesley	Willie Rheams
Donaldsonville	c	CM	7	(504) 473-4247	Leroy Sullivan	Charles Oatis	Bernard Francis	Sandra Cost	Kirk Landry	...	Gerard Joesph
Eunice	c	MC	11	(337) 457-7389	E. Lynn Lejeune	...	Doug Cart	...	Gerald Le Jeune	James Fontenot	...
Farmerville	t	MC	3	(318) 368-9242	...	...	...	...	...	...	...
Ferriday	t	MC	3	(318) 757-3411	...	...	...	...	...	...	...
Franklin *	c	MC	8	(337) 828-6316	Sam Jones	Lecia Verrette	...	Bianca Phillips	Boykin Bourgeois	Sabria McGuire	Jeremy Smith
Franklinton	t	MC	3	(985) 839-3569	Earle Brown	...	Faye Boyd	...	...	Lynn Armand	Cockern Linwood
Gonzales	c	MC	8	(985) 647-2841	...	...	...	...	...	...	...
Grambling	v	MC	4	(318) 247-6120	...	...	...	...	...	...	...
Gramercy	t	MC	3	(225) 869-4403	Eugene Louque	...	...	...	Andy Detillier	David Dufresne	...
Gretna	c	MC	17	(504) 363-1700	Beauregard Miller	Arthur Lawson	...	...	...	...	...
Hammond	c	MC	17	(985) 542-3400	Mayson Foster	Martis Jones	Lanita Johnson	Larry Francis	Paul Collura	Roddy Devall	...
Harahan	c	MC	9	(504) 737-6383	Paul Johnston	Margaret Broussard	Rena Sanders	...	Todd St. Cyr	Peter Dale	Leslie Lauricella
Haynesville	t	MC	2	(318) 624-0911	Tom Crocker	...	Marilyn Bush	...	Mark Furlow	...	Alvin Moss
Homer *	t	MC	3	(318) 927-3555	David Newell	...	Rita Mitchell	James Colvin	Dennis Butcher	Albert Mills	Lee Wells
Jackson	t	MC	4	(985) 634-7777	...	...	...	...	...	...	...
Jeanerette	t	MC	5	(318) 256-4587	...	...	...	...	...	...	...
Jena *	t	MC	2	(318) 992-2148	Murphy McMillin	...	Cory Floyd	...	Don Smith	M. Smith	Don Jones
Jennings	c	MC	10	(337) 821-5500	Gregory Marcantel	...	Norman Cain	...	Tommy Deshotel	Dalton Joseph	Cyril Charles
Jonesboro	t	MC	3	(318) 259-2385	Don Essmeier	...	Beatrice Rice	...	Tim Wyatt	G. Horton	Donald Davis
Jonesville	t	MC	2	(318) 339-8596	William Edwards	...	Robert Swayze	...	Ben Adams	Clyde Walker	Sim Nichols
Kaplan	c	MC	5	(337) 643-8600	Levi Schexnider	...	Darlene Labry	...	Donald Meaux	Stephen Perry	...
Kenner	c	MC	70	(504) 468-7207	Louis Congemi	Joseph Nicolosi	Michelle Sheeren	Duke McConnell	Michael Zito	Nick Congemi	Michael Scardino
Kentwood	t	MC	2	(985) 229-3451	Bobby Gill	...	Julia Forrest	...	Frankie Gehringer	James Rimes	David Sellers
Kinder	t	MC	2	(337) 738-2620	...	...	...	...	...	...	...
Lafayette Consolidated Government	c	MC	110	(337) 291-8300	Joey Durel	Dee Stanley	Norma Dugas	Rebecca Lalumia	Robert Benoit	Jim Craft	Tom Carrol
Lake Arthur *	t	MC	3	(337) 774-2211	Edley Giles	...	Cynthia Mallett	...	...	Cheryl Vincent	Conrad Whitman
Lake Charles	c	MC	71	(337) 491-1200	Willie Mount	...	Elizabeth Eastman	Ronald Kemerly	Emerson Peet	Samuel Ivey	...
Lake Providence	t	MC	5	(318) 559-2288	Isaac Fields	...	Barbara McDaniel	Leland Jong	Jimmy Coleman	Renee Jones	Frank Powell
Leesville	t	CM	6	(337) 239-2444	...	Delain Prewitt	...	...	Donny McKee	Bobby Hickman	Sunny Martin
Lutcher	t	MC	3	(225) 869-5823	Troas Poche	...	Patricia Lemoine	...	...	Corey Pittman	Nolan Scott
Mamou	t	MC	3	(337) 468-3272	...	...	Guy Pucheu	...	...	Adam Fruge	Spencer Long
Mandeville *	c	MC	10	(985) 626-3144	Edward Price	...	Erin Killeen	Milton Stiebing	...	Thomas Buell	David deGeneres
Mansfield	c	MC	5	(318) 872-0406	Harold Cornett	...	Judy Wilkerson	...	...	...	James Ruffin
Many	t	MC	2	(318) 256-3651	...	...	...	...	...	...	...
Marksville	c	MC	5	(318) 253-9500	Richard Michel	...	Myron Gagnard	...	Ned Bordelon	N. Greenhouse	Jerry Ducey

Jurisdiction	Type	Form of govern- ment	2000 Popu- lation (000)	Main telephone number	Chief elected official	Appointed administrator	Clerk of the governing board	Chief financial officer	Fire chief	Police chief	Public works director
LOUISIANA continued											
Minden	c	MC	13	(318) 377-2144	Bill Robertson	Robert Green	...	...	...	T. Bloxom	George Rolfe
Monroe	c	MC	53	(318) 329-2284	James Mayo	David Barnes	Carolus Riley	Stacey Haynie	Jimmy Bryant	Ronald Schleuter	C. Janway
Morgan City	c	MC	12	(985) 385-1770	Tim Tregle	Michael Loupe	...	Lorrie Braus	Richard Anderson	Claude Christy	Vincent Matherne
Natchitoches	c	MC	17	(318) 357-3826	Joseph Sampite	...	Maryann Nunley	Patrick Jones	Robert Hebert	Keith Thompson	Clyde Lacaze
New Iberia *	c	MC	32	(337) 369-2300	Hilda Curry	Amie Varnado	Elmire Brennan	...	Ronnie Bourque	...	James Russell
New Orleans	c	MC	484	(504) 565-6500	C. Ray Nagin	...	Peggy Crutchfield	Reginald Zeno	Warren McDaniels	Edwin Compass	...
New Roads	t	MC	4	(225) 638-5360	...	...	...	...	Leslie Lindsly	...	Robert Staehle
Oakdale	c	MC	8	(318) 335-3629	Robert Abrusley	Melissa Schaefer	...	...	Thomas Moore	Bobby Gordon	Ronald Turner
Opelousas	c	MC	22	(337) 948-2532	Anna Simmons	Monica Semien	Frances Carron	...	Lee Cahanin	Larry Caillier	...
Patterson	t	MC	5	(985) 395-5205	...	...	...	...	Gary Morrow	Jay Barber	Charles Moore
Pineville	c	MC	13	(318) 449-5659	Clarence Fields	...	Ellen Melancon	Kimberly Portier	Mackie Guillot	Orian Gulotta	Louis Guidry
Plaquemine	t	MC	7	(225) 687-3116	Mark Gulotta	...	Sheila Migliacio	Laurie Berthelot	...	Timothy Gideon	...
Ponchatoula	c	MC	5	(985) 386-6484	Julian Dufreche	...	...	E. LeSaicherre	...	...	...
Port Allen	c	MC	5	(504) 348-5670	...	...	...	...	...	...	...
Port Barre	t	MC	2	(337) 585-7646	John Fontenot	...	Juanita Hardy	...	...	Huey Guillory	Donald Robin
Rayne	c	MC	8	(318) 334-3121	...	...	...	...	...	...	...
Rayville	t	MC	4	(318) 728-7501	...	...	...	...	Donnie Watson	Randal Hermes	Thomas Love
Ruston	c	MC	20	(318) 251-8663	Dan Hollingsworth	George Byrnside	Arthur Thompson	E. Washington	Kelvin Cochran	Stephen Prator	...
Shreveport	c	MC	200	(318) 673-5150	Robert Williams	Thomas Dark	Thomas Reeves	Sharon Howes	...	Freddie Drennan	Michael Noto
Slidell *	c	MC	25	(985) 646-4377	Ben Morris	Robert Dunbar	Faye Farrar	...	...	Ronnie Coleman	Mike Dunaway
Springhill *	c	MC	5	(318) 539-5681	Carroll Breaux	...	Linda Jackson	Katrina Stewart	Floyd Sanchez	Patrick Nelson	W. Cushenberry
St. Gabriel	t	MC	5	(225) 642-9600	George Grace	Yolonda Mattaur	Darren Dore	...	...	Steve Champagne	Nolan Champagne
St. Martinville	c	MC	6	(337) 394-2230	Eric Martin	...	Arlene Blanchard	...	Danny Dupre	Kenneth Moss	Dennis Bergeron
Sulphur	c	MC	20	(337) 527-4500	Ronald LeLeux	...	...	Paree Prejean	...	Donnell Rose	...
Tallulah *	c	MC	9	(318) 574-0964	Eddie Beckwith	...	...	Gerald Odom	...	...	...
Thibodaux	c	MC	14	(985) 448-5848	Lucien Cailloet	Theresa Larose	...	Deborah Daigle	...	Howard Robertson	Kermit Kraemer
Vidalia	t	MC	4	(318) 336-5206	...	...	...	...	...	...	...
Ville Platte	t	MC	8	(337) 363-2939	Phillip Lemoine	...	Bryan Savant	...	Ted Demourelle	Romeo Hargrove	Clifford Fontenot
Vinton	t	MC	3	(337) 589-7453	Claude Lemaire	...	Melba Landry	...	...	Dennis Drouillard	Charles Guillory
Vivian *	t	MC	4	(318) 375-3856	H. McCormick	...	Diann House	...	...	Ronald Smith	Ronald Brown
Walker	t	MC	4	(225) 665-4356	Mike Grimmer	...	Janet Borne	Ronald Petty	...	Casey Grimes	Gary Green
Welsh	t	MC	3	(337) 734-2231	Edward Cormier	...	Linda Le Blanc	...	...	Ben Richard	James Ewing
West Monroe	c	MC	13	(318) 396-2600	...	...	...	...	...	...	...
Westlake	t	MC	4	(337) 433-0691	Dudley Dixon	...	Holly Fontenot	W. La Fleur	Robert McClelland	Gary Guillory	Doylin Kile
Westwego	c	MC	10	(504) 341-3424	Robert Billiot	C. Trosclair	Bonnie Pertuit	...	Doyle Guidroz	Roy Juncker	Robert Utley
Winnfield	c	MC	5	(318) 628-3939	...	...	...	...	...	...	...
Winnsboro	t	MC	5	(318) 435-9087	...	...	...	...	...	...	...
Zachary	c	MC	11	(504) 654-0287	John Womack	Stephen Nunnery	...	...	Douglas Gleason	John Wales	Chris Davezac
Zwolle	t	MC	1	(318) 645-6141	Marvin Frazier	...	Mindy Ezernack	...	...	...	...
MAINE											
Amity	t	CM	..	(207) 532-2485	...	Darrell Williams	...	...	...	...	...
Ashland	t	CM	1	(207) 435-2311	...	William Beaulier	...	...	Ned Labelle	Gary Ellis	...
Auburn	c	CM	23	(207) 333-6600	Normand Guay	...	Mary Magno	Ronald Farris	Russell Werts	Richard Small	Robert Belz
Augusta	c	CM	18	(207) 626-2353	William Dowling	William Bridgeo	Barbara Wardwell	...	...	Wayne McCamish	John Charest
Baileyville	t	TM	1	(207) 427-3442	...	...	...	...	...	...	...
Bangor	c	CM	31	(207) 992-4200	John Cashwell	Edward Barrett	Patti Dubois	Deborah Cyr	Jeffrey Cammack	Donald Winslow	Dana Wardwell
Bar Harbor	t	CM	4	(207) 288-4098	...	Dana Reed	Patricia Gray	Stanley Harmon	David Rand	Nathan Young	Charles Reeves
Bath	c	CM	9	(207) 443-8330	Bernard Wyman	William Giroux	Mary White	Abigail Yacoben	Stephen Hinds	Michael Field	Peter Owen
Belfast	c	CM	6	(207) 338-3370	...	Joseph Slocum	Roberta Fogg	...	James Richards	Jeffrey Trafton	Wesley Richards
Berwick	t	CM	6	(207) 698-1101	Thomas Fournier	Keith Trefethen	Judith Buckman	Janet Canney	Dennis Plante	Timothy Towne	Robert Perchy
Bethel	t	TM	2	(207) 824-2669	...	Scott Cole	Christen Mason	Nesta Littlefield	James Young	Darren Tripp	Robert Pilgrim
Biddeford	c	MC	20	(207) 284-9105	Jim Gratello	John Bubier	Clairma Matherne	Richard Lagarde	Raymond Gagne	Roger Beaupre	Mike Ostrosky
Blaine	t	TM	..	(207) 425-2611	...	...	...	...	...	...	...
Boothbay *	t	TM	2	(207) 633-2051	C. Cunningham	John Anderson	Bonnie Lewis	...	Richard Spofford	...	Anthony Goode
Boothbay Harbor *	t	TM	2	(207) 633-3671	Robert Jacobson	Carlo Pilgrim	Patricia Wheeler	Julia Latter	Glenn Townsend	Stephen Clark	Joseph Lewis
Bowdoinham	t	CM	2	(207) 666-5531	Brian Hobart	...	Cheryl Litchfield	...	Jack Tourtelotte	...	Kevin Prout
Brewer	c	CM	8	(207) 989-7500	Gayle Kelly	Stephen Bost	Arthur Verow	Karen McVey	Richard Bronson	Steve Barker	David Cote
Bridgewater	t	CM	..	(207) 429-9856	Amanda Dow	...	...	...	John Barker	...	Ralph Kinney
Bridgton	t	TM	4	(207) 647-8786	...	Mitchell Berkowitz	Laurie Chadbourne	...	Thomas Harriman	David Lyons	James Kidder
Brownville	t	CM	1	(207) 965-2561	Dennis Green	Sophia Wilson	Kathy White	...	David Preble	Todd Lyford	Kevin Black
Brunswick	t	CM	21	(207) 725-6659	Charles Priest	Donald Gerrish	Fran Smith	John Eldridge	Gary Howard	Jerry Hinton	John Foster
Bucksport	t	CM	4	(207) 469-7368	...	...	...	...	...	...	...
Buxton	t	TM	7	(207) 929-6171	Stephen Nichols	...	John Myers	...	Jeff Grinnell	Jody Thomas	Larry Owen
Calais	c	CM	3	(207) 454-2521	...	...	Theresa Porter	Pamela Bridges	Danny Carlow	Michael Milburn	Mark Magoon
Camden	t	CM	5	(207) 236-3353	Morton Strom	Roberta Smith	Carol Rogers	...	Steven Gibbons	...	Earl Weaver
Cape Elizabeth	t	CM	9	(207) 799-5251	...	Michael McGovern	Deborah Cabana	...	Philip McGouldrick	Neil Williams	Robert Malley
Caribou	c	CM	8	(207) 493-3324	...	Steven Buck	Judy Corrow	Wanda Ouellette	Roy Woods	Michael Gahagan	David Ouellette
Carmel	t	TM	2	(207) 848-3361	...	...	...	...	...	...	...
Carrabassett Valley	t	TM	..	(207) 235-2645	...	David Cota	Sherie McCatherin	...	Courtney Knapp	Ronald Moody	...
Casco	t	CM	3	(207) 627-4515	Calvin Nutting	David Morton	...	...	John Small	...	...
Castle Hill	t	CM	..	(207) 764-3754	...	John Edgecomb	Trudence Buck	...	Richard Wark	...	John Orcutt
Chelsea	t	TM	2	(207) 582-4802	Richard Danforth	Mary Sabins	Judith Jones	...	Shawn Ramage	...	...
Cherryfield	t	TM	1	(207) 546-2376	Randy Derry	George Hanington	...	...	Charles Curtis	...	...
China	t	TM	4	(207) 445-2014	Thomas Barber	...	Becky Cunningham	...	Richard Morse	James Lane	...
Clinton *	t	TM	3	(207) 426-8511	Jeffrey Towne	James Rhodes	Pamela Violette	...	Gary Petley	Randy Wing	...
Corinna	t	CM	2	(207) 278-4183	Galen McKenney	...	Tressa Gudroe	...	F. Clark	...	Stephen Lawson
Corinth	t	TM	2	(207) 285-3271	...	...	...	...	...	...	...
Crystal	t	TM	..	(207) 463-2770	...	Susan York	...	...	...	...	...
Cumberland	t	CM	7	(207) 829-2205	Jeffrey Porter	William Shane	Nadeen Daniels	Melody Main	Daniel Small	Joseph Charron	Adam Ogden
Danforth	t	CM	..	(207) 448-2321	...	...	...	...	...	...	...
Dexter	t	CM	3	(207) 924-7351	Peter Haskell	Judith Doore	Shelly Watson	Marilyn Curtis	Melvin Wyman	Arthur Roy	Michael Delaware
Dixfield	t	CM	2	(207) 562-8151	G. Daley	...	Vickie Cross	...	Scott Blaisdell	Richard Pickett	David Orr
Dover-Foxcroft	t	TM	4	(207) 564-3318	Elwood Edgerly	Owen Pratt	...	...	Joseph Guyotte	Dennis Dyer	...
Dyer Brook	t	TM	..	(207) 757-8302	David McLaughlin	...	...	...	...	...	...
Eagle Lake	t	CM	..	(207) 444-5125	...	...	...	...	...	...	...
East Millinocket *	t	TM	1	(207) 746-3376	Mark Scally	Shirley Tapley	Laura Ferguson	...	Leslie Brown	Garold Cramp	Danny Violette
Easton	t	TM	1	(207) 488-6652	Michael Corey	Jackalene Bradley	Cheryl Clark	...	Theodore White	...	...
Eastport	c	CM	1	(207) 853-2300	...	...	Helen Archer	...	Richard Clark	Matt Vinson	Rene O'Dell
Eliot	t	TM	5	(207) 439-1813	Stephen Beckert	Daniel Blanchette	Wendy Rawski	...	Richard Wood	Almon Boston	William Shapleigh
Ellsworth *	c	CM	6	(207) 667-2563	...	...	Heidi Grindle	...	Jonathan Marshall	John Deleo	Myron Grant
Exeter	t	CM	..	(207) 379-2191	James Crane	Tressa Gudroe	Jeanette Black	...	Alan Clark	...	...

Directory 1/9 continued — OFFICIALS IN U.S. MUNICIPALITIES 2,500 AND OVER IN POPULATION

Jurisdiction	Type	Form of govern-ment	2000 Popu-lation (000)	Main telephone number	Chief elected official	Appointed administrator	Clerk of the governing board	Chief financial officer	Fire chief	Police chief	Public works director
MAINE continued											
Fairfield	t	CM	6	(207) 453-7911	Richard Spear	Paul Blanchette	Tracey Stevens	...	Duane Bickford	John Emery	Bruce Williams
Falmouth	t	CM	10	(207) 781-5253	Paul Davis	Nathan Poore	Kathleen Babeu	John McNaughton	Cameron Martin	Edward Tolan	Anthony Hayes
Farmingdale	t	TM	2	(207) 582-2225	...	Phyllis Weeks	...	...	...	...	...
Farmington	t	CM	7	(207) 778-6539	...	Richard Davis	Leanne Pinkham	...	Terry Bell	Richard Caton	Mitchell Boulette
Fort Fairfield	t	CM	3	(207) 472-3800	...	Dan Foster	Mary Whitmore	...	Paul Durepo	Joseph Bubar	George Watson
Fort Kent	t	CM	4	(207) 834-3507	...	...	...	...	...	...	...
Freeport	t	CM	7	(207) 865-4743	...	Dale Olmstead	Beverly Curry	Gregory L'Heureux	Darrel Fournier	Jerry Schofield	James Plummer
Frenchville	t	CM	1	(207) 543-7301	...	...	...	...	...	...	...
Frye Island	t	CM	..	(207) 655-4551	...	Wayne Fournier	...	Calvin Nutting	Steve Persson	Dana Wessling	John Crosby
Fryeburg *	t	TM	3	(207) 935-2805	David Knapp	Phil Covelli	Theresa Shaw	...	Richard Sheaff	Wayne Brooking	...
Gardiner *	c	CM	6	(207) 582-4200	Andrew MacLean	Jeffrey Kobrock	Deirdre Berglund	Patricia Coty	Mark Kimball	James Toman	Chuck Applebee
Garland	t	CM	..	(207) 924-6615	Royce Butler	...	Dorothy Robinson	...	Norman Packard	...	...
Glenburn	t	CM	3	(207) 942-2905	...	...	Ruthena Brasslett	...	...	...	...
Gorham	t	CM	14	(207) 839-5041	Michael Phinney	David Cole	Christina Silberman	Maureen Finger	Robert Lefebvre	Ronald Shepard	Robert Burns
Gouldsboro	t	CM	1	(207) 963-7582	...	...	...	...	...	...	...
Gray	t	CM	6	(207) 657-3339	...	...	...	...	Jon Barton	...	Steve La Vallee
Greenbush	t	TM	1	(207) 826-2050	Albert Weatherbee	...	...	...	Edward Haverlock	...	...
Greene	t	CM	4	(207) 946-5146	Ron Grant	...	...	...	...	...	Kevin Doyle
Greenville	t	TM	1	(207) 695-2421	...	David Cota	Roxanne Lizotte	...	Michael Drinkwater	Duane Alexander	...
Guilford	t	TM	1	(207) 876-2202	William Thompson	Robert Littlefield	Joyce Burton	...	...	...	...
Hallowell	c	CM	2	(207) 623-4021	Barry Timson	James Rhodes	Deanna Hallett	...	Michael Grant	Eric Nason	Robert Rayot
Hampden	t	CM	6	(207) 862-3034	Ricky Briggs	Susan Lessard	Denise Hodsdon	Virgil Pratt	...	...	Greg Nash
Harpswell	t	TM	5	(207) 833-5771	Robert Webber	...	Laverne Vayo	...	William Beazley	...	Roland Berry
Hartland	t	TM	1	(207) 938-4401	...	...	...	...	...	...	...
Haynesville	t	TM	..	(207) 448-2090	...	Norma Malone	...	...	Steven Rouse	...	...
Hermon	t	CM	4	(207) 848-3485	...	Clinton Deschene	Carol Davis	...	Larry Willis	William Laughlin	...
Hodgdon	t	CM	1	(207) 532-6498	...	James Griffin	Cheryl Cameron	...	Dana Belyea	...	Roger Hutchinson
Holden	t	CM	2	(207) 843-5151	...	R. Varisco	Wanda Libbey	Deborah Given	...	Gene Worcester	Bruce Dowling
Hollis *	t	TM	4	(207) 929-8552	...	...	Claire Dunne	...	H. Carpenter	...	Robert Hanson
Houlton	t	CM	6	(207) 532-7111	Dale Flewelling	Margaret Daigle	Cathy O'Leary	...	Milton Cone	Daniel Soucy	Leigh Stilwell
Island Falls	t	TM	..	(207) 463-2246	Dwayne Hartin	Albert Clukey	Sandra Lane	...	Lewis Conrad	...	Cecil Given
Islesboro	t	TM	..	(207) 734-2253	...	...	...	...	...	...	...
Jackman	t	TM	..	(207) 668-2111	...	K. MacKenzie	Diane St. Hilaire	...	William Jarvis	...	...
Jay	t	TM	4	(207) 897-6785	William Harlow	Ruth Marden	Jill Gingras	Linda Brundage	Scott Shink	Larry White	John Johnson
Kennebunk	t	TM	10	(207) 985-2102	Boyd Long	Barry Tibbetts	Betty Emmons	...	Stephen Nichols	Matthew Baker	Michael Claus
Kennebunkport *	t	TM	3	(207) 967-4243	Mathew Lanagan	Larry Mead	April Dufoe	...	...	Joseph Bruni	John Hirst
Kittery *	t	CM	9	(207) 439-0452	Glenn Shwaery	Jonathan Carter	Maryann Place	...	David O'Brien	Edward Strong	Richard Rossiter
Lebanon	t	TM	5	(207) 457-1171	...	...	...	...	...	...	...
Levant	t	MC	2	(207) 884-7660	...	...	Amy Eaton	...	...	...	...
Lewiston *	c	CM	35	(207) 513-3000	Laurent Gilbert	James Bennett	Kathleen Montejo	Richard Metivier	Paul LeClair	William Welch	Paul Boudreau
Limestone	t	TM	2	(207) 325-4704	Steve Leighton	Paul Beaulieu	Marlene Durepo	...	Paul Durepo	Ronald Sprague	Dale Brooker
Lincoln	t	CM	5	(207) 794-3372	Roderick Carr	Glenn Aho	Lisa Goodwin	...	William Lee	...	David Lloyd
Lincolnville	t	TM	2	(207) 763-3555	David Kinney	...	...	Jodi Hanson	Michael Eugley	W. Labombarde	...
Linneus	t	CM	..	(207) 532-6182	...	Frances Hutchinson	...	...	Stephen Bither	...	...
Lisbon *	t	CM	9	(207) 353-3000	...	Stephen Eldridge	Twila Lycette	Rodney Moody	P. Galipeau	David Brooks	Elwood Beal
Litchfield	t	TM	3	(207) 268-4721	Elton Wade	Stephen Musica	Elaine McFee	...	Stanley Labbe	...	...
Littleton	t	TM	..	(207) 538-9862	...	Jennifer Gogan	...	...	...	...	William Dunbar
Livermore Falls	t	CM	3	(207) 897-2016	William Demaray	Martin Puckett	Kristal Flagg	...	Kenneth Jones	Ernest Steward	Kent Mitchell
Lubec	t	CM	1	(207) 733-2341	Harold Jackson	...	Diana Wilson	...	...	...	...
Ludlow	t	CM	..	(207) 532-7743	...	...	...	...	...	...	...
Lyman	t	TM	3	(207) 499-2925	...	...	...	...	...	...	...
Machias *	t	CM	2	(207) 255-6621	...	...	Donna Dzierzynski	Meghan Dennison	Joey Dennison	Grady Dwelley	Michael Gooch
Madawaska	t	CM	4	(207) 728-6351	...	...	...	Linda Cyr	Norman Cyr	Ron Pelletier	Yves Lizotte
Madison	t	TM	4	(207) 696-3971	...	Norman Dean	Kathy Estes	...	Roger Lightbody	Barry Moores	Glen Mantor
Manchester	t	TM	2	(207) 622-1894	Terri Watson	...	Marilyn Palmer	...	Allan Hewey	...	...
Mapleton	t	TM	1	(207) 764-3754	...	...	...	...	...	...	...
Mars Hill	t	CM	1	(207) 425-3731	Penny Rideout	R. Mersereau	...	...	...	...	Wallace Boyd
Masardis	t	CM	..	(207) 435-2841	Vernon Craig	Julia Mac Donald	...	...	Nelson Craig	...	Clive Bragdon
Mechanic Falls *	t	CM	3	(207) 345-2871	Dan Blanchard	...	...	Lisa Prevost	Fred Sturtevant	Jeffrey Goss	Scott Penney
Merrill	t	CM	..	(207) 757-8286	...	...	...	...	...	...	...
Mexico	t	TM	2	(207) 364-7971	Barbara Laramee	John Madigan	Penny Duguay	...	Gary Wentzell	James Theriault	David Errington
Milbridge	t	TM	1	(207) 546-2422	Gary Willey	...	Brienne Fraser	...	Peter Sawyer	Lewis Pinkham	...
Milford *	t	CM	2	(207) 827-2072	John Costigan	Barbara Cox	Dawn Adams	...	Christopher Matson	...	...
Millinocket	t	CM	5	(207) 723-7000	...	Eugene Conlogue	Roxanne Johnson	...	Wayne Campbell	Carlton Jones	Dennis Cox
Milo	t	CM	2	(207) 943-2202	Charles Buzzell	Jane Jones	Barbara Crider	...	...	...	Glenn Ricker
Monmouth	t	TM	3	(207) 933-2206	...	Curtis Lunt	...	...	...	...	...
Monroe	t	TM	..	(207) 525-5515	Jackie Robbins	...	Lois Aitken	...	Keith Nealley	...	...
Monson	t	TM	..	(207) 997-3641	...	Jeanne Reed	Julie Anderson	...	Robert Wilson	...	...
Monticello *	t	TM	..	(207) 538-9500	Terrence Wade	...	...	...	Edwin Ellis	...	Andrew Lynds
Mount Desert	t	TM	2	(207) 276-5531	Richard Savage	Michael MacDonald	Kimberly Parady	Jean Bonville	Christopher Farley	John Doyle	Anthony Smith
Naples	t	CM	3	(207) 693-6364	...	Derik Goodine	Judy Whynot	...	...	...	...
New Canada	t	CM	..	(207) 834-4004	Frank Jalbert	Rodney Pelletier	...	...	...	...	...
New Gloucester	t	CM	4	(207) 926-4126	Steven Libby	Rosemary Kulow	...	...	Gary Sacco	...	Kevin Doyle
New Portland	t	TM	..	(207) 628-4441	Peter Gardner	Andrea Reichert	Mary Hutchins	...	Jethro Poulin	...	...
Newcastle *	t	TM	1	(207) 563-3441	...	Sandra Blake	Lynn Maloney	...	Clayton Huntley	Mark Doe	Donald Hunt
Newport	t	TM	3	(207) 368-4410	Albert Worden	James Ricker	Paula Clark	...	...	Gary Morin	Jack Wilson
Norridgewock	t	TM	3	(207) 634-2252	Clyde Hendeson	John Doucette	Charlotte Gorman	...	David Jones	...	...
North Berwick	t	TM	4	(207) 676-3112	Gregg Drew	Dwayne Morin	Janet Belmain	...	James Moore	Randolph Jones	Michael Dunn
North Yarmouth	t	CM	3	(207) 829-3705	David Perkins	...	...	...	James Malorson	...	Donald Chaisson
Norway	t	TM	4	(207) 743-6651	...	David Holt	...	...	...	...	...
Oakfield	t	TM	..	(207) 757-8479	...	Dale Morris	...	...	...	...	...
Oakland	t	CM	5	(207) 465-7357	...	Steve Dyer	Janice Porter	Douglas Mather	Charles Pullen	Michael Tracy	Robert Laplante
Ogunquit	t	CM	..	(207) 646-5139	John Miller	...	J. Shaw-Kagiliery	...	Edward Smith	Patricia Arnaudin	Jonathan Webber
Old Orchard Beach *	t	CM	8	(207) 934-5714	...	...	Kim McLaughlin	Jill Eastman	John Glass	Dana Kelley	Mary Ann Conroy
Old Town	c	CM	8	(207) 827-3965	...	John Lord	Patricia Ramsey	Joseph Schlick	Charles Bruxh	Donald O'Halloran	David Wight
Orono	t	CM	9	(207) 866-2556	Geoffrey Gordon	Catherine Conlow	...	Annie Brown	Norman Webb	Gary Duquette	Calvin Smith
Orrington	t	CM	3	(207) 825-3340	Paul White	Dexter Johnson	Anita Demmons	...	Michael Spencer	Jon Carson	John Hodgins
Oxford	t	CM	3	(207) 539-4431	David Ivey	...	Elle Morrison	...	Ernest Knightly	Ronald Kugell	...
Paris *	t	TM	4	(207) 743-2501	...	Sharon Jackson	Elizabeth Larson	...	Bradley Frost	David Verrier	Frank Danforth
Patten	t	TM	1	(207) 528-2215	Carolyn Ryan	Paul Caruso	Lora Sleeper	...	...	...	...
Phillips	t	TM	..	(207) 639-3561	...	Laura Toothaker	...	...	...	...	Stephen Haines

Directory 1/9 continued **OFFICIALS IN U.S. MUNICIPALITIES 2,500 AND OVER IN POPULATION**

Jurisdiction		Type	Form of govern- ment	2000 Popu- lation (000)	Main telephone number	Chief elected official	Appointed administrator	Clerk of the governing board	Chief financial officer	Fire chief	Police chief	Public works director
MAINE continued												
Pittsfield		t	CM	4	(207) 487-3136	. . .	Kathryn Ruth	. . .	. . .	. . .	. . .	. . .
Plantation Of Reed	*	pl	CM	. .	(207) 456-7546	Ellen Mitchell	Mitch Lansky	Nyoka Irish	. . .	. . .	. . .	. . .
Poland		t	TM	4	(207) 998-4601	. . .	Richard Chick	Judith Akers	Debbie Taber	. . .	. . .	Jeffrey Chappell
Portage Lake		t	CM	. .	(207) 435-4361	Patrick Raymond	Rita Sinclair	Katherine Gagnon	. . .	David Bolsiridge	. . .	Vaughn Devoe
Portland		c	CM	64	(207) 874-8624	. . .	Joseph Gray	Linda Cohen	Duane Kline	F. Lamontagne	Michael Chitwood	Michael Bobinsky
Presque Isle		c	CM	9	(207) 764-2522	Donald Gardner	Thomas Stevens	Nancy Gervais	. . .	Darrell White	Naldo Gagnon	Gerry James
Rangeley		t	TM	1	(207) 864-3326	. . .	Perry Ellsworth	Kim Dolbier	. . .	Rudolph Davis	Phil Weymouth	Everett Quimby
Raymond		t	CM	4	(207) 655-4742	. . .	Donald Willard	Louise Lester	E. Cummings	Denis Morse	. . .	Nathan White
Readfield	*	t	CM	2	(207) 685-4939	Henry Clauson	Stefan Pakulski	Robin Lint	Teresa Shaw	Matthew Dunn	. . .	. . .
Richmond		t	CM	3	(207) 737-4305	David Thompson	David Peppard	Judy Savage	Laurie Boucher	Richard Emmons	Richard Heald	Richard Lachance
Rockland		c	CM	7	(207) 594-8431	Edward Mazurek	Thomas Hall	Stuart Sylvester	Robert Armelin	Raymond Wooster	Alfred Ockenfels	Greg Blackwell
Rockport	*	t	TM	3	(207) 236-0806	Robert Peabody	. . .	Linda Greenlaw	Virginia Lindsey	Bruce Woodward	Mark Kelley	Steve Beveridge
Rumford	*	t	CM	6	(207) 364-4576	Gregory Buccina	James Doar	Jane Gaisson	Debbie Laurinaitus	John Woulf	Stacy Carter	Eric Russell
Sabattus	*	t	MC	4	(207) 375-4331	William Henshaw	Gregory Gill	Suzanne Adams	. . .	. . .	Thomas Fales	John Hyde
Saco	*	c	CM	16	(207) 282-4191	Mark Johnston	Richard Michaud	Lucette Pellerin	Lisa Parker	Alden Murphy	Bradley Paul	Michael Bolduc
Sanford		t	RT	20	(207) 324-9100	Herbert Stone	Mark Green	Claire Morrison	Ronni Champlin	Raymond Parent	Thomas Jones	Richard Wilkins
Sangerville		t	TM	1	(207) 876-2814	Richard Pellerin	. . .	Alice Moulton	. . .	Jerry Rush	. . .	Ron Hall
Scarborough		t	CM	16	(207) 730-4031	Jeffery Messer	Ronald Owens	Yolanda Norton	Ruth Porter	B Michael Thurlow	Robert Moulton	Michael Shaw
Searsport		t	CM	2	(207) 548-6372	Bruce Mills	James Gillway	Marie Dakin	. . .	Derek Dunbar	. . .	Robert Seekins
Sebago	*	t	CM	1	(207) 787-2457	Ruth Douglas	Robert Nicholson	M. Bukoveckas	. . .	. . .	. . .	Theodore Shane
Sherman		t	TM	. .	(207) 365-4260	Robert Gould	Debra O'Roak	. . .	. . .	Harold Lane	. . .	. . .
Skowhegan		t	TM	8	(207) 474-6900	Lynda Quinn	Philip Tarr	Rhonda Stark	. . .	Stephen Miller	Butch Asselin	Gregory Dore
Smyrna		t	CM	. .	(207) 757-8286	. . .	. . .	. . .	. . .	. . .	. . .	. . .
South Berwick		t	CM	6	(207) 384-3300	David Webster	Jeffrey Grossman	Barbara Bennett	Fern Houliares	George Gorman	Dana Lajoie	Terry Oliver
South Portland		c	CM	23	(207) 767-3201	. . .	James Gailey	Susan Mooney	Robert Coombs	Kevin Guimond	. . .	Steven Johnson
Southwest Harbor	*	t	TM	1	(207) 244-5404	Trudy Bickford	Robin Bennett	Beatrice Grinnell	. . .	Sam Chisolm	David Chapais	Doug Monson
St. Agatha		t	TM	. .	(207) 543-7305	Dan LaBrie	Ryan Pelletier	Joan Ouellette	. . .	. . .	. . .	R. Chamberlain
St. Albans		t	CM	1	(207) 938-4568	Harlan Cooper	Larry Post	Stacey Desrosiers	. . .	Fred Cooper	. . .	Ronnie Finson
Stacyville		t	TM	. .	(207) 365-4195	. . .	. . .	. . .	. . .	. . .	. . .	. . .
Standish		t	CM	9	(207) 642-3461	. . .	Gordon Billington	Mary Chapman	Brenda Smith	Craig Butkus	. . .	Roger Mosley
Stockholm	*	t	TM	. .	(207) 896-5659	Gregory Landeen	. . .	. . .	. . .	Jeffrey Page	. . .	. . .
Stockton Springs		t	TM	1	(207) 567-3404	. . .	. . .	. . .	. . .	. . .	. . .	. . .
Stonington		t	CM	1	(207) 367-2351	James Bray	. . .	Lisa Gray	. . .	Adelbert Gross	. . .	Darran Eaton
Surry		t	TM	1	(207) 667-5912	Wilbur Saunders	. . .	. . .	. . .	Corey Esposito	. . .	. . .
Thomaston		t	CM	3	(207) 354-6107	Lee Upham	Valmore Blastow	Joan Linscott	. . .	Malcolm Hyler	James Hosford	David Taylor
Topsham	*	t	TM	9	(207) 725-5821	Donald Russell	. . .	Ruth Lyons	Debra Fischer	Ken Brillant	Tim Young	Welsey Thames
Tremont		t	CM	1	(207) 244-7204	Scott Grierson	. . .	McKenzie Clough	. . .	Brad Reed	William Clark	Jimmy Schlaefer
Turner	*	t	TM	4	(207) 225-3414	. . .	Eva Leavitt	. . .	. . .	. . .	. . .	. . .
Van Buren		t	CM	2	(207) 868-2886	Donald Dumond	Larry Cote	Kathleen Cyr	. . .	Ken Dumond	Jean Michaud	Robert Learnard
Vassalboro		t	TM	4	(207) 872-2826	. . .	Michael Vashon	Catherine St. Pierre	. . .	Eric Rowe	Richard Phippen	Eugene Field
Veazie		t	CM	1	(207) 947-2781	Joseph Friedman	William Reed	Beckie Woods	. . .	. . .	Mark Leonard	George Free
Vinalhaven		t	CM	1	(207) 863-4471	. . .	Marjorie Stratton	. . .	. . .	. . .	. . .	. . .
Waldoboro		t	TM	4	(207) 832-5369	Carleton Johnson	Lee Smith	Linda Perry	Eileen Dondlinger	Robert Maxey	Leroy Jones	John Daigle
Wallagrass		t	CM	. .	(207) 834-2263	James Gagnon	Bonnie Lamarre	. . .	. . .	. . .	. . .	. . .
Warren		t	CM	3	(207) 273-2421	E. La Flamme	Grant Wathough	Marsha Soule	. . .	Edward Grinnell	. . .	Marvin Lewis
Washburn		t	CM	1	(207) 455-8485	Rick Corey	Andrea Powers	Elizabeth Carter	. . .	Daryl Sperry	Dwight Wilcox	Harold Easley
Waterboro		t	TM	6	(207) 247-6166	Brenda Charland	. . .	Nancy Brandt	. . .	. . .	Steve Foglio	Fred Fay
Waterville		c	MC	15	(207) 873-7131	Nelson Madore	. . .	Patti Dubois	Clara Varney	Raymond Poulin	John Morris	Gregory Brown
Wells	*	t	TM	9	(207) 646-5113	Richard Clark	Jane Duncan	Jessica Keyes	. . .	Daniel Moore	Richard Connelly	. . .
West Bath		t	CM	1	(207) 443-4342	David Bourget	Pamela Hile	Susan Look	. . .	Michael Demers	. . .	James Whorff
Westbrook		c	MC	16	(207) 854-9105	Donald Esty	Jerre Bryant	. . .	Susan Rossignol	Gary Littlefield	. . .	Paul Boudreau
Wilton		t	CM	4	(207) 645-4961	Rodney Hall	Peter Nielsen	Linda Jellison	. . .	Frederick Hyde	James Parker	Kenneth Vining
Windham	*	t	CM	14	(207) 892-1907	John Mackinnon	Anthony Plante	Linda Morrell	Brian Wolcott	Charles Hammond	Richard Lewsen	Douglas Fortier
Winslow		t	CM	7	(207) 872-2776	Howard Mette	Michael Heavener	Pamela Smiley	. . .	William Page	Richard Grindall	John Girioux
Winter Harbor		t	TM	. .	(207) 963-2235	. . .	Roger Barto	Marianne Ray	. . .	Robert Webber	Warren Ahrens	. . .
Winterport		t	CM	3	(207) 223-5055	. . .	Leo La Chance	Kathy Selfridge	. . .	. . .	. . .	. . .
Winthrop	*	t	CM	6	(207) 377-7200	Patrice Putman	Cornell Knight	Lisa Gilliam	Jan Tewksbury	Dan Brooks	Joseph Young	Matt Burnham
Wiscasset	*	t	TM	3	(207) 882-8200	Duane Goud	Arthur Faucher	Sandra Johnson	. . .	Tim Merry	John Allen	Robert Blagden
Yarmouth		t	CM	8	(207) 846-9036	. . .	Nathaniel Tupper	Jennifer Doten	Maura Haliotis	Byron Fairbanks	Michael Morrill	Erik Street
York		t	CM	12	(207) 363-1000	David Marshall	Robert Yandow	M. A. Szenlawski	Elizabeth McCann	C. Balentine	Douglas Bracy	William Bray
MARYLAND												
Aberdeen		t	CM	13	(410) 272-1600	S. Simmons	Douglas Miller	. . .	Opiribo Jack	. . .	Randall Rudy	Matt Lapinsky
Accident		t	MC	. .	(301) 746-6346	. . .	Ruth Ann Hahn	. . .	. . .	. . .	. . .	. . .
Annapolis		c	MC	35	(410) 263-7998	Ellen Moyer	Robert Agee	Deborah Heinbuch	Timothy Elliott	Edward Sherlock	Joseph Johnson	Margaret Martin
Baltimore		c	MC	651	(410) 396-3100	Martin O'Malley	. . .	. . .	Edward Gallagher	Herman Williams	Robert Smith	. . .
Bel Air		t	CM	10	(410) 638-4550	David Carey	Christopher Schlehr	. . .	. . .	. . .	Leo Matrangola	. . .
Berlin	*	t	MC	3	(410) 641-2770	Thomas Cardinale	Linda Bambary	. . .	Joseph Davis	. . .	Arnold Downing	. . .
Berwyn Heights		t	MC	2	(301) 474-5000	Cheye Calvo	Edward Murphy	Kerstin Harper	. . .	. . .	Patrick Murphy	Joseph Coleman
Bladensburg		t	MC	7	(301) 927-7048	David Harrington	Doris Sarumi	. . .	. . .	. . .	Robert Zidek	Larry Goff
Bowie		c	CM	50	(301) 262-6200	George Robinson	David Deutsch	Pamela Fleming	Robert Patrick	. . .	. . .	Richard Henrikson
Brentwood		t	MC	2	(301) 927-3344	George Denny	Peter Jones	Linda Grigsby	. . .	. . .	. . .	. . .
Brunswick		t	MC	4	(301) 834-7500	Carroll Jones	David Dunn	. . .	. . .	. . .	Don Rough	Kevin Brawner
Cambridge	*	c	MC	10	(410) 228-4020	Cleveland Rippons	. . .	Edwin Kinnamon	. . .	Jeff Hurley	Kenneth Malik	Steven Johnson
Capitol Heights		t	CM	4	(301) 336-0626	Vivian Dodson	James Booth	. . .	. . .	. . .	William Harrison	. . .
Cecilton		t	MC	. .	(410) 275-2692	. . .	Shelley McDonald	Brenda Cochran	. . .	. . .	. . .	. . .
Centreville		t	CM	1	(410) 758-1180	Mary McCarthy	Robert McGrory	. . .	. . .	. . .	Dino Pignataro	. . .
Chesapeake City		t	MC	. .	(410) 885-2598	. . .	. . .	. . .	. . .	. . .	. . .	. . .
Chestertown		t	MC	4	(410) 778-0500	Margo Bailey	W. Ingersoll	. . .	. . .	. . .	Walter Coryell	Medford Capel
Cheverly	*	t	CM	6	(301) 773-8360	Julia Mosley	David Warrington	Christy Clark	. . .	. . .	Harry Robshaw	Juan Torres
Chevy Chase	*	t	CM	2	(301) 654-7144	. . .	Todd Hoffman	Andrea Silverstone	. . .	. . .	. . .	Larry Plummer
Chevy Chase		v	CM	2	(301) 654-7300	George Kinter	Geoffrey Biddle	. . .	Jacqueline Parker	. . .	Roy Gordon	Jerry Lesesne
College Park	*	c	CM	24	(301) 864-8666	Stephen Brayman	Joseph Nagro	Janeen Miller	Stephen Groh	. . .	. . .	Robert Stumpff
Crisfield		c	MC	2	(410) 968-1333	Donald Gerald	. . .	. . .	. . .	. . .	. . .	. . .
Cumberland		c	CM	21	(301) 722-2000	Lee Fiedler	Jeffrey Repp	Sharon Clark	Joseph Urban	William Herbaugh	Charles Hinnant	Kevin Hagerich
Delmar		t	CM	1	(410) 896-2777	Paul Niblett	Sara Bynum-King	Jessica Barnes	Wendy Brady	. . .	Harold Saylor	Robert Handy
Denton		t	MC	2	(410) 479-2050	. . .	Terry Fearins	. . .	. . .	. . .	Rodney Cox	Scott Getchell
District Heights		t	MC	5	(301) 336-1402	Jack Sims	Tamil Perry-Lloyd	Tamil Perry	. . .	. . .	Herbert Keeney	Brian Edwards
Easton		t	MC	11	(410) 822-2525	C. Butler	. . .	Robert Karge	. . .	. . .	Walter Chase	John Larrimore
Edmonston		t	MC	. .	(301) 699-8806	. . .	Guy Tiberio	. . .	. . .	. . .	. . .	. . .
Elkton		t	CM	11	(410) 398-0970	Joseph Fisona	Lewis George	. . .	. . .	. . .	William Ryan	Joseph Enrico
Emmitsburg		t	CM	2	(301) 447-2313	. . .	David Haller	Donna DesPres	. . .	. . .	. . .	. . .

Directory 1/9 continued — OFFICIALS IN U.S. MUNICIPALITIES 2,500 AND OVER IN POPULATION

Jurisdiction	Type	Form of government	2000 Population (000)	Main telephone number	Chief elected official	Appointed administrator	Clerk of the governing board	Chief financial officer	Fire chief	Police chief	Public works director
MARYLAND continued											
Fairmount Heights	t	MC	1	(301) 925-8585	L. Thompson-Martin	Jose Gonzalez	Alva Fields	. . .	. . .	David Rice	Carlton Whittingham
Forest Heights	t	MC	2	(301) 839-1030	Paula Noble	Cynthia Farrar	Bonita Anderson	. . .	. . .	Bernard Sewell	William Clarke
Frederick	c	MC	52	(301) 694-1440	. . .	Janel Flora	. . .	Gerald Kolbfleisch	. . .	R. Raffensberger	Fred Eisenhart
Friendship Heights	v	MC	8	(301) 650-2797	Alfred Muller	Julian Mansfield	. . .	. . .	. . .	. . .	. . .
Frostburg	c	CO	7	(301) 689-6000	James Cotton	. . .	. . .	Candace Sandvick	. . .	William Evans	C. Hovatter
Fruitland	c	CM	3	(410) 548-2800	Valerie Mann	John McDonnell	. . .	Amy Caton	Robin Townsend	Paul Jackson	P. Townsend
Gaithersburg	c	CM	52	(301) 258-6310	Sidney Katz	. . .	. . .	Harold Belton	. . .	Mary Viverette	James Arnoult
Galena	t	MC	. .	(410) 648-5151	. . .	Thomas Bass	. . .	. . .	. . .	. . .	. . .
Garrett Park	t	MC	. .	(301) 933-7488	. . .	Edwin Pratt	. . .	. . .	. . .	. . .	. . .
Glenarden	t	CM	6	(301) 773-2100	Donjuan Williams	Kimberly O'Neil	Brenda Leake	. . .	. . .	William Reese	Darvin Arnold
Greenbelt	c	CM	21	(301) 474-8000	Judith Davis	M. McLaughlin	Kathleen Gallagher	. . .	. . .	. . .	Kenneth Hall
Greensboro	t	CM	1	(410) 482-6222	. . .	David Kibler	Jeannette DeLude	. . .	. . .	. . .	. . .
Hagerstown	c	CM	36	(301) 790-3200	William Breichner	Bruce Zimmerman	Donna Spickler	Alfred Martin	Gary Hawbaker	Arthur Smith	Eric Deike
Hampstead	t	MC	5	(410) 239-7408	Haven Shoemaker	Kenneth Decker	Patricia Warner	. . .	. . .	R. Meekins	Roger Steger
Havre De Grace	c	MC	11	(410) 939-1800	David Craig	. . .	. . .	. . .	. . .	Randall Holt	Arthur Doty
Highland Beach	t	CO	. .	(410) 268-2956	Raymond Langston	Crystal Chissell	Patricia Butler	Craig Herndon	. . .	. . .	Geneza Hudson
Hyattsville	c	MC	14	(301) 985-5000	William Gardiner	Elaine Murphy	Douglas Barber	. . .	. . .	. . .	Margaret Mallino
Indian Head	t	CM	3	(301) 743-5511	Warren Bowie	Ryan Hicks	. . .	Dorothy Smith	. . .	. . .	James Chase
Kensington	t	MC	1	(301) 949-2424	. . .	Patricia McAuley	. . .	. . .	. . .	. . .	. . .
Kitzmiller	t	MC	. .	(301) 453-3449	. . .	. . .	Diane Paugh	. . .	. . .	. . .	. . .
La Plata	t	CM	6	(301) 870-3377	Gene Ambrogio	Daniel Mears	Judith Frazier	Joseph Norris	. . .	Cassin Gittins	Steve Murphy
Landover Hills	t	MC	1	(301) 773-6401	Lee Walker	Kathleen Tavel	Juanita Hood	. . .	. . .	Henry Norris	. . .
Laurel	c	MC	19	(301) 725-5300	Craig Moe	Kristie Mills	Kimberley Rau	Sandra Saylor	. . .	David Moore	Teddy Dulaney
Laytonsville	t	MC	. .	(301) 869-0042	Willard Oland	Dan Prats	Cathern Buit	. . .	. . .	. . .	. . .
Leonardtown	t	MC	1	(301) 475-9791	J. Norris	Laschelle Miller	Teri Dimsey	. . .	. . .	. . .	John Johnson
Manchester	t	MC	3	(410) 239-3200	. . .	Steve Miller	. . .	. . .	. . .	. . .	. . .
Middletown	t	CM	2	(301) 371-6171	. . .	Andrew Bowden	. . .	. . .	. . .	. . .	. . .
Mount Airy	t	MC	6	(301) 831-5768	James Holt	Monika Weierbach	Barbara Jean Dixon	. . .	. . .	. . .	. . .
Mount Rainier	c	MC	8	(301) 985-6585	Bryan Knedler	Jeannelle Wallace	. . .	. . .	. . .	Michael Scott	Edward Gabay
Mountain Lake Park *	t	MC	2	(301) 334-2250	Britten Martin	Richard Haynes	Judy Paugh	. . .	. . .	. . .	. . .
New Carrollton	c	MC	12	(301) 459-6100	Andrew Hanko	J. Michael Downes	Regina Robinson	Sharia Abraham	. . .	David Rice	Richard Robbins
New Windsor *	t	MC	1	(410) 635-6575	Sam Pierce	Lanny Mummert	Donna Alburn	. . .	. . .	. . .	. . .
North Chevy Chase	v	CM	. .	(301) 654-7084	. . .	Robert Weesner	. . .	. . .	. . .	. . .	. . .
North East *	t	MC	2	(410) 287-5801	Robert McKnight	M. Cook-Mackenzie	Anne Barker	. . .	. . .	Darrell Hamilton	Phillip Meekins
Ocean City	t	CM	7	(410) 289-8822	Richard Meehan	Dennis Dare	Carol Jacobs	Martha Bennett	Samuel Villani	Bernadette DiPino	Hal Adkins
Perryville *	t	MC	3	(410) 642-6066	James Eberhardt	Thomas Morsicato	Jackie Sample	. . .	Lloyd Beard	Chris Daly	Michael Caldwell
Pocomoke City	c	CM	4	(410) 957-1333	. . .	Russell Blake	. . .	. . .	. . .	. . .	. . .
Poolesville	t	CO	5	(301) 428-8927	. . .	D. Yost	. . .	. . .	. . .	. . .	. . .
Port Deposit	t	MC	. .	(410) 378-2121	Charles Flayhart	Sharon Weygand	. . .	. . .	Greg Miller	Marc Tomlin	Robert Rouselle
Princess Anne	t	CM	2	(410) 651-1818	. . .	John O'Meara	. . .	Brenda Benton	. . .	Russell Pecoraro	. . .
Ridgely	t	CO	1	(410) 634-2177	L. Epperly-Glover	Joseph Mangini	. . .	. . .	. . .	Merlin Evans	Robin Eaton
Rising Sun	t	CO	1	(410) 658-5353	Judith Cox	. . .	Sandra Didra	. . .	. . .	Al Michael	. . .
Riverdale Park	t	MC	5	(301) 927-6381	. . .	Patrick Prangley	. . .	. . .	. . .	. . .	. . .
Rock Hall	t	CM	1	(410) 639-7611	. . .	Ronald Fifhian	. . .	. . .	. . .	. . .	. . .
Rockville	c	CM	47	(240) 314-8470	Larry Giammo	Scott Ullery	Claire Funkhouser	Donna Boxer	. . .	Terrance Treschuk	Eugene Cranor
Salisbury *	c	MC	23	(410) 548-3100	Barrie Tilghman	John Pick	Brenda Colegrove	. . .	David See	Allan Webster	James Caldwell
Seat Pleasant	c	CM	4	(301) 336-2600	Eugene Kennedy	. . .	Sandra Yates	. . .	David McGill	Elliott Taylor	. . .
Sharpsburg	t	MC	. .	(301) 432-4428	Sidney Gale	. . .	. . .	. . .	. . .	. . .	. . .
Snow Hill	t	CM	2	(410) 632-2080	Stephen Mathews	Albert Cohen	Shirley Goodman	Jo Pruitt	. . .	Maurice Ames	James Doughty
St. Michaels	t	MC	1	(410) 745-9535	A. Dinkel	Cheril Thomas	. . .	. . .	. . .	. . .	. . .
Sudlersville	t	MC	. .	(410) 438-3465	William Faust	. . .	. . .	. . .	. . .	. . .	. . .
Sykesville	t	CM	4	(410) 795-8959	. . .	Matthew Candland	. . .	. . .	. . .	. . .	. . .
Takoma Park	c	CM	17	(301) 891-7100	Kathy Porter	Barbara Matthews	Jessie Carpenter	. . .	. . .	Edward Coursey	Daryl Braithwaite
Taneytown	c	CM	5	(410) 751-1100	Henry Heine	J. Schumacher	Linda Hess	. . .	. . .	Gregory Woelfel	Gary Hardman
Thurmont	t	MC	5	(301) 271-7313	Martin Burns	. . .	. . .	Richard May	. . .	. . .	. . .
University Park	t	MC	2	(301) 927-4262	John Brunner	. . .	Amy Headley	. . .	. . .	Michael Wynnyk	L. Bloomfield
Upper Marlboro	t	MC	. .	(301) 627-6905	Julian Tucker	Daithi Htun	Tracy Smith	. . .	. . .	Michael Gonnella	. . .
Walkersville	t	CM	5	(301) 845-4500	. . .	Gloria Rollins	. . .	. . .	. . .	. . .	Dennis Miller
Westernport	t	MC	2	(301) 359-3932	Donald Smith	. . .	Renee Morris	. . .	Timothy Dayton	. . .	. . .
Westminster	c	MC	16	(410) 848-9000	Kevin Dayhoff	. . .	Laurell Taylor	. . .	. . .	. . .	. . .
MASSACHUSETTS											
Abington	t	TM	14	(781) 982-2112	John Henderson	. . .	Patricia McKenna	Patricia Majenski	Malcolm Whiting	Richard Franey	Richard Burns
Acton	t	TM	20	(978) 264-9603	Walter Foster	Steven Ledoux	Edward Ellis	Stephen Barrett	Robert Craig	Francis Widmayer	. . .
Acushnet	t	TM	10	(508) 998-0200	. . .	Alan Coutinho	Richard Threlfall	Cathy Doane	Paul Cote	Michael Poitras	Richard Settele
Adams	t	RT	8	(413) 743-8300	. . .	William Ketcham	Paul Hutchinson	Mary Beverly	. . .	Donald Poirot	Thomas Satko
Agawam	t	CM	28	(413) 786-0400	Richard Cohen	. . .	Richard Theroux	Carol Taylor	David Pisano	Robert Campbell	John Stone
Amesbury	t	RT	16	(978) 388-8100	David Hildt	. . .	Bonnie Kitchin	Michael Basque	William Shute	Michael Cronin	Brian Gilbert
Amherst	t	RT	34	(413) 256-4004	Carl Seppala	Laurence Shaffer	Anna Maciaszek	Nancy Maglione	Keith Hoyle	Charles Scherpa	Guilford Mooring
Andover	t	CM	31	(978) 623-8200	. . .	R. Stapczynski	Randall Hansen	Anthony Torrisi	Charles Murnane	Brian Pattullo	John Petkus
Arlington	t	CM	42	(781) 316-3121	John Hurd	Brian Sullivan	Corinne Rainville	. . .	Allan McEwen	Frederick Ryan	John Sanchez
Ashburnham	t	TM	5	(978) 827-4104	Ronald Reed	Kevin Paicos	. . .	. . .	Paul Zbikowski	Roy Bourque	Stephen Neal
Ashland	t	CM	14	(508) 881-0100	Richard Desmarais	John Petrin	Anges Kelemen	. . .	William Kee	Roy Melnick	James Lefter
Athol	t	RT	11	(978) 249-2368	. . .	David Ames	Nancy Burnham	. . .	James Wright	Timothy Anderson	Doug Walsh
Attleboro	c	MC	42	(508) 223-2222	. . .	. . .	. . .	. . .	. . .	. . .	. . .
Auburn	t	RT	15	(508) 832-7721	David Briggs	. . .	Elizabeth Prouty	Edward Kazanovicz	Roger Belhumeur	Ronald Miller	Glenn Mitchell
Avon	t	TM	4	(508) 588-0414	Deborah Jencunas	. . .	. . .	Debra Morin	. . .	Warren Phillips	. . .
Ayer	t	TM	7	(978) 772-8216	. . .	. . .	Ann Callahan	Lisa Gabree	Paul Fillebrown	Richard Rizzo	Michael Madigan
Barnstable *	t	CM	40	(508) 862-4610	Gary Blazis	John Klimm	Linda Hutchenrider	Mark Milne	. . .	John Finnegan	Mark Ells
Barre	t	TM	5	(978) 355-2504	Richard Stevens	Lorraine Leno	Ellen Glidden	Daniel Haynes	Joseph Rogowski	James Thompson	Stephen Mansfield
Bedford *	t	TM	12	(781) 275-1111	Sheldon Moll	Richard Reed	Doreen Tremblay	Peter Naum	Kevin MacCaffrie	James Hicks	Richard Warrington
Belchertown	t	TM	12	(413) 323-0403	David Fredenburgh	Gary Brougham	. . .	. . .	Edward Bock	Robert Knight	. . .
Bellingham	t	TM	15	(508) 966-0040	. . .	Denis Fraine	. . .	. . .	. . .	. . .	. . .
Belmont	t	RT	24	(617) 489-8213	W. Brownsberger	Thomas Younger	Delores Keefe	Barbara Hagg	William Osterhaus	Andrew O'Malley	Peter Castanino
Berkley	t	TM	5	(508) 822-3348	Carol Mills	. . .	. . .	. . .	Kevin Partridge	Harold Ashley	. . .
Beverly *	c	MC	39	(978) 921-6000	William Scanlon	. . .	Frances MacDonald	John Dunn	Richard Pierce	Mark Ray	Michael Colllins
Billerica	t	RT	38	(978) 671-0942	James O'Donnell	Rocco Longo	Shirley Schult	Paul Watson	Anthony Capaldo	Daniel Rosa	. . .
Blackstone *	t	TM	8	(508) 883-1500	. . .	Ken Bianchi	Marianne Staples	. . .	Michael Sweeney	Ross Atstupenas	Thomas Devlin
Bolton	t	TM	4	(978) 779-2297	. . .	Jodi Ross	. . .	. . .	. . .	. . .	. . .
Boston	c	MC	589	(617) 635-3370	Thomas Menino	Dennis DiMarzio	Rosaria Salerno	. . .	Paul Christian	Paul Evans	Joseph Casazza

Directory 1/9 continued OFFICIALS IN U.S. MUNICIPALITIES 2,500 AND OVER IN POPULATION

Jurisdiction	Type	Form of govern-ment	2000 Popu-lation (000)	Main telephone number	Chief elected official	Appointed administrator	Clerk of the governing board	Chief financial officer	Fire chief	Police chief	Public works director
MASSACHUSETTS continued											
Bourne *	t	TM	18	(508) 759-0600	Linda Zuern	Thomas Guerino	Barry Johnson	Linda Marzelli	David Kingsbury	Earl Baldwin	Rickie Tellier
Boxborough	t	TM	4	(978) 263-1116	Simon Bunyard	Selina Shaw	Virginia Richardson	. . .	Kevin Lyons	Richard Vance	Kenneth March
Boxford	t	TM	7	(978) 352-8021	Barbara Jessel	Alan Benson	Patricia Shields	. . .	Peter Perkins	Gordon Russell	David Durkee
Boylston	t	TM	4	(508) 869-2234	Frank Reale	Suzanne Olsen	Sandra Bourassa	Daniel Haynes	Roger Wentzell	Anthony Sahagian	Donald Parker
Braintree	t	RT	33	(781) 848-1870	. . .	. . .	Saran Gillies	. . .	Richard Hull	Paul Frazier	Robert Brangiforte
Brewster	t	TM	10	(508) 896-3701	John Mitchell	Charles Sumner	Joanna Krauss	Lisa Souve	Roy Jones	James Ehrhart	Allan Tkaczyk
Bridgewater	t	TM	25	(508) 697-0926	Allan Chiocca	David Canepa	Ronald Adams	. . .	Roderick Walsh	George Gurley	Joseph Souto
Brockton	c	MC	94	(508) 580-7123	. . .	. . .	. . .	. . .	. . .	. . .	. . .
Brookline	t	CM	57	(617) 730-2000	Joseph Geller	Richard Kelliher	Patrick Ward	Harvey Beth	John Spillane	Daniel O'Leary	A. De Maio
Buckland	t	CM	1	(413) 625-6330	James Budrewicz	Robert Dean	Janice Purington	. . .	. . .	. . .	Steven Daby
Burlington *	t	RT	22	(781) 270-1600	Al Fay	Robert Mercier	Jane Chew	Paul Sagarino	Lee Callahan	Francis Hart	John Sanchez
Cambridge	c	CM	101	(617) 349-4000	Michael Sullivan	Robert Healy	Margaret Drury	Louis DePasquale	Gerald Reardon	Ron Watson	Lisa Peterson
Canton	t	TM	20	(781) 821-5000	. . .	William Friel	. . .	James Murgia	Thomas Ronayne	Peter Bright	Michael Trott
Carlisle	t	TM	4	(978) 369-6155	John Ballantine	M. McKenzie	Charlene Hinton	. . .	David Flannery	David Galvin	Gary Davis
Carver *	t	TM	11	(508) 866-3400	John Angley	Richard Lafond	Jean McGillicuddy	. . .	Craig Weston	Arthur Parker	William Halunen
Charlton	t	TM	11	(508) 248-2200	Kathleen Walker	Robin Craver	Susan Nichols	. . .	Ralph Harris	James Pervier	. . .
Chatham	t	TM	6	(508) 945-5100	Reginald Nickerson	William Hinchey	Joanne Holdgate	Donald Poyant	W. Schwerdtfeger	Kevin Fitzgibbons	Gilbert Borthwick
Chelmsford	t	CM	33	(978) 250-5201	Michael McCall	. . .	Elizabeth Delaney	. . .	John Parow	R. McCusker	James Pearson
Chelsea	c	CM	35	(617) 889-8294	. . .	Jay Ash	Robert Bishop	. . .	Louis Addonizio	Rafael Hernandez	Ted Sobolewski
Cheshire	t	TM	3	(413) 743-2826	. . .	. . .	. . .	. . .	. . .	. . .	. . .
Chicopee	c	MC	54	(413) 594-1510	Richard Kos	Erwin Hurley	Nancy Mulvey	Sharyn Riley	Stephen Burkott	John Ferraro	Stanley Kulig
Clinton *	t	TM	13	(978) 365-4120	Robert Pasquale	Michael Ward	Philip Boyce	Diane Magliozzi	Richard Hart	Mark Laverdure	C. McGown
Cohasset	t	TM	7	(781) 383-4105	Roseanne McMorris	William Griffin	Marion Douglas	John Buckley	Roger Lincoln	Robert Jackson	Carl Sestito
Concord *	t	TM	16	(978) 318-3025	Margaret Briggs	Christopher Whelan	Anita Tekle	Anthony Logalbo	Kenneth Willette	L. Wetherbee	Richard Reine
Dalton	t	CM	6	(413) 684-6100	Timothy Kirby	Kenneth Walto	Barbara Suriner	Richard Charon	. . .	Daniel Filiault	James Galliher
Danvers	t	RT	25	(978) 777-0001	. . .	Wayne Marquis	. . .	. . .	James Tutko	Stuart Chase	Don Dehart
Dartmouth *	t	RT	30	(508) 910-1883	. . .	Michael Gagne	Eleanor White	Edward Iacaponi	. . .	Mark Pacheco	Manuel Branco
Dedham	t	RT	23	(781) 751-9100	M. Louise Kehoe	William Keegan	Geraldine Pacheco	Mariellen Murphy	James Driscoll	Dennis Teehan	Paul Keane
Deerfield *	t	RT	4	(413) 665-2130	John Paciorek	Bernard Kubiak	. . .	. . .	. . .	M. Wozniakewicz	Harold Eaton
Dennis	t	TM	15	(508) 394-8300	Cleon Turner	Robert Canevazzi	. . .	Janet Gibson	Paul Tucker	Michael Whalen	Dennis Hanson
Dighton	t	TM	6	(508) 669-6431	Gene Nelson	. . .	. . .	Janice Boucher	Jeffrey Allie	Robert MacDonald	Paul DeMoura
Douglas	t	TM	7	(508) 476-4000	Shirley Mosczynski	Michael Guzinski	Christine Furno	Richard Mathieu	Donald Gonynor	Patrick Foley	. . .
Dover	t	TM	5	(508) 785-0032	Tobe Deutschmann	David Ramsay	Barrie Clough	. . .	John Hughes	Joseph Griffin	Craig Hughes
Dracut *	t	TM	28	(978) 452-1227	John Zimini	Dennis Piendak	Kathleen Graham	. . .	Leo Gaudette	Kevin Richardson	Michael Buxton
Dudley *	t	TM	10	(508) 949-8000	Paul Joseph	Peter Jankowski	Ora Finn	. . .	Jeffrey Phelps	Steven Wojnar	. . .
Duxbury	t	CM	14	(781) 934-1100	. . .	Richard MacDonald	Nancy Oates	. . .	Kevin Nord	Mark De Luca	Tom Daley
East Bridgewater	t	TM	12	(508) 378-1600	Eric Greene	George Samia	M. Weidenfeller	Frank Savino	Ryon Pratt	John Silva	. . .
East Longmeadow	t	TM	14	(413) 525-5400	. . .	. . .	Thomas Florence	Sandra Choquette	Preston Wallace	Walter Niznik	David Gromaski
Eastham	t	TM	5	(508) 240-5900	Linda Burt	Sheila Vanderhoef	Lillian Lamperti	Jane Wall	Glenn Olson	Richard Hedlund	Stephen Douglas
Easthampton *	t	RT	15	(413) 529-1466	Michael Tautznik	. . .	B. LaBombard	. . .	Kevin Croake	Bruce McMahon	Joseph Pipczynski
Easton	t	TM	22	(508) 230-0500	Colleen Corona	David Colton	Janet Linehan	Wendy Nightingale	Thomas Stone	Thomas Kominsky	Wayne Southworth
Essex	t	TM	3	(978) 768-6531	Rolf Madsen	Brendhan Zubricki	Sally Soucy	Brian Dagle	Richard Carter	David Harrell	Bruce Julian
Everett	c	MC	38	(617) 389-2100	David Raqucci	. . .	John Hanlon	Donald Andrew	David Butler	James Rogers	David Ravanesi
Fairhaven	t	RT	16	(508) 979-4026	Jeffrey Osuch	. . .	Eilleen Lowney	. . .	Timothy Francis	Gary Souza	Robert Carey
Fall River	c	MC	91	(508) 324-2000	Edward Lambert	. . .	Carol Valcourt	Douglas Fiore	Edward Dawson	John Souza	Terrance Sullivan
Falmouth	t	RT	32	(508) 495-7332	Kevin Murphy	Robert Whritenour	Michael Palmer	. . .	Paul Brodeur	David Cusolito	. . .
Fitchburg	c	MC	39	(978) 345-9556	Dan Mylott	Robert Pontbraind	Anna Farrell	Richard Sarasin	Kevin Roy	Edward Cronin	Denis Meunier
Foxborough	t	TM	16	(508) 543-1200	A. LaChapelle	Andrew Gala	Arlene Crimmins	Randy Scollins	Robert Gaulin	Edward O'Leary	Robert Swanson
Framingham	t	RT	66	(508) 620-4847	Charles Sisitsky	Julian Suso	Darcy Hawes	. . .	Michael Smith	Steven Carl	James Pianka
Franklin	t	CM	22	(508) 553-4810	. . .	Jeffrey Nutting	Deborah Pellegri	Susan Gagner	Gary McCarraher	Stephen Williams	William Fitzgerald
Freetown	t	TM	8	(508) 644-2204	John Ashley	Linda Remedis	Jacqueline Brown	. . .	Wayne Haskins	Carlton Abbott	Joseph Simmons
Gardner	c	MC	20	(978) 632-1900	Gerald St. Hilaire	. . .	Kathleen Lesneski	Calvin Brooks	Ronald Therrien	Neil Erickson	Dane Arnold
Georgetown *	t	TM	7	(978) 352-5755	Matthew Vincent	Stephen Delaney	Janice McGrane	. . .	Michael Anderson	James Mulligan	Peter Durkee
Gloucester	c	MC	30	(978) 281-9700	John Bell	James McKenna	Robert Whynott	. . .	Barry McKay	James Marr	Joseph Parisi
Grafton *	t	TM	14	(508) 839-5335	Craig Dauphinais	Natalie Lashmit	Maureen Clark	. . .	Michael Gauthier	Normand Crepeau	Roger Hammond
Granby	t	TM	6	(413) 467-7177	Patrick Curran	Christopher Martin	K. Kelly-Regan	. . .	Russell Anderson	. . .	David Desrosiers
Great Barrington	t	MC	7	(413) 528-1619	Edward Morehouse	Burke LaClair	Maryellen Siok	. . .	Michael Ordyna	William Walsh	Donald Chester
Greenfield	t	RT	18	(413) 772-1577	Christine Forgey	. . .	Maureen Winsick	Michael Kociela	Mark Cogswell	David Guilbault	John Bean
Groton	t	TM	9	(978) 448-9818	. . .	. . .	. . .	. . .	. . .	. . .	. . .
Groveland	t	TM	6	(978) 374-0470	William Dorke	N.Lewandowski	Richard Sciacca	Thomas Moses	John Clement	William Sargent	Robert Arakelian
Hadley	t	TM	4	(413) 586-0221	. . .	. . .	Joanna Devine	. . .	. . .	. . .	. . .
Halifax	t	TM	7	(781) 294-1316	Troy Garron	Charles Seelig	Marcia Cole	John Stanbrook	Lance Benjamino	Michael Manoogian	Ralph Hayward
Hamilton	t	TM	8	(978) 468-5572	. . .	Candace Wheeler	Jane Wetson	. . .	Philip Stevens	Walter Cullen	Steven Kenney
Hampden	t	TM	5	(413) 566-2151	Mark Casey	Pamela Courtney	Eva Wiseman	Clifford Bombard	Peter Hatch	Scott Trombly	Dana Pixley
Hanover	t	TM	13	(781) 826-2261	Viola Ryerson	Stephen Rollins	William Flynn	George Martin	Stephen Tucker	Paul Hayes	Frank Cheverie
Hanson	t	TM	9	(781) 293-2131	. . .	Earl Davis	Sandra Harris	Barbara Gomez	Allan Hoyt	Edward Savage	Richard Harris
Harvard	t	TM	5	(978) 456-4100	Richard Maiune	Timothy Bragan	Janet Vellente	. . .	. . .	. . .	James Smith
Harwich	t	TM	12	(508) 430-7513	Cyd Zeigler	. . .	Anita Doucette	M. Gallagher	Robert Peterson	William Mason	Alice Norgeot
Hatfield	t	TM	3	(413) 247-0481	Patrick Gaughan	William Szych	. . .	. . .	William Belden	David Hurley	James Reidy
Haverhill	c	MC	58	(978) 374-2300	. . .	. . .	. . .	. . .	. . .	. . .	. . .
Hingham	t	TM	19	(781) 741-1400	Mathew MacIver	Charles Cristello	Eileen McCracken	Ted Alexiades	Mark Duff	Steven Carlson	Joseph Stigliani
Holbrook	t	RT	10	(781) 767-4316	. . .	. . .	. . .	. . .	Edward O'Brien	. . .	. . .
Holden	t	CM	15	(508) 829-0225	Joseph Sullivan	Brian Bullock	Kathleen Peterson	. . .	Edward Stark	George Sherrill	L. Galkowski
Holliston	t	TM	13	(508) 429-0608	. . .	. . .	. . .	. . .	. . .	. . .	. . .
Holyoke	c	MC	39	(413) 534-2176	Michael Sullivan	. . .	Susan Egan	Brian Smith	David Lafond	Anthony Scott	William Fuqua
Hopedale *	t	TM	5	(508) 634-2203	Alan Ryan	Eugene Phillips	Janet Jacaruso	Linda Catanzariti	Scott Garland	Eugene Costanza	Robert DePonte
Hopkinton	t	TM	13	(508) 497-9700	. . .	Anthony Trioano	. . .	. . .	Gary Daugherty	Thomas Irvin	JT Gaucher
Hudson	t	TM	18	(978) 562-9963	Jo Forance	Paul Blazar	Deborah Boudreau	Christopher Pile	Thomas Garrity	. . .	Anthony Marques
Hull	t	TM	11	(781) 925-2000	. . .	. . .	. . .	. . .	. . .	. . .	. . .
Ipswich	t	CM	12	(978) 356-6600	Patrick McNally	Robert Markel	P. Carakatsane	Rita Negri	Arthur Howe	. . .	Robert Gravino
Kingston	t	CM	11	(781) 585-0500	Olavo DeMacedo	Kevin Donovan	Mary Lou Murzyn	Joan Paquette	David McKee	Gordon Fogg	. . .
Lakeville *	t	TM	9	(508) 946-8800	Richard LaCamera	Rita Garbitt	Janet Tracy	Cynthia McRae	Daniel Hopkins	Mark Sorel	Christopher Peck
Lancaster *	t	TM	7	(978) 365-3326	Stephen Kerrigan	Orlando Pacheco	D. S. Thompson	Bonnie Holston	John Fleck	Kevin Lamb	Jack Sonia
Lanesborough	t	TM	2	(413) 442-1167	Peter Gallant	Paul Boudreau	Judith Gallant	Phillip Abraham	Charles Durfee	Stanley Misiuk	William Decelles
Lawrence	c	MC	72	(978) 794-5858	Mary Kennedy	Jack McCarthy	P. Marchand	. . .	Richard Shafer	Robert Hayden	Raymond Difiore
Lee	t	CM	5	(413) 243-5500	Patricia Carlino	Robert Nason	Suzanne Scarpa	. . .	Ronald Driscoll	Ronald Glidden	Christopher Pompi
Leicester *	t	TM	10	(508) 892-7000	Douglas Belanger	. . .	Patricia Hartnett	Sandra Buxton	Robert Wilson	James Hurley	James Coughlin
Lenox	t	TM	5	(413) 637-5506	Robert Akroyd	Gregory Federspiel	Marie Colvin	. . .	Daniel Clifford	Timothy Face	Jeffrey Vincent
Leominster	c	MC	41	(978) 534-7500	Dean Mazzarella	Elizabeth Irvine	Lynn Bouchard	. . .	Ronald Pierce	Peter Roddy	Patrick LaPointe
Lexington *	t	CM	30	(781) 862-0500	Jeanne Krieger	Carl Valente	Donna Hooper	Robert Addelson	William Middlemiss	Christopher Casey	William Hadley
Lincoln Center	t	TM	8	(781) 259-2600	John Kerr	Timothy Higgins	Nancy Zuelke	Suzanne Marchand	Richard Goddard	Allen Bowles	Vincent De Amicis
Littleton	t	TM	8	(978) 952-2311	Paul Glavey	Keith Bergman	Mary Crory	Carol Wideman	Alexander McCurdy	. . .	Eric Durcing

Directory 1/9 continued — OFFICIALS IN U.S. MUNICIPALITIES 2,500 AND OVER IN POPULATION

Jurisdiction	Type	Form of govern-ment	2000 Popu-lation (000)	Main telephone number	Chief elected official	Appointed administrator	Clerk of the governing board	Chief financial officer	Fire chief	Police chief	Public works director
MASSACHUSETTS continued											
Longmeadow	t	TM	15	(413) 565-4110	Hal Haberman	Roberta Crosbie	...	Paul Pasterczyk	Eric Madison	Richard Marchese	Douglas Barron
Lowell	c	CM	105	(978) 970-4000	Eileen Donoghue	Bernard Lynch	Richard Johnson	James Kennedy	William Desrosiers	Edward Davis	Edward Walsh
Ludlow	t	RT	21	(413) 583-5600	...	Michael Szlosek	...	...	...	...	...
Lunenburg	t	TM	9	(978) 582-4130	Robert Bowen	Kerry Speidel	Linda Douglas	Karen Brochu	Scott Glenny	Daniel Bourgeois	John Rodriquenz
Lynn	c	MC	89	(781) 598-4000	Edward Clancy	...	...	John Pace	Curtis Numberg	John Suslak	Michael Donovan
Lynnfield	t	CM	11	(781) 334-3180	...	...	...	...	...	...	...
Malden	c	MC	56	(781) 397-7000	Richard Howard	...	Karen Anderson	Domenic Fermano	Joseph Mahoney	Kenneth Coye	Jeffery Manship
Manchester-By-The-Sea	t	CM	5	(978) 526-2000	Susan Thorne	Wayne Melville	Gretchen Wood	Charles Lane	Andrew Paskalis	Ronald Ramos	Robert Moroney
Mansfield	t	CM	22	(508) 261-7370	...	John D'Agostino	Helen Christian	...	Robert Bellavance	Arthur O'Neill	Ilidio Azinheira
Marblehead	t	TM	20	(781) 631-0528	Bill Conly	Anthony Sasso	Betty Brown	George Snow	Charles Maurais	John Palmer	William McLaughlin
Marion	t	CM	5	(508) 748-3550	Jonathan Dickerson	...	...	Karen Gomez	C. Davis	Lincoln Miller	Robert Zora
Marlborough	c	MC	36	(508) 460-3775	Nancy Stevens	...	...	...	...	...	Ron LaFreniere
Marshfield	t	TM	24	(781) 834-5563	James Fitzgerald	...	Sheila Sullivan	...	...	...	Makram Megalli
Mashpee	t	MC	12	(508) 539-1400	...	Joyce Mason	Deborah Dami	...	George Baker	Maurice Cooper	R. Taylor
Mattapoisett	t	TM	6	(508) 758-4100	Paul Lambalot	Carol Adams	Lois Ennis	Judith Mooney	Ronald Scott	James Moran	Wesley Bowman
Maynard	t	TM	10	(978) 897-1001	Anne Desmarais	Michael Gianotis	Judith Peterson	Harry Gannon	Ronald Cassidy	James Corcoran	Walter Sokolowski
Medfield	t	TM	12	(508) 359-8505	Ann Thompson	Michael Sullivan	Carol Mayer	...	William Kingsbury	Robert Meaney	Kenneth Feeney
Medford	c	CM	55	(781) 396-5500	Michael McGlynn	...	Edward Finn	...	...	...	...
Medway	t	TM	12	(508) 533-3264	Douglas Downing	Suzanne Kennedy	Maryjane White	Margery Sanford	Wayne Vinton	W. Lambirth	Lee Henry
Melrose	c	MC	27	(781) 979-4500	Robert Dolan	...	Mary Rita O'Shea	John Dunn	Kevin Walsh	Richard Smith	Robert Beshara
Mendon	t	TM	5	(508) 473-2312	Sharon Culter	Michael McCue	M. Bonderenko	...	...	Ernest Horn	...
Merrimac	t	TM	6	(978) 346-8862	...	...	...	...	...	...	...
Methuen	c	CM	43	(978) 794-3237	Sharon Pollard	Kathleen Healy	T. Touma Conway	Thomas Kelly	Kenneth Bourassa	Joseph Solomon	Ray DiFiore
Middleborough *	t	TM	19	(508) 947-0928	Marsha Brunelle	John Healey	Eileen Gates	...	Robert Silva	Gary Russell	Donald Boucher
Middleton	t	TM	7	(978) 777-3617	Nancy Jones	Ira Singer	Sarah George	Robert Murphy	David Leary	Paul Armitage	Robert LaBossiere
Milford	t	RT	26	(508) 634-2307	Brian Murray	Louis Celozzi	Joseph Arcudi	...	...	...	...
Millbury	t	TM	12	(508) 865-4710	E. Bernard Plante	...	Deborah Plante	Gerald Bleau	David Rudge	Richard Handfield	Joseph Chase
Millis	t	TM	7	(508) 376-2634	James McCaffrey	Charles Aspinwall	George Ford	...	W. Champagne	Albert Baima	...
Millville *	t	MC	2	(508) 883-8433	Diane McCutcheon	Helen Coffin	Susan McNamara	Marilyn Mathieu	John Mullaly	Ronald Landry	John Dean
Milton	t	RT	26	(617) 696-5604	...	...	James Mullen	David Grab	Malcolm Larson	Kevin Mearn	...
Monson	t	TM	8	(413) 267-4100	R. Blanchette	Gretchen Neggers	Nancy Morrell	Debi Mahar	Elmer Harris	Joseph Rebello	...
Montague	t	RT	8	(413) 863-3200	Patricia Pruitt	Frank Abbondanzio	Debra Bourbeau	Carolyn Olsen	Raymond Godin	Raymond Zukowski	Thomas Bergeron
Nahant	t	TM	3	(781) 581-0088	Jim Walsh	Mark Cullinan	Susan Behen	Deborah Cormier	Lee Fox	Joseph Manley	Robert Ward
Nantucket	t	TM	9	(508) 228-7255	...	C. Gibson	Catherine Stover	Constance Voges	Bruce Watts	William Pittman	Jeffrey Willett
Natick	t	RT	32	(508) 651-7230	Edward Dlott	Frederick Conley	Jane Hladick	Robert Palmer	Richard Fredette	Dennis Mannix	...
Needham	t	RT	28	(781) 455-7500	James Healy	Kate Fitzpatrick	Theodora Eaton	...	Robert Di Poli	Tom Leary	Richard Merson
New Bedford	c	MC	93	(508) 979-1444	Frederick Kalisz	Stephen Furtado	Michelle Ouellette	Daniel Patten	Paul Leger	Carl Moniz	Lawrence Worden
Newbury	t	TM	6	(978) 465-9241	Richard Joy	...	Donna Stefanile	...	...	Roger Merry	Timothy Leonard
Newburyport	c	MC	17	(978) 465-4413	...	...	...	...	John Cutter	John Connors	Dan Lynch
Newton	c	MC	83	(617) 796-1260	David Cohen	...	Edward English	David Wilkinson	Edward Murphy	Jose Cordero	Robert Rooney
Norfolk	t	TM	10	(508) 528-1408	James Lehan	John Hathaway	Marie Chiofolo	Jane Wall	Coleman Bushnell	Charles Stone	Remo Vito
North Adams	c	MC	14	(413) 662-3000	John Barrett	...	Maryann Abuisi	Beverly Cooper	Craig Rougeau	Ernest Morocco	Leo Senecal
North Andover *	t	TM	27	(978) 688-9510	James Xenakis	Mark Rees	Joyce Bradshaw	Lyne Savage	William Martineau	Richard Stanley	J. Hmurciak
North Attleborough	t	RT	27	(508) 699-0100	Donald Hart	...	William Moffitt	...	Robert Coleman	Michael Gould	Michael Stankovich
North Brookfield	t	TM	4	(508) 867-0200	Richard Chabot	Melanie Jenkins	Sheila Buzzell	Scott Usher	...	...	Raymond Blake
North Reading	t	CM	13	(978) 664-6010	Marcia Bailey	Greg Balukonis	Barbara Stats	Thomas Tracy	Edward O'Brien	Henry Purnell	David Hanlon
Northampton	c	MC	28	(413) 587-1258	Mary Higgins	...	...	John Musante	Brian Duggan	Russell Sienkiewicz	George Andrikidis
Northborough *	t	TM	14	(508) 393-5040	William Pantazis	Barry Brenner	Andrew Dowd	...	David Durgin	Mark Leahy	Kara Buzanoski
Northbridge *	t	CM	13	(508) 234-2095	C. Ampagoomian	Theodore Kozak	Muriel Barry	...	Gary Nestor	Walter Warchol	Richard Sasseville
Norton	t	TM	18	(508) 285-0200	...	James Purcell	Diane Casagni	...	...	Bruce Finch	Keith Silver
Norwell	t	TM	9	(781) 659-8000	John Mariano	James Boudreau	Janice Lawson	Donna Mangan	Paul Rosebach	Theodore Ross	Paul Foulsham
Norwood	t	CM	28	(781) 762-1240	Domenic Fruci	John Carroll	Robert Thornton	...	William Sullivan	Bartley King	Joseph Welch
Oak Bluffs *	t	TM	3	(508) 693-3554	...	Michael Dutton	...	Paul Manzi	Gilbert Forend	Erik Blake	Richard Combra
Orange	t	TM	7	(978) 544-1100	Robert Andrews	R. Kwiatkowski	Nancy Blackmer	N. Reibschlaegen	Dennis Annear	Brian Spear	...
Orleans	t	TM	6	(508) 240-3700	Jon Fuller	John Kelly	Cynthia May	David Withrow	Steven Edwards	Jeff Roy	...
Oxford	t	TM	13	(508) 987-6030	Henry LaMountain	...	...	Donald Kaminski	Jeffrey Wilson	Charles Noyes	John Phillips
Palmer	t	CM	12	(413) 283-2603	...	Richard Fitzgerald	Patricia Donovan	...	Alan Roy	Robert Frydryk	...
Paxton *	t	TM	4	(508) 754-7638	Michael Quinlivan	Charles Blanchard	Deirdre Malone	...	Jay Conte	Robert Desrosiers	Michael Putnam
Peabody	c	MC	48	(978) 532-3000	Peter Torigian	...	...	Patricia Schaffer	Joseph Mendonca	Robert Champayne	Richard Carnevale
Pembroke	t	TM	16	(781) 293-3844	Robert Demarco	Edwin Thorne	Donna Pratt	...	James Neenan	Gregory Wright	Michael Valenti
Pepperell	t	TM	11	(978) 433-0333	Scott Butcher	...	Lois Libby	Theresa Walsh	Wes Whittier	Alan Davis	Kim Spaulding
Pittsfield *	c	MC	45	(413) 499-9340	Sara Hathaway	...	Jody Phillips	Susan Carmel	Stephen Duffy	Anthony Riello	Bruce Collingwood
Plainville	t	TM	7	(508) 695-3142	Charles Smith	Joseph Fernandes	Kathleen Sandland	...	Edwin Harrop	Edward Merrick	Calvin Hall
Plymouth	t	RT	51	(508) 747-1620	Kenneth Tavares	Mark Sylvia	Laurence Pizer	Bruce Miller	James Pierson	Robert Pomeroy	George Crombie
Provincetown *	t	CM	3	(508) 487-7000	Mary-Jo Avellar	Sharon Lynn	Douglas Johnstone	Alexandra Hielala	Michael Trovato	Warren Tobias	David Guertin
Quincy	c	MC	88	(617) 376-1000	James Sheets	John Keenan	Joseph Shea	Michael McFarland	Thomas Gorman	Thomas Frane	...
Randolph	t	RT	30	(617) 961-0900	...	...	...	...	...	...	...
Raynham	t	TM	11	(508) 824-2707	Donald McKinnon	Randall Buckner	Helen Lounsbury	Belcher Stanley	George Andrews	Peter King	Roger Stolte
Reading *	t	CM	23	(781) 942-9001	James Bonazoli	P. Hechenbleikner	Cheryl Johnson	...	Gregory Burns	James Cormier	Edward McIntire
Rehoboth	t	TM	10	(508) 252-3758	Arthur Tobin	David Marciello	Kathleen Conti	...	Robert Pray	Gary Fiedler	Daniel Kelley
Revere	c	MC	47	(781) 286-8202	Thomas Ambrosino	...	John Henry	...	Eugene Doherty	Terrance Reardon	Donald Goodwin
Rochester	t	TM	4	(508) 763-3871	Richard Cutler	James Huntoon	Naida Parker	Claudette Coutu	Scott Ashworth	Walter Denham	Jeffrey Eldridge
Rockland	t	TM	17	(781) 871-1874	Keven Pratt	Bradley Plante	Mary Pat Kaszanek	Eric Hart	J. Michael Sammon	John Llewellyn	...
Rockport	t	TM	7	(978) 546-6894	Nicola Barletta	...	Frederick Frithsen	Dean Anderson	Russell Anderson	John McCarthy	John Tomasz
Rowley	t	TM	5	(978) 948-2705	Robert Morse	...	Jeanne Grover	Sue Bailey	...	Kevin Barry	Scott Leavitt
Rutland	t	TM	6	(508) 886-4104	James Leger	...	...	...	Thomas Ruchala	Joseph Baril	Carl Christianson
Salem	c	MC	40	(978) 745-9595	Stanley Usovicz	...	D. Burkinshaw	Bruce Guy	Robert Turner	Robert St. Pierre	Bruce Thibodeau
Salisbury	t	CM	7	(978) 465-2310	Henry Richenburg	Neil Harrington	Wilma McDonald	Andrew Gould	Richard Souliotis	Richard Simmons	Donald Levesque
Sandwich	t	CM	20	(508) 888-5144	Pamela Terry	George Dunham	Barbara Walling	Doreen Guild	Dennis Newman	...	Peter Tancredi
Saugus	t	CM	26	(781) 231-4126	...	...	...	...	...	...	...
Scituate	t	TM	17	(781) 545-8741	Shawn Harris	Richard Agnew	Barbara Maffucci	Mary Gallagher	Edward Hurley	Thomas Neilen	Anthony Antoniello
Seekonk	t	RT	13	(508) 336-2910	Dana Beal	...	Janet Parker	Robin Tavares	David Viera	Vito Scotti	James Tusino
Sharon	t	TM	17	(781) 784-1515	...	Benjamin Puritz	Marlene Chused	...	Dennis Mann	Joseph Bernstein	Eric Hooper
Sheffield	t	CM	3	(413) 229-2335	Janet Stanton	...	Natalie Funk	...	John Ullrich	...	Ronald Bassett
Sherborn	t	TM	4	(508) 651-7850	Paul DeRensis	Kristine Irving	Carole Marple	Ruth Hohenschau	Neil McPherson	Gary Hendron	Gary Kellaher
Shirley	t	TM	6	(978) 425-2600	Leonardo Guercio	Kyle Keady	Sylvia Shipton	Karen Kucala	Dennis Levesque	Paul Thibodeau	Albert Chevrette
Shrewsbury	t	CM	31	(508) 842-7471	Laurie Lindberg	Daniel Morgado	Ann Dagle	Mary Thompson	...	...	...
Somerset	t	TM	18	(508) 646-2800	Steven Moniz	John McAuliffe	Patricia Hart	Joseph Bolton	Stephen Rivard	Joseph Ferreira	Thomas Fitzgerald
Somerville	c	MC	77	(617) 625-6600	Michael Capuano	...	Arthur McCue	...	Kevin Kelleher	Donald Caliguri	Robert Trahan

Directory 1/9 continued OFFICIALS IN U.S. MUNICIPALITIES 2,500 AND OVER IN POPULATION

Jurisdiction	Type	Form of govern-ment	2000 Popu-lation (000)	Main telephone number	Chief elected official	Appointed administrator	Clerk of the governing board	Chief financial officer	Fire chief	Police chief	Public works director
MASSACHUSETTS continued											
South Hadley	t	RT	17	(413) 538-5017	Barbara Eckman	...	Lisa Napiorkowski	...	...	David LaBrie	...
Southampton	t	TM	5	(413) 529-0106	Thomas Cross	Marlene Michonski	Eileen Couture	K. Archambeault	William Barcomb	Eugene Lemoine	Edward Cauley
Southborough	t	TM	8	(508) 485-0710	Bonnie Phaneuf	Jean Kitchen	Paul Berry	...	John Mauro	William Webber	John Boland
Southbridge	t	CM	17	(508) 764-5405	Laurent McDonald	Clayton Carlisle	Helen Lenti	Dean Iacobucci	Leonard Laporte	Michael Stevens	Hamer Clarke
Southwick	t	TM	8	(413) 569-5995	David St. Pierre	Karl Stinehart	Paul Mormino	Linda Carr	Don Morris	Henry Labombard	Arthur Chevalier
Spencer	t	TM	11	(508) 885-7500	...	Carter Terenzini	Jean Mulhall	Alaine Boucher	Robert Parsons	David Darrin	Warren Ramsey
Springfield	c	MC	152	(413) 787-6068	Michael Albano	Nigel Spencer	William Metzger	Donna Williams	Gary Cassannelli	Paula Meara	Allan Chawlek
Sterling *	t	TM	7	(978) 422-8111	Donlin Murray	Terri Ackerman	Melanie Clark	...	David Hurlbut	Gary Chamberland	Charles Ripa
Stoneham	t	TM	22	(781) 279-2600	Robert Sweeney	Ronald Florino	John Hanright	Ronald Castignetti	Lawrence Lamey	Eugene Passaro	Robert Grover
Stoughton	t	CM	27	(781) 341-1300	Joseph Mokrisky	Mark Stankiewicz	...	Paul Leaver	William Stipp	Philip Dineen	Lawrence Barrett
Stow	t	TM	5	(978) 897-4514	...	William Wrigley	Linda Smart	...	David Soar	John Scichilone	Michael Clayton
Sturbridge	t	TM	7	(508) 347-2500	Arnold Wilson	James Malloy	Lorraine Murawski	...	Leonard Senecal	Thomas Button	Gregory Morse
Sudbury	t	TM	16	(978) 443-8891	Lawrence O'Brien	Maureen Valente	...	Suzanne Petersen	Kenneth MacLean	Peter Fadgen	William Place
Sunderland	t	TM	3	(413) 665-1441	Scott Bergeron	Margaret Nartowicz	Wendy Houle	Herb Sanderson	Robert Ahearn	Jeffrey Gilbert	...
Sutton	t	CM	8	(508) 865-8720	Robert Kneeland	James Smith	Laura Rodgers	Timothy Harrison	David Currier	John Hebert	Mark Brigham
Swampscott	t	RT	14	(781) 596-8850	...	Andrew Maylor	Jack Paster	...	Laurence Galante	Ronald Madigan	Silvio Baruzzi
Swansea	t	TM	15	(508) 678-2981	...	...	...	...	...	...	...
Taunton	c	MC	55	(508) 821-1000	Robert Nunes	Gill Enos	R. Marie Blackwell	...	Thomas Downey	Raymond O'Berg	Frederic Cornaglia
Templeton *	t	TM	6	(978) 939-8801	Gerald Skelton	Carol Skelton	Carol Harris	Scott Sawyer	Thomas Smith	David Whitaker	Francis Chase
Tewksbury	t	TM	28	(978) 640-4300	Charles Coppola	David Cressman	Elizabeth Carey	Donna Walsh	Thomas Ryan	John Mackey	William Burris
Tisbury	t	TM	3	(508) 696-4200	Edmond Coogan	John Bugbee	Marion Mudge	Timothy McLean	Richard Clark	...	Frederick Lapiana
Topsfield	t	TM	6	(978) 887-8571	...	...	...	...	...	...	...
Townsend	t	CM	9	(978) 597-1700	Robert Rebholz	Gregory Barnes	Daniel Murphy	Richard Choate	Donald Hurme	...	Edward Kukkula
Truro	t	CM	1	(508) 349-7004	Alfred Gaechter	Pamela Nolan	...	Gertrude Brazil	E. Thomas Prada	John Thomas	Paul Morris
Tyngsborough	t	TM	11	(978) 649-2300	J. Schnackerts	...	Joanne Shifres	Leon Cote	Timothy Madden	John Miceli	Frederick Flanagan
Upton *	t	TM	5	(508) 529-6901	James Bate	...	Martha Williams	...	Richard Henderson	Tom Stockwell	Bob Gilchrist
Uxbridge	t	TM	11	(508) 278-8600	Julie Woods	Jill Myers	Holly Gallerani	David Genereux	Peter Ostroskey	Scott Freitas	Larry Bombara
Wakefield	t	TM	24	(781) 246-6390	...	Thomas Butler	Virginia Zingarelli	Kevin Gill	David Parr	Stephen Doherty	Richard Stinson
Walpole *	t	RT	22	(508) 660-7294	Albert Denapoli	Michael Boynton	Ronald Fucile	Mark Good	Timothy Bailey	Richard Stillman	Robert O'Brien
Waltham	c	MC	59	(781) 893-4040	J. McCarthy	...	Rosario Malone	Dennis Quinn	Thomas Keough	Edward Drew	John Bradley
Ware	t	TM	9	(413) 967-9648	John Desmond	...	Nancy Talbot	John Hirbour	Thomas Coulombe	Dennis Healey	Gilbert Sorel
Wareham	t	CM	20	(508) 291-3100	Patrick Tropeano	...	MaryAnn Silva	Robert Bliss	...	Thomas Joyce	Mark Gifford
Warren	t	TM	4	(413) 436-5701	David Delanski	Jean McCaughey	Nancy Lowell	William Schlosstein	James Dolan	Ronald Syriac	...
Warwick *	t	TM	..	(978) 544-6315	...	John Columbus	...	...	...	...	...
Watertown *	t	CM	32	(617) 972-6465	Clyde Younger	Michael Driscoll	John Flynn	...	Mario Orangio	Edward Deveau	Gerald Mee
Wayland	t	CM	13	(508) 358-7755	Betsy Connolly	Frederic Turkington	Judith St. Croix	Robert Hilliard	Robert Loomer	Robert Irving	...
Webster	t	TM	16	(508) 949-3800	...	Raymond Houle	Regina Bugan	Pamela Leduc	...	Richard Bergeron	...
Wellesley *	t	RT	26	(781) 431-1019	...	Hans Larsen	Kathleen Nagle	Sheryl Strother	Kevin Rooney	T. Cunningham	Michael Pakstis
Wellfleet	t	TM	2	(508) 349-0300	Dale Donavon	...	Dawn Rickman	Patricia Eagar	Alan Hight	Richard Rosenthal	Jameson Bell
Wenham *	t	TM	4	(978) 468-5523	John Clemenzi	Jeffrey Chelgren	Frances Hart Young	...	Robert Blanchard	Kenneth Walsh	William Tyack
West Boylston *	t	CM	7	(508) 835-3490	Kevin McCormick	Leon Gaumond	Kim Hopewell	Michael Daley	Richard Pauley	Dennis Minnich	John Westerling
West Bridgewater	t	TM	6	(508) 894-1200	Victor Flaherty	Elizabeth Faricy	Marion Leonard	Marilyn Gordon	Leonard Hurt	Robert Kominsky	Thomas Green
West Brookfield *	t	TM	3	(508) 867-1421	Roland Gaboury	Johanna Barry	Sarah Allen	...	Ronald Gresty	C. O'Donnell	Jason Benoit
West Newbury *	t	TM	4	(978) 363-1100	Richard Cushing	...	Larry Murphy	Tracy Blais	Raymond Dower	Jonathon Dennis	Gary Bill
West Springfield *	t	RT	27	(413) 263-3232	Edward Gibson	...	Diane Foley	...	David Barkman	Thomas Burke	John Dowd
Westborough	t	TM	17	(508) 366-3030	Kristina Allen	Henry Danis	Nancy Yendriga	Leah Talbot	Walter Perron	Glenn Parker	John Walden
Westfield	c	MC	40	(413) 572-6200	...	...	...	...	...	...	...
Westford	t	CM	20	(978) 692-5500	...	...	Kari Tari	Suzanne Marchald	Richard Rochon	Bob Welch	...
Westminster *	t	TM	6	(978) 874-7400	John Fairbanks	Karen Murphy	Denise MacAloney	Donna Allard	Brenton MacAloney	Salvatore Albert	William Wintturi
Weston *	t	TM	11	(781) 893-7320	Michael Harrity	Donna VanderClock	M. Nolan	...	Joseph Daniele	Steven Shaw	Robert Hoffman
Westport	t	TM	14	(508) 636-1003	Steven Tripp	John Dolan	Marlene Samson	Katherine Benoit	William Tripp	Michael Healy	Paul Pereira
Westwood	t	TM	14	(781) 326-6450	Anthony Antonellis	Michael Jaillet	Edith McCracken	Pamela Dukeman	William Scoble	William Chase	J. Walsh
Weymouth	t	RT	53	(617) 335-2000	William Ryan	...	Franklin Fryer	Arthur Gallagher	David Madden	Thomas Higgins	Joseph Mazzotta
Whatley	t	CM	1	(413) 665-4400	...	...	...	...	...	...	...
Whitman	t	TM	13	(781) 447-7600	Daniel Holbrook	Francis Lynam	Pamela Martin	...	Timothy Travers	John Schnyer	John Pettinelli
Wilbraham	t	TM	13	(413) 596-8111	David Barry	Robert Weitz	Beverly Litchfield	Joanne Degray	Francis Nothe	Allen Stratton	Edmond Miga
Williamstown	t	CM	8	(413) 458-3500	John Madden	Peter Fohlin	Mary Kennedy	Charles St. John	Craig Pedercini	Arthur Parker	Timothy Kaiser
Wilmington *	t	CM	21	(978) 658-3311	Michael Newhouse	Michael Caira	Sharon George	Michael Morris	Daniel Stewart	Michael Begonis	Donald Onusseit
Winchendon	t	TM	9	(978) 297-0085	...	James Kreidler	Carly Antonellis	Elizabeth Gilman	Allen Lafrennie	Robert Harrington	Michael Murphy
Winchester	t	RT	20	(781) 721-7133	Stephen Powes	Melvin Kleckner	Carolyn Ward	Joseph Bonner	John Nash	Joseph Perritano	Anthony Celli
Winthrop	t	RT	18	(617) 846-1077	Tom Reily	Richard White	Claire Sheltry	Michael Bertino	J. Powers	David Goldstein	David Hickey
Woburn	c	MC	37	(781) 932-4400	T. McLaughlin	...	William Campbell	Gerald Surette	Paul Tortolano	Philip Mahoney	Frederick Russell
Worcester	c	CM	172	(508) 799-1031	Raymond Mariano	...	David Rushford	John Pranckevicius	Gerard Dio	James Gallagher	Robert Moylan
Wrentham	t	TM	10	(508) 384-5400	Mary Dunn	Steven Boudreau	Carol Mollica	Barry Yeaw	Robert Morrill	Joseph Collamati	Robert Reardon
Yarmouth	t	TM	24	(508) 398-2231	James Saben	Robert Lawton	Jane Hastings	Susan Milne	C. R. Sherman	Peter Carnes	George Allaire
MICHIGAN											
Adrian	c	CM	21	(517) 264-4883	Sam Rye	Dane Nelson	Marsha Rowley	Jeffrey Pardee	Paul Trinka	Mike Martin	...
Albion *	c	CM	9	(517) 629-5535	William Wheaton	Michael Herman	Kerry Helmick	...	...	...	Kevin Markovich
Algonac	c	CM	4	(810) 794-9361	Raymond Martin	Chris Wilson	Helen Hazuka	...	S. John Stier	Richard Torongeau	Paul Jarmolowicz
Allegan	c	CM	4	(616) 673-5511	Craig Van Melle	Robert Hillard	...	...	Joel Merchant	...	Victor Rose
Allen Park	c	MC	29	(313) 928-1400	Richard Huebler	Rocco Minghine	John Weise	Kristine Barann	Gregory Murphy	Dennis Gallow	David Boomer
Alma *	c	CM	9	(989) 463-8336	Melvin Nyman	Phillip Moore	Barbara Gager	Paul Borle	Richard Pratt	...	Ronald Turner
Almont *	v	CM	2	(810) 798-8528	Steven Schneider	Gerald Oakes	Sally McCrea	...	...	Eugene Bruns	Russell Kelley
Alpena	c	CM	11	(989) 354-1700	John Gilmet	...	Karen Hebert	...	...	Thad Taylor	...
Alpine *	tp	MC	13	(616) 784-1262	Marta Brechting	...	Jean Wahlfield	...	Ron Christians	...	...
Ann Arbor	c	CM	114	(734) 994-2803	John Hieftje	Roger Fraser	J. Beaudry	Tom Crawford	...	Daniel Oates	Sue McCormick
Au Gres	c	MC	1	(989) 876-8811	...	...	...	...	...	...	...
Auburn	c	MC	2	(989) 662-6761	...	Jo Ella Krantz	Lucille Wiesenauer	...	...	James Klann	Ronald Perry
Auburn Hills	c	CM	19	(248) 370-9440	M. Harvey-Edwards	Michael Culpepper	Linda Shannon	Gary Barnes	Mark Walterhouse	Doreen Olko	Ronald Melchert
Bad Axe	c	CM	3	(989) 269-7681	Herbert Williams	John Nugent	Kay Goebel	...	...	John Bodis	Scott Boshart
Bangor	c	CM	1	(269) 427-5831	George Sink	...	Adeline Starks	...	Michael Anchor	Gary Baker	Roy Hill
Baraga	v	MC	1	(906) 353-6237	Wendell Dompier	...	Dorothy Mayo	...	...	Harold Miron	William Marlor
Bath	tp	CM	7	(517) 641-6728	Valerie Shirey	...	Kathleen McQueen	...	Art Hosford	Jack Phillips	...
Battle Creek	c	CM	53	(616) 966-3300	...	Wayne Wiley	Deborah Owens	Jim Ritsema	Larry Hausman	David Headings	...
Bay City	c	CM	36	(989) 894-8246	Michael Buda	Robert Belleman	Connie Deford	Gary Fields	Gary Mueller	Linda Collier	...
Bear Creek	tp	MC	5	(231) 347-0592	Dennis Keiser	...	...	...	Norman Conklin	...	...
Belding	c	CM	5	(616) 794-1900	...	Randall DeBruine	Kareen Thomas	...	Gregg Moore	Dale Nelson	Ernest Thomas
Bellaire	v	MC	1	(231) 533-8213	...	Janet Person	...	...	...	...	...
Belleville	c	CM	3	(734) 697-9577	Thomas Fielder	...	Diana Kollmeyer	...	Darwin Loyer	Paul Davis	Keith Boc

Directory 1/9 continued **OFFICIALS IN U.S. MUNICIPALITIES 2,500 AND OVER IN POPULATION**

Jurisdiction	Type	Form of govern-ment	2000 Popu-lation (000)	Main telephone number	Chief elected official	Appointed administrator	Clerk of the governing board	Chief financial officer	Fire chief	Police chief	Public works director
MICHIGAN continued											
Benton Harbor	c	CM	11	(269) 927-8401	...	Dwight Mitchell	Joyce Taylor	Jacqueline Bell	...	Samuel Harris	Michael Dancer
Berkley	c	CM	15	(248) 546-2470	Marilyn Stephan	Jane Bais DiSessa	Karen Brown	...	...	...	Richard Shepler
Bessemer	c	CM	2	(906) 663-4311	Peter Matonich	Joseph Erickson	Bruce Carlson	...	...	...	Daniel Johnson
Beverly Hills *	v	CM	10	(248) 646-6404	Todd Stearn	Renzo Spallasso	...	Robert Wiszowaty	...	...	Tom Meszler
Big Rapids	c	CM	10	(231) 592-4000	Edward Burch	Stephen Sobers	Roberta Cline	...	...	...	Timothy Vogel
Birch Run *	v	MC	1	(989) 624-5711	Marianne Nelson	Paul Moore	Becky Walther	...	...	Al Swearengin	Terry Engelhardt
Birmingham *	c	CM	19	(248) 644-1800	Donald Carney	Thomas Markus	Nancy Weiss	B. Ostin	Timothy Wangler	Richard Patterson	Robert Fox
Blissfield	v	CM	3	(517) 486-4347	Jae Guetschow	James Wonacott	Laura Neuman	...	...	Jane Kelley	Mark Strahan
Bloomfield Hills	c	CM	3	(248) 644-1520	Benjamin Hoffiz	Jay Cravens	...	...	...	David Piche	Daniel Hamlin
Boyne City	c	CM	3	(231) 582-6597	Eleanor Stackus	Michael Cain	Sue Hobbs	...	Dennis Amesbury	Randall Howard	Michael Wiesner
Brandon *	tp	MC	14	(248) 627-4918	Ronald Lapp	...	B. McCreery	...	Robert McArthur	...	...
Breitung *	tp	MC	5	(906) 779-2050	...	Perry Franzoi	Samantha Coron	...	...	...	Guy Forstrom
Bridgman	c	MC	2	(616) 465-5144	...	Aaron Anthony	Elaine Thomas	...	Skip Munson	Harry Lenandson	Rich Knuth
Brighton	c	CM	6	(810) 227-1911	Kate Lawrence	Dana Foster	Tammy Allen	David Gajda	...	Mike Kinaschuk	M. Schindewolf
Brighton	tp	CM	17	(810) 229-0550	H. E. Prine	David Murphy	Ann Bollin	...	...	...	...
Bronson *	c	CM	2	(517) 369-7334	Thomas Rissman	David O'Rourke	Karen Smith	...	Brent Wilber	Richard Stout	Carl Ransbottom
Brooklyn	v	CM	1	(517) 592-2591	...	Victor Cardenas	...	...	...	...	...
Brown City *	c	CM	1	(810) 346-2325	Laura Carpenter	Clinton Holmes	Kelly Pavel	...	James Groat	Ronald Smith	David Kinney
Buchanan	c	CM	4	(616) 695-3844	Joe Scanlon	M. Mullendore	Gladys Bybee	...	Warren Weaver	William Marx	Rick Smigielski
Buena Vista	tp	CM	10	(989) 754-6536	Dwayne Parker	Martin Williams	B. Montgomery	Alan Bailey	John Parrott	Brian Booker	Victor Killingbeck
Burton	c	MC	30	(810) 743-1500	Charles Smiley	Charles Abbey	Gayle Webster	Bradley Becker	Douglas Halstead	Bruce Whitman	Jeffrey Major
Cadillac	c	CM	10	(231) 775-0181	Ronald Blanchard	Peter Stalker	Janice Nelson	...	...	...	Robert Johnson
Canton	tp	CM	76	(734) 394-5260	Thomas Yack	...	Terry Bennett	Anthony Minghine	M. Rorabacher	...	Joseph Teramino
Capac	v	MC	1	(810) 395-4355	Mark Klug	...	C. Franckowiak	...	...	Raymond Hawks	Donald Standel
Carleton	v	MC	2	(734) 654-6255	Glenn Goodnight	...	Lori Dahl	...	...	Larry Buckingham	...
Caro	v	CM	4	(989) 673-2226	Thomas Striffler	Donald Beavers	Karen Snider	...	David Mattlin	Benson Page	Charles Sundblad
Cascade Charter	tp	CM	15	(616) 949-1500	Michael Julien	...	M. Kleinheksel	...	John Sigg	...	...
Caseville	v	CM	..	(989) 856-2102	...	...	Nancy Moss	Forrest Williams	...	Jamie Learman	David Quinn
Caspian	c	CM	..	(906) 265-2514	Mark Stauber	Richard Frighetto	...	...	Jerry Anderson	Curt Soderbloom	Mark Ghiggia
Cass City	v	CM	2	(989) 872-2911	Lambert Althaver	Peter Cristiano	Nanette Walsh	...	...	Craig Haynes	Gary Barnes
Cassopolis	v	CM	1	(616) 445-8648	Julia Bell	...	Paula Beauchamp	...	William Fitzgerald	Frank Williams	Daniel Bates
Cedar Springs *	c	CM	3	(616) 696-1330	Linda Hunt	Christine Burns	Linda Branyan	Linda Lehman	Jerry Gross	Roger Gren	Gerald Hall
Center Line	c	CM	8	(586) 757-2297	...	Nancy Bourgeois	...	...	...	...	Dennis Tenniswood
Charlevoix *	c	CM	2	(231) 547-3270	Norman Carlson	Robert Straebel	Carol Ochs	...	Paul Ivan	Gerard Doan	Patrick Elliott
Charlotte *	c	CM	8	(517) 543-2750	Deb Shaugnessy	...	Catalina Beasley	Christine Mossner	Kevin Fullerton	William Callahan	Amy Schoonover
Charter Township Of Port Huron	tp	CM	8	(810) 987-6600	...	Michael Uskiewicz	...	...	...	...	...
Charter Township Of West Bloomfield	tp	MC	64	(248) 451-4800	...	...	...	...	...	...	...
Cheboygan	c	CM	5	(231) 627-9931	James Muschell	Scott McNeil	K. Kwiatkowski	...	David Lloyd	Kurt Jones	David LaCross
Chelsea	c	CM	4	(734) 475-1771	Ann Feeney	...	Teresa Burtch	...	...	...	...
Chesaning	v	CM	2	(989) 845-3800	Douglas Corwin	...	Denise Ebenhoeh	...	...	...	Joe Pacek
Clare	c	CM	3	(989) 386-7541	Pat Humphrey	Ken Hibl	Kay Haven	Neil Hammerbacher	Kent Randall	D. Miedzianowski	Robert Bonham
Clawson	c	CM	12	(248) 435-4500	Lisa Dwyer	Richard Haberman	G. Machele Kukuk	Mark Pollock	Douglas Ballard	Bruce Henderlight	Harry Drinkwine
Clinton	tp	MC	95	(586) 286-8000	Robert Cannon	...	Dennis Tomlinson	Norman Troppens	John Murphy	Al Ernst	George Westerman
Clio *	c	CM	2	(810) 686-5850	William Kovl	Thomas Yost	Michelle King	...	James Bronson	James McLellan	David Green
Coldwater *	c	CM	12	(517) 279-9501	Eugene Wallace	William Stewart	Ruth Ann Volkmer	Jeffrey Budd	...	...	David Sattler
Constantine	v	CM	2	(269) 435-2085	...	Mark Honeysett	...	Jody Boulette	...	Jeffrey Blough	J. Hamminga
Coopersville *	c	CM	3	(616) 997-9731	Kenneth Bush	Steven Patrick	Stephanie Pelkey	...	Lee Waldie	...	Ken Orquist
Corunna	c	MC	3	(989) 743-3650	Stephen Corey	Joseph Sawyer	...	...	Scott Johnson	Kim Williams	Timothy Crawford
Croswell	c	CM	2	(810) 679-2299	...	...	Suzanne Dobson	...	...	Dave Hall	Tom Dickensheets
Crystal Falls	c	CM	1	(906) 875-3212	Jeffrey Cram	Charles Nordeman	...	...	John Ahola	Jack Bicigo	Dennis Fabbri
Davison	c	CM	5	(810) 653-2191	Federick Rappuhn	Peter Auger	Cynthia Payton	...	Michael Wright	William Brandon	Scott Yaklin
De Witt	c	CM	4	(517) 669-2441	...	Brian Vick	Denice Smith	...	Robin Ballard	Larry Jerue	...
Dearborn	c	MC	97	(313) 943-2320	Michael Guido	Mark Guido	Kathleen Buda	James O'Connor	Michael Birrell	Timothy Strutz	Kurt Giberson
Dearborn Heights *	c	MC	58	(313) 791-3420	Daniel Paletko	...	Judy Dudzinski	Donald Barrow	Andy Gurka	Michael Gust	Jack Franzil
Decatur	v	CM	1	(616) 426-6114	Carl Wickett	Martin Super	Lou Ann Conklin	...	...	David McLeese	Dale Avery
Delhi	tp	CM	22	(517) 694-2137	Stuart Goodrich	John Elsinga	Evan Hope	...	Richard Royston	...	...
Delta *	tp	CM	29	(517) 323-8500	Joseph Drolett	Richard Watkins	Janice Vedder	Jeffrey Anderson	Victor Hilbert	...	Stanley Wegrzyn
Detroit	c	MC	951	(313) 224-3400	Dennis Archer	Nettie Seabrooks	Jackie Currie	Valerie Johnson	Harold Watkins	Isaiah McKinnon	Clyde Dowell
Dewitt *	tp	CM	12	(517) 668-0270	Rick Galardi	Rodney Taylor	Diane Mosier	...	Fred Koos	Brian Russell	...
Dexter	v	CM	2	(734) 426-8308	Jim Seta	Donna Dettling	David Boyle	...	...	...	Ed Lobdell
Dowagiac	c	CM	6	(616) 782-2195	Donald Lyons	Dale Martin	James Snow	David Pilot	Harold Munson	Thomas Atkinson	Donald Hallowell
Dundee *	v	CM	3	(734) 529-3430	Ted Norris	Patrick Burtch	D. Westbrook	Robin Moon	...	...	...
Durand	c	CM	3	(989) 288-3113	James Schuyler	Lynn Markland	Amy Roddy	...	...	Michael Tanner	Steven Mince
East Grand Rapids *	c	CM	10	(616) 949-2110	Cindy Bartman	Brian Donovan	Karen Brower	Laura Vanderwall	...	...	Ken Feldt
East Jordan	c	CM	2	(231) 536-3381	...	David White	Lori Campbell	...	...	Daniel Reece	William Breakey
East Lansing *	c	CM	46	(517) 337-1731	Samir Singh	Theodore Staton	Sharon Reid	Mary Haskell	Randall Talifarro	Thomas Wibert	Todd Sneathen
East Tawas *	c	CM	2	(989) 362-6161	Bruce Bolen	Ronald Leslie	Blinda Baker	...	William Deckett	Dennis Frank	Thomas Lixey
Eastpointe *	c	CM	34	(586) 445-5016	David Austin	Darwin Parks	...	Susan Mancani	Danny Hagen	Michael Lauretti	Gregory Brown
Eaton Rapids	c	CM	5	(517) 663-8118	Donald Colestock	William Lefevere	Kristy Reinecke	...	Roger McNutt	Carl Watkins	Howard Hillard
Ecorse	c	MC	11	(313) 386-2344	James Tassis	...	Phyllis Cook	William Barnett	Charles Lafferty	James Hunt	...
Edmore	v	CM	1	(989) 427-5641	...	...	Shirley Drain	...	...	Timber Irwin	Charles Burr
Elk Rapids	v	CM	1	(231) 264-9274	Joseph Yuchasz	Robert Peterson	Barbara Manley	...	...	Michael Miles	Ronald Ridge
Emmett	tp	MC	11	(269) 968-0241	...	...	...	...	...	...	...
Escanaba	c	CM	13	(906) 786-9402	Judith Schwalbach	...	Robert Richards	Michael Dewar	...	...	Bill Farrell
Essexville *	c	CM	3	(989) 893-0772	Thomas Rehmus	Dale Majerczyk	Cynthia Fournier	...	...	...	Daniel Hansford
Evart	c	CM	1	(231) 734-2181	...	Roger Elkins	Martha Pattee	...	Shane Helmer	Kirt Vink	James Ward
Farmington	c	CM	10	(248) 474-5500	James Mitchell	Vincent Pastue	...	Patsy Cantrell	...	...	Kevin Gushman
Farmington Hills	c	CM	82	(248) 474-6115	Nancy Bates	Steven Brock	Kathryn Dornan	Charles Rosch	Richard Marinucci	William Dwyer	Thomas Biasell
Fenton	c	CM	10	(810) 629-2261	Sue Osborn	Michael Senyko	Melinda Carrier	...	Dennis Smith	Richard Aro	Leslie Bland
Ferndale *	c	CM	22	(248) 546-2360	Robert Porter	Robert Bruner	J. C. Tallman	J. Hubanks	Roger Schmidt	Michael Kitchen	Byron Photiades
Ferrysburg *	c	CM	3	(616) 842-5803	Ray Tejchma	Craig Bessinger	Debbie Wierenga	...	Mike Olthof	Roger DeYoung	George Dunning
Flat Rock *	c	MC	8	(734) 782-2455	...	...	Lorene Butski	Richard Jones	William Vack	Stephen Tallman	...
Flint	c	MC	124	(810) 766-7280	Woodrow Stanley	Peggy Cook	Inez Brown	Marc Pockett	Theron Wiggins	Trevor Hampton	J. Jones
Flushing *	c	CM	8	(810) 659-3130	Janice Gensel	Dennis Bow	...	...	Ronald Downing	Mark Hoornstra	Bryan Sutton
Fowlerville	v	CM	2	(517) 223-3771	Julie Woodward	Joseph Merucci	Melissa Keniston	...	John Wright	Gary Krause	Anthony Casali
Frankenmuth *	c	CM	4	(989) 652-9901	Gary Rupprecht	Charles Graham	Phillip Kerns	...	...	Donald Mawer	Randy Braeutigam
Franklin	v	MC	2	(248) 626-9666	James Pikulas	Jon Stoppels	Eileen Pulker	...	Anthony Averbuch	Edward Glomb	...
Fraser	c	CM	15	(586) 293-3102	Marilyn Lane	Jeffrey Bremer	...	Patricia Jamison	...	...	B. Van Fleteren
Fremont	c	CM	4	(231) 924-2101	James Rynberg	Chris Yonker	Todd Blake	...	Rusty Boeskool	Philip Deur	Brian Hettinger

Directory 1/9 continued — **OFFICIALS IN U.S. MUNICIPALITIES 2,500 AND OVER IN POPULATION**

Jurisdiction		Type	Form of govern-ment	2000 Popu-lation (000)	Main telephone number	Chief elected official	Appointed administrator	Clerk of the governing board	Chief financial officer	Fire chief	Police chief	Public works director
MICHIGAN continued												
Garden City		c	CM	30	(734) 525-8800	...	David Harvey	Allyson Bettis	...	Michael Todd	...	Jack Barnes
Gaylord		c	CM	3	(989) 732-4060	Gladys Solokis	Joseph Duff	Rebecca Curtis	...	Tim Warren	Joseph Fitzgerald	Keith Roberts
Genoa		tp	MC	15	(810) 227-5225	Gary McCririe	Michael Archinal	Paulette Skolarus	...	...	...	...
Gibraltar		c	MC	4	(734) 676-3900	James Beaubien	Paul Lehr	Cynthia Ward	Barbara Meyer	Arthur Beauman	...	...
Gladstone		c	CM	5	(906) 428-2311	Thomas Simaeve	Brant Kucera	Linda Gray	...	...	...	Robert Johnson
Gladwin		c	MC	3	(989) 426-9231	Thomas Winarski	Robert Moffit	Shannon Greaves	...	George Alward	Charles Jones	...
Grand Blanc		c	MC	8	(810) 694-1118	Michael Matheny	Randall Byrne	...	Richard Saathoff	James Harmes	Mark Heidel	Matthew Wurtz
Grand Blanc		tp	MC	29	(810) 424-2600	...	...	...	...	...	...	...
Grand Haven		c	CM	11	(616) 842-3210	...	Patrick McGinnis	Leah Spinner	James Bonamy	...	...	Dan Czarnecki
Grand Haven	*	tp	CM	13	(616) 842-5988	Joanne Marcetti	William Cargo	Sue Buitenhuis	Gary Schreiber	Thomas Gerencer	...	Mark VerBerkmoes
Grand Ledge		c	CM	7	(517) 627-2149	Thomas Peek	Jon Bayless	Gregory Newman	...	John Cagle	Martin Underhill	James Eimer
Grand Rapids		tp	MC	14	(616) 361-7391	Michael DeVries	...	Janice Hulbert	...	...	...	...
Grand Rapids		c	CM	197	(616) 456-3166	George Heartwell	Kurt Kimball	Mary Hegarty	Scott Buhrer	Robert VanSolkema	Harry Dolan	Patrick Bush
Grandville		c	CM	16	(616) 531-3030	James Buck	Kenneth Krombeen	Mary Meines	...	Harvey Veldhouse	Vernon Snyder	Ron Carr
Grayling		c	CM	1	(989) 348-2131	...	Allen Lowe	Michele Moshier	...	...	Karl Schriener	Douglas Duby
Green Oak		tp	MC	15	(810) 231-1333	Jan Plas	...	...	...	...	...	...
Greenville		c	CM	7	(616) 754-5645	Lloyd Walker	George Bosanic	...	...	...	...	Thomas Ledger
Grosse Ile		tp	CM	10	(734) 676-4422	Douglas Jones	...	Ute O'Connor	Brian Kuchik	Duncan Murdock	William Barron	Tim Taylor
Grosse Pointe		c	CM	5	(313) 885-5800	Dale Scrace	Peter Dame	Julie Arthurs	Glenn Mach	...	...	Paul Weitzel
Grosse Pointe Farms		c	CM	9	(313) 885-6600	Ronald Kneiser	Shane Reeside	...	John Modzinski	...	Robert Ferber	Terry Brennan
Grosse Pointe Park		c	CM	12	(313) 822-6200	Palmer Heenan	Dale Krajniak	Jane Blahut	...	...	...	Christon Reimel
Grosse Pointe Shores		v	CM	2	(313) 881-6565	James Cooper	Michael Kenyon	Victoria Boyce	Rhonda Ricketts	...	...	Brett Smith
Grosse Pointe Woods		c	CM	17	(313) 343-2440	Robert Novitke	Mark Wollenweber	Lisa Hathaway	Clifford Maison	...	...	Joseph Ahee
Gun Plain		tp	CM	5	(616) 685-9471	Shelly Edgerton	Sherry Mason	Martha Meert	...	...	...	...
Hamtramck	*	c	CM	22	(313) 876-7700	Karen Majewski	Donald Crawford	Melanie Babij	Nevrus Nazarko	James Szafarczyk	James Doyle	Martin Ladd
Hancock		c	CM	4	(906) 482-2720	...	Glenn Anderson	Karen Haischer	...	...	Michael Beaudoin	Doug Hoyrynen
Harbor Beach	*	c	MC	1	(989) 479-3363	Bob Swartz	Tom Youatt	...	...	J. P. Lermont	...	Gary Shedd
Harbor Springs		c	CM	1	(231) 526-2104	...	Frederick Geuder	Ronald McRae	...	...	Daniel Branson	Fredrick Ward
Harper Woods		c	CM	14	(313) 343-2500	Kenneth Poynter	James Leidlein	Mickey Todd	Laura Stowell	Sean Gunnery	R. Skotarczyk	William Snyder
Hart		c	CM	1	(231) 873-2488	Robert Steen	Stanley Rickard	...	...	...	Daniel Leimback	David Dillingham
Hartford		c	CM	2	(616) 621-2477	Theodore Johnson	Yemi Akinwale	Roxann Isbrecht	...	Ed Riley	Ramon Beltran	Daniel Staunton
Hartland		tp	MC	10	(810) 632-7498	...	James Wickman	...	...	...	...	...
Hastings		c	CM	7	(616) 945-2468	Franklin Campbell	Jeffrey Mansfield	Everil Manshum	...	Roger Caris	Jerry Sarver	Timothy Girrbach
Hazel Park		c	CM	18	(248) 546-4064	Jack Lloyd	Edward Klobucher	Sharon Pinch	...	...	David Niedermeier	Michael Mazzuckelli
Highland Park		c	MC	16	(313) 252-0022	...	...	...	...	...	...	...
Hillsdale	*	c	CM	8	(517) 437-6441	Michael Sessions	...	Parke Hayes	Bonnie Tew	...	...	Rick Rose
Holland		c	CM	35	(616) 355-1300	Albert McGeehan	Soren Wolff	...	...	Danny Henderson	John Kruithoff	Timothy Morawski
Holly		v	CM	6	(248) 634-9571	Peter Clemens	...	Marsha Powers	...	Jack Hollands	Rollie Gackstetter	Marvin Swanson
Homer		v	CM	1	(517) 568-4321	Jerry Stonebraker	...	Lea Nowlin	Teresa Hayes	William Burkwalt	John Kirkbride	Donald Drumm
Houghton		c	CM	7	(906) 482-1700	Thomas Merz	Robert Macinnes	Kurt Kuure	...	James Lightfoot	Ralph Raffaelli	Mark Zenner
Howard City		v	MC	1	(231) 937-4311	...	Mark Rambo	...	...	...	...	...
Howell		c	CM	9	(517) 546-3500	...	Reid Charles	Rebecca Ruttan	...	...	Roger Goralski	Terry Wilson
Hudson		c	CM	2	(517) 448-8983	Lee Daugherty	Frank Goodroe	Kimberly Murphy	...	Terry Camp	Charles Weir	Philip Goodlock
Hudsonville		c	CM	7	(616) 669-0200	D. Van Doeselaar	Pauline Luben	Jan Wiersum	D. Van de Roovaart	Richard Mohr	Michael Wieringa	John Gorney
Huntington Woods		c	CM	6	(248) 541-4300	Ronald Gillham	Alex Allie	Ruth Franzoni	Richard Lehmann	...	...	Larry Harworth
Huron		tp	CM	13	(734) 753-4466	...	...	...	...	...	...	...
Imlay City		c	CM	3	(810) 724-2135	J. Rodney Warner	Amy Planck	Janice Zuhlke	...	Kip Reaves	...	Larry Lloyd
Independence	*	tp	MC	32	(248) 625-5111	Dave Wagner	...	S. VanderVeen	Susan Hendricks	Steve Ronk	...	Linda Richardson
Inkster	*	c	CM	30	(313) 563-4232	Hilliard Hampton	Joyce Parker	V. Gutierrez-Smith	Charles Stanhouse	Mark Hubanks	Gregory Gaskin	Archer Collins
Ionia		c	MC	10	(616) 527-4170	Daniel Balice	Jason Eppler	Karen Confer	Catherine Pearce	...	...	Gary Cunningham
Iron Mountain		c	CM	8	(906) 774-8530	James Petroff	John Marquart	Lou Ann Hagen	James Brinker	Daniel Johnson	Peter Flaminio	David Farragh
Iron River	*	c	CM	1	(906) 265-4719	C. Soderbloom	...	Peggy Shamion	...	...	Michael Goriesky	Richard Anderson
Ironwood		c	CM	6	(906) 932-5050	Thomas Yelich	Keith Johnson	Anita Zak	Julie Frederickson	...	Joseph Cayer	James Davis
Ishpeming	*	c	CM	6	(906) 485-1091	Patrick Scanlon	Alan Bakalaski	Jenifer Holli	...	R. Delongchamp	James Bjorne	James Bertucci
Ithaca		c	CM	3	(989) 875-3200	George Bailey	Bradley Heffner	Gayla Foster	...	David Nelson	Lee Schlappi	Neil Allen
Jackson	*	c	CM	36	(517) 788-4046	...	William Ross	Lynn Fessel	Philip Hones	Larry Bosell	...	Glenn Chinavare
Jonesville	*	v	MC	2	(517) 849-2104	David Steel	...	Betsy Brooks	...	Dean Adair	Robert Corbett	Claude Russell
Kalamazoo		c	CM	77	(269) 337-8052	Robert Jones	Kenneth Collard	Stephen French	Angie Bennett	...	...	...
Kalkaska		v	CM	2	(231) 258-9191	Jeffery Fitch	Bill Cousins	...	Leslie Belcher	...	Melvin Hill	Allen Smith
Keego Harbor	*	c	CM	2	(248) 682-1930	Barbara Kline	Dale Stuart	Linda Voll	...	...	Dennis Watkins	Tony Hale
Kentwood	*	c	MC	45	(616) 554-0732	Richard Root	...	Dan Kasunic	Thomas Chase	James Carr	Richard Mattice	Ron Woods
Kingsford		c	CM	5	(906) 774-3526	...	Darryl Wickman	...	...	...	...	Anthony Edlebeck
Lake Isabella		v	CM	1	(989) 644-8654	George Dunn	Timothy Wolff	Jeffrey Grey	...	...	...	...
Lake Orion	*	v	CM	2	(248) 693-8391	William Siver	Jo Ann Van Tassel	Arlene Nichols	Janet Adams	...	Jerry Narsh	Scott Baker
L'Anse		v	MC	2	(906) 524-6116	...	...	...	...	...	...	...
Lansing		c	MC	119	(517) 483-4004	...	...	Chris Swope	Douglas Rubley	Greg Martin	Mark Alley	David Berridge
Lapeer		c	CM	9	(810) 664-5231	William Sprague	Dale Kerbyson	Donna Cronce	Paul Boucher	Terrence Kluge	Todd Alexander	John Lyons
Lathrup Village		c	CM	4	(248) 557-2600	...	Jeffrey Mueller	Gloria Harris-Ford	...	...	Robert Jones	...
Laurium		v	CM	2	(906) 337-1600	Leonard Miller	Edward Vertin	Amber Small	...	Joseph Shaltz	James Lemler	...
Leslie	*	c	CM	2	(517) 589-8236	Ron Schmit	...	Vyrna Weideman	Cheryl Neu	Mike Fancher	Robert Delamarter	Martha Owen
Lexington	*	v	CM	1	(810) 359-8631	Daniel Maliniak	Reid Charles	Karolyn McEntee	...	Mike Sharon	Kirk Sasinowski	Gary Flannigan
Lincoln Park	*	c	MC	40	(313) 386-1800	Steven Brown	Steve Duchane	Donna Breeding	Lisa Santos	Kenneth Elmore	Thomas Karnes	Robert Bartok
Linden		c	CM	2	(810) 735-7980	James McIntyre	Christopher Wren	Martha Donnelly	...	Brian Will	P. Van Driessche	James Letts
Litchfield	*	c	CM	1	(517) 542-2921	Edwin Smith	Douglas Terry	Roger Sprague	...	Dan Pitts	Steve Marson	...
Livonia		c	MC	100	(734) 466-2530	Jack Engebretson	...	Val Vandersloot	Michael Slater	Shadd Whitehead	Robert Stevenson	...
Lowell		c	CM	4	(616) 897-8457	C. Jeanne Shores	David Pasquale	Betty Morlock	...	Frank Martin	James Valentine	Daniel DesJarden
Ludington	*	c	CM	8	(231) 845-6237	John Henderson	John Shay	Gerry Klaft	...	Jerry Funk	Mark Barnett	Shawn McDonald
Mackinaw City		v	CM	..	(231) 436-5351	Robert Heilman	Jeffrey Lawson	Sandra Krueger	...	F. Thompson	Patrick Wyman	James Tamlyn
Madison Heights	*	c	CM	31	(248) 583-0829	Edward Swanson	Jon Austin	Carole Corbett	...	Richard Donahue	Kevin Sagan	...
Manistee		c	CM	6	(231) 398-2801	Robert Goodspeed	Mitchell Deisch	Michelle Wright	Edward Bradford	Sid Scrimger	David Bachman	John Garber
Manistique		c	CM	3	(906) 341-2290	John Hoag	Sheila Aldrich	Deborah Dougovito	...	...	...	Nicholas Bosanic
Marine City		c	CM	4	(810) 765-8847	George Bukowski	...	Helen Hazuka	...	Richard Tucker	Ronald Krueger	Richard Ames
Marlette		c	CM	2	(989) 635-7448	Kenneth Babich	Steven Schaub	...	...	...	...	Robert Foster
Marquette	*	c	CM	19	(906) 228-0480	Thomas Tourville	Judy Akkala	David Bleau	Gary Simpson	Thomas Belt	Philip Siegert	Scott Cambensy
Marquette		tp	CM	19	(906) 228-6220	Max Muelle	Randell Girard	Kathleen Musolf	...	Robert Sims	...	Kirk Page
Marshall	*	c	CM	7	(269) 781-5183	Bruce Smith	Christopher Olson	Donna Kolodica	Gail Bradstreet	...	Brett Pehrson	Timothy Eggleston
Marysville		c	CM	9	(810) 364-6613	Gary Orr	Jack Schumacher	Carolyn East	...	James Czarnecki	Mark Thorner	Steven Kerr
Mason		c	CM	6	(517) 676-9155	...	Martin Colburn	...	Kathy Revels	David Scutt	John Stressman	Joe Dean
Mattawan		v	CM	2	(269) 668-2128	Claude Powers	...	Harriet Kucinich	...	...	Donald Verhage	Tom Anthony
Mayville		v	CM	..	...	...	...	...	...	...	...	...

Directory 1/9 continued — OFFICIALS IN U.S. MUNICIPALITIES 2,500 AND OVER IN POPULATION

Jurisdiction	Type	Form of govern-ment	2000 Popu-lation (000)	Main telephone number	Chief elected official	Appointed administrator	Clerk of the governing board	Chief financial officer	Fire chief	Police chief	Public works director
MICHIGAN continued											
Melvindale	c	MC	10	(313) 429-1040	James Kinard	Mark Kibby	Valerie Cadez	Michael Lofton	Samuel Pedron	John Difatta	Eric Witte
Menominee	c	CM	9	(906) 863-2656	George Krah	Eric Strahl	Thomas Denike	. . .	. . .	. . .	Michael Roach
Meridian *	tp	CM	39	(517) 853-4200	Susan McGillicuddy	Gerald Richards	Mary Helmbrecht	Diana Hasse	Fred Cowper	David Hall	Raymond Severy
Middleville	v	CM	2	(616) 795-3385	. . .	George Strand	. . .	. . .	. . .	. . .	. . .
Midland	c	CM	41	(989) 837-3300	Bruce Johnson	Jon Lynch	Selina Tisdale	David Keenan	Leonardo Garcia	James St. Louis	Martin McGuire
Milan	c	CM	4	(734) 439-1501	Owen Diaz	Daniel Bishop	. . .	. . .	Robert Burch	Michael Stuck	Todd Knepper
Milford *	v	CM	6	(248) 684-1515	Tom Nader	Arthur Shufflebarger	Ann Collins	Becky Jacques	. . .	Wayne Walli	Robert Calley
Monroe	c	MC	22	(734) 243-0700	C. Cappuccilli	George Brown	Charles Evans	Michael O'Connel	William Bert	John Michrina	Scott Davidson
Montague	c	CM	2	(231) 893-1155	. . .	John French	Melinda O'Connell	. . .	. . .	Robert Rought	Thomas Kroll
Montrose	c	CM	1	(810) 639-6168	Eldon Dunklee	Frank Crosby	. . .	. . .	. . .	. . .	Matthew Fejedelem
Mount Clemens *	c	CM	17	(586) 469-6818	Barb Dempsey	. . .	Lynne Kennedy	Marilyn Dluge	. . .	. . .	Douglas Anderson
Mount Morris	c	CM	3	(810) 686-2160	Robert Slattery	. . .	Lisa Baryo	. . .	Robert Meuhlen	Frederick Thorsby	Jeffrey Roth
Mount Pleasant	c	CM	25	(989) 779-5321	C. Bradley Kilmer	Kathie Grinzinger	Robert Flynn	Nancy Ridley	Greg Walterhouse	. . .	Duane Ellis
Munising	c	CM	2	(906) 387-2095	Rod DesJardins	Douglas Bovin	Sue Roberts	. . .	Dan Malone	Steven Swanberg	. . .
Muskegon	c	CM	40	(231) 724-6716	Steve Warmington	Bryon Mazade	Gail Kundinger	Timothy Paul	Mark Kincaid	. . .	Robert Kuhn
Muskegon Heights	c	CM	12	(231) 733-8870	Rillastine Wilkins	. . .	Kordilia Buckner	Lori Doody	David Alves	Clifton Johnson	Michael Smith
Negaunee	c	CM	4	(906) 475-7700	Ray Rappazini	Thomas Manninen	. . .	Joan Du Shane	Tom Gardyko	Paul Waters	Dave Palmer
New Baltimore *	c	MC	7	(586) 725-2151	T. Goldenbogen	Marc Levise	Marcella Shinksa	. . .	Ken Lawfield	John Bolgar	Thomas Gunst
New Buffalo	c	CM	2	(616) 469-1500	Raymond Wojdula	Thomas Johnson	Joan Jones	. . .	Billy Taylor	Thomas Harken	Donald Krause
Newaygo *	c	CM	1	(231) 652-1657	Ron Armstrong	Rich Blachford	. . .	. . .	Jim Uthe	Pat Hedlund	Ron Wight
Niles	c	CM	12	(269) 683-4700	Michael McCauslin	Terry Eull	Ruth Harte	David Flowers	Larry Lamb	Richard Huff	Neil Coulston
North Muskegon	c	CM	4	(231) 744-1621	Chris Witham	Dennis Stepke	Ann Becker	. . .	James Kersman	Thomas Korabik	Bruce Moore
Northville	c	CM	6	(248) 349-1300	C. Johnson	Patrick Sullivan	Dianne Massa	Nicolette Bateson	James Allen	Gary Goss	James Gallogly
Northville	tp	CM	21	(248) 449-5087	. . .	Marvin Snider	. . .	. . .	. . .	. . .	. . .
Norton Shores	c	MC	22	(231) 798-4391	Nancy Crandall	Mark Meyers	Lynne Fuller	. . .	David Purchase	Dan Shaw	Gerald Bartoszek
Norway	c	CM	2	(906) 563-9961	Edward Coates	Ray Anderson	Trisha Plante	. . .	David Bal	John Jarecki	. . .
Novi *	c	CM	47	(248) 347-0460	David Landry	Clay Pearson	Maryanne Cornelius	Kathy Roy	Frank Smith	Doug Shaeffer	William McCusker
Oak Park *	c	CM	29	(248) 691-7410	Gerald Naftaly	James Hock	Sandy Gadd	James Ghedotte	. . .	. . .	Kevin Yee
Oakland Charter	tp	CM	13	(248) 651-4440	. . .	James Creech	. . .	. . .	. . .	. . .	. . .
Ontonagon *	v	CM	1	(906) 884-2305	Scott Frazer	. . .	Joan Nygard	. . .	. . .	. . .	Jerry Roehm
Ortonville	v	CM	1	(248) 627-4976	Susan Bess	. . .	. . .	. . .	. . .	. . .	. . .
Oscoda	tp	CM	7	(989) 739-8299	. . .	Robert Stalker	. . .	. . .	. . .	. . .	. . .
Otisville	v	CM	. .	(810) 631-4680	Tom Bess	David Tatrow	Andrea Barden	. . .	. . .	Leo Johnsen	. . .
Otsego *	c	CM	3	(616) 692-3391	. . .	Thad Beard	Angela Cronen	. . .	. . .	Gordon Konkle	David Dutton
Owosso *	c	CM	15	(989) 725-0568	Linda Robertson	Joseph Fivas	Amy Kohagen	Richard Williams	Michael Bradley	Michael Rau	. . .
Oxford	tp	MC	14	(248) 628-9787	William Dunn	Deanna Burns	Clara Sanderson	Beverly Johnson	. . .	Lori Collier	Tracy Deveroux
Oxford	v	CM	3	(248) 628-2543	George Del Vigna	Kervin Young	. . .	. . .	Jack LeRoy	M. Neymanowski	Donald Brantley
Parchment	c	CM	1	(269) 349-3785	Daniel DeGraw	R. Fleckenstein	Curtis Flowers	. . .	Timothy Bourgeois	William Bongers	Thomas LeRoy
Paw Paw	v	CM	3	(616) 657-3148	Roman Plaszczak	Larry Nielsen	. . .	Ke Ven Richcreek	Trevor Carlson	Russell Reynnells	John Ruiter
Petoskey	c	CM	6	(231) 347-2500	. . .	George Korthauer	. . .	Alan Terry	. . .	Michael Vargo	Walter Goodwin
Pinconning	c	CM	1	(989) 879-2360	Michael Duranczyk	Richard Byrne	Terri Hribek	. . .	David Ramsay	Thomas Tober	Timothy Stalker
Pittsfield Charter Township	tp	MC	30	(734) 822-3101	James Walter	. . .	Feliziana Meyer	. . .	Alan D'Agostino	. . .	. . .
Plainfield *	tp	CM	30	(616) 364-8466	George Meek	Robert Homan	Susan Morrow	Warren Smith	David Peterson	. . .	. . .
Plainwell *	c	CM	3	(269) 685-6821	Richard Brooks	Erik Wilson	Noreen Farmer	. . .	. . .	. . .	Rick Updike
Pleasant Ridge	c	CM	2	(248) 541-2900	Ralph Castelli	Sherry Ball	Amy Porcs	. . .	. . .	Karl Swieczkowski	. . .
Plymouth *	c	CM	9	(734) 453-1234	Daniel Dwyer	Paul Sincock	Linda Langmesser	Mark Christiansen	Randy Maycock	. . .	Chris Porman
Plymouth	tp	MC	27	(734) 453-3840	Richard Reaume	. . .	Marilyn Massengill	. . .	Randy Maycock	Thomas Tiderington	James Anulewicz
Pontiac	c	MC	66	(248) 758-3000	Willie Payne	Leon Jukowski	Vivian Spann	J Edward Hannan	Wilburt McAdams	Rollie Gackstetter	Claudia Filler
Port Huron *	c	CM	32	(810) 984-9723	Alan Cutcher	Karl Tomion	Pauline Repp	John Ogden	Robert Eick	William Corbett	Robert Clegg
Portage	c	CM	44	(269) 329-4412	James Graham	Maurice Evans	James Hudson	Daniel Foecking	Randolph Lawton	Richard White	Jack Hartman
Portland	c	CM	3	(517) 647-7531	Peter Weeks	. . .	Yvonne Bailey	Brenda Schrauben	. . .	David Brown	Jon Hyland
Potterville	c	CM	2	(517) 645-7641	Brian Grosnickle	Ron Howell	R. Cwiertniewicz	. . .	Jack Fox	Van Johnson	Bradley Boyce
Reading	c	CM	1	(517) 283-2604	Michael Redenius	. . .	. . .	. . .	Michael McCauit	George Turchan	T. Stephenson
Redford	tp	MC	54	(313) 387-2700	Kevin Kelley	. . .	Garth Christie	J Cubba	Edwin Leonard	John Buck	Leo Snage
Reed City	c	CM	2	(231) 832-2245	Janet Campau	George Freeman	Jane Wekenman	. . .	Jim Decker	Charles Davis	Kevin Rambadt
Richland	tp	MC	. .	(989) 642-2097	Joel Wardin	Renee Herhold	Kevin Kreger	. . .	Gary Wade	Robert Dalton	Timothy Rohn
Richmond	c	CM	4	(586) 727-7571	Tim Rix	. . .	Karen Stagl	. . .	Jack Smith	Dennis Privette	Paul Fejedelem
River Rouge	c	MC	9	(313) 842-0801	Greg Joseph	. . .	Charles Manley	. . .	David Chirillo	John Birrbach	Cornelius Cooper
Riverview	c	CM	13	(734) 281-4201	Tim Durand	. . .	Judy Bratcher	Doug Daysdale	Robert Hale	Dean Workman	Gerald Perry
Rochester	c	CM	10	(248) 651-9061	David Katulic	Kenneth Johnson	Lee Ann O'Connor	. . .	Daniel Jacobson	Theodore Glynn	David Kowaleski
Rochester Hills	c	MC	68	(248) 656-4600	Patricia Somerville	. . .	Beverly Vasinski	Robert Spaman	G. Walterhouse	. . .	Roger Rousse
Rockford	c	CM	4	(616) 866-1537	. . .	Michael Young	Christine Bedford	Jeff Dood	Michael Reus	John Porter	Richard Johnston
Rockwood *	c	MC	3	(734) 379-9496	Philip Smalley	. . .	Patricia Roxberry	. . .	Daniel Mercure	R. VanWassehnova	Adam Grabetz
Rogers City	c	CM	3	(989) 734-2191	Beach Hall	Mark Slown	Theresa Heinzel	. . .	Timothy Luebke	Matthew Quaine	William Robin
Romeo	v	MC	3	(586) 752-3565	Paul Reiz	. . .	Marian McLaughlin	. . .	. . .	J. Vanderlinder	Rory Trowsse
Romulus	c	MC	22	(734) 942-7512	Alan Lambert	Besey Krampitz	Linda Choate	Debra Hoffman	David Allison	Charles Kirby	Richard Suiter
Roosevelt Park	c	CM	3	(231) 755-3721	Robert Young	William Boehm	Marcia Jeske	. . .	. . .	William Wiebenga	Matt Farrar
Roscommon *	v	CM	1	(989) 275-5743	Jesse Carlson	. . .	Kathryn Muphy	. . .	. . .	. . .	Dave Hodges
Roseville *	c	CM	48	(586) 445-5410	Harold Haugh	Stephen Truman	Rae Oldaugh	Peter Provenzano	Benjamin Foronato	Richard Heinz	Gary Bierl
Royal Oak *	c	CM	60	(248) 246-3000	James Ellison	Thomas Hoover	Mary Graver	. . .	Wil White	T. Quisenberry	Greg Rassel
Saginaw	c	CM	61	(989) 759-1480	. . .	Darnell Earley	Yolanda Olgine	. . .	Joe Dziuban	Gerald Cliff	Thomas Darnell
Saginaw	tp	CM	39	(989) 791-9800	Timothy Braun	Ronald Lee	Shirley Wazny	Michele Gadd	Jim Peterson	. . .	Herbert Grunwell
Saline	c	MC	8	(734) 429-4907	Gretchen Driskell	. . .	Dianne Hill	Lee Bourgoin	Craig Hoeft	Paul Bunten	George Danneffel
Sandusky	c	CM	2	(810) 648-4444	. . .	Lou LaPonsie	Laurie Thompson	Polly Frost	. . .	Paul Cowley	Phillip Klaus
Saugatuck	c	CM	1	(616) 857-4243	. . .	Kirk Harrier	. . .	. . .	. . .	. . .	. . .
Sault Ste. Marie *	c	CM	16	(906) 632-5705	Anthony Bosbous	Spencer Nebel	Lori Clarke	John Boger	Kenneth Eagle	Louis Murray	James Atkins
Schoolcraft	v	CM	1	(269) 679-4304	. . .	Cheri Lutz	. . .	. . .	. . .	. . .	. . .
Scio	tp	CM	15	(734) 665-2123	. . .	Darrell Fecho	. . .	. . .	. . .	. . .	. . .
Scottville	c	CM	1	(231) 757-4729	Leon Begue	Amy Hansen	Deborah Howe	. . .	Rick Gleason	Larry Nichols	James Kriesel
South Haven	c	CM	5	(269) 637-0700	Dale Lewis	Kevin Anderson	Amanda Sleigh	. . .	Randy VanWynen	Rod Somerlott	Robert Stickland
South Lyon	c	CM	10	(248) 437-1735	John Doyle	Rodney Cook	Julie Zemke	. . .	. . .	Lloyd Collins	Steve Renwick
Southfield *	c	CM	78	(248) 796-5000	Brenda Lawrence	. . .	Nancy Banks	James Scharret	Peter Healy	Joseph Thomas	Gary Mekjian
Southgate	c	MC	30	(734) 246-1305	Norma Wurmlinger	. . .	Tom Alexander	David Angileri	Randy Layton	. . .	Denny Gendron
Sparta *	v	MC	4	(616) 887-8251	Leonard Meyer	. . .	Greta Heugel	Sharon DeLange	Jerold Bolen	Andrew Milanowski	. . .
Spring Lake	v	CM	2	(616) 842-1393	William Filber	Ryan Cotton	Maribeth Lawrence	. . .	. . .	Roger DeYoung	. . .
Springfield	c	CM	5	(269) 965-2354	Susan Anderson	Franklin Peterson	Kristen Vogel	Jeannine Turner	. . .	. . .	Tom Matson
St. Charles *	v	CM	2	(989) 865-8287	Ray Cornford	Hal Mead	Deanna Koehler	. . .	. . .	Kevin McInerney	. . .
St. Clair *	c	CM	5	(810) 329-7121	William Cedar	Scott Adkins	Janice Winn	Michael Booth	. . .	Donald Barnum	Jeff Westrick
St. Clair Shores	c	CM	63	(586) 445-5200	. . .	Kenneth Podolski	Mary Kotowski	Timothy Haney	. . .	Francis Troester	Donald Hubler
St. Ignace	c	CM	2	(906) 643-9671	. . .	Gary Heckman	Renee Vonderwerth	. . .	John Robinson	Timothy Matelski	Les Therrian

Directory 1/9 continued — OFFICIALS IN U.S. MUNICIPALITIES 2,500 AND OVER IN POPULATION

Jurisdiction	Type	Form of govern-ment	2000 Popu-lation (000)	Main telephone number	Chief elected official	Appointed administrator	Clerk of the governing board	Chief financial officer	Fire chief	Police chief	Public works director
MICHIGAN continued											
St. Johns	c	CM	7	(989) 224-8944	Dana Beaman	Dennis LaForest	Mindy Seavey	. . .	Richard Cornwell	. . .	Jeffrey Stephens
St. Joseph	c	CM	8	(269) 983-5541	Mary Goff	Frank Walsh	Peggy Block	. . .	Kevin Luhrs	Mark Clapp	Roy Dost
St. Louis *	c	CM	4	(989) 681-2137	George Kubin	Robert McConkie	Nancy Roehrs	. . .	. . .	Patrick Herblet	Mark Abbott
Standish	c	CM	1	(989) 846-9588	Ray Koroliski	Tori Kelly	Becky Lakin	. . .	. . .	. . .	Greg Norgan
Sterling Heights *	c	CM	124	(586) 446-2489	Richard Notte	Mark Vanderpool	Walter Blessed	Brian Baker	John Childs	. . .	Guy Kebbe
Stevensville	v	MC	1	(616) 429-1802	Michele Getz	Bret Witkowski	Deb Warragen	. . .	. . .	. . .	. . .
Stockbridge	v	CM	1	(517) 851-7435	Daniel Dancer	. . .	Kristen Ottke	. . .	. . .	. . .	Shane Batdorff
Sturgis	c	CM	11	(269) 651-2321	C. S.-Horstman	Michael Hughes	Kenneth Rhodes	Michael Vance	Michael Houck	Eugene Alli	Rick Miller
Swartz Creek *	c	CM	5	(810) 635-4464	Richard Abrams	Paul Bueche	Juanita Aguilar	Mary Jo Clark	Brent Cole	Rick Clolinger	Thomas Svrcek
Sylvan Lake	c	CM	1	(248) 682-1440	. . .	John Martin	. . .	. . .	. . .	Richard Hummel	. . .
Tawas City	c	CM	2	(989) 362-8688	Edward Nagy	. . .	Kay Whitney	. . .	Steve Masiett	Dennis Frank	. . .
Taylor	c	MC	65	(734) 374-1491	Gregory Pitoniak	James Riddle	Dorothy West	Dean Philo	Kenneth Costella	Thomas Bonner	James Katona
Tecumseh	c	CM	8	(517) 423-2107	. . .	Kevin Welch	Laura Caterina	. . .	Joseph Tuckey	Mack Haun	Steven Johnston
Tekonsha	v	MC	. .	(517) 767-4204	Lisa Long	. . .	Howard Rigg	. . .	. . .	. . .	. . .
The Village Of Douglas	c	MC	2	(269) 857-1438	. . .	David Kowal	. . .	. . .	. . .	. . .	. . .
Thomas	tp	CM	11	(989) 781-0150	. . .	Russell Taylor	. . .	. . .	. . .	. . .	. . .
Three Oaks *	tp	MC	2	(269) 756-9801	Charles Sittig	. . .	E. Cummings	. . .	David Flick	. . .	. . .
Three Oaks	v	MC	1	(269) 756-9221	Philip Smith	. . .	Mary Nallenweg	. . .	. . .	Frank Nekvasil	Todd Noble
Three Rivers	c	CM	7	(269) 273-1075	Thomas Lowry	Joseph Bippus	Barbara Redford	W. Hochstedler	Danny Cross	Earl Stark	Mark Glessner
Tittabawassee	tp	CM	7	(989) 695-9512	. . .	Brian Kischnick	. . .	Brian Hofmeister	. . .	Robert Harken	. . .
Traverse City	c	CM	14	(231) 922-4440	Margaret Dodd	Richard Lewis	Debbra Curtiss	W. Twietmeyer	Edward Fisher	Michael Warren	Robert Cole
Trenton	c	MC	19	(734) 675-6500	Patricia Hartig	Robert Cady	Kyle Stack	David Flaten	Joseph Grutza	James Menna	Lawrence Dusincki
Troy *	c	CM	80	(248) 524-3300	Louise Schilling	Phillip Nelson	Tonni Bartholomew	John Lamerato	William Nelson	Charles Craft	Timothy Richnak
Union	tp	CM	3	(989) 772-4600	James Collin	Gwen Plowman	Susan Gilpin	. . .	. . .	. . .	Kimberly Smith
Union City	v	CM	1	(517) 741-8591	Gene Tassie	Keith Baker	Diane Smith	. . .	David Hughes	Tom Case	David Johnson
Utica	c	MC	4	(586) 739-1600	Jacqueline Noonan	. . .	M. McGrail	Philip Paternoster	Robert Beck	Michael Reaves	William Lang
Vassar *	c	CM	2	(989) 823-8517	Evart Stewart	Kevin Mackey	Tina Bacon	. . .	Gary Millerov	David Manier	. . .
Vicksburg *	v	CM	2	(616) 649-1919	Daniel Pryson	Matthew Crawford	. . .	. . .	. . .	M. Descheneau	Kenneth Schippers
Wakefield	c	CM	2	(906) 229-5132	. . .	. . .	. . .	. . .	. . .	. . .	. . .
Walker *	c	CM	21	(616) 453-6311	Robert VerHeulen	C. VanderMeulen	Sandy Wisniewski	Cindy Mielke	William Schmidt	C. Garcia-Lindstrom	Mark Koning
Walled Lake	c	CM	6	(248) 624-4847	. . .	Jerry Walker	Catherine Metevia	. . .	K. VanSparrentak	John Woychowski	Loyd Cureton
Warren	c	MC	138	(586) 574-4520	Mark Steenbergh	Michael Griner	. . .	Richard Fox	Henry Gesing	John Baird	Robert Slavko
Waterford	tp	CM	73	(248) 674-3111	Katherine Innes	. . .	Betty Fortino	. . .	Dennis Storrs	Paul Vallad	Terry Biederman
Wayland *	c	CM	3	(269) 792-2265	Burrell Stein	Deborah Nier	Sharon Baumgard	. . .	Joe Miller	Daniel Miller	Pierre Brazeau
Wayne	c	CM	19	(734) 722-2000	. . .	John Zech	Mary Carney	Thomas Norwood	Robert Dahlman	Michael Sumeracki	Gary Clark
West Branch	c	CM	1	(989) 345-0500	. . .	. . .	Jane Tennant	. . .	Brent Banning	Rodger Williams	Richard Dack
Westland	c	MC	86	(734) 467-3225	Sandra Cicirelli	. . .	Nancy Bonaparte	. . .	Michael Reddy	Dan Pfannes	Thomas Wilson
White Cloud *	c	CM	1	(231) 689-1194	Donald Barnhard	Robert Sullivan	Dick England	. . .	Duane Cruzan	Roger Ungrey	Gary Zatalokin
Whitehall *	c	CM	2	(231) 894-4048	Emery Hatch	Scott Huebler	Karen Helmlinger	Laurie Audo	. . .	Donald Hulbert	Brian Armstrong
Williamston	c	CM	3	(517) 655-2774	. . .	Lisa Hitchcock	. . .	. . .	. . .	Mark Hetfield	Gary Haney
Wixom	c	CM	13	(248) 624-0894	Michael McDonald	J. Dornan	Linda Kirby	Kevin Brady	George Spencer	. . .	Michael Howell
Wolverine Lake	v	CM	4	(248) 624-1710	. . .	Sharon Miller	Rita Irwin	. . .	. . .	Joseph George	Andrew Stone
Woodhaven	c	MC	12	(734) 675-4900	Richard Truskowski	David Flaten	Sheryl McGlynn	. . .	Jan Sikes	Roy Rook	Michael Kruse
Wyandotte	c	MC	28	(734) 324-4500	Leonard Sabuda	. . .	William Griggs	Todd Drysdale	. . .	William Lilienthal	. . .
Wyoming	c	CM	69	(616) 530-7241	Douglas Hoekstra	Curtis Holt	Heidi Isakson	Timothy Smith	Gerald Ball	E. Edwardson	William Dooley
Ypsilanti *	tp	MC	49	(734) 481-0617	Ruth Ann Jamnick	. . .	Brenda Stumbo	M. Olshelfske	Larry Morabito	Michael Radzik	. . .
Ypsilanti	c	CM	22	(734) 483-1100	Cheryl Farmer	Edward Koryzno	Cherry Lawson	Marilou Uy	James Roberts	George Basar	Harry Hutchison
Zeeland	c	MC	5	(616) 772-6400	Lester Hoogland	Timothy Klunder	Nancy Tuls	Audrey Brodzinski	William Gruppen	William Olney	David Walters
Zilwaukee *	c	CM	1	(989) 755-0931	Eugene Jolin	Patricia Hascall	Richard DeLong	. . .	Michael Bauer	Bruce King	Warren Davis
MINNESOTA											
Ada	c	MC	1	(218) 784-4536	. . .	. . .	. . .	. . .	. . .	. . .	. . .
Afton	c	CM	2	(651) 436-5090	Dave Engstrom	. . .	. . .	. . .	. . .	. . .	. . .
Albert Lea	c	CM	18	(507) 377-4300	. . .	Victoria Simonsen	Sandi Behrens	Rhonda Krcil	Paul Stieler	Thomas Menning	Steve Jahnke
Albertville	c	MC	3	(763) 497-3384	. . .	Larry Kruse	. . .	. . .	. . .	. . .	. . .
Alexandria	c	MC	8	(320) 763-6678	H. Dan Ness	. . .	. . .	. . .	Michael Donnay	Chuck Nettestad	Truman Hanson
Andover *	c	CM	26	(763) 755-5100	Michael Gamache	James Dickinson	Victoria Volk	. . .	Daniel Winkel	. . .	Francis Stone
Annandale	c	CM	2	(320) 274-3055	Marian Harmoning	. . .	Sylvia Onstad	. . .	Brian Haag	Myron Morris	William McNellis
Anoka	c	CM	18	(763) 576-2700	Bjorn Skogquist	T. Cruikshank	Amy Oehlers	James Knutson	Charles Thompson	Edward Wilberg	Craig Gray
Apple Valley	c	CM	45	(952) 953-2500	M. Hamann-Roland	M. Lawell	Mary Mueller	George Ballenger	Keith Wassmund	. . .	Neal Heuer
Arden Hills *	c	MC	9	(651) 792-7800	Stan Harpstead	Michelle Wolfe	. . .	Sue Iverson	. . .	. . .	Gregory Hoag
Aurora *	v	MC	1	(218) 229-2614	Mary Hess	. . .	. . .	Linda Cazin	Kent Dickinson	William Lesar	C. Vreeland
Austin	c	MC	23	(507) 437-9940	. . .	James Hurm	Lucy Johnson	. . .	Daniel Wilson	Paul Philipp	Jon Erichson
Barnesville	c	MC	2	(218) 354-2292	Ken Bauer	Michael Brethorst	. . .	. . .	. . .	Dean Ernst	. . .
Baxter	c	MC	5	(218) 454-5100	Darrel Olson	Dennis Coryell	Beva Olson	Jeremy Vacinek	. . .	James Exsted	Trevor Walter
Bayport	c	MC	3	(651) 275-4404	Rick Schneider	. . .	. . .	John Nash	Scott Radke	John Gannaway	Milan Horak
Becker	c	CM	2	(763) 261-4302	Kenneth Paulson	Harry Rudberg	Nancy Fiereck	Brenda Weller	Chad Stephens	. . .	Karla Eggink
Belle Plaine	c	MC	3	(612) 873-5553	Maynard Harms	Luayn Murphy	. . .	Dawn Meyer	Christopher Meyer	Steven Rost	Alan Fahey
Bemidji	c	CM	11	(218) 759-3560	Richard Lehmann	John Chattin	Shirley Sherman	Ron Eischens	Kelly Skime	. . .	Andy Mack
Benson	c	CM	3	(320) 843-4775	Paul Kittelson	Robert Wolfington	. . .	Glen Pederson	Gregory Lee	James Crace	Robert Flaws
Big Lake	c	CM	6	(763) 263-2107	Donald Orrock	. . .	Gina Wolbeck	Corey Boyer	. . .	Sean Rifenberick	Michael Goebel
Biwabik	c	CM	. .	(218) 865-4183	. . .	Pam Bertf	. . .	. . .	. . .	. . .	. . .
Blaine	c	CM	44	(763) 784-6700	. . .	. . .	Jane Hall	. . .	. . .	. . .	Mike Ulrich
Bloomington	c	CM	85	(952) 563-8700	Eugene Winstead	Mark Bernhardson	Thomas Ferber	L. E.-Scholler	Ulysses Seal	John Laux	Charles Honchell
Blue Earth	c	CM	3	(507) 526-7336	Robert Hammond	Benjamin Martig	. . .	Nancy Thompson	. . .	Dean Vereide	Richard LaMont
Brainerd	c	CM	13	(218) 828-2307	James Wallin	Daniel Vogt	. . .	Theresa Goble	Fred Underhill	John Bolduc	. . .
Breckenridge	c	MC	3	(218) 643-1431	. . .	. . .	Blaine Hill	. . .	. . .	Dennis Milbrandt	Paul Stollenwerk
Breezy Point *	c	MC	. .	(218) 562-4441	JoAnn Weaver	Bradley Scott	Kathy Millard	. . .	. . .	Steve Rudek	Tim Polipnick
Brooklyn Center	c	CM	29	(763) 569-3300	Myrna Kauth	Cornelius Boganey	Sharon Knutson	Daniel Jordet	Ronald Boman	Scott Bechthold	Todd Blomstrom
Brooklyn Park	c	CM	67	(763) 424-8000	Steven Lampi	Douglas Reeder	Devin Montero	Cory Kampf	Steven Schmidt	Greg Roehl (Acting)	Jon Thiel
Buffalo	c	CM	10	(763) 682-1181	Fred Naaktgeboren	Merton Auger	. . .	Mary Stubstad	Robin Barfknecht	Mitch Weinzetl	. . .
Buhl	c	CM	. .	(218) 258-3226	Craig Pulford	. . .	Patricia Marks	Mary Markas	Michael Lopac	. . .	John Markas
Burnsville	c	CM	60	(952) 895-4400	Elizabeth Kautz	Craig Ebeling	Susan Olesen	. . .	Ron Payne	David Farrington	. . .
Caledonia *	c	MC	2	(507) 725-3450	Michael Morey	Robert Nelson	. . .	Stephanie Mann	Charles Gavin	Randy Shefelbine	. . .
Cambridge	c	CM	5	(763) 689-3211	. . .	Stoney Hiljus	. . .	Jessie Hart	. . .	Michael Johnson	Steven Wegwerth
Cannon Falls *	c	MC	3	(507) 263-9300	. . .	. . .	. . .	. . .	John Miller	Jeffrey McCormick	Barry Underdahl
Carver	c	CM	1	(952) 448-5353	Jim Weygand	James Elmquist	Patricia Plekkenpol	. . .	Jerry Dauwalter	. . .	Paul Schultz
Centerville	c	MC	3	(651) 429-3232	Terry Sweeney	K. Moore-Sykes	Teresa Bender	Ellen Paulseth	Milo Bennett	. . .	Paul Palzar
Champlin	c	CM	22	(763) 421-8100	Steve Boynton	Bret Heitkamp	Jo Anne Brown	June Johnston	. . .	Alan Garber	. . .
Chanhassen	c	CM	20	(952) 227-1100	Thomas Furlong	Todd Gerhardt	. . .	Bruce DeJong	John Wolff	. . .	. . .
Chaska	c	CM	17	(952) 448-2851	Gary VanEyll	David Pokorney	Margo Steffel	. . .	Bruce Schueing	Scott Knight	Timothy Wiebe

Directory 1/9 continued — OFFICIALS IN U.S. MUNICIPALITIES 2,500 AND OVER IN POPULATION

Jurisdiction		Type	Form of govern-ment	2000 Popu-lation (000)	Main telephone number	Chief elected official	Appointed administrator	Clerk of the governing board	Chief financial officer	Fire chief	Police chief	Public works director
MINNESOTA continued												
Chisago City		c	CM	2	(651) 257-4162	C. DuBose	John Pechman	Paula Oehme	Gail Wilson	Bruce Peterson	W. Schlumbohm	Catherine Rude
Chisholm	*	c	MC	4	(218) 254-7900	Michael Jugovich	Garrison Hale	. . .	Gary Krampotich	Robert Brown	Scott Erickson	. . .
Circle Pines		c	CM	4	(763) 784-5898	Keith Perlich	James Keinath	. . .	Peggy Bauman	Milo Bennett	. . .	Richard Lavell
Clara City		c	MC	1	(320) 847-2142	Orville Meints	Sara Folsted	. . .	. . .	David Lieser	Ralph Bradley	Roger Knapper
Cloquet		c	MC	11	(218) 879-3347	. . .	Brian Fritsinger	Robert Norrgard	. . .	J. Langenbrunner	. . .	James Prusak
Cohasset		c	MC	2	(218) 328-6225	. . .	. . .	Debra Sakrison	. . .	. . .	. . .	. . .
Cokato		c	MC	2	(320) 286-5505	Bruce Johnson	Donald Levens	Peggy Carlson	. . .	Dennis Johnson	. . .	Kenneth Bakke
Cologne		c	MC	1	(952) 466-2064	. . .	John Douville	Laurel Jones	. . .	. . .	. . .	. . .
Columbia Heights		c	CM	18	(763) 706-3600	Gary Peterson	Walter Fehst	. . .	William Elrite	Gary Gorman	Thomas Johnson	Kevin Hansen
Coon Rapids	*	c	CM	61	(763) 755-2880	Tim Howe	Matthew Fulton	Joan Anderson	Sharon Legg	John Piper	Steve Wells	Steven Gatlin
Corcoran		c	MC	5	(763) 420-2288	Kenneth Guenthner	Susan Vergin	Kary Tillmann	. . .	. . .	Paul Schutte	Patrick Meister
Cottage Grove		c	CM	30	(651) 458-2800	. . .	Ryan Schroeder	Caron Stransky	Ronald Hedberg	Robert Byerly	. . .	Les Burshten
Cottonwood		c	CM	1	(507) 423-6488	Ellen Lenz	. . .	Gregory Isaackson	. . .	. . .	. . .	. . .
Crookston		c	MC	8	(218) 281-1232	Don Osborne	Aaron Parrish	Al Chesley	. . .	Dick Rock	Paul Monteen	Patrick Kelly
Crystal		c	CM	22	(763) 531-1000	. . .	Anne Norris	Janet Lewis	. . .	. . .	Harold Algyer	Thomas Mathisen
Dassel	*	c	CM	1	(320) 275-2454	Ava Flachmeyer	Myles Mc Grath	. . .	. . .	Dale Grochow	. . .	David Scepaniak
Dawson		c	CM	1	(320) 769-2154	Al Schacherer	David Bovee	Melva Larson	. . .	Jeff Olson	William Stock	Brent Powers
Dayton		c	CM	4	(763) 427-4589	James Jadwin	Samantha Orduno	Sandra Borders	. . .	. . .	Richard Pietrzak	Richard Hass
Deephaven		c	CM	3	(952) 474-4755	. . .	. . .	Sandra Langley	. . .	. . .	Harlan Johnson	Gerald Hudlow
Delano		c	MC	3	(763) 972-0550	John Jaunich	Philip Kern	Marlene Kittock	. . .	Bob Van Lith	. . .	Dan Alger
Detroit Lakes		c	CM	7	(218) 847-5658	Larry Buboltz	Robert Louiseau	. . .	Louis Guzek	Jeffrey Swanson	Kelvin Keena	. . .
Dilworth		c	MC	3	(218) 287-2313	Paul Marquart	Ken Parke	. . .	Gwynn Misialek	Dave Lamb	Michael Jacklovich	Donald Vogel
Dodge Center		c	CM	2	(507) 374-2575	Bill Ketchum	Lee Mattson	Julene Ellefson	. . .	. . .	. . .	Lee Fitzgerald
Duluth		c	MC	86	(218) 723-3291	Gary Doty	. . .	Jeffrey Cox	Les Bass	Daniel Haus	. . .	Richard Larson
Eagan		c	CM	63	(651) 675-5000	Pat Geagan	Thomas Hedges	Maria Petersen	Thomas Pepper	Michael Scott	James McDonald	Tom Colbert
Eagle Lake		c	MC	1	(507) 257-3218	Tim Auringer	Brad Potter	Kerry Rausch	. . .	. . .	Phil Wills	Richard Reinbold
East Bethel		c	MC	10	(763) 434-9569	. . .	Douglas Sell	Wendy Warren	Robert Sundberg	Arden Anderson	. . .	Jack Davis
East Grand Forks		c	MC	7	(218) 773-2483	Lynn Stauss	. . .	. . .	. . .	Randy Gust	Michael Lealos	John Thompson
Eden Prairie	*	c	CM	54	(952) 949-8300	Phil Young	. . .	Kitty Porta	Sue Kotchevar	George Esbensen	Rob Reynolds	Eugene Dietz
Edina	*	c	CM	47	(952) 927-8861	James Hovland	Gordon Hughes	Debra Mangen	John Wallen	Martin Scheerer	Michael Siitari	. . .
Elk River		c	MC	16	(763) 635-1000	Stephanie Klinzing	Lori Johnson	Joan Schmidt	. . .	Bruce West	Jeffrey Beahen	. . .
Elko New Market		c	MC	2	(952) 461-2777	. . .	Thomas Terry	. . .	. . .	. . .	. . .	. . .
Ely		c	CM	3	(218) 365-3224	Lolita Schnitzius	Lee Tessier	. . .	Bob Hedloff	Gary Klun	John Manning	Ken Hegman
Eveleth		c	MC	3	(218) 744-2501	Calvin Cassalter	J. Monahan-Junek	Sharon Stimac	. . .	. . .	Brian Lillis	Michael Wiskow
Excelsior	*	c	CM	2	(952) 474-5233	Nick Ruehl	. . .	Cheri Johnson	. . .	Scott Gerber	Bryan Litsey	Dave Wisdorf
Eyota	*	c	MC	1	(507) 545-2135	Wesley Bussell	. . .	Marlis Knowlton	Mike Bubany	Jeremy Newton	. . .	Brad Boice
Fairmont		c	CM	10	(507) 238-9461	Donna Holstine	James Zarling	Lois Cairns	Thomas Koeritz	Joe Rosol	Erwin Thiel	Larry Read
Falcon Heights	*	c	MC	5	(651) 792-7600	Susan Gehrz	Justin Miller	M. Shea Kodluboy	Roland Olson	Clem Kurhajetz	John Ohl	Tim Pittman
Faribault	*	c	CM	20	(507) 334-2222	Chuck Ackman	Timothy Madigan	. . .	Terry Berg	Michael Monge	Michael Lewis	Mark Knoff
Farmington	*	c	CM	12	(651) 463-7111	Kevan Soderberg	Peter Herlofsky	. . .	Robin Roland	Tim Pietsch	Brian Lindquist	. . .
Fergus Falls		c	MC	13	(218) 739-2251	Russell Anderson	Mark Sievert	. . .	William Sonmor	Mark Hovland	Timothy Brennan	Clifton Allen
Forest Lake		c	MC	6	(651) 464-3550	Terry Smith	Charles Robinson	Chantal Doriott	Ellen Paulseth	Gary Sigfrinius	Clark Quiring	Mike Tate
Fosston		c	MC	1	(218) 435-1959	. . .	Charles Lucken	. . .	. . .	. . .	. . .	. . .
Franklin		c	MC	. .	(507) 557-2259	Ronald Degner	. . .	Wendy Pederson	. . .	. . .	. . .	Kevin Kokesch
Fridley		c	CM	27	(763) 572-3507	Scott Lund	William Burns	Debra Skogen	Richard Pribyl	Charles McKusick	David Sallman	Jon Haukaas
Gilbert		c	MC	1	(218) 748-2232	Michael Skenzich	Gary Mackley	. . .	. . .	Richard Kohler	Mark Skelton	David Ochis
Glencoe		c	CM	5	(320) 864-5586	. . .	Mark Larson	Ruth Lange	Karla Kullman	Gary Vogt	Larry Aldape	Leroy Brelge
Glenwood		c	CM	2	(320) 634-5433	. . .	David Iverson	. . .	. . .	. . .	David Thompson	David Perryman
Golden Valley	*	c	CM	20	(763) 593-8000	Linda Loomis	Thomas Burt	. . .	Sue Virnig	Mark Kuhnly	. . .	Jeannine Clancy
Goodview	*	c	CM	3	(507) 452-1630	Jack Weimerskirch	. . .	Daniel Matejka	. . .	Rick Bambenek	La Vern Hauschildt	Greg Volkart
Grand Marais		c	MC	1	(212) 387-1848	Mark Sandbo	Michael Roth	. . .	Annette Dunsmoor	. . .	. . .	Russell Good
Grand Rapids	*	c	MC	7	(218) 326-7600	James Millis	Shawn Gillen	. . .	Shirley Miller	Dale Rosier	Leigh Serfling	Jeff Davies
Granite Falls		c	CM	3	(320) 564-3011	David Smiglewski	William Lavin	Joan Taylor	Darcy Mulvihill	Mike Ohliger	Russell Blue	Paul Krogstad
Ham Lake		c	MC	12	(763) 434-9555	. . .	. . .	. . .	. . .	. . .	. . .	. . .
Hanover		c	CM	1	(763) 497-3777	Joyce Paullin	Daniel Buchholtz	. . .	Melissa Barker	Tracey Franke	. . .	. . .
Harmony		c	CM	1	(507) 886-8122	. . .	. . .	. . .	. . .	. . .	. . .	. . .
Hastings		c	MC	18	(651) 480-2350	Michael Werner	David Osberg	. . .	Lori Webster	Mark Holmes	M. McMenomy	T. Montgomery
Hector	*	c	MC	1	(320) 848-2122	Jeff Heerdt	Matthew Jaunich	Barbara Johnson	. . .	Charlie Mathiowetz	Tony Faulid	Harold Carstens
Hermantown		c	CM	7	(218) 729-6331	Dan Urshan	Lynn Lander	Nancy Sirois	. . .	Ronald Minter	Terrance Ulshafer	James Olson
Hibbing	*	c	CM	17	(218) 262-3486	Rick Wolff	Brian Redshaw	Patrick Garrity	Sherri Lindstrom	Tony Pogorels	Barbara Mitchel	John Fairchild
Hopkins		c	CM	17	(952) 935-8474	Eugene Maxwell	Richard Getschow	Terry Obermaier	Christine Harkess	. . .	Craig Reid	Steven Stadler
Howard Lake		c	CM	1	(320) 543-3670	. . .	. . .	. . .	. . .	Joe Drusch	. . .	. . .
Hoyt Lakes	*	c	RT	2	(218) 225-2344	Marlene Pospeck	Richard Bradford	. . .	. . .	. . .	Steve Stoks	Mark Novosel
Hugo		c	CM	6	(651) 762-6300	Francis Miron	Michael Ericson	Mary Creager	Ronald Otkin	James Compton	. . .	Christopher Petree
Hutchinson		c	CM	13	(320) 587-5151	Steve Cook	Gary Plotz	. . .	Kenneth Merrill	Bradley Emans	Daniel Hatten	John Rodeberg
Independence		c	MC	3	(763) 479-0527	Marvin Johnson	Toni Hirsch	. . .	. . .	. . .	. . .	Daniel Koch
International Falls		c	MC	6	(218) 283-9484	Shawn Mason	Rodney Otterness	. . .	Mike Stanich	Jerry Jensen	Chris Raboin	. . .
Inver Grove Heights		c	CM	29	(651) 450-2500	George Tourville	Joseph Lynch	Cathy Iago	Ann Lanone	William McLean	. . .	Gary Johnson
Isanti	*	c	MC	2	(763) 444-5512	George Wimmer	Donald Lorsung	. . .	Rita Pierce	. . .	Ronald Sager	Patrick Meyer
Jackson	*	c	MC	3	(507) 847-4410	James Jasper	Dean Albrecht	. . .	Deb Mitchell	Larry Olson	Andre Schofield	. . .
Janesville		c	MC	2	(507) 234-6265	. . .	Clinton Rogers	. . .	. . .	. . .	David Ulmen	David Wheelock
Jordan	*	c	CM	3	(952) 492-2535	. . .	Edward Shukle	. . .	Tom Nikunen	Steve Kochlin	Bob Malz	Dave Bendzick
Kasson		c	MC	4	(507) 634-7071	Duane Burton	Randy Lenth	. . .	Lynne Erickson	Jeffrey Stevenson	David Johnson	Burton Fjerstad
Kenyon	*	c	MC	1	(507) 789-6415	Diane Barrett	Aaron Reeves	. . .	Sue Dodds	Doug Noah	Lee Sjolander	Thomas Bergeson
La Crescent		c	MC	4	(507) 895-2595	Mike Poellinger	Harris Waller	Phyllis Feiock	. . .	Bernie Buehler	Todd Nelson	. . .
Lake City	*	c	MC	4	(651) 345-5383	Katie Himanga	Ronald Johnson	Cindy Gosse	Barbara Pratt	Todd Hubbard	Lyle Schumann	Steve Kleeberger
Lake Elmo		c	MC	6	(651) 777-5510	Wyn John	Susan Hoyt	Sharon Lumby	Marilyn Banister	Richard Sachs	. . .	Dan Olinger
Lakefield		c	MC	1	(507) 662-5457	. . .	. . .	Kelly Rasche	Cheryl Ulferts	. . .	Jared Praska	Jim Koep
Lakeville	*	c	CM	43	(952) 985-4400	Robert Johnson	Steven Mielke	Charlene Friedges	Dennis Feller	Scott Nelson	Steven Strachan	Donald Volk
Lamberton		c	MC	. .	(507) 752-7601	Craig Wetter	. . .	Steven Flaig	. . .	. . .	James Clark	Wade Wellner
Lauderdale		c	CM	2	(651) 631-0300	Jeffrey Dains	Brian Heck	. . .	. . .	. . .	. . .	. . .
Le Sueur		c	CM	3	(507) 665-6401	Edward Rasmusen	Richard Almich	Laurie Swenson	Deborah Mediger	Le Roy Swenson	Bruce Kelly	Dean Kunze
Lexington	*	c	MC	2	(763) 784-2792	Donald Valenta	Dot Heifort	. . .	. . .	Paul Pechan	Robert Makela	. . .
Lino Lakes		c	MC	16	(651) 982-2400	. . .	Gordon Heitke	. . .	Al Rolek	. . .	David Pecchia	Rick De Gardner
Litchfield		c	CM	6	(320) 693-7201	Vernon Madson	Bruce Miller	Joyce Spreiter	. . .	Gale Smith	Bruce Dicke	. . .
Little Canada		c	CM	9	(651) 484-2177	William Blesener	Joel Hanson	. . .	Michele Ruechkert	. . .	. . .	Bill Dircks
Little Falls		c	CM	7	(320) 632-2341	. . .	. . .	. . .	. . .	Fred Tobatt	Michael Pender	Gerald Lochner
Long Lake		c	CM	1	(952) 473-6961	Randy Gilbert	Steven Stahmer	Jeanette Moeller	Terry Post	. . .	. . .	Marvin Wurzer
Long Prairie		c	CM	3	(320) 732-2167	. . .	. . .	. . .	. . .	. . .	. . .	. . .
Luverne		c	CM	4	(507) 449-2388	Glen Gust	John Call	Marianne Perkins	Barbara Berghorst	Donald Deutsch	. . .	Kenneth Vos

Directory 1/9 continued OFFICIALS IN U.S. MUNICIPALITIES 2,500 AND OVER IN POPULATION

Jurisdiction		Type	Form of govern-ment	2000 Popu-lation (000)	Main telephone number	Chief elected official	Appointed administrator	Clerk of the governing board	Chief financial officer	Fire chief	Police chief	Public works director
MINNESOTA continued												
Madison		c	CM	1	(320) 598-7373	Greg Thole	Garrison Hale	Kathleen Weber	Deloris Churness	Ken Fernholz	Stanley Ross	Harold Hodge
Madison Lake	*	c	MC	..	(507) 243-3011	Kenneth Reichel	...	Debra DeVlaeminck	...	Debb Pongratz	Daniel Bunde	Jeff Moe
Mahnomen		c	MC	1	(218) 935-2573	...	Mitchell Berg	...	...	...	...	...
Mahtomedi		c	CM	7	(651) 426-3344	...	Scott Neilson	...	Marlin Amundson	Todd Rogers	...	Keith Arboleda
Mankato		c	CM	32	(507) 387-8600	Jeffrey Kagermeier	Patrick Hentges	Cheryl Lindquist	...	Allen Ratzloff	James Franklin	George Rosati
Maple Grove		c	CM	50	(763) 494-6000	Mark Steffenson	Alan Madsen	...	Jim Knutson	Scott Anderson	Ramona Dohman	Gerald Butcher
Maple Plain	*	c	MC	2	(763) 479-0515	...	Jason Ziemer	...	...	Nate Jerde	...	...
Maplewood		c	CM	34	(651) 249-2000	Robert Cardinal	...	Karen Guilfoile	Daniel Faust	Steven Lukin	David Thomalla	R. Ahl
Marshall	*	c	MC	12	(507) 537-6763	Robert Byrnes	...	T. Meulebroeck	...	Marc Klaith	...	Glenn Olson
Medina	*	c	CM	4	(763) 473-4643	Thomas Crosby	Chad Adams	...	Jeanne Day	...	Ed Belland	...
Melrose	*	c	MC	3	(320) 256-4278	Eric Senager	Brian Beeman	Patti Haase	...	Jeremy Kraemer	John Jensen	John Harren
Mendota Heights		c	CM	11	(651) 452-1850	John Huber	James Danielson	Kathleen Swanson	Kristen Schabacker	John Maczko	Mike Aschenbrener	...
Milaca		c	CM	2	(320) 983-3141	...	Greg Lerud	...	...	...	Mike Mott	Steve Burklund
Minneapolis		c	MC	382	(612) 673-3344	...	...	Merry Keefe	Patrick Born	Bonnie Bleskachek	William McManus	...
Minnetonka	*	c	CM	51	(952) 939-8200	Jan Callison	John Gunyou	David Maeda	Merrill King	Joe Wallin	...	Brian Wagstrom
Minnetonka Beach Village		c	MC	..	(952) 471-8878	Jim Gaash	Jill Teetzel	...	...	...	...	...
Minnetrista	*	c	MC	4	(952) 446-1660	Cheryl Fischer	Michael Funk	...	Brian Grimm	...	Craig Anderson	Robin Bowman
Montevideo		c	CM	5	(320) 269-6575	Jim Curtiss	Steven Jones	La Vonne Sundlee	Jan Flaherty	...	Bruce Kann	Greg Schwaegerl
Monticello		c	CM	7	(763) 295-2711	Clint Herbst	Jeffrey O'Neill	Dawn Grossinger	...	Steve Joerg	...	John Simola
Moorhead	*	c	CM	32	(218) 299-5166	Mark Voxland	Michael Redlinger	Kaye Buchholz	Harlyn Ault	Joel Hewitt	Grant Weyland	...
Mora	*	c	CM	3	(320) 679-1511	Gregory Ardner	Joel Dhein	Mason Hjelle	...	Gene Anderson	Chris Olson	...
Morris		c	CM	5	(320) 589-3141	Carol Wilcox	Edward Larson	...	Gene Krosschell	Doug Storck	Jim Beauregard	Jim Dittbenner
Mound	*	c	CM	9	(952) 472-0609	Mark Hanus	Kandis Hanson	Bonnie Ritter	Gino Businaro	Greg Pederson	Jim Kurtz	Carlton Moore
Mounds View		c	MC	12	(763) 717-4000	Robert Marty	...	...	Mark Beers	Nyle Zickmund	...	...
Mountain Iron	*	c	MC	2	(218) 748-7570	Gary Skalko	Craig Wainio	...	...	Thomas Cvar	Rick Fiero	D. Kleinschmidt
New Brighton	*	c	CM	22	(651) 638-2100	Steve Larson	Dean Lotter	...	Daniel Maiers	...	...	Grant Wyffels
New Hope	*	c	CM	20	(763) 531-5100	Martin Opem	...	Valerie Leone	Julie Linnehan	...	Gary Link	Guy Johnson
New London		c	MC	1	(320) 354-2444	John Mack	...	Trudie Dubord	...	...	...	Loren Beck
New Prague		c	CM	4	(952) 758-4401	Craig Sindelar	Jerry Bohnsack	...	...	Jim Becker	Dennis Rohloff	Dennis Seurer
New Ulm		c	CM	13	(507) 359-8233	Joel Albrecht	Brian Gramentz	...	Reginald Vorwerk	Curt Curry	Ervin Weinkauf	Thomas Patterson
Newport		c	MC	3	(651) 459-5677	Kevin Chapdelaine	Lawrence Bodahl	Wanda Swarthout	...	Mark Mailand	Veidols Muiznieks	Bruce Hanson
North Branch		c	MC	8	(651) 674-8113	Gloria Karsky	...	Bridgitte Konrad	David Stutelberg	Donald Brown	Jules Zimmer	Gary Schaefer
North Mankato	*	c	CM	11	(507) 625-4141	Gary Zellmer	Wendell Sande	Nancy Gehrke	Steven Mork	Tim Pohlman	Michael Pulis	Richard Peterson
North Oaks	*	c	MC	3	(651) 792-7750	...	Jim March	...	...	...	...	...
North St. Paul	*	c	CM	11	(651) 747-2400	William Sandberg	Walter Wysopal	...	Al Mahlum	Scott Duddeck	Tom Lauth	Mark Bartholomew
Northfield		c	MC	17	(507) 645-8833	Lee Lansing	Albert Roder	...	Karl Huber	Gerry Franek	Gary Smith	Heidi Hamilton
Norwood Young America		c	MC	3	(952) 467-1800	LaVonne Kroells	Tom Simmons	Diane Frauendienst	...	...	...	Brent Aretz
Oak Grove	*	c	MC	5	(763) 753-1920	...	Chantell Knauss	Sheryl Fiskewold	...	Tony Hennemann	...	Timothy Smith
Oak Park Heights		c	CM	3	(651) 439-4439	David Beaudet	Eric Johnson	Julie Johnson	Judy Holst	...	Lindy Swanson	Jay Johnson
Oakdale	*	c	CM	26	(651) 739-5086	Carmen Sarrack	Craig Waldron	...	Suzanne Warren	Jeff Anderson	William Sullivan	Brian Bachmeier
Olivia	*	c	MC	2	(320) 523-2361	Bill Miller	Daniel Hoffman	Mary Halliday	Kathy Herndina	...	Donald Davern	...
Orono	*	c	MC	7	(952) 249-4600	...	Ronald Moorse	Linda Vee	...	...	Correy Farniok	...
Ortonville		c	MC	2	(320) 839-3428	David Ellingson	...	Roman Taffe	...	Dallas Hanson	Gary Dinnel	Roger Anderson
Osseo		c	MC	2	(763) 425-2624	John Hall	Gregory Withers	LeAnn Larson	Gary Braaten	Gary Current	Michael Haller	Donald Peterson
Ostego	*	c	CM	6	(763) 441-4414	Larry Fournier	Michael Robertson	Judy Hudson	Gary Groen	...	...	Brad Belair
Owatonna	*	c	MC	22	(507) 444-4300	Tom Kuntz	Kris Busse	...	Brad Svenby	Michael Johnson	Shaun LaDue	Jeffrey Johnson
Park Rapids		c	MC	3	(218) 732-3163	...	...	Margie Vik	...	Randy McFarren	Terry Eilers	Scott Burlingame
Perham	*	c	CM	2	(218) 346-4455	Kevin Keil	...	Fern Nundahl	Karla McCall	Tracy Schmidt	Brian Nelson	Merle Meece
Pine City		c	MC	3	(320) 629-2575	Jane Robbins	Donald Howard	...	...	...	...	Vern Smetana
Pine Island		c	MC	2	(507) 356-4591	Kenneth Markham	...	...	Nancy Decker	...	...	Mark Swarthout
Pipestone		c	MC	4	(507) 825-3324	...	...	...	...	...	...	...
Plainview		c	CM	3	(507) 534-2229	Neil Weaver	Steven Robertson	...	Nancy Richardson	Rich Klees	Randy Doughty	Michael Burgdorf
Plymouth	*	c	CM	65	(763) 509-5000	Kelli Slavik	Laurie Ahrens	Sandra Paulson	...	Richard Kline	Michael Goldstein	Doran Cote
Princeton		c	CM	3	(763) 389-2040	Brian Humphrey	Mark Karnowski	...	Steven Jackson	...	David Warneke	Thomas Mismash
Prior Lake	*	c	CM	15	(952) 447-9800	Jack Haugen	Francis Boyles	...	Ralph Teschner	Doug Hartman	Bill O'Rourke	Steve Albrecht
Proctor	*	c	MC	2	(218) 624-3641	Richard Kieren	...	...	...	John Benson	Walter Wubig	...
Ramsey	*	c	MC	18	(763) 427-1410	Thomas Gamec	Kurtis Ulrich	Jo Thieline	Diana Lund	Dean Kapler	James Way	Brian Olson
Red Lake Falls		c	CM	1	(218) 253-2684	Allen Ducharme	Marion Martell	...	...	...	...	...
Red Wing		c	CM	16	(651) 385-3600	V. Steffenhagen	Kay Kuhlmann	Kathy Johnson	Marshall Hallock	...	...	Dennis Tebbe
Redwood Falls		c	MC	5	(507) 637-5755	Sara Triplett	Keith Muetzel	Elaine Jenniges	...	Tom Stough	Mark Dressen	...
Renville		c	CM	1	(320) 329-8366	Loyal Fisher	Paul McLaughlin	LouAnn Ahrens	...	Brad Varpness	Ben Dehmlow	Peter Peterson
Richfield	*	c	CM	34	(612) 861-9700	Debbie Goettel	Steven Devich	Nancy Gibbs	...	Brad Sveum	...	Michael Eastling
Robbinsdale		c	CM	14	(763) 537-4534	Michael Holtz	Marcia Glick	...	Cory Kampf	Mark Fairchild	Wayne Shellum	...
Rochester		c	MC	85	(507) 285-8082	Ardell Brede	Stevan Kvenvold	Judy Scherr	Dale Martinson	David Kapler	Roger Peterson	Richard Freese
Rockford		c	CM	3	(763) 477-6565	Michael Beyer	Nancy Evers	...	...	...	...	...
Rosemount		c	CM	14	(651) 423-4411	...	James Verbrugge	Linda Jentink	Jeff May	...	Gary Kalstabakken	...
Roseville		c	CM	33	(651) 490-2200	John Kysylyczyn	William Malinen	Margaret Driscoll	Chris Miller	Rich Gasaway	Carol Sletner	Duane Schwartz
Rush City		c	CM	2	(320) 358-4743	Michael Skalsky	Daniel Hoffman	Susan Hochstatter	...	Robert Carlson	Scott Sellman	Raymond Benolken
Rushford	*	c	MC	1	(507) 864-2444	Les Ladewig	Winthro Block	Kathy Zacher	...	Mike Ebner	Sam Stensgard	Jeff Copley
Saint Michael		c	MC	9	(763) 497-2041	...	Robert Derus	Carol Beall	...	...	...	...
Sandstone		c	MC	1	(320) 245-5241	Douglas McGhee	Samuel Griffith	Jane Grundmeier	Wendy Nelson	Joe Drilling	...	Dennis Carlson
Sartell		c	MC	9	(320) 253-2171	...	Patti Gartland	Peggy Schupp	...	...	Robert Ringstrom	Brad Borders
Sauk Centre		c	MC	3	(320) 352-2203	Dennis Rykken	Vicki Willer	...	...	Joe Deters	James Metcalf	Harold Wessel
Sauk Rapids		c	MC	10	(320) 258-5300	Harold Jesh	Ross Olson	...	Jack Kahlhamer	...	Curtis Gullickson	Roger Schotl
Savage		c	CM	21	(952) 882-2660	...	Barry Stock	Jan Saarela	Shelly Kolling	Joel McColl	Gordon Vlasak	...
Scandia	*	c	MC	3	(651) 433-2274	Dennis Seefeldt	Anne Hurlburt	Brenda Eklund	...	Steve Spence	...	John Morrison
Shakopee		c	MC	20	(952) 233-3800	William Mars	Mark McNeill	Judith Cox	Gregg Voxland	...	Daniel Hughes	Bruce Loney
Sherburn		c	CM	1	(507) 764-4491	Gerald Jenkinson	Sack Thongvanh	...	...	...	...	...
Shoreview		c	CM	25	(651) 490-4600	Sandra Martin	Terry Schwerm	...	Jeanne Haapala	Tim Boehlke	George Altendorfer	Mark Maloney
Shorewood		c	MC	7	(952) 474-3236	C. Love	Craig Dawson	Jean Panchyshyn	Bonnie Burton	...	...	Lawrence Brown
Silver Bay		c	MC	2	(218) 226-4408	...	Thomas Smith	...	...	...	Wayne Billings	Douglas Peusetto
Sleepy Eye	*	c	MC	3	(507) 794-3731	James Broich	Mark Kober	Jeanne Tauer	...	...	David Sievert	Bob Elston
South St. Paul	*	c	MC	20	(651) 554-3200	...	Stephen King	Christy Wilcox	Brian Swanson	...	Michael Messerich	...
Spring Lake Park	*	v	MC	6	(763) 784-6491	Robert Nelson	Barbara Nelson	...	...	Nyle Zikmund	Dave Toth	Terry Randall
Spring Park	*	c	MC	1	(952) 471-9051	Jerome Rockvam	Sarah Friesen	...	...	...	...	David Goman
Spring Valley		v	MC	2	(507) 346-7367	Jim Struzyk	Michael Bubany	Deb Zimmer	...	Nevin Stender	...	Stu Smith
Springfield	*	c	CM	2	(507) 723-3500	Mark Brown	Malcolm Tilberg	Amy Vogel	...	Charles Baumann	John Nicholson	...
St. Anthony		c	CM	8	(612) 782-3301	Jerome Faust	Michael Mornson	Barbara Suciu	Roger Larson	John Malenick	Richard Engstrom	Jay Hartman
St. Augusta		c	MC	3	(320) 654-0387	Ollie Mondloch	Aaron Anderson	...	...	...	...	...

Directory 1/9 continued — OFFICIALS IN U.S. MUNICIPALITIES 2,500 AND OVER IN POPULATION

Jurisdiction	Type	Form of govern-ment	2000 Popu-lation (000)	Main telephone number	Chief elected official	Appointed administrator	Clerk of the governing board	Chief financial officer	Fire chief	Police chief	Public works director
MINNESOTA continued											
St. Charles	c	MC	3	(507) 932-3020	. . .	Jennifer Prentice	. . .	. . .	. . .	. . .	. . .
St. Cloud	c	MC	59	(320) 255-7200	John Ellenbecker	Michael Williams	Gregg Engdahl	. . .	William Mund	Dennis Ballantine	Stephen Gaetz
St. Francis	c	MC	4	(763) 753-2630	Randy Dressen	Matthew Hylen	Barb Held	. . .	Ken Pace	Byron Froh	. . .
St. James	c	CM	4	(507) 375-3241	Gary Sturm	Joseph McCabe	LeeAnn Nibbe	. . .	Jon Craig	Mark Carvatt	. . .
St. Joseph	c	MC	4	(320) 363-7201	Richard Carlbom	. . .	Judy Weyrens	. . .	. . .	Pete Jansky	Richard Taufen
St. Louis Park *	c	CM	44	(952) 924-2500	Jeff Jacobs	Thomas Harmening	Nancy Stroth	Bruce DeJong	Luke Stemmer	John Luse	Michael Rardin
St. Paul	c	MC	287	(651) 266-6500	Norm Coleman	. . .	Fred Owusu	Matt Smith	Timothy Fuller	William Finney	. . .
St. Paul Park	c	CM	5	(651) 459-9785	Donal Mullan	Barry Sittlow	. . .	. . .	Scott Gerry	Michael Monahan	Lee Flandrich
St. Peter	c	CM	9	(507) 931-0663	Jerry Hawbaker	Todd Prafke	. . .	Paula O'Connell	Windy Block	Matthew Peters	Lewis Gesking
Staples	c	MC	3	(218) 894-2550	. . .	. . .	. . .	. . .	. . .	. . .	. . .
Stewartville	c	MC	5	(507) 533-4745	Chris Gray	William Schimmel	Cheryl Roeder	. . .	. . .	. . .	Ron Robb
Stillwater *	c	MC	15	(651) 430-8800	Ken Harycki	Larry Hansen	Diane Ward	Sharon Harrison	Stuart Glaser	John Gannaway	Shawn Sanders
Thief River Falls *	c	MC	8	(218) 681-2943	Dale Wennberg	Jodie Torkelson	. . .	Lisa Johnson	Jerry Stenseth	Kim Murphy	Ron Lindberg
Thomson	tp	MC	1	(218) 879-9719	Ruth Janke	. . .	Rhonda Peleski	. . .	Jeffrey Juntunen	Thomas Foldesi	David Black
Tonka Bay *	c	CM	1	(952) 474-7994	. . .	Jessica Loftus	. . .	. . .	Scott Gerber	Bryan Litsey	Gregory Kluver
Tracy	c	MC	2	(507) 629-5528	S. Ferrazzano	. . .	Audrey Koopman	. . .	Dennis Vandeputte	Bryan Hillger	Richard Robinson
Two Harbors	c	CM	3	(218) 834-5631	. . .	Lee Klein	. . .	Jill Anderson	. . .	Richard Hogenson	Scott Johnson
Tyler	c	CM	1	(507) 247-5556	Douglas Hess	Jason Maxwell	Kristin Wibben	. . .	Allan Rensvold	. . .	Darwin Lu Herman
Vadnais Heights *	c	MC	13	(651) 204-6000	Susan Banovetz	Gerald Urban	. . .	Jeanne Vogt	Dave Hertog	. . .	. . .
Victoria *	c	CM	4	(952) 443-4210	. . .	. . .	Jennifer Kretsch	Jylan Johnson	Tim Walsh	Erick Boder	Bruce Osborn
Virginia	c	CM	9	(218) 748-7500	Carolyn Gentilini	John Tourville	Lois Roskoski	Ronald Lackner	. . .	. . .	. . .
Wabasha	c	CM	2	(651) 565-4568	. . .	David Schmidt	Darlene Wallerich	. . .	. . .	. . .	Ted Stearns
Waconia *	c	MC	6	(952) 442-2184	Don Johnson	Susan Arntz	Mary Johnson	. . .	. . .	. . .	Randall Sorensen
Wadena	c	MC	4	(218) 631-7707	Wayne Wolden	Bradley Swenson	. . .	Lloyd Lanz	Ray Beyer	Lane Waldahl	Ron Bucholz
Waite Park	c	MC	6	(320) 252-6822	Carla Schaefer	Shaunna Johnson	Jill Bauer	Keith Lindberg	Gary Curtis	James McDermott	William Schluenz
Warroad	c	CM	1	(216) 386-1454	. . .	. . .	. . .	. . .	. . .	. . .	. . .
Waseca	c	CM	8	(507) 835-9700	. . .	. . .	. . .	Julie Linnihan	Gary Conrath	Keith Hiller	. . .
Watertown	c	CM	3	(952) 955-2681	Stephen Sarvi	David Mandt	. . .	Steven Wallner	Ned Schroeder	. . .	K. Gulbrandson
Waterville	c	CM	1	(507) 362-8300	. . .	. . .	. . .	Teresa Hill	. . .	Max Venero	. . .
Wayzata	c	CM	4	(952) 404-5300	Barry Petit	Allan Orsen	Joan Smith	David Frischmon	Paul Klapprich	Kevin Kelleher	David Dudinsky
Wells	c	MC	2	(507) 553-6371	David Jacobson	. . .	. . .	. . .	Tim Orbell	Michael Iverson	. . .
West St. Paul *	c	CM	19	(651) 552-4100	John Zanmiller	Arbon Hairston	. . .	John Remkus	John Ehret	Maila Shaver	Matt Saam
White Bear Lake	c	CM	24	(651) 429-8526	Paul Auger	Mark Sather	. . .	Don Rambow	Timothy Vadnais	Todd Miller	Mark Burch
Willmar	c	CM	18	(320) 235-4913	. . .	Michael Schmit	. . .	Steven Okins	Marvin Calvin	. . .	Melvin Odens
Windom *	c	CM	4	(507) 831-6129	Tom Riordan	Steven Nasby	. . .	. . .	. . .	Jeff Shirkey	Mike Haugen
Winnebago *	c	CM	1	(507) 893-3217	Scott Owen	Nathan Mathews	Susan Lynch	. . .	Todd Enger	Robert Toland	Darold Nienhaus
Winona	c	CM	27	(507) 457-8234	Jerry Miller	Eric Sorensen	Monica Mohan	Mary Burrichter	Ed Krall	Frank Pomeroy	. . .
Winsted	c	MC	2	(320) 485-2366	. . .	Brent Mareck	Deborah Boelter	. . .	. . .	. . .	. . .
Woodbury	c	CM	46	(651) 714-3500	. . .	Clinton Gridley	. . .	Timothy Johnson	Mike Richardson	. . .	David Jessup
Worthington	c	MC	11	(507) 372-8600	Alan Oberloh	. . .	Karen Buchman	Brian Kolander	. . .	. . .	James Laffrencen
Wyoming	c	MC	3	(651) 462-0575	Sheldon Anderson	Craig Mattson	. . .	. . .	Dennis Berry	. . .	Bill Eisenmenger
Zumbrota	c	MC	2	(507) 732-7318	Richard Bauer	Neil Jensen	. . .	. . .	Ron Horsman	Gary Selness	Rick Lohmann
MISSISSIPPI											
Aberdeen	c	MC	6	(662) 369-8588	William Tisdale	Willie Howell	Susan Honeycutt	Glen Howell	Herbert Rieves	Brent Coleman	Louis Burroughs
Amory *	c	MC	6	(662) 256-5721	Howard Boozer	. . .	Suzanne Mobley	. . .	Jimmy Bost	Ronnie Bowen	Bobby Cox
Baldwyn	t	MC	3	(601) 365-2383	. . .	. . .	. . .	. . .	. . .	. . .	. . .
Batesville	c	MC	7	(662) 563-4576	Jerry Autrey	. . .	Laura Herron	. . .	Timothy Taylor	Gerald Legge	. . .
Bay St. Louis	c	MC	8	(228) 467-9092	Edward Favre	Robert Parker	. . .	. . .	Robert Gavagnie	Frank McNeil	Ronald Vanney
Belzoni	c	MC	2	(601) 247-1343	T Turner	. . .	Laura Anne Byars	. . .	Henry Outlaw	Richard McMillian	. . .
Biloxi	c	MC	50	(228) 435-6259	Andrew Holloway	. . .	Brenda Johnston	William Lanham	David Roberts	Tommy Moffett	Jerry Morgan
Booneville	t	MC	8	(662) 728-6810	. . .	. . .	. . .	. . .	. . .	. . .	. . .
Brandon	c	MC	16	(601) 825-5021	Carlo Martella	Mike Farrar	Angela Bean	. . .	James Rutland	Kenneth McBroom	Cathy Goolsby
Brookhaven *	c	MC	9	(601) 833-2362	Robert Massengill	. . .	Micahel Jinks	. . .	Bob Watts	Arlustra Henderson	Steve Moreton
Canton	c	MC	12	(601) 859-4331	. . .	. . .	. . .	. . .	. . .	. . .	. . .
Carthage	t	MC	4	(601) 267-8322	Bobbye Henderson	. . .	Elizabeth Hogue	. . .	Mike Faulkner	Jimmy Cook	Larry Hoye
Charleston	c	MC	2	(662) 647-5841	Robert Rowe	. . .	Diane Stanford	. . .	Phil Shook	Jerry Williams	Dizzy Prine
Clarksdale	c	CO	20	(662) 621-8100	Richard Webster	. . .	Sylvia Burton	. . .	S. Washington	Glenn Coker	James Butler
Cleveland	c	MC	13	(662) 846-1471	. . .	. . .	. . .	. . .	. . .	. . .	. . .
Clinton *	c	MC	23	(601) 924-5474	Rosemary Aultman	. . .	. . .	Russell Wall	Jonathan Burnside	Don Byington	. . .
Columbia *	c	MC	6	(601) 736-8201	Harold Bryant	Donna McKenzie	. . .	. . .	Larry Ratliff	Joe Van Parkman	. . .
Columbus	c	MC	25	(662) 328-7021	Jeffrey Rupp	. . .	. . .	. . .	Kenneth Moore	J. Sanders	Dan Mattick
Corinth	c	MC	14	(662) 286-6644	Jerry Latch	. . .	Vickie Roach	. . .	Gerald Horner	William Cregeen	Billy Glover
Crystal Springs	c	MC	5	(601) 892-1210	Walter Rielley	. . .	Linda Caston	. . .	Abra Hines	Richard Anderson	Robert Sims
D'Iberville	c	MC	7	(228) 392-7966	. . .	Richard Rose	Mary Lee Williams	Sharron Perkins	Gerald Smith	Wendy Swetman	Al Gombos
Drew	c	MC	2	(662) 745-8556	James Pettigrew	. . .	Bettie Dickey	. . .	. . .	. . .	Melvin Matthews
Durant	c	MC	2	(662) 653-3221	Johnny Pritchard	Rosie Hill	Linda McDonald	. . .	Houston Kyzer	Jerry Bankhead	Bernard Wright
Ellisville *	c	MC	3	(601) 477-3323	Tim Waldrup	. . .	Margaret Brewer	. . .	Ronnie McGilberry	Robert Russell	Stan Ishee
Forest	c	MC	5	(601) 469-2921	Nancy Chambers	. . .	Melissa Barnes	. . .	Clint Craig	Mike Lee	Randall George
Fulton	t	MC	3	(662) 862-4929	Charlie McCarthy	. . .	Lisa Russell	. . .	Charles Grimes	Ray Barrett	Dan Pate
Gautier	c	CM	11	(228) 497-8000	Ken Taylor	Christy Wheeler	Pearl Mercer	Linda Green	Michael Gray	Ed Williams	. . .
Greenville	c	MC	41	(601) 378-1551	Paul Artman	. . .	Ella Johnson	. . .	John Richardson	Lon Pepper	Brad Jones
Greenwood *	c	MC	18	(662) 453-2246	Sheriel Perkins	Nick Joseph	. . .	Deirdre Mayes	Larry Griggs	Henry Harris	Benny Herring
Grenada	c	CM	14	(601) 226-8820	John Hyneman	James Cummins	Douglas Ashmore	Valleria Blaylock	Eugene Doss	Curtis Liles	. . .
Gulfport	c	MC	71	(228) 868-5831	. . .	. . .	. . .	. . .	. . .	. . .	. . .
Hattiesburg	c	MC	44	(601) 545-4501	J. Morgan	. . .	Edgar Myers	Joseph Townsend	George Herrington	Charles Sims	Bennie Sellers
Hazlehurst	c	MC	4	(601) 894-3131	Randy Kimble	. . .	Sue Brown	. . .	James Harper	Ellis Stuart	. . .
Hernando	c	MC	6	(601) 429-9092	. . .	. . .	. . .	. . .	. . .	. . .	. . .
Hollandale	c	MC	3	(662) 827-2241	Willie Burnside	. . .	Helen Johnson	. . .	Mitchell Baugh	Jimmy Taylor	Lee Edwards
Holly Springs *	c	MC	7	(662) 252-4280	Andre Deberry	. . .	Belinda McDonald	. . .	Kenneth Holbrook	Robert Pearson	D. Hollingsworth
Horn Lake	c	MC	14	(662) 393-6178	. . .	. . .	Diane Stewart	. . .	Leroy Bledsoe	Darryl Whaley	James McKell
Houston	c	MC	4	(662) 456-2328	John Moore	. . .	Bobby Sanderson	. . .	. . .	Kevin Davis	Russell Lancaster
Indianola	c	MC	12	(662) 887-3101	Arthur Marble	. . .	Paul Correro	. . .	Eugene Snipes	Carver Randle	Jimmie Strong
Itta Bena	t	MC	2	(601) 254-7231	Thelma Collins	. . .	. . .	. . .	Curtis Purnell	J. Hudson	Jimmy Pittman
Iuka	c	MC	3	(601) 423-3781	. . .	. . .	. . .	. . .	. . .	. . .	. . .
Jackson	c	MC	184	(601) 960-1084	Harvey Johnson	Otha Burton	Eddie Carr	Cynthia Melvin	Raymond McNulty	Robert Moore	Ben Wolfe
Kosciusko	c	MC	7	(662) 289-1226	Jimmy Cockroft	. . .	Janet Baird	. . .	Duane Bardine	Ronnie Adams	Wallace Simmons
Laurel	c	CO	18	(601) 428-6423	Susan Vincent	Gary Suddith	. . .	Mary Hess	James Russell	John Waterson	Kenny Hogan
Leland	c	MC	5	(662) 686-4136	Kenny Thomas	Mickey Fratesi	. . .	. . .	Robert Johnson	Wade Burns	Fred Jones
Lexington	c	MC	2	(662) 834-1261	. . .	. . .	Pamela Williams	. . .	Jim Hughes	Jessie Joiner	Keith James
Long Beach	c	MC	17	(228) 863-1556	William Skellie	Rebecca Schruff	. . .	. . .	George Bass	Wayne McDowell	Derrell Wilson
Louisville	c	MC	7	(662) 773-9201	Daniel Yarbrough	. . .	Babs Fulton	. . .	Mike Stevenson	Ricky Peterson	Kenny Morris

Directory 1/9 continued — OFFICIALS IN U.S. MUNICIPALITIES 2,500 AND OVER IN POPULATION

Jurisdiction		Type	Form of govern-ment	2000 Popu-lation (000)	Main telephone number	Chief elected official	Appointed administrator	Clerk of the governing board	Chief financial officer	Fire chief	Police chief	Public works director
MISSISSIPPI continued												
Magee		c	MC	4	(601) 849-3344	...	...	...	...	...	...	...
Mc Comb		c	CM	13	(601) 684-4000	Thomas Walman	Sam Mims	Russell Wall	...	Vernell Felder	Billie Hughes	...
Mendenhall		t	MC	2	(601) 847-1212	Randall Neely	Tim Gray	Judi May	...	...	Jimbo Sullivan	...
Meridian		c	MC	39	(601) 485-1927	John Smith	Kenneth Storms	Lawrence Skipper	...	Henry Partridge	Benny Dubose	David Jackson
Moorhead		t	CM	2	(662) 246-5461	...	...	...	...	...	...	...
Morton	*	c	MC	3	(601) 732-8609	Greg Butler	...	Dorothy Redeemer	...	JOEL DAVIDSON	Jimmy Rogers	Terrell Harvey
Moss Point		c	MC	15	(228) 475-0300	Frank Lynn	Adlean Liddell	...	Shavay Gaines	Jimmy Harris	Michael Ricks	Robert Armstrong
Mound Bayou		c	MC	2	(662) 741-2193	...	...	...	...	...	...	...
Natchez		c	MC	18	(601) 445-7515	Phillip West	...	Donnie Holloway	...	Paul Johnson	Michael Mullins	Eric Smith
New Albany		c	MC	7	(662) 534-1010	Tim Kent	...	Anne Neal	...	Richard Hamric	David Grisham	...
Newton		c	MC	3	(601) 683-6181	Michael Pickens	...	Janice Bridges	...	...	Harvey Curry	Jerry Bounds
Ocean Springs		c	MC	17	(228) 875-4236	Seren Ainsworth	...	Adrienne Howell	...	Mark Hare	Kerry Belk	Andre Kaufman
Okolona		c	MC	3	(662) 447-5461	S. Carouthers	...	Anna Stovall	...	Edward Chapman	Tommie Ivy	Robert May
Oxford		c	MC	11	(662) 236-1310	Richard Howorth	...	Lisa Carwyle	...	Jerry Johnson	Stephen Bramlett	David Bennett
Pascagoula	*	c	CM	26	(228) 762-1020	Matthew Avara	Kay Johnson Kell	Brenda Reed	Lloyd Marshall	Robert O'Sullivan	Eddie Stewart	Brian Nelson
Pass Christian		c	MC	6	(228) 452-3310	William McDonald	...	Vicki Goff	Janet Dudding	Richard Marvil	John Dubuisson	Michael Pavlisick
Pearl	*	c	MC	21	(601) 932-2262	Jimmy Foster	...	Kay Lang	Ron Morgan	Robert Williams	Bill Slade	Bud Overby
Petal		c	MC	7	(601) 545-1776	Carl Scott	...	Jean Ishee	...	Richard Bryant	Lee Shelbourn	...
Philadelphia		c	MC	7	(601) 656-3612	...	...	...	...	...	...	...
Picayune		c	CM	10	(601) 798-9770	Gregory Mitchell	James Burns	...	...	Keith Brown	James Luke	Reginald Oliver
Pontotoc		c	MC	5	(662) 489-4321	Bill Rutledge	...	Patricia Clayton	...	Jerry Russell	Larry Poole	Tim Roberts
Poplarville		c	MC	2	(601) 795-8161	Billy Spiers	Francis Stuart	Linda DuPont	Jackie Davis	Chris Carr	Charles Fazende	Sam Hale
Quitman		t	MC	2	(601) 776-3728	...	...	...	...	...	...	...
Richland		c	MC	6	(601) 932-3000	Mark Scarborough	...	Donna Diffrient	...	Jim McClendon	Bruce Breland	Wade Overby
Ridgeland		c	MC	20	(601) 856-7113	...	...	Ina Byrd	M. McPhearson	Elmer Waits	...	...
Ripley		c	MC	5	(662) 837-0130	...	...	...	...	...	...	...
Rolling Fork		c	MC	2	(662) 873-2814	Gary Henderson	...	Dorothy Pearson	...	Robert McClendon	Eugene Bell	Billy Johnson
Ruleville		c	MC	3	(662) 756-2791	Shirley Edwards	...	Jane Ward	...	...	Larry Mitchell	John Downs
Senatobia		c	MC	6	(662) 562-4474	Alan Callicott	...	Kay Minton	...	Gary Copeland	Sammy Webb	Robert Morris
Shelby		c	MC	2	(601) 398-5156	...	...	...	...	...	...	...
Southaven		c	MC	28	(662) 280-2489	Gregory Davis	Christopher Wilson	Glenda Smallwood	Andrea Freeze	V. McCammon	Thomas Long	Ray Tarrance
Starkville		c	CM	21	(662) 324-4011	Mack Rutlege	...	Vivian Collier	Debbie Clark	William Grantham	David Lindley	...
Tupelo		c	MC	34	(662) 841-6487	Larry Otis	Darrell Smith	...	Daphne Holcombe	Michael Burns	Harold Chaffin	Thomas Rankin
Vicksburg		c	CO	26	(601) 634-4553	Laurence Leyens	...	Walter Osborne	Elvin Parker	Keith Rogers	Tommy Moffett	James Rainer
Water Valley		c	MC	3	(662) 473-2431	...	...	...	...	...	...	...
Waveland	*	c	MC	6	(228) 467-4134	John Longo	Lisa Planchard	...	...	David Garcia	James Varnell	Ron Calcagno
Waynesboro	*	t	MC	5	(601) 735-4874	Bobby Taylor	...	Sytrecia Hull	...	Willard Crocker	Leonard Frost	Harvey Hull
West Point		c	MC	12	(601) 494-2573	...	...	...	...	...	...	...
Wiggins		c	MC	3	(601) 928-7221	Ferris O'Neal	...	Teresa Ladner	...	Richard Tice	Reid Lowe	Jimmy Smith
Winona		c	MC	5	(601) 283-1232	H W Simmons	...	Bonita Smith	...	Booker Clay	Johnny Hargrove	Bain Hughes
Yazoo City		c	MC	14	(662) 746-1401	...	...	...	...	...	...	...
MISSOURI												
Albany	*	c	MC	1	(660) 726-3935	John Rieks	Derek Brown	Janet Sweat	...	...	...	...
Arnold		c	MC	19	(636) 296-2100	Ronald Voss	Matthew Unrein	Rita Thompson	Jo Anne Tietjens	...	Dale Fredeking	Robert Eade
Ashland	*	c	MC	1	(573) 657-2091	Mike Asmus	...	Darla Sapp	...	...	Scott Robbins	John Fraga
Aurora		c	CM	7	(417) 678-5121	Noelle Naillon	...	Kathie Needham	...	Robert Ward	Richard Batson	Steve Woods
Ava		c	MC	3	(417) 683-5516	Leon Harris	...	Marilyn Alms	...	...	Larry Smith	...
Ballwin		c	CM	31	(636) 227-8580	Robert Jones	Robert Kuntz	...	Glenda Loehr	...	James Biederman	Gary Kramer
Bellefontaine Neighbors	*	c	MC	11	(314) 867-0076	Martin Rudloff	...	Deni Donovan	...	...	Robert Pruett	Mike Welz
Bel-Ridge		v	MC	3	(314) 429-2878	...	...	...	...	...	...	...
Belton		c	CM	21	(816) 331-4331	Robert Gregory	Ronald Trivitt	Patti Ledford	Michael Wade	Steve Holle	James Person	Cliff Fain
Berkeley		c	CM	10	(314) 524-3313	K. McClendon	De'Carlon Seewood	Doris Jackson	Jean Holmes	Lloyd Vester	...	Jon Langerak
Bethany		c	MC	3	(660) 425-3511	Richard Graner	Tony Stonecypher	Marilyn Smith	...	John Gannan	Brian Groom	...
Black Jack		c	MC	6	(314) 355-0400	Norman McCourt	...	Monica Van Stratten	John Engelmeyer	Robert Coffman	...	Melvin Kosanchick
Blue Springs	*	c	CM	48	(816) 228-0110	Steven Steiner	Eric Johnson	Kathy Richardson	Christine Cates	...	Wayne McCoy	Oliver De Grate
Bolivar		c	MC	9	(417) 326-2489	Charles Ealy	...	Dale Newcomb	...	Patricia Head	Michael Seibert	...
Bonne Terre		c	CM	4	(573) 358-2254	...	Ron Thomure	Tina Miller	...	...	Charles Mallow	Clarence Keen
Boonville		c	CM	8	(660) 882-2332	Danielle Blanck	...	Kimberly Justus	...	Tim Carmichael	Jim Gholson	M. Cauthon
Bowling Green	*	c	MC	3	(573) 324-5451	Dana Portwood	JD Kehrman	Barb Allison	...	Mel Meyer	Steve Kruse	Patrick Stinnett
Branson		c	MC	6	(417) 334-3345	...	...	Lisa Westfall	Deanna Schlegel	Carl Sparks	Caroll McCullough	Larry Van Gilder
Breckenridge Hills		c	MC	4	(314) 427-6868	Archie Ledbetter	...	Pamela Price	...	...	Donald Kaley	...
Brentwood		c	MC	7	(314) 962-4800	Charles Kelly	C. Seemayer	...	Susan Zimmer	Robert Niemeyer	Frederick Knight	Gerald Wolf
Bridgeton		c	MC	15	(314) 739-7500	Conrad Bowers	Thomas Haun	Carole Stahlhut	Dennis Rainey	...	Walter Mutert	Richard Houchin
Brookfield		c	CM	4	(660) 258-3377	Richard Techau	Darrell Williams	...	...	Jerry Wine	David Hane	Robert Stufflebean
Buckner		c	MC	2	(816) 650-3191	James Parcel	...	...	...	Greg Pottberg	Charles Loring	Wilson Jones
Butler		c	MC	4	(660) 679-4182	Jerry Cook	Dennis Pyle	Janet Kirtley	...	James Henry	James Garnett	...
Cabool		c	MC	2	(417) 962-3136	Donald Wells	H. Swanson	Olive Wood	...	Jerry Miller	Lynn Jones	Joseph Engleman
California		c	MC	4	(573) 796-2500	Norris Gerhart	...	Brian Scrivner	...	Allen Smith	Fred Kirchoff	Gary Wells
Camdenton	*	c	MC	2	(573) 346-3600	Kerry Shannon	Elmer Meyer	Brenda Colter	Renee Kingston	Scott Frandsen	Laura Webster	William Jeffries
Cameron	*	c	CM	8	(816) 632-2177	Larry McCord	Phillip Lammers	Barbara O'Connor	...	Michael O'Donnell	Corey Sloan	Drew Bontrager
Cape Girardeau		c	CM	35	(573) 334-1212	Jay Knudtson	Douglas Leslie	Gayle Conrad	John Richbourg	Richard Ennis	Stephen Strong	Tim Gramling
Carl Junction		c	MC	5	(417) 649-7237	Mike Moss	James Whisenant	Maribeth Matney	...	...	Delmar Haase	Jimmy Chaligo
Carrollton		c	MC	4	(660) 542-1414	Sharon Metz	Mary McGinness	...	...	Curtis Shields	Donald King	...
Carthage		c	MC	12	(417) 237-7000	Kenneth Johnson	Thomas Short	Lynn Campbell	...	John Cooper	Dennis Veach	Chad Wampler
Caruthersville		c	CM	6	(573) 333-2142	Diane Sayre	...	Melinda Scifres	...	Charles Jones	Kenneth Chastain	...
Centralia	*	c	MC	3	(573) 682-2139	Tim Grenke	Lynn Behrns	...	Kathy Colvin	Marvin Rodgers	Larry Dudgeon	...
Chaffee		c	MC	3	(573) 887-3558	William Cannon	Ron Eskew	Diane Eftink	...	Mike Lee	...	Eric Hicks
Charleston		c	CM	4	(573) 683-3325	Brett Matthews	David Brewer	Marsha Hart	...	Michael Maness	Richard Couch	David Teeters
Chesterfield		c	CM	46	(636) 537-4000	John Nations	Michael Herring	Marty Demay	Jeremy Craig	...	Ray Johnson	Michael Geisel
Chillicothe		c	MC	8	(660) 646-2424	Todd Rodenberg	...	Rozanne Frampton	Theresa Kelly	Joseph Rinehart	Richard Knouse	Steve Svec
Clayton	*	c	CM	12	(314) 290-8449	Linda Goldstein	Michael Schoedel	June Waters	Donald Yucuis	George Thorp	Thomas Byrne	Paul Wojciechowski
Clinton	*	c	MC	9	(660) 885-6121	Gus Wetzel	Robert Bridges	Kelly Harrelson	...	Russell Ritchey	Kevin Miller	Gary Mount
Columbia	*	c	CM	84	(573) 874-7235	Darwin Hindman	H. Watkins	Sheela Amin	Lori Fleming	William Markgraf	Randy Boehm	John Glascock
Crestwood	*	c	CM	11	(314) 729-4700	Roy Robinson	Frank Myers	Tina Flowers	...	Karl Kestler	Michael Paillou	Jim Eckrich
Creve Coeur		c	CM	16	(314) 432-6000	Harold Dielmann	Mark Perkins	La Verne Collins	Daniel Smith	...	John Beardslee	Robert Gunn
Crystal City		c	MC	4	(636) 937-4614	Grant Johnston	Debbie Johns	...	...	Tony Picarella	...	Karry Friedmeyer
Dardenne Prairie		c	MC	4	(636) 561-1718	...	Robert Hussey	...	...	...	...	...
De Soto		c	CM	6	(636) 586-3326	...	David Dews	Arlene Burt	...	...	Donald Kraher	...
Dellwood		c	MC	5	(314) 521-4339	...	...	...	...	...	...	...
Des Peres		c	MC	8	(314) 835-6110	Richard Lahr	Douglas Harms	Linda Schulte	Andrew Reiter	Sean Quinn	Charles Milano	Denis Knock

Directory 1/9 continued **OFFICIALS IN U.S. MUNICIPALITIES 2,500 AND OVER IN POPULATION**

Jurisdiction		Type	Form of govern-ment	2000 Popu-lation (000)	Main telephone number	Chief elected official	Appointed administrator	Clerk of the governing board	Chief financial officer	Fire chief	Police chief	Public works director
MISSOURI continued												
Desloge		c	MC	4	(573) 431-3700	Gregory Camp	. . .	Linda Moore	. . .	. . .	James Bullock	Gary Momot
Dexter		c	MC	7	(573) 624-5959	Joe Weber	J Mark Stidham	Joann Steinbrueck	. . .	Alphonse Banken	Paul Haubold	Thomas Espey
East Prairie		c	CM	3	(573) 649-3057	Gene Ditto	Kathie Simpkins	Lori Lemons	. . .	John Gifford	Danny Lafferty	Joe Garner
Edmundson		c	CM	. .	(314) 428-7125	. . .	. . .	. . .	. . .	. . .	Ron Hawkins	. . .
El Dorado Springs		c	CM	3	(417) 876-2521	Gene Floyd	Bruce Rogers	Lisa Janes	Vi Clevenger	Eugene Elliott	Jimmy Luster	Eric McPeak
Eldon		c	CM	4	(573) 392-2291	Ron Bly	Gary Marriott	Charlotte Dolby	Deborah Guthrie	Randy Vernon	Robert Hurtubise	. . .
Ellisville	*	c	CM	9	(636) 227-9660	Matt Pirrello	Kevin Bookout	Catherine Demeter	Lori Helle	. . .	Tom Felgate	Bill Schwer
Eureka		c	MC	7	(636) 938-5233	Kevin Coffey	Craig Sabo	Ralph Lindsey	Karen Crayne	Gregory Brown	Michael Wiegand	Michael Schlereth
Excelsior Springs		c	CM	10	(816) 630-0750	James Nelson	David Haugland	. . .	Steven Marriott	William Stewart	John McGovern	Rex Brinker
Farmington		c	CM	13	(573) 756-1701	. . .	Gregory Beavers	Phyllis Hartrup	Gregory Stover	Phillip Johnson	Rick Baker	Jeffrey Blue
Fayette		c	MC	2	(660) 248-5246	Michael Hirsch	Gerard Bender	Robin Overstreet	. . .	James Hudson	Bryan Kunze	. . .
Fenton		c	MC	4	(636) 343-2080	Dennis Hancock	Mark Sartors	Diane Monteleone	Arthur DeWitt	. . .	. . .	Dale Oberhaus
Ferguson		c	CM	22	(314) 521-7721	Steve Weigert	John Shaw	K. Goodwin-Raftery	Jo Ann Bordeleau	. . .	. . .	Charles Feldman
Festus		c	MC	9	(636) 937-4694	Walter Doyle	. . .	Charlene Byers	. . .	Charles Cayce	Timothy Lewis	William Gray
Florissant		c	MC	50	(314) 921-5700	. . .	. . .	. . .	Randal McDaniel	. . .	William Karabas	Louis Jearls
Foristell	*	c	MC	. .	(636) 463-2123	Wanda Donnelly	Sandra Stokes	. . .	. . .	. . .	Douglas Johnson	. . .
Forsyth		c	CM	1	(417) 546-4763	. . .	. . .	. . .	. . .	James Single	. . .	. . .
Fredericktown		c	MC	3	(573) 783-3683	Philip Wulfert	C. Morgan	Caryn Sullivan	. . .	Darryl Asher	G. De Spain	. . .
Frontenac		c	MC	3	(314) 994-3200	Saundra Sobelman	. . .	Leesa Ross	Christine Harms	John Trout	Benjamin Branch	. . .
Fulton	*	c	CM	12	(573) 592-3111	Charles Latham	William Johnson	Carolyn Laswell	Kathleen Holschlag	Dean Buffington	Steve Myers	Darrell Dunlap
Gallatin		c	CM	1	(660) 663-2011	. . .	. . .	. . .	. . .	. . .	. . .	. . .
Gladstone		c	CM	26	(816) 436-2200	. . .	Kirk Davis	Cathy Swenson	Deborah Daily	. . .	. . .	Charles Williams
Glendale		c	MC	5	(314) 965-3600	John Schuster	Michael Pounds	M. Mackenberg	Daniel Lawrence	Larry Zeitzmann	Richard Black	Carl Politte
Grain Valley		c	CM	5	(816) 847-6200	Matthew Farlin	Gary Bradley	Carol Branson	Jill Shatto	. . .	Aaron Ambrose	Gary Hanson
Grandview		c	CM	24	(816) 316-4800	Harry Wilson	Cory Smith	Phoebe Cameron	Shirley Moses	Chuck Thacker	Larry Dickey	Lawrence Creek
Greenwood	*	c	MC	3	. . .	Richard DeCourcy	D. Carlyle	Tamara Woolford	. . .	. . .	Gary Bonine	Ryan Hunt
Hannibal		c	MC	17	(573) 221-0111	Roy Hark	Jeffrey Lagarce	Mary Baudendistel	. . .	John Hymers	Joey Runyon	James Burns
Harrisonville		c	CM	8	(816) 380-8900	Kevin Wood	Dianna Wright	Debbie Grant	. . .	Larry Francis	John Hofer	Robert Surber
Hayti		c	MC	3	(573) 359-0632	Richard Ashbaugh	. . .	. . .	. . .	Milford Chism	Paul Sheckell	Leonard Plunkett
Hazelwood		c	CM	26	(314) 839-3700	David Farquharson	Edwin Carlstrom	Colleen Klos	. . .	James Matthies	. . .	Thomas Manning
Hermann		c	MC	2	(573) 486-5400	Norbert Englert	JD Lester	D. Grannemann	. . .	. . .	Frank Tennant	. . .
Higginsville	*	c	CM	4	(660) 584-2106	Bill Kolas	Lee Barker	Richard Reyna	. . .	. . .	Shawn Smith	. . .
Holts Summit		c	MC	2	(573) 896-5600	Dan Cox	. . .	Cheryl Fletcher	. . .	Scott Brooks	Victor Pitman	. . .
Houston		c	MC	1	(417) 967-3348	. . .	Bill Bates	Lorraine Aye	. . .	. . .	Carloss Kirkman	. . .
Independence		c	CM	113	(816) 325-7000	Don Reimal	Robert Heacock	Bruce Lowrey	James Harlow	Larry Hodge	Fred Mills	Howard Penrod
Jackson		c	MC	11	(573) 243-3568	Paul Sander	Stephen Wilson	Mary Waller	. . .	Bradley Golden	Marvin Sides	Jim Roach
Jefferson City		c	CM	39	(573) 634-6310	John Landwehr	S. Rasmussen	Phyllis Powell	Stephen Schlueter	Robert Rennick	Roger Schroeder	Patrick Sullivan
Jennings		c	MC	15	(314) 388-1164	Benjamin Sutphin	Cheryl Balke	. . .	Beverly Roche	James Sutphin	John Judd	. . .
Joplin		c	CM	45	(417) 624-0820	Phil Stinnett	R. Rohr	Barbara Hogelin	Darelyn Cooper	Gary Trulson	Kevin Lindsey	David Hertzberg
Kansas City		c	CM	441	(816) 513-1408	Kay Barnes	Wayne Cauthen	Millie Crossland	Wanda Gunter	Richard Dyer	James Corwin	Stanley Harris
Kearney		c	CM	5	(816) 628-4142	Billy Dane	James Eldridge	Joan Updike	. . .	. . .	Thomas Carey	Richard Ritter
Kennett	*	c	CM	11	(573) 888-9001	Roger Wheeler	Ken Goslee	Brenda Privett	. . .	John Mallott	Barry Tate	Larry Jones
Kimberling City	*	c	MC	2	(417) 739-4903	George Quest	. . .	Elaine Kahler	. . .	. . .	Paul Howerton	Travis Tucker
Kinloch		c	MC	. .	(314) 521-3335	. . .	. . .	. . .	. . .	Lewis Miller	. . .	. . .
Kirksville	*	c	CM	16	(660) 627-1224	Martha Rowe	Mari Macomber	Vickie Brumbaugh	Laura Guy-Rice	Randy Behrens	James Hughes	Mark Gaugh
Kirkwood		c	CM	27	(314) 822-5802	Mike Swoboda	Michael Brown	Elizabeth Montano	John Adams	. . .	Jack Plummer	Kenneth Yost
Knob Noster		c	CM	2	(660) 563-2595	Stanley Hall	Douglas Kermick	Robert Niffen	. . .	Rick Johnson	Brian Kniskern	Steven Smith
La Grange		c	MC	1	(573) 655-4301	Timothy Rossiter	Mark Campbell	Patty Spindler	. . .	Henry Gunsauls	Larry Penn	Edward Ensor
La Plata		c	MC	1	(660) 332-7166	Gerald Lovingier	Ray Ivy	Betty Wheeler	. . .	Jerry Thomas	Kendrick Daniels	. . .
Ladue		c	MC	8	(314) 993-3439	Jean Quenon	. . .	John Williams	George Pelt	Robert Leroy	Don Wickenhauser	Dennis Bible
Lake Ozark		c	MC	. .	(573) 365-5378	. . .	. . .	Rachel Kelley	. . .	. . .	David Fair	Rick Sturgeon
Lake St. Louis		c	CM	10	(636) 625-1200	Michael Potter	Paul Markworth	Donna Daniel	Renee Roettger	. . .	Michael Force	. . .
Lake Tapawingo		c	CM	. .	(816) 229-3722	Reed Alberg	Carl Scarborough	Ty Saigh	. . .	. . .	. . .	. . .
Lamar		c	MC	4	(417) 682-5554	Keith Divine	Lynn Calton	Carolyn Taffner	Herbert Jett	Bill Rawlings	Ronald Hager	. . .
Lathrop	*	c	MC	2	(816) 740-4251	Rodney Greer	Donald Moore	Susie Freece	. . .	David Eads	Raymond Sprague	Dwight Adkison
Lawson		c	CM	1	(816) 580-3217	Robert Gill	. . .	Virgina Wickham	. . .	. . .	Raymond Sapp	Douglas Kessler
Lebanon		c	MC	12	(417) 532-2156	Stanley Allen	. . .	James Wilson	. . .	Samuel Schneider	Samuel Mustard	Scott Shumate
Lee's Summit		c	CM	70	(916) 969-7300	Karen Messeri	Stephen Arbo	Denise Chisum	Conrad Lamb	Thomas Solberg	Kenneth Conlee	Chuck Owsley
Lexington		c	CM	4	(660) 259-4633	Tom Hayes	. . .	. . .	. . .	Kirk Smith	Don Rector	Jim Knott
Liberty		c	CM	26	(816) 792-6000	Stephen Hawkins	Curtis Wenson	. . .	. . .	Richard Lehmann	Arthur Chevalier	Steven Hansen
Louisiana		c	MC	3	(573) 754-4132	James Yokem	Kelly Henderson	Sharon Kakouris	. . .	Mike Lesley	James Graham	. . .
Macon		c	MC	5	(660) 385-2632	. . .	. . .	Gerald Maloney	. . .	. . .	. . .	. . .
Malden	*	c	MC	4	(573) 276-4502	Ray Santie	Rick Murray	Marilyn Fiddler	. . .	Winford German	Jarrett Bullock	Ted Bellers
Manchester		c	CM	19	(636) 227-1385	Larry Miles	. . .	. . .	Marsha Knudtson	. . .	John Quinn	Edwin Blatther
Maplewood		c	CM	9	(314) 645-3600	Mark Langston	Martin Corcoran	. . .	. . .	Charlie Granda	James White	. . .
Marceline		c	CM	2	(660) 376-3528	Charles Dowell	Mike Leighton	Elizabeth Capp	. . .	Larry Ervie	Tom Bendure	Kirk Lockwood
Marshall		c	MC	12	(660) 886-2225	Mitchel Geisler	Charles Tryban	Janet French	Debbie Trimble	John Rieves	James Simmerman	Paul Jensen
Marshfield		c	MC	5	(417) 468-2310	. . .	. . .	. . .	. . .	. . .	. . .	. . .
Maryland Heights		c	CM	25	(314) 291-6550	Michael Moeller	Mark Levin	Marsha Jones	David Watson	. . .	Thomas O'Connor	Bryan Pearl
Maryville	*	c	CM	10	(660) 562-8001	Chad Jackson	Matthew LeCerf	Sheila Smail	. . .	. . .	. . .	Greg Decker
Mexico		c	CM	11	(573) 581-2100	. . .	Todd Thompson	Donna Barnes	Roger Haynes	. . .	. . .	. . .
Moberly	*	c	CM	11	(660) 263-4420	Don Burton	Andrew Morris	Diane Galloway	Greg Hodge	Kenny Brandow	Dennis Cupp	Doug Henry
Moline Acres	*	c	MC	2	(314) 868-2433	. . .	. . .	Nina Walker	Tina Minor	. . .	. . .	Dennis DeShay
Monett		c	CO	7	(417) 235-3763	Jerry Fulp	Rex Lane	Janie Knight	Lisa Crawford	Tom Jones	David Tatum	Pete Rauch
Monroe City		c	MC	2	(573) 735-4585	John Browning	James Burns	Gary Osbourne	. . .	Gary McElroy	Rick Stone	. . .
Montgomery City		c	MC	2	(573) 564-3160	Jeffrey Porter	Steven Deves	. . .	. . .	. . .	Michael Frye	Dorsey Stotler
Mount Vernon		c	MC	4	(417) 466-2122	Robert Walster	. . .	Mary Walker	. . .	Melvin Owens	W. Turk	Gene Stanton
Mountain Grove		c	CM	4	(417) 926-4162	Jake Slayton	Rick Outersky	Sandra Crisp	. . .	Paul Bushong	Tommy Gaddis	Michael Williams
Neosho		c	CM	10	(417) 451-8050	Howard Birdsong	Jan Blase	James Haddock	Cheryl Mosby	Michael Goldswortly	David McCracken	James Otten
Nevada		c	CM	8	(417) 448-2700	Jim Rayburn	William McGuire	Julie Stumpff	. . .	. . .	. . .	Joseph Charles
New Madrid		c	CM	3	(573) 748-2866	. . .	Furgison Hunter	Shelby Desmore	. . .	. . .	Claude McFerren	. . .
Nixa		c	CM	12	(417) 725-3788	Sharon Whitehill	Brian Bingle	. . .	Coralee Patrick	. . .	. . .	. . .
Normandy		c	MC	5	(314) 385-3300	James Murphy	Brent Bury	Pam Rogers	Kay Kulage	. . .	John Connolly	Rodney Jarrett
North Kansas City		c	MC	4	(816) 274-6000	Gene Bruns	Pamela Windsor	Marsha Wilson	Shirley Land	H David Williams	Glenn Ladd	Patrick Hawver
Northwoods		c	MC	4	(314) 385-8000	Errol Bush	. . .	Marvalda Howard	Renee Mayweather	. . .	Sylvester Jones	Lumis Kitchen
Oak Grove		c	CM	5	(816) 690-3773	Mark Fulks	Bryan Long	Cathy Smith	. . .	. . .	. . .	Joe Bobadilla
Odessa		c	MC	4	(816) 230-5577	Tom Murry	Steven Sanders	Margaret Howerton	. . .	. . .	Robert Kinder	Donald Elder
O'Fallon		c	CM	46	(636) 240-2000	Paul Renaud	Robert Lowery	Sandra Stokes	Vicki Boschert	. . .	Steve Talbott	Ken Morgan
Olivette	*	c	CM	7	(314) 993-0444	James Baer	T. McDowell	Myra Bennett	Alice Young	Robin Jobe	Richard Knox	Mike Gartenberg
Osage Beach		c	MC	3	(573) 302-2000	Penny Lyons	Nancy Viselli	Diann Warner	Karri Badolato	. . .	. . .	Rick King
Osceola	*	c	MC	. .	(417) 646-8421	Jerry Osborn	. . .	Lila Foster	. . .	. . .	Richard Gardner	. . .
Overland		c	MC	16	(314) 428-4321	Robert Dody	Linda Downs	. . .	Lisa Ridolfi	. . .	James Herron	. . .
Ozark		c	MC	9	(417) 581-2407	Donna McQuay	. . .	Lana Calley	. . .	. . .	Lyle Hodges	. . .

Directory 1/9 continued OFFICIALS IN U.S. MUNICIPALITIES 2,500 AND OVER IN POPULATION

Jurisdiction		Type	Form of govern- ment	2000 Popu- lation (000)	Main telephone number	Chief elected official	Appointed administrator	Clerk of the governing board	Chief financial officer	Fire chief	Police chief	Public works director
MISSOURI continued												
Pacific		c	MC	5	(636) 271-0500	Jeffrey Titter	Harold Selby	Joann Hoehne	. . .	. . .	Ronald Reed	Edward Gass
Pagedale	*	c	MC	3	(314) 726-1200	Mary Carter	Fran Stevens	. . .	Barbara Frierson	. . .	Albert Keys	. . .
Palmyra		c	MC	3	(573) 769-2223	Jim Browning	. . .	. . .	. . .	Charles Hoehne	James Beadle	. . .
Park Hills	*	c	MC	7	(573) 431-3577	John Clark	John Kennedy	Carla Johnson	. . .	Rick Whaley	William Holloway	Don Akers
Parkville		c	MC	4	(816) 741-7676	Charles Kutz	Joseph Turner	Barbara Lance	Justin Kuder	. . .	William Hudson	Jeff Rupp
Peculiar		c	MC	2	(816) 779-5212	George Lewis	Brad Ratliff	Nora Dodge	Karen Parrot	James Toone	Dean Kelly	Charlie Mohr
Perryville		c	CM	7	(573) 547-2594	Robert Miget	William Lewis	Marilyn Dobbelare	. . .	. . .	Keith Tarrillion	Charles La Rose
Pevely	*	c	MC	3	(636) 475-4452	John Knobloch	Happy Welch	Elizabeth Stackley	. . .	. . .	Ronnie Wicks	. . .
Pine Lawn		c	MC	4	(314) 261-5500	Adrian Wright	. . .	Charlotte Graham	. . .	. . .	Donald Hardy	George Prophete
Platte City		c	CM	3	(816) 858-3046	Dave Brooks	Keith Moody	Tanya Bates	Julie Pennington	. . .	. . .	Leonard Hendricks
Plattsburgh	*	c	CM	2	(816) 539-2148	James Kennedy	Dennis Gehrt	Mickey Streeter	. . .	. . .	Zephrey Bingham	Tom Eads
Pleasant Hill		c	CM	5	(816) 987-3135	Clarence Hall	Mark Randall	. . .	Sandra Beatty	Jeffrey Johnson	Robert Driscoll	Bob Kee
Poplar Bluff		c	CM	16	(573) 785-7474	. . .	Doug Bagby	. . .	. . .	. . .	. . .	. . .
Portageville		c	MC	3	(573) 379-5789	. . .	. . .	. . .	. . .	. . .	. . .	. . .
Potosi		c	MC	2	(573) 438-2767	Wayne Malugen	. . .	Doris Eye	Roger Bilderback	Richard Knight	Don Cooksey	. . .
Raymore		c	MC	11	(816) 331-0488	Juan Alonzo	Eric Berlin	Susan Gnefkow	. . .	. . .	Kris Turnbow	Mary Jaeger
Raytown		c	MC	30	(816) 737-6000	Jack Nesbitt	Michael Miller	Karlan Curtis	. . .	Rick Mawhirter	. . .	Mahesh Sharma
Republic		c	MC	8	(417) 732-6065	Keith Miller	James Krischke	Beth West	. . .	Don Murray	Mark Lowe	David Brock
Richland		c	MC	2	(573) 765-4421	Lucy Henson	. . .	Tana Mitschele	. . .	. . .	. . .	Claude Hill
Richmond		c	MC	6	(816) 776-5304	Thomas Morman	Stephen Kirk	Robin Milligan	. . .	Lonnie Quick	Theresa Williams	Allen Minnick
Richmond Heights		c	CM	9	(314) 645-0404	Betty Humphrey	Amy Hamilton	Patricia Villmer	Sara Fox	Charles Drexler	Rick Vilcek	Bruce Murray
Riverside		c	MC	2	(816) 741-3993	Betty Burch	David Blackburn	Louise Rusick	Terry Goodrich	. . .	Greg Mills	Larry Meyer
Riverview		v	CM	3	(314) 868-0700	Elizabeth Morris	. . .	Madonna Forrest	Jana Warmann	. . .	Roy Midkiff	Susan Kenkel
Rock Hill		c	CM	4	(314) 968-1410	Robert Salamone	George Liyeos	Penny Thomas	Don Cary	John Kriska	Terry Good	Ron Meyer
Rogersville	*	c	MC	1	(417) 753-2884	Jack Cole	Nancy Edson	Glenda Stegner	. . .	Richard Stirts	Leland McMasters	Scott Dorrell
Rolla	*	c	CM	16	(573) 426-6948	William Jenks	John Butz	Carol Daniels	Steffanie Rogers	Robert Williams	Mark Kearse	Steve Hargis
Salem		c	CM	4	(573) 729-4811	Gary Brown	. . .	Mary Happel	. . .	. . .	Clifford Jadwin	. . .
Savannah		c	CM	4	(816) 324-3315	Robert Wilson	Janice Hatcher	. . .	. . .	Steve Oliver	Derald Lammers	Kenny Lance
Scott City		c	MC	4	(573) 264-2157	Jim Parch	Ron Eskew	Nona Walls	. . .	James Cassout	Don Cobb	Jack Rasnic
Sedalia		c	MC	20	(660) 827-3000	Bob Wasson	Keith Riesberg	Arlene Silvey	Pamela Burlingame	Michael Ditzfeld	John DeGonia	Bill Beck
Shrewsbury		c	MC	6	(314) 647-5795	Bert Gates	Barry Alexander	. . .	Kathryn Wehner	William Fox	Jeffrey Keller	Tony Wagner
Sikeston		c	CM	16	(573) 471-2512	Michael Marshall	Kevin Friend	Carroll Couch	. . .	. . .	. . .	Tommy Bridger
Slater		c	MC	2	(660) 529-2271	. . .	. . .	. . .	. . .	. . .	. . .	. . .
Smithville		c	CM	5	(816) 532-3897	Charles Hitchborn	Gerry Vernon	Judy Clough	. . .	. . .	Ken Wilson	. . .
Springfield		c	CM	151	(417) 864-1000	Thomas Carlson	Robert Cumley	B. Cirtin Decker	Mary Mannix-	Dan Whisler	Lynn Rowe	Marc Thornsberry
St. Ann		c	MC	13	(314) 427-8009	Carrie Cafazza	. . .	Christina Santel	. . .	. . .	Robert Schrader	Kevin McCarthy
St. Charles		c	MC	60	(636) 949-3265	Patricia York	. . .	Marilyn McCoy	Karen McDermott	Ernest Rhodes	James Gooch	. . .
St. Clair	*	c	MC	4	(636) 629-0333	Ron Blum	James Arndt	Chris Fawe	. . .	Tim Wideman	. . .	James Terry
St. James	*	c	MC	3	(573) 265-7011	Dennis Wilson	. . .	Marilyn Woolsey	Paulette Craft	Bruce Parton	Kevin Friend	Mike Licklider
St. John		c	CM	6	(314) 427-8700	Lee Taylor	Terry Milam	Donna Davis	Marilyn Betkis	. . .	. . .	James Phillips
St. Joseph	*	c	CM	73	(816) 271-4674	Ken Shearin	Vincent Capell	Paula Heyde	Carolyn Harrison	Jack Brown	C. Connally	J. Woody
St. Louis		c	MC	348	(314) 622-3562	Francis Slay	Jeff Rainford	Parrie May	Darlene Green	Sherman George	Joseph Mokwa	David Visintainer
St. Peters		c	MC	51	(636) 477-6600	Shawn Brown	William Charnisky	Rhonda Shaw	. . .	. . .	. . .	Russell Batzel
Ste. Genevieve		c	CM	4	(573) 883-5400	. . .	. . .	Betty Seibel	. . .	. . .	Brian Clubb	Gene Thurman
Stockton		c	MC	1	(417) 276-5210	. . .	Kendel Goslee	. . .	. . .	. . .	. . .	. . .
Sugar Creek		c	MC	3	(816) 252-4400	Stanley Salva	Ronald Martinovich	Jana Dickerson	. . .	. . .	. . .	Edward Layton
Sullivan	*	c	CM	6	(573) 468-4612	James Schatz	Mark Falloon	Janice Nolie	. . .	. . .	George Counts	. . .
Sunset Hills	*	c	MC	8	(314) 849-3400	John Hunzeker	. . .	Laura Rider	. . .	. . .	William Lagrand	Anne Lamitola
Town & Country		c	MC	10	(314) 432-6606	Jonathan Dalton	John Copeland	Pamela Burdt	Betty Cotner	. . .	. . .	Douglas Hopkins
Trenton	*	c	CM	6	(660) 359-4310	Cathie Smith	Kerry Sampson	Cindy Simpson	. . .	Tony Ralston	Robert Lewis	. . .
Troy	*	c	MC	6	(636) 528-4712	Charles Kemper	. . .	Karen Hotfelder	. . .	. . .	Jeff Taylor	Robert Hembrock
Union	*	c	MC	7	(636) 583-3600	Michael Livengood	. . .	Jonita Copeland	. . .	. . .	Norman Brune	Harold Lampkin
University City	*	c	CM	37	(314) 862-6767	. . .	Julie Feier	Joyce Pumm	. . .	Steve Olshwanger	Charles Adams	E. Shields-Benford
Valley Park		c	MC	6	(314) 225-5171	Daniel Michel	. . .	Marguerite Wilburn	. . .	. . .	. . .	James McMullen
Vandalia		c	CM	2	(573) 594-6186	Ramon Barnes	Alan Winders	Karen Schutz	Sharon Myers	. . .	Raymond Laird	Aaron Rentfro
Warrensburg	*	c	CM	16	(660) 747-9131	Don Nimmer	J. Hancock	Cynthia Gabel	. . .	Phil Johnston	Bruce Howey	Robert Crumb
Warrenton	*	c	MC	5	(636) 456-3535	James Shores	Terri Thorn	Chris McCormick	. . .	. . .	Patrick Harney	Denneth Schwerdt
Warsaw		c	CM	2	(660) 438-5522	Lou Breshars	Randy Pogue	Betty Brumbaugh	. . .	. . .	James Hanik	. . .
Washington	*	c	MC	13	(636) 390-1000	Richard Stratman	James Briggs	Brenda Mitchell	Janet Braun	Willard Halmich	Kenneth Hahn	Gary Thornhill
Waynesville		c	MC	3	(573) 774-6171	Cliff Hammock	Bruce Harrill	Barbara Stinson	. . .	. . .	Donald McCulloch	. . .
Webb City	*	c	MC	9	(417) 673-4651	Glenn Dolence	Steven Garrett	Lorinda Southard	. . .	Ernie Goad	Donald Richardson	James Wallace
Webster Groves		c	CM	23	(314) 963-5300	Gerry Welch	Steven Wylie	Katie Nakazono	. . .	Michael Capriglione	Dale Curtis	Dennis Wells
Weldon Springs		c	MC	5	(636) 441-2110	Donald Licklider	. . .	M. Kwiatkowski	. . .	. . .	. . .	. . .
Wellston		c	MC	2	(314) 385-1015	James Harvey	Michael Evans	Diane Irvin	. . .	. . .	Robert Lewis	Eldright White
Wentzville	*	c	MC	6	(636) 327-5101	Paul Lambi	Andrew McCown	Vitula Skillman	. . .	. . .	Robert Noonan	William Bensing
West Plains	*	c	CO	10	(417) 256-7176	Joe Evans	Charles Fugate	Constance Shelton	. . .	James Bean	Charles Brotherton	Jim Davidson
Wildwood		c	CM	32	(636) 458-0440	Edward Marshall	Daniel Dubruiel	L. Greene-Beldner	Dawn Kaiser	. . .	. . .	Ryan Thomas
Willow Springs		c	CM	2	(417) 469-2107	David Wehmer	Ron Mersch	Darla Langford	. . .	Larry Foster	Danny Dunn	Paul Collins
Winchester		c	CM	1	(636) 391-0600	Fred Brenner	Barbara Beckett	. . .	. . .	. . .	. . .	. . .
Windsor		c	MC	3	(660) 647-3512	. . .	. . .	. . .	. . .	. . .	. . .	. . .
Woodson Terrace		c	MC	4	(314) 427-2600	William Ratchford	Lawrence Besmer	Margaret Wilson	. . .	. . .	Robert Dowling	Micah Jacquemin
MONTANA												
Anaconda–Deer Lodge		c	CM	9	(406) 563-4000	. . .	Gene Vuckovich	Susan McNeil	. . .	William Converse	John Sullivan	. . .
Belgrade		c	CM	5	(406) 388-4994	Lee Stevens	Joseph Menicucci	Marilyn Foltz	. . .	. . .	Gregory Waldon	Henry Hathaway
Billings		c	CM	89	(406) 657-8265	Charles Tooley	Christina Volek	Marita Herold	. . .	Marvin Jochems	Jerry Archer	David Mumford
Bozeman		c	CM	27	(406) 582-2300	Steven Kirchhoff	Chris Kukulski	Robin Sullivan	Miral Gamradt	. . .	. . .	Debra Arkell
Butte–Silver Bow		c	CO	33	(406) 497-6200	Judith Jacobson	. . .	Dinah McLeod	John Shea	Robert Armstrong	John Walsh	James Johnston
Columbia Falls		c	CM	3	(406) 892-4391	Susan Nicosia	William Shaw	. . .	Sybil Noss	Robert Webber	Dave Perry	Gary Stempin
Conrad	*	c	MC	2	(406) 271-3623	John Shevlin	. . .	. . .	Agnes Fowler	Kevin Moritz	Gary Dent	Richard Anderson
Cut Bank		c	MC	3	(406) 873-5526	William McCauley	. . .	Mary Embleton	. . .	. . .	. . .	Lorin Lowry
Deer Lodge	*	c	MC	3	(406) 846-3649	. . .	Mary Fraley	Chris Zawada	. . .	. . .	. . .	. . .
Dillon		c	MC	3	(406) 683-4245	Martin Malesich	. . .	Faye Jones	. . .	. . .	. . .	. . .
Forsyth		c	MC	1	(406) 356-2521	Dennis Kopitzke	. . .	Doris Pinkerton	. . .	Neil Donner	Tim Fulton	Richard Thompson
Glasgow		c	MC	3	(406) 228-2476	Wilmer Zeller	. . .	Kay Jackson	. . .	Neil Chouinard	Lyndon Erickson	Jon Bengochea
Glendive		c	MC	4	(406) 365-3318	. . .	. . .	. . .	. . .	. . .	. . .	. . .
Great Falls		c	CM	56	(406) 771-1180	. . .	John Lawton	Peggy Bourne	Coleen Balzarini	Randall McCamley	Robert Jones	Jim Rearden
Hamilton	*	c	MC	3	(406) 363-2101	Jessica Randazzo	Steve Green	Rose Allen	Cody Geddes	. . .	Ryan Oster	. . .
Hardin		c	MC	3	(406) 665-9293	Ronald Adams	. . .	Theresa Hert	Lori Dorn	. . .	. . .	Larry Vandersloot
Havre		c	MC	9	(406) 265-6719	Robert Rice	. . .	. . .	Lowell Swenson	Dave Sheppard	Mike Barthel	David Peterson
Helena	*	c	CM	25	(406) 447-8404	James Smith	Timothy Burton	Debbie Havens	. . .	Stephen Larson	Troy McGee	John Rundquist
Kalispell		c	CM	14	(406) 758-7757	Pamela Kennedy	James Patrick	Theresa White	Amy Robertson	Randy Brodehl	Frank Garner	James Hansz

Directory 1/9
continued

OFFICIALS IN U.S. MUNICIPALITIES 2,500 AND OVER IN POPULATION

Jurisdiction	Type	Form of government	2000 Population (000)	Main telephone number	Chief elected official	Appointed administrator	Clerk of the governing board	Chief financial officer	Fire chief	Police chief	Public works director
MONTANA continued											
Laurel	c	MC	6	(406) 628-7431	Kenneth Olson	...	Mary Embleton	...	Scott Wilm	Richard Musson	Steve Klotz
Lewistown	c	MC	5	(406) 538-2302	...	...	Kathy Wallingboro	...	Steve Cunningham	Kevin Mynre	Bill Bandel
Libby	c	MC	2	(406) 293-2731	Anthony Berget	...	...	...	Tom Wood	Clayton Coker	Daniel Thede
Livingston	* c	CM	6	(406) 823-6003	Steve Caldwell	Edwin Meece	...	Shirley Ewan	James Mastin	Darren Raney	Clint Tinsley
Miles City	c	MC	8	(406) 232-3462	Ernest Metzenberg	...	Patricia Huss	...	B. Christopherson	...	Patrick Rogers
Missoula	* c	MC	57	(406) 552-6130	John Engen	Bruce Bender	Martha Rehbein	Brent Ramharter	Thomas Steenberg	Roy Wickman	R. King
Polson	c	MC	4	(406) 883-8200	...	Jay Henry	Aggi Loeser	...	Thomas Maloney	Douglas Chase	...
Red Lodge	c	MC	2	(406) 446-1606	...	...	...	...	...	...	...
Shelby	c	MC	3	(406) 434-5222	Larry Bonderud	...	...	Teri Ruff	...	...	Bill Moritz
Sidney	c	MC	4	(406) 433-2809	Bret Smelser	...	Brenda Thogersen	...	Ken Volk	Frank Di Fonzo	Terry Meldahl
Whitefish	c	CM	5	(406) 863-2400	...	Gary Marks	Necile Lorang	Michael Eve	David Sipe	William Dial	John Wilson
Wolf Point	c	MC	2	(406) 653-1852	Matt Golik	...	...	...	Steve Harada	Jeff Harada	Richard Isle
NEBRASKA											
Ainsworth	c	MC	1	(402) 387-2494	...	Kristi Thornburg	...	...	...	...	...
Albion	c	MC	1	(402) 395-2428	James Tishammer	Jolynn Weber	...	...	Brent Lipker	James Vibsky	...
Alliance	c	CM	8	(308) 762-5400	Dan Kusek	Pamela Caskie	Linda Jines	...	David McCarty	E. Kiss	...
Ashland	c	CM	2	(402) 944-3387	Ronna Wiig	Jessica Preister	...	...	Rick Grauerholz	Mark Powell	Doug Peters
Auburn	* c	MC	3	(402) 274-3420	Robert Engles	...	Sherry Heskett	...	Randy Bennett	Dan White	David Hunter
Aurora	c	CM	4	(402) 694-6992	Kenneth Harter	Michael Bair	Erma Luth	...	Gary Gerdes	Charles Headley	William Vandeman
Beatrice	c	MC	12	(402) 223-3569	...	...	...	...	...	...	...
Bellevue	c	MC	44	(402) 293-3000	Jerry Ryan	Gary Troutman	Kay Dammast	...	Dale Tedder	John Stacey	Jerry Hare
Blair	c	MC	7	(402) 426-4191	James Realph	Rodney Storm	Brenda Taylor	...	Lonnie Penry	Joseph Lager	Allen Schoemacker
Bloomfield	c	MC	1	(402) 373-4396	Jim Cripe	...	Marilyn True	...	Rodger Freeman	Bryan Ruhr	Joe Kauth
Broken Bow	c	MC	3	(308) 872-5831	Jim Franssen	Steve Waring	Elaine Bayer	...	Kent Mallette	Steve Scott	Mike Lucas
Central City	c	MC	2	(308) 946-3806	Clayton Erickson	C. Anderson	David Rish	...	Tim Bolling	Dennis Wagner	...
Chadron	* c	CM	5	(308) 432-0505	Donnie Grantham	Sandra Powell	Donna Rust	Melany Hughes	Patrick Gould	Gerald Crews	Milo Rust
Chappell	c	MC	..	(308) 874-2401	...	...	Kim Johnson	...	Jim Riechman	Jeff Ortgies	...
Columbus	c	MC	20	(402) 564-8584	...	J. Mangiamelli	...	Anne Kinnison	...	William Gumm	...
Cozad	* c	MC	4	(308) 784-3907	Greg Tetley	Carl York	Susan Kloepping	...	Dave Cullers	Mark Montgomery	...
Crete	c	MC	6	(402) 826-4313	Judith Henning	...	Gary Yank	...	Mahlon Kohl	Steve Hensel	Tom Ourada
Dakota City	* c	MC	1	(402) 987-3448	Charmaine Cantrell	Robert Peters	...	...	Jerry Yacevich	...	Danny Fager
David City	c	MC	2	(402) 367-3135	H. Smith	Joseph Johnson	Joan Kovar	...	Michael Hiatt	Stephen Sunday	Jim McDonald
Fairbury	* c	MC	4	(402) 729-2476	E. Mueller	James Ferneau	Tami Arnold	...	Eric Voss	Brooks Bryan	Mick Hynek
Falls City	c	CM	4	(402) 245-2707	...	...	...	...	...	...	...
Fremont	c	MC	25	(402) 727-2630	...	Robert Hartwig	Kimberly Volk	...	...	Timothy Mullen	Clark Boschult
Fullerton	c	MC	1	(308) 536-2428	Gretchen Treadway	Wesley Nespor	...	...	...	...	Jerry Collins
Geneva	c	MC	2	(402) 759-3109	Rodney Norrie	Robert Higel	Barbara Whitley	...	Larry Waiss	Travis Cunningham	...
Gering	c	MC	7	(308) 436-5096	Starr Lehl	Lane Danielzuk	...	...	James Templar	Melvin Griggs	...
Gibbon	c	MC	1	(308) 468-6118	Monte Standage	Christopher Rector	Vicki Power	...	Gene Smith	...	Jerry Jergensen
Gordon	c	CM	1	(308) 282-0837	Nancy Russell	Fred Hlava	Toni Siders	...	Gary Paul	Loren Tesch	Michael Winter
Gothenburg	c	MC	3	(308) 537-3677	Larry Franzen	Bruce Clymer	Connie Dalrymple	...	Dale Franzen	Randy Olson	...
Grand Island	c	MC	42	(308) 385-5444	Ken Gnadt	Jeffrey Pederson	Cindy Johnson	Chuck Haase	...	Kyle Hetrick	Steven Riehle
Grant	c	MC	1	(308) 352-2100	William Wilson	Joseph Morris	DeAnn Zwickl	...	...	...	David Kedrowski
Hastings	* c	MC	24	(402) 461-2309	Matthew Rossen	Joe Patterson	Connie Hartman	...	Kent Gilbert	Larry Thoren	David Wacker
Hickman	c	MC	1	(402) 792-2212	...	B. Baker	...	...	...	...	David Hunter
Holdrege	c	CM	5	(308) 995-8681	Mark Rona	Robert Rager	Sheryl Nelson	...	...	Dennis DaMounde	...
Kearney	c	CM	27	(308) 233-3215	Bruce Blankenship	Michael Morgan	Michaelle Trembly	Wendell Wessels	...	Daniel Lynch	R. Wiederspan
Kimball	* c	CM	2	(308) 235-3639	Gregory Dinges	...	Pamela Richter	...	Rick Wynne	Douglas Provance	...
La Vista	c	MC	11	(402) 331-4343	Douglas Kindig	Brenda Gunn	...	Sheila Lindberg	Kirk Schuster	Robert Lausten	Joseph Soucie
Lexington	* c	CM	10	(308) 324-2341	Ted Cook	Joseph Pepplitsch	...	...	Bob Martin	Charles Clark	Glenn Hawks
Lincoln	c	MC	225	(402) 441-7888	Don Wesely	...	Joan Ross	Don Herz	Michael Spadt	Tom Casady	Allan Abbott
Madison	c	CM	2	(402) 454-2675	Darrel Lyon	...	...	...	...	Roddy Waterbury	Jim Lewis
Mc Cook	* c	CM	7	(308) 345-2022	Dennis Berry	Kurt Fritsch	Lea Doak	...	Marc Harpham	Isaac Brown	Kyle Potthoff
Minden	* c	MC	2	(308) 832-1820	Roger Jones	Brenton Lewis	...	...	Craig Space	James Huff	Gregg Hinrichsen
Nebraska City	* c	CO	7	(402) 873-5515	JoDee Adelung	Scott Bovick	Arnold Ehlers	...	Alan Viox	David Lacy	...
Norfolk	c	MC	23	(402) 844-2010	Gordon Adams	Michael Nolan	Beth Deck	Randy Gates	Shane Weidner	William Mizner	Dennis Smith
North Platte	c	MC	23	(402) 535-6724	G. Keith Richardson	James Hawks	...	...	Richard Pedersen	M. Gutschenritter	Wesley Meyer
Ogallala	* c	CM	4	(308) 284-6001	Paul Foy	...	Jane Skinner	...	Bill Fortune	David Kling	...
Omaha	c	MC	390	(402) 444-5300	Michael Fahey	...	Buster Brown	Carol Ebdon	Robert Dahlquist	Thomas Warren	Norman Jackman
O'Neill	c	MC	3	(402) 336-3640	William Price	...	Nikki Johnston	...	Rodney Ludemann	Benjamin Matchett	...
Ord	c	MC	2	(308) 728-5791	Roger Goldfish	...	Sandy Kruml	...	Charles Green	...	...
Papillion	c	MC	16	(402) 597-2000	James Blinn	Daniel Hoins	Jennifer Niemier	Nancy Purscell	Bill Bowes	Leonard Houloose	Marty Leming
Pierce	c	MC	1	(402) 329-4535	...	Chad Anderson	...	...	...	...	...
Plainview	c	CM	1	(402) 582-4928	...	John Vaughn	Jayne Gentzler	...	...	Bruce Yosten	...
Plattsmouth	c	MC	6	(402) 296-2522	R Paul Lambert	...	Rose Covert	...	Mike Wilson	Brian Paulsen	Gary Hellwig
Ralston	c	MC	6	(402) 331-6677	Donald Groesser	...	Dolores Costanzo	...	Kyle Ienn	Bill White	Daniel Freshman
Ravenna	c	MC	1	(308) 452-3273	...	...	Cindy Keslar	...	...	...	...
Red Cloud	c	MC	1	(402) 746-2215	...	...	...	...	...	...	...
Scottsbluff	* c	CM	14	(308) 630-4136	Randy Meininger	Rick Kuckkahn	Cindy Dickinson	Renae Griffiths	Dana Miller	Alex Moreno	Mark Bohl
Seward	c	MC	6	(402) 643-2928	Roger Glawatz	Daniel Berlowitz	...	Debra Schaefer	...	Alan Baldwin	Calvin Nordmeyer
Sidney	* c	MC	6	(308) 254-5300	Wendall Gaston	Gary Person	G. Anthony	...	Keith Stone	Larry Cox	Otto Hahnke
South Sioux City	* c	MC	11	(402) 494-7500	Robert Giese	Lance Hedquist	Sue Murray	...	Denis Campbell	Scot Ford	Paul Nolan
Springfield	* c	MC	1	(402) 253-2204	Dorothy Richards	...	Kathleen Fauver	...	Robert Roseland	...	Allen Post
Stanton	c	CM	1	(402) 439-2199	Harold Krumwiede	...	Nancy Morfeld	...	Richard Locke	...	...
Superior	c	MC	2	(402) 879-4713	Billy Maxey	...	Jan Diehl	Sam Clark	Todd Kroeger	Perry Freeman	Larry Brittenham
Sutton	c	MC	1	(402) 773-4225	John Hull	Virg Ulmer	...	...	Pat Merrick	...	Kevin Finnegan
Valentine	c	CM	2	(402) 376-2323	Wassace Balliet	...	John Hanzlicek	...	Terry Engles	Robert McLean	Scott Egelhoff
Wahoo	* c	MC	3	(402) 443-3222	Daryl Reitmajer	...	Melissa Harrell	...	Donald Jonas	Kenneth Jackson	James Gibney
Wakefield	c	MC	1	(402) 287-2080	Jim Clark	Jim Litchfield	Kathy Skinner	...	Dean Ulrich	...	...
Waverly	c	CM	2	(402) 786-2312	Ron Melbye	Douglas Rix	...	...	Aaron Hummel	...	Tracey Whyman
Wayne	c	CM	5	(402) 375-1733	Sheryl Lindau	Lowell Johnson	...	...	Robert Woehler	Lance Webster	...
West Point	c	MC	3	(402) 372-2466	Marlene Johnson	Thomas Goulette	Mary Kempf	...	Lyle Hansen	Michael Fisher	...
York	c	MC	8	(402) 363-2600	Greg Adams	Jack Vavra	C. Thiele	Susan Tonniges	Kevin Stuhr	Donald Klug	Orville Davidson
NEVADA											
Boulder City	c	CM	14	(702) 293-9202	Robert Ferraro	Vicki Mayes	Pamella Malmstrom	Robert Kenney	Dean Molburg	Thomas Finn	Scott Hansen
Carlin	c	MC	2	(775) 754-6354	Linda Bingaman	William Kohbarger	LaDawn Lawson	...	Will Johnston	William Bauer	Peter Aiazzi
Carson City	c	CM	52	(775) 887-2103	...	Linda Ritter	Alan Glover	Thomas Minton	Robert Giomi	Kenneth Furlong	Andrew Burnham
Elko	c	CM	16	(775) 777-7110	Michael Franzoia	...	Loralee Lynch	Dawn Stout	Alan Kightlinger	Clair Morris	...
Ely	c	MC	4	(775) 289-2430	...	Brent Hutchings	...	...	...	...	...

Directory 1/9 continued — OFFICIALS IN U.S. MUNICIPALITIES 2,500 AND OVER IN POPULATION

Jurisdiction		Type	Form of govern- ment	2000 Popu- lation (000)	Main telephone number	Chief elected official	Appointed administrator	Clerk of the governing board	Chief financial officer	Fire chief	Police chief	Public works director
NEVADA continued												
Fallon		c	MC	7	(775) 423-5104	Kenneth Tedford	. . .	Gary Cordes	. . .	. . .	Russell Brooks	Jerry Mayfield
Fernley		c	CM	9	(775) 575-5455	. . .	Gary Bacock	. . .	. . .	. . .	. . .	. . .
Gardnerville		t	CM	3	(775) 782-7134	. . .	James Park	. . .	. . .	. . .	. . .	. . .
Henderson	*	c	CM	175	(702) 267-2323	James Gibson	Mary Kay Peck	Monica Simmons	. . .	James Cavalieri	Richard Perkins	Robert Murnane
Las Vegas		c	CM	535	(702) 229-6011	Oscar Goodman	Douglas Selby	Barbara Ronemus	Mark Vincent	David Washington	Michael Sheldon	Richard Goecke
Laughlin		t	CM	4	(702) 298-0828	. . .	Jacquelyn Brady	. . .	. . .	. . .	. . .	. . .
Mesquite		c	CM	9	(702) 346-5295	Bill Nicholes	Timothy Hacker	Carol Woods	David Empey	Derek Hughes	Douglas Law	Bill Tanner
North Las Vegas		c	CM	115	(702) 633-1000	Michael Montandon	Gregory Rose	Karen Storms	Philip Stoeckinger	Al Gillespie	Mark Paresi	. . .
Pahrump		t	CM	7	(775) 727-5107	Tim Leavitt	Chuck Stidham	. . .	. . .	Barry Jennings	. . .	Gordon Scott
Reno		c	CM	180	(775) 334-2099	Robert Cashell	Charles McNeely	Lynette Jones	Andrew Green	Paul Wagner	Michael Poehlman	Neil Mann
Sparks		c	CM	66	(775) 353-2345	. . .	Shaun Carey	Deborine Dolan	Terri Thomas	. . .	John Dotson	Wayne Seidel
Wells		c	CM	1	(775) 752-3355	Rusty Tybo	Jolene Supp	Catherine Smith	Mary Ray	Randy Dedman	La Don Murray	David Linge
West Wendover		c	MC	4	(775) 664-3081	. . .	Chris Melville	Anna Bartlome	Leon Flinders	Jeffrey Knudtson	Ron Supp	Thomas Stratton
Winnemucca	*	c	CM	7	(775) 623-6333	Di An Putnam	Stephen West	Eddy Davis	. . .	Walt Johnstone	Robert Davidson	Eugenio Bernardi
NEW HAMPSHIRE												
Allenstown		t	TM	4	(603) 485-4276	Sandra McKenney	David Jodoin	Edward Cyr	. . .	Everett Chaput	James McGonigle	James Boisvert
Alton		t	MC	4	(603) 875-2161	James Washburn	Russell Bailey	Lisa Waterman	Paulette Wentworth	Alan Johnson	Kevin Iwans	Kenneth Roberts
Amherst		t	TM	10	(603) 673-6041	Jay Dinkel	. . .	Nancy Demers	Merri Howe	John DeSilva	Gary MacGuire	Bruce Berry
Antrim		t	CM	2	(603) 588-6785	Robert Flanders	William Prokop	Mary Hammond	. . .	Mike Beauchamp	Todd Feyrer	Jim Cruthers
Ashland	*	t	CM	1	(603) 968-4432	Glenn Dion	Richard Alpers	Patricia Tucker	. . .	Thomas Stewart	Joseph Chivell	Mark Ober
Atkinson		t	TM	6	(603) 362-5266	. . .	. . .	Linda Jetty	Sandra La Velle	Michael Murphy	Philip Consentino	Edward Stewart
Auburn	*	t	TM	4	(603) 483-5052	Harland Eaton	William Herman	Joanne Linxweiler	Adele Brown	Bruce Phillips	Edward Picard	Michael Dross
Barrington		t	TM	7	(603) 664-9007	George Bailey	Carol Reilly	Sheila Marquette	. . .	Richard Walker	Richard Conway	Peter Cook
Bedford	*	t	CM	18	(603) 472-5242	Paul Roy	Russell Marcoux	Wanda Jenkins	Crystal Dionne	Scott Wiggin	David Bailey	James Stanford
Belmont		t	TM	6	(603) 267-8300	. . .	. . .	. . .	. . .	. . .	. . .	. . .
Berlin		c	CM	10	(603) 752-7532	Robert Danderson	Patrick Macqueen	Debra Patrick	Blandine Shallow	Randall Trull	Peter Morency	. . .
Boscawen		t	RT	3	(603) 753-9188	Rhoda Hardy	Sherlene Fisher	. . .	. . .	Ray Fisher	David Croft	Richard Hollins
Bow		t	TM	7	(603) 228-1187	Leon Kenison	James Pitts	Jill Hadaway	. . .	Dana Abbott	Jeff Jaran	Leighton Cleverly
Bristol	*	t	MC	3	(603) 744-3354	Richard Alpers	Elizabeth Corrow	Raymah Simpson	Peggy Petraszewski	Norman Skantze	John Clark	Mark Bucklin
Canaan		t	TM	3	(603) 523-4501	Robert Reagan	. . .	Vicky McAlister	Gloria Koch	William Bellion	Samuel Frank	. . .
Candia		t	TM	3	(603) 483-8101	Gary York	. . .	Christine Dupere	. . .	Rudolph Cartier	Michael McGillen	. . .
Charlestown		t	RT	4	(603) 826-4400	Brenda Ferland	David Edkins	Debra Clark	Patricia Royce	Gary Stoddard	Edward Smith	. . .
Chesterfield		t	TM	3	(603) 363-4624	T. Butterworth	Ricky Carrier	Shirley Philbrick	. . .	. . .	Earl Nelson	Stephen Bevis
Claremont		c	CM	13	(603) 542-7002	Scott Pope	Guy Santagate	Gwendolyn Melcher	Mary Walter	Peter Chase	Alex Scott	Bruce Temple
Colebrook		t	CM	2	(603) 237-4070	Greg Placy	Donna Caron	Sheila Beauchemin	Camilla Stewart	Philip Ducret	Steve Cass	Kevin McKinnon
Concord		c	CM	40	(603) 225-8535	Michael Donovan	Thomas Aspell	Janice Bonenfant	James Howard	Christopher Pope	Jerome Madden	Earle Chesley
Conway		t	TM	8	(603) 447-3811	Gary Webster	Earl Sires	Rhoda Quint	. . .	. . .	Jeffrey Dicey	Paul Degliangeli
Derry	*	t	CM	34	(603) 432-6100	Craig Bulkley	Richard Stenhouse	Denise Neale	Frank Childs	George Klauber	Edward Garone	Michael Fowler
Dover		c	CM	26	(603) 516-6000	. . .	J. Joyal	Judy Gaouette	Jeffrey Harrington	Perry Plummer	William Fenniman	. . .
Durham		t	CM	12	(603) 868-5571	Malcom Sandberg	Todd Selig	Lorrie Pitt	Paul Beaudon	Ronald O'Keefe	David Kurz	Michael Lynch
Enfield	*	t	TM	4	(603) 632-5026	. . .	Steven Schneider	Ilene Reed	. . .	David Crate	Richard Crate	Timothy Jennings
Epping		t	TM	5	(603) 679-5441	Susan McGeough	. . .	Linda Foley	. . .	Henry Letourneau	Gregory Dodge	. . .
Epsom		t	TM	4	(603) 736-9002	Mary Frambach	. . .	Dawn Blackwell	Nancy Wheeler	R. Yeaton	Wayne Preve	. . .
Exeter		t	TM	14	(603) 778-0591	Paul Binette	Russell Dean	L. H.-Macomber	Jack Sheehy	Brian Comeau	Richard Kane	Keith Noyes
Farmington	*	t	TM	5	(603) 755-2208	Gerald McCarthy	Anthony Minscu	Kathy Seaver	. . .	Richard Fowler	Scott Roberge	Joel Moulton
Franklin	*	c	CM	8	(603) 934-3900	Anthony Giunta	Gregory Doyon	Gayle Cook	Dawn Ouellette	Scott Clarenbach	Brad Haas	Brian Sullivan
Gilford		t	RT	6	(603) 527-4700	Alice Boucher	Evans Juris	Denise Morrissette	. . .	Michael Mooney	. . .	Sheldon Morgan
Goffstown		t	MC	16	(603) 497-8990	Henry Boyle	S. Desruisseaux	. . .	Janice O'Connell	Paul Nault	Michael French	Carl Quiram
Gorham		t	TM	2	(603) 466-3322	. . .	William Jackson	Grace La Pierre	Denise Vallee	George Eichler	Ronald Devoid	Roger Guilmette
Grantham	*	t	MC	2	(603) 863-6021	. . .	Tina Stearns	. . .	. . .	Robert Seavey	Russell Lary	. . .
Hampstead		t	TM	8	(603) 329-4100	Richard Hartung	Laura Buono	Tina Harrington	. . .	Walter Hastings	Joseph Beaudoin	Jon Worthen
Hampton		t	TM	14	(603) 926-6766	James Workman	. . .	Arleen Andreozzi	Dawna Duhamel	Henry Lipe	William Wrenn	John Hangen
Hampton Falls		t	TM	1	(603) 926-4618	. . .	Eric Small	Holly Knowles	. . .	. . .	. . .	. . .
Hanover		t	TM	10	(603) 643-0742	Brian Walsh	Julia Griffin	. . .	. . .	Roger Bradley	Nicholas Giaccone	Peter Kulbacki
Haverhill		t	TM	4	(603) 787-6800	Robert Maccini	Glenn English	Bette Pollock	Jo Lacaillade	. . .	Jeffrey Williams	. . .
Henniker		t	RT	4	(603) 428-3221	J. Damour	Kelly Clark	K. Johnson	. . .	Ben Ayer	T. Russell	T. Woodley
Hillsborough		t	TM	4	(603) 464-3877	Robert Buker	James Coffey	Deborah McDonald	. . .	David Holmes	David Roarick	. . .
Hinsdale		t	RT	4	(603) 336-5710	Michael McGrath	Jill Collins	T.-Jean Akeley	. . .	Robert Johnson	Wayne Gallagher	Frank Podlenski
Hollis		t	RT	7	(603) 465-2780	. . .	C. Hallsworth	Nancy Jambard	Paul Calabria	Richard Towne	Russell Ux	Arthur Leblanc
Hooksett		t	CM	11	(603) 485-8472	Michael DiBitetto	David Jodoin	Leslie Nepveu	Diane Savoie	Michael Howard	Stephen Agrafiotis	. . .
Hopkinton		t	TM	5	(603) 746-3170	Barbara Unger	Edward Wojnowski	Sue Strickford	. . .	Peter Russell	Ira Midgal	David Story
Hudson		t	CO	22	(603) 886-6024	E. Madison	. . .	Cecile Nichols	Stephen Malizia	Francis Carpentino	Richard Gendron	Kevin Burns
Jaffrey		t	CM	5	(603) 532-7445	Franklin Sterling	Michael Hartman	Maria Chamberlain	Pamela Bernier	Francis McConnell	Martin Dunn	Randall Heglin
Keene	*	c	CM	22	(603) 357-9804	Michael Blastos	John MacLean	Patricia Little	Martha Landry	. . .	Arthur Walker	Kurt Blomquist
Kingston		t	TM	5	(603) 642-3342	Mark Heitz	. . .	Ann Sullivan	Cindy Kenerson	Bill Seaman	Donald Briggs	Richard St. Hilaire
Laconia		c	CM	16	(603) 524-3877	. . .	Eileen Cabanel	Ann Kaligian	Pamela Reynolds	Ken Erickson	Tom Oetinger	Frank Tilton
Lancaster		t	TM	3	(603) 788-2114	. . .	. . .	. . .	. . .	. . .	. . .	. . .
Lebanon		c	CM	12	(603) 448-4220	. . .	G. Mandsager	Sandi Allard	Leonard Jarvi	Stephen Allen	Randall Chapman	Michael Lavalla
Lincoln		t	CM	1	(603) 745-2757	. . .	. . .	. . .	. . .	. . .	. . .	. . .
Litchfield		t	TM	7	(603) 424-4046	. . .	. . .	. . .	. . .	. . .	. . .	. . .
Littleton		t	TM	5	(603) 444-3996	Burton Ingerson	Charles Connell	Judy White	Karen Noyes	Paul Lopes	Cameron Brown	Larry Jackson
Londonderry		t	TM	23	(603) 432-1100	. . .	David Caron	M. Seymour	Susan Hickey	Michael Carrier	Joseph Ryan	Janusz Czyzowski
Manchester		c	MC	107	(603) 624-6543	Robert Baines	. . .	Leo Bernier	Kevin Clougherty	Joseph Kane	John Jaskolka	Frank Thomas
Meredith		t	CM	5	(603) 279-4538	. . .	Carol Granfield	. . .	. . .	Charles Palm	John Curran	Michael Faller
Merrimack	*	t	TM	25	(603) 424-2331	Richard Hinch	Keith Hickey	Diane Pollock	Paul Micali	Michael Currier	Micheal Milligan	Edward Chase
Milford	*	t	TM	13	(603) 673-2257	Noreen O'Connell	Guy Scaife	Margaret Langell	Rosemarie Evans	Francis Fraitzl	Frederick Douglas	William Ruoff
Milton	*	t	MC	3	(603) 652-4501	Tom Gray	Edward Ryan	Carol Martin	. . .	Andy Lucier	Mark McGowan	Patrick Smith
Moultonborough		t	CM	4	(603) 476-2347	Ernest Davis	. . .	Barbara Wakefield	. . .	Richard Plaisted	Scott Kinmond	Wayne Richardson
Nashua		c	MC	86	(603) 589-3230	Bernard Streeter	. . .	Paul Bergeron	Carol Anderson	Roger Hatfield	Donald Gross	Richard Seymour
New Boston	*	t	CM	4	(603) 487-5504	Harold Strong	. . .	Margit Hooper	. . .	James Dodge	James McLaughlin	Lee Murray
New Durham		t	MC	2	(603) 859-2091	Paul Gelinas	. . .	Carole Ingham	. . .	. . .	Douglas Scruton	Mark Fuller
New London	*	t	TM	4	(603) 526-4821	Ruth Clough	Jessie Levine	Linda Hardy	Carolyn Fraley	Jason Lyon	David Seastrand	Richard Lee
Newbury		t	MC	1	(603) 763-4940	. . .	Dennis Pavlicek	. . .	. . .	. . .	. . .	. . .
Newmarket	*	t	CM	8	(603) 659-3617	. . .	. . .	Becky Benvenuti	Donald Parnell	. . .	Kevin Cyr	Richard Malasky
Newport		t	TM	6	(603) 863-1360	Gary Nichols	Daniel O'Neill	Karlene Stoddard	Paul Brown	John Marcotte	. . .	Larry Wiggins
Newton	*	t	TM	4	(603) 382-4405	John Ulcickas	Nancy Wrigley	. . .	. . .	William Ingalls	Lawrence Streeter	Frank Gibbs
North Hampton	*	t	TM	4	(603) 964-8087	Donald Gould	Stephen Fournier	Susan Uchanan	. . .	Thomas Lambert	Brian Page	Robert Strout
Northfield		t	TM	4	(603) 286-7039	. . .	Joyce Fulweiler	. . .	. . .	. . .	. . .	. . .
Northumberland		t	CM	2	(603) 636-1450	John Normand	Jeremiah Lamson	Melinda Kennett	. . .	Terrance Bedell	Lloyd Tippitt	Gregory Kenison

Directory 1/9 continued — OFFICIALS IN U.S. MUNICIPALITIES 2,500 AND OVER IN POPULATION

Jurisdiction	Type	Form of govern-ment	2000 Popu-lation (000)	Main telephone number	Chief elected official	Appointed administrator	Clerk of the governing board	Chief financial officer	Fire chief	Police chief	Public works director
NEW HAMPSHIRE continued											
Pelham	t	RT	10	(603) 635-8233	...	...	Dorothy Marsden	Robert Blanchette	David Fisher	Evan Haglund	Donald Foss
Pembroke *	t	TM	6	(603) 485-4747	Larry Preston	Troy Brown	James Goff	...	Harold Paulsen	Scott Lane	James Boisvert
Peterborough	t	TM	5	(603) 924-8000	Lawrence Ross	Pamela Brenner	Robert Lambert	Nancie Vaihinger	William Naugle	Scott Guinard	Edwin Betz
Pittsfield *	t	TM	3	(603) 435-6773	Arthur Morse	Jeremiah Lamson	Elizabeth Hast	...	Gary Johnson	Robert Wharem	George Bachelder
Plaistow	t	CM	7	(603) 382-8469	Barbara Hobbs	...	Barbara Tavitian	Susan Drew	Donald Petzold	Stephen Savage	Daniel Garlington
Plymouth	t	RT	5	(603) 536-1731	Timothy Naro	...	Kathleen Latuch	Karen Freitas	Brian Thibeault	Anthony Raymond	Michael Heath
Portsmouth *	c	CM	20	(603) 431-2000	Steve Marchand	John Bohenko	Kelli Barnaby	Judith Belanger	C. LeClaire	Michael Magnant	Steven Parkinson
Raymond *	t	TM	9	(603) 895-4735	Franklin Bishop	Christopher Rose	Doris Gagnon	Grace Collette	Kevin Pratt	David Salois	Dennis McCarthy
Rindge	t	TM	5	(603) 899-5181	David Collum	Edgar Gadbois	Nancy Martin	Julie Labonte	Richard Donovan	Michael Sebor	Peter Goewey
Rochester *	c	CM	28	(603) 332-1167	John Larochelle	John Scruton	Joseph Gray	...	Norman Sanborn	David Dubois	Melodie Esterberg
Rye	t	TM	5	(603) 964-5523	Joseph Mills	...	Jane Ireland	Cynthis Gillespie	Richard O'Brien	Alan Gould	Everett Jordan
Salem	t	CM	28	(603) 890-2000	...	Henry LaBranche	Barbara Lessard	Linda Casey	Arthur Barnes	Paul Donovan	Rodney Bartlett
Sanbornton	0	MC	2	(603) 286-4034	...	Bruce Kneuer	Jane Goss	...	Jerry Busby	Mark Barton	...
Seabrook *	t	CM	7	(603) 474-3311	Richard McCann	Scott Dunn	Bonnie Fowler	V. McGlaughlin	Jeffrey Brown	David Currier	John Starkey
Somersworth	c	CM	11	(603) 692-4262	James McLin	Robert Belmore	Nancy Liebson	Heather Briggs	Paul Vallee	Dean Crombie	John Jackman
Stratham *	t	TM	6	(603) 772-7391	Martin Wool	Paul Deschaine	Shirley Daley	...	Robert Law	Michael Daley	Fred Hutton
Sugar Hill	t	TM	..	(603) 823-8468	Richard Bielefield	Jennifer Gaudette	L. Boissonneault	...	Allan Clark	Jose Pequeno	Douglas Glover
Sunapee *	t	CM	3	(603) 763-2212	Emma Smith	Donna Nashawaty	Betty Ramspott	...	Daniel Ruggles	David Cahill	Anthony Bergeron
Sutton	t	CM	1	(603) 927-4416	Thomas Brooks	Elten Phillips	Janet Haines	...	Darrel Palmer	Patrick Tighe	...
Swanzey *	t	RT	6	(603) 352-7411	Bruce Tatro	Elizabeth Fox	Deirdre Geer	...	Robert Symonds	Richard Busick	Lee Dunham
Temple	t	TM	1	(603) 878-2536	...	Debra Harling	Kathleen Nolte	...	...	...	...
Tilton	t	TM	3	(603) 286-4521	...	...	...	...	Harold Harbour	...	...
Wakefield	t	CM	4	(603) 522-6205	Paul Morrill	Robin Frost	Cynthia Bickford	Kathleen Estabrook	Todd Nason	Tim Merrill	Dan Davis
Walpole	t	TM	3	(603) 756-3672	Sheldon Sawyer	...	Sandra Smith	Teresa Fernette	Richard Hurlburt	David Hewes	James Terell
Weare	t	TM	7	(603) 529-7525	Laura Buono	Fred Ventresco	Evelyn Connor	...	Robert Richards	Gregory Begin	Carl Knapp
Wilton	t	TM	3	(603) 654-9451	Jane Farrell	...	...	Barry Greene	Rene Houle	Robert Maguire	Charles McGettigan
Winchester	t	RT	4	(603) 239-4951	Gustave Ruth	John Stetser	...	...	Barry Kellom	Gary Phillips	Dale Gray
Windham	t	RT	10	(603) 432-7732	...	David Sullivan	...	Dana Call	Steven Fruchtman	...	...
Wolfeboro	t	TM	6	(603) 569-8161	Shirley Ganem	David Owen	Patricia Waterman	Scott Smith	Benjamin Bean	Richard Labell	Marty Bilafer
NEW JERSEY											
Aberdeen *	tp	CM	17	(732) 583-4200	David Sobel	Stuart Brown	Karen Ventura	Angela Morin	...	John Powers	James Lauro
Absecon	c	MC	7	(609) 641-0663	Peter Elco	Terry Dolan	Carie Crone	Jessica Thompson	Stan Kolbe	Charles Smith	Lloyd Jones
Allendale *	b	MC	6	(201) 818-4400	Vincent Barra	Leslie Shenkler	Gwen Gabbert	Paula Favata	Greg Andersen	Robert Herndon	George Higbie
Alpha	b	MC	2	(908) 454-0088	Thomas Fey	...	Bess Embardino	Peter Kowalick	Edward Hanics	John Haidu	Leo Pursell
Andover	tp	CM	6	(973) 383-4280	Bob Transue	Richard Stewart	Vita Thompson	Jeffrey Theriault	Jeff Schick	Phillip Coleman	Mike Insinga
Asbury Park	c	CM	16	(732) 775-2100	Kenneth Saunders	Terence Reidy	Stephen Kay	Ricardo Diaz	Joseph Mirarchi	Richard Lucherini	Garrett Giberson
Atlantic City	c	MC	40	(609) 347-5300	James Whelan	...	Benjamin Fitzgerald	Joanne Shepherd	Benjamin Brenner	Benn Polk	Richard Norwood
Atlantic Highlands	b	MC	4	(732) 291-1444	Michael Harmon	Adam Hubeny	David Palamara	Catherine Campbell	Russell Mount	Gerard Vasto	...
Audubon	b	CO	9	(856) 547-0711	...	...	...	...	...	...	...
Avalon	b	MC	2	(609) 967-8200	Martin Pagliughi	Andrew Bednarek	Amy Kleuskens	James Craft	...	Stephen Sykes	Harry DeButts
Barnegat	tp	MC	15	(609) 698-0080	...	...	...	...	...	...	...
Barrington *	b	MC	7	(856) 547-0706	...	...	Terry Shannon	Denise Moules	Wayne Robenolt	...	...
Bayonne	c	MC	61	(201) 858-6010	Len Kiczek	Harold Demellier	Robert Sloan	Terrance Malloy	William Kosakowski	Francis Pawlowski	Robert Kaminski
Beach Haven	b	MC	1	(609) 492-0111	Deborah Whitcraft	Richard Crane	Judith Howard	Diane Marshall	...	Stanley Markoski	Kim England
Beachwood	b	MC	10	(732) 286-6000	Harold Morris	...	...	...	...	...	...
Bedminster	tp	CM	8	(908) 234-0333	...	Susan Stanbury	Dorothy Wilkie	June Enos	...	William Stephens	Jon Mantz
Belleville	tp	CM	34	(973) 450-3300	Gerald DiGori	Victor Canning	Kelley Nash	...	Robert Caruso	Joseph Rotonda	James Messina
Bellmawr	b	MC	11	(609) 933-1313	...	...	...	...	...	...	...
Belmar	b	MC	6	(732) 681-3700	Kenneth Pringle	...	Margaret Plummer	Robbin Kirk	...	Richard Lynch	Anders Meuerle
Bergenfield	b	CM	26	(201) 387-4055	Kevin Clancy	Joseph Hess	...	John Mosca	Charles Hartung	Richard Baroch	Robert Bartley
Berkeley Heights *	tp	MC	11	(908) 464-2700	David Cohen	Angela Devanney	Patricia Rapach	Tracy Tedesco	Anthony Padovano	David Zager	...
Berlin	b	MC	6	(856) 767-7777	...	...	...	...	...	...	...
Bernards	tp	CM	24	(908) 766-2510	William Homes	...	Denise Szabo	Dorothy Stikna	...	Thomas Kelly	Michael Beale
Bernardsville	b	MC	7	(908) 766-3000	Hugh Fenwick	Ralph Maresca	...	...	Randy Steinkopf	Thomas Sciaretta	John Mac Dowall
Beverly	c	MC	2	(609) 387-1881	Robert Lowden	...	Barbara Sheipe	...	Cornell Hawkins	...	Daniel Schoen
Bloomfield	tp	MC	45	(973) 680-4000	James Norton	Louise Palagano	...	Wayne Hartmann	Joseph Intile	John McNiff	Anthony Marucci
Bloomingdale	b	MC	7	(973) 838-0778	...	...	Jane Febbi	Dave Hollberg	Duane Muldoon	William Alexander	Joe Luke
Bogota	b	MC	8	(201) 342-1736	Steven Lonegan	...	Frances Garlicki	...	David Hanley	Gary Kohles	Robert Stauffer
Boonton	t	MC	8	(973) 402-9410	Edward Bolcar	...	Cynthia Oravits	Jeffery Theriault	John Steinhauser	...	Michael Petonak
Bordentown	c	CO	3	(609) 298-0604	Zigmont Targonski	...	...	...	Steve McGowan	Philip Castagna	Robert Erickson
Bound Brook	b	MC	10	(732) 356-0833	Frank Gilly	Thomas Brodbeck	...	Kathryn Kinney	R. Colombaroni	K. Henderson	Mark Cassebaum
Bradley Beach	b	CO	4	(732) 776-2999	Stephen Schueler	Phyllis Quixley	Mary Ann Solinski	Joyce Wilkins	John Zech	Robert Denardo	Richard Bianchi
Branchburg	tp	CM	14	(908) 526-1300	...	Gregory Bonin	Sharon Brienza	Diane Salek	James McAleer	John Tamburini	Bruce Kosensky
Brick *	tp	MC	66	(732) 262-1050	Joseph Scarpelli	Scott Mac Fadden	George Cevasco	...	...	Ronald Dougard	John Nydam
Bridgeton *	c	MC	22	(856) 455-3230	James Begley	Arthur Liston	Darlene Richmond	Teresa Delp	David Schoch	...	Roy Burlew
Bridgewater	tp	MC	42	(908) 725-6300	James Dowden	William O'Neill	Bette Nuse	Kathryn Kinney	...	Richard Borden	John Laugel
Brielle *	b	MC	4	(732) 528-6600	Thomas Nicol	Thomas Nolan	...	Karen Brisben	Joe Harriman	Michael Palmer	William Burkhardt
Brigantine *	c	CM	12	(609) 266-7600	Philip Guenther	James Barber	Lynn Sweeney	Christian Johansen	Stanley Cwiklinski	Art Gordy	Ernie Purdy
Buena	b	MC	3	(856) 697-9393	...	...	...	...	...	...	...
Burlington	c	MC	9	(609) 386-0200	Darlene Scocca	Robin Snodgrass	Cindy Crivaro	Kenneth MacMillan	Ron Devlin	John Lazzarotti	Vincent Calisti
Butler	b	MC	7	(973) 838-7200	Ronald Assante	James Lampmann	Carol Ashley	James Kozimor	Daniel Canty	Dennis Passenti	Edward Becker
Byram *	tp	CM	8	(973) 347-2500	Eskil Danielson	...	Doris Flynn	Lisa Spring	Paul Conklin	Ray Rafferty	Adolf Steyh
Caldwell	tp	MC	7	(973) 226-6100	Paul Jemas	Maureen Ruane	...	...	...	...	...
Camden	c	MC	79	(856) 757-7000	Gwendolyn Faison	Christine Tucker	Luis Pastoriza	Richard Wright	Joseph Marini	Edwin Figueroa	Patrick Keating
Cape May	c	CM	4	(609) 884-9525	...	...	Virginia Petersen	Jack Jansen	Bruce Bieber	Robert Boyd	Robert Smith
Carlstadt	b	MC	5	(201) 939-2850	William Roseman	Jane Fontana	Claire Foy	D. Griancaspro	Chris Assenheimer	John Occhiuzzo	Paul Ritchie
Carteret	b	MC	20	(732) 541-3800	...	...	Kathleen Barney	Patrick Deblasio	Brian O'Connor	John Pieczyski	Ted Surick
Cedar Grove	tp	CM	12	(973) 239-1410	...	...	...	...	...	...	...
Chatham	b	MC	8	(973) 635-0674	...	...	Susan Caljean	Dorothy Klein	Peter Glogloida	John Drake	Robert Venezia
Cherry Hill	tp	MC	69	(856) 488-7800	...	...	...	...	...	...	...
Chester	b	MC	1	(908) 879-5361	Dennis Verbaro	...	Valerie Egan	Vidya Nayak	Angelo Bolio	Neil Logan	Tom Delmore
Cinnaminson	tp	MC	14	(856) 829-6000	Sandra Iaquinto	John Ostrowski	Grace Campbell	...	...	Michael Wallace	Carl Letterie
Clark	tp	MC	14	(732) 388-3600	Sal Bonaccorso	John Laezza	Kathleen Leonard	Robert Stanley	Andrew Beach	Anton Danco	Frances Brattole
Clayton	b	CM	7	(856) 881-2882	Patricia Gannon	Ted Taylor	Christine Newcomb	Donna Nestore	Harry Simpson	N. Winters	Edward Bell
Clementon	b	MC	4	(609) 783-0284	Frederick Busch	...	Patricia Porter	Stephen Considine	Randall Freiling	Robert Getz	Mark Williams
Cliffside Park	b	MC	23	(201) 945-3456	...	...	...	...	...	...	...
Clifton	c	CM	78	(973) 470-5800	...	Albert Greco	...	...	...	...	...
Clinton	t	MC	2	(908) 735-8616	...	...	...	...	...	...	...
Clinton	tp	MC	12	(908) 735-8800	Nick Corcodilos	Marvin Joss	...	Ulrich Steinberg	Marc Strauss	...	...
Closter	b	MC	8	(201) 784-0600	Fred Pitofsky	Erik Lenander	Loretta Castano	Joseph Luppino	Thomas Reineke	David Berrian	Rob Stauffer

Directory 1/9 continued OFFICIALS IN U.S. MUNICIPALITIES 2,500 AND OVER IN POPULATION

Jurisdiction	Type	Form of govern-ment	2000 Popu-lation (000)	Main telephone number	Chief elected official	Appointed administrator	Clerk of the governing board	Chief financial officer	Fire chief	Police chief	Public works director
NEW JERSEY continued											
Collingswood	b	CO	14	(856) 854-0720	M. Maley	Jean Di Gennaro	Alice Marks	Patrick Abusi	Michael Hall	Thomas Garrity	Brad Stokes
Colts Neck	t	MC	12	(732) 462-5470	Albert Yodakis	. . .	. . .	John Antonides	Michael Piotrowski	Kevin Sauter	Charles Buck
Commercial	tp	MC	5	(856) 785-3100	. . .	. . .	. . .	Judson Moore	. . .	. . .	. . .
Cranbury	tp	MC	3	(609) 395-0544	. . .	Christine Smeltzer	K. Cunningham	Kathleen Kovach	. . .	. . .	Thomas Witt
Cranford	tp	CM	22	(908) 709-7200	George Jorn	Marlena Schmid	R. Hellenbrecht	. . .	Leonard Dolan	Eric Mason	. . .
Cresskill *	b	MC	7	(201) 569-5400	. . .	Barbara Nasuto	. . .	Harold Laufeld	John Birnie	Steve Lillis	Kevin Terhune
Delanco *	tp	MC	3	(856) 461-0561	Kate Fitzpatrick	Steven Corcoran	Janice Lohr	Robert Hundell	Keith Mohrmann	Ed Parsons	. . .
Delran	tp	MC	15	(856) 461-7734	Joseph Stellwag	Jeffrey Hatcher	Bernadette McPhee	. . .	Joseph Bennett	Arthur Saul	. . .
Demarest	b	MC	4	(201) 768-0167	. . .	. . .	. . .	. . .	. . .	. . .	. . .
Dennis	tp	CM	6	(609) 861-9700	Ruth Blessing	. . .	Jacqueline Justice	Glenn Clarke	. . .	. . .	Clarence Ryan
Denville	tp	MC	15	(973) 625-8300	. . .	. . .	Donna Costello	Bernard Re	Tracey Egbert	Steven Boepple	Joseph Lowell
Deptford	tp	CM	26	(609) 845-5300	William Bain	Denise Rose	Dina Zawadski	Lois De More	. . .	William Underwood	Howard Johnson
Dover	t	MC	18	(973) 366-2200	James Dodd	Bibi Garvin	Marge Verga	Kelly Toohey	Edward Ridner	Harold Valentine	Louis Acevedo
Dover	tp	MC	89	(732) 341-1000	Paul Brush	Fred Ebenau	J. Mutter	Christine Manolio	. . .	M. Mastronardy	Robert Tully
Dumont	b	MC	17	(201) 387-5022	. . .	. . .	John Eckel	. . .	James Yelland	. . .	John Cook
Dunellen	b	MC	6	(732) 968-3033	Robert Seader	. . .	Mary Blue	Scott Olsen	William Scott	Thomas Ventriglia	Jerry Schaffer
East Brunswick	tp	MC	46	(732) 390-6810	William Neary	James White	Elizabeth Kiss	Louis Neely	. . .	. . .	. . .
East Hanover	tp	MC	9	(973) 428-3000	L. Colasurdo	C. Paduch	Marilyn Snow	Smruti Amin	George Busold	Stanley Hansen	Ray Grossmann
East Orange	c	MC	69	(973) 266-5100	Robert Bowser	Joseph Jenkins	Cynthia Brown	Linda Munro	Leonard McDaniel	Richard Wright	. . .
East Rutherford	b	MC	8	(201) 933-3444	James Cassella	. . .	Darlene Sawicki	Anthony Bianchi	Peter Hodge	. . .	Thomas Miller
East Windsor *	tp	CM	24	(609) 443-4000	Janice Mironov	Alan Fisher	Cindy Dye	Margaret Gorman	. . .	William Spain	William Askenstedt
Eastampton	tp	CM	6	(609) 267-5723	. . .	Thomas Czerniecki	. . .	. . .	. . .	. . .	. . .
Eatontown *	b	MC	14	(732) 389-7621	Gerry Tarantolo	. . .	Karen Naughton	Lesley Connolly	Bill Mego	George Jackson	Nathan Albert
Edgewater	b	MC	7	(201) 943-1700	Bryan Christiansen	Harvey Weber	Barbara Rae	. . .	. . .	Donald Martin	Peter Rambone
Edison	tp	MC	88	(732) 248-7299	George Spadoro	Anthony Cancro	Reina Murphy	G. Bobal	G Campbell	Edward Costello	Robert Heck
Egg Harbor	tp	MC	30	(609) 926-4000	James McCullough	Peter Miller	Patricia Indrieri	Charlene Canale	. . .	John Coyle	Lloyd Simerson
Egg Harbor City	c	MC	4	(609) 965-0081	. . .	Joseph Harney	Lillian Debow	Betty Wenzel	. . .	. . .	. . .
Elizabeth	c	MC	120	(908) 820-4000	J. C. Bollwage	Lorraine Dumke	Anthony Pillo	Anthony Zengaro	Edward Sisk	John Simon	John Papetti
Elmwood Park	b	MC	18	(201) 796-1457	Richard Mola	. . .	Dolores Camlet	. . .	Joseph Miklovic	G. Morgan	Joseph Mulligan
Emerson	b	MC	7	(201) 262-6099	Robert Menditto	Joseph Scarpa	Sandra Joaquin	Nancy Burns	Michael Cimino	Peter Mazzeo	Joseph Solimando
Englewood	c	CM	26	(201) 871-6660	Michael Wildes	Robert Gorman	Lenore Schiavelli	. . .	Robert Moran	John Banta	Clyde Sweatt
Englewood Cliffs	b	MC	5	(201) 569-5252	. . .	Joseph Favaro	. . .	Joseph Iannaconi	George Drimones	T. Bauernschmidt	Rodney Bialko
Essex Fells	tp	MC	2	(973) 226-3400	. . .	Francis Bastone	Francine Paserchia	Kerry Geisler	. . .	Daniel Tapper	Roger Kerr
Evesham	tp	CM	42	(856) 983-2900	Augustus Tamburro	Edward Sasdelli	Carmela Bonfrisco	Paul Thomas	Thaddeus Lowden	Joseph Cornely	Paul Tomasetti
Ewing	tp	MC	35	(609) 883-2900	Wendell Pribila	James McManimon	Charles Green	Shannon Keyes	. . .	Robert Coulton	. . .
Fair Haven *	b	MC	5	(732) 747-0241	Michael Halfacre	Mary Howell	A. Cinquegrana	Denise Jawidzik	Michael Reddy	. . .	Tom Curcio
Fair Lawn	b	CM	31	(201) 796-1700	David Ganz	J. Kwasniewski	. . .	Barry Eccleston	Dennis Gaul	Rodman Marshall	Joseph Maslo
Fairfield	tp	MC	7	(973) 882-2700	Rocco Palmieri	Joseph Catenaro	Patricia Fahy	. . .	. . .	Carolyn Centonze	M. deMontaigne
Fairview	b	MC	13	(201) 943-3300	Vincent Bellucci	Diane Testa	. . .	Joseph Rutch	David Masso	John Pinzone	. . .
Fanwood	b	MC	7	(908) 322-8236	. . .	. . .	. . .	. . .	. . .	. . .	. . .
Flemington	b	MC	4	(908) 782-8840	Austin Kutscher	. . .	Robert Hauck	Raymond Krov	Stephen Borucki	Peter Tirpok	Terry Pickering
Florence	tp	MC	10	(609) 499-2525	Michael Muchowski	Richard Brook	Joy Weiler	Sandra Blacker	Edward Kensler	Gordon Dawson	John Purakovics
Florham Park	b	MC	8	(973) 410-5300	Frank Tinari	. . .	Judith Beecher	Donna Mollineaux	Alban Kellogg	Raymond Smith	Carl Ganger
Fort Lee *	b	MC	35	(201) 592-3500	Jack Alter	Peggy Thomas	Neil Grant	Joseph Iannaconi	Jack Siccardi	Thomas Ripoli	Anthony Lione
Franklin	b	MC	5	(973) 827-9280	Douglas Kistle	Richard Wolak	Patricia Leasure	Grant Rome	Jason Doyle	Joseph Kistle	Mike Gunderman
Franklin	tp	MC	15	(856) 694-1234	David Ferrucci	. . .	Carol Coulbourn	Frances Carder	. . .	Michael DiGiorgio	William Nese
Franklin (Somerset) *	tp	CM	50	(732) 873-2500	Brian Levine	Kenneth Daly	Ann McCarthy	Vandana Khurana	. . .	Craig Novick	. . .
Franklin Lakes	b	MC	10	(201) 891-0048	G Thomas Donch	. . .	. . .	Harold Laufeld	. . .	. . .	Brian Peterson
Freehold	b	MC	10	(732) 462-1410	Michael Wilson	Joseph Bellina	Dolores Gibson	Nancy Forman	Forrest Woolford	William Burlew	. . .
Freehold	tp	CM	31	(732) 294-2000	Raymond Kershaw	Thomas Antus	Romeo Cascaes	Debrah Defeo	. . .	Ernest Schriefer	Richard Warren
Galloway	tp	CM	31	(609) 652-3700	Charles Endicott	Thomas Henshaw	Karen Bacon	Jill Gougher	. . .	Keith Spencer	Steve Bonanni
Garfield	c	CM	29	(201) 340-2001	Louis Aloia	Anthony Librizzi	Andrew Pavlica	Soe Myint	Joseph Dymarczyk	. . .	Munzio Santora
Garwood	b	MC	4	(908) 789-0710	Dennis McCarthy	. . .	Christina Ariemma	Sue Wright	Thomas Spera	Dennis Lesak	Jeffrey Atkinson
Gibbsboro	b	MC	2	(609) 783-6655	. . .	. . .	. . .	. . .	. . .	. . .	. . .
Glassboro	b	MC	19	(856) 881-9230	Leo McCabe	Joseph Brigandi	Patricia Frontino	Josephine Myers	Ralph Johnson	Alex Fanfarillo	Russell Clark
Glen Ridge	tp	MC	7	(973) 748-8400	Thomas Lincoln	Michael Rohal	. . .	. . .	. . .	R. Wohlgemuth	Jay Weisenbach
Glen Rock	b	MC	11	(201) 670-3956	Richard Hahn	. . .	Jacqueline Scalia	Lenora Benjamin	. . .	Steven Cherry	Richard Van Heest
Gloucester	tp	MC	64	(856) 228-4000	Sandra Love	Thomas Cardis	Rosemary DiJosie	Candace Prince	. . .	John Stollsteimer	Gabriel Busa
Gloucester City	c	MC	11	(856) 456-0205	Robert Gorman	Patrick Keating	Paul Kain	Frank Robertson	William Glassman	Theodore Howarth	James Johnson
Green Brook	tp	CM	5	(732) 968-1023	Patricia Walsh	. . .	. . .	David Dickinson	Allen Sprague	Martin Rasmussen	. . .
Guttenberg	t	MC	10	(201) 868-2315	David DelleDonna	. . .	Linda Martin	Patrick De Blasio	. . .	. . .	Michael Ronchi
Hackensack	c	CM	42	(201) 646-3980	John Zisa	. . .	Debra D'Auria	Louis Garbaccio	Richard Yannelli	Charles Zisa	Jesse D'Amore
Hackettstown	t	MC	10	(908) 852-3130	John Di Maio	. . .	William Kuster	Jeffrey Theriault	Edward Howell	Leonard Kunz	Thomas Kitchen
Haddon	tp	CO	14	(856) 854-1176	William Park	. . .	Denise White	James Clark	. . .	Joseph Gallager	. . .
Haddon Heights	b	MC	7	(856) 547-7164	Susan Griffith	. . .	Joan Moreland	Ernest Merlino	Steve Kinky	Ronald Shute	Donald Witzig
Haddonfield	b	CM	11	(856) 429-4700	Letitia Colombi	. . .	Deanna Speck	Terry Henry	Joseph Riggs	Richard Tsonis	Howard Frazier
Hainesport	tp	MC	4	(609) 267-2730	Ronald Corn	Paul Tuliano	Rita Schuster	Douglas Ayrer	William Wiley	. . .	Jay Jones
Haledon	b	MC	8	(973) 595-7766	James Van Sickle	. . .	Allan Susen	Janet Wolons	. . .	. . .	Angelo Passafaro
Hamilton	tp	MC	87	(609) 890-3500	Glen Gilmore	. . .	Christina Wilder	Richard Serini	. . .	James Collins	Jeffrey Moyer
Hamilton	tp	MC	20	(609) 625-1511	Frank Giordano	Edward Perugini	Joan Anderson	Richard Tuthill	. . .	Jay McKeen	Oliver Thies
Hammonton	t	MC	12	(609) 567-4300	. . .	. . .	. . .	. . .	. . .	. . .	. . .
Harding	tp	MC	3	(973) 267-8000	. . .	Lyn Evers	Linda Peralta	Himanshu Shah	. . .	K. Gaffney	Tracy Toribio
Hardyston	tp	CM	6	(973) 823-7020	Leslie Hamilton	Marianne Smith	Jane Bakalarczyk	Grant Rome	. . .	Keith Armstrong	Robert Schulz
Harrington Park	b	MC	4	(201) 768-1700	. . .	. . .	. . .	. . .	. . .	. . .	. . .
Harrison	t	MC	14	(973) 268-2425	. . .	. . .	. . .	. . .	. . .	. . .	. . .
Hasbrouck Heights	b	MC	11	(201) 288-0195	William Torre	Michael Kronyak	Rose Marie Sees	Paul Garbarini	Robert Thomasey	Michael Colaneri	Robert Heck
Haworth	b	MC	3	(201) 384-4785	John De Rienzo	Ann Fay	. . .	R. Overgaard	. . .	. . .	Martin Mahon
Hawthorne	b	MC	18	(973) 427-5555	Fred Criscinelli	. . .	P. Mele	MaryJeanne Hewitt	Joseph Speranza	Martin Boyd	. . .
Hazlet	tp	MC	21	(732) 264-1700	Michael Sachs	Margaret Margiotta	Evelyn Strelsky	C. Campbell	Frank Olivia	James Broderick	David Rooke
High Bridge	b	MC	3	(908) 638-6455	Alfred Schweikert	William Wahl	. . .	Bonnie Fleming	Craig Van Natta	Edward Spinks	Mark Banks
Highland Park	b	MC	13	(732) 572-3400	Meryl Frank	Karen Waldron	Janet Potenza	Nick Trasente	Jay Littman	. . .	Lloyd Young
Highlands	b	MC	5	(732) 872-1515	. . .	. . .	. . .	. . .	. . .	. . .	. . .
Hightstown *	b	MC	5	(609) 490-5100	Robert Patten	. . .	C. Gallagher	George Lang	John Archer	James Eufemia	Larry Blake
Hillsdale	b	MC	10	(201) 666-4800	Timothy O'Reilly	Harold Karns	Robert Sandt	Colleen Ennis	Kimberly Saul	Frank Mikulski	Keith Durie
Hillside	tp	MC	21	(973) 926-3000	K. McCoy Oliver	. . .	Janet Vlaisavljevic	. . .	Joe Behnke	Robert Quinlan	Scott Anderson
Hoboken	c	MC	38	(201) 420-2059	. . .	. . .	. . .	. . .	. . .	. . .	. . .
Ho-Ho-Kus	b	MC	4	(201) 652-4400	Rusty Thompson	C. Henderson	Judith Odo	. . .	. . .	G. Kallenberg	Michael Frank
Holmdel	tp	MC	15	(732) 946-2820	Larry Fink	. . .	M. Shepherd	J. Annecharico	Ronald Pontrelli	Robert Phillips	Jeffrey Smith
Hopatcong	b	MC	15	(973) 770-1200	. . .	. . .	. . .	. . .	. . .	. . .	. . .
Hopewell	tp	MC	16	(609) 737-0605	Francesca Bartlett	. . .	Annette Bielawski	Elaine Borges	. . .	Michael Chipowsky	. . .
Howell	tp	CM	48	(732) 938-4500	Joseph DiBella	Bruce Davis	. . .	Jeff Filiatreault	. . .	Ronald Carter	Mildred Bernier
Irvington	tp	MC	61	(973) 399-8111	Wayne Smith	. . .	Harold Wiener	D. Timothy Roberts	Donald Huber	Michael Damiano	Wayne Bradley

Directory 1/9 continued — **OFFICIALS IN U.S. MUNICIPALITIES 2,500 AND OVER IN POPULATION**

Jurisdiction	Type	Form of government	2000 Population (000)	Main telephone number	Chief elected official	Appointed administrator	Clerk of the governing board	Chief financial officer	Fire chief	Police chief	Public works director
NEW JERSEY continued											
Jackson	tp	CO	42	(732) 928-1281	Michael Broderick	...	Ann Eden	Lily Farley	...	...	Sergio Panunizo
Jamesburg	b	MC	6	(732) 521-2222	Joseph Dipierro	...	Gretchen Schauer	Jo Ann Olenik	John Miller	...	Wallace Fisher
Jefferson	tp	MC	19	(973) 697-1500	Russell Felter	James Leach	Lydia Magnotti	William Eagen	...	John Palko	David Hansen
Jersey City	c	MC	240	(201) 547-5000	Glenn Cunningham	Brian O'Reilly	Robert Byrne	Paul Soyka	Frederick Eggers	Robert Troy	John Yurchak
Keansburg	b	CM	10	(732) 787-0215	...	...	...	...	Andrew Murray	...	...
Kearny	* t	MC	40	(201) 955-7400	Alberto Santos	Joseph D'Arco	Jill Waller	Shuaib Firozvi	Steven Dyl	John Dowie	Gerald Kerr
Kenilworth	b	MC	7	(908) 276-9090	Michael Tripodi	...	Hedy Lipke	Dianne Marus	Lou Giordino	Don Tisch	Dan Ryan
Keyport	b	MC	7	(732) 739-3900	...	...	Judith Poling	Thomas Fallon	...	Theodore Gajewski	George Sappah
Kinnelon	b	MC	9	(973) 838-5401	Glenn Sisco	...	Mary Ricker	...	...	John Finkle	Jeffrey LaPooh
Lakehurst	b	CM	2	(732) 657-4141	...	...	...	...	...	...	...
Lakewood	tp	CM	60	(732) 364-2500	Marta Harrison	Frank Edwards	B. Standowski	William Rieker	...	...	John Franklin
Lambertville	c	MC	3	(609) 397-0110	David Del Vecchio	...	Mary Sheppard	Linda Monteverde	Robert Hayes	Bruce Cocuzza	Paul Cronce
Lawnside	b	MC	2	(856) 573-6202	...	Jessie Harris	Sylvia Van Nockay	...	...	...	Alex Barr
Lawrence	* tp	CM	29	(609) 844-7000	Gregory Puliti	Richard Krawczun	Kathleen Norcia	...	...	Daniel Posluszny	Gregory Whitehead
Leonia	b	MC	8	(201) 592-5743	...	...	...	...	...	...	...
Lincoln Park	b	MC	10	(973) 694-6100	David Baker	Joseph Maielle	Annette Smith	Dennis Gerber	Dan Moeller	Kenneth West	Tom Piorkowski
Linden	c	MC	39	(908) 474-8479	John Gregorio	...	Val Imbriaco	...	William Konecny	John Miliano	John Mesler
Lindenwold	b	MC	17	(609) 783-2121	Frank Delucca	...	Jane Barber	Helen Gielda	...	Frank McHenry	Robert Lodovici
Linwood	c	MC	7	(609) 927-4108	R. DePamphilis	Kenneth Mosca	Leigh Ann Napoli	Bonnie Tiemann	...	Charles Desch	Walter Jones
Little Egg Harbor	tp	MC	15	(609) 296-7241	...	...	...	...	...	...	...
Little Falls	tp	MC	11	(973) 256-0170	Janice Sandri	...	Joan Skal	Kathy Albanese	Edmond Pomponio	...	Phillip Simone
Little Ferry	b	MC	10	(201) 641-9234	...	C. Navarro-Steinel	B. Maldonado	...	...	...	John Bladek
Little Silver	b	TM	6	(732) 842-2400	...	...	...	...	...	...	...
Livingston	tp	CM	26	(973) 992-5000	David Katz	Michele Meade	Renee Green	...	Craig Dufford	Donald Jones	Michael Anello
Lodi	b	MC	23	(201) 365-4005	...	...	...	...	...	...	...
Long Branch	c	MC	31	(732) 222-7000	...	Howard Woolley	Irene Joline	Ronald Mehlhorn	...	...	Fred Migliaccio
Long Hill	tp	MC	8	(908) 647-8000	...	Richard Sheola	...	...	...	...	...
Lower	tp	CM	22	(609) 886-2005	Larry Starner	...	Claudia Kammer	Lauren Read	...	John Maher	Gary Douglass
Lyndhurst	tp	CO	18	(201) 804-2457	Richard DiLascio	...	Helen Polito	Deborah Ferrato	Keith Carroll	James O'Connor	Brian Haggerty
Madison	* b	MC	16	(973) 593-3042	...	...	Marilyn Schaefer	Robert Kalafut	Douglas Atchison	Vincent Chirico	David Maines
Magnolia	b	MC	4	(609) 783-1520	B. Cowling-Carson	...	P Joyce Harrum	Dorothea Jones	...	Robert Doyle	Steven Pacella
Mahwah	tp	MC	24	(201) 529-5757	Richard Martel	Brian Campion	Doris Perez	Kenneth Sesholtz	Elmore Wilson	...	Stanley Spiech
Manalapan	tp	MC	33	(732) 446-3200	Mary Cozzolino	...	Rose Ann Weeden	...	...	John McCormack	John Lewis
Manasquan	b	MC	6	(908) 223-0544	...	John Trengrove	Colleen Scimeca	Joanne Madden	...	Daniel Scimeca	James Coder
Manchester	tp	MC	38	(732) 657-8121	...	...	...	...	...	...	...
Manville	b	MC	10	(908) 725-9478	...	Kathryn Kinney	...	...	Vincent Albanese	Michael Moschak	Philip Petrone
Maple Shade	tp	CM	19	(856) 779-9610	Gerald Mornell	George Haeuber	Patricia Berger	Donna Gallagher	...	Edmund Vernier	Arthur Dees
Maplewood	* tp	CM	23	(973) 762-8120	Fred Profeta	Joseph Manning	Elizabeth Fritzen	Peter Fresulone	Dennis Carragher	Robert Cimino	Gary Lenci
Margate City	c	CO	8	(609) 822-2605	Vaughan Reale	Thomas Hiltner	...	Charles Beirne	John Kelley	David Wolfson	Sigmund Rimm
Marlboro	tp	MC	36	(732) 526-0200	...	...	...	...	...	...	...
Matawan	b	MC	8	(732) 290-2000	Bea Duffy	Frederick Carr	Jean Montfort	Monica Antista	James Bishop	Robert McGowan	Anthony Bucco
Maywood	b	MC	9	(201) 845-2900	Thomas Murphy	Jack Terhune	Mary Rampolla	...	John Gargagliano	Patrick Reynolds	...
Medford	tp	CM	22	(609) 654-2608	Lisa Post	Michael Achey	Joyce Frenia	Katherine Burger	...	James Kehoe	George Snyder
Medford Lakes	* b	CM	4	(609) 654-8898	Timothy Casey	Richard Knight	...	Donna Condo	Mark McIntosh	Frank Martine	Patrick McCorriston
Mendham	b	CM	5	(973) 543-7152	Richard Kraft	Ralph Blakeslee	Maureen Massey	Susan Giordano	Joseph Eible	Patricia Cameron	Thomas Miller
Mendham	tp	CM	5	(973) 543-4555	...	Stephen Mountain	Penny Newell	Heather Webster	...	Thomas Costanza	David Read
Merchantville	b	MC	3	(609) 662-2474	...	...	...	...	...	...	...
Metuchen	b	CM	12	(732) 632-8540	Edmund O'Brien	William Boerth	Bozena Lacina	Lori Majeski	Robert Donnan	...	Kenneth O'Brien
Middlesex	b	MC	13	(732) 356-7400	...	...	Kathleen Anello	...	Edward Winters	James Benson	Jerry Schaefer
Middletown	tp	CM	66	(732) 615-2000	Joan Smith	...	Heidi Abs	Robert Roth	William Hibell	John Pollinger	Lawrence Werger
Midland Park	* b	MC	6	(201) 445-5720	Ester Vierheilig	Michelle Dugan	Adeline Hanna	...	Peter Hook	John Cassone	Rudolph Gnehm
Millburn	tp	CM	19	(973) 564-7075	T. McDermott	Timothy Gordon	Joanne Monargue	Jason Gabloff	Michael Roberts	P. Boegershausen	Peter Gallitelli
Milltown	b	MC	7	(732) 828-2100	...	...	...	...	...	...	...
Millville	c	CO	26	(856) 825-7000	James Quinn	Lewis Thompson	...	R. Charlesworth	...	...	Vicki Marshall
Monmouth Beach	b	CO	3	(732) 229-2204	...	...	...	...	...	...	...
Montclair	* tp	CM	37	(973) 509-4939	Edward Remsen	Joseph Hartnett	Linda Wanat	Gordon Stelter	Kevin Allen	David Sabagh	Steven Wood
Montgomery	tp	CM	17	(908) 359-8211	Louise Wilson	Donato Nieman	Donna Kukla	Randy Bahr	...	Michael Beltranena	Jeffrey Williams
Montvale	b	CM	7	(201) 391-5700	George Zeller	John Doyle	Maureen Alwan	...	...	Joseph Marigliani	Robert Culvert
Montville	tp	CM	20	(973) 331-3300	Marie Cetrulo	...	Gertrude Atkinson	F. Vanderhoof	...	Richard Cook	...
Moonachie	b	MC	2	(201) 641-1813	Frederick Dresser	Paul Hansen	Jean Finch	...	Richard Behrens	Michael McGahn	Henry Van Saders
Moorestown	* tp	CM	19	(856) 235-0912	Kevin Aberant	Christopher Schultz	Patricia Hunt	Thomas Merchel	...	Harry Johnson	Kenneth Ewers
Morris Plains	b	MC	5	(973) 538-2224	...	...	June Uhrin	David Banks	...	Douglas Scherzer	Joseph Signorelli
Morristown	t	MC	18	(973) 292-6626	John Delaney	...	William Chambers	Robert Calise	David Barter	Carol Williams	Jeffrey Hartke
Mount Arlington	b	MC	4	(973) 398-6832	Arthur Ondish	Joanne Sendler	Linda DeSantis	Allan Dickinson	...	Richard Peterson	John Tappen
Mount Ephraim	b	CO	4	(856) 931-1546	...	...	Mildred Salamone	Dorothea Jones	Mario Scullan	Christopher Ferrari	Anthony Chambers
Mount Holly	tp	CM	10	(609) 267-0170	Brooke Tidswell	Kathleen Hoffman	...	Christina Chambers	David Gsell	...	Ronald Crain
Mount Laurel	tp	CM	40	(856) 234-0001	Mark Sanchirico	Patricia Halbe	...	Linda Lewis	...	David Haas	Everett Johnson
Mount Olive	* tp	MC	24	(973) 691-0900	David Scapicchio	Bill Sohl	Lisa Lashway	Sherry Jenkins	...	Mark Spitzer	Tim Quinn
Mountain Lakes	b	CM	4	(973) 334-3131	Jud Breslin	Gary Webb	Christina Whitaker	Dona Mooney	...	Robert Tovo	Mark Prusina
Mountainside	* b	MC	6	(908) 232-2400	...	...	Judith Osty	Jill Goode	...	James Debbie	Robert Farley
National Park	b	MC	3	(609) 845-3891	...	...	...	...	...	...	...
Neptune	tp	CM	27	(732) 988-5200	James Manning	Philip Huhn	Richard Cottrell	Michael Bascom	...	James Ward	Richard Bormann
Neptune City	b	MC	5	(732) 776-7224	Robert Deeves	Joel Popkin	...	William Folk	Mark Balzarano	William Geschke	Gerrit Devos
Netcong	b	MC	2	(973) 347-0252	Nicholas Pompilio	Marvin Joss	D. Dalessandro	Jason Gabloff	...	...	Robert Olivo
New Brunswick	c	MC	48	(732) 745-5008	Jim Cahill	Thomas Loughlin	Daniel Torrisi	Douglas Petix	...	...	...
New Hanover	tp	CO	9	(609) 758-7149	...	...	...	...	...	...	...
New Milford	b	MC	16	(201) 967-5044	Frank Debari	...	Kathy Sayers	...	...	J. Costello	Michael Giambrone
New Providence	b	MC	11	(908) 665-1400	Harold Weideli	Douglas Marvin	...	James Testa	Kevin Kennedy	James Venezia	John Meyer
Newark	c	MC	273	(973) 733-6400	Cory Booker	Richard Monteilh	Robert Marasco	Daniel Gonzalez	Lowell Jones	Anthony Ambrose	...
Newton	t	CM	8	(973) 383-3521	Philip Diglio	...	Lorraine Read	Eileen Kithcart	Christopher Blakely	John Tomasula	Christopher Bond
North Arlington	b	MC	15	(201) 991-6060	Russell Pitman	...	Martin Gobbo	Timothy Roberts	Mark Cunningham	Louis Ghione	James McCabe
North Bergen	tp	CO	48	(201) 392-2000	Nicholas Sacco	Christopher Pianese	Carol Fontana	Robert Pittfield	...	...	Timothy Grossi
North Brunswick	* tp	MC	36	(732) 247-0922	Francis Womack	Robert Lombard	Lisa Gerhartz	Ronald Amorino	Craig Snediker	Joseph Battaglia	Glenn Sandor
North Caldwell	tp	MC	7	(973) 228-6410	Melvine Levine	John Kosko	...	Richard Modelli	...	Joseph Clark	Frank Zichelli
North Haledon	b	MC	7	(973) 427-7793	Randy George	...	Lucille Debiak	...	...	Joseph Ferrante	...
North Plainfield	* b	MC	21	(908) 769-2902	Janice Allen	David Hollod	Gloria Pflueger	Patrick DeBlasio	William Eaton	William Parenti	James Rodino
North Wildwood	c	MC	4	(609) 522-2030	Aldo Palombo	...	Jane Parson	Helen Gielda	Thomas McGarry	Gary Sloan	Timothy O'Leary
Northfield	c	MC	7	(609) 641-2832	Frank Perri	...	Carol Raph	Marilyn Dolcy	...	Kenneth Adams	James Clark
Northvale	b	MC	4	(201) 767-3330	...	...	...	...	...	...	...
Norwood	b	MC	5	(201) 767-7200	Gus D'Ercole	...	Lorraine McMackin	Maureen Neville	Scott Roberts	Frank D'Ercole	Camilo DiRese
Nutley	tp	CO	27	(973) 284-4951	Joanne Cocchiola	...	E. Rosario-Garcia	Rosemary Costa	Thomas Peters	John Holland	Peter Scarpelli

Directory 1/9 continued — OFFICIALS IN U.S. MUNICIPALITIES 2,500 AND OVER IN POPULATION

Jurisdiction	Type	Form of govern-ment	2000 Population (000)	Main telephone number	Chief elected official	Appointed administrator	Clerk of the governing board	Chief financial officer	Fire chief	Police chief	Public works director
NEW JERSEY continued											
Oakland	b	CM	12	(201) 337-8111	J. Kendall	Charles Smiley	Lenore Tully	. . .	David Jeltes	James O'Connor	. . .
Oaklyn	b	MC	4	(609) 858-2457	Michael Lamaina	. . .	Marie Hawkins	. . .	Fred Garbrecht	Christopher Ferrari	Enrico Storino
Ocean	tp	CM	26	(732) 531-5000	William Larkin	Andrew Brannen	Deborah Smith	Stephen Gallagher	. . .	Antonio Amodio	Lawrence Iverson
Ocean City	c	MC	15	(609) 399-6111	Henry Knight	. . .	Angela Pileggi	John Hansen	Joe Foglio	Robert Blevin	George Savastano
Oceanport	b	MC	5	(732) 222-8221	. . .	. . .	. . .	. . .	. . .	. . .	. . .
Ogdensburg	b	MC	2	(973) 827-3444	J. Pietrodangelo	. . .	Phyllis Drouin	Michelle LaStarza	Michael Franek	George Lott	Kenneth Smith
Old Bridge	tp	CM	60	(732) 721-5600	James Phillips	Michael Jacobs	R. Marie Saracino	. . .	. . .	Thomas Collow	Rocco Donatelli
Old Tappan *	b	MC	5	(201) 664-1849	Victor Polce	Mary Carmenini	Jeanine Siek	Rebecca Overgaard	Kevin Dorney	Joseph Fasulo	Arthur Lake
Oradell *	b	MC	8	(201) 261-8200	Frederick LaMonica	Wolfgang Albrecht	Laura Graham	Roy Rossow	David Gangemi	Rhynie Emanuel	Robert Stauffer
Orange Township	c	MC	29	(973) 266-4245	Mims Hackett	. . .	Dwight Mitchell	John Kelly	. . .	Edward Lucas	Robert Corrado
Palisades Park	b	MC	17	(201) 585-4100	Sandy Farber	. . .	Martin Gobbo	Roy Riggitano	George Beck	John Genovese	James Burns
Palmyra	b	MC	7	(856) 829-6100	Robert Leather	Marianne Hulme	Grace Carr	. . .	Richard Derby	Robert Fow	Brian McCleary
Paramus	b	MC	25	(201) 265-2100	. . .	. . .	Ian Shore	Joseph Citro	. . .	Fred Corrubia	Brian Koenig
Park Ridge	b	MC	8	(201) 573-1800	Donald Ruschman	Gregory Franz	. . .	Ann Kilmartin	. . .	R. Oppenheimer	William Beattie
Parsippany–Troy Hills *	tp	MC	48	(973) 263-4294	Michael Luther	Jasmine Lim	Judith Silver	Ruby Malcolm	. . .	Michael Peckerman	Robert Schneider
Passaic	c	MC	67	(973) 365-5500	Samuel Rivera	G. Hill Shabaka	W. S.-Shabaka	. . .	Louis Imparato	Stanley Jarensky	Theodore Evans
Paterson	c	MC	149	(973) 321-1310	Jose Torres	Eli Burgos	J. Williams Warren	Margaret Cherone	James Pasquariello	Lawrence Spagnola	Manuel Ojeda
Paulsboro	b	MC	6	(856) 423-1500	John Burzichelli	. . .	Kathy Van Scoy	John Salvatore	Gary Stevenson	Kenneth Ridinger	. . .
Pemberton	tp	MC	28	(609) 894-8201	Robert McCullough	David Thompson	Mary Young	John Schoenberg	. . .	Stephen Emery	Frank Chapman
Pennington	b	MC	2	(609) 737-0276	. . .	. . .	. . .	. . .	. . .	. . .	. . .
Penns Grove	b	MC	4	(856) 299-0098	Paul Morris	. . .	Sharon Williams	Stephen Labb	Joseph Grasso	Gary Doubledee	Santiago Rosario
Pennsauken	tp	CM	35	(609) 665-1000	Jack Killion	Bob Cummings	Patrica Gudis	Ronald Crane	Gene Sheppard	John Coffey	John Fiqueroa
Pequannock	tp	CM	12	(973) 835-5700	Lawrence Blomberg	Kevin Boyle	Elizabeth Eley	David Hollberg	Bryan Daley	William Montono	Charles McKearnin
Perth Amboy	c	MC	47	(732) 826-0290	Joseph Vas	Donald Perlee	Elaine Kiczula	Jill Goldy	Lawrence Cattano	Michael Kohut	Kenneth Schwartz
Phillipsburg	t	MC	15	(908) 454-5500	Thomas Corcoran	Frank Tolotta	Michele Broubalow	Joseph Hriczak	. . .	James Mac Aulay	. . .
Pine Hill	b	MC	10	(609) 783-7400	Curtis Noe	. . .	Joan Schneebele	. . .	. . .	Judd Booker	Robert McGlinchey
Piscataway	tp	MC	47	(732) 562-2308	Brian Wahler	. . .	Ann Nolan	Victoria Miragliotta	. . .	Kevin Harris	Joseph Scranton
Pitman	b	MC	9	(609) 589-3522	Bruce Ware	. . .	. . .	Earl Kelly	Ray Kelley	Scott Campbell	Edward Lewis
Plainfield	c	CM	47	(908) 753-3219	Albert McWilliams	Marc Dashield	Laddie Wyatt	Peter Sepelya	Cecil Allen	Edward Santiago	Priscilla Castles
Plainsboro *	tp	MC	20	(609) 799-0909	Peter Cantu	Robert Sheehan	Patricia Hullfish	Wendy Wulstein	. . .	E. Bondurant	Jeff Cramer
Pleasantville	c	MC	19	(609) 484-3600	Ralph Peterson	Marvin Hopkins	Gloria Griffin	. . .	Leroy Borden	Duane Comeaux	Robert Oglesby
Point Pleasant	b	CM	19	(732) 892-3434	Martin Konkus	David Maffei	. . .	Judith Block	Daniel Mulligan	Raymond Hilling	Dennis Sears
Point Pleasant Beach	b	MC	5	(732) 892-1118	Thomas Vogel	. . .	MaryAnn Ellsworth	Christine Riehl	. . .	Daniel DePolo	Robert Meany
Pompton Lakes	b	MC	10	(973) 835-0144	John Murrin	Lawrence Pollex	Carol Kehoe	. . .	Albert Evangelista	Albert Ekkers	Ben Steltzer
Princeton	b	MC	14	(609) 924-3118	Marvin Reed	Robert Bruschi	Andrea Quinty	Decimus Marsh	. . .	Charles Davall	Wayne Carr
Princeton	tp	CM	16	(609) 924-5176	Phyllis Marchand	James Pascale	Linda McDermott	John Clawson	. . .	Anthony Gaylord	. . .
Prospect Park	b	MC	5	(973) 790-7902	William Kubofcik	B. Varcadipone	Yancy Wazirmas	Stephen Sanzari	Douglas Struyk	Frank Franco	Kenneth Valt
Rahway	c	MC	26	(732) 827-2000	James Kennedy	Bob Gorman	Jean Kuc	Frank Ruggiero	Edward Fritz	Kevin White	John Ross
Ramsey	b	MC	14	(201) 825-3400	John Scerbo	Nicholas Saros	Nancy Ecke	Richard Mathieson	George Sutherland	Joseph Delaney	William Horton
Randolph	tp	CM	24	(973) 989-7100	Jon Huston	John Lovell	Frances Bertrand	Michael Soccio	James Reynolds	James McLagan	. . .
Raritan *	b	MC	6	(908) 231-1300	Anthony Hudak	Daniel Jaxel	Pamela Heufner	Carolyn Gara	Carl Memoli	Michael Sniscak	A. DiGiuseppantonio
Raritan	tp	CM	19	(908) 806-6100	John King	Allan Pietrefesa	Dorothy Gooditis	. . .	Michael Mangin	Glenn Tabasko	Dirk Streuning
Red Bank	b	MC	11	(732) 530-2740	. . .	Stanley Sickels	Carol Vivona	Bruce Loversidge	. . .	James Clayton	J. Buonacquista
Ridgefield	b	MC	10	(201) 943-5215	Anthony Suarez	Roberta Stern	Stewart Veale	. . .	John Hoffman	John Bogovich	N. Gambardella
Ridgefield Park	v	CO	12	(201) 641-4950	. . .	. . .	. . .	. . .	. . .	. . .	. . .
Ridgewood *	v	CM	24	(201) 670-5500	David Pfund	James Ten Hoeve	Heather Mailander	Dorothy Stikna	James Bombace	William Corcoran	. . .
Ringwood	b	CM	12	(973) 962-7037	Theodore Taukus	. . .	. . .	. . .	. . .	Armando Dimuzio	Edward Haack
River Edge	b	MC	10	(201) 599-6300	James Kirk	. . .	Grace Gutekunst	. . .	George O'Connell	Ronald Starace	John Pusterla
River Vale	tp	MC	9	(201) 664-2346	George Paschalis	Bibi Stewart-Garvin	Roy Blumenthal	Roy Rossow	. . .	Aaron Back	Peter Wayne
Riverdale	b	MC	2	(973) 835-4060	. . .	. . .	. . .	. . .	. . .	. . .	. . .
Riverside	tp	CO	7	(856) 461-0284	James Ott	. . .	P. Collinsworth	Deborah Crowe	. . .	. . .	Eric March
Riverton	b	MC	2	(856) 829-0120	Robert Martin	. . .	Mary Longbottom	Marianne Hulme	Scott Reed	Robert Norcross	. . .
Rochelle Park	tp	CO	5	(201) 587-7730	. . .	. . .	Virginia De Maria	Joseph Manzella	Sal Antista	Richard Zavinsky	John Tanucilli
Rockaway	b	MC	6	(973) 627-2000	. . .	. . .	. . .	. . .	. . .	. . .	. . .
Rockaway *	tp	MC	22	(973) 627-7200	John Inglesino	Gregory Poff	Mary Cilurso	Charles Wood	Robert Jenkins	Walter Kimble	Edward Hollenbeck
Roseland	b	MC	5	(973) 403-6030	. . .	Thomas Kaczynski	. . .	M. Chumacas	Kent Yates	Richard McDonough	Gary Schall
Roselle	b	MC	21	(908) 245-5600	Garrett Smith	David Brown	Rhona Bluestein	Kenneth Blum	Robert Hill	Peter DeRose	Carl Bowles
Roselle Park	b	MC	13	(908) 245-6222	Joseph Delorio	. . .	Arlene Triano	Gregory Mayers	Joseph Signorello	Warren Wielgus	Frank Wirzbicki
Roxbury	tp	CM	23	(973) 448-2007	Fred Hall	Christopher Raths	Betty De Croce	Lisa Palmieri	Michael Piccitto	Mark Noll	. . .
Rumson	b	MC	7	(732) 842-3300	. . .	. . .	. . .	. . .	. . .	. . .	. . .
Runnemede	b	MC	8	(856) 939-5161	. . .	. . .	. . .	. . .	. . .	. . .	. . .
Rutherford	b	MC	18	(201) 460-3000	B. McPherson	. . .	Mary Kriston	Edward Cortright	Donald Tomko	Edward Caughey	Douglas Adamo
Saddle Brook	tp	MC	13	(201) 843-7100	R. Santalucia	. . .	Joyce Larena	. . .	Robert Lapari	Robert Kugler	Charles Cerone
Saddle River	b	MC	3	(201) 327-2609	Conrad Caruso	Charles Cuccia	Marie Macari	. . .	Brian Yates	Tim McWilliams	Bruce Mautz
Salem	c	MC	5	(856) 935-0372	. . .	. . .	Barbara Wright	David Crescenzi	John Ayars	Ronald Sorrell	Fred Mucci
Sayreville	b	MC	40	(732) 390-7000	Kennedy O'Brien	Jeffrey Bertrand	Theresa Farbaniec	Wayne Kronowski	Robert Lasko	John Garbowski	Bernard Bailey
Scotch Plains	tp	CM	22	(908) 322-6700	. . .	Thomas Atkins	Barbara Riepe	Lori Majeski	Jonathon Ellis	Marshall Nelson	Walter Di Nizo
Sea Girt *	b	MC	2	(732) 449-9433	Edward Ahern	. . .	Lorene Wright	. . .	. . .	Edward Sidely	Kevin Thompson
Sea Isle City	c	CO	2	(609) 263-4461	Leonard Desiderio	. . .	Theresa Tighe	. . .	. . .	H. Muller	. . .
Secaucus	t	MC	15	(201) 330-2000	Anthony Just	. . .	Geraldine Morgan	Margaret Barkala	Charles Oplach	Dennis Corcoran	Michael Gonnelli
Shrewsbury	b	MC	3	(732) 741-4200	Emilia Siciliano	. . .	Lynn Neil	Lesley Connolly	. . .	John Wilson	Robert Wentway
Somerdale	b	MC	5	(609) 783-6320	. . .	. . .	. . .	. . .	. . .	. . .	. . .
Somers Point	c	MC	11	(609) 927-9088	Tony Martin	William Swain	Carol Degrassi	John Hansen	Frank Denan	Orville Mathis	Richard Gray
Somerville	b	MC	12	(908) 725-2300	David Hollod	Ralph Sternadori	. . .	Janet Kelk	Bruce Kessler	Dennis Manning	Peter Hendershot
South Amboy	c	MC	7	(732) 727-4600	. . .	. . .	. . .	. . .	. . .	. . .	. . .
South Bound Brook	b	MC	4	(732) 356-0258	Jo Anne Schubert	. . .	Donald Kazar	Randy Bahr	Michael Tomaro	Robert Verry	Ken Pine
South Brunswick	tp	CO	37	(732) 329-4000	Frank Gambatese	Matthew Watkins	Barbara Gut	Ralph Palmieri	Robert Davidson	Michael Paquette	Raymond Olsen
South Orange Village	tp	CO	16	(973) 378-7715	William Calabrese	John Gross	Marjorie Smith	John Mosca	Jeffrey Markey	Anthony Coppola	Mario Luciani
South Plainfield	b	MC	21	(732) 754-9000	Daniel Gallagher	. . .	James Eckert	Ronald Zilinski	John Mocharski	. . .	Joseph Glowacki
South River	b	MC	15	(732) 257-1999	Robert Szegeti	Andrew Salerno	Albert Seaman	K. Sivananthan	Jonathan Magaw	Wesley Bomba	George Lyons
South Toms River	b	MC	3	(732) 349-0403	. . .	. . .	. . .	. . .	. . .	. . .	. . .
Southampton	tp	MC	10	(609) 859-2676	James Young	. . .	. . .	Nancy Gower	. . .	. . .	Charles Oatman
Sparta *	tp	CM	18	(973) 729-4493	James Henderson	Henry Underhill	Miriam Tower	Mike Ganrino	. . .	Ernie Reigstadt	Tom Spring
Spotswood	b	MC	7	(732) 251-0700	Barry Zagnit	Ron Fasanello	Patricia De Stefano	Barbara Petren	Jason Michels	Karl Martin	Patrick Pacyna
Spring Lake	b	MC	3	(732) 449-0800	Thomas Byrne	. . .	Mary Anne Coogan	Susan Schreck	. . .	Robert Dawson	Robert Winemiller
Spring Lake Heights	b	MC	5	(732) 449-3500	. . .	. . .	Claire Barrett	. . .	. . .	. . .	Arthur Herner
Springfield	tp	RT	13	(973) 912-2200	Sy Mullman	. . .	Kathleen Wisniewski	Marie Sedlak	William Gras	William Chisholm	Kenneth Homlish
Stafford	tp	CM	22	(609) 597-1000	Carl Block	Paul Shives	Bernadette Park	Suzanne Babcock	. . .	Larry Parker	Ronald Cop
Stanhope	b	MC	3	(973) 347-0159	Diana Kuncken	Teresa Massood	Antoinette Battaglia	Theresa Vervaet	Jeff Jozowski	Steven Pittigher	William Storms
Stratford	b	MC	7	(856) 783-0600	Thomas Angelucci	John Keenan	. . .	John Fabritiis	Stephen Gagliardi	John Brown	Frank Gagliardi
Summit *	c	MC	21	(908) 522-3600	Jordan Glatt	Christopher Cotter	David Hughes	Ronald Angelo	James Connelly	Robert Lucid	Paul Cascais

Directory 1/9 continued — OFFICIALS IN U.S. MUNICIPALITIES 2,500 AND OVER IN POPULATION

Jurisdiction	Type	Form of govern-ment	2000 Popu-lation (000)	Main telephone number	Chief elected official	Appointed administrator	Clerk of the governing board	Chief financial officer	Fire chief	Police chief	Public works director
NEW JERSEY continued											
Teaneck *	tp	CM	37	(201) 837-4807	...	Helene Fall	Robyn Lamorte	Anthony Bianchi	Robert Montgomery	Paul Tiernan	...
Tenafly	b	CM	13	(201) 568-6100	Peter Rustin	Joseph Di Giacomo	Nancy Hatten	Karen Palermo	Richard Philpott	Michael Bruno	J. Robert Beutel
Tinton Falls *	b	MC	15	(732) 542-3400	Peter Maclearie	William Dempsey	Karen Mount-Taylor	Stephen Pfeffer	...	Gerald Turning	John Bucciero
Totowa	b	MC	9	(973) 956-1000	...	...	...	...	...	...	...
Trenton *	c	MC	85	(609) 989-3000	Douglas Palmer	Renee Haynes	...	Ronald Zilinski	Richard Laird	Joseph Santiago	Eric Jackson
Union	tp	MC	50	(908) 688-2800	Joseph Florio	Frank Bradley	Eileen Birch	Debbie Cyburt	Frederic Fretz	Thomas Kraemer	...
Union Beach	b	MC	6	(732) 264-2277	...	...	...	...	...	...	...
Union City	c	CO	67	(201) 348-5754	Raul Garcia	...	Michael Licameli	Jorge Carmona	Thomas Tormey	Paul Hanak	Sergio Panunzio
Upper Saddle River	b	MC	7	(201) 327-2196	Nicholas Rotonda	Michael Mariniello	Rose Vido	...	...	Theodore Preusch	Craig Rossiter
Ventnor City	c	CO	12	(609) 823-7900	Timothy Kreischer	Andrew McCrosson	Sandra Biagi	William Johnson	Bertram Sabo	Stanley Wodazak	David Smith
Vernon	tp	CM	24	(973) 764-4055	...	Melinda Carlton	Patricia Lycosky	Monica Goscicki	...	Roy Wherry	David Pullis
Verona	tp	MC	13	(973) 239-3220	Robert Detore	...	Evelyn Hill	Dorothy Trimmer	Pat McEvoy	...	...
Vineland	c	MC	56	(856) 794-4000	Perry Barse	Paul Trivellini	Keith Petrosky	Mary Chalow	Peter Finley	Mario Brunetta	Joseph Bond
Waldwick *	b	MC	9	(201) 652-5300	Rick VanderWende	Gary Kratz	Paula Jaegge	Mary Viviani	Joseph Alvarez	Mark Messner	Joseph Agugliaro
Wall	tp	MC	25	(732) 449-8444	Edward Thompson	Joseph Verruni	Lorraine Kobacz	Stephen Mayer	...	Roy Hall	Kenneth Critchlow
Wallington	b	MC	11	(973) 777-0318	Walter Wargacki	Witold Baginski	...	Charles Cuccia	Ken Friedman	Anthony Benevento	...
Wanaque	b	MC	10	(973) 839-3000	Warren Hagstrom	Thomas Carroll	Katherine Falone	Maryann Brindisi	Scott Montegari	John Reno	...
Wantage	tp	MC	10	(973) 875-7192	Paul Grau	James Doherty	...	Michelle Lastarza	Parker Space	...	Bob Wagner
Warren	tp	RT	14	(908) 753-8000	Victor Sordillo	Mark Krane	Patricia DiRocco	S. Boswell	...	William Stahl	Ewald Friedrich
Washington	b	CM	6	(908) 689-3600	M. VanDeursen	...	Linda Hendershot	Kay Stasyshan	Joseph Fox	George Cortellesi	John Burd
Washington (Bergen)	tp	MC	9	(201) 664-4404	Rudolph Wenzel	...	...	...	...	...	...
Washington (Glcstr)	tp	MC	47	(856) 589-0520	Randy Davidson	John Lipsett	Leticia Lamonica	Mary Breslin	Everett Hoffman	Frances Burke	Kenneth Patrone
Washington (Morris)	tp	MC	17	(908) 876-3315	Kennethson Short	Dianne Gallets	...	Kevin Lifer	...	Ted Ehrenburg	Ralph DeFranzo
Washington (Warren) *	tp	MC	6	(908) 689-7200	John Horensky	...	Mary O'Neil	C. Gangaware	James Vergos	James McDonald	Peter De Boer
Watchung *	b	MC	5	(908) 756-0080	Albert Ellis	Laureen Fellin	...	William Hance	Steve Peterson	John Frosoni	Charles Gunther
Wayne	tp	MC	47	(973) 694-1800	David Waks	Neal Bellet	Katherine Pusterla	Robert Miller	...	Raymond Riga	...
Weehawken	tp	CO	12	(201) 319-6005	Richard Turner	James Marchetti	Theresa Ulrich	Laurie Cotter	Edward Flood	Jeffrey Welz	Orlando Giusto
West Caldwell	tp	MC	10	(973) 226-2300	Joseph Tempesta	Benedict Martorana	...	Russell Jarger	Charles Holden	Charles Tubbs	William Frint
West Deptford *	tp	CM	19	(856) 845-4004	Anna Docimo	...	Raymond Sherman	Richard Giuliani	...	Craig Mangano	Edward Phelps
West Long Branch	b	MC	8	(732) 229-1756	Janet Tucci	...	Lori Cole	Gail Watkins	Brian Kramer	Arthur Cosentino	Earl Reed
West Milford *	tp	CM	25	(973) 728-7000	...	Richard Kunze	Antoinette Battaglia	Arthur Magnotti	...	Paul Costello	Gerald Storms
West New York	t	CO	45	(201) 295-5100	Albio Sires	Richard Turner	Carmela Riccie	Darren Maloney	...	Silverio Vega	Lawrence Riccardi
West Orange	tp	MC	39	(973) 325-4050	John McKeon	John Sayers	Nancy O'Hara	Edward Coleman	...	James Abbott	Leonard Lepore
West Paterson	b	MC	10	(973) 345-8100	Pat Lepore	...	...	Joseph McCluskey	Joseph Macones	Joseph Renne	George Galbraith
West Windsor *	tp	MC	21	(609) 799-2400	Shing-Fu Hsueh	Christopher Marion	Sharon Young	Joanne Louth	...	Joseph Pica	George Spille
Westfield	t	MC	29	(908) 789-4040	...	James Gildea	...	...	...	...	...
Westville	b	MC	4	(856) 456-0030	William Packer	William Bittner	Richard Burr	...	...	Frederick Lederer	...
Westwood	b	MC	10	(201) 664-7100	Bernard Kelley	Robert Hoffmann	Eileen Sarubbi	Raymond Herr	John Domville	Frank Regino	Robert Woods
Wharton *	b	MC	6	(973) 361-8444	Leo Finnegan	Jon Rheinhardt	G. Voight-Cherna	...	Kyle Door	Anthony Fernandez	Walter VanKirk
Wildwood	c	MC	5	(609) 522-2444	Bernie Troiano	...	Patricia Rhodes	Jeanette Powers	Conrad Johnson	Joseph Fisher	...
Wildwood Crest	b	CO	3	(609) 522-3843	John Pantalone	Kevin Yecco	...	Stephen Ritchie	Jack Holland	T. Sinsheimer	Joyce Gould
Willingboro	tp	CM	36	(609) 877-2200	Eddie Campbell	...	Marie Annese	Joanne Diggs	Anthony Burnett	Donna Dimitri	Richard Brevogel
Woodbine	b	MC	2	(609) 861-2153	William Pikolycky	...	Frances Pettit	Sharon McCullough	Douglas Watkins	...	Clarence Ryan
Woodbridge *	tp	MC	97	(732) 634-4500	Frank Pelzman	Robert Landolfi	John Mitch	Margaret Gorman	...	William Trenery	Gerald MacIntyre
Woodbury	c	MC	10	(609) 845-1300	...	...	...	...	...	...	...
Woodbury Heights	b	MC	2	(856) 848-2832	...	...	...	...	...	...	...
Woodcliff Lake	b	MC	5	(201) 391-4977	...	...	Darlene Schnure	Gene Vinci	...	...	Edward Barboni
Woodlynne	b	MC	2	(856) 962-8300	J. Coyle	...	Veronica Gitto	...	...	John Ragan	...
Wood-Ridge	b	MC	7	(201) 939-0202	Paul Calocino	...	Diane Thornley	Doris Marek	Damian Cauceglia	John Frank	John Sabia
Woodstown	b	MC	3	(856) 769-2200	Richard Pfeffer	...	Jeanette Gerlack	James Hackett	Carl Castagliuolo	George Lacy	Frank Mitchell
Woolwich	tp	MC	3	(856) 467-2666	...	...	...	...	...	...	...
Wrightstown	b	MC	..	(609) 723-4450	Jozsef Farago	...	Donna Snyder	Barbara Petren	...	...	...
Wyckoff	tp	CM	16	(201) 891-7000	Joseph Fiorenzo	Robert Shannon	Joyce Santimauro	Diana Lindner	Rick Alnor	John Ydo	Scott Fisher
NEW MEXICO											
Alamogordo *	c	CM	35	(505) 439-4399	Donald Carroll	Pat McCourt	Renee Cantin	Lee Ann Nichols	...	...	Brian Cesar
Albuquerque	c	MC	448	(505) 768-3700	Martin Chavez	Bruce Perlman	Millie Santillanes	Anna Lamberson	Robert Ortega	Ray Schultz	Leonard Garcia
Angel Fire	v	MC	1	(505) 377-3232	Alvin Clanton	Melissa Vossmer	Elizabeth Sanchez	...	Orlando Sandoval	William Kitts	Marvin Sheriff
Artesia	c	MC	10	(505) 746-2122	Daniel Reyes	...	Barbara Kilough	...	...	...	...
Aztec *	c	CM	6	(505) 334-7600	Mike Arnold	David Velasquez	Rebecca Howard	John Gallegos	Burt Bennett	Michael Heal	Steve Christensen
Bayard	v	MC	2	(505) 537-3327	Rudolfo Martinez	...	Kristina Ortiz	...	...	Ascencion Manzano	Eddie Sedillos
Belen	t	CM	6	(505) 864-8221	Ronnie Torres	Sally Garley	...	Mildred Garley	Lenor Pena	Lawrence Romero	John Duran
Bernalillo	t	CM	6	(505) 867-3311	...	...	...	...	...	...	...
Bloomfield	c	MC	6	(505) 632-6300	...	Keith Johnson	Carol Miller	Kevin Rodolph	George Duncan	Andrew Standley	Curtis Lynch
Bosque Farms	v	MC	3	(505) 869-2358	Wayne Ake	...	...	...	Spencer Wood	Joe Stidham	Dominic Romero
Carlsbad	c	CM	25	(505) 887-1191	Gary Perkowski	Arthur Burgess	...	Pearlene Bradshaw	Thomas Duffin	James Koch	...
Clayton	t	CM	2	(505) 374-8331	Garth Boyce	...	Theresa Gard	...	Fred Sinclair	Scott Julian	Lynn Davis
Cloudcroft	v	MC	..	(505) 682-2411	David Venalbe	Michael Nivison	Patricia Taylor	...	...	Gene Green	...
Clovis	c	CM	32	(505) 769-7828	David Lansford	Joe Thomas	...	Leigh Melancon	Sam McCallie	Bill Carey	Harry Wang
Corrales *	v	MC	7	(505) 897-0502	Philip Gasteyer	Nora Scherzinger	...	...	Jim Fritts	Michael Tarter	Tony Tafoya
Deming	c	MC	14	(505) 546-8848	...	Richard McInturff	...	Stephen Duran	David Kinman	Michael Carillo	Louis Jenkins
Espanola	c	CM	9	(505) 747-6100	Richard Lucero	Gustavo Cordova	Veronica Martinez	...	Robert Shuttles	Wayne Salazar	Leroy Archuleta
Eunice	c	MC	2	(505) 394-2576	James Brown	Kenneth Weaver	Dawn Money	...	Jerry Harper	Kevin Burnam	Larry Haase
Farmington	c	CM	37	(505) 599-1132	William Standley	Michael Miller	Gina Morris	Herman Mason	Robert Martin	Mike Burridge	Joseph Schmitz
Gallup	c	CM	20	(505) 863-1221	Robert Rosebrough	...	Ruth Ruiz	...	Louis Chavez	Daniel Kneale	Stanley Henderson
Grants	c	CM	8	(505) 287-7927	...	...	...	...	...	...	...
Hobbs *	c	CM	28	(505) 397-9229	Monty Newman	Eric Honeyfield	Kristi Parker	Roger Hines	Brady Graham	Tony Knott	Scott Bussell
Jal	c	MC	1	(505) 395-3340	Mary Claiborne	...	Skeet Posey	...	Ronnie Walls	Larry Burns	Frederick Seifts
Las Cruces	c	CM	74	(505) 528-3401	William Mattiace	Terrence Moore	Shirley Clark	Mark Sutter	Adolf Zubia	Harry Romero	Michael Johnson
Las Vegas	c	CM	14	(505) 454-1401	Tony Martinez	...	Ronald Maestas	Ann Gallegos	Robert Gonzales	Albert Mares	Benny Romero
Lordsburg	c	CM	3	(505) 542-3421	Arthur Smith	...	Irene Galvan	...	...	John McDonald	...
Los Lunas	v	MC	10	(505) 865-9689	Louis Huning	Phillip Jaramillo	...	Monica Clarke	Atilano Chavez	Nick Balido	Betty Behrend
Los Ranchos De Albuquerque	v	MC	5	(505) 344-6582	Harry Stowers	Juan Vigil	Annabelle Martinez	Sylvia Pesce	...	...	Dale Addison
Lovington	c	CM	9	(505) 396-2884	...	Andrew Wise	Rhonda Jones	...	Perry Williams	Ron Black	...
Milan	v	CM	1	(505) 285-6694	Thomas Ortega	Carlos Montoya	...	...	Keith Austin	Jerry Stephens	Ben Chavez
Portales *	c	CM	11	(575) 356-6662	Orlando Ortega	Debi Lee	Joan Terry	...	John Bridges	Jeffrey Gill	Thomas Howell
Questa	v	CM	1	(505) 586-0694	Malaquias Rael	Brent Jaramillo	...	...	Max Ortega	Frank Gallegos	Joey Vigil
Raton	c	CM	7	(505) 445-9551	Joe Apache	...	Michael Lannon	...	Dave Pasquale	Vincent Mares	Pete Mileta
Rio Rancho	c	MC	51	(505) 891-5000	James Owen	James Payne	Christina Gonzales	Richard Kristof	...	...	Kenneth Curtis
Roswell	c	CM	45	(505) 624-6700	Sam LaGrone	John Capps	David Kunko	Larry Fry	Alan Warboys	John Balderston	John Miscavage
Ruidoso	v	CM	7	(505) 258-4343	Leon Eggleston	Dan Higgins	Irma Nava	Elaine Beltran	Virgil Reynolds	Lanny Maddox	Kenneth Mosley
Ruidoso Downs	c	MC	1	(505) 378-4422	Bob Miller	John Waters	...	...	...	...	Dan Gens

Directory 1/9 continued **OFFICIALS IN U.S. MUNICIPALITIES 2,500 AND OVER IN POPULATION**

Jurisdiction	Type	Form of govern-ment	2000 Popu-lation (000)	Main telephone number	Chief elected official	Appointed administrator	Clerk of the governing board	Chief financial officer	Fire chief	Police chief	Public works director
NEW MEXICO continued											
Santa Fe	c	CM	62	(505) 955-6601	Larry Delgado	Galen Buller	Yolanda Vigil	Kathryn Raveling	Chris Rivera	Beverly Lennen	...
Santa Rosa	c	MC	2	(505) 472-3404	Joseph Campos	Timothy Dodge	Carol Tapia	Yolanda Garcia	...	James Moncayo	...
Silver City	t	CM	10	(505) 538-3731	Terry Fortenberry	...	Jane Toumajanian	Alex Brown	Rudy Bencomo	John Calender	Peter Pena
Socorro	c	MC	8	(505) 835-0240	...	...	Pat Salome	...	Robert Brunson	Johnnie Trujillo	...
Sunland Park	c	MC	13	(505) 589-7565	...	...	Juan Fuentes	...	Robert Monsivaiz	Ricardo Perez	...
Taos	t	MC	4	(505) 751-2000	Bobby Duran	Tomas Benavidez	Renee Lucero	Marietta Fambro	Eric Montoya	Eddie Lucero	Francisco Espinoza
Taos Ski Valley	v	CM	..	(505) 776-8220	...	Susan Steele	...	...	...	...	...
Truth Or Consequences	c	CM	7	(505) 894-6674	...	...	...	...	...	...	...
Tucumcari *	c	CM	5	(505) 461-3451	Mary Mayfield	John Sutherland	J. Maddaford	John Garcia	Michael Cherry	...	...
Tularosa	v	MC	2	(505) 585-2771	Demetrio Montoya	...	Dianna Brusuelas	Louanne Garcia	Robert Chavez	Frank Sackman	Trinidad Guilez
NEW YORK											
Airmont	v	MC	7	(845) 357-8111	John Layne	...	Irene Murphy	...	...	...	Robert Kowalik
Akron	v	MC	3	(716) 542-9636	Ray Perkins	Daniel Borchert	...	...	...	Richard Lauricella	...
Albany	c	MC	95	(518) 434-5075	Gerald Jennings	Philip Calderone	John Marsolais	Christopher Hearley	James Larson	James Turley	...
Albion	v	MC	7	(585) 589-9176	...	...	Kathleen Ludwick	...	...	...	Douglas Long
Alfred *	v	MC	3	(607) 587-9188	Craig Clark	...	...	Linda Burlingame	...	Timothy O'Grady	James McNulty
Amherst *	t	MC	116	(716) 631-7000	Satish Mohan	...	Susan Jaros	Frank Belliotti	...	John Askey	...
Amityville *	v	MC	9	(631) 264-6000	Peter Imbert	Diane Sheridan	...	Donna Barnett	Arthur Smith	Woodrow Cromarty	Bruce Hopper
Amsterdam	c	MC	18	(518) 841-4300	John Duchessi	...	Jane Di Caprio	Kim Brumley	Richard Liberti	Thomas Brownell	Raymond Halgas
Ardsley *	v	CM	4	(914) 693-1550	Jay Leon	George Calvi	Barbara Berardi	...	Joseph Cippollone	Emil Califano	Louis Pascone
Attica	v	MC	2	(585) 591-0898	...	...	...	...	...	...	...
Auburn *	c	CM	28	(315) 255-4146	Timothy Lattimore	Mark Palesh	Debra McCormick	Lisa Green	Michael Quill	Gary Giannotta	Gerald Del Favero
Avon	v	MC	2	(585) 226-8118	Richard Burke	...	Robyn Harris	...	David Piampiano	John Braisington	John Barrett
Babylon	t	MC	211	(631) 957-3000	...	...	...	...	...	...	...
Babylon	v	MC	12	(631) 669-1500	E. Conroy	...	Patricia Carley	...	James Anderson	...	Charles Gardner
Baldwinsville	v	MC	7	(315) 635-3521	...	...	...	...	...	...	...
Ballston Spa	v	MC	5	(518) 885-5711	...	...	Patricia Bowers	Mary Munday	...	Charles Koenig	Joseph Thompson
Batavia	c	CM	16	(585) 345-6300	...	Jason Molino	...	...	...	...	B. Walker
Batavia *	t	MC	5	(585) 343-1729	...	...	Teressa Morasco	Gregory Post	...	...	...
Bath	v	MC	5	(607) 776-3811	...	...	Florence Mulcahy	...	...	David Rouse	Matthew Benesh
Bayville	v	MC	7	(516) 628-1439	...	...	...	...	...	...	...
Beacon	c	MC	13	(845) 838-5000	Clara Gould	Joseph Braun	Carla Eylers	Toni Tracy	Dennis Lahey	Richard Sassi	Robert Riley
Bedford	t	MC	18	(914) 864-0045	Lee Roberts	...	Lisbeth Fumagalli	Patricia Ploss	...	Chris Menzel	...
Bellport	v	MC	2	(631) 286-0327	Frank Trotta	...	Richard Semple	...	...	...	...
Binghamton	c	MC	47	(607) 772-7000	Matthew Ryan	...	Eric Denk	Beverly Palmer	Clifford Colgan	...	Lou Kelly
Blasdell	v	CM	2	(716) 822-1921	...	Ernest Jewett	Sandra Corcoran	...	...	...	Robert Bushen
Briarcliff Manor *	v	CM	7	(914) 944-2782	Peter Chatzky	Michael Blau	Christine Dennett	...	William Ventura	Ronald Trainham	Robert Ferreira
Brighton	t	MC	35	(585) 784-5250	Sandra Frankel	...	Susan Kramarsky	...	...	Thomas Voelkl	Thomas Low
Brightwaters	v	MC	3	(516) 665-1280	...	...	...	...	...	...	...
Brockport	v	MC	8	(585) 637-5300	Morton Wexler	Ian Coyle	Leslie Morelli	...	C. McCullough	Daniel Varrenti	Harry Donahue
Bronxville	v	CM	6	(914) 337-6500	Mary Marvin	Harold Porr	...	...	...	Brian Downey	Rocco Circosta
Brookville	v	MC	2	(516) 626-1792	Richard Goodwin	Nancy Graikoski	...	...	...	...	...
Buffalo	c	MC	292	(716) 851-4841	Anthony Masiello	...	...	...	Kevin Comerford	...	...
Camden	v	MC	2	(315) 245-0560	Cristen Harlander	...	Tamara Bonomo	...	...	Richard Paul	Jerry Williamson
Camillus	t	MC	23	(315) 488-1335	Mary Ann Coogan	...	Marilyn Smith	...	...	H. L. Perkins	...
Canandaigua *	c	CM	11	(585) 396-5000	Ellen Pomimeni	Stephen Cole	...	...	Robert Case	Patrick McCarthy	Louis Loy
Canastota	v	MC	4	(315) 697-7559	Mark Lavonas	B. Andaloro	Sena Clarke	...	Douglas Chandler	Guy Blazier	Ronald Bennett
Canisteo	v	MC	2	(607) 698-2711	...	...	...	...	...	...	...
Canton	v	MC	5	(315) 386-2871	...	...	...	...	...	...	...
Carthage	v	CO	3	(315) 493-1060	G. McIlroy	...	Linda Weir	...	William Blunden	Reevie Rockhill	Daniel Trembley
Catskill	v	MC	4	(518) 943-3830	...	...	Carolyn Pardy	...	...	Roger Masse	Lewis O'Connor
Cayuga Heights	v	MC	3	(607) 257-1238	Walter Lynn	...	Norma Manning	...	George Tamborelle	Ken Lansing	Brent Cross
Cazenovia *	v	MC	2	(315) 655-3041	Thomas Dougherty	...	Laura Abernathy	...	Samuel Usborne	David Amico	Steven McLaughlin
Cedarhurst	v	MC	6	(516) 295-5770	...	...	...	...	...	...	...
Chestnut Ridge *	v	MC	7	(914) 425-2805	Jerome Kobre	Florence Mandel	...	...	Walter Morris	...	...
Chittenango	v	MC	4	(315) 687-3936	Robert Freunscht	...	Jill Doss	...	...	Jeffrey Paul	Raymond Snyder
Cobleskill	v	MC	4	(518) 234-3891	William Gilmore	...	Sheila Hay-Gillespie	...	Douglas Angle	Michael O'Brien	Thomas Fissell
Cohoes	c	MC	15	(518) 237-7641	John McDonald	...	Lori Yando	Michael Durocher	Joseph Fahd	Bill Heslin	Kenneth Radliff
Colonie	t	MC	79	(518) 783-2734	...	...	...	...	...	...	...
Colonie	v	MC	7	(518) 869-7562	...	...	...	...	...	...	...
Corinth	v	MC	2	(518) 654-2012	...	...	...	...	...	...	...
Corning	c	CM	10	(607) 962-8148	Alan Lewis	Mark Ryckman	Rose Blackwell	Margaret Horn	William Cummings	Richard Faulisi	Richard Biggio
Cornwall-On-Hudson *	v	MC	3	(845) 534-4200	Joseph Gross	...	Jeanne Mahoney	...	Jeffrey Armitage	Charles Williams	...
Cortland	c	MC	18	(607) 756-7312	Mary Leonard	...	William Wood	William Damiano	Dennis Baron	James Nichols	C. Bistocchi
Cortlandt *	t	MC	38	(914) 734-1000	Linda Puglisi	...	Joann Dyckman	Glenn Cestaro	...	Robert Frank	Richard McIntyre
Coxsackie	v	MC	2	(518) 731-2718	Henry Rausch	...	Angela Wilsey	...	Robert Frank	...	John Halsted
Croton-On-Hudson *	v	CM	7	(914) 271-4848	Gregory Schmidt	Richard Herbek	Pauline DiSanto	...	Gary Diggs	Dennis Coxen	Kenneth Kraft
Dannemora *	v	MC	4	(518) 492-7000	Michael Bennett	...	Donna Taylor	...	Richard Akey	...	Thomas Tripp
Dansville *	v	MC	4	(585) 335-5330	William Dixon	Keith Petti	Donna Clark	...	...	...	...
Delhi	v	MC	2	(607) 746-2258	David Truscott	...	Margaret Reinman	...	Gerard Garofollow	Robert Walsh	David Curley
Depew	v	MC	16	(716) 683-1400	Robert Kucewicz	...	Joan Priebe	Elizabeth Melock	Michael Pelleterri	James Brennan	John Wojcik
Dobbs Ferry	v	MC	10	(914) 693-2203	Brian Monahan	Anthony Giaccio	Elizabeth Dreaper	...	Dennis Roth	George Longworth	James Dunn
Dolgeville	v	MC	2	(315) 429-3112	...	...	Tammy Chmielewski	...	...	Howard Lanphier	...
Dunkirk	c	MC	13	(716) 366-1600	Margaret Wuerstle	...	Kevin Mikula	...	Michael Edwards	John Yannie	Randy Woodbury
East Aurora *	v	CM	6	(716) 652-6000	David DiPierto	Kimberly LaMarche	...	...	Roger LeBlanc	Ronald Krowka	Matthew Hoeh
East Hills	v	MC	6	(516) 621-5600	Michael Koblenz	...	...	...	...	Barry Lamb	Carmine Ceriello
East Rochester	v	CM	6	(585) 586-3553	...	...	...	...	...	...	...
East Rockaway *	v	MC	10	(516) 887-6300	Edward Sieban	...	Sandra Torborg	...	Elvie Hickam	...	John Keating
East Syracuse	v	MC	3	(315) 437-3541	Lorene Dadey	...	Patricia Derby	...	...	Douglas Robertson	Ronald Russell
East Williston	v	MC	2	(516) 746-0782	Nancy Zolezzi	Jeanne Lyons	...	...	John McWhirk	...	Daniel Creighton
Ellenville	v	CM	4	(845) 647-7080	Jeffrey Kaplan	Elliott Auerbach	Ann Bowler	Linda Polkoski	...	Phil Mattracion	...
Elmira	c	CM	30	(607) 737-5644	Stephen Hughes	John Burin	Angela Williams	Joy Bates	Donald Harrison	James Waters	Ronald Hawley
Elmira Heights *	v	MC	4	(607) 734-7156	Arthur Caparula	...	...	...	...	Robert Hauptman	Jean Cazorla
Elmsford	v	MC	4	(914) 592-6555	...	...	...	...	...	...	...
Endicott	v	MC	13	(607) 757-2421	Joan Pulse	...	Jacquelyn Ingraham	Thomas Johnson	Thomas Murphy	Michael Cox	Richard Miller
Fairport	v	MC	5	(585) 223-0313	Clark King	Kenneth Moore	...	...	...	...	Douglas Waite
Falconer	v	MC	2	(716) 665-4400	David Krieg	...	Gloria Anderson	...	Wayne Oste	...	Samuel Ognibene
Fallsburg	t	CM	12	(845) 434-8810	Steven Levine	...	Patricia Haaf	Linda Kinney	...	Brent Lawrence	William Illing
Farmingdale	v	MC	8	(516) 249-0093	George Graf	David Smollett	...	...	...	...	Fred Zamparelle

Directory 1/9 continued — OFFICIALS IN U.S. MUNICIPALITIES 2,500 AND OVER IN POPULATION

Jurisdiction	Type	Form of govern-ment	2000 Popu-lation (000)	Main telephone number	Chief elected official	Appointed administrator	Clerk of the governing board	Chief financial officer	Fire chief	Police chief	Public works director
NEW YORK continued											
Fayetteville *	v	MC	4	(315) 637-9864	Mark Olson	...	Lorie Corsette	...	Paul Hildreth	...	James Craw
Floral Park	v	MC	15	(516) 326-6300	Steven Corbett	Nancy McCloughlin	...	...	V. Brooks	Michael Reid	Louis Di Sunno
Flower Hill	v	MC	4	(516) 627-2253	...	...	...	...	...	...	...
Fort Edward	v	MC	3	(518) 747-4023	Edward Ryan	...	...	Daniel Smatko	Matthew Altizio	Mitchell Suprenant	Robert Dickinson
Fort Plain	v	MC	2	(518) 993-4271	Guy Barton	...	Susanne Mahn	...	Bud Wainer	Robert Thomas	...
Frankfort	v	MC	2	(315) 895-7651	Frank Moracco	...	Sharon Carlesimo	...	Charles Conigliaro	Steven Conley	Ronald Vivacqua
Fredonia	v	MC	10	(716) 679-2302	Frank Pagano	James Sedota	...	...	Perry Mitchell	Daniel Johnson	Richard Lascola
Freeport	v	MC	43	(516) 377-2200	William Glacken	...	Anna Knoeller	Thomas Preston	Arthur Burdette	Michael Woodward	Louis Digrazia
Fulton *	c	MC	11	(315) 592-7330	Daryl Hayden	...	Joseph Tetro	James Laboda	Anthony Gorea	Mark Spawn	Daniel O'Brien
Garden City	v	MC	21	(516) 465-4000	Harold Hecken	Robert Schoelle	Joan Gallaer	...	Richard Chiarello	Ernest Cipullo	Robert Mangan
Gates	t	TM	29	(585) 247-6100	Ralph Esposito	...	Richard Warner	...	...	Thomas Roche	John Lathrop
Geneseo	v	MC	7	(585) 243-1177	Richard Hatheway	...	...	Marsha Merrick	Frank Manzo	Eric Osganian	Douglas Welch
Geneva	c	CM	13	(315) 789-4369	Donald Cass	Richard Rising	Margaret Cass	David Stowell	Ralph De Bolt	Frank Pane	Gordon Eddington
Glen Cove	c	MC	26	(516) 676-2000	...	...	Carolyn Willson	John Macari	Joseph Solomito	Timothy Edwards	Gerald Gardruits
Glens Falls	c	MC	14	(518) 761-3800	Robert Regan	...	Robert Curtis	Bruce Crouser	Ronald Cote	Richard Carey	Robert Schiavoni
Gloversville	c	MC	15	(518) 773-4500	...	...	...	...	...	...	...
Goshen	v	MC	5	(845) 294-6750	George Lyons	Ronald Bally	...	Helen Felter	...	John Egbertson	Michael Nuzzolese
Gouverneur	v	MC	4	(315) 287-1720	Alfred Netto	Karen Lancto	Sheryl Simmons	...	Vinnie Ferry	David Whitton	Glenn McCollum
Gowanda	v	MC	2	(716) 532-3353	Richard Klancer	...	Kathleen Mohawk	...	Steve Raiport	Joseph Alessi	Michael Hutchinson
Granville *	v	MC	2	(518) 642-2640	Jay Niles	...	...	Richard Roberts	Russel Bronson	Ernest Bassett	George Johnson
Great Neck *	v	MC	9	(516) 482-0019	Ralph Kreitzman	John Dominsky	...	...	...	...	Louis Massaro
Great Neck Estates	v	MC	2	(516) 482-8283	Lawrence Nadel	...	Kathleen Santelli	...	...	John McNulty	Sandor Schweiger
Great Neck Plaza	v	MC	6	(516) 482-4500	...	...	...	...	...	...	...
Green Island	v	MC	2	(518) 273-2201	Ellen McNulty-Ryan	Sean Ward	Anne Strizzi	...	David Carl	John Nardone	Ronald Rootes
Greenburgh	t	MC	86	(914) 993-1540	Paul Feiner	...	Alfreda Williams	Norah McAvoy	...	John Kapica	Al Regula
Greenwood Lake	v	MC	3	(914) 477-9215	Roger Jacobsen	Robert Langan	Doris Hawkins	...	...	E. Baldesweiler	Michael Batz
Hamburg *	v	MC	10	(716) 649-0200	Thomas Moses	Robert Pauley	...	...	George Utz	Dennis Gleason	Gerald Knoll
Hamilton	v	CM	3	(315) 824-1111	Sue McVaugh	Paul Kogut	Ronda Winn	...	Bob Holcomb	James Tilbe	Sean Graham
Harrison	v	MC	24	(914) 835-2000	Ronald Bianchi	...	Joan Walsh	Maureen MacKenzie	...	David Hall	Robert Wasp
Hastings-On-Hudson	v	CM	7	(914) 478-3400	William Lee Kinnally	Francis Frobel	...	...	Leslie Jenkins	Joseph Marsic	Michael Gunther
Haverstraw	v	MC	10	(914) 429-0300	Francis Wassmer	...	Deborah Smith	...	Carl Gitlan	John Reilly	Andrew Connors
Hempstead	t	MC	755	(516) 489-5000	Richard Guardino	...	Kate Murray	...	...	...	...
Hempstead	v	MC	56	(516) 489-3400	...	...	...	...	...	...	...
Herkimer	v	MC	7	(315) 866-3303	Mark Ainsworth	...	Bonnie Yatarola	...	Alfonso Varlaro	Joseph Malone	James Franco
Highland Falls	v	MC	3	(845) 446-3400	Joseph D'Onofrio	...	Regina Taylor	...	William Lee	Peter Miller	Gary Boyce
Hilton	v	MC	5	(585) 392-4144	William Carter	...	...	...	...	...	Thomas Tilebein
Homer *	v	MC	3	(607) 749-3322	Michael McDermott	...	Louanne Randall	...	Phil Hess	Daniel Mack	Michael Galeotti
Hoosick Falls	v	MC	3	(518) 686-7072	Donald Bogardus	...	Denise McMahon	Judy Vandemar	Paul Daverdonis	Royal Howard	Timothy Stratton
Hornell	c	MC	9	(607) 324-7421	Shawn Hogan	...	Bernard McAneney	Thelma Pelych	Vincent Kelly	...	David Oakes
Horseheads	v	CM	6	(607) 739-5691	Patricia Gross	...	S. Cunningham	...	Richard Sullivan	David Kole	Christopher Lawrick
Hudson	c	MC	7	(518) 828-1030	Kenneth Cranna	...	Bonita Colwell	Kevin Walsh	Patrick Colwell	Ellis Richardson	Charles Butterworth
Hudson Falls	v	MC	6	(518) 747-5426	C. Cronin	...	Kathryn Fitzpatrick	Marie Philo	...	James Clary	Michael Fiorillo
Huntington	t	MC	195	(631) 351-3014	...	...	...	...	...	...	...
Ilion	v	MC	8	(315) 895-7449	Charles Haggerty	Mark Cushman	...	Gale Hatch	Karl Tripple	Anthony Licari	...
Irondequoit	t	MC	52	(585) 467-8840	David Schantz	...	Lydia Dzus	John Bovenzi	...	Robert Longdue	Timothy Oakes
Irvington	v	MC	6	(914) 591-7070	Erin Malloy	Lawrence Schopher	Edward Ritter	...	James Ruffler	Louis Grieco	Gregory Nilsson
Island Park	v	MC	4	(516) 431-0600	...	...	...	...	...	...	...
Islandia	v	MC	3	(516) 348-1133	...	...	...	...	...	...	...
Islip	t	MC	322	(631) 244-5500	Pete McGowan	...	Joan Johnson	...	...	...	...
Ithaca	c	MC	29	(607) 274-6539	Alan Cohen	...	Julie Holcomb	Steven Thayer	Brian Wilbur	Victor Loo	William Gray
Jamestown	c	MC	31	(716) 483-7600	Samuel Teresi	...	Shirley Sanfilipo	James Olson	Lance Hedlund	...	Jeffrey Lehman
Johnson City	v	MC	15	(607) 798-7861	...	...	...	...	...	...	...
Johnstown	c	MC	8	(518) 736-4011	William Pollak	...	Marilyn Muzzi	Michael Gifford	Steven Hart	Gregory Horning	Christopher Foss
Kenmore	v	MC	16	(716) 873-5700	John Beaumont	Kathleen Johnson	...	...	Jeffrey Tamsen	Samuel Cammilleri	Charles Sottile
Kings Point	v	MC	5	(516) 482-7872	...	...	...	...	...	...	...
Kingston	c	MC	23	(845) 331-0080	James Sottile	...	Kathy Janeczek	Penny Radel	Richard Salzmann	Gerald Keller	Steven Gorsline
Lackawanna	c	MC	19	(716) 827-6464	Norman Polanski	...	Joseph Carnevale	Robert Marciniak	Reynold Jennetti	Dennis O'Hara	Leo Murphy
Lake Grove	v	MC	10	(516) 585-2000	Robert Henke	Leroy Heoffner	Carmela Constant	...	...	...	Douglas Colino
Lake Success	v	CM	2	(516) 482-4411	Roberta Chavis	...	...	...	...	William Roberts	Richard Faraci
Lakewood	v	MC	3	(716) 763-8557	...	...	...	...	...	...	...
Lancaster	v	MC	11	(716) 683-2105	William Carsdale	...	Tammy Derkovitz	...	...	...	William Natalzia
Lansing	v	MC	3	(607) 257-0424	Donald Hartill	...	...	...	...	...	John Courtney
Larchmont	v	MC	6	(914) 834-6230	Kenneth Bialo	...	Eileen Finn	...	Brian Payne	Stephen Rubeo	Joseph Bedard
Lawrence	v	MC	6	(516) 239-4600	...	...	...	...	...	...	...
Le Roy	v	CM	4	(585) 768-2527	William Horgan	...	...	...	...	Samuel Steffenilla	Robert Walters
Lewiston	v	MC	2	(716) 754-8271	Richard Soluri	...	...	...	William Fyfe	...	David Jacobs
Liberty	v	CM	3	(845) 292-2250	William Smith	...	Judy Zurawski	...	...	Michael DeFrank	Peter Parks
Lindenhurst	v	MC	27	(516) 957-7500	Lynda Distler	Shawn Cullinane	...	...	Henry Batz	...	...
Little Falls	c	MC	5	(315) 823-2400	...	...	...	...	James Staffo	...	...
Liverpool	v	MC	2	(315) 457-3441	Marlene Ward	...	Mary Ellen Sims	David Murray	...	Donald Morris	William Asmus
Lloyd Harbor	v	MC	3	(631) 549-8893	Leland Hairr	...	Kristi King	...	...	Bernard Welsh	George McCabe
Lockport	c	MC	22	(716) 439-6665	Michael Tucker	...	Richard Mullaney	...	Thomas Passoite	Neil Merritt	...
Long Beach	c	CM	35	(516) 431-1000	Michael Zapson	Glen Spiritis	Marcia Markowitz	Michael Barlotta	...	Thomas Browne	Robert Raab
Lowville *	v	MC	3	(315) 376-2834	Robert King	Eric Virkler	...	...	...	Eric Fredenburg	Mark Tabolt
Lynbrook	v	MC	19	(516) 599-8300	...	...	...	...	...	...	...
Lyons	v	MC	3	(315) 946-4531	John Cinelli	...	Diana Marro	...	Charles Witt	Michael Donalty	...
Malone	v	MC	6	(518) 483-4570	Joyce Tavernier	...	Elizabeth Bessette	...	...	Gerald Moll	Frank Riley
Malverne	v	MC	8	(516) 599-1200	Anthony Panzarella	Teresa Emmel	...	...	...	Glen Jacobson	Paul Jessup
Mamaroneck	t	CM	28	(914) 381-7810	...	Stephen Altieri	Patricia DiCioccio	...	...	Richard Rivera	Marco Gennarelli
Mamaroneck *	v	CM	18	(914) 777-7703	Philip Trifiletti	Leonard Verrastro	...	Agostino Fusco	Barry Casterella	Edward Flynn	Anthony Iacovelli
Manlius	v	MC	4	(315) 682-9171	...	Cheryl Haskins	...	...	...	...	John Maher
Manorhaven	v	MC	6	(516) 883-7000	...	...	...	...	...	...	...
Massapequa Park	v	MC	17	(516) 798-0244	James Altadonna	Peggy Caltabiano	...	...	...	...	John LaMarca
Massena	v	MC	11	(315) 769-8625	K. MacDonnell	...	Patricia Dumas	...	R. Gray	Timmy Currier	Hassan Fayad
Mechanicville	c	CO	5	(518) 664-8331	Thomas Higgins	...	Paul Guilianelle	Nicholas Forte	Charlie Wheeler	Peter Clements	Daniel Robens
Medina	v	MC	6	(716) 798-0710	Herbert Brant	...	E. Crowley	...	Gregory Barhite	Jose Avila	E. Houseknecht
Menands	v	MC	3	(518) 434-2922	John Bishop	...	William Smith	...	Donald Handerhan	Michael O'Brien	Timothy Boyd
Middletown	c	MC	25	(845) 346-4150	Joseph Destefano	Russell Russo	Charles Mitchell	...	...	Louis Ogden	Alfred Fusco
Mineola	v	MC	19	(516) 746-0750	Jack Martins	...	Michael Arens	...	Jack Gayson	...	Thomas Rini
Minoa	v	MC	3	(315) 656-3100	John Regan	...	Karen Curulla	...	...	...	Thomas Petterelli

Directory 1/9 continued — OFFICIALS IN U.S. MUNICIPALITIES 2,500 AND OVER IN POPULATION

Jurisdiction	Type	Form of govern-ment	2000 Popu-lation (000)	Main telephone number	Chief elected official	Appointed administrator	Clerk of the governing board	Chief financial officer	Fire chief	Police chief	Public works director
NEW YORK continued											
Mohawk	v	MC	2	(315) 866-4312	Irene Dibble	...	Judy Bray	...	Leo Kinville	Joseph Malone	Kevin Wheelock
Monroe	v	MC	7	(845) 782-8341	Joseph Mancuso	...	Virginia Carey	...	...	Dominic Giudice	Anthony Vaccaro
Montebello	v	MC	3	(914) 368-2211	Kathryn Ellsworth	...	Debra Mastroeni	...	...	...	...
Monticello	v	CM	6	(845) 794-6130	Gary Sommers	...	Edith Schop	...	Carl Houman	Michael Brennan	Steve Kozachuk
Morrisville *	v	MC	2	(315) 684-7007	Michelle Forward	...	Amy Will	...	Richard Gorton	...	Raymond Heh
Mount Kisco	v	CM	9	(914) 241-0500	Mark Farrell	James Palmer	...	...	Jack Marshall	Robert Dagostino	George Brown
Mount Morris	v	MC	3	(585) 658-4160	James Murray	...	Donald Scalia	...	...	Sherman Yates	Patsy Zingaru
Mount Vernon	c	MC	68	(914) 665-2300	Ernest Davis	...	Lisa Copeland	Maureen Walker	Al Everett	...	James Finch
Munsey Park	v	MC	2	(516) 365-7790	Harry Nicolaides	Helen Averso	...	...	...	...	...
Muttontown	v	MC	3	(516) 364-2240	...	...	...	...	...	...	...
New Castle	t	CM	17	(914) 234-4771	Janet Wells	Gennaro Faiella	Linda Peterson	...	...	Robert Breen	Gerard Moerschell
New Hempstead	v	MC	4	(845) 354-8100	Lawrence Dessau	...	Carole Vazquez	...	...	...	...
New Hyde Park	v	MC	9	(516) 354-0022	...	...	...	...	...	...	...
New Paltz *	v	MC	6	(845) 255-0130	Terry Dungan	...	Brittany Turner	...	David Weeks	Raymond Zappone	G. Bleu Terwilliger
New Rochelle	c	CM	72	(914) 654-2000	Timothy Idoni	Charles Strome	Dorothy Allen	Howard Rattner	Raymond Kiernan	Patrick Carroll	James Maxwell
New York	c	MC	8008	(212) 669-8090	Michael Bloomberg	...	...	...	Nicholas Scoppetta	Raymond Kelly	...
New York Mills	v	MC	3	(315) 736-9212	Michael Dubiel	...	Sharon Guca	...	Ron Roman	Stephen Verminski	Joseph Cotrupe
Newark	v	MC	9	(315) 331-4770	...	...	John Trickey	...	...	Richard Bogan	James Bridgeman
Newburgh	c	CM	28	(845) 569-7320	Andrew Marino	Jean McGrane	Lorene Vitek	Marie Gida	James Morrill	William Bloom	George Garrison
Niagara Falls	c	CM	55	(716) 286-4300	...	William Bradberry	Cynthia Baxter	Maria Brown	William Correa	Christopher Carlin	Paul Colangelo
North Hempstead	t	MC	222	(516) 627-0590	May Newburger	...	Michele Schimmel	...	...	...	Gil Anderson
North Syracuse	v	MC	6	(315) 458-0900	James Hotchkiss	...	Elizabeth Visell	...	Patrick Brennan	David Wilkinson	Michael Abruzzese
North Tonawanda	c	MC	33	(716) 695-8555	Mary Kabasakalian	...	Michael Cox	...	David Rogge	Carl Stiles	Gary Franklin
Northport	v	MC	7	(631) 261-7502	Peter Nolan	...	D. Smith	Dorothy Dugan	Anthony Graziano	...	Joseph Correia
Norwich	c	MC	7	(607) 334-1200	...	...	...	Brian Molinaro	John Tighe	Joseph Angelino	Carl Ivarson
Nyack	v	MC	6	(845) 358-0548	Terry Hekker	...	Berta Campbell	...	...	...	Joe Stach
Oakfield *	v	CM	1	(585) 948-5862	Raymond Cianfrini	...	Joyce Grazioplene	...	...	...	David Laney
Ocean Beach	v	MC	..	(631) 583-5940	Joseph Loeffler	Anne Minerva	...	...	Franklin Silsdorf	Edward Paradiso	Kevin Schelling
Ogdensburg *	c	CM	12	(315) 393-6100	William Nelson	Arthur Sciorra	Kathleen Bouchard	Philip Cosmo	Steven Badlam	Richard Polniak	Kit Smith
Old Westbury	v	MC	4	(516) 626-0800	...	...	Kenneth Callahan	...	...	William Doerrie	John Ingram
Olean *	c	MC	15	(716) 376-5615	John Ash	...	David John	Theodore Luty	John Gibbons	Patrick Brandow	Peter Marcus
Oneida	c	MC	10	(315) 363-4800	Leo Matzke	...	Jane Mariani	...	...	...	...
Oneonta *	c	MC	13	(607) 432-0670	Kim Muller	...	James Koury	David Martindale	Robert Barnes	Jack Donadio	...
Orangetown	t	MC	47	(845) 359-5100	...	...	...	...	...	...	...
Orchard Park	v	MC	3	(716) 662-9327	John Wilson	...	...	...	...	...	Paul Barker
Ossining	t	MC	36	(914) 762-6000	John Chervokas	...	...	...	...	Kenneth Donato	...
Ossining	v	CM	24	(914) 941-3554	Miguel Hernandez	...	Mary Ann Roberts	...	...	Joseph Burton	...
Oswego *	c	MC	17	(315) 342-8159	Randolph Bateman	...	Barbara Sugar	Deborah Coad	Edward Geers	Michael Dehm	Richard Bateman
Owego *	v	MC	3	(607) 687-3555	John Loftus	...	...	Lynne Mieczkowski	Thomas Taft	Edward McCulskey	Jeff Soules
Palmyra	v	MC	3	(315) 597-4849	Victoria Daly	...	...	...	...	David Dalton	...
Patchogue	v	MC	11	(631) 475-4300	Stephen Keegan	...	Mary Pontieri	...	John Parris	Jeffrey Kracht	Daniel Wirshup
Peekskill	c	CM	22	(914) 737-3400	John Testa	Daniel Fitzpatrick	Pamela Beach	...	...	Eugene Tumolo	David Greener
Pelham *	v	MC	6	(914) 738-2015	Edward Hotchkiss	Richard Slingerland	Terri Rouke	...	Richard Carfora	Joseph Benefico	Harry Pallett
Pelham Manor	v	CM	5	(914) 738-8820	Ferdinand Spucci	John Pierpont	...	...	Joseph Ruggerio	Dennis Carroll	...
Penfield	t	MC	34	(585) 340-8600	Channing Philbrick	...	Cassie Williams	Robert Beedon	...	...	Jim Fletcher
Penn Yan	v	MC	5	(315) 536-3015	D. Marchionda	...	Linda Banach	...	Kevin Pallar	Stephen Hill	Edward Balsley
Perry	v	MC	3	(585) 237-2216	Dennis Vergason	...	...	...	Arnold Wilson	...	Ryan Dure
Plattsburgh	c	MC	18	(518) 561-7701	Daniel Stewart	...	Keith Herkalo	James Buran	James Squires	Desmond Racicot	Kevin Murphy
Pleasantville	v	CM	7	(914) 769-1900	Bernard Gordon	Patricia Dwyer	Judith Weintraub	...	...	Anthony Chiarlitti	Stephen Johnson
Port Chester	v	CM	27	(914) 939-2200	Gerald Logan	William Williams	Richard Falanka	...	Joseph Publiese	Joseph Krzeminski	James Cole
Port Jefferson	v	MC	7	(516) 473-4724	...	...	...	...	...	...	...
Port Jervis	c	MC	8	(845) 858-4014	R. Worden	...	...	James Hinkley	Joseph Kowal	William Wagner	Vincent Lopez
Port Washington North	v	MC	2	(516) 883-5900	Thomas Pellegrino	...	Palma Torrisi	...	...	...	Edward Ratkoski
Potsdam	v	CM	9	(315) 265-7480	Ruth Garner	Michael Weil	Lori Queor	...	...	John Kaplan	Bruce Henderson
Poughkeepsie	c	MC	29	(845) 451-4035	Nancy Cozean	...	Felicia Santos	James Wojtowicz	Kenneth Boyd	Ronald Knapp	Stephen Miko
Queensbury	t	MC	25	(518) 761-8201	Dennis Brower	William Lavery	Darleen Dougher	Henry Hess	Steve Smith	...	Perley Rice
Ramapo *	t	MC	108	(845) 357-5100	C. St. Lawrence	...	Christian Sampson	Ilan Schoenberger	...	Peter Brower	Ted Dzurinko
Ravena	v	MC	3	(518) 756-8233	...	...	Nancy Warner	...	Joel Trombley	...	Bernard Persico
Rensselaer	c	MC	7	(518) 462-6424	Linda Ganance	...	Maureen Nardacci	Margaret VanDyke	Charles Mann	Fredrick Fusco	Donald Butler
Rhinebeck	v	MC	3	(845) 876-7015	John Costa	Valerie Kilmer	...	...	Donald Fingar	Steven Hanaburgh	Peter Sipperley
Rochester	c	MC	219	(585) 428-7115	William Johnson	Jeffrey Carlson	Carolee Conklin	Vincent Carfagna	Floyd Madison	Robert Duffy	Edward Doherty
Rockville Centre	v	MC	24	(516) 678-9300	...	...	...	...	...	John McKeon	Harold Weed
Rome	c	MC	34	(315) 336-6000	...	...	...	...	...	...	...
Rye	c	CM	14	(914) 967-4603	Steve Otis	O. Paul Shew	...	...	George Hogben	...	Louis Martirano
Rye Brook	v	CM	8	(914) 939-1121	Lawrence Rand	C. Bradbury	...	...	...	Theodore Sabato	...
Sag Harbor *	v	MC	2	(631) 725-0222	Gregory Ferraris	Sandra Schroeder	...	...	Philip Garypie	Thomas Fabiano	James Early
Salamanca	c	MC	6	(716) 945-3890	C. Vecchiarella	...	April Vecchiarella	Linda Rychcik	Barney Lee	Edward Gimbrone	Raymond Wilson
Sands Point	v	MC	2	(516) 883-3044	Leonard Wurzel	Randy Bond	...	Lynn Najman	...	Owen Kirby	Brian Gunderson
Saranac Lake	v	CM	5	(518) 891-4150	Thomas Michael	Martin Murphy	Kareen Tyler	...	Ed Woodard	Donald Perryman	Robert Martin
Saratoga Springs	c	CO	26	(518) 587-3550	J. O'Connell	...	Edward Valentine	Michael Lenz	Robert Cogan	Kenneth King	Joseph O'Neill
Saugerties	v	MC	4	(845) 246-2321	Robert Yerick	...	Mary Frank	Barbara Griffis	Brian Martin	William Kimble	Kevin Kiefer
Scarsdale	v	CM	17	(914) 722-1110	Beverly Sved	Alfred Gatta	Donna Conkling	James Heslop	Walter Felice	John Brogan	Benedict Salanitro
Schenectady	c	MC	61	(518) 382-5000	Albert Jurczynski	...	Carolyn Friello	Michael Strenka	Robert Farstad	Michael Geraci	Milton Mitchell
Scotia	v	MC	7	(518) 374-1071	...	...	...	...	...	...	...
Sea Cliff	v	MC	5	(516) 671-0080	Eileen Kriieb	Daniel Maddock	Peter Hesse	...	...	...	Tom Bellingham
Seneca Falls	v	CM	6	(315) 568-8107	Diana Smith	C. Sowards	...	...	...	Frederick Capozzi	William Gladis
Sherrill	c	CM	3	(315) 363-2440	Joseph Shay	David Barker	...	Michael Holmes	...	James Hastings	Gary Onyan
Sidney	v	MC	4	(607) 561-2324	James Warren	...	...	...	John Gilmore	Craig Whitten	David Stevens
Silver Creek	v	MC	2	(716) 934-3240	...	Thomas Postle	...	...	...	Louis Pelletter	Robert Groat
Skaneateles	v	MC	2	(315) 685-0730	James Rhinehart	...	Sally Sheehan	...	David Card	Jack McNeil	Robert Green
Sleepy Hollow	v	CM	9	(914) 631-1440	Sean Treacy	...	Angela Everett	Sanjay Shah	Lenny Rutigliano	...	Joe Defeo
Sloan *	v	MC	3	(716) 897-1560	Leonard Szymanski	...	Debra Smith	...	Barry Ping	...	Sean McGee
Sloatsburg *	v	MC	3	(845) 753-2727	Carl Wright	...	Thomas Bollatto	...	...	...	Michael Demartino
Smithtown	t	MC	115	(631) 360-7512	Patrick Vecchio	...	Vincent Puleo	Anthony Minerva	...	...	...
Solvay	v	MC	6	(315) 468-1651	...	...	Cheryl Libertone	...	...	Richard Cox	David Pettitt
Somers	t	MC	18	(914) 277-3323	Mary Beth Murphy	...	Kathleen Pacella	...	...	Michael Driscoll	Thomas Chiaverini
South Glens Falls	v	MC	3	(518) 793-1455	Robert Phinney	...	Karin Blood	...	Jake Losaw	Kevin Judd	John Dixon
South Nyack	v	MC	3	(845) 358-0287	Richard Helmke	...	Sara Seiler	...	...	Alan Colsey	James Johnson
Southampton	v	MC	3	(631) 283-0247	Mark Epley	J. Van Nostrand	...	...	Brian Cooke	Lars King	Gary Aldrich

Directory 1/9 continued — OFFICIALS IN U.S. MUNICIPALITIES 2,500 AND OVER IN POPULATION

Jurisdiction	Type	Form of govern-ment	2000 Popu-lation (000)	Main telephone number	Chief elected official	Appointed administrator	Clerk of the governing board	Chief financial officer	Fire chief	Police chief	Public works director
NEW YORK continued											
Spencerport	v	MC	3	(585) 352-6775	Theodore Walker	Alan Scheg	P. Cunningham	Linda Harissis	. . .	. . .	Thomas West
Spring Valley	v	MC	25	(845) 352-1100	George Darden	Barry Harris	Sherry Scott	. . .	Fred Thibault	Anthony Furco	John Ackerson
Springville	v	MC	4	(716) 592-4936	Gary Eppolito	. . .	Deborah Murphy	. . .	Dennis Dains	. . .	Karl Lux
Suffern	v	MC	11	(845) 357-2600	James Giannettino	. . .	Virginia Menschner	. . .	Donald Schreck	Frank Finch	Joseph Hornick
Syracuse	c	MC	147	(315) 448-8780	Matthew Driscoll	Kenneth Mokrzycki	John Copanas	Brian Roulin	John Cowin	Dennis Duval	James Collins
Tarrytown	v	CM	11	(914) 631-7873	Eileen Pilla	Stephen McCabe	Louise Camilliere	. . .	. . .	Scott Brown	. . .
Thomaston *	v	MC	2	(516) 482-3110	Robert Stern	Barbara Daniels	. . .	. . .	. . .	. . .	. . .
Ticonderoga	v	MC	2	(518) 585-6265	Robert Dedrick	. . .	Paula Buckman	. . .	. . .	Jeffrey Cook	Phillip Huestis
Tonawanda	c	MC	16	(716) 695-8645	Alice Roth	Donald Witkowski	Janice Bodie	. . .	Thomas Miller	Mark Winters	Neal Myers
Troy	c	MC	49	(518) 270-4401	Mark Patterson	James Conroy	Lawrence Quinn	Martin Dunbar	Thomas Garrett	Mark Whitman	. . .
Tuckahoe	v	MC	6	(914) 961-3100	Michael Martino	. . .	Susan Ciamarra	. . .	. . .	John Costanzo	Robert Mascianica
Tupper Lake	v	MC	3	(518) 359-3341	Sandra Strades	Mary Casagrain	Mary Kennedy	. . .	. . .	Ronald Cole	Michael Sparks
Union	t	MC	56	(607) 786-2915	John Cheevers	. . .	Gail Springer	Gary Leighton	. . .	. . .	Kenneth Del Bianco
Utica	c	MC	60	(315) 792-0300	. . .	. . .	. . .	. . .	. . .	. . .	. . .
Valley Stream *	v	MC	36	(516) 825-4200	Edward Cahill	Vincent Ang	. . .	John Mastromarino	. . .	. . .	. . .
Voorheesville *	v	MC	2	(518) 765-2692	Robert Conway	. . .	Linda Pasquali	. . .	Frank Papa	. . .	William Smith
Walden	v	CM	6	(845) 778-2177	. . .	James Politi	Nancy Mitchell	. . .	. . .	Jeffrey Holmes	Stefa Neuhaus
Walton *	v	MC	3	(607) 865-4358	Edward Snow	. . .	Virginia O'Dell	. . .	. . .	Melvin Woodin	Joseph Cetta
Wappingers Falls	v	MC	4	(845) 297-8773	. . .	. . .	. . .	. . .	. . .	. . .	. . .
Warsaw	v	MC	3	(585) 786-2120	Daniel Moran	. . .	Linda Hoffmeister	. . .	. . .	William Blythe	Gilbert Stearns
Warwick	v	MC	6	(845) 986-2031	Michael Newhard	. . .	Jacqueline Mongelli	. . .	. . .	. . .	Steven Sisco
Waterloo	v	MC	5	(315) 539-9131	. . .	. . .	. . .	. . .	. . .	. . .	. . .
Watertown	c	CM	26	(315) 785-7730	Jeffrey Graham	Mary Corriveau	Donna Dutton	James Mills	Daniel Gaumont	Joseph Goss	Eugene Hayes
Watervliet	c	CM	10	(518) 270-3800	Robert Carlson	Paul Murphy	Bruce Hidley	Robert Fahr	. . .	Gerald Beston	. . .
Waverly *	v	MC	4	(607) 565-8106	Kyle McDuffee	. . .	. . .	. . .	. . .	Grady Updyke	Michael Steck
Webster	v	MC	5	(585) 265-3770	. . .	. . .	. . .	. . .	. . .	. . .	. . .
Wellsville	v	MC	5	(585) 593-1121	Susan Goetschius	. . .	Janice Givens	. . .	David Sweet	James Cicirello	William Whitfield
Wesley Hills	v	MC	4	(845) 354-0400	Robert Frankl	Helen Schiela	. . .	Marvin Nyman	. . .	. . .	. . .
West Haverstraw	v	MC	10	(845) 947-2800	Edward Zugibe	. . .	O. Miller	. . .	. . .	. . .	David Barbera
West Seneca	t	MC	45	(716) 674-5600	. . .	. . .	. . .	. . .	. . .	. . .	. . .
Westbury	v	MC	14	(516) 334-1700	Ernest Strada	Thomas Savino	. . .	. . .	. . .	. . .	Dennis Maher
Westfield	v	MC	3	(716) 326-4961	Ronald Catalano	. . .	Vincent Luce	. . .	. . .	Ken Machemer	. . .
White Plains	c	MC	53	(914) 422-1200	Joseph Delfino	Paul Wood	Janice Minieri	G. Cuneo-Harwood	Richard Lyman	James Bradley	Joseph Nicoletti
Whitehall	v	MC	2	(518) 499-0871	Patricia Norton	. . .	. . .	Joan Douglas	. . .	Richard Rizzo	Donald Williams
Whitesboro	v	MC	3	(315) 736-1613	Richard Pugh	. . .	Susan Goding	. . .	. . .	Dominick Hiffa	Charles Tritten
Williamsville	v	CM	5	(716) 632-4120	F Hazlett	Sally Kuzon	. . .	. . .	James Zymanek	. . .	Anthony Grisanti
Williston Park	v	MC	7	(516) 746-2193	. . .	. . .	. . .	. . .	. . .	. . .	. . .
Woodridge	v	CM	. .	(845) 434-7447	Ivan Katz	. . .	Diane Garritt	. . .	Eric Akerley	John Calvello	Carl Garritt
Yonkers	c	MC	196	(914) 377-6180	John Spencer	Philip Amicone	Joan Deierlein	James La Perche	Anthony Pagano	Charles Cola	John Liszewski
Yorktown	t	MC	36	(914) 962-5722	. . .	. . .	Alice Roker	Joan Goldberg	. . .	Daniel McMahon	. . .
Yorkville	v	MC	2	(315) 736-9391	Michael Mahoney	. . .	Helen Petruccione	. . .	George Farley	Kirk Lanahan	Conrad Chaya
NORTH CAROLINA											
Aberdeen *	t	CM	3	(910) 944-1115	Elizabeth Mofield	William Zell	Nancy Matthews	Beth Wentland	Phillip Richardson	Michael Connor	Rickie Monroe
Ahoskie *	t	CM	4	(252) 332-5146	Linda Blackburn	Charles Hammond	Evelyn Howard	. . .	Kenneth Dilday	Troy Fitzhugh	Kirk Rogers
Albemarle	c	CM	15	(704) 984-9400	Roger Snyder	Raymond Allen	. . .	Colleen Jones	George McDaniel	Gerald Michael	James Coble
Angier	t	CM	3	(919) 639-2071	Wanda Gregory	Coley Price	Tina Westy	Jason Forelines	. . .	Anthony Poppler	Henry Cook
Apex	t	CM	20	(919) 249-3400	Keith Weatherly	Bruce Radford	Georgia Evangelist	Richard Smiley	Mark Haraway	Jack Lewis	Timothy Donnelly
Archdale *	c	CM	9	(336) 431-9141	Bertha Stone	Jerry Yarborough	. . .	Debbie Hinson	. . .	Gary Lewallen	Michael Shuler
Asheboro	c	CM	21	(336) 629-2037	David Jarrell	John Ogburn	Holly Hartman	Deborah Juberg	James Smith	Gary Mason	Robert Kivett
Asheville	c	CM	68	(828) 259-5695	Charles Worley	Gary Jackson	Magdalen Burleson	Benjamin Durant	Gregory Grayson	William Hogan	Franklin Combs
Atlantic Beach *	t	CM	1	(252) 726-2121	Joyce Vinson	David Harvell	Kelly Nash	. . .	Adam Snyder	Allen Smith	Marc Schulze
Ayden	t	CM	4	(252) 746-7030	Stephen Tripp	Adam Mitchell	Dorothy Bridges	Christopher Tucker	Barry Wood	Charles Crudup	Henry Hardison
Badin	t	CM	1	(704) 422-3470	James Harrsion	William Herms	Lorraine Tucker	. . .	. . .	Bryan Lambert	Floyd Carter
Bald Head Island	v	CM	. .	(910) 457-9700	Larry Lammert	Calvin Peck	Amy Candler	Shelia Boyd	Jerome Munna	Richard Herring	Wendell Liddle
Beaufort	t	CM	3	(252) 728-2141	Ann Carter	Terri Parker-Eakes	Della Knight	Betsy Gilchrist	James Lynch	Steve Lewis	John Young
Beech Mountain *	t	CM	. .	(828) 387-4236	Richard Owen	James Boaz	Reba Greene	Sally Rominger	. . .	Marvin Hefner	William Hatch
Belhaven	t	CM	1	(252) 943-3055	Charles Boyette	Timothy Johnson	Marie Adams	Robert Richardson	Tracy Logan	. . .	Carroll Hearring
Belmont	c	CM	8	(704) 825-5586	Richard Boyce	Barry Webb	Mozelle Lingafeldt	. . .	George Attice	David James	David Isenhour
Belville	t	CM	1	(910) 371-2456	. . .	Tracie Davis	. . .	. . .	. . .	. . .	. . .
Benson	t	CM	2	(919) 894-3553	. . .	Keith Langdon	Connie Sorrell	. . .	. . .	Kenneth Edwards	Billy Addison
Bermuda Run	t	CM	1	(336) 998-0906	John Ferguson	Joan Carter	. . .	. . .	. . .	. . .	. . .
Bessemer City	c	CM	5	(704) 629-2238	Allan Farris	. . .	Janice Costner	Mary Hook	. . .	. . .	James Ramsey
Beulaville *	t	CM	1	(910) 298-4647	Joseph Edwards	Scotty Summerlin	Lori Williams	. . .	. . .	Hal Williams	Earl Sanderson
Biltmore Forest	t	CM	1	(828) 274-0824	George Goosmann	Nelson Smith	. . .	. . .	. . .	Eugene Ray	Terry Crouch
Biscoe	t	CM	1	(910) 428-4112	James Blake	. . .	Lisa Cagle	. . .	Kelly Kellem	James Myrick	David Asbill
Black Mountain *	t	CM	7	(828) 669-9102	Carl Bartlett	Anthony Caudle	Shirley Raines	. . .	Timothy Rayburn	Kevin Pressley	Robert Watts
Bladenboro	t	CM	1	(910) 863-3655	. . .	Delane Jackson	. . .	. . .	. . .	. . .	. . .
Blowing Rock	t	CM	1	(828) 295-5200	James Lawrence	Scott Hildebran	Barbara Beach	. . .	Marcus Hickman	James Tolbert	Johnny Lentz
Boiling Spring Lakes	c	CM	2	(910) 845-2614	Joan Kinney	David Lewis	. . .	. . .	. . .	Richard White	Larry Modlin
Boiling Springs	t	CM	3	(704) 434-2357	Max Hamrick	Zach Trogdon	Kim Greene	Rhonda Allen	Neal McSwain	James Clary	Joey Gantt
Boone	t	CM	13	(828) 262-4530	Loretta Clawson	Gregory Young	Freida Van Allen	Amy Davis	Reginald Hassler	William Post	J. Brown
Brevard	c	CM	6	(828) 884-4123	James Harris	Joseph Albright	Glenda Sansosti	Terrell Scruggs	. . .	Dennis Wilde	Donald Owen
Bryson City	0	CM	1	(828) 488-3335	. . .	Larry Callicutt	. . .	. . .	. . .	. . .	. . .
Burgaw *	t	CM	3	(910) 259-2151	John James	Martin Beach	Sylvia Raynor	Michelle Grant	William George	Joseph Briley	Douglas Riseden
Burlington	c	CM	44	(336) 222-5000	Stephen Ross	Harold Owen	Jondeen Terry	Linda Hollifield	Jay Smith	Michael Gauldin	Gary Hicks
Canton	t	CM	4	(828) 648-2363	Patrick Smathers	William Stamey	Albert Matthews	. . .	James Smathers	William Guillet	Russell Teague
Carolina Beach *	t	CM	4	(910) 458-2992	William Clark	Timothy Owens	Lynn Prusa	Dawn Johnson	Brian Roberts	William Younginer	Steven Pagley
Carrboro	t	CM	16	(919) 942-8541	Mark Chilton	Steven Stewart	Sarah Williamson	. . .	Travis Crabtree	Carolyn Hutchison	George Seiz
Carthage *	t	CM	1	(910) 947-2331	William Walton	Carol Cleetwood	Melissa Adams	Linda Phillips	Christopher Tyner	C. McKenzie	Rocky Davis
Cary	t	CM	94	(919) 469-4070	Glen Lang	William Coleman	Sue Rowland	Karen Mills	Raymond Cain	Windy Hunter	Michael Bajorek
Caswell Beach	t	CM	. .	(910) 278-5471	. . .	David Hewett	Linda Bethune	Judy Williamson	. . .	. . .	. . .
Catawba *	t	CM	. .	(828) 241-2215	Thomas Jones	Jonathan Kanipe	Kathy Johnson	. . .	Donald Robinson	Cecil Cook	Cary Broadwell
Cedar Point *	0	CM	. .	(252) 393-7898	Harry Redfearn	C. Seaberg	Jackie Paylor	. . .	. . .	. . .	Donald Redfearn
Chadbourn	t	CM	2	(910) 654-4148	Leo Mercer	Dottie Thomas	. . .	. . .	Randy Guyton	Timothy Stoker	Michael Foss
Chapel Hill	t	CM	48	(919) 968-2700	Kevin Foy	Roger Stancil	Sabrina Oliver	Kay Johnson	Daniel Jones	Gregg Jarvies	William Letteri
Charlotte	c	CM	540	(704) 336-2285	Patrick McCrory	Curt Walton	Brenda Freeze	Greg Gaskins	Luther Fincher	Darrel Stephens	. . .
Cherryville *	c	CM	5	(704) 435-1709	Robert Austell	David Hodgkins	Kelly Sellers	Bonny Alexander	Jeff Cash	Woodrow Burgess	Brandon Abernathy
China Grove	t	CM	3	(704) 857-2466	Donald Bringle	Eric Davis	Gail Carter	Mary Jo Bopp	. . .	. . .	. . .
Claremont	c	CM	1	(828) 459-7009	Glenn Morrison	Doris Bumgarner	. . .	Stephanie Corn	Gary Sigmon	Gerald Tolbert	Thomas Winkler
Clayton	t	CM	6	(919) 553-5002	Douglas McCormac	R Biggs	Jessica Coutu	Marc Jones	Lee Barbee	. . .	. . .

Directory 1/9 continued **OFFICIALS IN U.S. MUNICIPALITIES 2,500 AND OVER IN POPULATION**

Jurisdiction	Type	Form of govern-ment	2000 Popu-lation (000)	Main telephone number	Chief elected official	Appointed administrator	Clerk of the governing board	Chief financial officer	Fire chief	Police chief	Public works director
NORTH CAROLINA continued											
Clemmons	v	CM	13	(336) 766-7511	Edward Brewer	Gary Looper	Marsha Sucharski	K. Stroud	. . .	. . .	Larry Kirby
Clinton	c	CM	8	(910) 299-4907	Luther Starling	John Connet	Elizabeth Fortner	Betty Brewer	Phillip Miller	Michael Brim	Chris Doherty
Columbus *	t	CM	. .	(828) 894-8236	Kathleen McMillian	Tim Holloman	Donna Butler	Kathy Gregory	. . .	Butch Kennedy	Wendell Pace
Concord	c	CM	55	(704) 920-5200	Jeffrey Padgett	W. Hiatt	Vickie Weant	Joyce Allman	Terry Holloway	Merlyn Hamilton	. . .
Conover	c	CM	6	(828) 464-1191	Bruce Eckard	Donald Duncan	Cara Reed	Vickie Schlichting	. . .	Gary Lafone	Jimmy Clark
Cornelius	t	CM	11	(704) 892-6031	Gary Knox	Anthony Roberts	Carolyn Sigmon	Jackie Huffman	Jim Barbee	Ronald McKinney	Ricky Overcash
Cramerton	t	CM	2	(704) 824-4337	Cathy Biles	Michael Peoples	LuAnn Ellis	. . .	. . .	David Young	. . .
Creedmoor	c	CM	2	(919) 528-3332	. . .	Robert Schaumleffel	Sandra Harper	Lenessa Hawkins	. . .	. . .	. . .
Dallas	t	MC	3	(704) 922-3176	Rick Coleman	Steven Miller	Maria Stroupe	. . .	David Callahan	Gary Buckner	John Ferguson
Davidson	t	MC	7	(704) 892-7591	Randall Kincaid	Leamon Brice	. . .	Peggy Smith	A. Hollingsworth	. . .	James Treadaway
Dobson	t	CM	1	(336) 386-8962	. . .	J Atkins	. . .	. . .	. . .	. . .	. . .
Drexel	t	CM	1	(828) 437-7421	Richard Propst	Matthew Settlemyer	Sherry Carswell	. . .	James Richards	Michael Swink	Johnny Rowe
Duck	t	CM	. .	(252) 255-1234	Donald Morrison	Christopher Layton	Lori Kopec	. . .	Donna Black	Alan Hamilton	. . .
Dunn *	c	CM	9	(910) 230-3500	William Elmore	Ronald Autry	Joyce Valley	Renee Daughtry	Austin Tew	Bernard Jones	Billy Addison
Durham	c	CM	187	(919) 560-4214	William Bell	Patrick Baker	Dorothy Gray	Kenneth Pennoyer	Otis Cooper	Jose Lopez	Kathryn Kalb
Eden *	c	CM	15	(336) 623-2110	John Grogan	Stephen Corcoran	Kim Scott	Tammie McMichael	Doug Cline	Gary Benthin	Dennis Asbury
Edenton	t	CM	5	(252) 482-7352	Roland Vaughan	A.-Marie Knighton	. . .	Janet Hines	Charlie Westbrook	Gregory Bonner	Jimmy Patterson
Elizabeth City *	c	CM	17	(252) 337-6677	Charles Foster	Richard Olson	Dianne Pierce	Sarah Blanchard	William Pritchard	Charles Crudup	Paul Fredette
Elizabethtown	t	MC	3	(910) 862-2066	Kenneth Kornegay	. . .	Patricia Stokes	Darlene Norris	Jamie Fulk	Robert Kinlaw	. . .
Elkin	t	CM	4	(336) 835-9800	Thomas Gwyn	Lloyd Payne	Catherine Tilley	John Holcomb	Thomas Wheeler	Carmel Wagoner	Robert Fuller
Elon College	t	CM	6	(336) 584-3601	Roxie Schmidt	Michael Dula	Sabrina Oliver	. . .	Walter King	Dan Ingle	Donald Wagoner
Emerald Isle *	t	CM	3	(252) 354-3424	Arthur Schools	Frank Rush	Rhonda Ferebee	Georgia Overman	William Walker	William Hargett	John Dunn
Enfield	t	CM	2	(252) 445-3146	Edward Jones	. . .	Jannie Burnette	Bobby Davis	. . .	. . .	Clyde Spence
Erwin	t	CM	4	(910) 897-5140	James Glover	M. Thornton	Joan Weeks	. . .	. . .	Thomas Chandler	Mark Byrd
Fairmont	t	CM	2	(910) 628-9766	Nedward Gaddy	H. Proctor	Jennifer Larson	Linda Vause	James Thompson	Samuel Hunt	Ronnie Seals
Farmville	t	CM	4	(252) 753-5774	Robert Evans	Richard Hicks	Amy Bryan	. . .	. . .	Robert Smith	David Shackleford
Fayetteville	c	CM	121	(910) 433-1635	Marshall Pitts	Dale Iman	Janet Jones	Lisa Smith	James Hall	Thomas McCarthy	. . .
Fletcher	t	CM	4	(828) 687-3985	Robert Parrish	Mark Biberdorf	Janice Sherlock	Carol Plack	. . .	John Moss	Ronnie Frady
Forest City	t	CM	7	(828) 245-0148	Grover Bradley	Charles Summey	Sandra Mayse	F. Walden	L. McCurry	Randy Chapman	Scott Hoyle
Franklin	t	MC	3	(828) 524-2516	. . .	Mike Decker	. . .	Janet Anderson	Howard Haithcock	Terry Bradley	Harry Gibson
Franklinton	t	CM	1	(919) 494-2520	J. Kearney	Sharon Garner	Kim Worley	. . .	Darrell Chalk	Ray Gilliam	. . .
Fremont	t	CM	1	(919) 242-6234	. . .	Kerry McDuffie	. . .	. . .	. . .	. . .	. . .
Fuquay-Varina	t	CM	7	(919) 552-3191	John Byrne	Andy Hedrick	Rose John	. . .	Anthony Mauldin	Larry Smith	. . .
Gamewell *	c	MC	3	(828) 754-1991	Jack Roberts	Mary Carter	. . .	. . .	. . .	. . .	. . .
Garner	t	CM	17	(919) 772-4688	F. Rohrbaugh	F. Watkins	. . .	Linwood Jones	. . .	. . .	Daniel Rudy
Gastonia	c	CM	66	(704) 866-6859	Jennifer Stultz	James Palenick	Virginia Creighton	Wilson Bradley	Robert Ridgeway	Rodney Parham	Matthew Jordan
Gibsonville	t	CM	4	(336) 449-4144	Leonard Williams	Robert Baxley	Laurie Yarbrough	Connie Woody	Clarence Owen	Anthony Cole	Coy May
Goldsboro	c	CM	39	(919) 735-6121	Alfonzo King	Joseph Huffman	Sandra Justice	Richard Durham	Bobby Greenfield	Timothy Bell	Karen Brashear
Graham	c	CM	12	(336) 570-6700	Bill Cooke	Chris Rollins	Eydie May	Sandra King	John Andrews	Milford Miller	Donnell Braxton
Granite Falls *	t	CM	4	(828) 396-3131	Barry Hayes	Linda Story	Judy Mackie	Brenda Poe	Thomas Laws	Richard Bolick	William Hamilton
Green Level	t	CM	2	(336) 578-3443	. . .	Quentin McPhatter	. . .	. . .	. . .	. . .	. . .
Greensboro	c	CM	223	(336) 373-2065	Keith Holiday	Mitchell Johnson	Juanita Cooper	Richard Lusk	Johnny Teeters	. . .	. . .
Greenville	c	CM	60	(252) 329-2489	Robert Parrott	Wayne Bowers	Wanda Elks	Bernita Demery	Mike Burton	William Anderson	Thomas Tysinger
Grifton	t	CM	2	(252) 524-5168	Timothy Bright	Shawn Condin	Patricia Bryan	. . .	Ed Meeks	Warren Morrisette	Robert Williams
Hamlet	c	CM	6	(910) 582-2651	William Garner	Marchell David	Tammy Kirkley	Michael Deese	David Knight	Robert Bristow	. . .
Harrisburg	t	MC	4	(704) 455-5614	. . .	. . .	. . .	. . .	. . .	. . .	. . .
Havelock *	c	CM	22	(919) 444-6402	Jimmy Sanders	James Freeman	Cindy Morgan	Lee Tillman	Rick Zaccardelli	Wayne Cyrus	. . .
Haw River *	t	CM	1	(336) 578-0784	Buddy Boggs	Jeffrey Earp	Misty Hagood	. . .	Ronnie Wade	Phillip Felts	Charles Allen
Henderson	c	CM	16	(252) 431-6000	Donald Seifert	Jerry Moss	Dianne White	. . .	Daniel Wilkerson	Glen Allen	James Morgan
Hendersonville	c	CM	10	(828) 697-3000	Fred Niehoff	Chris Carter	Tammie Drake	James Rudisill	. . .	Donnie Parks	Don Sides
Hickory *	c	CM	37	(828) 323-7412	G. Wright	Mick Berry	Pamela Tallent	Deanna Rios	Thomas Alexander	Thomas Adkins	Charles Hansen
High Point *	c	CM	85	(336) 883-3259	Rebecca Smothers	Stribling Boynton	Lisa Vierling	Jeffrey Moore	David Taylor	James Fealy	Chris Thompson
Hillsborough	t	CM	5	(919) 732-2104	Tom Stevens	Eric Peterson	Donna Armbrister	Greg Siler	. . .	Clarence Birkhead	. . .
Holden Beach	t	CM	. .	(910) 842-6488	. . .	Steven Wheeler	Joyce Shore	Kate White	. . .	Wallace Layne	J. Hickman
Holly Springs	t	CM	9	(919) 552-6221	Dick Sears	Carl Dean	Joni Powell	Drew Holland	. . .	. . .	Luncie McNeil
Hope Mills	t	CM	11	(910) 424-4555	. . .	Randy Beeman	Phyllis Register	David Stafford	Lee Sudia	John Hodges	James McLaurin
Hudson *	t	CM	3	(828) 728-8272	Billy Beane	Rebecca Bentley	Tamra Swanson	. . .	. . .	David Greene	Carl Henderson
Huntersville *	t	CM	24	(704) 875-6541	Kim Phillips	Gregory Ferguson	Janet Pierson	Janet Stoner	. . .	Philip Potter	. . .
Indian Trail	t	CM	11	(704) 821-8114	Sandy Moore	Edward Humphries	. . .	Janice Chandler	. . .	. . .	. . .
Jacksonville *	c	CM	66	(910) 938-5227	Jan Slagle	Kristoff Bauer	Carmen Miracle	. . .	Rick McIntyre	Michael Yaniero	Grant Sparks
Jamestown	t	CM	. .	(336) 454-1138	. . .	Kathryn Billings	. . .	. . .	. . .	. . .	. . .
Jonesville	t	CM	1	(336) 835-3426	Delos Martin	Ron Niland	. . .	Debbie Welborn	Keith Macy	Tim Gwyn	Roger Martin
Kannapolis *	c	CM	36	(704) 920-4300	R. Misenheimer	Michael Legg	Bridgette Bell	Michael Shinn	Cyde Hiers	. . .	Wilmer Melton
Kenly *	t	CM	1	(919) 284-2116	Herbert Hales	Elvin Shelton	Sharon Evans	. . .	Paul Whitehurst	Josh Gibson	Kenneth Thompson
Kernersville	t	CM	17	(336) 996-3121	Curtis Swisher	Roger Bryant	Dale Martin	. . .	Jimmy Barrow	Grady Stocktown	Timothy Shields
Kill Devil Hills *	t	CM	5	(252) 449-5300	Raymond Sturza	Debora Diaz	Mary Quidley	Beverly Gist	Thomas Penland	Raymond Davis	. . .
King	c	CM	5	(336) 983-8265	Jack Warren	John Cater	Tamara Hatley	Christine Whicker	Randy Williams	Tim Ledford	Ricky Lewis
Kings Mountain	c	CM	9	(704) 734-0333	Edgar Murphrey	Marilyn Sellers	. . .	Lori Hall	Frank Burns	Melvin Proctor	Jackie Barnette
Kinston *	c	CM	23	(252) 939-3120	Orice Ritch	Scott Stevens	Carol Barwick	Keith Fiaschetti	Bill Johnson	Annette Boyd	Rhonda Barwick
Kitty Hawk	t	CM	2	(252) 261-3552	William Harris	John Stockton	Lynn Morris	Mike Eubank	James Spivey	David Ward	Mark McKenzie
Knightdale	t	CM	5	(919) 217-2220	Jeanne Bonds	Gary McConkey	Rebecca Agner	Pamela Hinson	Timothy Guffey	. . .	Reed Alexander
La Grange	t	MC	2	(252) 566-3186	Woodard Gurley	John Craft	Phyllis Harrison	. . .	David Holmes	John Sullivan	Aubrey Rouse
Lake Lure	t	CM	1	(828) 625-9983	James Proctor	H. M. Place	Mary Flack	Sam Karr	Ron Morgan	Charles Hester	Tony Hennessee
Lake Waccamaw	t	CM	1	(910) 646-3700	Bolling McNeil	Darren Currie	. . .	. . .	. . .	Timothy Barrett	Mike Prostinak
Laurel Park *	t	CM	1	(828) 693-4840	Henry Johnson	James Ball	Kimberly Hensley	Dona Mennella	. . .	Donald Fisher	James Newman
Laurinburg	c	CM	15	(910) 276-8257	Ann Slaughter	Craig Honeycutt	Dee Hammond	Cynthia Carpenter	. . .	Robert Malloy	Harold Smith
Leland	t	CM	1	(910) 371-0148	Franky Thomas	. . .	. . .	Donna Strickland	. . .	Osey Sanders	Jimmy Strickland
Lenoir *	c	CM	16	(828) 757-2200	David Barlow	W. Bailey	Shirley Cannon	Danny Gilbert	Kenneth Briscoe	Joseph Reynolds	Charles Beck
Lewisville	t	CM	8	(336) 945-5558	Robert Stebbins	Cecil Wood	Joyce Walker	. . .	. . .	. . .	George Hauser
Lexington *	c	CM	19	(336) 243-2489	Richard Thomas	John Gray	Sara Lanier	Terra Greene	Thad Dickerson	John Lollis	Rick Comer
Liberty	t	CM	2	(336) 622-4276	John Stanley	. . .	Sandra Dixon	Nancy Granger	J. R. Beard	Jerry Brown	Roby Woods
Lillington *	t	CM	2	(910) 893-2654	Glenn McFadden	Tommy Burns	Vickie Wilder	Cherie Turner	John Bethune	Frank Powers	Tim Smith
Lincolnton *	c	CM	9	(704) 736-8980	Bobby Huitt	Jeff Emory	Donna Flowers	Georgetta Williams	Robert Gates	Harold Abernathy	Stephen Peeler
Long View	t	CM	4	(828) 322-3921	Norman Cook	David Epley	Denise Danielson	Peggy Willis	Eric Shepherd	Buck Rogers	Gary Workman
Louisburg	t	CM	3	(919) 496-3406	. . .	C. Gobble	Carolyn Patterson	Denise Harris	Timmy Smith	Tommy Leonard	Gary Cottrell
Lowell	c	MC	2	(704) 824-3518	. . .	Ben Blackburn	. . .	. . .	. . .	. . .	. . .
Lucama	t	CM	. .	(252) 239-0560	. . .	. . .	. . .	. . .	. . .	. . .	. . .
Lumberton	c	CM	20	(910) 671-3832	Ray Pennington	Thomas Horne	Laney Sapp	Rebecca Maynor	James Cox	Robert Grice	Henry Ivey
Madison	t	CM	2	(336) 427-0221	Kenneth Hawkins	Robert Scott	Lannette Johnson	. . .	Fred Butts	Perry Webster	Keith Tucker
Maggie Valley *	t	CM	. .	(828) 926-0866	Roger McElroy	Timothy Barth	Vickie Best	Shayne Wheeler	. . .	Scott Sutton	Michael McHaffey
Maiden	t	CM	3	(828) 428-5000	Zane Hudson	Kevin Sanders	Wendy Vanover	. . .	Burl Shieum	Kent Auton	Eddie Faulkner

Directory 1/9 continued — OFFICIALS IN U.S. MUNICIPALITIES 2,500 AND OVER IN POPULATION

Jurisdiction	Type	Form of govern- ment	2000 Popu- lation (000)	Main telephone number	Chief elected official	Appointed administrator	Clerk of the governing board	Chief financial officer	Fire chief	Police chief	Public works director
NORTH CAROLINA continued											
Manteo	t	CO	1	(252) 473-2133	...	Kermit Skinner	Rebecca Breiholz	Sally Defosse	...	...	James McClease
Marion *	c	CM	4	(828) 652-3551	A. Clark	J. Boyette	...	Harriett Thomas	James Neal	Mika Elliott	E Hollifield
Marshville *	t	CM	2	(704) 624-2515	Franklin Deese	Carl Webber	Shelley Maness	...	...	Mike Gaddy	Bivens Steele
Matthews	t	CM	22	(704) 847-4411	Royce Myers	Harley Blodgett	Jill Pleimann	...	...	Robin Hunter	Ralph Messera
Maxton *	t	MC	2	(910) 844-5231	Lillie McKoy	Katrina Tatum	...	Myra Tyndall	...	Paul McDowell	Leonard Green
Mayodan	t	CM	2	(336) 427-0241	Billy Smith	Debra Cardwell	Melessa Hopper	Marcia Pulliam	Bryant Garner	Lawrence Shelton	David Baker
Mebane	t	CM	7	(919) 563-5901	G. Stephenson	Robert Wilson	Elaine Hicks	...	Bob Louis	Gary Bumgarner	Jimmy Jobe
Mills River	t	CM	6	(828) 890-2901	Roger Snyder	Jaime Adrignola	Susan Powell	...	...	...	...
Mint Hill	t	MC	14	(704) 545-9726	...	Brian Welch	Beth Hamrick	...	...	Brian Barnhardt	Dwayne Dorton
Mocksville	t	CM	4	(336) 751-2259	Francis Slate	Christine Sanders	...	...	Phil Crowe	Jack Keller	Danny Smith
Monroe	c	CM	26	(704) 282-4500	...	F. Meadows	Jeanne Deese	Sonia Vizcaino	Ronald Fowler	Robert Haulk	...
Montreat	t	MC	..	(828) 669-8002	...	Ron Nalley	Misty Gedlinske	...	...	William McClintock	Charles Caldwell
Mooresville *	t	CM	18	(704) 663-3800	Al Jones	James Justice	Janet Pope	Maia Setzer	Wesley Greene	John Crone	...
Morehead City	t	CM	7	(252) 726-6848	...	Robert Martin	Jeanne Giblin	Ellen Sewell	Jerry Leonard	Sammie Turner	David McCabe
Morganton	c	CM	17	(828) 437-8863	...	Sally Sandy	Debbie Ogle	Karen Duncan	...	...	Joseph Lookadoo
Morrisville *	t	CM	5	(919) 463-6200	...	John Whitson	Diana Davis	Julia Ketchum	Todd Wright	Ira Jones	Maurice Gunn
Mount Airy	c	CM	8	(336) 786-3501	Jack Loftis	Donald Brookshire	...	John Overton	Benny Brannock	Ronald Hill	Jeffery Boyles
Mount Gilead	t	CM	1	(910) 439-5111	Earl Poplin	...	...	Mary Lucas	Tommy Gaddy	Ronnie Jarman	Curtis Speakman
Mount Holly	c	CM	9	(704) 827-3931	Robert Black	...	...	...	John Calder	C Benson	Donald Price
Mount Olive	t	CM	4	(919) 658-9537	Buster Huggins	Charles Brown	Arlene Talton	...	Steve Martin	Emmett Ballree	Ervin Holland
Murfreesboro *	t	MC	2	(252) 398-5904	Ben McLean	Cathy Davison	Stephanny Marshall	...	Bryant Cook	...	Gene Byrd
Nags Head	t	CM	2	(252) 441-5508	Robert Muller	...	Carolyn Morris	...	...	...	David Clark
Nashville	t	CM	4	(252) 459-4511	Warren Evans	Preston Mitchell	Cynthia Brake	Barbara Woodall	Timothy Pope	William Creech	Larry Williams
New Bern	c	CM	23	(252) 636-4000	Thomas Bayliss	Walter Hartman	Vickie Johnson	Mary Muraglia	Robert Aster	Frank Palombo	Danny Meadows
Newport *	t	CM	3	(252) 223-4749	Derryl Garner	Richard Casey	Penny Weiss	Gay Cox	Rob Holt	Jeffrey Clark	Marty Mensch
Newton	c	CM	12	(828) 695-4260	Robert Mullinax	Everette Clark	Beunice Roberts	James Baker	Kevin Yoder	David Dial	Martin Wilson
North Topsail Beach	c	CM	..	(910) 328-1349	Rodney Knowles	Bradley Smith	Loraine Carbone	Lydia King	...	Daniel Salese	Thomas Best
North Wilkesboro *	t	CM	4	(336) 667-7129	George Church	William Perkins	V Kay Minton	Patsy Billings	Niki Hamby	Randy Rhodes	Robert Bauguess
Norwood	t	CM	2	(704) 463-5423	...	Dwight Smith	...	...	...	...	...
Oak Island	t	CM	6	(910) 278-5011	Helen Cashwell	Jerry Walters	Patricia Brunell	Cathy Harvell	Alan Essey	Thomas Johnson	Gene Kudgus
Oak Ridge	t	CM	3	(336) 644-7009	Ray Combs	Bruce Oakley	Larry Harville	Sam Anders	...	...	...
Ocean Isle Beach	t	CM	..	(910) 579-2166	...	Daisy Ivey	...	...	...	...	...
Oriental	t	CM	..	(252) 249-0555	...	Wyatt Cutler	...	...	...	...	...
Oxford	c	CM	8	(919) 603-1100	Alvin Woodlief	Thomas Marrow	Barbara Rote	Kelway Howard	Lanny Dillehay	John Wolford	...
Pembroke	t	CM	2	(910) 521-9758	...	M. Cummings	...	...	...	...	...
Pilot Mountain	t	CM	1	(336) 368-2248	...	Blair Knox	...	...	...	...	...
Pinehurst	v	CM	9	(910) 295-1900	...	Andrew Wilkison	Linda Brown	...	Jimmy McCaskill	Ernest Hooker	Walter Morgan
Pinetops	t	CM	1	(252) 827-4435	J Cobb	Gregory Bethea	...	...	...	...	...
Pineville	t	CM	3	(704) 889-2291	George Fowler	Michael Rose	Sara Rodriguez	Ann Wilson	Billy Griffin	Robert Merchant	Bobby Howington
Pittsboro	t	CM	2	(919) 542-4621	Nancy May	William Terry	Alice Lloyd	...	...	Jerry Clapp	John Poteat
Plymouth	t	CM	4	(252) 793-9101	Jarahnee Bailey	James Tripp	...	...	Jack Barnes	Steve O'Neil	William Ehrenbeck
Princeville	t	CM	..	(252) 823-1057	P. Everette-Oates	Samuel Knight	Diana Draughn	Pamela Barlow	...	Gary Foxx	...
Raeford	c	CM	3	(910) 875-8161	John McNeill	Richard Douglas	...	Raymond Teal	Dickie Lippard	Kevin Locklear	Johnny Melton
Raleigh	c	CM	276	(919) 890-3315	Charles Meeker	J Allen	Gail Smith	Perry James	Earl Fowler	Jane Perlov	Carl Dawson
Randleman	c	CM	3	(336) 495-7500	...	Tony Sears	...	Nicole Belgarde	Martin Leonard	Steve Leonard	...
Red Springs *	t	CM	3	(910) 843-5241	George Paris	Billy Farmer	...	Regenia Humphrey	George Hall	Troy McDuffie	Philip Smith
Reidsville	c	CM	14	(336) 349-1058	...	Dennis Almond	Angela Stadler	Christopher Phillips	David Bracken	William Hunt	...
Rhodhiss *	t	CM	..	(828) 396-8400	...	...	...	...	...	...	...
Richlands	t	CM	..	(910) 324-3301	Marvin Trott	Gregg Whitehead	Eva Brown	...	...	Thomas Bennett	Jimmy Powell
River Bend	t	CM	2	(252) 638-3870	John Kirkland	Andrew Havens	Ann Katsuyoshi	Margaret Boggs	...	Earl Pratt	Thomas Datt
Roanoke Rapids	c	CM	16	(252) 533-2800	Drewery Beale	...	Lisa Vincent	Phyllis Lee	Kenneth Carawan	James Lawson	James Parnell
Rockingham	c	CM	9	(910) 997-5546	Eugene McLaurin	Monty Crump	Johnsye Lunsford	Hazel Tew	Curtis Bennett	Robert Voorhees	Richard Haugen
Rocky Mount *	c	CM	55	(252) 972-1111	John Turnage	Stephen Raper	Jean Bailey	Amy Staton	Keith Harris	John Manley	Jonathan Boone
Rolesville	t	CM	..	(919) 556-3506	Nancy Kelly	Matthew Livingston	Lynn House	...	...	Jimmy Green	...
Rose Hill	t	MC	1	(910) 289-3159	Clarence Brown	Thomas Drum	Jeannette Cloud	...	...	Michael O'Connell	Jerry James
Roxboro	c	CM	8	(336) 599-3116	Steve Joyner	Jonathan Barlow	Cheryl Barnette	James Overton	Jonathan Rorie	Jeffrey Insley	Lindsay Mize
Rutherfordton	t	MC	4	(828) 287-3520	Sally Lesher	Karen Andrews	Jennifer Armstrong	Rus Scherer	Charles Blanton	Kevin Lovelace	Keith Ward
Saint Pauls	t	CM	2	(910) 865-5164	Gordon Westbrook	...	Annie Espey	...	Evans Jackson	Tommy Hagens	Wayne McDuffie
Salisbury	c	CM	26	(704) 638-5270	Susan Kluttz	David Treme	Myra Heard	John Sofley	Samuel Brady	Lester Wilhelm	Vernon Sherrill
Sanford	c	CM	23	(919) 775-8348	Winston Hester	Phillip Hegwer	Bonnie White	Melissa Miller	Teddy Barber	Ronald Yarborough	Larry Thomas
Sawmills	t	CM	4	(828) 396-7903	Max Andrews	...	Wanda Reid	Deanna Rios	...	...	Arnold Arrowood
Scotland Neck	t	MC	2	(252) 826-3152	Robert Partin	Russell Tutor	Nancy Jackson	...	Bruce Josey	Doug Pilgreen	Doug Braddy
Selma	t	CM	5	(919) 965-9841	Charles Hester	Stan Farmer	Fran Davis	Erica Walters	Joe Price	Charles Bowen	Terry Keen
Seven Devils	t	CM	..	(828) 963-5343	...	Robert Lambert	Catherine Pinson	Steven Smith	Bobby Powell	Joe Buchanan	Kevin Aldridge
Shallotte	t	MC	1	(910) 754-4032	...	Paul Sabiston	...	Maria Gaither	...	Rodney Gause	Albert Hughes
Sharpsburg	t	CM	2	(252) 446-9441	...	Sonya Meeks	...	...	...	...	...
Shelby *	c	CM	19	(704) 484-6471	W Alexander	James Howell	B. Parduski	Ted Phillips	William Hunt	Tandy Carter	Brad Cornwell
Siler City	t	CM	6	(919) 742-4731	Charles Turner	Joel Brower	Karen Alman	Wanda Ingold	Mitch Vann	Lewis Phillips	Arthur Green
Smithfield	t	CM	11	(919) 934-2116	William Jordan	Peter Connet	Debra Holmes	Robert Plowman	Patrick Harris	Steven Gillikin	Marty Anderson
Southern Pines	t	CM	10	(910) 692-7021	Frank Quis	Reagan Parsons	...	Crystal Gabric	Hampton Williams	John Letteney	...
Southern Shores	t	CM	2	(252) 261-2394	Paul Sutherland	Webb Fuller	Carrie Gordin	...	...	Thaddeous Pledger	Glenn Alexander
Southport	c	CM	2	(910) 457-7929	Norman Holden	Robert Gandy	Regina Alexander	Patty Miller	Gregory Cumbee	Jerry Dove	Robert Grant
Spencer *	t	CM	3	(704) 633-2231	Alicia Bean	Larry Smith	Lisa Perdue	...	Joel Baker	Robert Bennett	Richard Paestella
Spindale	t	CM	4	(828) 286-3466	...	John Lewis	Teresa Curtis	Kathleen Swafford	Harton Turner	Charles Deviney	Benny Brooks
Spring Hope	t	CM	1	(252) 478-5186	James Gwaltney	John Holpe	...	...	...	Timothy Denton	George Meeks
Spring Lake	t	CM	8	(910) 436-0241	Ethel Clark	Edward Faison	Cora Nunes	Allen Coats	Robert Doberstein	Alvin Brown	Daniel Gerald
Stallings	t	CM	3	(704) 824-8557	...	Brian Matthews	...	...	...	...	...
Stanley	t	CM	3	(704) 263-4779	Judith Johnson	Robert Greback	Evyonne Smith	Reva Braswell	...	Heath Jenkins	Hildreth Miller
Stantonsburg	0	CM	..	(252) 238-3608	...	Gary Davis	...	...	...	...	...
Statesville *	c	CM	23	(704) 878-3550	Constantine Kutteh	Robert Hites	Mary Craddock	Lisa Salmon	...	Stephen Hampton	...
Stoneville	t	MC	1	(336) 573-9393	Sammy Tuggle	Robert Wyatt	Marilyn Smith	Amy Winn	Hugh Belton	Gary Walker	Jerry Whitt
Sugar Mountain	v	MC	..	(828) 898-9292	David Nixon	David Lane	Amy Keller	Kay Sudderth	...	David Henson	David Webb
Sunset Beach	t	CM	1	(910) 579-6297	Ronald Klein	Linda Fluegel	Kimberly Cochran	James Jones	Chris Barbee	Lisa Massey	John Hancock
Surf City	t	CM	1	(910) 328-4131	A. D. Guy	J. Moore	Patricia Arnold	Jane Kirk	Joey Rivenbark	Michael Halstrad	Dean Wise
Swansboro	t	CM	1	(910) 326-4428	Paul Edgerton	...	Paula Webb	Marina Williams	Max Powell	Harry Publiese	Daniel Crisman
Tabor City	t	CM	2	(910) 653-3458	...	Al Leonard	...	...	...	...	...
Tarboro *	t	CM	11	(252) 641-4200	Donald Morris	Samuel Noble	Pamela Pate	Janet Lewis	William Whitaker	Robert Cherry	David Cashwell
Taylorsville	t	CM	1	(828) 632-2218	Guy Barriger	David Odom	Yolanda Prince	...	...	Anthony Jones	David Robinette
Thomasville	c	CM	19	(336) 475-4210	Joe Bennett	...	Betty Almond	Tony Jarrett	Martin Dailey	Larry Murdock	...
Tobaccoville	v	CM	1	(336) 983-0029	Keith Snow	Leo Corder	Robin Key	...	...	...	Dale Hauser
Topsail Beach	t	CM	..	(910) 328-5841	Edward Parrish	Jim Carter	S. Rivenbark	...	Andy Cavender	Rickey Smith	Charles Derrick

Directory 1/9 **OFFICIALS IN U.S. MUNICIPALITIES 2,500 AND OVER IN POPULATION**
continued

Jurisdiction	Type	Form of govern- ment	2000 Popu- lation (000)	Main telephone number	Chief elected official	Appointed administrator	Clerk of the governing board	Chief financial officer	Fire chief	Police chief	Public works director
NORTH CAROLINA continued											
Trent Woods	t	MC	4	(252) 637-9810	J. Day	...	Tina Woolard	Glenda Bynum	...	Michael Register	Michael Haber
Trinity	c	CM	6	(336) 431-2841	...	Debbie Hinson	...	...	...	...	...
Troutman	t	CM	1	(704) 528-7600	Elbert Richardson	David Saleeby	Kim Davis	Steve Shealy	...	...	...
Troy	t	CM	3	(910) 572-3661	Roy Maness	Greg Zephir	...	Cathy Maness	Joe Huntley	E. Phillips	Gray Walls
Tryon	* t	CM	1	(828) 859-6654	J Peoples	James Fatland	Susan Bell	...	Joey Davis	Jeff Arrowood	Joel Burrell
Valdese	* t	CM	4	(828) 879-2120	James Hatley	Jeffrey Morse	Frances Hildebran	Jerry LaMaster	Charles Watts	John Suttle	Bryan Duckworth
Wadesboro	t	CM	3	(704) 694-5171	Lynn Horton	John Witherspoon	Nancy Huntley	...	Eddie Pope	...	Ben Barber
Wake Forest	t	CM	12	(919) 554-6100	Vivian Jones	Mark Williams	Joyce Wilson	Aileen Staples	...	...	Michael Barton
Walkertown	* t	CM	4	(336) 595-4212	Kenneth Davis	...	Carol McKinnie	...	...	...	...
Wallace	t	CM	3	(910) 285-4136	Charles Farrior	Roger Cornatzer	...	Anna Leary	Thomas Townsend	Bobby Maready	...
Walnut Cove	* t	CM	1	(336) 591-4809	...	Homer Dearmin	Leslie Falstreau	...	...	Barry Conaway	Kevin Webb
Warrenton	t	CM	..	(252) 257-3315	Walter Gardner	Larry Carver	...	...	...	Freddie Robinson	Paul Brown
Warsaw	t	MC	3	(910) 293-7814	Win Batten	Jason Burrell	...	Myra Mays	John Blackmore	Raymond Wood	Gerald Lanier
Washington	c	CM	9	(252) 975-9300	Lee Rumley	James Smith	Rita Thompson	Carol Williams	Nelson Pyle	Joseph Stringer	Raymond Lewis
Waxhaw	0	CM	2	(704) 843-2195	...	Francis McLaurin	...	...	...	...	...
Waynesville	t	CM	9	(828) 452-2491	Henry Foy	A. Galloway	Phyllis McClure	Eddie Caldwell	William Fowler	William Hollingsed	Fred Baker
Weaverville	t	CM	2	(828) 645-7116	Mary Stroud	Michael Morgan	Shelby Shields	Brenda Ayers	Fred Sims	Gregory Stephens	Lawrence Sprinkle
Weddington	* t	CM	6	(704) 846-2709	Nancy Anderson	...	Amy McCollum	Leslie Gaylord	...	...	...
Wendell	t	CM	4	(919) 365-4444	Lucius Jones	David Bone	...	Barbara Raper	...	Joseph Privette	Donnie Ayscue
West Jefferson	t	CM	1	(336) 246-3551	Dale Baldwin	Steven McGinnis	...	Katherine Howell	Calvin Green	James Williams	David Hamilton
Whiteville	c	CM	5	(910) 642-8046	Anne Jones	Joshua Ray	...	Douglas Palmer	Bill Poe	Robert Memory	...
Wilkesboro	* t	CM	3	(336) 838-3951	Norman Call	Kenneth Noland	Josephine Cass	...	Mike Testerman	Robert Bowlin	Jim Wyatt
Williamston	t	MC	5	(252) 792-5142	Tommy Roberson	Donald Christopher	Glinda Fox	Ronnie Wilson	James Peele	Mark Smith	Kerry Spivey
Wilmington	c	CM	75	(910) 341-7800	Harper Peterson	Sterling Cheatham	A. Spicer-Sidbury	William McAbee	Samuel Hill	John Cease	...
Wilson	* c	CM	44	(252) 399-2300	Calvin Rose	Grant Goings	Rebecca Rose	Gordon Baker	Donald Oliver	...	...
Windsor	t	CM	2	(252) 794-2331	...	Allen Castelloe	...	...	...	Scott Stroud	Mike Brower
Wingate	t	MC	2	(704) 233-4411	Tony Maye	Greyson Blanchard	Mildred Parks	...	...	...	...
Winston-Salem	c	CM	185	(336) 747-6800	Allen Joines	Lee Garrity	Renee Henderson	Denise Bell	John Gist	Patricia Norris	...
Winterville	t	CM	4	(252) 756-2221	Douglas Jackson	William Whisnant	Tangi Leary	Anthony Bowers	...	Billy Wilkes	Bobby Crawford
Woodfin	t	MC	3	(828) 253-4887	Alvin Honeycutt	Jason Young	Cheryl Mears	...	...	William Krause	Dewey Wills
Wrightsville Beach	t	CM	2	(910) 256-7900	James Roberts	Robert Simpson	Sylvia Holleman	Peggy Jones	...	John Carey	Michael Vukelich
Yadkinville	t	CM	2	(336) 679-8732	Hubert Gregory	Kenneth Larking	Nancy Hollar	...	...	William Parks	Perry Williams
Yanceyville	* t	CM	2	(336) 694-5431	Dan Printz	David Parrish	...	Carolyn Hall	...	Greg Gibson	Mark Guthrie
Youngsville	t	CM	..	(919) 556-5073	...	Brenda Robbins	...	...	...	...	...
Zebulon	t	CM	4	(919) 269-7455	Robert Matheny	Richard Hardin	Lisa Markland	Emily Thomas	Sidney Perry	Timothy Hayworth	Kenneth Waldroup
NORTH DAKOTA											
Beulah	c	MC	3	(701) 873-4637	...	...	...	...	...	...	...
Bismarck	* c	CO	55	(701) 222-6471	John Warford	William Wocken	...	Sheila Hillman	Joel Boespflug	Keith Witt	...
Bottineau	c	MC	2	(701) 228-3232	...	...	...	...	...	...	...
Carrington	c	MC	2	(701) 652-2911	Donald Frye	Vicky Triplett	...	...	...	Randy Munkeby	Doug Schroeder
Cavalier	* c	MC	1	(701) 265-8800	Ronald Storie	Thomas Trenbeath	Christal Schlecht	Katie Werner	...	David Peterson	Barry Walton
Devils Lake	c	CO	7	(701) 662-7600	Fred Bott	Terry Johnston	Carol Donnelly	...	James Moe	Bruce Kemmet	...
Dickinson	* c	CO	16	(701) 456-7744	Dennis Johnson	Greg Sund	Cindy Selinger	Tina Fisher	Robert Sivak	Chuck Rummel	...
Fargo	c	MC	90	(701) 241-1334	Bruce Furness	Patrick Zavoral	...	Kent Costin	Bruce Hoover	Keith Ternes	...
Grafton	c	MC	4	(701) 352-1561	...	...	...	...	...	...	...
Grand Forks	c	MC	49	(701) 746-2665	Michael Brown	Richard Duquette	...	John Schmisek	Peter O'Neill	John Packett	Todd Feland
Harvey	c	MC	1	(701) 324-2000	Wes Arnold	Kim Moen	...	...	Gary Troftgruben	Larry Hoffer	Robert Weninger
Jamestown	c	MC	15	(701) 252-5900	...	...	...	...	...	...	...
Mandan	c	CO	16	(701) 667-3210	Robert Dykshoorn	Kevin Christ	...	...	Pete Gartner	...	Pete Snider
Minot	c	CM	36	(701) 857-4756	Curt Zimbelman	David Waind	...	Cindy Hemphill	Harold Haugstad	Jeffrey Balentine	Alan Walter
Rugby	c	MC	2	(701) 776-6181	Dale Niewoehner	Howard Burns	Phyllis Johnson	...	William Hartl	Robert Walls	Jerome Voeller
Valley City	c	CO	6	(701) 845-1700	...	...	...	...	...	...	...
Wahpeton	c	MC	8	(701) 642-8448	Duane Schmitz	Shawn Kessel	...	Darcie Huwe	Don Klovstad	Scott Throsteinson	Randall Nelson
Watford City	c	MC	1	(701) 444-2533	...	Lowell Cutshaw	...	...	...	...	...
West Fargo	c	CO	14	(701) 282-3843	...	...	...	...	...	...	...
Williston	c	CO	12	(701) 572-8161	...	...	...	...	...	...	...
OHIO											
Ada	v	MC	5	(419) 634-4045	...	...	...	...	...	Ray Mumma	...
Akron	c	MC	217	(330) 375-2726	Donald Plusquellic	Jerry Holland	...	D. Miller-Dawson	Charles Gladman	Max Rothal	Paul Barnett
Alliance	c	MC	23	(330) 821-3110	Toni Middleton	John Blaser	...	Alexander Zumbar	James Reese	Lawrence Dordea	...
Amberley	v	CM	3	(513) 531-8675	Charles Kamine	Bernard Boraten	Patricia Eisenmann	Margaret Crowley	...	John Monahan	Stephen Rasfeld
Amherst	c	MC	11	(440) 988-4380	John Higgins	...	Olga Sivinski	Diane Eswine	Ralph Zilch	Lonnie Dillon	...
Anderson Township	* tp	MC	43	(513) 474-5560	...	Henry Dolive	Kenneth Dietz	Mark Ober	...	...	Richard Shelley
Anna	v	MC	1	(937) 394-3751	...	Jon Hulsmeyer	Kathleen Eshleman	...	...	Charles Shepherd	Daniel Patterson
Arcanum	v	MC	2	(937) 692-8500	Larry Foureman	Philip Courtright	...	Lori Huffman	Ken Williams	Dan Light	...
Archbold	v	MC	4	(419) 445-4726	James Wyse	Dennis Howell	Laurie Storrer	Joan Lovejoy	...	Martin Schmidt	...
Ashland	c	MC	21	(419) 289-3426	William Strine	...	...	Nancy Boyd	Mark Burgess	...	...
Ashtabula	* c	MC	20	(440) 992-7103	Robert Beacom	August Pugliese	La Vette Hennigan	Michael Zullo	Ron Pristera	...	Dominic Iarocci
Ashville	* v	CM	3	(740) 983-6367	Chuck Wise	Frank Christman	...	Nelson Embrey	...	Jerry Pennington	...
Athens	c	MC	21	(740) 592-3338	Richard Abel	Wayne Key	Debra Walker	Jimmy Stewart	Robert Troxel	Richard Mayer	James Norris
Aurora	c	MC	13	(330) 995-9100	Lynn McGill	...	Tracy Humbert	Robert Paul	David Barnes	Seth Riewaldt	John Trew
Avon	c	MC	11	(440) 937-7800	James Smith	...	Ellen Young	Robert Hamilton	Frank Root	John Vilagi	...
Avon Lake	c	MC	18	(440) 933-6141	Robert Berner	...	...	Joseph Newlin	Lawrence Grizzell	David Owad	John Kniepper
Baltimore	v	MC	2	(740) 862-4491	Robert Kalish	Terry McGrath	...	Florence Welker	...	Bret Rogers	...
Barberton	c	MC	27	(330) 753-6611	...	...	...	...	...	...	...
Barnesville	* v	CM	4	(740) 425-3444	Thomas Michelli	Roger Deal	...	Amy Jackson	Robert Smith	David Norris	...
Bay Village	c	MC	16	(440) 871-2200	Deborah Sutherland	...	Joan Kemper	Steven Presley	Gregory Jackson	David Wright	James Sears
Beachwood	* c	MC	12	(216) 464-1070	Merle Gorden	...	Carol Vinyard	David Pfaff	Patrick Kearns	Mark Sechrist	Dale Pekarek
Beavercreek	c	CM	37	(937) 427-5500	Robert Glaser	Michael Cornell	Lucia Ball	...	...	Arthur Scott	Ronald Huff
Bedford	* c	CM	14	(440) 232-1600	Daniel Pocek	Robert Reid	Kathleen Lynch	Frank Gambosi	David Nagy	Gregory Duber	Clinton Bellar
Bedford Heights	c	MC	11	(440) 439-1600	Debora Mallin	...	Patricia Stahl	Mark Cegelka	Ken Ledford	Tim Kalavsky	Nick Baucco
Bellaire	c	MC	4	(740) 676-6538	...	...	...	...	...	...	...
Bellbrook	c	CM	7	(937) 848-4666	...	David Hamilton	...	...	...	...	...
Bellefontaine	c	MC	13	(937) 592-4376	Robert Lentz	Garon Carmean	...	Tim Decker	James Holycross	Bradley Kunze	...
Bellevue	c	MC	8	(419) 484-8400	George Branco	Gary Haynes	Vickie Dauch	Linda Cooper-Smith	Sherrard Barr	Richard Englund	...
Belpre	c	MC	6	(740) 423-7592	Richard Thomas	Willis Neff	...	Patrick Hines	Wesley Walker	Ira Walker	Michael Betz
Berea	* c	MC	18	(440) 826-5800	J. Biddlecombe	...	...	Dana Kavander	Theodore Novak	Harry Bernhardt	R. Brown
Bethel	tp	CM	4	(937) 845-8472	...	Kathryn Reagan	Deborah Watson	...	F. Reittinger	...	...
Bethel	v	CM	2	(513) 734-2243	David Simpson	Michael Shiverski	...	...	...	...	...

Directory 1/9 continued — OFFICIALS IN U.S. MUNICIPALITIES 2,500 AND OVER IN POPULATION

Jurisdiction	Type	Form of govern-ment	2000 Popu-lation (000)	Main telephone number	Chief elected official	Appointed administrator	Clerk of the governing board	Chief financial officer	Fire chief	Police chief	Public works director
OHIO continued											
Bexley	c	MC	13	(614) 235-8694	David Madison	. . .	. . .	Beecher Hale	. . .	John Carruthers	Dorothy Pritchard
Blanchester	v	MC	4	(937) 783-4702	Harry Brumbaugh	. . .	James Walker	. . .	. . .	Robert Gable	Myers James
Blue Ash	c	CM	12	(513) 745-8500	Rick Bryan	David Waltz	. . .	Sherry Poppe	James Fehr	Chris Wallace	Dennis Albrinck
Bluffton	v	MC	3	(419) 358-2066	. . .	James Mehaffie	. . .	. . .	. . .	. . .	. . .
Botkins	v	MC	1	(937) 693-3856	James King	M. Van Brocklin	. . .	. . .	. . .	. . .	. . .
Bowling Green *	c	MC	29	(419) 353-6200	John Quinn	John Fawcett	Kay Scherreik	Brian Bushong	Stephen Meredith	Gary Spencer	Brian Craft
Brecksville *	c	MC	13	(440) 526-4351	Jerry Hruby	. . .	Mary Scullin	Virginia Price	Edwin Egut	Dennis Kancler	Robert Pech
Bridgeport	v	MC	2	(740) 635-9998	John Callarik	. . .	Betty Riley	. . .	Mark Subasic	William Frasher	. . .
Broadview Heights	c	MC	15	(440) 526-4357	Glenn Goodwin	. . .	Annette Phelps	Linda Pertz	Lee Ippolito	Robert Lipton	Raymond Mack
Brook Park	c	MC	21	(216) 433-1300	Thomas Coyne	. . .	Roseann Armstrong	Gregory Cingle	Neal Donnelly	Thomas Dease	. . .
Brooklyn	c	MC	11	(216) 351-2133	John Coyne	. . .	Nathan Felker	. . .	Daniel Smetana	James Maloney	T. Morgan
Brooklyn Heights *	v	MC	1	(216) 749-4300	Michael Procuk	. . .	. . .	. . .	Michael Lasky	Joseph Kocab	. . .
Brookville	c	CM	5	(937) 833-2135	. . .	John Wright	. . .	Sonja Keaton	James Nickel	Edgar Preston	. . .
Brunswick	c	CM	33	(330) 225-9144	. . .	Robert Zienkowski	Barb Ortiz	Bill White	Mark Schrade	Carl DeForest	Sam Scaffide
Bryan	c	MC	8	(419) 636-4232	Douglas Johnson	. . .	. . .	John Seele	Jerry Manon	Gregory Brillhart	Stephen Casebere
Buckeye Lake	v	MC	3	(740) 928-7100	Frank Foster	. . .	Tim Matheny	. . .	Pete Leindecker	Ronald Small	. . .
Bucyrus	c	MC	13	(419) 562-6767	Douglas Wilson	Jack Binnix	Regina Zornes	Carol Wagner	Daniel Ross	Michael Corwin	. . .
Byesville	v	MC	2	(740) 685-5901	Donald Gadd	Richard Rausch	Tracey Cain	. . .	Brian Sills	John Hornak	Thomas McVicker
Cadiz	v	MC	3	(740) 942-8844	Don Bethel	. . .	. . .	. . .	. . .	Dwight Spaar	Thomas Carter
Cambridge	c	MC	11	(740) 439-1240	Charles Schaub	. . .	Sharon Cassler	Sue Ellen Johnson	William Minter	Brian Neff	Jerry Williams
Campbell	c	MC	9	(330) 755-1451	. . .	Charles Terek	Judith Clement	Dennis Stephens	David Horvath	Nicholas Phillips	Robert Davis
Canal Fulton *	c	MC	5	(330) 854-2225	John Grogan	Mark Cozy	Tammy Marthey	Scott Svab	Ray Green	David Frisone	Daniel Mayberry
Canal Winchester	v	MC	4	(614) 837-7493	Jeffery Miller	. . .	. . .	Nanisa Osborn	. . .	. . .	. . .
Canfield	c	CM	7	(330) 533-1101	. . .	Charles Tieche	Patricia Matevich	Sandra Mayberry	. . .	David Blystone	Ronald Wiant
Canton	c	MC	80	(330) 489-3000	Richard Watkins	Michael Miller	Debra Vanckunas	Kim Perez	James Scott	Dean McKim	Kevin Monroe
Cardington *	v	MC	1	(419) 864-7607	Franklin Perry	Daniel Ralley	Darlene Wallace	Kathy Belcher	. . .	. . .	. . .
Carey	v	MC	3	(419) 396-7681	Dallas Risner	Roy Johnson	Antonia Ahlberg	. . .	Chad Snyder	Dennis Yingling	Todd Spurlock
Carlisle	v	CM	5	(937) 746-0555	Gerald Ellendar	. . .	Flo Cracraft	. . .	Gregory Wallace	Timothy Boggess	Gaylon Brown
Carrollton *	v	MC	3	(330) 627-2411	Stan Bright	Robert Fowler	. . .	Judi Noble	Robert Herron	Ronald Yeager	. . .
Cedarville	v	MC	3	(937) 766-2061	James Phipps	Paul Terrell	. . .	. . .	. . .	Keith Stigers	. . .
Celina	c	MC	10	(419) 586-6464	Craig Klopfleisch	Thomas Schwartz	Barbara Belknap	Patrick Smith	Douglas Kuhn	David Slusser	Dennis Zahn
Centerville	c	CM	23	(937) 433-7151	Mark Kingseed	Gregory Horn	Marilyn McLaughlin	Mark Schlagheck	. . .	Stephen Walker	Robert James
Chagrin Falls *	v	MC	4	(440) 247-5050	Thomas Brick	Benjamin Himes	. . .	David Bloom	James Leffler	James Brosius	. . .
Chardon	c	CM	5	(440) 286-2600	John Park	David Lelko	. . .	Jeffrey Smock	. . .	Tim McKenna	Gayland Moore
Cheviot	c	MC	9	(513) 661-2700	J. Laumann	Steven Neal	. . .	Debra Gooch	. . .	. . .	Thomas Braun
Chillicothe	c	MC	21	(740) 774-1185	Margaret Planton	. . .	. . .	William Morrissey	Bruce Vaughan	. . .	Richard Johnson
Cincinnati *	c	CM	331	(513) 352-2400	Mark Mallory	Milton Dohoney	Melissa Autry	William Moller	Robert Wright	Thomas Streicher	Andrew Glenn
Circleville	c	MC	13	(740) 477-2551	Pat Radabaugh	. . .	Linda Chancey	Gayle Spangler	. . .	. . .	. . .
Clayton	c	MC	13	(937) 836-3500	Joyce Deitering	David Rowlands	Wilbur Sussman	Ferris Brown	. . .	. . .	Jim Percival
Cleveland	c	MC	478	(216) 664-2000	Frank Jackson	Darnell Brown	. . .	Sharon Dumas	. . .	. . .	. . .
Cleveland Heights *	c	CM	49	(216) 291-4444	. . .	Robert Downey	. . .	Thomas Malone	Kevin Mohr	Martin Lentz	Alex Mannarino
Clyde	c	CM	6	(419) 547-6898	. . .	Daniel Weaver	Tami Steinbauer	Christine May	James Andrews	Bruce Gower	. . .
Coal Grove	v	MC	2	(740) 533-0102	Bernard McKnight	Mark Dean	Juanita Markel	. . .	. . .	John Goldcamp	. . .
Coldwater	v	MC	4	(419) 678-4881	Vern Stammen	. . .	Clyde Bellinger	. . .	. . .	Gery Thobe	John Moorman
Colerain Township *	tp	MC	60	(513) 385-7500	Keith Corman	David Foglesong	. . .	Heather Harlow	G. Smith	Steven Sarver	Bruce McClain
Columbiana	v	CM	5	(330) 482-2173	Lowell Schloneger	Keith Chamberlin	Deann Davis	Mary Dicken	Charles Flohr	John Krawchyk	Jay Groner
Columbus	c	MC	711	(614) 645-8100	Michael Coleman	. . .	T. McSweeney	Joel Taylor	Ned Pettus	James Jackson	Linda Page
Conneaut *	c	CM	12	(440) 593-7401	James Jones	Douglas Lewis	Pamela Harper	John Williams	Bim Orrenmaa	John Arcaro	Bob Howland
Copley *	tp	MC	13	(330) 666-1853	Dale Panovich	Peggy Spraggins	. . .	Janice Marhall	. . .	Michael Mier	. . .
Cortland	v	MC	6	(330) 637-3916	Curt Moll	. . .	Donna Lyden	Fran Moyer	William Novakovich	Gary Mink	Don Wittman
Coshocton *	c	MC	11	(740) 622-1465	Timothy Turner	Jerry Stenner	. . .	Lois Murphy	Mike Layton	. . .	. . .
Covington	v	MC	2	(937) 473-2102	Lowell Yingst	. . .	. . .	Kay McKinney	C. Westfall	Rick Wright	Michael Manson
Crestline	c	MC	5	(419) 683-3800	Peter Dzugan	Eugene Toy	Annette Johnston	Jody Wagoner	David Bauer	Edward Wilhite	. . .
Crooksville	v	MC	2	(740) 982-2656	Douglas Cannon	Thomas Collins	Kathy Campbell	. . .	Kenneth Alexander	Robin Zinn	. . .
Cuyahoga Falls	c	MC	49	(330) 971-8000	Don Robart	. . .	. . .	Joseph Brodzinsky	Mark Snyder	John Conley	Valerie Wax Carr
Dayton	c	CM	166	(937) 333-4047	Rhine McLin	Rashad Young	Leonard Roberts	Cheryl Garrett	Larry Collins	Julian Davis	Frederick Stovall
Deer Park *	c	MC	5	(513) 794-8860	David Collins	Michael Berens	. . .	John Applegate	. . .	Michael Schlie	. . .
Defiance *	c	MC	16	(419) 782-3193	. . .	Jeff Leonard	. . .	John Seele	Mark Marentette	Norman Walker	. . .
Delaware *	c	CM	25	(740) 203-1000	Windell Wheeler	R. Homan	Cindy Dinovo	Dean Stelzer	John Donahue	Russell Martin	Tim Browning
Delhi	tp	MC	30	(513) 922-3111	Jerome Luebbers	Gerard Schroeder	Kenneth Ryan	. . .	Harold Edwards	Thomas Bauer	Robert Bass
Delphos	c	MC	6	(419) 695-4010	Gerald Neumeier	Gregory Berquist	. . .	Tom Jettinghoff	David McNeal	David Wagner	. . .
Delta	v	CM	2	(419) 822-4500	. . .	. . .	Valerie Edwards	. . .	. . .	Garry Chamberlin	. . .
Dennison	v	MC	2	(740) 922-4072	. . .	. . .	. . .	. . .	Charles Pulley	. . .	. . .
Dover	c	MC	12	(330) 343-6395	R. Homrighausen	. . .	. . .	Mary Fox	Russell Volkert	Ronald Johnson	. . .
Dublin	c	CM	31	(614) 410-4400	Thomas McCash	Jane Brautigam	Anne Clarke	Marsha Grigsby	. . .	. . .	. . .
East Cleveland	c	MC	27	(216) 681-5020	Eric Brewer	. . .	. . .	. . .	Bobby Jenkins	Mitchell Guyton	R. Kenniebrew
East Liverpool	c	MC	13	(330) 385-3381	Dolores Satow	Paul Wise	. . .	Kim Woomer	Gerald Barcus	Michael McVay	Robert Disch
East Palestine	c	CM	4	(330) 426-4367	Raymond Hull	Gary Clark	Cindy Clark	Constance Robinson	Brett Todd	Clyde Hoffmeister	John Jurjaucic
Eastlake	c	MC	20	(440) 951-1416	Dan Dilberto	. . .	Deborah Cendvoski	John Masterson	Richard Sabo	John Ruth	William Philipp
Eaton	c	CM	8	(937) 456-4125	Robert Ball	Martin Gabbard	. . .	Leslie Renner	Richard Crowe	Jeff Fuller	John Hornbrook
Elmwood Place	v	MC	2	(513) 242-2578	Richard Ellison	. . .	Ronald Hamm	. . .	Terry Zimmerman	Douglas Herberger	. . .
Elyria	c	MC	55	(440) 326-1404	William Grace	. . .	. . .	Thaddeus Pileski	John Zielinski	Michael Medders	Thomas Brand
Englewood *	c	CM	12	(937) 836-5106	Michael Bowers	Eric Smith	. . .	Robert Fortman	Elmer Bergman	Mark Brownfield	. . .
Enon	v	MC	2	(937) 864-7870	Jerry Crane	Timothy Howard	Stephen Trout	. . .	. . .	Paul Wilmer	. . .
Euclid	c	MC	52	(440) 289-2700	. . .	. . .	. . .	. . .	. . .	. . .	. . .
Evendale *	v	MC	3	(513) 563-2244	Don Apking	. . .	Michelle Ficke	George Snyder	John Vail	Gary Foust	Jim Bothe
Fairborn *	c	CM	32	(937) 754-3021	. . .	Deborah McDonnell	. . .	. . .	Michael Riley	Terry Barlow	Robert Sowers
Fairfield	c	CM	42	(513) 867-5300	Ronald D'Epifanio	Arthur Pizzano	Dena Morsch	Mary Hopton	Donald Bennett	Michael Dickey	David Bock
Fairfield	tp	MC	15	(513) 887-4400	Joe McAbee	Kate Earley	Chris Fontaine	. . .	Dave Downie	D. Kirsch	. . .
Fairlawn	c	MC	7	(330) 668-9500	William Roth	. . .	Tonja Caldwell	Jerry Apple	Glenn Goodrich	Kenneth Walsh	John Sellars
Fairport Harbor	v	MC	3	(440) 352-3620	Frank Sarosy	Thomas Hilston	. . .	. . .	Jeffrey Hogya	Mark Kish	. . .
Fairview Park	c	MC	17	(440) 333-2200	Eileen Patton	. . .	Traci Waldron	Ted Kowalski	David Simon	Patrick Nealon	. . .
Fayette	v	CM	1	(419) 237-2116	Anita VanZile	Thomas Spiess	. . .	Lisa Zuver	Tom Franks	Rick Kline	. . .
Findlay	c	MC	38	(419) 424-7137	John Stozich	Robert Ruse	Sally Cassidy	Janet Wobser	Roy De Vore	Tom Renninger	. . .
Forest Park	c	CM	19	(513) 595-5200	. . .	Ray Hodges	Kathy Lives	Lois Reynolds	Patricia Brooks	Kenneth Hughes	Dave Buesking
Fort Shawnee *	v	MC	3	(419) 991-2015	Dennis Shaffer	. . .	. . .	Twyla Overman	. . .	Benjamin Kehres	. . .
Fostoria	c	MC	13	(419) 435-8282	John Davoli	Ronald Reinhard	Paul Allison	. . .	Russell Rite	Phil Hobbs	. . .
Franklin *	c	CM	11	(937) 746-9921	Todd Hall	James Lukas	Jane McGee	Mike Robinette	J. Westendorf	Gordon Ellis	Howard Lewis
Fremont	c	MC	17	(419) 334-2687	Terry Overmyer	. . .	. . .	. . .	Daniel De Vanna	Monte Huss	Kenneth Myers
Gahanna	c	MC	32	(614) 342-4000	R. Stinchcomb	. . .	Connie McGlish	W. Isler	Dennis Murphy	. . .	Roland Hall
Galion *	c	CM	11	(419) 468-1680	. . .	David Oles	. . .	James Graff	Michael Christini	Brian Saterfield	. . .

Directory 1/9 continued — OFFICIALS IN U.S. MUNICIPALITIES 2,500 AND OVER IN POPULATION

Jurisdiction	Type	Form of govern-ment	2000 Popu-lation (000)	Main telephone number	Chief elected official	Appointed administrator	Clerk of the governing board	Chief financial officer	Fire chief	Police chief	Public works director
OHIO continued											
Gallipolis	c	CM	4	(740) 446-1789	Dow Saunders	R Jenkins	. . .	Annette Landers	W Poling	Roger Brandeberry	. . .
Garfield Heights	c	MC	30	(216) 475-1100	Thomas Longo	. . .	. . .	Richard Obert	Anthony Collova	Thomas Murphy	Timothy McLaughlin
Geneva	c	CM	6	(440) 466-4675	Dennis Brown	James Pearson	Laurie Donatone	Juanita Stuetzer	Doug Starkey	Daniel Dudik	Gary Hydinger
Georgetown	v	CM	3	(937) 378-6395	John Jandes	Kelly Jones	Vickie Bradley	. . .	. . .	Forrest Coburn	. . .
Germantown	c	CM	4	(937) 855-7255	Theodore Landis	Randy Bukas	Anna Casto	Rebecca Jamison	Scott Anding	Roy McGill	. . .
Girard	c	MC	10	(330) 545-3879	. . .	. . .	. . .	. . .	. . .	. . .	. . .
Glenwillow	v	MC	. .	(440) 232-8788	. . .	. . .	. . .	. . .	. . .	. . .	. . .
Golf Manor	v	MC	3	(513) 531-7491	Donna Faulk	Stephen Tilley	Gregory Doening	. . .	Gregory Bollmon	. . .	. . .
Grandview Heights	c	MC	6	(614) 488-3159	N. Sexton	Patrik Bowman	. . .	James Nicholson	Henry Kauffman	Rollin Kiser	Sam Troiano
Granville	v	CM	3	(740) 587-0707	Melissa Hartfield	Donald Holycross	Beverly Adzic	Molly Roberts	. . .	. . .	Terry Hopkins
Green	c	MC	22	(330) 896-6602	Daniel Croghan	. . .	Molly Kapeluck	Laurence Rush	Robert Calderone	. . .	. . .
Green	tp	MC	55	(513) 574-4848	William Seitz	Kevin Celarek	Stephen Grote	. . .	. . .	. . .	Adam Goetzman
Greenfield	c	MC	4	(937) 981-3048	Betty Jackman	William Lynch	. . .	Jaclyn Emerick	Steven Campbell	Robin Roche	. . .
Greenhills	v	CM	4	(513) 825-2100	Oscar Hoffmann	David Moore	. . .	Kathryn Brokaw	Anthony Spaeth	Thomas Doyle	. . .
Greenville *	c	MC	13	(937) 548-1482	Richard Rehmert	. . .	. . .	Nancy Myers	Mark Wolf	Dennis Butts	. . .
Grove City	c	MC	27	(614) 277-3000	Cheryl Grossman	. . .	Tami Kelly	Robert Behlen	. . .	James McKean	James Blackburn
Groveport	v	MC	3	(614) 836-5301	Lance Westcamp	Jon Crusey	Julie Fisher	Kenneth Salak	. . .	Bary Murphy	Dennis Moore
Hamilton	c	CM	60	(513) 785-7030	Donald Ryan	Michael Samoviski	Ina Allen	George Gordon	Joseph Schutte	Neil Ferdelman	R. Reigelsperger
Hanover	tp	MC	7	(513) 896-9059	. . .	Bruce Henry	. . .	. . .	. . .	. . .	. . .
Harrison	c	MC	7	(513) 367-2111	Daniel Gieringer	. . .	. . .	James Satger	Alan Kinnett	. . .	James Lauver
Harrison Township	tp	MC	2	(937) 890-5611	George Curry	Marlyn Flee	Linda Pickard	. . .	Ronald Casey	. . .	Randy Brooks
Heath	c	MC	8	(740) 522-1420	Daniel Dupps	. . .	Lynn Hunt	Carolyn Broyles	Rick Taylor	Gordon Ellis	. . .
Hebron	v	MC	2	(740) 928-2261	Clifford Mason	Michael Mcfarland	Vicky Fulk	. . .	Randy Weekly	Mike Carney	. . .
Hicksville	v	MC	3	(419) 542-6138	Janis Meyer	Kent Miller	Diane Collins	. . .	. . .	Laurie Szabo	. . .
Highland Heights	c	MC	8	(440) 461-2440	Scott Coleman	. . .	. . .	Anthony Ianiro	Edward Berrcin	James Cook	Thomas Evans
Hilliard	c	MC	24	(614) 876-7361	Donald Schonhardt	. . .	Judith Perry	M. Kelly-Underwood	David Long	Rodney Garnett	Clyde Seidle
Hillsboro	c	MC	6	(937) 393-5219	Dick Zink	Ralph Holt	Beverly Brown	Rosemary Ryan	Gerald Powell	Nicholas Thompson	. . .
Hubbard	c	MC	8	(330) 534-3090	George Praznik	William Colletta	Linda Green	Michael Villano	. . .	Raymond Moffitt	. . .
Huber Heights	c	CM	38	(937) 233-1423	. . .	Catherine Armocida	. . .	. . .	Charles Ford	Sherwood Eldredge	Alexander Hynds
Hudson *	c	CM	22	(330) 650-1799	William Currin	Anthony Bales	Maryann George	Jeffrey Knoblauch	Robert Carter	David Robbins	Priscilla Blanchard
Huron	c	CM	7	(419) 433-5000	. . .	Andrew White	. . .	Catherine Ramey	Paul Berlin	Randy Glovinsky	. . .
Independence	c	MC	7	(216) 524-4131	Fred Ramos	. . .	Angela Zeleznik	John Veres	Peter Nelson	Michael Dugan	David Snyderburn
Indian Hill	v	CM	5	(513) 561-6500	Stella Hassan	Michael Burns	Paul Riordan	. . .	. . .	Willis McQueen	Richard Robinson
Ironton	c	MC	11	(740) 532-3833	John Elam	. . .	Janet Hieronimus	Cynthia Anderson	Thomas Runyon	James Carey	John McCabe
Jackson	c	MC	6	(740) 286-3224	John Evans	. . .	Tara Taylor	Carl Barnett	Richard Eubanks	Carl Eisnaugle	. . .
Jackson	tp	MC	32	(614) 875-2742	. . .	Michael Lilly	. . .	. . .	. . .	. . .	. . .
Jefferson	v	MC	3	(440) 576-3941	Judy Maloney	Terry Finger	. . .	. . .	John Wayman	Steve Febel	. . .
Johnstown	v	MC	3	(740) 967-3177	Karl VanDeest	Sarah Phillips	Regina Hunt	Sandra Berry	. . .	Donald Corbin	Jack Liggett
Kent	c	CM	27	(330) 678-8100	John Fender	David Ruller	Linda Copley	Barbara Rissland	James Williams	James Peach	David Merleno
Kenton	c	MC	8	(419) 674-4850	Gary Ritzler	Ronald Shaffer	Brenda Keckler	Cynthia Layman	Russell Blue	John Vermillion	Burl Helton
Kettering	c	CM	57	(937) 296-2400	Marilou Smith	Mark Schwieterman	Connie Gaw	Nancy Gregory	Robert Zickler	James O'Dell	. . .
Kirtland	c	MC	6	(440) 256-3332	Edward Podojil	. . .	Valerie Beres	Keith Martinet	Anthony Hutton	Wayne Baumgart	Carmelo Catania
Lake	tp	MC	25	(330) 877-9479	Don Myers	Carolyn Casey	Ben Sommers	. . .	. . .	Don Hensley	. . .
Lakemore	v	MC	2	(330) 733-6125	Richard Humm	William Bookman	Sandra Stafford	. . .	Clarence Bittner	Rodney Sands	. . .
Lakewood	c	MC	56	(216) 521-7580	Madeline Cain	. . .	Mary Hagan	Glenda Blasko	Lawrence Mroz	Timothy Malley	William Boag
Lancaster	c	MC	35	(740) 687-6676	Arthur Wallace	Earl Strawn	. . .	Mary Green	Steven Sells	Randall Lutz	. . .
Lebanon	c	CM	16	(513) 932-3060	Amy Brewer	George Clements	. . .	Sharee Dick	Michael Hannigan	Kenneth Burns	. . .
Leipsic	v	CM	2	(419) 943-2009	Kevin Benton	James Russell	R. Schortgen	. . .	David Herring	Chad Schmersal	. . .
Lexington	v	MC	4	(419) 884-0765	Eugene Parkison	Charles Pscholka	Brenda Wilson	James Banks	Charles Rahall	Brett Pauley	. . .
Liberty	tp	MC	22	(513) 759-7500	. . .	Dina Minneci	. . .	Roger Reynolds	Paul Stumpf	. . .	. . .
Liberty	tp	MC	15	(740) 881-4467	. . .	David Anderson	. . .	. . .	. . .	. . .	. . .
Lima	c	MC	40	(419) 221-5125	David Berger	Catherine Garlock	Sally Clemans	Eugene Reaman	Ted Brookman	Joseph Garlock	J. Elstro
Lincoln Heights	v	CM	4	(513) 733-5900	Lovey Andrews	. . .	Elizabeth Smith	Carnell Mathews	. . .	Earnest McCowen	Alan Blackwell
Lisbon	v	MC	2	(330) 424-5503	Michael Lewis	. . .	. . .	. . .	David Lewton	John Higgins	Mike Ours
Lockland	v	MC	3	(513) 761-1124	. . .	. . .	Wayne Poe	Charlene Case	Gary Wehmeyer	Kenneth Johnson	. . .
Lodi	v	MC	3	(330) 948-2040	Tom Longsdorf	. . .	. . .	. . .	. . .	Steve Sivard	Donald Eaken
Logan	c	MC	6	(740) 385-4060	Paula Tucker	. . .	Bridget Brandon	Kim Miller	Brian Robertson	Aaron Miller	. . .
London	c	MC	8	(740) 852-3243	David Eades	. . .	. . .	Kathy McClelland	Matthew Noble	Michael Creamer	. . .
Lorain	c	MC	68	(440) 204-2005	Joseph Koziura	George Koury	Steve Bansek	Ronald Mantini	Phillip Dore	Cel Rivera	Robert De Santis
Lordstown	v	MC	3	(330) 824-2507	Arno Hill	. . .	Judith Hall	. . .	James Wishart	Brent Milhoan	Lee Davis
Loudonville	v	MC	2	(419) 994-3214	John Burkhart	. . .	Jane Hollinger	Sandra Lavengood	. . .	Scott Shoudt	Keith Edgington
Louisville	c	CM	8	(330) 875-3321	Cynthia Kerchner	Edmund Ault	. . .	William Rouse	Dennis Myers	James Miller	James McBeath
Loveland	c	CM	11	(513) 683-0150	Brad Greenberg	Thomas Carroll	. . .	William Taphorn	. . .	Dennis Rees	Larry Moreland
Lyndhurst	c	MC	15	(440) 442-5777	Joseph Cicero	. . .	. . .	Mary Kovalchik	Gerald Telzrow	Anthony Adinolfi	Frederick Glady
Macedonia	c	MC	9	(330) 468-8300	Barbara Kornuc	. . .	. . .	Joseph Mirtel	Timothy Black	Jon Golden	. . .
Madeira	c	CM	8	(513) 561-7228	. . .	Thomas Moeller	. . .	. . .	. . .	. . .	. . .
Mansfield	c	MC	49	(419) 755-9695	Lydia Reid	. . .	. . .	Sandra Converse	Michael Hartson	Philip Messer	Francis Fisher
Maple Heights	c	MC	26	(216) 587-9008	. . .	. . .	Linda Sigado	Keith Schuster	James Castelucci	Richard Maracz	. . .
Mariemont	v	MC	3	(513) 271-3246	Charles Lemon	. . .	Stanley Bahler	. . .	James Fordyce	Richard Pope	J. Schreckenhofer
Marietta	c	MC	14	(740) 373-1387	Joe Matthews	Robert Boersma	Susan Joyce	Sharon Adams	Ted Baker	Brett McKitrick	. . .
Marion	c	MC	35	(614) 387-2020	. . .	. . .	. . .	. . .	. . .	. . .	. . .
Martins Ferry	c	MC	7	(740) 633-2876	. . .	. . .	. . .	. . .	. . .	. . .	. . .
Marysville	c	MC	15	(937) 642-6015	Steven Lowe	. . .	Connie Patterson	John Morehart	Gary Johnson	Eugene Mayer	. . .
Mason	c	CM	22	(513) 229-8510	Peter Beck	Eric Hansen	Terry Schulte	. . .	Rich Fletcher	Ronald Ferrell	David Riggs
Massillon	c	MC	31	(330) 830-1700	Francis Cicchinelli	Alan Climer	Sharon Howell	. . .	Tommy Matthews	Mark Weldon	. . .
Maumee	c	MC	15	(419) 897-7115	Timothy Wagener	John Jezak	. . .	David Hazard	Richard Monto	Robert Zink	Larry Gamble
Mayfield *	v	MC	3	(440) 461-2210	Bruce Rinker	. . .	Mary Betsa	Philip Brett	David Mohr	Patrick Dearden	Douglas Metzung
Mayfield Heights *	c	MC	19	(440) 442-2626	M. Egensperger	. . .	. . .	Robert Tribby	Michael Forte	Joseph Donnelly	Andrew Fornaro
Mc Donald	v	MC	3	(330) 530-5472	Thomas Hannon	. . .	Barbara Urban	. . .	Michael Badila	Jimmy Tyree	E. Dometrovich
Medina	c	MC	25	(330) 725-8861	Jane Leaver	. . .	Catherine Horn	Keith Dirham	William Herthneck	Dennis Hanwell	Serafino Piccoli
Mentor *	c	CM	50	(440) 255-1100	Ray Kirchner	John Konrad	Elizabeth Limestahl	David Malinowski	Richard Harvey	Daniel Llewellyn	Matthew Schweikert
Mentor-On-The-Lake	c	MC	8	(440) 257-7216	John Rogers	Kip Molenaar	. . .	. . .	Robert Mahoney	James Lyons	Dwayne Bailey
Miami	tp	CM	36	(513) 248-3725	Joseph Uecker	David Duckworth	Eric Ferry	. . .	James Whitworth	Steven Bailey	Walter Fischer
Miami	tp	CM	45	(937) 433-9969	David Coffey	Gregory Hanahan	. . .	Robert Fowler	David Fulmer	John Krug	James Woolf
Miamisburg	c	CM	19	(937) 866-3303	Richard Church	William Nelson	Judith Barney	George Perrine	Robert Bobbitt	Thomas Schenck	Stephen Morrison
Middleburg Heights	c	MC	15	(440) 234-8811	Gary Starr	Jeffrey Minch	Mary Meola	Timothy Pope	Bernard Benedict	John Maddox	Frank Castelli
Middleport	v	MC	2	(740) 992-2705	Sandy Iannarelli	. . .	. . .	Susan Baker	David Hoffman	Bruce Swift	Bradford Anderson
Middletown *	c	CM	51	(513) 425-7766	David Schiavone	Judith Gilleland	Betsy Parr	John Lyons	Steven Botts	Mark Hoffman	Ginger Smith
Milan	tp	CO	3	(419) 499-2354	. . .	. . .	James Verbridge	. . .	Larry Doerner	. . .	. . .
Milan	v	MC	1	(419) 499-2944	Michael Bagnato	Gene Rospert	. . .	Mary Bruno	. . .	James Ward	. . .
Milford *	c	CM	6	(513) 831-4192	Lou Bishop	Loretta Rokey	Joanne Trilety	Harry Steger	John Cooper	Mark Machan	Michael Haight
Millersburg	v	CM	3	(330) 674-1886	. . .	Andrew Jones	. . .	Karen Shaffer	. . .	S. Vaughn	. . .

Directory 1/9 continued — OFFICIALS IN U.S. MUNICIPALITIES 2,500 AND OVER IN POPULATION

Jurisdiction	Type	Form of govern-ment	2000 Popu-lation (000)	Main telephone number	Chief elected official	Appointed administrator	Clerk of the governing board	Chief financial officer	Fire chief	Police chief	Public works director
OHIO continued											
Minerva	v	CM	3	(330) 868-7705	...	David Harp	Gail Bender	...	Richard McClellan	Robert First	Steve Jackson
Mingo Junction	v	MC	3	(740) 535-1616	...	Keith Murtland	...	...	John Brettell	Michael Maguschak	...
Minster	v	MC	2	(419) 628-3497	Dennis Kitzmiller	Donald Harrod	John Stechschulte	...	Dale Dues	Donald Bergman	Carl Wuebker
Mogadore	v	MC	3	(330) 628-4896	Fred Farina	...	Juliann McCulley	...	Don Adams	David Quillen	...
Monroe *	c	CM	7	(513) 539-7374	Robert Routson	William Brock	...	Kacey Waggaman	Mark Neu	Gregory Homer	Bradley Collins
Monroeville	v	MC	1	(419) 465-4443	Sharon Miller	Joshua Eggleston	Bonnie Beck	...	...	...	...
Montgomery	c	CM	10	(513) 891-2424	Gary Blomberg	Cheryl Hilvert	Susan Hamm	...	Paul Wright	Kirk Nordbloom	L. Nikula
Montpelier	v	CM	4	(419) 485-5543	William Shatzer	Pamela Lucas	...	Kelly Hephner	Dail Fritsch	Bill Noethen	...
Moraine	c	CM	6	(937) 535-1000	Roger Matheney	David Hicks	Rita Krell	Jim Kimmel	Steve Kirby	Thomas Schenck	...
Moreland Hills	v	MC	3	(440) 248-1188	Alvin Croucher	...	Claudette Pesti	Thomas Zammikiel	...	Frank Swanek	James Borsi
Mount Gilead	v	MC	3	(419) 946-4861	Thomas Whiston	Neil Rogers	...	Sue Mermann	Donald Staiger	Brian Zerman	...
Mount Healthy	c	MC	7	(513) 931-8840	Terry Todd	...	Becky Ramey	James Roy	Tom Harris	Albert Schaefer	...
Mount Vernon	c	MC	14	(740) 393-9521	Richard Mavis	...	Janet Brown	Terry Scott	...	...	David Carpenter
Munroe Falls	v	MC	5	(330) 688-7491	Brad Sisak	...	Amy Locy	Theodore Gordon	James Bowery	Steve Stahl	...
Napoleon	c	CM	9	(419) 599-1235	J. Small	Jon Bisher	...	Gregory Heath	Lynn Hancock	Robert Weitzel	...
Nelsonville	c	CM	5	(740) 753-1314	Clinton Stanley	Fred Holmes	Susan Harmony	Aileen Lehman	...	David Heineking	...
New Albany *	v	CM	3	(614) 855-3913	Nancy Ferguson	Joseph Stefanov	...	James Nicholson	...	Mark Chaney	Mark Nemec
New Boston	c	MC	2	(740) 456-4103	James Warren	...	Kathy Kammerer	...	Chris Bender	Darrold Clark	...
New Bremen	v	MC	2	(419) 629-2447	Jeffrey Pape	...	Diane Gast	...	Robert Kuck	Douglas Harrod	...
New Carlisle	c	CM	5	(937) 845-9492	...	James Caplinger	...	Debi Heiligenberg	...	...	Robert Bender
New Lebanon	v	CM	4	(937) 687-1341	Larry Shock	George Markus	...	E. Grimmett	...	Rickey Daulton	...
New Lexington	c	MC	4	(740) 342-0401	Janine Conrad	John McCort	Jennifer Dennis	Teri Moore	Mike Bringardner	Jeff Newlon	Chuck Hicks
New Miami	v	MC	2	(513) 896-7337	Kenneth Cheek	...	...	Joseph Ebbing	Gerald Cook	Gary Vaughn	Jamie Cook
New Philadelphia	c	MC	17	(330) 364-4491	Ronald Brodzinski	...	Diane Roudebush	...	Robert Snyder	Jeffrey Urban	...
New Richmond	v	MC	2	(513) 553-4146	Terry Durette	David Kennedy	...	...	...	Karl Hassebrock	Leo Hurst
Newark	c	MC	46	(740) 349-6605	Frank Stare	...	Diana Hufford	Stephen Johnson	Jack Stickradt	Herman Pennington	Timothy Matheny
Newburgh Heights	v	MC	2	(216) 641-4650	Paul Ruggles	...	Debra Malinowski	...	Richard Pugsley	Michael McKeon	...
Newcomerstown	v	MC	4	(740) 498-5881	Jimmie Carr	...	...	...	...	Brian Hursey	...
Newton Falls	c	CM	5	(330) 872-0806	T. Moorehead	Jack Haney	Kathleen King	Marcia Cunningham	Richard Bauman	Robert Carlson	Harry Shaver
Niles	c	MC	20	(330) 544-9000	Ralph Infante	...	...	Neil Buccino	Charles Semple	Bruce Simeone	Samuel Natoli
North Baltimore	v	MC	3	(419) 257-2394	Ned Sponsler	...	Richard Van Mooy	Chasity McCartney	Donald Baltz	Gerald Perry	...
North Canton	c	MC	16	(330) 499-8223	Thomas Rice	Michael Miller	...	Julie Herr	John Bacon	Michael Grimes	...
North College Hill	c	MC	10	(513) 521-7413	Daniel Brooks	...	Collen Bens	Carol Wullkotte	Michael Lotz	John Fulmer	John Knuf
North Kingsville	v	MC	2	(440) 224-0091	Ronald McVoy	...	...	...	Brian Lehtonen	Robert Houser	...
North Olmsted	c	MC	34	(440) 777-8000	Thomas O'Grady	...	Barbara Seman	Carrie Copfer	Thomas Klecan	George Ruple	Dan Driscoll
North Ridgeville	c	MC	22	(440) 353-0819	Deanna Hill	Thomas Sweeney	Beverly Gillock	Chris Costin	Rick Miller	Ronald Bauer	...
North Royalton	c	MC	28	(440) 237-5686	Cathy Luks	...	Laura Haller	Karen Fegan	Michael Fabish	Paul Bican	William Mayer
Northfield	v	MC	3	(330) 467-7139	Victor Milani	...	Cheryl Kennon	Robert Riedel	...	Mark Wentz	Anthony Fiorilli
Northwood	c	MC	5	(419) 693-9327	Mark Stoner	Patricia Bacon	Lynn Goertz	Toby Schroyer	Tim Romstadt	Gerald Herman	Craig Meier
Norton	c	MC	11	(330) 825-7815	Joseph Kernan	Claude Collins	Jim Mitchell	John Moss	James Calco	Greg Carris	...
Norwalk	c	MC	16	(419) 663-6700	Brooks Hartmann	James Koch	Kascie Horrigan	Diane Eschen	Robert Bores	Kevin Cashen	Ralph Seward
Norwood	c	MC	21	(513) 396-8150	Joseph Hochbein	Jeff Miller	...	Donnie Jones	...	Tim Brown	Larry Moreland
Oak Harbor	v	MC	2	(419) 898-5561	Peter Macko	Timothy Wilkins	...	S. Baumgartner	...	Larry St. Clair	...
Oakwood	c	CM	9	(937) 298-0600	Dorothy Cook	Norbert Klopsch	Cathy Blum	Brad Beachdell	...	...	Kevin Weaver
Oakwood	v	MC	3	(440) 232-9988	Gary Gottschalk	...	...	...	...	Robert Semik	Thomas Haba
Oberlin	c	CM	8	(440) 775-7206	...	Eric Norenberg	Eugene Simon	Salvatore Talarico	Dennis Kirin	Thomas Miller	Jeffrey Baumann
Obetz	v	MC	3	(614) 491-1080	Louise Crabtree	...	D. Hubner Smith	...	...	Richard Minerd	...
Olmsted Falls	c	MC	7	(440) 235-5550	...	...	...	...	...	...	...
Ontario	v	MC	5	(419) 529-3818	D. Kreisher	Calvin Miller	...	Shirley Bowman	...	Timothy McClaran	...
Oregon	c	MC	19	(419) 698-7095	James Haley	Kenneth Filipiak	Mary Finger	Sandra Bihn	R. Walendzak	Thomas Gulch	Michael White
Orrville	c	MC	8	(330) 684-5000	Dennis Steiner	Becky Jewell	...	James Leggett	Robert Ballentine	Joseph Routh	Dan Preising
Ottawa	v	MC	4	(419) 523-5020	Kenneth Maag	John Williams	Barbara Doepker	...	John Love	Richard Knowlton	Karen Kovolo
Ottawa Hills	v	CM	4	(419) 536-1111	Jean Youngen	Marc Thompson	Gay Macarthur	Karen Urbanik	Donald Farley	Ronald Jand	...
Oxford	c	CM	21	(513) 524-5200	Jerome Conley	Douglas Elliott	...	Harlita Robinson	Leonard Endress	Stephan Schwein	Michael Dreisbach
Painesville	c	CM	17	(440) 392-5786	William Horvath	Rita McMahon	Jennifer Bell	Timothy Petric	Mark Mlachak	Gary Smith	Kevin Lynch
Parma	c	MC	85	(440) 885-8000	Dean DePiero	...	Michael Hughes	Dennis Kish	John French	Daniel Hoffman	Brian Higgins
Parma Heights *	c	MC	21	(440) 884-9600	Martin Zanotti	...	...	Terrence Hickey	Bryan Sloan	Daniel Teel	Joseph Tal
Pataskala	c	CM	10	(740) 927-2021	...	Timothy Boland	...	...	...	...	...
Paulding *	v	MC	3	(419) 399-4011	Greg White	Harry Wiebe	...	Melissa Tope	Todd Weidenhamer	Randy Crawford	...
Pepper Pike	c	MC	6	(216) 831-8500	Bruce Akers	...	Sue Molnar	Prashant Shah	Thomas Hartman	Eugene Sokol	Robert Girardi
Perrysburg	c	MC	16	(419) 872-8010	Timothy McCarthy	John Alexander	...	David Creps	Ronn Thompson	Nelson Evans	Jon Eckel
Pickerington	c	CO	9	(614) 837-3974	Mitch O'Brien	...	Lynda Yartin	Linda Fersch	...	Michael Taylor	Edward Drobina
Pierce *	tp	MC	12	(513) 752-6262	Bonnie Batchler	Dave Elmer	...	Karen Register	Aaron Boggs	James Smith	Daryl Berry
Pioneer	v	MC	1	(419) 737-2614	David Thompson	...	...	...	Dennis Fackler	Judith Lineberger	William Rains
Piqua	c	CM	20	(937) 778-2053	Robert DeBrosse	Fredrick Enderle	Rebecca Cool	Cynthia Holtzapple	Gary Connell	...	Thomas Zechman
Plain	tp	MC	51	(330) 492-4689	Pamela Bossart	...	Claude Shriver	Jo Reikowski	John Sabo	...	...
Plain City	v	MC	2	(614) 873-5040	...	...	...	...	...	...	...
Poland	v	MC	2	(330) 757-2112	...	...	...	...	...	...	...
Pomeroy	v	MC	1	(740) 992-2246	...	John Anderson	Kathy Hysell	...	...	Mark Proffitt	...
Port Clinton	c	MC	6	(419) 734-5522	Thomas Brown	Richard Babcock	...	Nancy O'Neal	John Morton	Thomas Blohm	...
Portsmouth *	c	CM	20	(740) 354-8807	James Kalb	...	Jo Aeh	M Trent Williams	...	Charles Horner	Christopher Murphy
Powell	v	CM	6	(614) 885-5380	Dan Wiencek	Stephen Lutz	Dawn Nauman	Nanette Metz	...	Gary Vest	...
Ravenna	c	MC	11	(330) 296-3864	Paul Jones	...	Kathryn Halay	Kimble Cecora	James Dipaola	Randall McCoy	Donald Kainrad
Reading	c	MC	11	(513) 733-3725	Robert Bemmes	Albert Elmlinger	Miriam Lapple	Douglas Sand	Kevin Kaiser	Gregory Hilling	Darrell Courtney
Reynoldsburg *	c	MC	32	(614) 322-6808	Robert McPherson	...	Nancy Frazier	Richard Harris	...	David Suciu	...
Richfield	v	MC	3	(330) 659-9201	Michael Lyons	...	Joyce Remec	Eleanor Lukovics	Joseph Stopak	Dale Canter	...
Richmond Heights	c	MC	10	(216) 486-2474	Daniel Ursu	...	Betsy Traben	Lynda Rossiter	Michael Cek	Gene Rowe	Donald Lazar
Rittman *	c	CM	6	(330) 925-2045	William Robertson	Larry Boggs	Barbara Brooks	Cindy Mann	Don Sweigert	...	David Simpson
Riverside	c	CM	23	(937) 233-1801	Kenneth Curp	Bryan Chodkowski	MaryAnn Brane	Robert Gillian	Dan Alig	George Brown	Terrence Nealy
Rocky River	c	MC	20	(440) 331-0600	William Knoble	...	...	...	Christopher Flynn	Donald Wagner	...
Rossford *	c	MC	6	(419) 666-0210	William Verbosky	Edward Ciecka	Robert Watrol	Karen Freeman	James Verbosky	Robert Vespi	David Jones
Sabina	v	MC	2	(937) 584-2123	...	Karma Henson	...	...	...	Tim Tyree	Rob Dean
Salem *	c	MC	12	(330) 332-4241	Larry DeJane	...	...	James Armeni	Walter Greenamyer	Robert Floor	Donald Weingart
Sandusky	c	CM	27	(419) 627-5844	Frank Valli	Michael Will	Joyce Brown	...	Ken Gilliam	Kim Nuesse	Randy Whitman
Sebring	v	CM	4	(330) 938-9340	John Smith	Douglas Burchard	Malea Sanor	...	James Cannell	Ray Heverly	Bill Sanor
Seven Hills	c	MC	12	(216) 524-4421	Gerald Trafis	...	...	Albert Lippucci	Anthony Hosta	John Fechko	John Miller
Shadyside	c	MC	3	(740) 676-5972	...	Richard Melanko	...	...	Mark Badia	Russell Patt	Howard Heslop
Shaker Heights *	c	MC	29	(216) 491-1427	Judith Rawson	Jeri Chaikin	...	John Lehman	Donald Barnes	Walter Ugrinic	William Boag
Sharonville	c	MC	13	(513) 563-1144	Virgil Lovitt	Al Ledbetter	Martha Funk	...	Dale Duermit	Michael Schappa	Audrey Privett
Sheffield Lake	c	MC	9	(440) 949-7141	John Piskura	...	Dorothy Fantauzzi	Tammy Smith	Mike Conrad	Larry Shepherd	William Gardner
Shelby	c	MC	9	(419) 347-5131	James Hunter	Brad Harvey	...	Larry Paxton	Scott Hartman	Michael Bennett	...

Directory 1/9 continued — OFFICIALS IN U.S. MUNICIPALITIES 2,500 AND OVER IN POPULATION

Jurisdiction	Type	Form of govern-ment	2000 Popu-lation (000)	Main telephone number	Chief elected official	Appointed administrator	Clerk of the governing board	Chief financial officer	Fire chief	Police chief	Public works director
OHIO continued											
Sidney	c	CM	20	(937) 498-2335	Frank Mariano	Steven Stilwell	Jocele Fahnestock	Thomas Judy	Stan Crosley	Steven Wearly	S. Gosciewski
Silver Lake	v	MC	3	(330) 923-5233	Bernie Hovey	. . .	Teresa Spohn	. . .	. . .	Gary DeMoss	Richard Fenwick
Silverton *	c	MC	5	(513) 936-6240	James Siegel	Mark Wendling	Meredith George	. . .	Donald Newman	Michael Daudistel	. . .
Solon *	c	MC	21	(440) 248-1155	Kevin Patton	. . .	C. McConoughey	Duane Weber	William Shaw	Wayne Godzich	Jim Stanek
South Charleston	v	CM	1	(937) 462-7167	Marilyn Jarvis	Sarah Wildman	. . .	Bonnie White	. . .	Beryl McCloud	Ralph Cook
South Euclid	c	MC	23	(216) 381-0400	Georgine Welo	. . .	. . .	Joseph Filippo	Thomas Cannell	Matthew Capadona	Ed Gallagher
South Lebanon	v	MC	2	(513) 494-2296	James Smith	John Louallen	. . .	Debra Humston	. . .	Derrick Hollon	Larry Easterly
South Point	v	MC	3	(740) 377-4838	William Gaskin	Patrick Leighty	. . .	Scott Thomas	Richard Stevens	Carl Vance	. . .
South Russell	v	MC	4	(440) 338-7843	William Young	. . .	Nancy Gallagher	. . .	. . .	. . .	. . .
Springboro	c	CM	12	(937) 748-4343	John Agenbroad	Christine Thompson	Lori Martin	Robyn Brown	. . .	Jeffrey Kruithoff	Barry Conway
Springdale *	c	MC	10	(513) 346-5700	Doyle Webster	Cecil Osborn	Edward Knox	Jeff Williams	Dan Shroyer	Mike Laage	David Butsch
Springfield *	c	CM	65	(937) 324-7700	Warren Copeland	Matthew Kridler	Connie Chappell	Mark Beckdahl	J Beers	Stephen Moody	James Mann
Springfield	tp	CM	13	(513) 522-1410	Tom Bryan	M. Hinnenkamp	John Waksmundski	. . .	Robert Leininger	David Heimpold	John Musselman
St. Bernard	c	MC	4	(513) 242-7770	Barbara Siegel	. . .	Carol Ungruhe	C. Vonder Meulen	James Dwertman	Allen Rusche	Herb Siegel
St. Clairsville	c	MC	5	(740) 695-1324	Robert Vincenzo	. . .	Kathy Kaluger	Jill Lucidi	. . .	Martin Kendzora	Dennis Bigler
St. Marys *	c	MC	8	(419) 394-3303	Gregory Freewalt	Thomas Hitchcock	. . .	Douglas Riesen	Kenneth Cline	Greg Foxhoven	. . .
Steubenville	c	CM	19	(740) 283-6133	Domenick Mucci	Bruce Williams	Pamela Orlando	Michael Marshall	Terri Kovach	Jerry McCartney	. . .
Stow	c	MC	32	(330) 689-2700	Lee Schaffer	. . .	Bonnie Emahiser	John Baranek	Steven Groves	Louis Dirker	Dano Koehler
Streetsboro	c	MC	12	(330) 626-4942	Sally Henzel	. . .	Pamela Hejduk	D. Weber	Gerald Vicha	Ronald Schmid	Robert Langham
Strongsville *	c	MC	43	(440) 580-3151	Thomas Perciak	. . .	Leslie Seefried	Donald Batke	Robert Moody	Charles Goss	Joseph Walker
Struthers	c	MC	11	(330) 755-2181	Daniel Mamula	. . .	Toni Constantino	Tina Morell	Harold Milligan	Robert Norris	John Sveda
Sugarcreek	tp	MC	6	(937) 848-8426	. . .	Barry Tiffany	. . .	. . .	. . .	. . .	. . .
Sunbury	v	MC	2	(740) 965-2684	. . .	Dave Martin	. . .	. . .	. . .	. . .	. . .
Swanton	v	CM	3	(419) 826-9515	Tandy Grubbs	John Syx	Mary Lou Perrin	Barbara Guess	James Guy	Homer Chapa	. . .
Sycamore	tp	CM	19	(513) 791-8447	Richard Kent	Lori Thompson	Robert Porter	. . .	. . .	. . .	. . .
Sylvania	c	MC	18	(419) 885-8998	Craig Stough	. . .	Margaret Rauch	John Plock	Christopher Maurer	Gerald Sobb	Jeffrey Ballmer
Sylvania *	tp	CM	44	(419) 882-0031	Deidre Leidel	Hugh Thomas	David Simko	Devon Klofta	. . .	Robert Metzger	Greg Huffman
Tallmadge *	c	MC	16	(330) 633-0145	Christopher Grimm	. . .	Susan Wilson	Jill Stritch	Dennis Crossen	Mike Duvall	David Kline
Thornville	v	MC	. .	(740) 246-6020	. . .	. . .	. . .	. . .	. . .	. . .	. . .
Tiffin	c	MC	18	(419) 448-5401	Bernard Hohman	Wayne Stephens	. . .	Debora Souder	William Ennis	David Lagrange	Susan Kuhn
Tipp City	c	CM	9	(937) 667-8425	Bill Beagle	. . .	Misty Cox	Richard Drennen	Steve Kessler	Thomas Davidson	Milton Eichman
Toledo	c	CO	313	(419) 245-1500	Carleton Finkbeiner	Robert Reinbolt	Gerald Dendinger	John Sherburne	Michael Bell	Michael Navarre	Robert Williams
Toronto	c	MC	5	(740) 537-3743	John Geddis	Susan Kulstad	Linda Burkey	Robert Owen	David Solomon	Danny Mosti	John Skrabak
Trenton	c	CM	8	(513) 988-6304	Roy Wilham	Robert Leichman	Julie Muterspaw	Michael Engel	Thomas Puckett	Rodney Hale	. . .
Trotwood	c	CM	27	(937) 837-7771	Donald McLaurin	Michael Lucking	Lois Singleton	Jon Stoops	Paul Hutsonpillar	Michael Etter	Thomas Odenigbo
Troy *	c	MC	21	(937) 335-1725	Michael Beamish	Patrick Titterington	Sue Knight	Richard Cultice	C. Boehringer	Charles Phelps	Steven Leffel
Twinsburg	c	MC	17	(330) 425-7161	Katherine Procop	. . .	Cynthia Kaderle	Jo Anne Terry	Richard Racine	Richard Deal	Chris Campbell
Uhrichsville	c	MC	5	(740) 922-1242	. . .	. . .	. . .	. . .	. . .	. . .	. . .
Union	c	CM	5	(937) 836-8624	. . .	John Applegate	. . .	Denise Winemiller	. . .	Michael Blackwell	. . .
Union	tp	CM	42	(513) 752-1741	. . .	Doug Walker	. . .	. . .	Stanley Deimling	Terry Zinser	. . .
Union City	v	MC	1	(937) 968-4305	Scott Stahl	. . .	. . .	Judy Henry	. . .	Harold Schafer	Mike Grimes
University Heights	c	MC	14	(216) 932-7800	Beryl Rothschild	. . .	Nancy English	Arman Ochoa	John Pitchler	Gary Stehlik	. . .
Upper Arlington *	c	CM	33	(614) 583-5040	Edward Seidel	Virginia Barney	Beverly Clevenger	C. Armstrong	Mitchell Ross	Brian Quinn	Larry Helscel
Upper Sandusky	c	MC	6	(419) 294-3862	K. Richardson	. . .	. . .	Jean Hollanshead	Tom Fox	Robert Hollis	. . .
Urbana *	c	MC	11	(937) 652-4300	Ruth Zerkle	. . .	. . .	Dale Miller	James McIntosh	Pat Wagner	. . .
Van Wert	c	MC	10	(419) 238-1237	Stephen Gelves	Jay Fleming	. . .	Martha Balyeat	James Steele	Joel Hammond	. . .
Vandalia	c	CM	14	(937) 898-5891	William Loy	Jeffrey Hoagland	. . .	James Bell	John Sands	Douglas Knight	. . .
Vermilion *	c	MC	10	(440) 204-2400	Jean Anderson	. . .	Gwen Fisher	. . .	Chris Stempowski	. . .	Dan Squires
Versailles	v	CM	2	(937) 526-3294	. . .	. . .	. . .	. . .	. . .	. . .	. . .
Wadsworth	c	MC	18	(330) 335-1521	Caesar Carrino	William Lyren	. . .	John Moss	Ralph Copley	David Singleton	. . .
Walbridge	v	MC	2	(419) 666-1830	Daniel Wilczynski	Steve Smith	. . .	Patricia Crawford	. . .	Richard Solether	. . .
Walton Hills	v	MC	2	(440) 232-7800	Marlene Anielski	. . .	. . .	Vic Nogalo	. . .	Gary Rhines	Dan Stucky
Wapakoneta	c	MC	9	(419) 738-3011	Donald Wittwer	Rex Katterheinrich	Carlene Koch	Gail Walter	Christopher Agnew	David Harrison	Meril Simpson
Warren	c	MC	46	(330) 841-2610	Michael O'Brien	William Franklin	Darla Neugebauer	David Griffing	Kenneth Nussle	John Mandopoulos	Robert Davis
Warrensville Heights	c	MC	15	(216) 587-6500	Marcia Fudge	. . .	Yvonne McMillion	Rubin Moultrie	. . .	. . .	. . .
Washington	c	CM	13	(740) 636-2340	. . .	. . .	. . .	Tom Riley	Dan Fowler	Larry Mongold	Joe Burbage
Washington	tp	CM	7	(937) 433-0152	. . .	Gary Huff	Thomas Zobrist	Michael Barlow	Kenneth Parks	. . .	. . .
Waterville	v	CM	4	(419) 878-8100	Charles Peyton	James Bagdonas	Claudia Guimond	Dale Knepper	Steven Parons	Robert Selders	Kenneth Blair
Wauseon	c	MC	7	(419) 335-9022	Jerry Dehnbostel	. . .	Margaret Murphy	Jon Schamp	Marvin Wheeler	Keith Torbett	Dennis Richardson
Waverly	c	MC	4	(740) 947-5162	William Kelly	. . .	. . .	Harvey Whaley	R. Armbruster	Larry Roe	. . .
Waynesville	v	CM	2	(513) 897-8015	Ernie Lawson	Bruce Snell	. . .	Linda Jones	. . .	Kenny McCloud	. . .
Wellington	v	MC	4	(440) 647-4626	. . .	Robert Dupee	Karen Webb	. . .	. . .	Richard Rollins	Robert Box
Wellston	c	MC	6	(740) 384-2720	Edgar Hayburn	. . .	Mary Jarvis	J. Glass	Dan Gill	Mark Jacobs	Larry Walburn
Wellsville	c	MC	4	(330) 532-2510	. . .	. . .	. . .	. . .	. . .	. . .	. . .
West Carrollton *	c	CM	14	(937) 859-5183	Maxine Gilman	Bradley Townsend	Nancy Trimble	Thomas Reilly	John Keister	Richard Barnhart	Richard Norton
West Chester	tp	CM	54	(513) 777-5900	George Lang	Judith Boyko	Patricia Williams	. . .	James Detherage	John Bruce	. . .
West Jefferson	v	MC	4	(614) 879-7363	. . .	. . .	Jack Herrel	. . .	. . .	Frank Cox	Robert Carter
West Milton	v	CM	4	(937) 698-1500	. . .	Martin Gabbard	. . .	Jill Grise	Dennis Frantz	Tracey Hendricks	. . .
West Salem	v	MC	1	(419) 853-4400	Elmer Toth	Kathryn Reagan	. . .	Patricia Foradori	. . .	Don Sims	. . .
West Union	v	MC	2	(937) 544-5326	Harold Dryden	Richard Potter	Ruth Young	. . .	John Bradford	Harry Baldwin	. . .
Westerville *	c	CM	35	(614) 901-6400	Damian Wetterauer	David Collinsworth	Mary Johnston	John Winkel	Bernard Ingles	Joseph Morbitzer	Frank Wiseman
Westlake	c	MC	31	(440) 871-3300	Dennis Clough	. . .	. . .	Anne Fritz	Richard Pietrick	Richard Walling	Donald Glauner
Whitehall	c	MC	19	(614) 237-9803	John Wolfe	Kathy Crandall	Dawn Williams	Kim Maggard	Timothy Tilton	James Stacy	. . .
Whitehouse *	v	MC	2	(419) 877-5383	Stanley Wielinski	Dennis Recker	Susan Miller	Linda Snyder	Daryl McNutt	Edward Kaplan	Mark Weber
Wickliffe	c	MC	13	(440) 943-7100	Thomas Ruffner	. . .	C. Theophylactos	Martin Germ	Daniel Helsel	James Fox	Daniel Paschke
Willard	c	CM	6	(419) 933-2591	Michael Elmlinger	Brian Humphress	Jo Ann Jones	Jody Wagoner	Richard Myers	Thomas King	. . .
Williamsburg *	v	MC	2	(513) 724-6107	Mary Ann Lefker	Patti Bates	. . .	Denise Wehrum	. . .	Michael Gregory	Jeremy Fite
Willoughby	c	MC	22	(440) 951-2800	David Anderson	. . .	Loretta Radebaugh	R. Rogowski	Al Zwegat	Conrad Straube	Angelo Tomaselli
Willoughby Hills	c	MC	8	(440) 946-1234	Mort O'Ryan	Jim Teknipp	Terri Poppy	. . .	Rich Harmon	George Malec	. . .
Willowick *	c	MC	14	(440) 585-3700	Richard Bonde	. . .	. . .	Cheryl Killen	Robert Posipanka	Michael Lazor	Joseph Dominick
Wilmington	c	MC	11	(937) 382-5458	David Raizk	L. Reinsmith	. . .	. . .	Fred Shutts	Michael Hatten	. . .
Windham	v	MC	2	(330) 326-2622	Jess Starkey	Kevin Knight	. . .	Shelley Craine	Clair Simpson	Jacob DeSalvo	William Szymanski
Wintersville	v	MC	4	(740) 266-3175	. . .	. . .	. . .	. . .	. . .	Edward Laman	Perry Poole
Woodlawn	v	CM	2	(513) 771-6130	. . .	Evonne Kovach	Brenda Love	R Hardy	Richard Mynatt	Walter Obermeyer	Terry Meadows
Woodsfield	v	MC	2	(740) 472-0418	Lester Bolon	. . .	Patricia Templeton	. . .	Michael Young	Manifred Keylor	. . .
Wooster	c	MC	24	(330) 263-5200	James Howey	Michael Sigg	Sheila Stanley	Andrei Dordea	Stanley Brown	Steven Thornton	Michael Hunter
Worthington	c	CM	14	(614) 436-3100	. . .	Matthew Greeson	D. Kay Thress	Steven Gandee	Scott Highley	Michael Mauger	David Groth
Wyoming	c	CM	8	(513) 821-7600	David Savage	Robert Harrison	. . .	. . .	. . .	Timothy World	. . .
Xenia	c	CM	24	(937) 376-7232	John Saraga	Kenneth Johnson	. . .	Mark Bazelak	Jeffrey Leaming	Donald Person	. . .
Yellow Springs *	v	CM	3	(937) 767-7202	Karen Wintrow	Eric Swansen	Deborah Benning	. . .	. . .	John Grote	. . .
Youngstown	c	MC	82	(330) 742-8995	. . .	Richard Groucutt	. . .	. . .	. . .	. . .	. . .
Zanesville	c	MC	25	(740) 455-0603	Howard Zwelling	. . .	Joan Ziemer	Dale Raines	Dave Lacy	Eric Lambes	Michael Sims

Directory 1/9 continued — OFFICIALS IN U.S. MUNICIPALITIES 2,500 AND OVER IN POPULATION

Jurisdiction	Type	Form of govern-ment	2000 Popu-lation (000)	Main telephone number	Chief elected official	Appointed administrator	Clerk of the governing board	Chief financial officer	Fire chief	Police chief	Public works director
OKLAHOMA											
Ada *	c	CM	15	(580) 436-6300	Frank Stout	David Hathcoat	Sally Pool	Donna Doolen	Marion Harris	Michael Miller	. . .
Altus	c	MC	21	(580) 481-2200	T. Gramling	Michael Nettles	La June White	Shirley Norton	Kenneth Ward	Mike Patterson	Robert Stephenson
Alva *	c	MC	5	(580) 327-1340	Lynn Chaffee	Steven Tomberlin	Wayne Lane	. . .	Allen Schwerdtfeger	Arlo Darr	Randy Rhodes
Anadarko	c	CM	6	(405) 247-2481	Marilyn Shannon	. . .	Karen Thomsen	Robert Brooks	Dennis Wilkerson	Keith Tillis	Bill Rowton
Antlers	c	CM	2	(580) 298-3756	Brent Franks	Mike Winningham	Athelta Gay	Robin Byrum	Randy Janoe	Dwayne Morgan	Craig Wilson
Ardmore	c	CM	23	(580) 226-2100	. . .	Dan Parrott	. . .	Penny Long	J. Spohn	. . .	Robert Whitaker
Atoka	c	CM	2	(580) 889-3341	Bill Miller	Martha Allen	Donna Guinn	Joann Duckworth	Donnie Allen	John Smithart	Stephen Smith
Bartlesville	c	CM	34	(918) 338-4200	. . .	. . .	. . .	. . .	Robert Hasbrook	Leo Willey	Edgar Gordon
Bethany	c	CM	20	(405) 789-2146	Bryan Taylor	John Shugart	. . .	Sandra Kimerer	David Beck	Neal Troutman	Jim McGill
Bixby	c	CM	13	(918) 366-4430	Joe Williams	Micky Webb	Cheryl Sasser	. . .	Steve Abel	Anthony Stephens	Bea Aamodt
Blackwell	c	CM	7	(580) 363-7250	Eugene Braly	Sara Norris	Teresa Moses	. . .	Tommy Beliel	Lauren Johnson	. . .
Blanchard	c	CM	2	(405) 485-9392	Tom Sacchieri	Bill Edwards	Camille Dowers	. . .	. . .	Henry Weber	Monte Ketcham
Boise City	c	CM	1	(580) 544-2271	. . .	Rodney Avery	. . .	. . .	. . .	. . .	. . .
Bristow	c	MC	4	(918) 367-2237	Leon Pinson	. . .	Sabrina Mounce	. . .	Bob Grant	Perry Low	Fred Wesley
Broken Arrow	c	CM	74	(918) 259-2400	Richard Carter	James Twombly	Linda Fagundes	Thomas Caldwell	Dennis McIntire	Todd Wuestewald	. . .
Broken Bow *	c	CM	4	(580) 584-2885	Jerry Smith	Mark Guthrie	Vickie Pieratt	. . .	Roger Ross	Hurschel Thomas	Gary Swift
Catoosa	c	MC	5	(918) 266-2505	Curtis Conley	. . .	Judy Scullawl	. . .	. . .	Raymond Rodgers	. . .
Chandler *	c	CM	2	(405) 258-3200	Tom Knight	James Melson	Kay Pentecost	. . .	Bobby Johnson	Kevin Towler	David Nickell
Checotah	c	MC	3	(918) 473-5411	James Hayes	. . .	Shirley Fox	Bette Sanders	Raymon Webster	Terry Cossey	Wayne Williams
Cherokee *	c	CM	1	(580) 596-3052	Rosemary Whittet	Brandon Wright	Roberta Berry	. . .	Kevin Lingemann	Paul Michael	. . .
Chickasha	c	CM	15	(405) 222-6020	. . .	Larry Shelton	Sharon Chapman	. . .	Greg Gibson	Lynn Williams	Larry Fuchs
Choctaw	c	CM	9	(405) 390-8198	Bobbie Freeman	Robert Floyd	Linda Bomgren	. . .	Loren Bumgarner	William Carter	Bernie Nauheimer
Claremore	c	CM	15	(918) 341-2365	. . .	Troy Powell	Carlene Webber	. . .	Bradd Clark	Michael Perry	Charles Andrle
Cleveland	c	CM	3	(918) 358-3506	Dale Norrid	Elizie Smith	Viriginia Masters	. . .	Jo Burger	Marvin Howard	Les Taber
Clinton *	c	CM	8	(580) 323-0261	Lynn Norman	Grayson Bottom	. . .	. . .	Price Anders	David Crabtree	. . .
Coalgate *	c	CM	2	(580) 927-3914	Michael Elkins	Roger Cosper	. . .	. . .	David Holt	Kenny Pebworth	Walter Roebuck
Collinsville *	c	MC	4	(918) 371-1010	Stan Sallee	Pamela Polk	Kelly Young	. . .	Russell Young	Charlie Annis	. . .
Comanche	c	CM	1	(580) 439-8832	. . .	Rodney Love	Janice Willis	. . .	David Coder	Jack Shutts	. . .
Commerce	c	MC	2	(918) 675-4373	Jim Mullen	. . .	Vicki Turner	. . .	. . .	. . .	David Creason
Cordell	c	MC	2	(580) 832-3825	K Damon	R. McClanathan	. . .	. . .	Tom Merrill	Gary Coburn	. . .
Coweta	c	CM	7	(918) 486-2189	Robert Morton	Steven Whitlock	. . .	. . .	Craig Hinton	Derrick Palmer	Frank Dailey
Crescent	c	CM	1	(405) 969-2538	. . .	. . .	Tiffany Tillman	. . .	. . .	Kris Kelley	Frank De Fuentes
Cushing	c	CM	8	(918) 225-0277	Rodger Floyd	Andrew Katz	Cindy Vickers	. . .	John Henckel	William Myers	. . .
Davis	c	CM	2	(580) 369-3333	. . .	Donald Brittin	Paula Pollard	. . .	. . .	Darryl McCurtain	Ralph Thomasson
Del City	c	CM	22	(405) 671-3015	Brian Linley	Mark Edwards	. . .	Carol Noble	Terry Guinn	James Taylor	William Graham
Dewey	c	CM	3	(918) 534-2272	Joe Franco	. . .	Annette Breshears	. . .	Earl James	Bill Breshears	Chester Williams
Drumright	c	CM	2	(918) 352-2631	. . .	. . .	Susan White	Holly Maschino	Cam Bookout	Loren Guyer	Rick Dillard
Duncan	c	CM	22	(580) 252-0250	Gene Brown	Clyde Shaw	. . .	Gerald Morris	Larry Sullins	Jeff Johnson	R. Vaughn
Durant	c	CM	13	(580) 924-7205	Jerry Tomlinson	. . .	Leta McNatt	. . .	Steve Dow	Gary Rudick	Jerry Yandell
Edmond	c	CM	68	(405) 348-8830	S. Gragg-Naifeh	Larry Stevens	Nancy Nichols	Ross VanderHamm	Gilbert Harryman	Bob Ricks	Roger Coldiron
El Reno	c	CM	16	(405) 262-4070	James Moore	Antonio Rivera	. . .	Guy Love	Ronald Martin	Stephen Almon	Don Goucher
Elk City	c	CM	10	(580) 225-3230	Teresa Mullican	Guy Hylton	Cheryl Sipes	. . .	Rick Shelton	William Putman	. . .
Enid	c	CM	47	(580) 234-0400	Irv Honigsburg	William Gamble	Linda Parks	Kerrie Slayter	Philip Clover	Rick West	William Beck
Eufaula	c	MC	2	(918) 689-2534	Dean Smith	. . .	Donna Hysell	. . .	Thomas Foresee	Anthony Garrett	Vernon Hysell
Fairview	c	CM	2	(580) 227-4416	Kenneth Carmack	Dale Sides	Anita Gifford	. . .	Greg Harmon	Hank Weber	Curt Martin
Fort Gibson	t	CM	4	(918) 478-3551	Bob Peebles	Kathryn Carson	Deborah Daniels	. . .	Larry Cooper	Richard Slader	. . .
Frederick	c	CM	4	(580) 335-7551	Pete Wylie	Robert Johnston	Maria Arumugan	Joe Dunham	Bobby Givens	Ricky Guill	Jimmy Tyler
Glenpool	c	CM	8	(918) 322-5409	. . .	H. Tinker	. . .	. . .	. . .	. . .	. . .
Grandfield	c	CM	1	(580) 479-5215	. . .	. . .	. . .	. . .	. . .	. . .	. . .
Grove	c	CM	5	(918) 786-6107	Carolyn Nuckolls	Bruce Johnson	F Ivonne Buzzard	. . .	D Lee Dollarhide	James Wall	Ken Crowder
Guthrie	c	CM	9	(405) 282-0493	Jon Gumerson	. . .	Wanda Calvert	. . .	Rodney Davison	Damon Devereaux	Darryl Hughes
Guymon	c	CM	10	(580) 338-3396	Peggy Keenan	Micheal Shannon	Melissa Bond	. . .	Chris Purdy	Garrett Helton	. . .
Harrah	c	CM	4	(405) 454-2951	Davee Davis	Earl Burson	Alice Davis	Michele Cogdill	Murrel Coleman	Eddie Holland	Joe Morgan
Healdton	c	CM	2	(580) 229-1283	David Smith	Dale Milam	Vivian Glenn	. . .	. . .	. . .	Ray Glenn
Heavener	c	CM	3	(918) 653-2217	Mark Morris	Mike Kennerson	Sharon Loar	. . .	Max Roberts	Don Richards	Carroll Smallwood
Henryetta	c	CM	6	(918) 652-3348	. . .	. . .	Donna White	. . .	Raymond Eldridge	Audie Cole	Richard Kramer
Hobart	c	CM	3	(580) 726-3100	Tom Talley	Willard Brown	Nancy Ledford	. . .	Jerry Lankford	Dale Uptergrove	Jerry Gather
Holdenville	c	MC	4	(405) 379-3397	. . .	. . .	. . .	. . .	Dwight Barnett	. . .	. . .
Hollis	c	CM	2	(580) 688-2167	. . .	. . .	. . .	. . .	. . .	. . .	. . .
Hominy	c	CM	2	(918) 885-2164	R. Tex Bayouth	Patricia Wikel	Melissa Cupp	. . .	Steven Pitts	. . .	. . .
Hugo	c	CM	5	(580) 326-7755	Bill Cavner	. . .	. . .	. . .	Tom Pence	Layton Cox	Gary Lippard
Idabel *	c	MC	6	(580) 286-7608	Jerry Shinn	. . .	Tina Foshee	. . .	Billy Loftin	Jim Coffman	Steve Surratt
Jenks *	c	CM	9	(918) 299-5883	Vic Vreeland	. . .	. . .	Kenda Rice	Bob Douglas	Don Selle	. . .
Kingfisher	c	CM	4	(405) 375-3705	Roger Phillips	Reuben Pulis	Jack Graham	. . .	Kenneth Bengs	Tom Jones	. . .
Konawa	c	CM	1	(580) 925-3775	. . .	B. Dye	Wanda Lowry	. . .	. . .	. . .	. . .
Lawton	c	CM	92	(580) 581-3392	. . .	Larry Mitchell	. . .	Richard Endicott	Barton Hadley	Harold Thorne	Gerald Ihler
Lindsay	c	CM	2	(405) 756-2019	. . .	. . .	. . .	. . .	. . .	. . .	. . .
Lone Grove	c	CM	4	(580) 657-3111	Dickie Welch	Harrell Kennedy	Terri Downs	. . .	Billy Christian	Robert Oldham	Charles Gilbert
Madill	c	CM	3	(580) 795-5586	Leesa Stanley	Robert Watts	Carol Painter	. . .	J Keith Pruitt	James Fullingim	Bobby Kaney
Mangum	c	CM	2	(580) 782-2250	Robert Zinn	. . .	Staci Goode	. . .	Steven Slaton	Dale Rogers	Terry Warren
Mannford	c	MC	2	(918) 865-4314	. . .	Mike Nunneley	Joyce Martin	Cecilia Ward	Bob Evans	Virgil Reed	John Anson
Marlow	c	CM	4	(580) 658-5401	Gary Vining	Janice Cain	Michael Bullard	Donald Green	. . .	Robert Hill	. . .
Mc Alester *	c	CM	17	(918) 423-9300	Dale Covington	Mark Roath	Bobbie Lanz	. . .	Joe Benson	Dale Nave	. . .
Mc Loud	t	MC	3	(405) 964-5264	. . .	. . .	Patricia Morris	. . .	. . .	Dennis Samples	Billie Sneed
Medford	c	CM	1	(580) 395-2823	. . .	Dea Kretchmar	. . .	. . .	. . .	Roger Christman	Dennis Brittain
Miami	c	MC	13	(918) 542-6685	Harrell Post	Michael Spurgeon	. . .	Charles Tomlin	Kevin Trease	Gary Anderson	Tim Wilson
Midwest City	c	CM	54	(405) 739-1232	Russell Smith	John Henson	Rhonda Atkins	Judy Redman	Randall Olsen	Robert Clabes	. . .
Moore	c	CM	41	(405) 793-5000	Lewis Glenn	Stephen Eddy	. . .	Jim Corbett	Charles Stephens	Ted Williams	Richard Sandefur
Muldrow	t	MC	3	(918) 427-3226	Carl Fugett	David Taylor	. . .	Dorothy Chandler	Jim Mabray	Tony Lewis	Joe Shamblin
Muskogee	c	CM	38	(918) 682-6602	James Buschnell	Walter Beckham	Pamala Bush	. . .	Robert Hutson	Rex Eskridge	Don Younger
Mustang	c	CM	13	(405) 376-4521	Chad McDowell	David Cockrell	Patricia Winham	Brenda Wright	Alvin McClung	Monte James	. . .
Newcastle	c	CM	5	(405) 387-4427	James Wilson	Hank York	Shirley Guffey	. . .	Steven Bowers	Larry Hodges	Bill Canary
Newkirk	c	CM	2	(580) 362-2117	Michael Gibson	Harold Harris	Jane Thomas	. . .	Jerry Evans	John Hobbs	Jack Bagg
Nichols Hills	c	CM	4	(405) 843-6637	Kathy Walker	David Poole	. . .	Cathy Keller	Keith Bryan	Richard Mask	Charles Hooper
Nicoma Park	t	MC	2	(405) 769-5673	William Green	. . .	Beverly McManus	. . .	James Shonts	Eric Crews	. . .
Noble	t	CM	5	(405) 872-9251	Dee Downer	Harry Hill	Sarita Scott	. . .	James Stufflebean	Paul Boyd	Elza Harris
Norman *	c	CM	95	(405) 366-5487	Cindy Rosenthal	Steven Lewis	Mary Hatley	Anthony Francisco	James Fullingim	Phil Cotten	Shawn O'Leary
Nowata	c	CM	3	(918) 273-3538	John Carroll	Dave Neely	Tracy Mitchell	. . .	Randy Lawson	Bill Tate	Donald Lewis
Okeene	t	CM	1	(580) 822-3035	Angela Ohman	Mary Jac Rauh	. . .	. . .	. . .	Robert Cancemi	Keith Richardson
Okemah	c	CM	3	(918) 623-1050	Luna Burnett	Robert Baxter	Roberta Rutland	. . .	. . .	Edward Smith	Jerry Turner
Oklahoma City *	c	CM	506	(405) 297-2530	Mick Cornett	James Couch	Frances Kersey	Laura Johnson	Keith Bryant	William Citty	Dennis Clowers
Okmulgee	c	CM	13	(918) 756-4060	Everett Horn	Robert Baxter	Ronnia Andrews	. . .	Richard Mitchell	Joe Prentice	Charles Miller
Owasso	c	CM	18	(918) 376-1500	Craig Theondel	Rodney Ray	. . .	Sherry Bishop	Lenny Fisher	Dan Yancey	F. Carr

Directory 1/9 continued — OFFICIALS IN U.S. MUNICIPALITIES 2,500 AND OVER IN POPULATION

Jurisdiction	Type	Form of govern-ment	2000 Popu-lation (000)	Main telephone number	Chief elected official	Appointed administrator	Clerk of the governing board	Chief financial officer	Fire chief	Police chief	Public works director
OKLAHOMA continued											
Pauls Valley	c	CM	6	(405) 238-3308	Tim Gamble	. . .	Barbara Plummer	. . .	Joe Eddy	James Frizell	. . .
Pawhuska *	c	CM	3	(918) 287-3040	. . .	. . .	Virginia Kelderman	. . .	Laban Miles	Kevin St. Peter	Mark Chamberlain
Perkins	c	CM	2	(405) 547-2445	. . .	Peter Seikel	. . .	. . .	. . .	. . .	. . .
Perry *	c	MC	5	(580) 336-4241	Charles Hall	Roy Rainey	. . .	Randolph Meachan	Paul Hinchey	Michael Thomas	Jim Davis
Piedmont *	c	CM	3	(405) 373-2621	Mike Drea	Michael Vaughn	Amanda Percival	. . .	Mike Southard	. . .	Bud Stuber
Pocola	t	MC	3	(918) 436-2388	John Farris	. . .	Glenda Harris	. . .	Joe Pendleton	Russell Nichols	. . .
Ponca City	c	CM	25	(580) 767-0323	Richard Stone	Gary Martin	. . .	Marc La Bossiere	. . .	Clayton Johnson	. . .
Poteau	c	MC	7	(918) 647-4191	Jeff Shockley	. . .	Cindy Pollard	. . .	Jon Pickel	Billy Smith	Mark Collins
Prague	c	CM	2	(405) 567-2270	J. McBride	Louis Devereaux	Christi Riddle	. . .	Starland Davis	Jim Bartlett	. . .
Pryor	c	MC	8	(918) 825-0888	Jimmy Tramel	. . .	Eva Smith	. . .	David Harrison	Dennis Nichols	. . .
Purcell	c	CM	5	(405) 527-6561	Albert Hudson	B Darlene Duncan	Tina Allison	. . .	Michael Clifton	David Tompkins	. . .
Sallisaw	c	CM	7	(918) 775-6241	Shannon Vann	Bill Baker	Robert Park	. . .	Michael Tubbs	Gary Philpot	. . .
Sand Springs *	c	CM	17	(918) 246-2500	Mike Burdge	D. Enevoldsen	Bruce Ford	. . .	Mark Joslin	Daniel Bradley	Wayne Morgan
Sapulpa	c	CM	19	(918) 224-3040	Douglas Haught	Thomas DeArman	Shirley Burzio	Pamela Vann	Jackie Carner	James Wall	Tim White
Sayre	c	MC	4	(580) 928-2260	Jack Ivester	Jack McKennon	Elaine Barker	. . .	Sammy Green	Jeff Lambert	. . .
Seminole	c	CM	6	(405) 382-4330	Vicki Spears	Steven Saxon	Diane Johnson	. . .	Roy Lemmings	Christopher Mills	Michael Grant
Shawnee *	c	CM	28	(405) 878-1669	. . .	James Collard	. . .	Neva Treiber	. . .	William Mathis	Jim Bierd
Skiatook	t	CM	5	(918) 396-2797	Don Branscum	R. McClanathan	. . .	Shirley Lett	Jeff Perry	Richard Davis	. . .
Spencer	c	CM	3	(405) 771-3226	Earl Syth	Nicole Mukes	Evrett White	. . .	Ron Kelley	Olan Boydstun	Larry Mathews
Stigler	c	CM	2	(918) 967-2164	Larry Godfrey	Pete Bass	Leann Lassiter	. . .	Jim Pearson	Richard Dickson	Roger Edwards
Stillwater	c	CM	39	(405) 372-0025	Melvin Lacy	Dan Galloway	Clara Welch	Marcy Alexander	Larry Mulliken	Norman McNickle	. . .
Stroud *	c	CM	2	(918) 968-2890	Joseph Hankins	Steve Gilbert	Gayle Thornton	. . .	Berry McCammon	Brett Gipson	. . .
Sulphur *	c	MC	4	(580) 622-5096	Mitch Hull	William Holley	Shannon Couch	. . .	Dayton Burnside	David Shores	Keith Woodell
Tahlequah	c	MC	14	(918) 456-0651	Jenny Cook	Kevin Smith	Deb Corn	. . .	Mike Swim	Norman Fisher	. . .
Tecumseh	c	CM	6	(405) 598-2188	Greg Wilson	David Johnson	Joanne Medley	. . .	Jimmy Stokes	Gary Crosby	. . .
The Village	c	CM	10	(405) 751-8861	Stanley Alexander	Bruce Stone	. . .	. . .	Dewayne Price	Michael Robinson	Larry Walton
Tishomingo	c	CM	3	(580) 371-2369	Rex Morrell	Jack Yates	Geneva Carr	. . .	Tom Winkler	Wayne Solomon	Wayne Taylor
Tonkawa	c	CM	3	(580) 628-2508	. . .	John Ramey	Deborah Miner	. . .	Kirk Henderson	Bill Jordan	Darrell Steelmon
Tulsa	c	MC	393	(918) 596-7440	Kathy Taylor	. . .	. . .	Michael Kier	Alan LaCroix	David Been	Charles Hardt
Tuttle	c	CM	4	(405) 381-2335	Lonnie Paxton	Jerry Taylor	Cheryl LaFerney	. . .	Gerald Cook	Donald Cluck	Tommy Chester
Vinita *	c	MC	6	(918) 256-8552	Jesse Johnson	Charles Enyart	Linda Scott	. . .	Jimmie Butcher	George Hicks	. . .
Wagoner *	c	MC	7	(918) 485-4586	Joshua Hughes	Larry Morgan	Linda Gaylor	. . .	Kelly Grooms	Terry Hornbuckle	Kenneth Peters
Walters	c	CM	2	(580) 875-3337	. . .	John Sheppard	Dollie Glenn	. . .	Richard Lewallen	Mike Carter	. . .
Warr Acres	c	MC	9	(405) 789-2892	Tommy Pike	. . .	Nancy Jones	. . .	Bob Cunningham	David Smith	Gerald Wright
Watonga	c	MC	4	(580) 623-4669	. . .	. . .	. . .	. . .	. . .	. . .	. . .
Waurika	c	CM	1	(580) 222-2713	Dana Eck	Kenneth Ferreira	Donna Brown	. . .	Harold Winton	James Jones	. . .
Waynoka	c	MC	. .	(580) 824-2261	Charlene Bixler	. . .	. . .	Sharlotte Bolar	Larry Milledge	Kermit Criswell	. . .
Weatherford	c	MC	9	(580) 772-7451	Gary Rader	Tony Davenport	. . .	. . .	Dean Brown	Byron Cox	Arnold Miller
Wetumka	c	CM	1	(405) 452-3251	Bob Fansher	Don Kardokus	J. Smith	Pat Griggs	Robert Spradlin	. . .	. . .
Wewoka	c	CM	3	(405) 257-2413	. . .	David Fuqua	. . .	. . .	. . .	. . .	. . .
Wilburton	c	MC	2	(918) 465-5361	Danny Baldwin	. . .	Denise Brunk	. . .	. . .	. . .	. . .
Woodward	c	CM	11	(580) 256-2280	Bill Fanning	D. Riffel	Catherine Coleman	Doug Haines	Steve Day	Harvey Rutherford	Thomas Goff
Wynnewood	c	CM	2	(405) 665-2307	John Warren	. . .	Beverly Collier	. . .	Jeff Green	Troy Bishop	Don Harmon
Yale	c	CM	1	(918) 387-2405	James Matlock	Joe Johnson	Sharon Crisjohn	. . .	Jeff Morphew	Rick Gibson	Wes Thurman
Yukon	c	CM	21	(405) 354-1895	John Alberts	James Crosby	Patricia Hargis	. . .	Jeff Lara	Ike Shirley	Jerry Reed
OREGON											
Adair Village	c	MC	. .	(541) 745-5507	. . .	James Minard	. . .	. . .	. . .	. . .	. . .
Albany *	c	CM	40	(541) 917-7500	Doug Killin	Roland Hare	Betty Langwell	Stewart Taylor	Kevin Kreitman	Edward Boyd	D. Taniguchi-Dennis
Amity	c	CM	1	(503) 835-3711	. . .	. . .	Heidi Blaine	. . .	. . .	. . .	. . .
Ashland	c	MC	19	(541) 488-6002	. . .	Martha Bennett	. . .	Lee Tuneberg	Keith Woodley	. . .	Paula Brown
Astoria	c	CM	9	(503) 325-5824	Willis VanDusen	Paul Benoit	. . .	John Snyder	Lenard Hansen	Robert Deu Pree	William Mitchum
Aumsville	c	CM	3	(503) 749-2030	Harold White	Maryann Hills	. . .	Dianne Pursell	. . .	Michael Andall	Steve Oslie
Baker City	c	CM	9	(541) 523-6541	Karen Yeakley	Stephen Brocato	. . .	Roger Dexter	. . .	Jim Tomlinson	Dick Fleming
Bandon	c	MC	2	(541) 347-2437	Mary Schamehorn	Matt Winkel	Marie Ducharme	Carolyn Stephens	. . .	Bob Webb	Richard Anderson
Banks	c	MC	1	(503) 324-5112	Mike Lyda	James Hough	Jolynn Becker	. . .	. . .	. . .	. . .
Beaverton	c	MC	76	(503) 526-2201	Rob Drake	. . .	. . .	Patrick O'Claire	. . .	David Bishop	. . .
Bend	c	CM	52	(541) 388-5502	Oran Teater	Harold Anderson	Patricia Stell	M. Escheveste	Larry Langston	Andrew Jordan	Michael Elmore
Boardman	c	CM	2	(541) 481-9252	. . .	. . .	Lila Killingbeck	Kenneth Fleck	. . .	Mark Calbick	Jeffrey Hayzlett
Brookings *	c	CM	5	(541) 469-2163	Pat Sherman	Gary Milliman	. . .	. . .	William Sharp	Christopher Wallace	John Cowan
Brownsville	c	CM	1	(541) 466-5666	C. Shipley-Kalupa	. . .	. . .	. . .	. . .	. . .	Kurt Riemer
Burns *	c	CM	3	(541) 573-5255	Laura Van Cleave	David Boone	Dauna Wensenk	. . .	Bill Guindon	Rob Nou	David Cullens
Canby	c	CM	12	(503) 266-4021	Melody Thompson	Mark Adcock	Kim Scheafer	. . .	. . .	Ken Pagano	Roy Hester
Cannon Beach	c	CM	1	(503) 436-1581	Dave Rouse	Richard Mays	. . .	. . .	. . .	Gene Halliburton	Joy Gannon
Canyonville *	c	MC	1	(541) 839-4258	Charles Spindel	Cheryl Masotto	. . .	. . .	. . .	. . .	Tony Lakey
Carlton *	c	MC	1	(503) 852-7575	Kathie Oriet	Steven Weaver	Apryl Denman	. . .	Terry Lucich	Frank Butler	Bryan Burnham
Cascade Locks	c	CM	1	(541) 374-8484	Ralph Hesgard	Bernard Seeger	. . .	Katherine Mast	. . .	. . .	Richard McCulley
Central Point	c	CM	12	(541) 664-3321	Henry Williams	Phillip Messina	. . .	Jill Turner	. . .	Michael Sweeny	Robert Pierce
Clatskanie	c	CM	1	(503) 728-2622	Chip Waisanier	Preston Polasek	Tina Hendricks	Arlene Long	. . .	Marvin Hoover	. . .
Coburg	c	MC	. .	(541) 682-7850	. . .	William Hudson	. . .	. . .	. . .	. . .	. . .
Condon	c	MC	. .	(541) 384-2711	N Dale Thompson	Kathryn Greiner	. . .	. . .	. . .	William Gubser	Larry Durfrey
Coos Bay	c	CM	15	(541) 269-1181	Joe Benetti	Charles Freeman	. . .	Janell Howard	Stan Gibson	Eura Washburn	Jim Hossley
Coquille	c	CM	4	(541) 396-2115	. . .	Terence O'Connor	. . .	. . .	Dave Waddington	Michael Reaves	John Higgins
Cornelius *	c	CM	9	(503) 357-9112	William Bash	David Waffle	Debby Roth	Nancy McClain	Chris Asanovic	Paul Rubenstein	Mark Crowell
Corvallis	c	CM	52	(541) 766-6902	Helen Berg	Jon Nelson	Sue Mariner	Nancy Brewer	Dan Campbell	Gary Boldizsar	Steve Rogers
Cottage Grove	c	CM	8	(541) 942-5501	Gary Williams	Richard Meyers	Joan Hoehn	Roberta McClintock	. . .	Michael Grover	Robert Sisson
Creswell	c	MC	3	(541) 895-2531	Ron Petitti	Mark Shrives	. . .	Layli Nichols	. . .	. . .	Roy Sprout
Dallas *	c	CM	12	(503) 623-2338	Jim Fairchild	. . .	. . .	Marcia Baragary	Bill Hahn	Jim Harper	Fred Braun
Damascus	c	CM	9	(503) 658-8545	. . .	James Bennett	. . .	Dan O'Dell	. . .	. . .	. . .
Dayton	c	MC	2	(503) 864-2221	. . .	Sue Hollis	. . .	. . .	. . .	. . .	. . .
Dundee	c	CM	2	(503) 538-3922	C. Ragsdale	. . .	Debra Manning	Sheryl Hartman	John Stock	. . .	. . .
Durham	c	CM	1	(503) 639-6851	Gery Schirado	Roland Signett	. . .	. . .	. . .	. . .	. . .
Eagle Point	c	MC	4	(541) 826-4212	. . .	David Hussell	Dena Roberts	Melissa Owens	. . .	David Strand	Robert Miller
Enterprise	c	MC	1	(541) 426-4196	. . .	Michele Young	. . .	. . .	. . .	. . .	. . .
Estacada	c	CM	2	(503) 630-8270	Robert Austin	Randy Ealy	Denise Carey	. . .	. . .	. . .	William Strawn
Eugene	c	CM	137	(541) 682-5061	James Torrey	. . .	. . .	Cindi Hamm	Thomas Tallon	Thad Buchanan	Kurt Corey
Fairview *	c	MC	9	(503) 665-7929	Mike Weatherby	Joseph Gall	. . .	Laura Zentner	. . .	Ken Johnson	Bob Cochran
Florence	c	CM	7	(541) 997-3436	Phil Brubaker	. . .	Barbara Miller	David Armstrong	. . .	Lynn Lamm	. . .
Forest Grove	c	CM	17	(503) 359-3200	. . .	Michael Sykes	Catherine Jansen	Paul Downey	Robert Davis	Thomas Lowther	Robert Foster
Gearhart	c	MC	. .	(503) 738-5501	. . .	Dennis McNally	. . .	. . .	William Eddy	. . .	. . .
Gervais	c	CM	2	(503) 792-4222	. . .	M. Davis	. . .	. . .	. . .	. . .	. . .

Directory 1/9 continued — OFFICIALS IN U.S. MUNICIPALITIES 2,500 AND OVER IN POPULATION

Jurisdiction		Type	Form of govern-ment	2000 Popu-lation (000)	Main telephone number	Chief elected official	Appointed administrator	Clerk of the governing board	Chief financial officer	Fire chief	Police chief	Public works director
OREGON continued												
Gladstone		c	CM	11	(503) 656-5225	Wade Byers	Ron Partch	. . .	. . .	Charles Ames	Frank Grace	. . .
Gold Beach	*	c	CM	1	(541) 247-7029	Karl Popoff	. . .	Heather Wainscott	Jodi Hatfield	Bruce Floyd	Russ Merkley	Jeff Denney
Granite	*	c	MC	. .	(541) 755-5100	Fred Corbin	. . .	. . .	. . .	. . .	. . .	Paul Schnitzer
Grants Pass		c	CM	30	(541) 474-6360	Len Holzinger	David Frasher	. . .	. . .	. . .	. . .	Dave Wright
Gresham		c	CM	90	(503) 661-3000	Charles Becker	Erik Kvarsten	Debbie Jermann	Terrance McCall	Scott Lewis	Carla Piluso	David Rouse
Happy Valley	*	c	CM	4	(503) 760-3325	Rob Wheeler	Catherin Daw	. . .	Barbara Muller	. . .	. . .	. . .
Harrisburg		c	CM	2	(541) 995-6655	. . .	Bruce Cleeton	. . .	. . .	. . .	. . .	. . .
Heppner	*	c	CM	1	(541) 676-9618	Tim VanCleave	Dave DeMayo	. . .	. . .	. . .	. . .	Bruce Nelson
Hermiston		c	CM	13	(541) 567-5521	Bob Severson	Edward Brookshier	. . .	. . .	. . .	Daniel Coulombe	. . .
Hillsboro		c	CM	70	(503) 681-6100	Tom Hughes	Sarah Jo Chaplen	Gail Waibel	. . .	Gary Seidel	Ronald Louie	Roy Gibson
Hood River		c	CM	5	(541) 386-1488	Paul Cummings	Robert Francis	Anita Smith	Steven Everroad	Gary Willis	Richard Younkins	. . .
Hubbard		c	MC	2	(503) 981-9633	. . .	. . .	. . .	. . .	. . .	. . .	. . .
Independence		c	CM	6	(503) 838-1212	Larry Dalton	Greg Ellis	Charlotte Townsend	David Gephart	. . .	Vernon Wells	Kenneth Perkins
Jacksonville		c	CM	2	(541) 899-8910	James Lewis	Paul Wyntergreen	Kathy Hall	. . .	Tracy Shaw	David Towe	Jeff Alvis
Jefferson		c	MC	2	(541) 327-2768	Michael Myers	. . .	Janet Powell	. . .	. . .	. . .	Steve Human
Joseph		c	MC	1	(541) 432-3832	Peggy Kite-Martin	. . .	. . .	Noma McDaniel	Herman Ortmann	. . .	James Lewis
Junction City		c	MC	4	(541) 998-2153	Jon Edwards	David Clyne	. . .	Barbara Scott	. . .	Laddie Hancock	David Renshaw
Keizer		c	CM	32	(503) 390-3700	. . .	Christopher Eppley	. . .	Susan Gahlsdorf	. . .	Marc Adams	Rob Kissler
King City		c	CM	1	(503) 639-4082	. . .	David Wells	. . .	Bhavana Nesargi	. . .	Charles Fessler	. . .
Klamath Falls		c	CM	19	(541) 883-5317	Todd Kellstrom	Jeffrey Ball	. . .	Phyllis Shidler	. . .	Jim Hunter	Mike Kuenzi
La Grande	*	c	CM	12	(541) 962-1302	. . .	. . .	Alexandra Lund	Eldon Slippy	Bruce Weimer	John Courtney	Danny Chevalier
Lafayette		0	MC	2	(503) 864-2451	. . .	Diane Rinks	Jamie Rhodes	. . .	. . .	. . .	. . .
Lake Oswego	*	c	CM	35	(503) 635-0215	Judie Hammerstad	Douglas Schmitz	Robyn Christie	Richard Seals	Ed Wilson	Dan Duncan	E. Papadopoulos
Lakeview		t	MC	2	(541) 947-2029	. . .	Raymond Simms	. . .	Marlisa Jameson	Kenneth Chartier	David King	Ronald Wilkie
Lebanon		c	CM	12	(541) 451-7476	Kenneth Tombs	John Hitt	. . .	Casey Cole	. . .	Michael Healy	James Ruef
Lincoln City		c	CM	7	(541) 996-2152	Lori Hollingsworth	David Hawker	Oneita McCalman	Ron Tierney	. . .	Mike Holden	Lance Burke
Lowell		c	CM	. .	(541) 937-2157	. . .	Charles Spies	. . .	. . .	. . .	. . .	. . .
Madras		c	CM	5	(541) 475-2344	Richard Allen	Mike Morgan	Karen Coleman	Brenda Black	. . .	Tommy Adams	Gus Burril
Manzanita		c	CM	. .	(503) 368-5343	Joyce Raker	Jerald Taylor	Judith New	. . .	. . .	. . .	Bret Siler
Mc Minnville	*	c	CM	26	(503) 434-7301	Edward Gormley	Kent Taylor	. . .	Carole Benedict	Jay Lilly	Ron Noble	Mike Bisset
Medford		c	CM	63	(541) 774-2000	Gary Wheeler	Michael Dyal	. . .	Alison Chan	Dave Bierweiler	Eric Mellgren	Cory Crebbin
Mill City		c	CM	1	(503) 897-2302	Tim Kirsch	Deborah Hogan	Stacie Cook	Renee Short	. . .	. . .	John Dickinson
Milton-Freewater	*	c	CM	6	(541) 938-5531	Lewis Key	Delphine Palmer	. . .	Dave Richmond	Shane Garner	Mike Gallaher	Howard Moss
Milwaukie		c	CM	20	(503) 786-7555	Carolyn Tomei	Michael Swanson	Pat Duval	Steve Smith	. . .	Brent Collier	James Brink
Molalla		c	CM	5	(503) 829-6855	Mike Clarke	John Atkins	. . .	Peggy Johnson	. . .	Jerry Giger	Dean Madison
Monmouth		c	CM	7	(503) 838-0722	Larry Dalton	Scott McClure	Phyllis Bolman	Jeff White	Darrell Patterson	Darrell Tallan	Craig Johns
Monroe		c	MC	. .	(541) 847-5175	. . .	Aaron Palmquist	. . .	. . .	. . .	. . .	James Hickey
Mount Angel		c	CM	3	(503) 845-9291	. . .	James Hunt	Carrie Huff	Tracy Grambusch	Don Fleck	Brent Earhart	Daniel Bernt
Myrtle Creek		c	CM	3	(541) 863-3171	Jerry Pothier	Aaron Cubic	Charity Hays	Jeanne Babcock	Bill Leming	Cecil Earp	Steven Johnson
Myrtle Point	*	c	CM	2	(541) 572-2626	Ed Cook	Randall Whobrey	B. Kirkpatrick	Amy McCall	Dan Gardner	Rock Rakossi	Randy Whobrey
Nehalem		c	CM	. .	(503) 368-5627	Shirley Kalkhoven	Michael Nitzsche	Dee Anne Stockton	. . .	Steve Van Dyke	. . .	Don Davidson
Newberg	*	c	CM	18	(503) 538-9421	Robert Andrews	. . .	Norma Alley	Elizabeth Comfort	Al Blodgett	Brian Casey	Dan Danicic
Newport	*	c	CM	9	(541) 574-0603	William Bain	Michael O'Neal	Margaret Hawker	Janice Riessbeck	Richard Crook	Mark Miranda	Lee Ritzman
North Bend		c	CM	9	(541) 756-8500	Rick Wetherell	Jan Willis	Angie Kellar	Juana Bell	Scott Graham	Steve Scibelli	. . .
Nyssa	*	c	CM	3	(541) 372-2264	Bob Fehlman	Roberta Donovan	Hilda Contreras	Helen Holtz	Pedro Vasquez	Dennis Francis	Myra Harley
Oakridge	*	c	CM	3	(541) 782-2258	Don Hampton	G. Zimmerman	. . .	Chantell Hayson	Tim Demers	Louis Gomez	Kevin Urban
Ontario		c	CM	10	(541) 889-7684	M. Cammack	. . .	Tori Ankrum	Rachel Hopper	Terry Mairs	Mike Kee	Steve Gaschler
Oregon City	*	c	CM	25	(503) 657-0891	Alice Norris	Larry Patterson	Nancy Ide	David Wimmer	. . .	. . .	Nancy Kraushaar
Pendleton	*	c	CM	16	(541) 966-0201	Phillip Houk	Lawrence Lehman	. . .	Linda Carter	John Fowler	Stuart Roberts	Robert Patterson
Philomath		c	CM	3	(541) 929-6148	. . .	Randy Kugler	Ruth Post	. . .	. . .	Ken Eluer	Beau Vencill
Phoenix		c	MC	4	(541) 535-1955	. . .	M. Shaddox	. . .	. . .	. . .	. . .	. . .
Pilot Rock		c	CM	1	(541) 443-2811	. . .	Jackie Carey	Amanda Howard	. . .	. . .	Ronnie Layton	Steve Draper
Port Orford		c	CM	1	(541) 332-3681	. . .	. . .	Patricia Clark	Robert Ewalt	. . .	William Rush	David Pace
Portland		c	CO	529	(503) 823-3572	Vera Katz	. . .	Karla Moore-Love	. . .	. . .	Charles Moose	Felicia Trader
Prineville		c	CM	7	(541) 447-5627	Mike Wendel	Robb Corbett	Patricia Hepperle	Liz Schutte	. . .	Eric Bush	Jim Mole
Rainier	*	c	CM	1	(503) 556-7301	Jerry Cole	Kenneth Knight	. . .	. . .	. . .	. . .	. . .
Redmond	*	c	CM	13	(541) 923-7739	Alan Unger	. . .	Patricia Leymaster	Chris Earnest	Tim Moor	Ronnie Roberts	Chris Doty
Reedsport	*	c	CM	4	(541) 271-3603	Keith Tymchuk	Rick Hohnbaum	. . .	Vera Koch	Tom Anderson	Shawn Essex	Floyd Dollar
Roseburg	*	c	CM	20	(541) 672-7701	Larry Rich	P. Swanson	Sheila Cox	Cheryl Guyett	Jack Cooley	Mark Nickel	Clay Baumgartner
Salem		c	CM	136	(503) 588-6162	Janet Taylor	. . .	. . .	Glen Merritt	Marcus Knode	Walter Myers	Timothy Gerling
Sandy		c	CM	5	(503) 668-5533	Linda Malone	Scott Lazenby	. . .	Larry Stohosky	. . .	Harold Skelton	Mike Walker
Scappoose		c	CM	4	(503) 543-7146	Glenn Dorschler	Jon Hanken	Susan Pentecost	Jill Herr	. . .	Douglas Greisen	Terry Andrews
Seaside		c	CM	5	(503) 738-5511	Donald Larson	Mark Winstanley	. . .	. . .	Joseph Dotson	Robert Gross	Neal Wallace
Shady Cove	*	c	MC	2	(541) 878-2225	Ruth Keith	Elise Smurzynski	Margaret Borgen	. . .	. . .	Richard Mendenhall	George Bostic
Sheridan		c	CM	3	(503) 843-2347	Robert White	Francis Sheridan	Patricia Henderson	Joel Wade	. . .	. . .	Lonnie Hinchcliff
Sherwood		c	CM	11	(503) 625-5522	Keith Mays	Ross Schultz	Sylvia Murphy	Chris Robuck	. . .	William Middleton	Craig Sheldon
Silverton	*	c	CM	7	(503) 873-5321	Ken Hector	Bryan Cosgrove	. . .	Kathleen Zaragoza	. . .	Richard Lewis	Richard Barstad
Sisters		c	MC	. .	(541) 549-6022	M.David Elliot	Eileen Stein	. . .	Emma Sivers	. . .	. . .	Gary Frazee
Springfield		c	CM	52	(541) 726-3700	Sidney Leiken	Gino Grimaldi	Amy Sowa	Robert Duey	Dennis Murphy	Jerry Smith	Dan Brown
St. Helens		c	MC	10	(503) 397-6272	Randy Peterson	Chad Olsen	. . .	Marilyn Peterson	. . .	Steve Salle	Timothy Homann
Stayton		c	CM	6	(503) 769-3425	Gerry Aboud	Christopher Childs	. . .	. . .	. . .	Don Eubank	Michael Faught
Sutherlin		c	CM	6	(541) 459-2856	Joe Mongiovi	Arthur Schmidt	. . .	David Harker	Joel King	Thomas Boggs	Michael Gray
Sweet Home		c	CM	8	(541) 367-8969	Craig Fentiman	Craig Martin	. . .	Patricia Gray	. . .	Robert Burford	Michael Adams
Talent		c	CM	5	(541) 535-1566	Marian Telerski	Betty Wheeler	. . .	Holly Haviland	. . .	Robert Rector	Lester Naught
The Dalles		c	CM	12	(541) 296-5481	David Beckley	Nolan Young	Julie Krueger	Robert Moody	. . .	Jay Waterbury	Brian Stahl
Tigard		c	CM	41	(503) 639-4171	. . .	Craig Prosser	Catherine Wheatley	. . .	. . .	William Dickinson	Edward Wegner
Tillamook		c	CM	4	(503) 842-2472	Robert McPheeters	Mark Gervasi	Susan Huntsman	B. Sorensen	. . .	Terrence Wright	Michael Mahoney
Toledo		c	CM	3	(541) 336-2247	. . .	Peter Wall	Renee Ballinger	. . .	William Ewing	Donald Denison	Herbert Jennings
Troutdale		c	CM	13	(503) 665-5175	Paul Thalhofer	John Anderson	Debbie Stickney	Kathy Leader	. . .	David Nelson	James Galloway
Tualatin	*	c	CM	22	(503) 692-2000	Lou Ogden	Sherilyn Lombos	Maureen Smith	. . .	. . .	Kent Barker	Daniel Boss
Turner		c	CM	1	(503) 743-2155	Carly Strauss	Richard Van Orman	Betty Jensen	Patty Dunn	. . .	Gary Will	Terry Rust
Umatilla		c	CM	4	(541) 922-3226	David Trott	Lawrence Clucas	Linda Gettmann	. . .	. . .	Darla Huxel	Roger Frances
Veneta		c	MC	2	(541) 935-2191	Tim Brooker	Ric Ingham	. . .	. . .	. . .	. . .	. . .
Vernonia		c	MC	2	(503) 429-5291	Sally Harrison	. . .	Kate Conley	Cindy Naillon	. . .	Mathew Workman	Jeff Burch
Waldport		c	CM	2	(541) 563-3561	Scott Beckstead	Nancy Leonard	Reda Quinlan	. . .	. . .	. . .	Rick McClung
Warrenton		c	CM	4	(503) 861-2233	Paul Rodriguez	. . .	Linda Engbretson	Laurie Sawrey	Frank Ames	Robert Maxfield	. . .
West Linn		c	CM	22	(503) 657-0331	David Dodds	Christopher Jordan	Nancy Davis	Elizabeth Carlson	. . .	John Ellison	Ronald Hudson
Wilsonville		c	CM	13	(503) 682-1011	. . .	Arlene Loble	Sandy King	Gary Wallis	. . .	. . .	Jeff Bauman
Winston		c	CM	4	(541) 679-6739	Rex Stevens	David Van Dermark	. . .	Ann Munson	. . .	Scott Gugel	. . .
Wood Village	*	c	CM	2	(503) 667-6211	David Fuller	Sheila Ritz	. . .	Wyatt Parno	Scott Lewis	Bernie Guisto	Randall Jones
Woodburn	*	c	CM	20	(503) 982-5228	Kathryn Figley	John Brown	Mary Tennant	David Gillespie	. . .	Scott Russell	. . .

Directory 1/9 continued **OFFICIALS IN U.S. MUNICIPALITIES 2,500 AND OVER IN POPULATION**

Jurisdiction	Type	Form of govern-ment	2000 Popu-lation (000)	Main telephone number	Chief elected official	Appointed administrator	Clerk of the governing board	Chief financial officer	Fire chief	Police chief	Public works director
PENNSYLVANIA											
Abington	tp	MC	1	(570) 586-0111	Jeff Thurston	William White	Jacqueline Bisch	...	...	Daniel Mooney	Thomas James
Abington	tp	MC	56	(267) 536-1000	Barbara Ferrara	Burton Conway	...	Susan Matiza	Kenneth Clark	William Kelly	Ed Micciolo
Akron	b	MC	4	(717) 859-1600	John McBeth	Reed Imhoff	...	...	Larry Hanke	...	Kenneth Gestewitz
Aldan	b	MC	4	(610) 626-3553	...	...	...	...	...	...	...
Aleppo *	tp	MC	1	(412) 741-6555	Frank Bialek	Gwen Patterson	...	...	William Davis	Norbert Micklos	Mark Kerr
Aliquippa	b	CO	11	(724) 375-5188	James Mansueti	...	...	Dennis Panagitsas	Darryl Jones	Ralph Pallante	Bernie Hall
Allegheny	tp	MC	8	(724) 842-4641	Kathy Starr	David Soboslay	Susan Teagarden	Carol Waronsky	...	Timothy Solla	Steven Kanas
Allentown	c	MC	106	(610) 437-7523	Roy Afflerbach	Francis Dougherty	Michael Hanlon	Lawrence Hilliard	Scott Lindenmuth	Roger MacLean	Peter Wernsdorfer
Altoona	c	CM	49	(814) 949-2410	Thomas Martin	Joseph Weakland	Linda Rickens	Omar Strohm	Reynold Santone	...	David Diedrich
Ambler	b	CM	6	(215) 646-1000	Bud Wahl	Rocco Wack	...	...	Charles Baily	...	James Wack
Ambridge	b	CM	7	(724) 266-4070	...	Kristen Denne	Joanne Trella	...	David Drewnowski	David Sabol	...
Amity	tp	CM	8	(610) 689-6000	Leslie Sacks	Charles Lyon	Linda McCue	...	...	Noel Roy	...
Archbald	b	MC	6	(570) 876-1800	Kenneth Propst	Fred Donnini	Peggy Adams	Chester Jezerski	Robert Harvey	George Iyoob	Joseph Chindemi
Arnold	c	MC	5	(412) 337-4441	...	...	...	...	...	...	...
Ashland	b	MC	3	(570) 875-2411	Rosemarie Noon	Edward Wallace	...	...	Thomas Towers	Adam Bernodin	...
Ashley	b	MC	2	(570) 824-1364	George Oravic	Kathleen Krofchok	...	...	Joseph McGlynn	David Cerski	Robert Hess
Aspinwall	b	MC	2	(412) 781-0213	John Lovey	Edward Warchol	Georgene Veltri	...	...	Charles Clouse	Lee Albacker
Aston	tp	CM	16	(610) 494-2915	James McGinn	Richard Lehr	...	...	Thomas Morgan	Albert Fasano	Russell Palmore
Athens	b	MC	3	(570) 888-2120	...	...	...	...	...	C. Hutchinson	...
Avalon *	b	CM	5	(412) 761-5820	Edward Kildare	Harry Dilmore	...	David Pfeiffer	William Carney	Robert Howie	Keith Lorey
Avoca	b	MC	2	(570) 457-4947	Joseph Satkowski	Ann Backlasky	S. Yokimishyn	...	...	Edward Lukowich	Keith Patterson
Baden	b	MC	4	(724) 869-3700	Carol Sambol	Susan Blum	Michael Miketa	Michael Stuban	David Trzcianka	...	John Peoples
Baldwin	b	MC	19	(412) 882-9600	Alexander Bennett	Timothy Little	Judy Assad	...	...	...	Mark Stephenson
Bally	b	MC	1	(610) 845-2351	...	Toni Hemerka	Brenda Sturdevant	...	...	Kenneth Norton	...
Bangor	b	MC	5	(610) 588-2216	Bonnie La Bar	Lynn Martocci	Linda Paynter	Cynthia Weiss	Robert Owens	H. Schollhammer	...
Barnesboro	b	MC	2	(814) 948-8230	Eva Wargo	Fred Nastasi	...	...	Dave Hassen	Kevin Stanek	Dave Suchar
Beaver	b	MC	4	(724) 773-6700	...	...	...	...	...	...	...
Beaver Falls *	c	CO	9	(724) 847-2800	Karl Boak	Richard Janus	Paula Burdine	Leonard Chiappetta	Mark Stowe	Gary Minnitte	Ted Krzemienski
Beavertown	b	MC	..	(570) 658-2505	David Hassinger	Chris Weller	...	...	William Mattern	...	...
Bedford	b	MC	3	(814) 623-8192	William Leibfreid	John Montgomery	Beverly Fisher	...	Rocky Fetter	C. Reicheldorfer	...
Bedminster	tp	MC	4	(215) 795-2190	...	...	...	...	...	...	...
Bellefonte	b	CM	6	(814) 355-1501	Joseph Heidt	Ralph Stewart	Suzanne Egli	...	...	Duane Dixon	William Comly
Bellevue	b	CM	8	(412) 766-6164	Paul Cusick	David Golebiewski	Marsha Smith	Lori Forbes	Charles Amrhein	Michael Bookser	Murl Thompson
Bensalem *	tp	CM	58	(215) 633-3600	Joseph Digirolamo	William Cmorey	...	John McGinley	Joseph Scanlon	...	James Ryan
Bentleyville	b	MC	2	(724) 239-2112	Lena Greenfield	...	Sheryl Hreha	...	Ronald Sicchitano	...	Arthur Blackburn
Benzinger	tp	MC	8	(814) 781-1274	...	...	...	...	...	...	...
Berwick *	b	CM	10	(570) 752-2723	Gary Pinterich	Shane Pepe	...	...	Bill Coolbaugh	Frank Brennan	Robert Markle
Bethlehem *	c	MC	71	(610) 865-7000	John Callahan	...	Cynthia Biedenkopf	Dennis Reichard	George Barkanic	Randall Miller	Michael Alkhal
Bethlehem *	tp	CM	21	(610) 814-6400	Allan Robertson	Jon Hammer	Judy Todaro	Andrew Freda	...	Daniel Pancoast	Richard Grube
Big Beaver	b	MC	2	(724) 827-2416	...	...	...	...	...	...	...
Birdsboro	b	CM	5	(610) 582-6030	Robert Myers	Randall Miller	Michelle Cramer	...	...	Theodore Roth	...
Blairsville	b	CM	3	(412) 459-9100	Raymond Baker	Edward Smith	Mary Brown	...	Daniel Duralli	...	Joseph Spiaggi
Blakely *	b	MC	7	(570) 383-3340	Robert Klinko	Harold McCusker	...	...	Walter Yankovitch	Joseph Williams	...
Bloomsburg	t	MC	12	(570) 784-7703	Charles Coffman	Carol Mas	...	...	Hugh Gross	Leo Sokoloski	John Barton
Blossburg	b	MC	1	(570) 638-2452	John Backman	George Lloyd	Sally Ward	...	...	...	...
Boyertown	b	CM	3	(610) 367-2688	...	...	...	...	...	...	...
Brackenridge	b	CM	3	(724) 224-0800	...	...	Carol Jones	...	...	Jamie Bock	Joseph Chifulini
Braddock	b	CM	2	(412) 271-1018	Pauline Abdullah	...	Clara Jones	...	Thomas Petrovic	William Moore	...
Braddock Hills	b	CM	1	(412) 241-5080	...	...	...	...	Robert Henkel	Frank Gardone	Thomas McQuade
Bradford	c	CM	9	(814) 362-3884	Michele Corignani	John Peterson	...	Katherine Graff	William McCormack	Roger Sager	Gary Alcock
Brentwood	b	MC	10	(412) 884-1500	...	George Zboyovsky	...	...	...	...	...
Bridgeport	b	MC	4	(610) 272-1811	...	...	...	...	Steven Wanczyk	...	...
Bridgeville	b	CM	5	(412) 221-6012	...	...	...	...	...	...	...
Brighton	tp	CM	8	(724) 774-4803	Jack Erath	Bryan Dehart	...	...	...	Stanley Guza	...
Bristol	b	MC	9	(215) 788-3828	...	...	...	...	...	...	...
Bristol	tp	CM	55	(215) 785-5884	Samuel Fenton	Suzanne Newsome	...	Sharon Rendeiro	Edward Copper	Thomas Mills	Steven McClain
Brookhaven	b	MC	7	(610) 874-2557	...	...	...	...	...	...	...
Brookville	b	MC	4	(814) 849-5321	Chip Wonderling	...	Stephen Rowan	...	Denny Allgiver	Kenneth Dworek	...
Brownsville	b	MC	2	(724) 785-5761	...	...	...	...	...	...	...
Buckingham	tp	CM	16	(215) 794-8834	...	Raymond Stepnoski	...	...	...	Steven Daniels	...
Butler	c	CO	15	(724) 285-4124	Leonard Pintell	...	Robert Brehm	Joseph Bratkovich	Larry Christy	Timothy Fennell	Mitch Ufner
Butler	tp	MC	17	(724) 283-3430	...	Gerald Patterson	...	...	...	...	...
Butler	tp	MC	7	(570) 788-3547	Ramson Young	Steven Hahn	...	Erin Braddock	...	...	...
California	b	MC	5	(724) 938-8878	John Greenlief	...	Diane Pagac	Edwin Glab	Thomas Hartley	Joseph Dochinez	John Mariscotti
Callimont	b	MC	..	(814) 634-0010	Arlene Feeney	...	...	...	...	...	...
Caln	tp	MC	11	(610) 384-0600	Arnold Kring	Gregory Prowant	...	Eliza Derring	David Aberts	John Bennett	Michael Fowler
Cambridge Springs	b	CM	2	(814) 398-2311	Joseph Tuminello	Peggy Lewis	Sandra Pude	...	Richard Massung	Eugene Woznicki	Kenneth Dine
Camp Hill	b	CM	7	(717) 737-3456	Philip Murren	Edward Knittel	...	Natalie Lee	Rob Kozicki	Gregory Ammons	Tim Maro
Canonsburg	b	CM	8	(724) 745-1800	Anthony Colaizzo	Terry Hazlett	...	...	Harold Coleman	R.T. Bell	Chester Osiecki
Canton	tp	CM	8	(724) 225-8990	...	...	Lori Castle	...	...	...	...
Carbondale	c	MC	9	(570) 282-4110	John Jordan	Fred Moase	Michele Bannon	...	Robert Wright	Dominick Andidora	...
Carlisle	b	CM	17	(717) 249-4422	Kirk Wilson	...	Susan Armstrong	John O'Neill	Robert Kennedy	Stephen Margeson	Michael Keiser
Carnegie	b	CM	8	(412) 276-1414	...	...	Lori Ritter	...	John Kandracs	...	Leonard Mitkoski
Carroll Valley	b	MC	3	(717) 642-8269	Grady Edwards	David Hazlett	Barbara Hertz	...	...	Richard Hileman	...
Castle Shannon	b	CM	8	(412) 885-9200	Regis Zezulewicz	Thomas Hartswick	Linda Karlovich	...	William Reffner	Harold Lane	...
Catasauqua	b	CM	6	(610) 264-0571	Barbara Schlegel	Eugene Goldfeder	...	...	Samuel Burrows	Douglas Kish	Jeffrey MacHose
Center	tp	MC	11	(724) 774-0271	Tony Amadio	...	...	Rachael Del Tondo	Dennis Morrison	Barry Kramer	...
Centerville	b	MC	3	(724) 785-9206	Patsy Ricciuti	...	...	...	...	David Simon	...
Chalfont	b	MC	3	(215) 822-7295	Robert Cleland	Melissa Shafer	Barbara Qualteria	...	Randy Teschner	Frank Campbell	J. Michael Bishop
Chambersburg	b	CM	17	(717) 264-5151	William McLaughlin	Eric Oyer	Tanya Mickey	Casimir Rzomp	...	Michael Defrank	Robert Wagner
Chanceford	tp	CM	5	(717) 927-6401	Eric Bacon	Brenda Gohn	Amie Baldwin	...	Ronald Witmer	...	...
Charleroi	b	MC	4	(724) 483-6011	Edward Paluso	Robert Hodgson	Carl Minkovich	...	Robert Whiten	Armand Costantino	Thomas Santoro
Chartiers	tp	CM	7	(724) 745-3415	Harlan Shober	Alice Derian	Wendy Williams	...	...	James Horvath	Lloyd Bard
Cheltenham	tp	CM	36	(215) 887-6200	Jeffrey Mauldower	David Kraynik	...	Rosemary Poppert	Michael Moonblatt	John Scholly	Richard Young
Chester	c	MC	36	(610) 447-7700	...	...	Sara Bingnear	Monir Ahmed	Joseph Cliffe	...	Patricia West
Chippewa	tp	CM	7	(724) 843-8177	...	...	...	...	...	Robert Berchtold	...
Churchill *	b	MC	3	(412) 241-7113	Richard Farrell	Craig Robinson	...	...	...	Allen Park	Ralph Zatlin
Clairton	c	CM	8	(412) 233-8113	Dominic Serapiglia	Ralph Imbrogno	Frances Jones	Scott Andrejchak	John Lattanzi	...	Perry Ohm
Clarion	b	CM	6	(814) 226-7707	Ronald Wilshire	Nancy Freenock	...	...	...	Mark Hall	Bradley Stutzman
Clarks Summit	b	CM	5	(570) 586-9316	Harold Kelly	Barbara Grabfelder	...	...	...	...	...
Clearfield *	b	CM	6	(814) 765-7817	Patty Gilliland	...	...	Pamela Peters	Brett Owens	Jeffrey Rhone	William Beveridge
Clifton Heights	b	MC	6	(610) 623-1000	Mike Galantino	...	Shannon Ostien	...	Jim Kneass	Walter Senkow	John Grace

Directory 1/9 continued — OFFICIALS IN U.S. MUNICIPALITIES 2,500 AND OVER IN POPULATION

Jurisdiction		Type	Form of govern-ment	2000 Popu-lation (000)	Main telephone number	Chief elected official	Appointed administrator	Clerk of the governing board	Chief financial officer	Fire chief	Police chief	Public works director
PENNSYLVANIA continued												
Coaldale	*	b	RT	2	(570) 645-6310	Claire Remington	...	...	...	Richard Marek	Timothy Delaney	Kenneth Hankey
Coatesville		c	CM	10	(610) 384-0300	Stephon Hines	...	...	E. McQuiston	Glen Davis	Dominic Bellizzi	Donald Wilkinson
Colebrookdale	*	tp	MC	5	(610) 369-1362	Todd Gamler	Cindy Conrad	...	...	...	Christopher Schott	Bruce Sands
College		tp	CM	8	(814) 231-3021	...	Adam Brumbaugh	...	Robert Long	...	...	Garry Williams
Collegeville		b	MC	8	(610) 489-9208	Dennis Parker	Geoffrey Thompson	Donna Artiuch	...	Jeffrey Wentworth	Barton Bucher	Joseph Hastings
Collingdale		b	CM	8	(610) 586-0500	...	...	...	...	...	...	...
Columbia	*	b	CM	10	(717) 684-2467	...	...	...	G. Schreck	Chuck Anderson	Joseph Greenya	Ron Miller
Colwyn		b	CM	2	(610) 461-2000	James McAnamy	Daniel McEnhill	Kelly Winter	Earl Reed	Rahn Monreal	Bryan Hills	Martha Van Auken
Concord	*	tp	CM	9	(610) 459-8911	Dominic Pileggi	Robert Willert	...	...	Frederick Field	...	Harry Shire
Connellsville		c	MC	9	(724) 628-2020	...	...	...	...	...	...	...
Conshohocken		b	MC	7	(610) 828-1092	Gerald McTamney	Francis Marabella	...	...	Robert Zinni	James Dougherty	C. Buek
Conway	*	b	MC	2	(724) 869-5550	...	Diane McKay	...	...	Robert Charlovich	Anthony Blum	Brian Giles
Coopersburg	*	b	MC	2	(610) 282-3307	Joseph Volk	Daniel Stonehouse	Carol Anderson	...	Thomas Reinhard	Daniel Trexler	Dennis Nace
Coplay		b	MC	3	(610) 262-6088	William Leiner	Sandra Gyecsek	Carol Schleder	...	David Buskaritz	Vincent Genovese	Daniel Pavelko
Coraopolis		b	MC	6	(412) 264-3002	Mary Sike	Thomas Cellante	...	...	Larry Byrge	Alan DeRusso	...
Cornwall		b	MC	3	(717) 274-3436	...	...	...	...	...	...	...
Corry		c	CO	6	(814) 663-7041	...	...	...	...	...	...	...
Coudersport		b	MC	2	(814) 274-9776	George Hults	Marlin Moore	Gwendolyn Bretz	...	Brian Wilson	Lee Gross	...
Crafton		b	MC	6	(412) 921-0752	Charles Wooster	...	...	...	William Finlay	Harold Rost	Joseph Pitnaro
Cranberry	*	tp	CM	23	(724) 776-4806	John Milius	Jerry Andree	...	Vanessa Gleason	...	...	...
Cranberry Township		tp	CM	7	(814) 676-8812	Patrick Andres	Frank Pankratz	Margaret Allaman	...	...	...	Mike Erwin
Crescent		tp	CM	2	(724) 457-8100	David Hays	Patrica Moser	...	...	...	Todd Miller	...
Cross Roads		b	CM	..	(717) 993-6669	...	...	...	...	...	...	...
Cumberland		tp	CM	5	(717) 334-6485	...	Florence McLeish	...	...	...	...	...
Cumru		tp	CO	13	(610) 777-1343	Ray Henry	James Sigworth	Jeanne Johnston	Peggy Carpenter	G. Kellenberger	Brian Hiester	Robert McNichols
Curwensville		b	MC	2	(814) 236-1840	...	...	...	...	...	...	...
Dallas		b	CM	2	(570) 675-1389	John Oliver	Joseph Moskovitz	...	...	Harry Vivian	James Drury	John Cybulski
Dallastown		b	MC	4	(717) 244-6626	Beverly Scott	Connie Stokes	Melody Hess	...	Dennis List	...	Brett Patterson
Danville		b	MC	4	(570) 275-3091	Ed Coleman	Thomas Graham	Kathleen Creasy	Shannon Berkey	Brian Witmer	Rae Leighow	Robert Haas
Darby		b	MC	10	(610) 586-1102	Angela Maskart	Joseph Possenti	Rita Tucker	...	Edward Gannon	Robert Smythe	Aaron Ockimey
Darby		tp	CO	10	(610) 586-1514	Lawrence Patterson	John Ryan	...	...	...	Robert Thompson	Charles Joyner
Delta	*	b	CM	..	(717) 456-6248	Jenalyn Williams	...	...	...	...	...	William Ailes
Denver	*	b	CM	3	(717) 336-2831	Danny Rabold	Michael Hession	Joan High	...	Matt Martzall	George Beever	George Whetsel
Derry		b	MC	2	(724) 694-2030	Ronald Bolen	...	...	...	William Woods	Charles Dyche	...
Derry		tp	CM	21	(717) 533-2057	Frank O'Connell	James Negley	...	...	...	William Smith	Thomas Clark
Dickson City		b	MC	6	(717) 489-4758	Bob Wilitshire	Ken Novack	Kathy Simone	...	Tony Zalewski	Bill Stadnitski	...
Dillsburg		b	CM	2	(717) 432-9969	...	...	...	...	...	...	...
Donora		b	MC	5	(412) 379-6600	...	...	...	...	...	...	...
Dormont	*	b	MC	9	(412) 561-8900	Thomas Lloyd	...	Vickie McGurk	Sherri Pruce	Dennis Davis	...	Anthony Kobistek
Dover		tp	CM	18	(717) 292-3634	...	Michael Morris	...	...	...	...	...
Downingtown		b	CM	7	(610) 269-0344	Michael Menna	Anthony Gambale	...	...	Gregg Nelms	James McGowan	Steve Sullins
Doylestown		b	CM	8	(215) 345-4140	Tom Jarret	John Davis	...	Caroline Leiter	Michael Wood	James Donnelly	Daniel Lightcap
Doylestown	*	tp	CM	17	(215) 348-9915	Barbara Lyons	Stephanie Mason	...	William Wightman	Robert Lanetti	Stephen White	Richard John
Dravosburg		b	MC	2	(412) 466-5200	...	...	Brenda Honick	...	...	Ken Holland	Ron Vezzani
Du Bois	*	c	CM	8	(814) 371-2000	William Reay	...	...	DeLean Wagner	Joe Bigar	Ronald LaRotonda	Steve Swope
Dublin		b	CM	2	(215) 249-3310	Kent Moore	Eleanor Sadorf	Marybeth Cody	...	...	Brian Lehman	Stefan Green
Duncannon		b	CM	1	(717) 834-4311	...	Dan Rapp	...	...	...	...	...
Dunmore		b	CM	14	(570) 344-4590	Patrick Loughney	Richard Carr	...	Mary Rice	Vincent Arnone	Mecca Salvatore	Maglio Salvatore
Dupont		b	MC	2	(570) 666-6216	Ann Marie O'Malley	William Riccetti	...	...	Charles Tetlak	Anthony De Mark	Paul Houdyshell
Duquesne		c	MC	7	(412) 469-3770	...	...	...	...	...	...	...
Duryea		b	MC	4	(570) 655-2829	...	...	...	...	...	...	...
East Caln		tp	CM	2	(610) 269-1989	...	Robert Glisson	...	...	...	Brian Gallagher	...
East Conventry		tp	CM	4	(610) 495-5443	David Leinbach	...	...	...	Joel McMillan	John Theobald	Ray Kolb
East Goshen		tp	CM	16	(610) 692-7171	...	Louis Smith	Marie Clevenger	...	...	C. Mac Intyre	Mark Miller
East Hempfield	*	tp	CM	21	(717) 898-3100	Susan Bernhardt	Robert Krimmel	...	Gary Kline	...	Douglas Bagnoli	Perry Madonna
East Hopewell		tp	CM	2	(717) 993-6529	...	...	...	...	...	...	...
East Lampeter	*	tp	CM	13	(717) 393-1567	Glenn Eberly	Ralph Hutchison	...	Jeanne Glick	...	John Bowman	Charles Thomas
East Lansdowne		b	CM	2	(610) 623-7131	James France	George Bobnak	Julie McDevitt	Lindsay Crosby	Larry Mellon	Thomas Pearlingi	Robert Kleinberg
East Mc Keesport	*	b	MC	2	(412) 824-2531	Robert Howard	C. Rosenbayger	...	William Daugherty	Paul Marcoz	Richard Michaels	...
East Nantmeal		tp	TM	1	(610) 458-5780	Virginia Devaney	...	...	...	...	...	Raymond Nestorick
East Norriton		tp	CM	13	(610) 275-2800	Donald Gracia	Helmuth Baerwald	...	William Scurry	George Myers	John McGowan	Joseph Sorgini
East Pennsboro		tp	CO	18	(717) 732-0711	George DeMartyn	Robert Gill	...	...	...	Dennis McMaster	...
East Petersburg		b	CM	4	(717) 569-9282	Cathleen Panus	James Williams	...	...	...	...	Herbert Mattern
East Rockhill		tp	MC	5	(215) 257-9156	...	Anne Klepfer	...	...	...	...	...
East Stroudsburg	*	b	CM	9	(570) 421-8300	Roger Delarco	James Phillips	...	Berrill Dennis	John Fahl	John Baujan	...
East Vincent	*	tp	CM	5	(610) 993-4424	Ryan Costello	Mary Flagg	Edward Miller	Sheila Mauger	...	William Demski	Darwin Schafer
East Whiteland		tp	CM	9	(610) 648-0600	Virginia McMichael	Terry Woodman	...	...	Darin Fitzgerald	Eugene Dooley	William Steele
Easton		c	MC	26	(610) 250-6600	Thomas Goldsmith	Michael McFadden	Thomas Hess	Pat Vulcano	Francis Chisesi	Lawrence Palmer	Kristie Miers
Easttown		tp	CM	10	(610) 644-9000	...	...	...	...	...	...	...
Ebensburg		b	CM	3	(814) 472-7166	Charles Moyer	Daniel Penatzer	Theresa Chaffin	Sharon Burkett	...	George Brady	Charles Voyda
Economy		b	MC	9	(724) 869-4779	Kenneth Campbell	Randy Kunkle	...	Marie Hagg	John Thomas	Tom Harrington	Earl Fitzgerald
Eddystone		b	MC	2	(610) 874-1100	Charles Rowles	Patricia Rodden	...	...	...	Raymond Rodden	Tom Belton
Edgewood		b	CM	3	(412) 242-4824	Joseph Young	Kurt Ferguson	Michael Bowen	David Amatangelo	Edward Bechtold	...	Richard Christenson
Edgeworth		b	CM	1	(412) 741-2866	Robert McGinnis	Martin McDaniel	...	...	...	...	Fred Gregorich
Edinboro		b	CM	6	(814) 734-1812	Clifford Allen	Taras Jemetz	...	...	...	Jeffrey Craft	Butch Shafer
Edwardsville	*	b	MC	4	(570) 288-6484	Bernard Pubaskas	Charles Szalkowski	...	...	Ray King	David Souchick	Michael Wozniak
Elizabeth	*	tp	MC	13	(412) 751-2880	Joanne Beckowitz	Malisa Migliori	...	...	...	Robert Wallace	Keith Shaffer
Elizabethtown		b	CM	11	(717) 367-1700	Douglas Pfautz	Peter Whipple	...	...	...	Dennis Landvater	Wayne Devan
Ellwood City	*	b	CM	8	(724) 758-7777	David Stramella	...	...	...	Connie Mac Donald	Joseph Santillo	Henry Turner
Emmaus		b	CM	11	(610) 965-9292	Craig Neely	...	Johanna Green	Alan France	Robert Reiss	David Faust	Daniel Delong
Emporium		b	CM	2	(814) 486-0768	James Slusarick	Robert Aversa	Joyce Beichner	...	Raymond Housler	Allen Neyman	Timothy Leydig
Emsworth		b	MC	2	(412) 761-1161	Keith Johnston	David Venturella	Cathy Jones	...	Robert Bennett	...	Steven Ference
Ephrata		b	CM	13	(717) 738-9232	Fred Thomas	Gary Nace	...	Gail Bare	...	Steven Annibali	Robert Thompson
Erie		c	MC	103	(814) 870-1234	Joyce Savocchio	...	James Klemm	Charles Herron	Gregory Martin	Paul De Dionisio	John Barzano
Etna		b	CM	3	(412) 781-0569	Peter Ramage	Mary Ellen Ramage	Patricia Ruby	...	Gregory Porter	William Grover	Keith Olash
Exeter		b	MC	5	(570) 654-6816	Richard Murawski	...	...	John Petrucci	Donald Skursky	John McNeil	...
Exeter		tp	CM	21	(610) 779-5660	Lachlan MacBean	Troy Bingaman	Nancy Jack	...	David Janiszewski	Gerard Radke	Clarence Hamm
Fairview Township		tp	CM	14	(717) 901-5200	Perry Albert	Paula Tezik	John Mickle	...	William Carlisle	Bernard Dugan	Michael Fleming
Falls		tp	CM	34	(215) 949-9000	Allen Wilson	Wayne Bergman	...	Peter Gray	Edward Copper	Arnold Conoline	Walter Almond
Farrell		c	CM	6	(724) 983-2703	Eugene Pacsi	Lavon Saternow	Nadine Shimshock	...	Joseph Santell	...	Gerald Multari
Felton	*	b	CM	..	(717) 246-6493	Craig Wood	Joy Flinchbaugh	...	...	Scott Gingrich	...	...
Ferguson		tp	CM	14	(814) 238-4651	...	Mark Kunkle	...	Eric Endersen	Stan Clouser	Diane Conrad	David Modricker

Directory 1/9 continued — OFFICIALS IN U.S. MUNICIPALITIES 2,500 AND OVER IN POPULATION

Jurisdiction	Type	Form of govern-ment	2000 Popu-lation (000)	Main telephone number	Chief elected official	Appointed administrator	Clerk of the governing board	Chief financial officer	Fire chief	Police chief	Public works director
PENNSYLVANIA continued											
Findlay *	tp	CM	5	(724) 695-0500	Thomas Gallant	Gary Klingman	...	...	Robert Lambert	...	John O'Neal
Fleetwood	b	MC	4	(610) 944-8220	Alexander Szoke	...	Lois Geist	...	Steve Bleiler	Ray Nester	Robert Weidner
Folcroft	b	MC	6	(610) 522-1305	Kathleen Kelly	...	Judith Serratore	...	Frank Foglio	Edward Christie	Daniel Falcone
Ford City	b	MC	3	(724) 763-3081	Jeff Pyle	...	Lisa Bittner	...	...	Jan Lysakowski	...
Forest Hills *	b	CM	6	(412) 351-7330	Michael Belmonte	Steven Morus	Roberta McGreevy	...	Ray Heller	William Fabrizi	Jim Theilacker
Forks *	tp	CM	8	(610) 252-0785	Dave Hoff	Richard Schnaedter	Barbara Bartek	James Farley	Bryan Weis	Gregory Dorney	Mark Roberts
Forty Fort	b	MC	4	(717) 287-8586	Andy Tuzinski	...	Paula Lucas	Denise Syms	James Shedlarski	Eric Morgantini	Robert Barnard
Foster	tp	CO	4	(814) 362-4656	Robert Slike	...	Donna Griesbaum	...	Scott Hannahs	Jeffrey Wolbert	Joseph Sweet
Fountain Hill	b	MC	4	(610) 867-0301	...	...	...	...	...	...	...
Fox Chapel	b	CM	5	(412) 963-1100	Nathan Parker	William Gordon	Dana Abate	Joy Hardt	...	David Laux	Albert Biernesser
Frackville	b	MC	4	(570) 874-3860	...	...	...	...	...	...	...
Franconia	tp	CM	11	(215) 723-1137	Steven Barndt	Kevin Baver	...	David Bernhauser	...	Joseph Kozeniewski	Paul Nice
Franklin *	c	CM	7	(814) 437-1485	Robert Heller	E. Gabrys	...	Cheryl Carson	James Wetzel	Jeff Storm	...
Franklin Park	b	CM	11	(412) 364-4115	L. Shupe	Ambrose Rocca	...	...	...	Donald Dorsch	Ronald Merriman
Freeland	b	CM	3	(570) 636-0111	Paul Thomas	...	...	...	Mark Sosar	...	...
Geistown	b	MC	2	(814) 266-8313	Louis Valle	Sandra Porada	Karen Giebfried	...	Richard Kyler	James McGrath	Dennis Ryan
Gettysburg	b	CM	7	(717) 334-1160	John Eline	...	Sara Stull	...	Larry Weikery	Frederick Gantz	John Lawver
Girard	b	CM	3	(814) 774-9683	Alfred Noble	Richard Higley	...	...	Robert Orr	Daniel Bucho	Guy McDonald
Glassport	b	MC	4	(412) 672-7400	Anthony Pepe	Nancy Piazza	Andrea Foster	...	...	Bernard Dworek	Dan Kunf
Glenolden *	b	MC	7	(610) 583-3221	Thomas Danzi	Brian Hoover	Donna Williams	...	Joseph Locke	Michael Donohue	...
Green Tree	b	CM	4	(412) 921-1110	...	...	...	...	...	...	...
Greencastle	b	CM	3	(717) 597-7143	...	Kenneth Myers	...	...	...	Terry Sanders	...
Greensburg *	c	MC	15	(724) 838-4324	Karl Eisaman	Susan Trout	...	Mary Perez	John Hutchinson	Walter Lyons	Rick Hoyle
Greenville	b	CM	6	(724) 588-4193	Clifford Harriger	Ryan Eggleston	...	...	Stephen Thompson	Dennis Stephens	Paul Boyer
Grove City	b	CM	8	(724) 458-7060	George Pokrant	...	...	...	Jeffrey Badger	Dean Osborne	Barry Spiker
Halfmoon Township	tp	CM	2	(814) 692-9800	D. C. Bracken-Piper	Karen Brown	Gregory Love	...	...	...	Scott Brown
Hamburg	b	CM	4	(610) 562-7821	...	Lynda Albright	...	...	...	...	Richard Pickel
Hampden	tp	CM	24	(717) 761-0119	Melvyn Finkelstein	Michael Gossert	...	Janice Jensen	Richard Flinn	Michael Andreoli	Steven Campbell
Hampton	tp	CM	15	(412) 486-0400	...	W. Lochner	Susan Bernet	Albert Presto	...	...	Alex Zarenko
Hanover	b	CM	14	(717) 637-3877	Gary Brown	Bruce Rebert	Joyce Zimmerman	Judith Lee	James Roth	Margret Hormel	Randal Baugher
Hanover	tp	CM	1	(610) 264-1069	Bruce Paulus	Sandra Pudliner	Josephine Romano	...	Robin Yoder	...	Bruce Pudliner
Harmony	tp	CO	3	(724) 266-1910	...	...	...	...	...	...	...
Harris *	tp	CM	4	(814) 466-6228	...	Amy Farkas	Suzanne Shirvani	Walter Cheatle	...	...	Allen Klinger
Harrisburg	c	MC	48	(717) 255-6475	Stephen Reed	Linda Lingle	Vicki Williams	Robert Kroboth	Donald Konkle	Charles Kellar	James Close
Harrison	tp	CO	11	(724) 226-1393	George Conroy	Faith Payne	...	...	...	Michael Klein	Robert Hines
Hatboro	b	CM	7	(215) 443-9100	Thomas McMackin	...	...	...	Steve Plum	Frank Campbell	W. Stauch
Hatfield *	b	CM	2	(215) 855-0781	John Weierman	Robert Ihlein	Scott Smith	...	Robert Kahler	Mark Toomey	Gerald Heffner
Hatfield	tp	CM	16	(215) 855-0900	John Norman	Stephanie Teoli	...	John Hall	Steve Walt	...	Nick DeMeno
Haverford	tp	CM	48	(610) 446-1000	...	Michael English	...	George Rementer	James Marino	Gary Hoover	...
Hazleton *	c	MC	23	(717) 459-4961	Louis Barletta	Samuel Monticello	Lisa Shema	...	Donald Leshko	Robert Ferdinand	Robert Dougherty
Hellertown *	b	CM	5	(610) 838-7041	Thomas Opsatnick	Charles Luthar	Janice Unangst	T.-L. Krasnansky	Rickey Delmore	Robert Balum	Thomas Henshaw
Hempfield	tp	CO	40	(724) 834-7232	...	Rob Ritson	...	...	David Roddy	...	Michael Volpe
Hermitage *	c	CM	16	(724) 981-0800	Duane Piccirilli	Gary Hinkson	...	Jami Kirila	Robert Goeltz	Patrick McElhinney	...
Highspire	b	CM	2	(717) 939-3303	Wayne Shank	John McHale	...	...	Justin Varnicle	Mark Stonbraker	John Ingiosi
Hilltown	tp	CM	12	(215) 453-6000	John McIlhinney	K. Bennington	Lynda Seimes	...	...	C. Engelhart	Thomas Buzby
Hollidaysburg	b	CM	5	(814) 695-7543	James Shoemaker	...	Ann Andrews	Robert Kuntz	Brian Seiler	David Shiffler	David Zeek
Homer City	b	CM	1	(724) 479-8005	Arlene Barker	Stanley Buggey	Karen Valyo	...	Carl Filler	John Griffith	Butch Hiner
Homestead	b	CM	3	(412) 461-1340	Lloyd Cunningham	Richard Sharkey	Jacquelyne Tomko	...	William Purfory	Mark Zeger	Daniel Kelly
Honesdale	b	MC	4	(717) 253-0731	H Richard Osborne	...	...	...	...	Frank Rosler	William Corcoran
Honey Brook	tp	CM	6	(610) 273-3970	...	Michael Brown	...	...	...	...	...
Hopewell	tp	CM	5	(717) 933-2027	William Streett	Patricia Schaub	...	...	...	...	...
Hopewell	tp	CO	13	(412) 378-1460	Tim Force	...	Pat Owens	Andy Brunette	Steve Seaman	Eugene Ungarean	Chas Srafin
Horsham	tp	CM	24	(215) 643-3131	James Doherty	Michael McGee	...	...	...	Robert Ruxton	William Pietzsch
Hughesville	b	CM	2	(717) 584-5272	D. Davis	...	...	...	...	...	...
Hummelstown	b	MC	4	(717) 566-2555	...	Michael O'Keefe	Donna Spittle	...	Charles Cogan	Charles Dowell	Rich Engle
Huntingdon	b	CM	6	(814) 643-3966	Foster Ulrich	Daniel Varner	...	...	...	...	...
Indian Lake	b	CM	..	(814) 754-8161	...	...	...	...	...	...	...
Indiana	b	MC	14	(724) 465-6691	...	...	...	...	...	...	...
Indiana	tp	CM	6	(412) 767-5333	...	Daniel Anderson	...	...	...	Robert Wilson	John Carson
Industry	b	MC	1	(724) 643-4360	...	...	Jeannie Caffro	...	...	...	...
Ingram	b	CM	3	(412) 921-3625	Frank Petrell	Cindy Dzadovsky	Chrissy Testa	...	George Beerhalter	George Jak	Tom Dzadovsky
Irwin	b	CM	4	(724) 864-3100	Daniel Rose	...	Connie Serman	...	...	John Karasek	Randy Altman
Jackson	tp	CM	3	(724) 452-5581	Ralph DeLuigi	Richard Crown	Sarah Richards	...	Tim Sapienza	Len Keller	Robert Russell
Jackson *	tp	CM	6	(717) 225-5661	...	William Conn	...	...	...	...	...
Jeannette	c	MC	10	(724) 527-4000	...	Ronald Dinsmore	...	...	...	...	...
Jefferson Hills	b	CM	9	(412) 655-7735	Kevin McFarland	John Shepherd	Saundra Mortle	...	...	John Maple	William McVicker
Jenkintown	b	CM	4	(215) 885-0700	Vincent McCabe	Edwin Geissler	Tricia Anderson	...	Gary Bachman	Albert Divalentino	Mike Micciolo
Jersey Shore *	b	CM	4	(570) 398-0104	Cheryl Brungard	...	...	Martha Gottschall	...	Martin Jeirles	Randy Stover
Jessup	b	MC	4	(717) 489-0411	...	...	...	...	...	...	...
Jim Thorpe	b	MC	4	(717) 325-3025	Michael Sofranko	...	Louise McClafferty	...	Patrick McGinley	Barry Andrews	...
Johnsonburg	b	CM	3	(814) 965-5682	Hudnell Caldwell	Mary Polaski	...	...	Jack Fowler	...	Louis Cherry
Johnstown	c	CM	23	(814) 533-2001	...	Curtis Davis	...	Joseph Bunk	Michael Huss	Craig Foust	Darby Sprincz
Kane	b	CM	4	(814) 837-9240	Edgar James	Michael Holtz	...	...	David Silvis	William Osmer	...
Kenhorst	b	CM	2	(610) 777-7327	...	...	...	...	...	...	...
Kennett Square	b	CM	5	(610) 444-6020	...	David Fiorenza	...	Kathy Holliday	...	Albert McCarthy	Joseph Scalise
Kingston	c	MC	13	(570) 288-4576	...	Paul Keating	...	Carol Urban	Robert Cannon	Daniel Beky	Russel Kratz
Kingston	tp	CM	7	(570) 696-3809	Jeffrey Box	Kelly Cook	Kathleen Sebastian	...	...	James Balavage	Donald Fritzges
Kittanning	b	MC	4	(412) 543-2091	...	...	...	...	...	...	...
Kulpmont	b	MC	2	(570) 373-1521	Robert Slaby	Frank Chesney	...	Ann Martino	Matthew Siko	Edward Grego	George Malakoski
Kutztown	b	CM	5	(610) 683-6131	Carl Mantz	Jaymes Vettraino	...	Eric Ely	Robert Hauck	Theodore Cole	...
Lancaster	c	MC	56	(717) 291-4711	Charles Smithgall	Carol Roland	Janet Spleen	...	Jeffrey Pierce	William Heim	C. Katzenmoyer
Lancaster	tp	CM	13	(717) 291-1213	...	David Clouser	...	Diana Hess	...	...	J. Eckenrode
Lansdale	b	CM	16	(215) 368-1691	Carl Guenst	F. Mangan	...	Carolyn McCreary	Jay Daveler	Joseph McGuriman	Jacob Ziegler
Lansdowne	b	CM	11	(610) 623-7300	A. Campuzano	...	...	...	Tom Young	Daniel Kortan	William Johnson
Lansford	b	MC	4	(570) 645-3900	Robert Gaughan	...	...	...	Joe Cannon	James Strauss	...
Larksville	b	MC	4	(570) 714-9846	Robert Wallace	...	...	...	Andrew Kachmark	Tony Kopko	Paul Kachinko
Latrobe *	c	MC	8	(724) 539-8548	Tom Marflak	Richard Stadler	...	Barbara Buck	John Brasille	Charles Huska	Joseph Bush
Laureldale	b	MC	3	(610) 929-8700	...	...	...	...	...	...	...
Lebanon	c	CO	24	(717) 273-6711	Robert Anspach	Trish Ward	Cheryl Gibson	Gerald Weise	Barry Fisher	William Harvey	Jonathan Beers
Leechburg	b	MC	2	(724) 842-8511	...	...	...	...	...	...	...
Lehighton	b	CM	5	(610) 377-4002	Wilbur Bauchspies	John Hanosek	Carol Clay	...	John Kuller	Dennis Wentz	Alton Steigerwalt

Directory 1/9 continued **OFFICIALS IN U.S. MUNICIPALITIES 2,500 AND OVER IN POPULATION**

Jurisdiction	Type	Form of govern-ment	2000 Popu-lation (000)	Main telephone number	Chief elected official	Appointed administrator	Clerk of the governing board	Chief financial officer	Fire chief	Police chief	Public works director
PENNSYLVANIA continued											
Lemoyne	b	CM	3	(717) 737-6843	James Yates	Howard Dougherty	...	Jan Boyer	Ronald Frank	...	John Paden
Lewisburg	b	CM	5	(570) 523-3614	Peter Bergonia	Chad Smith	Debra Depew	...	...	Paul Yost	George Stump
Lewistown	b	CM	8	(717) 248-1361	Fred Saxton	David Frey	...	...	Robert McCaa	...	Frank Hernandez
Liberty	b	MC	2	(717) 324-3461	Darrie Mase	Beverly Mase	...	...	Tony Baker	...	John Zeafla
Limerick	tp	CM	13	(610) 495-6432	Thomas DiBello	Daniel Kerr	Karen Willman	...	Dennis Rumler	W. Weaver	William Bradford
Lititz	b	CM	9	(717) 626-2044	Timothy Snyder	Sue Barry	...	...	...	Douglas Shertzer	Gary Rynier
Littlestown	b	MC	3	(717) 359-5101	Charles Bridinger	Yvette Kreitz	Dorothy King	...	Michael Sneeringer	Donald Baker	Michael Dillman
Lock Haven	c	CM	9	(570) 893-5900	Richard Vilello	...	...	...	Robert Neff	Elwood Hocker	...
Logan *	tp	MC	11	(814) 944-5349	...	Bonnie Lewis	...	Tiffany Noonan	...	Ronald Heller	David Lynch
London Grove *	tp	CM	5	(610) 345-0100	...	Steven Brown	...	...	...	...	...
Londonderry	tp	CM	5	(717) 944-1803	...	Steve Letavic	...	...	...	...	...
Lower Allen *	tp	CM	17	(717) 975-7575	John Titzel	Thomas Vernau	...	Nancy Dietel	...	...	Gary Frazer
Lower Burrell	c	MC	12	(724) 335-9875	Donald Kinosz	Edward Kirkwood	...	Brian Eshbaugh	...	Tracy Lindo	Richard Kotecki
Lower Chanceford	tp	CM	2	(717) 862-3589	J. Taylor	...	...	...	...	...	...
Lower Frederick	tp	CM	4	(610) 287-8857	...	...	...	...	...	...	...
Lower Gwynedd	tp	CM	10	(215) 646-5302	Edward Brandt	Larry Comunale	Carole Culberth	Karen Yeutter	...	Gerrard Gray	Robert Pierson
Lower Macungie	tp	MC	19	(610) 966-4343	...	Ricky Prill	...	...	...	...	...
Lower Makefield	tp	CM	32	(215) 493-3646	...	Terry Fedorchak	...	Brian McCloskey	...	Kenneth Coluzzi	James Coyne
Lower Merion	tp	CM	59	(610) 645-6120	Matthew Comisky	Douglas Cleland	Eileen Trainer	Dean Dortone	Charles McGarvey	Joseph Daly	Donald Cannon
Lower Moreland	tp	MC	11	(215) 947-3100	Kurt Mayer	Alison Rudolf	...	Marion Marucci	...	Peter Hasson	H. Lawrence
Lower Paxton	tp	CM	44	(717) 657-5600	William Hawk	George Wolfe	...	Donna Speakman	...	...	Joseph Sutor
Lower Pottsgrove	tp	MC	11	(610) 323-0436	Bruce Foltz	Rodney Hawthorne	...	...	Dennis Miller	Raymond Bechtel	Richard Yoder
Lower Providence	tp	CM	22	(610) 539-8020	Craig Dininny	...	...	Julie Dechnik	Bryan McFarland	Francis Carroll	David Shafter
Lower Salford Township	tp	CM	12	(215) 256-8087	...	J. Plank	...	...	...	...	...
Lower Saucon	tp	CM	9	(610) 865-3291	...	Jack Cahalan	...	Martha Chase	...	Guy Lesser	Roger Rasich
Lower Southampton	tp	CO	19	(215) 357-7300	Steven Pizzollo	Susanne McKeon	Janet Hude	Raymond Schaefer	Richard Noon	Edward Donnelly	Randy Behmke
Lower Swatara	tp	CM	8	(215) 939-9377	...	...	...	...	...	...	...
Lower Windsor *	tp	CM	7	(717) 244-6813	Gerald Kellner	...	Tricia Smeltzer	...	...	David Sterner	Kim Miller
Luzerne	b	MC	2	(570) 287-7633	Rosemary Sigmond	Bonnie Arnone	Linda Ziegenfus	...	David White	Charles Urban	Howard Fox
Mahanoy City	b	CM	4	(570) 773-2150	Michael Di Baggio	...	Sonia Hiney	...	Frank Bedisky	Mark Wiekrykas	John Wilner
Malvern	b	CM	3	(610) 644-2602	Henry Briggs	Sandra Kelley	Lois Thorpe	...	Gerald Vaughn	Michael McMahon	Ira Dutter
Manchester	b	MC	2	(717) 266-1022	...	...	...	...	...	...	...
Manchester *	tp	CM	12	(717) 764-4646	John D'Ottavio	David Raver	...	...	Richard Shank	Carl Segatti	Kenneth Goodyear
Manheim	b	CM	4	(717) 665-2461	Thomas Showers	Robert Stoner	...	...	Rick Houser	Barry Weidman	Barry Bracken
Manheim	tp	CM	33	(717) 569-6408	...	James Martin	Linda DiPerna	Valerie Calhoun	...	Paul Rager	Carl Neff
Mansfield	b	CM	3	(570) 662-2315	...	...	...	...	...	...	...
Marcus Hook	b	MC	2	(610) 485-1341	...	Bruce Dorbian	...	...	...	...	...
Marietta	b	MC	2	(717) 426-4143	Oliver Overlander	Jody Shaffner	...	...	Paul Armold	...	...
Marple	tp	MC	23	(610) 356-4040	Martin Nash	Joseph Flicker	...	...	...	...	...
Marysville	b	CM	2	(717) 957-3110	Joseph Raisner	Marita Kelley	...	...	Kenneth Seitz	Jacob Stoss	George Sponsler
Masontown	b	MC	3	(412) 583-7731	...	...	...	...	...	...	...
Mc Adoo	b	MC	2	(570) 929-1182	Gregory Kurtz	...	Margie Rodgers	Joseph Jevitt	...	Joseph Litchko	Ed Wanyo
Mc Candless *	t	CM	28	(412) 364-0616	Robert Powers	Tobias Cordek	...	...	...	Gary Anderson	Mark Sabina
Mc Donald	b	MC	2	(724) 926-8711	Marilou Ritchie	...	Gloria Stroop	...	...	Mark Dorsey	...
Mc Kees Rocks	b	MC	6	(412) 331-2498	Richard Keenan	William Beck	Charlotte Myers	...	Nicholas Radoycis	Robert Martineau	Richard Naughton
Mc Keesport	c	MC	24	(412) 675-5050	...	...	...	...	...	...	...
Mc Sherrystown	b	MC	2	(717) 637-1838	...	...	...	...	...	...	...
Meadville	c	CM	13	(814) 724-6000	Richard Friedberg	Joseph Chriest	Ronald Rushton	Timothy Groves	Larndo Hedrick	David Acker	...
Mechanicsburg	b	CM	9	(717) 691-3310	Brian Rider	Jonathan Stough	...	...	Larry Seagrist	David Spotts	...
Media	b	MC	5	(610) 566-5210	Joan Hagan	Jeffrey Smith	Marianne States	Jordan Blane	James Jeffery	Martin Wusinich	Ralph De Rosa
Mercer *	b	MC	2	(724) 662-3980	Ted Isoldi	Debbie Scruci	...	...	William Finnley	David Fockler	Dennis Heasley
Mercersburg	b	CM	1	(717) 328-3116	Robert Brindle	James Leventry	Thelma Corrales	...	...	Larry Thomas	Lee Beck
Meyersdale	b	CM	2	(814) 634-5110	Paul Fuller	...	Patricia Ackerman	...	David Lauver	Vernon Bowman	...
Middlesex *	tp	CM	5	(724) 898-3571	George Phillips	Scot Fodi	...	...	Dave Vanatta	Randy Ruediger	Jim Benninger
Middletown	b	CM	9	(717) 948-3000	Dale Sinniger	Jeffrey Stonehill	...	Karen Casciotti	Kenton Whitebread	Keith Reismiller	Solomon Swartz
Middletown	tp	CM	16	(610) 565-2700	...	W. Clark	...	Timothy Sander	...	...	...
Middletown (Levittown)	tp	CM	44	(215) 750-3800	Robert McMonagle	Richard Gestrich	...	Jean Reukauf	...	Frank McKenna	Kenneth Banks
Midland *	b	CM	3	(724) 643-4170	Angela Adkins	Diane Kemp	Erma Di Renzo	...	James Ulizio	Ronald Bongivengo	Michael Miller
Mifflinburg	b	CM	3	(570) 966-1013	Donald Bitner	Margaret Metzger	...	...	...	...	Steven Benner
Millcreek	tp	MC	46	(814) 833-1111	...	...	...	...	...	...	...
Millersburg *	b	MC	2	(717) 692-2389	...	...	...	...	...	...	...
Millersville	b	MC	7	(717) 872-4645	Richard Moriarty	Edward Arnold	...	...	Keith Eshleman	John Rochat	Andrew Boxleitner
Millvale	b	MC	4	(412) 821-2777	Jim Burn	Virginia Heller	...	Don Gillespie	Gary Witkowski	...	...
Milton	b	CM	6	(717) 742-8759	Scott Jones	Lawrence Wilver	Wanda Walls	...	Fred Kurtz	Michael Warns	Charles Beck
Minersville	b	MC	4	(570) 544-2149	...	...	...	...	...	...	...
Monaca	b	CM	6	(724) 775-9600	Thomas Ely	Stephen Vincenti	Georgina Wilson	...	...	Frank Primo	Dan Colville
Monessen	c	MC	8	(412) 684-9712	Robert Leone	John De Luca	...	Ernest Wisyanski	Tim Billick	John Bachinski	Ed Burdock
Monongahela *	c	MC	4	(412) 258-5500	Kenneth Cole	...	Carole Foglia	Thomas Caudill	Frank Hnatik	Dennis Mendicino	Robert Kepics
Monroeville	b	CM	29	(412) 856-1000	Sean Logan	Marshall Bond	...	Susan Werksman	...	George Polnar	Eugene Mezeutch
Montgomery	b	CM	1	(717) 547-1671	...	...	...	...	...	...	...
Montgomery	tp	CM	22	(215) 393-6900	Warren Greenberg	John Nagel	...	...	David Vasconez	Richard Brady	Kevin Costello
Montoursville	b	CM	4	(570) 368-2486	...	...	...	...	...	...	...
Moon	tp	CM	22	(412) 262-1700	A. Ropelewski	Gregory Smith	...	...	Charles Belgie	H. Krance	James Henkemeyer
Moosic	b	MC	5	(717) 457-5480	...	...	...	...	...	...	...
Morrisville	b	CM	10	(215) 295-8181	...	Victoria Keller	...	...	...	...	...
Mount Carmel	b	CM	6	(570) 339-4486	John Jones	Joseph Bass	...	...	Jack Williams	Brian Shurock	...
Mount Joy	b	CM	6	(717) 653-2300	...	Terry Kauffman	...	...	...	John Sweigart	Scott Hershey
Mount Joy	tp	CM	7	(717) 367-8917	Robert Miller	Charles Kraus	...	...	...	...	David Hummer
Mount Lebanon *	c	CM	33	(412) 343-3400	David Humphreys	Stephen Feller	...	William McKain	Nicolas Sohyda	Thomas Ogden	Tom Kelley
Mount Oliver	b	MC	3	(412) 431-8107	Martin Palma	Joanne Malloy	...	...	...	Frank Mosesso	...
Mount Penn	b	MC	3	(610) 799-5151	Josh Nowotarski	Ann Ftorski	...	...	Timothy Waldman	...	...
Mount Pleasant	b	MC	4	(724) 547-6745	Steven Fontanazza	Margene Wilczynski	...	...	Gerald Lucia	Gregory Smolka	...
Mount Union	b	MC	2	(814) 542-4051	Herbert Kidd	Eric Powell	...	...	Michael Goodman	Douglas Gummo	Robert Himes
Muncy	b	MC	2	(570) 546-3952	Michael Fornwalt	Edward Coup	...	...	...	Richard Sutton	Dave Alexander
Munhall	b	MC	12	(412) 464-7310	...	...	...	...	...	...	...
Municipality Of Bethel Park *	c	CM	33	(412) 831-6800	Clifford Morton	William Spagnol	...	Mark Romito	...	John Mackey	Robert Cygrymus
Murrysville *	c	MC	18	(724) 327-2100	Joyce Somers	John Barrett	...	Diane Heming	...	Thomas Seefeld	Richard Connors
Myerstown	b	MC	3	(717) 866-5038	Ellsworth Troutman	John Brown	Denise Krall	Lee Smith	Mitch Hemperly	Phillip Stark	Randall Brown

Directory 1/9
continued

OFFICIALS IN U.S. MUNICIPALITIES 2,500 AND OVER IN POPULATION

Jurisdiction	Type	Form of govern-ment	2000 Popu-lation (000)	Main telephone number	Chief elected official	Appointed administrator	Clerk of the governing board	Chief financial officer	Fire chief	Police chief	Public works director
PENNSYLVANIA continued											
Nanticoke	c	MC	10	(717) 735-2200	Wasil Kobela	Kenneth Johnson	Michael Yurkowski	Donna Wall	William Ives	Chester Zaremba	Joseph Mikilonis
Nanty-Glo	b	MC	3	(814) 749-0331	T. Cunningham	...	Melissa Weekes	...	Joseph Lamantia	Richard Miller	...
Narberth	b	CM	4	(610) 664-2840	Dennis Sharkey	William Martin	...	...	John Thomas	Art Pauoni	...
Nazareth	b	CM	6	(610) 264-1069	...	Sandra Pudliner	Pina Romano	...	...	...	Bruce Pudliner
Nesquehoning	b	MC	3	(570) 669-9588	Eugene Hrebik	Jillian Hoppel	Suzanne Nothstein	...	John McArdle	Sean Smith	Nicholas Degiglio
Nether Providence *	tp	CO	13	(610) 566-4516	...	...	...	April Reeser	...	Richard Slifer	John Ellis
New Brighton	b	CM	6	(724) 846-1870	Paul Spickerman	Larry Morley	Marleen Ionta	...	Jeff Bolland	Dale Nicholson	William Caplinger
New Britain	t	CM	3	(215) 348-4586	...	Robin Trymbiski	...	...	...	David Sempowski	...
New Britain	tp	CM	10	(215) 822-1391	Robert Piccone	...	...	...	Randal Teschner	Robert Scafidi	Mark Roberts
New Castle	c	MC	26	(412) 656-3500	...	...	...	...	...	...	...
New Cumberland	b	CM	7	(717) 774-0404	John Murray	S. Sultzaberger	...	...	Michael Kann	Oren Kauffman	...
New Eagle	b	MC	2	(412) 258-4477	...	...	...	...	...	...	...
New Hanover *	tp	CM	7	(610) 323-1008	Martin Dyas	...	Maryann Brennan	Janice Reid	...	Michael Dykie	R. Batchelder
New Holland	b	CM	5	(717) 354-4567	...	James Fulcher	...	...	...	...	...
New Hope *	b	CM	2	(215) 862-3347	Richard Hirschfield	John Burke	Joann Connell	...	Craig Forbes	Rick Pasqualini	Tom Carroll
New Kensington	c	CO	14	(412) 337-4523	...	...	...	...	...	...	...
New Stanton	b	MC	1	(724) 925-9700	Joseph Kazan	...	Anita Hoffman	Todd Bartlow	Bob Liberty	...	Melvin Steele
New Wilmington	b	MC	2	(412) 946-8167	...	...	...	...	...	...	...
Newtown	b	MC	2	(215) 968-2109	...	...	...	...	...	...	...
Newtown	tp	CM	11	(610) 356-0200	Peter DeLiberty	James Sheldrake	...	...	Doug Everlof	Leon Hunter	Charles Steinmetz
Newtown Township	tp	CM	18	(215) 968-2800	Scott Harp	Joseph Czajkowski	Judy Setar	Elaine Gibbs	Donald Harris	Martin Duffy	...
Newville	b	CM	1	(717) 776-7633	Jerry Gilbert	Fred Potzer	...	...	...	...	...
Norristown	b	MC	31	(610) 272-8080	Theodore LeBlanc	David Forrest	S. Felice-Grubb	Monica DeCaro	...	...	Joseph Picard
North Braddock	b	CM	6	(412) 271-1306	...	...	...	...	...	...	...
North Catasauqua	b	MC	2	(610) 264-1504	William McGinley	Francis Roberts	Helen Hutt	...	Francis Hadik	Kim Moyer	Gregory Loch
North Codorus	tp	CM	7	(717) 225-4812	John Rebert	...	Mary Aikens	...	Larry Wildasin	...	Laverne Oversmith
North Cornwall	tp	CM	4	(717) 273-9200	Randy Hoffman	John Primus	Stacey Kindt	...	...	Thomas Gates	Thomas Long
North Coventry	tp	CM	7	(610) 323-1694	William Deegan	...	...	...	Randall Richter	Michael Benyo	Joseph Wood
North East	b	MC	4	(814) 725-8611	...	Benjamin Breniman	...	...	...	...	...
North Fayette	tp	CM	12	(724) 693-9601	Daniel Fink	Robert Grimm	Carol Stenzel	...	...	...	Victor Rogale
North Huntingdon *	tp	CM	29	(724) 863-3806	Thomas Kerber	Kelly Wolfe	...	...	...	Michael Daugherty	Richard Albert
North Londonderry *	tp	MC	6	(717) 838-1373	Ronald Fouche	Gordon Watts	Judy Miller	Lisa Daubert	...	Kevin Snyder	...
North Middleton	tp	MC	10	(717) 243-8550	William Myers	Deborah Ealer	Dana Dunkle	...	Dave Dick	Jeffrey Rudolph	Lester Brickner
North Strabane	tp	CM	10	(724) 745-8880	Brian Spicer	Frank Siffrinn	...	Jamie Schaller	Gary Zimak	Dan Strimel	Harry Hayman
North Versailles	tp	MC	12	(412) 823-6602	...	...	...	...	...	...	...
North Wales	b	CM	3	(215) 699-4424	Jocelyn Tenney	Susan Patton	Sandra Rhoads	...	William Goltz	Barry Hackert	Thomas Costella
Northampton	b	MC	9	(610) 262-2576	Thomas Reenock	Gene Zarayko	B. Matuczinski	...	Robert Siegfried	Laird Brownmiller	Stephen Gerny
Northampton *	tp	CM	39	(215) 357-6800	Peter Palestina	Robert Pellegrino	...	...	Robert Sutherland	M. Pilla	Pasquale Giradi
Northumberland	b	MC	3	(570) 473-3414	Bryan Wolfe	Janice Bowman	J. Sanders-Ressler	...	Brian Crebs	Timothy Fink	Nathan Fisher
Norwood	b	MC	5	(610) 586-5800	...	...	...	...	...	...	...
Oakmont	b	CM	6	(412) 828-3232	William Benusa	...	...	...	William Peoples	David DiSanti	...
O'Hara	tp	CM	9	(412) 782-1400	...	...	...	...	...	James Farringer	Loren Kephart
Ohio	tp	CO	3	(412) 364-6321	Herbert Hartle	John Sullivan	Eleanor Owens	...	...	Norbert Micklos	Danny Weigle
Ohioville	b	CM	3	(724) 643-1920	Linda Wells	Diane Kemp	Debra Doughty	...	Clarence Dawson	Ronald Lutton	Bruce Thorne
Oil City	c	CM	11	(814) 678-3012	Malachy McMahon	Thomas Rockovich	...	Michelle Hoovler	John Huey	Robert Wenner	Miles Truitt
Old Forge	b	MC	8	(717) 457-8852	...	...	...	...	...	...	...
Olyphant	b	MC	4	(570) 489-2135	Michael Wargo	Stephen Klem	Patricia Angradi	Frank Campbell	Dave Kurkovitz	James Foley	Peter Kolcharno
Orwigsburg	b	MC	3	(570) 366-3103	...	...	...	...	...	...	...
Oxford	b	MC	4	(610) 932-2500	John Ware	...	Virginia Holt	...	Percy Reynolds	Paul Stolz	Thomas Hindman
Palmer	tp	CM	16	(610) 253-7191	David Colver	Robert Anckaitis	...	Sheri Young	Delmar Grube	Bruce Fretz	Thomas Adams
Palmerton	b	MC	5	(610) 826-2505	John Neff	Rodger Danielson	Anita Harry	...	Christopher Kegel	George Taptich	Joseph Kercsmar
Palmyra	b	CM	7	(717) 838-6361	Richard Mazzocca	Sherry Capello	...	...	...	Stanley Jasinski	Craig Campbell
Parkesburg *	b	MC	3	(610) 857-2616	K. Knickerbocker	Lester Thomas	Wendy Keegan	David Jones	Richard Klingler	Brian Sheller	...
Patton	tp	CM	11	(814) 234-0271	...	Douglas Erickson	...	Kim Wyatt	...	John Petrick	...
Peach Bottom	tp	CM	4	(717) 456-5083	...	...	...	...	...	...	...
Pen Argyl *	b	MC	3	(610) 863-4119	Judith Piper	Robin Zmoda	...	...	Dean Parson	Philip Viglione	Steven Bender
Penbrook	b	MC	3	(717) 232-3733	Richard Stottlemyer	...	Linda Losh	Michael Goodman	Joe Nickle	David Hiester	Frederick Pace
Penn	tp	CM	14	(717) 632-7366	Michael Rishel	Jeffrey Garvick	...	...	Jan Cromer	Samuel Gilbert	Kevin Mahan
Penn	tp	CM	1	(724) 586-1165	...	Gregory Primm	Linda Furka	...	...	Cheryl Cranmer	Douglas Roth
Penn Hills	c	MC	46	(412) 798-2100	Anthony DeLuca	...	Diane Fitzhenry	E. Schrecengost	John Mason	Howard Burton	Mohammed Rayan
Penndel	b	MC	2	(215) 757-5153	Arlene Harms	Barbara Vasquez	Michelle Nigra	...	...	Stephen Burke	...
Perkasie	b	CM	8	(215) 257-5065	Eadie Burke	Daniel Olpere	...	...	...	Paul Dickinson	Phil Ivins
Peters	tp	CM	17	(724) 941-4180	Robert Lewis	Michael Silvestri	...	...	Daniel Coyle	Harry Fruecht	Peter Overcashier
Philadelphia	c	MC	1517	(215) 686-2331	John Street	Pedro Ramos	Patricia Rafferty	Vincent Jannetti	Lloyd Ayers	Lynne Abraham	Richard Tustin
Philipsburg	b	MC	3	(814) 342-3440	Sandra Martin	John Knowles	Barbara Godissart	...	...	William Stouffer	...
Phoenixville *	b	CM	14	(610) 933-8801	Louis Amici	A. DiGirolomo	Susan Dinato	Steven Nease	James Gable	John Kalavik	Brian Watson
Pine	tp	CM	7	(724) 625-1591	Richard Brant	Gary Koehler	...	...	Kenneth Young	T. Amann	Jack Fasick
Pitcairn	b	MC	3	(412) 372-6500	Orelio Vecchio	...	Judy Shipley	Josephine Higgins	...	David McIntyre	Rocco Trunzo
Pittsburgh	c	MC	334	(412) 255-2519	Luke Ravenstahl	...	Linda Wasler	Ellen McLean	Peter Michali	Robert McNeilly	Guy Costa
Pittston *	c	CO	8	(570) 654-0513	Michael Lombardo	...	Ronald Mortimer	Chris Latona	James Rooney	Jeffrey Tayoun	George Renfer
Pleasant *	tp	MC	2	(814) 723-5240	Marshall Gern	...	...	...	...	...	...
Pleasant Hills	b	MC	8	(412) 655-3300	...	...	...	...	...	...	...
Plum	b	CM	26	(412) 795-6800	...	...	...	...	...	Terry Focareta	William Berchick
Plumstead	tp	CM	11	(215) 766-8914	Frank Froio	...	...	...	...	Duane Hasenauer	Alan Bleam
Plymouth	b	MC	6	(717) 779-1011	Frank Coughlin	Joseph Mazur	Dorothy Woodruff	...	Jason Ravert	Myles Collins	James Hunlock
Plymouth	tp	CM	16	(610) 277-4100	Alexander Fazzini	Karen Weiss	...	Timothy Creelman	...	Carmen Pettine	Timothy Boyd
Port Allegany	b	MC	2	(814) 642-2526	Joseph Demott	John Gaydeski	Barbara Fink	...	Tom Johnson	...	...
Port Carbon	b	MC	2	(570) 622-2255	Thomas Pavlick	...	Luanne Kruss	Michael Sninsky	Michael Welsh	Jon Bowman	...
Port Vue	b	MC	4	(412) 664-9323	...	...	...	...	...	...	...
Portage	b	MC	2	(814) 736-4330	Joyce French	...	...	...	...	Donald Kehn	Donald Squillario
Pottstown *	b	CM	21	(610) 970-6510	Jack Wolf	Raymond Lopez	...	Robert Armelin	Richard Lengel	Mark Flanders	Douglass Yerger
Pottsville	c	CM	15	(570) 622-1234	John Reiley	Thomas Palamar	Julie Rescorla	Michael Halcovage	Todd March	Joseph Murton	James Muldowney
Prospect Park	b	MC	6	(610) 532-1007	Donald Cook	...	Deborah Luty	Peter Subers	James Simmonds	John Saddic	Glen Schwenke
Punxsutawney	b	CM	6	(814) 938-4480	Susan Glessner	Benjamin White	Jill Carey	...	Donald Bosak	Thomas Fedigan	Joseph DeFelice
Quakertown	b	CM	8	(215) 536-5001	Raymond Fulmer	...	...	...	...	James McFadden	Joseph Murgia
Radnor	tp	CM	30	(610) 688-5600	...	David Bashore	Concetta Clayton	...	...	John Rutty	John Stauffer
Rankin	b	MC	2	(412) 271-1027	...	...	...	...	...	...	...
Reading	c	MC	81	(610) 655-6012	Paul Angstadt	...	Linda Kelleher	Tammie Kipp	William Rehr	Keith Mooney	D. Mucha
Red Lion	b	CM	6	(717) 244-3475	...	...	...	...	...	...	...
Reynoldsville	b	MC	2	(814) 653-2110	...	...	...	...	...	...	...

Directory 1/9 continued — OFFICIALS IN U.S. MUNICIPALITIES 2,500 AND OVER IN POPULATION

Jurisdiction	Type	Form of govern-ment	2000 Popu-lation (000)	Main telephone number	Chief elected official	Appointed administrator	Clerk of the governing board	Chief financial officer	Fire chief	Police chief	Public works director
PENNSYLVANIA continued											
Richland *	tp	CM	9	(215) 536-4066	Craig Staats	Stephen Sechriest	Tracey Virnelson	. . .	. . .	Lawrence Cerami	Thomas Roeder
Richland	tp	CM	12	(814) 266-2922	. . .	. . .	. . .	. . .	. . .	. . .	. . .
Richland (Allegheny)	tp	MC	9	(412) 443-5921	. . .	Dean Bastianini	. . .	. . .	. . .	. . .	Lee Geortz
Ridgway	b	CM	4	(814) 776-1125	. . .	Martin Schuller	. . .	. . .	John Wygant	Ralph Tettis	. . .
Ridley *	tp	CM	30	(610) 534-4800	Robert Willert	Anne Howanski	. . .	Chris Betlzer	. . .	Charles Howley	Louis De Pietro
Ridley Park	b	MC	7	(610) 532-2100	Henry Eberle	Robert Poole	C. Heimbacher	. . .	. . .	Robert Marks	Richard Miles
Roaring Spring	b	MC	2	(814) 224-4814	. . .	. . .	. . .	. . .	. . .	. . .	. . .
Robinson	tp	CM	12	(412) 788-8120	. . .	Richard Charnovich	Mildred Cvengros	. . .	. . .	Dale Vietmeier	Paul Kashmer
Rochester	b	CM	4	(724) 775-1200	. . .	. . .	. . .	. . .	. . .	. . .	. . .
Rockledge	b	MC	2	(215) 379-8572	Joseph Denelsbeck	Michael Hartey	Debora Flanagan	. . .	Russell Hellyer	Paul Kittredge	George Praediger
Ross	tp	CM	32	(412) 931-7055	. . .	Thomas Lavorini	. . .	Virginia Finnegan	Frank Stright	Gregory Tenos	James Stack
Rostraver *	tp	MC	11	(724) 929-8877	Nick Lorenzo	. . .	Pamela Beard	. . .	. . .	Greg Resetar	Thomas Backstrom
Royersford	b	CM	4	(610) 948-3737	. . .	. . .	. . .	. . .	. . .	. . .	. . .
Salisbury	tp	CM	13	(610) 797-4000	James Kozuch	Gabriel Khalife	. . .	Cathy Bonaskiewich	. . .	Allen Stiles	John Andreas
Sandy	tp	CM	11	(814) 371-4220	. . .	M. Stojek	Barbara Hopkins	. . .	. . .	. . .	. . .
Saxonburg *	b	MC	1	(724) 352-1400	William Gillespie	Mary Papik	Linda Kovacik	. . .	Gary Cooper	Erik Bergstrom	Thomas Grech
Sayre	b	CM	5	(570) 888-7739	Henry Farley	David Jarrett	. . .	. . .	. . .	Kevin Guinane	Blane Lathrop
Schuylkill Haven	b	CM	5	(570) 385-2841	John Dudley	. . .	. . .	. . .	. . .	Robert Schaeffer	. . .
Scott	tp	CM	17	(412) 276-5300	Donald Diebold	Denise Fitzgerald	. . .	Sandy Novelli	. . .	Stanley Butkus	Randy Lubin
Scottdale	b	CM	4	(724) 887-8220	Eugene Beran	Barry Whoric	. . .	. . .	Scott Rollinson	Tony Martin	. . .
Scranton	c	MC	76	(570) 348-4100	C. Doherty	Leonard Kresefski	J. Wintermantel	R. Novembrino	Harvey Appelgate	James Klee	Rocco Damiano
Selinsgrove	b	CM	5	(570) 374-2311	. . .	John Bickhart	. . .	. . .	. . .	Thomas Garlock	Gary Klingler
Sellersville	b	CM	4	(215) 257-5075	. . .	. . .	. . .	. . .	. . .	. . .	. . .
Seven Fields	b	CM	1	(724) 776-3090	. . .	Thomas Smith	. . .	. . .	. . .	. . .	Bret Cole
Sewickley	b	CM	3	(412) 741-4015	John Wise	Kevin Flannery	Fran Frynkewicz	. . .	Jeff Neff	John Mook	. . .
Sewickley Heights	b	CM	. .	(412) 741-5119	S. Phil Hundley	William Rohe	Julienne Giuliani	. . .	Bill Davis	Herbert Ford	Jeff Marek
Shaler *	tp	CM	29	(412) 486-9700	Thomas McElhane	Timothy Rogers	. . .	Judith Kording	. . .	Jeffrey Gally	James Henderson
Shamokin	c	MC	8	(570) 644-0876	James Yurick	William Strausser	. . .	Ed O'Donnell	Richard Jilinski	Richard Nichols	Ronald Bradley
Sharon	c	MC	16	(724) 983-3220	Robert Lucas	. . .	Sharronda Faber	Michael Gasparich	Terence Whalen	Thomas Burke	. . .
Sharon Hill	b	MC	5	(610) 586-8200	Joseph Botta	William Scott	Connie Hamond	. . .	William Benecke	Joseph Kelly	. . .
Sharpsburg *	b	MC	3	(412) 781-0546	Joseph Panza	Ronald Borczyk	. . .	. . .	Lawrence Trozzo	Leo Rudzki	. . .
Sharpsville	b	CM	4	(412) 962-7896	Kenneth Robertson	. . .	. . .	. . .	Andrew Totin	Willard Thompson	Dale Bulcher
Shenandoah	b	MC	5	(717) 462-1918	. . .	. . .	. . .	. . .	. . .	. . .	. . .
Shillington	b	CM	5	(610) 777-1338	C. Yetter	Michael Mountz	Jan Boyd	. . .	Bruce Squibb	Andrew Hivner	Earl Bare
Shippensburg	b	CM	5	(717) 532-2147	Mark Buterbaugh	William Wolfe	. . .	. . .	Jamie White	. . .	W. Del Grande
Shrewsbury	b	MC	3	(717) 235-4371	. . .	. . .	. . .	. . .	. . .	. . .	. . .
Silver Spring	tp	MC	10	(717) 766-0178	Wayne Pecht	William Cook	Karen Dunlevy	. . .	. . .	James Sadler	. . .
Sinking Spring	b	MC	2	(610) 678-4903	. . .	. . .	. . .	. . .	. . .	. . .	. . .
Skippack Township	tp	CM	6	(610) 454-0909	. . .	Theodore Locker	Peggy White	. . .	Ronald Wilkie	. . .	William Parkins
Slatington	b	CM	4	(610) 767-2131	Clayton Snyder	. . .	Bertha Griffith	. . .	Jeff Schmick	Richard Dorward	Daniel Freed
Slippery Rock	b	MC	3	(724) 794-6391	Ronald Steele	. . .	. . .	. . .	Dave Taggert	Frederick Emigh	Paul Dickey
Solebury	tp	CM	7	(215) 297-5656	. . .	. . .	. . .	. . .	. . .	. . .	. . .
Somerset	b	CM	6	(814) 443-2661	Paul Urbain	Benedict Vinzani	. . .	Brett Peters	Pete Barnhart	Randolph Cox	George Svirsko
Souderton	b	CM	6	(215) 723-4371	. . .	P. Coll	. . .	. . .	. . .	. . .	. . .
South Fayette	tp	CM	12	(412) 221-8700	. . .	Michael Hoy	. . .	. . .	. . .	. . .	. . .
South Greensburg	b	MC	2	(724) 837-8858	. . .	. . .	. . .	. . .	. . .	. . .	. . .
South Hanover	tp	MC	4	(717) 566-0224	. . .	Brian Engle	Kay Stare	. . .	. . .	. . .	Scott Plouse
South Lebanon	tp	CM	8	(717) 274-0481	. . .	. . .	. . .	. . .	. . .	. . .	. . .
South Park	tp	CM	14	(412) 831-7000	George Smith	Mark Schroyer	Lisa Schmigel	Deborah Petrovich	. . .	Joseph Ferrelli	Brian Farmer
South Strabane	tp	CM	7	(724) 225-9055	. . .	John Stickle	. . .	. . .	Scott Reese	Donald Zofchak	D. Mankey
South Whitehall	tp	CO	18	(610) 398-0401	Gary Search	Gerald Gasda	. . .	Linda Perry	. . .	Thomas Toth	James Weber
South Williamsport	b	CM	6	(570) 322-0158	. . .	. . .	. . .	. . .	. . .	. . .	. . .
Southmont	b	MC	2	(814) 255-3104	Kevin Pile	. . .	Mary Magistro	Loretta Spak	Chet Borosky	Andy Havas	Jan Bosley
Southwest Greensburg	b	MC	2	(724) 834-0360	Shaun Teacher	. . .	. . .	. . .	Edward Milliron	James Santmyer	John Warren
Spring	tp	MC	21	(610) 678-5393	Alan Kreider	. . .	Sheryl Kressler	. . .	John Schach	Michael Messner	. . .
Spring City	b	CM	3	(610) 948-3660	. . .	Dennis Rittenhouse	. . .	. . .	. . .	. . .	. . .
Spring Garden	tp	CM	11	(717) 848-2858	David Meckley	Gregory Maust	Wendy Stermer	Mary Yonker	Barry Emig	George Swartz	Edward Salabsky
Springdale *	b	MC	3	(724) 274-6800	Pete Mazak	April Winklmann	. . .	. . .	Kevin Wilhelm	Joseph Naviglia	Bill Cadamore
Springettsbury	tp	CM	23	(717) 757-3521	William Schenck	John Holman	. . .	Jack Hadge	Andrew Stern	David Eshbach	Charles Lauer
Springfield	tp	CM	24	(215) 544-1300	E. Lehman	Michael Lefevre	. . .	. . .	. . .	. . .	. . .
Springfield	tp	CM	19	(215) 836-7600	Kenneth Bradley	Donald Berger	Carol Holcomb	. . .	. . .	Randall Hummel	John Connor
Springfield	tp	CM	4	(610) 346-6700	. . .	. . .	. . .	. . .	. . .	. . .	. . .
St. Clair	b	MC	3	(527) 429-0640	Michael McCord	Roland Price	. . .	. . .	. . .	Michael Carey	Don Hosler
St. Marys *	c	CM	14	(814) 781-1718	David Meier	David Greene	Tammy Lang	Carol Yost	Mike Kraus	Todd Caltagarone	. . .
State College *	b	CM	38	(814) 234-7100	William Welch	Thomas Fountaine	Cynthia Hanscom	Michael Groff	. . .	Thomas King	Mark Whitfield
Steelton	b	MC	5	(717) 939-9842	Michael Rozman	Michael Musser	. . .	. . .	Eugene Vance	Kenneth Lenker	Joseph Conjar
Stewartstown	b	CM	1	(717) 993-2963	. . .	. . .	. . .	. . .	. . .	. . .	. . .
Stowe	tp	CO	6	(412) 331-4050	Frank Carpellotti	. . .	Marie Incorvati	. . .	Martin Jacobs	Stephen Homer	Nick Pegorelli
Strasburg	b	CM	2	(717) 687-7732	. . .	. . .	. . .	. . .	. . .	. . .	. . .
Stroudsburg *	b	CM	5	(570) 421-5444	Kim Diddio	Barbara Quarantello	. . .	. . .	Clement Kochanski	John Baujan	Jack Lesoine
Sugar Creek	b	CM	5	(814) 432-4717	Tom Sloss	Bonnie Beightol	. . .	. . .	Stephen McElhaney	. . .	Richard Phillips
Sugarcreek	tp	MC	1	(724) 526-3261	. . .	. . .	. . .	. . .	. . .	. . .	. . .
Summit Hill	b	MC	2	(570) 645-2305	. . .	. . .	. . .	. . .	. . .	. . .	. . .
Sunbury	c	CO	10	(717) 286-7820	David Persing	. . .	Theresa Nichols	William Mackey	Richard Neff	Charles McAndrew	. . .
Susquehanna	tp	MC	21	(717) 545-4751	Graffus Johnston	. . .	. . .	. . .	. . .	. . .	. . .
Swarthmore	b	CM	6	(610) 543-4599	Elisabeth Aaron	Jane Billings	Cathy Van Sant	. . .	Cris Hansen	Brian Craig	Charles Rowles
Swatara	tp	CM	22	(717) 564-2551	Gregory Ricci	Paul Cornell	. . .	. . .	George Bittinger	Ronald Mellott	A. Hammer
Swissvale	b	MC	9	(412) 271-7101	Charles Martoni	Thomas Esposito	Elizabeth Deluca	. . .	Ken Johnston	Henry Ohrman	Michael Viglietta
Swoyersville	b	MC	5	(717) 288-6602	Fred Romanowski	Gene Breznay	Shirley Gavlick	. . .	. . .	John Shemo	Edward Volack
Tamaqua	b	CM	7	(570) 668-0300	Kenneth Smulligan	Kevin Steigerwalt	Georgia Depos	. . .	Thomas Schlorf	George Woodward	. . .
Tarentum	b	CM	4	(724) 224-1818	Tim Cornuet	C. Turner	Ann Conroy	. . .	. . .	David Sieber	David Hilliard
Taylor	b	MC	6	(570) 562-1400	. . .	. . .	. . .	. . .	. . .	. . .	. . .
Telford *	b	CM	4	(215) 723-5000	Jay Stover	Mark Fournier	. . .	Daphne Hollowbush	Raymond Fegley	Douglas Bickel	Donald Beck
Thornbury	tp	MC	2	(610) 399-1425	. . .	Cary Vargo	. . .	. . .	. . .	. . .	. . .
Throop *	b	MC	4	(570) 489-8311	Stanley Lukowski	. . .	Elaine Morrell	. . .	Jeff Granza	Neil Furiosi	Robert Kalinoski
Titusville	c	CM	6	(814) 827-5300	Brian Sanford	Mary Nau	. . .	Julie Clowes	John Crotty	Michael Simmons	Randall Nebel
Tobyhanna	tp	CM	6	(570) 646-1212	John Kerrick	. . .	. . .	. . .	Troy Counterman	John Lamberton	. . .
Towamencin *	tp	CM	17	(215) 368-7602	H. Charles Wilson	. . .	James Sinz	Beth DiPrete	James Geslak	Joseph Kirschner	Dennis Carney
Towanda	b	CM	3	(717) 265-2696	Richard Snell	Thomas Fairchild	Mary Harris	. . .	Arthur Johnson	Dale Cole	Fred Johnson

Directory 1/9 continued **OFFICIALS IN U.S. MUNICIPALITIES 2,500 AND OVER IN POPULATION**

Jurisdiction	Type	Form of government	2000 Population (000)	Main telephone number	Chief elected official	Appointed administrator	Clerk of the governing board	Chief financial officer	Fire chief	Police chief	Public works director
PENNSYLVANIA continued											
Trafford	b	CM	3	(412) 372-7652	Thomas Babes	Lisa Mallik	Diane Bonifati	...	...	Ronald Troy	...
Tredyffrin	tp	CM	29	(610) 644-1400	Judy DiFilippo	Marie Gleason	...	David Brill	...	Richard Harkness	William Bryant
Troy	b	CM	1	(570) 297-2966	Jerry May	Alan Roloson	Debra Hulslander	...	Roy Vargson	Greg Hostettler	...
Turtle Creek	b	MC	6	(412) 824-2500	...	Dolores Porter	...	...	John Osman	Dale Kraeer	Nick Laurito
Tyrone *	b	CM	5	(814) 684-1330	James Kilmartin	Sharon Dannaway	...	Phyllis Garhart	...	Joseph Beachem	...
Union	tp	MC	3	(717) 935-2890	I. Esh	...	...	...	...	...	...
Union	tp	MC	3	(610) 582-3769	...	Cindy Schweitzer	...	...	...	...	...
Union City	b	CM	3	(814) 438-2331	Brian Tufts	Cheryl Capela	...	...	Robert Seitz	Marvin Tubbs	Raymond Rhodes
Uniontown	c	MC	12	(724) 430-2900	James Sileo	...	Grace Giachetti	Robert Lloyd	James Wood	Kyle Sneddon	Donald Miller
Upland	b	MC	2	(610) 874-7317	...	...	...	...	...	...	...
Upper Allen	tp	CM	15	(717) 766-0756	...	Richard Laskey	...	Laurel Yohe	...	...	Donald Worden
Upper Chichester	tp	MC	16	(610) 855-5881	...	...	...	...	...	...	...
Upper Darby *	tp	MC	81	(610) 734-7622	F. Raymond Shay	Thomas Judge	Richard Nolan	James Smith	Edward Cubler	Michael Chitwood	Joseph Vasturia
Upper Dublin	tp	CM	25	(215) 643-1600	Robert Pesavento	Paul Leonard	...	...	C Samtmann	Terrence Thompson	Charles Oyler
Upper Gwynedd	tp	MC	14	(215) 699-7777	James Santi	Leonard Perrone	...	Michael Sultanik	Jeffrey Mullaly	Robert Freed	Willard Troxel
Upper Hanover	tp	CM	4	(215) 679-4401	...	Stanley Seitzinger	...	...	...	...	...
Upper Leacock *	tp	CM	8	(717) 656-9755	Richard Heilig	Michael Morris	...	...	...	...	Denny Millhouse
Upper Makefield *	tp	CM	7	(215) 968-3340	Daniel Worden	...	...	Sandra Wenitsky	...	Mark Schmidt	Robert Johnson
Upper Merion *	tp	CM	26	(610) 265-2600	Ralph Volpe	R. Wagenmann	...	Nickolas Hiriak	...	Ronald Fonock	Robert Norman
Upper Moreland	tp	CM	24	(215) 659-3100	Richard Booth	David Dodies	...	...	...	William Moffett	Jack Snyder
Upper Pottsgrove *	tp	CM	4	(610) 323-8675	Elwood Taylor	Jack Layne	...	Cynthia Saylor	Tom Mattingly	Bryan Ross	Frank Quinter
Upper Providence *	tp	CM	9	(610) 565-4944	William O'Donnell	Anthony Hamaday	...	Joanne Moore	Donald Wilkins	Thomas Davis	David Pyser
Upper Providence	tp	CM	15	(610) 933-9179	Robert Fieo	George Waterman	Kathleen Stuehler	...	Donald Stiteler	Donald Sherid	Thomas Broadbelt
Upper Saucon	tp	CM	11	(610) 282-1171	Stephen Wagner	Thomas Beil	...	Robert Kassel	Charles Castetter	Robert Coyle	Donald Eck
Upper Southampton	tp	MC	15	(215) 322-9700	John Held	...	...	Anoop Tolani	Mark Showmaker	David Schultz	Wayne Crompton
Upper St. Clair	tp	CM	19	(412) 831-9000	...	Douglas Watkins	...	August Stache	...	Ronald Pardini	F. Robinson
Upper Uwchlan	tp	CM	6	(610) 458-9400	...	John Roughan	Elaine Benson	...	...	John DeMarco	Michael Heckman
Upper Yoder	tp	CM	5	(814) 255-5243	...	...	...	...	...	...	...
Uwchlan	tp	CM	16	(610) 363-9450	John Pribanic	Douglass Hanley	Rebecca Wethman	...	Richard Ruth	J. Davis	James Peterson
Vandergrift	b	CM	5	(724) 567-7818	Jack Jewart	S. Delledonne	Melissa Holmes	...	Thomas Holmes	Louis Purificato	...
Vernon	tp	MC	5	(814) 337-8126	...	David Stone	...	...	...	...	...
Verona	b	MC	3	(412) 828-8080	...	...	Annette Bracken	...	Thomas Tihey	Guy Truby	Robert Gaggie
Warminster	tp	MC	31	(215) 443-5414	...	Robert Tate	...	Ginnie Gehring	James Krueger	Michael Murphy	George Mullen
Warren *	c	CM	11	(814) 723-6300	Mark Phillips	James Nelles	...	...	Sam Pascuzzi	Raymond Zydonik	Brent Ordiway
Warrington *	tp	CM	17	(215) 343-9350	Glenn McKay	Timothy Tieperman	...	...	Christopher Harvey	James Miller	Carl Sames
Warwick	tp	CM	15	(717) 626-8900	...	Daniel Zimmerman	...	...	...	...	Dean Saylor
Warwick	tp	CM	11	(215) 343-6100	...	Gail Weniger	...	Rosemarie Christie	...	Joseph Costello	Robert Benninghoff
Washington	c	MC	15	(724) 223-4200	Kenneth Westcott	Samuel Stockton	Cathy Voytek	Matt Staniszewski	Linn Brookman	John Haddad	Robert Nicolella
Watsontown	b	CM	2	(570) 538-1000	Harriet Miller	Paul Kreckel	Polly Keefer	...	Mark Burrows	Dennis Derr	...
Waynesboro	b	CM	9	(717) 762-2101	...	Lloyd Hamberger	...	...	...	...	...
Waynesburg	b	CM	4	(724) 627-8111	Charles Berryhill	G. Howard	Bonnie Baily	Murray Hoy	Larry Marshall	Timothy Hawfield	Danny Scott
Weatherly	b	CM	2	(570) 427-8640	...	Harold Pudliner	Eloise Hinterleiter	...	Richard Knepper	Brian Cara	Arthur Michael
Wellsboro	b	CM	3	(717) 724-3186	R. Decamp	Susan Leedy	Florence Martino	...	Mark Cooper	John Wheeler	Mark Dieffenbach
Wesleyville	b	MC	3	(814) 899-9124	Terry St. Denny	Peter Nye	...	...	Earl Clark	George Hooker	Clayton Smith
West Bradford	tp	CM	10	(610) 269-4174	John Haiko	Jack Hines	...	Nancy Althouse	...	...	Steven Becker
West Caln	tp	CM	7	(610) 384-5643	...	...	...	...	...	...	...
West Chester	b	CM	17	(610) 692-7574	Robert Whetstone	Ernie McNeely	...	Douglas Kapp	Kevin Corcoran	John Green	Robert Wilpizeski
West Conshohocken	b	CM	1	(610) 828-9747	Patricia Barr	Michael Leonard	Terry Fox	...	Dennis Frankenfield	Joseph Clayborne	Michael McGuire
West Deer	tp	CM	11	(724) 265-3680	...	Jason Dailey	...	...	...	...	...
West Goshen	tp	CM	20	(610) 696-5266	Robert White	Casey LaLonde	Sandra Turley	Jeanne Denham	Andrea Testa	Michael Carroll	R. Halvorsen
West Hanover	tp	CM	6	(717) 652-4841	...	Michael Rimer	...	...	Brian Cassell	...	Harold Harman
West Hazleton	b	MC	3	(570) 455-3695	Daniel Guydish	...	...	...	Robert Ward	Thomas Wallace	Paul Swinesburg
West Homestead	b	MC	2	(412) 461-1844	John Dindak	...	Elsie Fekety	...	...	...	...
West Lampeter	tp	CM	13	(717) 464-3731	James Kalenich	R. D'Agostino	...	...	Sean Alexander	James Walsh	James Kreider
West Manchester	tp	CM	17	(717) 792-3505	...	Jan Dell	...	Betty Keller	David Nichols	Arthur Smith	R. Haifley
West Mifflin	b	CM	22	(412) 466-8170	William Welsh	Howard Bednar	...	...	...	Frank Diener	James Hess
West Newton	b	MC	3	(724) 872-6860	...	...	...	...	...	...	...
West Norriton	tp	CO	15	(610) 631-0450	...	Joseph Hein	...	...	...	Robert Adams	Thomas Cinaglia
West Pikeland *	tp	MC	3	(610) 827-7660	...	Jeri Diesinger	...	...	...	...	...
West Pittston	b	MC	5	(570) 655-7782	Carl Rosencrance	Rick Melvin	Ellen Riddle	...	John Janczewski	Ralph Zezza	Robert Dovin
West Pottsgrove	tp	MC	3	(610) 323-7717	...	...	...	...	...	...	...
West Reading	b	CM	4	(610) 374-8273	R. Shuttlesworth	Lorri Swan	Rosalie Loeper	...	Sherry Fabriziani	Edward Fabriziani	...
West Rockhill *	tp	CM	4	(215) 257-9063	John Mann	...	Lora Sulahian	...	...	...	Randy Lemon
West View	b	MC	7	(412) 931-2800	...	...	...	...	...	...	...
West Whiteland	tp	CM	16	(610) 363-9525	Diane Snyder	...	Patricia Launi	Elizabeth Butch	George Turner	Ralph Burton	Joseph Roscioli
West Wyoming	b	MC	2	(717) 693-1311	...	...	...	...	...	...	...
West York	b	MC	4	(717) 846-8889	...	...	...	...	...	...	...
Westmont	b	MC	5	(814) 255-3865	...	...	...	...	...	...	...
Westtown	tp	CM	10	(610) 692-1930	...	Robert Layman	Sandra Preston	...	...	...	Mark Gross
White	tp	CM	1	(724) 843-2819	Tom Bozic	Antoinette Wiley	...	...	...	Lou Adrian	Charles Currie
White *	tp	CM	14	(724) 463-8585	Robert Overdorff	Larry Garner	...	...	...	...	...
White Oak	b	CM	8	(412) 672-9727	Margaret Kadar	...	Nancy Greenland	...	...	Bruce Greenland	Ron Baldridge
Whitehall	b	MC	14	(412) 884-0505	...	James Leventry	Marilyn Moore	Beverly Weikel	Hobart Moore	J. Schmitt	David King
Whitehall	tp	MC	24	(610) 437-5524	Glenn Solt	Jack Meyers	...	Deborah Bowman	Robert Benner	Theodore Kohuth	John Rackus
Whitemarsh *	tp	CM	16	(610) 825-3535	Joseph Corcoran	C. van De Velde	...	Thomas Mullin	Calvin Bononborger	Eileen Behr	Jerry Breitmayer
Whitpain	tp	CM	18	(610) 277-2400	Leigh Narducci	Phyllis Lieberman	...	John Crawford	...	Joseph Stemple	Ronald Cione
Wilkes-Barre	c	MC	43	(570) 826-8222	Thomas McGroarty	John Murphy	James Ryan	John Koval	James Delaney	Anthony George	Albert Clocker
Wilkins	tp	CM	6	(412) 824-6650	Peter Wychis	Rebecca Bradley	Mae Franc	...	Leonard Hill	Keith Guthrie	Paul Vargo
Wilkinsburg	b	CM	19	(412) 244-2900	Astrid Ware	Marla Marcinko	...	...	Owen McAfee	Mark Springer	Arthur Comer
Williamsport	c	MC	30	(717) 327-7500	Phillip Preziosi	...	Diane Ellis	Robert Fox	Harold Anthony	William Miller	George Holliday
Willistown	tp	CM	10	(610) 647-5300	David Rawson	Hugh Murray	Donna Monardo	...	...	Jay Molvie	John Di Mascio
Wilson	b	MC	7	(610) 258-6142	David Perruso	Walter Boran	Lisa Guth	...	Michael Collins	Richard Nace	Gregory Drake
Wind Gap	b	MC	2	(610) 863-7288	...	...	...	...	...	...	...
Windber	b	CM	4	(814) 467-9014	...	Richard Wargo	Christine Mulcahy	...	...	Richard Skiles	...
Windsor	tp	CM	12	(717) 244-3512	...	...	...	...	...	...	...
Woodard	tp	CM	3	(814) 378-8178	...	...	...	...	...	...	...
Wormleysburg	b	CM	2	(717) 763-4483	Thomas Kargams	Gary Berresford	...	...	...	...	...
Wyoming	b	MC	3	(717) 693-0291	Michael Podwika	Patricia Carter	...	...	...	John Gilligan	Larry Selenski
Wyomissing *	b	CM	8	(610) 376-7481	Ronald Stanko	Kevin Tobias	Rosemar Schnable	...	Bruce Longenecker	Jeffrey Biehl	James Baab

Directory 1/9 continued **OFFICIALS IN U.S. MUNICIPALITIES 2,500 AND OVER IN POPULATION**

Jurisdiction	Type	Form of govern-ment	2000 Popu-lation (000)	Main telephone number	Chief elected official	Appointed administrator	Clerk of the governing board	Chief financial officer	Fire chief	Police chief	Public works director
PENNSYLVANIA continued											
Yardley	b	MC	2	(215) 493-6832	S.Edward Johnson	Chris Harding	...	...	...	James O'Neill	...
Yeadon *	b	CM	11	(610) 284-1606	Jacqueline Mosley	...	...	Joseph Bartley	Craig Jeffries	Donald Molineux	...
York	c	MC	40	(717) 849-2301	John Brenner	Michael O'Rourke	Dianna Thompson	Carol Brown	John Senft	Mark Whitman	James Gross
York	tp	MC	23	(717) 741-3861	David Hamberger	E. Heathcote	...	Joseph Robinson	Paul Reichenbach	Thomas Gross	Mark Clark
Youngsville	b	CM	1	(814) 563-4604	Bruce Williams	Ronald Bosworth	Sherry Martin	...	Wallace Tydus	Gerald Calaldo	...
Youngwood	b	MC	4	(724) 925-3660	...	...	...	...	...	...	...
Zelienople	b	CM	4	(724) 452-6610	Charles Underwood	Donald Pepe	...	...	Andrew Mathew	Jim Miller	Mark Matscherz
RHODE ISLAND											
Barrington *	t	CM	16	(401) 247-1900	Jeffrey Brenner	Peter Deangelis	Lorraine Derois	Dean Huff	Gerald Bessette	John La Cross	Alan Corvi
Bristol	t	TM	21	(401) 253-7000	Joseph Parella	...	Diane Mederos	John Day	David Sylvaria	Russel Serpa	Paul Romano
Burrillville	t	CM	15	(401) 568-4300	Kevin Menard	Michael Wood	Nancy Faford	John Mainville	...	Bernard Gannon	Richard St. Sauveur
Central Falls *	c	MC	18	(401) 727-7400	Charles Moreau	...	Elizabeth Crowley	John Kuzmiski	Rene Coutu	Joseph Moran	Joseph Nield
Charlestown	t	CM	7	(401) 364-1210	...	...	Jodi LaCroix	...	...	Thomas Sharkey	Alan Arsenault
Coventry	t	CM	33	(401) 821-6400	...	...	...	Warren West	...	...	Sheila Patnode
Cranston	c	MC	79	(401) 461-1000	Stephen Laffey	...	Maria Wall	Jerome Baron	Robert Warren	Michael Chalek	Marco Schiappa
Cumberland	t	MC	31	(401) 728-2400	David Iwuc	David Fernandes	Patricia Skurka	Thomas Bruce	...	John Desmarais	Robert Joyal
East Greenwich *	t	CM	12	(401) 886-8676	...	William Sequino	Deidra Kettelle	Thomas Mattos	Thomas Rowan	David Desjarlais	Joseph Duarte
East Providence *	c	CM	48	(401) 435-7762	Isadore Ramos	Richard Brown	Virginia Nunes	James McDonald	Joseph Klucznik	Hubert Paquette	Stephen Coutu
Exeter	t	RT	6	(401) 294-3891	Richard Kenyon	...	Cheryl Chorney	...	Scott Kettelle	Richard Brown	John Sullivan
Foster	t	CM	4	(401) 392-9200	Janet Dannecker	...	Anne Irons	...	...	Donald Kettelle	Bradford Gove
Glocester	t	MC	9	(401) 568-6206	Charles Poirier	...	Jean Fecteau	Thomas Mainville	...	Jamie Hainsworth	Alan Whitford
Hopkinton	t	TM	7	(401) 377-7777	Linda DiOrio	William DiLibero	Elizabeth Martin	Janice Bergeron	...	John Scuncio	Charles Niles
Jamestown	t	CM	5	(401) 423-7220	Kenneth Littman	Bruce Keiser	Arlene Petit	...	James Bryer	Thomas Tighe	Steven Goslee
Johnston	t	MC	28	(401) 553-8855	William Macera	...	Robin Pimental	...	Victor Cipriano	Richard Tamburini	Anthony Venditelli
Lincoln	t	MC	20	(401) 333-1100	Sue Sheppard	...	Karen Allen	Stephen Woerner	John McCaughey	Robert Kells	John MacQueen
Little Compton	t	MC	3	(401) 635-4400	Robert Mushen	...	Carol Wordell	...	Harry Hallgring	Sidney Wordell	Michael Mello
Middletown *	t	CM	17	(401) 846-5781	Paul Rodrigues	...	Barbara Nash	Shawn Brown	Stephen Martin	Anthony Pesare	Thomas O'Loughlin
Narragansett	t	CM	16	(401) 789-1044	Anne-Marie Silveira	...	Carol Robbins	David Krugman	James Cotter	J Smith	David Ousterhout
New Shoreham	t	CM	1	(401) 466-3200	Richard Kiley	...	Susan Shea	Mary Balser	Kirk Littlefield	William McCombe	...
Newport *	c	CM	26	(401) 845-5444	Stephen Waluk	Edward Lavallee	Kathleen Silvia	Laura Sitrin	Edward McCarthy	Michael McKenna	Julia Forgue
North Kingstown	t	CM	26	(401) 294-3331	Anthony Miccolis	Michael Embury	James Marques	...	David Murray	E. Charboneau	Philippe Bergeron
North Providence *	t	MC	32	(401) 232-0900	A. Mollis	John Fleming	M. DeAngelus	Maria Vallee	Alfred Bertoncini	Ernest Spaziano	Glenn Corrente
North Smithfield	t	MC	10	(401) 767-2202	Robert Lowe	...	Debra Todd	Jill Gemma	Joel Jillson	Steven Reynolds	...
Pawtucket *	c	MC	72	(401) 728-0500	James Doyle	Harvey Goulet	Janice LaPorte	Ronald Wunschel	Timothy McLaughlin	George Kelley	John Carney
Portsmouth *	t	MC	17	(401) 683-9118	Dennis Canario	Robert Driscoll	K. Viera Beaudoin	David Faucher	Jeffrey Lynch	Lance Hebert	David Kehew
Providence	c	MC	173	(401) 421-7740	David Cicilline	...	...	Alexander Prignano	James Rattigan	Richard Sullivan	Ferdinand Ihenacho
Richmond	t	RT	7	(401) 539-2497	Michael Sullivan	...	Mary Morgan	...	...	Raymond Driscoll	Scott Barber
Scituate	t	MC	10	(401) 647-2822	...	...	Margaret Long	...	...	William Mack	Richard Iverson
Smithfield	t	CM	20	(401) 233-1000	Alberto La Greca	...	...	Dennis Finlay	Joseph Mollo	William McGarry	...
South Kingstown	t	CM	27	(401) 789-9331	Barbara Hackey	Stephen Alfred	Dale Holberton	Alan Lord	...	Vincent Vespia	Jon Schock
Tiverton	t	CM	15	(401) 625-6700	Donald Bollin	W Steckman	Hannibal Costa	...	Alan Jack	George Arruda	John Ratcliffe
Warren	t	CM	11	(401) 245-7554	...	Mike Abruzzi	Rita Galinelli	...	Alexander Galinelli	Thomas Gordon	John Massed
Warwick	c	MC	85	(401) 738-2000	Scott Avedisian	Barbara Caniglia	Marie Bennett	Ernest Zmyslinski	John Chartier	Stephen McCartney	Edmund Sarno
West Greenwich	t	TM	5	(401) 392-3800	Thaylen Waltonen	Kevin Breene	Janet Olsson	...	...	Gary Malikowski	David Andrews
West Warwick *	t	CM	29	(401) 822-9219	J.-M. DiMasi	Wolfgang Bauer	David Clayton	Malcolm Moore	Charles Hall	Peter Brousseau	Paul Thomas
Westerly	t	CM	22	(401) 348-2500	...	Joseph Turo	Donna Giordano	...	David Sayles	J. Smith	...
Woonsocket	c	MC	43	(401) 762-6400	Susan Menard	M. Annarummo	Pauline Payeur	...	Henry Renaud	Robert Morris	...
SOUTH CAROLINA											
Abbeville *	c	CM	5	(864) 459-5017	Harold McNeill	Nolan Wiggins	Kathy Wilson	Fran Strickland	George Speer	Patrick Henderson	Franklin Lewis
Aiken	c	CM	25	(803) 642-7654	F. Cavanaugh	Roger LeDuc	Sara Ridout	Anita Lilly	...	...	Larry Morris
Allendale	t	MC	4	(803) 584-4619	Chuck Cochran	DeWayne Ennis	...	Marilyn Leonard	...	James Youse	Maner Blackwood
Anderson	c	CM	25	(864) 231-2200	Richard Shirley	John Moore	...	Peggy Maxwell	Jack Abraham	Derrill McConnell	Tony Norris
Andrews	t	MC	3	(803) 264-8666	...	...	...	...	...	...	...
Atlantic Beach	t	CM	..	(843) 272-5287	Irene Armstrong	Carolyn Montomery	Cheryl Pereira	Rolanda McDuffie	...	...	...
Awendaw	t	MC	1	(843) 928-3100	...	Dan Martin	...	...	...	...	...
Bamberg	c	MC	3	(803) 245-5128	...	...	...	...	...	...	...
Barnwell	c	MC	5	(803) 259-3266	...	...	...	...	...	...	...
Batesburg-Leesville	t	CM	5	(803) 532-4601	James Wiszowaty	Joan Taylor	Judy Edwards	...	Tommy Shealy	William Oswald	...
Beaufort	c	CM	12	(843) 525-7070	William Rauch	Scott Dadson	Beverly Gay	...	Wendell Wilburn	Jeff Dowling	Isiah Smalls
Belton	c	MC	4	(864) 338-7773	...	David Watson	...	...	Alan Sims	David Dockins	Derrall Foster
Bennettsville	c	CM	9	(843) 479-9001	...	Max Alderman	...	Wesley Park	Harvey Odom	Larry McNeil	Thomas Bostick
Bishopville	t	MC	3	(803) 484-9418	Thomas Alexander	William McCutchen	Hannah Tention	Suzette Robinson	...	Altagracia Simon	Luther Bramlett
Blackville *	t	MC	2	(803) 284-2444	David Kenner	...	Harriett McKnight	...	Charles Epps	Kenneth Bamberg	Edward Rockwell
Bluffton	t	MC	1	(843) 706-4500	Henry Johnston	William Workman	Sandra Lunceford	Michael Nolte	...	John Brown	Harold Cooler
Calhoun Falls	t	CM	2	(864) 418-8512	Johnnie Waller	A. Harris	Peggy Waters	...	Darrell Manning	Mike Alewine	...
Camden	c	CM	6	(803) 432-2421	Mary Clark	G. Broom	Betty Slade	Mel Pearson	John Bowers	Joseph Floyd	Tom Couch
Cayce	c	CM	12	(803) 796-9020	...	John Sharpe	...	...	...	...	Frank Robinson
Central *	t	MC	3	(864) 639-6381	Mac Martin	Phillip Mishoe	Sandra Brown	Jerri Martin	Ben Smith	Kerry Avery	Dean Martin
Charleston	c	MC	96	(843) 577-6970	Joseph Riley	...	Vanessa Maybank	Stephen Bedard	Russell Thomas	Reuben Greenberg	...
Cheraw	t	MC	5	(843) 537-8401	Andrew Ingram	J. Taylor	...	...	John Melton	J. A. Graves	James Lewis
Chester	c	CM	6	(803) 581-2123	...	...	...	...	David McAbee	Anthony Staten	Raymond Douglas
Clemson *	c	MC	11	(864) 653-2030	Larry Abernathy	Richard Cotton	Beverly Coleman	Tom Sparacino	...	James Dixon	David Conner
Clinton	c	CM	8	(864) 833-2790	Myra Nichols	Joshua Kay	Tammy Templeton	...	...	A. Barker	Ralph Lewis
Clover	t	MC	4	(803) 222-9495	Donnie Burris	Allison Harvey	Shannon Nix	...	Charlie Love	Legrand Guerry	Mark Geouge
Columbia *	c	CM	116	(803) 545-3000	Bob Coble	Charles Austin	Erika Salley	Lisa Rolan	Bradley Anderson	Harold Crisp	Melissa Gentry
Conway	c	CM	11	(803) 248-1760	Gregory Martin	...	Cyndi Gore	Michael Hardee	Darrel McDowell	Samuel Hendrick	Jerry Barnhill
Darlington	c	MC	6	(843) 398-4000	James Ward	Rodney Langley	Gloria Pridgen	...	James Stone	Jay Cox	Dale Freeze
Denmark	t	MC	3	(803) 793-3734	Linda Davis	Thomas Robertson	...	...	...	...	Timothy Freeman
Dillon	c	CM	6	(843) 774-0040	J Davis	Richard Wagner	Lynn Bowman	...	Michael Goodwin	Joe Rogers	Hardy Jackson
Easley *	c	MC	17	(864) 855-7900	M. Christopherson	Jonathan Simons	Dianne Carter	...	Huey Womack	William Traber	Lamar Hunnicutt
Edgefield *	t	MC	4	(803) 637-4014	Ken Durham	...	C. Cheatham	...	Roger Ellis	Ronald Carter	David Coleman
Edisto Beach	t	MC	..	(843) 869-2505	Burley Lyons	Linda Woods	...	...	William Simmons	H. Trent Canady	Robert Doud
Florence	c	CM	30	(843) 665-3158	Frank Willis	David Williams	...	Thomas Chandler	Joseph Robertson	Anson Shells	Andrew Griffin
Folly Beach	c	CM	2	(843) 588-2447	Vernon Knox	Toni Connor-Rooks	Marlene Estridge	Charles McManus	...	...	Steve Robinson
Forest Acres	c	CM	10	(803) 782-9475	J. Rowe	Mark Williams	...	...	...	Marion Sealy	Dominic Poeta
Fort Mill	t	CM	7	(803) 547-2116	Charles Powers	David Hudspeth	April Beachum	Chantay Bouler	Kenneth Kerber	Jeffrey Helms	William Broom
Fountain Inn	t	MC	6	(864) 862-4421	Gary Long	...	Sandra Woods	...	Dale Watson	Anthony Morton	Roger Case

Directory 1/9 continued — OFFICIALS IN U.S. MUNICIPALITIES 2,500 AND OVER IN POPULATION

Jurisdiction	Type	Form of govern-ment	2000 Popu-lation (000)	Main telephone number	Chief elected official	Appointed administrator	Clerk of the governing board	Chief financial officer	Fire chief	Police chief	Public works director
SOUTH CAROLINA continued											
Gaffney	* c	MC	12	(864) 206-3303	Henry Jolly	James Taylor	Leighann Smuggs	. . .	Nathan Ellis	John O'Donald	. . .
Georgetown	c	MC	8	(843) 545-4000	Lynn Wilson	Steven Thomas	Ann Mercer	Jessica Miller	Joseph Tanner	Dan Furr	Sterling Geathers
Goose Creek	c	CM	29	(843) 797-6220	Michael Heitzler	Dennis Harmon	Kelly Lovette	Ronald Faretra	Steve Chapman	Harvey Becker	Steven Price
Great Falls	t	MC	2	(803) 482-2055	H. Starnes	. . .	Julie Blackwell	Don Camp	John Hipp	John Brown	Gary McManus
Greenville	c	CM	56	(864) 467-4530	Knox White	James Bourey	Cheryle Ratliff	Stephen Keef	William McDowell	Willie Johnson	Daniel Durig
Greenwood	c	CM	22	(864) 942-8414	Floyd Nicholson	Steven Brown	. . .	Steffanie Dorn	Ronald Strange	Gerald Brooks	Billy Allen
Greer	c	CM	16	(864) 848-2150	Rick Danner	Edward Driggers	Lucia Polson	Mary Greer	Christopher Harvey	Harold Crisp	James Johnson
Hampton	t	MC	2	(803) 943-2951	John Rhoden	. . .	Michelle Brown	. . .	Wade Freeman	Perry McAlheney	Walter Barefoot
Hanahan	c	MC	12	(843) 554-4221	William Cobb	Stephen Mason	Debra Lewis	K. Armstrong	Jerry Barham	Donald Wilcox	Kenneth Prosser
Hardeeville	t	CM	1	(843) 784-2231	Rodney Cannon	R. Shane Haynes	Jessica Louden	S. Henderson	John Ekaitis	James Hubbard	James Hatter
Hartsville	c	CM	7	(843) 383-3018	William Gaskins	James Pennington	. . .	Renee Douglas	William Heathman	L Tim Kemp	Mike Welch
Hemingway	t	MC	..	(843) 558-2824	Grady Richardson	Joseph Lee	Cindy Owens	. . .	George Sutton	Sandy Thompson	Ken Laster
Hilton Head Island	* t	CM	33	(843) 341-4600	Thomas Peeples	Stephen Riley	Betsy Mosteller	Susan Simmons	Thomas Fieldstead	. . .	. . .
Hollywood	t	MC	3	(843) 889-3222	Gerald Schuster	. . .	Wendy Ward	. . .	. . .	. . .	. . .
Honea Path	t	CM	3	(864) 369-2466	. . .	. . .	. . .	. . .	. . .	. . .	. . .
Irmo	t	CM	11	(803) 781-7050	John Gibbons	John Hanson	. . .	P. McMahon	. . .	. . .	. . .
Isle Of Palms	c	MC	4	(843) 886-6428	F. Sottile	Linda Tucker	Janet Mauldin	. . .	Ann Marie Graham	T. Buckhannon	David Mobley
Johnston	* t	MC	2	(803) 275-2488	Willie Campbell	. . .	. . .	. . .	John Clark	Chris Aston	Stuart Smith
Kershaw	t	MC	1	(803) 475-6065	Tommy Baker	Tony Starnes	Sandra Morgan	. . .	Tracy Caldwell	Jeff Jackson	Don Rutledge
Kiawah Island	t	MC	1	(843) 768-9166	James Piet	Tumiko Rucker	Pat Wallis	. . .	. . .	. . .	. . .
Kingstree	t	CM	3	(843) 355-7484	James Kirby	Bradley Smith	Patricia Graham	. . .	Curtis Graham	Robert Ford	James Tisdale
Lake City	c	CM	6	(843) 374-5421	Arthur Martin	. . .	Cherline Miles	Jaunita Bradley	. . .	Lev Brown	. . .
Lancaster	c	CM	8	(803) 286-8414	. . .	. . .	Brenisha Wells	. . .	Dennis Cole	Jimmy Balkcum	. . .
Landrum	c	MC	2	(864) 457-3712	E. Brannon	James Edwards	. . .	. . .	. . .	. . .	. . .
Laurens	c	MC	9	(864) 984-0144	James Goss	A. Madden	. . .	. . .	William Hughes	Robin Morse	Oscar Tribble
Lexington	* t	CM	9	(803) 951-4164	randy halfacre	James Duckett	Becky Hildebrand	Kathy Roberts	. . .	Terrence Greene	Alan Lutz
Liberty	c	MC	3	(864) 850-3505	Eddie Hughes	. . .	Dawn Lewis	. . .	Kevin McClain	Robert Griffin	Raymond Jones
Loris	c	MC	2	(843) 756-4004	David Stoudenmire	. . .	Martha Dorman	. . .	Jerry Hardee	Marshall Russell	Rodney Hardee
Manning	c	CM	4	(803) 435-8477	Kevin Johnson	Mary Adger	. . .	C. Hemingway	Mitchell McElveen	Randy Garrett	Lowell Hardy
Marion	t	MC	7	(843) 423-5961	Bobby Gerald	Tim Harper	Lakesha Shannon	. . .	Alan Ammons	Willie Smith	Mike Shall
Mauldin	c	MC	15	(864) 288-4910	R. Jones	Raymond Eubanks	Cindy Miller	. . .	Russell Sapp	John Davidson	Thomas Lynn
Mc Coll	t	MC	2	(843) 523-5341	. . .	. . .	Sandra Brewer	. . .	. . .	Thomas Langley	Marshall Grooms
Moncks Corner	t	MC	5	(843) 761-6650	William Peagler	. . .	Marilyn Baker	. . .	David Miller	Chad Caldwell	James Bodiford
Mount Pleasant	t	MC	47	(843) 884-8517	Harry Hallman	Robert Burdette	Carol Hunter	Colleen Jernigan	Harry Mims	Ronald Perry	Joseph Peele
Mullins	t	MC	5	(803) 464-9583	Joseph George	J. C. Richardson	Brenda Ivey	. . .	. . .	Jimmy Alford	Kenneth Johnson
Myrtle Beach	c	CM	22	(843) 918-1114	Mark McBride	Thomas Leath	Joan Grove	Michael Shelton	James Payne	Warren Gall	Everett Andrews
Newberry	c	CM	10	(803) 321-1000	. . .	Eric Budds	. . .	Marie Hickman	Joseph Palmer	Lewis Swindler	Arnold Hiller
North Augusta	* c	CM	17	(803) 441-4202	Lark Jones	Charles Bennett	Donna Young	John Potter	. . .	. . .	Thomas Zeaser
North Charleston	c	MC	79	(843) 740-2501	R. Summey	Raymond Anderson	Ellen Clark	Edward Newton	Larry Waddle	John Zumalt	Michael Hendrick
North Myrtle Beach	c	CM	10	(843) 280-5555	Marilyn Hatley	John Smithson	. . .	Randy Wright	Thomas Barstow	. . .	Kevin Blayton
Orangeburg	c	CM	12	(803) 533-6000	Paul Miller	John Yow	. . .	Carrie Johnson	. . .	Wendell Davis	Durwood Bowder
Pageland	t	MC	2	(843) 672-7292	Carroll Faile	. . .	Linda Long	. . .	. . .	Johnny Sowell	Wesley Miles
Pendleton	t	MC	2	(864) 646-9409	Carol Burdette	Theresa Perry	Amber Barnes	. . .	. . .	. . .	Richard Bork
Pickens	c	MC	3	(864) 878-6421	David Owens	C. Eldridge	. . .	. . .	David Porter	Tommy Ellenburg	Henry Anthony
Port Royal	t	MC	3	(843) 986-2200	Samuel Murray	Van Willis	Tanya Payne	. . .	Wendell Wilburn	James Cadien	Jeff Coppinger
Ridgeland	t	MC	2	(843) 726-7500	Ralph Tuten	Jason Taylor	Penelope Daley	. . .	John Mingledorff	Richard Zareva	James Mixson
Rock Hill	* c	CM	49	(803) 329-7000	Doug Echols	Carey Smith	. . .	. . .	Kenneth Blackmon	John Gregory	Bobby Banks
Saluda	* t	MC	3	(864) 445-3522	Frank Addy	Randy Cole	Claudia Cochran	. . .	Edwin Riley	David Farmer	Robert Langford
Seneca	t	MC	7	(864) 885-2700	John Fields	Gregory Dietterick	. . .	Walter Smith	. . .	. . .	Benny Burrell
Simpsonville	c	MC	14	(864) 967-9526	Dennis Waldrop	Russell Hawes	. . .	Robert Harrison	Jess Majors	Charles Reece	Joseph Carter
Spartanburg	c	CM	39	(864) 596-2000	William Barnet	Mark Scott	Connie Littlejohn	Dennis Locke	Phillip Caruso	Jennifer Kindall	. . .
Springdale	t	CM	2	(803) 794-0408	Pat Smith	Natalie McKelvey	. . .	. . .	. . .	Matthew Johnson	Terry Montgomery
Summerville	t	MC	27	(843) 871-6000	Berlin Myers	Dennis Pieper	. . .	Kristina Plymel	. . .	Roy Whitehead	Matthew Halter
Sumter	c	CM	39	(803) 436-2583	Stephen Creech	Deron McCormick	Sherry Evans	David Brown	Douglas Mathis	Harold Johnson	Al Harris
Surfside Beach	t	MC	4	(843) 913-6111	Roy Hyman	. . .	Debra Herrmann	Diana King	Robert Packard	. . .	Terry Grady
Tega Cay	c	MC	4	(803) 548-3512	. . .	Grant Duffield	Dora Perry	. . .	. . .	Rick Evelsizer	John Lathan
Travelers Rest	c	CM	4	(864) 834-7958	Roy Reynolds	Dianna Gracely	Gail Braziel	. . .	Richard Johnson	Timothy Christy	Francis Allen
Trenton	t	MC	..	(803) 275-2538	. . .	W. Welborn	. . .	. . .	. . .	. . .	. . .
Union	c	MC	8	(864) 429-1702	Bruce Morgan	. . .	Gloria Rogers	Walker Gallman	Phillip Moore	. . .	Perry Harmon
Walhalla	t	MC	3	(864) 638-4343	Julian Stoudemire	. . .	Nancy Goehle	Karen Burgess	Greg Fowler	. . .	James Moore
Walterboro	c	CM	5	(843) 549-2548	W Harry Cone	Ernest Mc Connell	Betty Hudson	Jeffrey Lord	Jack Lyons	Michael Devin	Charlie Chewning
Ware Shoals	t	CM	2	(864) 456-7478	. . .	. . .	Sherry Busbee	. . .	. . .	. . .	. . .
West Columbia	c	CM	13	(803) 791-1880	Wyman Rish	J. Cunningham	Marta McKinnon	. . .	Ronald Scarboro	Dennis Tyndall	Joseph Owens
Westminster	t	MC	2	(864) 647-3200	Vera Duke	. . .	Donna Owen	. . .	Bobby Williams	William Strachan	Gary Cobb
Williamston	* t	MC	3	(864) 847-7473	Phillip Clardy	. . .	Mahala Cochran	. . .	Steve Ellison	David Baker	Timothy Hood
Williston	t	MC	3	(803) 266-7015	Thomas Rivers	. . .	Patricia Fowler	. . .	. . .	Roger Kaney	John Melton
Winnsboro	* t	CM	3	(803) 635-4943	Roger Gaddy	Don Wood	Anne Stewart	Kathy Belton	. . .	. . .	Leon Adams
Woodruff	c	CM	4	(864) 476-8154	Jerald Craig	Jeffrey Slatton	. . .	. . .	J. Westmoreland	Michael Cromer	Gerald Bailey
York	c	CM	6	(803) 684-2341	W. Connolly	. . .	Nelle Pittman	. . .	Domenico Manera	Ronnie Roberts	Charles Helms
SOUTH DAKOTA											
Aberdeen	c	CM	24	(605) 626-7025	Tim Rich	. . .	. . .	Karl Alberts	John Stahl	. . .	Robin Bobzien
Belle Fourche	c	MC	4	(605) 892-2494	Bill Schmidt	. . .	. . .	Gloria Landphere	Ken Firnen	Larry Roberdeau	Leslie Snoozy
Beresford	c	CM	2	(605) 763-2008	Brent Palmer	Jerry Zeimetz	. . .	Kathy Moller	Tarz Mullinix	Larry Christensen	Dan Andre
Box Elder	c	MC	2	(605) 923-1403	William Maher	Paula Carpenter	Kelley Kadlecek	James Schwegerdt	Roger Williams	Bradford Phillips	Vince Finkhouse
Brandon	c	MC	3	(605) 582-6515	Michael Schultz	Dennis Olson	Janell Boor	Ellaine Henriksen	Larry Johnson	Phil Youngdale	Wayne Fletcher
Brookings	* c	CO	18	(605) 692-6281	. . .	Jeffrey Weldon	Shari Thornes	Rita Thompson	Darrell Hartmann	Bryan Gums	. . .
Canton	c	CO	3	(605) 987-2881	Patrick Van Wyhe	Daniel Amert	Karen Leffier	. . .	Trevor Erle	Stephan Warnock	Palmer Ericksen
Custer	c	MC	1	(605) 673-4824	. . .	. . .	. . .	. . .	. . .	. . .	. . .
Dell Rapids	c	CM	2	(605) 428-3595	Scott Fiegen	Jeffrey Traill	. . .	Vicky Haskell	. . .	. . .	Larry Schildhauer
Elk Point	c	MC	1	(605) 356-2141	Isabel Trobaugh	. . .	. . .	. . .	Jason Welch	Ryan Fleek	Mark Rubida
Hartford	c	MC	1	(605) 528-3427	. . .	R. VanDerWerff	. . .	. . .	. . .	. . .	. . .
Hot Springs	c	MC	4	(605) 745-3135	. . .	. . .	. . .	. . .	. . .	. . .	. . .
Huron	c	CO	11	(605) 353-8502	Mary Pearson	. . .	Carol Tschetter	Paullyn Carey	John Coughlin	Douglas Schmitt	. . .
Lead	c	CO	3	(605) 584-1401	Thomas Nelson	Patrick Milos	Jeneen Mack	. . .	Ray Bubb	John Wainman	John Bunch
Lennox	c	MC	2	(605) 647-2286	. . .	Justin Weiland	. . .	. . .	. . .	. . .	. . .
Madison	c	CO	6	(605) 256-4586	. . .	. . .	. . .	Jeff Heinemeyer	Jerald Johnson	Ken Scott	Dick Birk
Milbank	* c	MC	3	(605) 432-9575	Dale Aesoph	Jason Kettwig	Pat Berkner	C. Schumacher	Ron Bjerke	Tim Kwasniewski	Larry Tietjen
Mitchell	c	MC	14	(605) 995-8420	Louis Sebert	. . .	. . .	Marilyn Wilson	Steve Willis	Lyndon Overweg	Tim McGannon
Mobridge	* c	MC	3	(605) 845-3509	Taylor Oster	Steve Gasser	. . .	Lori Heil	. . .	Michael Nehls	Brad Milliken
Pierre	c	CO	13	(605) 773-7407	Dennis Eisnach	. . .	. . .	Kenneth Hericks	Tom Kurtenbach	Allen Aden	Rodney Liesinger

Directory 1/9 continued **OFFICIALS IN U.S. MUNICIPALITIES 2,500 AND OVER IN POPULATION**

Jurisdiction		Type	Form of govern- ment	2000 Popu- lation (000)	Main telephone number	Chief elected official	Appointed administrator	Clerk of the governing board	Chief financial officer	Fire chief	Police chief	Public works director
SOUTH DAKOTA continued												
Rapid City	*	c	MC	59	(605) 394-4110	Jerome Munson	. . .	. . .	James Preston	Gary Shepherd	Craig Tieszen	. . .
Redfield		c	MC	2	(605) 472-4550	Duane Sanger	. . .	. . .	Joan Marlette	Richard Gruenwald	. . .	James Haider
Sioux Falls		c	CO	123	(605) 367-8740	Dave Munson	. . .	Dianne Metli	E. Rowenhorst	Donald Hill	Doug Barthel	. . .
Sisseton		c	CM	2	(605) 698-3391	. . .	. . .	. . .	. . .	. . .	. . .	. . .
Spearfish		c	MC	8	(605) 642-1325	. . .	. . .	. . .	Elizabeth Benning	. . .	Pat Rotert	Cheryl Johnson
Sturgis		c	MC	6	(605) 347-4422	. . .	. . .	. . .	. . .	Ron Koan	. . .	. . .
Vermillion	*	c	CM	9	(605) 677-7050	Dan Christopherson	John Prescott	. . .	Michael Carlson	Douglas Brunick	Art Mabry	Harold Holoch
Watertown		c	MC	20	(605) 882-6200	Brenda Barger	. . .	. . .	Tracy Turbak	Larry Anderson	Terry Lohr	Herbert Blomquist
Winner	*	c	MC	3	(605) 842-2606	Richard Lewis	. . .	R. Augspurger	Jack Day	Glen McCready	Paul Schueth	Dennis Schroeder
Yankton	*	c	CM	13	(605) 668-5200	Curt Bernard	. . .	. . .	Al Viereck	Tom Kurtenbach	Duane Heeney	Kevin Kuhl
TENNESSEE												
Adams		t	CM	. .	(615) 696-2593	Omer Brooksher	. . .	. . .	. . .	Ray Brown	. . .	. . .
Alamo		t	MC	2	(731) 696-4551	. . .	. . .	Melinda East	Sharon Kail	. . .	Jimmy Irvin	Steve Hughes
Alcoa		c	CM	7	(865) 380-4700	Donald Mull	Mark Johnson	. . .	Ray Richesin	Larry Graves	Wayne Chodak	Kenneth Wiggins
Algood		c	MC	2	(931) 537-9545	. . .	. . .	. . .	. . .	Lloyd Norris	. . .	. . .
Ashland City		t	CM	3	(615) 792-4211	Gary Norwood	. . .	Phyllis Schaeffer	. . .	James Walker	Curtis Bennett	Christopher Cherry
Athens	*	c	CM	13	(423) 744-2703	John Proffitt	Mitchell Moore	Kaye Burton	Brad Harris	Robert Miller	Charles Ziegler	Shawn Lindsey
Atoka	*	t	MC	3	(901) 837-5300	Charles Walker	Mark Johnson	Juanita Ayers	. . .	Jay Bonson	Jessie Poole	Walter Billings
Bartlett		c	MC	40	(901) 385-6400	A. Keith McDonald	Jay Rainey	Gail Russo	Mark Brown	James Graves	Marcus Hopper	Toby Adkison
Beersheba Springs		t	CM	. .	(931) 692-3314	. . .	. . .	. . .	. . .	. . .	. . .	. . .
Belle Meade		c	CM	2	(615) 297-6041	. . .	Beth Reardon	. . .	. . .	. . .	Jimmy Binkley	George Bartlett
Berry Hill		c	CM	. .	(615) 292-5531	William Spray	Joseph Baker	Cheri Thompson	. . .	. . .	Robert Bennett	Kennith Bush
Bolivar		c	MC	5	(731) 658-2020	. . .	. . .	. . .	. . .	. . .	. . .	. . .
Brentwood		c	CM	23	(615) 371-0060	Brian Sweeney	Michael Walker	Roger Horner	Carson Swinford	Kenny Lane	Ricky Watson	Ray Mize
Bristol		c	CM	24	(423) 989-5500	James Messimer	Jeffrey Broughton	. . .	Tara Musick	Phil Vinson	Blaine Wade	Charles Robinette
Brownsville		t	MC	10	(731) 772-1212	Webb Banks	. . .	. . .	. . .	Mark Foster	Gill Kendrick	Bobby Mayer
Camden		t	MC	3	(731) 584-4656	James Travis	. . .	Phyllis Woodard	. . .	Tom Bordonaro	George Smith	. . .
Carthage		c	MC	2	(615) 735-1881	David Bowman	. . .	Brenda McKinley	Joyce Rash	. . .	Jimmy Williams	Charles Massey
Centerville		t	MC	3	(931) 729-4246	Ronnie Martin	. . .	. . .	Patricia Skelton	. . .	Roger Livengood	Danny Hudgins
Charleston		t	CM	. .	(423) 336-1483	. . .	. . .	. . .	. . .	. . .	. . .	. . .
Chattanooga		c	CO	155	(423) 757-5200	Ron Littlefield	Dan Johnson	Carol O'Neal	Daisy Madison	Jim Coppinger	J. Dotson	William McDonald
Church Hill		t	MC	5	(423) 357-6161	. . .	. . .	. . .	. . .	. . .	. . .	. . .
Clarksville		c	MC	103	(931) 645-7444	. . .	. . .	Sylvia Skinner	Wilbur Berry	Michael Roberts	Mark Smith	Dwight Luton
Cleveland		c	CO	37	(423) 559-3313	John Rowland	Joseph Cate	Janice Casteel	. . .	Chuck Atchley	Wesley Snyder	Tom Grant
Clifton		c	CM	2	(931) 676-3370	Wayne Brandon	Dana Deem	Miranda Burcham	. . .	Jerry Warren	Byron Skelton	. . .
Clinton		c	MC	9	(865) 457-0424	Winfred Shoopman	James Jones	Regina Ridenour	Vickie Fagan	. . .	Richard Scarbrough	Robert Murphy
Collegedale	*	c	CM	7	(423) 396-3135	John Turner	Ted Rogers	Jamie Bialeschki	Michelle Brown	. . .	Dennis Cramer	Rodney Keeton
Collierville		t	MC	31	(901) 457-2200	Linda Kerley	James Lewellen	Deborah Carmack	Mary Bevill	Jerry Crawford	Lawrence Goodwin	Wilbur Betty
Collinwood		c	CM	1	(931) 724-9107	Jasper Brewer	Ryan Tyhuis	. . .	. . .	Sherman Martin	Daniel Farris	Ricky Bratton
Columbia	*	c	CM	33	(931) 560-1510	William Gentner	Paul Boyer	. . .	Patti Baltzer	Donald Martin	Barry Crotzer	Ken Donaldson
Cookeville		c	CM	23	(931) 526-9591	Charles Womack	Jim Shipley	Cathy McClain	Mike Davidson	John Kendrick	Bob Terry	Greg Brown
Covington		c	MC	8	(901) 476-9613	. . .	. . .	. . .	. . .	. . .	. . .	. . .
Crossville		c	CM	8	(931) 484-5113	J. Graham	Jack Miller	Sam Oglesby	Amanda Houston	Michael Turner	David Beaty	Richard Campbell
Dandridge		t	CM	2	(865) 397-7420	George Gantte	James Hutchins	. . .	. . .	Chuck McSpadden	Carson Williams	Gregg Gann
Dayton		c	CM	6	(423) 775-1817	. . .	Victor Welch	. . .	. . .	Jack Arnold	Kenneth Walker	. . .
Dickson		t	MC	12	(615) 441-9508	Don Weiss	Tom Waychoff	Dianne Eubank	. . .	Eugene Tidwell	Ricky Chandler	Lee Mathis
Dover		t	MC	1	(931) 232-5907	. . .	James Scurlock	. . .	. . .	. . .	. . .	. . .
Dunlap		c	MC	4	(423) 949-2115	George Wagner	. . .	Mary Phipps	. . .	. . .	Clinton Huth	Clayton Smith
Dyersburg		c	MC	17	(731) 286-7607	. . .	. . .	. . .	. . .	. . .	. . .	. . .
East Ridge		t	CO	20	(423) 867-7711	Fred Pruett	David Mays	. . .	. . .	. . .	Steve Mize	. . .
Elizabethton		c	CM	13	(423) 547-6200	Pat Bowers	. . .	Sidney Cox	. . .	Michael Shouse	. . .	Ted Leger
Erwin		t	MC	5	(423) 743-6231	William Lewis	Randy Trivette	Jan Day	. . .	James Bailey	James Hicks	Carroll Mumpower
Etowah	*	c	CM	3	(423) 263-2202	Joel Blair	Andrew Hyatt	. . .	Melissa Henderson	Daniel Ammons	June Parham	. . .
Fairview		c	CM	5	(615) 799-2484	. . .	Shirley Forehand	. . .	Kathleen Daugherty	. . .	Terry Harris	. . .
Farragut	*	t	CM	17	(865) 966-7057	Eddy Ford	Daniel Olson	. . .	. . .	. . .	. . .	William McKelvey
Fayetteville		c	MC	6	(931) 433-6154	John Underwood	Kevin Helms	. . .	. . .	Robert Strope	Doug Carver	Joe Abernathy
Forest Hills		c	CM	4	(615) 383-8447	Charles Evers	Alan Deck	. . .	. . .	. . .	. . .	. . .
Franklin		t	MC	41	(615) 791-3216	Jerry Sherber	James Johnson	. . .	Judy Kennedy	Donald Claiborne	Jackie Moore	. . .
Gallatin		c	MC	23	(615) 452-5400	Don Wright	Suzan Nickerson	Connie Kittrell	Matthew Stewart	Joe Womack	Walter Tangel	Thomas Murray
Gatlinburg	*	c	CM	3	(865) 436-1400	Mike Werner	Cindy Ogle	. . .	David Beeler	Gregory Patterson	Randall Brackins	Ronald Greene
Germantown		c	MC	37	(901) 757-7200	. . .	Patrick Lawton	Judy Simerson	John Dluhos	Dennis Wolf	Richard Hall	Sam Beach
Goodlettsville	*	c	CM	13	(615) 851-2200	Jerry Garrett	James Thomas	Ann Crawford	Julie High	Phillip Gibson	Terry Hutcherson	Bill Brasier
Greenbrier		t	MC	4	(615) 643-4531	Billy Wilson	. . .	. . .	. . .	. . .	. . .	William Maitland
Greeneville		t	MC	15	(423) 639-7105	. . .	. . .	. . .	. . .	. . .	. . .	. . .
Halls		t	MC	2	(731) 836-9653	. . .	. . .	. . .	. . .	. . .	. . .	Alan Cherry
Harriman	*	c	MC	6	(865) 882-9414	Jerry Davis	Bob Tidwell	Tracey Bolden	. . .	Wayne Best	Randy Heidel	Darrell Langley
Hartsville–Trousdale County		c	MC	2	(615) 374-2461	Jerry Clift	. . .	Harold Gregory	. . .	. . .	Ray Russell	. . .
Henderson	*	c	MC	5	(731) 983-5000	Charles Patterson	Jim Garland	Darian Denton	. . .	Jimmy Carter	Tommy Davis	Jerry King
Hendersonville		c	MC	40	(615) 822-1000	James Fuqua	. . .	Connie Bilbrey	Marylou Piper	Jamie Steele	David Key	James Harrison
Hohenwald		c	MC	3	(931) 796-2231	. . .	. . .	. . .	. . .	. . .	. . .	. . .
Humboldt		c	MC	9	(731) 784-2511	Allen Barker	. . .	Stacey Williamson	Howard Hadley	Chester Owens	Simmons Raymond	David Sikes
Huntingdon		t	MC	4	(731) 986-2900	Dale Kelley	Martha Taylor	. . .	. . .	Robert Brewer	Joe Parker	Jerry Nolen
Jackson		c	MC	59	(731) 425-8252	Charles Farmer	. . .	. . .	Alan Laffoon	Michael Morgan	Richard Staples	Johnny Williams
Jasper		t	MC	3	(423) 942-3180	. . .	. . .	. . .	. . .	. . .	. . .	. . .
Jefferson City		c	CM	7	(865) 475-9071	Darrell Helton	John Johnson	. . .	. . .	Robert Turner	William Clark	Michael Jones
Jellico		c	MC	2	(423) 784-6351	John Clifton	. . .	. . .	Linda Meadors	John Perkins	Ned Smiddy	Gene Beck
Johnson City		c	CM	55	(423) 434-6001	Steven Darden	M. Denis Peterson	. . .	Janet Jennings	Paul Greene	John Lowry	Phil Pindzola
Jonesborough		t	CM	4	(423) 753-1030	Tobie Bledsoe	Robert Browning	. . .	Abbey Miller	Bobby Freeman	Steve Wheat	Jeff Thomas
Kingsport	*	c	CM	44	(423) 229-9401	Dennis Phillips	John Campbell	Elizabeth Gilbert	James Demming	J. Craig Dye	Gale Osborne	Ryan McReynolds
Kingston		c	CM	5	(865) 376-6584	W. Troy Beets	James Pinkerton	Eleanor Neal	Carolyn Brewer	Saul Gordon	James Washam	Tim Clark
Knoxville		c	MC	173	(865) 215-2106	. . .	. . .	. . .	Randy Vineyard	H. Hamlin	Phillip Keith	Bob Whetsel
La Follette		c	CM	7	(423) 562-4961	Clifford Jennings	David Young	Debbie Pierce	Terry Sweat	. . .	Jack Widner	Connie Robinson
La Vergne		c	CM	18	(615) 793-6295	. . .	Mark Moshea	. . .	. . .	. . .	Steve Lindsay	Robert Burns
Lafayette	*	c	MC	3	(615) 666-2194	Bill Wells	Annette Morgan	Deneshia Hesson	. . .	Keith Scruggs	Jerry Dallas	. . .
Lake City		t	CO	2	(865) 426-2838	Graydon Lovely	. . .	. . .	Jean Hayton	Ricky Ferguson	James Shetterly	James Wills
Lakeland	*	c	CM	6	(901) 867-2717	Scott Carmichael	Robert Wherry	Sontidra Franklin	. . .	. . .	. . .	. . .
Lakesite		c	MC	1	(423) 842-2533	. . .	David Edwards	. . .	. . .	. . .	. . .	. . .
Lakewood		c	CM	2	(615) 847-2187	Charles Gann	. . .	Alysia Prince	. . .	. . .	Jackie Camp	. . .
Lawrenceburg		c	CO	10	(931) 762-4459	Allen Chapman	Ken Hinson	. . .	. . .	Barry Kelley	Terry Shay	. . .

Directory 1/9 continued — **OFFICIALS IN U.S. MUNICIPALITIES 2,500 AND OVER IN POPULATION**

Jurisdiction	Type	Form of govern-ment	2000 Popu-lation (000)	Main telephone number	Chief elected official	Appointed administrator	Clerk of the governing board	Chief financial officer	Fire chief	Police chief	Public works director
TENNESSEE continued											
Lebanon	c	MC	20	(615) 443-2839	Don Fox	. . .	. . .	Hal Bittinger	Wayne Driver	Scott Bowen	Jeff Baines
Lenoir City	c	MC	6	(865) 986-2715	Charles Eblen	Walter Hurst	. . .	. . .	Richard Martin	Jack Fine	John Johnson
Lewisburg	c	CM	10	(931) 359-1544	Robert Phillips	Gordon Fuller	. . .	. . .	John Redd	Mike Hunter	Bill Wheat
Lexington	c	MC	7	(731) 968-6657	David Jowers	Sue Wood	. . .	. . .	Danny Barker	Roger Loftin	. . .
Livingston	t	MC	3	(931) 823-1269	Frank Martin	. . .	Phyllis Looper	. . .	Rocky Dial	Roger Phillips	Tim Coffee
Loudon *	c	CM	4	(865) 458-2033	Bernie Swiney	Lynn Mills	Stephanie Putkonen	. . .	Michael Brubaker	James Webb	Billy Fagg
Madisonville	t	MC	3	(423) 442-9416	Alfred McClendon	Ted Cagle	Connie White	V. Watson-Sisco	John Talent	Gregg Breeden	Donnie Chambers
Manchester	c	CM	8	(931) 728-4652	Johnnie Brown	. . .	. . .	Nina Moffitt	. . .	. . .	Ed Anderson
Martin	c	MC	10	(731) 587-3126	Randy Brundige	Richard Tidwell	. . .	. . .	. . .	. . .	Charles Vowell
Maryville *	c	CM	23	(865) 273-3425	Joe Swann	Gregory McClain	. . .	Debbie Caughron	Marvin Mitchell	Tony Crisp	Angie Luckie
Maynardville	c	CM	1	(865) 992-3821	Herbert Richardson	Porter Massengill	. . .	Hazel Gillenwater	Darrell Whits	Gerald Simmons	. . .
Mc Kenzie *	c	MC	5	(731) 352-2292	Walter Winchester	. . .	Charlie Beal	. . .	Brian Tucker	Harry Cooper	Tim Waldrup
Mcminnville	c	MC	12	(931) 473-1200	Royce Davenort	David Rutherford	Shirley Durham	. . .	Kevin Lawrence	. . .	William Brock
Memphis	c	MC	650	(901) 576-6569	Willie Herenton	Rick Masson	. . .	Charles Williamson	. . .	. . .	. . .
Milan	t	MC	7	(731) 686-3301	. . .	. . .	. . .	. . .	. . .	. . .	. . .
Millersville *	c	MC	5	(615) 859-0880	Dan Toole	Robert Mobley	. . .	Holly Murphy	Kirt Brinkley	Ronnie Williams	Frank Wilkerson
Millington	c	MC	10	(901) 872-4051	Terry Jones	. . .	Carolyn Madill	Richard Almond	Charles Carter	Richard Jewell	Jack Huffman
Monterey	t	MC	2	(931) 839-3770	John Bowden	. . .	Linda Sproles	. . .	. . .	Bruce Breedlove	Claude Reams
Morristown	c	CM	24	(423) 581-0100	Gary Johnson	James Crumley	Nellie Spradling	Dynise Robertson	William Honeycutt	Roger Overholt	. . .
Mount Carmel	t	MC	4	(423) 357-8125	. . .	. . .	Deborah Perry	. . .	. . .	Jeffery Jackson	Carl Cradic
Mount Juliet	c	CM	12	(615) 754-2552	Kevin Mack	Randy Robertson	. . .	Shelia Luckett	. . .	Charles McCrary	Hatton Wright
Mount Pleasant	c	CM	4	(931) 379-7717	Willie Baker	. . .	. . .	Debora McMullin	Tim Smith	James Wilson	James Holden
Mountain City	c	MC	2	(423) 727-0696	. . .	David Kitchell	. . .	. . .	. . .	. . .	. . .
Murfreesboro *	c	CM	68	(615) 893-5210	John Bragg	Roger Haley	. . .	. . .	David Baxter	Glenn Chrisman	. . .
Nashville-Davidson	c	MC	510	(615) 862-6640	William Purcell	Billy Phillips	Marilyn Swing	David Manning	Stephen Halford	Emmett Turner	. . .
Newbern	c	MC	2	(731) 627-3221	Thomas Parnell	Steve Anderson	. . .	. . .	Bill Berry	Harold Dunivant	K. Dennison
Newport	t	CM	7	(423) 623-7323	Connie Ball	H. Moffitt	Amanda White	. . .	Wayne Butler	Maurice Schults	Ben Hicks
Norris *	c	CM	1	(865) 494-7645	George Dyer	. . .	. . .	. . .	. . .	Danny Humphrey	Shirley Walker
Oak Hill	c	CM	4	(615) 371-8291	R. Throckmorton	William Kraus	. . .	. . .	. . .	. . .	. . .
Oak Ridge	c	CM	27	(865) 425-3550	David Bradshaw	James O'Connor	Jacquelyn Bernard	Janice McGinnis	William Bailey	David Beams	. . .
Oliver Springs *	t	CM	3	(865) 435-7722	Chris Hepler	David Bolling	Karen Campbell	Ramona Walker	Terry Phillips	Kenneth Morgan	Troy Burney
Oneida	t	MC	3	(423) 569-4295	. . .	. . .	. . .	. . .	. . .	. . .	. . .
Paris	c	CM	9	(731) 641-1402	David Travis	Jack Tarkington	. . .	David Smith	Don Cox	Thomas Cooper	Billy King
Pigeon Forge *	c	CM	5	(865) 453-9061	Keith Whaley	Earlene Teaster	Mable Ellis	Dennis Clabo	Tony Watson	Jack Baldwin	Jerol Miller
Pittman Center	t	MC	. .	(865) 436-5499	. . .	S. Spicer-Dudley	. . .	. . .	. . .	. . .	. . .
Portland	t	MC	8	(615) 325-6776	Jim Calloway	. . .	. . .	. . .	. . .	. . .	Kenneth Wilber
Pulaski	c	MC	7	(931) 561-7228	Daniel Speer	Terry Harrison	Donna Goens	. . .	Jimmy Thompson	Stanley Newton	Floyd Poppenhouse
Red Bank	c	CM	12	(423) 877-1103	Pat Brown	Christopher Dorsey	. . .	Carolyn Lewis	Mark Mathews	Larry Sneed	Wayne Hamill
Ripley	c	MC	7	(731) 635-4000	Richard Douglas	Donna Buckner	. . .	. . .	Jim Jarrett	Dennis King	Leamon Pennington
Rockwood	c	CO	5	(865) 354-0163	Michael Miller	James Hines	. . .	. . .	Robert Wertz	James Cisson	Tom Pierce
Rogersville	t	MC	4	(423) 272-7497	Jim Sells	William Lyons	. . .	. . .	Hal Price	Larry Lawson	. . .
Samburg	t	CM	. .	(731) 538-3235	Larry Davis	. . .	Carrie Hogg	. . .	Guy Hogg	. . .	. . .
Savannah	c	CM	6	(731) 925-3300	Nancy Davis	Garry Welch	. . .	. . .	Willie Benson	Donald Cannon	Warren Higgins
Selmer	t	MC	4	(731) 645-3241	Jimmy Whittington	. . .	Ann Henderson	. . .	. . .	R. Leonard	Floyd Hawkins
Sevierville	c	CM	11	(865) 453-5504	Bryan Atchley	Douglas Bishop	Kimberly Graves	Lynn McClurg	Michael Rawlings	Don Myers	Bryon Fortner
Shelbyville	c	CM	16	(931) 684-2691	Geneva Smith	Edward Craig	Alicia Holliman	Gary Cantrell	John Habel	Austin Swing	Mark Clanton
Signal Mountain	t	CM	7	(423) 886-2177	James Althaus	Diana Campbell	. . .	. . .	. . .	Larry Eddings	Mitchell Lawson
Smithville	t	MC	3	(615) 597-4745	Cecil Burger	. . .	. . .	Robert Vandergriff	Charlie Parker	Richard Jennings	. . .
Smyrna	t	MC	25	(615) 459-2553	Paul Johns	Mark O'Neal	J. Woods	Jeanne Nolan	William Culbertson	Kevin Arnold	Chuck Boyett
Soddy-Daisy	c	CM	11	(423) 332-5323	Tommy Shipley	Janice Cagle	. . .	Sara Burris	. . .	Allen Branum	Bill Renfro
South Fulton	c	CM	2	(731) 479-2151	David James	Kathy Dillon	Debra Beadles	. . .	Tommy Smith	Andy Crocker	Hubert Maynard
South Pittsburg	c	CM	3	(423) 837-5000	. . .	. . .	Carolyn Case	. . .	. . .	Ronald Lancaster	Ronald Myers
Sparta	c	MC	4	(931) 836-3248	. . .	Marty Carmichael	. . .	. . .	. . .	. . .	. . .
Spring City	t	CM	2	(423) 365-6441	. . .	Woody Evans	. . .	. . .	. . .	. . .	. . .
Spring Hill	c	MC	7	(931) 486-2252	Ray Williams	. . .	April Goad	. . .	Clyde Farmer	Reggie Pope	John McCord
Springfield	c	CM	14	(615) 382-2200	Dave Fisher	Paul Nutting	Connie Watson	Bobby Lehman	David Greer	Mike Wilhoit	Allan Ellis
St. Joseph	c	CM	. .	(931) 845-4141	. . .	Robert Cheekwood	. . .	. . .	. . .	. . .	. . .
Sweetwater	c	MC	5	(423) 337-6979	. . .	. . .	. . .	. . .	. . .	. . .	. . .
Tennessee Ridge	t	CM	1	(931) 721-3385	Kenneth Dunavant	Larry Laxton	Leslie Rucker	Woodrow Adams	Spencer Bryant	. . .	Jerry Bryant
Trenton	c	MC	4	(731) 855-2013	Tommy Litton	. . .	. . .	Sammy Dickey	Barry Green	William Sanders	Terry Bailey
Tullahoma	c	CM	17	(931) 455-2648	Troy Bisby	Louis Baltz	. . .	Susan Wilson	William Watkins	JC Ferrell	Wayne Limbaugh
Tusculum *	c	CM	1	(423) 638-6211	John Foster	. . .	Eva Sams	. . .	. . .	Danny Greene	Warren Cutshall
Union City	c	CM	10	(731) 885-1341	Terry Hailey	Don Thornton	. . .	. . .	Kelly Edmison	Joe Garner	Dean Laird
Watauga	c	CM	. .	(423) 928-3490	Kenneth Ray	Hattie Skeans	Shirley Fair	. . .	. . .	. . .	. . .
Waverly	t	MC	4	(931) 296-2101	David Vaughn	W Frazier	Kathy Camuzie	Sarah Tinnell	. . .	C. Frazier	Johhny Whitfield
Waynesboro *	c	CM	2	(931) 722-5458	William White	Victor Lay	. . .	. . .	Douglas Gobbell	Thomas Seitz	Howard Riley
White House	c	MC	7	(615) 672-4350	Stan McAfee	Angela Carrier	Anne Love	C. Soporowski	Joesph Palmer	Stan Hilgadiack	Edward Hickman
Whitwell	c	CM	1	(423) 658-5151	Glenn Henry	Jim Trayer	Angela Cookston	Tina Seagroves	Debbie Suggs	Ryan Meeks	. . .
Winchester	t	MC	7	(931) 967-4771	. . .	Beth Rhoton	. . .	. . .	. . .	. . .	. . .
TEXAS											
Abernathy	c	CM	2	(806) 298-2546	Shane Cunningham	Frank Russell	Heilda Cannon	. . .	Kelley Vandygriff	Chris Lopez	Michael Grimsley
Abilene	c	CM	115	(325) 676-6267	Norm Archibald	Larry Gilley	Jo Moore	David Wright	Brad Fitzer	Melvin Martin	Paul Knippel
Addison *	t	CM	14	(972) 450-2817	Joseph Chow	Ronald Whitehead	. . .	Randolph Moravec	Noel Padden	Ron Davis	Nancy Cline
Alamo	c	MC	14	(956) 787-0006	. . .	Luciano Ozuna	. . .	Enrique Guzman	Rolando Espinosa	Arturo Espinosa	Jose Villescas
Alamo Heights	c	MC	7	(210) 822-3331	Louis Cooper	Rebecca Waldman	. . .	Cynthia Barr	Darren Smith	Giles Fortson	Jim Gray
Alice *	c	CM	19	(361) 668-7210	Grace Saenz-Lopez	Albert Uresti	Rene Marshall	Hector Hinojosa	Dean Van Nest	Daniel Bueno	. . .
Allen	c	CM	43	(214) 509-4100	Steven Terrell	Peter Vargas	Shelley George	Kevin Hammeke	William Hawley	William Rushing	Stephen Massey
Alpine	c	CM	5	(432) 837-3301	Mickey Clouse	Jesse Garcia	Margaret Taylor	Ricky Chavez	. . .	. . .	Hector Ramirez
Alton *	c	CM	4	(956) 581-2733	Salvador Vela	Jorge Arcaute	. . .	. . .	Elias Saldivar	Jose Vela	Rudy Garza
Alvarado *	c	MC	3	(817) 790-3351	Tom Durington	Mary Daly	. . .	Kelle Whitfill	Richard Van Winkle	John Allen	Michael Dwiggins
Alvin *	c	CM	21	(281) 388-4295	Gary Appelt	Paul Horn	Thomas Peebles	Suzy Kou	Rex Klesel	Michael Merkel	David Kocurek
Amarillo	c	CM	173	(806) 378-3000	Trent Sisemore	Alan Taylor	Donna Deright	Dean Frigo	Steve Ross	Jerry Neal	Michael Rice
Andrews	c	CM	9	(915) 523-4820	Greg Sweeney	Len Wilson	. . .	Kitty Bristow	Joe Harper	Dolphus Jones	Larry Fleming
Angleton	c	CM	18	(979) 849-4364	Matt Sebesta	. . .	David Emswiler	Susie Hernandez	. . .	David Ashburn	Robert Heinemeyer
Anna	c	. . .	1	(972) 924-3325	. . .	Philip Sanders	. . .	. . .	. . .	. . .	. . .
Anson	c	CM	2	(915) 823-2411	E. Spraberry	. . .	Lou Wilson	. . .	Bill Cromeens	Bobby Evans	Freddy Elkins
Anthony	t	MC	3	(915) 886-3944	. . .	. . .	Myriam Uribe	. . .	. . .	Edward Miranda	Jesus Almaraz
Aransas Pass	c	CM	8	(361) 758-5301	Jesus Galvan	Thomas Ginter	Karen Mayer	Marie Roddell	Gilbert Ritz	Darryl Jones	Darren Gurley
Argyle	c	MC	2	(940) 464-7273	Richard Tucker	Lyle Dresher	. . .	. . .	. . .	. . .	. . .
Arlington	c	CM	332	(817) 459-6869	Robert Cluck	James Holgersson	Barbara Heptig	. . .	Robin Paulsgrove	Theron Bowman	Robert Lowry

Directory 1/9 continued — OFFICIALS IN U.S. MUNICIPALITIES 2,500 AND OVER IN POPULATION

Jurisdiction	Type	Form of govern-ment	2000 Popu-lation (000)	Main telephone number	Chief elected official	Appointed administrator	Clerk of the governing board	Chief financial officer	Fire chief	Police chief	Public works director
TEXAS continued											
Athens	c	CM	11	(903) 675-5131	Jerry King	Pam Burton	Pam Watson	David Hopkins	Dan Barnes	Dave Harris	Don Herriage
Atlanta	c	CM	5	(903) 796-2192	Keith Crow	Mike Ahrens	Janice Elliott	Jacqueline Jones	David Burden	Mike Dupree	Tom Townsend
Austin	c	CM	656	(512) 974-3215	William Wynn	Toby Futrell	Shirley Brown	John Stephens	...	Stanley Knee	Peter Rieck
Azle *	c	CM	9	(817) 444-2541	Russ Braudis	Craig Lemin	...	...	Thomas Scott	Stephen Myers	...
Balch Springs	c	CM	19	(972) 557-6070	Brenda Haas	Kandi Hubert	Cindy Gross	...	Richard Woodham	Gary Moore	William McDonald
Balcones Heights	c	MC	3	(210) 735-9148	James Craven	...	...	JoAnn Vidal	Benjamin Hoeffner	Kenneth Menn	...
Ballinger	c	CM	4	(325) 365-3511	Joe Shelby	Tommy New	...	...	Lonnie Bishop	JC Gore	Carl Williams
Bastrop	c	CM	5	(512) 303-7305	Tom Scott	Michael Talbot	Teresa Valdez	Lamar Ozley	Henry Perry	David Board	Lee Weatherford
Bay City	c	MC	18	(979) 245-6550	Charles Martinez	...	...	...	...	...	Jon Abshier
Baytown	c	CM	66	(281) 422-8281	Pete Alfaro	Garrison Brumback	Eileen Hall	L. Daws	...	Charles Shaffer	Herbert Thomas
Beaumont	c	CM	113	(409) 880-3716	Guy Goodson	James Hayes	Rose Jones	Max Duplant	Michel Bertrand	Frank Coffin	Thomas Warner
Bedford	c	CM	47	(817) 952-2100	Richard Hurt	Beverly Queen	Rita Frick	Thomas Ross	Stephen Bass	David Flory	James Wood
Bee Cave	c	CM	..	(512) 767-6600	Caroline Murphy	James Fisher	Sherry Mashburn	...	...	Steven Gonzalez	...
Beeville	c	CM	13	(361) 358-4641	...	Ford Patton	Tomas Saenz	Robert Aguilar	...	Joe Salinas	John Standlea
Bellaire	c	CM	15	(713) 662-8222	Mary Ann Goode	Bernard Satterwhite	Tracy Dutton	Louise Richman	Joe Bettega	Randall Mack	...
Bellmead	c	CM	9	(254) 799-2436	...	S Radcliffe	...	...	James Karl	Robert Harold	Michael Willis
Bellville	c	CM	3	(979) 865-3136	James Bishop	J. Johnston	Cheryl Robertson	...	Warren Klump	...	...
Belton *	c	CM	14	(254) 933-5800	Jim Covington	Sam Listi	Connie Torres	Cristy Daniell	Roy Harmon	Michael Sleeth	Les Hallbuaer
Benbrook *	c	CM	20	(817) 249-3000	Jerry Dittrich	Andrew Wayman	Joanna King	David Ragsdale	Tommy Davis	James Mills	Walter Shumac
Big Lake	c	MC	2	(915) 884-2511	...	Evelyn Ammons	...	...	Alan Garner	...	Troy Kuykendall
Big Spring	c	CM	25	(915) 264-2400	...	...	...	...	Brian Jensen	Lonnie Smith	Russell Darden
Bishop	t	CM	3	(361) 584-2567	Geraldine Rypple	Cynthia Contreras	Delma Salinas	...	...	Larry Lawrence	Albert Guajardo
Boerne	c	CM	6	(830) 249-9511	...	Ronald Bowman	Linda Zartler	Sandra Mattick	Doug Meckel	Gary Miller	Michael Mann
Bonham	c	CM	9	(903) 583-7555	Roy Floyd	Corby Alexander	Janell Cain	...	William Palya	Mike Bankston	Ronald Ford
Booker	c	MC	1	(806) 658-4579	Lois Sheets	Donald Kerns	Jaque Stephens	...	Roger Almenroad	...	...
Borger *	c	CM	14	(806) 273-0903	Jeff Brain	Wanda Klause	...	Glynn Carlock	Bob Watson	Jimmy Adams	Henry Veach
Bovina	c	CM	1	(806) 251-1116	Stan Miller	Ernest Terry	...	...	...	Leon Saddler	Andres Garcia
Bowie	c	CM	5	(940) 872-1114	Brandon Earp	James Cantwell	Mitzi Wallace	Renee Lawson	Doug Page	David Scruggs	...
Boyd	c	MC	1	(940) 433-5166	...	...	...	...	...	...	...
Brady *	c	CM	5	(915) 597-2152	James Stewart	Merle Taylor	...	Lisa Remini	Johnnie Elliott	Tommy Payne	Rufus Beam
Brazoria	c	CM	2	(979) 798-2489	Ken Corley	Teresa Borders	...	...	Marcus Rabren	Neal Longbotham	John Jordan
Breckenridge *	c	CM	5	(254) 559-8287	Jim McKay	Gary Ernest	...	...	Roger McMullen	Larry Mahan	Tim Williams
Brenham	c	CM	13	(979) 337-7200	Milton Tate	Terry Roberts	Doris Seilheimer	Carolyn Baker	Robert Weiss	Gary Buchanan	John Baker
Bridge City	c	CM	8	(409) 735-6801	John Dubose	...	Terry Jordan	...	...	Stephen Faircloth	Donald Fields
Bridgeport *	c	MC	4	(940) 683-3400	Donald Majka	Van James	...	Amy Standard	Michael McComis	Randall Singleton	David Turnbow
Brownfield	c	CM	9	(806) 637-4547	Nancy Wade	Eldon Jobe	...	Mary Collins	Marvin Dawson	Roy Rice	Willie Herrera
Brownsville	c	CM	139	(956) 548-6000	Blanca Vela	...	Melissa Morales	Pete Gonzalez	Ramiro Torres	Ben Reyna	Carlos Ayala
Brownwood *	c	CM	18	(915) 646-5775	Bert Massey	Bobby Rountree	...	Walter Middleton	Del Albright	Virgil Cowin	Keith Pulaski
Bryan	c	CM	65	(979) 209-5000	Jay Watson	David Watkins	Mary Stratta	Kathy Davidson	Michael Donoho	Michael Strope	...
Buda	c	CM	2	(512) 312-0084	...	Jeff Coffee	...	Sarah Mangham	Clay Huckaby	...	Everett Conner
Bullard	c	MC	1	(903) 894-7223	C. R. Vaughan	Larry Morgan	Deborah Jessup	...	...	...	...
Bulverde	c	MC	3	(830) 438-3612	...	John Hobson	...	...	...	...	...
Bunker Hill Village	c	MC	3	(713) 467-9762	...	Ruthie Sager	Valerie Cantu	...	Cleve Calagna	Gary Brye	Ron Garrison
Burkburnett	c	CM	10	(940) 569-2263	Bill Vincent	Michael Slye	Patricia Holley	...	...	Curtis Salyer	Gordon Smith
Burleson *	c	CM	20	(817) 447-5400	Ken Shetter	Curtis Hawk	Mary Kayser	Charles Harris	Gary Wisdom	Thomas Cowan	Morris Stringer
Burnet *	c	CM	4	(512) 756-6093	Dennis Kincheloe	Michael Steele	Christy Fath	J. Laudenschlager	Mark Ingram	...	Danny Lester
Caldwell	c	CM	3	(979) 567-3271	Bernard Rychlik	...	...	...	Doug Beavers	Virgil Hurt	...
Cameron	c	MC	5	(254) 697-6646	William Meacham	Fred Stephens	Amy Kopriva	...	...	Leonard Doskocil	...
Canadian	t	CM	2	(806) 323-6473	...	...	...	...	...	...	...
Canton	c	CM	3	(903) 567-2826	...	Cliff Bowden	...	...	...	...	...
Canyon	c	CM	12	(806) 655-5000	Lois Rice	Glen Metcalf	...	Howard Morris	Joe Rice	Bobby Griffin	Dan Reese
Carrizo Springs	c	CM	5	(830) 876-2476	Ralph Salinas	Mario Martinez	P. Garcia Vargs	Nicolas Cardona	Jose Rodriguez	...	Ruben Garcia
Carrollton	c	CM	109	(972) 466-3001	...	Leonard Martin	Pamela Schmidt	...	Bruce Varner	David James	Stephen Jenkins
Carthage	c	CM	6	(903) 693-3868	Carson Joines	Brenda Samford	Joyce Whitehead	Debbie Pierce	...	Duane Baushke	William McMillan
Castle Hills	c	CM	4	(210) 342-2341	Marcy Harper	Michael Rietz	Linda Gill	...	Gerald Riedel	Donald Davis	Rick Harada
Castroville	c	MC	2	(830) 931-4070	Jesse Byars	...	...	Cheryl Peery	...	Lee McVay	Bruce Alexander
Cedar Hill	c	CM	32	(972) 291-5100	Rob Franke	Alan Sims	Frankie Lee	William Browder	Stephen Pollock	Steve Rhodes	Ruth Antebi
Cedar Park *	c	CM	26	(512) 401-5000	Bob Lemon	Brenda Eivens	Leann Barnes	Joyce Herring	Chris Connealy	Henry Fluck	...
Celina *	c	MC	1	(972) 382-2682	Corbett Howard	Jason Gray	Vicki Faulkner	...	Jerry Duffield	Joe Williams	...
Center	c	CM	5	(936) 598-2941	John Windham	Chad Nehring	Terre Noble	Robin Andrews	Vernon Byndom	Walter Shofner	John Holt
Childress	c	CM	6	(940) 937-3684	...	Jerry Cummins	...	Charlene Smith	Steve Jones	Reece Bowen	Gilbert Bailey
Cibolo *	c	MC	3	(210) 658-9900	Charles Ruppert	Todd Parton	Yvonne Griffin	...	...	Mark Riffe	Richard Arenas
Cisco *	c	CM	3	(254) 442-2111	Joe Wheatley	Jim Baker	Virginia Dill	Peggy Ledbetter	...	...	Cecil Boles
Clarksville	c	CM	3	(903) 427-3834	Ann Rushing	Belinda Peek	Rosalind Rosser	Lorene Beers	Allan Thompson	Weldon Warren	...
Clear Lake Shores	c	CM	1	(281) 334-2799	Katherine McIntyre	Karen McDaniel	Christy Stroup	...	Larry Steed	Paul Shelley	...
Cleburne	c	CM	26	(817) 645-0900	Ted Reynolds	Chester Nolen	Joy Doty	Thomas Wilmore	John Ishmael	Terry Powell	Larry Barkman
Cleveland	c	CM	7	(281) 592-2667	...	...	Kelly McDonald	Rebecca Roseberry	Steve Wheeler	Ike Hines	Mike Ulbig
Clifton *	c	MC	3	(254) 675-8337	Raymond Zuehlke	Charles McLean	...	Pamela Harvey	Russell Jenkins	Rex Childress	Jim Burch
Clute	c	CM	10	(979) 265-2541	Jerry Adkins	Kyle McCain	Sarah Oakes	...	...	Mark Wicker	Robert Ray
Clyde	t	MC	3	(325) 893-4234	Steve Livingston	Tim Atkinson	C. Jean Gilmore	...	Billy Dezern	Jerome Chaney	Phillip McDowell
Cockrell Hill	c	MC	4	(214) 330-6333	Luis Carrera	...	...	...	Mike Burns	C. Smith	Danny Thomas
Coleman *	c	CM	5	(325) 625-5114	Nick Poldrack	Larry Weise	...	...	Richard Hensley	Jay Moses	Bob Ray
College Station	c	CM	67	(979) 764-3500	Ronald Silvia	Glenn Brown	Connie Hooks	Charles Cryan	R. B. Alley	Edgar Feldman	Mark Smith
Colleyville	c	CM	19	(817) 503-1000	David Kelly	William Lindley	Cynthia Singleton	Terrell Leake	Mike Johnston	Tommy Ingram	Keith Fisher
Colorado City	c	CM	4	(325) 728-3464	Jim Baum	Paul Catoe	Connie Baker	Connie Ponko	Rufino Martinez	Shawn Myatt	Rick Carver
Columbus	c	MC	3	(979) 732-2366	Paula Frnka	...	Jill Ready	...	Robert Walla	Robert Connor	Michael Poncik
Comanche	c	MC	4	(915) 356-2616	...	...	...	...	...	...	...
Commerce *	c	CM	7	(903) 886-1100	Sheryl Zelhardt	Bill Shipp	Marty Cunningham	...	Tommy Eaton	Kerry Crews	Tracy Lunceford
Conroe	c	MC	36	(936) 539-4431	Tommy Metcalf	Jerry McGuire	Marla Porter	Stephen Williams	...	John Lindon	L. Towery
Converse *	c	CM	11	(210) 658-5356	Al Suarez	Samuel Hughes	...	Gerald Wilson	Richard Wendt	Richard Jamison	Lupe Perez
Coppell	c	CM	35	(972) 462-0022	...	James Witt	Elizabeth Ball	Jennifer Miller	...	...	Kenneth Griffin
Copper Canyon	t	MC	1	(940) 241-2677	Sue Tejnl	...	Virginia Moore	...	...	...	...
Copperas Cove	c	CM	29	(254) 547-4221	J. Darossett	Andrea Gardner	Rose Mansfield	...	...	...	David Brinegar
Corinth *	c	CM	11	(940) 498-3200	Victor Burgess	Clovia English	Kimberly Pence	Kathy DuBose	Jason Collier	Darrell Brown	Don Locke
Corpus Christi	c	CM	277	(361) 880-3315	...	George Noe	Armando Chapa	...	Juan Adame	Pedro Alvarez	...
Corsicana *	c	CM	24	(903) 654-4800	Clifford Brown	...	...	Cathy McMullan	Donald McMullan	G. Cox	Ron Lynch
Cotulla	c	MC	3	(830) 879-2367	...	Higinio Martinez	...	...	...	...	...
Crandall	c	CM	2	(972) 427-3771	Joe Baker	Judy Bell	...	...	...	Larry Davis	Todd Weber
Crane	c	MC	3	(432) 558-3563	...	...	...	...	...	...	...
Crockett	c	CM	7	(936) 544-5156	Wayne Mask	Ronald Duncan	Mitzi Thompson	...	Darrell Deckard	Jimmy Fisher	...
Crowley	c	CM	7	(817) 297-2201	Billy Davis	Truitt Gilbreath	Martha Najera	Cathy Coffman	Robert Loftin	Kirk Nemitz	Jim McDonald
Crystal City	c	CM	7	(830) 374-3477	...	Diana Palacios	...	Emma Flores	Delwin Hale	Luis Contreras	...
Cuero	c	CM	6	(361) 275-3476	W. Edge	Corlis Riedesel	...	Sandra Oehlke	William Tolbert	Glenn Mutchler	...

Directory 1/9 continued OFFICIALS IN U.S. MUNICIPALITIES 2,500 AND OVER IN POPULATION

Jurisdiction		Type	Form of govern-ment	2000 Popu-lation (000)	Main telephone number	Chief elected official	Appointed administrator	Clerk of the governing board	Chief financial officer	Fire chief	Police chief	Public works director
TEXAS continued												
Daingerfield		c	CM	2	(903) 645-3906	Lou Slaughter	Marty Byers	Margie Hargrove	Heide Edmonson	. . .	Joseph Farino	. . .
Dalhart		c	CM	7	(806) 249-5511	. . .	Greg Duggan	. . .	. . .	. . .	. . .	. . .
Dallas		c	CM	1188	(214) 670-3120	Laura Miller	Mary Suhm	Shirley Acy	De McCombs	. . .	. . .	. . .
Dayton		t	CM	5	(936) 258-2642	Steve Stephens	David Douglas	Terry Brown	Chris Contreras	Terry Boyett	Pete Douzat	Toby Stroughter
De Soto		c	CM	37	(972) 230-9601	Michael Hurtt	James Baugh	Mary Shipman	Camelia Browder	Fred Hart	William Brodnax	Thomas Johnson
Decatur	*	c	MC	5	(940) 627-2741	Joe Lambert	Brett Shannon	Diane Cockrell	. . .	Mike Richardson	Rex Hoskins	Earl Smith
Deer Park	*	c	CM	28	(281) 479-2394	Wayne Riddle	Ronald Crabtree	Michelle Combs	H. Nelson	Greg Bridges	William Young	. . .
Del Rio		c	CM	33	(830) 774-8616	Dora Alcala	. . .	Juanita Douglas	Frances Rodriguez	Harold Bean	Manuel Herrera	Alejandro Garcia
Denison		c	CM	22	(903) 465-2720	Wayne Cabaniss	Larry Cruise	Nina Jones	Andy Wilkins	Bill Taylor	Jimmy Lovell	Jerry White
Denton		c	CM	80	(940) 349-8200	Euline Brock	George Campbell	Jennifer Walters	L. Langley	Edward Chadwick	Charles Wiley	. . .
Denver City	*	t	MC	3	(806) 592-5426	David Bruton	Stan David	Beverly Prather	. . .	Carl Whittaker	Jack Miller	Perry Ham
Devine		c	MC	4	(830) 663-2804	Steve Lopez	. . .	Dora Rodriguez	. . .	. . .	Robert Flores	Ed Gentry
Diboll	*	c	MC	5	(936) 829-4757	Bill Brown	Kenneth Williams	Tina Cavazos	Elvia Garza	Charlie Mann	Kent Havard	Doug McCoy
Dickinson		c	MC	17	(281) 337-2489	Julie Masters	Julie Johnston	Rena Hardage	Usha Mathew	Jasper Liggio	Ron Morales	Kellis George
Dilley		c	MC	3	(830) 965-1624	Russell Foster	Felix Arambula	Juanita Gonzalez	Irma Rodriguez	J. C. Molina	. . .	Rudy Olivarez
Dimmitt		t	MC	4	(806) 647-2155	. . .	Don Sheffy	. . .	. . .	. . .	Ray Aleman	Saul Arce
Donna		c	CM	14	(956) 464-3314	Ricardo Morales	Juan Ortiz	Martha Alvarado	Daniel Downs	David Simmons	Ruben De Leon	. . .
Dublin		c	MC	3	(254) 445-3331	Brian Boudreaux	James Seigars	Rhonda Keilers	. . .	James Fritts	Lannie Lee	Jimmy Williams
Dumas	*	c	MC	13	(806) 935-4101	Johnnie Rhoades	Vince DiPiazza	Kim Rehkopf	Dorothy Williams	Paul Jenkins	Dale Alwan	Tommy Raper
Duncanville		c	CM	36	(972) 780-5000	David Green	J. Cagle	. . .	Frank Trando	Terry Webb	Jack Long	Dennis Schwartz
Eagle Lake		c	CM	3	(979) 234-2640	Mike Morales	Ronald Holland	Sylvia Rucka	. . .	Howard Wilkerson	William Lattimore	Thurston Webb
Eagle Pass		c	CM	22	(830) 773-1111	Joaquin Rodriguez	Roberto Gonzalez	. . .	Manuel Contreras	Rogelio Dela Cruz	Jose Castaneda	Hector Chavez
Early		c	CM	2	(915) 643-5451	David Brooks	Ken Thomas	. . .	. . .	Travis Eoff	Audie Pinson	Stephen Walker
Eastland		c	CM	3	(254) 629-8321	Jerry Mathews	David Maddox	Shirley Stuart	Leslie Zander	Phillip Arther	Cecil Funderburgh	Bobby Jacoby
Edcouch		t	CM	3	(956) 262-2140	. . .	. . .	. . .	. . .	. . .	. . .	. . .
Edgecliff Village		t	MC	2	(817) 293-4313	Ed Lucas	. . .	Sherrie Rundle	. . .	Kevin Davis	. . .	Bob Parker
Edinburg	*	c	CM	48	(956) 383-5661	Joe Ochoa	W. Smith-Sturgis	Myra Garza	Ascencion Alonzo	Shawn Snider	Quirino Munoz	Daniel Tijerina
Edna	*	c	CM	5	(361) 782-3122	Joe Hermes	Kenneth Pryor	. . .	Olga Salomon	Wendel Hamilton	Clinton Wooldridge	Brad Ryan
El Campo	*	c	CM	10	(979) 541-5000	Kenneth Martin	John Steelman	. . .	Courtney Sladek	Jimmy George	Jimmy Elliott	Brad Ramsey
El Lago		c	MC	3	(281) 326-1951	Brad Emel	. . .	. . .	. . .	Ray Cook	. . .	. . .
El Paso	*	c	CM	563	(915) 541-4509	John Cook	Joyce Wilson	Richarda Momsen	C. A.-Candelaria	Roberto Rivera	Richard Wiles	. . .
Electra		c	CM	3	(940) 495-2146	Glen Branch	S. Giesbrecht	Kim Cryer	. . .	Greg Lynn	Johnny Morris	Tex Owen Simpson
Elgin		c	MC	5	(512) 285-5721	Eric Carlson	. . .	Shirley Garvell	. . .	Mike Carter	Steven Huckabay	Joe Marten
Elsa		c	CM	5	(956) 262-2127	Ramiro Alvarado	. . .	Frieda Reyes	. . .	Gregorio Ramirez	Gerald Senk	Severo Trevino
Ennis		c	CM	16	(972) 875-1234	Russell Thomas	Stephen Howerton	. . .	Shirley Trull	David Hopkins	Dale Holt	Roy Callahan
Euless	*	c	CM	46	(817) 685-1475	Mary Saleh	Gary McKamie	Susan Crim	Vicki Rodriquez	Lee Koontz	Mike Brown	Ron Young
Everman		c	MC	5	(817) 293-0525	James Stephenson	Donna Anderson	Judy Thompson	Scott Holoway	Donnie Hurd	Randy Sanders	Michael Box
Fair Oaks Ranch	*	c	MC	4	(210) 698-0900	Boots Gaubatz	. . .	Carole Vanzant	Kristin Hansen	. . .	Scott Rubin	Ronald Emmons
Fairfield		c	MC	3	(903) 389-2633	. . .	. . .	. . .	. . .	. . .	. . .	. . .
Fairview	*	t	MC	2	(972) 562-0522	Sim Israeloff	John Godwin	M. Lewis-Sirriani	Teresa Ramirez	Dick Price	Granver Tolliver	Aron Holmgren
Falfurrias		c	CO	5	(361) 325-2420	J. Guerra	Aurora Rodriguez	Leocadia Benavides	. . .	. . .	Baldemar Rivera	Kenneth Martin
Farmers Branch	*	c	CM	27	(972) 247-3131	Bob Phelps	Gary Greer	Cindee Peters	Charles Cox	Kyle King	Sidney Fuller	. . .
Farmersville		c	CM	3	(972) 782-6151	Robbin Lamkin	Alan Hein	. . .	Daphne Hamlin	Kim Morris	Wayne Pickett	. . .
Fate		c	CM	. .	(972) 771-4601	. . .	. . .	. . .	. . .	. . .	. . .	. . .
Ferris	*	c	CM	2	(972) 544-2110	Jim Parks	. . .	Patricia Bradley	Elizabeth Saegert	Eddie Duran	Michael Braly	Charlie James
Flatonia		t	CM	1	(361) 865-3548	Lori Berger	. . .	Melissa Brunner	. . .	. . .	Leonard Cox	Jack Daulas
Floresville		c	MC	5	(830) 393-3105	Raymond Ramirez	Gary Pelech	. . .	Evelyn Grimes	. . .	Daniel Martinez	Vincent Griego
Flower Mound		t	CM	50	(972) 874-6000	Jody Smith	Harlan Jefferson	Paula Lawrence	. . .	Eric Metzger	Kenneth Brooker	Kenneth Parr
Floydada		t	CM	3	(806) 983-2834	Bobby Gilliland	Gary Brown	Karen Lawson	. . .	. . .	Darrell Gooch	Jack Alaniz
Forest Hill	*	c	CM	12	(817) 568-3000	James Gosey	David Miller	Jacquelyn Allen	Debbie Maness	Pat Ekiss	Rex Phelps	. . .
Forney		c	CM	5	(972) 552-2291	. . .	Brian Brooks	. . .	. . .	. . .	. . .	. . .
Fort Stockton	*	c	CM	7	(432) 336-8525	Ruben Falcon	Rafael Castillo	Delma Gonzalez	Penny Smith	Melvin Thomas	Juan Castro	Brad Newton
Fort Worth		c	CM	534	(817) 871-8900	. . .	Charles Boswell	Gloria Pearson	Karen Montgomery	. . .	Ralph Mendoza	Robert Goode
Fredericksburg		t	MC	8	(830) 997-7521	Tim Crenwelge	Gary Neffendorf	Shelley Britton	Brad Kott	. . .	Paul Oestreich	Jerry Bain
Freeport	*	c	CM	12	(979) 233-3526	Larry McDonald	. . .	Delia Munoz	Gary Beverly	John Stanford	Jeff Pynes	Larry Fansher
Freer		c	MC	3	(512) 394-6612	Arnoldo Cantu	Cynthia Lackey	Nelia Alaniz	. . .	James Finney	John Spillers	. . .
Friendswood		c	CM	29	(281) 996-3200	David Smith	Robert McDaniel	Deloris McKenzie	. . .	. . .	Robert Wieners	Kazem Hamidian
Friona	*	c	CM	3	(806) 250-2761	John Taylor	Terri Johnson	Rachel Douglas	Patricia Phipps	Jim Taylor	Fraustino Salinaz	Kenneth Ford
Frisco		c	CM	33	(972) 335-5555	Michael Simpson	George Purefoy	Nan Parker	Nell Lange	Mack Borchardt	Todd Renshaw	Gary Hartwell
Fritch		c	CM	2	(806) 857-3143	Kevin Keener	Dottie Williams	Emily West	. . .	Calvin Nickell	Terry Cox	Alvin Clark
Gainesville		c	CM	15	(940) 668-4500	Glenn Loch	. . .	Rita Gray	Daniel Parker	Steven Boone	Carl Dunlap	James Gray
Galena Park		c	MC	10	(713) 672-2556	Robert Barrett	Margaret Stevens	Janie Guerrero	Rae Moreau	Paul Grider	Robert Pruett	John Cooper
Galveston		c	CM	57	(409) 797-3500	Lyda Thomas	Steven Leblanc	Barbara Lawrence	. . .	. . .	Robert Pierce	Brandon Wade
Garland		c	CM	215	(972) 205-2000	. . .	William Dollar	Linda Larson	George Kauffman	Daniel Grammer	Larry Wilson	Jack May
Gatesville	*	c	CM	15	(254) 865-8951	David Byrom	Roger Mumby	Darleen Hodges	Brenda Kiphen	Billy Vaden	Nathan Gohlke	Doyle Barton
George West		c	CM	2	(361) 449-1556	August Caron	Terri Garza	Jacquelyn Harborth	. . .	Lloyd Clifton	Ray Garcia	Benjamin Tanguma
Georgetown		c	CM	28	(512) 930-3652	Gary Nelon	Paul Brandenburg	Sandra Lee	Micki Rundell	Anthony Lincoln	David Morgan	. . .
Giddings		c	CM	5	(979) 540-2710	James Arndt	Paul Kipp	Dianne Schneider	. . .	James Garner	. . .	Serapio Garza
Gilmer		c	CM	4	(903) 843-2552	R Cross	Ron Stephens	Heather Steelman	Mary Bates	J Steelman	James Grunden	Brian Rodgers
Gladewater		c	CM	6	(903) 845-2196	John Tallent	James Stokes	. . .	Melba Haralson	Wayne Smith	Jimmy Davis	. . .
Glenn Heights		c	CM	7	(972) 223-1690	Alvin DuBois	Joseph Portugal	. . .	Patsy Ragland	Chris Shook	. . .	Drew Roberts
Goldthwaite		c	CM	1	(915) 648-3186	Danny Hammond	Bobby Rountree	Tammy Clifton	. . .	. . .	. . .	. . .
Goliad		c	MC	1	(361) 645-3454	. . .	Kenneth Bays	. . .	. . .	. . .	. . .	. . .
Gonzales		c	CM	7	(830) 672-2815	Bobby O'Neal	Buddy Drake	. . .	Joe Cavazos	. . .	Tim Crow	Raymie Zella
Graham		c	CM	8	(940) 549-3324	Douglas Strond	Larry Fields	. . .	Hugh Nanny	Terry Watkins	Jim Nance	Chester Smith
Granbury		c	CM	5	(817) 573-1114	David Southern	. . .	Dee Arcos	Bob Evart	H. Robertson	Randy Jaquess	Richard English
Grand Prairie		c	CM	127	(972) 237-8012	Charles England	Thomas Hart	Catherine DiMaggio	Diana Ortiz	Clifton Nelson	Glen Hill	Ron McCuller
Grand Saline		c	MC	3	(903) 962-3122	. . .	. . .	. . .	. . .	Robert Coffman	Daniel Zajac	Gene Putman
Granite Shoals		c	MC	2	(830) 598-2424	Pat Crochet	. . .	Ronda Reichle	. . .	George Cambanis	J. P. Wilson	. . .
Grapevine		c	CM	42	(817) 410-3000	William Tate	Bruno Rumbelow	Linda Huff	Fred Werner	David Anderson	Richard Wilkins	Jerry Hodge
Greenville	*	c	CM	23	(903) 457-3100	Tom Oliver	Steven Alexander	Debra Newell	. . .	. . .	Harold Roseberry	Massoud Ebrahim
Gregory		c	MC	2	(361) 643-6562	. . .	Norma Garcia	. . .	. . .	. . .	Robert Garza	Cesario Vela
Groesbeck	*	c	MC	4	(254) 729-3293	Jackie Levingston	Martha Stanton	Brenda Jackson	. . .	Charles Bratcher	Jerri Almy	Keith Tilley
Groves		c	CM	15	(409) 962-4471	Brad Bailey	D. Sosa	Kimbra Caldwell	Jeri Rainey	Dale Jackson	Stephen Savoy	. . .
Groveton		c	MC	1	(936) 642-1122	. . .	. . .	Carolyn Davis	. . .	. . .	Jon Archer	. . .
Hallettsville	*	c	MC	2	(361) 798-3681	Warren Grindeland	Tom Donnelly	Elizabeth Woytek	. . .	Anthony Ludwig	Randal Schlauch	Ervin Kolacny
Haltom City	*	c	CM	39	(817) 222-7700	William Lanford	Thomas Muir	Brenda Staab	Calvert Welch	Robert Rhodes	Kenneth Burton	David Fain
Hamilton		c	MC	2	(254) 386-8116	. . .	Bill Funderburk	Jane Dodson	. . .	. . .	. . .	Ronnie Harris
Hamlin		c	MC	2	(915) 576-2711	Jack Shields	. . .	. . .	. . .	. . .	Mike Middleton	. . .
Harker Heights	*	c	CM	17	(254) 953-5600	Mary Gauer	Steve Carpenter	. . .	Alberta Barrett	Leon Charpentier	Michael Gentry	Mark Hyde
Harlingen	*	c	CM	57	(956) 216-5020	Chris Boswell	Craig Lonon	Sylvia Trevino	Roel Gutierrez	Mike Rinaldi	Daniel Castillo	Dan Serna
Haskell		c	CM	3	(940) 864-2355	Ken Land	. . .	Loretta Gray	. . .	Bill Steele	Tom Bassett	Dave Miller

Directory 1/9 continued

OFFICIALS IN U.S. MUNICIPALITIES 2,500 AND OVER IN POPULATION

Jurisdiction	Type	Form of government	2000 Population (000)	Main telephone number	Chief elected official	Appointed administrator	Clerk of the governing board	Chief financial officer	Fire chief	Police chief	Public works director
TEXAS continued											
Hearne	c	CM	4	(979) 279-3461	...	Ruben Gomez	Anna Leslie Ely	Marcus Hilton	Robert Parsley	Cowboy Poole	...
Heath	c	CM	4	(972) 771-6228	...	Edward Thatcher	...	...	...	...	...
Hedwig Village	* c	MC	2	(713) 465-6009	Sue Speck	Beth Staton	...	...	...	David Barber	Lane Standley
Helotes	c	CM	4	(210) 695-8877	Jonathan Allan	Marie Gelles	Theresa Helbert	...	Walton Daugherty	Mort Ault	...
Hempstead	c	MC	4	(979) 826-2486	...	...	...	...	...	...	...
Henderson	* c	CM	11	(903) 657-6551	John Fullen	Randall Freeman	Kelly Poovey	Trina Freeman	Dwayne Pirtle	John Waldie	Davis Brown
Henrietta	c	CM	3	(940) 538-4316	...	...	Carol Loucks	...	...	...	James Scarber
Hereford	c	CM	14	(806) 363-7100	...	Rick Hanna	...	Steve Bartels	...	David Wagner	Paul Kilpatrick
Hewitt	c	CM	11	(254) 666-6171	Charles Turner	Dennis Woodard	Becky Frels	Lee Garcia	Glenn Arthur	James Barton	Paul Holroyd
Hico	* c	MC	1	(254) 796-4620	...	Lambert Little	...	...	...	...	...
Hidalgo	c	CM	7	(956) 843-2286	...	Joe Vera	...	Xavier Moron	Juan Reyes	Vernon Rosser	Ruben Puente
Highland Park	t	CM	8	(214) 521-4161	William White	George Patterson	...	...	...	...	James Fisher
Highland Village	c	CM	12	(972) 317-2558	Dianne Costa	Michael Leavitt	Alicia Richardson	Kenneth Heerman	Lonnie Tatum	Edward O'Bara	Matthew Kite
Hill Country Village	* c	MC	1	(210) 494-3671	Kirk Francis	...	...	...	...	Francisco Morales	...
Hillsboro	* c	CM	8	(254) 582-3271	John Erwin	Jack Harper	Betty Harrell	...	Burney Baskett	Carl Cain	...
Hitchcock	c	MC	6	(409) 986-5591	Lee Sander	...	Rose Marie Theiler	...	Scott Fleming	Glen Manis	John Dieringer
Hollywood Park	c	MC	2	(210) 494-2023	Ellen Alkire	...	Barbara Haddock	...	Javier Garcia	Frank Ballard	Jimmy Arroyo
Hondo	c	CM	7	(830) 426-3378	Norman Fisher	Robert Herrera	...	...	...	Don Berger	...
Houston	* c	MC	1953	(713) 837-0311	Bill White	Anthony Hall	Anna Russell	Judy Johnson	Phil Boriskie	Harold Hurtt	Michael Marcotte
Hudson Oaks	c	MC	1	(817) 596-4899	Pat Deen	Robert Hanna	...	...	...	Kenneth West	...
Humble	c	MC	14	(281) 446-3061	Donald McMannes	William Boeske	Stella Daniel	Dixie Kellum	Gary Outlaw	Gary Warman	Barry Brock
Hunters Creek Village	c	MC	4	(713) 465-2150	...	...	...	...	...	...	...
Huntsville	* c	CM	35	(936) 291-5401	J. Turner	...	Dana Welter	Winston Duke	Tom Grisham	...	Glenn Isbell
Hurst	c	CM	36	(817) 281-6160	...	W. Weegar	...	Anita Thetford	...	...	...
Hutchins	* c	MC	2	(972) 225-6121	Mary Washington	Donna Holder	Cheryl Wesley	Joe Wallace	Stacey Hickson	Rick Hutcherson	Curley White
Hutto	* c	CM	1	(512) 759-4030	Kenneth Love	Edward Broussard	Debbie Chelf	Laurie Brewer	...	...	Scot Stromsness
Ingleside	c	CM	9	(361) 776-2517	Gene Stewart	...	Kimberly Drysdale	Terry LeBlanc	Robert Richardson	Stan Bynum	Donald Paty
Iowa Park	c	CM	6	(940) 592-2131	Randy Catlin	Michael Price	Janice Newman	Tammy Persick	Danny Skinner	Steve Klempa	Kenneth Lytle
Irving	c	CM	191	(972) 721-2600	Joe Putnam	...	Catherine Duncan	Jack Hickey	William Cannaday	Jack Angel	
Jacinto City	c	CM	10	(713) 674-8424	Mike Jackson	Jack Maner	Joyce Raines	...	Lon Squyres	Joe Ayala	Kyle Reed
Jacksboro	* c	CM	4	(940) 567-6321	Jerry Craft	Shawna Dowell	Shirley Grantham	Eddie Peacock	Jeremy Jennings	Frank Mooney	...
Jacksonville	c	CM	13	(903) 586-3510	Kenneth Durrett	Mo Raissi	Betty Thompson	Jan Tomlinson	Rodney Kelley	Mark Johnson	...
Jamaica Beach	c	CM	1	(409) 737-1142	Victor Pierson	John Brick	...	...	...	Debbie Kershaw	...
Jasper	c	CM	8	(409) 389-4651	R. Horn	Alan Grindstaff	Betty Glenn	Judy Nash	...	Stanley Christopher	Joe Matthews
Jefferson	c	MC	2	(903) 665-3922	Ned Fratangelo	James Gibson	Anita Perot	...	...	...	...
Jersey Village	c	CM	6	(713) 466-2100	Ed Heathcott	Norbert Castro	Deborah Loesch	Stephen Lawrenz	Kathleen Hutchens	C. Wedemeyer	Roderick Hainey
Jones Creek	v	MC	2	(979) 233-2700	Howard Rape	Linda Shepard	Arevelia Ortiz	...	...	...	...
Joshua	c	MC	4	(817) 558-7447	...	Paulette Hartman	...	...	...	...	...
Jourdanton	c	CM	3	(830) 769-3589	Tammy Clark	Daniel Nick	Cindy Trevino	...	David Prasifka	Ronald Lawson	...
Junction	c	CO	2	(915) 446-2622	...	Kathleen Saiz	Maria Alvarado	...	...	Steven Brown	Audren Tomlinson
Karnes City	t	MC	3	(830) 780-3422	...	...	...	...	...	...	...
Katy	c	MC	11	(281) 391-9181	...	...	...	...	...	...	...
Kaufman	c	CM	6	(972) 932-2216	Paula Bacon	Curtis Snow	Jo Ann Talbot	Cathy Cummins	Eddie Brown	James Smith	Richard Underwood
Keene	* c	MC	5	(817) 641-3336	Roy Robinson	James Minor	Juanita Gold	...	Matt Gillin	Rocky Alberti	Mike Baze
Keller	* c	CM	27	(817) 743-4000	Pat McGrail	...	Sheila Stephens	Johnny Phifer	Kelly King	Mark Hafner	Gregory Dickens
Kemp	c	CM	1	(903) 498-3191	...	Melinda Oliver	Jimmie Lou Webb	...	...	Richard Arnold	Joe Villareal
Kenedy	* c	MC	3	(512) 583-2230	Ruhman Franklin	Reggie Winters	...	...	Steven Leal	Dwight DeBose	Rusty Snyder
Kennedale	* c	CM	5	(817) 478-5418	Bryan Lankhorst	Bob Hart	Kathy Turner	Clifford Blackwell	Scott Raven	Tommy Williams	Mark White
Kermit	* c	CM	5	(915) 586-3460	Ted Westmoreland	Sam Watson	Gloria Sanez	Frankie Rolfe	...	Ron Hoge	John Shepard
Kerrville	c	CM	20	(830) 257-8000	...	Paul Hofmann	...	...	Raymond Holloway	...	...
Kilgore	* c	CM	11	(903) 984-5081	Joe Parker	Jeffrey Howell	Karen Custer	Lawanna Chrisman	...	...	David Hackley
Killeen	* c	CM	86	(254) 501-7831	Timothy Hancock	Connie Green	...	...	Jerry Gardner	Dennis Reed	James Butler
Kingsville	c	CM	25	(361) 595-8017	Sam Fugate	...	Edna Lopez	...	Alonzo Lopez	Ricardo Torres	...
Kirby	c	CM	8	(210) 661-3198	...	Zina Tedford	Alva Gardner	Timothy Bolda	Kevin Riedel	Marvin Ivy	Sidney Lankford
Kountze	c	MC	2	(409) 246-3463	Charles Bilal	James Davis	Abbe Overstreet	Dee Zimmerman	Dale Williford	Michael Parrish	Ervin Jordan
Kyle	c	CM	5	(512) 268-5341	...	Thomas Mattis	...	...	...	...	...
La Feria	c	MC	6	(956) 797-2261	...	Sunny Philip	Olga Oberwetter	...	...	Donato Garcia	Javier Martinez
La Grange	* c	CM	4	(979) 968-5805	Janet Moerbe	Shawn Raborn	Lisa Oltmann	Frances Wied	...	Jackie Skelton	...
La Marque	* c	CM	13	(409) 938-9200	Larry Crow	Robert Ewart	...	Susan Lang	Todd Zacherl	Richard Price	Michael Morgan
La Porte	c	CM	31	(281) 471-5020	Alton Porter	Ronald Bottoms	Martha Gillett	...	Mike Boaze	Richard Reff	Steve Gillett
Lacy-Lakeview	c	MC	5	(254) 799-2458	Calvin Hodde	Michael Nicoletti	...	Connie Foreman	...	...	Keith Bond
Lago Vista	c	CM	4	(512) 267-1155	...	...	Joyce Stapleton	...	...	Danny Smith	Bill Angelo
Laguna Vista	* t	CM	1	(956) 943-1793	...	Iris Hill	...	...	Mike Meyn	Robert McGinnis	...
Lake Dallas	c	MC	6	(940) 497-2226	Marjory Johnson	Earl Berner	Beverly Weikum	...	Jason Collier	Nick Ristagno	Johnny Webber
Lake Jackson	* c	CM	26	(979) 415-2400	Bob Sipple	William Yenne	...	Pamela Eaves	...	Paul Hromadka	Jesse Nisbett
Lake Worth	c	MC	4	(817) 237-1211	Walter Bowen	Joey Highfill	...	Vicki Mikel	Mark Cone	Ron Wadkins	Jamye Sexton
Lakeway	c	CM	4	(512) 314-7500	Charles Edwards	Steve Jones	Linda Winn	Nancy Klingman	...	Rick DeLong	David Ferry
Lamesa	c	CM	9	(806) 872-2124	...	Fernando Vera	Maria Aguayo	...	Geno Todd	Richard Garcia	Arbie Taylor
Lampasas	c	CM	6	(512) 556-6831	Jack Calvert	Michael Stoldt	Stacy Brack	Vicki Kinsey	Terry Lindsey	T. Angermann	Randy Clark
Lancaster	c	CM	25	(972) 227-2111	Joe Tillotson	Rickey Childers	...	Maria Joyner	Richard Knopf	Daniel Shiner	James Smith
Laredo	c	CM	176	(956) 795-2192	Elizabeth Flores	Carlos Villarreal	Gustavo Guevara	Rosario Cabello	Luis Sosa	Agustin Dovalina	Jose Guerra
League City	c	CM	45	(281) 332-3431	...	Chris Reed	...	Monica Kohlenberg	...	Michael Jez	Chris Peifer
Leander	c	CM	7	(512) 528-2712	John Cowman	Anthony Johnson	Debbie Haile	Zelmar Tovar	Jerry Williams	...	...
Leon Valley	* c	CM	9	(210) 684-1391	Chris Riley	Lanny Lambert	Marie Feutz	Vickie Wallace	Stan Irwin	Randall Wallace	Fred Stolz
Levelland	* c	CM	12	(806) 894-0113	Hugh Bradley	Rick Osburn	Beth Walls	...	Marvin Brewer	...	Pat Riley
Lewisville	c	CM	77	(972) 219-3400	Gene Carey	Claude King	Julie Heinze	Joe Barrett	Richard Lasky	Steve McFadden	Don Locke
Liberty	c	CM	8	(936) 336-3684	Bruce Halstead	Ronald Wood	Aneisha Nugent	Naomi Herrington	...	Wlliam Griffin	...
Lindale	c	MC	2	(903) 882-3422	...	...	...	...	...	...	...
Little Elm	* t	CM	3	(214) 975-0400	Frank Kastner	Ivan Langford	Kathy Phillips	Ryan Adams	Joe Florentino	Waylan Rhodes	Doug Peach
Littlefield	c	CM	6	(806) 385-9202	Shirley Mann	Danny Davis	Concha Aleman	...	Jamie Grey	Bill McMinn	Michael Williamson
Live Oak	c	CM	9	(210) 653-9140	Henry Edwards	...	Naomi Cox	Richard Middleton	Brian Elbel	Mark Jackley	Mark Wagster
Livingston	c	CM	5	(936) 327-4311	Ben Ogletree	Sam Gordon	Irene Nicks	...	Corky Cochran	Dennis Clifton	William Haecker
Llano	c	MC	3	(915) 247-4158	C. Bauman	F. deGraffenried	Martha Box	Lynda Kuder	...	...	...
Lockhart	c	CM	11	(512) 398-3461	Ray Sanders	...	Connie Ortiz	Stephanie House	Jerry Doyle	...	Vance Rodgers
Longview	c	CM	73	(903) 237-1000	Jay Dean	David Willard	Lois McCaleb	Angela Coen	Michael Pruitt	J. B. McCaleb	Keith Bonds
Lorena	* c	CM	1	(254) 857-4641	Chuck Roper	John Moran	Monica Hendrix	Linda Klump	James Menefee	Morris Colyer	...
Lubbock	c	CM	199	(806) 775-3000	Marc McDougal	Lee Dumbauld	Rebecca Garza	Jeffrey Yates	Steven Hailey	Claude Jones	Terry Ellerbrook
Lufkin	c	CM	32	(936) 633-0228	...	Paul Parker	Atha Martin	Douglas Wood	Fenton Prewitt	Larry Brazil	Kenneth Williams
Luling	c	CM	5	(830) 875-2481	Mike Hendricks	E. T. Gibson	Ruby White	Sonny Rougeou	Paul Stahl	John Cochran	Chris Powell
Madisonville	c	CM	4	(936) 348-2748	Scott Singletary	...	Joyce Shiflet	Ruth Smith	Thom Jones	George Sweetir	Vivian Sheffield
Malakoff	c	CM	2	(903) 489-0699	Patricia Isaacson	Thomas Caffall	...	...	David Files	...	...

Directory 1/9 continued OFFICIALS IN U.S. MUNICIPALITIES 2,500 AND OVER IN POPULATION

Jurisdiction	Type	Form of govern-ment	2000 Popu-lation (000)	Main telephone number	Chief elected official	Appointed administrator	Clerk of the governing board	Chief financial officer	Fire chief	Police chief	Public works director
TEXAS continued											
Mansfield	c	CM	28	(817) 473-9371	David Harry	Clayton Chandler	. . .	Peter Phillis	A. Rodriguez	Steven Noonkester	Bud Ervin
Manvel	c	MC	3	(281) 489-0630	Delores Martin	. . .	Florence Schumann	. . .	. . .	Ralph Garcia	Fred White
Marble Falls	c	CM	4	(830) 693-3615	Nona Fox	Judy Miller	Christina Laine	Margie Cardenas	Jack Floyd	Mark Whitacre	Perry Malkemus
Marlin	c	MC	6	(254) 883-5542	Tom Black	. . .	Dora Vaughan	. . .	Roderick Robinson	Marion Humphrey	Dewey Lee
Marshall	c	CM	23	(903) 935-4416	. . .	Frank Johnson	. . .	. . .	. . .	. . .	. . .
Mathis	c	MC	5	(361) 547-3343	Vicente Gonzalez	Manuel Lara	. . .	Kalee Webb	. . .	Oscar Maldonado	Lucio Munoz
Mc Allen	c	CM	106	(956) 972-7160	Leo Montalvo	Mike Perez	Annette Villarreal	Jerry Dale	. . .	Victor Rodriguez	. . .
Mc Gregor	c	CM	4	(254) 840-2806	Felix Morris	Dennis McDuffie	. . .	Christine Otter	Ronnie Spradley	Jeff Straub	Jerry Lowrance
Mc Kinney	c	CM	54	(972) 547-7500	Bill Whitfield	. . .	Jennifer Sproull	Jennifer Fung	Mark Wallace	Douglas Kowalski	. . .
Meadows	c	MC	4	(806) 539-2377	. . .	. . .	. . .	. . .	Jim Dewbre	. . .	Roberto Camdos
Melissa	c	CM	1	(972) 838-2338	David Dorman	Jason Little	Linda Bannister	Gail Dansby	David Wright	Duane Smith	Mark Maulding
Memphis *	c	MC	2	(806) 259-3001	Joe Rollo	Nelwyn Ward	Cindy Woodard	. . .	James Edwards	William Nowlin	Kirby Gardenhire
Menard	c	CM	1	(915) 396-4706	. . .	Sharon Key	Lupe McSherry	. . .	. . .	. . .	Rhome Hill
Mercedes	c	CM	13	(956) 565-3114	Joel Quintanilla	. . .	Arcelia Felix	Gilda Cordova	. . .	Omar Lucio	Jesse Villarreal
Mesquite	c	CM	124	(972) 288-7711	Mike Anderson	Ted Barron	Judy Womack	Donald Simons	Jim Stark	Gary Westphal	Tim Tumulty
Mexia	c	CM	6	(254) 562-4100	Steve Brewer	. . .	. . .	Carolyn Martin	Clayton Shivers	Richard Hawthorne	Fred Samford
Midland	c	CM	94	(432) 685-7100	Mike Canon	Rick Menchaca	Kaylah McCord	Robert McNaughton	Andrew Mehl	John Urby	Charles Swallow
Midlothian	c	CM	7	(972) 775-3481	Boyce Whatley	Ronald Stephens	Lou Jameson	Jimmie McClure	David Schrodt	William Campbell	Adam Mergener
Mineola	c	MC	4	(903) 569-6183	N. Smith	Dion Miller	David Stevenson	. . .	. . .	Charles Bittner	. . .
Mineral Wells	c	CM	16	(940) 328-1211	Earl Medlin	Lance Howerton	Juanita Formby	Scott Blasor	Robert Spears	Jerry White	. . .
Mission	c	CM	45	(956) 580-8650	Norberto Salinas	Julio Cerda	Anna Carrillo	Janie Flores	Ricardo Saldana	Leonardo Longoria	Francisco Flores
Missouri City	c	CM	52	(281) 261-4260	. . .	. . .	. . .	. . .	Russell Sander	. . .	David Dorger
Monahans	c	CM	6	(915) 943-4343	David Cutbirth	David Mills	. . .	Shirlan Turner	Billy Riley	David Watts	. . .
Morton	c	MC	2	(806) 266-8850	Edward Akin	Brenda Shaw	. . .	. . .	Edward Amalla	. . .	Frank Enriquez
Mount Pleasant	c	CM	13	(903) 575-4000	Jerry Boatner	Courtney Sharp	. . .	Brenda Reynolds	Larry McRae	. . .	Darrell Grubbs
Muenster *	c	CM	1	(940) 759-2236	John Pagel	Stan Endres	Micallee Matson	. . .	Herbie Knabe	Robert Stovall	. . .
Muleshoe	c	CM	4	(806) 272-4528	Victor Leal	David Brunson	LeAnn Gallman	. . .	Richard Ronek	Don Carter	Ramon Sanchez
Munday	c	MC	1	(940) 422-4331	. . .	John Weeks	. . .	. . .	. . .	. . .	. . .
Murphy	c	MC	3	(972) 424-6021	. . .	Craig Sherwood	Aimee Nemer	. . .	. . .	Billy Myrick	Johnny Boles
Nacogdoches *	c	CM	29	(936) 559-2567	Bob Dunn	James Jeffers	Lila Fuller	Jack Sparks	Keith Kiplinger	Jimmie Sevey	Wayne Shepherd
Nassau Bay	c	CM	4	(281) 333-4211	Donald Matter	John Kennedy	Patsy Jones	David Quick	. . .	Ronald Wrobleski	Phil Briscoe
Navasota *	c	CM	6	(936) 825-6475	Patricia Gruner	Brad Stafford	. . .	Geraldine Binford	Jason Katkoski	. . .	Gary Johnson
Nederland	c	CM	17	(409) 723-1500	R. A. Nugent	Andre' Wimer	La Donna Floyd	. . .	Gary Collins	Darrell Bush	Steve Hamilton
New Boston	t	MC	4	(903) 628-5596	Johnny Branson	Carol Ensey	Gladys Nelson	. . .	. . .	Kerry Pinkham	R. Thomas
New Braunfels *	c	CM	36	(830) 221-4000	Bruce Boyer	Michael Morrison	Michael Resendez	D. Korinchock	John Herber	Ron Everett	. . .
Nocona	c	MC	3	(940) 825-3282	Paul Gibbs	Minnie Walker	Revell Hardison	. . .	. . .	Kent Holcomb	Lynn Henley
North Richland Hills	c	CM	55	(817) 427-6000	Tommy Brown	Larry Cunningham	Patricia Hutson	. . .	Andrew Jones	Jerry McGlasson	Gregory Dickens
Oak Leaf *	c	MC	1	(972) 617-2660	. . .	. . .	Patricia Cortes	. . .	. . .	. . .	. . .
Oak Point *	c	CM	1	(972) 294-2312	Duane Olson	Richard Martin	Mary Beth Thomas	. . .	. . .	. . .	Mike Sloggett
Oak Ridge North	c	CM	2	(281) 292-4648	. . .	Paul Mendes	Su Powell	. . .	. . .	Andrew Walters	Lawrence Bienvenu
Odessa	c	CM	90	(432) 335-3200	Larry Melton	Richard Morton	Norma Aguilar	James Zentner	Richard Dietz	Chris Pipes	Matt Squyres
Olmos Park	c	CM	2	(210) 824-3281	Gerald Dubinski	Amy Buckert	. . .	. . .	Mark Medbury	Louis Alcoser	. . .
Olney	c	CM	3	(940) 564-2102	Mary Schoonover	Danny Parker	Lee Campbell	Wanda Clifton	Garry Keeter	Scott Given	Ronnie Stroud
Orange	c	CM	18	(409) 886-3611	William Claybar	. . .	Kerry Kittrell	Susan English	David Frenzel	Sam Kittrell	James Wolf
Ovilla	c	CM	3	(972) 617-7262	William Turner	. . .	Tammy McCoy	. . .	Donnie Pickard	Michael Moon	Tony Bumpus
Palacios	c	MC	5	(361) 972-3605	John Connor	Charles Winfield	Patsy Gibson	. . .	Don Kopecky	Bernando Gurrerro	John Martinez
Palestine	c	CM	17	(903) 731-8400	George Foss	R Brown	Ann Pesce	Robert Sherrill	Henry York	Charles Edge	Ron Sullivan
Pampa	c	CM	17	(806) 669-5750	Lonny Robbins	John Horst	Phyllis Jeffers	. . .	Kim Powell	Trevlyn Pitner	Richard Morris
Panhandle	c	CM	2	(806) 537-3517	Les McNeill	Loren Brant	Connie McKiernan	. . .	Roy Tarpley	Jeffery Oldham	Lenro Jennings
Pantego	t	CM	2	(817) 274-1381	Dorothy Aderholt	Doug Davis	Norma Zenk	Fitzhugh Newsome	Thomas Griffith	Jon Coulter	Ronald Edwards
Paris *	c	CM	25	(903) 785-7511	Jesse Freelen	Kevin Carruth	Janice Ellis	Warren Anderson	Ronnie Grooms	Roger Louis	Shawn Napier
Pasadena	c	MC	141	(713) 477-1511	John Manlove	. . .	Linda Rorick	Wayne Long	Jerry Gardner	Mike Massey	Melvin Embry
Pearland	c	CM	37	(281) 652-1600	. . .	William Eisen	. . .	Claire Manthei	. . .	Chris Doyle	Jerry Burns
Pearsall	c	CM	7	(830) 334-3676	Roland Segovir	Jose Trevino	Amy Padilla	. . .	Steve Parsons	Ray Talamarto	Alex Hernandez
Pecos	c	CM	9	(915) 445-2421	Dot Stafford	. . .	Geneva Martinez	Steve McCormick	Doug Cox	Troy Moore	Octavio Garcia
Perryton	c	CM	7	(806) 435-4014	. . .	David Landis	. . .	. . .	. . .	. . .	. . .
Pflugerville *	c	CM	16	(512) 990-4363	Scott Winton	David Buesing	Karen Thompson	. . .	. . .	. . .	James Wills
Pharr	c	CO	46	(956) 702-5335	Ricardo Medina	Fred Sandoval	Dora Garza	Juan Guerra	Jaime Guzman	Jesse Medina	Frank Vecchio
Pinehurst	c	CM	2	(409) 886-2221	. . .	C. Nash	. . .	. . .	. . .	. . .	. . .
Piney Point Village *	c	MC	3	(713) 782-0271	Carol Fox	Lorena Briel	Samantha Watts	. . .	Anthony Calagna	Gary Brye	Bob Peach
Pittsburg	c	CM	4	(903) 856-3621	D. Abernathy	. . .	Margaret Jackson	. . .	David Abernathy	Martin Pessink	Wayne Hadderton
Plainview	c	CM	22	(806) 296-1100	John Anderson	Greg Ingham	Belinda Hinojosa	Jack Keller	H. Glass	William Mull	John Berry
Plano	c	CM	222	(972) 941-7000	Pat Evans	T. Muehlenbeck	Elaine Bealke	John McGrane	Hugo Esparza	Greg Rushin	Jimmy Foster
Pleasanton *	c	CM	8	(830) 569-3867	William Carroll	Kathy Coronado	Cynthia Urrabazo	. . .	. . .	Gary Soward	Juan Martinez
Port Aransas *	c	CM	3	(361) 749-4111	Claude Brown	Michael Kovacs	. . .	Judy Lyle	Scott Mack	Samuel Russell	Eluterio Moreno
Port Arthur	c	CM	57	(409) 983-8100	Oscar Ortiz	S. Fitzgibbons	E. Van Green	Rebecca Underhill	Larry Richard	. . .	John Comeaux
Port Isabel	c	CM	4	(956) 943-2682	Pat Marchan	Robert Garcia	Nancy Davalos	Pete Capistran	Hector Bennett	Joel Ochoa	Baldemar Alaniz
Port Lavaca	c	CM	12	(361) 552-9795	Allen Tharling	Gary Broz	. . .	Gerald Durocher	Raymond Tennisen	John Stewart	. . .
Port Neches	c	CM	13	(409) 727-2182	Glenn Johnson	A. Kimler	Patty Faulk	Linda Richardson	Steve Curran	Clois Marsh	Taylor Shelton
Portland	c	CM	14	(361) 643-6501	David Krebs	Michael Tanner	Annette Rodriguez	Sandra Clarkson	James Nelson	Randy Wright	Kim Parker
Post	c	CM	3	(806) 495-2811	Archie Gill	. . .	Deana Gunn	. . .	Ivan Line	. . .	John Rudd
Poteet	c	MC	3	(830) 742-3574	Diana Martinez	. . .	Cathy Leal	. . .	Pete Ramirez	Frank Leal	Adolfo Rodriguez
Pottsboro	c	CM	1	(903) 786-2281	. . .	Jerry Guillory	. . .	. . .	. . .	. . .	. . .
Prairie View	c	MC	4	(936) 857-3711	Frank Jaconson	. . .	. . .	. . .	Frank Jackson	Wilbert White	Scott Spidale
Premont	c	MC	2	(361) 348-2022	Mario Rodriguez	. . .	Iris Flores	. . .	Jerry Larue	. . .	Lorenzo Cabrera
Princeton	c	MC	3	(972) 736-2416	Kathy Davis	. . .	Thomas Wyatt	Lara Feagins	Mike Woody	Rick Cantrell	. . .
Progreso	c	MC	4	(956) 565-0241	Arturo Valdez	. . .	Ana Delgado	Ponciano Garcia	. . .	Xavier Martinez	. . .
Prosper	t	CM	2	(972) 346-2640	Charles Niswanger	Douglas Mousel	Matthew Denton	Ron Butler	Ronnie Tucker	Kirk McFarlin	Rick Bogle
Quanah	c	CM	3	(940) 663-5536	Jess Adkins	. . .	Paula Wilson	Patricia Elliott	Ricky Burton	Guy Smith	Tony Tallant
Ranger *	c	CO	2	(254) 647-3522	John Casey	. . .	Twila Dobson	Margaret Green	Louis Fox	Elton McCoy	Marty Williamson
Raymondville	c	CM	9	(956) 689-2443	C. Crowell	Eleazar Garcia	. . .	. . .	. . .	. . .	Octavio Correa
Red Oak *	c	CM	4	(972) 617-3638	Todd Little	Scott Albert	Judy Grant	. . .	Eric Thompson	Donald Fullerton	. . .
Refugio	c	MC	2	(512) 526-5361	Ray Jaso	. . .	C. Shreckengost	. . .	Don Pullin	Chris Brock	Clifford Lynn
Richardson *	c	CM	91	(972) 744-4000	Steve Mitchell	William Keffler	Pamela Schmidt	Kenton Pfeil	Alan Palomba	David Zacharias	Jerry Ortega
Richland Hills	c	CM	8	(817) 299-1800	David Ragan	James Quin	Kim Sutter	Barbara Mann	Davis Anderson	Barbara Childress	Michael Barnes
Richmond *	t	CM	11	(281) 342-5456	Hilmar Moore	Robert Gilmore	Ramona Matak	Terri Vela	Stephen Noto	William Whitworth	Lenert Kurtz
Richwood	c	MC	3	(979) 265-2082	Sandra Boykin	. . .	Karen Schrom	. . .	Mark Guthrie	Glenn Patton	Don Malone
Rio Grande City	c	CM	11	(956) 487-0672	Kevin Hiles	Juan Zuniga	Holly Guerrero	Mary Barrera	Ricardo Reyes	Guadalupe Marquez	Fernando Guerra
River Oaks	c	MC	6	(817) 626-5421	Herman Earwood	Linda Ryan	. . .	. . .	David Hubbard	Daniel Chisholm	Marvin Gregory
Roanoke	c	CM	2	(817) 491-2411	. . .	James Stathatos	. . .	. . .	. . .	. . .	. . .
Robinson *	c	MC	7	(254) 662-1415	Bryan Ferguson	Richard Fletcher	Linda Vranich	Karen Sanchez	Gerald Groppe	Rusty Smith	Dale Pattillo

Directory 1/9 continued **OFFICIALS IN U.S. MUNICIPALITIES 2,500 AND OVER IN POPULATION**

Jurisdiction	Type	Form of govern-ment	2000 Popu-lation (000)	Main telephone number	Chief elected official	Appointed administrator	Clerk of the governing board	Chief financial officer	Fire chief	Police chief	Public works director
TEXAS continued											
Robstown	c	MC	12	(361) 387-4589	Rodrigo Ramon	Paula Wakefield	. . .	Isabel Barrientes	Richard Gonzalez	Carlos Pena	Roy Gutierrez
Rockdale	c	CM	5	(512) 446-2511	John Shoemake	T. Flemming	Shelli Turner	. . .	Elvis McQuinn	Thomas Harris	Eddie Zapata
Rockport *	c	CM	7	(361) 729-2213	Todd Pearson	Thomas Blazek	Irma Parker	Jacky Cockerham	. . .	Tim Jayroe	Billy Dick
Rockwall	c	CM	17	(972) 771-7700	Ken Jones	Julie Couch	Belinda Page	. . .	Mark Poindexter	William Watkins	Chuck Todd
Roma	c	CM	9	(956) 849-1411	Fernando Pena	Rogeio Salinas	Josie Hinojosa	Marco Soto	Jose Garcia	Emilio Montalvo	Jorge Munoz
Rosebud	c	CM	1	(254) 583-7926	Ken Hensel	Megan Henderson	Kim Kennedy	. . .	Rick Trubee	Earl Winebrenner	Rudy Reyna
Rosenberg	c	CM	24	(832) 595-3310	Joe Gurecky	Jack Hamlett	Linda Cernosek	Mindi Snyder	. . .	Robert Gracia	Kenneth Jansky
Round Rock	c	CM	61	(512) 218-5490	Nyle Maxwell	James Nuse	Christine Martinez	Cindy Demers	Lynn Bizzell	Paul Conner	Tom Word
Rowlett	c	CM	44	(972) 412-6100	C. Johnson	Craig Owens	Janita Quinn	Brian Funderburk	Lawrence Wright	James Walling	Patrick Baugh
Royse City	c	MC	2	(972) 636-2250	Jim Mellody	Connie Goodwin	Brenda Craft	. . .	Richard Bell	Dana Thomason	. . .
Rusk	c	CM	5	(903) 683-2213	. . .	. . .	. . .	. . .	Wayne Morgan	Ronny Miller	Gene Kelley
Sachse	c	CM	9	(972) 495-1212	Mike Felix	Allen Barnes	Terrence Smith	Alan Dickerson	Doug Kendrick	Richard Benedict	Joey Crase
Saginaw	c	CM	12	(817) 232-4640	Gary Brinkley	Nan Stanford	Nelda Mays	. . .	Bob Harvey	Roger Macon	Terry Highfill
San Angelo	c	CM	88	(915) 657-4221	. . .	Harold Dominguez	Kathy Keane	Michael Dane	Brian Dunn	Joe Gibson	Will Wilde
San Antonio	c	CM	1144	(210) 207-2030	. . .	Sheryl Sculley	Leticia Vacek	Milo Nitschke	Robert Ojeda	Albert Ortiz	Thomas Wendorf
San Augustine	c	MC	2	(936) 275-2121	. . .	Duke Lyons	Cinda Garner	. . .	. . .	Ken Delaserda	. . .
San Benito	c	CM	23	(956) 361-3800	Cesar Gonzalez	Victor Trevino	Lupita Passenent	. . .	. . .	. . .	. . .
San Diego	c	MC	4	(361) 279-3341	Alfredo Cardenas	Ramon Tanguma	Isabel Trevino	Ernesto Sanchez	. . .	Abelizario Escalan	. . .
San Juan *	c	CM	26	(956) 702-6400	. . .	Guillermo Seguin	. . .	Steven Austin	Tirso Garza	Juan Garza	John Avielz
San Marcos	c	CM	34	(512) 393-8000	R. Habingreither	Daniel O'Leary	Janis Womack	James Gonzales	Todd Derkacz	. . .	Richard Mendoza
Sanger	c	MC	4	(940) 458-7930	Tommy Kincaid	Michael Brice	Rose Chavez	. . .	Jeff Morris	Benny Erwin	Chuck Tucker
Sansom Park Village	c	MC	4	(817) 626-3791	Mike Wasser	Deana McMullen	. . .	. . .	. . .	. . .	. . .
Santa Fe	c	CM	9	(409) 925-6412	Robert Cheek	Joe Dickson	. . .	. . .	. . .	. . .	Chris Beanland
Schertz *	c	CM	18	(210) 619-1000	Hal Baldwin	Donald Taylor	Judy Tokar	Juan Santova	Glen Outlaw	Stephen Starr	Sam Willoughby
Seabrook	c	CM	9	(281) 474-3201	. . .	. . .	. . .	. . .	. . .	Robert Kerber	Gary Jones
Seagoville	c	CM	10	(972) 287-2050	Calvin Travers	. . .	Ruth Sorrells	Shirley Booth	Tommy Lemond	I. Smith	Michael Hitt
Seagraves	c	MC	2	(806) 387-2593	. . .	Catherine Mitchell	Jacqueline Orum	. . .	. . .	Richard Cordell	James Fischer
Sealy	c	CM	5	(979) 885-3511	Betty Reinbeck	. . .	Krisha Langton	Steven Kutra	. . .	Brad Murray	Larry Mayberry
Seguin *	c	CM	22	(830) 379-3212	Betty Matthies	Douglas Faseler	. . .	Susan Caddell	Scott Mycue	Luis Collazo	Ruben Perez
Selma	c	CM	. .	(210) 651-6661	Jim Parma	Kenneth Roberts	. . .	. . .	Ric Braun	Sydnor Hall	. . .
Seminole	c	CM	5	(915) 758-3676	Wayne Mixon	Tommy Phillips	. . .	. . .	. . .	. . .	. . .
Seymour	c	MC	2	(940) 889-3148	Dan Craighead	Joe Shephard	. . .	Mary Griffin	Randy Coltharp	Tommy Duncan	. . .
Shamrock	c	CM	2	(806) 256-3281	. . .	. . .	. . .	. . .	. . .	. . .	. . .
Shavano Park	c	CM	1	(210) 493-3478	Pete Fleischhacker	H Smith	Brian Harrison	James Percival	Linc Surber	Leo Stewart	Rogelio Quiroqa
Shenandoah *	c	MC	1	(281) 298-5522	Becky Altemus	Chip Vansteenberg	Susan Hensley	. . .	. . .	John Chancellor	Manuel DeLaRosa
Sherman *	c	CM	35	(903) 892-7201	Bill Magers	George Olson	Linda Ashby	. . .	Jeffrey Jones	Tom Watt	Jeffrey Miller
Shoreacres	c	CM	1	(281) 471-2244	Nancy Edmonson	David Stall	. . .	. . .	. . .	Randall French	Eloy Gonzalez
Silsbee	c	CM	6	(409) 385-2863	Dean Robinson	Tommy Bartosh	. . .	. . .	Berl Slaydan	Robert Nelson	Roger Fussell
Sinton	t	CM	5	(361) 364-2381	. . .	Ira Knox	Betty Wood	. . .	. . .	Eugene Deleon	Beverly Agomuo
Slaton	c	CM	6	(806) 828-2000	Laura Wilson	Roger McKinney	Toni Chrestman	. . .	Joe Scott	Jeff Creager	Doyce Field
Smithville	c	CM	3	(512) 237-3282	Renee Blaschke	Price Middlebrook	Brenda Page	. . .	. . .	Delvin Dockery	Jack Page
Snyder	c	CM	10	(325) 573-4957	F. Allen Noah	Jared Miller	Teresa Wall	Jeanne Johnson	P. Westmoreland	Steve Warren	. . .
Sonora *	c	MC	2	(325) 387-2558	Gloria Lopez	James Polonis	Patti Prather	. . .	Rick Cearley	Edward House	. . .
Sour Lake	c	MC	1	(409) 287-3573	. . .	Ricky Jorgensen	. . .	. . .	. . .	. . .	. . .
South Houston	c	MC	15	(713) 947-7700	Joe Soto	. . .	Maria Vega	. . .	Jesse Garcia	Herbet Gilbert	. . .
South Padre Island *	t	CM	2	(956) 761-6456	Robert Pinkerton	Dewey Cashwell	Joyce Adams	Darla Honea	. . .	Robert Rodriguez	. . .
Southlake	c	CM	21	(817) 481-1653	Andy Wambsganss	Shana Yelverton	Lori Farwell	Sharon Elam	Robert Finn	Marlin Price	Pedram Farahnak
Southside Place	c	MC	1	(713) 668-2341	Richard Rothfelder	David Moss	. . .	. . .	. . .	. . .	. . .
Spearman	c	CM	3	(806) 659-2524	. . .	Edward Hansen	Cheryl Salgado	. . .	. . .	. . .	Danny Parker
Spring Valley	c	MC	3	(713) 465-8308	Tammy Canon	R. Rockenbaugh	Betty Lusk	. . .	. . .	John Cook	. . .
Stafford	t	MC	15	(281) 261-3900	Leonard Scarcella	. . .	. . .	Karen Austin	Mike Melton	Bonny Krahn	Lawrence Vaccaro
Stamford	c	CM	3	(915) 773-2723	Oscar Armstrong	. . .	Liz Rodriquez	Jerry Pingle	Wyatt Oakley	Glenn Smith	Mark Routon
Stephenville	c	CM	14	(254) 918-1220	Rusty Jergins	Mark Kaiser	Cindy Stafford	Donald Ives	Jimmy Chew	Mark Johnson	. . .
Sugar Land *	c	CM	63	(281) 275-2700	David Wallace	Allen Bogard	G. Gundermann	Linda Symank	Dannie Smith	Steve Griffith	Tommy Haynes
Sulphur Springs	c	CM	14	(903) 885-7541	Brad Burgin	Marc Maxwell	Sharon Ricketson	Peter Karstens	Gerry Cleaver	James Bayuk	. . .
Sundown	c	CM	1	(806) 229-3131	Jim Winn	. . .	Toni Wilson	. . .	Doug Barry	Jerry Escobar	Barry Stephens
Sunnyvale	t	CM	2	(972) 226-7177	Jim Phaup	Hugh Campbell	. . .	. . .	. . .	. . .	. . .
Sunray	c	CM	1	(806) 948-4111	. . .	Greg Smith	. . .	Kathy Lee	. . .	Tommy Bogart	K Perry
Sweeny	c	CM	3	(979) 548-3321	Larry Piper	Tim Moss	Reatta Minshew	. . .	Billy Ward	Gary Stroud	Homer Toscano
Sweetwater *	c	CM	11	(915) 236-6313	. . .	Edward Brown	. . .	Jeanie McPherson	. . .	. . .	Ray Adames
Taft	c	MC	3	(512) 528-3512	. . .	Florencio Sauceda	. . .	. . .	. . .	David Wood	Ruth Robertson
Tahoka	c	CM	2	(806) 998-4211	Mike Mensch	Jerry Webster	Cheryl Krey	. . .	Steve Miller	Doyle Lee	David Graves
Taylor *	c	CM	13	(512) 352-3675	Benito Gonzales	Frank Salvato	Susan Brock	Rosemarie Dennis	Bruce Watson	Jeffrey Straub	Danny Thomas
Taylor Lake Village	c	MC	3	(281) 326-2843	Natalie O'Neill	. . .	. . .	. . .	. . .	. . .	. . .
Teague	c	MC	4	(254) 739-2547	Blelve Bridges	. . .	Todd Solley	. . .	Robert Knight	. . .	Gerald Horton
Temple	c	CM	54	(254) 298-5700	William Jones	David Blackburn	C. Entzminger	Tracie Barnard	Lonzo Wallace	Gary Smith	. . .
Terrell	c	CM	13	(972) 551-6600	Frances Anderson	Torry Edwards	. . .	John Rounsavall	James Harper	Michael Shewmake	Robert Rogers
Terrell Hills	c	CM	5	(210) 824-7401	J. Camp	James Browne	Betty Gover	. . .	. . .	L. Semander	Jimmy Phelps
Texarkana	c	CM	34	(903) 798-3915	James Bramlett	George Shackelford	Geri Haddock	Charles Bassett	Harry Simms	Danny Alexander	Philip Ball
Texas City	c	MC	41	(409) 643-5930	Matthew Doyle	. . .	Pamela Lawrence	Cheryl Hunter	Gerald Grimm	Robert Burby	Thomas Kessler
The Colony	c	CM	26	(972) 624-3100	John Dillare	Dale Cheatham	Christie Wilson	Rebecca Koo	James Nolen	Joseph Clark	Stephen Eubanks
Tomball *	c	CM	9	(281) 351-5484	Gretchen Fagan	. . .	Doris Speer	. . .	Randall Parr	Gregory Blake	Rod Haney
Trophy Club	t	MC	6	(682) 831-4600	Scott Smith	Donna Welsh	Diane Cockrell	Roger Unger	. . .	. . .	. . .
Tulia	c	CM	5	(806) 995-3547	John Emmitt	Ricky Crownover	Barbara Cabe	. . .	Wayne Nevins	Jimmy McCaslin	Roy Campbell
Tyler *	c	CM	83	(903) 531-1112	Joey Seeber	Robert Turner	Cassandra Brager	Daniel Crawford	Neal Franklin	Gary Swindle	Gregory Morgan
Universal City	c	CM	14	(210) 659-0333	. . .	Kenneth Taylor	Alene Patton	Karl McCormick	Ross Wallace	Floyd Bryant	Antonio Rivas
University Park *	c	CM	23	(214) 363-1644	James Holmes	T. Livingston	. . .	Kent Austin	David Ledbetter	Gary Adams	Bud Smallwood
Uvalde	c	CM	14	(830) 278-3315	Gus Neutze	John Harrell	. . .	Jorge Trevino	Jimmy Howard	Joel Sanchez	. . .
Van Alstyne	c	CM	2	(903) 482-5426	. . .	. . .	. . .	. . .	. . .	. . .	. . .
Van Horn	t	MC	2	(432) 283-2050	. . .	Rebecca Brewster	Virginia Carrasco	Jodi Corrales	. . .	. . .	Raquel Mendez
Venus	t	MC	. .	(972) 366-3348	. . .	Jerry Reed	. . .	. . .	. . .	. . .	. . .
Vernon	c	CM	11	(940) 552-2581	R Couch	James Murray	. . .	Jerry Rogers	Charles Stewart	. . .	Ronnie Richie
Victoria *	c	CM	60	(361) 485-3500	Will Armstrong	Charles Windwehen	Scarlet Swoboda	Gilbert Reyna	Vance Riley	Howard Ure	John Johnston
Vidor *	c	MC	11	(409) 769-5473	Joe Hopkins	Ricky Jorgensen	Rhonda Haskins	Lorrie Taylor	. . .	Steve Conroy	Byron Richard
Waco	c	CM	113	(254) 750-5600	Mike Morrison	Larry Groth	Patricia Ervin	Janice Andrews	Jon Fasana	Gilbert Miller	. . .
Wake Village	c	MC	5	(903) 838-0515	Mike Huddleston	Bob Long	Wanda Sandlin	. . .	Bruce Dinsmore	Tony Estes	. . .
Watauga	c	CM	21	(817) 514-5819	Harry Jeffries	Kerry Lacy	Kathleen Wedell	Janina Jewell	. . .	. . .	Johnnie Reagan
Waxahachie *	c	CM	21	(972) 937-7330	. . .	Paul Stevens	Nancy Ross	Carl Wessels	David Hudgins	Charles Edge	Jeff Chambers
Weatherford	c	CM	19	(817) 598-4000	Joe Tison	Jennifer Fadden	Angie Winkle	Renita Bishop	George Teague	Jerry Blaisdell	. . .
Webster	c	CM	9	(281) 332-1826	Floyd Myers	. . .	Pauline Small	Debra Wennagel	Bruce Ure	Mike Keller	Jim Williams
Weimar	c	CM	1	(979) 725-8554	. . .	Randal Jones	Dolores Stoever	Wade Cernosek	. . .	Bill Livingston	. . .

Directory 1/9 continued **OFFICIALS IN U.S. MUNICIPALITIES 2,500 AND OVER IN POPULATION**

Jurisdiction	Type	Form of govern-ment	2000 Popu-lation (000)	Main telephone number	Chief elected official	Appointed administrator	Clerk of the governing board	Chief financial officer	Fire chief	Police chief	Public works director
TEXAS continued											
Wellington	c	CM	2	(806) 447-2544	...	...	...	...	...	...	...
Weslaco	c	CM	26	(956) 968-3181	...	Anthony Covacevich	...	James Hiebert	Arturo Avila	Juan Martinez	Juan Flores
West Columbia	c	CM	4	(979) 345-3123	David Foster	...	...	Rhonda Weems	Jimmy Chafin	Don Fairrel	...
West Lake Hills	c	MC	3	(512) 327-3628	...	Robert Wood	Janet Rogers	...	...	...	...
West Orange *	c	MC	4	(409) 883-3468	Roy McDonald	...	Theresa Van Meter	...	Randy Veitch	Michael Stelly	Ron Garrison
West Tawakoni	c	MC	1	(903) 447-2285	Bill Stausing	Cloy Richards	Annette Lemons	Susan Roberts	...	Jack Schultz	Ken Newville
West University Place	c	CM	14	(713) 668-4441	Richard Ballanfant	Michael Ross	Kaylynn Holloway	Walter Thomas	Terry Stevenson	...	Ronald Wicker
Westlake *	t	CM	..	(817) 430-0941	Scott Bradley	...	Kim Sutter	Debbie Piper	Don Wilson	...	...
Westworth Village	c	MC	2	(817) 738-3673	Andy Foutenot	Gary Robinson	Shelli Branson	...	Don Day	Doug Reim	...
Wharton *	c	CM	9	(979) 532-2491	Bryce Kocian	Andres Garza	...	Joyce Vasut	Anthony Abbott	Timothy Guin	Phillip Bush
White Oak	c	MC	5	(903) 759-3936	Tim Vaughn	Ralph Weaver	Lisa Blount	...	Jimmy Nall	...	Kelly Mitchell
White Settlement	c	CM	14	(817) 246-4971	...	Jimmie Burnett	Lucy Polk	...	...	David Place	Mark White
Whitesboro *	t	MC	3	(903) 564-3311	W. D. Welch	Michael Marter	Brenda Goldsmith	...	Kevin Walton	Scott Taylor	Donald Zielke
Wichita Falls	c	CM	104	(940) 761-7404	Lanham Lyne	Darron Leiker	Lydia Toress	James Dockery	Earl Foster	Dennis Bachman	John Taylor
Willis	c	MC	3	(936) 856-4611	Leonard Reed	James McAlister	Brenda Burns	...	...	James Nowak	Jerry Humphreys
Wills Point	c	CM	3	(903) 873-2578	Roy Caldwell	Carman Girdley	Carla Oldacre	...	Robert Tisdale	Rickey Willis	Scott Drake
Windcrest	c	MC	5	(210) 655-0022	Jack Leonhardt	F. Cain	Tracy Freimarck	...	Tom Winn	Rick Pruitt	Byron Vick
Winnsboro	c	MC	3	(903) 342-3654	Carolyn Jones	Ronny Knight	Nina Browning	Wanda Renshaw	...	James Whittiker	...
Winters	c	CM	2	(915) 754-4424	Dawson McGuffin	Mir Hassan	Saffron Gibbs	...	Jack Davis	L. Balentine	Charles Grenwelge
Woodville *	t	MC	2	(409) 283-2234	Tony Castillo	George Jones	Terri Bible	...	Tommy Shane	Scott Yosko	Charles Comte
Woodway	c	CM	8	(254) 772-4480	Donald Baker	Yousry Zakhary	Jennifer Canady	William Klump	...	...	...
Wylie	c	CM	15	(972) 442-8100	...	Mindy Manson	Carole Ehrlich	Larry Williamson	Noe Flores	Jeffrey Butters	Mike Sferra
Yoakum *	c	CM	5	(361) 293-6321	Anita Rodriguez	Calvin Cook	Theresa Bowe	Charlotte Morrow	Phillip Baker	William Formolo	...
UTAH											
Alpine	c	MC	7	(801) 756-6347	Don Watkins	Ted Stillman	Janis Williams	...	...	...	Jay Healey
Alta	t	MC	..	(801) 742-3522	Tom Pollard	John Guldner	Katherine Black	...	...	Jerry Larson	...
American Fork	c	MC	21	(801) 763-3000	Ted Barratt	Carl Wanlass	Richard Colborn	...	Paul Peters	John Durrant	...
Blanding	c	CM	3	(435) 678-2791	Calvin Balch	Chris Webb	Patricia Bartlett	...	Gordon Hawkins	Melvin Halliday	Jeff Black
Bluffdale	c	CM	4	(801) 254-2200	...	...	...	...	...	...	...
Bountiful	c	CM	41	(801) 298-6118	Joe Johnson	Thomas Hardy	...	Kim Coleman	George Sumner	Paul Rapp	...
Brian Head	t	CM	..	(435) 677-2029	H. Deutschlander	Judy Gubler	...	...	...	Wade Carpenter	Randy Rasmussen
Brigham City	c	MC	17	(435) 734-2001	David Kano	...	...	Dennis Sheffield	Art Petersen	James Paine	Bruce Leonard
Cedar City	c	MC	20	(435) 586-2950	Harold Shirley	Ronald Chandler	Bonnie Moritz	Jace Bunting	Paul Irons	Glen Miller	Kit Wareham
Cedar Hills	c	MC	3	(801) 785-9668	Michael McGee	Konrad Hildebrandt	Kim Holindrake	Richard Knapp	Craig Carlisle	...	...
Centerville	c	CM	14	(801) 295-3477	Michael Deamer	Steve Thacker	Marilyn Holje	Blaine Lutz	George Sumner	Neal Worsley	Randy Randall
Clearfield	c	CM	25	(801) 525-2700	Thomas Waggoner	Christopher Hillman	...	Bob Wylie	...	Jim Schilling	Scott Hodge
Clinton	c	CM	12	(801) 774-2600	Lane Adams	...	...	...	Floyd Petersen	Bill Chilson	Michael Child
Draper	c	CM	25	(801) 576-6500	Richard Alsop	Layne Long	Barbara Sadler	Ron Patera	David Limberg	...	...
Eagle Mountain	t	CM	2	(801) 789-5990	Kelvin Bailey	John Hendrickson	Janet Valentine	Kent Parker	Robert Dekover	...	Mark Sovine
Ephraim *	c	MC	4	(435) 283-4631	Clifford Birrell	Richard Anderson	Leigh Ann Warnock	Nevin Holmberg	...	Ronald Rasmussen	Chad Parry
Farmington	c	CM	12	(801) 451-2383	Dave Connors	Max Forbush	Margy Lomax	Keith Johnson	Larry Gregory	Wayne Hansen	Walt Hokanson
Fruit Heights	c	MC	4	(801) 546-0861	Richard Harvey	Richard Marchant	...	...	...	...	Jack Palmer
Grantsville	c	MC	6	(435) 884-3411	Merle Cole	Wendy Palmer	...	...	Lowell Anderson	Danny Johnson	...
Gunnison	c	MC	2	(435) 528-7969	...	...	...	...	...	...	...
Heber	c	MC	7	(435) 654-0757	David Phillips	Mark Anderson	Paulette Thurber	...	...	Edward Rhoades	Stephen Tozier
Helper	c	MC	2	(435) 472-5391	Joseph Bonacci	Jona Skerl	...	...	Mike Zamantakis	George Zamantakis	...
Highland	c	MC	8	(801) 756-5751	Jesse Adamson	Damon Edwards	Winifred Jensen	Lynn Ruff	...	...	Lloyd Hansen
Hurricane	c	CM	8	(435) 635-2811	...	Clark Fawcett	...	...	Ed Campbell	Lynn Excell	Mac Hall
Hyrum	c	MC	6	(435) 245-6033	...	...	...	...	...	...	...
Ivins	t	MC	4	(435) 674-5503	...	...	...	...	...	...	...
Kaysville	c	CM	20	(801) 546-1235	...	John Thacker	...	...	...	...	...
La Verkin	c	MC	3	(435) 625-2581	...	...	...	...	...	...	...
Layton	c	CM	58	(801) 336-3800	Jerry Stevenson	Alex Jensen	...	Steven Ashby	Kevin Ward	Terry Keefe	Terry Coburn
Lehi *	c	MC	19	(801) 768-7100	Howard Johnson	James Davidson	Connie Ashton	...	Dale Ekins	Chad Smith	James Hewitson
Lindon	c	CM	8	(801) 785-5043	Jeff Acerson	Ott Dameron	...	Kristen Colson	...	...	Don Peterson
Logan	c	MC	42	(435) 716-9043	Douglas Thompson	...	Lois Price	...	Mark Meaker	Richard Hendricks	Mark Nielsen
Manila	t	CM	..	(435) 784-3143	Chuck Dickison	...	Judy Archibald	...	...	...	Jerry Muir
Mapleton	c	MC	5	(801) 489-5655	Dean Allan	Robert Bradshaw	Debbie Walser	...	...	Mike Roberts	M. Bird
Midvale *	c	MC	27	(801) 567-7200	JoAnn Seghini	Kane Loader	...	...	Stephen Higgs	...	...
Moab	c	CM	4	(435) 259-5121	David Sakrison	Donna Metzler	Rachel Ellison	...	...	Mike Navarre	Brent Williams
Monticello	c	CM	1	(435) 587-2271	C Pehrson	C. Schafer	Rita Walker	...	...	Kent Adair	Nathan Langston
Murray	c	MC	34	(801) 264-2656	Daniel Snarr	Jan Wells	Carol Heales	Donald Whetzel	Gilbert Rodriguez	Peter Fondaco	Douglas Hill
Nephi	c	MC	4	(435) 623-0822	Chad Brough	J. McKnight	...	R. Painter	...	Chad Bowles	Edwin Park
North Ogden	c	MC	15	(801) 782-7211	...	Richard Nelson	S A. Spendlove	Terri Marsh	Lynn Froerer	Polo Afuvai	Melvin Blanchard
North Salt Lake	c	MC	8	(801) 936-3877	Kay Briggs	Collin Wood	LaRae Dillingham	Brian Passey	...	Steve Harder	Rod Wood
Ogden City *	c	MC	77	(801) 629-8730	Matthew Godfrey	John Patterson	Cindi Mansell	A. Arrington	Michael Mathieu	Jon Greiner	...
Orem *	c	CM	84	(801) 229-7035	Jerry Washburn	James Reams	...	...	Scott Gurney	...	Bruce Chesnut
Panquitch	c	CM	1	(435) 676-8585	Janet Oldham	Allen Henrie	Cindy Johnson	...	...	...	Dave Owens
Park City	c	MC	7	(435) 615-5241	...	Thomas Bakaly	...	...	...	Lloyd Evans	Jerry Gibbs
Payson	c	CM	12	(801) 465-5200	Bernall Evans	Gary Hall	Cheryl Hobbs	Jeanette Curtis	Scott Spencer	Franklyn Rowland	...
Pleasant Grove	c	MC	23	(801) 785-5045	Lloyd Ash	...	Charmaine Childs	K. Driggs	Mark Hales	...	Frank Mills
Pleasant View	c	MC	5	(801) 782-8529	...	...	...	...	...	...	...
Price	c	MC	8	(435) 637-5010	Joe Piccolo	...	Joanne Lessar	Pat Larsen	Kent Boyack	Aleck Shilaos	Gary Sonntag
Providence	c	MC	4	(435) 752-9441	Alma Leonhardt	Brent Speth	Peggy Giles	...	...	...	Leroy Barnes
Provo	c	MC	105	(801) 852-6000	Lewis Billings	Wayne Parker	Marilyn Perry	George Karlsven	Scott Alvord	...	Merril Bingham
Richfield	c	CM	6	(435) 896-6439	...	Renald Farnsworth	Michele Jolley	Michael Langston	...	...	...
Riverdale *	c	MC	7	(801) 394-5541	J. Bruce Burrows	Larry Hansen	Marilyn Hansen	Lynn Fortie	Doug Illum	Dave Hansen	Lynn Moulding
Riverton	c	MC	25	(801) 254-0704	R. Mont Evans	...	Stacie Olson	...	...	...	Culas Hutchinson
Roosevelt	c	MC	4	(435) 722-5001	Dennis Jenkins	Dallas Hancock	Carolyn Wilcken	Justin Johnson	Kenny McDonald	Rick Harrison	Roger Eschler
Roy *	c	CM	32	(801) 774-1000	Joe Ritchie	Christopher Davis	...	...	Jon Ritchie	Greg Whinham	Mike Mansfield
Salem	c	MC	4	(801) 423-2770	...	...	...	...	...	...	...
Salina *	c	MC	2	(435) 529-7304	Jim Reynolds	...	Sherri Westbrook	...	J. R. Carter	Greg Harwood	Jim Casto
Salt Lake City	c	MC	181	(801) 535-7704	Ross Anderson	...	...	Gordon Hoskins	Charles Querry	Charles Dinse	Richard Graham
Sandy City	c	MC	88	(801) 568-7100	Thomas Dolan	Byron Jorgenson	Dianne Aubrey	...	Donald Chase	Stephen Chapman	Rick Smith
Santa Clara *	c	CM	4	(435) 673-6712	Rick Rosenberg	Matthew Brower	...	Wally Ritchie	...	...	Jack Taylor
Santaquin	c	MC	4	(801) 754-3211	...	Stefan Chatwin	...	...	...	...	...
Saratoga Springs	c	CM	1	(801) 766-9793	Timothy Parker	Kenneth Leetham	Lori Yates	...	Dave Vickers	...	George Leatham
Smithfield	c	MC	7	(435) 563-6226	Archy Winn	James Gass	Connie Gittins	...	Jay Downs	Johnny McCoy	Doug Petersen
South Jordan	c	MC	29	(801) 254-3743	William Money	Ricky Horst	Mary Ann Dean	...	Chris Evans	...	Donald Bruey
South Ogden *	c	CM	14	(801) 622-2700	George Garwood	J. Darrington	Dana Pollard	Steve Liebersbach	Brian Minster	...	Paul Tippets
South Salt Lake	c	MC	22	(801) 483-6000	Wes Losser	...	Dawn Deakin	Gail Carlson	Steven Foote	Theresa Garner	Kyle Kingsbury

Directory 1/9 continued **OFFICIALS IN U.S. MUNICIPALITIES 2,500 AND OVER IN POPULATION**

Jurisdiction	Type	Form of government	2000 Population (000)	Main telephone number	Chief elected official	Appointed administrator	Clerk of the governing board	Chief financial officer	Fire chief	Police chief	Public works director
UTAH continued											
South Weber	c	MC	4	(801) 479-3177	...	Matthew Dixon	...	...	...	...	...
Spanish Fork	c	CM	20	(801) 798-5000	Dale Barney	David Oyler	...	Kent Clark	Clyde Johnson	...	Richard Heap
Springdale	t	CM	..	(435) 772-3434	Bruce VanderWerff	Richard Wixom	Fay Cope	Lynn Smith	...	Kurt Wright	Dale Harris
Springville *	c	MC	20	(801) 489-2700	Gene Mangum	Troy Fitzgerald	Venla Gubler	David Allen	Phil Whitney	Scott Finlayson	Brad Stapley
St. George	c	MC	49	(435) 634-5800	Dan McArthur	Gary Esplin	Gay Cragun	Phil Peterson	Robert Stoker	...	Larry Bulloch
Sunset	c	MC	5	(801) 825-1628	Janice Galbraith	...	Susan Hale	...	Neil Coker	Ken Eborn	Mickey Hennessee
Syracuse *	c	MC	9	(801) 825-1477	Fred Panucci	J. Moyes	Cassie Brown	Lamar Holt	Craig Cottrell	Brian Wallace	Michael Waite
Taylorsville	c	MC	57	(801) 963-5400	Janice Auger	John Morgan	Virginia Loader	Gerry Orr	...	...	...
Tooele	c	MC	22	(435) 882-0110	Charlie Roberts	...	Patrick Dunlavy	Sam Woodruff	...	...	Gerald Webster
Tremonton	c	MC	5	(435) 257-2625	Max Weese	Richard Woodworth	Darlene Hess	...	Blair Westergard	S. Hodges	Paul Fulgham
Vernal	c	CM	7	(435) 789-2255	William Kremin	Kenneth Bassett	...	Harley Hales	Dennis Paulson	Michael Hamner	...
Washington	c	CM	8	(435) 628-1666	...	Roger Carter	...	...	Charles Tandy	...	...
Washington Terrace *	c	MC	8	(801) 393-8681	...	Mark Christensen	Marci Heil	Shari Garrett	Brett Felter	...	Richard Taylor
West Bountiful	c	MC	4	(801) 292-4486	James Behunin	Wendell Wild	Beverly Haslam	Brian Passey	...	Randy Lloyd	Blake Anderson
West Jordan	c	CM	68	(801) 569-5000	...	Gary Luebbers	Melanie Briggs	David Hales	Jacob Nielson	Ken McGuire	...
West Point	c	CM	6	(801) 776-0971	John Petroff	Richard Davis	Joann Stoddard	...	Roger Bodily	Bud Cox	Paul Rochelle
West Valley City	c	CM	108	(801) 966-3600	Dennis Nordfelt	Wayne Pyle	Sheri McKendrick	James Welch	Vannie Summers	Thayle Nielsen	Russell Willardson
Woods Cross	c	CM	6	(801) 292-4421	Jerry Larrabee	Gary Uresk	Alan Low	...	...	Paul Howard	Scott Anderson
VERMONT											
Barre	c	CM	9	(802) 476-0240	Harry Monti	John Craig	Eugene Stratton	...	Peter John	Trevor Whipple	Reginald Abare
Barre	t	CM	7	(802) 479-9331	...	Carl Rogers	Donna Kelty	...	...	Michael Stevens	...
Barton *	t	TM	2	(802) 525-6222	Robert Croteau	...	...	...	...	...	...
Bellows Falls	v	CM	3	(802) 463-3964	K. Hennesey	John Schempf	Ann Dibernardo	...	William Weston	Frederick Gardy	...
Bennington	t	CM	15	(802) 442-1037	Sharyn Brush	Stuart Hurd	Timothy Corcoran	David Essaff	Phil Frasier	Richard Gauthier	...
Bethel *	t	CM	1	(802) 234-9340	Neal Fox	Delbert Cloud	Jean Burnham	...	Robert Dean	James Bennett	...
Brandon	t	CM	3	(802) 247-3635	Lynn Saunders	...	William Dick	Denise Mahoney	...	...	...
Brattleboro	t	CM	12	(802) 254-4541	Stephen Steidle	Barbara Sondag	Annette Cappy	Barbara Vinci	David Emery	John Martin	Stephen Barrett
Bristol	t	CM	3	(802) 453-2410	...	...	...	...	...	...	...
Bristol	v	CM	1	(802) 453-2410	...	...	...	...	...	...	...
Burlington	c	MC	38	(802) 865-7145	Peter Clavelle	...	JoAnne LaMarche	...	...	Alana Ennis	Steven Goodkind
Castleton	t	CM	4	(800) 468-5319	Patrick Eagan	Beverly Davidson	Ellen La Fleche	Melanie Combs	C. Mulholland	Douglas Norton	Clarence Decker
Cavendish	t	CM	1	(802) 226-7291	Sandra Stearns	Richard Svec	...	...	...	...	...
Charlotte	t	TM	3	(802) 425-3071	Ellie Russell	Gloria Warden	Mary Mead	...	Chris Davis	...	...
Chester	t	TM	3	(802) 875-2173	...	Susan Spaulding	...	...	...	...	...
Colchester *	t	CM	16	(802) 264-5500	...	Albin Voegele	Karen Richard	Joan Boehm	...	Charles Kirker	Bryan Osborne
Derby	t	TM	4	(802) 766-4906	Thomas Bailey	...	Elizabeth Lahar	...	Craig Ellam	Bruce Warner	William Duma
Dorset	t	CM	2	(802) 362-4571	William Mahlmann	Peter Webster	Denise Veillette	...	...	...	...
Essex	t	TM	18	(802) 878-1341	...	Patrick Scheidel	Cheryl Moomey	Douglas Fisher	Howard Rice	Leo Nadeau	Dennis Lutz
Essex Junction *	v	CM	8	(802) 878-6944	...	...	Susan Hill	Lauren Morrisseau	Chris Gaboriault	...	James Jutras
Fair Haven	t	CM	2	(802) 265-3010	John Lulck	...	Suzanne Dechame	...	Donald Howard	Raymond Viger	John Eaton
Hardwick	t	TM	3	(802) 472-6120	...	Daniel Hill	...	...	...	James Dziobek	Alan May
Hartford	t	CM	10	(802) 295-9353	Leonard Berliner	Hunter Rieseberg	Mary Hill	William Hall	Mark Miller	...	Richard Menge
Hartland	t	TM	3	(802) 436-2444	Thomas White	Robert Stacey	Clyde Jenne	Carolyn Trombly	Mark Cote	Anthony Leonard	...
Hinesburg *	t	TM	4	(802) 482-2096	Robert Bast	Jeanne Wilson	Melissa Ross	...	...	...	...
Jericho	t	TM	5	(802) 899-4936	...	...	...	...	...	...	...
Johnson	t	TM	3	(802) 635-2611	...	...	...	...	...	...	...
Killington	t	CM	..	(802) 422-3241	...	David Lewis	...	...	...	...	...
Ludlow	t	CM	2	(802) 228-2841	Keith Arlund	...	Nettie Gruber	...	...	...	David Norton
Lyndon	t	TM	5	(802) 626-5785	...	...	...	...	...	...	...
Manchester	t	CM	4	(802) 362-1313	Ivan Beattie	...	Linda Spence	Ruth Woodard	...	Manfred Wessner	...
Middlebury	t	CM	8	(802) 388-8107	John Tenny	William Finger	Ann Webster	...	Richard Cole	Thomas Hanley	Daniel Werner
Milton	t	TM	9	(802) 893-6655	Kenneth Nolan	Sanford Miller	John Cushing	...	Donald Turner	Brett Van Noordt	...
Montpelier	c	CM	8	(802) 223-9502	Charles Karparis	William Fraser	Charlotte Hoyt	Michael Welch	Norman Lewis	Douglas Hoyt	Stephen Gray
Morristown	t	TM	5	(802) 888-5147	Shaun Bryer	David Crawford	Mary Ann Wilson	Carol Bradley	Wallace Reeve	Richard Keith	Robert Melfy
Newport	c	CM	5	(802) 334-5136	Richard Baraw	John Ward	...	...	Robert George	Paul Duquette	Thomas Bernier
North Troy	v	CM	..	(802) 988-4700	...	...	Jim Wentworth	...	...	...	...
Northfield	t	CM	3	(802) 485-6121	Donald Wallace	Nanci Allard	Kimberly Pombar	...	...	Jeffrey Shaw	William Lyon
Norwich	t	CM	3	(802) 649-0127	Alison May	Stephen Soares	Bonnie Munday	Roberta Robinson	...	...	...
Pittsford	t	CM	3	(802) 483-6500	Margaret Flory	...	Gordon Delong	...	Tom Hooker	Joseph Warfle	Shawn Erickson
Poultney	t	CM	3	(802) 287-9751	...	...	...	...	...	...	...
Poultney	v	CM	1	(802) 287-4003	...	...	...	...	...	...	...
Pownal	t	TM	3	(802) 823-7757	...	...	...	...	...	...	...
Randolph	t	CM	4	(802) 728-5433	...	Peter Butterfield	Joyce Mazzucco	...	...	James Krakowiecki	Joseph Voci
Richmond	t	TM	4	(802) 434-5170	...	Ronald Rodjenski	Velma Ploufee	...	...	William Miller	Kendall Chamberlin
Rockingham	t	CM	5	(802) 463-3964	Lamont Barnett	John Schempf	Doreen Aldrich	Deane Haskell	Denis Jeffrey	...	Everett Hammond
Rutland	c	MC	17	(802) 773-1800	Jeffrey Wennberg	...	Rosemary Finley	...	Craig Shelly	Anthony Bossi	Warren Conner
Rutland	t	TM	4	(802) 773-2528	...	...	Marie Hyjek	...	Joseph Denardo	Brian Abbey	...
Shaftsbury *	t	TM	3	(802) 442-4043	...	Aaron Chrostowsky	Judith Stratton	...	Joe Vadakin	...	Ronald Daniels
Shelburne	t	CM	6	(802) 985-5111	Chris Neme	Paul Bohne	Colleen Haag	Peter Frankenburg	Craig Wooster	James Warden	Bernie Gagnon
South Burlington	c	CM	15	(802) 846-4105	James Condos	Charles Hafter	Donna Kinville	...	Douglas Brent	Lealand Graham	Bruce Hoar
Springfield	t	CM	9	(802) 885-2104	John Follett	Robert Forquittes	Bonnie Reynolds	Jeffrey Mobus	...	Douglas Johnston	Harry Henderson
St. Albans	c	CM	7	(802) 524-1500	Peter Des Lauriers	...	Dianna Baraby	Jacques Bergeron	Gary Palmer	Gary Taylor	Allen Robtoy
St. Albans	t	CM	5	(802) 524-2415	...	...	...	...	Harold Cross	...	K. Barkyoumb
St. Johnsbury	t	CM	7	(802) 748-3926	...	Michael Welch	Sandra Grenier	...	Troy Ruggles	Richard Leighton	Larry Gadapee
Stowe	t	CM	4	(802) 253-7350	Richard Marron	Charles Safford	...	Karla Spaulding	Wendall Mansfield	Ken Kaplan	...
Swanton	t	TM	6	(802) 868-4421	Mark Hojaboom	Richard Thompson	Doris Raleigh	...	...	...	...
Swanton	v	CM	2	(802) 868-3397	Neal Speer	George Lague	Christine Davis	...	Peter Prouty	Michael McCarthy	Michael Menard
Troy	t	TM	1	(802) 988-2663	...	...	...	...	...	...	...
Vergennes	c	CM	2	(802) 877-3637	Thelma Oxholm	Reynold Perry	Joan Devine	...	Ralph Jackman	Mike Lowe	Carroll O'Connor
Wallingford	t	TM	1	(802) 446-2336	...	Christine O'Gorman	...	...	...	...	...
Waterbury	t	CM	4	(802) 244-7033	Edward Steele	William Shepeluk	Donna Centonze	...	...	...	...
Weathersfield *	t	CM	2	(802) 674-2626	Henry Cobb	Laurence Melen	Flora Ann Dango	Christopher Adams	...	Richard Brown	Westley Hazeltine
West Rutland	t	TM	2	(802) 438-2263	Edward Gilman	...	Jayne Pratt	...	Joe Skaza	...	...
Westminster	t	CM	3	(802) 722-4255	William Noyes	Glenn Smith	Penny Muzzey	...	...	...	...
Williamstown	t	TM	3	(802) 433-6671	Linda Riddell	...	Deborah Palmer	...	Ed Eaton	...	Bernie Duff
Williston *	t	TM	7	(802) 878-0919	Virginia Lyons	Richard McGuire	Deborah Beckett	Susan Lamb	Kenneth Morton	James Dimmick	Neil Boyden
Wilmington	t	TM	2	(802) 464-8591	Frederick Skwirut	...	Susan Manton	Laurie Boyd	Troy Johnson	Joseph Szarejko	...
Windsor	t	CM	3	(802) 674-6786	...	...	...	...	...	...	...
Winhall	t	MC	..	(802) 297-2119	Randy Ameden	Dennis McCarthy	Elizabeth Jenks	...	Harold Coleman	Jeffery Whitesell	Randy Kimball
Winooski	c	CM	6	(802) 655-6410	C. Bissonnette	Joshua Handverger	...	...	David Bergeron	Steve McQueen	Steve Woodworth
Woodstock	t	TM	3	(802) 457-3456	...	Philip Swanson	Jerome Morgan	...	...	...	Glenn Frederick
Woodstock	v	CM	..	(802) 457-3456	...	...	...	...	...	Byron Kelly	...

Directory 1/9 continued — OFFICIALS IN U.S. MUNICIPALITIES 2,500 AND OVER IN POPULATION

Jurisdiction	Type	Form of govern- ment	2000 Popu- lation (000)	Main telephone number	Chief elected official	Appointed administrator	Clerk of the governing board	Chief financial officer	Fire chief	Police chief	Public works director
VIRGINIA											
Abingdon *	t	CM	7	(276) 628-3167	Lois Humphreys	Gregory Kelly	Cecile Rosenbaum	Mark Godbey	Joey Burke	Phillip Sullivan	Claude Vernon
Alexandria	c	CM	128	(703) 838-4696	William Euille	James Hartmann	J. Henderson	...	Thomas Hawkins	Charles Samarra	Richard Baier
Altavista *	t	CM	3	(434) 369-5001	James Burgess	J. Coggsdale	...	...	John Tucker	Thomas Neal	John Tomlin
Amherst	t	CM	2	(434) 946-7885	...	Jack Hobbs	...	...	...	...	...
Appalachia	t	CM	1	(276) 565-3900	Gary Bush	Bobby Dorton	...	...	Robert Anderson	Roy Munsey	Bobby Reynolds
Appomattox	t	MC	1	(434) 352-8268	Ronald Spiggle	David Garrett	Bobbie Mullins	...	Timothy Garrett	...	Jeff Elder
Ashland	t	CM	6	(804) 798-9219	Angela LaCombe	Charles Hartgrove	Carolyn Barnett	...	...	Frederic Pleasants	Michael Davis
Bedford	c	CM	6	(540) 587-6001	E. Messier	Charles Kolakowski	Teresa Hatcher	Rosemarie Jordan	Todd Stone	Milton Graham	Clarke Gibson
Berryville *	t	CM	2	(540) 955-1099	Richard Sponseller	Keith Dalton	Celeste Heath	...	...	Neal White	...
Big Stone Gap	t	CM	4	(276) 523-0115	William Cole	George Polly	Joyce Page	...	Billy Chandler	Larry Mohn	...
Blacksburg	t	CM	39	(540) 961-1100	Roger Hedgepeth	Marc Verniel	Donna Caldwell	Susan Kaiser	B. Bolte	William Brown	Kelly Mattingly
Blackstone	t	CM	3	(434) 292-7251	...	James Palmore	Joan Palmore	Charles Wells	...	Wayne Shields	John Lee
Bluefield	t	CM	5	(276) 322-4626	William King	Daryl Day	Patricia Douthat	...	James Hardy	Jack Asbury	...
Bowling Green	t	CM	..	(804) 633-6212	Frank Benser	...	Virginia Brooks	...	...	Robert Hall	Dan Curran
Bridgewater	t	CM	5	(540) 828-3390	Hallie Dinkel	Bob Holton	Carleen Loveless	Theodore Flory	...	Robert Hill	Jeffrey Riddleberger
Bristol	c	CM	17	(276) 645-7300	Paul Hurley	Paul Spangler	...	Steven Allen	Walt Ford	William Price	...
Broadway	t	CM	2	(540) 896-5152	...	Kyle O'Brien	Maria Kline	...	...	Jay Lantz	...
Brookneal	t	MC	1	(434) 376-3124	Phyllis Campbell	Joseph Williams	Beth Elder	...	...	Jim Hires	Mike Crews
Buena Vista *	c	CM	6	(540) 261-8600	James Jones	...	Janie Coffey	Timothy Dudley	Tommy Keiser	Lewis Plogger	Dewey Tyree
Cape Charles	t	CM	1	(757) 331-3259	Frank Lewis	Cela Burge	Jennie Moore	...	...	David Eder	Mike Thornes
Charlottesville	c	CM	45	(434) 970-3490	Virginia Daugherty	Gary O'Connell	Jeanne Cox	Aubrey Watts	Julian Taliaferro	Julian Rittenhouse	Judith Mueller
Chase City	t	CM	2	(434) 372-5136	A. Reid	Rickey Reese	Cynthia Gordon	...	Winthy Hatcher	J. Jordon	Stanley Duckworth
Chatham	t	CM	1	(434) 432-9515	L. Elton Pruitt	...	...	...	Landon Worsham	Floyd Poindexter	Robert Hanson
Chesapeake	c	CM	199	(757) 382-6151	William Ward	William Harrell	Dolores Moore	Nancy Tracy	R. Best	Richard Justice	Patricia Biegler
Chincoteague	t	CM	4	(757) 336-6519	...	...	...	...	...	...	...
Christiansburg *	t	CM	16	(540) 382-6128	Harold Linkous	Robert Terpenny	Michele Stipes	...	James Epperly	Mark Sisson	Wayne Nelson
Clarksville	t	CM	1	(434) 374-8177	Benjy Burnett	Melinda Moran	...	Tara Glover	Robert Wilkerson	...	Terry Hite
Clifton Forge	c	CM	4	(540) 863-2500	Daryl Rhodes	...	Nellie Friel	LeeAnna Tyler	...	Barry Balser	...
Coeburn	t	CM	1	(276) 395-3323	G. Wells	Loretta Mays	...	...	Cliff Hawkins	Willie Stout	Danny Jordan
Colonial Beach	t	CM	3	(804) 224-7181	George Bone	John Barkley	Barbara Goff	Mary Bowen	...	Courtlandt Turner	...
Colonial Heights	c	CM	16	(804) 520-9265	J. Kollman	Richard Anzolut	Kimberly Rollinson	William Johnson	Allan Moore	Richard Schurman	Charles Loving
Covington *	c	CM	6	(540) 965-6300	Harrison Scott	Claire Collins	Edith Wood	Linda Brown	Wes Walker	J. Broughman	Jack Munsey
Crewe	t	CM	2	(434) 645-9453	Wilfred Wilson	William Walker	...	...	...	William Abel	Ralph Shelton
Culpeper	t	CM	9	(540) 829-8250	Pranas Rimeikis	...	Donna Foster	...	...	Daniel Boring	Robert Thornhill
Danville	c	CM	48	(434) 799-5240	John Hamlin	Jerry Gwaltney	Annette Crane	Barbara Dameron	B. Lewis	Phillip Broadfoot	R. Drazenovich
Dublin	t	CM	2	(540) 674-4731	Benny Skeens	William Parker	...	...	...	Jay Vest	Garnett Lyons
Dumfries *	t	CM	4	(703) 221-3400	Fred Yohey	David Whitlow	Donna Johnson	...	...	Calvin Johnson	Greg Tkac
Elkton	t	CM	2	(540) 298-1951	...	...	Richard Carey	...	...	Richard Pullen	Jarrod Shifflett
Emporia	c	CM	5	(434) 634-3332	Samuel Adams	...	Andrea Hines	Ann Magee	Warren Rawlings	Mallory Daughtry	Linwood Pope
Fairfax	c	CM	21	(703) 293-7120	Robert Lederer	Robert Sisson	...	...	...	Richard Rappoport	John Veneziano
Falls Church	c	CM	10	(703) 248-5000	Daniel Gardner	F. Shields	Kathleen Buschow	...	...	Robert Murray	Moe Wadda
Farmville	t	CM	6	(434) 392-5686	Sydnor Newman	Gerald Spates	Lisa Hricko	...	...	Stuart Dunnavant	Robin Atkins
Franklin	c	CM	8	(757) 562-8550	...	Rowland Taylor	...	...	Vincent Holt	Steven Wills	Jamie Weist
Fredericksburg *	c	CM	19	(540) 372-1010	Thomas Tomzak	Phillip Rodenberg	Mary Smith	Clarence Robinson	Edwin Allen	David Nye	P. Fawcett
Front Royal *	t	CM	13	(540) 635-8007	James Eastham	James Graham	Jennifer Berry	Kim Gilkey-Breeden	...	...	George Shadman
Galax *	c	CM	6	(276) 236-5773	C Mitchell	Keith Holland	...	Nikki Shank	David Hankley	Richard Clark	Charles Joyce
Gate City	t	CM	2	(276) 386-3831	...	...	...	...	...	...	...
Glasgow	t	CM	1	(540) 258-2246	Sam Blackburn	...	...	...	Richard Spangler	Damon Propst	Armond Falgoust
Gordonsville	t	MC	1	(540) 832-2233	Robert Coiner	Sabrina Martyn	Ethel Hutchinson	...	...	Christopher Spare	Vincent Seal
Grundy	t	CM	1	(276) 935-2551	John Fleenor	Chuck Crabtree	...	...	Donnie Compton	Barney Stiltner	...
Hampton	c	CM	146	(757) 727-8311	Mamie Locke	Jesse Wallace	Diana Hughes	Karl Daughtrey	Robert Green	Thomas Townsend	Edward Henifin
Harrisonburg *	c	CM	40	(540) 432-8920	Rodney Eagle	Kurt Hodgen	Yvonne Ryan	Lester Seal	Larry Shifflett	Donald Harper	James Baker
Haymarket	t	CM	..	(703) 753-2600	...	Mason Swearingen	Jennifer Preli	James Naradzay	...	...	...
Herndon	t	CM	21	(703) 787-7368	Michael O'Reilly	Arthur Anselene	Victoria Wellershaus	Mary Tuohy	...	Toussaint Summers	Robert Boxer
Hillsville *	t	CM	2	(276) 728-2128	Randall Gravley	Larry South	Vickie Yonce	...	...	Steven Williams	Terry Cole
Hopewell	c	CM	22	(804) 541-2245	James Patterson	Edwin Daley	Ann Romano	Elesteen Hager	Steve Brown	Rex Marks	Phillip Elliott
Kilmarnock	t	CM	1	(804) 435-1552	...	Lara Burleson	...	...	...	...	...
Lebanon	t	CM	3	(276) 889-7200	...	...	...	...	...	...	...
Leesburg	t	CM	28	(703) 777-2420	Kristen Umstattd	...	Judith Ahalt	Norman Butts	...	Joseph Price	Thomas Mason
Lexington *	c	CM	6	(540) 462-3700	John Knapp	T. Ellestad	Sharon Edwards	Curtis Higgins	Dave Clark	Steve Crowder	David Woody
Louisa	t	CM	1	(540) 967-1400	Charles Rosson	Brian Marks	Jessica Ellis	...	...	Stan Batten	...
Lovettsville *	t	CM	..	(540) 822-5788	Elaine Walker	Keith Markel	Judy Kromholz	Lance Gladstone	...	...	...
Luray	t	CM	4	(540) 743-5511	Ralph Dean	...	...	...	...	Page Campbell	Lynn Mathews
Lynchburg *	c	CM	65	(434) 455-3990	Joan Foster	L. Payne	Patricia Kost	Donna Witt	Steven Ferguson	Charles Bennett	David Owen
Manassas	c	CM	35	(703) 257-8200	...	Lawrence Hughes	Kimberly Allen	Patricia Weiler	...	John Skinner	Michael Moon
Manassas Park	c	CM	10	(703) 335-8800	Frank Jones	Mercury Payton	Lana Conner	Gary Fields	John O'Neal	John Evans	Kathleen Gammell
Marion	t	CM	6	(276) 783-4113	...	John Clark	Dixie Sheets	...	...	Michael Roberts	Roy Eurke
Martinsville *	c	CM	15	(276) 403-5000	Kimble Reynolds	...	...	...	Clarence Monday	Michael Rogers	Leon Towarnicki
Middleburg	t	CM	..	(540) 687-5152	Betsy Davis	Jerry Schiro	...	...	...	Steven Webber	...
Narrows	t	CM	2	(540) 726-2423	...	...	...	...	...	Thomas Gautier	...
New Market	t	CM	1	(540) 740-3432	Thomas Constable	Evan Vass	Deborah Ritchie	...	...	Steven Crisman	Orville Ryman
Newport News	c	CM	180	(757) 926-8000	Joe Frank	Randy Hildebrandt	Mabel Washington	LaVerne Lovett	Kenneth Jones	James Fox	H. Fowler
Norfolk	c	CM	234	(757) 664-4486	Paul Fraim	Regina Williams	Robert Daughtrey	Steven de Mik	Paul Savage	Bruce Marquis	John Keifer
Norton	c	CM	3	(276) 679-1160	B. Raines	Ernest Ward	Mary Brown	Teresa Belcher	David Mullins	Samuel Mongle	Richard Hurt
Orange *	t	CM	4	(540) 672-5005	Henry Carter	Cole Hendrix	Wendy Chewning	Lydia Hadley	...	James Fenwick	Jeffrey Dodson
Pearisburg	t	CM	2	(540) 921-0340	Barabara Stafford	Kenneth Vittum	Judy Harrell	...	Richard Stump	Jackie Marlin	Rickie Tawney
Petersburg *	c	CM	33	(804) 733-2324	Annie Mickens	B. Canada	Nykesha Jackson	Thomas Blount	Thomas Hairston	Lee Crowell	Michael Briddell
Poquoson *	c	CM	11	(757) 868-3000	Gordon Helsel	Charles Burgess	...	Lisa Dessoffy	Robert Holloway	Clifford Bowen	J. Montgomery
Portsmouth	c	CM	100	(757) 393-8000	James Holley	Kenneth Chandler	Debra White	...	...	Frank Kitzerow	James Spacek
Pulaski *	t	CM	9	(540) 994-8696	Charles Wade	John Hawley	Patricia Cruise	...	Bill Webb	Gary Roche	...
Purcellville	t	MC	3	(540) 338-7421	William Durhan	Robert Lohr	Richmond Coburn	...	...	...	Karin McKnight
Radford	c	CM	15	(540) 731-3603	Thomas Starnes	Anthony Cox	...	...	Robert Simpkins	Gary Harmon	Jimmy Dean
Richlands *	t	CM	4	(276) 964-2566	Kenneth Wysor	Timothy Taylor	Elva Vandyke	...	William Vance	William Puckett	Jim Taylor
Richmond	c	MC	197	(804) 646-7000	Rudolph McCollum	Harry Black	Edna Keys-Chavis	Andrew Rountree	Robert Creecy	Andre Parker	Jeffrey Powell
Roanoke	c	CM	94	(540) 853-2231	Ralph Smith	Darlene Burcham	Mary Parker	Jesse Hall	...	Atlas Gaskins	Robert Bengtson
Rocky Mount	t	CM	4	(540) 483-7660	Mark Newbill	Clifton Ervin	Patricia Hooke	Linda Woody	...	R Jenkins	Cecil Mason
Round Hill *	t	MC	..	(540) 338-7878	Francis Etro	Bradley Polk	...	...	...	...	Alan Wolverton
Rural Retreat	t	MC	1	(276) 686-4221	Timothy Litz	Raymond Matney	...	...	David Evans	Robert Lewis	...
Salem *	c	CM	24	(540) 375-3060	Howard Packett	Forest Jones	Krystal Coleman	Frank Turk	Chester Counts	James Bryant	Melvin Doughty
Scottsville	t	MC	..	(434) 286-9267	...	Clark Draper	Amy Moyer	...	...	...	...

Directory 1/9 continued — OFFICIALS IN U.S. MUNICIPALITIES 2,500 AND OVER IN POPULATION

Jurisdiction	Type	Form of govern-ment	2000 Popu-lation (000)	Main telephone number	Chief elected official	Appointed administrator	Clerk of the governing board	Chief financial officer	Fire chief	Police chief	Public works director
VIRGINIA continued											
Shenandoah	t	CM	1	(540) 652-8164	Clinton Lucas	Larry Dovel	. . .	Cindy Breeden	. . .	Peter Monteleone	Mark Armentrout
Smithfield *	t	CM	6	(757) 365-4200	James Chapman	Peter Stephenson	Sharon Thomas	. . .	Mickie Stallings	Mark Marshall	. . .
South Boston *	t	CM	8	(434) 575-4200	Carroll Thackston	Ted Daniel	Jane Jones	Lester Scott	Steve Phillips	James Binner	Alan Auld
South Hill *	t	CM	4	(434) 447-3191	Earl Horne	. . .	Anna Cratch	Heidi Porter	Rosser Wells	Norman Hudson	Bill Wilson
Staunton	c	CM	23	(540) 332-3800	Lacy King	Stephen Owen	Deborah Sutton	Jeanne Colvin	Michael Myers	James Williams	Thomas Sliwoski
Strasburg	t	CM	4	(540) 465-9197	Harry Applegate	Kevin Fauber	Amy Keller	Mary Price	. . .	Marshall Robinson	John Rhodes
Suffolk *	c	CM	63	(757) 923-2070	Curtis Milteer	James Vacalis	Henry Murden	M. Ledford	. . .	Jimmy Wilson	Eric Nielsen
Tappahannock	t	CM	2	(804) 443-3336	Roy Gladding	George Belfield	Patsy Bryant	. . .	. . .	James Barrett	Kenneth Gillis
Tazewell	t	CM	4	(276) 988-2501	Charles Green	Jerry Wood	. . .	. . .	A. Buchanan	Roy Brewster	Danny Whitt
Victoria	t	CM	1	(434) 696-2343	Carol Watson	. . .	Diane Harding	. . .	. . .	James Dayton	M Carl Ashworth
Vienna	t	CM	14	(703) 255-6300	M. Seeman	John Schoeberlein	Carol Orndorff	Philip Grant	. . .	. . .	Dennis King
Vinton	t	CM	7	(540) 983-0607	Bradley Grose	Kevin Boggess	Darleen Bailey	Barry Thompson	. . .	Herbert Cooley	Michael Kennedy
Virginia Beach	c	CM	425	(757) 427-8374	Meyera Oberndorf	James Spore	Ruth Smith	Patricia Phillips	Gregory Cade	Alfred Jacocks	Edgar Block
Warrenton *	t	CM	6	(540) 347-1101	George Fitch	Kenneth McLawhon	Evelyn Weimer	Richard Heartley	. . .	. . .	Edward Tucker
Waynesboro	c	CM	19	(540) 942-6719	Thomas Reynolds	Douglas Walker	Bonnie Hamby	S. Hash-Rodgers	Charles Scott	Douglas Davis	Brian McReynolds
West Point *	t	MC	2	(804) 843-3330	Jame Hudson	Trenton Funkhouser	Karen Barrow	. . .	. . .	William Hodges	Walter Feurer
Williamsburg *	c	CM	11	(757) 220-6100	Jeanne Zeidler	Jackson Tuttle	Shelia Crist	Philip Serra	T Weiler	James Yost	Daniel Clayton
Winchester	c	CM	23	(540) 667-1815	Elizabeth Minor	J. Godfrey	Leticia Chavez	Mary Blowe	Frank Wright	Eric Varnau	. . .
Windsor	t	CM	. .	(757) 242-4288	Wesley Garris	Kurt Falkenstein	Patricia Mann	. . .	William Copeland	. . .	. . .
Wise	t	CM	3	(276) 328-6013	Clifton Carson	Beverly Owens	. . .	. . .	Conley Holbrook	Anthony Bates	Gregory Jefferson
Woodstock	t	CM	3	(540) 459-3621	William Moyers	Larry Bradford	Dorothy Hutchinson	. . .	Warren Schennum	Jerry Miller	James Didawick
Wytheville *	t	CM	7	(276) 223-3321	Trenton Crewe	Curtis Sutherland	Sharon Hackler	. . .	James Davidson	Harry Ayers	Dennis Hackler
WASHINGTON											
Aberdeen	c	MC	16	(360) 533-4100	Chuck Gurrad	. . .	. . .	Fred Thurman	Steve Mitchell	Robert Maxfield	Jim Robertson
Airway Heights	c	MC	4	(509) 244-5578	Dale Perry	. . .	. . .	. . .	John Schoen	Lee Bennett	. . .
Anacortes	c	MC	14	(360) 299-1970	Dean Maxwell	. . .	. . .	. . .	Richard Curtis	Michael King	Robert Hyde
Arlington	c	MC	11	(360) 403-3421	Margaret Larson	Allen Johnson	. . .	Kathy Peterson	Jim Rankin	John Gray	Len Olive
Auburn	c	MC	40	(253) 288-3000	Peter Lewis	. . .	Danielle Daskam	Shelley Coleman	Robert Johnson	James Kelly	Dennis Dowdy
Bainbridge Island	c	MC	20	(206) 842-2545	Darlene Kordonowy	Mary Jo Briggs	Susan Kasper	Elray Konkel	. . .	Matt Haney	Randy Witt
Battle Ground *	c	MC	9	(360) 342-5000	John Idsinga	Dennis Osborn	Claire Lider	. . .	. . .	James McDaniel	Rob Charles
Bellevue	c	CM	109	(425) 452-6800	Connie Marshall	Steven Sarkozy	Myrna Basich	. . .	Mario Trevino	James Montgomery	Lloyd Warren
Bellingham	c	MC	67	(360) 676-6960	Mark Asmundson	. . .	. . .	Therese Holm	Mike Leigh	Randall Carroll	Richard McKinley
Black Diamond	c	MC	3	(360) 886-2560	. . .	Gwendolyn Voelpel	. . .	Mayene Miller	Greg Smith	Rick Luther	Dan Dal Santo
Blaine	c	CM	3	(360) 332-8311	John Liebert	Gary Tomsic	Sheri Sanchez	Meredith Riley	Tom Fields	Mike Haslip	Steve Banham
Bonney Lake *	c	MC	9	(253) 862-8602	Neil Johnson	Don Morrison	Harwood Edvalson	. . .	. . .	Mike Mitchell	Dan Grigsby
Bothell	c	CM	30	(425) 489-3437	Mark Lamb	Robert Stowe	Jo Anne Trudel	Tami Schackman	. . .	Forrest Conover	Doug Jacobson
Bremerton	c	MC	37	(360) 473-5846	Cary Bozeman	. . .	Paula Johnston	. . .	Allison Duke	Robert Forbes	Phil Williams
Brier	c	MC	6	(425) 775-5440	Gary Starks	. . .	. . .	. . .	. . .	Don Lane	. . .
Buckley	c	MC	4	(360) 829-1960	John Blanusa	Dave Schmidt	Alice Money	Sheila Bazzar	Alan Predmore	Art McGehee	P. Brendel
Burien *	c	CM	31	(206) 241-4647	Joan McGilton	Michael Martin	. . .	Scott Hardin	. . .	. . .	Stephen Clark
Burlington	c	MC	6	(360) 755-0531	Roger Tjeerdsma	Jon Aarstad	Judith Sheahan	Richard Patrick	Mark Anderson	Gerald Bowers	. . .
Camas	c	MC	12	(360) 834-6864	Paul Dennis	Lloyd Halverson	. . .	Joan Durgin	Leo Leon	Donald Chaney	Monte Brachmann
Carnation	c	CM	1	(425) 333-4192	Yvonne Funderburg	Candice Bock	Mary Otness	. . .	. . .	Glenn Merryman	James Dorsey
Castle Rock	c	MC	2	(360) 274-8181	Barbara Larsen	. . .	Ryana Covington	. . .	Eric Koreis	Robert Heuer	David Vorse
Centralia *	c	CM	14	(360) 330-7670	Timothy Browning	J. D. Fouts	Deena Bilodeau	Bradley Ford	Jim Walkowski	Robert Berg	Richard Southworth
Chehalis	c	CM	7	(360) 748-6664	Anthony Ketchum	Merlin MacReynold	Judy Schave	Jim Larson	Bill Nacht	. . .	Tim Grochowski
Chelan	c	MC	3	(509) 682-4037	W Mitchell Atkinson	. . .	Linda Allison-Liles	Heidi Kollmeyer	. . .	Edwin Bush	Dwane Van Epps
Cheney	c	MC	8	(509) 498-9203	Amy Sooy	. . .	. . .	. . .	John Montague	Jeff Sale	Donald Mac Donald
Clarkston	c	CO	7	(509) 758-5541	Donna Engle	. . .	Vickie Storey	. . .	Steven Cooper	Joel Hastings	James Martin
Cle Elum	c	CM	1	(509) 674-2262	Gary Berndt	Lars Gare	DeLiela Bannister	. . .	. . .	Brennen Milloy	Jim Leonhard
Clyde Hill *	c	MC	2	(425) 453-7800	George Martin	Mitchell Wasserman	. . .	John Gagan	. . .	William Archer	Allan Newbill
Colfax	c	MC	2	(509) 397-3861	Norma Becker	Emily Adams	Carol Larson	. . .	Carl Thompson	Barney Buckley	. . .
College Place	c	MC	7	(509) 529-1200	Edward Ammon	. . .	. . .	Robert Zielfelder	Patrick Shipp	Dennis Lepiane	Paul Hartwig
Colville	c	MC	4	(509) 684-5094	Duane Scott	. . .	Holly Pannell	. . .	Rick Naff	D. Meshishnek	Harlan Elsasser
Connell	c	MC	2	(509) 234-2701	Gary Walton	Arthur Tackett	Joan Eckman	. . .	. . .	Rick Rochleau	Patrick Munyan
Covington *	c	CM	13	(253) 638-1110	Margaret Harto	Derek Matheson	Jacqueline Cronk	Rob Hendrickson	. . .	Kevin Klason	David Delph
Davenport *	c	MC	1	(509) 725-4352	Charles Johnston	. . .	. . .	. . .	Eugene Johnson	. . .	Fred Bell
Dayton	c	MC	2	(509) 382-2361	William Graham	Sheila McCaw	. . .	. . .	Robert Allbee	. . .	Jim Costello
Des Moines	c	CM	29	(206) 878-4595	Robert Sheckler	Anthony Piasecki	Denis Staab	Paula Henderson	Al Church	Roger Baker	Grant Fredricks
Dupont	c	MC	2	(253) 964-8121	Steve Young	William McDonald	. . .	. . .	Chris Jensen	Mike Pohl	. . .
East Wenatchee	c	MC	5	(509) 884-9515	Steven Lacy	. . .	Dana Barnard	. . .	. . .	John Harrison	Robert Goodman
Edgewood	c	CM	9	(253) 952-3299	. . .	Henry Lawrence	. . .	. . .	. . .	Robert Santoro	. . .
Edmonds	c	MC	39	(425) 775-2525	Barbara Fahey	. . .	Sandra Chase	Peggy Hetzler	Tom Tomberg	Robin Hickok	Noel Miller
Ellensburg	c	CM	15	(509) 962-7204	Obie O'Brien	Theodore Barkley	Coreen Reno	Ade' Ariwoola	Richard Elliott	Dale Miller	John Akers
Elma	t	MC	3	(360) 482-2212	David Osgood	. . .	Diana Easton	. . .	Ken Evans	Jean Wilson	James Starks
Enumclaw	c	MC	11	(360) 825-3591	John Wise	Mark Bauer	Marcia Hopkins	Mark Turley	Joseph Kolisch	Bruce Weigel	Christopher Searcy
Ephrata	c	CM	6	(509) 754-4601	Chris Jacobson	James Cherf	Leslie Trachsler	. . .	James Burns	Joseph Varick	William Sangster
Everett	c	MC	91	(425) 257-8700	. . .	Jim Langus	Sharon Marks	. . .	Terry Ollis	James Scharf	Clair Olivers
Federal Way	c	CM	83	(253) 835-2604	Dean McColgan	Neal Beets	Christine Green	. . .	. . .	Anne Kirkpatrick	Cary Roe
Ferndale *	c	CM	8	(360) 384-4302	Jerry Landcastle	Gregory Young	Linda Knutson	. . .	. . .	Michael Knapp	Bob Ceicle
Fife *	c	MC	4	(253) 922-2489	. . .	Steve Worthington	. . .	Steven Marcotte	. . .	Brad Blackburn	Russell Blount
Fircrest *	c	CM	5	(253) 564-8901	David Viafore	Bill Brandon	Rick Rosenbladt	Colleen Corcoran	. . .	John Cheesman	Bill Larkin
Forks	c	MC	3	(360) 374-5412	Nedra Reed	. . .	. . .	Daniel Leinan	. . .	Michael Powell	David Zellar
Gig Harbor *	c	MC	6	(253) 851-8136	Charles Hunter	Robert Karlinsey	Molly Towslee	David Rodenbach	. . .	Mitchell Barker	. . .
Goldendale	c	CM	3	(509) 773-3771	Mark Sigfrinius	Larry Bellamy	. . .	. . .	Lawrence Browning	David Hill	David Griffin
Grandview	c	MC	8	(509) 882-9200	Norm Childress	Scott Staples	Anita Palacios	. . .	Pat Mason	David Charvet	Castulo Arteaga
Hoquiam	c	MC	9	(360) 532-5700	Jack Durney	. . .	. . .	Michael Folkers	Ray Pumphrey	Rick Thomas	M. Parsons
Issaquah	c	MC	11	(425) 837-3020	Ava Frisinger	Leon Kos	Tina Eggers	James Blake	. . .	Dave Draveling	Bob Brock
Kelso	c	CM	11	(360) 423-1371	Donald Gregory	Paul Brachvogel	Veryl Anderson	. . .	. . .	Wayne Nelson	David Sypher
Kenmore *	c	CM	18	(425) 398-8900	Randy Eastwood	Stephen Anderson	Lynn Batchelor	. . .	. . .	Cliff Sether	Theodore Carlson
Kennewick	c	CM	54	(509) 585-4200	James Beaver	Robert Hammond	Valerie Loffler	Marie Mosley	Bobby Kirk	Ken Hohenberg	E. Russ Burtner
Kent	c	MC	79	(253) 856-5700	James White	John Hodgson	Brenda Jacober	. . .	James Schneider	Edward Crawford	Don Wickstrom
Kirkland	c	CM	45	(425) 828-1100	Lawrence Springer	David Ramsay	. . .	. . .	Jeffery Blake	Stanley Aston	James Arndt
La Conner *	t	MC	. .	(360) 466-3125	Wayne Everton	Shani Taha	. . .	Lorraine Taylor	Dan Taylor	. . .	Brian Lease
Lacey	c	CM	31	(360) 491-3214	Graeme Sackrison	Greg Cuoio	Charlotte Taylor	Blaine Martin	. . .	Lawrence Dickerson	Dennis Ritter
Lake Forest Park	c	MC	13	(206) 368-5440	David Hutchinson	David Cline	Susan Stine	. . .	. . .	. . .	Frank Zenk
Lake Stevens *	c	MC	6	(425) 334-1012	Vern Little	. . .	Norma Scott	Jan Berg	. . .	Randy Celori	David Ostergaard
Lakewood	c	CM	58	(253) 589-2489	Claudia Thomas	Andrew Neiditz	Alice Bush	Galen Kidd	. . .	Larry Saunders	Don Wickstrom

Directory 1/9 continued — OFFICIALS IN U.S. MUNICIPALITIES 2,500 AND OVER IN POPULATION

Jurisdiction	Type	Form of government	2000 Population (000)	Main telephone number	Chief elected official	Appointed administrator	Clerk of the governing board	Chief financial officer	Fire chief	Police chief	Public works director
WASHINGTON continued											
Leavenworth	c	MC	2	(509) 548-5275	William Bauer	...	Cheryl Grant	...	...	...	Mike Deason
Liberty Lake	c	MC	4	(509) 755-6702	...	...	...	...	...	...	...
Long Beach	c	MC	1	(360) 642-4421	...	Eugene Miles	...	...	...	...	...
Longview	c	CM	34	(360) 442-5004	Mark McCrady	Robert Gregory	...	Kurt Sacha	Daryl McDaniel	Alex Perez	Jeff Cameron
Lynden	c	CM	9	(360) 354-4270	Jack Louws	William Verwolf	...	Teresa Camfield	Gary Baar	Jack Foster	Duane Huskey
Lynnwood	c	MC	33	(425) 775-1971	Michael McKinnon	...	...	John Moir	Gary Olson	Steven Jensen	William Franz
Maple Valley *	c	CM	14	(425) 413-8800	Laure Iddings	Anthony Hemstad	Irvalene Moni	Laurence McCarthy	Timothy Lemon	...	Bill Guenzler
Marysville	c	MC	25	(360) 363-8000	Dennis Kendall	Mary Swenson	Gerry Becker	Sandy Langdon	...	Robert Carden	Paul Roberts
Medical Lake	c	MC	3	(509) 565-5000	Delmar Harland	Curtis Kelling	...	Pamela McBroom	Gino Palomino	Anthony Harbolt	John Ross
Medina *	c	CM	3	(425) 454-6400	Miles Adam	Mark Weinberg	Rachel Baker	Jan Burdue	...	Jeffrey Chen	Joe Willis
Mercer Island	c	CM	22	(206) 236-5300	Alan Merkle	Richard Conrad	Christine Eggers	Chip Corder	Walter Mauldin	Ronald Elsoe	Glenn Boettcher
Mill Creek *	c	CM	11	(425) 745-1891	Donna Michelson	Timothy Burns	Kelly Hennessey	Joanne Gregory	...	Robert Crannell	...
Milton	t	MC	5	(253) 922-8733	John Williams	...	Kathleen Browning	Gene Bray	Steve McKeen	Stan Jack	Mark Burlingame
Monroe	c	MC	13	(360) 794-7400	Bob Holman	James Southworth	Betty King	Carol Grey	...	Colleen Wilson	Gene Brazel
Montesano *	c	MC	3	(360) 249-3021	Richard Stone	...	...	...	Ken Walkington	Raymond Sowers	Mike Wincewicz
Moses Lake *	c	CM	14	(509) 766-9201	Ron Covey	Joseph Gavinski	...	Ronald Cone	Tom Taylor	Dean Mitchell	Gary Harer
Mount Vernon	c	MC	26	(360) 336-0630	Skye Richendrfer	...	...	Alicia Huschka	Stephen Abel	Mike Barsness	John Buckley
Mountlake Terrace	c	CM	20	(425) 776-1161	Jerry Smith	John Caulfield	Virginia Olsen	Sonja Springer	...	Scott Smith	Lawrence Water
Mukilteo *	c	MC	18	(425) 355-4141	Joe Marine	Lee Walton	C. Boughman	Scott James	Michael Springer	Michael Murphy	Larry Waters
Newcastle	c	CM	7	(425) 649-4444	...	John Starbard	Laura Hathaway	...	...	...	James Walker
Normandy Park	c	CM	6	(206) 248-7603	John Wiltse	Douglas Schulze	Ronald Moore	...	...	...	Karl Franta
North Bend *	c	MC	4	(425) 888-1211	Kenneth Hearing	Duncan Wilson	Cheryl Proffitt	Elena Montgomery	...	Joseph Hodgson	Ron Garrow
Oak Harbor	c	MC	19	(360) 679-5551	Steve Dernbach	Earl Silvers	Rosemary Morrison	Douglas Merriman	Mark Soptich	Antonio Barge	Cathy Rosen
Ocean Shores	c	CM	3	(360) 289-2488	Terry Veitz	Richard McEachin	Diane Houston	...	David Cowardin	...	John Gow
Olympia	c	CM	42	(360) 753-8447	Mark Foutch	Steven Hall	Debbie Krumpols	Jane Kirkemo	Larry Dibble	Gary Michel	D Mucha
Omak	c	MC	4	(509) 826-1170	Dale Sparber	...	...	Trish Butler	Kevin Bowling	L. Schreckengast	Fred Sheldon
Orting *	c	MC	3	(360) 893-2219	Cheryl Temple	Mark Bethune	Susan Davis	...	Randy Shelton	...	Dean Kaelin
Othello *	c	MC	5	(509) 488-5686	Shannon McKay	Ehman Sheldon	Debbie Kudrna	Michael Bailey	...	Alvia Dunnagan	Jay Van Ness
Pacific	c	MC	5	(253) 929-1100	Richard Hildreth	...	Sandy Paul-Lyle	Lynne Simons	Harold Philbin	...	John Walsh
Pasco *	c	CM	32	(509) 545-3404	Joyce Olson	Gary Crutchfield	...	...	Greg Garcia	Denis Austin	Bob Alberts
Port Angeles	c	CM	18	(360) 457-0411	...	Mark Madsen	Becky Upton	G. Ziomkowski	Daniel McKeen	Thomas Riepe	Glenn Cutler
Port Orchard	c	MC	7	(360) 876-4407	Kim Abel	...	...	...	...	Alan Townsend	...
Port Townsend	c	MC	8	(360) 379-4404	Catharine Robinson	David Timmons	Pamela Kolacy	Michael Legarsky	Michael Mingee	Connor Daily	Kenneth Clow
Poulsbo	c	MC	6	(360) 779-3901	Donna Bruce	...	Karol Jones	Nanci Lien	...	Jeff Doran	Jeff Lincoln
Prosser	c	MC	4	(509) 786-2332	...	Frederick Stouder	...	Regina Williams	Douglas Merritt	Win Taylor	L. J. Da Corsi
Pullman *	c	MC	24	(509) 338-3207	Mitchell Chandler	John Sherman	...	Troy Woo	Patrick Wilkins	William Weatherly	Mark Workman
Puyallup	c	CM	33	(253) 841-5550	Kathy Turner	James Bacon	Barbara Price	Scott McCarty	Merle Frank	Robin James	Thomas Heinecke
Quincy	c	MC	5	(509) 787-3523	R. Zimbelman	...	...	Sue Miller	...	William Gonzales	Dan Frazier
Raymond	c	CO	2	(360) 942-4100	...	...	Janet Jarvi	...	Tom Betrozoff	William Wilson	Rebecca Chaffee
Redmond	c	MC	45	(425) 556-2900	Rosemarie Ives	...	Bonnie Mattson	Lenda Crawford	John Ryan	Steven Harris	Carol Osborne
Renton *	c	MC	50	(425) 430-7650	K. Keolker-Wheeler	Jay Covington	Bonnie Walton	Michael Bailey	Ira Daniels	Kevin Milosevich	Gregg Zimmerman
Richland	c	CM	38	(509) 942-7390	Larry Haler	Cynthia Johnson	...	...	Glenn Johnason	David Lewis	Pete Squires
Ridgefield	c	MC	2	(360) 887-3557	...	George Fox	...	Kay Kammer	...	Bruce Hall	Justin Clary
Roslyn	c	MC	1	(509) 649-3105	Jeri Porter	...	Maria Fischer	Shannon Johansen	Steve Wynn	...	...
Sammamish *	c	CM	34	(425) 295-0500	Mark Cross	Bunyamin Yazici	Melonie Anderson	...	John Murphy	Brad Thompson	...
Seatac *	c	CM	25	(206) 973-4800	Gene Fisher	Craig Ward	Kristina Gregg	Mike McCarty	Bob Meyer	Jim Graddon	Dale Schroeder
Seattle	c	MC	563	(206) 684-4000	Gregory Nickels	...	Judith Pippin	Dwight Dively	Gregory Dean	R. Kerlikowske	...
Sedro-Woolley	c	MC	8	(360) 855-1661	Sharon Dillon	...	Patsy Nelson	...	Dean Klinger	Dave Cooper	Rick Blair
Selah	c	MC	6	(509) 698-7327	Robert Jones	Frank Sweet	Dale Novobielski	...	Jerry Davis	Rick Gutierrez	Joseph Henne
Sequim	c	CM	4	(360) 683-4139	Walter Schubert	William Elliott	Karen Kuznek	...	...	Robert Spinks	James Bay
Shelton *	c	CO	8	(360) 426-4491	John Tarrant	Michael O'Leary	...	Cathy Beierle	Jim Ghiglione	Terry Davenport	Jay Ebbeson
Shoreline	c	CM	53	(206) 546-1700	Robert Ransom	Robert Olander	Scott Passey	Debra Tarry	...	...	Paul Haines
Snohomish	c	CM	8	(360) 568-3115	...	Larry Bauman	Torchie Corey	...	...	...	Dan Takasugi
Snoqualmie *	c	MC	1	(425) 888-1555	Matthew Larson	Robert Larson	Joann Warren	Harry Oestreich	Bob Rowe	James Schaffer	Kirk Holmes
Spokane	c	MC	195	(509) 625-6250	Dennis Hession	John Pilcher	Terri Pfister	Gavin Cooley	Robert Williams	Anne Kirkpatrick	Dave Mandyke
Spokane Valley	c	CM	82	(509) 921-1000	...	David Mercier	...	Ken Thompson	...	...	Neil Kersten
Stanwood	c	MC	3	(360) 629-2181	Matthew McCune	...	Linda Jeffries	Landy Manuel	...	...	William Beckman
Steilacoom	t	MC	6	(253) 581-1912	Ron Lucas	Paul Loveless	Susan Wilson	...	...	...	Johnny Bednarczyk
Sultan	c	CM	3	(360) 793-2231	Ben Tolson	...	Laura Koenig	...	...	Fred Walser	Connie Dunn
Sumas	c	MC	..	(360) 988-5711	...	...	...	...	...	...	...
Sumner	c	MC	8	(253) 863-8300	David Enslow	John Doan	Susan Clary	Mary Ann Norquist	Dan Packer	Colleen Wilson	William Shoemaker
Sunnyside	c	CM	13	(509) 837-3997	Edward Prilucik	...	...	Scott James	Aaron Markham	Ed Radder	Jim Bridges
Tacoma	c	CM	193	(253) 591-5000	William Baarsma	Eric Anderson	Doris Sorum	...	Eileen Lewis	Donald Ramsdell	William Pugh
Toledo	c	MC	..	(360) 864-4564	...	...	Michelle Whitten	...	...	...	...
Toppenish *	c	CM	8	(509) 865-6319	William Rogers	William Murphy	...	Linda Mead	...	...	Lance Hoyt
Tukwila	c	MC	17	(206) 433-1800	Steve Mullet	...	Jane Cantu	Alan Doerschel	Nick Olivas	Keith Haines	James Morrow
Tumwater	c	MC	12	(360) 754-5855	Ralph Osgood	Doug Baker	...	Gayla Gjertsen	Rich Ridgeway	H. Vandiver	Jay Eaton
Union Gap	c	MC	5	(509) 248-0432	...	...	...	...	...	...	...
University Place *	c	CM	29	(253) 566-5656	Gerald Gehring	Robert Jean	Sarah Ortiz	David Layden	...	Jim Andrews	Gary Cooper
Vancouver	c	CM	143	(360) 619-1005	Royce Pollard	Patrick McDonnell	...	...	Don Bivins	Brian Martinek	Brian Carlson
Walla Walla	c	CM	29	(509) 527-4522	Dominick Elia	Duane Cole	Kammy Hill	...	Terrence Thomas	Charles Fulton	Harold Thomas
Wapato	c	MC	4	(509) 877-2334	Jesse Farias	...	Rosie Rumsey	...	Jose Valdez	Richard Sanchez	Gary Potter
Washougal	c	MC	8	(360) 835-8501	Jeff Guard	Nabiel Shawa	...	Rebecca Hasart	Ronald Caster	Robert Garwood	...
Wenatchee	c	CO	27	(509) 664-3300	...	...	...	Mark Calhoun	...	...	...
West Richland	c	MC	8	(509) 967-3431	Jerry Peltier	...	Julie Richardson	Howard Roberts	...	Mark Panther	Denise Wright
Woodinville *	c	CM	9	(425) 489-2700	...	Richard Leahy	Jennifer Kuhn	Jim Katica	Steve Smith	Ken Wardstrom	Mick Monken
Woodland	c	MC	3	(360) 225-8281	Doug Monge	...	...	...	Anthony Brentin	Robert Stephenson	R. VanderZanden
Yakima	c	CM	71	(509) 575-6090	...	Richard Zais	Karen Roberts	Rita Debord	Dennis Mayo	Samuel Granato	C. Waarvick
Yelm *	c	MC	3	(360) 458-3244	Ron Harding	Shelly Badger	Janine Schnepf	Tanya Robacker	...	Todd Stancil	Tim Peterson
WEST VIRGINIA											
Barboursville	v	MC	3	(304) 736-8994	Nancy Cartmill	...	...	Charles Woolcock	Paul Ritchie	Frank Simpson	Steve Parsons
Beckley	c	MC	17	(304) 256-1768	...	...	...	...	...	...	...
Bethlehem	v	MC	2	(304) 242-4180	...	...	...	...	...	...	...
Bluefield *	c	CM	11	(304) 327-2401	Linda Whalen	Mark Henne	Drema Shireman	Larkin Calhoun	Tony Hodges	Joe Wilson	Dallas Fowler
Bridgeport	c	CM	7	(304) 842-8217	Leonard Timms	A. Kim Haws	Judith Lawson	Keith Boggs	J. Vanlandingham	Jack Clayton	Daniel Ferrell
Buckhannon	c	MC	5	(304) 472-1651	E. Poundstone	...	...	...	Larry Mackey	Frederic Gaudet	...
Charles Town	c	MC	2	(304) 725-2311	Peggy Smith	...	...	...	...	...	...
Charleston *	c	MC	53	(304) 348-8015	Daniel Jones	David Molgaard	James Rieshman	Joseph Estep	Randy Stanley	Brent Webster	Donald Carr
Chester	c	MC	2	(304) 387-2820	...	...	...	...	...	...	...
Clarksburg	c	CM	16	(304) 624-1600	Sam Lopez	Martin Howe	Annette Wright	Frank Ferrari	Joe Gonzalez	John Walker	Frank Scercelli

Directory 1/9
continued

OFFICIALS IN U.S. MUNICIPALITIES 2,500 AND OVER IN POPULATION

Jurisdiction	Type	Form of govern-ment	2000 Popu-lation (000)	Main telephone number	Chief elected official	Appointed administrator	Clerk of the governing board	Chief financial officer	Fire chief	Police chief	Public works director
WEST VIRGINIA continued											
Dunbar	c	MC	8	(304) 766-0222	...	...	...	...	...	...	...
Elkins	c	MC	7	(304) 636-1414	...	...	Philip Graziani	...	...	Mike Taylor	...
Fairmont	c	CM	19	(304) 366-6211	Nick Fantasia	Bruce McDaniel	Janet Keller	Eileen Layman	Gregg Freme	Stephen Cain	Michael DeMary
Fayetteville	t	CM	2	(304) 574-0101	James Murdock	Cecil Gibson	Paula Ballard	...	John Vernon	Paul Tygrett	...
Follansbee	c	CM	3	(304) 527-1330	Anthony Paesano	Kevin Diserio	David Kurcina	...	Larry Rea	John Schwertfeger	Steve Meca
Grafton	c	CM	5	(304) 265-1412	Jeffery Tansill	Kevin Stead	Larry Richman	...	Richard Beall	Jeffrey Leach	Gerald Weber
Hinton	c	CM	2	(304) 466-3255	Cleo Matthews	C. Meadows	Sherry Allen	...	Leon Pivont	Richard Poe	Ralph Trout
Huntington	c	MC	51	(304) 696-5580	David Felinton	Conrad Thornburgh	Barbara Nelson	Robert Wilhelm	Gregory Fuller	A. Baumgardner	George McClennen
Hurricane	c	MC	5	(304) 562-5896	Raymond Peak	...	...	...	...	Lawrence Foster	...
Kenova	c	MC	3	(304) 453-1571	Larry Smith	...	Sheila Wheeler	...	Steve Salyers	Ronnie Dickerson	...
Keyser	c	MC	5	(304) 788-1511	Roger Newlin	Kathy Merrill	...	...	...	Karen Shoemaker	...
Kingwood	t	MC	2	(304) 329-1225	Fred Peddicord	...	Eleanor Williams	...	Thomas Martin	Claude Waugerman
Lewisburg *	c	MC	3	(304) 645-2080	John Manchester	...	S. Ninnemann	...	Wayne Pennington	Tim Stover	Mark Carver
Logan	t	MC	1	(304) 752-4044	Claude Ellis	...	Dolores Lopes	Jeff Vallet	Vernon Beckett	David White	...
Madison	c	MC	2	(304) 369-2762	...	...	...	...	...	...	...
Mannington	t	MC	2	(304) 986-2700	Orval Price	...	Michele Fluharty	...	Joel McCann	David James	Richard Stevens
Martinsburg	c	CM	14	(304) 264-2131	George Karos	Mark Baldwin	...	Mark Spickler	Paul Bragg	Theodore Anderson	Ben Leonard
Montgomery	t	MC	2	(304) 442-5181	...	...	...	...	...	...	...
Morgantown	c	CM	26	(304) 284-7405	Ronald Justice	Dan Boroff	Linda Little	Denise White	David Fetty	Robert Lucci	Terry Hough
Moundsville	c	CM	9	(304) 845-3394	...	Allen Hendershot	Sondra Hewitt	...	Noel Clark	James Kudlak	James Richmond
Mullens	t	MC	1	(304) 294-7132	S. Brewer	...	William Mongeni	...	Rick Rice	James Miller	James Roop
New Martinsville	c	MC	5	(304) 455-9120	James Herrick	...	Bonnie Shannon	...	Kent Longwell	Timothy Cecil	Gary Lemons
Nitro	t	MC	6	(304) 755-0701	...	...	...	...	...	...	...
Oak Hill	c	CM	7	(304) 469-9541	...	...	...	...	...	...	...
Paden City	t	MC	2	(304) 337-2295	Anthony Sapp	...	Judy Lyons	Ginger Wilcox	James Richmond	Scott Dalrymple	Clifford Duke
Parkersburg	c	MC	33	(304) 424-8400	Jimmy Colombo	...	Connie Shaffer	Randall Craig	John Knapp	Robert Newell	William Slater
Philippi	c	CM	2	(304) 457-3700	Caton Hill	Karen Weaver	Tamula Stemple	Whitni Kines	John Green	...	Buddy Shreve
Point Pleasant *	c	MC	4	(304) 675-2360	Charles McCann	...	Donald Whitten	...	Vernon Quintrell	James Scites	...
Princeton *	c	CM	6	(304) 487-5020	Dewey Russell	Wayne Shumate	Kenneth Clay	Kelly Davis	Shawn Vest	William Harman	Kenneth Rose
Ranson	c	MC	2	(304) 725-1010	A. Hamill	Paul Mills	Elizabeth Stroop	Stephen Hudson	...	William Roper	James Spradley
Ravenswood *	c	CM	4	(304) 273-2621	Lucy Harbert	...	Kendra Liegey	...	Terry Drennen	Paul Hesson	Edwin Flinn
Richwood	c	MC	2	(304) 846-2596	Jeromy Rose	...	Emily Williams	Ronnie Bragg	John Greer	Larry Tinney	Frank White
Ripley	c	MC	3	(304) 372-3482	Ollie Harvey	...	...	...	...	Tom McCrady	Tim King
Ronceverte *	c	MC	1	(304) 647-5455	Gail White	Blaine Oborn	...	...	...	...	...
Salem	c	CM	2	(304) 782-1318	...	...	...	...	...	...	...
Shinnston	c	CM	2	(304) 592-2126	Sammy De Marco	...	Debra Herndon	...	...	Michael Secreto	...
South Charleston	c	MC	13	(304) 744-5301	Richard Robb	...	Jack Woolwine	Rodger Raybourn	Claude Sigman	David Dunlap	Franklin Mullens
Spencer	c	MC	2	(304) 927-1640	...	...	...	...	...	...	...
St. Albans	c	MC	11	(304) 722-3391	Jack Gessel	...	B. Cunningham	...	Dwight Pettry	Homer Clark	Orville Browning
St. Marys *	c	CM	2	(304) 684-2401	L. Paul Ingram	Thomas Painter	Linda Wilson	...	Lee Ogdin	William Stull	Ron Cokeley
Summersville	t	MC	3	(304) 872-1211	Stanley Adkins	...	Michael Brown	Ronald Hancock	Joe Boso	Ray Moore	Robert Hilleary
Vienna	c	MC	10	(304) 295-4541	David Nohe	...	Carla Starcher	...	Daniel Goodwin	Gary Deem	Craig Metz
Weirton	c	CM	20	(304) 797-8501	William Miller	Gary Dufour	Dolores Ostrander	Valerie Means	Kessler Cole	Lance Scott	Brae Bryant
Welch	c	CM	2	(304) 436-3113	Martha Moore	...	Robin Owens	...	Dennie Hale	Robert Bowman	Robert Lee
Wellsburg *	c	CM	2	(304) 737-2104	Wayne Campbell	...	Mary Blum	...	...	Stanley Kins	...
Weston	c	MC	4	(304) 269-6141	Jon Tucci	Frank Robinette	...	Rebecca Swisher	Michael Young	Roger Clem	...
Westover	c	MC	3	(304) 296-6860	Suzanne Kenney	Jim Rutledge	Lahomma Brock	...	David Clawges	James Smith	Roger Malone
Wheeling *	c	CM	31	(304) 234-3819	Nick Sparachane	Robert Herron	Janice Jones	Michael Klug	Stephen Johnston	Kevin Gessler	Russell Jebbia
White Sulphur Springs *	c	MC	2	(304) 536-1454	Debra Fogus	...	...	L. Coleman-Barker	Paul Fogus	James Hylton	...
Williamson	c	MC	3	(304) 235-1510	Sam Kapourales	...	...	...	Grover Phillips	Roby Pope	Dewey Dingess
Williamstown	c	MC	2	(304) 375-7761	Marvin Stead	...	Susan Wooddell	...	...	...	Robert Kimble
WISCONSIN											
Adams	c	MC	1	(608) 339-6516	Kenneth Romell	Robert Ellisor	Linda Ritchie	...	...	James Gold	David Mead
Algoma	c	MC	3	(920) 487-5203	Virginia Haske	Thomas Romdenne	...	...	Thomas Ackerman	Daniel Brusky	Gary Paape
Allouez	v	CM	14	(920) 448-2800	Camron McCain	Susan Foxworthy	...	...	...	...	Tom Meier
Altoona	c	CM	6	(715) 839-6092	Larry Sturz	Ronald Rusmussen	...	...	...	...	Henry Gleason
Amery	c	MC	2	(715) 268-7486	...	J. Riemenschneider	...	...	R. Van Blaricom	Thomas Marson	John Frisco
Antigo *	c	MC	8	(715) 623-3633	Michael Matousek	...	Kaye Matucheski	...	Robert Donohue	William Brandt	...
Appleton	c	MC	70	(920) 832-6400	Timothy Hanna	...	Cynthia Hesse	Lisa Maertz	Neil Cameron	Richard Myers	Paula Vandehey
Ashland	c	MC	8	(715) 682-7071	Fred Schnoor	...	Rae Buckwheat	Michael Screnock	Keith Tveit	Daniel Crawford	James Struck
Ashwaubenon	v	MC	17	(920) 492-2327	Norbert DeCleene	...	Dawn Collins	Greg Wenholz	Paul Hawley	...	Keith Watermolen
Baraboo *	c	MC	10	(608) 355-2700	Patrick Liston	Edward Geick	Cheryl Giese	...	Kevin Stieve	Craig Olsen	Robert Koss
Barron	c	MC	3	(715) 537-5631	...	...	Tony Slagstad	...	...	...	David Hanson
Bayside *	v	CM	4	(414) 351-8811	Samuel Dickman	Andrew Pederson	...	...	...	Bruce Resnick	Joel Hawkins
Beaver Dam	c	MC	15	(920) 885-5541	...	...	...	...	...	...	...
Bellevue	v	CM	9	(920) 468-5225	...	Aaron Oppenheimer	Karen Simons	...	...	...	Ronald Umentum
Beloit	c	CM	35	(608) 364-6610	...	Larry Arft	Carol Alexander	...	Bradley Liggett	Sam Lathrop	David Botts
Beloit	t	CM	7	(608) 364-2980	Cosmo Daguanno	Robert Museus	...	...	Joseph Holomy	John Wilson	Howard Hemmer
Berlin	c	CM	5	(920) 361-5400	Roberta Erdmann	...	Jodie Olson	...	John Stetter	Dennis Plantz	Brian Freimark
Black River Falls	c	MC	3	(715) 284-5514	Joseph Hunter	William Arndt	...	...	Steven Schreiber	Donald Gilberg	Todd Gomer
Bloomer	c	MC	3	(715) 568-3032	Randy Summerfield	...	...	...	...	Michael Bungartz	...
Boscobel *	c	MC	3	(608) 375-5001	Stephen Wetter	Arlie Harris	...	...	Jeff Boughton	James Reynolds	Michael Reynolds
Brillion	c	MC	2	(920) 756-2250	Gerald Sonnabend	Lori Gosz	...	...	Richard Janke	Scott Kaphingst	...
Bristol *	t	MC	4	(262) 857-2368	Richard Gossling	Randall Kerkman	Amy Klemko	Kathleen Gerretsen	Mike Moran	...	...
Brodhead	c	MC	3	(608) 897-4018	William Wellnitz	...	Nancy Schoeller	...	...	Richard Bennett	Randy Rosheisen
Brookfield	c	MC	38	(262) 796-6642	Jeffrey Speaker	...	Kris Schmidt	Robert Scott	John Dahms	Daniel Tushaus	Thomas Grisa
Brookfield	t	CM	6	(262) 796-3788	...	Richard Czopp	Jane Carlson	...	...	...	...
Brown Deer	v	CM	12	(414) 371-3000	Margaret Jaberg	R. Van Gompel	...	...	...	Steven Rinzel	Larry Neitzel
Burlington	c	CM	9	(262) 342-1172	Claude Lois	Kevin Lahner	...	Terri Padgett	...	David Walsh	Connie Wilson
Butler	v	MC	1	(262) 783-2525	Walter Woloszyk	Tim Rhode	...	...	Ron Worgull	Ernie Rosenthal	...
Caledonia	v	CM	23	(262) 835-4451	J. Delagrave	Thomas Lebak	Wendy Christensen	Larry Borchert	Peter Waselchuk	Jeffrey Meier	Robert Wittke
Cedarburg *	c	MC	10	(262) 375-7600	Gregory Myers	Christy Mertes	Constance McHugh	...	Richard Van Dinter	Thomas Frank	Thomas Wiza
Cedarburg	t	MC	5	(262) 377-4509	Dave Valentine	James Culotta	Karen Behrens	...	...	...	Thomas Marquardt
Chenequa	v	CM	..	(262) 367-2239	Bryce Styza	Robert Douglas	Bonita Zimdars	...	Richard Hagemann	...	Jeff Kante
Chilton	c	MC	3	(920) 849-2451	Bill Engler	...	...	...	Jim Kurtz	Dennis Plantz	Todd Schwarz
Chippewa Falls *	c	MC	12	(715) 726-2719	Daniel Hedrington	...	Frank Braswell	...	Edward Mishefske	Joseph Coughlin	John Allen
Clayton	t	MC	2	(920) 836-2007	...	Craig Clark	...	...	...	...	...
Clinton	v	MC	2	(608) 676-5304	Mary Jensen	Philip Rath	...	...	John Rindfleisch	James Korth	Roger Johnson
Clintonville	c	MC	4	(715) 823-7600	Robert Gay	Lisa Kuss	Chris Vollrath	...	John Krubsack	Terry Lorge	Michael McCord

Directory 1/9 continued **OFFICIALS IN U.S. MUNICIPALITIES 2,500 AND OVER IN POPULATION**

Jurisdiction	Type	Form of govern-ment	2000 Popu-lation (000)	Main telephone number	Chief elected official	Appointed administrator	Clerk of the governing board	Chief financial officer	Fire chief	Police chief	Public works director
WISCONSIN continued											
Columbus	c	MC	4	(920) 623-5900	William Wendt	Boyd Kraemer	Anne Donahue	. . .	Glenn Dykstra	Gerald Sallmann	Michael Healy
Combined Locks	v	MC	2	(920) 788-2059	Ed Wulgaert	Mark Van Thiel	. . .	. . .	Rick Strick	Steve Wulgaert	Mark Ristau
Coon Valley	v	MC	. .	(608) 452-3168	Michael Johnson	. . .	Michael Borgen	. . .	. . .	Michael Raasch	John Langaard
Cottage Grove	v	MC	4	(608) 839-4704	Kenneth Dahl	. . .	Kim Manley	. . .	. . .	John Gould	James Hessling
Cudahy	c	MC	18	(414) 769-2203	Raymond Glowacki	. . .	Philip Brannon	. . .	Richard Demien	Mark Hayes	Michael Clark
De Forest	v	CM	7	(608) 846-6751	Jeffrey Miller	JoAnn Miller	Susan Harper	Steve Fahlgren	David Arnold	Robert Henze	P. Vander Sanden
De Pere	c	CM	20	(920) 339-4044	Mike Walsh	Lawrence Delo	Dave Minten	Joseph Zegers	Robert Kiser	Derek Beiderwieden	Roy Simonson
Delafield	c	MC	6	(262) 646-6220	Paul Craig	Matthew Carlson	Marilyn Czubkowski	. . .	Allyn Swayze	Scott Taubel	Thomas Hafner
Delavan *	c	MC	7	(262) 728-5585	Melvin Nieuwenhuis	Joseph Salitros	Susan Kitzman	. . .	Neil Flood	Tim O'Neill	Mark Wendorf
Delavan	t	CM	4	(262) 728-3471	Marvin Herman	. . .	Colleen Endish	. . .	. . .	Andrew Mayer	James Wolfgram
Denmark	v	MC	1	(920) 863-6400	. . .	Gordon Ellis	. . .	. . .	. . .	. . .	. . .
Dodgeville	c	MC	4	(608) 935-5228	. . .	. . .	. . .	. . .	. . .	. . .	. . .
East Troy	v	CM	3	(262) 642-6255	William Loesch	. . .	. . .	. . .	Mike Barutha	David Fox	Tom Rossmiller
Eau Claire	c	CM	61	(715) 839-4921	Mark Lewis	Michael Huggins	Donna Austad	Rebecca Noland	. . .	. . .	William Bittner
Edgerton	c	MC	4	(608) 884-3341	Erik Thompson	Ramona Flanigan	Cinthia Hegglund	. . .	. . .	Thomas Klubertanz	Tom Hartzell
Elkhorn	c	MC	7	(262) 723-2219	Paul Ormson	Samuel Tapson	Nancy Jacobson	Samuel West	Dennis Hommen	John Giese	Terry Weter
Elm Grove	v	CM	6	(262) 782-6700	Susan Freedy	David DeAngelis	Mary Stredni	Monica Hughes	. . .	Jeffrey Haig	Charles Armao
Elroy *	c	MC	1	(608) 462-2400	Don Baldwin	. . .	. . .	. . .	. . .	Dave Wagner	Ed Gashi
Evansville *	c	MC	4	(608) 882-2266	Sandy Decker	Dan Wietecha	Judy Walton	Eric Jepperson	. . .	Scott McElroy	David Wartenweiler
Fitchburg *	t	MC	20	(608) 270-4200	Thomas Clauder	Anthony Roach	Linda Cory	Nancy Solberg	Randall Pickering	Thomas Blatter	Paul Woodard
Fond Du Lac	c	CM	42	(920) 322-3623	Marty Ryan	Thomas Herre	Theresa Hochrein	Hal Wortman	Joe Clow	Duane Johnson	Mark Lentz
Fontana-On-Geneva Lake	v	CM	1	(262) 275-6136	. . .	K. Hayden-Staggs	Phyllis Smith	. . .	. . .	Steven Olson	Craig Workman
Fort Atkinson	c	CM	11	(920) 563-7760	Loren Gray	John Wilmet	Faith Elford	. . .	Thomas Emrick	Tony Brus	Tom Kramp
Fox Lake	c	MC	1	(920) 928-2280	Richard Klomsten	William Petracek	Susan Hollnagel	. . .	William Frank	Patrick Lynch	Douglas Buchda
Fox Point	v	CM	7	(414) 351-8900	Michael West	Susan Robertson	. . .	. . .	. . .	Thomas Czaja	Scott Brandmeier
Franklin	c	MC	29	(414) 858-1100	. . .	. . .	Sandi Wesolowski	Cal Patterson	James Martins	Richard Oliva	Jerry Schaefer
Germantown	v	CM	18	(262) 250-4750	Charles Hargan	David Schornack	Jane Wilms	Kim Rath	Gary Pollpeter	Raymond Van Male	Allan Caverson
Glendale	c	MC	13	(414) 228-1700	. . .	Richard Maslowski	. . .	. . .	. . .	Tom Czarnyszka	Dave Eastman
Grafton	v	CM	10	(262) 375-5300	James Brunnquell	Darrell Hofland	Teri Dylak	. . .	David Harvey	Charles Wenten	David Murphy
Grand Chute	t	CM	18	(920) 832-1573	Michael Marsden	Mark Rohloff	Judith Christjohn	. . .	Todd Farley	Edgar Kopp	. . .
Green Bay *	c	MC	102	(920) 448-3147	Jim Schmitt	. . .	Sue Badeau	Doug Daul	Jeff Stauber	James Arts	Carl Weber
Green Lake *	c	MC	1	(920) 294-6912	Joseph Parise	. . .	Barbara Dugenske	. . .	William Wagner	Stephen Huber	Glen McCarty
Greendale	v	CM	14	(414) 423-2100	Scott Leonard	. . .	. . .	. . .	Gary Fedder	Robert Dams	Carl Tisonik
Greenfield	c	MC	35	(414) 329-5208	Timothy Seider	. . .	Donna Rynders	M. Vandermeuse	Roland Poppy	Francis Springob	Richard Sokol
Greenville	t	MC	6	(920) 757-5151	. . .	David Tebo	. . .	. . .	Glenn Kelly	. . .	. . .
Hales Corners	v	CM	7	(414) 529-6161	James Ryan	Michael Weber	. . .	. . .	David Bialk	Kent Bieganski	Michael Martin
Hartford	c	CM	10	(262) 673-8204	Scott Henke	. . .	Marjorie Savana	Gary Koppelberger	Robert Baus	Thomas Jones	. . .
Hartland	v	CM	7	(262) 367-2714	David Lamerand	Wallace Thiel	Constance Casper	Joicelyn Schwager	Allen Wilde	Robert Rosch	James Wilson
Hillsboro	c	CM	1	(608) 489-2521	. . .	Mark Lynch	. . .	. . .	. . .	. . .	. . .
Hobart	v	MC	5	(920) 869-1011	Len Teresinski	Joseph Helfenberger	. . .	. . .	. . .	. . .	. . .
Holman	v	CM	6	(608) 526-4336	. . .	Catherine Schmit	. . .	. . .	. . .	Mike McHugh	Phil Scholze
Horicon *	c	MC	3	(920) 485-3500	James Grigg	. . .	David Pasewald	. . .	James Bandsma	Joseph Adamson	S. Bogenschneider
Hortonville	v	CM	2	(920) 779-6011	Roger Retzlaff	J. Mitchell	Lynne Mischker	. . .	. . .	Michael Sullivan	Ronald Austreng
Howard *	v	CM	13	(920) 434-4640	Carlene Felmer	Joshua Smith	. . .	. . .	John O'Connor	. . .	Robert Bartelt
Hudson	c	MC	8	(715) 386-4765	Jack Breault	Devin Willi	Nancy Norvold	Betty Caruso	James Frye	Richard Trende	James Eulberg
Jackson	v	CM	4	(262) 677-9001	. . .	Delmore Beaver	. . .	. . .	John Skodinski	Jed Dolnick	Brian Kober
Janesville	c	CM	59	(608) 755-3080	. . .	Steven Sheiffer	Jean Wulf	Herbert Stinski	Larry Grorud	Burton Mahan	Jack Messer
Jefferson	c	MC	7	(920) 674-7700	Arnold Brawders	. . .	Tanya Stewart	. . .	. . .	. . .	Daniel Ludwig
Johnson Creek	v	MC	1	(920) 699-2296	. . .	Paul Moderacki	Joan Dykstra	. . .	. . .	. . .	. . .
Kaukauna	c	MC	12	(920) 766-6300	John Lambie	. . .	Susan Duda	Steve Giebel	Paul Hirte	John Manion	John Sundelius
Kenosha	c	MC	90	(262) 653-4130	John Antaramian	Nick Arnold	Jean Morgan	Carol Stancato	Joseph Kiser	Daniel Wade	Ronald Bursek
Kewaskum	v	CM	3	(262) 626-8484	. . .	Jay Shambeau	. . .	. . .	Mark Groeschel	Richard Knoebel	Jerry Gilles
Kewaunee	c	MC	2	(920) 388-5000	Jerome Zelten	. . .	. . .	. . .	Greg Hlinak	David Decramer	Michael Ley
Kiel	c	MC	3	(920) 894-2909	. . .	. . .	. . .	. . .	. . .	. . .	. . .
Kimberly	v	CM	6	(920) 788-7500	Charles Kuen	Rick Hermus	Sandra Haas	. . .	. . .	David Peterson	D. V. Boogaard
Kronenwetter	v	CM	5	(715) 693-4200	Rick Smith	W. Bierma	Krystal Bokelman	. . .	Roger James	Daniel Joling	Lisa Myles
La Crosse	c	MC	51	(608) 789-7595	Mark Johnsrud	. . .	Teri Lehrke	Eugene Pfaff	Gregg Cleveland	Edward Kondracki	Dale Hexom
La Pointe	t	MC	. .	(715) 747-6914	. . .	B. Cunningham	. . .	. . .	. . .	. . .	. . .
Ladysmith	c	MC	3	(715) 532-2600	Ronald Moore	Alan Christianson	Kathleen Stewart	Joel Dutenhoefer	Scott Bingham	Norman Rozak	W. Christianson
Lake Geneva	c	MC	7	(262) 248-3673	Charles Rude	Dennis Jordan	Diana Dykstra	Sandra Kulik	James Binkert	Richard Meinel	Daniel Winkler
Lake Mills	c	CM	4	(920) 648-2344	Danny Stevens	Steven Wilke	James Heilman	. . .	Richard Heinz	Kathleen Hansen	John Tremain
Lancaster *	c	MC	4	(608) 723-4246	Jerome Wehrle	Scot Simpson	David Kurihara	. . .	Robert Little	Dan Jacobson	Jerry Carroll
Little Chute *	v	CM	10	(920) 788-7380	Charles Fischer	Charles Kell	Vicki Karch	Dale Haug	R. Vanden Heuvel	David Peterson	Roy Van Gheem
Long Lake	t	MC	. .	(715) 674-6974	Wally Cooper	. . .	J. Behrmann	. . .	. . .	. . .	. . .
Madison	c	MC	208	(608) 266-4611	Dave Cieslewicz	. . .	Ray Fisher	Dean Brasser	Debra Amesqua	Richard Williams	. . .
Manitowoc	c	MC	34	(920) 686-6950	Kevin Crawford	. . .	Jennifer Hudon	Brian Ruechel	Charles Herzog	Perry Kingsbury	William Handlos
Maple Bluff *	v	CM	1	(608) 244-3048	John Larson	. . .	. . .	. . .	Eric Dahl	Timothy Krueger	Thomas Schroeder
Marinette	c	MC	11	(715) 732-5141	Douglas Oitzinger	. . .	James Anderson	Yuzhen Liu	Joseph Giver	Jeffery Skorik	Brian Miller
Marshfield	c	MC	18	(715) 387-6597	Michael Meyers	Michael Brehm	Debbie Hall	Keith Strey	Gregg Cleveland	Joseph Stroik	Daniel Knoek
Mauston	c	MC	3	(608) 847-6676	Brian McGuire	Harlin Owens	Renee Hazelton	. . .	Kim Hale	Mark Messer	Rob Nelson
Mayville *	c	MC	4	(920) 387-7900	Ronald Sternat	. . .	Kathie Wild	. . .	Roger Williams	W. Linzenmeyer	Vern Hilker
Mc Farland	v	CM	6	(608) 838-3153	Erik Thoresen	. . .	Donald Peterson	. . .	Gary Garmon	Greg Leck	Dennis Dancker
Medford	c	MC	4	(715) 748-4321	Michael Wellner	John Fales	Virginia Brost	. . .	. . .	Ted Bever	. . .
Menasha	c	MC	16	(920) 967-5117	Joseph Laux	. . .	Joan Smogoleski	Thomas Stoffel	Patrick O'Brien	Robert Stanke	Mark Radtke
Menasha *	t	CM	15	(920) 720-7101	Arden Tews	Jeffrey Sturgell	Karen Tweedie	Myra Piergrossi	Keith Kiesow	Rod McCants	. . .
Menomonee Falls *	v	CM	32	(262) 532-4200	Richard Rechlicz	Mark Fitzgerald	. . .	Mary Datka	Robert Coon	. . .	Frank Paulus
Menomonie	c	CM	14	(715) 232-2187	Dennis Kropp	Lowell Prange	JoAnn Kadinger	. . .	Jack Baus	Dennis Beety	Randy Eide
Mequon	c	MC	21	(262) 242-3100	C. Nuernberg	Lee Szymborski	Maureen Murphy	Douglas Bates	Curtis Witzlib	E. Barker	Jon Garms
Merrill	c	MC	10	(715) 536-5594	Douglas Williams	Tony Chladek	William Heideman	Katherine Unertl	Norm Hanson	Neil Strobel	. . .
Middleton	c	MC	15	(608) 827-1050	. . .	Michael Davis	. . .	Tim Studer	Mark Rauls	Larry Fass	Hank Simon
Middleton *	t	CM	4	(608) 833-5887	Milo Breunig	David Shaw	. . .	. . .	. . .	. . .	. . .
Milton *	c	MC	5	(608) 868-6900	Nathan Bruce	Todd Schmidt	Nancy Zastrow	. . .	Loren Lippincott	Thomas Gilland	Howard Robinson
Milwaukee	c	MC	596	(414) 286-3387	John Norquist	Steven Jacquart	Ronald Leonhardt	Waldemar Morics	William Wentlandt	Arthur Jones	M. Schifalacqua
Mondovi	c	MC	2	(715) 926-3866	S. Beauchamp	. . .	Daniel Lauersdorf	. . .	Dennis Brion	Terry Pittman	Randy Gruber
Monona	c	CM	8	(608) 222-2525	V. Metcalfe	Patrick Marsh	Nanette Ursino	. . .	Robert Van Etten	Brad Keil	Gary Weinert
Monroe	c	MC	10	(608) 329-2500	William Ross	Mark Vahlsing	James Myers	Kathie Lindsay	Thomas Casey	Frederick Kelley	Nathan Klassy
Mosinee *	c	CM	4	(715) 693-2275	Alan Erickson	Jeff Gates	. . .	. . .	. . .	Kenneth Muelling	Kevin Breit
Mount Horeb	v	MC	5	(608) 437-6884	John Zimmel	Patrick Dann	Cheryl Sutter	. . .	Charles Himsel	Scott Sterland	Laurel Grindle
Mount Pleasant	v	CM	23	(262) 554-8750	Mark Gleason	. . .	Juliet Edwards	Dancy Bugni	William Bouma	James Madjoch	. . .

Directory 1/9 continued — OFFICIALS IN U.S. MUNICIPALITIES 2,500 AND OVER IN POPULATION

Jurisdiction	Type	Form of govern-ment	2000 Popu-lation (000)	Main telephone number	Chief elected official	Appointed administrator	Clerk of the governing board	Chief financial officer	Fire chief	Police chief	Public works director
WISCONSIN continued											
Mukwonago	t	TM	6	(262) 363-4555	David Dubey	...	...	...	...	Grant Turner	...
Mukwonago	v	MC	6	(262) 363-6420	James Wagner	...	Steve Braatz	...	Jeffrey Rolfe	Fred Winchowky	T. Brandemuehl
Muskego	c	MC	21	(262) 679-5675	Mark Slocomb	...	Jean Marenda	Dawn Gunderson	...	John Johnson	Wayne Delikat
Neenah	c	MC	24	(920) 751-4604	...	...	...	...	...	...	...
Neillsville *	c	MC	2	(715) 743-2105	Diane Murphy	...	...	...	Matt Meyer	Bradley Lindner	David Flynn
Nekoosa *	c	MC	2	(715) 886-3811	Gordon Freeman	...	...	...	Ken Hartje	...	Terry Shymanski
New Berlin *	c	MC	38	(262) 786-8610	Jack Chiovatero	...	Marilyn Gauger	Michael Holzinger	Edward Dobernig	Joseph Rieder	...
New Glarus *	v	CM	2	(608) 527-2510	...	Nicholas Owen	Lynne Erb	...	...	Steven Allbaugh	Scott Jelle
New Holstein	c	MC	3	(920) 898-5766	...	...	...	...	...	...	...
New Lisbon	c	MC	1	(608) 562-5213	Lloyd Chase	...	...	...	Lynn Willard	Brent Granger	...
New London *	c	MC	7	(920) 982-8500	Wayne Toltzman	Kent Hager	...	James Villiesse	Wayne Wilfuer	Kevin Wilkinson	Carol Radtke
New Richmond	c	MC	6	(715) 246-4268	...	Dennis Horner	Helen Demulling	...	James Vanderwyst	Mark Samelstad	John Berends
Niagara	c	MC	..	(715) 251-3235	Joseph Stern	Donald Novak	...	...	...	Randy Wodenka	Dennis Payette
North Fond Du Lac	v	MC	4	(920) 929-3765	James Moon	...	...	...	...	William Lamb	Michael Tolvstad
Oak Creek	c	MC	28	(414) 768-6500	Richard Bolender	Patrick DeGrave	Beverly Buretta	R. Ann Underberg	Brian Satula	Thomas Bauer	...
Oconomowoc *	c	MC	12	(262) 569-3235	Maurice Sullivan	Diane Gard	Diane Coenen	Sarah Kitsembel	Glenn Leidel	...	Mark Frye
Oconomowoc	t	MC	7	(262) 567-0251	...	...	Nancy Lins	...	...	...	...
Oconto	c	MC	4	(920) 834-7711	D. Nerenhausen	...	Linda Belongia	...	Michael Hoppe	Dale Carper	...
Oconto Falls *	c	CM	2	(920) 846-4505	Don Osborne	John Dougherty	...	Eve Wallace	Tim Magnim	Mike Roberts	Gerry Lemirande
Omro *	c	MC	3	(920) 685-7000	Bob Breu	Linda Kutchenriter	...	...	...	James Reed	Gary Marks
Onalaska	c	MC	14	(608) 781-9530	James Bialecki	...	Cari Burmaster	Fred Buehler	...	Randy Williams	C. Jarrod Holter
Onalaska	t	TM	5	(608) 783-4958	...	...	...	...	...	...	...
Oregon	v	MC	7	(608) 835-3118	Gerald Luebke	Michael Gracz	Georgia Johnson	Renee Hoeft	...	...	Mark Below
Osceola *	v	CM	2	(715) 294-3498	Charles Jensen	Neil Soltis	...	...	Don Stark	Tim Lauridsen	James Schmidt
Oshkosh *	c	CM	62	(920) 236-5000	Frank Tower	Richard Wollangk	Pamela Urbrig	Edward Nokes	Tim Franz	Scott Greuel	David Patek
Paddock Lake	v	MC	3	(262) 843-2400	David Buehn	Ernest Mooney	Doris Raditz	...	...	...	...
Palmyra *	v	MC	1	(262) 495-8316	Timothy Gorsegner	...	Laurie Mueller	...	Ryan Meyers	Charles Warren	Scott Halbrucker
Park Falls *	c	MC	2	(715) 762-2436	...	...	Arla Homann	...	George Schneider	Scott Straetz	Dennis Wartgow
Peshtigo *	c	MC	3	(715) 582-3041	Thomas Strouf	...	Mary Wills	...	Steven Anderson	Thomas Hartwig	...
Pewaukee *	c	CM	11	(262) 691-0770	Scott Klein	Tammy LaBorde	Kelly DeMotto	...	Matthew Pinter	Gary Bach	Jeffrey Weigel
Pewaukee	v	MC	8	(262) 691-5660	Charles Nichols	Scott Gosse	Susan Atherton	...	...	Edward Baumann	David White
Platteville	c	CM	9	(608) 348-9741	Ed White	David Berner	Annette Dutcher	Duane Borger	Bob Leighty	Doug McKinley	Howard Crofoot
Pleasant Prairie	v	MC	16	(262) 694-1400	John Steinbrink	Michael Pollocoff	Jane Romanowski	...	Paul Guilbert	Brian Wagner	...
Plover	v	CM	10	(715) 345-5250	Daniel Schlutter	Daniel Mahoney	Karen Swanson	...	Tim Kluck	Roger Zebro	Bill Konkol
Plymouth	c	MC	7	(920) 893-1271	William Kiley	...	Patricia Huberty	...	Ronald Nicolaus	Donn Davis	William Immich
Port Washington	c	MC	10	(262) 284-5585	Scott Huebner	Mark Grams	...	...	Marc Eernisse	Edward Rudolph	Rob VandenNoven
Portage	c	MC	9	(608) 742-2176	Jeff Grothman	Laurence Plaster	Marie Moe	...	Curtis Ray	Kenneth Manthey	...
Poynette	v	MC	2	(608) 635-2122	Arthur Bredeson	Dennis Linn	...	...	...	Donald White	Michael Paulcheck
Prairie Du Chien	c	MC	6	(608) 326-6406	MaryJane Faas	...	...	...	Mark Hoppenjan	Michael King	...
Prairie Du Sac	v	CM	3	(608) 643-2421	Cheryl Sherman	Alan Wildman	...	...	James Hambrecht	Gerald Strunz	Patrick Drone
Prescott	c	CM	3	(715) 262-5544	Sheila Wojtowicz	Lloyd Matthes	...	...	...	James Schneider	Jeffrey Kittleson
Princeton *	c	MC	1	(920) 295-6612	Matt Schneider	...	...	...	George Jachthuber	Don Metoxen	Joshua Schoemann
Pulaski	v	CO	3	(920) 822-5182	Ronald Kryger	...	Karen Ostrowski	...	...	Randal Dunford	Thomas Holewinski
Racine	c	MC	81	(262) 636-9175	James Smith	Benjamin Hughes	Karen Norton	Jerome Maller	John Hilmer	...	Richard Jones
Reedsburg	c	MC	7	(608) 524-6404	Carl Stolte	Lori Curtis	Anna Meister	...	...	Wilbur Abel	William Meyer
Rhinelander	c	MC	7	(715) 365-8607	Richard Johns	Philip Parkinson	Mary Raith	Peggy Lass	Donald Knutson	Glenn Parmeter	Randolph Knuth
Rib Mountain	t	CM	6	(715) 842-0983	...	Gaylene Rhoden	Patricia Jahns	...	...	...	...
Rice Lake *	c	MC	8	(715) 234-7088	Lawrence Jarvela	Curtis Snyder	Kathleen Morse	...	James Resac	John Sommerfeld	Gary Neuman
Richfield	t	CM	..	(262) 628-2260	Diane Pedersen	Toby Cotter	Pam Spranger	...	John Schmidt	Brian Rahn	Gary Wolf
Richland Center	c	MC	5	(608) 647-3466	Larry Fowler	...	Jude Elliott	...	Robert Bindl	John Annear	Richard Wilson
Ripon *	c	MC	6	(920) 748-4916	Aaron Kramer	Steven Barg	...	...	...	David Lukoski	...
River Falls *	c	MC	12	(715) 425-0900	Don Richards	B. Van Osdale	...	...	Robert Schwalen	Roger Leque	...
River Hills	v	CM	1	(414) 352-8213	Robert Brunner	Thomas Tollaksen	C. Toms-Neary	...	David Berousek	Tom Rischmann	Kurt Fredrickson
Rothschild	v	MC	4	(715) 359-3660	Neal Torney	...	...	...	William Padiram	William Schremp	George Peterson
Sauk City	v	CM	3	(608) 643-3932	...	Vicki Breunig	...	...	...	Gerald Strunz	Herman Mack
Saukville	v	CM	4	(262) 284-9423	Barbara Dickmann	Dawn Wagner	...	...	Gilly Schultz	William Meloy	Roy Wilhelm
Seymour *	c	MC	3	(920) 833-2209	...	...	Susan Garsow	...	Steve Krabbe	Edwin Janz	Michael Pepin
Shawano	c	MC	8	(715) 524-4611	Russell Schmidt	James Stadler	Marlene Brath	...	Douglas Knope	Norman Jahn	Rick Stautz
Sheboygan	c	MC	50	(920) 459-3373	James Schramm	...	Patricia Lohse	Richard Gebhart	Mark Zeier	David Kirk	Thomas Holtan
Sheboygan Falls	c	MC	6	(920) 467-7900	...	...	...	...	...	...	...
Sherwood	v	MC	1	(920) 989-1589	...	Randall Friday	...	...	...	...	...
Shorewood	v	CM	13	(414) 847-2700	Mark Kohlenberg	M. Swartz	Kathleen Greig	...	...	David Banaszynski	James Bartnicki
Shorewood Hills	v	CM	1	(608) 267-2680	Peter Hans	Karl Frantz	Jennifer Anderson	...	Thomas De Meuse	Jerry Jansen	Dennis Lybeck
Sister Bay	v	MC	..	(920) 854-4118	Denise Bhirdo	Robert Kufrin	Christy Sully	Juliana Neuman	Chris Hecht	...	Steve Jacobson
Slinger *	v	MC	3	(262) 644-5265	Russell Brandt	Maureen Murphy	...	...	...	Dean Schmidt	...
South Milwaukee	c	MC	21	(414) 762-2222	David Kieck	Tamara Mayzik	Kathleen Lisowski	...	Jay Behling	Ann Wellens	Richard Davidoff
Sparta	c	MC	8	(608) 269-4340	John Gomez	Kenneth Witt	Janice Foss	...	Scott Lindemann	Ray Harris	Jordan Skiff
Spring Green *	v	CM	1	(608) 588-2335	Greg Prem	...	Wendy Crary	...	Lin Gunderson	Kevin Wilkins	Greg Wipperfurth
St. Croix Falls *	c	MC	2	(715) 483-3929	Brad Foss	Ed Emerson	Bonita Leggitt	...	Dale Anderson	Jack Rydeen	Scott Brust
St. Francis	c	MC	8	(414) 481-2300	...	Ralph Voltner	...	...	...	...	...
Stevens Point	c	MC	24	(715) 346-1569	Gary Wescott	...	Victoria Zdroik	John Schlice	Mark Barnes	Douglas Carpenter	...
Stoughton	c	MC	12	(608) 873-6677	Helen Johnson	...	Judy Kinning	...	Marty Lamers	Patrick O'Connor	Karl Manthe
Sturgeon Bay	c	MC	9	(920) 746-2900	...	Kevin O'Donnell	...	...	Terry Mac Donald	Daniel Trelka	Anthony Depies
Sturtevant	v	MC	5	(262) 886-7201	Steven Jansen	...	Donna Deuster	...	...	...	...
Suamico *	v	MC	8	(920) 434-2212	Elizabeth Sheedy	Karen Matze	Bonnie Swan	...	Thomas Hussin	Dennis Kocken	Timothy Krause
Sun Prairie *	c	MC	20	(608) 825-1192	Joseph Chase	Patrick Cannon	D. Hermann Brown	William Burns	Steve Knaus	Frank Sleeter	Larry Herman
Superior *	c	MC	27	(715) 395-7210	David Ross	...	Margaret Ciccone	Jean Vito	Tad Matheson	Floyd Peters	Jeffrey Vito
Sussex	v	CM	8	(262) 246-5200	Patricia Bartlett	Evan Teich	...	...	Thomas Schlei	...	Raymond Grzys
Thiensville	v	CO	3	(262) 242-3720	Donald Molyneux	Dianne Robertson	...	...	William Rausch	Richard Preston	Robert Gehrke
Thorp	c	MC	1	(715) 669-5371	Richard Wnek	Randall Reeg	...	...	...	Sharon Verges	T. McCredden
Tomah	c	MC	8	(608) 374-7422	Charles Ludeking	John Rusch	Jo Ann Cram	...	...	Chris Anderson	Kenneth Patterson
Tomahawk	c	MC	3	(715) 453-4040	Jonathan Rose	...	Paul Garner	...	John Peeters	Mike Smitley	Mark Dochnahl
Trempealeau *	v	MC	1	(608) 534-6434	...	Travis Cooke	Vicki Freeman	...	...	Stanley Ridgeway	Todd Lakey
Turtle Lake *	v	MC	1	(715) 986-2134	Laurie Tarman	William Bell	Frances Duncanson	...	...	Al Gabe	Cory Davis
Twin Lakes	v	MC	5	(262) 877-2858	Cathleen Zamazal	David Cox	Dorothy Sandona	...	Bruce Haase	Robert O'Hallen	...
Two Rivers *	c	CM	12	(920) 793-5525	...	Gregory Buckley	...	...	Kevin Timm	Joseph Collins	Bill Scola
Union Grove	v	CM	4	(262) 878-1818	Robert Orre	C. Rademacher	Janice Winget	...	...	...	L. Behling
Verona *	c	MC	7	(608) 845-6495	Jon Hochkammer	Shawn Murphy	JoAnn Wainwright	...	...	Bernard Coughlin	Ronald Rieder
Viroqua	c	MC	4	(608) 637-7154	Larry Fanta	...	...	...	Steve Skrede	Mark Rahr	Thomas Henry
Washburn	c	MC	2	(715) 373-6130	Ralph Brzezinski	Pete Mann	Vickie Swanson	...	...	Ken Johnson	Charlie Guski
Washington	t	MC	..	(920) 847-2522	...	...	...	...	...	...	...
Washington	t	CM	6	(715) 834-3257	...	...	...	...	...	...	...

Jurisdiction	Type	Form of govern-ment	2000 Popu-lation (000)	Main telephone number	Chief elected official	Appointed administrator	Clerk of the governing board	Chief financial officer	Fire chief	Police chief	Public works director
WISCONSIN continued											
Waterford	v	MC	4	(262) 534-7912	Dave Richmond	Rebecca Ewald	Michelle Allender	...	Steve Denman	John Schanning	Randall Niewolny
Watertown	c	MC	21	(920) 262-4000	Frederick Smith	...	Michael Hoppenrath	...	Dick Olson	Chuck McGee	Brian Field
Waukesha	c	MC	64	(262) 524-3500	Larry Nelson	...		Steve Neaman	Allen LaConte	Leslie Sharrock	Paul Feller
Waunakee	v	CM	8	(608) 850-8500	...	Ronald Wilde	Julee Helt	David Ferris	...	Kevin Plendl	Kevin Even
Waupaca	c	MC	5	(715) 258-4411	Brian Smith	Henry Veleker	...	...	Jeff Olson	Timothy Goke	John Edlebeck
Waupun	c	MC	10	(920) 324-7900	Jodi Steger	Gary Rogers	Kyle Clark	...	Jeff Berry	Dale Herringa	Richard Flynn
Wausau	c	MC	38	(715) 261-6610	Linda Lawrence	...	K. Michaels-Sagger	Maryanne Groat	Gary Buchburger	William Brandimore	John Hess
Wauwatosa	c	MC	47	(414) 479-8915	...	James Archambo	Carla Ledesma	Ronald Braier	Dean Redman	...	William Kappel
West Allis	c	MC	61	(414) 302-8200	Jeannette Bell	Paul Ziehler	...	Gary Schmid	Steven Hook	Dean Puschnig	Michael Pertmer
West Bend *	c	MC	28	(262) 335-5114	Kristine Deiss	Dennis Melvin	Barbara Barringer	...	James Vest	Kenneth Meuler	Terry Kiekhaefer
West Milwaukee	v	MC	4	(414) 645-1530	Ronald Hayward	Patrick Casey	...	...	...	Eugene Oldenburg	James Stenzel
West Salem	v	CM	4	(608) 786-1858	...	Teresa Schnitzler	...	...	...	Dennis Abbott	Wade Peterson
Weston	v	CM	12	(715) 359-6114	Vilas Machmueller	Dean Zuleger	Sherry Weinkauf	John Jacobs	Loren White	Daniel Vergin	Keith Donner
Weyauwega *	c	MC	1	(920) 867-2635	...	S. Scheuermann	...	...	...	...	...
Whitefish Bay	v	CM	14	(414) 962-6690	Kathleen Pritchard	James Grassman	...	...	...	Gary Mikulec	...
Whitewater	c	CM	13	(262) 473-0500	...	Kevin Brunner	Michele Smith	Doug Saubert	Howard Higgins	James Coan	Dean Fischer
Winneconne	v	CM	2	(920) 582-4381	John Rogers	Stephen McNeil	Jacquin Jensen	...	...	Peter Running	Carroll Vizecky
Winsdor	t	MC	5	(608) 846-3854	...	...	...	...	...	...	...
Wisconsin Dells	c	MC	2	(608) 254-2012	Ben Borcher	...	Dale Darling	...	Mark Hamm	Dean Edgington	Michael Horkan
Wisconsin Rapids *	c	MC	18	(715) 421-8200	Mary Jo Carson	...	Shane Blaser	Timothy Desory	Mitchell Waite	Kurt Keuer	...
Wittenberg	v	MC	1	(715) 253-6063	...		...	...	...	...	...
Wrightstown	v	MC	1	(920) 532-5567	...	Daniel Guild	...	...	...	...	...
WYOMING											
Afton	t	MC	1	(307) 885-9831	Chad Jensen	Gregg Wilkes	Lisa Hokunson	...	Allan Sessions	Tim Heggenstaller	Blake Robinson
Buffalo	t	MC	3	(307) 684-5566	Bruce Hepp	...	Kay Wertz	...	Gomer Gammon	Mike Dahmer	Leslie Hook
Casper	c	CM	49	(307) 235-8400	Barbara Peryam	Thomas Forslund	...	Velton McDonald	Mark Young	Thomas Pagel	Philip Stuckert
Cheyenne	c	MC	53	(307) 637-6300	Leo Pando	...	Carol Intlekofer	...	Dennis Piester	John Powell	Jackie Smith
Cody	c	MC	8	(307) 527-7511	Ken Stockwell	McFerrin Whiteman	...	...	...	Perry Rockvam	Stephen Payne
Douglas	c	CM	5	(307) 358-3462	Sherri Mullinnix	Bobbe Fitzhugh	...	Janice Lampert	...	Lori Emmert	Brian Sweeney
Evanston	c	MC	11	(307) 783-6307	Mark Harris	James Davis	...	...	...	...	Brian Honey
Evansville	t	MC	2	(307) 234-6530	...	...	...	...	...	...	...
Gillette	c	CM	19	(307) 686-5200	Duane Evenson	Bret Jones	Karlene Abelseth	Nadine Ireland	...	Richard Paul	George Haines
Glenrock *	t	MC	2	(307) 436-9294	Steven Cielinski	...	Donna Geho	...	...	Michael Colling	Dave Andrews
Green River	c	MC	11	(307) 872-0500	David Gomez	Barry Cook	Jeff Nieters	...	George Nomis	Greg Gillen	Michael Nelson
Jackson	t	CM	8	(307) 733-3932	Mark Barron	Robert McLaurin	...	Kevin Watson	Rusty Palmer	Dan Zivkovich	Larry Pardee
Kemmerer	c	CM	2	(307) 828-2350	Jim Carroll	John Roberts	Glenda Young	...	...	Jay Phillips	...
Lander	c	MC	6	(307) 332-2870	Mick Wolfe	...	Sharon Anderson	...	...	Richard Currah	Mickey Simmons
Laramie	c	CM	27	(307) 721-5200	Fred Homer	Janine Jordan	R. Sue Jones	Malea Brown	Randy Vickers	...	Terry Haugen
Lovell	t	CM	2	(307) 548-6551	...	...	...	...	...	...	...
Lyman	t	MC	1	(307) 787-6595	Oliver Moretti	...	Lynn Arnell	...	...	Dean Iannelli	Andrew Spray
Mills	t	MC	2	(307) 234-6679	Robert Goff	...	Sue Regennas	...	Ronald Schindler	Jerry Endresen	Robert McPherson
Newcastle	c	MC	3	(307) 746-3535	Edward Wagoner	...	Gregory James	...	Donny Munger	Andrew Macke	Douglas Sankey
Powell	c	CM	5	(307) 754-5106	James Milburn	...	Ardyce Busboom	...	...	Timothy Feathers	...
Rawlins *	c	CM	8	(307) 328-4500	Kenneth Klouda	David Derragon	Marla Brown	...	Scott Hannum	James Reed	...
Riverton	c	CM	9	(307) 856-2227	John Vincent	James Napier	Gloria Leadbetter	...	...	John Snell	William Urbigkit
Rock Springs	c	MC	18	(307) 352-1500	Timothy Kaumo	...	...	...	Brad Sarff	Michael Lowell	Paul Kauchich
Sheridan *	c	MC	15	(307) 674-6483	Dave Kinskey	...	Arthur Elkins	...	Patrick Reitz	Mike Card	Rod Liesinger
Thermopolis	t	MC	3	(307) 864-3838	...	...	Tracey Van Huele	...	...	James Weisbeck	Earnest Slagle
Torrington	t	MC	5	(307) 532-5666	Mike Varney	...	Sandy Pittman	...	Dennis Estes	Billy Janes	Jim Foster
Wheatland	t	MC	3	(307) 322-2962	Joel Dingman	...	Cindy Kahler	...	...	Steve Gilmore	...
Worland *	c	MC	5	(307) 347-2486	Lawrence Shearer	...	Tracy Glanz	...	...	Robert Richardson	Gene Cliame

Directory 1/10

OFFICIALS IN U.S. COUNTIES 2,500 AND OVER IN POPULATION

Data collection

The names appearing in this directory were obtained from the ICMA database of local government employees. Local governments that have provided updated information are designated by an asterisk (∗). For those that have not, the directories show the names of officials from the most recent update.

As noted in "Inside the *Year Book*," there are certain unorganized areas of some states that have a county designation from the Census Bureau for strictly administrative purposes and are not included in the *Year Book* databases. Along with 12 areas in Alaska, 2 areas in South Dakota, and 1 area in Montana, these comprise all 8 areas in Connecticut and all 5 areas in Rhode Island.

Form of government

CM   Council-manager
CE   Council–elected executive
C   Commission

Population

Population figures are rounded; 14,500 will appear as 15.

(. .) Less than 500 population

Other codes

. . . Data not reported or not applicable

Jurisdiction	Form of govern- ment	2000 Popu- lation (000)	Main telephone number	Chief elected official	Appointed administrator	Clerk of the governing board	Chief financial officer	Director of personnel	Chief law enforcement official
ALABAMA									
Autauga	C	43	(334) 361-3701	Clyde Chambliss	Steven Golsan	. . .	. . .	. . .	. . .
Baldwin	∗ CM	140	(251) 937-9561	Wayne Gruenloh	Michael Thompson	. . .	Locke Williams	Susan Lovett	Hoss Mack
Barbour	C	29	(334) 775-3203	. . .	. . .	. . .	. . .	. . .	. . .
Bibb	C	20	(205) 926-3114	. . .	Mark Tyner	. . .	. . .	. . .	Keith Hannah
Blount	C	51	(205) 274-9111	. . .	. . .	. . .	. . .	. . .	. . .
Bullock	C	11	(334) 738-3883	Ronald Smith	Lillie Hall	Marion Milbry	Janne Brabham	. . .	Raymond Rodgers
Butler	C	21	(334) 382-3612	. . .	. . .	Diane Kilpatrick	. . .	. . .	Diane Harris
Calhoun	C	112	(256) 241-2800	. . .	Kenneth Joiner	. . .	. . .	. . .	Larry Amerson
Chambers	C	36	(334) 864-4341	Jack Bunn	James Simms	Regina Norris	. . .	. . .	Calvin Lockhart
Cherokee	C	23	(256) 927-3009	. . .	. . .	. . .	. . .	. . .	. . .
Chilton	C	39	(205) 755-1551	. . .	Sharon Sumrall	Edith Gentry	. . .	Cathy Martin	Billy Fulmer
Choctaw	C	15	(205) 459-2100	. . .	. . .	. . .	. . .	. . .	. . .
Clarke	C	27	(251) 275-3507	. . .	. . .	. . .	. . .	. . .	. . .
Clay	C	14	(256) 354-7888	Ricky Burney	Lou Hanners	Jeffery Colborn	. . .	. . .	Charlie Toland
Cleburne	C	14	(256) 463-7130	Ryan Robertson	Steven Swafford	Mary Thomas	Melissa Wood	. . .	Joe Jacks
Coffee	∗ C	43	(251) 894-5556	. . .	Kathryn Lolley	. . .	. . .	. . .	Dave Sutton
Colbert	CM	54	(256) 386-8500	. . .	. . .	. . .	. . .	. . .	. . .
Conecuh	C	14	(251) 578-2095	. . .	. . .	. . .	. . .	Sandra Smith	Dudley Godwin
Coosa	C	12	(205) 377-2420	. . .	Sherrie Kelley	. . .	. . .	. . .	. . .
Covington	C	37	(334) 222-3613	. . .	. . .	. . .	. . .	. . .	. . .
Crenshaw	∗ C	13	(334) 335-6568	Ronnie Hudson	David Smyth	. . .	Annette Sipper	. . .	Charles West
Cullman	C	77	(205) 739-3530	. . .	. . .	. . .	. . .	. . .	. . .
Dale	C	49	(334) 774-6262	C. Johnston	. . .	. . .	. . .	Peggy Roper	James Mixon
Dallas	C	46	(334) 877-4803	Roy Moore	. . .	. . .	. . .	Marilyn Riddle	Harris Huffman
De Kalb	CM	64	(256) 845-8500	Sidney Holcomb	Matt Sharp	. . .	. . .	. . .	. . .
Elmore	∗ C	65	(334) 567-1156	Joe Faulk	Lera Medders	. . .	. . .	. . .	William Franklin
Escambia	CM	38	(251) 867-0828	. . .	. . .	. . .	. . .	. . .	. . .
Etowah	C	103	(256) 549-5393	. . .	. . .	. . .	. . .	James Naugher	James Hayes
Fayette	C	18	(205) 932-4510	. . .	John Gordon	. . .	. . .	Bobbie Kemp	Richard White
Franklin	C	31	(205) 332-8850	Mike Green	Gail Estis	. . .	. . .	. . .	. . .
Geneva	C	25	(334) 684-5600	. . .	. . .	. . .	. . .	. . .	. . .
Greene	C	9	(205) 372-3349	Chris Beeker	. . .	. . .	. . .	. . .	Johnny Isaac
Hale	∗ C	17	(334) 624-4257	Leland Avery	Tricia Galbreath	. . .	. . .	. . .	Kenneth Ellis
Henry	CM	16	(334) 585-3257	. . .	. . .	. . .	. . .	. . .	. . .
Houston	C	88	(334) 677-4777	Mark Culver	Roy Roberts	Karen Price	. . .	Jeff Baker	Lamar Glover
Jackson	C	53	(256) 574-9280	James Tidmore	Terry West	Valerie Harris	. . .	Shirley Morris	Terry Wells
Jefferson	C	662	(205) 325-5523	Gary White	Orville Ifill	. . .	Steve Sayler	Ben Payton	Mike Hale
Lamar	C	15	(205) 695-7333	. . .	. . .	. . .	. . .	. . .	. . .
Lauderdale	C	87	(256) 760-5750	Dewey Mitchell	. . .	. . .	. . .	. . .	Charles Townsend
Lawrence	C	34	(256) 974-0663	. . .	. . .	. . .	. . .	. . .	. . .
Lee	C	115	(334) 745-9767	Bill English	Roger Rendleman	. . .	. . .	Kim Oas	. . .
Limestone	C	65	(256) 233-6400	Charles Seibert	. . .	Pamela Ball	Emily Ezzell	Anita Jewell	Michael Blakely
Lowndes	C	13	(334) 548-2331	Charlie King	Jacquelyn Thomas	Geraldine Ingram	. . .	. . .	Willie Vaughner
Macon	C	24	(334) 727-5120	Jesse Upshaw	. . .	. . .	Susan Thomas	Gertrude Benjamin	David Warren
Madison	C	276	(256) 532-3492	Mike Gillespie	Edsel Baites	. . .	Judy Teague	Gail Medley	Blake Dorning
Marengo	C	22	(334) 295-2200	. . .	. . .	. . .	. . .	John Marler	. . .
Marion	CM	31	(205) 921-3172	Bobby Burleson	. . .	Gearldean Lindsey	. . .	. . .	E. B. Purser
Marshall	CE	82	(256) 571-7701	. . .	Nancy Willson	. . .	. . .	Christy Kelley	. . .
Mobile	CE	399	(251) 574-5077	Mike Dean	John Pafenbach	. . .	Michelle Herman	. . .	Jack Tillman
Monroe	C	24	(251) 743-3782	. . .	. . .	. . .	. . .	. . .	. . .
Montgomery	∗ CE	223	(334) 832-1259	Todd Strange	Donald Mims	. . .	Sandra Johnson	Barbara Montoya	D. T. Marshall
Morgan	C	111	(256) 351-4600	. . .	. . .	. . .	. . .	. . .	. . .
Perry	C	11	(334) 683-2200	Johnny Flowers	. . .	Walta Kennie	. . .	. . .	James Hood
Pickens	C	20	(205) 367-2020	Tony Junkin	Cheryl Gary	Marva Gipson	. . .	. . .	David Abston
Pike	C	29	(334) 566-6374	Willie Thomas	Harry Sanders	. . .	. . .	. . .	Russell Thomas
Randolph	C	22	(256) 357-4980	Mack Diamond	. . .	Kathy Breed	Cindy Arrington	Lisa Green	. . .
Russell	C	49	(334) 298-6426	Clifford Lee	. . .	. . .	. . .	. . .	. . .
Shelby	C	143	(205) 669-3740	. . .	Alex Dudchock	. . .	William Burbage	Jennifer Ray	Christopher Curry
St. Clair	∗ C	64	(205) 594-2100	Stanley Batemon	Kim McPherson	. . .	Donna Wood	Judith Abernathy	Terry Surles
Sumter	C	14	(205) 652-2731	. . .	. . .	. . .	. . .	. . .	. . .
Talladega	C	80	(205) 362-1357	. . .	. . .	. . .	. . .	. . .	. . .
Tallapoosa	C	41	(256) 825-4268	Johnny Allen	. . .	. . .	. . .	Deborah Dobbs	James Abbett
Tuscaloosa	C	164	(205) 349-3870	C. McCollum	. . .	Robert Johnston	William Lamb	Melvin Vines	Edmund Sexton
Walker	C	70	(205) 384-7230	Bruce Hamrick	Jill Farris	. . .	. . .	Edith Duncan	John Tirey
Washington	C	18	(251) 847-2208	John Armstrong	Mary Carpenter	. . .	. . .	. . .	William Wheat
Wilcox	C	13	(334) 682-9112	Mark Curl	Clarissa Dear	. . .	. . .	Demetria Turk	Prince Arnold
Winston	C	24	(205) 489-5026	Roger Hayes	. . .	Joanie Wright	. . .	. . .	David Sutherland
ALASKA									
Aleutians East	CM	2	(907) 383-2699	Dick Jacobsen	Robert Juettner	Tina Anderson	Cynthia Samuelson	. . .	. . .
Bristol Bay	CM	1	(907) 246-4224	. . .	David Soulak	. . .	. . .	. . .	Jerry Castleberry
Denali	∗ C	1	(907) 683-1330	David Talerico	. . .	Gail Pieknik	. . .	. . .	. . .
Fairbanks North Star	C	82	(907) 459-1000	Rhonda Boyles	. . .	Mona Drexler	Michael Lamb	Sallie Stuvek	. . .

Directory 1/10 continued

OFFICIALS IN U.S. COUNTIES 2,500 AND OVER IN POPULATION

Jurisdiction	Form of government	2000 Population (000)	Main telephone number	Chief elected official	Appointed administrator	Clerk of the governing board	Chief financial officer	Director of personnel	Chief law enforcement official
ALASKA continued									
Haines	CE	2	(907) 766-2711	...	...	Jacqueline Lawson	...	Jerry Lapp	...
Kenai Peninsula	CE	40	(907) 262-4441	Dale Bagley	...	Linda Murphy	...	Richard Campbell	...
Ketchikan Gateway	CM	14	(907) 228-6625	Mike Salazar	Dan Bockhorst	Harriett Edwards	Alvin Hall	...	Jerry Cegelske
Kodiak Island	CE	13	(907) 486-9301	Jerome Selby	Rick Gifford	Donna Smith	Karleton Short	Rachael Nelson	...
Lake and Peninsula	* CM	1	(907) 246-3421	Glen Alsworth	Jeff Currier	Sheila Bergey	George Castaneda	...	...
Matanuska Susitna	* CM	59	(907) 745-4801	Curt Menard	John Duffy	Michelle McGehee	...	Patricia Von Ah	...
North Slope	CM	5	(907) 852-2611	Edward Itta	George Olemaun	...	John Ames	Jeri Cleveland	Don Grimes
Northwest Arctic	CM	7	(907) 442-2500	Reggie Cleveland	Chuck Greene	Valarie Romane	Judith Hassinger	Linda Joule	...
Yakutat	CM	..	(907) 784-3323	David Stone	...	Catherine Bremner	Constance Klushkan	...	...
ARIZONA									
Apache	CE	69	(928) 337-4364	Joe Shirley	Delwin Wengert	Sue Hall	Karla Rogers	...	C. Lee
Cochise	CM	117	(520) 432-9700	Pat Call	Jody Klein	Nadine Parkhurst	Lois Klein	Ken Wallace	Larry Dever
Coconino	CM	116	(928) 779-6702	Paul Babbitt	Steven Peru	Wendi Escoffier	Holly Lindfors	Jane Emberty	Joseph Richards
Gila	CM	51	(928) 425-3231	Ron Christensen	John Nelson	...	Dave Patterson	Susan Mitchell	John Armer
Graham	CE	33	(928) 428-3250	...	...	Terry Cooper	Clel Flake	...	Frank Hughes
Greenlee	CE	8	(928) 865-2072	Hector Ruedas	Deborah Gale	...	...	...	Richard McCluskey
La Paz	CE	19	(928) 669-6115	Clifford Edey	...	Donna Hale	Ava Alcaida	...	Hal Collett
Maricopa	CM	3072	(602) 506-3223	Janice Brewer	David Smith	Fran McCarrol	Thomas Manos	Gwynn Simpson	Joseph Arpaio
Mohave	CE	155	(928) 753-0729	Tom Sockwell	Ronnie Walker	Barbara Bracken	John Timko	Geoff Riches	Thomas Sheahan
Navajo	C	97	(928) 524-4000	Percy Deal	James Jayne	Judy Jones	Clinton Shreeve	Gilbert Gonzales	Gary Butler
Pima	CM	843	(520) 740-8672	...	Chuck Huckelberry	Lori Godoshian	Thomas Burke	Gwendolyn Hatcher	Clarence Dupnik
Pinal	CM	179	(520) 866-6228	Lionel Ruiz	Terry Doolittle	...	Victoria Prins	Michael Arnold	Chris Vasquez
Santa Cruz	CM	38	(520) 761-7800	Manuel Ruiz	Gregory Lucero	Melinda Meek	Jennifer St. John	Carlos Rivera	Marco Estrada
Yavapai	* CE	167	(928) 771-3252	...	Julie Ayers	...	John Zander	Alan Vigneron	...
Yuma	CE	160	(928) 373-1013	Lenore Stuart	Robert Pickels	...	Douglas Allen	Alonzo Strange	Ralph Ogden
ARKANSAS									
Arkansas	C	20	(870) 673-3181	...	...	...	...	...	...
Ashley	C	24	(870) 853-2000	Larry Kinnaird	...	Genie Kersten	...	...	James Robinson
Baxter	C	38	(870) 425-2755	Joe Bodenhamer	...	Rhonda Porter	...	...	...
Benton	C	153	(479) 271-1000	Gary Black	Travis Harp	Mary Slinkard	Richard McComas	Janie Robinson	Andrew Lee
Boone	C	33	(870) 741-9724	Mike Moore	...	Kristie Blevins	Linda Brown	...	Dan Hickman
Bradley	CE	12	(870) 226-3464	Noel Rice	...	Janet Kimbrell	...	...	William Belin
Calhoun	C	5	(870) 798-4818	Arthur Jones	...	Alma Davis	...	...	John Ables
Carroll	CE	25	(870) 423-2967	...	...	...	...	...	...
Chicot	CE	14	(870) 265-8015	Fred Zieman	...	Pam Donaldson	...	...	Floyd White
Clark	C	23	(870) 246-5847	Ron Daniell	...	Rhonda Williams	...	...	Troy Tucker
Clay	C	17	(870) 598-2667	...	Gary Howell	Sharon Williams	...	...	Ronnie Cole
Cleburne	* CE	24	(501) 362-8141	Claude Dill	Patsy McNeese	Dana Guffey	...	...	Marty Moss
Cleveland	C	8	(870) 325-6521	Vernon Dollar	...	Sharon Gray	...	...	Joe King
Columbia	CE	25	(870) 234-2542	...	...	...	...	...	...
Conway	CE	20	(501) 354-9640	Jimmy Hart	Rebecca Spires	Debra Hartman	...	...	Mark Flowers
Craighead	C	82	(870) 933-4500	...	...	...	...	...	James Ballard
Crawford	C	53	(479) 474-1312	Harold Loyd	...	Patti Hill	...	...	Richard Busby
Crittenden	C	50	(870) 739-4434	Melton Holt	...	Ruth Trent	...	...	...
Cross	C	19	(870) 238-3373	...	...	...	...	...	Donny Ford
Dallas	C	9	(870) 352-3317	Jimmy Jones	...	Janice Mc Daniel	...	...	...
Desha	C	15	(870) 877-2426	...	...	...	...	...	...
Drew	* CE	18	(870) 460-6200	Damon Lampkin	...	Lyna Gulledge	...	...	...
Faulkner	C	86	(501) 450-4900	...	...	...	...	...	...
Franklin	C	17	(479) 667-4726	Joe Powell	Kathy McDonald	Sharon Needham	Donna Vaughn	...	Reed Hayes
Fulton	C	11	(870) 895-3341	Curren Everett	...	Gene Maguffee	...	...	...
Garland	CE	88	(501) 622-3600	Larry Williams	...	Vicki Rima	...	Valerie Dodge	...
Grant	C	16	(870) 942-2551	Dan Nall	...	Carol Ewing	...	...	Sammy Pruitt
Greene	C	37	(870) 239-6300	...	...	...	...	...	Jerry Crane
Hempstead	C	23	(870) 777-2241	Charles Martin	...	Jackie Ridling	...	...	...
Hot Spring	C	30	(501) 332-2261	...	...	Shirley Dildy	...	...	Butch Morris
Howard	C	14	(870) 845-7500	Max Tackett	...	Margaret Boothby	...	...	Ron Webb
Independence	CE	34	(870) 793-8800	David Wyatt	Rita Potts	Rhonda Halbrook	...	...	Joe Martz
Izard	C	13	(870) 368-4328	Eddie Cooper	...	Pamela Graham	Marilyn Downing	...	David Lucas
Jackson	CE	18	(870) 523-7400	Jerry Carlew	...	Pamela Ratliff	Dottie Calhoun	...	W. Brassell
Jefferson	C	84	(870) 541-5360	Jack Jones	Winnie Eastman	...	...	...	...
Johnson	C	22	(479) 754-3967	...	...	Diane Fletcher	...	...	Danny Ormond
Lafayette	C	8	(870) 921-4858	Frank Scroggins	...	Tina Stowers	...	...	Dan Ellison
Lawrence	C	17	(870) 886-1110	Alex Latham	...	...	...	...	...
Lee	C	12	(870) 295-2339	...	...	...	...	...	...
Lincoln	C	14	(870) 628-4147	...	...	...	...	...	...
Little River	C	13	(870) 898-7202	Carolyn Coleman	...	Linda Coleman	Deanna Bishop	...	Danny Russell
Logan	C	22	(479) 963-3601	...	...	...	...	...	...
Lonoke	C	52	(501) 676-6403	Don Bevis	...	Myrtle Finch	...	...	J. Isaac
Madison	C	14	(479) 738-6721	...	...	...	...	...	...
Marion	C	16	(870) 449-6231	...	...	...	...	...	...
Miller	CE	40	(870) 774-1501	Hubert Easley	...	Ann Nicholas	...	...	H. Phillips
Mississippi	C	51	(870) 763-3212	...	...	...	...	...	...
Monroe	C	10	(870) 747-3632	Tom Catlett	...	Janet Tweedle	...	...	Larry Morris
Montgomery	C	9	(870) 867-3521	Ted Elder	...	Debbie Baxter	...	...	Barry Spivey
Nevada	C	9	(870) 887-3115	James Brown	...	Julie Stockton	Sydney De Charme	...	Steve Otwell
Newton	C	8	(870) 446-5127	Harold Smith	Carolyn McCutcheon	Hubert Robinson	...	...	Mark Rupp
Ouachita	C	28	(870) 837-2210	Mike Hesterly	...	Britt Williford	...	...	Paul Lucas
Perry	* C	10	(501) 889-5128	True Robinson	...	Barbara Lovell	...	...	...
Phillips	CM	26	(870) 338-5500	...	...	...	...	...	...
Pike	C	11	(870) 285-2743	Donald Baker	...	Sandy Campbell	...	...	Jerry Jones
Poinsett	C	25	(870) 578-4412	William Craft	...	Fonda Condra	...	...	Larry Mills
Polk	C	20	(479) 394-8100	Ray Stanley	...	Terri Harrison	...	...	Mike Oglesby
Pope	C	54	(479) 968-6064	...	...	Karan Tate	...	...	...
Prairie	C	9	(870) 256-3741	Butch Calhoun	...	...	...	...	Randy Raper
Pulaski	CE	361	(501) 340-6110	Floyd Villines	...	...	Ron Quillin	Temperlene Smith	Randy Johnson
Randolph	C	18	(870) 892-5264	Michael Davis	...	Janis Mock	...	...	Rob Samons
Saline	C	83	(501) 303-5600	Lanny Fite	...	Freddy Burton	...	...	Judy Pridgen
Scott	CE	10	(479) 637-2155	Charlie Vaughan	Edna Piles	James Owens	...	...	Buck Byford

Directory 1/10
continued

OFFICIALS IN U.S. COUNTIES 2,500 AND OVER IN POPULATION

Jurisdiction	Form of govern- ment	2000 Popu- lation (000)	Main telephone number	Chief elected official	Appointed administrator	Clerk of the governing board	Chief financial officer	Director of personnel	Chief law enforcement official
ARKANSAS continued									
Searcy	C	8	(870) 448-3807	Paul Lee	. . .	Wesley Smith	. . .	. . .	George Sutterfield
Sebastian	CE	115	(479) 783-6139	David Hudson	Tom Minton	Nancy Brewer	Virginia Reed	. . .	Paul Atkinson
Sevier	CE	15	(870) 642-2425	Dick Tallman	. . .	Sandra Dunn	. . .	. . .	John Partain
Sharp	C	17	(870) 994-7338	Joe Stidman	. . .	Tommy Estes	. . .	. . .	Dale Weaver
St. Francis	C	29	(870) 261-1700	Carl Cisco	. . .	. . .	. . .	. . .	Dave Partman
Stone	C	11	(870) 269-3351	. . .	. . .	Donna Wilson	. . .	. . .	. . .
Union	C	45	(870) 864-1910	. . .	. . .	. . .	. . .	. . .	. . .
Van Buren	C	16	(479) 745-2443	Robert Bramlett	Pam Baugus	Ester Bass	. . .	Bobbye Bennett	Dennis Bradley
Washington	C	157	(479) 444-1728	Jerry Hunton	John Gibson	Marilyn Edwards	. . .	Naomi Mitchell	Steve Whitmill
White	CE	67	(501) 279-6233	. . .	. . .	. . .	. . .	. . .	. . .
Woodruff	CM	8	(870) 347-5206	William Simmons	Erlene Sawyer	Becky Hicks	. . .	. . .	Jack Caperton
Yell	* C	21	(479) 495-4860	Jimmy Witt	. . .	Carolyn Morris	. . .	. . .	Bill Gilkey
CALIFORNIA									
Alameda	CM	1443	(510) 272-6471	. . .	Susan Muranishi	Crystal Hishida	Patrick O'Connell	Denise Eaton-May	Charles Plummer
Alpine	CE	1	(530) 694-2287	Herman Zellmer	. . .	Barbara Jones	Marilyn McKenzie	. . .	Henry Veatch
Amador	* C	35	(209) 223-6456	Louis Boitano	Terri Daly	Sheldon Johnson	Joe Lowe	. . .	Martin Ryan
Butte	CE	203	(530) 538-7651	. . .	. . .	Candace Grubbs	David Houser	Jeanne Gravette	Perry Reniff
Calaveras	CE	40	(209) 754-6303	. . .	Thomas Mitchell	Karen Varni	. . .	. . .	Dennis Downum
Colusa	* CE	18	(530) 458-0420	Christy Scofield	. . .	Kathleen Moran	Peggy Scroggins	. . .	Scott Marshall
Contra Costa	CM	948	(925) 335-1080	John Gioia	. . .	Stephen Weir	. . .	Lori Gentles	Warren Rupf
Del Norte	C	27	(707) 464-7214	Jack Reese	Jeannine Galatioto	Donna Walsh	Christie Babich	. . .	Dean Wilson
El Dorado	CM	156	(530) 621-5530	. . .	Laura Gill	Cindy Keck	Joe Harn	Mark Gregerson	Jeffrey Neves
Fresno	* CM	799	(559) 488-3266	Bob Waterston	Bart Bohn	Victor Salazar	. . .	Ralph Jimenez	Margaret Mims
Glenn	C	26	(530) 934-6451	Denny Bungarz	David Shoemaker	. . .	Don Santoro	John Greco	Robert Shadley
Humboldt	CM	126	(707) 445-7266	Roger Rodoni	Loretta Nickolaus	Lora Canzoneri	Michael Giacone	Richard Haeg	Gary Philp
Imperial	CM	142	(760) 482-4488	Gary Wyatt	Robertta Burns	Dolores Provencio	Douglas Newland	Nellie Lerma	Harold Carter
Inyo	CE	17	(760) 878-0373	. . .	Ronald Juliff	. . .	. . .	. . .	. . .
Kern	CM	661	(661) 868-3480	. . .	. . .	Ann Barnett	Kay Madden	Mack Wimbish
Kings	CM	129	(559) 582-3211	Jon Rachford	Larry Spikes	Catherine Venturella	Darrell Warnock	Allison Picard	Ron Calhoun
Lake	C	58	(707) 263-2213	Walter Wilcox	Kelly Cox	Sharon Lewis	Judy Murray	Glenn Walters	. . .
Lassen	* CM	33	(530) 251-8349	. . .	John Ketelsen	Julie Bustamante	M. Karen Fouch	Ronald Vossler	Steven Warren
Los Angeles	CM	9519	(213) 974-1101	Yvonne Burke	David Janssen	Conny McCormack	J. Tyler McCauley	Michael Henry	Leroy Baca
Madera	* CE	123	(559) 661-5455	. . .	Stell Manfredi	Rebecca Martinez	Robert DeWall	Kathy Taylor	John Anderson
Marin	CE	247	(415) 499-6111	. . .	Matthew Hymel	Diane Sauer	Richard Arrow	Laura Armor	Robert Doyle
Mariposa	CE	17	(209) 966-3222	Robert Stewart	Mike Coffield	Margie Williams	Don Phillips	. . .	Roger Matlock
Mendocino	CM	86	(707) 463-4441	Richard Shoemaker	Albert Beltrami	Marsha Wharff	Dennis Huey	Sue Campbell	Anthony Craver
Merced	CE	210	(209) 385-7682	. . .	Demitrios Tatum	. . .	James Ball	Beverly Morse	Gary Carlson
Modoc	C	9	(530) 233-6400	. . .	Michael Maxwell	Stephanie Northrup	. . .	. . .	. . .
Mono	CE	12	(760) 932-5410	Mary Pipersky	David Wilbrecht	Renn Nolan	Lauretta Cochran	Stephanie Kentala	Dan Paranick
Monterey	CE	401	(831) 755-5115	Dave Potter	Lew Bauman	Darlene Drain	Rosie Pando	. . .	Mike Kanalakis
Napa	CE	124	(707) 253-4303	Brad Wagenknecht	Nancy Watt-Collins	Pamela Miller	Pamela Kindig	Dennis Morris	Gary Simpson
Nevada	CM	92	(530) 265-7040	Samuel Dardick	Richard Haffey	Cathy Thompson	Bruce Bielefelt	Lori Walsh	Keith Royal
Orange	CM	2846	(714) 834-5315	. . .	Thomas Mauk	Gary Granville	Gary Burton	Jan Walden	Michael Carona
Placer	* CE	248	(530) 889-4060	. . .	Thomas Miller	Jim McCauley	Kathy Martinis	Nancy Nittler	Edward Bonner
Plumas	C	20	(530) 283-6444	Bobby Pearson	Jack Ingstad	Kathleen Williams	Michael Tedrick	Gayla Trumbo	Terry Bergstrand
Riverside	CM	1545	(909) 955-3500	. . .	David Parrish	Gary Orso	Charles Corser	Ronald Komers	Robert Doyle
Sacramento	CM	1223	(916) 440-7097	. . .	Terry Schutten	. . .	. . .	Mike DeBord	. . .
San Benito	* CM	53	(831) 636-4000	. . .	Susan Thompson	John Hodges	. . .	. . .	. . .
San Bernardino	CM	1709	(909) 387-4811	Jerry Eaves	. . .	. . .	Errol Mackzum	Barbara Musselman	Gary Penrod
San Diego	CM	2813	(619) 531-5100	. . .	Walter Ekard	. . .	William Kelly	Carlos Arauz	William Kolender
San Joaquin	CE	563	(209) 468-3113	. . .	Manuel Lopez	Lois Sabyoun	Adrian Van Houten	Cynthia Clays	Steve Moore
San Luis Obispo	CM	246	(805) 781-5011	Harry Ovitt	David Edge	Julie Rodewald	Gere Sibbach	. . .	James Hedges
San Mateo	CM	707	(650) 363-4000	Rose Jacobs Gibson	John Maltbie	. . .	Tom Huening	Mary Welch	Donald Horsley
Santa Barbara	CM	399	(805) 568-3400	Joni Gray	Michael Brown	Brenda Davis	Robert Geis	Ann Goodrich	Jim Thomas
Santa Clara	CM	1682	(408) 299-5830	. . .	Peter Kutras	Brenda Davis	John Guthrie	. . .	Laurie Smith
Santa Cruz	CM	255	(831) 454-2600	Ellen Pirie	Susan Mauriello	Richard Bedal	Gary Knutson	Dania Wong	Mark Tracy
Shasta	CE	163	(530) 225-5561	Glenn Hawes	Lawrence Lees	. . .	Richard Graham	Harry Albright	Jim Pope
Sierra	C	3	(530) 289-3295	. . .	. . .	. . .	Van Maddox	. . .	Leland Adams
Siskiyou	CM	44	(530) 842-8017	. . .	Howard Moody	Colleen Baker	Leanna Dancer	. . .	Charles Byrd
Solano	* CM	394	(707) 421-6170	William Carroll	Michael Johnson	Chuck Lomeli	William Eldridge	Yolanda Ivigon	Rick Hulse
Sonoma	CM	458	(707) 565-2331	Paul Kelley	Robert Deis	Eeve Lewis	Rodney Dole	Ray Myers	William Cogbill
Stanislaus	CM	446	(209) 525-6341	. . .	Richard Robinson	Lee Lundrigan	Larry Haugh	. . .	Mark Puthuff
Sutter	CE	78	(530) 822-7100	. . .	Larry Combs	Joan Bechtel	Robert Stark	Joann Dobelbower	James Denney
Tehama	* CM	56	(530) 527-4655	. . .	Williams Goodwin	Beverly Ross	LeRoy Anderson	Michelle Schafer	Clay Parker
Trinity	C	13	(530) 623-1325	Billie Millie	. . .	Dero Forslund	David Nelson	. . .	Lorrac Craig
Tulare	CM	368	(559) 733-6266	James Maples	. . .	Gregory Hardcastle	Jerry Messinger	Tim Huntley	Bill Wittman
Tuolumne	CE	54	(209) 533-5511	Mark Thornton	Craig Pedro	Alicia Jamar	Deborah Russell	Eric Larson	James Mele
Ventura	* CM	753	(805) 654-5129	Linda Parks	John Johnston	Richard Dean	Christine Cohen	Barry Zimmerman	Bob Brooks
Yolo	CM	168	(530) 666-8055	Lynnel Pollock	Sharon Jensen	Fredericka Oakley	Howard Newens	. . .	Ed Prieto
Yuba	CE	60	(530) 741-6281	Don Schrader	Robert Bendorf	Donna Stottlemeyer	Dean Sellers	Beverly Barnes	Virginia Black
COLORADO									
Adams	CM	363	(303) 654-6070	Elaine Valente	Terry Funderburk	Carol Snyder	Richard Lemke	Stuart Shepard	Douglas Darr
Alamosa	CM	14	(719) 589-3841	Robert Zimmerman	Harold Andrews	Holly Lowder	. . .	Peggy Curto	David Stone
Arapahoe	CE	487	(303) 795-4400	. . .	. . .	Donnetta Davidson	Charles Green	Ann Harden	Patrick Sullivan
Archuleta	* C	9	(970) 264-8555	Eugene Crabtree	. . .	June Madrid	Donald Warn	Kathy Wendt	William Richards
Baca	C	4	(719) 523-4521	. . .	Candy Briles	. . .	. . .	. . .	Gerry Oyen
Bent	C	5	(719) 456-1600	James Coffielo	Gary Pritchard	Patricia Nickell	Molly Riddock	. . .	Gerry Oyen
Boulder	C	291	(303) 441-3131	Paul Danish	. . .	. . .	. . .	Peggy Jackson	Joseph Pelle
Chaffee	CM	16	(719) 539-2218	Timothy Glenn	Kathy Leinz	Joyce Reno	Dan Short	. . .	Timothy Walker
Cheyenne	CM	2	(719) 767-5872	Ronald Rehfeld	Lara Crowell	Kay Feyh	. . .	. . .	Virgil Drescher
Clear Creek	* C	9	(303) 679-2300	Joan Drury	Selby Myers	Pam Phipps	Carl Small	Cate Camp	Don Krueger
Conejos	C	8	(719) 376-5772	Le Roy Valasquez	Tressesa Maltinez	Andrew Perea	. . .	. . .	Isaac Gallegos
Costilla	C	3	(719) 672-3372	Edward Vigil	. . .	Delores Burns	Julie Gallegos	. . .	Roger Benton
Crowley	* C	5	(719) 267-3248	T. E. Allumbaugh	. . .	Lucile Nichols	Michael Apker	. . .	Miles Clark
Custer	C	3	(719) 783-9067	. . .	Francis Ferron	. . .	. . .	. . .	. . .
Delta	C	27	(970) 874-2100	Jim Ventrello	Susan Hansen	Lela McCracken	Margaret Davey	Wade Hall	William Blair
Dolores	C	1	(970) 677-2383	Leroy Gore	. . .	Earlene White	. . .	. . .	Jerry Martin
Douglas	* CM	175	(303) 660-7427	. . .	Douglas DeBord	Jack Arrowsmith	. . .	Jessica McCoy	David Weaver
Eagle	C	41	(970) 328-8600	Michael Gallagher	. . .	Teak Simonton	Michael Roeper	Carla Budd	Joe Hoy

Directory 1/10 continued

OFFICIALS IN U.S. COUNTIES 2,500 AND OVER IN POPULATION

Jurisdiction	Form of govern-ment	2000 Popu-lation (000)	Main telephone number	Chief elected official	Appointed administrator	Clerk of the governing board	Chief financial officer	Director of personnel	Chief law enforcement official
COLORADO continued									
El Paso	C	516	(719) 520-6426	. . .	Jeffrey Greene	Eileen Gilbert	. . .	Imad Karaki	Terry Maketa
Elbert	C	19	(303) 621-3199	John Metli	Suzie Graeff	Amy Fordyce	. . .	Kathi Lancaster	. . .
Fremont	C	46	(719) 276-7333	. . .	. . .	Norma Hatfield	Dana Angel	George Overstreet	. . .
Garfield	C	43	(970) 945-1377	John Martin	Ed Green	Mildred Alsdorf	Patsy Hernandez	Judith Osman	Lou Vallario
Gilpin	C	4	(303) 582-5214	Jeanne Nicholson	Roger Baker	Jessica Lovingier	Clorinda Smith	Susie Allen	Bruce Hartman
Grand	CM	12	(970) 725-3347	Robert Anderson	Lurline Curran	Sara Rosene	Denise Harvey	. . .	Rodney Johnson
Gunnison	* CM	13	(970) 641-0248	Hap Channell	Matthew Birnie	Stella Dominguez	Linda Nienhueser	Debbie Moore	Rick Murdie
Hinsdale	* C	. .	(970) 944-2225	. . .	Laurie Vierheller	Linda Ragle	. . .	. . .	William Denison
Huerfano	C	7	(719) 738-2370	. . .	. . .	. . .	. . .	. . .	. . .
Jackson	C	1	(970) 723-4660	Richard Wyatt	William Crowder	Charlene Geer	. . .	. . .	Rick Rizor
Jefferson	C	527	(303) 271-6511	. . .	James Moore	Faye Griffin	. . .	. . .	Theodore Mink
Kiowa	C	1	(719) 438-5810	Rodney Brown	Debra Immer	Betty Crow	Gary Woodward	. . .	Forrest Frazee
Kit Carson	C	8	(719) 346-8139	Jim Whitmore	Lyn Brownfield	Della Calhoon	. . .	Erva Carpenter	Steve Goering
La Plata	CE	43	(970) 382-6200	Robert Lieb	Joanne Spina	Linda Daley	Wayne Bedor	Kelli Ganevsky	Sydney Schirard
Lake	C	7	(719) 486-1410	Bill Hollenback	. . .	. . .	. . .	. . .	Edward Holte
Larimer	CE	251	(970) 498-7010	Kathay Rennels	Frank Lancaster	Scott Doyle	Carol Block	Wynette Cerciello	James Alderden
Las Animas	C	15	(719) 846-2081	Robert Valdez	William Cordova	Bernard Gonzales	Leeann Fabec	Kimberly Chavez	James Casias
Lincoln	* C	6	(719) 743-2810	Ted Lyons	Roxie Devers	Corinne Lengel	. . .	. . .	Tom Nestor
Logan	C	20	(970) 522-0888	Eugene Meisner	. . .	Roberta Perry	. . .	. . .	Robert Bollish
Mesa	CM	116	(970) 244-1856	. . .	Jon Peacock	Janice Ward	Marcia Arnhold	Nancie Flenard	Stanley Hilkey
Mineral	C	. .	(719) 658-2331	. . .	Les Cahill	. . .	. . .	. . .	. . .
Moffat	* CE	13	(970) 824-5517	Saed Tayyara	. . .	Elaine Sullivan	. . .	Lynnette Running	Timothy Jantz
Montezuma	C	23	(970) 565-8317	G. Story	Thomas Weaver	Evalena Ritthaler	Mary Sanders	. . .	Sherman Kennell
Montrose	C	33	(970) 249-7755	Betsey Hale	Joseph Kerby	Carol Kruse	Nita Emerson	Nancy Eloe	Warren Waterman
Morgan	C	27	(970) 542-3505	Mike Harms	. . .	Connie Ingmire	Michelle Covelli	David Bute	James Crone
Otero	CE	20	(719) 383-3000	Robert Bauserman	George Shioshita	Sharon Sisnroy	. . .	. . .	Christopher Johnson
Ouray	C	3	(970) 325-7320	. . .	Connie Hunt	Michelle Olin	. . .	. . .	Dominick Mattiui
Park	C	14	(719) 836-4201	Leni Walker	. . .	Debra Green	Kathy Boyce	Cynthia Gharst	Fred Wegener
Phillips	C	4	(970) 854-3778	Quentin Biesemeier	Randy Schafer	Beth Cumming	. . .	. . .	Rob Urbach
Pitkin	CM	14	(970) 920-5200	. . .	Hilary Smith	Janice Vos Caudill	Deborah Nelson	Phylis Mattice	Bob Braudis
Prowers	CE	14	(719) 336-8025	Leroy Mauch	. . .	Dorothy McCaslin	. . .	. . .	James Faull
Pueblo	C	141	(719) 583-6000	Matt Peulen	. . .	Christella Munoz	Aimee Tihonovich	Myrna Gibson	Dan Corsentino
Rio Blanco	C	5	(970) 878-3627	Forrest Nelson	. . .	Nancy Amick	Thomas Judd	Teresa Anderson	Si Woodruff
Rio Grande	CE	12	(719) 657-2744	Ralph Rominger	. . .	Sandra Jackson	Suzanne Benton	. . .	Brian Norton
Routt	* CE	19	(970) 879-0108	Nancy Stahoviak	Thomas Sullivan	Karen Weinland	Daniel Strnad	Christine Hensen	Gary Wall
Saguache	* CM	5	(719) 655-2231	Mike Spearman	. . .	Marlene Pruitt	. . .	April Quintana	Michael Norris
San Juan	C	. .	(970) 387-5766	Ernest Kuhlman	William Norman	Dorothy Zanoni	. . .	. . .	Greg Leithauser
San Miguel	C	6	(970) 327-3844	Art Goodtimes	Lynn Black	Doris Ruffe	Gordon Glockson	. . .	William Masters
Sedgwick	C	2	(970) 474-3346	. . .	. . .	Patrice Carter	. . .	. . .	Rick Ingwersen
Summit	* CM	23	(970) 453-2951	Bob French	. . .	Cheri Brunvand	Martina Ferris	Scott Vargo	John Minor
Teller	* C	20	(719) 689-2988	James Ignatius	Sheryl Decker	Patricia Crowson	Laurie Litwin	Lindsey Chapman	Kevin Dougherty
Washington	* CE	4	(970) 345-2701	Dennis Everhart	Scott Harold	Garland Wahl	Debra Cooper	. . .	Larry Kuntz
Weld	C	180	(970) 336-7220	David Long	. . .	Steve Moreno	Donald Warden	. . .	John Cooke
Yuma	* C	9	(970) 332-5796	Robin Wiley	Linda Briggs	Beverly Wenger	Vicky Southards	. . .	Sam McCoy
DELAWARE									
Kent	* C	126	(302) 744-2305	P. Brooks Banta	M. Petit de Mange	Loretta Wootten	Susan Durham	Allan Kujala	James Higdon
New Castle	CE	500	(302) 395-5555	Christopher Coons	Jeffrey Bullock	Betsy Gardner	Michael Strine	Charlotte Crowell	David McAllister
Sussex	CM	156	(302) 855-7700	Dale Dukes	Robert Stickels	Robin Griffith	David Baker	Dennis Cordrey	. . .
FLORIDA									
Alachua	CE	217	(352) 374-5219	Rodney Long	Randall Reid	J. Irby	Walter Barry	Kim Baldry	Stephen Oelrich
Baker	* C	22	(904) 259-3613	. . .	Joseph Cone	Al Fraser	Debbie Perryman	Cathy Williams	Joey Dobson
Bay	CM	148	(850) 784-4013	Michael Ropa	. . .	Harold Bazzel	Joseph Rogers	. . .	Guy Tunnell
Bradford	C	26	(904) 964-6280	. . .	. . .	Ray Norman	James Farrell	. . .	Robert Millner
Brevard	CM	476	(321) 633-2000	Ron Pritchard	Peggy Busacca	. . .	. . .	Frank Abbate	. . .
Broward	* CM	1623	(954) 357-6001	Kristin Jacobs	. . .	. . .	Phillip Allen	James Acton	. . .
Calhoun	C	13	(904) 674-4545	. . .	. . .	. . .	. . .	. . .	. . .
Charlotte	CM	141	(941) 743-1200	. . .	Bruce Loucks	. . .	. . .	Magali Kain	. . .
Citrus	CM	118	(352) 527-5400	Vicki Phillips	. . .	Betty Strifler	Catherine Taylor	Richard Petitt	Jeffrey Dawsey
Clay	* CM	140	(904) 269-6387	. . .	Fritz Behring	James Jett	Donald Moore	Richard O'Connell	Scott Lancaster
Collier	CM	251	(941) 774-8460	John Norris	James Mudd	Dwight Brock	Crystal Kinzel	Jennifer Edwards	Don Hunter
Columbia	CE	56	(386) 755-4100	Ronald Williams	Dale Williams	. . .	P. Cason	Debi Dyal	Frank Owens
De Soto	* CM	32	(863) 993-4808	Delma Allen	Craig Coffey	Mitzie McGavic	Jan Brewer	Paul Erickson	Vernon Keen
Dixie	C	13	(352) 498-1205	John Driggers	. . .	. . .	. . .	. . .	. . .
Escambia	CM	294	(850) 595-4900	James Dickson	George Touart	Ernie Magaha	Wanda McBrearty	Rod Powell	Ron McNesby
Flagler	CE	49	(386) 437-7480	James Darby	. . .	Gail Wadsworth	Phil Pulliam	Joe Mayer	Don Fleming
Franklin	C	11	(850) 653-8861	. . .	Alan Pierce	Marcia Johnson	. . .	. . .	Mike Mock
Gadsden	CM	45	(850) 875-8660	Bill McGill	Marlon Brown	Nicholas Thomas	. . .	Arthur Lawson	W. Woodham
Gilchrist	C	14	(352) 463-3170	Randy Durden	Ronald McQueen	Joseph Gilliam	Samuel Ferguson	. . .	David Turner
Glades	CM	10	(863) 946-6000	Robert Giesler	Wendell Taylor	Joseph Flint	Jerry Beck	. . .	James Rider
Gulf	* C	13	(850) 229-6106	Billy Traylor	Donald Butler	Becky Norris	Carla Hand	. . .	Joe Nugent
Hamilton	* C	13	(386) 792-1288	Lewis Vaughn	Danny Johnson	. . .	Greg Godwin	. . .	. . .
Hardee	CM	26	(863) 773-2161	William Lambert	Lexton Albritton	B. Bradley	Kathy Crawford	Jane Long	Loren Cogburn
Hendry	C	36	(941) 675-5352	Janet Taylor	D. O'Neal	. . .	Christine Pratt	Ellen Strickland	. . .
Hernando	CE	130	(352) 754-4000	Betty Whitehouse	Gary Kuhl	Karen Nicolai	George Zoettlein	Barbara Dupre	Richard Nugent
Highlands	CM	87	(863) 402-6809	Chester Maxcy	Carl Cool	Luke Brooker	Robert Jameson	Fred Carino	Howard Godwin
Hillsborough	CM	998	(813) 272-5660	Dorothy Berger	Patricia Bean	Pat Frank	Eric Johnson	George Williams	David Gee
Holmes	C	18	(850) 547-1100	. . .	. . .	. . .	. . .	. . .	. . .
Indian River	CM	112	(561) 567-8000	. . .	Joseph Baird	. . .	. . .	Ron Baker	. . .
Jackson	* C	46	(850) 482-9633	Chuck Lockey	Ted Lakey	Dale Guthrie	Lucretia Farris	Lennetta Greene	John McDaniel
Jefferson	CE	12	(850) 342-0218	. . .	. . .	. . .	. . .	Annie Charron	. . .
Lafayette	C	7	(386) 294-1600	. . .	. . .	James Watkins	. . .	. . .	. . .
Lake	CM	210	(352) 343-9694	Welton Cadwell	. . .	. . .	Barbara Minkoff	Michael Milanowski	George Knupp
Lee	* CM	440	(941) 533-2245	Bob Janes	Donald Stilwell	. . .	William Bergquist	. . .	. . .
Leon	CM	239	(850) 488-9962	. . .	Parwez Alam	. . .	. . .	Reginald Ofuani	. . .
Levy	C	34	(352) 486-5100	. . .	. . .	. . .	. . .	. . .	. . .
Liberty	* C	7	(850) 643-2215	. . .	. . .	Robert Hill	. . .	. . .	Harrell Revell
Madison	C	18	(850) 973-3179	Michael Salls	. . .	. . .	Tim Sanders	Karen Botino	Joe Peavy
Manatee	CM	264	(941) 748-4501	Jonathan Bruce	Edwin Hunzeker	R. B. Shore	James Seuffert	Garry Dye	. . .
Marion	CM	258	(352) 620-3340	Parnell Townley	Patrick Howard	. . .	. . .	Andrew Adams	. . .

Directory 1/10
continued

OFFICIALS IN U.S. COUNTIES 2,500 AND OVER IN POPULATION

Jurisdiction	Form of government	2000 Population (000)	Main telephone number	Chief elected official	Appointed administrator	Clerk of the governing board	Chief financial officer	Director of personnel	Chief law enforcement official
FLORIDA continued									
Martin	CE	126	(772) 288-5515	Michael DiTerlizzi	Duncan Ballantyne	Marsha Ewing	...	Linda Skelton	Robert Crowder
Miami-Dade	C	2076	(305) 375-5311	...	George Burgess	Harvey Ruvin	David Morris	Donald Allen	Carlos Alvarez
Monroe	CM	79	(305) 294-4641	...	Thomas Willi	...	Salvatore Zappulla	Teresa Aguiar	...
Nassau	C	57	(904) 321-5908	...	Edward Sealover	...	...	Chili Pope	...
Okaloosa	CM	170	(850) 689-5870	Sherry Campbell	James Curry	Don Howard	Gary Stanford	Kay Godwin	Charles Morris
Okeechobee	CM	35	(863) 763-6441	Clif Betts	...	Sharon Robertson	Edward Sizemore	...	O. Raulerson
Orange	CM	896	(407) 836-5661	Richard Crotty	Ajit Lalchandani	...	...	James Daye	...
Osceola	CM	172	(407) 343-2200	Paul Owen	Michael Freilinger	Paula Carpenter	Tom Klinker	Mary Cooper	Robert Hansell
Palm Beach	CM	1131	(561) 616-6888	Karen Marcus	Robert Weisman	...	Richard Roberts	Janis Brunell	...
Pasco	CM	344	(727) 847-8103	...	John Gallagher	...	Michael Nurrenbrock	Barbara De Simone	...
Pinellas	CM	921	(727) 464-3367	Kenneth Welch	...	Kenneth Burke	...	David Libby	Jim Coats
Polk	CE	483	(863) 534-6030	Neil Combee	Robert Herr	...	...	Percy Harden	...
Putnam	* C	70	(386) 329-0200	...	Rick Leary	John Smith	Michael Anderson	Kenneth McClinton	Dean Kelly
Santa Rosa	CM	117	(850) 983-1863	Robert Cole	W. Walker	...	Joel Haniford	Devann Cook	...
Sarasota	* CM	325	(941) 861-5000	David Mills	James Ley	Karen Rushing	Peter Ramsden	Joanie Whitley	Geoffrey Monge
Seminole	CM	365	(407) 665-7945	Daryl McLain	Cynthia Coto	Maryanne Morse	Robert Wilson	Janet Davis	Don Eslinger
St. Johns	CM	169	(904) 823-2460	...	Michael Wanchick	Cheryl Strickland	Michael Givens	K. Van Volkinburg	Neil Perry
St. Lucie	CM	192	(561) 462-1546	Doug Coward	Douglas Anderson	Jo Ann Holman	Marie Govin	Carl Holeva	Ken Mascara
Sumter	* C	53	(352) 793-0200	Michael Francis	Lyndon Bonner	Gloria Hayward	Gary Reynolds	Kitty Fields	Bill Farmer
Suwannee	C	34	(386) 364-3400	Eddy Hillhouse	Edward Allen	...	W. Henderson	...	Al Williams
Taylor	C	19	(850) 838-2097	Daryll Gunter	Wayne Humphries	Annie Murphy	Tammy Taylor	Amy Cooper	...
Union	C	13	(386) 496-3711	Regina Parrish	...	...	Donna Jackson	...	Jerry Whitehead
Volusia	CM	443	(386) 736-5951	Frank Bruno	James Dinneen	Susan Whitaker	Charlene Weaver	Michael Lary	Ben Johnson
Wakulla	* CM	22	(850) 926-0919	Maxie Lawhon	Benjamin Pingree	Brent Thurmond	Tim Barden	...	David Harvey
Walton	C	40	(850) 892-8115	William Young	Ronnie Bell	Daniel Bodiford	...	Lynda Robinson	Quinn McMillian
Washington	CE	20	(850) 638-6200	Hulan Carter	Peter Herbert	Linda Cook	...	Jennifer Cook	...
GEORGIA									
Appling	* C	17	(912) 367-8100	Virgil Carter	Mike Phillips	Chrissy Harris	...	Yvonne Sellers	Benny DeLoach
Atkinson	CE	7	(912) 422-3391	Edwin Davis	...	Joyce Taylor	...	Judith Mancil	Herman Tucker
Augusta–Richmond County	CE	199	(706) 821-2850	Bob Young	Fredrick Russell	Lena Bonner	David Persaud	Brenda Byrd-Pelaez	Ronald Strength
Bacon	C	10	(912) 632-5214	Eugene Dyal	...	Mary Wheeler	...	...	Richard Foskey
Baker	C	4	(229) 734-3000	...	...	...	...	...	...
Baldwin	C	44	(478) 445-4791	Collins Lee	Joan Minton	Cynthia Cunningham	Linda Zarkowsky	...	William Massee
Banks	CE	14	(706) 677-6200	Gene Hart	Angela Sheppard	Regina Gailey	...	Judy Greer	Charles Chapman
Barrow	CE	46	(770) 307-3114	Walter Elder	Larry Price	Michelle Sims	Jeanne Horacek	Tammy Esco	Joel Robinson
Bartow	* C	76	(770) 387-5020	Clarence Brown	Stephen Bradley	Kathy Gill	Jo Taylor	Sandra Southern	Clark Millsap
Ben Hill	* C	17	(229) 426-5112	Larry Davis	David McCranie	Paula Jones	...	Donna Lampkin	Bobby McLemore
Berrien	CM	16	(229) 686-5421	Delma Roberts	Elaine Shiver	Darlene Nix	...	...	Gerald Brogdon
Bibb	CE	153	(478) 621-6343	Charles Bishop	Steve Layson	Shelia Thurmond	Deborah Martin	Tommy Brown	Jerry Modena
Bleckley	CE	11	(478) 934-3200	Billy Smith	...	Sandra Higgins	...	...	Harold Lancaster
Brantley	C	14	(912) 462-5256	...	...	...	...	...	...
Brooks	CM	16	(229) 263-5561	Wayne Carroll	Robert O'Barr	Patricia Wright	...	...	...
Bryan	C	23	(912) 653-3839	H. Warnell	Waverly Jones	Donna Waters	...	...	Clyde Smith
Bulloch	CM	55	(912) 764-6245	Garrett Nevil	Thomas Couch	Evelyn Wilson	...	Kymberly Kuebler	Arnold Akins
Burke	CE	22	(706) 554-2324	Jimmy Dixon	C. Hopper	...	...	...	Gregory Coursey
Butts	CM	19	(770) 775-8200	Gerald Kersey	Van Whaler	Margaret Holloway	Deborah Upshaw	...	Joseph Pope
Calhoun	C	6	(229) 849-4835	...	...	...	...	...	...
Camden	CM	43	(912) 576-5601	...	...	...	Michael Fender	Penny Woodard	William Smith
Candler	C	9	(912) 685-2835	Kent Campbell	Milton Futch	Doris Strickland	...	...	Charles Bell
Carroll	* CE	87	(770) 830-5800	William Chappell	...	Susan Mabry	Don Johnson	Anne Lee	Terry Langley
Catoosa	C	53	(706) 965-2500	William Clark	Michael Mahn	Martha Davis	Carl Henson	...	Phil Summers
Charlton	C	10	(912) 496-2549	Steve Nance	...	Jenifer Nobles	...	...	...
Chatham	* CM	232	(912) 652-7878	Pete Liakakis	Russell Abolt	Sybil Tillman	Linda Cramer	Michael Kaigler	Al St. Lawrence
Chattahoochee	C	14	(706) 929-3602	Larry Dillard	W Elvin Hardy	Ann Sills	...	...	Glynn Cooper
Chattooga	C	25	(706) 857-0700	James Parker	...	Martha Tucker	...	...	R. Kellett
Cherokee	* CM	141	(678) 493-6000	Leavitt Ahrens	Jerry Cooper	Sheila Corbin	Amy Davis	Kay Bolick	Roger Garrison
Clay	* CM	3	(229) 768-3238	Gerald Anderson	Pamela Ward	Teresa Smith	...	...	Roger Shivers
Clayton	CE	236	(770) 477-3208	Crandle Bray	...	Margarette Swaim	P. Martin	Renee Bright	Ronnie Clackum
Clinch	C	6	(912) 487-2667	...	...	...	...	...	...
Cobb	C	607	(770) 528-2600	Sam Olens	David Hankerson	Carol Granger	Brad Bowers	Tony Hagler	Lee New
Coffee	* C	37	(912) 384-4799	Jimmy Kitchens	...	Joann Metts	Wesley Vickers	Princess Leggett	...
Colquitt	CM	42	(229) 891-7400	Maxwell Hancock	Jack Byrd	Deborah Cox	Miriam Smith	...	Charles Whittington
Columbia	CM	89	(706) 868-3379	Ron Cross	Steven Szablewski	Phebe Dent	Leanne De Loach	Marcia Lowry	Clay Whittle
Cook	CM	15	(229) 896-2266	...	Faye Hughes	...	...	...	...
Coweta	CM	89	(770) 254-2604	Kathryn Schlumper	L. Gay	Roxie Clark	Rickey Smoot	Rick Watson	Michael Yeager
Crawford	C	12	(478) 836-3328	...	Martha Leary	...	...	...	...
Crisp	C	21	(229) 276-2672	Ferrell Henry	Lester Crapse	...	Sherrie Leverett	...	Donnie Haralson
Dade	C	15	(706) 657-4625	Ted Rumley	Jason Ford	Larry Cooper	...	...	Philip Street
Dawson	C	15	(706) 344-3501	Mike Berg	Ross Hubbard	Cathy Maher	Lowayne Craig	Jay Sessions	Billy Carlisle
De Kalb	CE	665	(404) 371-2000	Vernon Jones	...	...	Michael Bell	Richard Conley	Thomas Brown
Decatur	C	28	(229) 248-3030	Marvin Rentz	...	Faye Gunn	...	...	Wiley Griffin
Dodge	C	19	(478) 374-4361	Dan McCranie	Kelly Bowen	Linda Lowery	...	...	Lawton Douglas
Dooly	C	11	(229) 268-4228	...	...	...	...	...	...
Dougherty	CM	96	(229) 431-2122	Jeff Sinyard	Richard Crowdis	Barbara Russell	Gail Kohler	Alice Jenkins	Donald Cheek
Douglas	CM	92	(770) 920-7435	Rita Rainwater	G. Linton	Aida Tullis	Robert Harshbarger	Raymond Martin	Phil Miller
Early	C	12	(229) 723-4304	...	Kathy English	...	...	...	...
Echols	* C	3	(229) 559-6538	...	...	Brenda Stalvey	...	...	...
Effingham	* C	37	(912) 754-2153	Verna Phillips	Ed Williams	Patrice Morris	Joanna Floyd	...	Jimmy McDuffie
Elbert	C	20	(706) 283-2000	...	...	Phyllis Thompson	...	...	Barry Haston
Emanuel	C	21	(478) 237-3881	...	Ezra Price	...	...	...	...
Evans	C	10	(912) 739-1141	...	Caughey Hearn	Liz Lynn	Bryan Rodgers	...	Marvin Bradley
Fannin	C	19	(706) 632-2203	Richard Vollrath	...	Diane Thomas	...	Janice Bailey	George Ensley
Fayette	* CM	91	(770) 460-5730	Jack Smith	Jack Krakeel	...	Mary Holland	Connie Boehnke	Randall Johnson
Floyd	CM	90	(706) 291-5111	...	Kevin Poe	Michele Fountain	Alexander Leonard	Larry Johnson	James Free
Forsyth	* CE	98	(770) 781-3088	C. Laughinghouse	...	Douglas Sorrells	...	Patricia Carson	Ted Paxton
Franklin	C	20	(706) 384-2483	Samuel Elrod	...	Laverne Hilley	Franklin Ginn	Elaine Evans	Steve Thomas
Fulton	CM	816	(404) 730-6710	Mike Kenn	Thomas Andrews	Mark Massey	Patrick O'Connor	Robert Brandes	Jacquelyn Barrett
Gilmer	C	23	(706) 635-4361	Rayburn Smith	...	Kimberly Rogers	...	...	Carl Bernhart
Glascock	C	2	(706) 598-2671	Thomas Chalker	...	...	...	...	Bryan Bopp

Directory 1/10
continued

OFFICIALS IN U.S. COUNTIES 2,500 AND OVER IN POPULATION

Jurisdiction		Form of govern-ment	2000 Popu-lation (000)	Main telephone number	Chief elected official	Appointed administrator	Clerk of the governing board	Chief financial officer	Director of personnel	Chief law enforcement official
GEORGIA continued										
Glynn		CM	67	(912) 554-7170	...	...	Vanessa Mincey	Phyllis McNicoll	Rebecca Rowell	Wayne Bennett
Gordon		CM	44	(706) 629-3795	...	Randall Dowling	Annette Berry	Brent Burdette	Garah Childers	Jerry Davis
Grady	*	CM	23	(229) 377-1512	Robert Burns	Rusty Moye	Ann Mobley	Betty Rawls	...	Harry Young
Greene		C	14	(706) 453-7716	Vincent Duvall	Byron Lombard	Elna Hutchinson	Amanda Smith	Yalonde Reese	Chris Houston
Gwinnett		CM	588	(770) 822-7900	Wayne Hill	Jock Connell	Brenda Maddox	Lisa Johnsa	Roderick Powell	William Dean
Habersham	*	CM	35	(706) 754-6264	Jim Butterworth	...	Janeann Allison	William Tinsley	Lynn Merritt	DeRay Fincher
Hall		CM	139	(770) 531-6712	Tom Oliver	James Shuler	Michelle Smallwood	Carl Stephens	Charley Nix	Steve Cronic
Hancock		C	10	(706) 444-5746	...	...	...	...	...	...
Haralson		C	25	(770) 646-2002	Amos Sparks	Charles Walker	Charlene Smith	...	...	Ronnie Kimball
Harris	*	CM	23	(706) 628-4958	...	Carol Silva	Nancy McMichael	Jennie Shelhorse	...	Robert Jolley
Hart		C	22	(706) 376-2024	Joey Dorsey	Jon Caime	Lawana Kahn	...	...	Mike Cleveland
Heard	*	C	11	(706) 675-3821	June Jackson	...	Patty Jiles	...	...	Ross Henry
Henry		CM	119	(770) 954-2400	Leland Maddox	Robert Magnaghi	Susan Craig	James Schuster	Alice Oliver	Mac Nale
Houston		C	110	(478) 542-2115	Ned Sanders	...	...	Sandi Stalnaker	Harold Wilson	Cullen Talton
Irwin		C	9	(229) 468-9441	Armond Morris	...	Angela Thompson	...	...	Donnie Youghn
Jackson	*	C	41	(706) 367-1199	Pat Bell	Richard Hampton	Erica Johnson	John Hulsey	Melanie Thomas	Stanley Evans
Jasper		C	11	(706) 468-4900	Jerry Crow	Phil Peevy	...	...	...	...
Jeff Davis		CM	12	(912) 375-6611	Clyde McCall	James Carter	Sherri Lytle	...	...	...
Jefferson		CM	17	(478) 625-3332	Gardner Hobbs	James Rodgers	Mary Lamb	...	...	...
Jenkins	*	C	8	(478) 982-5252	James Henry	Carol Cates	Joyce Mixon	...	...	Timothy Fields
Johnson		C	8	(478) 864-3388	Billy Dudley	K. Strange	Ann Buxton	Betty Watkins	...	Michael Morris
Jones		C	23	(478) 986-6405	J. Hawkins	James Washburn	Leila Land	...	G. Henderson	Robert Reece
Lamar		C	15	(770) 358-5146	Bobby Burnette	Patricia Stephens	...	...	...	Joseph Buice
Lanier	*	C	7	(229) 482-2088	George Hamm	Albert Studstill	Donna Studstill	...	...	Charles Norton
Laurens		C	44	(478) 272-4755	...	Bryan Rogers	...	Scott Bourassa	...	Kenneth Webb
Lee		C	24	(229) 759-6000	Billy Mathis	Alan Ours	Christi Dockery	Darlow Maxwell	...	Harold Breeden
Liberty		C	61	(912) 876-2164	John McIver	Joseph Brown	Deanna Pflieger	Kimberly McGlothlin	...	James Martin
Lincoln		CE	8	(706) 359-4444	Tommy Drew	...	Bruce Beggs	...	...	Edwin Bentley
Long		C	10	(912) 545-2494	Randall Wilson	Lisa Long	Mary Odum	...	Crystal Knowles	...
Lowndes		CM	92	(229) 671-2400	...	Joseph Pritchard	Phyllis Waters	Stephanie Black	Mickey Tillman	Ashley Paulk
Lumpkin		C	21	(706) 864-3742	...	Stanley Kelley	...	...	...	...
Macon		C	14	(478) 472-7021	Charles Allen	...	Roselyn Starling	...	...	...
Madison	*	C	25	(706) 795-5664	Wesley Nash	C. Fortson	...	...	Connie Benge	Clayton Lowe
Marion		C	7	(229) 649-2603	...	...	...	...	...	...
Mc Duffie		C	21	(706) 595-2100	Charlie Newton	Donald Norton	Annette Finley	Jimmy Whitaker	Ruthie Thomas	Logan Marshall
Mc Intosh		C	10	(912) 437-6671	...	Luther Smart	...	...	...	Steve Whitlock
Meriwether	*	C	22	(706) 672-1314	Charles Neely	Paul Penn	Beverly Thomas	...	...	Herbert Glass
Miller		C	6	(229) 758-4104	India Taylor	...	Debbie Cox	...	...	William Bozeman
Mitchell		C	23	(229) 336-2000	Benjamin Hayward	Bennett Adams	Shelia Cannon	...	...	John Bittick
Monroe	*	C	21	(478) 994-7000	Harold Carlisle	...	Cindy Crowley	Barbara Baswell	...	...
Montgomery		C	8	(912) 583-2363	...	...	...	...	...	...
Morgan		CM	15	(706) 342-0725	William Nabors	Michael Lamar	...	...	...	Robert Markley
Murray		C	36	(706) 517-1400	Jim Welch	Tom Starnes	...	Tommy Parker	Christy Capehart	Howard Ensley
Newton	*	C	62	(678) 625-1210	R. Aaron Varner	John Middleton	Jackie Smith	Marsha Allen	Becky Heisten	Joseph Nichols
Oconee	*	C	26	(706) 769-3938	Melvin Davis	Alan Theriault	Gina Lindsey	Jeff Benko	Malinda Smith	Scott Berry
Oglethorpe	*	C	12	(706) 743-5270	Robert Johnson	...	Sheila Arnold	...	...	Mike Smith
Paulding		C	81	(770) 443-7514	Jerry Shearin	...	...	Pat Brannum	Lillian Norton	...
Peach		C	23	(478) 825-2535	James Khoury	...	Marcia Johnson	...	...	Terry Deese
Pickens	*	C	22	(706) 253-8809	Robert Jones	...	Deborah Watson	Mechelle Champion	...	Billy Wofford
Pierce	*	CE	15	(912) 449-2022	James Dennison	Nicole Wood	Mollie Howard	...	Tina White	Richard King
Pike		C	13	(770) 567-3406	Bobby Blount	Stephen Marro	Tabitha Weaver	...	...	James Thomas
Polk	*	C	38	(770) 749-2100	Billy Croker	...	Dawn Turner	Muriel Dulaney	...	Bobby Sparks
Pulaski		C	9	(478) 783-4154	...	...	...	...	...	...
Putnam		C	18	(706) 485-5826	Howard McMichael	William Clack	Helen Carnes	...	...	Howard Sills
Quitman		C	2	(229) 334-0903	C. Redding	...	Carolyn Wilson	...	...	Lon Ming
Rabun		C	15	(706) 782-5271	...	Jimmy Bleckley	Debra Westberg	...	...	Michael Carnes
Randolph		C	7	(229) 732-6440	Charles Simmons	...	Keisha Burkes	...	...	...
Rockdale		C	70	(770) 929-4000	...	William Sands	Jennifer Rutledge	Deb Dobbs	...	Thomas Wigington
Schley		C	3	(229) 937-2609	...	...	...	...	...	...
Screven		CM	15	(912) 564-7535	...	Rick Jordan	Frankie Kirkland	...	Dee Cail	R. Kile
Seminole	*	C	9	(229) 524-2878	Tommy Rogers	Marty Shingler	Donna Jones	...	...	Jerry Godby
Spalding	*	CM	58	(770) 467-4200	...	William Wilson	Nancy Downs	...	William Gay	James Stewart
Stephens		C	25	(706) 886-9491	Steve Chitwood	...	...	Phyllis Ayers	...	Eugene Sorrells
Stewart		C	5	(229) 838-6769	John Patterson	...	...	...	...	Larry Jones
Sumter	*	C	33	(229) 928-4500	William Bowen	Lynn Taylor	Rayetta Floyd	Ann Barefoot	Christopher Ryan	Pete Smith
Talbot	*	C	6	(706) 665-3220	Franklin Holmes	S. Higginbotham	Teresa Callaway	Brenda Crawford	...	John Johnson
Taliaferro		CE	2	(706) 456-2494	Charles Ware	...	Ruby Randolph	...	...	James Leslie
Tattnall		C	22	(912) 557-4335	John Parker	...	Faye Hussey	...	...	Quinton Rush
Taylor		C	8	(478) 862-3336	Clinton Perry	Lenda Taunton	...	...	Vera Moore	Jeff Watson
Telfair		C	11	(229) 868-5688	Roy Selph	...	Gwen Wilmoth	...	...	Jim Williamson
Terrell		CE	10	(229) 995-4476	Wilbur Gamble	...	Beth Parnacott	...	...	John Bowens
Thomas		CM	42	(229) 225-4100	Josh Herring	M. Stephenson	Monnette Monahan	...	...	R. Carlton Powell
Tift		CM	38	(229) 386-7850	James Spurlin	...	...	...	Deborah Benson	Gary Vowell
Toombs		C	26	(912) 526-3311	Charles Rustin	...	Sara Taylor	Louie Powell	...	Alvie Light
Towns		C	9	(706) 896-2276	...	...	...	...	...	...
Treutlen		CE	6	(912) 529-3664	George McLendon	...	Sylvia Norris	...	...	Wayne Hooks
Troup	*	CM	58	(706) 883-1610	Richard Wolfe	Michael Dobbs	...	Stewart Mills	Lavelle Barnes	Donny Turner
Turner		C	9	(229) 567-4313	...	...	...	...	...	...
Twiggs		C	10	(478) 945-3629	Ray Bennett	Glenn Barton	...	...	...	Darion Mitchum
Union		C	17	(706) 439-6000	Lamar Paris	...	...	Patti Holder	...	Scott Stephens
Upson	*	CE	27	(706) 647-7012	Glenn Collins	...	...	...	...	Don Peacock
Walker	*	C	61	(706) 638-1437	Bebe Heiskell	...	Briggitt Garrett	Gregory McConnell	...	Steven Wilson
Walton		C	60	(770) 267-1401	Kevin Little	...	Leta Talbird	Merridy McDaniel	Janice Holland	Fred Yarbrough
Ware		CM	35	(912) 287-4300	Ralph Tyson	Gail Boyd	Pam Gibson	Harrison Tillman	JoAnn Drawdy	Ronnie McQuaig
Warren		C	6	(706) 465-2171	...	...	...	...	...	...
Washington		C	21	(478) 552-2325	...	Lee Lord	...	...	...	...
Wayne		CM	26	(912) 427-5900	...	Nancy Jones	Angie Parker	...	...	John Carter
Webster		C	2	(229) 828-5775	Dave Wills	...	Margie Everett	Joyce Starrak	...	Robbie Wells
Wheeler		C	6	(912) 568-7135	...	...	...	...	...	...
White		CM	19	(706) 865-2235	Chris Nonnemaker	Alton Brown	Jean Welborn	Vickie Neikirk	...	Neal Walden

Directory 1/10 continued — OFFICIALS IN U.S. COUNTIES 2,500 AND OVER IN POPULATION

Jurisdiction		Form of govern-ment	2000 Popu-lation (000)	Main telephone number	Chief elected official	Appointed administrator	Clerk of the governing board	Chief financial officer	Director of personnel	Chief law enforcement official
GEORGIA continued										
Whitfield	*	CE	83	(706) 275-7500	Brian Anderson	Robert McLeod	Barbara Love	Melva Smith	Jackie Palacios	Scott Chitwood
Wilcox		C	8	(229) 467-2737	Homer Conner	. . .	Hazel Keen	. . .	. . .	. . .
Wilkes		C	10	(706) 678-2511	. . .	David Tyler	. . .	. . .	. . .	. . .
Wilkinson	*	C	10	(478) 946-2236	Dennis Holder	. . .	. . .	. . .	. . .	Richard Chatman
Worth	*	C	21	(229) 776-8200	Dan Miller	. . .	. . .	. . .	Buffy Walker	Freddie Tompkins
HAWAII										
Hawaii	*	CE	148	(808) 961-8361	Harry Kim	Dixie Kaetsu	Casey Jarmin	William Takaba	Michael Ben	Lawrence Mahuna
Kauai		CE	58	(808) 241-6595	Maryanne Kusaka	. . .	Peter Nakamura	Wallace Rezentes	Allan Tanigawa	George Freitas
Maui		CE	128	(808) 244-7855	Charmaine Tavares	Sheri Morrison	. . .	Kalbert Young	Lynn Krieg	Thomas Phillips
IDAHO										
Ada		C	300	(208) 287-6990	Judy Peavey-Derr	. . .	J. Navarro	. . .	Terry Johnson	Vaughn Killeen
Adams		C	3	(208) 253-4561	Ray Bennett	. . .	Michael Fisk	. . .	. . .	Rich Green
Bannock	*	C	75	(208) 236-7217	. . .	. . .	Dale Hatch	Patricia Wilson	Bobette Wilson	Lorin Nielsen
Bear Lake		C	6	(208) 945-2212	. . .	. . .	. . .	. . .	. . .	. . .
Benewah	*	C	9	(208) 245-3212	Jack Buell	. . .	J. Michele Reynolds	. . .	. . .	Robert Kirts
Bingham		C	41	(208) 785-8040	. . .	. . .	Judie Hampton	. . .	Steven Barton	Dayle Holm
Blaine		C	18	(208) 788-5505	C Dennis Wright	Michael McNees	Marsha Riemann	. . .	. . .	Jerry Femling
Boise		C	6	(208) 392-4431	. . .	. . .	C. Swearingen	Patricia Coleman	. . .	Drew Bodie
Bonner		CE	36	(208) 265-1438	Dale Van Stone	. . .	Marie Scott	Karen Weldon	Jan Morrison	Evan Roos
Bonneville		C	82	(208) 529-1350	Roger Christensen	. . .	Ronald Longmore	. . .	Dan Byron	Byron Stommel
Boundary		C	9	(208) 267-7212	Ronald Smith	. . .	Diane Cartwright	. . .	Michael Weland	George Voyles
Butte		C	2	(208) 527-3021	Judith Bailey	. . .	Anna Perez	. . .	. . .	Cary Van Etter
Camas		C	. . .	(208) 764-2242	. . .	. . .	Rollie Bennett	. . .	. . .	D. Rast
Canyon		C	131	(208) 454-7300	. . .	. . .	. . .	. . .	. . .	. . .
Caribou		C	7	(208) 547-4324	Max Rigby	. . .	Edie Izatt	Linda Godfrey	. . .	Ray Van Vleet
Cassia		C	21	(208) 878-7302	John Adams	Timothy Hurst	Darrell Roskelley	Cara Petterson	. . .	Billy Crystal
Clark	*	CE	1	(208) 374-5304	Greg Shenton	. . .	Lisa Black	. . .	. . .	Craig King
Clearwater		C	8	(208) 476-3615	Don Ebert	. . .	Robin Christensen	. . .	. . .	Alan Hengen
Custer		C	4	(208) 879-2360	Ted Strickler	. . .	Ethel Peck	. . .	. . .	Micky Rosskelley
Elmore		C	29	(208) 587-2130	Larry Rose	. . .	Gail Best	Merrilee Hiler	Linda Pickett	Rick Layher
Franklin		C	11	(208) 852-1090	Brad Smith	. . .	V. Larsen	Rae Lajohnson	. . .	Don Beckstead
Fremont		C	11	(208) 624-7332	Bill Forbush	. . .	Abbie Mace	. . .	. . .	Thomas Stegelmeier
Gem		C	15	(208) 365-4561	Edward Mansfield	. . .	Susan Howard	. . .	. . .	Clint Short
Gooding		C	14	(208) 934-4841	. . .	. . .	Helen Edward	. . .	. . .	Shaun Gough
Idaho		C	15	(208) 983-2751	Patricia Holmberg	. . .	Rose Gehring	. . .	. . .	Lawrence Dasenbrock
Jefferson		C	19	(208) 745-7756	. . .	. . .	A. Christine Boulter	. . .	Marilyn Vanderbeek	Blair Olsen
Jerome		C	18	(208) 324-8811	Veronica Lienman	. . .	Cheryl Watts	. . .	Jerome	Jim Weaver
Kootenai		C	108	(208) 446-1640	Gus Johnston	. . .	Daniel English	David McDowell	. . .	Rocky Watson
Latah		C	34	(208) 882-8580	John Nelson	. . .	Susan Peterson	. . .	. . .	Wayne Rausch
Lemhi	*	C	7	(208) 756-2815	Richard Snyder	. . .	Terri Morton	. . .	. . .	Sam Slavin
Lewis		C	3	(208) 937-2661	Joe Leitch	. . .	Cathy Larson	. . .	. . .	Don Fortney
Lincoln		C	4	(208) 886-7641	Jerry Nance	. . .	Liz Kime	. . .	. . .	Kent McBride
Madison		C	27	(208) 356-3662	. . .	. . .	Marilyn Rasmussen	. . .	. . .	Roy Klingler
Minidoka		C	20	(208) 436-9511	Daniel Stapelman	. . .	Duane Smith	. . .	. . .	Kevin Halverson
Nez Perce		C	37	(208) 799-3090	Ron Wittman	. . .	Patricia Weeks	. . .	. . .	Jim Dorion
Oneida		C	4	(208) 766-4116	Gerald Goodenough	. . .	Shirlee Blaisdell	. . .	. . .	Jeff Semrad
Owyhee		C	10	(208) 495-2421	. . .	. . .	Cynthia Eaton	. . .	. . .	Gary Aman
Payette		C	20	(208) 642-6000	Rudolph Endrikat	. . .	Betty Dressen	. . .	. . .	Charles Huff
Power		C	7	(208) 226-7611	Kenneth Estep	. . .	Christine Steinlight	. . .	. . .	Howard Sprague
Shoshone		C	13	(208) 752-3331	. . .	. . .	. . .	. . .	. . .	. . .
Teton		C	5	(208) 354-2905	. . .	. . .	. . .	. . .	. . .	. . .
Twin Falls	*	C	64	(208) 736-4000	Gary Grindstaff	. . .	Kristina Glascock	. . .	Elaine Molignoni	Wayne Tousley
Valley		C	7	(208) 382-7100	. . .	. . .	Leland Heinrich	. . .	. . .	Patti Bolen
Washington		C	9	(208) 414-2092	Diana Thomas	. . .	Sharon Widner	. . .	. . .	Marvin Williams
ILLINOIS										
Adams		C	68	(217) 223-6300	. . .	. . .	. . .	. . .	. . .	. . .
Alexander		C	9	(618) 734-7000	. . .	. . .	. . .	. . .	. . .	. . .
Bond		C	17	(618) 664-1966	. . .	. . .	Randy Reitz	. . .	. . .	Jeff Brown
Boone		CE	41	(815) 547-4770	Donald Meier	Kenneth Terrinoni	Sylvia Schroeder	. . .	. . .	. . .
Brown		CE	6	(217) 773-3421	Eugene Kerr	. . .	Judy Woodworth	. . .	. . .	Gerald Kempf
Bureau		C	35	(815) 875-0373	James Lilley	. . .	Kami Hieronymus	. . .	. . .	John Thompson
Calhoun		C	5	(618) 576-2351	Vince Tepen	. . .	Lucille Kress	. . .	. . .	Richard Meyer
Carroll		C	16	(815) 244-0221	. . .	. . .	. . .	. . .	. . .	. . .
Cass		C	13	(217) 452-7217	. . .	. . .	. . .	. . .	. . .	. . .
Champaign		CM	179	(217) 384-3776	Barbara Wysocki	. . .	Mark Shelden	. . .	. . .	Daniel Walsh
Christian		CE	35	(217) 824-4011	John Curtin	. . .	Linda Curtin	. . .	. . .	Robert Kindermann
Clark		C	17	(217) 826-8311	William Weaver	. . .	William Downey	. . .	. . .	Jerry Parsley
Clay		C	14	(618) 665-3626	. . .	. . .	Phyllis Miller	. . .	. . .	Lee Ryker
Clinton		C	35	(618) 594-2464	. . .	. . .	Thomas La Caze	. . .	. . .	Mike Kreke
Coles	*	C	53	(217) 348-0595	. . .	. . .	. . .	. . .	. . .	. . .
Cook		CE	5376	(312) 603-5500	John Stroger	Mark Kilgallon	David Orr	Barbara Sutton	. . .	. . .
Crawford		CE	20	(618) 546-1212	Joe Bliss	. . .	Patty Lycan	. . .	. . .	Tom Weger
Cumberland	*	C	11	(217) 849-2631	. . .	. . .	Julie Gentry	. . .	. . .	Stephen Ozier
De Kalb		CE	88	(815) 895-7189	. . .	Ray Bockman	Sharon Holmes	Gary Hanson	. . .	Roger Scott
De Witt		CM	16	(217) 935-5917	Duane Harris	. . .	Jayne Usher	. . .	. . .	Roger Massey
Douglas		C	19	(217) 253-2411	. . .	. . .	. . .	. . .	. . .	. . .
Du Page		CE	904	(630) 407-6300	. . .	. . .	Gary King	George Kouba	Cara Perrone	John Zaruba
Edgar	*	C	19	(217) 466-7433	James Keller	. . .	Rebecca Kraemer	. . .	. . .	Tim Crippes
Edwards	*	C	6	(618) 445-2115	. . .	. . .	Mary Smith	. . .	. . .	Scott Meserole
Effingham	*	C	34	(217) 342-4990	Carolyn Willenburg	. . .	Kerry Hirtzel	. . .	. . .	John Monnet
Fayette	*	C	21	(618) 283-5000	Dean Black	. . .	Terri Braun	. . .	. . .	Aaron Lay
Ford	*	C	14	(217) 379-2721	Debbie Smith	. . .	Linda Kellerhals	. . .	. . .	Mark Doran
Franklin	*	C	39	(618) 438-3221	Randall Crocker	. . .	Dave Dobill	. . .	. . .	Bill Wilson
Fulton	*	C	38	(309) 547-3041	. . .	. . .	James Nelson	Doug Manock	. . .	Jeff Standard
Gallatin		C	6	(618) 269-3025	Randy Drone	. . .	Elizabeth Wrangel	. . .	. . .	Raymond Martin
Greene		C	14	(217) 942-5443	. . .	. . .	. . .	. . .	. . .	Michael Fry

Directory 1/10 continued   **OFFICIALS IN U.S. COUNTIES 2,500 AND OVER IN POPULATION**

Jurisdiction		Form of government	2000 Population (000)	Main telephone number	Chief elected official	Appointed administrator	Clerk of the governing board	Chief financial officer	Director of personnel	Chief law enforcement official
ILLINOIS continued										
Grundy	*	C	37	(815) 941-3400	Francis Halpin	. . .	Lana Phillips	. . .	Amanda Andreano	Terry Marketti
Hamilton	*	C	8	(618) 643-2721	James Deen	. . .	Lovella Craddock	Keith Botsch	. . .	Gregory Brenner
Hancock		C	20	(217) 357-3911	David Walker	. . .	Kerry Asbridge	. . .	. . .	Karen Andrews
Hardin	*	C	4	(618) 287-2251	Wendell Brownfield	. . .	Mary Denton	. . .	. . .	Tom Seiner
Henderson		C	8	(309) 867-2911	Barbara Lumbeck	. . .	Joyce Meloan	. . .	. . .	Daryl Thompson
Henry		C	51	(309) 937-3574	Marvin Gradert	Dick Erickson	. . .	. . .	. . .	Gilbert Cady
Iroquois		C	31	(815) 432-6963	Ronald Schroeder	. . .	Mark Henrichs	. . .	. . .	Eldon Sprau
Jackson	*	C	59	(618) 687-7240	John Evans	. . .	Larry Reinhardt	Michelle Tweedy	. . .	Robert Burns
Jasper		C	10	(618) 783-3124	. . .	. . .	. . .	. . .	. . .	. . .
Jefferson	*	C	40	(618) 244-8000	Ted Buck	. . .	Connie Simmons	. . .	. . .	Paul Cunningham
Jersey		C	21	(618) 498-5571	Howard Landon	. . .	Linda Crotchett	. . .	. . .	Leo Hefel
Jo Daviess	*	CM	22	(815) 777-6557	Marvin Schultz	Dan Reimer	Jean Dimke	. . .	. . .	Elry Faulkner
Johnson		C	12	(618) 658-3611	Max Ray	. . .	Robin Whitehead	. . .	. . .	. . .
Kane		C	404	(630) 232-3560	. . .	. . .	Bruce Clark	. . .	. . .	Timothy Bukowski
Kankakee		CE	103	(815) 937-3642	Karl Kruse	. . .	Paul Anderson	Steven McCarty	. . .	Richard Randall
Kendall		C	54	(630) 553-4171	. . .	Jeffrey Wilkins	Scott Erickson	. . .	. . .	Jim Thompson
Knox	*	C	55	(309) 345-3840	Sally Keener	. . .	. . .	. . .	. . .	. . .
La Salle		C	111	(815) 434-8242	. . .	. . .	Willard Helander	. . .	. . .	Gary Del Re
Lake		CE	644	(847) 377-2000	Suzanne Schmidt	Barry Burton	Teresa Linton	Gary Gordon	. . .	Russell Adams
Lawrence	*	C	15	(618) 943-2346	Charles Gillespie	. . .	Nancy Nelson	. . .	. . .	Tim Bivins
Lee		C	36	(618) 288-5676	James Seeberg	. . .	Kristy Masching	. . .	Linda Daniels	Robert McCarty
Livingston		CM	39	(815) 844-6378	Bill Flott	Alina Hartley	. . .	. . .	. . .	. . .
Logan		C	31	(217) 732-6400	. . .	. . .	Steve Bean	Amy Stockwell	. . .	Jerry Dawson
Macon	*	C	114	(217) 424-1470	Robert Sampson	. . .	John Saracco	. . .	. . .	Jim Zirkelbach
Macoupin		C	49	(217) 854-3214	Don Denby	. . .	Mark Von Nida	H. Frandsen	Christine Sillery	Bob Churchich
Madison		CE	258	(618) 692-7040	Rudolph Papa	Joseph Parente	Cliff Neudecker	. . .	. . .	Gerald Benjamin
Marion		C	41	(618) 548-3400	Ralph Johnnie	. . .	A. Mahoney Platt	. . .	. . .	E. Webster
Marshall		CE	13	(309) 246-3667	. . .	. . .	. . .	. . .	. . .	. . .
Mason		C	16	(309) 543-6661	. . .	. . .	John Taylor	Deborah Beal	Terri Johnston	Sam Dunning
Massac		C	15	(618) 524-5213	Doris Vogt	. . .	. . .	. . .	. . .	. . .
Mc Donough		CE	32	(309) 837-2308	. . .	. . .	Katherine Schultz	Ralph Sarbaugh	. . .	Keith Nygren
Mc Henry		CM	260	(815) 334-4220	Kenneth Koehler	Peter Austin	Peggy Milton	. . .	. . .	Mike Emery
Mc Lean	*	CE	150	(309) 888-5110	Michael Sweeney	John Zeunik	Gene Treseler	. . .	. . .	Larry Smith
Menard		C	12	(217) 632-3201	. . .	. . .	Tom Hanson	. . .	. . .	. . .
Mercer		C	16	(309) 582-7021	Kevin Basala	. . .	Dennis Knobloch	. . .	. . .	Daniel Kelley
Monroe		C	27	(618) 939-8681	Robert Rippelmeyer	Grace Miller	Sandy Leitheiser	. . .	. . .	Jim Vazzi
Montgomery		C	30	(217) 532-9530	. . .	. . .	Barbara Gross	. . .	. . .	James Robson
Morgan		C	36	(217) 245-4619	Virgil Smith	Dan Little	Georgia England	Ron White	Earline Reed	Jeff Thomas
Moultrie		C	14	(217) 728-4389	. . .	. . .	Rebecca Huntley	. . .	. . .	Gregory Beitel
Ogle		C	51	(815) 732-3201	Ed Rice	Jim Mielke	JoAnn Thomas	. . .	Kate VanBeek	Michael McCoy
Peoria		CE	183	(309) 672-6947	David Williams	F. Urich	Don Hirsch	. . .	. . .	Keith Kellerman
Perry		C	23	(618) 357-5116	Danny Wildermuth	. . .	Pat Rhoades	. . .	. . .	Robert Manint
Piatt		C	16	(217) 762-7009	Robert Scheffer	. . .	Roger Yaeger	Melisa Borrowman	. . .	Mike Lord
Pike		CE	17	(217) 285-6812	Allen Seiler	. . .	Connie Gibbs	Ann Ferrell	. . .	John Crabb
Pope		C	4	(618) 683-4466	David Bramlet	. . .	Tanna Goins	. . .	. . .	Kenneth Moore
Pulaski		C	7	(618) 748-9400	. . .	. . .	Daniel Kuhn	. . .	. . .	Kevin Doyle
Putnam		C	6	(815) 925-7129	Duane Calbow	. . .	Alice Mullinax	. . .	. . .	. . .
Randolph		C	33	(618) 826-5000	. . .	. . .	Richard Leibovitz	. . .	Mindi Nelson	Andrew Hires
Richland	*	C	16	(618) 392-3111	. . .	. . .	Willie McClusky	. . .	. . .	Michael Grchan
Rock Island		C	149	(309) 558-3605	James Bohnsack	. . .	Joseph Aiello	Joseph Cavanagh	. . .	. . .
Saline		C	26	(618) 252-6228	Kermit Coffee	. . .	Linda Ward	. . .	. . .	Don Schieferdecker
Sangamon		C	188	(217) 753-6630	Andy Vanmeter	Ryan McCrady	Barbara McDade	. . .	. . .	. . .
Schuyler	*	C	7	(217) 322-4734	Brian Peak	. . .	Kathy Lantz	. . .	. . .	Michael Miller
Scott		C	5	(217) 742-5532	. . .	. . .	. . .	. . .	. . .	. . .
Shelby	*	C	22	(217) 774-4421	. . .	. . .	Linda Pyell	. . .	. . .	Jimmie Dison
St. Clair		CE	256	(618) 277-6600	. . .	. . .	Vici Otte	. . .	. . .	David Snyders
Stark	*	C	6	(309) 286-5901	Michael Bigger	. . .	Christie Webb	. . .	. . .	Robert Huston
Stephenson	*	C	48	(815) 235-8277	John Blum	Russell Mulnix	. . .	. . .	. . .	. . .
Tazewell		C	128	(309) 477-2272	James Unsicker	David Jones	Lynn Foster	Linda Anstey	Nancy Boose	William Hartshorn
Union		C	18	(618) 833-5711	. . .	. . .	Marie Kolb	. . .	. . .	Terry McWilliams
Vermilion		CE	83	(217) 431-2550	Todd Lee	. . .	Janet Hammond	. . .	. . .	Richard Hart
Wabash		C	12	(618) 262-4561	Charles Sanders	. . .	. . .	. . .	. . .	. . .
Warren		C	18	(309) 734-8592	William Reichow	Mike Pearson	Donna Endsley	. . .	. . .	Jerry Joslin
Washington		C	15	(618) 327-8314	. . .	. . .	. . .	. . .	. . .	Douglas Maier
Wayne		C	17	(618) 842-5182	. . .	. . .	Dan Heusinkveld	. . .	Deborah Workman	Roger Schipper
White		C	15	(618) 382-7211	Ronnie Wooten	. . .	N. Schultz Voots	Stephen Weber	J. Gregory Pike	Paul Kaupas
Whiteside		CE	60	(815) 772-5100	Tony Arduini	Michael Zurn	Barney Boren	. . .	. . .	Tom Cundiff
Will		CE	502	(815) 722-5753	Joseph Mikan	. . .	. . .	. . .	. . .	. . .
Williamson		C	61	(618) 997-1301	Rex Piper	. . .	Debbie Harms	. . .	. . .	James Pierceall
Winnebago		CE	278	(815) 987-3034	. . .	Steven Chapman	. . .	. . .	. . .	. . .
Woodford		C	35	(309) 467-7344	. . .	Gregory Jackson	. . .	. . .	. . .	. . .
INDIANA										
Adams		C	33	(260) 724-2600	Michael Ripley	. . .	D. O'Shaunessey	. . .	. . .	. . .
Allen	*	C	331	(260) 449-7217	Linda Bloom	. . .	Therese Brown	. . .	Brian Dumford	Kenneth Fries
Bartholomew		CE	71	(812) 379-1513	Larry Kleinhenz	. . .	Norma Trimpe	Nancy McKinney	. . .	Kenneth Whipker
Benton	*	C	9	(765) 884-0760	Mel Budreau	. . .	Janet Hasser	Joan Schluttenhofer	. . .	. . .
Blackford	*	C	14	(765) 348-1620	Fred Walker	. . .	Laura Coons	Kathy Bantz	. . .	John Lancaster
Boone	*	C	46	(765) 482-2940	. . .	. . .	Penny Bogan	Gretchen Smith	. . .	Ken Campbell
Brown	*	C	14	(812) 988-5485	James Gredy	. . .	Benita Fox	Mari Miller	. . .	Robert Stogsdill
Carroll		C	20	(765) 564-3172	William Brown	. . .	Laura Sterrett	Robert Baker	. . .	Dennis Randle
Cass		CE	40	(574) 753-7727	. . .	. . .	Linda Crimmins	Dawn Conner	. . .	Gene Isaacs
Clark		C	96	(812) 285-6400	Ralph Guthrie	. . .	Keith Groth	. . .	. . .	Michael Becher
Clay		C	26	(812) 448-9005	Angela Modesitt	Susan Kellum	Mary Brown	. . .	. . .	. . .
Clinton		C	33	(765) 659-6300	. . .	. . .	. . .	. . .	. . .	. . .
Crawford		C	10	(812) 338-2601	Randy Gilmore	. . .	Peggy Bullington	Terry Stroud	. . .	Richard Scott
Daviess		C	29	(812) 254-1090	. . .	. . .	Rosemary Abel	. . .	. . .	. . .
De Kalb		C	40	(260) 925-2362	William Ort	. . .	Marilyn Miller	Mary Bowman	. . .	Jay Oberholtzer
Dearborn	*	C	46	(812) 537-1040	. . .	. . .	. . .	. . .	. . .	. . .
Decatur		C	24	(812) 663-2570	Thomas Menkedick	. . .	Beverly Stiers	Mary Doggett	. . .	. . .
Delaware		C	118	(765) 747-7730	Tom Bennington	. . .	Steven Craycraft	. . .	Julie Hillgrove	George Sheridan

Directory 1/10
continued

OFFICIALS IN U.S. COUNTIES 2,500 AND OVER IN POPULATION

Jurisdiction		Form of govern-ment	2000 Popu-lation (000)	Main telephone number	Chief elected official	Appointed administrator	Clerk of the governing board	Chief financial officer	Director of personnel	Chief law enforcement official
INDIANA continued										
Dubois		C	39	(812) 481-7000	Lawrence Vollmer	. . .	Kathleen Hopf	. . .	. . .	Jerry Breeding
Elkhart		C	182	(574) 535-6725	Terry Rodino	Thomas Byers	Stephanie Burgess	David Hess	Floyd Hindbaugh	Michael Books
Fayette		C	25	(765) 825-8987	. . .	. . .	Melinda Sudhoff	. . .	. . .	Frank Jackson
Floyd		C	70	(881) 294-8549	Larry Denison	. . .	Betty Hammond	William Jenks	William Burkhart	Leland Watson
Fountain	*	C	17	(765) 793-2243	. . .	. . .	Patricia Gritten	Colleen Chambers	. . .	Robert Bass
Franklin		C	22	(765) 647-4985	Louis Linkel	. . .	Marlene Flaspohler	. . .	. . .	Dale Maxie
Fulton	*	C	20	(574) 223-2912	Richard Powell	. . .	Letty McKee	Denise Bonnell	Penny Bramble	Walker Conley
Gibson		C	32	(812) 385-4927	. . .	. . .	Debbie Wethington	. . .	. . .	R. Allen Harmon
Grant		C	73	(765) 668-8871	. . .	. . .	Carolyn Mowery	Judith Carmichael	. . .	. . .
Greene		C	33	(812) 384-8658	Thomas Britton	. . .	Thomas Franklin	David Bailey	. . .	William Allen
Hamilton		C	182	(317) 776-8401	. . .	. . .	Tamela Baitz	Robin Mills	Sheena Randall	Larry Cook
Hancock	*	C	55	(317) 477-1105	. . .	. . .	Sharon Burris	. . .	. . .	Calvin Gray
Harrison		C	34	(812) 738-8241	Terry Miller	. . .	Carole Gaither	Karen Engleman	. . .	C. Wendell Smith
Hendricks		C	104	(317) 745-9221	. . .	. . .	Cindy Spence	. . .	. . .	. . .
Henry		CE	48	(765) 529-4705	. . .	. . .	Patricia French	Linda Ratcliff	. . .	Kim Cronk
Howard		C	84	(765) 456-7010	Paul Raver	Lawrence Murrell	Mona Myers	Ann Wells	Wanda McKillip	Marshall Talbert
Huntington	*	C	38	(260) 358-4822	. . .	. . .	Vicki Stoffel	Donald Schoeff	. . .	Kent Farthing
Jackson	*	C	41	(812) 358-6161	Gary Darlage	. . .	Sarah Benter	Debra Eggeman	. . .	. . .
Jasper		C	30	(219) 866-4930	Richard Maxwell	. . .	Arlene Castongia	Rita Steele	. . .	James Wallace
Jay		CE	21	(260) 726-4951	. . .	. . .	. . .	. . .	. . .	. . .
Jefferson	*	C	31	(812) 265-8944	. . .	. . .	Kim Smith	Sandra Shelton	. . .	William Andrews
Jennings		C	27	(812) 352-3016	. . .	. . .	Janice Ramey	Edwin Judd	. . .	Earl Taggart
Johnson		CE	115	(317) 736-5000	James Rhoades	. . .	Jill Jackson	Deborah Shutta	. . .	Terry McLaughlin
Knox	*	C	39	(812) 885-2502	Dodi Blackburn	. . .	Brenda Hall	. . .	. . .	Jerry Mooney
Kosciusko		C	74	(574) 372-2475	. . .	Ronald Robinson	. . .	. . .	. . .	Aaron Rovenstine
La Grange		C	34	(260) 499-6310	Richard Strayer	. . .	June Prill	Kay Myers	. . .	Greg Dhaene
La Porte		C	110	(574) 326-6808	Clay Turner	. . .	Ann Sperak	Kenneth Layton	. . .	Robert Blair
Lake		C	484	(219) 755-3200	Rudolph Clay	John Dull	Anna Anton	Dante Rondelli	. . .	John Buncich
Lawrence		C	45	(812) 275-3111	. . .	. . .	Julie Brinegar	. . .	. . .	. . .
Madison		C	133	(765) 642-0186	. . .	. . .	. . .	. . .	. . .	. . .
Marion		CE	860	(317) 327-4622	Philip Borst	. . .	Doris Sadler	Martha Womacks	. . .	Frank Anderson
Marshall		CE	45	(574) 935-8555	Kevin Overmyer	. . .	Janice Fisher	Jan Quivey	. . .	Robert Ruff
Martin		C	10	(812) 247-3731	. . .	. . .	John Hunt	. . .	. . .	. . .
Miami		C	36	(765) 472-3901	Brenda Weaver	. . .	Trudy McCrae	. . .	. . .	Charles McCord
Monroe		C	120	(812) 349-2550	. . .	. . .	. . .	Barbara Clark	. . .	. . .
Montgomery		C	37	(765) 364-6400	Stephen Hester	G. Plunkett	Cindy Edmiston	Janet Harris	Carrie Hocking	Dennis Rice
Morgan		C	66	(765) 342-1025	. . .	. . .	. . .	. . .	. . .	. . .
Newton	*	C	14	(219) 474-6081	Russell Collins	. . .	Janice Wilson	Patricia Carlson	. . .	Donald Hartman
Noble		C	46	(260) 636-2658	J Hal Stump	. . .	Diann Bortner	Michelle Mawhorter	Connie Smith	Douglas Dukes
Ohio	*	C	5	(812) 438-2062	Connie Brown	. . .	Constance Althoff	. . .	. . .	Eldon Fancher
Orange		C	19	(812) 723-3600	. . .	. . .	Beth Jones	. . .	. . .	Doyle Cornwell
Owen		C	21	(812) 829-5000	Nick Robertson	. . .	Julie Bandy	Bobby Hall	. . .	Stephen Cradick
Parke		C	17	(765) 569-3422	. . .	. . .	Vickie White	Diana Hazlett	. . .	Charles Bollinger
Perry		C	18	(812) 547-2758	L. Fortwendel	Diane Gebhard	Deborah Weatherholt	Deborah Elder	. . .	Jon Deer
Pike		C	12	(812) 354-6451	Stephen Stidd	. . .	Shirley Van Meter	Sharon Booth	. . .	Todd Meadors
Porter		C	146	(219) 465-3355	Larry Sheets	. . .	Pamela Mishler Fish	James Murphy	. . .	David Reynolds
Posey		C	27	(812) 838-1306	. . .	. . .	. . .	. . .	. . .	. . .
Pulaski		C	13	(574) 946-3653	Richard Sommers	. . .	Janet Kennedy	Thomas Shank	Christi Hoffa	Paul Grandstaff
Putnam		C	36	(765) 653-5513	. . .	. . .	Opal Sutherlin	Kristina Warren	. . .	Mark Frisbie
Randolph	*	C	27	(765) 584-6700	. . .	. . .	Claudia Thornburg	David Kelly	. . .	Jay Harris
Ripley		C	26	(765) 689-6311	. . .	. . .	Ginger Bradford	Mary McCoy	. . .	William Davison
Rush		CE	18	(765) 932-2077	Marvin Cole	. . .	Linda Sheehan	. . .	. . .	James Owens
Scott		C	22	(812) 752-8408	Billy Comer	. . .	Karen Roth	. . .	Marsha Miller-Smith	Thomas Herald
Shelby		C	43	(317) 392-6310	Robert Wade	. . .	Carol Stohry	Margaret Brunk	Michael Flynn	Tom DeBaum
Spencer	*	C	20	(812) 649-4376	Dan Rininger	. . .	Ann Jochim	. . .	. . .	Kermitt Lindsey
St. Joseph	*	C	265	(574) 235-9547	. . .	. . .	Rita Glenn	Mike Eby	Phyllis Emmons	Frank Canarecci
Starke		C	23	(574) 772-9101	Daniel Bau	. . .	Rhonda Milner	Michaelene Houston	. . .	Robert Sims
Steuben		C	33	(260) 668-1000	F Mayo Sanders	. . .	Debra Arnett	Kim Koomler	. . .	Richard Lewis
Sullivan		C	21	(812) 268-4491	Ray McCammon	. . .	Rochelle Parris	. . .	. . .	John Waterman
Switzerland		C	9	(812) 427-3302	Brian Morton	. . .	Ginger Peters	Janice Ramsey	. . .	Nathan Hughes
Tippecanoe	*	CE	148	(765) 423-9215	K Benson	. . .	Linda Phillips	. . .	Shirley Mennen	Tracy Brown
Tipton		CE	16	(765) 675-2795	. . .	. . .	. . .	. . .	. . .	. . .
Union		C	7	(765) 458-5464	Allen Paddock	. . .	Patricia Hensley	Virginia Bostick	. . .	Steve Leverton
Vanderburgh		C	171	(812) 435-5241	. . .	. . .	Susan Kirk	. . .	. . .	Brad Ellsworth
Vermillion		C	16	(765) 492-3570	Timothy Wilson	. . .	Martha Padish	Ruth Ann Swinford	. . .	Kim Hawkins
Vigo		C	105	(812) 462-3000	William Bryan	. . .	William Mansard	Raymond Watts	. . .	William Harris
Wabash	*	C	34	(260) 563-0661	Lester Templin	Jim Dils	Lori Draper	Bob Fuller	. . .	Leroy Striker
Warren		C	8	(765) 762-3275	Thomas Hetrick	. . .	Carolyn Weston	Michelle Hetrick	. . .	Russell Hart
Warrick		C	52	(812) 897-6160	. . .	. . .	Shannon Weisheit	Richard Kixmiller	. . .	Marvin Heilman
Washington	*	C	27	(812) 883-4805	. . .	. . .	Rita Martin	Sarah Bachman	. . .	Claude Combs
Wayne		C	71	(765) 973-9209	Mary Heyob	. . .	SueAnne Lower	. . .	Vickie Hill	Matt Strittmatter
Wells		C	27	(260) 824-6470	. . .	. . .	Betsy Noe	. . .	. . .	Brooks Mounsey
White	*	C	25	(574) 583-5761	Mary Pool	Julie McKenzie	Bruce Lambert	. . .	. . .	John Roberts
Whitley	*	C	30	(260) 248-3100	James Argerbright	. . .	Cindy Greer	Linda Gerig	Paula Reimers	Mark Hodges
IOWA										
Adair	*	CM	8	(641) 743-2546	Bill Lamb	. . .	Jenice Wallace	. . .	. . .	Randy Marchant
Adams		C	4	(641) 322-3340	Mark Olive	. . .	. . .	Donna West	. . .	Bill Lyddon
Allamakee		C	14	(563) 568-3522	Kathy Campbell	. . .	Mary O'Neill	. . .	. . .	Tim Heiderscheit
Appanoose		C	13	(641) 856-6191	Wayne Sheston	. . .	Linda Demry	. . .	. . .	. . .
Audubon		C	6	(712) 563-2584	LaVerne Deist	. . .	Kim Johnson	Lisa Frederiksen	. . .	Todd Johnson
Benton		C	25	(319) 472-4869	Jason Sanders	. . .	. . .	. . .	. . .	Kenneth Popenhagen
Black Hawk	*	C	128	(319) 833-3009	Tom Little	. . .	. . .	Grant Veedor	June Watkins	Michael Kubic
Boone		C	26	(515) 433-0502	Albert Sorensen	David Reed	Philippe Meier	. . .	Sara Behn	Ronald Fehr
Bremer		C	23	(319) 352-0340	. . .	. . .	. . .	Kathy Thoms	. . .	Duane Hildebrandt
Buchanan		C	21	(319) 334-3578	Leo Donnelly	. . .	Vicki Brasch	Cynthia Witt	. . .	Bill Wolfgram
Buena Vista	*	C	20	(712) 749-2542	Herb Crampton	. . .	Shari O'Bannon	Karen Strawn	. . .	Chuck Eddy
Butler	*	C	15	(319) 267-2670	Holly Fokkena	. . .	. . .	. . .	. . .	Jason Johnson
Calhoun		C	11	(712) 297-7741	. . .	. . .	. . .	Judy Howrey	. . .	Bill Davis
Carroll	*	C	21	(712) 792-9802	. . .	. . .	. . .	. . .	. . .	Douglas Bass
Cass		C	14	(712) 243-4570	Don Volk	. . .	Joyce Jensen	Dale Sunderman	. . .	Bill Sage

Directory 1/10
continued

OFFICIALS IN U.S. COUNTIES 2,500 AND OVER IN POPULATION

Jurisdiction	Form of govern-ment	2000 Popu-lation (000)	Main telephone number	Chief elected official	Appointed administrator	Clerk of the governing board	Chief financial officer	Director of personnel	Chief law enforcement official
IOWA continued									
Cedar	C	18	(563) 886-3168	...	...	...	Betty Ellerhoff	...	Dan Hannes
Cerro Gordo	* C	46	(641) 421-3021	Jay Urdahl	...	Michelle Rush	Heather Mathre	...	Kevin Pals
Cherokee	C	13	(712) 225-6704	Ronald Wetherell	...	Dawn Coombs	Bonnie Ebel	...	Dave Scott
Chickasaw	* CE	13	(641) 394-2100	Virgil Pickar	...	Cindy Messersmith	...	...	Patrick Wegman
Clarke	* C	9	(641) 342-3315	Myron Manley	...	Marsha Parsons	Judy Church	...	Bill Kerns
Clay	C	17	(712) 262-1569	Kenneth Chalstrom	...	Shirley Goyette	Marjorie Pitts	...	Randy Krukow
Clayton	C	18	(563) 245-1106	Neil Meyer	...	...	...	...	Robert Hamann
Clinton	C	50	(563) 244-0560	Lewis Todtz	...	...	...	...	Michael Wolf
Crawford	* C	16	(712) 263-3045	Daniel Muhlbauer	...	...	Cecilia Fineran	...	Thomas Hogan
Dallas	C	40	(515) 993-5814	Mark Hanson	Connie Kinnard	...	Gene Krumm	Joni Fagen	Brian Gilbert
Davis	* C	8	(641) 664-2101	...	...	Judith Brunk	...	...	Monte Harsch
Decatur	C	8	(641) 446-4382	...	...	...	...	...	...
Delaware	C	18	(563) 927-2515	William Skinner	...	...	Sharon McCrabb	...	Ronald Wilhelm
Des Moines	C	42	(319) 753-8232	Edgar Blow	...	K. Waterhouse	Carol Copeland	...	William Johnstone
Dickinson	C	16	(712) 336-3356	...	...	...	...	...	...
Dubuque	C	89	(563) 589-4441	Donna Smith	Mary Ann Specht	...	Denise Dolan	...	Ken Runde
Emmet	C	11	(712) 362-4261	Beverly Juhl	Ronald Smith	...	Vickie Jurrens	...	Larry Lamack
Fayette	* CE	22	(563) 422-3497	...	...	...	Larry Popenhagen	...	Martin Fisher
Floyd	C	16	(641) 257-6131	Warren Dunkel	...	Barb Fuls	...	Gloria Carr	Rick Lynch
Franklin	* C	10	(641) 456-5622	Corey Eberling	...	...	Michelle Giddings	...	Larry Richtsmeier
Fremont	* C	8	(712) 374-2031	Chuck Larson	Earl Hendrickson	Marsha Smith	Joan Kirk	...	...
Greene	* C	10	(515) 386-5680	Guy Richardson	...	Mary Gilley	Jane Heun	...	Thomas Heater
Grundy	C	12	(319) 824-3122	Mark Schildroth	...	...	...	...	Rick Penning
Guthrie	C	11	(641) 747-3619	James Petersen	...	...	John Rutledge	...	Roger Baird
Hamilton	* C	16	(515) 832-9510	Doug Bailey	...	Kim Schaa	...	...	Dennis Hagenson
Hancock	C	12	(641) 923-3163	Florence Greiman	...	...	...	...	Scott Dodd
Hardin	C	18	(641) 939-8113	Jim Johnson	...	...	Renee McClellan	...	Timothy Smith
Harrison	* C	15	(712) 644-2401	Larry King	...	Dean Rodwald	...	...	Terry Baxter
Henry	* C	20	(319) 385-0756	...	...	Christine Brakeville	Hettie Maschmann	...	Allen Wittmer
Howard	C	9	(563) 547-2880	Mary Jo Wilhelm	...	Cherri Caffrey	...	Craig Fencl	Mark Grinhaug
Humboldt	* C	10	(515) 332-1571	Jerry Haverly	...	Peggy Rice	...	...	Dean Kruger
Ida	C	7	(712) 364-2626	Robert Paulstud	...	...	Lorna Steenbock	...	Wade Harriman
Iowa	C	15	(319) 642-3923	...	...	...	...	...	...
Jackson	C	20	(563) 652-3144	John Willey	...	...	...	...	Russell Kettmann
Jasper	C	37	(641) 787-1024	Max Worthington	...	...	Dennis Parrott	Brian Sims	Michael Balmer
Jefferson	C	16	(641) 472-2840	...	...	...	...	...	Frank Bell
Johnson	C	111	(319) 356-6000	Mike Lehman	...	...	...	Lora Shramek	Lonny Pulkrabek
Jones	C	20	(319) 462-2282	Joe Cruise	...	...	Janine Sulzner	...	Mark Denniston
Keokuk	C	11	(641) 622-2320	William Deitrich	...	Marilyn Wells	...	...	Ron George
Kossuth	* C	17	(515) 295-2718	Laurel Anderson	...	Audrey Haverly	Joann Bormann	...	Kevin Van Otterloo
Lee	C	38	(319) 372-6557	...	...	...	...	...	...
Linn	C	191	(319) 892-5120	Lu Barron	...	Linda Langenberg	Stephen Tucker	Thomas Flanders	Donald Zeller
Louisa	C	12	(319) 523-3371	David Wilson	...	...	Sylvia Belzer	Kay Smith	Curtis Braby
Lucas	C	9	(641) 774-4512	Larry Davis	...	...	G. Patterson	...	Delbert Longley
Lyon	C	11	(712) 472-3713	Kenneth Mellema	...	...	Richard Heidloff	...	Kevin Hammer
Madison	C	14	(515) 462-3914	...	...	...	...	...	...
Mahaska	* C	22	(641) 673-7148	Henry VanWeelden	...	...	Kay Swanson	...	Paul DeGeest
Marion	C	32	(641) 828-2217	William Shepherd	...	Joan Noftsger	Dody Devries	...	Marv Van Haaften
Marshall	C	39	(641) 754-6330	Gordie Johnson	...	...	...	...	Ted Kamatchus
Mills	C	14	(712) 527-4729	...	...	...	...	...	Mack Taylor
Mitchell	C	10	(641) 732-5861	...	...	...	...	...	...
Monona	C	10	(712) 433-2191	Richard Merritt	...	Karen Kahl	Benita Davis	...	Jeffrey Pratt
Monroe	C	8	(641) 932-7706	Dennis Ryan	...	C. Brothers	...	...	William Owens
Montgomery	C	11	(712) 623-5127	Glen Benskin	...	...	...	...	Tony Updegrove
Muscatine	* C	41	(563) 263-5287	Kas Kelly	Nancy Schreiber	...	Leslie Soule	...	R. Orr
O'Brien	C	15	(712) 757-3225	Dan Struve	...	Jeff Roos	Barb Rohwer	...	...
Osceola	CE	7	(712) 754-2241	Barbara Echter	...	Eileen Grave	...	...	Edward Harskamp
Page	C	16	(712) 542-5018	...	...	...	...	...	...
Palo Alto	* C	10	(712) 852-2924	Ronald Graettinger	...	Gary Leonard	...	...	Dennis Goeders
Plymouth	* C	24	(712) 546-6100	Jim Henrich	...	...	...	Karen Meyer	Mike Van Otterloo
Pocahontas	C	8	(712) 335-3361	...	...	Carol Williams	Margene Bunda	...	Robert Lampe
Polk	CM	374	(515) 286-3000	John Mauro	Ronald Olson	Thomas Parkins	Larry Millang	Diana Williams	...
Pottawattamie	* C	87	(712) 328-5700	Melvyn Houser	...	...	Marilyn Drake	Mary Davis	Jeff Danker
Poweshiek	C	18	(641) 623-5723	...	...	...	...	...	...
Ringgold	* CE	5	(641) 464-3239	Wayne Kemery	...	...	...	...	Michael Sobotka
Sac	C	11	(712) 662-7401	...	...	...	...	...	...
Scott	CE	158	(563) 326-8611	Larry Minard	Ray Wierson	...	...	...	Denny Conard
Shelby	C	13	(712) 755-3831	...	...	...	Marsha Carter	...	Gene Cavenaugh
Sioux	C	31	(712) 737-2216	...	...	...	Dennis Lange	...	Daniel Altena
Story	* C	79	(515) 382-6581	Wayne Clinton	...	Mary Mosiman	...	Sherry Howard	Paul Fitzgerald
Tama	C	18	(641) 484-2740	James Ledvina	...	Ann Hendricks	...	...	Mike Richardson
Taylor	* C	6	(712) 523-2280	...	...	Lori Reed	Bonny Baker	...	Lonnie Weed
Union	C	12	(641) 782-7218	Michael King	...	...	Sandy Hysell	...	Rick Piel
Van Buren	* C	7	(319) 293-3129	Marvin Philips	...	Jon Finney	...	...	Dan Tedrow
Wapello	* C	36	(641) 683-0025	...	...	Phyllis Dean	...	...	Donald Kirkendall
Warren	* C	40	(515) 961-1001	G. Middleswart	...	...	Traci Vandealinden	...	...
Washington	C	20	(319) 653-7715	Jack Dillon	...	Julie Johnson	William Fredrick	...	Jerry Dunbar
Wayne	CE	6	(641) 872-2242	Jerry O'Dell	...	Sue Ruble	...	...	Keith Davis
Webster	C	40	(515) 573-7175	...	...	...	Carol Messerly	...	Charles Griggs
Winnebago	C	11	(641) 585-3412	Jennifer Fjelstad	...	...	...	...	Thomas Lillquist
Winneshiek	* C	21	(563) 382-5085	Dean Darling	...	G. Schweinefus	...	...	Leon Bohr
Woodbury	CE	103	(712) 279-6480	Maurice Welte	...	...	Patrick Gill	John Pellersels	David Amick
Worth	* C	7	(641) 324-2316	...	...	...	...	...	David Gentz
Wright	* C	14	(515) 532-2771	Rodney Toftey	Betty Ellis	Sue Harson	P. Schluttenhofer	...	Paul Schultz
KANSAS									
Allen	* C	14	(620) 365-1407	...	...	Sherrie Riebel	...	...	Thomas Williams
Anderson	CE	8	(785) 448-6841	Dean Register	...	Phyllis Gettler	...	...	Darin Dalsing
Atchison	C	16	(913) 367-1653	Susie Pick	...	Pauline Lee	...	...	...
Barber	C	5	(620) 886-3961	Mike Thomas	...	Debbie Wesley	...	...	Tommy Tomson
Barton	CE	28	(620) 793-1800	Kirby Krier	...	Donna Zimmerman	...	...	Buck Causey
Bourbon	C	15	(620) 223-3800	Gary Houston	...	Joanne Long	...	Kendell Mason	Harold Coleman
Brown	* C	10	(785) 742-2581	Steve Roberts	...	Debbie Parker	...	...	Lamar Shoemaker
Butler	CE	59	(316) 322-4300	...	William Johnson	Ronald Roberts	...	...	Craig Murphy

Directory 1/10 continued   **OFFICIALS IN U.S. COUNTIES 2,500 AND OVER IN POPULATION**

Jurisdiction		Form of government	2000 Population (000)	Main telephone number	Chief elected official	Appointed administrator	Clerk of the governing board	Chief financial officer	Director of personnel	Chief law enforcement official
KANSAS continued										
Chase		C	3	(620) 273-6423	Alan Phipps	...	Nadine Buell	...	...	Gerald Ingalls
Chautauqua		C	4	(620) 725-5800	Mike Champlin	...	Lori Martin	Peggy McAfee	...	...
Cherokee	*	C	22	(620) 429-2042	...	...	Sandra Soper	...	Melody Sanderson	Steven Norman
Cheyenne		C	3	(785) 332-8800	Tim Raile	...	Terry Miller	...	...	Eddie Dankenbring
Clark		C	2	(620) 635-2813	Betty Jo Denton	...	Rebecca Mishler	...	...	N. Brad Harris
Clay		C	8	(785) 632-2552	David Thurlow	...	Mary Brown	...	...	Charles Dunn
Cloud	*	C	10	(785) 243-8110	Bill Garrison	...	Linda Bogart	...	...	Larry Bergstrom
Coffey		C	8	(620) 364-2191	Gene Merry	...	Vernon Birk	...	...	Randy Rogers
Comanche		C	1	(620) 582-2361	Velma Basnett	...	Alice Smith	...	...	Dave Timmons
Cowley		C	36	(620) 221-5400	...	Leroy Alsup	Carmelita Clarkson	...	...	Robert Odell
Crawford	*	C	38	(620) 724-6115	...	...	Don Pyle	Heather Hurt	...	Sandy Horton
Decatur	*	C	3	(785) 475-8102	...	...	Marilyn Horn	...	...	Ken Badsky
Dickinson		C	19	(785) 263-3774	...	...	...	...	...	...
Doniphan		C	8	(785) 985-3513	Paul Scott	...	Peggy Franken	...	...	Michael Batchelder
Douglas		CM	99	(785) 831-5100	Charles Jones	G. Weinaug	Jamie Shew	...	...	Ken McGovern
Edwards		C	3	(620) 659-3000	...	...	...	...	...	...
Elk		C	3	(620) 374-2490	...	...	Donna Kaminska	...	...	Doug Hanks
Ellis	*	C	27	(785) 628-9410	Vernon Berens	...	Alberta Klaus	...	...	Ed Harbin
Ellsworth		C	6	(785) 472-4161	...	...	...	...	...	...
Finney		C	40	(620) 272-3500	Cliff Mayo	Peter Olson	Elsa Ulrich	...	Debra Hays	Kevin Bascue
Ford		C	32	(620) 227-4550	T. Kim Goodnight	Edward Elam	...	Victoria Wells	...	Carl Bush
Franklin	*	C	24	(785) 229-3485	Roy Dunn	John Harris	Shari Perry	...	Gayla Stofko	Craig Davis
Geary		C	27	(785) 238-4300	Florence Whitebread	...	R. Bossemeyer	Therese Hoff	Lisa Eickholt	William Deppish
Gove	*	C	3	(785) 938-2300	Manlen Tuttle	...	Julie Hawkey	...	...	Allan Weber
Graham		C	2	(785) 421-3453	Barbara Bell	...	...	...	...	Don Scott
Grant		CE	7	(620) 356-1335	Madison Traster	...	Linda McHenry	...	...	Lance Babcock
Gray	*	C	5	(620) 855-3618	...	...	Bonnie Swartz	...	...	Bernard Kramer
Greeley		C	1	(620) 376-4256	Michael Thon	...	Linda Firner	...	...	Bradley Clark
Greenwood		C	7	(620) 583-8121	...	...	Debbie Wyckoff	...	...	Rory Kenneson
Hamilton	*	C	2	(620) 384-5629	Jamie Cheatum	...	Marcia Ashmore	...	...	Bethanie Popejoy
Harper		CE	6	(620) 842-5555	Harold Pearl	...	Cheryl Adelhardt	...	...	Kirk Rogers
Harvey	*	CE	32	(316) 284-6806	Max Graber	...	Margaret Wright	Charles Summers	...	Byron Motter
Haskell		C	4	(620) 675-2263	...	...	Sharon Hinkle	...	...	Larry Phoenix
Hodgeman		C	2	(620) 357-6421	...	...	...	...	...	...
Jackson		C	12	(785) 364-2891	Jerry Harter	...	...	...	Kathy Mick	...
Jefferson	*	C	18	(785) 863-2272	David Christy	...	...	Linda Buttron	...	Roy Dunnaway
Jewell		C	3	(785) 378-4020	Frank Langer	...	Carla Waugh	...	...	John Owen
Johnson	*	CM	451	(913) 715-5000	Annabeth Surbaugh	Michael Press	Beverly Baker	...	...	Frank Denning
Kearny		C	4	(620) 355-6551	...	...	...	...	...	...
Kingman	*	C	8	(620) 532-2521	Garry Smith	...	Inge Luntsford	...	...	Randy Hill
Kiowa		C	3	(620) 723-3366	Earl Liggett	...	Evelyn Grimm	...	...	Galen Marble
Labette		C	22	(620) 795-2138	Brian Kinzie	Jim Cook	Linda Schreppel	...	...	William Blundell
Lane		C	2	(620) 397-5653	Thomas Bennett	...	Crysta Torson	...	...	Donald Wilson
Leavenworth		C	68	(913) 684-0400	...	...	...	...	...	John Lamar McLeod
Lincoln		C	3	(785) 524-4757	Doug Gomel	...	Dawn Harlow	...	...	Marvin Stites
Linn		C	9	(913) 795-2668	Herbert Pemberton	...	David Lamb	...	...	...
Logan		C	3	(785) 672-4244	...	...	...	...	...	Gary Eichorn
Lyon		C	35	(620) 342-4950	...	Marshall Miller	Karen Hartenbower	Larry Tucker	...	Lee Becker
Marion	*	C	13	(620) 382-2185	Randy Dallke	...	Carol Maggard	...	...	Kenneth Coggins
Marshall		C	10	(785) 562-5361	Charles Loiseau	...	Gayle Landoll	...	...	Larry Powell
McPherson		C	29	(620) 241-1800	...	Richard Witte	Susan Meng	...	...	Michael Cox
Meade		C	4	(620) 873-8700	Max Johannsen	Harold Rickers	Dannice Meyer	...	...	Frank Kelly
Miami		CM	28	(913) 294-9500	Jim Wise	Shane Krull	Kathy Peckman	...	Brenda Carlson	Douglas Daugherty
Mitchell		C	6	(785) 738-3652	Terry Collins	...	Chris Treaster	...	...	...
Montgomery		C	36	(620) 330-1111	...	...	...	...	...	Roy Meierhoff
Morris		C	6	(620) 767-5518	Robert Mark	...	Michelle Garrett	Patty Carson	...	...
Morton		C	3	(620) 697-2157	...	...	Mary Gilmore	...	Julie Wares	...
Nemaha		C	10	(785) 336-2170	...	...	...	...	...	...
Neosho	*	C	16	(620) 244-3800	John Edwards	Roger Daniels	Randal Neely	...	...	James Keath
Ness		C	3	(785) 798-2401	Frederick Flax	...	Ramona Meis	...	...	Larry Tittel
Norton		C	5	(785) 877-5710	Lloyd Ritter	...	Dorothy Shearer	Valerie Babcock	...	...
Osage		C	17	(785) 828-4812	...	Delton Gilliland	Rhonda Beets	...	...	Kenneth Lippert
Osborne		C	4	(785) 346-2431	...	...	...	...	...	Curtis Miner
Ottawa		C	6	(785) 392-2279	Kathy Luthi	...	Mary Arganbright	...	...	Kenneth White
Pawnee		C	7	(620) 285-3721	Arlis Atteberry	...	Ruth Searight	...	...	...
Phillips		C	6	(785) 543-6825	Rodger VanLoenen	...	Linda McDowell	...	...	Le Roy Stephen
Pottawatomie		C	18	(785) 457-3314	Barbara Kolde	Robert Reece	Susan Figge	...	...	Greg Riat
Pratt	*	C	9	(620) 672-4110	...	...	Sherry Kruse	...	...	Vernon Chinn
Rawlins	*	C	2	(785) 626-3351	Don Marshall	...	Meredith Hrnchir	...	...	William Finley
Reno	*	C	64	(620) 694-2982	Frances Garcia	...	Shari Gagnebin	Tim Davies	Kristie Evans	Randy Henderson
Republic	*	C	5	(785) 527-7231	Linda Holl	...	Vickie Hall	...	...	Ronald Blad
Rice		C	10	(620) 257-2232	Bill Oswalt	...	Joan Davison	...	...	Steve Bundy
Riley		C	62	(785) 537-6200	...	...	Rich Vargo	Johnette Horne	Cindy Volanti	...
Rooks	*	C	5	(785) 425-6391	Patrick Hageman	...	Clara Strutt	...	...	Roger Mongeau
Rush	*	C	3	(785) 222-2731	Larry Wiedeman	...	Barbara Matal	...	...	Ward Corsair
Russell		C	7	(785) 483-3418	...	Lenny Tyson	Simone Ginther	...	...	John Fletcher
Saline	*	C	53	(785) 309-5812	Craig Stephenson	Rita Deister	Donald Merriman	...	Marilyn Leamer	Glen Kochanowski
Scott		C	5	(620) 872-2420	...	...	Pamela Faurot	...	...	Alan Stewart
Sedgwick		CE	452	(316) 660-7057	Ben Sciortino	William Buchanan	Don Brace	Chris Chronis	Jo Templin	Gary Steed
Seward		C	22	(620) 626-3212	...	...	Stacia Long	...	April Warden	Bill McBryde
Shawnee		C	169	(785) 233-8200	Victor Miller	...	Cynthia Beck	Marti Leisinger	Richard Davis	Richard Barta
Sheridan		C	2	(785) 675-3361	...	...	...	...	...	...
Sherman		C	6	(785) 899-4800	...	...	...	...	...	Alvin Gaines
Smith		C	4	(785) 282-5110	Roger Allen	...	Lela Rogers	...	...	Jeff Parr
Stafford		C	4	(620) 549-3509	...	...	Dorothy Stites	...	...	Edward Bezona
Stanton		C	2	(620) 492-2140	Martie Floyd	...	Sharon Dimitt	...	...	Ted Heaton
Stevens		C	5	(620) 544-2541	...	...	Pamela Bensel	...	...	Shawn DeJarnett
Sumner		C	25	(620) 326-3395	...	...	Shane Shields	...	...	Thomas Jones
Thomas		C	8	(785) 462-4500	Ron Evans	...	...	...	...	Richard Schneider
Trego		C	3	(785) 743-5773	Toby Lynd	...	Lori Augustine	...	...	...

Directory 1/10 continued

OFFICIALS IN U.S. COUNTIES 2,500 AND OVER IN POPULATION

Jurisdiction	Form of government	2000 Population (000)	Main telephone number	Chief elected official	Appointed administrator	Clerk of the governing board	Chief financial officer	Director of personnel	Chief law enforcement official
KANSAS continued									
Wabaunsee	C	6	(785) 765-3414	Fred Howard	. . .	Jennifer Savage	. . .	. . .	Craig Spomer
Wallace *	C	1	(785) 852-4282	Bruce Buck	. . .	Melody Fulton	. . .	. . .	Larry Townsend
Washington	C	6	(785) 325-2974	Marcia Funke	. . .	Louella Kern	. . .	. . .	Verni Overbeck
Wichita	C	2	(620) 375-2731	Dan Nickelson	. . .	Karla Ridder	. . .	. . .	Randy Keeton
Wilson	C	10	(620) 378-4337	Fred Rinne	Kris Marple	Maurine Burns	. . .	. . .	Paul Ammann
Woodson	C	3	(620) 625-2179	. . .	. . .	. . .	. . .	. . .	. . .
Wyandotte County–Kansas City	CM	157	(913) 573-5000	Joe Reardon	Dennis Hays	Thomas Roberts	John Manahan	Patty Knoll	Ronald Miller
KENTUCKY									
Adair	C	17	(502) 384-2801	Jerry Vaughan	. . .	. . .	. . .	. . .	. . .
Allen	C	17	(502) 237-3631	. . .	. . .	. . .	. . .	. . .	. . .
Anderson *	C	19	(502) 839-3471	Steve Cornish	. . .	Harold Ritchie	Renee Evans	. . .	Troy Young
Ballard	C	8	(502) 335-5176	Bill Graves	. . .	Lynn Lane	Belinda Sullivan	. . .	Todd Cooper
Barren	CE	38	(270) 651-3338	Davie Greer	. . .	Pamela Browning	. . .	. . .	Barney Jones
Bath	C	11	(606) 674-6346	Ray Bailey	Sandra Crouch	Glen Thomas	. . .	. . .	Randall Armitage
Bell	C	30	(606) 337-3076	. . .	. . .	. . .	. . .	. . .	. . .
Boone	C	85	(606) 334-2100	Larry Burcham	Jeffrey Earlywine	Jerry Rouse	Lisa Buerkley	Marilyn Rouse	Edward Ammann
Bourbon	C	19	(859) 987-2135	Charles Hinkle	. . .	Richard Eads	. . .	. . .	. . .
Boyd	C	49	(606) 739-4134	Billy Ross	Jesse Ross	Debbie Jones	Linda Cassity	. . .	. . .
Boyle	C	27	(606) 238-1118	Anthony Wilder	. . .	Denise Curtsinger	Mary Lynn	. . .	Karl Luttrell
Bracken	C	8	(606) 735-2300	Lovell Jett	Tina Cummins	. . .	. . .	. . .	Michael Nelson
Breathitt	C	16	(606) 666-3810	. . .	. . .	Jill Irwin	. . .	. . .	. . .
Breckinridge *	C	18	(270) 756-2269	Tom Moorman	. . .	Jill Irwin	Lisa Hoskins	. . .	Todd Pate
Bullitt	C	61	(502) 543-2262	Kenneth Rigdon	. . .	Nora McCawley	. . .	. . .	Paul Parsley
Butler	C	13	(270) 526-3433	. . .	. . .	. . .	. . .	. . .	. . .
Caldwell	CE	13	(502) 365-6660	Gerald Knight	. . .	Toni Watson	Betty Holt	. . .	. . .
Calloway	C	34	(502) 753-2920	. . .	. . .	. . .	. . .	. . .	. . .
Campbell *	C	88	(859) 292-3838	Steve Pendery	Robert Horine	Susan Prather	Jim Seibert	Naguanda Deaton	Keith Hill
Carlisle	C	5	(270) 628-5451	. . .	. . .	. . .	. . .	. . .	. . .
Carroll	CE	10	(502) 732-7000	Gene McMurry	Traci Courtney	Marketta Brock	. . .	. . .	. . .
Carter	C	26	(606) 474-5366	Charles Wallace	. . .	Hugh McDavid	. . .	. . .	Kevin McDavid
Casey *	C	15	(606) 787-8311	Ronald Wright	Judy Allen	Eva Miller	. . .	. . .	. . .
Christian	C	72	(270) 887-4100	Steve Tribble	. . .	Michael Kem	. . .	. . .	William Gloyd
Clark	C	33	(859) 745-0200	John Myers	Liz Elswick	Anita Jones	. . .	. . .	Ray Caudill
Clay	C	24	(606) 598-2071	Carl Sizemore	. . .	Freddy Thompson	Diana Roberts	. . .	. . .
Clinton	CE	9	(606) 387-5234	. . .	. . .	Jim Elmore	. . .	. . .	. . .
Crittenden *	C	9	(270) 965-5251	Fred Brown	. . .	Carolyn Byford	Daphenia Downs	. . .	Wayne Agent
Cumberland	C	7	(270) 864-3444	Tim Hicks	. . .	. . .	Eugenia Ferguson	. . .	James Pruitt
Daviess	C	91	(270) 685-8424	Louis Haire	. . .	. . .	. . .	Marsha Hardesty	. . .
Edmondson	C	11	(270) 597-2819	N. E. Reed	. . .	Larry Carroll	. . .	. . .	Billy Joe Honeycutt
Elliott	C	6	(606) 738-5821	D. Blair	. . .	Kyle Faulkner	. . .	. . .	Elwood Flannery
Estill *	C	15	(606) 723-7524	Wallace Taylor	Teresa Sparks	Sherry Fox	Christine Brandenburg	. . .	Gary Freeman
Fleming	C	13	(606) 845-8801	. . .	. . .	. . .	. . .	. . .	. . .
Floyd	CE	42	(606) 886-9193	Paul Thompson	. . .	Carla Boyd	Turner Campbell	. . .	John Blackburn
Franklin	CE	47	(502) 875-8751	Robert Roach	. . .	Shirley Brown	Susan Laurenson	. . .	Ted Collin
Fulton	C	7	(270) 236-2594	. . .	. . .	Leslie LaRue	. . .	. . .	. . .
Gallatin	C	7	(859) 567-5691	George Zubaty	. . .	Tracy Miles	Elaine Lillard	. . .	. . .
Garrard	C	14	(859) 792-3531	Ray Hammonds	. . .	Shelton Moss	. . .	Rita Hinds	. . .
Grant *	CE	22	(859) 823-7561	Darrell Link	Evalene Davis	Judith Fortner	. . .	Connie McClure	Randall Middleton
Graves	C	37	(502) 247-3626	Tony Smith	. . .	Glen Bruce	. . .	. . .	Robert Morgan
Grayson	CE	24	(270) 259-3024	. . .	. . .	. . .	. . .	. . .	Joe Hudson
Green	C	11	(270) 932-4024	Mary Baron	. . .	Alice Clark	. . .	. . .	. . .
Greenup	C	36	(606) 932-6564	. . .	. . .	. . .	. . .	. . .	. . .
Hancock	C	8	(270) 927-8137	. . .	. . .	. . .	. . .	. . .	. . .
Hardin	C	94	(270) 765-2350	Harry Berry	Steve Smith	Kenneth Tabb	. . .	Lisa Pearman	Charles Williams
Harlan	C	33	(606) 573-4771	Joseph Grieshop	. . .	Wanda Clem	. . .	. . .	Stephen Duff
Harrison	CE	17	(859) 234-7136	Dean Peak	Wanda Jones	Linda Fucnish	Judy Cunningham	. . .	Bruce Hampton
Hart	C	17	(270) 524-5219	. . .	. . .	. . .	. . .	. . .	. . .
Henderson	C	44	(270) 826-3971	Sandy Watkins	. . .	Renny Matthews	Rebecca Carroll	. . .	Dennis Clary
Henry	CE	15	(502) 845-5707	Thomas Bryant	Peggy Bryant	Rhonda Carpenter	. . .	. . .	Ray Powell
Hickman	C	5	(270) 653-6195	Gregory Pruitt	Carol Malugin	Sophia Barclay	Nancy Pruitt	Scott Smith	J. Moran
Hopkins *	C	46	(270) 821-8294	Donald Carroll	. . .	Kim Blue	. . .	. . .	. . .
Jackson	C	13	(606) 287-8562	. . .	. . .	. . .	. . .	. . .	. . .
Jessamine	C	39	(859) 885-4500	. . .	. . .	. . .	. . .	. . .	. . .
Johnson	C	23	(606) 789-2550	. . .	. . .	. . .	. . .	. . .	. . .
Kenton	C	151	(859) 491-2800	Richard Murgatroyd	R. Kimmich	William Aylor	. . .	Joseph Shriver	William Dorsey
Knott	C	17	(606) 785-5592	. . .	. . .	. . .	. . .	. . .	. . .
Knox	C	31	(606) 546-6192	Raymond Smith	Bruce Murphy	Mike Corey	Tammy Mays	. . .	John Pickard
Larue	C	13	(270) 358-4400	Tommy Turner	Brenda Miller	. . .	Janet Propes	. . .	Merle Edlin
Laurel	C	52	(606) 864-5158	Lawrence Kuhl	. . .	Dean Johnson	. . .	. . .	. . .
Lawrence	CE	15	(606) 638-4102	Phillip Carter	. . .	. . .	. . .	. . .	. . .
Lee	C	7	(606) 464-4100	. . .	. . .	. . .	. . .	. . .	. . .
Leslie	C	12	(606) 672-3200	. . .	. . .	. . .	. . .	. . .	. . .
Letcher	C	25	(606) 633-2129	Carroll Smith	. . .	Winston Meade	. . .	. . .	Stephen Banks
Lewis	C	14	(606) 796-2722	. . .	. . .	Shirley Hinton	Robert Blaine	. . .	William Lewis
Lincoln	C	23	(606) 365-2534	. . .	. . .	. . .	. . .	. . .	. . .
Livingston	C	9	(502) 928-2105	Joe Ward	. . .	James Jones	Nerva Richards	. . .	. . .
Logan	C	26	(270) 726-3116	. . .	. . .	. . .	. . .	. . .	. . .
Lyon	C	8	(502) 388-7311	. . .	. . .	. . .	. . .	. . .	. . .
Madison	C	70	(859) 624-4702	Kent Clark	Linda Ginter	Mary Ginter	Shirl Cross	. . .	Cecil Cochron
Magoffin	C	13	(606) 349-2313	Paul Salyer	Marcella Salyer	Haden Arnett	. . .	Tammy Mullins	Pat Montgomery
Marion	C	18	(270) 692-3451	John Mattingly	. . .	Karen Spalding	. . .	. . .	Carroll Kirkland
Marshall	C	30	(270) 527-4740	. . .	. . .	. . .	. . .	. . .	. . .
Martin	C	12	(606) 298-2800	. . .	. . .	. . .	. . .	. . .	. . .
Mason	C	16	(606) 564-6706	James Gallenstein	. . .	Frances Cotterill	. . .	. . .	Tony Wenz
Mc Cracken	C	65	(270) 444-4707	Danny Orazine	Steve Doolittle	Randy Otey	Angie Brown	. . .	Frank Augustus
Mc Creary	C	17	(660) 376-2413	Jimmie Green	Bruce Murphy	Jo Kidd	Sue Kidd	. . .	Regal Bruner
Mc Lean	C	9	(270) 273-3213	Larry Whitaker	. . .	Linda Johnson	Betty Ray	. . .	Lester Stratton

Directory 1/10
continued

OFFICIALS IN U.S. COUNTIES 2,500 AND OVER IN POPULATION

Jurisdiction	Form of govern-ment	2000 Popu-lation (000)	Main telephone number	Chief elected official	Appointed administrator	Clerk of the governing board	Chief financial officer	Director of personnel	Chief law enforcement official
KENTUCKY continued									
Meade	C	26	(270) 422-3967	William Haynes	...	...	...	...	Clifford Wise
Menifee *	C	6	(606) 768-3482	Hershell Sexton	...	Joann Spencer	...	...	Rodney Coffey
Mercer	C	20	(859) 734-5135	...	...	...	...	...	...
Metcalfe	C	10	(270) 432-3181	Don Butler	...	Carol England	Lorrie Boston	...	Rondal Shirley
Monroe	C	11	(502) 487-5505	Wilbur Graves	...	...	...	...	Jerry Gee
Montgomery	C	22	(859) 498-8707	B. Wilson	Casey Jones	Judy Witt	...	...	Fred Shortridge
Morgan	C	13	(606) 743-3898	...	...	...	...	...	...
Muhlenberg	C	31	(270) 338-2520	Rodney Kirtley	...	Gaylan Spurlin	...	...	Jerry Mayhugh
Nelson	C	37	(502) 348-1801	...	...	...	...	...	...
Nicholas	C	6	(859) 289-2404	...	...	...	...	...	...
Ohio	C	22	(502) 298-4402	Wayne Hunsaker	...	Les Johnson	Carolyn Johnson	...	Elvis Doolin
Oldham	CE	46	(502) 222-9357	Mary Ellen Kinser	James Morse	Ann Brown	Shawn Boyle	...	Michael Griffin
Owen	C	10	(502) 484-3405	William O'Banion	Cindy Ellis	Eugene Young	Pam Miller	...	Zemer Hammond
Owsley	C	4	(606) 593-6202	...	...	...	...	...	...
Pendleton	C	14	(859) 654-4321	Henry Bertram	...	...	Vicky King	...	...
Perry	C	29	(606) 436-4513	Denny Noble	...	Haven King	Kay Spicer	...	Les Borgett
Pike	C	68	(606) 432-6247	William Deskins	Karen Ratliff	Rose Farley	...	Paul Maynard	...
Powell	C	13	(606) 663-2834	Bobby Drake	...	Rhonda Barnett	...	...	Joe Martin
Pulaski	C	56	(606) 678-4856	Louie Floyd	Dale Weddle	Willard Hansford	Ethel Vanhook	Joan Muse	...
Robertson	C	2	(606) 724-5615	Gordon Buckler	Tara McCord	S. Hendricks	...	...	Randy Insko
Rockcastle	C	16	(606) 256-2856	Buzz Carloftis	...	Norma Houk	Joseph Clontz	...	Shirley Smith
Rowan	CE	22	(606) 784-5151	Clyde Thomas	Timothy Gibbs	Jean Bailey	Maryann Stevens	Becky Banks	Jack Carter
Russell	C	16	(270) 343-2112	Charles Smith	...	Brigette Popplewell	...	...	...
Scott	C	33	(502) 863-7850	George Lusby	Michael Wright	Donna Perry	...	...	...
Shelby	C	33	(502) 633-1220	Bobby Stratton	R. Rothenburger	Sue Perry	Karen Blake	Gail Renfro	Mike Armstrong
Simpson	C	16	(270) 586-7184	...	...	Bobby Phillps	...	...	...
Spencer	C	11	(502) 477-3211	David Jenkins	Karen Curtsinger	Robin Waldridge	Judy Puckett	...	Steve Coulter
Taylor	C	22	(270) 465-7729	Eddie Rogers	...	Randall Phillips	Alice Lee	...	John Shipp
Todd *	C	11	(270) 265-2451	Arthur Green	...	Jennifer Shemwell	...	...	Billy Stokes
Trigg	CE	12	(270) 522-8459	Berlin Moore	...	Wanda Thomas	...	...	Randy Clark
Trimble	C	8	(502) 255-7196	...	...	Jerry Powell	...	...	Dennis Long
Union	C	15	(270) 389-1081	Larry Jenkins	...	...	Vicki O'Nan	...	James Girten
Warren	C	92	(270) 843-4146	Michael Buchanon	Sue Greathouse	Dorothy Owens	Vicki Duckett	...	Jerry Gaines
Washington	C	10	(859) 336-5410	John Settles	William Logsdon	A. H. Robertson	Carla Hardin	...	Tommy Bartley
Wayne	C	19	(606) 348-4241	Bruce Ramsey	...	...	...	Sue Thompson	James Hill
Webster	C	14	(270) 639-5042	James Townsend	...	Valerie Franklin	Janice Marks	...	Frankie Springfield
Whitley	C	35	(606) 549-6000	Leroy Gilbert	...	...	Tracy Davis	...	...
Wolfe	C	7	(606) 668-3040	Raymond Hurst	...	...	Barbara Phillips	...	...
Woodford	C	23	(859) 873-4139	...	...	...	...	...	...
LOUISIANA									
Acadia	CE	58	(337) 788-8800	Cecelia Broussard	Katry Martin	...	...	...	Kenneth Goss
Allen	C	25	(337) 639-4328	Kenneth Hebert	...	Sandria Goodman	...	...	...
Ascension	CE	76	(225) 621-5700	Harold Marchand	Randall Anderson	Suzanne Patterson	Gwen LeBlanc	Gaye Ambeau	...
Assumption	C	23	(985) 369-7435	Martin Triche	Bettie Monson	Lawrence Bergeron	...	Calvin James	Thomas Mabile
Avoyelles	C	41	(318) 253-9208	Kirby Roy	Allison Laborde	...	...	...	...
Beauregard	C	32	(337) 463-7019	Jerry Kern	...	Pauline Marshall	...	...	...
Bienville	C	15	(318) 263-2019	...	...	...	...	...	Larry Deen
Bossier	CM	98	(318) 965-2329	Edwin Shell	William Altimus	Cindy Dodson	...	...	...
Caddo	CE	252	(318) 226-6906	...	William Hanna	Jerry Spears	Erica Bryant	Maria Eades	...
Calcasieu	CE	183	(337) 437-3500	...	S. McMurry	...	Jerry Milner	Cheryl Heisser	...
Caldwell	C	10	(318) 649-2681	...	Monty Adams	...	...	...	...
Cameron	C	9	(337) 775-5718	Charles Sandifer	Earnestine Horn	Carl Broussard	Darrell Williams	...	James Savoie
Catahoula	CE	10	(318) 744-5435	...	...	...	...	...	...
Claiborne	C	16	(318) 927-9601	...	...	...	...	...	Randy Maxwell
Concordia	CE	20	(318) 336-5953	Rodney Smith	Russell Wagoner	Clyde Webber	...	...	Hugh Bennett
De Soto	C	25	(318) 872-0738	Marlin Caston	Don Edington	Shirley Wheless	Betty Woods	S. Mayweather	...
East Carroll	C	9	(318) 559-2256	Joseph Jackson	Major Watson	...	...	...	...
East Feliciana	C	21	(225) 683-8577	James Hunt	Clarence Payne	...	Judith Kelly	...	T. Maglone
Evangeline	C	35	(337) 363-5651	William Guidry	...	...	...	...	...
Franklin	CE	21	(318) 435-9429	Carey Stevens	Emmett Book	Jenny Curtis	Sherri Wiltshire	...	...
Grant	C	18	(318) 627-3246	...	...	...	...	...	...
Iberia	C	73	(337) 365-8246	...	...	...	...	...	...
Iberville	CM	33	(985) 687-5190	...	...	...	...	...	...
Jackson	C	15	(318) 259-5680	...	...	...	...	...	...
Jefferson	C	455	(504) 736-6400	Timothy Coulon	Tim Whitmer	Terrie Rodrigue	Nancy Cassagne	Martin Schwegmann	Harry Lee
Jefferson Davis	C	31	(337) 824-4792	...	...	...	...	...	...
La Salle *	C	14	(318) 992-2101	...	...	...	...	...	...
Lafourche	CM	89	(985) 446-8427	Gerald Breaux	...	Joel Pierce	Veronica Gonzales	Kristy Chiasson	...
Lincoln *	C	42	(318) 513-6200	Joyce Huntington	Richard Durrett	...	...	Annie Hamlin	...
Livingston	C	91	(985) 686-2266	Dewey Ratcliff	...	Mary Kistler	Tracie Eisworth	...	...
Madison	C	13	(318) 574-3451	Thomas Williams	Margarett Smith	Rhonda Brooks	...	...	Earl Pinkney
Morehouse	C	31	(318) 281-4132	...	...	...	...	...	...
Natchitoches	C	39	(318) 352-2714	...	Bobby Dean	...	...	...	...
Ouachita	CE	147	(318) 327-1340	Daryll Berry	Tom Janway	...	...	La Quita Danna	...
Plaquemines	CE	26	(504) 682-0081	...	...	...	...	...	...
Pointe Coupee	C	22	(225) 638-9556	Owen Bello	David Cifreo	Gerrie Patin	...	Bertell Dixon	Paul Smith
Rapides	C	126	(318) 473-6660	Jerry Wood	...	Angie Richmond	Bruce Kelly	...	William Hilton
Red River	C	9	(318) 932-5719	...	...	...	...	...	...
Richland	C	20	(318) 728-2061	Ronnie Gilley	...	...	...	...	...
Sabine	CE	23	(318) 256-5637	...	...	...	...	...	...
St. Bernard	CE	67	(504) 278-4200	Charles Ponstein	Danny Menesses	...	Barbara Bench	Kevin Clark	...
St. Charles	CE	48	(985) 783-5000	Albert Laque	Timothy Vial	...	Lorrie Toups	Sandra Zimmer	...
St. Helena	C	10	(225) 222-4549	Thomas Wicker	Deborah Strickland	...	...	...	Ronald Ficklin
St. James	CE	21	(225) 562-2387	Dale Hymel	John Lubrano	G. Schexnayder	Arile Laiche	Sidney Oubre	...
St. John The Baptist	CE	43	(985) 652-9569	...	Natalie Robottom	...	...	...	...
St. Landry	CE	87	(337) 948-3688	...	...	...	...	...	...
St. Martin	CE	48	(337) 394-2200	Guy Cormier	Gerard Durand	...	...	Claire Lastrapes	...
St. Mary	CE	53	(337) 828-4100	William Cefalu	Henry La Grange	Kimberly Pusateri	...	Leslie Long	...
St. Tammany	CM	191	(985) 898-2362	Kevin Davis	William Oiler	Diane Hueschen	Leslie Long	Sherri Mederos	Rodney Strain
Tangipahoa	CE	100	(985) 748-3211	Gordon Burgess	Jeffery McKneely	Margie Allen	Melissa Cowart	Virginia Baker	...

Directory 1/10
continued

OFFICIALS IN U.S. COUNTIES 2,500 AND OVER IN POPULATION

Jurisdiction	Form of govern-ment	2000 Popu-lation (000)	Main telephone number	Chief elected official	Appointed administrator	Clerk of the governing board	Chief financial officer	Director of personnel	Chief law enforcement official
LOUISIANA continued									
Tensas	C	6	(318) 766-3542	...	...	...	...	...	...
Terrebonne Parish Consolidated	CE	104	(985) 873-6474	Robert Bergeron	Al Levron	Paul Labat	...	William Torres	Pat Boudreaux
Union	CE	22	(318) 368-8687	...	Dennis Reeves	Peggy Tate	...	...	...
Vermilion	C	53	(337) 898-4300	Donald Sagrera	Clay Menard	...	...	...	Michael Couvillion
Vernon	C *	52	(337) 238-1384	...	...	...	...	...	...
Washington	C	43	(985) 839-7825	M. Taylor	...	Sylvia Forbes	Carole McMillan	...	...
Webster	C	41	(318) 377-7564	Charles Walker	Ronda Carnahan	...	...	...	...
West Baton Rouge	CE	21	(225) 383-4755	Riley Berthelot	Joseph Delapasse	Sharon Zito	...	...	...
West Carroll	C	12	(318) 428-3390	Richard Strong	Martha Stephens	...	...	...	...
West Feliciana	C	15	(985) 635-3794	...	...	...	...	...	...
Winn	C	16	(318) 628-5824	Lamar Tarver	Thelma Jarnagin	...	...	...	James Jordan
MAINE									
Androscoggin	C	103	(207) 786-8390	...	...	...	...	...	...
Aroostook	CM	73	(207) 493-3318	Paul Adams	Douglas Beaulieu	...	...	...	James Madore
Cumberland	CM	265	(207) 775-6809	Esther Clenott	Peter Crichton	Barbara Buckley	Victor LaBrecque	Wanda Pettersen	Mark Dion
Franklin	CM	29	(207) 778-6614	...	...	...	...	...	...
Hancock	C	51	(207) 667-9542	Dennis Damon	Ray Bickford	...	...	...	William Clark
Kennebec	C	117	(207) 622-0971	George Jabar	Robert Devlin	...	...	...	Everett Flannery
Knox	C *	39	(207) 594-0420	...	William Post	...	...	...	Donna Dennison
Lincoln	CM *	33	(207) 882-6311	William Blodgett	James McMahon	...	...	...	Todd Brackett
Oxford	C	54	(207) 743-6359	...	...	...	...	...	...
Penobscot	C	144	(207) 942-8535	...	William Collins	...	...	...	Glenn Ross
Piscataquis	C	17	(207) 564-2161	W. Bartley	Michael Henderson	...	...	...	John Goggin
Sagadahoc	C *	35	(207) 443-8200	Alan Houston	Pamela Corrigan	...	Sheila Leavitt	...	Mark Westrum
Somerset	C	50	(207) 474-9861	Dorothy Canelli	...	...	...	...	Barry De Long
Waldo	C	36	(207) 338-3282	John Hyk	...	Barbara Arseneau	...	Michelle Adams	Scott Story
Washington	CE *	33	(207) 255-3127	Christopher Gardner	L. Pagels-Wentworth	...	...	...	Donald Smith
York	C	186	(207) 324-1572	William Layman	David Adjutant	Rachel Sherman	...	April Powell	Philip Cote
MARYLAND									
Allegany	CM *	74	(301) 777-2190	James Stakem	Vance Ishler	Carol Gaffney	Jerry Frantz	Brian Westfall	David Goad
Anne Arundel	CE	489	(410) 222-1831	Janet Owens	...	...	John Hammond	Randall Schultz	Larry Tolliver
Baltimore	CE	754	(410) 887-2004	James Smith	Anthony Marchione	...	Fred Homan	Theresa Hill	Terrence Sheridan
Calvert	C *	74	(410) 535-1600	Wilson Parran	A Douglas Parran	Corinne Cook	Terry Shannon	Gail Bourdon	Edward Evans
Caroline	CE	29	(410) 479-0660	John Cole	Charles Cawley	Katherine Sands	...	...	Philip Brown
Carroll	CE *	150	(410) 386-2400	Julia Gouge	Steven Powell	K. Rauschenberg	Eugene Curfman	Carole Hammen	Kenneth Tregoning
Cecil	C	85	(410) 996-5250	...	Alfred Wein	...	...	Donna Nichols	Rodney Kennedy
Charles	CE	120	(301) 645-0585	Murray Levy	Paul Comfort	Linda Rollins	Richard Winkler	Ann Pokora	...
Dorchester	C	30	(410) 228-1700	Glenn Bramble	Jane Baynard	...	Michael Spears	Becky Dennis	James Phillips
Frederick	CE	195	(301) 694-9000	...	Ronald Hart	...	John Kroll	Mitchell Hose	James Hagy
Garrett	CE *	29	(301) 334-8970	Ernest Gregg	R. Pagenhardt	...	Wendy Yoder	...	P. Sanders
Harford	CE	218	(410) 638-3201	James Harkins	John O'Neill	...	...	James Richardson	Howard Walter
Howard	CE	247	(410) 313-2300	James Robey	Raquel Sanudo	...	Dale Neubert	Jimmie Saylor	Wayne Livesay
Kent	C	19	(410) 778-4595	William Pickrum	Susanne Hayman	Janice Fletcher	Patricia Merritt	Marty Hale	John Price
Montgomery	CE	873	(240) 777-1000	Douglas Duncan	Timothy Firestine	...	...	Joseph Adler	...
Prince George's	CE	801	(301) 883-6330	Jack Johnson	Jacqueline Brown	Redis Floyd	Gail Francis	...	Gerald Wilson
Queen Annes	CM	40	(410) 758-4098	Ted Moeller	Paul Comfort	Lynda Palmatary	Joseph Zimmerman	Richard Mayer	Charles Crossley
Somerset	CE	24	(410) 651-0320	Charles Boston	Charles Massey	...	Charles Muir	Deborah Mahan	Robert Jones
St. Marys	CE *	86	(301) 475-4200	Francis Russell	John Savich	...	Elaine Kramer	Susan Sabo	Timothy Cameron
Talbot	CE *	33	(410) 770-8010	...	R. Hollis	Susan Moran	John Lehner	...	Dallas Pope
Washington	CE	131	(240) 313-2216	Gregory Snook	Gregory Murray	Joni Bitner	Debra Murray	Dave Hankinson	Charles Mades
Wicomico	CE	84	(410) 334-3105	...	Theodore Shea	...	Patricia Petersen	Edward Cox	Hunter Nelms
Worcester	CM	46	(410) 632-1194	...	Gerald Mason	...	Harold Higgins	Deirdre Rouse	Charles Martin
MASSACHUSETTS									
Barnstable	C	222	(508) 362-2511	Robert O'Leary	...	Marc Santos	...	...	Thomas Hodgson
Bristol	C	534	(508) 824-9681	Maria Lopes	...	Marc Santos	P. Harrington	...	Thomas Hodgson
Dukes	C	14	(508) 696-3840	Paul Strauss	E. Winn Davis	Joseph Sollitto	...	...	Michael McCormack
Norfolk	C	650	(781) 461-6105	...	Henry Ainslie	Nicholas Barbadoro	Robert Hall	Ann Brown	Michael Bellotti
Plymouth	C	472	(508) 830-9100	John Riordan	Rosalie Rodick	Francis Powers	...	...	Joseph McDonough
MICHIGAN									
Alcona	C	11	(989) 724-6807	Kevin Boyat	...	Gayle Simmons	...	...	Douglas Ellinger
Alger	C *	9	(906) 387-2076	...	...	Mary Ann Froberg	...	...	David Cromell
Allegan	CM	105	(269) 673-0205	Larry Jones	Robert Sarro	Joyce Watts	D. Van de Roovaart	Debbie Daniels	Frederick Anderson
Alpena	C *	31	(989) 354-9500	Mark Hall	Jeff Thornton	Bonnie Friedrichs	...	Cam Habermehl	Steven Kieliszewski
Antrim	C	23	(616) 533-8607	...	...	Laura Sexton	...	...	Dale Roggenbeck
Arenac	C *	17	(989) 846-4626	Raymond Daniels	...	Rickey Rockwell	...	...	Ronald Bouldin
Baraga	C	8	(906) 524-6183	Michael Koskinen	...	Nelda Bishop	...	...	Bob Teddy
Barry	CM	56	(269) 945-1400	Clare Tripp	...	Debbie Smith	Michael Brown	...	Darrin Leaf
Bay	CM	110	(989) 895-4000	Brian Elder	Thomas Hickner	Cynthia Luczak	Michael Regulski	Kenneth Petersen	John Miller
Benzie	C	15	(616) 882-9671	...	Charles Clarke	Dawn Olney	Linda Wilson	...	Robert Blank
Berrien	CE	162	(269) 983-7111	...	William Wolf	M. Stine	...	...	James Cherry
Branch	C	45	(517) 279-8411	Charlene Burch	Daniel Kaepp	Judy Elliott	Sandy Thatcher	John Dean	Ted Gordon
Calhoun	CE	137	(269) 781-0980	...	Greg Purcell	Anne Norlander	...	Alexander Lamm	Allen Byam
Cass	CM	51	(269) 445-4420	Robert Wagel	Terry Proctor	Barb Wilson	Becky Moore	...	Victor Fitz
Charlevoix	C	26	(231) 547-7200	...	...	Jane Brannon	...	...	George Lasater
Cheboygan	C *	26	(231) 627-8855	Linda Socha	Michael Overton	Mary Ellen Tryban	Kari Kortz	Timothy Garey	Dale Clarmont
Chippewa	C	38	(906) 635-6300	...	...	...	...	...	...
Clare	C	31	(989) 539-2510	Karen Lipovsky	...	Carol McAulay	...	...	Jeffery Goyt
Clinton	C	64	(989) 224-5120	John Arehart	Ryan Wood	Diane Zuker	Craig Longnecker	...	Chuck Sherman
Crawford	C	14	(989) 348-2841	Lynette Corlew	Paul Compo	Sandra Moore	...	...	Kirk Wakefield
Delta	C	38	(906) 789-5100	...	...	...	...	...	...
Dickinson	C	27	(906) 774-2573	Frank Smith	Kathryn Pascoe	Dolly Cook	...	...	Donald Charlevoix
Eaton	C	103	(517) 543-7500	Leonard Peters	James Stewart	Fran Fuller	John Fuentes	...	Rick Jones
Emmet	C	31	(231) 348-1702	Jim Tamlyn	...	Irene Granger	Cynthia Van Allen	...	Peter Wallin
Genesee	CE	436	(810) 257-3034	...	...	Michael Carr	George Martini	Steven Stratton	Robert Pickell
Gladwin	C *	26	(989) 426-7351	Terry Whittington	...	Laura Flach	...	...	Michael Shea
Gogebic	CE	17	(906) 667-0411	...	Juliane Giackino	Gerald Pelissero	...	...	Larry Sanders

Directory 1/10
continued

OFFICIALS IN U.S. COUNTIES 2,500 AND OVER IN POPULATION

Jurisdiction		Form of government	2000 Population (000)	Main telephone number	Chief elected official	Appointed administrator	Clerk of the governing board	Chief financial officer	Director of personnel	Chief law enforcement official
MICHIGAN continued										
Grand Traverse		C	77	(231) 922-4599	Wayne Schmidt	Dennis Aloia	Linda Coburn	Dean Bott	Brenda Ransom	Scott Fewins
Gratiot		CE	42	(989) 875-5282	...	Brian Smith	Carol Vernon	...	...	...
Hillsdale		C	46	(517) 437-3391	...	...	Thomas Mohr	...	...	Stanley Buchardt
Houghton		C	36	(906) 482-8307	Jackie Niemi	John Kelly	Mary Schoos	...	...	...
Huron		C	36	(989) 269-8242	...	...	...	...	...	...
Ingham		CE	279	(517) 887-4327	Mark Grebner	...	Michael Bryanton	Giamcomo Restuccia	...	Gene Wriggelsworth
Ionia		C	61	(616) 527-5300	...	Mark Howe	...	...	...	...
Iosco		C	27	(989) 362-4212	Larry Erickson	...	Michael Welsch	Elite Shellenbarger	...	Craig Herriman
Iron		CM	13	(906) 875-3301	Patti Peretto	Jan Huizing	Joan Luhtanen	Thomas Lesandrini	...	Robert Remondini
Isabella	*	CE	63	(989) 772-0911	David Ling	Timothy Dolehanty	Joyce Swan	...	...	Larry Burdick
Jackson	*	CE	158	(517) 788-4000	James Shotwell	...	Amanda Riska	Gerard Cyrocki	Joni Johnson	Henry Zavislak
Kalamazoo		CE	238	(269) 384-8087	David Buskirk	Peter Battani	Timothy Snow	William Dundon	Jo Woods	Michael Anderson
Kalkaska		C	16	(231) 258-3304	Michael Cox	...	Patricia Rodgers	Frank Wright	...	Jerry Cannon
Kent		C	574	(616) 632-7500	David Morren	Daryl Delabbio	Mary Hollinrake	Robert White	Don Clack	Lawrence Stelma
Keweenaw		C	2	(906) 337-2229	Frank Stubenrauch	...	Marilyn Winquist	...	...	Ronald Lahti
Lake		CM	11	(231) 745-2725	James Clark	...	Shelly Myers	...	Lori DeWolf	Robert Hilts
Lapeer		C	87	(810) 667-0366	David Taylor	John Biscoe	Marlene Bruns	Craig Horton	...	Byron Konschuh
Leelanau		C	21	(616) 256-9711	...	David Gill	...	...	...	...
Lenawee		C	98	(517) 264-4508	Larry Gould	William Bacon	Lou Bluntschly	Kathy Bernardo	...	Larry Richardson
Livingston		C	156	(517) 546-1010	David Domas	Robert Block	Margaret Dunleavy	Belinda Peters	Barbara Brooks	Donald Homan
Luce		C	7	(906) 293-5521	Beth Gibson	...	Kathy Mahar	Deborah Johnson	...	Kevin Erickson
Mackinac		C	11	(906) 643-7300	...	...	Mary Tamlyn	...	...	Scott Strait
Macomb		CM	788	(586) 469-5100	...	...	Carmella Sabaugh	David Diegel	Ted Cwiek	Mark Hackel
Manistee		CM	24	(231) 398-3500	Allan O'Shea	Thomas Kaminski	Marilyn Kliber	Russell Pomeroy	Karen Fredricks	Dale Kowalkowski
Marquette		CM	64	(906) 225-8151	Gerald Corkin	Steven Powers	Connie Branam	Susan Vercoe	John Greenberg	Gary Walker
Mason	*	C	28	(231) 843-7999	Thomas Posma	...	Jim Riffle	...	...	Laude Hartrum
Mecosta	*	C	40	(616) 796-2505	Ray Steinke	Paul Bullock	Marcee Purcell	Julia Tetsworth	...	John Sonntag
Menominee		C	25	(906) 863-7779	...	Brian Neumeier	Barbara Morrison	...	...	Edward Powell
Midland		CE	82	(989) 832-6775	Otis Wilson	David Benda	Karen Holcomb	...	Richard Busch	John Reder
Missaukee	*	C	14	(231) 839-4967	Susan Rogers	...	Carolyn Flore	...	...	James Bosscher
Monroe		CE	145	(734) 240-7295	V Roe	...	Geraldine Allen	Charles Londo	Peggy Howard	Tilman Crutchfield
Montcalm		CE	61	(989) 831-7300	Patrick Carr	...	Kristen Millard	Chris Hyzer	Brenda Taeter	William Barnwell
Montmorency	*	C	10	(989) 785-8000	...	Robert Goodall	Cheryl Neilsen	...	...	Douglas Baum
Muskegon		CE	170	(231) 724-6442	James Derezinski	James Borushko	Karen Buie	John Niemiec	...	George Jurkas
Newaygo		CM	47	(231) 689-7200	Stanley DeKuiper	Tobi Lake	Laurel Breuker	...	Laurie Gracik	Michael Mercer
Oakland		CE	1194	(248) 858-0535	L. Patterson	Douglas Williams	G. Caddell	Jeffrey Pardee	Judith Eaton	Michael Bouchard
Oceana		CE	26	(231) 873-4835	Larry VanSickle	Paul Inglis	Rebecca Griffin	...	...	Terry Shaw
Ogemaw		C	21	(989) 345-0215	...	...	Gary Klacking	...	...	Howard Hanft
Ontonagon		C	7	(906) 884-4255	...	...	Judith Roehm	...	...	John Gravier
Osceola		C	23	(231) 832-3261	...	...	Karen Bluhm	...	...	James Crawford
Oscoda	*	C	9	(989) 826-1109	...	...	Jeri Winton	...	...	Michael Larrison
Otsego	*	CM	23	(989) 731-7520	Paul Beachnau	John Burt	Susan DeFeyter	Rachel Frisch	Trisha Adam	James McBride
Ottawa		CM	238	(616) 738-4800	Dennis Swartout	Alan Vanderberg	Daniel Krueger	Rosemary Zink	Rich Schurkamp	Gary Rosema
Presque Isle		C	14	(989) 734-3288	...	Gary Nowak	Susan Rhode	...	Gary Wozniak	Terry Flewelling
Roscommon	*	C	25	(989) 275-7861	Larry Mead	...	Ann Bonk	Cheryl Mollard	Abby Roth	Fran Staley
Saginaw		C	210	(989) 790-5210	Robert Fish	Michael Thompson	Susan Kaltenbach	Nathan Baldermann	Larry Polk	Charles Brown
Sanilac		CM	44	(810) 648-2933	Robert Wood	John Males	Linda Kozfkay	...	...	James Young
Schoolcraft		C	8	(906) 341-3618	Ernest Hoholik	...	Sigrid Hedberg	...	...	Gary Maddox
Shiawassee		C	71	(989) 743-2223	...	Margaret McAvoy	...	...	...	Dean Porter
St. Clair		CM	164	(810) 989-6910	...	Shaun Groden	Marilyn Dunn	Robert Kempf	Terry Pettee	Edward Lane
St. Joseph		CM	62	(269) 467-5500	...	Judy West-Wing	Pattie Bender	Daniel Carey	Charles Cleaver	Matthew Lori
Tuscola	*	CE	58	(989) 672-3700	...	Michael Hoagland	M. White-Cormier	...	Carrie Krampits	Thomas Kern
Van Buren		C	76	(269) 657-8200	...	...	Shirley Jackson	...	...	Dale Gribler
Washtenaw		CE	322	(734) 222-6800	Leah Gunn	Robert Guenzel	Peggy Haines	Peter Ballios	...	Daniel Minzey
Wayne		CE	2061	(313) 224-5901	...	Robert Ficano	Kathy Garrett	Carla Sledge	Mark Ulicny	...
Wexford	*	C	30	(231) 779-9453	Leslie Housler	Cynthia Stambaugh	Elaine Richardson	...	...	Gary Finstrom
MINNESOTA										
Aitkin		CM	15	(218) 927-7276	...	Dennis Berg	...	Kirk Peysar	Cindi Hills	Scott Turner
Anoka	*	CM	298	(763) 421-4760	...	Terry Johnson	...	...	Melanie Ault	Bruce Andersohn
Becker		CM	30	(218) 846-7309	Roger Winter	Brian Berg	Sonia Johnson	...	Nancy Grabanski	Tim Gordon
Beltrami		C	39	(218) 759-4156	Vicki Haugen	Anthony Murphy	...	Kay Mack	Marilyn Nelson	Keith Winger
Benton		C	34	(320) 968-5000	Duane Grandy	Rick Speak	...	Dona Pederson	...	Jim McMahon
Big Stone		C	5	(320) 839-2525	Doug Tomschin	...	...	Michelle Knutson	Sue Schultz	John Haukos
Blue Earth		C	55	(507) 389-8100	...	Dennis McCoy	...	...	...	...
Brown		CM	26	(507) 233-6603	Charles Guggisberg	Charles Enter	...	Marlin Helget	Leah Crabtree	Timothy Brennan
Carlton		C	31	(218) 384-4281	...	...	...	Paul Gassert	R. Stafford	Kelly Lake
Carver	*	CM	70	(952) 361-1500	...	David Hemze	...	David Frischmon	Doris Krogman	Byron Olson
Cass		C	27	(218) 547-3300	Bob Stranne	Robert Yochum	Norma Geinert	Larry Wolfe	Jack Paul	Jim Dowson
Chippewa		C	13	(320) 269-7447	Gene VanBinsbergen	...	...	...	...	Stacy Tufto
Chisago		CM	41	(651) 213-1300	Bennett Montzka	John Moosey	Deanna Lilientham	Dennis Freed	Renee Kirchner	Todd Rivard
Clay		CM	51	(218) 299-5002	John Evert	Vijay Sethi	...	Lori Johnson	Terry Jacobson	William Bergquist
Clearwater		C	8	(218) 694-6130	...	...	...	Daniel Stenseng	...	Dennis Trandem
Cook		C	5	(218) 387-2282	Wesley Hedstrom	...	...	Carol Gresczyk	Janet Simonen	...
Cottonwood	*	C	12	(507) 831-1905	Charles Severson	...	...	J Johnson	...	Jason Purrington
Crow Wing	*	C	55	(218) 824-1067	Dewayne Tautges	David Hamilton	...	Michael Carlson	Tami Laska	Todd Dahl
Dakota	*	CM	355	(651) 437-3191	Michael Tuner	Brandt Richardson	Mary Scheide	Richard Neumann	Will Volk	Donald Gudmundson
Dodge		CM	17	(507) 635-6239	Klaus Alberts	David McKnight	...	Thomas Olney	Lisa Hager	Guy Thompson
Douglas		C	32	(320) 762-2381	Harvey Tewes	...	...	...	William Schalow	William Ingebrigtsen
Faribault		C	16	(507) 526-6211	...	...	...	...	...	...
Fillmore	*	C	21	(507) 765-4566	Marc Prestby	Karen Brown	...	...	...	Daryl Jensen
Freeborn	*	CM	32	(507) 377-5241	Glen Mathiason	John Kluever	...	William Helfritz	Susan Phillips	Mark Harig
Goodhue		C	44	(651) 385-3001	...	Scott Arneson	...	Brad Johnson	Melissa Cushing	Dean Albers
Grant		C	6	(218) 685-4502	...	Chad Van Santen	...	...	Zelda Avery	Dwight Walvatne
Hennepin		CM	1116	(612) 348-3000	...	Richard Johnson	Kay Mitchell	...	Rafael Viscasillas	Patrick McGowan
Houston	*	C	19	(507) 725-5822	...	Pete Johnson	Char Mieners	...	Timothy Comstock	Doug Ely
Hubbard		C	18	(218) 732-9023	...	Jack Paul	Luann Boltan	Pam Heeren	...	Gary Mills
Isanti		CE	31	(763) 689-3859	George Laison	Jerry Tvedt	...	T. Treichel	...	L. Southerland
Itasca		C	43	(218) 327-2847	...	Robert Olson	...	Robert Zuehlke	...	Patrick Medure
Jackson	*	C	11	(507) 847-4182	Craig Rubis	Janice Fransen	...	Ben Pribyl	...	Roger Hawkinson

Directory 1/10 continued   **OFFICIALS IN U.S. COUNTIES 2,500 AND OVER IN POPULATION**

Jurisdiction		Form of govern- ment	2000 Popu- lation (000)	Main telephone number	Chief elected official	Appointed administrator	Clerk of the governing board	Chief financial officer	Director of personnel	Chief law enforcement official
MINNESOTA continued										
Kanabec	*	C	14	(320) 679-5367	...	Alan Peterson	...	...	...	Steve Schulz
Kandiyohi		C	41	(320) 231-6215	Richard Larson	Wayne Thompson	...	Sam Modderman	Marilyn Johnson	Dan Hartog
Kittson		C	5	(218) 843-2655	Marilyn Gustafson	...	...	...	...	Ray Hunt
Koochiching	*	C	14	(218) 283-1152	Charles Lepper	Teresa Jaksa	...	Robert Peterson	...	Brian Youso
Lac Qui Parle	*	C	8	(320) 598-7444	...	...	...	Stanton Bjorgan	...	Graylen Carlson
Lake	*	CE	11	(218) 834-8300	Larry Larson	...	Wilma Rahn	Steven McMahon	Julie Svir-Peters	Carey Johnson
Lake Of The Woods		C	4	(218) 634-2430	...	Alan Christensen	...	John Hoscheid	...	Dallas Block
Le Sueur	*	C	25	(507) 357-2251	Joseph Connolly	Peggy Donovan	...	...	Cindy Westerhouse	Dave Gliszinski
Lincoln		C	6	(507) 694-1529	...	...	...	Kathy Schreurs	...	Jack Vizecky
Lyon		CM	25	(507) 537-6980	Philip Nelson	Loren Stomberg	...	...	...	Joel Dahl
Mahnomen		C	5	(218) 935-5669	Franklin Thompson	...	...	...	...	Richard Rooney
Marshall		C	10	(218) 745-4851	...	...	...	...	...	...
Martin		C	21	(507) 238-3126	Steve Pierce	Scott Higgins	...	...	...	Robert Meschke
Mcleod		C	34	(320) 864-5551	Ray Bayerl	Nan Crary	...	Cindy Schultz	Mary Jo Wieseler	Wayne Vinkemeier
Meeker	*	C	22	(320) 693-5200	Stephanie Beckman	Paul Virnig	...	...	...	Mike Hirman
Mille Lacs	*	C	22	(320) 983-8218	...	...	...	Philip Thompson	Roxy Traxler	Brent Lindgren
Morrison		CE	31	(320) 632-2941	Bill Block	Timothy Houle	...	Russ Nygren	...	Paul Tschida
Mower		CM	38	(507) 437-9549	Richard Cummings	Craig Oscarson	Susan Davis	Sherwood Vereide	Allan Cordes	Barry Simonson
Murray		C	9	(507) 836-6148	William Sauer	...	...	Gary Spaeth	Robert Klingle	Steve Telkamp
Nicollet	*	C	29	(507) 931-6800	...	Robert Podhradsky	Margo Brown	Bridgette Kennedy	...	David Lange
Nobles		CM	20	(507) 372-8241	...	Melvin Ruppert	...	...	...	Kent Wilkening
Norman		C	7	(218) 784-5471	Lee Ann Hall	...	Kari Aanenson	...	...	Myron Thronson
Olmsted		CM	124	(507) 285-8115	Kenneth Brown	Richard Devlin	...	Robert Bendzick	David Mueller	Steven Borchardt
Otter Tail		C	57	(218) 998-8000	...	Larry Krohn	...	...	...	...
Pennington	*	C	13	(218) 683-7000	...	...	...	Kenneth Olson	...	Michael Hruby
Pine		CM	26	(320) 629-6781	Alan Hancock	John Stieben	...	Kaye Jorgensen	...	Mark Mansavage
Pipestone	*	C	9	(507) 825-6760	...	Sharon Hanson	...	...	Judy Oldemeyer	Dan Delaney
Polk		CE	31	(218) 281-5408	Lyle Eisert	John Schmalenberg	...	...	...	Douglas Qualley
Pope	*	C	11	(320) 634-5029	Dean Paulson	Riaz Aziz	...	Donna Quandt	...	Thomas Larson
Ramsey	*	CM	511	(651) 266-8000	Tony Bennett	David Twa	Bonnie Jackelen	Julianne Kleinschmidt	Gail Blackstone	Robert Fletcher
Red Lake		C	4	(218) 253-2598	Robert Schmitz	...	...	...	...	Mitch Bernstein
Redwood	*	C	16	(507) 637-4016	Brian Kletscher	...	...	Larry Bunting	Vicki Knoblach	Richard Morris
Renville		CE	17	(320) 523-3710	...	William Wells	...	...	...	...
Rice		CM	56	(507) 332-6100	...	Gary Weiers	...	...	...	Richard Cook
Rock		C	9	(507) 283-4173	...	...	...	...	...	...
Roseau		C	16	(218) 463-2541	...	...	...	...	...	...
Scott		CM	89	(952) 445-7750	Robert Vogel	David Unmacht	Tracy Cervenka	Kevin Ellsworth	Jack Kemme	Dave Menden
Sherburne		CM	64	(763) 241-2700	Felix Schmiesing	Brian Bensen	...	Ramona Doebler	Roxanne Chmielewski	Bruce Anderson
Sibley		CE	15	(507) 237-4070	Leo Bauer	...	...	Lisa Pfarr	Roseann Nagel	Bruce Ponath
St. Louis		CM	200	(218) 726-2422	Stephen Raukar	Dana Frey	Paul Tynjala	...	Anthony Bruno	Ross Litman
Stearns		CE	133	(320) 656-3600	Vince Schaefer	George Rindelaub	...	Randy Schreifels	Jennifer Thorsten	John Sanner
Steele		CE	33	(507) 444-7400	Bruce Kubicek	Dave Severson	...	...	...	Gary Ringhofer
Stevens	*	C	10	(320) 589-7417	Paul Watzke	James Thoreen	...	Neil Wiese	...	Randal Willis
Swift	*	C	11	(320) 843-4069	Douglas Anderson	...	...	Byron Giese	...	Scott Mattison
Todd		C	24	(320) 732-4467	Anthony Haasser	...	...	Kathy Gresser	...	David Kircher
Traverse		C	4	(320) 563-4652	David Naatz	...	...	John Muellenbach	...	Donald Montonye
Wabasha	*	CM	21	(651) 565-3001	Eugene McNallan	Bambridge Peterson	...	Patrick Moga	...	Rodney Bartsh
Wadena	*	C	13	(218) 631-7650	Charleen West	...	...	...	...	Michael Carr
Waseca		CM	19	(507) 835-0630	Wendell Armstrong	Bruce Boyce	...	Joan Manthe	...	Timothy Dann
Washington		CM	201	(651) 430-6081	Dennis Hegberg	James Schug	Patricia Raddatz	Edison Vizuete	Kay McAloney	James Frank
Watonwan		C	11	(507) 375-1298	Lester Reckow	...	Lisa Schumann	Donald Kuhlman	...	Gary Menssen
Wilkin		C	7	(218) 643-7165	...	...	Wayne Bezenek	...	...	Tom Matejka
Winona	*	CM	49	(507) 457-6353	Dwayne Voegeli	Robert Reinert	...	Blake Pickart	Maureen Holte	David Brand
Wright		CM	89	(763) 682-3900	...	...	Richard Norman	...	...	Gary Miller
Yellow Medicine	*	C	11	(320) 564-5841	...	Ryan Krosch	...	Lois Bonde	...	Bill Flaten
MISSISSIPPI										
Adams		C	34	(601) 446-6684	...	...	...	...	...	...
Alcorn		C	34	(601) 286-7702	...	...	...	...	...	...
Amite		C	13	(601) 657-8022	...	...	...	...	...	...
Attala		C	19	(601) 289-2921	Sam Lewis	...	Gerry Taylor	...	...	Troy Steed
Benton		C	8	(601) 224-6305	...	...	...	...	...	...
Bolivar		CE	40	(662) 846-5877	...	...	...	...	...	...
Calhoun		C	15	(601) 412-3117	...	...	...	...	...	...
Carroll		C	10	(601) 237-9274	...	...	...	...	...	...
Chickasaw		C	19	(601) 456-2513	...	...	...	...	...	...
Choctaw		C	9	(601) 285-6329	...	...	...	...	...	...
Claiborne		C	11	(601) 437-4992	...	...	...	Gloria Dotson	...	Frank Davis
Clarke		C	17	(601) 776-2126	...	...	...	...	...	...
Clay		C	21	(601) 494-3124	...	...	...	...	...	...
Coahoma		C	30	(662) 624-3000	Eddie Smith	Hugh Stubbs	...	Linda Humber	...	Andrew Thompson
Copiah		C	28	(601) 894-1858	...	...	...	...	...	...
Covington		C	19	(601) 765-4242	...	...	...	...	...	...
De Soto		C	107	(601) 429-5011	Jessie Medlin	Michael Garriga	...	Dale Thompson	Ginger Allison	James Riley
Forrest		C	72	(601) 545-6000	Lynn Cartlidge	Betty Carlisle	Jimmy Havard	Penny Steed	...	Billy McGie
Franklin		C	8	(601) 384-2670	...	...	...	...	...	...
George		C	19	(601) 947-7506	...	...	...	...	...	...
Greene		C	13	(601) 394-2394	...	...	...	...	...	...
Grenada		C	23	(601) 226-1821	...	...	...	...	...	...
Hancock		C	42	(228) 467-0712	Timothy Kellar	...	...	Patty Greer	...	Ronnie Peterson
Harrison		CM	189	(228) 865-4207	Larry Benefield	Pamela Ulrich	John McAdams	Jenel Tompkins	Gene Evans	Joe Price
Hinds		C	250	(601) 968-6501	...	Anthony Brister	...	...	...	...
Holmes		C	21	(662) 834-2508	...	...	...	...	...	...
Humphreys		C	11	(601) 247-1740	...	...	...	...	...	...
Issaquena		C	2	(662) 873-2761	...	...	...	...	...	...
Itawamba		C	22	(662) 862-3421	Danny Holley	Gary Franks	...	Jim Witt	...	Leon Hayes
Jackson		C	131	(228) 769-3000	...	...	...	...	...	...
Jasper		C	18	(601) 764-3368	...	...	...	...	...	...
Jefferson		C	9	(601) 786-3021	...	...	...	...	...	...
Jefferson Davis		C	13	(601) 792-4204	Bennie Polk	...	Jack Berry	...	Faye Bedwell	Henry McCullan

Directory 1/10
continued

OFFICIALS IN U.S. COUNTIES 2,500 AND OVER IN POPULATION

Jurisdiction	Form of govern-ment	2000 Popu-lation (000)	Main telephone number	Chief elected official	Appointed administrator	Clerk of the governing board	Chief financial officer	Director of personnel	Chief law enforcement official
MISSISSIPPI continued									
Jones	C	64	(601) 428-3139	...	...	...	...	...	...
Kemper	C	10	(601) 743-4477	...	...	...	...	...	...
Lafayette	C	38	(601) 234-2131	...	...	...	...	...	...
Lamar	C	39	(601) 794-8504	Fred Hatten	George Fries	Sandra Morris	Cary Hartfield	...	Danny Rigel
Lauderdale	CE	78	(601) 482-9701	...	Rex Hiatt	...	...	...	...
Lawrence	C	13	(601) 587-7351	Calvin Fortenberry	Kelly Miller	Shelia Smithie	...	...	Joel Thames
Leake	C	20	(601) 267-7371	...	...	...	...	Margaret Smith	...
Lee	C	75	(662) 841-9100	...	...	...	...	...	...
Leflore	C	37	(601) 453-6203	...	...	...	...	...	...
Lincoln	C	33	(601) 835-3412	...	...	...	...	...	...
Lowndes	C	61	(601) 329-5800	...	...	...	...	...	...
Madison	C	74	(601) 855-5500	...	Donnie Caughman	Arthur Johnston	...	...	...
Marion	C	25	(601) 736-2691	...	...	...	...	...	...
Marshall	C	34	(601) 252-7903	...	...	...	...	...	...
Monroe	C	38	(601) 369-8143	...	...	...	...	...	...
Montgomery	C	12	(601) 283-2333	Ron Wood	...	...	...	...	...
Neshoba	C	28	(601) 656-3581	...	...	...	...	...	...
Newton	C	21	(601) 635-4150	Charles Moulds	Steve Seale	George Hayes	Debra Jackson	Pam Upton	Jackie Knight
Noxubee	CE	12	(662) 726-4243	...	...	...	...	...	...
Oktibbeha	C	42	(601) 323-5834	...	...	...	...	...	...
Panola	C	34	(662) 563-6200	Robert Avant	David Chandler	Sally Fisher	...	...	David Bryan
Pearl River	C	48	(601) 798-8013	...	Adrian Lumpkin	...	...	...	...
Perry	C	12	(601) 964-8370	...	...	...	...	...	...
Pike	C	38	(601) 783-5289	Aubrey Matthews	Chuck Lambert	Joel Barr	...	Dorothy Parker	...
Pontotoc	C	26	(662) 489-3900	Billy Simmons	...	Reggie Collums	...	...	...
Prentiss	C	25	(662) 728-8151	...	...	...	...	...	...
Quitman	C	10	(662) 326-2661	...	T. H. Scipper	...	...	...	...
Rankin	C	115	(601) 825-2217	...	Norman McLeod	Leonard Adkins	...	...	...
Scott	C	28	(601) 469-1926	...	...	...	...	...	...
Sharkey	C	6	(662) 873-2755	...	...	...	...	...	...
Simpson	C	27	(601) 847-1418	...	...	...	...	...	...
Smith	C	16	(601) 782-4000	...	...	...	...	...	...
Stone	C	13	(601) 928-5266	...	...	...	...	...	...
Sunflower	C	34	(662) 887-4703	...	...	...	...	...	...
Tallahatchie	C	14	(662) 647-5551	...	...	...	...	...	...
Tate	C	25	(662) 562-5661	...	...	...	...	...	...
Tippah	CE	20	(662) 837-7374	...	...	Daniel Shackelford	...	...	C. L. Crum
Tishomingo	C	19	(601) 423-7032	...	...	...	...	...	...
Tunica	C	9	(662) 363-1465	Cedric Burnett	Kenneth Murphree	Susie White	Clifton Johnson	...	Calvin Hamp
Union	C	25	(662) 534-1900	...	...	...	...	...	...
Walthall	C	15	(601) 876-3553	...	...	...	...	...	...
Warren	C	49	(601) 634-8073	Michael Mayfield	Rick Polk	Beth Britt	...	...	William Pace
Washington	C	62	(601) 332-8355	...	...	...	...	...	...
Wayne	C	21	(601) 735-3414	Fred Andrews	...	Brenda Ainsworth	Sylvia Chancellor	...	...
Webster	C	10	(662) 258-4131	Larry Crowley	...	Lady Doolittle	...	Charla Griffin	Robert Cooksey
Wilkinson	C	10	(601) 888-4381	...	...	...	...	...	...
Winston	C	20	(662) 773-3631	...	...	...	...	...	...
Yalobusha	C	13	(601) 473-2091	...	...	...	...	...	...
Yazoo	C	28	(662) 746-2661	...	...	...	...	...	...
MISSOURI									
Adair	C	24	(660) 665-3350	Gary Jones	...	Jim Lymer	...	...	Leonard Clark
Andrew *	C	16	(816) 324-3624	Larry Atkins	...	Daniel Hegeman	...	...	N. Howard
Atchison	C	6	(660) 744-6214	...	...	Susette Taylor	...	...	Dennis Martin
Audrain	C	25	(573) 473-5822	...	...	...	...	...	Donald Bolli
Barry	C	34	(417) 847-2561	...	...	...	...	...	...
Barton *	C	12	(417) 682-3529	Mike Davis	...	Kristina Crockett	...	...	Shannon Higgins
Bates	C	16	(660) 679-3371	...	...	...	...	...	...
Benton	C	17	(660) 438-7326	...	...	...	...	...	...
Bollinger	C	12	(573) 238-1900	Wayne Johnson	...	Diane Holzum	...	...	Terry Wiseman
Boone	C	135	(573) 886-4395	Keith Schnarre	...	Wendy Noren	June Pitchford	Betty Dickneite	Dwayne Carey
Buchanan	C	85	(816) 271-1503	Thomas Mann	...	Pat Conway	William Bennett	Kendra Ezzell	...
Butler	C	40	(573) 686-8050	Joseph Humphrey	...	John Dunivan	...	...	...
Caldwell	C	8	(816) 586-2571	Raymond Hartley	...	Shari Lee	...	...	Kirby Brelsford
Callaway	C	40	(573) 642-0730	Emil Fritz	...	Linda Love	...	Serena Morgan	Harry Lee
Camden	C	37	(573) 346-4440	...	...	Kara Clark	David Ludwig	...	...
Cape Girardeau *	C	68	(573) 243-3547	...	...	Kara Clark	David Ludwig	...	...
Carroll	C	10	(660) 542-0615	Nelson Heil	...	Peggy McGaugh	...	...	Joseph Arnold
Carter	CE	5	(573) 323-4527	Gene Oakley	...	Rebecca Gibbs	...	...	Greg Melton
Cass	C	82	(816) 380-8102	Gary Mallory	...	Janet Burlingame	Julie Cooper	...	Dwight Diehl
Cedar	C	13	(417) 276-6700	Kenneth Whitesell	...	Sheryl Swopes	...	...	Aaron Spillman
Chariton *	C	8	(660) 288-3273	Tony McCollum	...	Susan Littleton	...	...	Christopher Hughes
Christian	C	54	(417) 581-6369	John Grubaugh	...	Kay Brown	Susan Yarnell	...	Michael Robertson
Clark *	C	7	(660) 727-3283	Paul Allen	John Heinze	Leih Hayden	...	...	Roy Gilbert
Clay *	C	184	(816) 407-3600	Ed Quick	Alexa Barton	Tom Brandom	Vic Hulbert	Lisa Farr	Paul Vescovo
Clinton	C	18	(816) 539-3713	...	...	...	...	...	...
Cole	C	71	(573) 634-9100	Robert Jones	...	William Deeken	James LePage	L. Steinkuehler	John Hemeyer
Cooper	C	16	(660) 882-2114	...	...	...	...	...	...
Crawford	C	22	(573) 775-2376	...	...	Connie Smith	...	...	...
Dade	C	7	(417) 637-2724	Rex Wilkinson	...	Larry McGuire	...	...	Wayne Spain
Dallas	C	15	(417) 345-2632	...	...	...	...	...	...
Daviess	C	8	(660) 663-2641	...	...	...	...	...	...
De Kalb	C	11	(816) 449-5402	David Lippold	...	Mary Berry	...	Joan Pearl	...
Dent	C	14	(573) 729-3044	...	...	Janet Inman	...	...	...
Douglas *	C	13	(417) 683-4714	Donald Potter	...	Karry Davis	...	...	Gary Koop
Dunklin	C	33	(573) 888-2796	...	...	...	...	...	...
Franklin	C	93	(636) 583-6355	Gene Scott	...	Tom Herbst	Ralph Sudholt	...	...
Gasconade	C	15	(573) 486-5427	Charles Schlottach	...	Roger Prior	...	...	Glenn Ebker
Gentry	C	6	(660) 726-3525	...	...	...	...	...	...
Greene *	C	240	(417) 868-4116	David Coonrod	...	Richard Struckhoff	...	Hillary Murray	Jack Merritt
Grundy	C	10	(660) 359-6305	Kenneth Roberts	...	Kristi Urich	Colleen Kidd	...	Rodney Herring

Directory 1/10
continued

OFFICIALS IN U.S. COUNTIES 2,500 AND OVER IN POPULATION

Jurisdiction	Form of govern-ment	2000 Popu-lation (000)	Main telephone number	Chief elected official	Appointed administrator	Clerk of the governing board	Chief financial officer	Director of personnel	Chief law enforcement official
MISSOURI continued									
Harrison	C	8	(660) 425-6424	Steve Francis	Mick Parkhurst	Barbara Gates	...	...	Richard Stratton
Henry	C	21	(660) 885-6963	...	...	...	...	...	...
Hickory ✴	C	8	(417) 745-6450	...	...	Jeanne Lindsey	...	...	Ray Tipton
Holt	C	5	(660) 446-3303	...	...	...	...	...	...
Howard	C	10	(660) 248-2193	William Eaton	...	William Hiu	Kathryne Harper	...	Charles Polson
Howell	C	37	(417) 256-2591	...	...	...	...	...	...
Iron	C	10	(573) 546-2912	Terry Nichols	...	Norma Owens	...	...	Allen Mathes
Jackson	CE	654	(816) 881-3135	Michael Saunders	...	...	Q. Troy Thomas	Joanne Mossie	Thomas Phillips
Jasper	CE	104	(417) 358-0421	...	...	...	...	...	...
Jefferson	C	198	(636) 797-5381	Samuel Rauls	Mark Abel	Eleanor Rehm	Dorothy Stafford	Joan Masters	Oliver Boyer
Johnson	C	48	(660) 747-2633	William Brenner	...	Gilbert Powers	Cheryl Dolan	Lisa Shore	Charles Heiss
Knox	C	4	(660) 397-2184	...	...	...	...	...	...
Laclede	C	32	(417) 532-5471	...	...	Linda Niendick	Cherie Mason	...	Kerrick Alumbaugh
Lafayette	C	32	(660) 259-4315	...	...	Gary Emerson	...	...	Ed Weisacosky
Lawrence	C	35	(417) 466-2638	Joe Ruscha	...	Sharon Schlager	...	...	David Parrish
Lewis	C	10	(573) 767-5205	Nancy Goehl	...	...	...	...	...
Lincoln	C	38	(636) 528-6300	...	...	...	...	...	Tom Parks
Linn	C	13	(660) 895-5417	Rick Solomon	Randy Wade	...	...	...	...
Livingston	C	14	(660) 646-2200	...	...	Pat Clarke	...	...	...
Macon	C	15	(660) 385-2913	Roger Kohl	...	Joan Whitener	Danny Thompson	...	David Lewis
Madison	C	11	(573) 783-2176	Robert Mooney	...	...	...	...	...
Maries	C	8	(573) 422-3388	...	...	Robert Ravenscraft	...	Valerie Dornberger	John Waldschlager
Marion	CE	28	(573) 769-2549	Lyndon Bode	...	Joye Helm	...	...	Don Schlessman
Mc Donald	C	21	(417) 223-4717	Bill Wilson	...	Carolyn Kost	Ray Woodward	...	...
Mercer	C	3	(660) 748-3425	Russell Hobbs	...	...	...	...	...
Miller	C	23	(573) 369-2317	...	...	Hubert De Lay	...	...	Larry Turley
Mississippi	C	13	(573) 683-2146	Jim Blumenberg	...	...	...	...	Kenneth Jones
Moniteau	C	14	(660) 796-2213	Robert Hogge	...	Sandra Carter	...	...	Gary Tawney
Monroe	C	9	(660) 327-5106	Donald Simpson	...	...	...	...	...
Montgomery	C	12	(573) 564-3357	...	...	Cathy Daniels	...	...	James Petty
Morgan	C	19	(573) 378-4643	Rodney Schad	...	...	...	...	...
New Madrid	C	19	(573) 748-2524	...	...	Kay Baum	...	...	Ron Doerge
Newton	C	52	(417) 451-8220	Glenn Wilson	...	John Zimmerman	...	...	Ben Espey
Nodaway	C	21	(660) 582-2251	Lester Keith	...	...	...	...	...
Oregon	C	10	(417) 778-7475	...	...	...	...	...	...
Osage ✴	C	13	(573) 897-2139	...	...	...	...	...	...
Ozark	C	9	(417) 679-3516	...	...	...	...	...	...
Pemiscot	C	20	(573) 333-4203	...	...	...	...	...	Gary Schaaf
Perry	C	18	(573) 547-4242	Thomas Sutterer	...	Randy Taylor	...	...	Gary Starke
Pettis	C	39	(660) 826-5395	Todd Smith	Larry Wilson	Pam Doane	...	...	Don Blankenship
Phelps	C	39	(573) 458-6000	Randy Verkamp	...	Carol Bennett	...	...	Jim Wells
Pike	C	18	(573) 324-2412	Clark Pointer	...	Jim Ford	...	...	Richard Anderson
Platte	C	73	(816) 858-2232	Betty Knight	...	Sandra Krohne	Sandra Thomas	Rita Rubick	Steve Bruce
Polk	C	26	(417) 326-4031	Roy Harms	...	Sue Entlicher	...	...	James King
Pulaski ✴	C	41	(573) 774-4701	Bill Ransdall	...	Diana Linnenbringer	...	...	...
Putnam	C	5	(660) 947-2674	...	...	...	...	...	Bernard Berghager
Ralls	C	9	(573) 985-7111	George Lane	...	Ernest Duckworth	...	...	...
Randolph	C	24	(660) 277-4717	...	...	...	...	...	Sam Clemens
Ray	C	23	(816) 776-4502	Jeff Adams	...	Paul Rogers	...	...	Gary Barton
Reynolds	C	6	(573) 648-2494	Paul Wood	...	Mike Harper	...	...	...
Ripley	C	13	(573) 996-3215	...	...	...	...	...	Wally George
Saline	C	23	(660) 886-9050	Becky Plattner	...	Ken Bryant	...	...	...
Schuyler	C	4	(660) 457-3842	...	...	...	...	...	Wayne Winn
Scotland	C	4	(660) 465-7027	Mike Stephenson	...	Betty Lodewegen	...	...	...
Scott	C	40	(573) 545-3549	...	...	Shelly McAfee	...	...	Clinton Reeves
Shannon ✴	C	8	(573) 226-3414	Charles Orchard	...	Tracy Smith	...	...	Daniel Parshall
Shelby ✴	C	6	(573) 633-2181	Glennon Eagan	...	...	Rebecca Craig	William Kauffman	Timothy Swope
St. Charles	C	283	(636) 949-7320	Joseph Ortwerth	...	Donna Houston	...	...	Ronald Snodgrass
St. Clair	C	9	(417) 646-2315	Jay Knight	...	...	...	...	...
St. Francois	C	55	(573) 756-3623	...	...	S. Richeda-Pratl	Glenn Pearl	Kirk McCarley	Ronald Battelle
St. Louis	CE	1016	(314) 615-5000	George Westfall	James Baker	Kay Basler	...	...	Gary Stolzer
Ste. Genevieve ✴	C	16	(573) 883-5589	Albert Fults	...	...	...	...	...
Stoddard	C	29	(573) 568-3339	...	...	...	...	...	...
Stone	C	28	(417) 357-6127	...	...	...	...	...	...
Sullivan	C	7	(660) 265-3786	...	...	Donna Neeley	Rick Findley	...	Jimmie Russell
Taney	C	39	(417) 546-7201	Chuck Pennel	Tressa Luttrell	Don Troutman	...	...	Carl Watson
Texas ✴	C	23	(417) 967-2112	Don Shelhammer	...	Tammi Beach	...	...	Ron Peckman
Vernon	C	20	(417) 448-2500	C. David Darnold	...	Barbara Daly	...	...	Kevin Harrison
Warren	C	24	(636) 456-3331	Fred Vahle	...	Janet Adams	...	...	...
Washington	C	23	(573) 438-4901	Robert Reed	...	Alan Lutes	...	...	Phillip Burton
Wayne ✴	C	13	(573) 224-3011	Brian Polk	...	...	...	...	...
Webster	C	31	(417) 468-2223	...	...	Lisa Hargrave	...	...	...
Worth	C	2	(660) 564-2219	Billy Mozingo	...	Tony Dugger	...	...	Garrell Mitchell
Wright	C	17	(417) 741-6661	Rex Epperly	...	...	...	...	...
MONTANA									
Beaverhead	C	9	(406) 683-5245	...	...	...	...	...	...
Big Horn	C	12	(406) 665-3520	...	...	Sandra Boardman	...	...	Theron Paulsen
Blaine	C	7	(406) 357-3250	...	...	Elaine Graveley	Natalie Tomeo	...	Rich Thompson
Broadwater ✴	C	4	(406) 266-3443	James Hohn	...	...	...	...	...
Carbon	C	9	(406) 446-1595	...	...	Pamela Castleberry	...	...	Rusty Jardee
Carter	C	1	(406) 775-8749	Milton Markuson	...	Rita Hudak	Tom Meech	Richard Letang	John Shandell
Cascade	C	80	(406) 454-6810	...	...	...	...	...	...
Chouteau	C	5	(406) 622-3631	...	...	Beth Milligan	...	...	Tony Harbaugh
Custer	C	11	(406) 233-3343	Duane Mathison	...	Kristy Jones	...	...	Myron Baldry
Daniels ✴	C	2	(406) 487-5561	Lalon Trang	...	Maurine Lenhardt	...	...	John Kahl
Dawson	C	9	(406) 365-3058	Harold Skartved	...	Brenda Wood	...	...	Timothy Barkley
Fallon	C	2	(406) 778-7107	Roddy Rost	...	Kathy Fleharty	...	...	Ronald Rowton
Fergus	C	11	(406) 538-5119	Kathie Bailey	...	Paula Robinson	...	RaeAnn Campbell	...
Flathead	C	74	(406) 758-5522	Robert Watne	...	Shelley Vance	Ed Blackman	Randy Kuyath	Jim Cashell
Gallatin	C	67	(406) 582-3045	William Murdock	Earl Mathers				

Directory 1/10
continued

OFFICIALS IN U.S. COUNTIES 2,500 AND OVER IN POPULATION

Jurisdiction		Form of govern- ment	2000 Popu- lation (000)	Main telephone number	Chief elected official	Appointed administrator	Clerk of the governing board	Chief financial officer	Director of personnel	Chief law enforcement official
MONTANA continued										
Garfield		C	1	(406) 557-2760	...	...	...	Janet Sherer	...	Kelly Pierson
Glacier		C	13	(406) 873-5063	...	...	...	...	...	...
Golden Valley	*	C	1	(406) 568-2231	...	...	Mary Lu Ringler	...	...	...
Granite		C	2	(406) 859-3771	...	...	...	...	...	Stephen Immenschuh
Hill		C	16	(406) 265-5481	Kathleen Bessette	...	Diane Mellem	...	Cyndee Peterson	Gregory Szudera
Jefferson		C	10	(406) 225-4000	Leonard Wortman	...	Bonnie Ramey	Sue Miller	Chuck Notbohm	Thomas Dawson
Judith Basin		C	2	(406) 566-2277	Richard Cervenka	Henry Vaskey	Amanda Kelly	Sandra Weaver	...	John Shilling
Lake	*	C	26	(406) 883-7211	Paddy Trusler	...	Ruth Hodges	Sandra Weaver	...	...
Lewis & Clark		CM	55	(406) 447-8304	Ed Tinsley	Ronald Alles	...	Nancy Everson	Sheila Cozzie	Cheryl Liedle
Liberty		C	2	(406) 759-5365	Paul Johnson	...	Maureen Cicon	...	...	Richard Burrows
Lincoln		C	18	(406) 293-7781	Gerald Criner	Bill Bischoff	...	Coral Cummings	...	...
Madison		C	6	(406) 843-4277	...	...	...	...	...	...
Mc Cone		C	1	(406) 485-3505	...	...	Kae Fritz	...	...	Dave Harris
Meagher		C	1	(406) 547-3612	...	...	...	...	...	...
Mineral		C	3	(406) 822-3520	...	...	...	...	...	...
Missoula		C	95	(406) 721-5700	...	...	...	Dale Bickell	Steve Johnson	Doug Chase
Musselshell	*	C	4	(406) 323-1104	Larry Lekse	...	Jane Mang	...	...	Woodrow Weitzeil
Park		C	15	(406) 222-4100	Dan Gutebier	...	Denise Nelson	Joe Morse	...	Clark Carpenter
Petroleum		CM	..	(406) 429-5551	...	Stephanie Downs	Linda Gershmel	Mary Brindley	...	William Troutwine
Phillips	*	C	4	(406) 654-2423	...	...	...	Lauren Hines	...	Thomas Miller
Pondera		CE	6	(406) 278-4000	...	...	...	...	...	...
Powder River	*	C	1	(406) 436-2361	Ray Traub	...	Karen Amende	Valli Gaskill	...	John Blain
Powell	*	C	7	(406) 846-3680	Ralph Mannix	...	Diane Grey	...	...	Scott Howard
Prairie		C	1	(406) 637-5575	...	...	...	...	...	...
Ravalli		C	36	(406) 375-6500	Greg Chilcott	...	Nedra Taylor	...	...	Christopher Hoffman
Richland		C	9	(406) 482-1706	Mark Rehbein	...	Penni Lewis	...	...	Brad Baisch
Roosevelt		C	10	(406) 653-1590	...	...	...	...	...	...
Rosebud		C	9	(406) 356-2251	...	...	...	...	...	...
Sanders	*	CE	10	(406) 827-6942	...	...	Jennine Robbins	...	...	Gene Arnold
Sheridan		C	4	(406) 765-2310	Gordon Kampen	Robert Nikolaisen	Milton Hovland	...	...	Mike Overland
Stillwater		C	8	(406) 322-8010	Maureen Davey	...	Pauline Mishler	Joseph Morse	...	Clifford Brophy
Sweet Grass		C	3	(406) 932-5152	...	...	Shery Bjorndal	Victoria Uehling	...	Daniel Tronrud
Teton		C	6	(406) 466-2693	Robert Krause	...	Shirley Jensen	Diane Ameline	...	Michael Lamey
Toole	*	C	5	(406) 424-8300	Ben Ober	...	Mary Ann Harwood	...	Jewel Moritz	Wayne Robison
Treasure		C	..	(406) 342-5547	Norris Cole	...	Ruth Baker	...	...	Richard Wessler
Valley		C	7	(406) 228-8221	Eleanor Pratt	...	Lynne Nyquist	...	...	Steve Riveland
Wheatland		C	2	(406) 632-4891	Richard Moe	...	Carol Clark	...	...	...
Wibaux		C	1	(406) 796-2481	Thomas Nelson	...	...	Patricia Zinda	...	George Zorzakis
Yellowstone		CM	129	(406) 256-2705	James Reno	...	...	Scott Turner	Dwight Vigness	Chuck Maxwell
NEBRASKA										
Adams	*	CE	31	(402) 461-7107	Larry Woodman	...	Chrisella Lewis	...	...	Gregg Magee
Antelope		C	7	(402) 887-4410	...	...	...	...	...	...
Arthur		C	..	(308) 764-2203	...	...	...	...	...	...
Banner		C	..	(308) 436-5265	George Van Pelt	...	Sharon Sandberg	...	...	Kenneth Mooney
Blaine		C	..	(308) 547-2222	...	...	April Wescott	...	...	Timothy Sierks
Boone		C	6	(402) 395-2055	...	...	...	...	...	...
Box Butte		C	12	(308) 762-6565	...	...	...	...	...	...
Boyd		C	2	(402) 775-2391	Kenneth Boettcher	...	Phyllis Black	Joseph Hostert	...	...
Brown		C	3	(402) 387-2705	...	...	...	...	...	...
Buffalo		C	42	(308) 236-1226	...	...	Judy Jobman	...	...	Neil Miller
Burt		C	7	(402) 374-1955	...	...	...	...	...	...
Butler	*	C	8	(402) 367-7430	David Mach	...	C. Meysenburg	...	...	Mark Hecker
Cass		C	24	(402) 296-9300	Richard Stone	...	Alan Wohlfarth	Richard Wassinger	...	William Brueggemann
Cedar		C	9	(402) 254-7411	Richard Donner	...	David Dowling	...	...	Larry Koranda
Chase		C	4	(308) 882-7500	Don Weiss	...	Debra Clark	...	...	Tim Sutherland
Cherry		C	6	(402) 376-2420	...	...	...	...	...	...
Cheyenne		C	9	(308) 254-2141	...	...	...	...	...	...
Clay		CE	7	(402) 762-3463	Kendall Ham	...	Janet Hajny	...	...	Jeffrey Franklin
Colfax		C	10	(402) 352-8504	Earl Wendt	...	Sharon Bohaboj	...	...	Lynn Blum
Cuming		C	10	(402) 372-6002	...	...	Bonnie Vogltance	...	...	Bradley Boyum
Custer		C	11	(308) 872-5701	...	...	Constance Gracey	...	...	...
Dakota		C	20	(402) 987-2125	...	...	Theodore Piepho	...	...	James Wagner
Dawes		C	9	(308) 432-0102	...	...	...	...	...	...
Dawson		C	24	(308) 324-2127	...	...	...	...	...	...
Deuel		C	2	(308) 874-3308	...	...	...	...	...	...
Dixon		C	6	(402) 755-2208	Russell Fleury	...	Diane Mohr	...	...	Dean Chase
Dodge		C	36	(402) 727-2767	...	...	Fred Mytty	...	...	Dan Weddle
Douglas		C	463	(402) 444-7000	Carole Woods-Harris	Kathleen Kelley	Thomas Cavanaugh	Steve Walker	John Taylor	Timothy Dunning
Dundy		C	2	(308) 423-2058	Boyd Blair	...	Tony Lutz	...	...	...
Fillmore	*	C	6	(402) 759-4931	Robert Mueller	...	Amy Nelson	...	...	William Burgess
Franklin		C	3	(308) 425-6202	...	...	...	...	...	...
Frontier		C	3	(308) 367-8641	...	...	...	...	...	...
Furnas		C	5	(308) 268-4145	...	...	...	...	...	...
Gage		C	22	(402) 223-1300	Harvey Spilker	...	Sandra Eltiste	...	...	Jerry Dewitt
Garden		C	2	(308) 772-3924	Ron Klemke	William Campbell	Lorie Koester	...	...	Jim Winn
Garfield		C	1	(308) 346-4161	Martin Robbins	Daniel Hruza	...	...	...	Larry Donner
Gosper		C	2	(308) 785-2611	...	...	Cynthia Evans	...	...	David Schutz
Grant		C	..	(308) 458-2488	Frances Davis	...	Tonchita Ring	Sharon Applegarth	...	Mark Crouse
Greeley		C	2	(308) 428-2965	Thomas Smith	...	Catherine Sweeney	...	...	David Weeks
Hall		C	53	(308) 385-5080	Irene Abernethy	...	Marla Conley	...	...	Jerome Watson
Hamilton		CE	9	(402) 694-3443	Steven Jacobsen	...	Donita Friesen	...	...	Kirk Handrup
Harlan	*	C	3	(308) 928-2173	Douglas Horwart	...	Shirley Bailey	...	...	Chris Becker
Hayes		C	1	(308) 286-3413	Cletis Walker	...	Joan Lauenroth	...	...	Donald Miller
Hitchcock		C	3	(308) 334-5646	...	...	Margaret Pollmann	...	...	D. Leggott
Holt		C	11	(402) 336-1762	...	...	...	...	...	...
Hooker		C	..	(308) 546-2244	...	...	...	...	...	...
Howard	*	C	6	(308) 754-4343	...	...	Marge Palmberg	...	...	Harold Schenck
Jefferson		CE	8	(402) 729-2323	Tony Likens	...	Sandra Stelling	...	...	Nels Sorensen
Johnson		C	4	(402) 335-6300	Terry Keebler	...	Kathleen Nieveen	...	...	James Wenzl
Kearney		C	6	(308) 832-2723	...	...	...	...	...	...

Directory 1/10
continued

OFFICIALS IN U.S. COUNTIES 2,500 AND OVER IN POPULATION

Jurisdiction	Form of govern- ment	2000 Popu- lation (000)	Main telephone number	Chief elected official	Appointed administrator	Clerk of the governing board	Chief financial officer	Director of personnel	Chief law enforcement official
NEBRASKA continued									
Keith	CE	8	(308) 284-4726	...	...	...	...	...	...
Keya Paha	C	..	(402) 497-3791	Dewey Peterson	Ted Eichenberger	Karen Hallock	...	...	Wayne Crome
Kimball	C	4	(308) 235-2241	...	...	...	...	...	...
Knox	C	9	(402) 288-4282	...	...	...	...	...	...
Lancaster	C	250	(402) 441-7447	Ray Stevens	Kerry Eagan	Bruce Medcalf	David Kroeker	Don Taute	Terry Wagner
Lincoln	C *	34	(308) 534-4350	Joe Hewgley	...	Rebecca Rossell	...	...	Jerome Kramer
Logan	C	..	(308) 636-2311	...	...	Pat Harvey	...	...	Dan Kramer
Loup	C	..	(308) 942-3135	...	...	...	...	...	...
Madison	C	35	(402) 454-3311	...	...	Nancy Scheer	...	...	Vern Hjorth
Mc Pherson	C	..	(308) 587-2363	...	...	...	...	...	...
Merrick	C *	8	(308) 946-2881	...	...	Gloria Broekemeier	...	...	Anthony McPhillips
Morrill	C	5	(308) 262-1760	...	...	...	...	...	...
Nance	C	4	(308) 536-2331	Vernon Olson	...	Dianne Carter	...	...	...
Nemaha	C	7	(402) 274-4213	...	...	...	...	...	...
Nuckolls	C *	5	(402) 225-4361	...	...	Jackie Kassebaum	...	...	James Marr
Otoe	C *	15	(402) 873-9500	...	...	Janene Bennett	...	...	James Gress
Pawnee	C	3	(402) 852-2380	...	...	Carol Young	...	...	Arthur Baldridge
Perkins	C	3	(308) 352-4643	...	...	...	...	...	...
Phelps	C	9	(308) 995-4469	Eldon Steinbrink	...	Sally Fox	...	...	Thomas Nutt
Pierce	C	7	(402) 329-4225	Marvin Elwood	...	Carol Peters	...	...	...
Platte	C	31	(402) 563-4904	Ronald Pfeifer	...	Diane Pinger	...	...	Jon Zavadil
Polk	C	5	(402) 747-5431	Michael Simonsen	...	Debra Girard	...	...	Jim Davis
Red Willow	C *	11	(308) 345-1552	Earl McNutt	...	Pauletta Gerver	...	...	Gene Mahon
Richardson	C	9	(402) 245-2911	...	...	...	...	...	...
Rock	C	1	(402) 684-3933	...	... *	...	...	...	...
Saline	C	13	(402) 821-2374	Willis Luedke	...	Linda Kastanek	...	...	Alan Moore
Sarpy	C	122	(402) 593-4486	Tim Gay	Mark Wayne	Debra Houghtaling	Brian Hanson	Renee Lansman	Patrick Thomas
Saunders	C	19	(402) 443-8101	...	...	...	...	...	...
Scotts Bluff	C	36	(308) 436-6600	Mark Masterton	...	Vera Dulaney	Gwen Greely	Ernest Griffiths	Jim Lawson
Seward	C	16	(402) 643-2883	Leslie Nelson	...	Sherry Schweitzer	Bob Dahms	...	Roger Anderson
Sheridan	C	6	(308) 327-2633	...	...	...	...	...	...
Sherman	C	3	(308) 745-1513	Eldon Kieborz	...	Debra Mitteis	...	...	James Kugler
Sioux	C	1	(308) 668-2443	Harold Keener	...	Wendi McCormick	...	...	...
Stanton	C	6	(402) 439-2222	Glen Steffensmeier	...	Rita Roenfeldt	...	...	Mike Unger
Thayer	C	6	(402) 768-6126	Lawarence Traudt	...	Marie Rauner	...	...	Davie Lee
Thomas	C	..	(308) 645-2261	Stan Pettit	...	Wendy Rinestine	...	...	Randy Barnes
Thurston	C	7	(402) 385-2343	Teri Lamplot	...	Tammy Moore	...	...	Charles Obermeyer
Valley	C *	4	(308) 728-3700	...	...	Jenette Lindsey	...	...	Larry Ronzzo
Washington	CE *	18	(402) 426-6822	...	...	Merry Truhlsen	...	...	Michael Robinson
Wayne	CE	9	(402) 375-2288	...	...	Debra Finn	...	...	LeRoy Janssen
Webster	C	4	(402) 746-2716	...	...	...	...	...	...
Wheeler	C	..	(308) 654-3235	...	...	...	...	...	...
York	C	14	(402) 362-7759	Bob Wolfe	...	Patricia Bredenkamp	...	...	Dale Radcliff
NEVADA									
Churchill	C	23	(775) 428-1311	Gwen Washburn	Brad Goetsch	Gloria Venturacci	Alan Kalt	Geof Stark	Richard Ingram
Clark	CM	1375	(702) 455-3530	Bruce Woodbury	Virginia Valentine	Shirley Parraguirre	George Stevens	Raymond Visconti	Jerry Keller
Douglas	CE	41	(775) 782-9821	Stephen Weissinger	Daniel Holler	Barbara Reed	Claudette Springmeyer	Sheila Dugan	Ronald Pierini
Elko	CM	45	(775) 738-4375	...	Robert Stokes	Winifred Smith	Cash Minor	...	Arthur Harris
Esmeralda	CE	..	(775) 485-3406	R. J. Gillum	...	LaCinda Elgan	Karen Scott	...	Ken Elgan
Eureka	C	1	(775) 237-5263	Peter Goicoechea	...	Joan Shangle	Michael Rebaleati	...	Kenneth Jones
Humboldt	C	16	(775) 623-6300	John Milton	William Deist	Tami Spero	Bruce Brooks	...	Gene Hill
Lander	C	5	(775) 635-2885	Jimmie Fouts	...	Gladys Burris	Raye Fagg	...	Kenny Moore
Lincoln	C	4	(775) 962-5495	Timothy Perkins	...	Alice Hogan	Leslie Boucher	...	Dahl Bradfield
Lyon	CM	34	(775) 463-6531	Phyllis Hunewill	Dennis Stark	Nikki Bryan	Rita Evasovic	Steve Englert	Sid Smith
Mineral	C	5	(775) 945-3676	...	...	...	...	...	...
Nye	CE	32	(775) 482-8191	Henry Neth	...	Sandra Merlino	Charles Rodewald	James Allan	Anthony Demeo
Pershing	C	6	(775) 273-2208	Dave Ayoob	...	Donna Giles	Darlene Moura	...	Ron Skinner
Storey	C	3	(775) 847-0968	Henry Bland	Marilou Walling	Doreen Bacus	...	...	Robert Del Carlo
Washoe	CM	339	(775) 328-2081	Bonnie Weber	Katy Singlaub	Amy Harvey	John Sherman	Joanne Ray	Dennis Balaam
White Pine	C	9	(775) 289-8841	...	...	Donna Bath	...	...	Bernie Romero
NEW HAMPSIRE									
Belknap	CM	56	(603) 527-5400	Mark Thurston	Nancy Cook	...	...	...	Dan Collis
Carroll	C	43	(603) 539-2428	Brenda Presby	Marjorie Webster	...	...	...	Scott Carr
Cheshire	C	73	(603) 352-8215	...	John Wozmak	...	Sheryl Trombly	...	Richard Foote
Coos	C	33	(603) 246-3321	...	...	...	...	...	...
Grafton	C	81	(603) 787-6941	...	Julie Clough	Raymond Burton	...	Karen Clough	...
Hillsborough	C	380	(603) 627-5600	...	Gregory Wenger	...	...	Virginia Chandler	...
Merrimack	CE	136	(603) 228-0331	...	...	...	...	Sara Lewko	...
Rockingham	C	277	(603) 679-5335	Maureen Barrows	...	...	Theresa Young	Martha Roy	Daniel Linehan
Strafford	C	112	(603) 742-1458	...	...	...	...	...	...
Sullivan	C	40	(603) 863-2560	...	Edward Gil de Rubio	...	...	...	...
NEW JERSEY									
Atlantic	CE	252	(609) 345-6700	Dennis Levinson	Helen Walsh	Michael Garvin	...	Donna Lee	Jeffrey Blitz
Bergen	CE	884	(201) 336-6200	William Schuber	Timothy Dacey	...	...	...	Jack Schmidig
Burlington	C	423	(609) 265-5020	James Wujcik	Frederick Galdo	Philip Haines	Kurt Brock	Daniel Hornickel	Jean Stanfield
Camden	CE	508	(856) 225-5000	Jeffrey Nash	Mark Lonetto	Lee Sasse	David McPeak	Richard Dodson	Michael McLaughlin
Cape May	C	102	(609) 465-1060	Daniel Beyel	...	Angela Pulvino	Edmund Grant	Eileen Ballinghoff	James Plousis
Cumberland	CE	146	(856) 453-2125	Douglas Fisher	David Gray	Clair Miller	Gerald Seneski	Ralph Brownlee	...
Essex	C	793	(973) 621-4977	James Treffinger	Ronald Manzella	Patrick McNally	Anthony Abbaleo	Lucille Davino	Armando Fontoura
Gloucester	CE	254	(856) 853-3264	Stephen Sweeney	...	James Hogan	Gary Schwarz	...	Andrew Yurick
Hudson	CE	608	(201) 795-6255	Robert Janiszewski	Abraham Antun	Janet Haynes	Wade Frazee	Larry Henderson	Joseph Cassidy
Hunterdon	CE	121	(908) 788-1102	...	Cynthia Yard	Denise Doolan	...	Cheryl Wieder	J. Patrick Barnes
Mercer	CE	350	(609) 989-6676	Robert Prunetti	Andrew Mair	C. Dicostanzo	David Miller	Harris Kline	Daniel Giaquinto
Middlesex	CE	750	(732) 745-3090	David Crabiel	Walter De Angelo	Margaret Pemberton	Albert Kuchinskas	J. Cross	...
Monmouth	CE	615	(732) 431-7300	Harry Larrison	Robert Czech	M French	Mark Acker	Fredrica Brown	Joseph Oxley
Morris	CE	470	(973) 285-6000	Douglas Cabana	James Rosenberg	Ilene St. John	Glenn Roe	Herman Hoopes	John Dangler
Ocean	C	510	(732) 244-2121	John Bartlett	Steven Pollock	M. Haines	Julie Tarrant	Keith Goetting	William Polhemus
Passaic	CE	489	(973) 881-4402	...	...	...	...	...	...
Salem	C	64	(856) 935-7510	C. Sparks	Earl Gage	Gilda Gill	Joanne Bell	Robin Weinstein	John Cooksey

Directory 1/10 continued

OFFICIALS IN U.S. COUNTIES 2,500 AND OVER IN POPULATION

Jurisdiction	Form of govern-ment	2000 Popu-lation (000)	Main telephone number	Chief elected official	Appointed administrator	Clerk of the governing board	Chief financial officer	Director of personnel	Chief law enforcement official
NEW JERSEY continued									
Somerset	CE	297	(908) 231-7000	Peter Palmer	Richard Williams	Barbara Lucas	Brian Newman	Susan Dobrinsky	Wayne Forrest
Sussex	CM	144	(973) 579-0350	. . .	John Eskilson	Elaine Morgan	Doris Bush	Connie Sutton	Robert Untig
Union	CM	522	(908) 527-4100	Deborah Scanlon	George Devanney	Joanne Rajoppi	Lawrence Caroselli	Gregory Hardoby	Daniel Vaniska
Warren	CM	102	(908) 475-6500	Susan Dickey	Steve Marvin	. . .	Charles Houck	Jerry Coyle	Don Kelley
NEW MEXICO									
Bernalillo	CM	556	(505) 768-4000	. . .	. . .	Mary Herrera	Daniel Mayfield	Renetta Torres	Darren White
Catron	* C	3	(505) 533-6423	Ed Wehrheim	William Aymar	Sharon Armijo	. . .	. . .	Ian Fletcher
Chaves	CM	61	(505) 624-6600	. . .	. . .	Rhoda Coakley	Mary Chacon	Sheila Nunez	. . .
Cibola	C	25	(505) 287-9431	Isaac Padilla	David Ulibarri	Eileen Martinez	John Alexander	Syble Valles	Manuel Lujan
Colfax	* C	14	(505) 445-9661	Whitney Hite	. . .	Rayetta Trujillo	. . .	. . .	Patrick Casias
Curry	C	45	(505) 763-6016	Tim Ashley	Richard Smith	Mario Trujillo	. . .	Lance Pyle	Roger Hatcher
De Baca	C	2	(505) 355-2601	. . .	. . .	Nancy Sparks	. . .	. . .	Brent Sena
Dona Ana	CE	174	(505) 647-7200	William McCamley	Brian Haines	Rita Torres	Jaime Bari	Arturo Rodriguez	Todd Garrison
Eddy	CE	51	(505) 887-9511	Lucky Briggs	Stephen Massey	V. Blenden	Debbie Penaluna	Susan Collins	D. Waller
Grant	CM	31	(505) 574-0000	Henry Torres	Jon Saari	Jeff Carbajal	Erlinda Vasquez	. . .	. . .
Guadalupe	CE	4	(505) 472-3306	. . .	. . .	. . .	. . .	. . .	. . .
Harding	CM	. .	(505) 673-2301	Michael Lewis	Arlene Aragon	Elizabeth Martinez	Lucille Quintana	. . .	Freddie Gift
Hidalgo	CM	5	(505) 542-9428	Louise Peterson	Roger Ellis	Carmen Acosta	Connie Corbell	. . .	Robert Hall
Lea	CM	55	(505) 396-8521	Troy Teague	. . .	Melinda Hughes	Rick Bruce	Anne Behl	Ronald Rice
Lincoln	CE	19	(505) 648-2385	Rex Wilson	Thomas Stewart	Tammie Maddox	Glenna Robbins	. . .	Thomas Sullivan
Los Alamos	CM	18	(505) 662-8080	Geoffrey Rodgers	Max Baker	. . .	Steve Lynne	Denise Cassel	Richard Melton
Luna	CM	25	(505) 546-0494	Dennis Armijo	Scott Vinson	Natalie Pacheco	. . .	Danny Gonzales	Gary Ciccotelli
Mc Kinley	CE	74	(505) 722-3868	Earnest Becenti	Irvin Harrison	Carol Sloan	Judie Karuklis	. . .	Frank Gonzales
Mora	C	5	(505) 387-5279	Juan Espinoza	Phillip Cantu	Charlotte Duran	Doris Casados	Geraldine Martinez	John Sanchez
Otero	* CE	62	(505) 437-7427	. . .	Martin Moore	Robyn Holmes	Donna Brandon	. . .	John Blansett
Quay	C	10	(505) 461-2112	Glenn Briscoe	Bob Lamm	Jeannette Maddaford	Nadine Angel	Donna Dominguez	Jack Huntley
Rio Arriba	CE	41	(505) 588-7254	. . .	Lorenzo Valdez	Fred Vigil	Charlene Sanchez	Jessica Madrid	Joe Mascarenas
Roosevelt	CM	18	(505) 356-5307	Gene Creighton	Charlene Hardin	Janet Collins	Tammy Lee	. . .	Thomas Gossett
San Juan	CE	113	(505) 334-4502	. . .	Keith Johns	Fran Hanhardt	Robert Wasson	Charlene Scott	Bob Melton
San Miguel	C	30	(505) 425-9333	. . .	Les Montoya	Paul Maez	Melinda Gonzalez	. . .	Chris Najar
Sandoval	C	89	(505) 867-7500	. . .	Debbie Hays	Victoria Dunlap	Leroy Arquero	Tammie Gerrard	Ray Rivera
Santa Fe	CE	129	(505) 986-6369	. . .	Roman Abeyta	Valerie Espinoza	Katherine Miller	Helen Quintana	Raymond Sisneros
Sierra	C	13	(505) 894-6215	Russell Peterson	Janet Carrejo	Janice Sanchez	. . .	Janette Monsibaiz	Ronald Brown
Socorro	CE	18	(505) 835-0589	. . .	Matejka Ray-Olguin	Carmen Gallegos	. . .	. . .	. . .
Taos	CM	29	(505) 737-6300	Gabriel Romero	. . .	Elaine Montano	Edwin Fernandez	James Dennis	Charlie Martinez
Torrance	CE	16	(505) 246-4752	James Frost	Robert Ayre	Linda Kayser	Tracy Sedillo	. . .	Pete Golden
Union	C	4	(505) 374-8896	Thomas Gonzales	Della Wetsel	Freida Birdwell	. . .	. . .	Albert Johnston
Valencia	CE	66	(505) 866-2004	. . .	. . .	. . .	. . .	. . .	. . .
NEW YORK									
Albany	CE	294	(518) 447-7040	Charles Houghtaling	Michael Breslin	Thomas Clingan	Michael Conners	Joyce Timmons	James Campbell
Allegany	C	49	(585) 268-9217	. . .	John Margeson	. . .	. . .	. . .	. . .
Broome	CE	200	(607) 778-2109	. . .	. . .	James Griffith	Joseph Keller	. . .	Ernest Dustman
Cattaraugus	CE	83	(716) 938-9111	Gerard Fitzpatrick	John Searles	James Griffith	Joseph Keller	Howard Peterson	Ernest Dustman
Cayuga	CM	81	(315) 253-1273	Herbert Marshall	. . .	Susan Dwyer	. . .	. . .	C. Outhouse
Chautauqua	CE	139	(716) 753-4000	Mark Thomas	. . .	John Dillenburg	Robert Beckman	Joseph Porpiglia	Joseph Gerace
Chemung	CE	91	(607) 737-2918	G. Tranter	. . .	Katherine Hughes	Steven Hoover	Joycelyn Bermingham	Christopher Moss
Chenango	CE	51	(607) 337-1770	Richard Decker	. . .	Thomas Whittaker	William Evans	Bonnie Carrier	Thomas Loughren
Clinton	CE	79	(518) 565-4600	Donald Garrant	William Bingel	John Zurlo	Greg Bell	Alan Gibson	. . .
Columbia	C	63	(518) 828-1527	Gerald Simons	. . .	Gladys Goesch	. . .	Barbara Haywood	James Bertram
Cortland	C	48	(607) 753-5048	Scott Steve	Scott Schrader	Carletta Edwards	. . .	. . .	Duane Whiteman
Delaware	C	48	(607) 746-2603	. . .	. . .	. . .	. . .	. . .	. . .
Dutchess	CE	280	(845) 486-2169	William Steinhaus	. . .	William Paroli	Rita Brannen	Douglas McHoul	Fred Scoralick
Erie	CE	950	(716) 858-8500	. . .	. . .	. . .	. . .	. . .	. . .
Essex	CM	38	(518) 873-3360	Teresa Sayward	Clifford Donaldson	Deborah Weber	. . .	Ruth McDonough	Henry Hommes
Franklin	CM	51	(518) 481-1675	Earl Lavoie	James Feeley	Wanda Murtagh	. . .	Donna Barnes	Jack Pelkey
Fulton	C	55	(518) 736-5540	Peter Stone	Jon Stead	William Eschler	. . .	Edith Pashley	Thomas Lorey
Genesee	* CE	60	(585) 344-2550	. . .	Jay Gsell	Carolyn Pratt	. . .	Karen Marchese	Gary Maha
Greene	CE	48	(518) 943-3080	Frank Stabile	. . .	Donald Olson	. . .	Audrey Adrezin	Richard Hussey
Hamilton	C	5	(518) 548-6651	. . .	William Farber	Laura Abrams	. . .	Kimberly Parslow	Douglas Parker
Herkimer	C	64	(315) 867-1002	Leonard Hendrix	James Wallace	Sylvia Rowan	Bernard Decker	Jeffrey Whittemore	Christopher Farber
Jefferson	* C	111	(315) 785-3147	Kent Burto	Robert Hagemann	Jo Ann Wilder	. . .	Stephen Miller	John Burns
Lewis	C	26	(315) 376-5356	. . .	Sharon Cihocki	Teresa Kenealy	. . .	Mary Van Brocklin	Louis Tabolt
Livingston	CM	64	(585) 243-7000	Dennis House	Dominic Mazza	James Culbertson	Arlene Johnston	Tish Lynn	. . .
Madison	C	69	(315) 366-2011	. . .	. . .	. . .	. . .	. . .	. . .
Monroe	C	735	(585) 753-1000	Maggie Brooks	James Smith	Cheryl Dinolfo	Steve Gleason	Brayton Connard	Patrick O'Flynn
Montgomery	C	49	(518) 853-3431	. . .	. . .	. . .	. . .	. . .	. . .
Nassau	CE	1334	(516) 535-3131	. . .	Thomas Suozzi	Karen Murphy	Arthur Gianelli	Jo-Ann Goldson	. . .
Niagara	C	219	(716) 439-7177	Bradley Erck	Gregory Lewis	Paul Oates	Sharon Sacco	Bruce Fenwick	Thomas Beilein
Oneida	CE	235	(315) 798-5725	Ralph Eannace	. . .	Richard Allen	Anthony Carvelli	Mary Berie	Daniel Middaugh
Onondaga	CE	458	(315) 435-3537	Nicholas Pirro	Edward Kochian	Cynthia Miano	Joe Mareane	Elaine Walter	Kevin Walsh
Ontario	CE	100	(585) 396-4465	Carmen Orlando	Geoffrey Astles	Karen DeMay	Catherine Bentzoni	John Garvey	Philip Povero
Orange	CE	341	(845) 294-5151	Joseph Rampe	Chris Dunleavy	Donna Benson	Joel Kleiman	J. Dan Bloomer	Francis Phillips
Orleans	CE	44	(585) 589-7053	Marcia Tuohey	Stanley Dudek	Kathleen Ahlberg	. . .	Sandra Bower	Scott Hess
Oswego	CE	122	(315) 349-8367	. . .	John Tierney	George Williams	. . .	Maurice Hurd	Reuel Todd
Otsego	C	61	(607) 547-4200	. . .	. . .	. . .	. . .	. . .	. . .
Putnam	* CE	95	(845) 225-0860	Robert Bondi	. . .	Dennis Sant	William Carlin	Paul Eldridge	Donald Smith
Rensselaer	CE	152	(518) 270-2700	. . .	. . .	Doreen Connolly	Thomas Mannix	Susan Martin	. . .
Rockland	CE	286	(845) 638-5000	C. Vanderhoef	David Wickerham	Edward Gorman	George Rene	Patricia Prendergast	James Kralic
Saratoga	CE	200	(518) 885-2225	Robert Stokes	. . .	. . .	. . .	William Baker	James Bowen
Schenectady	CM	146	(518) 388-4233	Susan Savage	Kathleen Rooney	John Woodward	George Davidson	Kathleen Heap	Harry Buffardi
Schoharie	C	31	(518) 295-8347	James Brown	. . .	David Hallock	William Cherry	Lorrie Gordon	John Bates
Schuyler	C	19	(607) 535-8179	Thomas Gifford	Timothy O'Hearn	Linda Compton	. . .	Gail Hughey	Michael Maloney
Seneca	CM	33	(315) 539-5655	Robert Favreau	. . .	Christina Lotz	Nicholas Sciotti	. . .	Thomas Fox
St. Lawrence	CE	111	(315) 379-2210	Alex MacKinnon	. . .	Patricia Ritchie	. . .	Natalie Aldrich	Gary Jarvis
Steuben	C	98	(607) 776-9631	DeWitt Baker	Mark Alger	Christine Kane	. . .	Robert Biehl	Richard Tweddell
Suffolk	CE	1419	(631) 853-4000	Robert Gaffney	Eric Kopp	Edward Romaine	Joseph Sawicki	Alan Schneider	John Gallagher
Sullivan	CE	73	(845) 794-3000	Leni Binder	David Fanslau	. . .	Richard La Condre	Pamela Rourke	Daniel Hogue
Tioga	* C	51	(607) 687-8203	. . .	. . .	. . .	Ronald McEwen	Bethany O'Rourke	Gary Howard
Tompkins	CE	96	(607) 274-5526	Tim Joseph	Stephen Whicher	Catherine Covert	David Squires	Anita Fitzpatrick	Peter Meskill
Ulster	CE	177	(845) 340-3800	David Donaldson	Michael Hein	Nina Postupack	. . .	Randall Roth	J. Richard Bockelmann

Directory 1/10 continued

OFFICIALS IN U.S. COUNTIES 2,500 AND OVER IN POPULATION

Jurisdiction	Form of govern- ment	2000 Popu- lation (000)	Main telephone number	Chief elected official	Appointed administrator	Clerk of the governing board	Chief financial officer	Director of personnel	Chief law enforcement official
NEW YORK continued									
Warren	C	63	(518) 761-6535	. . .	. . .	. . .	. . .	. . .	. . .
Washington *	C	61	(518) 746-2250	JoAnn Trinkle	Kevin Hayes	Debra Prehoda	Kenneth Talkington	Barbara Winchell	Roger Le Claire
Wayne	C	93	(315) 946-7483	Marvin Decker	James Marquette	. . .	. . .	Peter Stirpe	Richard Pisciotti
Westchester	CE	923	(914) 995-2114	Andrew Spano	. . .	Leonard Spano	Peter Pucillo	Paula Zeman	Louis D'Aliso
Wyoming	C	43	(585) 786-8830	. . .	. . .	Jean Krotz	. . .	Sally Wing	Allen Capwell
Yates	CM	24	(315) 536-5112	Robert Multer	Sarah Purdy	Connie Hayes	. . .	Sherri Shoff	Ronald Spike
NORTH CAROLINA									
Alamance	CM	130	(910) 228-1312	John Patterson	David Smith	Patricia Jones	. . .	Joanne Garner	Terry Johnson
Alexander	CM	33	(828) 632-9332	. . .	Richard French	Jamie Starnes	Jennifer Herman	Sandra Gregory	Hayden Bentley
Alleghany	CE	10	(336) 372-4179	Robert Edwards	J. Adams	Karen Evans	Joy Hines	. . .	Mike Caudill
Anson	CM	25	(704) 694-3342	Bill Thacker	Andrew Lucas	Bonnie Huntley	Dorothy Tyson	. . .	James Sellers
Ashe	CE	24	(336) 219-2501	Larry Rhodes	Daniel McMillan	Ann Clark	Sandra Long	. . .	Jim Hartley
Avery *	CE	17	(828) 733-8201	Kenny Poteat	Robert Wiseman	Nancy Cook	Timothy Greene	Nancy Johnson	Kevin Frye
Beaufort	CM	44	(252) 946-0079	. . .	Paul Spruill	Sharon Singleton	Angela Andrew	. . .	Alan Jordan
Bertie *	CE	19	(252) 794-5300	Robert Harrell	Zee Lamb	Misty Edwards	Lydia Hoggard	Carolyn Fornes	Charles Atkins
Bladen	CM	32	(910) 862-6700	Gregory Taylor	Gregory Martin	Kathy Britt	Lisa Coleman	Stephanie Moultrie	Stephen Bunn
Brunswick *	CE	73	(910) 253-2000	David Sandifer	Marty Lawing	Deborah Gore	Ann Hardy	Margaret Grissett	Ronald Hewett
Buncombe	CM	206	(828) 250-4166	Nathan Ramsey	Wanda Greene	Kathy Hughes	Donna Clark	Robert Thornberry	Bobby Medford
Burke	CM	89	(828) 439-4356	Wayne Abele	Ronald Lewis	Vicki Craigo	. . .	Judith Catron	John McDevitt
Cabarrus	CM	131	(704) 920-2200	Carolyn Carpenter	John Day	Susie Bonds	. . .	Donald Cummings	David Riley
Caldwell	CM	77	(828) 757-1300	Herb Greene	William White	Kathy Myers	Laurie Faw	David Hill	Gary Clark
Camden	CM	6	(252) 338-1919	Jeff Jennings	Randell Woodruff	. . .	Clarann Mansfield	. . .	Tony Perry
Carteret *	CM	59	(252) 728-8450	Douglas Harris	John Langdon	Jeanette Deese	. . .	Myles McLoughlin	Asa Buck
Caswell *	CM	23	(336) 694-4193	George Ward	Kevin Howard	Wanda Smith	Gwendolyn Vaughn	Nichole McLaughlin	Michael Welch
Catawba	CM	141	(828) 465-8200	Katherine Barnes	Tom Lundy	Barbara Morris	Rodney Miller	Debbie Bradley	L. Huffman
Chatham	CM	49	(919) 542-8200	Margaret Pollard	Charles Horne	Sandra Lee	Vicki McConnell	Kim Bush	Donald Whitt
Cherokee	CE	24	(828) 837-5527	Barbara Vicknair	David Badger	R. Lindsay	William Block	. . .	Kevin Lovin
Chowan *	CM	14	(252) 482-8431	Ralph Cole	Luther Copeland	Susanne Stallings	Lisa Jones	. . .	Dwayne Goodwin
Clay	CE	8	(704) 389-0089	. . .	. . .	. . .	. . .	. . .	. . .
Cleveland *	CM	96	(704) 484-4800	Mary Accor	David Dear	Kerri Melton	Chris Crepps	R. Pearson	Raymond Hamrick
Columbus	CE	54	(910) 640-6600	Kippling Godwin	Jimmy Varner	. . .	Gayle Godwin	Debbie Long	Jimmy Ferguson
Craven	CE	91	(252) 636-6602	George Brown	Harold Blizzard	Gwendolyn Bryan	Richard Hemphill	. . .	Jerry Monette
Cumberland	CE	302	(910) 678-7653	Talmadge Baggett	James Martin	Marsha Fogle	. . .	James Lawson	Earl Butler
Currituck	CE	18	(252) 232-2075	Paul O'Neal	Daniel Scanlon	Gwendolyn Tatem	Sandra Hill	Derinda Leary	Susan Johnson
Dare	CM	29	(252) 475-5555	Warren Judge	Terry Wheeler	Frances Harris	John Clawson	Thomas O'Neal	Rodney Midgett
Davidson	CM	147	(336) 242-2000	Fred Sink	Robert Hyatt	. . .	Jane Kiker	Keli Greer	Gerald Hege
Davie *	CM	34	(336) 753-6001	John Frye	. . .	Brenda Hunter	James Stockert	. . .	. . .
Duplin	CE	49	(910) 296-2100	Larry Howard	. . .	. . .	Teresa Lanier	. . .	Blake Wallace
Durham	CM	223	(919) 560-0000	Ellen Reckhow	Michael Ruffin	Garry Umstead	George Quick	Marqueta Welton	Worth Hill
Edgecombe	CE	55	(252) 641-7834	Charlie Harrell	Lorenzo Carmon	Carolyn Hedgepeth	JoAnne Harrell	. . .	James Knight
Forsyth *	CM	306	(336) 703-2400	Gloria Whisenhunt	J. Watts	Jane Cole	Paul Fulton	Carol Gearhart	William Schatzman
Franklin	CM	47	(919) 496-5994	Harry Foy	. . .	. . .	Charles Murray	Ursula Hairston	Jerry Jones
Gaston	CM	190	(704) 866-3100	. . .	Jan Winters	Martha Jordan	Ronald Courtney	Charles Vinson	Leroy Russell
Gates *	CE	10	(252) 357-1240	William Harrell	Melinda Hoggard	Timothy Russell	. . .	. . .	Edward Webb
Graham	CM	7	(828) 479-7961	Joey Cody	. . .	Janice Millsaps	Sharon Crisp	. . .	Steven Odom
Granville	CM	48	(919) 693-4182	James Lumpkins	. . .	Bobbie Wilson	Michael Felts	. . .	David Smith
Greene	CE	18	(252) 747-3446	Bennie Heath	Donald Davenport	. . .	Deborah Gay	. . .	Ernest Smith
Guilford	CM	421	(336) 641-3383	Robert Landreth	W. McNeill	Efthemia Varitimidis	Brenda Jones	Sharisse Fuller	B. Barnes
Halifax	CE	57	(252) 583-1688	Carolyn Johnson	Matthew Delk	Lynne Simeon	Linda Taylor	. . .	Jeff Frazier
Harnett	CE	91	(910) 893-7555	Teddy Byrd	Neil Emory	Kay Blanchard	Vanessa Young	Charles Hill	Larry Rollins
Haywood	CE	54	(828) 452-6625	Mark Swanger	David Cotton	. . .	Julia Davis	La Neah Parton	Richard Alexander
Henderson *	CE	89	(828) 697-4669	. . .	Steven Wyatt	Elizabeth Corn	James McLelland	Janice Prichard	Rick Davis
Hertford	CM	22	(252) 358-7805	Johnnie Farmer	Loria Williams	. . .	Robbin Stephenson	. . .	Juan Vaughan
Hoke	CM	33	(910) 875-8751	Robert Wright	Michael Wood	Linda Revels	Leo Hunt	Edward Crutchfield	Hubert Peterkin
Hyde	CM	5	(252) 926-4178	Beatrice Emmert	Kevin Howard	. . .	Emily Thomas	. . .	L Johnson
Iredell *	CM	122	(704) 878-3000	Marvin Norman	Joel Mashburn	. . .	Susan Blumenstein	Carolyn Harris	Phillip Redmond
Jackson	CE	33	(828) 586-4055	K. Buchanan	K. Westmoreland	Evelyn Baker	Darlene Fox	. . .	James Ashe
Johnston	CE	121	(919) 989-5100	James Langdon	Rick Hester	Joyce Ennis	John Massey	Joseph LaCarter	Roger Bizzell
Jones	C	10	(252) 448-7571	Horace Phillips	Larry Meadows	Cora Davenport	Judy Smith	. . .	Robert Mason
Lee	CM	49	(919) 718-4615	Herbert Hincks	. . .	Gaynell Lee	Lisa Minter	Joyce McGehee	William Bryant
Lenoir	CE	59	(252) 559-6450	George Graham	Mike Jarman	Lashanda Aytch	Tommy Hollowell	. . .	William Smith
Lincoln *	CE	63	(704) 736-8471	Jerry Cochrane	. . .	Amy Long	Leon Harmon	Audrey Setzer	Barbara Pickens
Macon	CE	29	(828) 349-2000	Allan Bryson	Sam Greenwood	. . .	Evelyn Southard	Charles Nicholson	Robert Holland
Madison	CE	19	(828) 649-2521	Anthony Willis	. . .	Bruce Briggs	Beverly Wyatt	Karen Ensley	James Brown
Martin *	CM	25	(252) 789-4300	Tommy Bowen	Russell Overman	Linda Hardison	Cindy Ange	. . .	Dan Gibbs
Mc Dowell	CM	42	(828) 652-7121	Andrew Webb	Charles Abernathy	Carrie Padgett	Alison Morgan	Lesa Silver	Jackie Turner
Mecklenburg	CM	695	(704) 336-7600	Tom Cox	Harry Jones	Janice Paige	J. Weatherly	Susan Hutchins	James Pendergraph
Mitchell	CE	15	(828) 688-2139	Bill Slagle	Ryan Whitson	. . .	Mavis Parsley	. . .	Ken Fox
Montgomery	CM	26	(910) 576-4221	Billy Maness	Lance Metzler	. . .	Janice Shaw	. . .	Jeff Jordan
Moore	CE	74	(910) 947-6362	David Cummings	Thomas McSwain	Carol Thomas	Lisa Hughes	Teri Alesch	Lane Carter
Nash	CE	87	(252) 459-9800	J. Mayo	Robert Murphy	. . .	Lynne Anderson	Sheila Freeman	Jimmy Grimes
New Hanover	CM	160	(910) 798-7178	Robert Davis	Chris Coudriet	Sheila Schult	Avril Pinder	. . .	Sidney Causey
Northampton	CM	22	(252) 574-0236	Virginia Spruill	Wayne Jenkins	Kay Flythe	Dorothy Vick	Marcenda Rogers	Wardie Vincent
Onslow	CM	150	(910) 347-4717	Delma Collins	Frank Clifton	Beth Purcell	Alvin Barrett	Wayne Morris	Edward Brown
Orange *	CM	118	(919) 732-8181	Margaret Brown	Laura Blackmon	Donna Baker	Kenneth Chavious	. . .	Lindy Pendergrass
Pamlico	CM	12	(252) 745-3133	. . .	Timothy Buck	Kathy Cayton	. . .	Sherry Watts	Danny Pugh
Pasquotank	CM	34	(252) 337-6648	William Trueblood	Randy Keaton	Karen Jennings	Sheri Bulman	Margaret Jones	Randy Cartwright
Pender	CE	41	(910) 259-1513	Stephen Holland	Lori Brill	. . .	David McCole	. . .	Carson Smith
Perquimans *	C	11	(252) 426-8484	Mack Nixon	Bobby Darden	Mary Hunnicutt	Sharon Ward	. . .	Eric Tilley
Person	CM	35	(336) 597-1720	S. Knott	Steve Carpenter	Faye Fuller	Andrew Davenport	. . .	Dennis Oakley
Pitt	CM	133	(252) 902-3050	. . .	Donald Elliott	Susan Banks	Melonie Bryan	Florida Hardy	Mac Manning
Polk	CM	18	(828) 894-3301	Timothy McCormack	. . .	Pamela Thomas	Sandra Hughes	. . .	David Satterfield
Randolph *	CE	130	(336) 318-6600	Harold Holmes	Richard Wells	Cheryl Ivey	William Massie	Kim Newsom	Maynard Reid
Richmond	CM	46	(910) 997-8211	Kenneth Robinette	James Haynes	Marian Savage	Mac Steagall	. . .	Dale Furr
Robeson	CM	123	(910) 671-3016	Johnny Hunt	Kenneth Windley	Tamala Freeman	Kellie Blue	. . .	Kenneth Sealey
Rockingham	CM	91	(336) 342-8100	Harold Hoover	Thomas Robinson	Pamela Robertson	Michael Apple	. . .	Samuel Page
Rowan	CE	130	(704) 216-8100	Arnold Chamberlain	. . .	Carolyn Athey	Leslie Heidrick	Darlene Boling	George Wilhelm
Rutherford	CM	62	(828) 287-6145	Charles Hill	John Condrey	Hazel Haynes	Robert Bole	Judith Toney	Daniel Good
Sampson	CE	60	(910) 592-6308	Norman Naylor	Scott Sauer	. . .	Sylvia Blinson	. . .	O. L. McCullen
Scotland	CM	35	(910) 277-2406	J. D. Willis	John Crumpton	Ann Kurtzman	Kevin Patterson	Susan Butler	James Blalock
Stanly	CM	58	(704) 986-3600	Tony Dennis	Jerry Myers	Nancy Litaker	Charles Mashburn	. . .	Tony Frick

Directory 1/10
continued

OFFICIALS IN U.S. COUNTIES 2,500 AND OVER IN POPULATION

Jurisdiction	Form of govern-ment	2000 Popu-lation (000)	Main telephone number	Chief elected official	Appointed administrator	Clerk of the governing board	Chief financial officer	Director of personnel	Chief law enforcement official
NORTH CAROLINA continued									
Stokes	CE	44	(336) 593-2811	. . .	Rick Morris	. . .	. . .	. . .	. . .
Surry	* CM	71	(336) 401-8201	Craig Hunter	Macon Sammons	Conchita Atkins	Betty Taylor	Sandra Snow	Graham Atkinson
Swain	* CE	12	(828) 488-9273	Glenn Jones	Linda Cable	Cindi Woodard	Vida Cody	Elise Bryson	Curtis Cochran
Transylvania	CE	29	(828) 884-3100	Raymond Miller	Arthur Wilson	Kimberly Conover	Gay Poor	Sheila Cozart	Robert Orr
Tyrrell	C	4	(252) 796-1371	Thomas Spruill	James Brickhouse	Connie Hopkins	. . .	. . .	Harry Hemilright
Union	CM	123	(704) 283-3500	. . .	. . .	. . .	. . .	William Watson	. . .
Vance	CM	42	(252) 738-2001	J. Pegram	Jerry Ayscue	Kelly Grissom	Jerry Tucker	Argretta Reid	R. Breedlove
Wake	CM	627	(919) 856-6090	Linda Coleman	David Cooke	Gwendolyn Reynolds	David Frazier	John Kuhls	John Baker
Warren	CE	19	(252) 257-3115	Ulysses Ross	Linda Jones	Angelena Dunlap	Gloria Edmonds	Katherine Williamson	Johnny Williams
Washington	* CE	13	(252) 793-5823	Billy Corey	David Peoples	Lois Askew	Gayle Critcher	. . .	Janice Spruill
Watauga	CE	42	(828) 265-8000	Jim Deal	Robert Nelson	Anita Fogle	Doris Isaacs	. . .	Mark Shook
Wayne	CE	113	(919) 731-1435	. . .	William Smith	Marcia Wilson	E Norman Ricks	Harriett Guy	Carey Winders
Wilkes	CE	65	(336) 651-7300	Charles Sink	Gary Page	Alene Faw	Jerry Shepherd	. . .	Dane Mastin
Wilson	CM	73	(252) 399-2803	. . .	Ellis Williford	. . .	Phyllis Vick	. . .	Wayne Gay
Yadkin	CE	36	(336) 679-4200	DC Swaim	. . .	Melinda Vestal	Sheron Church	. . .	Mike Cain
Yancey	CE	17	(828) 682-3971	David McIntosh	Michele Lawhern	Todd Bailey	Jean Buchanan	Brandi Adkins	Kermit Banks
NORTH DAKOTA									
Adams	C	2	(701) 567-4363	Ramon Barnes	. . .	Ginger Dangerud	. . .	. . .	Eugene Molbert
Barnes	C	11	(701) 845-8500	Palmer Paulson	. . .	. . .	Edward McGough	Linda Anderson	Randy McClaflin
Benson	* C	6	(701) 473-5458	Curtis Hvinden	. . .	. . .	. . .	. . .	Steve Rohrer
Billings	* C	. .	(701) 623-4377	. . .	. . .	Donna Adams	Joan Jurgens	. . .	David Jurgens
Bottineau	C	7	(701) 228-2225	Ronald Block	. . .	. . .	Mae Streich	. . .	. . .
Bowman	C	3	(701) 523-3130	. . .	. . .	Annetta Anderson	. . .	. . .	. . .
Burke	* C	2	(701) 377-2861	Terry Nelson	. . .	. . .	Teri Baumann	. . .	Barry Jager
Burleigh	* C	69	(701) 222-6669	Kevin Glatt	. . .	. . .	Clyde Thompson	Renae Gall	Patrick Heinert
Cass	* C	123	(701) 241-5720	Scott Wagner	Bonnie Johnson	Dorothy Howard	Mike Montplaisir	. . .	Paul Laney
Cavalier	C	4	(701) 256-2229	Jerome Dosmann	. . .	. . .	. . .	. . .	David Zeis
Dickey	C	5	(701) 349-3249	Jerry Walsh	. . .	. . .	Lawrence Hoffman	. . .	Jim Bohannon
Divide	* C	2	(701) 965-6351	Gerald Brady	. . .	Penny Hagen	Gayle Jastrzebski	. . .	Lauren Throntveit
Dunn	C	3	(701) 573-4448	. . .	. . .	. . .	. . .	. . .	. . .
Eddy	C	2	(701) 947-2434	. . .	. . .	. . .	Wanda Kurtz	. . .	Lawrence Schagunn
Emmons	C	4	(701) 254-4807	Harvey Reamann	. . .	Anna Dockter	. . .	. . .	Rueben Richter
Foster	C	3	(701) 652-2441	. . .	. . .	. . .	Roger Schlotman	. . .	John Statema
Golden Valley	C	1	(701) 872-4331	. . .	. . .	. . .	Cecilia Stedman	. . .	DaLane Stedman
Grand Forks	C	66	(701) 780-8415	Greg Malm	Edward Nierode	. . .	Doris Bring	. . .	Dan Hill
Grant	* C	2	(701) 622-3275	Daniel Stewart	. . .	Joyce Stern	. . .	. . .	Steve Bay
Griggs	* C	2	(701) 797-3117	. . .	. . .	. . .	Cynthia Anton	Janet Tenneson	Paul Hendrickson
Hettinger	C	2	(701) 824-2073	. . .	. . .	. . .	. . .	. . .	. . .
Kidder	C	2	(701) 475-2632	. . .	. . .	. . .	. . .	. . .	. . .
La Moure	C	4	(701) 883-5301	Richard Aberle	. . .	. . .	Michial Johnson	. . .	Gary Jensen
Logan	C	2	(701) 754-2425	Mike Vetter	. . .	. . .	Blanche Schumacher	. . .	Steve Engelhardt
Mc Henry	C	5	(701) 537-5724	. . .	. . .	. . .	Darlene Carpenter	. . .	Marvin Sola
Mc Intosh	CE	3	(701) 288-3347	Gina Ketterling	. . .	. . .	Lanette Blumhardt	. . .	Paul Peters
Mc Kenzie	* C	5	(701) 444-3616	Richard Cayko	. . .	Ann Johnsrud	Frances Olson	. . .	Ron Rankin
Mc Lean	CE	9	(701) 462-8541	. . .	. . .	Mary Ann Anderson	Marlan Hvinden	. . .	Don Charging
Mercer	C	8	(701) 745-3292	Leora Retterath	Wayne Enze	. . .	. . .	Lynn Amsden	Ronald Kessler
Morton	C	25	(701) 667-3414	. . .	. . .	. . .	Paul Trauger	Paula Graner	Robert Erhardt
Mountrail	C	6	(701) 628-2145	Robert Wheeling	. . .	Karen Eliason	. . .	. . .	Kenneth Halvorson
Nelson	C	3	(701) 247-2463	. . .	. . .	Ruth Stevens	W. Davidson	. . .	Dale Quam
Oliver	C	2	(701) 794-8721	Barbara Fleming	. . .	Kim Wilkens	. . .	. . .	David Hilliard
Pembina	C	8	(701) 265-4231	Dorothy Robinson	. . .	Nancy Johnson	. . .	. . .	Joe Martindale
Pierce	* C	4	(701) 776-5225	Karin Fursather	. . .	Carla Marks	. . .	. . .	Robert Graber
Ramsey	* C	12	(701) 662-7009	Bill Mertens	. . .	. . .	Elizabeth Fischer	. . .	Steve Nelson
Ransom	C	5	(701) 683-5823	Connie Gilbert	Kathy Schultz	Valorie Lukes	. . .	. . .	Conrad Steinhaus
Renville	C	2	(701) 756-6301	. . .	. . .	. . .	Susan Ritter	. . .	Brent Johnson
Richland	C	17	(701) 642-7700	Perry Miller	. . .	. . .	Harris Bailey	. . .	Larry Leshovsky
Rolette	C	13	(701) 477-5665	Robert Leonard	. . .	. . .	Judith Boppre	. . .	Tony Sims
Sargent	C	4	(701) 724-6241	. . .	. . .	. . .	. . .	. . .	. . .
Sheridan	C	1	(701) 363-2205	Shirley Murray	. . .	. . .	. . .	. . .	Lawrence Gessner
Sioux	C	4	(701) 854-3481	Larry Silbernagel	. . .	. . .	Barbara Hettich	. . .	Frank Landeis
Slope	* C	. .	(701) 879-6276	Paul Brooks	. . .	. . .	Lorrie Buzalsky	. . .	Pat Lorge
Stark	C	22	(701) 456-7630	George Nodland	. . .	Carol Beckert	. . .	. . .	Clarence Tuhy
Steele	C	2	(701) 524-2110	David Washburn	. . .	. . .	Ruth Gullicks	. . .	Wayne Beckman
Stutsman	C	21	(701) 252-9035	Mark Klose	. . .	Karen Samek	Lary Olson	. . .	David Orr
Towner	* C	2	(701) 968-4340	David Lagein	. . .	. . .	Kent Haugen	. . .	Vaughn Klier
Traill	C	8	(701) 636-4458	. . .	. . .	. . .	Rebecca Braaten	. . .	Michael Crocker
Walsh	C	12	(701) 352-2851	. . .	. . .	. . .	. . .	. . .	. . .
Ward	* C	58	(701) 857-6420	Darlene Watne	. . .	. . .	Devra Smesatd	Colleen Houmann	Vern Erck
Wells	C	5	(701) 547-3521	. . .	. . .	. . .	. . .	. . .	. . .
Williams	C	19	(701) 577-4500	Daniel Kalil	. . .	. . .	Beth Innis	. . .	Scott Busching
OHIO									
Adams	C	27	(937) 544-3286	Paul Rothwell	. . .	Linda Mendenhall	Carroll Newman	. . .	. . .
Allen	CE	108	(419) 228-3700	Gregory Sneary	Rebecca Saine	Kelli Singhaus	Ben Diepenbrock	Crystal Balo	Daniel Beck
Ashland	C	52	(419) 289-0000	Matt Miller	. . .	Gail Crossen	Philip Leibolt	. . .	Estel Risner
Ashtabula	CE	102	(440) 576-9090	. . .	Joseph Pedro	. . .	. . .	. . .	. . .
Athens	C	62	(740) 592-3224	Bill Theisen	. . .	Crystal Mitchell	David Lovett	. . .	. . .
Auglaize	* C	46	(419) 739-6710	Ivo Kramer	Joseph Lenhart	Sue Ellen Kohler	Janet Schuler	. . .	Allen Solomon
Belmont	CE	70	(614) 425-1118	. . .	. . .	Jayne Long	. . .	. . .	. . .
Brown	C	42	(937) 378-3956	. . .	. . .	Beverly Gallimore	Doug Green	. . .	Dwayne Wenninger
Butler	CE	332	(513) 887-3000	Michael Fox	Derek Conklin	Flora Butler	Timothy Williams	Douglas Duckett	Don Gabbard
Carroll	C	28	(330) 627-5122	. . .	. . .	Sonja Leggett	E Leroy Van Horne	. . .	Ralph Lucas
Champaign	C	38	(937) 772-7001	. . .	Carolyn Poe	Howard Dugo	. . .	. . .	Joseph Lynch
Clark	CE	144	(937) 328-2405	Roger Tackett	W. Howard	Michelle Noble	George Sodders	Cathy Balas	Gene Kelly
Clermont	CE	177	(513) 732-7300	Mary Walker	David Spinney	Judith Kocica	Susanne Scheetz	Robert Sander	Albert Rodenberg
Clinton	C	40	(937) 382-2054	. . .	Mark Brooker	. . .	. . .	. . .	. . .
Columbiana	C	112	(330) 424-9511	. . .	. . .	. . .	. . .	. . .	. . .
Coshocton	C	36	(740) 622-1753	Alice Moore	. . .	Mary Beck	Richard Tompkins	. . .	. . .
Crawford	C	46	(419) 562-4602	Barbara Blackford	Mary Jo Allan	Glory Chaney	Donald Long	. . .	Ronald Shawber

Directory 1/10
continued

OFFICIALS IN U.S. COUNTIES 2,500 AND OVER IN POPULATION

Jurisdiction	Form of government	2000 Population (000)	Main telephone number	Chief elected official	Appointed administrator	Clerk of the governing board	Chief financial officer	Director of personnel	Chief law enforcement official
OHIO continued									
Cuyahoga	CE	1393	(216) 443-7190	Tim McCormack	Dennis Madden	...	...	...	...
Darke	C	53	(937) 547-7312	...	Maragret Hile	Robin Blinn	Janice Anderson	...	Toby Spencer
Defiance	C	39	(419) 782-4761	Richard Cromwell	Rebecca Wagner	Alison Grimes	...	...	David Westrick
Delaware	C	109	(740) 833-2100	Roy Jackson	David Cannon	...	Jon Peterson	Myra Williamson	...
Erie	CM	79	(419) 627-7678	Nancy McKeen	Michael Bixler	Carolyn Hauenstein	Jude Hammond	James Sennish	Terry Lyons
Fairfield	C	122	(740) 687-7190	...	Patrick Harris	Carri Brown	Jon Slater	Aundrea Cordle	Gary Demastry
Fayette	C	28	(740) 335-0720	Bob Peterson	...	Judy Rambo	Penny Johnson	...	Vernon Stanforth
Franklin	* CE	1068	(614) 462-6224	...	Don Brown	Debra Willaman	Kenneth Wilson	Margaret Snow	Jim Karnes
Fulton	C	42	(419) 337-9255	Jack Graf	Vond Hall	Mary Gype	John Trudel	...	Darrell Merillat
Gallia	C	31	(614) 446-4612	Harold Montgomery	Karen Sprague	Connie Johnson	Ronald Canaday	...	James Taylor
Geauga	CE	90	(440) 285-2222	William Repke	David Lair	...	Tracy Jemison	...	George Simmons
Greene	CM	147	(937) 562-5004	Reed Madden	Howard Poston	Judy Minton	L. Delaney	Marsha Jordan-Smart	Gene Fischer
Guernsey	C	40	(740) 432-9200	...	...	Cheryl Edwards	...	...	...
Hamilton	CM	845	(513) 946-4700	Phil Heimlich	Patrick Thompson	Jacqueline Panioto	...	Gary Berger	Simon Leis
Hancock	C	71	(419) 424-7044	...	...	...	...	...	...
Hardin	C	31	(419) 674-2240	Gerald Potter	...	...	Michael Bacon	...	Craig Leeth
Harrison	C	15	(740) 942-8861	...	...	Barbara Yoho	Patrick Moore	...	Mark Miller
Henry	C	29	(419) 592-4876	Richard Bennett	Anita Smith	Vicki Glick	Kevin Nye	...	John Nye
Highland	C	40	(937) 393-1911	...	...	...	...	...	...
Hocking	C	28	(740) 385-2127	Gary Starner	Roger Hinerman	...	Kenneth Wilson	...	Lanny North
Holmes	C	38	(330) 674-4901	...	...	...	...	...	...
Huron	CE	59	(419) 668-3092	Karen Wilhelm	Mary Cain	Ann Winters	...	...	Richard Sutherland
Jackson	C	32	(740) 286-3301	Ponney Cisco	...	Angela Cemini	Edward Jarvis	...	Gregg Kiefer
Jefferson	C	73	(740) 283-8500	...	...	...	...	...	...
Knox	C	54	(740) 393-6703	Robert Durbin	...	Rochelle Shackle	Margaret Ruhl	...	Daniel Dunlap
Lake	CE	227	(440) 350-2524	Mildred Teuscher	Kenneth Gauntner	Lynn Mazeika	Dale Langbehn	...	Roy Smith
Lawrence	C	62	(740) 533-4300	Carl Baker	Tammy Meade	...	Ray Dutey	...	...
Licking	C	145	(740) 349-6117	Albert Ashbrook	Michael Smith	...	George Buchanan	...	...
Logan	C	46	(937) 599-7823	...	...	Kacy Kirby	...	...	...
Lorain	C	284	(440) 329-5000	David Moore	James Cordes	Theresa Upton	John Rokasy	Jeff Fogt	Martin Mahony
Lucas	CE	455	(419) 213-4500	Sandy Isenburg	Michael Beazley	Nancy Poskar	Larry Kaczala	Gwen Moore	James Telb
Madison	C	40	(740) 852-2972	David Dhume	...	Regina Bogenrife	...	...	Jim Sabin
Mahoning	C	257	(330) 740-2130	...	George Tablack	...	...	J. Sellards	...
Marion	CE	66	(740) 223-4001	Andy Appelfeller	Lenora Mayes	Sylvia Almendinger	Joesph Campbell	...	John Butterworth
Medina	C	151	(330) 723-3641	Sharon Ray	John Stricker	Pamela Terrill	Michael Kovak	Patricia Larsen	Neil Hassinger
Meigs	C	23	(740) 992-2698	...	...	...	...	...	...
Mercer	C	40	(419) 586-3178	...	Kim Everman	...	Mark Giesige	...	Jeff Gray
Miami	* C	98	(937) 440-5910	John Evans	...	...	Chris Peeples	Teresa Clegg	Charles Cox
Monroe	C	15	(740) 472-0873	Gary Hudson	...	Kitty Kahrig	...	...	Glen Schwaben
Montgomery	CM	559	(937) 225-4000	Vickie Pegg	Deborah Feldman	Juanita Hunn	Tom Black	Leon Walker	...
Morgan	C	14	(740) 962-4752	...	...	...	...	...	...
Morrow	C	31	(419) 946-4085	Donald Weaver	...	Shirley Fissel	Mary Holtrey	...	...
Muskingum	* CE	84	(740) 455-7100	...	...	Susan Culbertson	Anita Adams	Michelle Campbell	Robert Stephenson
Noble	C	14	(740) 732-2969	...	...	...	...	...	...
Ottawa	C	40	(419) 734-6700	...	Jere Witt	...	...	...	...
Paulding	C	20	(419) 399-8215	Tony Burkley	Stanley Searing	Joanne Goerlitz	Bill Bolenbaugh	...	David Harrow
Perry	C	34	(740) 342-2074	John Altier	...	Timothy Wollenberg	Joann Hankinson	...	William Barker
Pickaway	C	52	(740) 474-6093	...	Daniel Bradhurst	...	...	...	...
Pike	C	27	(740) 947-4817	...	...	...	...	...	...
Portage	CE	152	(330) 297-3600	Charles Keiper	...	Deborah Mazanec	Eric Sponseller	Lynn Leslie	Duane Kaley
Preble	C	42	(937) 456-8143	...	Kenneth Moreland	Connie Crowell	...	...	...
Putnam	C	34	(419) 523-3656	...	...	Mary Wiener	Marlene Lahey	...	Ronald Diemer
Richland	C	128	(419) 755-5500	...	...	...	...	...	...
Ross	C	73	(740) 702-3085	James Caldwell	Kelly Shelton	Letitia Dobbins	Stephen Neal	...	Ronald Nichols
Sandusky	CE	61	(419) 332-2657	...	...	...	...	Tim Grabenstetter	...
Scioto	C	79	(740) 355-8356	Thomas Reiser	...	Inez Bloomfield	David Green	...	Marty Donini
Seneca	C	58	(419) 447-4550	Kenneth Estep	Robert Anderson	Ashley Reinhart	Larry Beidelschies	...	Tom Steyer
Shelby	C	47	(937) 498-7226	Dale Deloye	...	Judy Snodgrass	...	...	...
Stark	CE	378	(330) 451-7371	...	...	...	...	...	...
Summit	CE	542	(330) 643-2500	James McCarthy	...	John Thomas	...	Stephen Engler	Richard Warren
Trumbull	C	225	(330) 675-2589	Joseph Angelo	...	Paulette Godfrey	David Hines	James Keating	Thomas Altiere
Tuscarawas	C	90	(330) 364-8811	William Ress	...	Jane Clay	J Matt Judy	...	Walter Wilson
Union	C	40	(937) 645-3012	...	...	...	...	...	...
Van Wert	C	29	(419) 238-0843	Gary Adams	...	Carol Speelman	Nancy Dixon	Jane Harris	Stan Owens
Vinton	C	12	(740) 596-4571	Michael Bledsoe	Brande Minton	...	Cindy Owings	...	David Hickey
Warren	C	158	(513) 695-1250	C. Michael Kilburn	David Gully	Tina Davis	Tiffany Ferrell-Sauer	Susan Spencer	William Arris
Washington	C	63	(740) 373-6623	Sandra Matthews	...	Judy Van Dyk	Janet Seaman	...	Robert Schlicher
Wayne	C	111	(330) 287-5400	...	Patrick Herron	...	...	...	...
Williams	C	39	(330) 636-2059	...	...	...	...	...	...
Wood	* CE	121	(419) 354-9000	James Carter	Andrew Kalmar	Kristy Muir	Michael Sibbersen	...	Mark Wasylyshyn
Wyandot	C	22	(419) 294-3836	...	Martha Shrider	...	...	...	...
OKLAHOMA									
Adair	C	21	(918) 696-7198	...	...	...	...	...	...
Alfalfa	C	6	(580) 596-2392	...	...	...	...	...	...
Atoka	C	13	(580) 889-5157	...	...	...	...	...	...
Beaver	C	5	(580) 625-3418	Robby Westenhaver	...	Karen Schell	...	...	Reuben Parker
Beckham	C	19	(580) 928-2457	Carl Simon	...	Clydene Manning	...	...	Scott Jay
Blaine	C	11	(580) 623-5890	Farrol Boyd	...	Sharon Gates	...	...	Ricky Ainsworth
Bryan	C	36	(580) 924-2201	Tony Simmons	Quinton Jones	Patricia Brady	...	...	Bill Sturch
Caddo	CE	30	(405) 247-3105	Carlos Squires	Craig Gibson	Patrice Dolch	...	...	Gene Cain
Canadian	C	87	(405) 262-1070	...	...	...	...	...	...
Carter	C	45	(580) 223-8162	...	...	...	...	...	...
Cherokee	* C	42	(918) 456-3171	...	...	Marshel Benentt	...	...	...
Choctaw	* C	15	(580) 326-3778	Danny Antwine	...	Emily Vanworth	...	...	Lewis Collins
Cimarron	C	3	(580) 544-3420	Kenneth Maness	...	Dwilene Holbert	...	...	Ken Miller
Cleveland	C	208	(405) 366-0200	...	...	Dorinda Harvey	...	...	Dewayne Beggs
Coal	C	6	(580) 927-3122	John Ward	...	Marie Depasse	...	Alvin Rebworth	Tony Taylor
Comanche	C	114	(580) 353-3717	...	...	...	...	...	...
Cotton	C	6	(580) 875-3026	Elmer Beisch	...	Linda Thompson	...	...	Paul Jeffrey

Directory 1/10
continued

OFFICIALS IN U.S. COUNTIES 2,500 AND OVER IN POPULATION

Jurisdiction	Form of govern-ment	2000 Popu-lation (000)	Main telephone number	Chief elected official	Appointed administrator	Clerk of the governing board	Chief financial officer	Director of personnel	Chief law enforcement official
OKLAHOMA continued									
Craig	C	14	(918) 256-2507	James Smith	. . .	Tammy Malone	. . .	. . .	Jimmie Sooter
Creek	C	67	(918) 224-0278	Dana Hudgins	Johnny Burke	Betty Rentz	. . .	. . .	Steve Toliver
Custer	C	26	(580) 323-4420	. . .	. . .	. . .	. . .	. . .	. . .
Delaware	C	37	(918) 253-4520	. . .	. . .	Carol Fortner	. . .	. . .	. . .
Dewey	C	4	(580) 328-5361	Darrell Balfour	. . .	Sandra Clendenny	. . .	. . .	Robert Prentice
Ellis	C	4	(580) 885-7301	Terry Fagala	. . .	Lynn Smith	. . .	. . .	DeWayne Miller
Garfield	C	57	(580) 237-0225	Wendell Vencl	. . .	Kathy Hughes	. . .	. . .	Bill Winchester
Garvin	C	27	(580) 268-2685	Rex Carlton	. . .	Gina Cottrell	. . .	Evelyn Bradley	Bobby Davis
Grady	CE	45	(405) 224-7388	Jack Porter	. . .	Sharon Shoemake	. . .	. . .	Kieran McMullen
Grant	C	5	(580) 395-2214	Max Hess	John Futhey	Debbie Kretchmar	. . .	. . .	Roland Hula
Greer	C	6	(580) 782-2329	. . .	. . .	. . .	. . .	. . .	. . .
Harmon	C	3	(580) 688-3658	. . .	. . .	. . .	. . .	. . .	. . .
Harper	C	3	(580) 735-2870	. . .	. . .	. . .	. . .	. . .	. . .
Haskell	C	11	(918) 967-4352	. . .	. . .	. . .	. . .	. . .	. . .
Hughes	C	14	(405) 379-5487	Jerry Martin	. . .	Joquita Walton	. . .	. . .	Houston Yeager
Jackson	C	28	(580) 482-4420	. . .	. . .	. . .	. . .	. . .	. . .
Jefferson	C	6	(580) 228-2029	Cleo Tipton	. . .	Doris Pilgreen	. . .	. . .	. . .
Johnston	C	10	(580) 371-3184	. . .	. . .	Delores Muse	. . .	. . .	. . .
Kay	C	48	(580) 362-2537	Wayne Leven	. . .	Pamela Goodno	. . .	. . .	Craig Countryman
Kingfisher	C	13	(405) 375-3887	Judge Pritchett	. . .	Jane Hightower	Albert Post	. . .	. . .
Kiowa	C	10	(580) 726-5286	Robert Boelte	. . .	Geanea Watson	. . .	. . .	Buck Jones
Latimer	C	10	(918) 465-3543	John Medders	. . .	Shirley Brinkley	. . .	. . .	Melvin Holly
Le Flore	C	48	(918) 647-2527	. . .	. . .	. . .	. . .	. . .	. . .
Lincoln	C	32	(405) 258-1264	Ted O'Donnell	. . .	Debbie Greenfield	. . .	. . .	A. Brixey
Logan	C	33	(405) 282-0266	Kevin Leach	Mark Sharpton	Mary Lou Orndorff	. . .	. . .	Randy Richardson
Love	C	8	(580) 276-3059	Don Reed	. . .	Dora Jackson	. . .	. . .	Joe Russell
Major	C	7	(580) 227-4732	Kelly Wahl	. . .	. . .	. . .	. . .	Tom Shaffer
Marshall	* C	13	(580) 795-3165	David Brown	. . .	Ann Hartin	. . .	. . .	Robert Wilder
Mayes	C	38	(918) 825-0639	Jim Montgomery	. . .	Lori Parsons	. . .	. . .	Frank Cantey
Mc Clain	C	27	(405) 527-3360	Charles Foster	. . .	Lois Hawkins	. . .	. . .	Don Hewett
Mc Curtain	C	34	(580) 286-7428	Aubrey Thompson	Eugene Burke	Karen Conaway	Tom Porton	. . .	Richard McPeak
Mc Intosh	C	19	(918) 689-3375	Glen Coleman	. . .	Diana Curtis	. . .	. . .	Bobby Gray
Murray	C	12	(580) 622-2854	. . .	. . .	. . .	. . .	. . .	. . .
Muskogee	C	69	(918) 682-9601	Gene Wallace	. . .	Karen Anderson	. . .	. . .	Charles Pearson
Noble	C	11	(580) 336-2141	. . .	. . .	Ronita Coldiron	. . .	. . .	Jerry Cook
Nowata	C	10	(918) 273-2480	Dale Epperson	. . .	Teresa Jackson	. . .	. . .	James Hallett
Okfuskee	C	11	(918) 623-1724	. . .	. . .	Dianne Flanders	. . .	. . .	Jack Choate
Oklahoma	C	660	(405) 278-1500	Stuart Earnest	Blair Schoeb	Carolynn Caudill	John Rahhal	. . .	John Whetsel
Okmulgee	C	39	(918) 756-3836	. . .	. . .	. . .	. . .	. . .	. . .
Osage	C	44	(918) 287-3136	Clarence Brantley	Scott Hilton	Toby Bighorse	Sharon Casebolt	. . .	Russell Cottle
Ottawa	C	33	(918) 542-9408	James Leake	. . .	Carol Randall	. . .	. . .	Jack Harkins
Pawnee	C	16	(918) 762-2732	Royce Brien	. . .	Marcelee Welch	. . .	. . .	Dwight Woodrell
Payne	C	68	(405) 624-9300	Carl Moreland	. . .	Sherri Schieffer	. . .	. . .	Carl Hiner
Pittsburg	* C	43	(918) 423-6865	Randy Crone	. . .	Debbie Burch	. . .	. . .	Jerome Amaranto
Pontotoc	C	35	(580) 332-1425	. . .	. . .	. . .	. . .	. . .	. . .
Pottawatomie	C	65	(405) 273-4305	Bob Guinn	. . .	Nancy Bryce	Steve Sanders	. . .	Weldon Cantrell
Pushmataha	C	11	(580) 298-2512	Eddy McIntosh	. . .	Albert Brown	. . .	. . .	Elvin Flood
Roger Mills	C	3	(580) 497-3365	. . .	. . .	. . .	. . .	. . .	. . .
Rogers	C	70	(918) 341-0585	. . .	. . .	. . .	. . .	. . .	. . .
Seminole	C	24	(405) 257-2501	Herbert Williams	. . .	Tim Anderson	. . .	. . .	Charles Sisco
Sequoyah	C	38	(918) 775-5539	. . .	. . .	. . .	. . .	. . .	. . .
Stephens	C	43	(580) 255-8460	. . .	. . .	. . .	. . .	. . .	. . .
Texas	C	20	(580) 338-3233	Gary Winters	. . .	. . .	. . .	. . .	Arnold Peoples
Tillman	CE	9	(580) 335-2156	Joe Don Dickey	. . .	Jerri Boyd	. . .	. . .	Billy Hanes
Tulsa	C	563	(918) 596-5000	. . .	. . .	. . .	. . .	Terry Tallent	. . .
Wagoner	C	57	(918) 485-7780	Jim Hargrove	. . .	Carolyn Kusler	. . .	. . .	Johnny Cannon
Washington	C	48	(918) 337-2820	. . .	. . .	. . .	. . .	. . .	. . .
Washita	C	11	(580) 832-5016	. . .	. . .	. . .	. . .	. . .	. . .
Woods	C	9	(580) 327-0998	. . .	. . .	. . .	. . .	. . .	. . .
Woodward	C	18	(580) 256-8097	. . .	. . .	. . .	. . .	. . .	. . .
OREGON									
Baker	C	16	(541) 523-8200	. . .	. . .	. . .	. . .	. . .	. . .
Benton	C	78	(541) 766-6081	Linda Modrell	. . .	James Morales	Mary Otley	Libet Hatch	James Swinyard
Clackamas	CE	338	(503) 655-8459	. . .	Jonathan Mantay	Sherry Hall	Marc Gonzales	Nancy Drury	Craig Roberts
Clatsop	CE	35	(503) 325-1000	Joe Bakkensen	Scott Derickson	Lori Davidson	Michael Robison	Robin Young	John Raichl
Columbia	C	43	(888) 397-7210	Tony Hyde	. . .	Elizabeth Huser	Paul Downey	Jean Ripa	Phil Derby
Coos	C	62	(541) 396-3121	Beverly Owen	. . .	Terri Turi	. . .	Janis Falcon	Andy Jackson
Crook	C	19	(541) 447-6555	Fred Rodgers	. . .	Dee Berman	Mary Johnson	. . .	. . .
Curry	C	21	(541) 247-7011	Marlyn Schafer	. . .	Renee Kolen	Geoffrey Buchheim	Julie Swift	Lyle Owens
Deschutes	* C	115	(541) 388-6570	. . .	David Kanner	. . .	Marty Wynne	. . .	. . .
Douglas	C	100	(541) 440-4405	Doug Robertson	. . .	Barbara Nielsen	Sandee Correll	Jim Bruce	Chris Brown
Gilliam	C	1	(541) 384-2311	Laura Pryor	. . .	Rena Kennedy	. . .	. . .	Paul Barnett
Grant	CE	7	(541) 575-0059	Dennis Reynolds	William Gibbs	Kathy McKinnon	Kathy Smith	. . .	. . .
Harney	* C	7	(541) 573-6356	Steven Grasty	. . .	Maria Turriaga	. . .	La Dene Hurd	David Glerup
Hood River	CM	20	(541) 386-3970	Chuck Thomsen	David Meriwether	Sandra Berry	Sandra Borowy	Denise Ford	Joe Wampler
Jackson	CM	181	(541) 774-6036	Jack Walker	Danny Jordan	Kathy Beckett	Gary Cadle	. . .	Michael Winters
Jefferson	* C	19	(541) 475-2449	John Hatfield	Jeffrey Rasmussen	Kathy Marston	Kathie Rohde	. . .	Jack Jones
Josephine	C	75	(541) 474-5217	Jim Brock	. . .	Georgette Brown	. . .	Kent Granat	David Daniel
Klamath	CE	63	(541) 883-4296	. . .	. . .	Linda Smith	Michael Long	E. Johnson	Tim Evinger
Lake	C	7	(541) 947-6006	. . .	. . .	Stacie Geaney	DeEtta Vincent	. . .	Phillip McDonald
Lane	CM	322	(541) 682-5606	. . .	William Van Vactor	Annette Newingham	Kaylene Blackburn	Greta Utecht	Russel Burger
Lincoln	C	44	(541) 265-4157	Jean Cowan	. . .	Dana Jenkins	James Weider	. . .	Dennis Dotson
Linn	* C	103	(541) 967-3825	Roger Nyquist	Ralph Wyatt	Steven Druckenmiller	. . .	. . .	Tim Mueller
Malheur	C	31	(541) 473-5183	Russell Hursh	Nancy Moore	Deborah Delong	. . .	. . .	Andrew Bentz
Marion	C	284	(503) 589-3295	. . .	John Lattimer	Alan Davidson	. . .	Theresa Van Dusen	Raul Rameriz
Morrow	* CE	10	(541) 676-5620	Terry Tallman	. . .	Bobbi Childers	Fred Carlson	Karen Wolff	Ken Matlack
Multnomah	C	660	(503) 248-3100	Dianne Lynn	Tony Mounts	Debora Boystad	Dave Boyer	Gail Parnell	Bernie Guisto
Polk	C	62	(503) 623-8173	Mike Propes	Gregory Hansen	Val Unger	. . .	Kim Wallace	Robert Wolfe
Sherman	C	1	(541) 565-3416	Gary Thompson	. . .	Linda Cornie	. . .	. . .	Brad Lohrey
Tillamook	C	24	(503) 842-3403	Gina Firman	. . .	Josephine Veltri	. . .	Craig Schwinck	Tom Dye

Directory 1/10 continued **OFFICIALS IN U.S. COUNTIES 2,500 AND OVER IN POPULATION**

Jurisdiction	Form of govern-ment	2000 Popu-lation (000)	Main telephone number	Chief elected official	Appointed administrator	Clerk of the governing board	Chief financial officer	Director of personnel	Chief law enforcement official
OREGON continued									
Umatilla	C	70	(541) 276-7111	Emile Holeman	Marcia Wells	Jean Hemphill	Dan Leighty	James Barrow	John Trumbo
Union	C	24	(541) 963-1001	John Howard	Marlene Perkins	Nellie Hibbert	Phil Kohfeld	...	Stephen Oliver
Wallowa	C	7	(541) 426-4543	Mike Hayward	Gail Tally	Charlotte McIver	...	...	Fred Steen
Wasco	C	23	(541) 296-2276	...	...	...	...	...	...
Washington	* CM	445	(503) 846-8685	Tom Brian	Robert Davis	...	...	...	Robert Gordon
Wheeler	C	1	(541) 763-2400	Jeanne Burch	Jean Perry	Marilyn Garcia	...	...	Craig Ward
Yamhill	C	84	(503) 472-9371	Mary Stern	John Krawczyk	Jan Coleman	...	Steven Mikami	Jack Crabtree
PENNSYLVANIA									
Adams	C	91	(717) 334-6781	Harry Stokes	Brenda Constable	...	Kathy Fissel	David Zobel	Bernard Miller
Allegheny	CE	1281	(412) 350-5300	Jim Roddey	Robert Webb	...	Carmen Torockio	Allison Lee-Mann	Kenneth Fulton
Armstrong	C	72	(724) 543-2500	...	...	...	...	...	...
Beaver	C	181	(724) 728-5700	Beatrice Schulte	Robert Cyphert	...	Connie Javens	S. Richard Darbut	Felix Deluca
Bedford	C	49	(814) 623-4807	...	...	...	...	...	...
Berks	C	373	(610) 478-6119	...	William Dennis	...	...	...	...
Blair	C	129	(814) 695-5541	...	...	...	...	...	...
Bradford	C	62	(717) 265-1727	...	...	...	...	...	...
Bucks	CM	597	(215) 348-6100	Michael Fitzpatrick	David Steinbach	...	Stanley Allen	Jerry Fuqua	Lawrence Michaels
Butler	CE	174	(724) 285-4731	...	...	...	...	Lori Altman	...
Cambria	C	152	(814) 472-1606	Fred Soisson	...	Edward Sholtis	Michael Gelles	...	Robert Kolar
Cameron	C	5	(814) 486-2315	...	...	...	...	...	...
Carbon	CM	58	(570) 325-3611	Wayne Nothstein	Randall Smith	...	Robert Crampsie	...	Dwight Nothstein
Centre	C	135	(814) 355-6748	Vicki Wedler	...	...	Denise Elbell	Francis Bogert	Dennis Nau
Chester	C	433	(610) 344-6280	Colin Hanna	Karen Martynick	Edward Schmid	Caroline Cassels	Thomas Czulewicz	Anthony Sarcione
Clarion	C	41	(814) 226-4000	Donna Hartle	...	Sharon Roxbury	R. Keefer	...	William Peck
Clearfield	C	83	(814) 765-2641	Michael Lytle	...	Lisa McFadden	Claudia Read	Mary Mood	Chester Hawkins
Clinton	C	37	(570) 893-4000	Daniel Vilello	Kathy Conrad	...	...	Gloria Stinson	Charles Ankney
Columbia	C	64	(717) 389-5600	Leroy Diehl	Gail Kipp	...	Norma Beyers	Janet Weeks	Harry Roadarmel
Crawford	C	90	(814) 333-7400	Morris Waid	Marlene Robertson	...	Robyn Sye	...	Francis Schultz
Cumberland	CM	213	(717) 240-6100	Nancy Besch	John Byrne	John Connolly	Gay McGeary	Dan Hartnett	Thomas Kline
Dauphin	C	251	(717) 780-6230	Jeffrey Haste	Robert Burns	...	...	Faye Fisher	Edward Marsico
Delaware	CM	550	(610) 891-4852	...	...	...	...	...	...
Elk	C	35	(814) 776-1161	June Sorg	Peggy Aharrah	...	...	...	...
Erie	CE	280	(814) 451-6000	Rick Schenker	...	...	Tom Lyons	Peter Callan	Robert Merski
Fayette	CE	148	(724) 430-1202	Vincent Vicites	Warren Hughes	Judith Bodkin	Mark Roberts	...	Gary Brownfield
Forest	C	4	(814) 755-3537	Basil Huffman	Virginia Call	...	...	...	Robert Wolfgang
Franklin	C	129	(717) 261-3154	...	...	...	...	...	...
Fulton	* C	14	(717) 485-3691	...	...	...	...	...	...
Greene	C	40	(724) 852-5210	Dave Coder	Gene Lee	...	John Stets	Tracy Zivkovich	Richard Ketchem
Huntingdon	* C	45	(814) 643-3091	R. Dean Fluke	Cinnamon Bair	...	Sherri Rogers	...	William Walters
Indiana	C	89	(724) 465-3805	Bernie Smith	Helen Hill	...	...	Margaret Karp	Donald Beckwith
Jefferson	C	45	(814) 849-1653	Ira Sunderland	...	Julie Coleman	...	Debbie Rodriguez	Thomas Demko
Juniata	C	22	(717) 436-8991	...	...	...	...	...	...
Lackawanna	C	213	(925) 963-6771	Joseph Corcoran	William Jenkins	...	Vince Wiercinski	Anthony Bernardi	Michael Barrasse
Lancaster	CE	470	(717) 299-8000	Paul Thibault	Mark Esterbrook	...	Benjamin Hess	J. Myers	Philip Bomberger
Lawrence	C	94	(412) 656-2164	Daniel Vogler	James Gagliano	...	Maryann Reiter	Susan Quimby	...
Lebanon	C	120	(717) 274-2801	William Carpenter	Jamie Wolgemuth	...	Robert Mettley	Gary Robson	Deirdre Eshleman
Lehigh	CE	312	(717) 782-3130	Jane Ervin	...	Stephen Samuelson	Brian Kahler	...	...
Luzerne	C	319	(570) 825-1500	...	...	Samuel Guesto	...	...	...
Lycoming	CE	120	(570) 327-2200	Rebecca Burke	Fred Marty	William Burd	David Raker	...	Michael Dinges
Mc Kean	* C	45	(814) 887-5571	Clifford Lane	...	Audrey Irons	Dustin Laurie	...	John Pavlock
Mercer	CM	120	(724) 662-3800	Cloyd Brenneman	Kenneth Ammann	...	Tresa Templeton	...	James Epstein
Mifflin	C	46	(717) 248-6733	Susan McCartney	...	Peggy Finkenbiner	...	...	Joseph Bradley
Monroe	CE	138	(570) 420-3434	Mario Scavello	Robert Gress	...	Kenneth Sztukowski	Daniel Hite	Todd Martin
Montgomery	C	750	(610) 278-3052	Michael Marino	Robert Graf	...	Jon Ganser	Peter Leis	Bruce Caster
Montour	C	18	(717) 271-3000	...	...	...	...	...	...
Northampton	CE	267	(610) 559-3000	...	John Conklin	Frank Flisser	...	Peter Regina	Alfred Diomedo
Northumberland	C	94	(570) 988-4100	Allen Cwalina	William Stesney	...	Edward Zack	Walter Kalinoski	Anthony Rosini
Perry	C	43	(717) 582-2131	Mark Keller	...	Sharon Charles	Kathleen Penn	...	Carl Nace
Pike	C	46	(570) 296-7613	Karl Wagner	...	Gary Orben	...	...	Phil Bueki
Potter	C	18	(814) 274-8290	Kenneth Wingo	Cora Thompson	...	...	...	Kenneth Sauley
Schuylkill	* C	150	(570) 622-5570	Frank Staudenmeier	...	Jean Heffner	Gary Hornberger	S. Thomas White	Francis McAndrew
Snyder	C	37	(570) 837-0691	...	...	...	...	...	...
Somerset	C	80	(814) 443-1434	Robert Will	...	...	...	...	Carl Brown
Sullivan	C	6	(570) 946-5201	Betty Reibson	Lynne Strabryla	Naomi English	Kathy Robbins	...	Burton Adams
Susquehanna	C	42	(570) 278-4600	Roberta Kelly	Suzanne Brainard	Mary Evans	...	Sylvia Beamer	Lance Benedict
Tioga	* C	41	(570) 723-8191	Mark Hamilton	Derek Williams	...	...	Brian Morral	John Perry
Union	C	41	(570) 524-8631	William Haas	Diana Robinson	...	...	...	John Schrawder
Venango	C	57	(814) 432-9500	Robert Murray	Denise Jones	...	Tamara Varsek	Connie Hazelton	E. Price
Warren	C	43	(814) 723-7550	...	...	...	...	...	...
Washington	C	202	(724) 228-6738	John Bevec	...	Cathi Kresh	Roger Metcalfe	Michelle Miller-Kotula	Larry Maggi
Wayne	C	47	(717) 253-5970	...	...	...	...	...	...
Westmoreland	CE	369	(724) 830-3780	Richard Vidmer	...	Lana August	Dennis Adams	Betsy Griffin	John Peck
Wyoming	C	28	(570) 836-3200	Tony Litwin	William Gaylord	...	...	...	...
York	C	381	(717) 771-9214	...	Charles Noll	Vickie Glatfelter	...	Sharon Luker	William Hose
SOUTH CAROLINA									
Abbeville	* C	26	(864) 366-6690	Ernest Gunnells	Timothy Moulder	Lynn Sopolosky	Barry Devore	...	Charles Goodwin
Aiken	CM	142	(803) 642-2012	Ronnie Young	J. Killian	...	Terry Bodiford	Dorothy Powell	...
Allendale	C	11	(803) 584-3438	J. Wall	...	Sue Welch	...	...	Frances Coath
Anderson	CM	165	(864) 260-4031	...	Joey Preston	Cathy Phillips	Rita Davis	Kathy Fullbright	Gordon Taylor
Bamberg	CM	16	(803) 245-5191	John Williamson	Lawrence Clark	Rose Shepherd	Booker Patrick	Ruthie Brown	J. Darnell
Barnwell	CM	23	(803) 541-1000	Thomas Williams	Frank Williams	Verger Ashley	Hugh Quattlebaum	...	Joseph Zorn
Beaufort	CM	120	(843) 470-2650	William Newton	Gary Kubic	Suzanne Rainey	Thomas Henrikson	Suzanne Gregory	Phennis Tanner
Berkeley	C	142	(843) 761-6900	...	...	...	Lee Moulder	...	...
Calhoun	CM	15	(803) 874-2435	...	...	...	...	...	...
Charleston	CM	309	(843) 958-4700	Barrett Lawrimore	...	Beverly Craven	Keith Bustraan	Barbara Demarco	James Cannon
Cherokee	CE	52	(864) 487-2560	Lemuel Parris	...	Katie Baines	Michael Vassey	Betty Vernon	Billy Blanton
Chester	CE	34	(803) 385-5133	...	...	...	...	...	...
Chesterfield	CE	42	(843) 623-2535	Bruce Rivers	William Frick	Elizabeth Eddins	...	Peggy Smith	Kenny Welch
Clarendon	CE	32	(803) 435-9654	Dwight Stewart	William Houser	Betty Pritchard	Lynden Anthony	Linda Lemon	Keith Josey

Directory 1/10
continued

OFFICIALS IN U.S. COUNTIES 2,500 AND OVER IN POPULATION

Jurisdiction	Form of govern-ment	2000 Popu-lation (000)	Main telephone number	Chief elected official	Appointed administrator	Clerk of the governing board	Chief financial officer	Director of personnel	Chief law enforcement official
SOUTH CAROLINA continued									
Colleton	C	38	(803) 549-5221	Steven Murdaugh	Douglas Burns	Ruth Mayer	Jeanne Griffin	...	George Malone
Darlington	CE	67	(843) 398-4104	...	...	Jessie Bishop	Phyllis Griffitts	...	Walter Campbell
Dillon	* CE	30	(843) 774-1400	Clarence McRae	William Young	Lisa Gray	...	Winna Miller	Harold Grice
Dorchester	CM	96	(843) 563-0242	Randy Scott	Jason Ward	Sandy Lawley	Tommi Garrick	Anne Ayer	...
Edgefield	* CE	24	(803) 637-4000	Charles Kneece	...	Barbara Stark	Teresa Strom	Lee Anderson	Adell Dobey
Fairfield	CE	23	(803) 635-1415	David Brown	Philip Hinely	Shryll Brown	Annie McDaniel	Callie Bell	Herman Young
Florence	CE	125	(843) 665-3099	...	Richard Starks	Connie Haselden	Kevin Yokim	Bonita Andrews	James Gregg
Georgetown	CE	55	(843) 546-4189	Johnny Morant	Thomas Edwards	Karen Scott	David Parks	...	A. Cribb
Greenville	CM	379	(864) 467-7150	Phyllis Henderson	Joseph Kernell	Theresa Kizer	...	Vivian Anthony	Stephen Loftis
Greenwood	CM	66	(864) 942-8501	...	James Kier	...	...	...	T. C. Smalls
Hampton	* CE	21	(803) 914-2100	Hugh Gray	Sabrena Graham	Aline Newton	Mike Meyer	...	...
Horry	CM	196	(843) 915-5230	Chandler Prosser	Danny Knight	Patricia Hartley	Beth Fryar	Patrick Owens	...
Jasper	CE	20	(843) 726-7702	Avery Cleland	Andrew Fulghum	Judith Frank	Ronald Malphrus	Edith Drayton	Benjamin Riley
Kershaw	CE	52	(803) 425-1500	Steve Kelly	Robert Boland	Mamie Jones	Steve Bratton	...	Stephen McCaskill
Lancaster	* CM	61	(803) 285-1565	Rudy Carter	Steve Willis	Irene Plyler	Veronica Thompson	Lisa Robinson	John Cauthen
Laurens	C	69	(864) 984-5484	...	Ernest Segars	Betty Walsh	...	Columbus Stephens	James Moore
Lee	CE	20	(803) 484-5341	...	...	...	...	...	...
Lexington	CM	216	(803) 785-8000	Todd Cullum	William Brooks	Diana Burnett	Larry Porth	Katherine Doucett	James Metts
Marion	CE	35	(843) 423-8201	...	...	...	...	...	...
Marlboro	C	28	(803) 479-4462	...	Robert Kimrey	William Funderburk	Thomas Carabo	Grover McQueen	William Simon
McCormick	CM	9	(864) 465-2231	Alonzo Harrison	Bruce Cooley	Sheree Bowick	Peggy Trammel	...	George Reid
Newberry	CE	36	(803) 321-2100	Mike Hawkins	...	Jackie Bowers	Debbie Cromer	Tommy Shields	James Foster
Oconee	* C	66	(864) 638-4252	...	Dale Surrett	Elizabeth Hulse	Phyllis Lombard	Kay Olbon	James Singleton
Orangeburg	CM	91	(803) 533-6151	Harry Wimberly	Joseph Clark	Jacqueline Turner	Gloria Breland	Marion Boyd	Larry Williams
Pickens	CE	110	(864) 898-5900	Jennifer Willis	...	Donna Owen	Ralph Guarino	Jennifer Graham	David Stone
Richland	CM	320	(803) 929-6000	...	J. Milton Pope	Barbara Scott	Carrie Neal	T. Hanna	...
Saluda	* C	19	(864) 445-4500	Thomas Horne	Sandra Padget	Karen Whittle	...	Miriam McCoy	Jason Booth
Spartanburg	CE	253	(864) 596-2525	Jeff Horton	Darryl Breed	Deborah Ziegler	Alfred Rickett	Tony Bell	Chuck Wright
Sumter	CE	104	(803) 773-1581	...	...	...	...	...	...
Union	CM	29	(864) 429-1600	...	...	...	...	...	...
Williamsburg	C	37	(843) 354-9321	...	Richard Treme	Lisha Graham	Liz Brown	Jacquelyn Hailes	Kelvin Washington
York	CM	164	(803) 684-8511	Charles Short	...	Rebecca Sellers	Anne Bunton	Lisa Davidson	Bruce Bryant
SOUTH DAKOTA									
Aurora	C	3	(605) 942-7752	...	...	...	...	...	...
Beadle	C	17	(605) 353-8400	Roger Chase	...	...	Connie Muth	...	Tom Beerman
Bennett	C	3	(605) 685-6931	...	...	...	...	...	...
Bon Homme	C	7	(605) 589-4212	Allen Sternhagen	...	Katherine Horacek	...	...	...
Brookings	C	28	(605) 696-8205	...	...	Janet Willmott	...	Stephanie Vogel	Marty Stanwick
Brown	C	35	(605) 626-7110	Tom Fischbach	...	...	...	...	Mark Milbrandt
Brule	* CE	5	(605) 234-4430	Judd Lindquist	...	Judy Busack	Pamela Petrak	...	Darrell Miller
Buffalo	C	2	(605) 293-3217	Lloyd Lutter	...	...	...	Elaine Wulff	Wayne Willman
Butte	C	9	(605) 892-4485	Donald Kivimaki	...	...	Sally Pflaumer	...	Richard Davis
Campbell	C	1	(605) 955-3366	Arlene Odde	...	...	...	Lisa Schaefbauer	Lacey Perman
Charles Mix	C	9	(605) 487-7131	...	...	Monica Walder	Norman Cihak	...	Ray Westendorf
Clark	C	4	(605) 532-5921	Francis Hass	...	Nancy Worth	Kay Mahlen	...	Rob McGraw
Clay	* C	13	(605) 677-7120	Gerald Sommervold	Leo Powell	Ruth Bremer	Kathryn Heles	Carrie Crum	Andrew Howe
Codington	C	25	(605) 882-6297	Ed Spevak	...	Cindy Brugman	Carol Maloney	...	Keith Olson
Corson	* C	4	(605) 273-4229	Dorothy Schuh	...	Jessie VanLishout	...	...	Keith Gall
Custer	* C	7	(605) 673-8173	Joe McFarland	...	...	Chris Schutt	...	...
Davison	C	18	(605) 995-8608	...	...	...	Kathy Goetsch	...	David Miles
Day	C	6	(605) 345-9500	...	...	...	...	...	Douglas Nelson
Deuel	C	4	(605) 874-2330	Darold Hunt	...	...	Pam Lynde	...	Lynn Pederson
Dewey	C	5	(605) 865-3672	Adele Enright	...	Jean Tehle	...	...	Jim Fisher
Douglas	C	3	(605) 724-2423	...	...	...	...	...	...
Edmunds	C	4	(605) 426-6762	...	...	...	...	...	...
Fall River	* C	7	(605) 745-5130	Glen Reaser	...	...	...	...	Jeffrey Tarrell
Faulk	C	2	(605) 598-6224	...	...	...	...	...	...
Grant	C	7	(605) 432-6711	Richard Berens	...	Karen Hooth	Karen Layher	...	Michael McKernan
Gregory	C	4	(605) 775-2664	...	...	...	James Waterbury	...	Charles Wolf
Haakon	* C	2	(605) 859-2800	...	Rita O'Connell	Carol Schofield	Patricia Freeman	...	Larry Hanes
Hamlin	C	5	(605) 783-3201	...	...	...	...	...	...
Hand	C	3	(605) 853-2182	Larry Hurd	...	...	Betty Morford	...	Kurt Hall
Hanson	C	3	(605) 239-4714	...	...	...	...	...	...
Harding	C	1	(605) 375-3313	...	...	...	...	...	...
Hughes	C	16	(605) 773-7451	...	...	...	Shellie Baker	...	Mike Leidholt
Hutchinson	C	8	(605) 387-4212	Gillas Stern	...	Jerome Hoff	...	...	Jack Holden
Hyde	C	1	(605) 852-2519	...	...	Duane Johnson	Connie Conrad	...	Mike Volek
Jackson	C	2	(605) 837-2422	...	...	Harvey Byrd	Vicki Wilson	...	Arlo Madsen
Jerauld	C	2	(605) 539-1202	...	...	...	...	...	...
Jones	C	1	(605) 669-2242	...	...	...	...	...	...
Kingsbury	C	5	(605) 854-3832	Diane Schultz	...	...	...	...	Charles Smith
Lake	C	11	(605) 256-7600	George Vanhove	...	...	Kay Schmidt	...	Roger Hartman
Lawrence	C	21	(605) 578-1941	...	...	...	...	...	Dennis Johnson
Lincoln	C	24	(605) 764-2581	Jim Schmidt	...	...	Paula Feucht	...	Donald Manger
Lyman	C	3	(605) 869-2247	Pam Michalek	...	Tracy Brakke	...	...	Dale Elsen
Marshall	C	4	(605) 448-2401	...	...	Julie Hagen	...	...	Eugene Taylor
Mc Cook	C	5	(605) 425-2791	...	...	...	Geralyn Sherman	...	David Ackerman
Mc Pherson	* C	2	(605) 439-3314	Steven Serr	...	...	...	...	...
Meade	C	24	(605) 347-2360	...	...	...	...	...	...
Mellette	C	2	(605) 259-3291	Alvin Huber	...	...	Julie Dimond	...	Tate Mallory
Miner	C	2	(605) 772-4671	Rollin Schulz	...	...	Cindy Callies	...	Lanny Klinkhammer
Minnehaha	* CM	148	(605) 367-4206	Carol Twedt	Ken McFarland	Sue Roust	...	Nora Buckman	Mike Milstead
Moody	C	6	(605) 997-3161	...	...	...	Jean Larson	...	Jerry Hoffman
Pennington	C	88	(605) 394-2153	Ken Davis	Ron Buskerud	...	Julie Pearson	...	Don Holloway
Perkins	C	3	(605) 244-5624	Mike Schweitzer	...	...	Fern Brockel	...	Kelly Serr
Potter	C	2	(605) 765-9408	...	...	...	...	...	...
Roberts	C	10	(605) 698-7336	Wayne Johnson	...	...	...	...	Neil Long
Sanborn	* C	2	(605) 796-4513	Diane Larson	...	...	...	...	Thomas Fridley
Shannon	* C	12	(605) 745-3996	...	...	...	...	...	Jeff Not Help Him
Spink	* C	7	(605) 472-4580	Gerald Zerbel	...	...	Barbara Lenling	...	Leslie Helm

Directory 1/10 **OFFICIALS IN U.S. COUNTIES 2,500 AND OVER IN POPULATION**
continued

Jurisdiction	Form of govern- ment	2000 Popu- lation (000)	Main telephone number	Chief elected official	Appointed administrator	Clerk of the governing board	Chief financial officer	Director of personnel	Chief law enforcement official
SOUTH DAKOTA continued									
Stanley .... *	C	2	(605) 223-7780	Donald Jacobson	. . .	Beverly Stoeser	Lola Scott	. . .	Brad Rathbun
Sully	C	1	(605) 258-2541	. . .	. . .	. . .	. . .	. . .	. . .
Todd	C	9	(605) 842-3727	Gregg Grimshaw	. . .	Louise Flisram	Kathleen Flakus	. . .	Patrick Swallow
Tripp	C	6	(605) 842-3727	Ray Petersek	. . .	. . .	. . .	. . .	Clifford Schroeder
Turner	CM	8	(605) 297-3153	. . .	. . .	Sheila Hagemann	. . .	. . .	Byron Nogelmeier
Union .... *	C	12	(605) 356-2101	. . .	. . .	. . .	Carol Klumper	. . .	Dan Limoges
Walworth .... *	C	5	(605) 649-7878	. . .	. . .	Susan Eisemann	Gwenn Ackerman	. . .	Duane Mohr
Yankton	C	21	(605) 260-4400	Jerome Bienert	. . .	. . .	Paula Jones	. . .	Dave Hunhoff
Ziebach	C	2	(605) 365-5157	Clinton Farlee	. . .	. . .	Cindy Longbrake	. . .	Robert Menzel
TENNESSEE									
Anderson	CE	71	(865) 457-5400	Rex Lynch	. . .	Jeff Cole	Gail Cook	. . .	Bill White
Bedford	C	37	(931) 684-7944	Jimmy Woodson	. . .	. . .	Angie Petty	. . .	R. Parker
Benton .... *	C	16	(731) 584-6011	Jimmy Wiseman	. . .	. . .	. . .	. . .	Tony King
Bledsoe	C	12	(423) 447-6855	Bill Wheeler	Sheri Pendergrass	. . .	. . .	. . .	Bob Swafford
Blount	C	105	(865) 982-1302	. . .	. . .	. . .	. . .	. . .	. . .
Bradley	C	87	(423) 476-0502	D. Davis	. . .	Donna Simpson	. . .	Michael Willis	Daniel Gilley
Campbell	C	39	(423) 562-2526	Jeff Hall	J. Willoughby	Sue Nance	Jeff Marlow	. . .	Gary Perkins
Cannon	C	12	(615) 563-2320	Robert Gannon	. . .	. . .	. . .	. . .	Kenneth Wetzell
Carroll	C	29	(731) 986-1936	Kenny McBride	. . .	. . .	. . .	. . .	Bendall Bartholomew
Carter	C	56	(423) 542-1801	Raymond Fair	. . .	Mary Gouge	Jason Cody	. . .	John Henson
Cheatham	C	35	(615) 792-4316	William Orange	. . .	William Hall	Franklin Luppe	Clyde White	John Holder
Chester	C	15	(731) 989-5672	Troy Kilzer	. . .	Johnny Garner	Lance Beshires	. . .	Paul Hodges
Claiborne	C	29	(423) 626-5236	. . .	. . .	. . .	. . .	. . .	. . .
Clay	CE	7	(931) 243-2161	Frank Halsell	. . .	Patricia Hix	. . .	. . .	Cecil Anderson
Cocke	C	33	(423) 623-8791	Charles Moore	Bettye Carver	Janice Butler	Anne Williams	. . .	David Ramsey
Coffee	C	48	(931) 723-5100	David Pennington	. . .	. . .	Marianna Edinger	. . .	Stephen Graves
Crockett	C	14	(731) 696-5460	E. Dove	. . .	. . .	Gary Spraggins	. . .	Troy Klyce
Cumberland	C	46	(931) 484-6165	Brock Hill	. . .	Pete Stubbs	Nathan Brock	. . .	Butch Burgess
De Kalb	C	17	(615) 597-5175	. . .	Larry Webb	John Thweatt	. . .	. . .	Kenneth Pack
Decatur	C	11	(731) 852-2131	Kenneth Broadway	. . .	Randy Pope	. . .	. . .	Ronald Kenner
Dickson	C	43	(615) 789-7003	Linda Frazier	. . .	Phillip Simons	. . .	. . .	Tom Wall
Dyer	C	37	(731) 286-7800	. . .	. . .	. . .	. . .	. . .	. . .
Fayette	C	28	(901) 465-5202	Rhea Taylor	. . .	Dell Graham	. . .	. . .	Bill Kelley
Fentress	C	16	(931) 879-7713	. . .	. . .	. . .	. . .	. . .	. . .
Franklin	C	39	(931) 967-2905	Montgomery Adams	. . .	Nina Tucker	Joyce Miller	. . .	Mike Foster
Gibson	C	48	(731) 855-7613	Ronnie Riley	. . .	. . .	. . .	. . .	Joe Shepard
Giles	C	29	(931) 363-5300	William Wakefield	. . .	Carol Wade	Judy Roberts	. . .	Eddie Bass
Grainger	C	20	(865) 828-3513	Michael Hammer	. . .	Barbara Jackson	. . .	. . .	Richard McElhaney
Greene	C	62	(423) 798-1775	. . .	. . .	. . .	. . .	. . .	. . .
Grundy	C	14	(931) 692-3718	Michael Partin	. . .	Jimmy Rogers	Beverly Myers	. . .	Robert Meeks
Hamblen	C	58	(423) 586-1931	David Purkey	. . .	Linda Wilder	. . .	Sonia Miller	Otto Purkey
Hamilton	C	307	(423) 209-6180	Claude Ramsey	Jeannine Alday	William Knowles	Louis Wright	Rebecca Hunter	William Long
Hancock	C	6	(423) 733-4341	. . .	. . .	. . .	. . .	. . .	. . .
Hardeman	C	28	(731) 658-3266	. . .	. . .	. . .	. . .	. . .	. . .
Hardin	C	25	(731) 925-9078	Kevin Davis	. . .	Connie Stephens	. . .	. . .	Sammy Davidson
Hawkins	C	53	(423) 272-7359	Crockett Lee	. . .	Carroll Jenkins	. . .	. . .	William Rimer
Haywood	C	19	(731) 772-1432	John Sharpe	. . .	Ann Medford	William Howse	. . .	Melvin Bond
Henderson	C	25	(731) 968-0122	. . .	. . .	. . .	. . .	. . .	. . .
Henry	C	31	(731) 642-5212	Brent Greer	Faye Scott	Jerry Bomar	. . .	. . .	David Bumpus
Hickman	C	22	(931) 729-2492	. . .	. . .	. . .	. . .	. . .	. . .
Houston	C	8	(931) 289-3633	George Clark	Ann Lewis	Robert Brown	Annette Baggett	. . .	Kenneth Barnes
Humphreys	C	17	(931) 296-7795	. . .	. . .	. . .	. . .	. . .	. . .
Jackson	C	10	(931) 268-9888	. . .	. . .	. . .	. . .	. . .	. . .
Jefferson	C	44	(865) 397-3800	Gary Holiway	Doug Moody	Rick Farrar	. . .	. . .	David Davenport
Johnson	C	17	(423) 727-9696	Dick Grayson	. . .	. . .	Peggy Doine	. . .	. . .
Knox	C	382	(865) 215-2321	Michael Ragsdale	William Arms	. . .	John Werner	Frances Fogerson	Timothy Hutchison
Lake	C	7	(731) 253-7382	Macie Roberson	. . .	Jo Ann Mills	. . .	. . .	Paul Jones
Lauderdale	C	27	(731) 635-3500	. . .	. . .	. . .	. . .	. . .	. . .
Lawrence	C	39	(931) 762-7700	Ametra Bailey	. . .	Chuck Kizer	Teresa Purcell	. . .	William Dorning
Lewis	CE	11	(931) 796-3378	Kenneth Turnbow	Johnny Clayton	Sandra Clayton	. . .	. . .	Dwayne Kilpatrick
Lincoln	C	31	(931) 433-2454	. . .	. . .	. . .	. . .	. . .	. . .
Loudon	C	39	(865) 458-4664	. . .	. . .	Riley Wampler	. . .	. . .	. . .
Macon	C	20	(615) 666-2363	Shelvy Linville	Tammy Russell	. . .	Anita Hesson	Alecia King	Mark Gammons
Madison	C	91	(865) 397-3800	James Leech	Regetta Nelson	Freddie Pruitt	Gary Ligon	Tony White	David Woolfork
Marion	C	27	(423) 942-2552	Howell Moss	. . .	Patsy Hudson	. . .	. . .	Jim Webb
Marshall	CE	26	(931) 359-1279	. . .	. . .	. . .	. . .	. . .	. . .
Maury .... *	C	69	(931) 375-2400	James Bailey	. . .	Nancy Thompson	Malinda Stanford	Shirley Harmon	Enoch George
Mc Minn	CE	49	(423) 745-7634	Ronald Banks	. . .	Helen Haskins	Ed Fiegle	. . .	Steve Frisbie
Mc Nairy	C	24	(731) 645-3472	Mike Smith	Fairy Hunter	Ronnie Price	Billy Wolfe	. . .	Paul Ervin
Meigs	C	11	(423) 334-5850	Ken Jones	. . .	Janie Rowland	. . .	. . .	Walter Hickman
Monroe	C	38	(423) 442-3981	Allan Watson	Jean Samples	LouAnn Carmley	Brian Tallent	. . .	Doug Watson
Montgomery	C	134	(931) 648-5715	Douglas Weiland	. . .	. . .	Rachel Reddick	Michael Moore	Norman Lewis
Moore	C	5	(931) 759-7076	. . .	. . .	. . .	. . .	. . .	. . .
Morgan	CE	19	(423) 346-6288	Larry Kilby	. . .	. . .	Brian Leopper	. . .	. . .
Obion	C	32	(731) 885-9611	. . .	. . .	. . .	. . .	. . .	. . .
Overton	CE	20	(931) 823-5639	. . .	. . .	. . .	. . .	. . .	. . .
Perry	C	7	(931) 589-2216	. . .	. . .	. . .	. . .	. . .	. . .
Pickett	C	4	(931) 864-3798	. . .	. . .	. . .	. . .	. . .	. . .
Polk	C	16	(423) 338-2841	. . .	. . .	. . .	. . .	. . .	. . .
Putnam .... *	CE	62	(931) 526-2161	. . .	. . .	. . .	. . .	. . .	. . .
Rhea	C	28	(423) 775-7803	Billy Patton	Lorraine Phillips	Linda Shaver	. . .	. . .	Mike Neah
Roane	C	51	(865) 376-5578	Kenneth Yager	. . .	Dorothy Marshall	. . .	. . .	David Haggard
Robertson	C	54	(615) 384-0202	Howard Bradley	. . .	Susan Atchley	. . .	. . .	Gene Bollinger
Rutherford	C	182	(615) 898-7795	Nancy Allen	Paul Long	Georgia Lynch	. . .	. . .	Truman Jones
Scott	C	21	(423) 663-2355	. . .	. . .	. . .	. . .	. . .	. . .
Sequatchie	C	11	(423) 949-3479	David Barker	. . .	Charlotte Cagle	. . .	. . .	Ronnie Hitchcock
Sevier	C	71	(865) 453-6136	. . .	. . .	. . .	. . .	. . .	. . .
Shelby	CE	897	(901) 545-4342	A. C. Wharton	John Fowlkes	Jayne Creson	James Huntzicker	Paul Boyd	Mark Luttrell
Smith .... *	C	17	(615) 735-2294	Michael Nesbitt	. . .	James Norris	. . .	. . .	Ronnie Lankford
Stewart	C	12	(931) 232-3100	Rickie Joiner	. . .	Jimmy Fitzhugh	. . .	. . .	John Vinson

Directory 1/10
continued

OFFICIALS IN U.S. COUNTIES 2,500 AND OVER IN POPULATION

Jurisdiction		Form of govern-ment	2000 Popu-lation (000)	Main telephone number	Chief elected official	Appointed administrator	Clerk of the governing board	Chief financial officer	Director of personnel	Chief law enforcement official
TENNESSEE continued										
Sullivan	*	C	153	(423) 323-6417	Steve Godsey	...	Jean Gammon	Larry Bailey	Gayvern Moore	J Wayne Anderson
Sumner	*	C	130	(615) 442-1160	R. J. Thompson	...	...	Rachel Nichols	Ann Whiteside	Bob Barker
Tipton		C	51	(901) 476-0219	...	...	...	...	...	...
Unicoi		C	17	(423) 743-9391	Larry Rose	...	...	...	...	David Harris
Union		CE	17	(865) 992-3061	...	...	...	...	...	...
Van Buren		C	5	(931) 946-2314	...	...	...	...	...	...
Warren		C	38	(931) 473-2505	...	...	...	...	...	...
Washington		C	107	(423) 753-1666	...	...	...	...	...	...
Wayne		C	16	(931) 722-3653	Gilda Collie	...	Joey Horton	...	...	Carl Skelton
Weakley		C	34	(731) 364-5413	...	...	...	...	...	...
White		C	23	(931) 836-3216	Herd Sullivan	...	Connie Jolley	Keith Ryder	...	James O'Conner
Williamson		C	126	(615) 790-5700	Rogers Anderson	...	...	David Coleman	Michael Weber	Ricky Headley
Wilson		C	88	(615) 443-2630	...	...	...	...	...	...
TEXAS										
Anderson		C	55	(903) 723-7402	...	...	Wanda Burke	...	...	...
Andrews		C	13	(915) 524-1401	Richard Dolgener	...	Bubba Hoermann	Rod Noble	...	Sam Jones
Angelina		C	80	(936) 634-5413	Joe Berry	...	JoAn Chastain	Jesse Austin	...	David Henson
Aransas		CE	22	(361) 790-0124	Glenn Guillory	...	Peggy Friebele	...	...	Mark Gilliam
Archer		C	8	(940) 574-4811	Paul Wylie	...	Jane Ham	...	...	Melvin Brown
Armstrong		C	2	(806) 226-3221	Edwin Reed	...	Joe Reck	Ronald Patterson	...	Carmella Jones
Atascosa	*	C	38	(830) 769-3093	Diana Bautista	...	Diane Gonzales	Staci Jones	...	Tommy Williams
Austin		C	23	(979) 865-5911	Carolyn Bilski	...	Carrie Gregor	Betty Jez	...	R. Burger
Bailey		C	6	(806) 272-3077	Marilyn Cox	...	Sherri Harrison	...	...	Richard Wills
Bandera		C	17	(830) 796-3781	Richard Evans	...	Bernice Bates	...	...	James MacMillan
Bastrop		C	57	(512) 332-7201	Ronnie McDonald	...	Shirley Wilhelm	Jim Wither	Robert Pena	Richard Hernandez
Baylor		C	4	(940) 888-3553	James Coltharp	...	Clara Coker	...	...	Bob Elliott
Bee		C	32	(361) 362-3200	...	...	Mirella Davis	Susana Moron	...	Carlos Carrizales
Bell		C	237	(254) 933-5118	Jon Burrows	...	Vada Sutton	Donna Eakin	...	Dan Smith
Bexar		C	1392	(210) 335-2545	Nelson Wolff	...	M. Montemayor	David Smith	Veronica Sauceda	Ralph Lopez
Blanco		C	8	(830) 868-4266	George Byars	...	Dorothy Uecker	Doris Cage	...	William Elsbury
Borden		C	..	(806) 756-4391	...	...	...	...	...	...
Bosque		C	17	(254) 435-2382	Cole Word	Jane Murphey	Betty Outlaw	...	...	Charles Jones
Bowie		C	89	(903) 628-6700	James Carlow	...	...	...	...	James Prince
Brazoria		C	241	(979) 849-5711	...	...	...	...	...	...
Brazos		C	152	(979) 775-7400	Alvin Jones	...	...	John Reynolds	...	Christopher Kirk
Brewster		C	8	(915) 837-2412	...	...	...	...	...	...
Briscoe		C	1	(806) 823-2131	Loyd Nance	...	Bena Hester	...	...	Jeff Fuston
Brooks	*	C	7	(361) 325-5604	Raul Ramirez	Mary Ann Pulido	Frutoso Garza	Corina Molina	...	Baldemar Lozano
Brown		C	37	(915) 643-3254	...	...	...	...	...	...
Burleson		C	16	(979) 567-2305	...	...	...	...	...	...
Burnet		C	34	(512) 756-5420	Martin McLean	...	Janet Parker	...	...	Joe Pollock
Caldwell		C	32	(512) 398-1828	H Wright	...	Nina Sells	...	...	Daniel Law
Calhoun		C	20	(361) 553-4610	Arlene Marshall	...	Janice Paul	Ben Comiskey	...	Burnard Browning
Callahan		C	12	(915) 854-1399	Roger Corn	...	Jeanie Bohannon	...	...	Eddie Curtis
Cameron		C	335	(956) 544-0827	Gilberto Hinojosa	...	...	Xavier Villarreal	Manuel Villarreal	...
Camp		C	11	(903) 856-3845	Preston Combest	...	Elaine Young	...	...	Charles Elonger
Carson		C	6	(806) 537-3622	...	...	...	...	...	...
Cass		C	30	(903) 756-5181	Charles McMichael	...	Jannis Mitchell	Carol Cox	...	Paul Boone
Castro		CE	8	(806) 647-3338	Irene Miller	...	Joyce Thomas	Maretta Smithson	...	C. D. Fitzgerald
Chambers		C	26	(409) 267-8295	Frank Sylvia	Robert Sparks	Norma Rowland	Bonita McMurrey	...	Monroe Kreuzer
Cherokee		CM	46	(903) 683-2350	...	...	...	...	...	...
Childress		C	7	(940) 937-2221	...	...	...	...	...	...
Clay		C	11	(940) 538-5001	Kenneth Liggett	...	Kay Hutchison	...	...	Paul Benning
Cochran		C	3	(806) 266-5508	Robert Yeary	...	Rita Tyson	Danny Wiseley	...	Wallace Stalcup
Coke		C	3	(915) 453-2641	...	Stover Taylor	Mary Grim	...	...	Rick Styles
Coleman		C	9	(915) 625-4218	...	...	...	...	...	...
Collin		C	491	(972) 548-4606	Ronald Harris	Bill Bilyeu	...	Rodney Rhoades	Cynthia Jacobson	Terry Box
Collingsworth		C	3	(806) 447-2408	...	...	Jackie Johnson	...	...	Russell Lee
Colorado		C	20	(979) 732-2604	Al Jamison	Raymie Kana	Darlene Hayek	...	...	Reinhard Wied
Comal		CE	78	(830) 620-5510	Danny Scheel	...	Joy Streater	David Renken	Bob Grazioli	Bob Holder
Comanche		C	14	(915) 356-2466	...	...	...	...	...	...
Concho		C	3	(915) 732-4321	...	...	Barbara Hoffman	...	...	William Fiveash
Cooke		C	36	(940) 668-5433	...	...	...	...	...	...
Coryell		C	74	(254) 865-5911	...	...	Jan Irons	...	...	Kenneth Burns
Cottle		C	1	(806) 492-3613	...	...	Jan Irons	...	...	Kenneth Burns
Crane		CE	3	(432) 558-1100	John Farmer	...	Judy Crawford	Mindy Edmiston	...	Danny Simmons
Crockett		C	4	(915) 392-2965	...	...	...	...	...	...
Crosby	*	C	7	(806) 675-2241	Davey Abell	...	Betty Pierce	David Burke	...	Lavoice Riley
Culberson		C	2	(915) 283-2059	...	John Conoly	Linda McDonald	Francisco Gomez	...	Glenn Humphries
Dallam		C	6	(806) 244-2450	David Field	...	Lu Taylor	...	...	Bruce Scott
Dallas		C	2218	(214) 653-6067	Margaret Keliher	Jon Clemson	Paula Stephens	Ryan Brown	Mattye Taylor	James Bowles
Dawson		C	14	(806) 872-7544	Sam Saleh	Don Stephens	Gloria Vera	Gene Defee	...	John Garcia
De Witt		C	20	(361) 275-2116	Ben Prause	...	Elva Petersen	Barbara Martin	...	Gary Edwards
Deaf Smith		C	18	(806) 364-1451	...	...	...	...	...	...
Delta		C	5	(903) 395-3030	Hugh Whitney	Clarica Burns	Patsy Barton	...	...	Benny Fisher
Denton		C	432	(940) 349-3080	Mary Horn	Patricia Larson	Cynthia Mitchell	James Wells	Amy Phillips	Weldon Lucas
Dickens		C	2	(806) 623-5532	...	...	...	...	...	...
Dimmit		CE	10	(830) 876-3569	...	...	...	...	...	...
Donley		C	3	(806) 874-2328	Jack Hall	...	Fay Vargas	...	...	Jimmy Thompson
Duval		C	13	(361) 279-3322	...	...	...	...	...	...
Eastland		C	18	(254) 629-1263	...	...	Cathy Jentho	Loretta Key	...	...
Ector		C	121	(915) 498-4025	James Jordan	...	Barbara Bedford	David Austin	Patricia Mac Allister	Reginald Yearwood
Edwards		C	2	(830) 683-2235	...	...	...	...	...	...
El Paso		C	679	(915) 546-2218	Dolores Briones	James Manley	Waldo Alarcon	Edward Dion	Robert Almanzan	Leo Samaniego
Ellis		C	111	(972) 825-5126	Chad Adams	...	...	Michael Navarro	...	...
Erath		C	33	(254) 965-1452	Tab Thompson	James Young	Nelda Crockett	...	...	Tommy Bryant
Falls		C	18	(254) 883-1426	Thomas Sehon	...	Frances Braswell	...	...	Benell Kirk
Fannin	*	C	31	(903) 583-7451	Butch Henderson	...	Tammy Rich	...	...	Kenneth Moore
Fayette		C	21	(979) 968-6469	Edward Janecka	...	Carolyn Roberts	Dan Von Rosenberg	...	Keith Korenek

OFFICIALS IN U.S. COUNTIES 2,500 AND OVER IN POPULATION

Jurisdiction	Form of govern-ment	2000 Popu-lation (000)	Main telephone number	Chief elected official	Appointed administrator	Clerk of the governing board	Chief financial officer	Director of personnel	Chief law enforcement official
TEXAS continued									
Fisher	C	4	(325) 776-3257	Marshal Bennett	Betty Vaught	Patricia Thomson	...	...	Mickey Counts
Floyd	C	7	(806) 983-4900	William Hardin	...	Marilyn Holcomb	...	...	Billy Gilmore
Foard	* C	1	(940) 684-1365	Charlie Bell	...	Pat Aydelott	...	...	...
Fort Bend	C	354	(281) 341-8619	...	...	...	...	...	...
Franklin	C	9	(903) 537-2342	Gerald Hubbell	...	Betty Crane	...	...	...
Freestone	C	17	(903) 389-2635	...	...	...	...	...	...
Frio	C	16	(830) 334-2154	Carlos Garcia	...	Gloria Cubriel	...	...	...
Gaines	* CE	14	(432) 758-5411	Tom Keyes	...	...	...	...	Jon Key
Galveston	C	250	(409) 762-8621	...	...	...	...	Rosa Franco	...
Garza	* C	4	(888) 257-1287	Lee Norman	...	James Plummer	...	...	Cliff Laws
Gillespie	C	20	(830) 997-7502	Mark Stroeher	...	Mary Lynn Rusche	Nathan Craddock	...	Milton Jung
Glasscock	C	1	(915) 354-2415	...	...	...	...	...	...
Goliad	C	6	(512) 645-3337	...	...	...	...	...	...
Gonzales	C	18	(830) 672-6397	David Bird	...	Lee Riedel	...	...	Glen Sachtleben
Gray	C	22	(806) 669-8001	Richard Peet	Elaine Morris	Wanda Carter	...	...	Don Copeland
Grayson	C	110	(903) 813-4091	...	...	...	James Rivers	Lee Salinas	J. Keith Gary
Gregg	C	111	(903) 758-6181	...	...	...	...	...	...
Grimes	C	23	(936) 873-2111	...	...	David Pasket	Joy Dymke	Phillis Allen	Donald Sowell
Guadalupe	CE	89	(830) 303-4188	Mike Wiggins	...	Teresa Kiel	Kristen Klein	...	...
Hale	C	36	(806) 291-5210	...	...	Deborah Williams	...	...	David Mull
Hall	C	3	(806) 259-2511	Kenneth Dale	...	...	...	...	Robert McGuire
Hamilton	C	8	(254) 386-3518	...	...	...	...	...	...
Hansford	* C	5	(806) 659-4100	Benny Wilson	Cindy Scribner	Kim Vera	...	...	Gary Evans
Hardeman	C	4	(940) 663-2911	Kenneth McNabb	...	Linda Walker	...	...	Randy Akers
Hardin	C	48	(409) 246-5130	Billy Caraway	...	Glenda Alston	Freddie Barclay	...	Ed Cain
Harris	C	3400	(713) 755-8140	Robert Eckels	...	Beverly Kaufman	Barbara Schott	Joyce Cambric	Tommy Thomas
Harrison	* C	62	(903) 923-4018	Wayne McWhorter	Marc Palmer	Patricia Cox	...	Velma McGlothin	William McCool
Hartley	CE	5	(806) 235-3572	Ronnie Gordon	...	Diane Thompson	...	...	Johnny Williams
Haskell	C	6	(940) 864-2851	David Davis	...	Rhonda Moeller	...	...	...
Hays	C	97	(512) 393-2215	...	...	...	...	...	...
Hemphill	C	3	(806) 323-6521	Bob Gober	...	Davene Hendershot	...	...	Billy Bowen
Henderson	C	73	(903) 675-6119	David Holstein	Wesley Johnston	Gwen Moffeit	Karen Smith	...	Ronny Brownlow
Hidalgo	C	569	(956) 318-2660	...	...	...	...	...	...
Hill	C	32	(254) 582-4060	Kenneth Davis	Susan Swilling	Ruth Pelham	...	...	Brent Button
Hockley	C	22	(806) 894-6070	Larry Sprowls	Gene Rush	Donna Stanley	...	...	Donald Caddell
Hood	C	41	(817) 579-3208	Don Cleveland	...	Lynn Dewberry	Lawrence Levine	...	William Hardin
Hopkins	C	31	(903) 885-1178	...	...	...	...	...	...
Houston	C	23	(936) 544-3255	R. Von Doenhoff	Louis Cook	Bridgett Lamb	...	...	Darrel Bobbitt
Howard	* C	33	(432) 264-2218	Mark Barr	...	...	Jackie Olson	...	Dale Walker
Hudspeth	C	3	(915) 369-3511	Billy Love	...	Patricia Bramblett	James Peace	...	Jerry Kresta
Hunt	C	76	(903) 408-4100	...	...	Linda Brooks	...	...	...
Hutchinson	C	23	(806) 878-4010	Jack Worsham	...	Beverly Turner	...	...	Guy Rowh
Irion	C	1	(915) 835-4361	...	...	Riba Criner	...	...	Jimmy Mortin
Jack	C	8	(940) 567-2241	...	...	...	...	...	...
Jackson	C	14	(361) 782-3402	Albert Stafford	Carole Darilek	Kenneth McElveen	...	...	Andy Louderback
Jasper	C	35	(409) 384-2461	Joe Folk	Druscilla Miller	Judith Wright	...	Donna Kelley	Ronald McBride
Jeff Davis	C	2	(915) 426-3968	Peggy Robertson	...	Sue Blackley	...	...	Steve Bailey
Jefferson	C	252	(409) 835-8400	Carl Griffith	...	Sandra Walker	James Swain	Cary Erickson	George Woods
Jim Hogg	C	5	(512) 527-3015	...	...	...	...	...	...
Jim Wells	C	39	(361) 668-5706	...	...	...	...	...	...
Johnson	C	126	(817) 556-6305	...	...	...	...	...	...
Jones	C	20	(915) 823-3741	...	...	...	...	...	...
Karnes	C	15	(830) 780-3938	Alfred Pawelek	...	Elizabeth Swize	Arline Matthews	...	...
Kaufman	C	71	(972) 932-4331	...	...	...	...	...	...
Kendall	* C	23	(830) 249-9343	James Gooden	...	Darlene Herrin	...	...	Henry Hodge
Kenedy	C	..	(512) 294-5224	...	...	...	...	...	...
Kent	C	..	(806) 237-3381	...	...	...	...	...	...
Kerr	C	43	(830) 792-2215	...	...	Jannett Pieper	...	...	William Hierholzer
Kimble	C	4	(915) 446-2724	Delbert Roberts	...	Haydee Torres	...	...	...
King	C	..	(806) 596-4411	Royce McLaury	...	Linda Lewis	...	...	Terry Lambeth
Kinney	C	3	(830) 563-2401	Herbert Senne	...	Dora Sandoval	Sandra Fitzpatrick	...	Leland Burgess
Kleberg	C	31	(361) 595-8585	Pete De La Garza	...	Sam Deanda	...	...	Winston Kelly
Knox	C	4	(940) 454-2191	...	...	...	...	...	...
La Salle	C	5	(830) 879-2117	...	...	...	...	...	...
Lamar	C	48	(903) 737-2410	M. Superville	...	Kathy Marlowe	Kevin Parsons	...	B. McCoy
Lamb	* C	14	(806) 385-4222	Wayne Whiteaker	...	Bill Johnson	...	...	Jerry Collins
Lampasas	* C	17	(512) 556-8271	...	W. Boultinghouse	Connie Hartmann	...	...	Gordon Morris
Lavaca	C	19	(512) 798-2301	...	...	...	...	...	...
Lee	C	15	(979) 542-3178	Evan Gonzales	...	Carol Dismukes	...	...	Joe Goodson
Leon	C	15	(903) 536-2331	Byron Ryder	...	Carla McEachern	Donald Doucet	...	Larry Watson
Liberty	C	70	(936) 336-8071	...	...	...	...	...	...
Limestone	C	22	(254) 729-3314	Daniel Burkeen	...	Peggy Beck	Deborah Watson	...	Dennis Wilson
Lipscomb	C	3	(806) 862-3821	Willis Smith	...	Kimberly Blau	...	...	James Robertson
Live Oak	C	12	(361) 449-2733	James Huff	Traginia Smith	Mildred James	Violet Person	...	Larry Busby
Llano	C	17	(325) 247-7730	R. G. Floyd	...	Bette Hoy	...	...	Nathan Garrett
Loving	C	..	(915) 377-2362	Donald Creager	Janie Parker	Beverly Hanson	...	...	Richard Putnam
Lubbock	C	242	(806) 775-1097	Thomas Head	...	Anna Davidson	...	...	Charles Bartley
Lynn	C	6	(806) 561-4222	John Brandon	...	Susan Tipton	...	...	Charles Smith
Madison	C	12	(936) 348-2670	Cecil Neely	Melissa Mosley	...	...	...	Daniel Douget
Marion	C	10	(903) 665-3261	Gene Terry	Shanna Fuquay	Betty Smith	...	...	William McCay
Martin	C	4	(915) 756-3631	Charles Blocker	...	Susan Hull	H. Howard	...	C. Welling
Mason	C	3	(325) 347-5556	Jerry Bearden	...	B. Langehennig	...	...	Clint Low
Matagorda	C	37	(979) 244-7680	...	...	...	...	...	...
Maverick	C	47	(830) 773-3824	Rogelio Escobedo	...	Sara Montemayor	Carlos Pereda	...	Salvador Rios
Mc Culloch	C	8	(915) 597-0733	Randy Young	...	Tina Smith	...	...	Clyde Howell
Mc Lennan	C	213	(254) 757-5158	James Lewis	...	...	Steve Moore	Terrence Powers	Jack Harwell
Mc Mullen	C	..	(512) 274-3341	...	...	Nell Hodgin	...	Elaine Franklin	W. Potts
Medina	C	39	(830) 741-6000	David Montgomery	Jennifer Adlong	Elva Miranda	...	...	Gilberto Rodriguez
Menard	C	2	(915) 396-4789	Charles Childers	...	Elsie Maserang	...	...	Clay Wagner
Midland	CE	116	(432) 688-4310	William Morrow	...	Shauna Brown	...	...	Gary Painter

Directory 1/10
continued

OFFICIALS IN U.S. COUNTIES 2,500 AND OVER IN POPULATION

Jurisdiction	Form of govern-ment	2000 Popu-lation (000)	Main telephone number	Chief elected official	Appointed administrator	Clerk of the governing board	Chief financial officer	Director of personnel	Chief law enforcement official
TEXAS continued									
Milam	C	24	(254) 697-6596	Frank Summers	...	La Verne Soefje	Jeanie Hrozek	...	Charles West
Mills	* C	5	(325) 648-2222	Robert Lindsey	...	Carolyn Foster	...	...	Douglas Storey
Mitchell	C	9	(325) 728-8356	Ray Mayo	...	Debby Carlock	Susan Buckalew	...	Patrick Toombs
Montague	C	19	(940) 894-2401	James Kittrell	...	Gayle Edwards	Brenda Milligan	...	Chris Hamilton
Montgomery	C	293	(936) 756-0561	Alan Sadler	...	Mark Turnbull	Linda Breazeale	Diane Bass	Tommy Gage
Moore	C	20	(806) 935-5588	Kari Campbell	...	Brenda McKanna	...	...	J. DeArmond
Morris	C	13	(903) 645-3691	J. Jennings	...	Vicki Camp	...	...	Charles Blackburn
Motley	C	1	(806) 347-2334	Ed Smith	...	Kate Hurt	...	...	Jim Meador
Nacogdoches	C	59	(936) 560-7755	Susan Kennedy	Clara Flores	Carol Wilson	...	...	Thomas Kerss
Navarro	C	45	(903) 654-3090	...	...	...	...	...	...
Newton	C	15	(409) 379-5691	Truman Dougharty	...	Mary Cobb	...	...	Wayne Powell
Nolan	C	15	(915) 235-2263	Tim Fambrough	...	Pat McGowan	Judy Kasper	...	Jim Kelly
Nueces	C	313	(361) 888-0111	Richard Borchard	Edward Castoria	Ernest Briones	Margaret Hayes	Elsa Saenz	Larry Olivares
Ochiltree	C	9	(806) 435-8075	...	...	...	...	...	...
Oldham	C	2	(806) 267-2607	Don Allred	...	Rebecca Groneman	...	...	David Medlin
Orange	C	84	(409) 883-7740	Carl Thibodeaux	...	...	...	...	Michael White
Palo Pinto	C	27	(940) 659-1253	Mickey West	...	...	Sharon Allen	...	Larry Watson
Panola	C	22	(903) 693-3091	John Cordray	...	Mickey Dorman	Sidney Burns	...	Paul Ellett
Parker	C	88	(817) 599-6591	Mark Riley	...	Alice Brunson	...	Jim Thorp	Leonard Brown
Parmer	C	10	(806) 481-3383	...	...	...	...	...	...
Pecos	C	16	(432) 336-3461	Joe Shuster	Kay Hardwick	Judy Deerfield	...	...	Clifton Harris
Polk	* C	41	(936) 327-6802	John Thompson	...	Barbara Middleton	Ray Stelly	Jeanette Montgomery	Kenneth Hammack
Potter	C	113	(806) 349-4835	Arthur Ware	...	Sue Daniel	Kerry Hood	Janie Brown	Michael Shumate
Presidio	C	7	(915) 729-4452	...	...	...	...	...	...
Rains	C	9	(903) 474-9999	Joe Dougherty	...	Linda Wallace	...	...	Richard Wilson
Randall	C	104	(806) 468-5500	Ernie Houdashell	...	Sue Bartolino	Bob Raef	...	Joel Richardson
Reagan	C	3	(915) 884-2233	Mike Elkins	Jane Gay	Terri Pullig	...	...	Efrain Gonzales
Real	C	3	(830) 232-5304	W. Sansom	...	Bella Rubio	...	...	James Brice
Red River	C	14	(903) 427-2401	...	...	...	...	...	...
Reeves	C	13	(915) 445-4503	Jimmy Galindo	...	Dianne Florez	Lynn Owens	Belinda Salcido	Arnulfo Gomez
Refugio	C	7	(361) 526-4223	Roger Fagan	...	Ruby Garcia	Diana Moss	...	James Hodges
Roberts	C	..	(806) 868-3721	Vernon Cook	...	Donna Goodman	DeAnn Williams	...	Dana Miller
Robertson	C	16	(979) 828-3542	...	...	...	...	...	...
Rockwall	C	43	(972) 882-0200	Bill Bell	...	Lisa Constant	John Blackwood	...	Harold Eavenson
Runnels	C	11	(325) 365-2633	Marilyn Egan	...	Elesa Ocker	Darlene Smith	...	William Baird
Rusk	* C	47	(903) 657-0302	Sandra Hodges	Carolyn Walters	Joyce Lewis	Ronald Moody	...	Glenn Deason
Sabine	CE	10	(409) 787-3543	...	...	...	...	...	...
San Augustine	C	8	(936) 275-2762	...	...	...	...	...	...
San Jacinto	C	22	(936) 653-4331	Fritz Faulkner	...	Charlene Vann	...	...	...
San Patricio	C	67	(361) 364-6272	...	...	...	...	Norma Rivera	...
San Saba	C	6	(915) 372-3635	Harlen Barker	...	Kim Wells	...	...	John Wells
Schleicher	C	2	(915) 853-2766	Johnny Griffin	...	Peggy Williams	...	...	David Doran
Scurry	C	16	(915) 573-5332	...	...	...	...	...	...
Shackelford	C	3	(915) 762-2232	Ross Montgomery	...	Cheri Hawkins	...	...	Larry Bonner
Shelby	C	25	(936) 598-3535	Floyd Watson	...	Allison Harbison	Tracey Strong	...	Newton Johnson
Sherman	C	3	(806) 396-2021	...	...	...	...	...	...
Smith	C	174	(903) 590-2600	Larry Raig	...	Judy Carnes	Nancy Braswell	Denise Rebolini	...
Somervell	C	6	(254) 897-2322	...	...	...	...	...	...
Starr	C	53	(956) 487-5221	Jose Martinez	Bernardo Garcia	Maria Gutierrez	Mario Lopez	Elisa Beas	Rene Fuentes
Stephens	C	9	(254) 559-2190	...	...	...	...	...	...
Sterling	C	1	(915) 378-8511	Robert Browne	...	Diane Haar	...	...	Charlie Howard
Stonewall	C	1	(254) 989-3393	...	...	...	...	...	...
Sutton	C	4	(915) 387-2711	Carla Garner	...	Bobbie Smith	Charles Graves	...	Bill Webster
Swisher	CM	8	(806) 995-3504	Harold Keeter	...	Brenda Hudson	...	...	Larry Stewart
Tarrant	CM	1446	(817) 884-1111	Tom Vandergriff	G. Maenius	Suzanne Henderson	S. Tidwell	Gerald Wright	Dee Anderson
Taylor	C	126	(915) 674-1380	...	...	Janice Lyons	B. McDowell	...	...
Terrell	C	1	(432) 345-2391	...	...	...	...	...	...
Terry	C	12	(806) 637-6421	Douglas Ryburn	Alan Bayer	Ann Willis	...	...	...
Throckmorton	C	1	(940) 849-3081	...	...	...	...	...	...
Titus	C	28	(903) 572-8101	Danny Crooks	...	Sherry Mars	Carl Johnson	Milly Wilson	Arvel Shepard
Tom Green	C	104	(915) 659-5202	Michael Brown	...	Elizabeth McGill	Ed Sturivant	Dan Gray	Dan Gray
Travis	C	812	(512) 854-9020	Samuel Biscoe	...	Dana Debeavoir	Christian Smith	Linda Moore Smith	Margo Frasier
Trinity	C	13	(936) 642-1443	...	...	...	...	...	...
Tyler	* C	20	(409) 283-3054	Jacques Blanchette	...	Donece Gregory	...	...	Jessie Wolf
Upshur	C	35	(903) 843-3083	...	...	...	...	...	...
Upton	* C	3	(432) 693-2321	Vikki Bradley	...	Monetta Sides	Elizabeth Craig	...	Dan Brown
Uvalde	C	25	(830) 278-3216	William Mitchell	Valerie Ramos	Lucille Hutcherson	Alice Chapman	Lydia Steele	Beaumont Watkins
Val Verde	C	44	(830) 774-7543	Mike Fernandez	...	Elena Cardenas	Frank Lowe	Gloria Villarreal	D' Wayne Jernigan
Van Zandt	C	48	(903) 567-2551	Jeffrey Fisher	...	Elizabeth Everitt	...	...	R. Burnett
Victoria	C	84	(361) 578-0752	Helen Walker	...	Val Havar	Judy McAdams	Joyce Dean	Michael Ratcliff
Walker	C	61	(936) 436-4910	Sherri Pegoda	...	James Patton	Dan Clower	...	Victor Graham
Waller	C	32	(979) 826-3357	...	...	...	...	...	...
Ward	C	10	(915) 943-3209	...	...	...	...	...	...
Washington	CE	30	(979) 277-6200	...	...	...	...	...	...
Webb	C	193	(956) 721-2500	...	...	Sanra Sanders	Donna Thorton	...	...
Wharton	C	41	(979) 532-4612	Lawrence Naiser	...	Sanra Sanders	Donna Thorton	...	Jess Howell
Wheeler	C	5	(806) 826-5544	...	...	...	...	...	...
Wichita	C	131	(940) 766-8100	Woodrow Gossom	...	Lloyd Lueck	Deborah Stevens	Michele Arseneau	Thomas Callahan
Wilbarger	C	14	(940) 553-2300	Gary Streit	...	Fran McGee	...	...	David Quisenberry
Willacy	C	20	(956) 689-2710	...	...	...	...	...	...
Williamson	C	249	(512) 930-4300	John Doerfler	...	...	...	...	James Wilson
Wilson	C	32	(830) 393-3126	...	...	Eva Martinez	...	...	...
Winkler	C	7	(915) 586-2526	Bonnie Leck	Kay Warren	Sonja Fullen	...	...	Robert Roberts
Wise	C	48	(940) 627-5743	Dick Chase	...	S. Parker-Lemmon	Ann McCuiston	...	David Walker
Wood	C	36	(903) 763-4186	William Alexander	Becky Burford	Brenda Taylor	...	...	Billy Skinner
Yoakum	C	7	(806) 456-8794	Dallas Brewer	Hazel Lowrey	Deborah Rushing	...	...	Don Corzine
Young	C	17	(940) 362-4301	...	...	...	...	...	...
Zapata	C	12	(956) 765-9920	Norma Ramirez	Maria Villarreal	Consuelo Villarreal	Alejandro Ramirez	Sylvia Mendoza	Sigifredo Gonzalez
Zavala	C	11	(830) 374-2442	Joe Luna	...	Oralia Trevino	Carlos Pereda	...	...

OFFICIALS IN U.S. COUNTIES 2,500 AND OVER IN POPULATION

Jurisdiction		Form of govern-ment	2000 Popu-lation (000)	Main telephone number	Chief elected official	Appointed administrator	Clerk of the governing board	Chief financial officer	Director of personnel	Chief law enforcement official
UTAH										
Beaver		C	6	(801) 438-6463	. . .	. . .	. . .	. . .	Peggy Madsen	. . .
Box Elder		C	42	(435) 734-3347	Clark Davis	. . .	LuAnn Adams	Tom Bennett	James Smith	J. Yeates
Cache		C	91	(435) 755-1850	M. Lemon	. . .	Jill Zollinger	Tamra Stones	. . .	G. Nelson
Carbon		C	20	(435) 637-4700	. . .	. . .	. . .	. . .	RaNae Wilde	. . .
Daggett		C	. .	(435) 784-3210	Chad Reed	. . .	Vicky McKee	. . .	G. Baker	Allen Campbell
Davis		C	238	(801) 451-3415	Carol Page	. . .	. . .	Steve Rawlings	Carrie Mascaro	Mervin Gustin
Duchesne		C	14	(435) 738-1144	Larry Ross	. . .	Diane Freston	. . .	. . .	. . .
Emery		C	10	(435) 381-2119	. . .	. . .	. . .	. . .	. . .	. . .
Garfield		C	4	(435) 676-8826	. . .	. . .	. . .	. . .	. . .	Jim Nyland
Grand		C	8	(435) 259-1321	. . .	Judy Bane	Fran Townsend	. . .	. . .	David Benson
Iron		C	33	(435) 477-8332	Dennis Stowell	. . .	David Yardley	Joseph Gubler	Claire Dalton	Alden Orme
Juab		C	8	(435) 623-3410	William Howarth	Michael Seely	Patricia Ingram	. . .	. . .	Lamont Smith
Kane		C	6	(435) 644-2458	Norman Carroll	. . .	. . .	. . .	. . .	. . .
Millard		C	12	(801) 743-6223	. . .	. . .	. . .	. . .	. . .	Gene Ercanbrack
Morgan		C	7	(801) 845-4018	Reed Wilde	. . .	. . .	Stacy Lafitte	Eileen Nelson	. . .
Piute		C	1	(435) 577-2840	. . .	. . .	. . .	. . .	. . .	Dale Stacey
Rich		C	1	(435) 793-2415	Norman Weston	. . .	. . .	Pamela Shaul	. . .	. . .
Salt Lake		C	898	(801) 468-3000	Nancy Workman	Doug Willmore	Sherrie Swensen	Craig Sorensen	Felix McGowan	Mike Lacy
San Juan		C	14	(435) 587-3225	J. Lewis	Richard Bailey	Norman Johnson	John Fellmeth	. . .	Kevin Holman
Sanpete	*	C	22	(435) 835-2142	Claudia Jarrett	. . .	Sandy Neill	Ilene Frischknecht	. . .	Neldon Torgerson
Sevier	*	C	18	(435) 893-0400	Ralph Okerlund	. . .	. . .	Steven Wall	Patricia Langston	David Edmunds
Summit	*	C	29	(435) 336-3247	Sally Elliot	Anita Lewis	Kent Jones	Blake Frazier	Brian Bellamy	Frank Park
Tooele		C	40	(435) 843-3100	Dennis Rockwell	. . .	Dennis Ewing	Michael Jensen	Pamela Ayala	. . .
Uintah		C	25	(435) 781-0770	. . .	. . .	. . .	Danene Jackson	Lana Jensen	James Tracy
Utah		C	368	(801) 851-8158	Jerry Grover	. . .	Kim Jackson	. . .	. . .	Michael Spanos
Wasatch		C	15	(435) 654-3211	. . .	. . .	Brent Titcomb	. . .	. . .	Glenwood Humphries
Washington		C	90	(801) 634-5700	Gayle Aldred	. . .	Calvin Robison	. . .	Alis Ritz	. . .
Wayne		C	2	(435) 836-2731	Clenn Okerlund	. . .	. . .	. . .	. . .	. . .
Weber		C	196	(801) 399-8408	Glen Burton	. . .	Linda Lunceford	. . .	Brad Dee	Brad Slater
VERMONT										
Addison		C	35	(802) 388-7741	. . .	. . .	. . .	. . .	. . .	. . .
Bennington		CE	36	(802) 442-8528	. . .	. . .	. . .	. . .	. . .	. . .
Caledonia		C	29	(802) 748-6600	Roy Vance	. . .	Kathleen Pearl	Edward Senecal	. . .	Michael Bergeron
Chittenden		C	146	(802) 863-3467	. . .	. . .	Diane Lavallee	. . .	. . .	. . .
Essex		C	6	(802) 676-3910	. . .	. . .	. . .	. . .	. . .	. . .
Franklin		C	45	(802) 524-3863	. . .	. . .	. . .	. . .	. . .	. . .
Grand Isle		C	6	(802) 372-8350	. . .	. . .	. . .	. . .	. . .	. . .
Lamoille		C	23	(802) 888-2207	. . .	. . .	. . .	. . .	. . .	. . .
Orange		C	28	(802) 685-4610	Patricia Davis	Donald Hisey	Rodney Ackerman	. . .	. . .	Dennis McClure
Orleans		C	26	(802) 334-5136	Karin Zisselsberger	Kenneth Magoon	Charles Blake	. . .	. . .	David Winslow
Rutland		C	63	(802) 775-4394	. . .	. . .	. . .	. . .	. . .	. . .
Washington		C	58	(802) 828-2091	. . .	. . .	. . .	. . .	. . .	. . .
Windham		C	44	(802) 365-7979	. . .	. . .	. . .	. . .	. . .	. . .
Windsor		C	57	(802) 457-2121	. . .	. . .	. . .	. . .	. . .	. . .
VIRGINIA										
Accomack	*	CE	38	(757) 787-5700	. . .	Steven Miner	Samuel Cooper	Reed Ennis	Linda Warner	Robert Crockett
Albemarle		CM	79	(434) 296-5841	Charlotte Humphris	Robert Tucker	Ella Carey	Melvin Breeden	J. Jennings	John Miller
Alleghany	*	CM	12	(540) 863-6600	Cletus Nicely	John Strutner	Melissa Landis	Susan Myers	. . .	Dale Muterspaugh
Amelia		CE	11	(804) 561-3039	. . .	Thomas Harris	. . .	. . .	. . .	. . .
Amherst		CE	31	(434) 946-9400	Leon Parrish	. . .	Roy Mayo	. . .	. . .	L. J. Ayers
Appomattox	*	C	13	(434) 352-2637	Samuel Carter	Aileen Ferguson	Barbara Williams	. . .	. . .	Oscar Staples
Arlington		CM	189	(703) 228-3000	Paul Ferguson	Ron Carlee	Antoinette Copeland	Jeffrey Bergin	Marcia Foster	Michael Scott
Augusta	*	CE	65	(540) 245-5600	. . .	Patrick Coffield	John Davis	Joseph Davis	Faith Souder	Randall Fisher
Bath		CM	5	(540) 839-7221	Percy Nowlin	. . .	. . .	. . .	. . .	Charles Black
Bedford		CE	60	(540) 586-7601	. . .	Kathleen Guzi	. . .	Susan Crawford	Cheryl Dean	Michael Brown
Bland	*	C	6	(276) 688-4622	Karen Hodock	Jonathan Sweet	. . .	. . .	Carol Hall	Jerry Thompson
Botetourt		CE	30	(540) 473-8220	Terry Austin	Gerald Burgess	. . .	Anthony Zerrilla	. . .	Ronald Sprinkle
Brunswick		CE	18	(434) 848-3107	J. Martin	Charlette Woolridge	Tammy Newcomb	Marilyn Brammer	. . .	James Woodley
Buchanan		CE	26	(276) 935-6500	. . .	. . .	James Berins	Vonda Slone	Correna Roark	Paul Crouse
Buckingham		CE	15	(434) 969-4242	Joe Chambers	Rebecca Carter	. . .	Karl Carter	. . .	Danny Williams
Campbell	*	CM	51	(434) 332-9525	J. D. Puckett	R. Laurrell	Deborah Hughes	Alan Lane	Shameka Wright	Terry Gaddy
Caroline		CE	22	(804) 633-5380	Calvin Taylor	Percy Ashcraft	Ray Campbell	John Sieg	. . .	Homer Johnson
Carroll	*	CE	29	(276) 728-3331	. . .	. . .	Ronald Newman	. . .	. . .	Beverley Washington
Charles City		CM	6	(804) 829-2401	Michael Holmes	. . .	. . .	. . .	. . .	Thomas Jones
Charlotte		CM	12	(434) 542-5117	. . .	Russell Clark	Stuart Fallen	Norma Tuck	. . .	Thierry Dupuis
Chesterfield		CE	259	(804) 748-1551	Arthur Warren	. . .	Lisa Elko	Barry Condrey	Karla Gerner	Clifford Davidson
Clarke		CM	12	(540) 955-5100	A. Dunning	David Ash	James Wood	Thomas Judge	. . .	Harlan Hart
Craig		CE	5	(540) 864-5010	Zane Jones	Richard Flora	. . .	. . .	. . .	Claude Meinhard
Culpeper		CM	34	(540) 727-3427	John Coates	Frank Bossio	. . .	Valerie Lamb	Susanne Taylor	Bobby Hammons
Cumberland		C	9	(804) 492-3625	William Osl	Judy Ownby	. . .	. . .	. . .	Samuel Shands
Dickenson		CE	16	(276) 926-1676	James Moore	Keith Viers	Joseph Tate	Ronald Triplett	Betty Hill	Stanley Clarke
Dinwiddie	*	CE	24	(804) 469-4500	Harrison Moody	. . .	Alma Russell	Glenice Townsend	. . .	John Manger
Essex		CE	9	(804) 443-4331	Margaret Davis	R. Allen	. . .	. . .	. . .	Charlie Fox
Fairfax		CM	969	(703) 324-2000	. . .	Anthony Griffin	Nancy Vehrs	. . .	Peter Schroth	Shannon Zeman
Fauquier		CE	55	(540) 347-8600	Henry Atherton	Paul McCulla	. . .	Janice Bourne	Francine Bouldin	Ryant Washington
Floyd		CE	13	(540) 745-9300	David Ingram	. . .	. . .	Brenda Browning	. . .	W. Overton
Fluvanna		CE	20	(434) 591-1910	Andrew Sheridan	. . .	Alice Jones	Vincent Copenhaver	Phyllis Scott	Robert Williamson
Franklin	*	CM	47	(540) 483-3030	W. Angell	Richard Huff	Alice Hall	Cheryl Shiffler	Paula Nofsinger	Larry Falls
Frederick		CM	59	(540) 665-5600	Richard Shickle	John Riley	Rebecca Hogan	. . .	Patricia Michura	Robin Stanaway
Giles		CE	16	(540) 921-2525	Howard Morris	John Talbott	Scarlet Ratcliffe	Nickie Champion	Cynthia Clements	James Agnew
Gloucester	*	CM	34	(804) 693-4042	. . .	. . .	Dale Burrell	. . .	. . .	Jerry Wilson
Goochland		CM	16	(804) 556-5300	Andrew Pryor	Gregory Wolfrey	. . .	Charles Sturgill	. . .	Scott Haas
Grayson		CM	17	(276) 773-2471	. . .	Donald Young	Marie Durer	Tracy Morris	. . .	Donald Oakes
Greene		CE	15	(434) 985-5201	Steve Catalano	. . .	. . .	Brenda Parson	Alice Whitby	V. Cook
Greensville	*	CM	11	(434) 348-4205	Peggy Wiley	Kenneth Whittington	. . .	. . .	Nan Eddleton	Henry Stanley
Halifax		CE	37	(434) 476-3300	William Fitzgerald	Bryan Foster	. . .	Terry Stone	. . .	Frank Cassell
Hanover		CE	86	(804) 537-6000	John Gordon	Cecil Harris	. . .	. . .	George Cauble	. . .
Henrico		CM	262	(804) 501-4628	David Kaechele	Virgil Hazelett	Barry Lawrence	Reta Busher	. . .	Wyatt Lee
Henry		CE	57	(276) 634-4601	. . .	Ralph Summerlin	. . .	Jimmie Wright	. . .	. . .
Highland		C	2	(540) 468-2447	. . .	. . .	. . .	. . .	. . .	. . .

Directory 1/10 continued   **OFFICIALS IN U.S. COUNTIES 2,500 AND OVER IN POPULATION**

Jurisdiction		Form of govern-ment	2000 Popu-lation (000)	Main telephone number	Chief elected official	Appointed administrator	Clerk of the governing board	Chief financial officer	Director of personnel	Chief law enforcement official
VIRGINIA continued										
Isle Of Wight		CM	29	(757) 357-3191	Stan Clark	W. Caskey	. . .	Liesl DeVary	Emily Haywood	Charles Phelps
James City	*	CM	48	(757) 253-6728	Jay Harrison	Sanford Wanner	. . .	John McDonald	Carol Luckam	Emmett Harmon
King & Queen		CE	6	(804) 785-5975	. . .	Ronald Hachey	. . .	. . .	. . .	Earnest Walton
King George		CE	16	(540) 775-9181	James Howard	R. David	. . .	Donita Harper	. . .	C. Dobson
King William	*	CM	13	(804) 769-4926	C. Thomas Redd	Frank Pleva	Marian White	. . .	. . .	Jeffrey Walton
Lancaster	*	CM	11	(804) 462-5129	Patrick Frere	William Pennell	Constance Kennedy	. . .	. . .	Ronald Crockett
Lee		CM	23	(276) 346-7714	James Sutphin	David Poe	Beverly Anderson	. . .	. . .	Gary Parsons
Loudoun		CM	211	(703) 777-0213	Scott York	Kirby Bowers	Gary Clemens	Mark Adams	Susan Hack	Stephen Simpson
Louisa		CM	25	(540) 967-0401	Fitzgerald Barnes	C. Lintecum	Susan Hopkins	. . .	Sherry Vena	Ashland Fortune
Lunenburg	*	C	13	(434) 696-2142	. . .	Catherine Giorgetti	. . .	. . .	. . .	Wesley Adams
Madison		C	12	(540) 948-6700	. . .	Stephen Utz	. . .	Teresa Jones	. . .	Robert Russell
Mathews	*	CE	9	(804) 725-7172	Geneva Putt	Stephen Whiteway	Eugene Callis	. . .	. . .	Danny Howlett
Mecklenburg		CE	32	(434) 738-6191	. . .	Polly Johnson	. . .	. . .	. . .	. . .
Middlesex		CE	9	(804) 758-4330	. . .	. . .	. . .	. . .	. . .	. . .
Montgomery	*	CM	83	(540) 382-5700	Steve Spradling	B. Goodman	Vickie Swinney	Angela Hill	Karen Edmonds	James Whitt
Nelson		CM	14	(434) 263-7000	Thomas Harvey	Stephen Carter	Judith Smythers	Debra McCann	. . .	Gary Brantley
New Kent	*	CE	13	(804) 966-9861	. . .	John Budesky	. . .	Mary Altemus	Darla Stanley	Farrar Howard
Northampton		CM	13	(757) 678-0440	. . .	Katherine Nunez	Kenneth Arnold	Glenda Miller	. . .	John Robbins
Northumberland		CE	12	(804) 580-7666	Daniel Pritchard	Kenneth Eads	J. Steve Thomas	. . .	. . .	L. Middleton
Nottoway		CE	15	(434) 645-8696	. . .	Ronald Roark	James King	. . .	. . .	Larry Parrish
Orange		CE	25	(540) 672-3313	Roderic Slayton	William Rolfe	Linda Timmon	Valerie Lamb	. . .	Charles Feldman
Page		CE	23	(540) 743-4142	Tommy LaFrance	Mark Belton	. . .	. . .	. . .	Daniel Presgraves
Patrick	*	CE	19	(276) 694-6094	David Young	. . .	Susan Gasterini	. . .	. . .	. . .
Pittsylvania		CE	61	(434) 432-7700	Michael Irby	William Sleeper	. . .	Kimberly Vanderhyde	. . .	Grover Plaster
Powhatan		CM	22	(804) 598-5610	Robert Cosby	Carolyn Cios	. . .	. . .	Stephanie Davis	Lynn Woodcock
Prince Edward		CM	19	(434) 392-8837	William Fore	Mildred Hampton	Machelle Eppes	. . .	. . .	Travis Harris
Prince George	*	CM	33	(804) 722-8600	Joseph Leming	Brenda Garton	Teresa Knott	Sheila Minor	Rose Ford	Edward Frankenstein
Prince William		CM	280	(703) 792-6640	Sean Connaughton	Craig Gerhart	. . .	Christopher Martino	Cleil Fitzwater	Charlie Deane
Pulaski	*	CE	35	(540) 980-7705	Joseph Sheffey	Peter Huber	Gena Hanks	Gordon Jones	. . .	James Davis
Rappahannock	*	C	6	(540) 675-5330	Robert Anderson	John McCarthy	L. Bruce	. . .	. . .	Larry Sherertz
Richmond		CE	8	(804) 333-3415	C. Gray	William Duncanson	. . .	. . .	. . .	Gene Sydnor
Roanoke		CM	85	(540) 772-2006	. . .	Elmer Hodge	Mary Allen	Diane Hyatt	Joe Sgroi	John Cease
Rockbridge		CE	20	(540) 463-4361	W. Edwards	. . .	D. Patterson	R. E. Claytor	. . .	Robert Day
Rockingham	*	CM	67	(540) 564-3000	. . .	Joseph Paxton	. . .	James Allmendinger	Stephen Riddlebarger	Donald Farley
Russell		CE	30	(276) 889-8000	Frank Horton	James Gillespie	Joseph Gilmer	. . .	. . .	Trigg Fields
Scott		CM	23	(276) 386-6521	. . .	. . .	. . .	. . .	. . .	Jerry Broadwater
Shenandoah		CE	35	(540) 459-6165	Beverley Fleming	Vincent Poling	. . .	Garland Miller	. . .	Larry Green
Smyth		CM	33	(276) 783-3298	Joseph Staley	Edwin Whitmore	. . .	. . .	. . .	R. Bradley
Southampton	*	CE	17	(757) 653-3015	Dallas Jones	Michael Johnson	. . .	Julia Williams	. . .	Vernie Francis
Spotsylvania		CE	90	(540) 582-7192	Mary Carter	James Wheeler	. . .	Tammy Petrie	Theresa O'Quinn	Ronald Knight
Stafford		CE	92	(540) 658-8603	. . .	Anthony Romanello	Marsha Beard	. . .	Tammi Ellis	Charles Jett
Surry		CM	6	(757) 294-5271	Reginald Harrison	Tyrone Franklin	. . .	Melissa Motton	. . .	Harold Brown
Sussex		CE	12	(434) 246-5511	Rufus Tyler	Mary Jones	Gary Williams	. . .	. . .	E. Kitchen
Tazewell		CE	44	(276) 988-1200	Donnie Lowe	James Spencer	. . .	Arlene Matney	. . .	Henry Caudill
Warren		CM	31	(540) 636-4600	. . .	Douglas Stanley	. . .	Carolyn Stimmel	Anita Mabie	Daniel McEathron
Washington		CM	51	(276) 676-6204	Joe Derting	Mark Reeter	. . .	. . .	. . .	Fred Newman
Westmoreland		CE	16	(804) 493-0130	William Sydnor	Norman Risavi	Gwynne Chatham	Victor Nash	. . .	Charles Jackson
Wise		CM	40	(276) 328-2321	John Peace	Glen Skinner	Annette Underwood	. . .	Jeffery Gilliam	Ronald Oakes
Wythe		CE	27	(276) 223-6020	Wythe Sharitz	R. Dalton	. . .	. . .	Patti Mills	Doug King
York		CM	56	(757) 890-3320	James Burgett	James McReynolds	Mary Simmons	MaryCarol White	Laurie Blanton	Joseph Diggs
WASHINGTON										
Adams		C	16	(509) 659-0090	. . .	. . .	Paulette Gibler	. . .	. . .	Douglas Barger
Asotin		C	20	(509) 243-4160	. . .	. . .	. . .	. . .	. . .	. . .
Benton		C	142	(509) 737-2777	. . .	. . .	. . .	. . .	. . .	. . .
Chelan		C	66	(509) 664-5216	. . .	. . .	. . .	. . .	. . .	. . .
Clallam	*	CE	64	(360) 471-2233	Michael Chapman	James Jones	Trish Holden	Stanton Creasey	Marjorie Upham	William Benedict
Clark	*	CE	345	(360) 397-2456	Betty Sue Morris	Glyn Barron	Jo Anne McBride	John Ingram	Francine Reis	Garry Lucas
Columbia		C	4	(509) 382-4541	. . .	. . .	D. Lynne Leseman	. . .	. . .	Michael Berglund
Cowlitz		C	92	(360) 577-3065	. . .	. . .	Teri Nielsen	Claire Hauge	. . .	Bill Mahoney
Douglas		C	32	(509) 884-9444	Dane Keane	. . .	Marilyn Northrop	Karen Goodwin	. . .	Daniel Laroche
Ferry		C	7	(509) 775-5200	Michael Blankenship	. . .	Jean Booher	Joyce Schertenleib	. . .	Pete Werner
Franklin		C	49	(509) 545-3535	Robert Koch	Fred Bowen	Michael Killian	Thomas Westerman	. . .	Richard Lathim
Garfield		C	2	(509) 843-1411	Dean Burton	. . .	Donna Deal	. . .	. . .	Larry Bowles
Grant		C	74	(509) 754-2011	Le Roy Allison	. . .	Gordon Harris	Robert Mosher	. . .	William Wiester
Grays Harbor		C	67	(360) 249-3731	. . .	. . .	Cheryl Brown	. . .	. . .	. . .
Island		C	71	(360) 679-7372	William McDowell	. . .	Sharon Franzen	. . .	Richard Toft	Michael Hawley
Jefferson	*	C	25	(360) 385-9100	Phil Johnson	John Fischbach	Ruth Gordan	. . .	Lorna Delaney	Mike Brasfield
King	*	CE	1737	(206) 296-1737	Ron Sims	James Buck	Anne Noris	Steve Call	Anita Whitfield	Sue Rahr
Kitsap		C	231	(360) 337-7146	. . .	. . .	David Peterson	Karen Flynn	Penny Starkey	Stephen Boyer
Kittitas		C	33	(509) 962-7508	Perry Huston	. . .	. . .	. . .	Kirk Eslinger	. . .
Klickitat		C	19	(509) 773-7171	Donald Struck	. . .	Saundra Olson	. . .	Lori Walford	Chris Mace
Lewis		C	68	(360) 748-9121	Richard Graham	Connie Robins	Nettie Jungers	Larry Grove	. . .	John McCroskey
Lincoln		C	10	(509) 725-4971	Mason Hopkins	. . .	Peggy Semprimoznik	. . .	. . .	John Coley
Mason		C	49	(360) 427-9670	. . .	. . .	Rebecca Rogers	. . .	Charles Wright	Steve Whybark
Okanogan		C	39	(509) 422-7100	Mary Lou Peterson	. . .	Jackie Bradley	. . .	Nanette Kallunki	Frank Rogers
Pacific		C	20	(360) 875-9337	Jon Kaino	Vyrle Hill	Virginia Leach	Ida Taylor	. . .	John Didion
Pend Oreille		CE	11	(509) 447-4119	Mike Hanson	. . .	Fawneil Opp	. . .	. . .	Gerald Weeks
Pierce	*	C	700	(253) 798-7272	. . .	. . .	Kevin Stock	Patrick Kenney	Betsy Sawyers	Paul Pastor
San Juan		C	14	(360) 378-2163	. . .	Donald Rose	Joan White	. . .	. . .	. . .
Skagit		CM	102	(360) 336-9300	. . .	Gary Rowe	. . .	David Cunningham	Kathy Brown	. . .
Skamania		C	9	(509) 427-9447	Robert Talent	. . .	Rena Hollis	. . .	. . .	Dave Brown
Snohomish		C	606	(425) 388-3411	Kirke Sievers	Aaron Reardon	Pam Daniels	Roger Neumaier	Bridget Clawson	Rick Bart
Spokane		CE	417	(509) 477-5750	. . .	. . .	Tom Fallquist	Marshall Farnell	Cathy Malzahn	Mark Sterk
Stevens	*	C	40	(509) 684-3751	. . .	. . .	Patty Chester	Tim Gray	. . .	Craig Thayer
Thurston		CE	207	(360) 754-3800	Bob MacLeod	Donald Krupp	Betty Gould	John Bartz	Bill Kenny	Gary Edwards
Wahkiakum		C	3	(360) 795-3219	Daniel Cothren	. . .	Barbara Blix	. . .	. . .	Daniel Bardsley
Walla Walla		C	55	(509) 527-3200	David Carey	. . .	Connie Vinti	Gordon Heimbigner	Jay Winter	Mike Humphreys
Whatcom		CE	166	(360) 676-6802	Pete Kremen	. . .	N. F. Jackson	Brad Bennett	Karen Doens	William Elfo
Whitman	*	C	40	(509) 397-6205	. . .	Sharron Cunningham	. . .	. . .	. . .	. . .
Yakima		C	222	(509) 574-2210	Ron Gamache	. . .	Kim Eaton	Craig Warner	Linda Dixon	Kenneth Irwin

Directory 1/10 continued

OFFICIALS IN U.S. COUNTIES 2,500 AND OVER IN POPULATION

Jurisdiction	Form of govern-ment	2000 Popu-lation (000)	Main telephone number	Chief elected official	Appointed administrator	Clerk of the governing board	Chief financial officer	Director of personnel	Chief law enforcement official
WEST VIRGINIA									
Barbour	C	15	(304) 457-2232	...	...	...	...	...	...
Berkeley	C	75	(304) 267-3000	Steven Teufel	...	John Small	...	...	William Randy Smith
Boone	C	25	(304) 369-7301	...	...	...	...	...	...
Braxton	C	14	(304) 765-2833	Roy Huffman	...	John Jordan	...	...	...
Brooke	C	25	(304) 737-3661	...	...	...	...	...	...
Cabell	C	96	(304) 526-8634	...	...	...	...	...	...
Calhoun	C	7	(304) 354-6725	...	...	...	...	...	...
Clay	C	10	(304) 587-4259	R. Sizemore	...	Judy Moore	...	...	...
Doddridge	C	7	(304) 873-2631	...	...	...	...	...	...
Fayette	C	47	(304) 574-1200	John Witt	Charlotte Holly	Kelvin Holliday	...	...	William Laird
Gilmer	C	7	(304) 462-7641	Charles Hess	...	Beverly Marks	...	...	Mickey Metz
Grant	C	11	(304) 257-4550	...	...	...	...	...	Roger Sheppard
Greenbrier	C	34	(304) 647-6603	Betty Crookshanks	...	W. J. Livesay	Joyce Moody	...	...
Hampshire	C	20	(304) 822-5112	O. Bradfield	...	Nancy Feller	...	...	...
Hancock	C	32	(304) 564-3311	David Cline	Sharon Ulbright	Eleanor Straight	Cindy Jones	Carol Kaser	...
Hardy	C	12	(304) 538-2929	...	...	...	...	...	James Jack
Harrison	C	68	(304) 624-8500	Conrad Diaz	Robert Andre	Susan Thomas	...	...	...
Jackson	C	28	(304) 372-2011	...	...	...	...	...	...
Jefferson	C	42	(304) 725-9761	James Knode	Leslie Smith	Jennifer Maghan	...	...	...
Kanawha	C	200	(304) 357-0101	...	Brent Pauley	...	...	Debra Hull	Joseph Wagoner
Lewis *	C	16	(304) 269-8200	Samuel Hicks	Phyllis Corathers	Mary Myers	...	...	James Scites
Lincoln	C	22	(304) 824-3336	...	...	Greg Stowers	...	...	Wavle Hunter
Logan *	C	37	(304) 792-8600	Arthur Kirkendall	...	...	N. Wooten	...	Junior Slaughter
Marion	C	56	(304) 367-5400	James Sago	Sharon Shaffer	Barbara Core	Janice Cosco	...	...
Marshall	C	35	(304) 845-1220	...	...	...	...	...	...
Mason	C	25	(304) 675-1110	...	...	...	...	...	...
Mc Dowell	C	27	(304) 436-8344	...	...	...	...	...	Darrell Bailey
Mercer *	C	62	(304) 487-8306	Joe Coburn	...	Rudolph Jennings	...	...	Paul Sabin
Mineral	C	27	(304) 788-3924	Jack Bowers	Michael Bland	Carl Thomas	...	Debra Weasenforth	...
Mingo	C	28	(304) 235-0348	...	...	...	...	...	...
Monongalia	CM	81	(304) 291-7257	Robert Bell	Diane Demedici	Michael Oliverio	Joseph Bartolo	...	...
Monroe	C	14	(304) 772-3096	...	...	...	...	...	...
Morgan	C	14	(304) 258-8547	Glen Stotler	William Clark	Debra Kesecker	Cathy Payne	...	...
Nicholas	C	26	(304) 872-3630	...	...	...	...	...	...
Ohio	C	47	(304) 234-3628	David Sims	Gregory Stewart	Chester Kloss	...	...	...
Pendleton	C	8	(304) 358-2505	...	...	...	...	...	...
Pleasants *	C	7	(304) 684-3542	Joe Reckard	Tina Oldfield	Sue Morgan	Julie Richard	...	Ted Maston
Pocahontas	C	9	(304) 799-4549	...	...	...	...	...	...
Preston	C	29	(304) 329-1805	...	...	...	...	...	...
Putnam	C	51	(304) 586-0202	...	...	...	...	...	...
Raleigh	C	79	(304) 255-9146	...	...	...	...	...	...
Randolph	C	28	(304) 636-2057	...	...	...	...	...	...
Ritchie	C	10	(304) 643-2164	Samuel Rogers	...	Susan Scott	...	...	...
Roane	C	15	(304) 927-2860	...	...	...	...	...	...
Summers	C	12	(304) 466-7100	Lonnie Mullins	...	Mary Merritt	...	...	Garry Wheeler
Taylor	C	16	(304) 265-1401	...	...	...	...	...	...
Tucker	C	7	(304) 478-2866	Jerome Di Bacco	C. Tuesing	Linda Cale	...	...	...
Tyler	C	9	(304) 758-2103	Arthur Mason	...	Lora Thomas	...	...	Sherman Baxa
Upshur	CE	23	(304) 472-0535	Kenneth Davidson	William Parker	Debbie Wilfong	...	...	...
Wayne	C	42	(304) 272-6369	William Wellman	...	Robert Pasley	...	...	Dwayne Vandevender
Webster	C	9	(304) 847-5780	William Armentrout	...	Terry Payne	...	...	Thomas Shepherd
Wetzel	C	17	(304) 455-8224	Donald Mason	...	Carol Haught	...	...	...
Wirt	C	5	(304) 275-4271	...	...	...	...	...	...
Wood *	CE	87	(304) 424-1984	Robert Tebay	Marty Seufer	Jamie Six	...	...	Ken Merritt
Wyoming	C	25	(304) 732-8000	...	...	...	...	...	...
WISCONSIN									
Adams	CE	18	(608) 339-4267	...	...	Beverly Ward	...	Nicholas Funkhouser	Larry Warren
Ashland	C	16	(715) 682-7000	Kenneth Lindquist	Thomas Kieweg	Patricia Somppi	...	...	John Kovach
Barron	C	44	(715) 537-6200	Ole Severude	Duane Hebert	Clarice Fall	Jeffrey French	...	Thomas Richie
Bayfield *	C	15	(715) 373-6181	William Kacvinsky	Mark Abeles-Allison	Scott Fibert	...	...	Robert Follis
Brown	CE	226	(920) 448-4065	Carol Kelso	Roger De Groot	Darlene Marcelle	...	...	Dennis Kocken
Buffalo	C	13	(608) 685-6234	David Ernst	Del Twidt	Roxann Halverson	...	...	Michael Schmidtknecht
Burnett	C	15	(715) 349-2181	...	Candace Fitzgerald	Helen Steffen	...	...	Timothy Curtin
Calumet	C	40	(920) 849-2361	...	William Craig	Beth Hauser	Daniel DeBonis	Patrick Glynn	Gerald Pagel
Chippewa *	C	55	(715) 726-7969	...	William Reynolds	Kathleen Bernier	George McDowell	Shirley Ring	Douglas Ellis
Clark *	C	33	(715) 743-5148	Wayne Hendrickson	...	Christina Jensen	Terri Domaszek	Wendy Bautch	Louis Rosandich
Columbia	C	52	(608) 742-9668	Susan Martin	...	Jean Miller	Lois Schepp	...	Steven Rowe
Crawford	C	17	(608) 326-0201	Robert Dillman	...	Janet Geisler	...	...	Robert Ostrander
Dane	CE	426	(608) 266-4125	Kathleen Falk	...	Joseph Parisi	Chuck Hicklin	...	Gary Hamblin
Dodge	C	85	(920) 386-3600	Charles Swain	...	Karen Gibson	G. Gorst	Joseph Rains	Todd Nehls
Door	C	27	(920) 746-5511	Leo Zipperer	Michael Serpe	Nancy Bemmann	...	James Jetzke	...
Douglas *	C	43	(715) 395-1429	Douglas Finn	Steve Koszarek	Susan Sandvick	Ann Doucette	...	Charlie Law
Dunn	CM	39	(715) 232-2429	Jane Hoyt	Eugene Smith	Lorraine Hartung	...	Heather Baker	Dennis Smith
Eau Claire *	C	93	(715) 839-5106	...	J. McCarty	Janet Loomis	Scott Rasmussen	Robert Anderson	Ronald Cramer
Florence	C	5	(715) 528-3201	Edwin Kelley	...	...	...	...	Jeffrey Rickaby
Fond Du Lac	CE	97	(920) 929-3000	Allen Buechel	...	Joyce Buechel	Karen Kuehl	Richard Brzozowski	Gary Pucker
Forest	C	10	(715) 478-2422	...	...	Chris Carl	...	Joyce Roling	Keith Govier
Grant	C	49	(608) 723-2711	Eugene Bartels	...	...	...	...	...
Green	C	33	(608) 328-9430	Robert Hoesly	...	Michael Doyle	Rhonda Hunter	...	Mark Podoll
Green Lake *	CM	19	(920) 294-4005	Orrin Helmer	...	Margaret Bostelmann	...	...	...
Iowa	C	22	(608) 935-9752	Richard Scallion	Randolph Terronez	David Meudt	...	Annette Goldthorpe	Thomas De Voss
Iron	C	6	(715) 561-3375	...	...	Alice Larson	...	James De Gracie	...
Jackson	C	19	(715) 284-0201	Steve Dickinsen	...	Donna Oleson	...	Terri Palm-Kostroski	...
Jefferson	CE	74	(920) 674-7101	Sharon Schmeling	Gary Petre	Edna Highland	...	Barbara Hoile	Paul Milbrath
Juneau	C	24	(608) 847-9344	...	...	...	...	...	...
Kenosha	CE	149	(262) 653-6422	...	...	...	David Geertsen	Brooke Koons	...
Kewaunee	C	20	(920) 388-7164	Gerald Novickis	Edward Dorner	Linda Teske	...	...	John Cmeyla
La Crosse *	C	107	(608) 785-9640	Steven Doyle	Steven O'Malley	Marion Naegle	Gary Ingvalson	Robert Taunt	Steven Helgeson
Lafayette	C	16	(608) 776-4850	Wilson Wayne	...	...	Joy Galle	...	Scott Pedley
Langlade	C	20	(715) 627-6200	Alfred Schultz	...	Kathryn Jacob	Jeff Mundinger	...	Dave Stegar

Directory 1/10
continued

OFFICIALS IN U.S. COUNTIES 2,500 AND OVER IN POPULATION

Jurisdiction		Form of govern-ment	2000 Popu-lation (000)	Main telephone number	Chief elected official	Appointed administrator	Clerk of the governing board	Chief financial officer	Director of personnel	Chief law enforcement official
WISCONSIN continued										
Lincoln	*	CM	29	(715) 536-0310	Curtis Powell	John Mulder	Robert Kunkel	Dan Leydet	...	Jeff Jaeger
Manitowoc		C	82	(920) 683-4060	...	...	Daniel Fischer	Todd Reckelberg	Sharon Cornils	Thomas Kocourek
Marathon	*	CM	125	(715) 261-1451	Keith Langenhahn	Mort McBain	Nanette Kottke	Kristi Kordus	Frank Matel	Randall Hoenisch
Marinette		C	43	(715) 732-7406	...	Steven Corbeille	Katherine Brandt	...	...	Michael Kessler
Marquette		C	15	(608) 297-9173	...	...	James Thalacyer	...	Brent Miller	Rick Fullmer
Menominee		CE	4	(715) 799-3024	...	Ron Corn	Carol Latender	...	...	Bryan Lepscier
Milwaukee		CE	940	(414) 278-4143	Scott Walker	Linda Seemeyer	Mark Ryan	Scott Manske	Charles McDowell	David Clarke
Monroe		C	40	(608) 269-8719	Lavern Betthauser	...	Susan Matson	...	Ken Kittleson	Peter Quirin
Oconto		CE	35	(920) 834-6800	Leland Rymer	Kevin Hamann	Judy Ferris	Terry Hinds	...	Michael Jansen
Oneida		C	36	(715) 369-6154	...	...	...	...	...	...
Outagamie		CE	160	(920) 832-1672	James Schuette	...	James Hensel	Edward Czaja	Robert Sunstrom	Bradley Gehring
Ozaukee		C	82	(262) 284-8321	Leroy Biey	Thomas Meaux	Harold Dobberpuhl	...	Michael Puksich	Maurice Straub
Pepin		C	7	(715) 672-8704	Peggy Schlosser	Lawrence Kromar	Carol Forster	...	Darlene Brunner	John Andrews
Pierce		C	36	(715) 273-3531	Richard Wilhelm	Curt Kephart	Jamie Feuerhelm	Julie Brickner	Sandra Langer	Everett Muhlhausen
Polk		C	41	(715) 485-9270	Robert Blake	...	Cathy Albrecht	...	Rodney Beyer	Ann Hraychuck
Portage		CE	67	(715) 346-1327	Clarence Hintz	...	Roger Wrycza	Daryl De Deker	...	Stanley Potocki
Price		C	15	(715) 339-3325	...	...	Clarence Cvengros	...	Lori Blair-Hill	Wallace Krenzke
Racine		CE	188	(262) 636-3118	William McReynolds	...	Joan Rennet	Douglas Stansil	Karen Galbraith	Robert Carlson
Richland		C	17	(608) 647-2197	...	...	...	...	...	...
Rock		CM	152	(608) 757-5520	...	Craig Knutson	Kay O'Connell	Jeffrey Smith	John Becker	Eric Runaas
Rusk		C	15	(715) 532-2100	...	...	Denise Nelson	Rosemary Schmit	Dave Willingham	Dean Meyer
Sauk		CM	55	(608) 355-3286	Marty Krueger	Kathryn Schauf	Beverly Mielke	Kerry Beghin	Michelle Koehler	Randy Stammen
Sawyer		C	16	(715) 634-4866	...	...	Kris Mayberry	...	Carol Larson	James Meier
Shawano		C	40	(715) 526-9135	Marshal Giese	Frank Pascarella	Rosemary Bohm	Diane Rusch	Judith Rank	Robert Schmidt
Sheboygan		C	112	(920) 459-3003	Daniel LeMahieu	Adam Payne	Julie Glancey	Timothy Finch	Louella Conway	Alonna Koenig
St. Croix		CM	63	(715) 386-4600	...	Charles Whiting	...	...	...	...
Taylor		CM	19	(715) 748-1400	Herbert Bergmann	...	Roger Emmerich	...	Charles Rude	William Breneman
Trempealeau		C	27	(715) 538-2311	Barbara Semb	...	Paul Syverson	...	Beverly Monahan	Randall Niederkorn
Vernon		C	28	(608) 637-5302	Lee Nerison	...	Ronald Hoff	...	Lisa Berg	Gene Cary
Vilas		C	21	(715) 479-3600	...	...	...	...	...	...
Walworth	*	CM	93	(262) 741-3400	Nancy Russell	David Bretl	Kimberly Bushey	Nicole Andersen	...	David Graves
Washburn		C	16	(715) 468-4624	Michael Bobin	...	John Brown	Michael Keefe	...	Terrence Dryden
Washington	*	C	117	(262) 335-4489	Thomas Sackett	Douglas Johnson	Brenda Jaszewski	Susan Haag	Peter German	Dale Schmidt
Waukesha		CE	360	(262) 548-7902	James Dwyer	Daniel Vrakas	Kathy Nickolaus	...	Susan Zastrow	Daniel Trawicki
Waupaca		C	51	(715) 258-6210	Duane Brown	Mary Robbins	...	James Bernhagen	Amanda Welch	Steven Liebe
Waushara	*	C	23	(920) 787-0431	Norman Weiss	Debra Behringer	John Benz	...	...	David Peterson
Winnebago		CE	156	(920) 236-4800	Jane Vandehey	...	Susan Ertmer	Charles Orenstein	Frederick Bau	Michael Brooks
Wood		C	75	(715) 421-8457	Charles Gurtler	...	Cynthia Meyers	Michael Martin	Edward Reed	Thomas Reichert
WYOMING										
Albany	*	C	32	(307) 721-5535	Tim Chesnut	...	Jackie Gonzales	...	...	James Pond
Big Horn		C	11	(307) 568-2357	...	...	...	...	...	...
Campbell		C	33	(307) 682-7283	Craig Mader	...	Susan Saunders	...	Charlotte Terry	...
Carbon		C	15	(307) 328-2668	...	...	William Harshman	...	...	Jerry Colson
Converse	*	C	12	(307) 358-2244	James Willox	Ed Werner	Lucile Taylor	...	...	Clint Becker
Crook		C	5	(307) 283-1323	Floyd Canfield	...	...	...	...	Steve Stahla
Fremont		C	35	(307) 332-1063	Lanny Applegate	...	Julia Freese	...	...	Skip Hornecker
Goshen		C	12	(307) 532-4051	...	...	...	...	...	...
Hot Springs		C	4	(307) 864-3515	...	...	...	...	...	...
Johnson		C	7	(307) 684-7555	...	...	...	...	...	...
Laramie		C	81	(307) 633-4355	...	...	...	...	...	...
Lincoln		C	14	(307) 877-9056	Kathy Davison	...	Jeanne Wagner	...	...	Lee Gardner
Natrona		C	66	(307) 235-9206	...	...	Mary Collins	...	...	Mark Benton
Niobrara		C	2	(307) 334-2211	Tom Wasserburger	...	Becky Freeman	...	...	Rick Zerbe
Park		C	25	(307) 527-8600	Timothy Morrison	...	Karen Carter	...	...	David Doyle
Platte		C	8	(307) 322-2315	Alden Prosser	...	Jean Dixon	...	...	Steve Keigley
Sheridan		C	26	(307) 674-2900	Lawrence Durante	Maria Kennah	Audrey Koltiska	...	...	Dave Hoefmeier
Sublette		C	5	(307) 367-4372	Betty Fear	...	Mary Lankford	...	...	Bardy Bardin
Sweetwater		C	37	(307) 872-6400	John Pallesen	Robert Gordon	Loretta Bailiff	...	Garry McLean	David Gray
Teton		C	18	(307) 733-8094	Andy Schwartz	Janice Friedlund	S. Daigle	...	...	Bob Zimmer
Uinta		C	19	(307) 783-1700	Craig Welling	Brent Morris	Lynne Fox	...	...	Forrest Bright
Washakie		C	8	(307) 347-6491	Alice Lass	...	Mary Strauch	...	...	...
Weston		C	6	(307) 746-4744	...	...	...	...	...	...

Professional, Special Assistance, and Educational Organizations Serving Local and State Governments

This article briefly describes 80 organizations that provide services of particular importance to cities, counties, and other local and state governments. Most of the organizations are membership groups for school administrators, health officers, city planners, city managers, public works directors, city attorneys, and other administrators who are appointed rather than elected. Several are general service and representational organizations for states, cities, counties, and administrators and citizens. Some organizations provide distinctive research, technological, consulting, and educational programs on a cost-of-service basis and have been established to meet specific needs of state and local governments. The others support educational activities and conduct research in urban affairs or government administration, thereby indirectly strengthening professionalism in government administration.

The assistance available through the secretariats of these national organizations provides an excellent method of obtaining expert advice and actual information on specific problems. The information secured in this way enables local and state officials to improve administrative practices, organization, and methods and thus improve the quality of services rendered. Many of these organizations also are active in raising the professional standards of their members through in-service training, special conferences and seminars, and other kinds of professional development.

Research on current problems is a continuing activity of many of these groups, and all issue a variety of publications ranging from newsletters and occasional bulletins to diversified books, monographs, research papers, conference proceedings, and regular and special reports.

These organizations provide many of the services that in other countries would be the responsibility of the national government. They arrange annual conferences, answer inquiries, provide in-service training and other kinds of professional development, provide placement services for members, and develop service and cost standards for various activities. Most of the organizations listed have individual memberships, and several also have agency or institutional memberships. Some of these organizations have service

memberships that may be based on the population of the jurisdiction, the annual revenue of the jurisdiction or agency, or other criteria that roughly measure the costs of providing service. In addition to these kinds of membership fees, some of the organizations provide specialized consulting, training, and information services both by annual subscription and by charges for specific projects.

LISTING OF ORGANIZATIONS

Academy for State and Local Government
444 North Capitol Street, N.W., Suite 345
Washington, D.C. 20001-1512
(202) 434-4850
Chief Consult: Richard Ruda
Publication list available on request

Purpose: To coordinate cooperative efforts among federal, state, and local governments; the private sector; and the country's research community in addressing key issues facing state and local governments. Also serves as a policy center for joint projects and programs of ICMA and the Council of State Governments, National Association of Counties, National Conference of State Legislatures, National Governors Association, National League of Cities, and U.S. Conference of Mayors. The State and Local Legal Center, an arm of the academy, is devoted to the interests of state and local governments in the Supreme Court. Established 1971.

Airports Council International–North America (ACI-NA)
1775 K Street, N.W., Suite 500
Washington, D.C. 20006
(202) 293-8500; fax (202) 331-1362
Web site: aci-na.org
President: Greg Principato
Major publications: *Airport Highlights,* studies, surveys, reports

Purpose: To promote sound policies dealing with the financing, construction, management, operations, and development of airports; to provide reference and resource facilities and information for airport operators; and to act as the "voice" of airports to governmental agencies, officials, and the public on problems and solutions concerning airport operations. Established 1948.

American Association of Airport Executives (AAAE)
601 Madison Street, Suite 400
Alexandria, Virginia 22314
(703) 824-0500; fax (703) 820-1395
Web site: airportnet.org
President: Charles M. Barclay
Major publications: *Airport Report; Airport Magazine*

Purpose: To assist airport managers in performing their complex and diverse responsibilities through an airport management reference library; a consulting service; publications containing technical, administrative, legal, and operational information; an electronic bulletin board system; a professional accreditation program for airport executives; and Aviation News and Training Network, a private satellite broadcast network for airport employee training and news. Established 1928.

American Association of Port Authorities (AAPA)
1010 Duke Street
Alexandria, Virginia 22314-3589
(703) 684-5700; fax (703) 684-6321
E-mail: info@aapa-ports.org
Web site: aapa-ports.org
President: Kurt J. Nagle

Purpose: To promote the common interests of the port community and provide leadership on trade, transportation, environmental, and other issues related to port development and operations. As the alliance of ports of the Western Hemisphere, AAPA furthers public understanding of the essential role fulfilled by ports within the global transportation system. It also serves as a resource to help members accomplish their professional responsibilities. Established 1912.

American Association of School Administrators (AASA)

801 North Quincy Street, Suite 700
Arlington, Virginia 22203
(703) 528-0700; fax (703) 841-1543
Web site: aasa.org
Executive Director: Paul D. Houston
Major publications: *The School Administrator, Leadership News,* Critical Issues Series

Purpose: To develop qualified educational leaders and support excellence in educational administration; to initiate and support laws, policies, research, and practices that will improve education; to promote programs and activities that focus on leadership for learning and excellence in education; and to cultivate a climate in which quality education can thrive. Established 1865.

American College of Healthcare Executives (ACHE)

One North Franklin Street, Suite 1700
Chicago, Illinois 60606-3491
(312) 424-2800; fax (312) 424-0023
Web site: ache.org
President/CEO: Thomas C. Dolan, PhD, FACHE, CAE
Major publications: *Journal of Healthcare Management; Healthcare Executive; Frontiers of Health Services Management;* miscellaneous studies and task force, committee, and seminar reports

Purpose: To be the professional membership society for health care executives; to meet its members' professional, educational, and leadership needs; to promote high ethical standards and conduct; and to advance health care leadership and management excellence. Established 1933.

American Institute of Architects (AIA)

1735 New York Avenue, N.W.
Washington, D.C. 20006
(202) 626-7300; fax (202) 626-7547
(800) 242-3837
Web site: aia.org
Executive Vice President/CEO: Christine McEntee
Major publication: *AIArchitect*

Purpose: To organize and unite in fellowship the members of the architectural profession; to promote the aesthetic, scientific, and practical efficiency of the profession; to advance the science and art of planning and building by advancing the standards of architectural education, training, and practice; to coordinate the efforts of the building industry and the profession of architecture to ensure the advancement of living standards for people through improved environment; and to make the profession of architecture one of ever-increasing service to society. Established 1857.

American Library Association (ALA)

50 East Huron Street
Chicago, Illinois 60611
(312) 280-1392; fax (312) 944-3897
(800) 545-2433
Also at 1615 New Hampshire Avenue, N.W.
Washington, D.C. 20009-2520
(202) 628-8410; fax (202) 628-8419
Web site: www.ala.org
Executive Director: Keith Michael Fiels
Major publications: *American Libraries, Booklist, Book Links*

Purpose: To assist libraries and librarians in promoting and improving library service and librarianship. Established 1876.

American Planning Association (APA), including the American Institute of Certified Planners (AICP)

1776 Massachusetts Avenue, N.W.
Washington, D.C. 20036-1904
(202) 872-0611; fax (202) 872-0643
Also at 122 South Michigan Avenue, Suite 1600
Chicago, Illinois 60603
(312) 431-9100; fax (312) 431-9985
Web site: planning.org
Executive Director/CEO: Paul Farmer, FAICP
Major publications: *Journal of the APA, Planning, Planning and Environmental Law, Zoning Practice, The Commissioner, Practicing Planner, Interact, APA Advocate,* Planning Advisory Service (PAS) Reports

Purpose: To advance the art and science of urban and regional planning; to promote effective techniques for development in cities, regions, and states; to provide research for planners and information on new developments; and to bring together the professional planner, citizen, elected official, developer, and private practitioner. AICP provides an examination for certification, promotes professional continuing education, establishes ethical standards, and sponsors accreditation of university planning programs. Established 1909.

American Public Gas Association (APGA)

201 Massachusetts Avenue, N.E., Suite C-4
Washington, D.C. 20002
(202) 464-2742; fax (202) 464-0246
E-mail: bkalisch@apga.org
Web site: apga.org
President: Bert Kalisch
Major publications: *Public Gas News* (biweekly newsletter), *Publicly Owned Natural Gas System Directory* (annual)

Purpose: To provide professional assistance to publicly owned natural gas systems. Established 1961.

American Public Health Association (APHA)

800 I Street, N.W.
Washington, D.C. 20001-3710
(202) 777-2742; fax (202) 777-2534
Web site: apha.org
Executive Director: Georges Benjamin, MD
Major publications: *American Journal of Public Health, The Nation's Health*

Purpose: To protect the health of the public through the maintenance of standards for scientific procedures, legislative education, and practical application of innovative health programs. Established 1872.

American Public Human Services Association (APHSA)

810 First Street, N.E., Suite 500
Washington, D.C. 20002
(202) 682-0100; fax (202) 289-6555
Web site: aphsa.org
Executive Director: Jerry W. Friedman
Major publications: *Policy and Practice* magazine, *Public Human Services Directory, This Week in Washington, W-Memo, This Week in Health, Working for Tomorrow*

Purpose: To develop and promote policies and practices that improve the health and well-being of families, children, and adults. Established 1930.

American Public Power Association (APPA)

2301 M Street, N.W.
Washington, D.C. 20037-1484
(202) 467-2900; fax (202) 467-2910
Web site: appanet.org
President and CEO: Alan H. Richardson
Major publications: *Public Power* (bimonthly magazine), *Public Power Weekly* (newsletter), *Public Power Daily*

Purpose: To promote the efficiency and benefits of publicly owned electric systems; to achieve cooperation among public systems; to protect the interests of publicly owned utilities; and to provide service in the fields of management and operation, energy conservation, consumer services, public relations, engineering, design, construction, research, and accounting practice. APPA represents more than 2,000 community-owned electric utilities and provides services in the areas of government relations, engineering and operations, accounting and finance, energy research and development, management, customer relations, and public communications. The association represents public power interests before Congress, federal agencies, and the courts; provides educational programs and energy planning services in technical and management areas; and collects, analyzes, and disseminates information on public power and the electric utility industry. APPA publishes a weekly newsletter, bimonthly magazine, and many specialized publications; funds energy research and development projects; recognizes utilities and individuals for excellence in management and operations; and serves as a resource for federal, state, and local policy makers and officials, news reporters, public interest and other organizations, and the general public on public power and energy issues. Established 1940.

American Public Transportation Association (APTA)

1666 K Street, N.W., Suite 1100
Washington, D.C. 20006
(202) 496-4800; fax (202) 496-4321
Web site: apta.com
President: William W. Millar
Major publications: *Passenger Transport, Public Transportation Fact Book*

Purpose: To represent the operators of and suppliers to public transit; to provide a medium for discussion, exchange of experiences, and comparative study of industry affairs; and to research and investigate methods to improve public transit. The association also assists public transit entities with special issues, and collects and makes available public transit–related data and information. Established 1882.

American Public Works Association (APWA)

2345 Grand Boulevard, Suite 700
Kansas City, Missouri 64108-2641
(816) 472-6100; fax (816) 472-1610
Also at 1401 K Street, N.W., 11th Floor
Washington, D.C. 20005
(202) 408-9541; fax (202) 408-9542
Web site: apwa.net
Executive Director: Peter B. King
Major publications: *APWA Reporter* (12 issues), research reports, technical publications and manuals

Purpose: To serve its members by promoting professional excellence and public awareness through education, advocacy, and the exchange of knowledge. Established 1894.

American Society for Public Administration (ASPA)

1301 Pennsylvania Avenue, N.W., Suite 840
Washington, D.C. 20004
(202) 393-7878; fax (202) 638-4952
Web site: aspanet.org
Executive Director: Antoinette A. Samuel
Major publications: *Public Administration Review, PA Times*

Purpose: To improve the management of public service at all levels of government; to advocate on behalf of public service; to advance the science, processes, and art of public administration; and to disseminate information and facilitate the exchange of knowledge among persons interested in the practice or teaching of public administration. Established 1939.

American Water Works Association (AWWA)

6666 West Quincy Avenue
Denver, Colorado 80235
(303) 347-6135; fax (303) 795-1440
Also at 1300 I Street, N.W., Suite 701 West
Washington, D.C. 20005
(202) 628-8303
Web site: awwa.org
Executive Director: Jack W. Hoffbuhr, PE, DEE
Major publications: *AWWA Journal, MainStream, OpFlow, WaterWeek*

Purpose: To promote public health and welfare in the provision of drinking water of unquestionable and sufficient quality. Founded 1881.

Association of Public-Safety Communications Officials— International, Inc.

351 North Williamson Boulevard
Daytona Beach, Florida 32114-1112
(386) 322-2500; fax (386) 322-2501
Also at 1725 DeSales Street, N.W., Suite 808
Washington, D.C. 20036
(202) 833-2700; fax (202) 833-5700
Web site: apcointl.org
Executive Director: George S. Rice Jr.
Major publications: *APCO BULLETIN, The Journal of Public Safety Communications, Public Safety Operating Procedures Manual,* APCO training courses

Purpose: To promote the development and progress of public safety telecommunications through research, planning, and training; to promote cooperation among public safety agencies; to perform frequency coordination for radio services administered by the Federal Communications Commission; and to act as a liaison with federal regulatory bodies. Established 1935.

Association of Public Treasurers (APT) (formerly the Municipal Treasurers' Association)

962 Wayne Avenue, Suite 910
Silver Spring, Maryland 20910
(301) 495-5560; fax (301) 495-5561
Web site: aptusc.org
Executive Director: Kelley Noone
Major publications: *Technical Topics, Treasury Notes*

Purpose: To enhance local treasury management by providing educational training, technical assistance, legislative services, and a forum for treasurers to exchange ideas and develop policy papers and positions. Established 1965.

Building Officials and Code Administrators International (BOCA)
See **International Code Council (ICC)**

Canadian Association of Municipal Administrators (CAMA)

P.O. Box 128, Station A
Fredericton, New Brunswick E3B 4Y2
(866) 771-2262; fax (506) 460-2134
Web site: camacam.ca
Executive Secretary: Jennifer Goodine

Purpose: To achieve greater communication and cooperation among municipal managers across Canada, and to focus the talents of its members on the preservation and advancement of municipal government by enhancing the quality of municipal management in Canada. Established 1972.

Council of State Community Development Agencies (COSCDA)

1825 K Street, Suite 515
Washington, D.C. 20006
(202) 293-5820; fax (202) 293-2820
Web site: coscda.org
Executive Director: Dianne Taylor
Major publications: *The National Line; Financing Water and Waste Disposal Systems in Rural Areas; Holistic Community Development; Transforming Community Development Policy and Practice; Promoting Economic Opportunity: The CDBG Program, Empowerment, and Welfare Reform*

Purpose: To help state agencies keep abreast of state and federal initiatives in community and economic development, housing, public facilities, and local assistance, and to improve state programs through interstate coordination. Established 1974.

Council of State Governments (CSG)

2760 Research Park Drive
P.O. Box 11910
Lexington, Kentucky 40578-1910
(859) 244-8000; fax (859) 244-8001
Web site: csg.org
Executive Director/CEO: Daniel M. Sprague
Major publications: *Book of the States, State Government News* magazine, *CSG State Directories*

Purpose: To prepare states for the future by interpreting changing national and international trends and conditions; to promote the sovereignty of the states and their role in the American federal system; to advocate multistate problem solving and partnerships; and to build leadership skills to improve decision making. CSG is a multibranch and regionally focused association of the states, U.S. territories, and commonwealths. Established 1933.

Federation of Canadian Municipalities (FCM)

24 Clarence Street
Ottawa, Ontario K1N 5P3
(613) 241-5221; fax (613) 241-7440
E-mail: federation@fcm.ca
Web site: fcm.ca
Chief Executive Officer: Brock Carlton,
Major publications: *Forum* (national magazine), *Crossroads: The Newsletter for the International Centre for Municipal Development*

Purpose: To represent the interests of all municipalities on policy and program matters within federal jurisdictions. Policy and program priorities are determined by FCM's board of directors, standing committees, and task forces. Issues include payments in lieu of taxes, goods and service taxes, economic development, municipal infrastructure, environment, transportation, community safety and crime prevention, quality-of-life social indicators, housing, race relations, and international trade and aid. FCM members include Canada's largest cities, small urban and rural communities, and the 18 major provincial and territorial municipal associations; together these members represent more than 20 million Canadians. Established 1937.

Government Finance Officers Association (GFOA)

203 North LaSalle Street, Suite 2700
Chicago, Illinois 60601-1210
(312) 977-9700; fax (312) 977-4806
Also at 1301 Pennsylvania Avenue, N.W.,
Suite 309
Washington, D.C. 20004
(202) 393-8020; fax (202) 393-0780
Web site: gfoa.org
Executive Director/CEO: Jeffrey L. Esser
Major publications: GFOA *Newsletter; Government Finance Review Magazine; Public Investor; GAAFR Review; Pension & Benefits Update; Governmental Accounting, Auditing, and Financial Reporting; Investing Public Funds; Elected Official's Series; Local Government Finance: Concepts and Practices*

Purpose: To enhance and promote the professional management of governmental financial resources by identifying, developing, and advancing fiscal strategies, policies, and practices for the public benefit. Established 1906.

Government Management Information Sciences Users Group (GMIS)

P.O. Box 365
Bayville, New Jersey 08721
(973) 632-0470; fax (732) 606-9026
(800) 460-7454
Web site: gmis.org
GMIS Listserv: Headquarters@GMIS.org
Executive Secretary: Kay Randall

Purpose: To provide a forum for the exchange of ideas, information, and techniques; and to foster enhancements in hardware, software, and communication developments as they relate to government activities. State and local government agencies are members represented by their top computer or information technology professionals. The GMIS Annual Educational Conference promotes sharing of ideas and the latest technology. GMIS sponsors an annual "Professional of the Year" program, publishes a newsletter, and provides organizational support to 19 state chapters. State chapters enable member agencies within a geographical area to develop close relationships and to foster the spirit and intent of GMIS through cooperation, assistance, and mutual support. GMIS is affiliated with KommITS, a sister organization of local governments in Sweden; SOCITM in the United Kingdom; ALGIM in New Zealand; VIAG in Netherlands; MISA/ASIM in Ontario, Canada; LOLA-International (Linked Organisation of Local Authority ICT Societies); and V-ICT-OR in Belgium.

Governmental Accounting Standards Board (GASB)

401 Merritt 7
P.O. Box 5116
Norwalk, Connecticut 06856-5116
(203) 847-0700; fax (203) 849-9714
Web site: gasb.org
Chairman: Robert Attmore
Major publications: Governmental Accounting Standards Series; Codification of Standards; implementation guides; exposure drafts; Preliminary Views documents; *The GASB Report* (monthly newsletter); plain-language user guides

Purpose: To establish standards of financial accounting and reporting for state and local governmental entities. GASB standards guide the preparation of those entities' external financial reports so that users of the reports can obtain the state and local government financial information needed to make economic, social, and political decisions. Interested parties are encouraged to read and comment on discussion documents of proposed standards, which can be downloaded free of charge from the GASB Web

site. Final standards, guides to implementing standards and using government financial reports, as well as subscriptions to the GASB's publications, can be ordered through the Web site as well. GASB's Web site also provides up-to-date information about current projects, forms for submitting technical questions and signing up for e-mail news alerts, a section devoted to financial report users, and a link to its Performance Measurement for Government Web site. Established in 1984, the GASB is overseen by the Financial Accounting Foundation's Board of Trustees.

Governmental Research Association (GRA)

P.O. Box 292300
Samford University
Birmingham, Alabama 35229
(205) 726-2482; fax (205) 726-2900
Web site: graonline.org
President: Ran Coble
Major publications: *Directory of Organizations and Individuals Professionally Engaged in Governmental Research and Related Activities* (annual); *GRA Reporter* (quarterly)

Purpose: To promote and coordinate the activities of governmental research agencies; to encourage the development of effective organization and methods for the administration and operation of government; to encourage the development of common standards for the appraisal of results; to facilitate the exchange of ideas and experiences; and to serve as a clearinghouse. Established 1914.

ICMA

777 North Capitol Street, N.E., Suite 500
Washington, D.C. 20002-4201
(202) 289-4262; fax (202) 962-3500
Web site: icma.org
Executive Director: Robert J. O'Neill Jr.
Major publications: *Effective Supervisory Practices, The Ethics Edge* (2nd ed.), *Managing Local Government Services, Budgeting: A Guide for Local Governments, A Revenue Guide for Local Government, How Effective Are Your Community Services?* (3rd ed.), "Green" Books, *The Municipal Year Book, Public Management (PM)* magazine, *IQ Reports, ICMA Newsletter;* self-study courses, training packages

Purpose: To create excellence in local governance by developing and advocating professional management of local government worldwide. ICMA provides member support; publications, data, and information; peer and results-oriented assistance; and training and professional development to more than 9,000 city, town, and county experts and other individuals throughout the world. The management decisions made by ICMA's members affect 185 million individuals living in thousands of communities, from small villages and towns to large metropolitan areas. Established 1914.

ICMA Retirement Corporation (ICMA-RC)
777 North Capitol Street, N.E.
Washington, D.C. 20002
(202) 962-4600; fax (202) 962-4601
(800) 669-7400
Web site: icmarc.org
President/CEO: Joan McCallen

Purpose: To provide and administer low-cost retirement plans to units of government in their overall benefits programs and to educate public employees as investors. Included are defined contribution plans and deferred compensation programs for all personnel. Also offers IRAs to public employees. Now serving 650,000 participants and 6,000 public employers nationwide. Established 1972.

Institute of Internal Auditors, Inc., (The IIA)
247 Maitland Avenue
Altamonte Springs, Florida 32701-4201
(407) 937-1100; fax (407) 937-1101
Web site: theiia.org
President: David A. Richards, CIA
Major publications: *Internal Auditor, Tone at the Top* (quarterly corporate governance newsletter)

Purpose: To provide comprehensive professional development and standards for the practice of internal auditing; and to research, disseminate, and promote education in internal auditing and internal control. The IIA offers the Certified Government Auditing Professional (CGAP) to distinguish leaders in public sector auditing. In addition to offering quality assessment services, the IIA performs custom on-site seminars for government auditors and offers educational products that address issues pertaining to government auditing. An international professional association with global headquarters in Altamonte Springs, Florida, The IIA has more than 140,000 members in internal auditing, governance, internal control, information technology audit, education, and security. With representation from more than 165 countries, The IIA is the internal audit profession's global voice, recognized authority, acknowledged leader, chief advocate, and principal educator worldwide. Established 1941.

Institute of Public Administration (IPA)
180 Graham Hall
University of Delaware
Newark, Delaware 19716-7380

(302) 831-8971; fax (302) 831-3488
Web site: ipa.udel.edu/
President: Jerome R. Lewis
Major publications: IPA *Report* (semiannual), newsletter, conference proceedings

Purpose: To provide research, training, education, consulting, and advisory services in the United States and abroad in areas of public policy, government structure, public authorities, public enterprises, government procurement, personnel management and training, public/private sector improvements, economic development, charter revision, local government legislative bodies, planning and management, intergovernmental program responsibilities and relationships, and public ethics. Established 1906.

Institute of Transportation Engineers (ITE)
1099 14th Street, N.W., Suite 300 West
Washington, D.C. 20005-3438
(202) 289-0222; fax (202) 289-7722
Web site: ite.org
Executive Director: Thomas W. Brahms
Major publications: *Trip Generation, Parking Generation; Innovative Bicycle Treatments; Transportation and Land Use Development; Transportation Engineering Handbook; Transportation Planning Handbook; Parking Handbook for Small Communities; Manual of Transportation Engineering Studies; Traffic Safety Toolbox, A Primer on Traffic Safety; Manual of Uniform Traffic Control Devices, 2003; Traffic Control Devices Handbook; ITE Journal*

Purpose: To promote professional development in the field through education, research, development of public awareness, and exchange of information. Established 1930.

International Association of Assembly Managers (IAAM)
635 Fritz Drive, Suite 100
Coppell, Texas 75019-4442
(972) 906-7441; fax (972) 906-7418
Web site: iaam.org
Executive Director: Dexter King, CFE
Major publications: *Facility Manager, IAAM Guide to Members and Services, IAAM E-News, Venue Safety & Security* magazine

Purpose: To promote professional development in the public assembly field and provide assistance to members. Membership consists of the managers of arenas, convention centers, auditoriums, exhibit halls, amphitheaters, performing arts venues, and stadiums. Established 1925.

International Association of Assessing Officers (IAAO)
314 West 10th Street
Kansas City, Missouri 64105

(816) 701-8100; fax (816) 701-8149
Web site: iaao.org
Executive Director: Lisa J. Daniels
Major publications: *Journal of Property Tax Assessment and Administration; Property Appraisal and Assessment Administration; Property Assessment Valuation,* 2nd ed. (1996); *Mass Appraisal of Real Property* (1999); *GIS Guidelines for Assessors,* 2nd ed. (with URISA) (1999); Assessment Standards

Purpose: To provide leadership in accurate property valuation, property tax administration, and property tax policy throughout the world. Established 1934.

International Association of Chiefs of Police (IACP)
515 North Washington Street
Alexandria, Virginia 22314-2357
(703) 836-6767; fax (703) 836-4543
(800) THE IACP
Web site: theiacp.org
Executive Director: Daniel N. Rosenblatt
Major publications: *Police Chief, Training Keys*

Purpose: To advance the art of police science through the development and dissemination of improved administrative, technical, and operational practices, and to promote the use of such practices in police work. Fosters police cooperation through the exchange of information among police administrators, and encourages all police officers to adhere to high standards of performance and conduct. Established 1893.

International Association of Fire Chiefs (IAFC)
4025 Fair Ridge Drive, Suite 300
Fairfax, Virginia 22033-2868
(703) 273-0911; fax (703) 273-9363
Web site: iafc.org
Executive Director Mark Light, CAE
Major publication: *On Scene* (twice-monthly newsletter)

Purpose: To enhance the professionalism and capabilities of career and volunteer fire chiefs, chief fire officers, and managers of emergency service organizations throughout the international community through vision, services, information, education, and representation. Established 1873.

International Code Council
500 New Jersey Avenue, N.W., 6th Floor
Washington, D.C. 20001-2070
(888) 422-7233; fax (202) 783-2348
Web site: iccsafe.org
Chief Executive Officer: Richard P. Weiland
Major publication: *The International Codes*

Purpose: The ICC, a membership association dedicated to building safety and fire prevention, develops the codes used to construct residential and commercial buildings, including homes and schools. Most U.S. cities, counties, and states that adopt codes choose the international codes developed by the ICC.

International Economic Development Council (IEDC)

734 15th Street, N.W., Suite 900
Washington, D.C. 20005
(202) 223-7800; fax (202) 223-4745
Web site: iedconline.org
President/CEO: Jeffrey A. Finkle
Major publications: *Economic Development Journal, Economic Development Now, Federal Review, Federal Directory, Budget Overview*

Purpose: To help economic development professionals improve the quality of life in their communities. With more than 4,000 members, IEDC represents all levels of government, academia, and private industry, providing a broad range of member services that includes research, advisory services, conferences, professional certification, professional development, publications, and legislative tracking. Established 2001.

International Institute of Municipal Clerks (IIMC)

8331 Utica Avenue, Suite 200
Rancho Cucamonga, California 91730
(909) 944-4162; fax (909) 944-8545
(800) 251-1639
Web site: iimc.com
Executive Director: Chris Shalby
Major publications: *IIMC News Digest, Meeting Administration Handbook, The Language of Local Government, Role Call: Strategy for a Professional Clerk, Parliamentary Procedures in Local Government,* "Partners in Democracy" video, case study packets, technical bulletins

Purpose: To improve the administration of state, provincial, county, and local governments by maintaining central facilities for study and research devoted to the improvement of methods and procedures relating to the municipal clerk's, secretary's, or recorder's duties; and by sponsoring professional career development institutes in 46 universities. IIMC also sponsors an annual conference, distance learning programs, a monthly magazine, and a resource center; offers a self-study course in supervision and records and information management; and administers a professional certification program. Established 1947.

International Municipal Lawyers Association (IMLA)

7910 Woodmont Avenue, Suite 1440
Bethesda, Maryland 20814
(202) 466-5424; fax (202) 785-0152
E-mail: info@imla.org
Web site: imla.org
General Counsel/Executive Director: Chuck Thompson
Major publications: *Municipal Lawyer, The IMLA Model Ordinance Service*

Purpose: IMLA is a membership organization of U.S. and Canadian city and county attorneys that provides continuing legal education events, publications, research, legal advocacy assistance, and excellent networking opportunities for the local government legal community. Established 1935.

International Public Management Association for Human Resources (IPMA-HR)

1617 Duke Street
Alexandria, Virginia 22314
(703) 549-7100; fax (703) 684-0948
Web site: ipma-hr.org
Executive Director: Neil E. Reichenberg
Major publications: *Public Personnel Management, HR Bulletin, IPMA-HR News*

Purpose: To improve service to the public by promoting quality human resource management in the public sector. Established 1973.

League of Women Voters (LWV)

1730 M Street, N.W., Suite 1000
Washington, D.C. 20036-4508
(202) 429-1965; fax (202) 429-0854
Web site: lwv.org
Executive Director: Nancy Tate
Major publications: *Looking for Sunshine: Protecting Your Right to Know, Local Voices: Citizen Conversation on Civil Liberties and Secure Communities, Choosing the President: A Citizen's Guide to Electoral Process, Citizens Building Communities: ABC's of Public Dialogue, For the Public Record: A Documentary History of the League of Women Voters, The National Voter* magazine

Purpose: To encourage informed and active participation in government and to influence public policy through education and advocacy. The league's current advocacy priorities are campaign finance, lobbying, and election reform; civil liberties; and nonpartisan redistricting. The League of Women Voters Education Fund, a separate but complementary organization, provides research and public education services to the public to encourage and enable citizen participation in government. Current public education programs include voter outreach and education, the Vote 411.net Web site, election reform, judicial independence, and international forms and exchange activities. The league is a nonpartisan political organization. Established 1920.

Maritime Municipal Training and Development Board (MMTDB)

114 Woodlawn Road, Suite 516
Dartmouth, Nova Scotia B2W 2S7
(902) 439-8092; fax: (902) 484-6113
E-mail: munisource@munisource.org
Web site for municipal government information: munisource.org
Executive Director: A. Donald Smeltzer

Purpose: To improve municipal governance and service delivery. Located at Dalhousie University, the MMTDB was established by the Council of Maritime Premiers and is widely recognized for its key role in providing for municipal training and distance education programming; the development of decision-making resources; improvements made in information sharing and professionalism in municipal public service; and its leadership, since 1990, in promoting the Internet as an important networking, decision-making, and training resource for municipal government. Worldwide interest in the MMTDB's municipal information Web site, munisource. org, contributes to the board's growing international reputation as a leader in its field and as an important municipal government information provider. A certificate course in Basic HTML Programming for the municipal public sector is now available online through the MMTDB's training and education Web site, distance-ed.com. Additional programs of online training are planned. Established 1974.

National Animal Control Association (NACA)

P.O. Box 480851
Kansas City, Missouri 64148-0851
(913) 768-1319; fax (913) 768-1378
Web site: nacanet.org
President: Mark Kumpf
Major publications: *The NACA News* newsletter, *The NACA Training Guide*

Purpose: To provide training for animal control personnel; consultation and guidance for local governments on animal control ordinances, animal shelter design, budget and program planning, and staff training; and public education. Established 1978.

National Association of Counties (NACo)

25 Massachusetts Avenue, N.W., 5th Floor
Washington, D.C. 20001-1431
(202) 393-6226; fax (202) 393-2630
Web site: naco.org
Executive Director: Larry Naake
Major publication: *County News*

Purpose: To serve as the voice of county government at the national level; to improve county government; to serve as a liaison between counties and other levels of government; to achieve public understanding of the role of counties in the intergovernmental system; and to provide information and analysis of data. Two-thirds of the nation's counties are members of NACo and its 25 affiliated organizations. Through the National Association of Counties Research Foundation, Inc. (NACoR, Inc.), NACo undertakes grant- and contract-funded research and maintains expertise in major problems and programs of county government. Established 1935.

National Association of County and City Health Officials (NACCHO)

1100 17th Street, 2nd Floor
Washington, D.C. 20036
(202) 783-5550; fax (202) 783-1583
Web site: naccho.org
Executive Director: Patrick M. Libbey
Major publications: *Who's Who in Local Public Health* (annual), *Public Health Dispatch* (newsletter), *NACCHO Exchange* (quarterly), research briefs and videos

Purpose: To support efforts that protect and improve the health of all people and all communities by promoting national policy, developing resources and programs, seeking health equity, and supporting effective local public health practice and systems. Established 1960s.

National Association for County Community and Economic Development (NACCED)

2025 M Street, N.W., Suite 800
Washington, D.C. 20036-3309
(202) 367-1149; fax (202) 367-2149
Web site: nacced.org
Executive Director: John Murphy

Purpose: To help develop the technical capacity of county agencies in administering community development, economic development, and affordable housing programs. Created as an affiliate of the National Association of Counties (NACo), NACCED is a nonprofit national organization that also serves as a voice within NACo to articulate the needs, concerns, and interests of county agencies. Established 1978.

National Association of Development Organizations (NADO)

400 North Capitol Street, N.W., Suite 390
Washington, D.C. 20001
(202) 624-7806; fax (202) 624-8813
Web site: nado.org
Executive Director: Matthew Chase
Major publications: *Regional Development Digest, NADO News, EDFS Reporter*

Purpose: To provide training, information, and representation for regional development organizations serving small metropolitan and rural America. Building on nearly four decades of experience, the association offers its members exclusive access to a variety of services and benefits—all of which are crafted to enhance the activities, programs, and prospects of regional development organizations. Established 1970s.

National Association of Housing and Redevelopment Officials (NAHRO)

630 I Street, N.W.
Washington, D.C. 20001
(202) 289-3500; fax (202) 289-8181
(877) 866-2476
Web site: nahro.org
Executive Director: Saul N. Ramirez
Major publications: *Journal of Housing and Community Development, NAHRO Monitor, Directory of Local Agencies, Commissioners Dictionary, The NAHRO Public Relations Handbook, Commissioners Handbook*

Purpose: To serve as a professional membership organization representing local housing authorities; community development agencies; and professionals in the housing, community development, and redevelopment fields. Divided into eight regions and 43 chapters, NAHRO works to provide safe, decent, and affordable housing for low- and moderate-income persons. NAHRO provides its 15,000 members with information on federal policy, legislation, regulations, and funding. It also provides professional development and training programs in all phases of agency operations, including management, maintenance, and procurement. In addition, NAHRO sponsors a legislative conference, a summer conference, and a national conference and exhibition every year. Established 1933.

National Association of Regional Councils (NARC)

1666 Connecticut Avenue, N.W., Suite 300
Washington, D.C. 20009-1038
(202) 986-1032; fax (202) 986-1038
Web site: narc.org
Executive Director: Cameron Moore

Purpose: To promote regional approaches and collaboration in addressing diverse development challenges. A nonprofit membership organization and public interest group, NARC has represented the interests of its members and has advanced regional cooperation through effective interaction and advocacy with Congress, federal officials, and other related agencies and interest groups for more than 40 years. Its member organizations are composed of multiple local government units that work together to serve American communities, large and small, urban and rural. Among the issues it addresses are transportation, homeland security and regional preparedness, community and economic development, the environment, and a variety of community issues of interest to member organizations. NARC provides its members with valuable information and research on key national policy issues, federal policy developments, and best practices; in addition, it conducts enriching training sessions, conferences workshops, and satellite telecasts. Established 1967.

National Association of Schools of Public Affairs and Administration (NASPAA)

1029 Vermont Avenue, N.W., Suite 1100
Washington, D.C. 20005
(202) 628-8965; fax (202) 626-4978
E-mail: naspaa@naspaa.org
Web site: naspaa.org
Executive Director: Laurel McFarland
Major publications: *Journal of Public Affairs Education (J-PAE), Newsletter, MPA Accreditation Standards, MPA/MPP Brochure,* peer review and accreditation documents

Purpose: To serve as a national and international center for information about programs and developments in the area of public affairs and administration; to foster goals and standards of educational excellence; to represent members' concerns and interests in the formulation and support of national, state, and local policies for public affairs education and research; and to serve as a specialized accrediting agency for MPA/MPP degrees. Established 1970.

National Association of State Chief Information Officers (NASCIO)

c/o AMR Management Services
201 East Main Street, Suite 1405
Lexington, Kentucky 40507
(859) 514-9171; fax (859) 514-9166
Web site: nascio.org
Executive Director: Douglas Robinson
Major publications: *NASCIO Exchange* (newsletter), *Issues Focus Reports*

Purpose: To represent state chief information officers and be the leading forum for addressing the opportunities, implications, and challenges of improving the business of government through the application of information technology. Established 1969.

National Association of Towns and Townships (NATaT)

1130 Connecticut Avenue, N.W., Suite 300
Washington, D.C. 20036
(202) 454-3954; fax (202) 331-1598
Web site: natat.org
Federal Director: Jennifer Imo
Major publication: *Washington Report*

Purpose: To strengthen the effectiveness of town and township government by educating lawmakers and public policy officials about how small-town governments operate and by advocating policies on their behalf in Washington, D.C. Established 1976.

National Career Development Association (NCDA)

305 North Beech Circle
Broken Arrow, Oklahoma 74012
(918) 663-7060; fax (918) 663-7058
Web site: ncda.org
Executive Director: Deneen Pennington
Major publications: *The Internet: A Tool for Career Planning, A Counselor's Guide to Career Assessment Resources, Experiential Activities for Teaching Career Development Courses and Facilitating Work Groups, Adult Career Development, The Career Counseling Casebook*

Purpose: To promote career development of all people throughout the lifespan. A division of the American Counseling Association, NCDA provides services to the public and to professionals involved with or interested in career development; services include professional development activities, publications, research, public information, professional standards, advocacy, and recognition for achievement and service. Established 1913.

National Civic League (NCL)

1445 Market Street, Suite 300
Denver, Colorado 80202-1717
(303) 571-4343; fax (303) 571-4404
E-mail: kristins@ncl.org
Web site: ncl.org
President: Gloria Rubio-Cortés
Major publications: *National Civic Review, Model City Charter, Model County Charter, The Community Visioning and Strategic Planning Handbook, New Civic Index*

Purpose: To strengthen democracy by increasing the capacity of our nation's people to fully participate in and build healthy and prosperous communities across America. We are good at the science of local government, the art of public engagement, and the celebration of the progress that can be achieved when people work together. NCL is the home of the All-America City Awards.

National Community Development Association (NCDA)

522 21st Street, N.W., #120
Washington, D.C. 20006
(202) 293-7587; fax (202) 887-5546
Web site: ncdaonline.org
Executive Director: Cardell Cooper
Purpose: To serve as a national clearinghouse of ideas for local government officials and federal policy makers on pertinent national issues affecting America's communities. NCDA is a national nonprofit organization comprising more than 550 local governments across the country that administer federally supported community and economic development, housing, and human service programs, including those of the U.S. Department of Housing and Urban Development (HUD), the Community Development Block Grant program, and HOME Investment Partnerships. NCDA provides timely, direct information and technical support to its members in their efforts to secure effective and responsive housing and community development programs. Established 1968.

National Conference of State Legislatures (NCSL)

7700 East First Place
Denver, Colorado 80230
(303) 364-7700; fax (303) 364-7800
Also at 444 North Capitol Street, N.W., Suite 515
Washington, D.C. 20001-1201
(202) 624-5400; fax (202) 737-1069
Web site: ncsl.org
Executive Director: William T. Pound
Major publications: *State Legislatures, Federal Update, Capitol to Capitol*

Purpose: To improve the quality and effectiveness of state legislatures; to ensure that states have a strong, cohesive voice in the federal decision-making process; and to foster interstate communication and cooperation. Established 1975.

National Environmental Health Association (NEHA)

720 South Colorado Boulevard, Suite 1000-N
Denver, Colorado 80246-1925
(303) 756-9090; fax (303) 691-9490
E-mail: staff@neha.org
Web site: neha.org
Executive Director: Nelson E. Fabian
Major publications: *Journal of Environmental Health* and more than 200 other publications

Purpose: To advance the professional in the environmental field through education, professional meetings, and the dissemination of information. The association also publishes information relating to environmental health and protection and promotes professionalism in the field. Established 1937.

National Fire Protection Association (NFPA)

One Batterymarch Park
Quincy, Massachusetts 02169-7471
(617) 770-3000; fax (617) 770-0700
Web site: nfpa.org
President/CEO: James M. Shannon
Major publications: *National Electrical Code®, National Fire Codes®, Fire Protection Hand-book, Life Safety Code®, Risk Watch™, Learn Not to Burn® Curriculum, NFPA Journal, Fire Technology,* textbooks, manuals, training packages, detailed analyses of important fires, fire officers guides, and more

Purpose: To reduce the worldwide burden of fire and other hazards on the quality of life by providing and advocating scientifically based consensus codes and standards, research, training, and education. Established 1896.

National Governors Association (NGA)

Hall of the States
444 North Capitol Street, Suite 267
Washington, D.C. 20001-1512
(202) 624-5300; fax (202) 624-5313
Web site: nga.org
Executive Director: Raymond C. Scheppach
Major publications: *The Fiscal Survey of States, Policy Positions,* reports on a wide range of state issues

Purpose: To act as a liaison between the states and the federal government, and to serve as a clearinghouse for information and ideas on state and national issues. Established 1908.

National Housing Conference (NHC)

1801 K Street, N.W., Suite M-100
Washington, D.C. 20006-1301
(202) 466-2121; fax (202) 466-2122
Web site: nhc.org
President/CEO: Conrad Egan
Major publications: *NHC at Work, New Century Housing, NHC Affordable Housing Policy Review, Washington Wire*

Purpose: To promote better communities and affordable housing for Americans through education and advocacy. Established 1931.

National Institute of Governmental Purchasing (NIGP)

151 Spring Street
Herndon, Virginia 20170-5223
(703) 736-8900; fax (703) 736-2818
(800) FOR NIGP (367-6447)
Web site: nigp.org
Chief Executive Officer: Rick Grimm, CPPO, CPPB
Industry-specific publications: *The Source,* a quarterly e-magazine for the membership of NIGP; *NIGP BuyWeekly,* an e-newsletter for public procurement professionals; *NIGP Dictionary of Purchasing Terms*

Purpose: To develop, support, and promote the public procurement profession through premier educational and research programs, professional support, and advocacy initiatives that benefit members and constituents. As a vibrant international association, NIGP seeks to create a world in which public procurement practitioners are highly regarded members of a respected professional order. NIGP offers resources and seminars that address current industry issues and trends affecting the way governments do business. The Learning and Education to Advance Procurement (LEAP) curriculum is the basis for all educational offerings. NIGP also offers procurement management auditing and consulting services; the Government Contractor Certificate program, a training/certificate program to enhance partnerships with industry and ensure quality proposals in the government contracting process; a procurement information exchange that includes an online library of specifications, research projects, and reports; the NIGP Commodity/Service Coding System, a universal language identifying commodities and services; an accreditation program; formal award recognition in public purchasing based on standards to enhance purchasing operations and credibility; and E-Net, an electronic network for members. Additionally, NIGP supports the Universal Public Purchasing Certification Council (UPPCC) and its two-level certification program for public purchasing personnel: CPPB (Certified Professional Public Buyer) and CPPO (Certified Public Purchasing Officer). Established 1944.

National League of Cities (NLC)

1301 Pennsylvania Avenue, N.W., Suite 550
Washington, D.C. 20004-1763
(202) 626-3000; fax (202) 626-3043
Web site: nlc.org
Executive Director: Donald J. Borut
President: Council member James Hunt
Major publications: *Nation's Cities Weekly,* guide books, directories, and research reports
Purpose: To strengthen and promote cities as centers of opportunity, leadership, and governance; to serve as an advocate for its members in Washington in the legislative, administrative, and judicial processes that affect them; and to develop and pursue a national urban policy that meets the present and future needs of the nation's urban communities and the people who live in them. The league also offers training, technical assistance, and information to local government and state league officials to help them improve the quality of local government, and it researches and analyzes policy issues of importance to urban America. Established 1924.

National Public Employer Labor Relations Association (NPELRA)

1012 South Coast Highway, Suite M
Oceanside, California 92054
(760) 433-1686; fax (760) 433-1687
E-mail: info@npelra.org
Web site: npelra.org
Executive Director: Michael T. Kolb
Purpose: The premier organization for public sector labor relations and human resources

professionals, NPELRA is a network of state and regional affiliates. Its more than 3,000 members around the country represent public employers in a wide range of areas, from employee-management contract negotiations to arbitration under grievance and arbitration procedures. NPELRA strives to provide its members with high-quality, progressive labor relations advice that balances the needs of management, employees, and the public. It also works to promote the interests of public sector management in the judicial and legislative arenas, and to provide opportunities for networking among members by establishing state and regional organizations throughout the country. The governmental agencies represented in NPELRA employ more than 4 million workers in federal, state, and local government.

National Recreation and Park Association (NRPA)

22377 Belmont Ridge Road
Ashburn, Virginia 20148-4501
(703) 858-0784; fax (703) 858-0794
Web site: nrpa.org
Executive Director: John A. Thorner, CAE
Major publications: *Parks & Recreation Magazine; Journal of Leisure Research; Therapeutic Recreation Journal; Park, Recreation and Leisure Facilities Site Planning Guidelines; The Proximate Principle: The Impact of Parks, Open Space, and Water Features on Residential Property Values and the Property Tax Base*
Purpose: To advance parks, recreation, and environmental conservation efforts that enhance the quality of life for all people.

National School Boards Association (NSBA)

1680 Duke Street
Alexandria, Virginia 22314-3493
(703) 838-6722; fax (703) 683-7590
Web site: nsba.org
Executive Director: Anne L. Bryant
Major publications: *American School Board Journal, School Board News, Technology Leadership News, Inquiry and Analysis, Leadership Insider*
Purpose: To work with and through all of its federation members to foster excellence and equity in public education through school board leadership. Established 1940.

Police Executive Research Forum (PERF)

1120 Connecticut Avenue, N.W., Suite 930
Washington, D.C. 20036
(202) 466-7820; fax (202) 466-7826
Web site: policeforum.org
Executive Director: Chuck Wexler
Major publications: *Subject to Debate* (monthly newsletter)

Purpose: To improve policing and advance professionalism through research and involvement in public policy debate. Incorporated in 1977, PERF is a national membership organization of progressive police executives from the largest city, county, and state law enforcement agencies. Its primary sources of operating revenues are government grants and contracts, and partnerships with private foundations and other organizations.

Police Foundation

1201 Connecticut Avenue, N.W.
Washington, D.C. 20036-2636
(202) 833-1460; fax (202) 659-9149
E-mail: pfinfo@policefoundation.org
Web site: policefoundation.org
President: Hubert Williams
Major publications: *Ideas in American Policing* series, *Crime Mapping News,* and research and technical assistance reports on a wide range of law enforcement and public safety issues; a publications list and many foundation publications are available online
Purpose: To improve American policing through research, evaluation, training, field experimentation, technical assistance, technology, and information. Objective, nonpartisan, and nonprofit, the foundation assists federal, state, and local governments in such areas as community policing, strategic planning, crime mapping, civil disorder preparedness and response, police use of force, police misconduct, ethics, operational and administrative review, program evaluation, police-community relations, and police chief selection. The foundation's Crime Mapping and Problem Analysis Laboratory works to advance the understanding and pioneer new applications of computer mapping, and it provides training and technical assistance to police agencies. Established 1970.

Public Entity Risk Institute (PERI)

11350 Random Hills Road, Suite 210
Fairfax, Virginia 22030
(703) 352-1846; fax (703) 352-6339
E-mail: ghoetmer@riskinstitute.org
Web site: riskinstitute.org
Executive Director: Gerard J. Hoetmer
Major publications: *Emergency Management: The American Experience 1900–2005, Risk Management Resource Guide, Risk Identification and Analysis: A Guide for Small Public Entities, Community Leadership in a Risky World, Limiting Small Town Liability: A Risk Management Primer, Characteristics of Effective Emergency Management Structures, Are You Ready? What Lawyers Need to Know about Emergency Preparedness and Disaster Recovery, Holistic Disaster Recovery: Ideas for Building Local Sustainability after a Natural Disaster, Surviving Extreme*

Events: A Guide to Help Small Businesses and Not-for-Profit Organizations Prepare for and Recover from Extreme Events, PERIScope Newsletter

Purpose: A nonprofit, nonmembership organization, PERI provides risk management education and training resources for local governments and school districts, small businesses, and nonprofits. PERI's Web site, riskinstitute.org, serves as a resource center and clearinghouse with information on a wide range of topics, including disaster management and hazard mitigation, risk financing and insurance, safety and health, workers' compensation, and technology risks. PERI also operates a national benchmarking database, known as the PERI Data Exchange, which allows local governments to compare their liability and workers' compensation losses with those of their peers and to identify strategies to reduce losses and control costs. Local governments that submit data to the database receive prime benchmarking reports at no cost.

Public Risk Management Association (PRIMA)

500 Montgomery Street, Suite 750
Alexandria, Virginia 22314-1516
(703) 528-7701; fax (703) 739-0200
E-mail: info@primacentral.org
Web site: primacentral.org
Executive Director: Lisa Lopinsky
Major publications: *Public Risk Magazine, Public Sector Risk Management Manual;* special reports: *Cost of Risk Evaluation in State and Local Government, 1998 Tort Liability Today: A Guide for State and Local Governments;* videos: *Shaping a Secure Future*

Purpose: To promote effective risk management in the public interest as an essential component of administration. Established 1978.

Public Technology Institute (PTI)

1301 Pennsylvania Avenue, N.W., Suite 830
Washington, D.C. 20004
(202) 626-2400; fax (202) 626-2498
E-mail: press@pti.nw.dc.us
Web site: pti.org
Executive Director: Alan R. Shark
Major publications: *Online* magazine (www.prismonline.org); *Winning Solutions* (annual); *Slow Down, You're Going Too Fast: A Local Official's Guide to Traffic Calming; Roads Less Traveled: Intelligent Transportation Systems for Sustainable Communities; Sustainable Building Technical Manual; Smart Moves: A Decision Maker's Guide to the Intelligent Transportation Infrastructure; gis://the next management tool; Mission Possible: Strong Governance Structures for the Integration of Justice Information Sys-*

tems; E-Government: Factors Affecting ROI; E-Government: A Strategic Planning Guide for Local Officials; Why Not Do It Ourselves? A Resource Guide for Local Government Officials and Citizens Regarding Public Ownership of Utility Systems; Greening the Fleet: A Local Government Guide to Alternative Fuels and Vehicles; numerous case studies on energy and environmental technology development and sustainable management

Purpose: To identify and test technologies and management approaches that help all local governments provide the best possible services to citizens and business communities. With ICMA, NLC, and NACo, PTI works with progressive member cities and counties to (1) make communities "well-connected" by advancing communication capabilities; (2) develop tools and processes for wise decision making; and (3) promote sustainable approaches that ensure a balance between economic development and a clean, quality environment. The PTI member program engages cities and counties as laboratories for research, development, and public enterprise to advance technology applications in telecommunications, energy, the environment, transportation, and public safety. To disseminate member research, PTI provides print and electronic resources, and peer consultation and networking. PTI offers several technology products and services through partnerships with private vendors; these help local governments save money by bypassing rigorist RFP requirements, as they are competitively bid and chosen for superior quality and competitive pricing. PTI's research and development division continues to examine information and Internet technology, public safety, geographic information systems, energy-conserving technologies, sustainable management, and intelligent transportation systems. Established 1971.

Sister Cities International (SCI)

1301 Pennsylvania Avenue, N.W., Suite 850
Washington, D.C. 20004
(202) 347-8630; fax (202) 393-6524
E-mail: info@sister-cities.org
Web site: sister-cities.org
Executive Director: Patrick Madden
Major publications: Sister Cities International Membership Directory, *Sister Cities News, Report to the Membership* (bimonthly)

Purpose: To promote sustainable development, youth involvement, cultural understanding, and humanitarian assistance, and to increase global cooperation at the local level by creating and strengthening partnerships among U.S. and international communities. With its international headquarters in Washington, D.C., SCI is a nonprofit, citizen diplomacy network that officially certi-

fies, represents, and supports partnerships between U.S. cities, counties, states, and similar jurisdictions in other countries to ensure their continued commitment and success. The SCI network represents nearly 700 U.S. communities and over 1,800 international communities, making up more than 2,500 partnerships in 126 countries around the world. Established 1967.

Solid Waste Association of North America (SWANA)

P.O. Box 7219
Silver Spring, Maryland 20907-7219
(301) 585-2898; fax (301) 589-7068
(800) 467-9262
E-mail: info@swana.org
Web site: swana.org
Executive Director: John H. Skinner, PhD

Purpose: To advance the practice of environmentally and economically sound municipal solid waste management in North America. Established 1961.

Southern Building Code Congress International, Inc. (SBCCI)

See **International Code Council (ICC)**

Special Libraries Association (SLA)

331 South Patrick Street
Alexandria, Virginia 22314-3501
(703) 647-4900; fax (703) 647-4901
E-mail: sla@sla.org
Web site: sla.org
Chief Executive Officer: Janice R. Lachance
Major publications: *Information Outlook*

Purpose: To further the professional growth and success of its membership. Headquartered in Alexandria, Virginia, SLA is the international association representing the interests of thousands of information professionals in 84 countries. The association offers a variety of programs and services designed to help its members serve their customers more effectively and succeed in an increasingly challenging global information arena. Established 1909.

Universal Public Purchasing Certification Council (UPPCC)

151 Spring Street
Herndon, Virginia 20170
(800) 367-6447 Fax: (703) 796-9611
E-mail: certification@uppcc.org
Web site: uppcc.org
Program Administrator: Ann Peshoff

Purpose: To more effectively promote and ensure professionalism in public sector procurement, the National Institute of Governmental Purchasing (NIGP) and the National Association of State Procurement Officials (NASPO) jointly established the Universal Public Purchasing Certification Council

(UPPCC). UPPCC is charged with identifying and establishing a standard of competency for the public procurement profession; establishing and monitoring eligibility requirements of those interested in achieving certification; and furthering the cause of certification in the public sector. The UPPCC certification programs have been established to meet the requirements of all public purchasing personnel in federal, state, and local governments. Certification, which reflects established standards and competencies for those engaged in governmental purchasing and attests to the purchaser's ability to obtain maximum value for the taxpayer's dollar, is applicable to all public and governmental organizations, regardless of size. The council offers two credentials: the Certified Professional Public Buyer (CPPB), which applies to individuals who have demonstrated prescribed levels of professional competency as buyers in governmental purchasing, and the Certified Public Purchasing Officer (CPPO), which applies to similar individuals who also assume managerial functions within their jurisdiction or agency. As the trend in governmental purchasing is for mandatory certification of procurement professionals, these credentials communicate to the taxpayer that the public employee who manages tax dollars has reached a level of education and practical experience within government purchasing to be recognized by the UPPCC. Established 1978.

Urban Affairs Association (UAA)
298 Graham Hall
University of Delaware
Newark, Delaware 19716
(302) 831-1681; fax (302) 831-4225
Web site: udel.edu/uaa
Executive Director: Dr. Margaret Wilder
Major publications: *Journal of Urban Affairs, Urban Affairs* (a newsletter)

Purpose: To encourage the dissemination of information and research findings about urbanism and urbanization; to support the development of university education, research, and service programs in urban affairs; and to foster the development of urban affairs as a professional and academic field. Established 1969.

Urban Institute (UI)
2100 M Street, N.W.
Washington, D.C. 20037
(202) 833-7200
Web site: urban.org
President: Robert D. Reischauer
Publications: Research papers, policy briefs, and books on various social and economic issues, including health care, welfare reform, immigration policy, tax reform, prisoner reentry, housing policy, retirement, charitable giving, school accountability, economic development, and community revitalization; most publications available online

Purpose: To respond to needs for objective analyses and basic information on the social and economic challenges confronting the nation and for nonpartisan evaluation of the government policies and programs designed to alleviate such problems. Established 1968.

Urban and Regional Information Systems Association (URISA)
1460 Renaissance Drive, Suite 305
Park Ridge, Illinois 60068
(847) 824-6300; fax (847) 824-6363
Web site: urisa.org
Executive Director: Wendy Nelson
Major publications: *URISA Journal, URISA News,* Quick Studies, books and compendiums, salary surveys, conference proceedings, videos

Purpose: URISA is the premier organization for the use and integration of spatial information technology to improve the quality of life in urban and regional environments. Through its international, national, and local chapter operations, URISA serves nearly 7,000 professionals worldwide. Established 1963.

U.S. Conference of Mayors (USCM)
1620 I Street, N.W.
Washington, D.C. 20006
(202) 293-7330; fax (202) 293-2352
E-mail: info@usmayors.org
Web site: usmayors.org
Executive Director: J. Thomas Cochran
Major publications: *U.S. Mayor, Mayors of America's Principal Cities*

Purpose: To act as the official nonpartisan organization of cities with populations of 30,000 or more; to aid the development of effective national urban policy; to ensure that federal policy meets urban needs; and to provide mayors with leadership and management tools. Each city is represented in the conference by its mayor. Established 1932.

Water Environment Federation (WEF)
601 Wythe Street
Alexandria, Virginia 22314-1994
(703) 684-2400; fax (703) 684-2492
(800) 666-0206
Web sites: wef.org and weftec.org
Executive Director: William Bertera
Major publications: *Water Environment Research, Water Practice, Water Environment and Technology, Operations Forum, Water Environment Regulation Watch, Biosolids Technical Bulletin, Utility Executive Technical Bulletin,* series of Manuals of Practice

Purpose: To develop and disseminate technical information concerning the preservation and enhancement of the global water environment. As an integral component of its mandate, the federation has pledged to act as a source of education to the general public as well as to individuals engaged in the field of water pollution control. Established 1928.

Authors and Contributors

David R. Berman is a senior research fellow at the Morrison Institute for Public Policy and a professor emeritus of political science at Arizona State University. His research has been supported by numerous grants and contracts, and along with being a regular contributor to *The Municipal Year Book,* he has produced eight books and more than 60 published papers, book chapters, or referred articles dealing with state and local government, politics, and public policy; among his works are *Local Government and the States: Autonomy, Politics, and Policy* (2003) and, most recently, *Radicalism in the Mountain West* (2007). Before coming to Arizona State, he was a research associate with the National League of Cities. Professor Berman has also served as a consultant for the U.S. Advisory Commission on Intergovernmental Relations and on the executive committees of the American Political Science Association's Federalism and Intergovernmental Section and of the American Society for Public Administration's Section on Intergovernmental Administration and Management. He holds a bachelor's degree from Rockford College in Rockford, Illinois, and both a master's degree and a doctorate from the American University in Washington, D.C.

Lydia Bjornlund is a private consultant and freelance writer, working primarily on training materials and topics related to local government, land conservation, and industrial design. She has also written a series of books on American history and government for middle-school students. Before beginning Bjornlund Communications of Oakton, Virginia, in 1996, she was senior curriculum specialist at ICMA. She holds a bachelor of arts degree from Williams College and a master's degree in education from Harvard University.

Shea Riggsbee Denning is assistant professor of public law and government at the School of Government of the University of North Carolina (UNC) at Chapel Hill, where she focuses on the law of property tax listing, assessment, and collection and other local taxes such as privilege license, occupancy, prepared food and beverage, rental car excise, local ABC, and motor vehicle license. She earned her A.B. in journalism and mass communication and her J.D. from UNC at Chapel Hill.

Stephen Goldsmith, Daniel Paul Professor of Government at Harvard University's Kennedy School of Government, is a nationally recognized expert on government management, reform and innovation. He is the author of several books—most recently, *Governing by Network: The New Face of the Public Sector*—and his columns have often been published in such papers as the *Wall Street Journal* and the *New York Times*. While serving two terms as mayor of Indianapolis, he earned a national reputation for innovations in government. Mr. Goldsmith was chief domestic policy advisor to President George W. Bush in the 2000 campaign and then served as special advisor to the president on faith-based and not-for-profit initiatives. He currently serves as chairman of the Corporation for National and Community Service.

Jodi Harrison is an attorney with the Jail Health Law Project at the School of Government of the University of North Carolina at Chapel Hill. Prior to joining the School of Government, she spent ten years as a trial lawyer defending municipalities in law enforcement and corrections cases. She received her undergraduate and law degrees from the University of Montana.

Robert P. Joyce, a specialist in the law of education, the law of elections, and the law of employment, is professor of public law and government at the School of Government of the University of North Carolina at Chapel Hill (UNC). He has practiced law in New York City and in North Carolina. His undergraduate degree is from UNC and his law degree is from Harvard.

Laurie L. Mesibov is professor of public law and government at the School of Government of the University of North Carolina at Chapel Hill (UNC). She specializes in all aspects of public elementary and secondary school law except personnel law. Her undergraduate degree is from Stanford University and her law degree is from UNC.

Evelina R. Moulder, director of ICMA's survey research, is responsible for the development of survey instruments, design of the sample, design of logic checks, quality control, and analysis of survey results. Among the surveys conducted by ICMA under her supervision are economic development, e-government, financing infrastructure, homeland security, labor-management relations, parks and recreation, police and fire personnel and expenditures, service delivery, technology, and SARA Title III. She has also directed several survey projects funded by other organizations. With more than 20 years of experience in local government survey research, Ms. Moulder has collaborated extensively with government agencies, professors, the private sector, and other researchers in survey development, and she has played a key role in ICMA's homeland security and emergency response initiatives, including concept and proposal development.

Karl Nollenberger is the academic director of the Graduate Program in Public Administration at the Illinois Institute of Technology. Prior to taking this position, he served 30 years in local government positions and 5 years as a consultant to local governments. His local government service includes city and county management positions in five states as well as positions in financial management in local government. An accomplished practitioner in public administration, Professor Nollenberger served as president of ICMA in 1994–1995, representing more than 8,300 local government management professionals in 32 countries. He is also a Fellow in the congressionally chartered National Academy of Public Administration (NAPA). Professor Nollenberger received his M.P.A. from the University of Colorado and will receive his Ph.D. from the University of Illinois at Chicago this year.

Joyce C. Powell serves as a senior consultant in compensation systems with the Waters Consulting Group in Dallas, Texas, helping clients develop custom compensation programs to meet their corporate philosophy and overall compensation strategy. A certified compensation professional with 18 years of hands-on experience, she has served as an independent consultant working for major corporations in a myriad of industries, including energy and oil, health care, and information services. She also served as the supervisor of compensation and human resources for a major company in Garland, Texas.

Christine Shenot joined ICMA as a project manager on the Livable Communities team in January 2006. She oversees ICMA's technical assistance and other work on active living and healthy eating, funded by the Robert Wood Johnson Foundation as part of its Leadership for Healthy Communities initiative As part of ICMA's ongoing strategic partnership with CIGNA, which focuses on the leadership role of local government managers in health care, Ms. Shenot has also helped develop ICMA events and materials designed to examine how local governments can address the rising costs of health benefits. In addition to her health-related work, Ms. Shenot is active in ICMA's Sustainable Communities Leadership Initiative. Prior to joining ICMA, she worked for the Maryland Governor's Office of Smart Growth; before that she was a newspaper reporter covering sprawl and growth-related issues in Orlando, Florida.

Rollie O. Waters is president and founder of the Waters Consulting Group, Inc., in Dallas, Texas. Since 1976, he has been a management consultant to private and public sector clients, both national and international, and has given various lectures and seminars for organizations in the areas of compensation design and performance management. Known nationwide as one of the foremost authorities in compensation and performance management system design for the public sector, he has spoken before such organizations as the American Management Association, Southern Methodist University, the University of Maryland, California Institute of Technology, the Texas Municipal League, and the International Personnel Management Association, as well as before several international companies based in Great Britain.

Richard B. Whisnant is associate professor of public law and government at the School of Government of the University of North Carolina (UNC) at Chapel Hill, where he specializes in environmental law. He founded and continues to work with the UNC Environmental Finance Center. His 2003 publication, *Cleanup Law of North Carolina: A Guide to a State's Environmental Cleanup Laws,* received the Silver Magnum Opus award for outstanding achievement in corporate and custom publications. He earned his bachelor of arts degree from UNC and his master of public policy and law degrees from Harvard University.

Cumulative Index, 2004–2008

The cumulative index comprises the years 2004 through 2008 of *The Municipal Year Book*. Entries prior to 2004 are found in earlier editions.

How to Use This Index. Entries run in chronological order, starting with 2004. The **year** is in **boldface** numerals, followed by a colon (e.g., **04:**); the relevant page numbers follow. Years are separated by semicolons.